P9-DWJ-586

# REDEEMING
# THE
# TIME

# A
# PEOPLE'S HISTORY
# OF THE
# 1920S
# AND THE NEW DEAL

# REDEEMING THE TIME

## Page Smith

VOLUME EIGHT

McGRAW-HILL BOOK COMPANY

New York / St. Louis / San Francisco

Toronto / Hamburg / Mexico

1 2 3 4 5 6 7 8 9 DOCDOC 8 7 6

ISBN 0-07-058575-X

LIBRARY OF CONGRESS CATALOGING-IN-PUBLICATION DATA

Smith, Page.
  Redeeming the time.
  "Volume eight" of the author's history of the United States.
  Includes index.
  1. United States—History—1919–1933.  2. New Deal,
1933–1939.  3. United States—History—1933–1945.
I. Title.
E784.S65   1986        973.91        86–2922

*For our grandchildren,*
*Cary, Page, Levi, Noah, Sara, Robert, and Matthew*

ALSO BY PAGE SMITH:

# Contents

*Introduction (and Farewell)*     *xi*

1. *The Twenties*     *1*
2. *The Other America*     *27*
3. *Europe*     *55*
4. *The South in the Twenties*     *70*
5. *Coolidge's Election, 1924*     *101*
6. *The Sacco-Vanzetti Case*     *117*
7. *Lindbergh*     *146*
8. *1927*     *164*
9. *The Left*     *182*
10. *Black Americans*     *211*
11. *Election of 1928*     *263*
12. *Hoover and the Depression*     *282*
13. *The Democratic Convention*     *317*
14. *Roosevelt Prior to the Campaign of 1932*     *342*
15. *Roosevelt's Philosophy*     *362*
16. *Roosevelt as Governor*     *377*
17. *The Campaign of 1932*     *391*
18. *The New Deal Begins*     *406*

19. Roosevelt's Special Session of Congress     437
20. The White House     463
21. The United States and the World     481
22. Communism and the Intellectuals     505
23. The Scottsboro Boys and Angelo Herndon     539
24. Black America and the Communist Party     575
25. 1934     597
26. On the Fringe     618
27. 1935     634
28. The Election of 1936     659
29. The Court-Packing Fight     682
30. The CIO     703
31. The Autoworkers     727
32. The Last Campaigns     751
33. The Spanish Civil War     767
34. Federal Project No. 1     789
35. The South Stirs     814
36. The New Deal     840
37. Religion     851
38. Education     884
39. Medicine     904
40. The Popular Arts     918
41. Art and Architecture     947
42. The Literary Scene     966
43. The Clouds of War     1025
44. The Election of 1940     1050
45. War     1073
46. The Evaluation of Roosevelt     1093
47. Postwar America: Suppressing the Left     1108
48. The Path to the Future     1127
     Acknowledgments     1149
     Index     1151

Our passions give life to the world. Our collective passions constitute the history of mankind.

—Eugen Rosenstock-Huessy

Man is man only because he remembers.

—Anatole France

Whatever may have been the case in years gone by, the true use for the imaginative faculty of modern times is to give ultimate vivification to facts, to science, and to common lives, endowing them with the glows and glories and final illustriousness which belong only to every real thing, and to real things only.

—Walt Whitman

# Introduction
# (and Farewell)

This eighth and final volume of my *People's History of the United States* brings to an end a venture that began some fifteen years ago. At the suggestion of Oliver Allen, then an editor with *Time-Life Books,* I began, in 1970, a "Bicentennial" history of the American Revolution. That history, completed in 1973 and published in two volumes by McGraw-Hill in 1976, dealt with the formation of the character and the ideas of the colonial American subjects of the British crown and the events leading up to the armed conflict, as well as with the politics and campaigns of the Revolution itself. The two volumes turned out to have, mysteriously, 1976 pages, or, as printers put it, "signatures," that is to say, unnumbered as well as numbered pages; it was thus a kind of secret between me and my publisher.

After idling about for several years, the notion suddenly struck me one morning after breakfast to carry the narrative account of our past as a people on up to the present. My idea was that I could do this in three additional volumes, each volume covering some sixty years. My publisher entered, a little nervously I suspect, into an agreement for an additional volume to run from the Revolution through the Civil War and was understandably alarmed when the volume, *Shaping the*

*Nation,* turned out to be much longer than anticipated and to get no further than 1826. It was evident that the history was going to be on a much larger scale than any of us had thought. McGraw-Hill rallied manfully (or I should say, womanfully, since my editor was Gladys Justin Carr). The fact that the Book-of-the-Month Club took a kindly interest in the enterprise was also of crucial importance, since it encouraged us all to think that it might "fly" despite its ambitious scale.

To make a long history short, it turned out, quite unexpectedly, to take six additional volumes to cover the period from the end of the Revolution to the beginning of World War II (not of course to mention the original notion of bringing the story "up to the present"—about which more at the end of this volume).

Since my academic "field" is "early American history," a phrase variously defined but generally taken to run from the period of exploration to, say, 1800, the greater part of the period covered by what might be called Phase II of the history was relatively unfamiliar to me. It was thus a voyage of exploration, endlessly fascinating and absorbing. I staggered from revelation to revelation in a perpetual state of wonder and awe, a frame of mind which I'm sure seemed merely naïve to the more knowledgeable "experts" in the various fields over which I cruised so recklessly. I had stated it in any event as my purpose to take American history away from its jealous guardians, the academic historians, and return it to its proper heirs and guarantors, the American people, the public; to make it, hopefully, a useful part of the common wealth.

In the course of that attempt, I cheered myself up considerably. As I noted in the introduction to the third volume, I was not at all sure that I was not, like the Roman historian, Livy (or, much later, Gibbon) writing about a "decline" that might well be followed by a "fall." That of course is still a very present danger but I grew more optimistic as I progressed through the past decades of our history. With all the dismaying aspects of late-twentieth-century American life— drugs, crime in high and low places, infidelity of various kinds, greed, luxury, imperial arrogance, and other such matters, I am convinced that we are a more just and humane people than we were even a relatively few decades ago. I do not believe that progress is automatic or inevitable or irreversible (who now does?) but I believe that we have wellsprings of kindness, decency, and trust to draw on, provided in large part through the faith and generosity of those of our forebears who devoted their lives to trying to realize the ideals expressed in our Ur documents, most significantly the Declaration of Independence. The true question for every historian is: What must we remember? What dare we not forget? This is a work about what, I believe, we must not forget if we (and of course the rest of mankind) are to have a future worthy of the best in our past.

# 1

# The Twenties

The repressive spirit born out of the bitter conflicts occasioned by the World War threatened, during the 1920s, to become a permanent aspect of American life. In the Senate Thomas Walsh, the sturdy old Progressive from Montana, inveighed against "Palmerism" or the "White Terror," as the Department of Justice's witch-hunting was sometimes called. "Ever since World War I," William O. Douglas wrote, "our government has been increasingly lawless as it caters to popular fears, and indeed generates them by cries of 'subversion' and 'un-Americanism.' "

Charles Evans Hughes, in an address at the Harvard Law School in 1920, urged Americans not "to ignore the indications that, perhaps to an extent unparalleled in our history, the essentials of liberty are being disregarded. Very recently information has been laid by responsible citizens at the bar of public opinion of violations of personal rights which savor of the worst practices of tyranny."

Felix Frankfurter joined Roscoe Pound, Zechariah Chafee, and nine other liberal lawyers in a "Report upon the Illegal Practices . . . of the United States Department of Justice." The report was a withering denunciation of "the continued violation of [the] Constitution and the breaking of [the laws of the United States] by the Department of

Justice. . . . Wholesale arrests both of aliens and citizens have been made without warrant or any process of law; men and women have been jailed and held *incommunicado* without access to friends or counsel; homes have been entered without search-warrants and property seized and removed; other property has been wantonly destroyed; working-men and workingwomen suspected of radical views have been shamefully abused and maltreated. Agents of the Department of Justice have been introduced into radical organizations for the purpose of informing upon their members or inciting them to activities. . . . In support of these illegal acts, and to create sentiment in its favor, the Department of Justice has also constituted itself a propaganda bureau, and has sent to newspapers and magazines of this country quantities of material designed to excite public opinion against radicals, all at the expense of the government and outside of the scope of the Attorney General's duties."

Many wealthy Harvard alumni, indignant at the liberal opinions of Chafee and Frankfurter, declared that they would not contribute to the university as long as the two men were on the faculty. Chafee's attacks on the injustice of the Justice Department led to the appointment of a special committee by the Harvard Board of Overseers to pass on his "fitness to teach" at the law school. He was judged "fit" by a six to five margin, with Associate Justice of the Supreme Court Benjamin Cardozo casting the deciding vote. The argument against Chafee was the by now familiar one that he mixed too much in controversial political issues to be wholly "objective" in his teaching. It was the same argument that William Harper, the president of the University of Chicago, had used in 1896 to oust the pesky Edward Bemis, who had annoyed John D. Rockefeller by supporting public ownership of municipal utilities.

The same spirit was manifested by the State Department, which was assiduous in protecting the country from subversive intruders. A notorious case involved a Hungarian countess denied a visa on the ground that she was a subversive. Count Michael Károlyi had been briefly president of the Hungarian Republic. He had later been expelled from Italy by Benito Mussolini on the ground that he was a Bolshevik. When his wife tried to come to the United States to continue a lecture tour that had been interrupted by illness, the State Department refused to issue a visa. In the Senate Burton K. Wheeler introduced a resolution demanding to know the reasons for the countess's exclusion. Roger Baldwin and the Civil Liberties Union took up the case. Walter Lippmann and the *World* and a number of academics, among them John Dewey and Charles Beard, joined in the protest. Frank Kellogg, the secretary of state, declared that the countess had been denied a visa in order to maintain the "priceless heritage of liberty" which "came from the struggles of our ancestors through centuries."

The British novelist D. H. Lawrence had difficulty obtaining a visa on the ground that his book *Lady Chatterley's Lover* was an obscene and corrupting work.

Among the efforts to defend the constitutional rights of American citizens the most notable was that by Roger Baldwin, the elegant young Socialist who went to prison as a conscientious objector rather than serve in the army. After his release Baldwin rallied a handful of liberal friends to found the American Civil Liberties Union. Felix Frankfurter was one of the members of the National Advisory Committee.

The most disheartening symptom of the country's mood of fear and repression was undoubtedly the Ku Klux Klan. In the midst of what William Allen White referred to as "the economic revolution" following the war, the Ku Klux Klan staged an astonishing comeback. Apparently dead, it revived on a platform of anti-Catholicism and racism in general. To hostility to blacks it added anti-Semitism, which was, quite independently of the Klan, in its heyday. The great banking houses of the Rothschilds in France and England and the Loebs and Kuhns in America had become symbols of the money manipulation associated in the popular mind with capitalism. But the malady obviously had deeper roots. They lay in the odoriferous soil of nativism in general, a tradition as old as the Republic. Anti-Semitism was stimulated by the identification of Jews with socialism, which came increasingly under attack as a disguised ally of bolshevism, and with the communism of the Soviet Union, where Russian Jews were prominent in positions of leadership. Reform in general was under a cloud, and a disproportionate number of Jews were active in reform movements.

Suddenly it seemed that the Klan was everywhere: in the South where it concentrated its attention on blacks, in the Midwest, where Catholics and Jews were the enemy, and even in the Far West, where Orientals were the objects of hatred and persecution.

The William Allen Whites returned to Emporia, Kansas, in the spring of 1923 to find that the city hall had been captured by candidates who had publicly declared their belief in the principles of the Klan.

In White's mind the movement was somehow related to the nation's apparent preoccupation with material things and a nasty, small-spirited resentment of anyone defined by the leaders of the Klan as "un-American." The town was experiencing a building and business boom, and its lower classes were rapidly ascending to the middle class. "Old America, the America of 'our Fathers' pride,' the America wherein a frugal people had grown great through thrift and industry," White wrote, "was disappearing before the new machine age." But that was simply an observation and not a very accurate one at that; certainly it was not an explanation.

White took on the Klan in Emporia with characteristic zest. "To make a case against a birthplace, a religion, or a race, is wicked, un-American and cowardly," he wrote in the *Gazette*, . . . "for a self-constituted body of moral idiots who would substitute the findings of the Ku Klux Klan for the processes of law . . . would be a most un-American outrage which every good citizen should resent. . . . It is an organization of cowards. It is an institution of traitors to American institutions. . . ."

But a year later Emporia had a Ku Klux Klan mayor. It seemed more than ironic to White that Kansas, the state of emancipation, of profound radical impulse, of free lovers and freethinkers, should be hospitable to a "hooded gang of masked fanatics, ignorant and tyrannical. . . . It is a national menace, this Klan," he wrote. "It knows no party, it knows no country. It knows only bigotry, malice and terror. . . . This Klan is preaching and practising terror and force. Its only prototype is the Soviet of Russia."

The Klan successfully penetrated the state's Republican Party and its councils, and a thoroughly dismayed White denounced the "dragons, Kleagles, Cyclops and Furies," the "Terrors, Genii and Whangdoodles . . . parading in the Kansas cow pastures. . . ." He entered the gubernatorial race as an anti-Klan independent against the Klan-endorsed Republican candidate, and while his opponent won the election, White was pleased by the 150,000 or so votes he garnered.

Arthur Capper, Senator from Kansas, told the black leader, James Weldon Johnson, that as opposed as he was to the Klan, he dared not speak out publicly against it for fear of being defeated in the next election. In Indiana, at the Republican State Convention, the head of the state's chapter of the Klan walked down the aisle with a pistol strapped to his waist. Hiram Wesley Evans, the leader of the Klan in Georgia, put himself forward as a presidential candidate. In Texas it was estimated that the Klan controlled two-thirds of the state's county conventions.

Near the end of 1922 the governor of Kansas, charging that a state of insurrection existed, banned the Klan but was defied by its members. In Williamson County and the town of Herrin, Illinois, the war between the Klan drys and the anti-Klan wets resulted in numerous deaths. Several times the governor was forced to call on the national guard to restore order in the county. Finally, early in 1925, a shoot-out between the Klan leader and the deputy sheriff resulted in the deaths of the two adversaries and the wounding of six of their supporters.

When the Ku Klux Klan surfaced in Colorado in 1924, Judge Benjamin Lindsey was in the forefront of the fight against it, "speaking night and day," as George Creel put it, "at the risk of his life." In the face of the Klan's opposition Lindsey won reelection to his judgeship, but a corrupt member of the State Supreme Court nullified his election. The judge had meanwhile made himself more vulnerable by writing a book on "companionate marriage." What Lindsey recommended, among other things, was a kind of trial marriage, rather like the ancient New England custom of bundling—sexual relations undertaken prior to marriage with the understanding that marriage would eventuate if the girl became pregnant. It was Lindsey's view that many marriages ended in divorce because of sexual incompatibility; compatibility or incompatibility should therefore be determined before marriage. Lindsey was bitterly attacked in press and pulpit for promoting "legalized free love," "pal marriage," and "weekend marriage." He further outraged public opinion by advocating birth control, divorce by mutual consent by couples without children after efforts by courts of domestic relations to effect reconciliations had failed, and sex education. Lindsey's unorthodox views on sex and marriage made him a special target of the Klan.

In Oklahoma Oscar Ameringer battled the Klan, denouncing its anti-Semitism. What, Ameringer asked the citizens of Clinton, had the Jews done to deserve such obloquy? "They have given us Moses, the Prophets, Christ and his disciples. If it were not for the Jews hell-fire would be our future. Besides all that, you can't down God's chosen people. Always remember that Moses died, and the Jews are still in business, and I've a hunch they will be in business for many years after this Klan craze blows over."

Ameringer wrote of the Oklahoma Socialists: "The struggle against the Klan almost cooked our goose." Rather than continue the fight in a cause that seemed lost, Ameringer and his fellow Socialists decided to throw their weight into another attempt to form a farm-labor alliance. They settled on a "five-point program," ratified at a meeting of 751 delegates at Shawnee, Oklahoma. Perhaps, Ameringer thought, the day had come for a potent new anti-Eastern establishment party, founded in the heart of the Midwest. Its name, adopted as enthusiastically as its platform, was the Farm-Labor Reconstruction League. It was modeled after North Dakota's Nonpartisan League and had its counterpart in half a dozen other Western and Midwestern states. "Our Jack" Walton, former mayor of Oklahoma City, had been chosen as the league's standard-bearer and candidate for governor. After a spirited and at times bitter campaign, in which the charge of "Red" influence was constantly aired, "Our Jack" was elected governor by 60,000 votes. A gigantic barbecue celebrated his victory. The occasion was notably "democratic"; Indians, sharecroppers, miners, and cowboys mixed with wool-hat farmers and gorged themselves with slabs of beef. But the victory proved hollow. "Our Jack" was hardly settled in the governor's mansion when it became clear that he had sold out to the interests. Worse, he had, it turned out, become a member of the Klan, and he gave a number of political plums to Klansmen, receiving from the emperor of the Invisible Empire himself a letter commending him for his "constant loyalty, unwavering devotion and splendid service to the Knights of the Ku Klux Klan."

The message of the Klan, in Ameringer's words, was: "Unless these people are driven out of the country or are shown their proper places, the Reds will raise the red flag of Socialism over the Capitol in Washington, the Negroes will marry our sisters, the unions wipe out what little business peace is left to us, the Jews foreclose the mortgage they hold on the United States and the Catholics install the Pope in the White House. . . . Just see what this latest lunacy is doing to your town," Ameringer told a political rally. "Catholics are boycotting Protestant stores, Protestants are boycotting Jewish and Catholic stores. Everybody is afraid of everybody else. Everybody is looking under the bed at night for bolsheviks, Reds, Socialists, papists, klansmen and landsmen of Jesus Christ."

Gerald Johnson, the Southern journalist, seemed to view the Ku Klux Klan as a natural by-product of democracy. "In the voice of the organizer [the prospective Klansman] hears a clarion call to knightly and selfless service. It strikes him as in no wise strange that he should be so summoned; is he not, as an American citizen, of the nobility? . . . The klansman has already been made, in his own estimation, politically a monarch, socially a peer of the realm, spiritually a high priest . . . [F]or the trifling consideration of ten dollars he is made a Roland, a Lancelot, a knight-errant vowed to the succor of the oppressed, the destruction of ogres and magicians, the defense of the faith."

In the words of W. J. Cash, the ranks of the Klan in the South "swarmed with little business men . . . the rural clergy belonged to it or had traffic with it almost *en masse* . . . It was . . . at once anti-Negro, anti-Alien, anti-Red, anti-Catholic, anti-Jew, anti-Darwin, anti-Modern, anti-Liberal, Fundamentalist, vastly Moral, militantly Protestant." The Klansman, Cash wrote, not only relieved his "personal frustration and itches . . . but [enjoyed] also the old coveted, splendid sense of being an heroic blade, a crusader sweeping up mystical slopes for White Supremacy, religion, morality, and all that had made up the faith of the Fathers. . . ."

The spirit of repression did not, of course, stop with the Klan. It was amply manifested in the Federal government, in many state and municipal jurisdictions, in Chambers of Commerce, the American Legion, the Daughters of the American Revolution, and such service organizations as the Lions, Elks, Moose, and Rotarians.

To the unhappy consequences of World War I must be added the American Legion, an organization of ex-soldiers that became a byword for reaction. Its intentions were doubtless good, but it might be argued that only the Ku Klux Klan was more incompatible with the constitutional principles on which the nation had been founded. The American Legion at its convention in 1919 had resolved to combat "all anti-American tendencies, activities, and propaganda . . . to organize immediately for the purpose of meeting the insidious propaganda of Bolshevism, IWWism, radicalism, and all other anti-Americanisms by taking up the problem of . . . detecting anti-American activities everywhere and seizing every opportunity to speak plainly and openly for 100 percent Americanism and for nothing else." The Legion further concluded that there were in the country "various organizations and isms whose ultimate aim is the destruction of the principles of law, order, and true democracy." Moreover, the Department of Justice had "a great mass of facts and evidence regarding these activities, especially those of the so-called parlor socialists and Bolsheviki, which our organization considers by far the most dangerous, for they, under a mask of respectability, insidiously inject infamous teachings into the minds and thoughts of our citizens." The American Legion, in effect, appointed itself a vigilante body to police the thoughts of its fellow citizens, confident that it could measure loyalty and treason as precisely as a jeweler's scale.

The Elks, Rotarians, and Lions were determined not to be outdone by the American Legion in hunting down subversives. An item from the *Tucson Citizen* glorified the Elks: "There is nothing as responsive as an Elk's heart. In the social sense he is the courier, the gallant knight of modern times. There is more day-to-day Christianity in the practices of Elkdom than in many a monumental cathedral."

The Rotarians were no more reluctant than the Elks or the Optimists to boast of their virtues. An article in the *Rotarian* magazine proclaimed: "Had an Optimist, Co-operative, Exchange, Lions, Kiwanis or a Rotary Club flourished in the days of the Exodus with old Moses as president, the children of Israel would have reached the promised land in forty days instead of forty years. Would not any of these clubs in the days of Sodom and Gomorrah have saved those cities?"

The *Philadelphia Evening Bulletin* noted: "Several members of the Chester Rotary Club left the meeting last night after a speaker had made several bitter attacks on the United States, and had praised the I.W.W. At the end of his speech he removed a set of false whiskers and revealed himself as . . . chairman of the educational committee of the American Legion. He then addressed the Rotarians on the perils of Socialism, and told what the American Legion was doing to protect the government from its enemies."

The Daughters of the American Revolution, determined not to be outdone in patriotism by the American Legion or the Klan, issued its own index of Communist sympathizers, a noble list which included William Allen White; Dean Roscoe Pound of the Harvard Law School; Mary Woolley, the pious president of Mount Holyoke College; Felix Frankfurter; Clarence Darrow; Rabbi Stephen Wise; Norman Hapgood; and David Starr Jordan, perhaps the country's leading pacifist and former president of Stanford University. William Allen White had a word for the "nice old girls of the . . . D.A.R." who had been "hypnotized by the brass buttons of the retired army officers and lured into this red-baiting mania by the tea-gladiators of Washington . . . The D.A.R. has yanked the Klan out of the cow pasture and set it down in the breakfast room of respectability. . . ."

The agitation in advanced circles for complete sexual freedom brought, inevitably, a strong reaction from the citadels of conservatism. The YWCA in Albuquerque, New Mexico, had a chilling warning on its bulletin board: "Remember that these diseases can be contracted from kissing or dancing with a man who is diseased. . . . Never forget that at least 25 percent, *or one out of every four* men who you know, are diseased." Dancing was as demoralizing as jazz and bobbed hair; the wife of a Wheaton College biology professor announced: "I disapprove of our co-eds bobbing their hair because it is against the teachings of the Bible."

Jazz came to be listed by fundamentalist preachers along with dancing, smoking, and drinking as a major cause of sin. Mrs. E. M. Whittemore reported in an article entitled "From the Ballroom to Hell" that 70 percent of the prostitutes of New York City had been ruined by jazz. In Los Angeles the figures were even higher: 163 out of 200. In Cleveland public dance halls were governed by a municipal injunction that read in part: "Dancers are not permitted to take either exceptionally long or short steps. . . . Don't dance from the waist up; dance from the waist down. Flirting, spooning, and rowdy conduct of any kind is absolutely prohibited."

In Oshkosh, Wisconsin, a municipal ordinance forbade men and women from "looking into each other's eyes while dancing." In Okmulgee, Oklahoma, an oil field worker named T. H. Harvey was arrested and fined $10 for "walking down the street with a questionable woman." His defense—that she was an old friend whom he had met coming out of a movie house—was waved aside.

In California Lincoln Steffens and Clarence Darrow, along with Fremont Older, made a final effort to secure the release of Tom Mooney, the labor leader who had been convicted, on the basis of perjured testimony, of having been responsible for a bomb that killed several San Franciscans in 1916. They received a chilly reception from the governor of the state and his staff. "They talked of justice, their right, their honesty," Steffens wrote. "I knew what they meant: no generosity, no mercy, no human understanding, and no wise politics." It was as though the war had obliterated all generous impulses in the nation's collective heart.

The twenties were grim days for organized labor. Membership in the International Ladies' Garment Workers' Union dropped from 110,000 at the beginning of the decade to 40,000 by the time of the

Wall Street crash. Its finances had been depleted and its spirit badly bruised, if not broken, by a disastrous twenty-six-week-long strike in 1926 that failed.

There was a stubborn indisposition among most mill, mine, and factory owners even to discuss grievances with their workers. To meet in the same room with them would, the owners believed, be an admission that they had some rights, would be a kind of *de facto* recognition if not of a union then of the workers' rights to bargain over such issues as wages, hours, or working conditions. This fear of conceding, or appearing to concede, something to the rights of workers as opposed to the rights of owners and stockholders extended from such corporate giants as General Motors to relatively modest enterprises employing a few hundred or a few thousand workers. When some 4,400 copper workers in Rome, New York, employed by four factories went on strike in 1919 for shorter hours and higher pay, the factory owners refused to communicate with leaders of the strike by any means, direct or indirect. The most intractable employer, John Spargo (no relation apparently to the Socialist of the same name), tore up the strikers' request for a meeting and sent it back accompanied by the message "Kiss my ass and go to hell." For weeks Frances Perkins and other members of the New York State Industrial Commission tried to mediate between the strikers and the owners, but the owners remained obdurate while the strikers secretly collected dynamite to blow up the plants. From his hunting lodge in the Adirondacks Spargo sent the strike committee a letter so obscene that the other owners, rather than have the Industrial Commission make the letter public, agreed to negotiate with the strikers.

The first substantial effect of the Federal Reserve Board's mandate to manipulate the nation's currency was felt in 1921, when the board adopted a policy of deflation. The left-wing critics of the board were outraged; they charged that the action was in essence a punitive one, directed at labor, which in the view of capital had been given grandiose notions by the wartime boom. As interest rates soared, the immediate effect of deflation designed to restore "normalcy" (which may be interpreted as reducing the excessive expectations of the workingman and workingwoman) was to bring on a crisis in many Midwestern farm communities. Cattlemen, who depended heavily on loans to tide them over, were especially hard hit. Small towns felt the impact as banks and stores closed and railroad loadings dropped sharply.When railroads cut wages in 1922, railroad shopmen went out on strike.

Strikebreakers were called in. Everywhere the cry was raised of the "Red menace." Reds were as ubiquitous as German spies had been a few years earlier. Any repressive action by authorities was justified on the ground that it was necessary to meet the threat posed by the Reds.

In Wichita, Kansas, when railroad shopmen went on strike, Governor Henry Allen, one of the early Kansas Progressives and a close friend and political ally of William Allen White, forbade the strikers to walk out on the ground that they had been stirred up by "agitators." Allen called on the national guard to back up his order, but the strikers defied him, and violence flared. Strikers printed up signs for merchants to place in their windows that read: "We are for the strikers 100 per cent." Allen ordered them removed on the ground that they encouraged the strikers in their intransigence. William Allen White responded by printing a sign that read: "As long as the strikers maintain peace and use peaceful means in this community, the Gazette is for them 50 per cent, and every day which the strikers refrain from violence, we shall add 1 per cent more of approval." White believed that the actions of his old friend were not only unfair but unconstitutional. He wrote an editorial in the *Gazette* in the form of an open letter to Allen, entitled "To an Anxious Friend." To the argument that "freedom of utterance" must bow before the law, White warned "that you can have no wise laws nor free enforcement of wise laws unless there is free expression of the wisdom of the people—and, alas, their folly with it. But if there is freedom, folly will die of its own poison, and the wisdom will survive. That is the history of the race." Peace bought at the cost of suppressing dissent was no peace at all. "Peace without justice is tyranny, no matter how you may sugar-coat it with expediency. . . . So, dear friend, put fear out of your heart. This nation will survive, this state will prosper, the orderly business of life will go forward if only men can speak in whatever way given them to utter what their hearts hold—by voice, by post card, by letter, or by press. Reason never has failed men. Only force and repression have made wrecks in the world."

Joseph Leiter was a graduate of Harvard who had opened up the coalfields of southern Illinois, an area known as Egypt. (His wife was a famous Mrs. Malaprop who was reported to have said that she was going to a fancy-dress ball in "the garbage of a nun.") When Leiter attempted to import Southern strikebreakers, many of them blacks, into his mines, one of the bitterest labor wars of that much fought-over region broke out. By the mid-twenties, Egypt had become one of the most thoroughly organized sections of the country. Its "labor temples,"as they were called, were as much the centers of social life as the churches. May Days were observed with giant barbecues, parades, and fiery speeches that anticipated the day of emancipation for the "workers of the world." A good speech might run several hours, and Oscar Ameringer remembered hearing some that lasted four hours or more without visibly wearying the listeners. Two of the most popular speakers were Eugene Debs and Mother Jones.

When a young miner was shot and killed by a company guard, a fierce conflict broke out. The mine guards mounted a machine gun while the miners, many of them in oddments of their World War uniforms and armed with rifles and dynamite, laid siege to the mine. After some casualties on both sides the miners captured the mine, dynamited a number of railroad cars, and rounded up some 300 strikebreakers, ostensibly to ship them back to Chicago. But mob psychology got the upper hand, and 23 guards and strikebreakers were killed, and many more wounded.

The massacre of the strikebreakers and guards was utilized effectively by the enemies of organized labor to discredit the entire union movement and the closed shop. Lawyers, newspapermen by the score, and the curious descended on Egypt. A dozen union officials were chosen more or less at random to be prosecuted for the murders, and their trial dragged on for months. The lawyer for the miners, Angus Kerr, and his aide, Acquilla Lewis, got the miners acquitted by showing that no evidence linking them or indirectly to the killings had been produced. No Williamson County jury was inclined to convict its friends and neighbors on charges of killing strikebreakers.

One of the greatest threats to the labor movement and to workingmen in general was the rapid development of laborsaving machines that caused what was soon being referred to as technological unemployment. Men displaced by machines often found their working years at an end. Oscar Ameringer believed that the opening up of new mines in southern Illinois and Ohio would lead to a sharp increase in the 50,000 miners employed in the region. The reverse was true. While the output of the coal rose sharply, the number of miners declined to 30,000 in two decades. Ameringer set out to resettle the unemployed miners in a subsistence agricultural community on a 5,500-acre tract on the Mississippi delta in eastern Louisiana.

The reaction of old-line union leaders to the assault on the labor movement was primarily defensive and reactionary. The American Federation of Labor (AFL) opposed state and Federal legislation to improve working conditions or establish a wages and hours law on the ground that such measures discouraged unionization. If workers had decent working conditions and fair pay, they obviously had less incentive to join a union. The union argument was that such enlightened measures as those for which reformers like Florence Kelley and Frances Perkins were fighting might at any time be repealed (or simply ignored), and then the workers, without a union to represent them, would be at the mercy of their employers. Many unions became "closed." These unions typically had won high pay and favorable conditions for their members. Like exclusive clubs, they turned away job seekers; jobs were jealously guarded and given through the union to friends and relatives, most typically the latter. For an immigrant or a black to apply was futile. The AFL was dominated by individuals like William Hutcheson of the carpenters and John L. Lewis of the coal miners, jobholders and timeservers more interested in their power and prerogatives than in the needs of the members of their union and seemingly indifferent to the plight of nonunion workers. Even Henry Mencken, no friend of labor, wrote of "the gradual wearing down of labor . . . by capital's vigorous and well-planned war of attrition." Between 1920 and 1923 it was estimated that the American Federation of Labor had lost 1,152,272 members, or some 30 percent of its membership. More radical unions lost even larger numbers.

Working-class men and women (in modern parlance blue-collar workers) not only had to cope with aggressive efforts on the part of many employers to destroy unions, but had to contend with a government that almost invariably threw its support to the "capitalists" in any conflict with the "workers." In the 1920s the Supreme Court invalidated more state legislation than during the fifty years preceding. By such decisions, the Court in effect pitted the states against the Federal government, with the latter in the role of stubborn reaction. Senator Robert La Follette's remedy was a constitutional amendment that would give Congress the power to override a Supreme Court ruling by a two-thirds majority. Most liberal lawyers were alarmed by the prospect of such an amendment. Felix Frankfurter spoke for them when he placed his hopes in "a broader and more conscious legal education."

With the backing of President Warren G. Harding, Attorney General Harry Daugherty had used the injunction with devastating effect against strikers, especially in the coal and iron mines. Everywhere the cry arose for the open shop as the owner's principal weapon against the unions. Pinkerton agents, backed by police and deputy sheriffs, clubbed strikers and beat up pickets "from the railroad shops in Jersey City," Ameringer wrote, "to the Colorado coal pits." It seemed to Emma Goldman, writing her remarkable autobiography in 1927, that the "ideals of the Revolution" were dead in America—"Mummies that must not be touched. Hence the hatred and condemnation which meet the social and political rebel in the United States."

In the changed atmosphere of the United States Lincoln Steffens found "none of the old stress on the conflict between capital and labor." Instead, William Green, the successor to Samuel Gompers as president of the American Federation of Labor, talked about high wages for the workers. Like the socialists, the unions and their leaders "listened sympathetically to denunciations of Bolshevik Russia. . . . What it meant to me," Steffens wrote, "was the revolutionary spirit was dead or quiescent."

Ironically, the union movement was handicapped, especially after the recession of 1924, by the feverish prosperity of the country. From 1924 to the crash of 1929 real wages, as well as productivity, increased dramatically. Though workers, as always, profited less than others from the boom, the mood of optimism lessened their zeal for militant union activity. The same could not be said of the farmer. He lost ground. In September, 1927, some 38 percent of American farmers lived in counties where the average value of an acre of land was less than $40. They were, for all practical purposes, nonconsumers in the nation's consumer society. The farmer found himself, in numerous respects, an outsider. While farmers made up two-fifths of the population (down from half at the turn of the century), they were far behind city dwellers in those comforts which many Americans took to be as important as their citizenship, indeed symbols of the citizenship they so prized.

The fact that the wave of immigration was slowed and then virtually halted meant that industry began looking to farm children as workers to replace the stream of immigrants, many of whom had, to be sure, found their way to farms. The consequent rise in farm wages, coupled with the gradual decline of prices, squeezed the farmer further. A stream of statistics that poured from the Department of Agriculture demonstrated his constantly worsening situation. For example, "a suit of clothes which cost the farmer in North Dakota 21 bushels of wheat in July, 1913, cost him 31 bushels ten years later." Farm wages, at the same time, were 60 percent higher than they had been in 1913, and day wages at harvesttime had risen 82 percent. The cost of farm implements was almost 60 percent higher. The taxes on farmlands in Kansas had increased by 171 percent; in South Dakota, 129 percent. Freight rates were up some 50 percent, and the price of wheat, along with corn, the basic farm commodities, had risen only slightly above prewar levels.

By 1925 Western farms were showing a decreasing yield per acre as the effects of overtaxing the thin soil became more apparent. Pastureland was also growing thinner from overgrazing, and the subsurface water level in the Mississippi Valley was dropping at an alarming rate. Floods were growing more serious as forest growth grew sparser.

Many Oklahoma farmers who had mortgaged their farms to the banks refused even to pick their cotton when the market price fell below the cost of production; they left it to rot in the field. The result was a rash of bank failures. "A small town bank in Oklahoma, and in the South and Southwest generally," Burton Rascoe wrote, "was, properly speaking, not a bank, at all. It was primarily a firm engaged in real-estate speculation, horse-trading and mortgage foreclosing on defaulted notes bearing usurious rates of interest. The farmers were not depositors; they had nothing to deposit, most of them; they were borrowers at the banks. . . ."

The farmer's constant need was for credit at reasonable interest rates. The Intermediate Credit Act of 1923 attempted to make credit available to the farmer at low interest. It, too, proved ineffective and led to the McNary–Haugen farm relief bill, designed to control surpluses and stabilize farm prices. The idea was for the government to buy and store farm surpluses in years when high production threatened to drive prices below production costs and then to hold the crops until prices rose or to sell them on the world market at prevailing prices. Brought to the floor of Congress year after year, from January, 1924, on, it was defeated each year. It finally passed in 1927, whereupon President Calvin Coolidge vetoed it on the grounds that it was special-interest legislation and that its price-fixing provision was inconsistent with free-market principles. Rascoe, whose father was a successful farmer in Oklahoma until oil was found on his property and he became a millionaire overnight, was convinced that many of the problems of the farmers of the South and Southwest were of their own making. "The average farmer," Rascoe wrote, "is woefully ignorant, clannishly mistrustful of townfolks, independent to the point of brutish pigheadedness and unenlightened selfishness. He is narrow and bigoted. Field workers from the Department of Agriculture stand ready to help him, instruct him in scientific farming, in conservation of his resources; but most farmers will have none of this even though it is free of charge; they refuse to change their ancient and wasteful ways of doing things. . . ."

Few farmers were as resourceful as Burton Rascoe's father, who tried unsuccessfully to convert his Oklahoma fellow farmers to soil conservation, contour plowing, crop rotation, and diversified crops. He grew alfalfa, milo, maize, popcorn, wheat, barley, sugarcane, watermelons, cantaloupes, Irish potatoes, sweet potatoes, sage, and even tobacco to demonstrate the variety of uses of the land. His neighbors preferred to grow cotton. But whether farmers were progressive or reactionary in regard to their farming methods seemed in the long run to make little difference. Farm production increased greatly during the decade of the twenties, so the farmers must have been doing something right, but whether they did well or ill, they were time and again the victim of the unpredictability of the market.

There were subtler and more demoralizing psychological forces at work as well in the farm communities. The farm and especially the rural town were constantly held up to ridicule by the new city literati. The *American Mercury* was the most notorious heaper of ridicule. Sinclair Lewis's *Main Street* and *Babbitt* were aimed at the small towns of the Midwest, but most of those towns depended on adjacent farms, and the image of the rube and the yokel was no more encouraging than that of the small-town booster.

There was also the matter of cash wages. Farms provided reasonably comfortable housing, wholesome food in abundance, lots of fresh air, and, for the men, hunting and fishing and a reassuring sense of community. But there was little hard money, and in a society increasingly abundant in alluring *things* to buy, cash money, provided weekly by a factory paymaster, seemed more and more attractive. Finally, there was the new consciousness, or whatever we wish to call it: a sense of larger human possibilities, of new and freer and more exciting ways of living. The rumble seat of the Ford or Chevrolet roadster hinted at some of those possibilities. There were other places to court besides the front porch or the barn, other places to make the first groping attempts at sex besides the local bawdy house.

Basic to any understanding of America in the mid-twenties was the boom. When Frazier Hunt, the journalist, arrived back in New York in 1925 after a stay in Europe, he found the country in the midst of a financial orgy. Once-sober bankers and once-solid banks were engaged in giddy speculations in 6 percent South American and European bonds. "Talented young amateur confidence men, nurtured under the low moral codes of our universities," Hunt wrote, "were buying up honest industrial establishments and drowning them in watered stock, issued up to ten and twenty times their real value." Hunt discovered, somewhat to his surprise, that he had "ceased being a crusader." His Socialist ideals had gone glimmering. He poured his own savings and much of his earnings into a stock market guaranteed to make everyone rich. He found himself moving in a circle of the newly rich. "Amusing, entertaining, lavishly open-handed men and women, most of them in some area of editorial, publishing or advertising" they were a far cry from the friends of his prewar years: "newspaper and magazine men . . . artists, dreamers, seers, doers, enjoying a beautiful and eager world." It seemed to Hunt, reflecting upon the money mania, a madness that possessed the country and obscured every other issue, that the "last stand of the native-born American . . . against the onslaught of the tough, determined, and intelligent foreign-born pioneers—and particularly of that most vital of all races, the Jews"—had been made by "Midwesterners and Far Westerners." It was, he felt, his own generation that had made that "final but futile battle against the inevitable." The blood of the old pioneers had become too thinned out; they could no longer effectively contest the field against the new pioneers. "There had been too much energy used up in the very act of conquest and nation building. And there had been far too much personal ambition, and not enough thought for the continuity of family and clan. . . . Individuals won fame and fortune, but paid for it by lost blood streams. Their names would go with the wind."

By 1927 even such Socialist war-horses as John Spargo were eager to recant their youthful political heresies. "Today," Spargo wrote in a paper he entitled "Confession of Faith," "I am thoroughly convinced that the Socialist philosophy is unsound, the Socialist program dangerous and reactionary, and the Socialist movement a mischievous illusion." The capitalist system, he added, "seemed . . . to hold the greatest hope for mankind." A seasoned reformer, Abraham Epstein, wrote in 1928: "No longer are the voices of the early Isaiahs heard in the demand for justice. Vital social reforms are left to languish and social workers as a group take but little interest in them. Except for campaign purposes social work no longer proclaims itself as pure altruism. . . . It has lost its spiritual equilibrium and it has become too practical to be passionate. . . . Its only crusades are community chest drives which it conducts with the zip-zip of a successful team's cheerleader."

One young woman described the attitude of her generation: "We're not out to benefit society . . . or to make industry safe. We're not going to suffer over how the other half lives." Selfishness and self-indulgence, including extramarital sex, seemed to have replaced the ideal of unselfish service.

It was perhaps inevitable that the moral disarray of the country should give rise, at least among intellectuals and theorists, to serious doubts about the viability of democracy itself.

By the end of the 1920s Walter Lippmann was convinced that the "most important task of those who care for liberty" was "to limit the power of majorities, to dispute their moral authority, to deflect their impact, to dissolve their force. . . . The herd instinct . . . has surreptitiously acquired the sanction of conscience in democracy." It seemed to an increasingly conservative Lippmann that "the more or less unconscious and unplanned activities of businessmen are for once more novel, more daring, and in a sense more revolutionary than the theories of the progressives." He wrote to Judge Learned Hand in 1925: "My own mind is getting steadily anti-democratic. The size of the electorate, the impossibility of educating it sufficiently, the fierce ignorance of these millions of semi-literate, priest-ridden and parson-ridden people have gotten me to the point where I want to confine the actions of majorities."

The world was far from the place that Lippmann and his friends had dreamed and planned for in the prewar years and in fact all through the war and the months of the Paris Peace Conference. Lippmann's reaction to the Versailles Treaty was, as we have seen, to blame Wilson, but now it seemed the problem was more fundamental: It was the people themselves, the electorate, the masses, who were at fault. They were greedy and selfish, narrow-minded and parochial. They denied the constitutional rights of their fellow Americans—blacks, women, Orientals, Jews. They accused all those who differed from them of being un-American or of being Communists.

In his book *Public Opinion* Lippmann argued that the so-called public was a "mere phantom." The role of the public was limited to simply selecting which of those parties competing for its favor it wished to have run its affairs. "With the substance of the problem it can do nothing but meddle ignorantly or tyrannically." All the hopes of popular government which had been represented most dramatically by the movement for initiative and referendum were illusory. "Only the insider," Lippmann argued, "can make the decision, not because he is inherently a better man, but because he is so placed that he can understand and act. . . . The public must be put in its place so that it can exercise its powers, but no less and perhaps even more, so that each of us may live free of the trampling and roar of a bewildered herd." The central issue was not where power was derived from but the "use made of power. The problems that vex democracy seem to be unmanageable by democratic methods." In the words of Lippmann's biographer Ronald Steel, *Public Opinion* represented a startling change in Lippmann's own thinking. "First went socialism, then his faith in science, then his belief that the majority was fit to rule. Last to go . . . was his trust in experts. No longer did he assume that they might know best; only that they might know better than the common folk."

Graham Wallas, the British socialist who had been Lippmann's mentor, chided him for offering young men and women no hope for achieving a more just and humane world. A young man would get no clue from Lippmann on "how to make his brains and energy and love and pity for his fellows most effective, through different kinds of services and experiences, for the good of mankind."

When the *New York World* floundered, Lippmann was persuaded to write a signed column for the conservative Republican newspaper the *Herald Tribune,* owned by Ogden and Helen Reid. William Allen White wrote to congratulate and warn him: "You are a vogue. Your leadership is unquestioned among people who think. . . . I want you to know how proud I am of you, and to caution you to watch your step. Don't let the Bankers get you." The advice came too late. At least one banker, the liberally inclined Thomas Lamont of the House of Morgan, had "got" him. The Lippmanns were among the tycoon's closest friends. He lent them his special railroad car and took them touring through the Mediterranean on his lavish yacht.

In the war between capital and labor Lippmann's sympathies seemed clearly on the side of capital. The problem was "to civilize and rationalize these corporate organizations." The old notion that there was an inherent opposition between "the people and big business" was obsolete. The people themselves were "so deeply involved in big business" that the two forces could not be disentangled. Those politicians who called for a crusade of some kind by means of which the people might curtail the powers of the business world were hopelessly out of date. Lippmann had become, if not precisely a champion of states' rights, an enemy of "centralization," which amounted to pretty much the same thing. He opposed a child labor amendment and Federal intervention to protect the rights of citizens in particular states. The proposal to give pensions to the widows and orphans of war veterans seemed to Lippmann a "menace not only to the budget but to popular government itself." He lamented that Americans had "no firm and convincing standards by which to control the growth of their appetites for material things." The observation was a little disingenuous since Lippmann had conspicuously accumulated those material things associated with wealth and power. His old friend Harold Laski wrote Justice Oliver Wendell Holmes: "I think wealth has done two things to him [Lippmann]. A good deal of his sensitiveness is gone. He is interested in external things, queer little worthless comforts. . . . And he has arrived at the stage where he is not eager to take intellectual risks."

Norman Thomas complained that the "old reformer has become the Tired Radical, and his sons and daughters drink at the fountain of the *American Mercury*. They have no illusions but one, and that is that they can live like Babbitt and think like Mencken." William Allen White wrote in 1926 (rather in the middle of it): "What a sordid decade is passing! It will be known in American history fifty years hence as the time of terrible reaction." Harding and Coolidge had been only symptoms of a deeper spiritual malaise. The people had "gone out and lived riotously and ended up by feeding among the swine. Corruption is rampant in high places. Special privilege is unleashed and shameless. The fourth-rater is coming into prestige and power in business, in politics, in religion. . . ." White came to doubt that even Theodore Roosevelt, if he had lived, could have changed the course of things.

If there was disillusionment among reformers and an attitude of rather self-conscious despair in literary and intellectual circles, American business was in a euphoric mood. It was tireless in praising itself. "After all," Earnest Elmo Calkins, the advertising tycoon, wrote, "the captains of industry are as admirable by any ethical standard as the men who have been celebrated all these years in song and story. They have been and are self-seeking, but so are priests and kings. They have done their particular job better, on the average, than those other leaders of mankind." They had thus earned the right to take over management of the world's affairs. "That eternal job of administering this planet must," Calkins concluded, "be turned over to the despised business man. The work that religion, government, and war have failed in must be done by business. There is no country in the world so efficiently governed as the American Telephone and Telegraph Company or the General Electric Company. Business has become the world's greatest benefactor." In the words of William Allen White, "the national Chamber of Commerce, organizing all these [business] pressure groups, became the super-lobbyist of the land. In a nation whose head declared 'the business of America is business,' it was something more than a coincidence that the United States Chamber of Commerce housed itself during the administration in an imposing marble palace across Jackson Park from the White House."

Certainly America's material accomplishments were impressive. The sculptor Jo Davidson, one of Lincoln Steffens's closest friends, felt it. He wrote letters "about the energy and the adventure he felt, of the prosperity, the industry, the mass movement, which was so alive with fearless imagination that he himself was stirred by business. He wrote Steffens: "You must come and see it." And Steffens noted proudly that even the Russians were fascinated by America. "They coveted, not our reformers and good men," he wrote, "but our big, bad captains of industry; and they envied and planned to imitate our mass production, not our Constitution, laws, and customs, not our justice, liberty, and democracy, not our respectability, good intentions, and law-abiding morality—none of our ideals, not even our business ideals, but only our machinery, our big business production, our chain stores and other beginnings of mass distribution."

When Lincoln Steffens and his young English wife, Ella Winter, returned to the United States from the Riviera in 1926, they, too, were impressed by the booming economy. The cars of the laborers who came to build an addition to their house were the ultimate expression of the success of American industry. "This country," Ella Steffens declared, "has what the socialists in Europe have always said they wanted, and more. You have food, shelter, and clothing for the workers and—and a car!"

Lincoln Steffens's own prediction was that the new struggle would be between the owners of the great industries—the stockholders—and the management. He also foresaw the decline and eventual disappearance of the "leisure class," the substantial segment of the upper-middle and upper classes that lived on unearned income, usually in the form of dividends. "The good people whom I have found to be 'no good,' " Steffens wrote, "who carry through no reforms, who oppose all change as soon as they understand it—these, the great obstacle to all progress, whose incomes are a wasteful graft on business, in which they are a useless hindrance, whose 'moral' influence in art, literature, education, culture, and business is as 'bad' as it is in politics, these people are doomed . . . as they are in—Russia." Still, it was Russia that seemed to Steffens the best hope. "The preparation in America for the dawning future is not," he wrote, "so intelligent, conscious, and purposeful, but it is evident. The old arts of the theater, literature, painting, have got too far ahead of the crowds to be understood by them, but business is doing its blind best by what we call commercial art to show the work of painters, for example, in all kinds of advertising." He believed that "The United States is making an experiment second in hopefulness only to Russia, a revelation of evolution as against revolution." Steffens dared hope that the United States was, like Russia, though in a very different manner, trying so to "arrange the conditions of social living and . . . adjust the forces of economic life that not the cunning, grasping possessors of things, but the generous, industrious producers and the brave, imaginative leaders of the race shall be the fit to survive. . . . The world which I tried so hard, so honestly, so dumbly, to change has changed me. It took a war, a peace, and a couple of revolutions to do it, but it is done."

America was an "experimenting country," Ella Steffens pointed out. "Anybody can see anybody. Everybody is willing 'to try anything once' as they say. Nothing is final or fixed. Everything from high buildings to automobiles, from railroad coaches to cooking stoves and factory equipment—all but your Constitution—is tentative, temporary, to be scrapped someday for the next good thing." Steffens agreed. "I felt afresh," he wrote, "the power, the momentum of America as a going concern. The force of us had increased. There could be no stopping or turning us now. We were on the way; we might not know where we were going, but, for better or worse, we were going, going, going." It seemed clear to Steffens that big business was becoming not only domesticated but smart, that it was "absorbing science, the scientific attitude and the scientific method."

Frederick Taylor's teachings, now that the efficiency expert was dead and labor's suspicions of him were allayed, were coming into their own. "Cocksureness, unconscious ignorance, were giving way to experiment," in Steffens's opinion. Henry Ford's $5-a-day minimum wage had done more to change the general conception of the relation of capital to labor than all the tracts of all the reformers. "Research" was the magic new word. The head of General Motors told E. A. Filene, the Boston department store tycoon, "We don't think any more in business. . . . We may think up a theory, but we don't act on our theories any more. We send our theory or our need into the laboratory and so have it tried out. If it doesn't work, we change the theory, scrap it." If it worked, it was put into a car and tried out "in the market," but even then it was "only a sort of working hypothesis."

"This is revolutionary," Steffens wrote. If it were true that "this spirit had got out of the science laboratories into business in a business country," it must "seal the doom of our old Greek-Christian culture. It would spill over into politics, economics, life. No more thinking; no more right thinking; no more believing or logical reasoning from premises to conclusions. . . . Wondering would supplant convictions; insight inspiration; experiment would blow up argument. . . . No wonder my old liberal friends were sore and obstinate," Steffens concluded. "A new, new culture was sweeping down over us, and big business, and the root of all evil!" The "root of all evil" was clearly outmoded convictions, passionately and irrationally held to.

As William Allen White put it, "The corporation owned the machines of industry—the tools of trade. It represented the whole organized, aggrandized, acquisitive and possessive forces of society. The corporation sought to control and some did control politics." But there was, beneath the hectic surface of American life, White pointed out, a new spirit forming. "Sheer sense of justice was growing in the hearts of the liberalized masses," he noted. "Thus by reason of creative forces in man's heart and by reason of dynamic expansion of man's possessive forces, deep social changes were moving in the world. . . . The middle class was multiplying. In its upper reaches, it was absorbing corporate wealth. In its lower range it was enjoying higher wages, better food, better housing, wearing better clothes and educating its children with a prodigality that no middle class generation before had known."

An attitude common to most Americans was expressed by the mother of William O. Douglas. When he pressed her about why she supported a reactionary Republican candidate, she declared that the Republicans represented the rich, "who hired the entire labor force. If the Rich are disenchanted, then we are all unemployed."

*Business the Civilizer* was the title of a book written by Earnest Elmo Calkins and published in 1928 by the prestigious Atlantic Monthly Press. The theme, clear enough from the title, was underlined by a quotation from Ralph Waldo Emerson: "After all, the greatest meliorator of the world is selfish, huckstering trade."

There was a vast literature dealing with the romance of knights and round tables, Calkins declared, but little dealing with the heroes of business. The knight might seem picturesque, but on closer inspection he was revealed as "quarrelsome, ignorant, superstitious, cruel." The statesman likewise seldom bore close inspection. The priest was too often like Brigham Young. The businessman, on the other hand, "with all his meanness, his sordidness, his devotion to the selfish side of gain . . . is beyond and above them all immeasurably. . . . We need more Whitmans and Henleys to sing the modern man." Calkins quoted the advertising chief who was asked by a young idealist if advertising was "all bunk." The man replied, "There is just as much bunk in advertising as there is in law or medicine, or for that matter in literature and life, but it is never necessary to use bunk to practice advertising successfully." It was business which had brought America most of its blessings. It had lightened the housewife's labors in ways too numerous to list, it had encouraged cooperation, and perhaps most notably, it had embraced the arts.

The same theme was developed by the French journalist André Siegfried, whose book *America Comes of Age* was a best-seller in the United States. Siegfried noted that "the demand for . . . culture is today nowhere more insistent than in the executive circles of New York, Boston, or Chicago."

Advertising was the great new field for business enterprise. In the words of William Allen White, "Advertising is the genie which is transforming America into a place of comfort, luxury, and ease for millions. Advertising in the last twenty years has changed the economic status of at least one fifth and probably one fourth of our people, raising them from a lower to a higher standard, increasing their wants, increasing their ambitions, and hence their capacities and also their purchasing power. Advertising is the Archimedean lever that is moving the world."

A public with money in its pockets waited to be courted by the producers of consumer goods. Advertising geniuses rivaled, if they did not replace, engineers as the heroes of capitalism. Not only were advertising agencies tireless in promoting the products of the companies that hired them, but they were ingenious in promoting capitalism itself.

The striking advances in advertising Earnest Elmo Calkins credited to the recruitment of superior young men from colleges and universities. "Such men now realize that business is the true field of high adventure where opportunities are greater and rewards larger than in law, architecture, medicine, or any of the other intellectual professions. These men," Calkins continued "have taken their brains and their

ideals—especially their ideals, for business did not entirely lack brains—
into the selling end of business, and, with the open-mindedness that
only the outside view can give, have promptly adopted advertising as
a means of selling." Selling was, in essence, sportsmanship. "Good will,
fair play, welfare work, are all results of a higher code of business
ethics just as surely as they are a source of greater profits. . . . For
advertising is inherently a young man's work. It requires faith, courage,
vision, imagination. . . ." Calkins pointed to the evolution of the automobile as proof of the aesthetic element in advertising, the "remarkable turn of the industrial world toward beauty in design and
color." From having been, at least for most Americans, simply means
of conveyance, automobiles had become things of opulence and beauty.

As industry penetrated and perpetrated art, so art in turn entered
"business by the door of advertising," finding "new forms in which to
express the spirit of modern industrialism." The new art, soon to be
identified as Art Deco, now adorned buildings and offices so that art
was no longer confined to the home but enhanced public places.

Certainly it was true that design received a renewed attention,
which recalled the early days of machine design, when the machine
was treated unabashedly as an art object and elaborately painted and
embellished. In New York City Ethel Traphagen's School of Design
taught its students to rummage through the furniture and costumes
of past ages to create clothes for the prosperous middle and upper
classes.

Calkins made much of the fact that the large corporations, aware
of the value of educated executives, "sent scouts to the principal colleges at commencement time to spy out the land and appraise the
human material coming through, offering openings in their industries
to promising young men who are well spoken of by the college authorities." The Harvard Business School was a monument to the new
spirit of cooperation between the cloistered academic halls and the
corporate office. "Business as it is now conducted," Calkins wrote, "is
the supreme field of endeavor, calling for every quality of mind that
success in the most idealized profession demands, brains, energy,
and imagination, and as such it draws men to it for the sheer love of
doing it."

Owen D. Young, a prominent figure at Harvard Business School
ceremonies, declared, "To-day and here business formally assumes the
obligations of a profession, which means responsible action as a group,

devotion to its own ideals, the creation of its own codes, the capacity for its own discipline, the award of its own honors, the responsibility for its own service."

Millionaires seemed, perhaps for understandable reasons, especially attracted to journalists. Bernard Baruch, it was said, had enabled Herbert Bayard Swope (as well as Charles A. Lindbergh) to become a rich man by giving him inside market tips. Several prominent journalists benefited from the generosity of the House of Morgan along the same lines. Walter Lippmann, as we have noted, was a close friend of the Thomas Lamonts, traveled with them, and stayed at their various homes in the United States and abroad. Herbert Collins, founder of the United Cigar stores, through his managment of a few thousand dollars, enabled Burton Rascoe to accumulate a comfortable financial estate. Matthew Josephson, the exposer of robber barons, made enough money in the stock market to provide himself with a comfortable income.

Robert Hutchins, the brilliant young president of the University of Chicago, described the principal American delusions: The budget must be balanced annually, whatever the cost to the economy; the gold standard was sacred and must be preserved at all costs; socialism was the nation's greatest menace, and "free enterprise," if left alone, would provide jobs for everyone; the states were supreme and the Federal government subordinate to the states, except insofar as it undertook such measures as high tariffs to assist business. And, finally, of course, business should run the country. When James W. Gerard gave the newspapers a list of "fifty-nine men who rule the United States," the list significantly omitted every elected official but included John D. Rockefeller, Jr., J. P. Morgan, a number of Du Ponts, and Andrew Mellon. "These men rule by virtue of their ability," Gerard declared. "They are too busy to hold public office, but they determine who shall hold such office."

# 2

# The Other America

It was a commonplace, at least among intellectuals, that there were "two Americas," a phrase John Dos Passos used in his novel *The Big Money*. One was the repressive "puritanical" America hostile to immigrants, suspicious of "workers," inhibited in all matters concerning sex and the body generally, rigid in its Protestant fundamentalism—in short, the America we have just described.

The other America was the America of intellectuals, of artists, of writers, of liberals and radicals, and, above all (at least prospectively), of the "workers."

The decade of the 1920s was one of the more bizarre in our history. It is perhaps best comprehended by listing its contrarieties. It was the decade of triumphant capitalism which, having shaken off the attempts of Theodore Roosevelt and Woodrow Wilson to impose some constraints on its exploitative tendencies, embarked on a binge that ended only with the crash. It was a time of loosened morals or uninhibited freedom in sexual matters, depending on one's point of view. It was a time of severe hardship and repression for working-class men and women and of great growth and prosperity for the middle and upper classes. It was a time of deep personal confusion and distress for the members of the newly formed (or still forming) intellectual class and, at the same time, a period of almost unparalleled literary creativity the only rival of which was the decade of the 1850s. It was the era of the triumph of the new consciousness and, in some ways, the end of that consciousness.

What I have called the new consciousness, a consciousness made up of many various strands—literary, political, social, and, perhaps above all, sexual—a consciousness at the birth of which Theodore Dreiser might best claim to have been midwife with his *Sister Carrie* and Sherwood Anderson an attending physician, defied the country's generally reactionary mood. Vast schemes of social reform dwindled to intensely personal preoccupations. Lincoln Steffens lingered on the Riviera, uncertain whether or not to return to the United States. Brand Whitlock had been a friend and ally of Steffens during the prewar years, when both men had become famous as ardent, uncompromising reformers, but when he read the *Autobiography* on the Riviera, his only response was to criticize the "poor writing." A friend who visited Whitlock in Europe wrote: "In default of an economic philosophy he was apparently devoting himself to living, in a very debonair way. . . . About his tables were members of the aristocracy. . . . He was scrupulously dressed; careful in his habits; detached in his emotions. . . . Living was a thing to be finished off in a refined, artistic . . . way, possibly unsoiled by what was going on without."

The death of his father and an inheritance freed reformer-journalist Hutchins Hapgood from the most pressing economic needs. Like so many of his contemporaries, he found himself without a task or a direction. He used the word "rudderless" on several occasions to describe this feeling of aimlessness and depression. He turned to religion, to psychology, to introspection and meditation. "Since the patent failure of that burst of idealism which took place in America before the War," he wrote, "I have not come in contact with any social or political things which arouse my imagination." He and his wife, Neith, sold their beautiful old mansion in Dobbs Ferry in 1922 and headed for Europe, where so many of their friends were drifting about from one splendid ancient city to another, from Nice to Cannes to Florence, to Paris, to Geneva, to London, wherever fancy took them, refugees from an America they could hardly bear to contemplate. Hapgood saw a posturing Mussolini in Rome, strutting about "like a bombastic and self-conscious Napoleon," in the words of Hapgood's friend Guy Hickok, another American refugee.

Hapgood joined the migration back to the United States with his wife and children in 1924, but he was haunted by a strange sense that history had somehow ceased. "There seems to be no history, in any successive way, from that time to this," he wrote in the late 1930s. He had the "queer sensation of having in a sense completed my life as a Victorian struggling to let in upon it the new light. . . ." He was now "merely living . . . in this modern world. . . ." Like Frederic Howe and, indeed, Lincoln Steffens and dozens of others of his generation, he was increasingly preoccupied with his "own inner life."

Hapgood's friend Bayard Boyesen, himself a friend of Emma Goldman and Alexander Berkman, of Big Bill Haywood and Mabel Dodge, and a pioneer in educational reform, retired to a remote New England farm "and there tried to console himself for the loss of his illusions about teaching and revolutionary anarchism, with horses and dogs." He created a new romantic image: the "unhappy member of a superior race." Moreover, he drank to excess.

Soon abandoned farms in rural New England became the particular abodes of itinerant intellectuals. A subculture developed in such places as Peacham and Stowe in Vermont, Woodstock, New York, and Woodstock, New Hampshire, and a dozen other fading towns and villages. It was a culture made possible by the automobile, which linked what otherwise would have been depressingly isolated farms with each other and with adjacent towns. It soon included, in the summers, stockbrokers, bankers, professors, lawyers, and other refugees from city life as well as the original settlers, the artists, journalists, and writers, for the city was increasingly perceived not as a center of vital life and energy, of revolutionary hopes and aspirations but as crowded, dirty, noisy, and dangerous. Above all, there was a new or revived cult of nature. Refugees from the city wrote lyrical accounts of country life, of the sturdy character of the natives; they attended town meetings and celebrated the virtues of small-town democracy where they had once praised revolution.

Wading River, Long Island, was one of those literary-political-social enclaves where city dwellers fled for rural weekends and vacations. Among the luminaries who gathered there were Alexander Woollcott; most of the stars of the *New York World,* such as Edna Ferber, George S. Kaufman, and Franklin P. Adams; the British socialist Harold Laski; the golfer Bobby Jones; Dwight Morrow, a prominent liberal businessman and Morgan partner; Felix Frankfurter; and, most famous of all, Harry Houdini, the great magician and escape artist. Cornish, New Hampshire, was another retreat for city intellectuals:

Learned Hand; Herbert Croly; Charles Platt, the architect; the painter Maxfield Parrish; Augustus Saint-Gaudens, the sculptor; and the novelist Winston Churchill.

Hutchins and Neith Hapgood returned to Provincetown, Massachusetts, hoping to find there some of the gaiety and joy in life that had been so evident before the war. Instead, they found tourists and historians "researching" the great days so recently past. There were other ghosts there, and life was "a perpetual round of drinking-parties, drunken parties." There were numerous gaps in the ranks. George Cram "Jig" Cook, founder of the orginal Provincetown Playhouse in Greenwich Village, was gone, dead in Greece of some run-of-the-mill but inadequately treated infection. John Dos Passos was accepted into the Hapgoods' circle. He separated Kate Smith from her husband, Bill, and married her. Dancing became a favored form of social activity. To Hutchins Hapgood it was "the one element" in the Prohibition era "that meant greater health." The fox-trot with its "barbaric" rhythms and "oriental suggestions" helped mitigate the "curse of Prohibition. Without the dance, the gloom and darkness of Prohibition would have had an expression still more ugly. The dance was a relief in that tortured and uncivilized moment." Dancing "modified to a definite extent the picture I had formed of myself through years of self-consciousness," Hapgood wrote. "It was a great relief that I was part of the unindividualized rhythm of life. My moral breathing was deepened and my social responses were fuller and revivifying." Dancing inspired Hapgood to buy a Model T Ford and learn rather painstakingly to drive it. He discovered a "sense of almost romantic adventure," a "feeling of the acquisition of a new element in my life . . . a feeling of greater solidarity. . . ." In the midst of family conflicts and discords, "periodic violent quarrelings of a romantic character with my wife," and clashes with his younger daughter, "who belonged with a vengeance to the youthful school," Hapgood could mount his tin lizzie and rush off, "with a feeling perhaps like that of a free bird sailing through the air. . . ." Thus he could escape the sometimes stifling world of domestic concerns "with added proud consciousness of my control over the world of machinery!" As he raced along in his car, Hapgood "had the sense almost of the infinite in those marvelous suggestions" of unfolding landscapes.

Frederic Howe, Tom Johnson's lieutenant in the great reforming days of Cleveland, found his way back to the Baltimore psychiatrist who had advised him to speak out about his frustrations, fears, and anxieties. The psychiatrist urged him to follow his "instinctive desires." Men could not change the world. To have the illusion that they could would only increase the normal human quota of fears and anxieties. "He had induced a number of my friends to quit the government service after the war," Howe wrote, "to change their vocations and follow their instinctive desires. He had a philosophy of healthy living . . . [and] he talked about mental conflict, bad adjustments, a war that men had within themselves when they were not doing what they wanted to do." Howe was advised to let his subconscious or suppressed desires rise to the level of consciousness and then obey them. He decided that his subconscious desire, his "reverie," was to lead the life of a gardener-farmer in a Nantucket fishing village among "simple fisherfolk with whom I felt at ease." He joined the migration of Hutchins Hapgood and thousands of others to the rural towns of New England. Gradually he collected a little circle of fellow intellectuals who came to talk "about science, philosophy, literature and art, politics and international relations." Another year, and there was a ten-week "school enrolling several hundred young people." It was christened the School of Opinion. In the School of Opinion the subconscious and the theories of Freud received rather more attention than the highly depressing state of current politics. With the outer life a shambles, the inner life took on new importance. A new vocabulary appeared—words like "desire," "impulse," "adjustment." Howe still believed in liberalism, but he was less concerned "with the poverty of others" than "with the poverty of my own undeveloped experiences." He still believed in reform, but he was more concerned with reforming himself than reforming the world; he sought "harmony within," tried to repair "gaps in [his] personality," and achieve a "comradeship with myself such as I had never known before."

The fact that so many American writers and intellectuals fled to Europe after the war had important consequences; American cultural life became "internationalized." John Dos Passos described the spring of 1919 in an introduction to a new edition of his war novel *Three Soldiers*. "Americans in Paris were groggy with theatre and painting and music; Picasso was to rebuild the eye, Stravinsky was cramming the Russian steppes into our ears, currents of energy seemed bursting out everywhere as young guys climbed out of their uniforms, imperial America was all shiny with the new ideas of Ritz, in every direction the countries of the world stretched out starving and angry, ready for anything turbulent and new, whenever you went to the movies you saw Charlie Chaplin."

American artists and intellectuals in revolt against the excesses of industrial capitalism were startled to find that many of their European counterparts, notably the French Dadaists and the Italian Futurists, were ecstatic over the power and beauty of the machine and had erected a whole aesthetic based on its triumph. Matthew Josephson returned from Europe in the mid-twenties, celebrating American industry, and started a magazine entitled *Broom* in which to propound the new theories. "Whatever we may think of the social injustice wrought by the machine, it certainly has turned up an amazing store of artistic material," he wrote. The real strength of the nation lay in its "economic organization, and expresses itself in quantity production and national sales. It creates an inspiring enough spectacle for poets and novelists to ruminate over." Charles Sheeler began to paint oil refineries and grain elevators, but *Broom* failed after a few issues, and Josephson began to move to the left.

The year 1924 witnessed, among other notable literary events, the founding of the *American Mercury* by Henry Mencken and George Jean Nathan. Just as Sam McClure had caught the nation's mood for reform (or at least for revelation of wrongdoing) at the turn of the century with *his* magazine, and Steffens and Ida Tarbell had done the same almost equally successfully a few years later with the *American Magazine,* so Mencken and Nathan exactly transcribed the prevailing cynicism and mockery of the liberal-intellectual class that was emerging as such an influential element on the American scene. The principal targets of the *American Mercury* were politicians and preachers—organized religion in general and missionaries and Protestant fundamentalists in particular. Gerald Johnson, writing in the *American Mercury,* described the evangelist as a modern medicine man. "The roll of the tom-tom in the Congo jungles, the rhythm of the Hopi snake-dancers' stampings and yells—these he makes use of, but slightly modified, in his preliminary song-service."

The official position of the *American Mercury* on theological studies was that they were undertaken only by the "somewhat lazy and incompetent" because they offered "a quicker and easier route to an assured job and public respect. The sacred sciences," the editors wrote, "may be nonsensical bores, but they at least have the vast virtue of short-circuiting, so to speak, the climb up the ladder of security." The "Americana" department of the *American Mercury* scoffed at the venerated Professor William Lyon Phelps of Yale, who had declared: "Everyone who has a thorough knowledge of the Bible may truly be called educated; and no other learning or culture, no matter how extensive or elegant, can form a proper substitute."

American politicians, the *American Mercury* declared, were "plainly and depressingly inferior, both in common sense and in common decency," to their constituents. "These men," Mencken wrote, "in point of fact, are seldom if ever moved by anything rationally describable as public spirit; there is actually no more public spirit among them than among so many burglars or street-walkers. Their purpose, first, last and all the time, is to promote their private advantage, and to that end, and that end alone, they exercise all the vast powers that are in their hands." The case was no better with foreign nations. France, Mencken wrote, was in the hands of "the most corrupt and cynical politicians ever seen in the world. The experience of the Russians and Germans is even more eloquent."

The public officeholder was "indistinguishable from . . . a child-stealer, a well-poisoner or a Sunday-school superintendent." These "apostles of Service" were a "horde growing daily, vastly and irresistibly, in numbers, impudence, power and pay . . . nowhere else in Christendom, save perhaps in France, is government more extravagant, nonsensical, unintelligent and corrupt than here. . . ." Americans would remain the victims rather that the masters of government until they were able to "differentiate clearly between government as a necessary device for maintaining order . . . and government as a device for maintaining the authority and prosperity of predatory rascals and swindlers." That would come with the "Resurrection Morn."

The labor leader could expect no more mercy than the preacher or politician. The first issue of the *American Mercury* contained a portrait of a labor leader by James M. Cain. The typical union official saw himself, Cain wrote, as "a powerful, crafty fellow, a fellow of infinite brawn and terrifying jaw, a fellow of big shoulders and unfoolable shrewdness; in short, a sort of combination of Jack Dempsey and William John Burns," without a trace of impractical idealism.

Mencken's own sardonic reflections were contained in a department headed "Clinical Notes." There he indulged in what he called "nostalgia" for "the photographs of German lieutenants feeding Belgian babies into sausage-machines; for the daily bulls and ukases of the eloquent Woodrow, with their uplifting, lascivious phrases, . . . for

the Liberty Loans drives and the wholesale blackmailing of stenographers, book-keepers, waiters, yokels . . . for the thrilling bulletins
of the Creel Press Bureau . . . for the enchanting dawn of the Ku Klux
Klan, 100% Americanism and the American Legion . . . for the tall talk
about self-determination, saving the world for democracy, breaking
the heart of humanity." Mencken was especially bitter because as a
German-American who opposed the entry of the United States in the
war, he had experienced prejudice both directly and vicariously.

Mary Alden Hopkins, in an aritcle in the *American Mercury* entitled
"The Righteous Perish," described the movement of immigrants onto
New England farms the original owners of which had withered away
from the blighting influence of Puritanism. Unfortunately, in her view,
the newcomers were herded into schools still taught by New England
"schoolmarms," who influenced them toward those unlovely doctrines
of duty and repression "which have decimated the race of New Englanders." In school the defenseless immigrant children were "exposed
to the native passion for spiritual excellence." When they had been
indoctrinated with the ethic of work, thrift, and self-denial instead of
their natural "wants" of "land and sex," they would develop into classic
New Englanders, and then their days, too, would be numbered.

The "Americana" department was a regular feature of the *American Mercury*. It contained without comment newspaper items from
about the country illustrating the general benightedness of Americans
in general. It loved such items as the fact that the mayor of Pomona,
Kansas, had forbidden the pitching of horseshoes within the city limits
on Sunday.

Mencken's sharpest barbs were reserved for the "anthropoid rab-
ble," the mass of citizens of the Republic. His tone was iconoclastic;
Walter Lippmann congratulated him for destroying the "democratic
tradition of the American pioneers" by revealing them as the greedy
and uncultivated individuals that they were.

In one issue of the *American Mercury* Mencken summarized the
conclusions of the experts on the cause of the high rate of divorce or,
in his words, "the rapid decay of Christian monogamy." Some contended that "the movies, with their lascivious suggestions, are to
blame. . . . That the cause lies in the decline of belief in the literal
authority of the Holy Scriptures. . . . That the multiplication of deli-
catessen shops had destroyed home cooking, and so made for unbearable unhappiness at the domestic hearth. . . . That no woman truly
loves her husband until she has had eight children. . . . That the steady

fall in the price of Fords has enormously facilitated adultery. . . . That jazz is responsible. . . . That it is too easy for women to get good jobs. . . . That cheap sex magazines have done it. . . . That God is punishing the Republic for not joining the League of Nations. . . . That the education of women has caused them to take marriage lightly. . . . That the Republic is in decay, like Rome, and that the high divorce rate is but one symptom of it, others being bootlegging, the Ku Klux Klan, cheek-to-cheek dancing, mah jong, birth control and cocaine sniffing."

The sympathies of the *American Mercury,* if it could be said to have *any* sympathies, did not extend to black Americans. Gerald Johnson, editor of a Greensboro, North Carolina, paper and a frequent contributor to the magazine, assailed Northerners in classic fashion for meddling with the business of the South and especially for putting "uppity ideas" into the hands of young blacks, "who would otherwise spend their lives as humble toilers in the cotton-fields. . . ." Instead, given ideas above their station in life, they often enjoyed "a dignified and impressive end, quietly seated in the electric chair." Johnson added: "Yankeedom is lunatic, has been for years, and appears to be growing wilder every hour. Dismiss its attitude toward the South entirely. Conduct the clinic along other lines. Examine its politics, religion, business, sport, manner and customs, social intercourse, speech, deportment in public. The stigmata of insanity are numerous, conspicuous and unmistakable." The North "had written into the supreme law of the land that the Negro is only a sun-burnt white man, and must be treated accordingly. This lunatic provision the South had to accept to humor the maniac, who was then armed to the teeth and in a homicidal frenzy; but of course without the slightest illusion to the hopelessness of attempting to make it true." Prohibition, Johnson concluded, was the South's revenge on the North for giving blacks "ideas above their station in life."

In view of the mood of the times, it was not surprising that when Woodrow Wilson died in February, 1924, his reputation was at its lowest ebb. Hamilton Fish Armstrong was with Colonel Edward M. House and his wife when the news of Wilson's death reached them. The lunch was "dismal and awkward," and House obviously much shaken. Mrs. Wilson barred House from the funeral. William Allen White wrote a trenchant four-line epitaph for Wilson:

> God gave him a great vision.
> The Devil gave him an imperious heart.

The proud heart is still.
The vision lives.

An article in the *American Mercury* written by Charles Willis Thompson compared Wilson to Taft. Taft's blunders had hurt only himself, "whereas Wilson's blunders were disastrous to the United States, to Europe, and to remote communities not yet heard of. Taft's blunders are mainly forgotten. Wilson's will never cease to reverberate until the Resurrection morn."

In a similar spirit, a journalist named Parkhurst Whitney traced the decline of the Republic from the glory days of progressivism. "Then Wilson, then the war, then. . . . The Bolsheviks Are Coming! So Is Christ! Japan Preparing to attack the U.S.! So Is Russia! So Is Everybody! U.S. Getting Drier, Says Anti-Saloon Leaguer! Strikes Ruining Industry! Petting Parties Ruin Younger Generation! Minister Ruins Epworth League! . . . Anglo-Saxon Supremacy Menaced by Inferior Race! . . . Minister Flays Obscene Literature! Minister Held on Statutory Charge! Rotary Speaker Says Business Is Service! Bryan Bans Evolution!"

There was, of course, much more to the *American Mercury* than scoffing. Mencken had an excellent nose for undeveloped or unknown talent. He, after all, had been one of Theodore Dreiser's earliest and most enthusiastic supporters and remained one of that odd man's closest friends, a not inconsiderable achievement in itself. His magazine reviewed the latest plays and books discriminatingly and published scholarly articles on Whitman, John Brown, heredity, and a score of other serious topics.

There seemed much truth in Edmund Wilson's observation in a book called, significantly, *The American Jitters,* "that at the present time the optism of the Americans is flagging, that the morale of our society is weak . . . [and] a dreadful apathy, unsureness and discouragement seem to have fallen upon our life. It is as if people were afraid to go on with what they have been doing or as if they no longer had any real heart for it."

For those expatriates who made their way back to the United States, the final insult, the symbol of a reawakened American Puritanism, was Prohibition. Prohibition was, after all, the revenge that rural America had taken on urban America, that the native-born, the old stock, had taken upon the immigrants, that the yahoos, the philistines, Henry Mencken's booboisie had taken on the bohemians and intellectuals. An older, more simple America, the America of the Populists and William Jennings Bryan, which longed for redemption, had sought it in Prohibition. Mencken wrote: "Reduced to its essentials it is no more than a legal realization of the Methodist's hatred of the civilized man. Yet we are all asked to submit to it on the ground that it is the law, and that the law is remote . . . and impeccable. With all due respect, blah!"

Prohibition not only made the United States the object of ridicule in more sophisticated portions of the globe, but bred crime on an unprecedented scale and dramatized, as perhaps nothing else could have, the division between the two Americas, one (among other things) wet, the other dry. It made drinking almost obligatory for those who considered themselves free and emancipated. It made drinking an act of political and moral significance, defiance of the puritanical and repressive America. Rotgut, bootleg booze, took on something of the character of a sacrament of protest.

Equally demoralizing was the fact that Prohibition was impossible; it simply would not work. Enforcement became, increasingly, a farce eroding respect for the law, poisoning the streams of social intercourse. The state prohibition director of Illinois published figures showing "that 2,289,600 persons applied for, obtained and succeeded in having filled prescriptions for whisky, gin and other alcoholic 'medicines' during 1922." It was estimated that Illinois doctors who were willing to write such prescriptions made approximately $7,000,000 in that year while druggists made a profit of $2,500,000 by filling them.

"Every adult male in New York except teetotalers," the journalist Burton Rascoe wrote, "had cards to a dozen or more restaurants which served liquor at bars or tables during Prohibition." If that was somewhat of an exaggeration, it was certainly not difficult for a middle- or upper-middle-class business or professional male to get a card; one had only to be vouched for by a "member." When the so-called speakeasies had worked out the system of "protection" from the law, they became, in Rascoe's words, "not only safe places for public dining but the best places to eat. Good food was the attraction. . . ." Meals were often served at cost or below because the profit margin on bootleg liquor was so high. "Big Pigs" were fly-by-night drinking places which dispensed often dangerously diluted spirits. In addition, there were innumerable "clubs," some sponsored by employers for their employees, with names like Artists and Writers, Manufacturers and Engineers, Brokers and Bankers, Pen and Pencil, Bowling and Boxing. Even when raids were considered unlikely because of a sympathetic attitude on the part of the police toward the lawbreakers, liquor was often served in teacups, which made it all seem more daring. Sometimes concealed drains were located near bars or tables so that in the event of a raid, the evidence could be poured down them. Waiters were often insolent or thievish since they knew that managers dare not fire them for fear they would revenge themselves by informing the police.

Texas Guinan, a famous tough blonde, ran the El Fay Club, bankrolled by Larry Fay, one of New York's best known racketeers (later assassinated). Guinan offered an elaborate floor show for her customers and greeted them with the cheerful salutation "Hello, sucker!" Rascoe wrote: "The night clubs were ill-ventilated, stuffy, noisy, garish, vulgar, overcrowded, cheap, shoddy, and expensive. . . ." They were, in other words, just the kind of place tourists as well as New Yorkers loved to visit. If a nightclub could keep open a week without being raided, it might make as much as a quarter of a million dollars.

A rival night spot to Texas Guinan's was Gilda Gray's Piccadilly Rendezvous, where the hostess did the hula-hula. It became a favorite night out for Harvard, Princeton, and Yale students who were enthusiastic watchers but poor spenders.

There was, of course, another side of Prohibition. As any reader of these volumes knows well, temperance and/or prohibition had been a burning issue for reformers since the earliest days of the Republic. The great women leaders—Lucretia Mott and Susan B. Anthony, to name only two out of hundreds—started their careers as temperance lecturers. In addition to the women's rights movement, abolition was born out of the fires of the temperance movement. Abraham Lincoln was, for a time, a temperance lecturer. There was hardly a state in the Union that had not tried prohibition (and given it up) by the time of the Volstead Act. For families like the Beechers, temperance was, generation after generation, as much a sacred issue as the emancipation of the slaves or child labor laws. Frances Willard, head of the Woman's Christian Temperance Union, was one of the great women of the nineteenth century. Most Spiritualists, freethinkers, and advocates of free love were also teetotalers. Teetotalism and prohibition were prominent in the Populist movement, and the socialists flirted with it, taking the line that intemperance would disappear with capitalism.

For such individuals to observe the legal and moral shambles created by Prohibition (among other things the spawning of a great empire of organized crime) was extremely demoralizing. The failure hardened their hearts toward those who flouted the law. Instead of wiping out drunkenness and ushering in the new day of redeemed humanity, Prohibition clearly made the problem more acute. More people drank to excess after Prohibition had been instituted than before, and if there was less public drunkenness, there was more illness and death from poisonous liquor. The fact that the most conspicuous defiers of the law were, in the main, the self-appointed guardians of American culture and the untiring critics of the middle-class morality of the booboisie did nothing to endear the intellectual class to its countrymen.

Undoubtedly the most notorious by-product of Prohibition was gangsters, such famous public figures as Larry Fay, Dutch Schultz, and Al Capone. In ceaseless wars to control the distribution of liquor they slaughtered each other by the dozen, providing the newspapers with lurid headlines and presenting to the world one of the least edifying spectacles in the history of the Republic.

One of the names proposed for the era was the Age of Flaming Youth. Certainly the revolt of the youth from their elders was one of the most distinctive features of the period. In *Our America* Waldo Frank wrote that young men and women from the hinterland "pour into New York. . . . They are seekers of a world nearer their heart. Invariably, they are the artists and the writers. For such are the men and women who desire to create a world of their own to live in. . . . The vast horizontal Stream that fertilized a continent strains now to become vertical, in order to fertilize a heaven. . . . One great Hate they brought, in their retracing steps—one Hate from Vermont and from Ohio and from Arizona; the Hate of Puritan ideals. And here were the minds of Europe coming to teach them how to love! . . . What a leaven!"

Edna St. Vincent Millay had come to New York to seek fame as an actress. She lived, Floyd Dell wrote, "in that gay poverty which is traditional of the village." Her poems caught perfectly the spirit of her generation:

> We were very tired, we were very merry—
> We had gone back and forth all night on the ferry.
> It was bare and bright, and smelled like a stable—
> But we looked into a fire, we leaned across a table,
> We lay on a hill-top underneath the moon;
> And the whistles kept blowing, and the dawn came soon.

Her friend Edmund Wilson wrote in praise of her in the 1923 *Vanity Fair,* "because she wrote her first and one of her most extraordinary poems, 'Renascence,' at the age of nineteen; because she is half Irish, half New England, and has beautiful red hair; because she is a witty and charming prose writer . . . but chiefly because her lyric poems—combining austerity with emotional intensity—are among the best ever written by an American."

Josephine Herbst was another of those of whom Frank wrote. Herbst was born in 1897 in Sioux City, Iowa. She was graduated from the University of California in 1919 and then went to New York to make her way as a journalist and writer. Her first job was on Henry Mencken's and George Jean Nathan's *Smart Set,* the precursor of the *American Mercury.* "A sense of fatalism fed the anarchistic heart. . . ." Herbst wrote. "A pessimistic outlook was countered by a buoyant confidence in the precious moment. If we had abandoned the safe lives our parents had fancied so valuable, we seemed to have gained an insight into the creative fissures of the world. The fires and smoke steamed up from volcanoes, old and new . . . [and] the era that gave the Model-T Ford to the farmers opened the world to its literary young on a scale never before ventured and not equalled since. . . . Young women who in an earlier era might be getting the kids ready for school fancied themselves as Aspasias and counted the number of their 'affairs' as their mothers might have added up the household linen. . . .

"The bottom had dropped out of the old world and it was a truism that the 'old men had not only bungled the peace' but had screwed up the works. President Harding had been a stooge, the highest government officials had been crooks, and Coolidge, lulled by the booming stock market, took long naps every afternoon in the White House. The biggest city in the world had a playboy for mayor who had danced the can-can in a homosexual dive in Berlin. Disenchantment was not only a necessity, it was a joy. . . . The lovely and beautiful," Herbst added, "became for our generation a term of contempt; the grounds for complacency held by the parents, despised." The "sword of Picasso's analytical cubism" had ripped apart "a stifling overstuffed world of cushions and divans."

In *A Farewell to Arms* Hemingway's hero declared: "I was always embarrassed by the words sacred, glorious, and sacrifice and the expression in vain. We had heard them, sometimes standing in the rain, almost out of earshot, so that only the shouted words came through, and had read them, on proclamations that were slapped up by bill-posters over other proclamations, now for a long time, and I had seen no glory and the sacrifices were like the stockyards at Chicago if nothing was done with the meat except to bury it."

In New York Herbst's best friend was Genevieve Taggard, an aspiring poet from California who lived in Greenwich Village. Taggard—Jed to her friends—lived with Robert Wolf, who was also a writer and a rather self-consciously free spirit. In the words of Herbst's biographer Elinor Langer, "As a couple they were romantic and modern. They wanted love and work, freedom and commitment, involvement with people and absorption in themselves." It proved, in the atmosphere of the times, as difficult for them as for so many others. Wolf deteriorated until he had, finally, to be placed in a mental institution. "We knew we were in a period of evolution," Herbst wrote, "and called it a transitional time." There was a transient literary journal called *transition* to make the point. *transition* published an article on the "Revolt of the Philistines." The philistine was "a serf." Dominated "by his egotism and his sentimentality, he is incapable of hatred or love. He is not interested in the arts, save in their scandals. Dully he travels through his little world, devoid of any fresh impulse, hypocritically ecstatic at cultural phenomena, and, after his little sensation, goes back to his cocktail swilling and his self-sufficiency. His loves are whoremongering impulses, for he lacks the courage of his emotions."

New York was rather a shock to the girl from Sioux City. "Thousands & hundreds of thousands of people live in N.Y. in the most terrrible acute unbearable *unbelievable* discomfort. . . . And the few live in such insolent magnificence on 5th Avenue and the Drive," Herbst wrote her mother. The more she saw of the masses of poor, "the more I believe in revolution and the class war," she added. Soon Herbst had a married lover, an ambitious young playwright with a small-town upbringing named Maxwell Anderson. Anderson had been married to his high school sweetheart for nine years. Like Herbst, he was a radical of indeterminate breed, he had been fired from two teaching jobs for his pacifism. In the spirit of the times Herbst expected no more of the relationship than a "blinding exquisite moment of companionship," but she became pregnant and suffered considerable disillusionment when Anderson told her she must have an abortion for *his* sake.

Spending the winter of 1925 in a Connecticut village with her new lover, John Herrmann, while both of them pressed on with their writing, Herbst met the fascinating Southern belle Katherine Anne

Porter and her painter companion, Ernest Stock. Josephine Herbst and Katherine Anne Porter fell almost at once into one of those mysterious feminine friendships that begin with the most intimate revelations and often last a lifetime. "The two talkingest women I ever met" Malcolm Cowley called them.

While Katherine Anne Porter looked so much like a high-bred Southern girl that one could easily imagine a white-columned plantation behind her, she was as wild and restless and radical as Herbst. She had married at sixteen, left her husband, been married and divorced again. Indeed, it was difficult to be sure exactly what she had done; she changed stories constantly as though her life were itself a novel and she were experimenting with a variety of plots.

Herbst recalled that "a good deal of social existence eddied around 'corners' where in little nests scooped out of old tenements, in basements, the newly arrived youth had stripped themselves to modest requirements. . . . They put a substantial distance between themselves and their, commonly, small-town Mid-Western, antecedents," she noted. "The real expatriates were the Southerners in New York who came with the bloom of other lands more remote than modern France. . . . The Southerners reminded you of the fluctuations of time. . . ." Allen Tate was a fugitive Fugitive. The Tates made their Bank Street basement apartment a haven of Southern hospitality; Tate stoked the apartment house furnace, and Caroline Gordon, his talented novelist wife, supervised the cleaning. Ford Madox Ford's "imposing white walrus presence, (Herbst's description again) held forth on the top floor, while Katherine Anne Porter lived on the third floor of a ramshackle house on Hudson Street. Toiling up to her friend Porter's gingham-curtained apartment, Herbst could see Dorothy Day's infant daughter in her highchair, eating a bowl of bread and milk, an incongruous sight in a world almost devoid of children.

Greenwich Village, from having been a decade earlier the rather obscure refuge of would-be artists and writers, many from the Midwestern small towns, became a tourist mecca where rubes went to be scandalized. It developed a tourist-scandalizing industry which featured such acts as Eli Siegel, a young poet, reading Vachel Lindsay's "The Congo" and smashing the furniture —slam poetry in effect. One of the most prominent institutions of the Village was Eva Le Gallienne's Fourteenth Street Civic Repertory Theater, which produced excellent plays, favoring Anton Chekhov and Henrik Ibsen. The recently opened

Whitney Museum of Art on Eighth Street, which featured the work of contemporary American artists, was another attraction.

In an astonishingly short time young Edmund Wilson, only a few years out of Princeton, made himself one of the leading arbiters of the literary scene. Wilson had been born in Talcottsville, New York, and graduated from Princeton. Herbst described Edmund "Bunny" Wilson's "plump but graceful figure, the scholar's high brow, the luminous brown eyes, and the face delicately larded with baby-fat that might never wear off. There was about him something of the air of an oriental voluptuary or a choirboy."

Djuna Barnes was a conspicuous literary figure. Burton Rascoe called her "one of the handsomest women I have ever seen and one of the most amusing." He added, "I never saw her wear anything except a tailored black broadcloth suit with a white ruffled collar, a tight-fitting black hat, and high-heeled black shoes." In addition, she carried a shepherd's crook.

Barnes wrote a highly acclaimed and modestly enduring novel entitled *Nightwood*. But her real gift was as a journalist interviewing such figures as Florenz Ziegfeld, D. W. Griffith, and Billy Sunday. When Barnes interviewed Mother Jones, the great old labor leader was in her eighties. To Barnes's question about what impulse had started her on her career as a champion of the oppressed, "She rose abruptly to her feet, she swept her arms wide in a passionate gesture. It was the universal gesture of the powerful person, it proclaimed disgust and contempt.

" 'And you ask me that?' she said. 'That is the question that forty million other fools before you have asked. How does thunder or lightning have its start? How does the world start—it has its birth in struggle. I was born of the struggle and the torment and the pain. A child of the wheel, a brat of the cogs, a woman of the dust. For even iron has its dust, and when a laborer sweats his sweat of blood and weeps his tears of blood a remedy is thrust upon the world. I am the remedy. . . .

" 'I'm living—God has sent me to do this work and before it's done I can't die, and after it's done I can't die too soon. I don't care which place I go; I shall serve. They need more than Gunga Din in hell, anyway.' "

What was valued above everything else was eccentricity. Cornelia Street was crowded with artists, the most exotic of whom was Alice Neel, who painted her Village friends. She was more famous for her lovers than her portraits. Her first, a Cuban, fled to Cuba with their fifteen-month-old daughter. Neel suffered a nervous breakdown and tried to commit suicide. She then married a sailor, a drug addict named Kenneth Doolittle, who, in Jerre Mangione's words, "fascinated some twenty guests by trying to have sex with an artist in their presence." When Neel was pursued by a wealthy Harvard man, Doolittle, in a fury, destroyed sixty of her canvases, ripped up most of her clothes, and set fire to her apartment. Leaving the sailor and the Harvard man, Neel took up with a Puerto Rican singer in Spanish Harlem and had her first son by him.

One of Neel's favorite subjects was Joe Gould, another Harvard graduate—Harvard turned out a far higher proportion of eccentric radicals than its Ivy League sisters—who was busy writing a "universal history" on odd scraps of paper. One of Gould's diversions was challenging male guests at Village parties to compare the lengths of their penises with his. He carried a tape measure to verify respective sizes and claimed to have never been beaten. Alice Neel painted his portrait in the nude with multiple penises in recognition of his odd obsession.

Another familiar figure in the Village was Otis Ferguson, who wrote book reviews for the *New Republic*. His apartment was unfurnished and unheated. To keep warm, he slept in a tent with a coal stove in front of it. Maxwell Bodenheim was perhaps the Village's most enthusiastic advocate, in his novels and poems, of free love, which was by now old hat in the Village, if not in the middle ranges of America. Bodenheim's preoccupation with sex attracted nubile young women who wished to be initiated into its more arcane mysteries. Bodenheim was, as they say, "into bondage," and he paraded one of his mistresses, wearing a skintight tiger-skin dress, up and down lower Fifth Avenue on a leash.

There was something decidedly incestuous about the New York literary scene. Friends married each other's ex-wives and slept with their present ones. Malcolm Cowley married Orrick Johns's ex-wife, Peggy. Cowley's friend Kenneth Burke divorced his first wife and married her sister, Libby. The sisters lived within a short distance of each other in Andover, New Jersey, in "an atmosphere of accomplishment and conviviality," according to Jerre Mangione, who was a kind of permanent houseguest.

As the elder statesman of American letters Theodore Dreiser began a series of literary Thursdays which he presided over in "a soiled smock." It was there that Claude Bowers first met Elinor Wylie, poet and biographer of Shelley. She had begun to write poetry after an unhappy marriage broke up. Married subsequently to William Rose Benét, she appeared, in Bowers's words, "Beautiful, very girlish, a little wild in her exuberance. . . ." She stood in the middle of the living room, "displaying a new gown with the delight of a child, fairly glowing in response to the compliments her dress and manner invited." Other prominent members of the Dreiser circle were the Van Dorens, Carl and Mark; Joseph Wood Krutch, drama critic of the *Nation* and celebrator of nature's delights; Ernest Boyd, the novelist; and, a particular luminary by virtue of his influence as a publisher, Horace Liveright. Liquor of dubious quality was usually abundant, as were clusters of handsome young women, so much a part of New York bohemia. Max Reinhardt, the Berlin producer, appeared on his frequent visits to the city. Frank Walsh, reformer of Kansas City with George Creel and chairman of the Commission on Industrial Relations, was a member of the circle, conspicuous by his handsome ancient head and booming laugh. Deems Taylor joined forces with Edna St. Vincent Millay to write and produce *The King's Henchman.* Jakob Wassermann, German author of the internationally successful novel *The World's Illusion,* appeared, looking for the world like a Gypsy and surrounded by a bevy of admiring women. One of Dreiser's first Thursday evenings featured Abraham Brill, the principal interpreter of Freud in America. When Dreiser invited the visiting British critic and author Llewelyn Powys to meet some of his literary friends, including Mencken and Carl Van Vechten, F. Scott Fitzgerald was also invited, although Dreiser had not met him. According to Burton Rascoe, who was one of the guests, the party was an extremely stiff and awkward one. Suddenly Fitzgerald appeared, deep in his cups and bearing a precious gift of French champagne for his host, whom he had difficulty picking out among the guests.

As befitted a hedonistic era, the twenties was, as much as anything, the age of parties. Although New York was the international capital of parties, they also sprouted forth in places as remote and unlikely as Tulsa, Oklahoma, and Reno, Nevada, not, of course, to mention Hollywood. There was a considerable circulating "literature" on parties. The emphasis was not, as it had been earlier, on lavishness and expense as much as on originality and imagination, on "outrageousness." Parties of the rich, like the culminating party in *The Great Gatsby,* were as lavish and ostentatious as ever. Others were what might be called floating parties. Carl Van Vechten was famous for his New York parties. In London he and his wife took several floors of the Savoy Hotel and held a kind of open house for several days and nights for members of the English literary scene and Americans in London.

In February, 1926, Earl Carroll gave for a Texas millionaire who had backed his musicals what was the most famous party of the era at his theater. Rascoe, who was present, noted that the stately show girls of Carroll's *Vanities* "mingled with the guests and made themselves available for dances." Among the more notorious guests was Harry K. Thaw, who had been convicted of murdering the architect Stanford White over his attentions to Thaw's chorus girl wife, Evelyn Nesbit. The party featured vaudeville skits and a Charleston contest between scantily clad chorines. The main event was to be a champagne bath by a nude chorus girl with the guests invited to step up to the stage and drink champagne out of her tub. Unfortunately the bather fainted; whether because of excitement or chill was never determined. That ended the party, but a reporter wrote up the whole sensational story. Witnesses appeared to testify that Carroll had served his guests liquor and he was tried and sentenced to a year in the Federal penitentiary at Atlanta.

Another famous party giver was Robert Winthrop Chandler, scion of an old New York family who claimed descent from John Winthrop (you could hardly get much older than that). Chandler, who was an able painter, prevailed on Lina Cavalieri, the Metropolitan Opera star, to marry him by making a prenuptial settlement of $150,000. That was the last he saw of his bride or his money. He collected assorted noblemen, anarchists, revolutionists, royalists, Cubists, Expressionists, Dadaists, and academics. His studio was a four-story house on East Nineteenth Street. A guest who entered the front door found himself or herself surrounded by murals of exotic animals painted by Chandler. This room served as the dance floor, where a jazz orchestra provided the music and Japanese servants passed about a mildly alcoholic punch. The second floor was filled with couches, upholstered chairs, divans, and tables, rather in the manner of a restaurant. Here Chandler, dressed in exotic robes and sitting in a Renaissance chair on a dais, greeted guests, calling out, "Papa! Papa!" at each new arrival. There was serious booze in abundance. Chandler's bedroom, also on the second floor, featured a huge bed and a mirrored ceiling for sexual romps. He had a kind of retinue of White Russian exiles, some of whom slept on the third floor when they had no other habitat and lent an exotic tone to his social functions. The top floor was a large, bare, skylighted room which served as Chandler's studio. Not infrequently he abandoned his guests in the later hours of the night or early morning and ascended to his studio to paint. "The parties were conglomerates," Burton Rascoe wrote, "with guests in all sorts of costumes, from full evening dress to sweaters and corduroy trousers, from Russian smocks and baggy pantaloons to gypsy garb; one overheard conversations in French, Russian, Italian, Danish, Spanish, and German." A Japanese servant, trained in jujitsu, evicted quarrelsome or unruly guests. Charming young Miguel Covarrubias, the artist and illustrator, was a frequent guest along with the publisher Konrad Bercovici and Tommy Smith, Horace Liveright's editor. Helena Rubinstein, the artist John Sloan, and the sculptor Jo Davidson were also habitués along with "singers, composers, or writers." Rascoe attended a party at Chandler's for the Prince of Wales. When Rascoe left at five in the morning, he left behind not only the prince but the prince of the American stage, John Barrymore, and the English painter Augustus John.

Condé Nast, the publisher, gave small parties for 300 or 400 and large ones for 1,000 or more. Socialite Lee Meader entertained in his penthouse in the West Thirties with professional entertainment. Everyone was required to wear evening clothes, champagne was served, and the entertainment varied from fights between professional boxers to ballets and one-act plays, followed by dancing.

Carl Van Vechten was a dance critic married to a ballerina, Fania Marinoff. They were host and hostess to Bill "Bojangles" Robinson, the famous tap dancer; Bessie Smith, the blues singer; Salvador Dali; and Somerset Maugham, among hundreds of other celebrities, black and white. In Langston Hughes's words, guests appeared "from Hollywood, Broadway, London, Paris or Harlem." He remembered one party "when Chief Long Lance of the cinema did an Indian war dance, while Adelaide Hall of *Blackbirds* played the drums, and an international assemblage crowded around to cheer."

The Harlem "drag balls" were a favorite for blacks and whites alike. Men paid as high as $500, the black singer, Taylor Gordon, reported, for dresses to wear to the balls.

The Edmund Wilsons gave a party at which "about midnight," Wilson reported proudly to Allen Tate, "the guests began very slowly breaking phonograph records over each other's heads. It was like a slowed-up moving picture." Such events were treasured as striking instances of spontaneous, uninhibited, or "surreal" behavior, above all totally unbourgeois.

Nude bathing parties were almost a required exercise for the emancipated. Edmund Wilson, who was apparently inclined to nudity, learned from Henry Mencken in the spring of 1922 that Scott Fitzgerald and his wife, Zelda, "were reveling nude in the orgies of Westport . . . while Van Wyck Brooks might at the same time have been grinding out his sober plaint against the sterile sobriety of the country."

Tess Slesinger, a beautiful and talented young woman whose first novel, *The Unpossessed,* was a best-seller, gave a party for William Saroyan, whose *Daring Young Man on the Flying Trapeze* had brought him instant literary fame. Jerre Mangione was greeted by his hostess: "Come right in, sir. Will you have me? Or would you prefer a martini?"

Burton Rascoe was at a party for Bertrand Russell given by Horace Liveright and presided over by Tommy Smith as Liveright's majordomo. There was a four-piece black jazz combo, along with Mayor Jimmy Walker, Dreiser, Edna Ferber, Max Bodenheim, Sinclair Lewis, and vivid young Lillian Hellman. Tallulah Bankhead was a prominent figure at many literary parties as well as at Hollywood "orgies," at one of which, Anita Loos reported, she took off all her clothes and stretched out beside a swimming pool with a lily over her pubic region.

It was a generation as migratory as birds. If most expatriate Americans had returned to the United States by the mid-twenties, they would be off again at the drop of a hat, flying here and there—Hemingway and his circle, of which Josephine Herbst and her husband, John Herrmann, became a part, to Key West, Florida; others to San Francisco or Carmel, or to Mexico—above all, to Mexico. To Cuba, Haiti, Spain, Moscow, Paris, Berlin, London, Bucks County, or rural Connecticut or Vermont. There were way stations and checkpoints where friends brushed past each other in their various hegiras. In Paris Burton Rascoe encountered the circle of Nancy Cunard, Hadley and Ernest Hemingway, E. E. Cummings, the great enemy of capitals and punctuation, and Ford Madox Ford.

Sex was, of course, a crucial issue, and here the generation gap was most evident. Jerre Mangione, a young Sicilian-American who yearned for a literary career, recalled a friend, Tom Coolahan, who boasted that his therapist had prescribed sexual intercourse twice daily for Coolahan and his friend, Mary. Coolahan kept by his bed a chart on which he recorded their orgasms and displayed it proudly for his friends as evidence of his potency. Hutchins Hapgood, one of the "founding fathers" of the original Village and a pioneer in sexual liberation who had written a book on the relationship between love and revolution, was dismayed by the attitude of the younger generation toward sex. "Modern youth are neither so emphatic about the simplicities of sex, nor so spiritual in its further meaning" as he and his generation had been, he noted. It seemed to him that this was because "the sexual act, to them, is more natural, so they are not obsessed as the Victorian was." He wrote: "In the person in whom Victorianism persists still exist the mystic realities; so that to us sex still remains a mystic symbol. A girl *qua* girl, was a girl to be sure; but much more than a girl." Hapgood had tried to "make my sexuality casual," but he had not succeeded. Sex could never be mechanics, the exploration of the perfect orgasm—"his or her ultimate possibilities of sensation." It was, above all, a "spiritual emotion." Hapgood's daughters and their friends "lived lives at school and at home," he wrote, "which were full of gin and irregular sex-experience, often involving abortions and relations with men—which in my time could not exist without moral and physical deterioration if not destruction."

In the immediate aftermath of the war, Scott Fitzgerald noted, "petting in its more audacious manifestations was confined to the wealthier classes—among other young people the old standard prevailed . . . and a kiss meant that a proposal was expected." But soon the "veil" fell. "A whole race going hedonistic, deciding on pleasure. The precious intimacies of the younger generation would have come about with or without prohibition—they were implicit in the attempt to adapt English customs to American conditions." He wrote of one of his characters: "Like so many girls of that day Dolly was slackly and indiscreetly wild."

Fitzgerald noted: "The word jazz in its progress toward respectability has meant first sex, then dancing, then music. It is associated with a state of nervous stimulation, not unlike that of big cities behind the lines of a war. . . . By 1926 the universal preoccupation with sex had become a nuisance (I remember a perfectly mated, contented young mother asking my wife's advice about 'having an affair right away,' though she had no one especially in mind, 'because don't you think it's sort of undignified when you get much over thirty?')"

Floyd Dell, early friend and supporter of Sherwood Anderson's and of whom much had been expected, was caught in a kind of time-warp between the early promise of the new consciousness and the desperate realities of the postwar world. Like Hapgood, he deplored the debasing of sex and lamented the days of the "real" Village. "The war," he wrote poignantly, "has scattered and divided us; friend was set against old friend; and even if that had not been unhappily true, the war would inevitably have brought to an end that glorious intellectual playtime in which art and ideas, free-expression and the passion of propaganda, were for one moment happily mated."

In a short story entitled "A Piece of Slag," Dell wrote of a Greenwich Village couple, Kitty and Paul, who decide to defy convention by getting married but, once married, dare not go so far as to suggest that their marriage should be a monogamous one. They pledge each other not to be possessive. Just because they are married, "we needn't become like everybody else. We can keep our freedom," Paul insists. The narrator, Terence, who is clearly Dell himself, thinks, "[T]oo bad: these lovely young people—surely they aren't going to inflict upon each other the horrid cruelty of trying to live up to that ideal!" But Paul persists. "We all know," he says, "that marriage has no supernatural magic to keep people from being interested, emotionally and physically, in others." Terence tries to comfort an unhappy Kitty, who is prepared to have an unwanted affair simply to prove to Paul that she is as emancipated as he is and that she loves him. Such notions made Dell feel old and reactionary. "Gradually," he wrote, "one discovered in oneself certain bourgeois traits—the desire for, say, a house in the country, and children, and settled life—for one becomes tired even of freedom! Then let the bourgeoisie take Greenwich Village, by all means! We would move to the country and become respectable!" But even that turned out to present difficulties. There was a painful absence of nobility. "There's nothing to be noble for," Dell wrote. "We aren't fooling ourselves about Art or Revolution or Truth. We know we're out to have a good time. . . . It's a mistake to suppose one can't be happy in a meaningless world. Because at the end of all one's thinking is the question, 'Well, what of it?' And there isn't any answer, and there's nothing to do but live and enjoy life. . . . The Village—our Village—was dead and gone." But the Village refused to die. To claim it, there were other young people, "as gay and eager. . . . For them the world would never suddenly go blank of meaning. They were accustomed to its not having any meaning. I saw ourselves in retrospect," Dell added, "as touched with a miraculous naïveté, a Late Victorian credulousness, a faith, happy and absurd, in the goodness of this chaotic universe. These young people know better."

There was too much sex for even such a hardened old cynic as H. L. Mencken. "Today," he (or George Jean Nathan) wrote, "the newsstands are piled mountain high with magazines devoted frankly and exclusively to sex. Hundreds of writers make their livings producing this garbage; its merchandising has become one of the largest of American industries." Respectable magazines carried articles that would have been banned from the *Police Gazette* twenty years earlier. The characters in Dreiser's novels, Mencken complained, "imitate the colossal adulteries of a guinea pig, a movie star or a Wall Street broker," or (Mencken might have added, since he was the keeper of Dreiser's diary of his sexual adventures) Dreiser himself. Mencken was driven to appeal to writers for a "genuinely realist novel about a happy marriage." Sinclair Lewis, he decided, would be the best prospect. He should write a novel about a happy marriage "as aloof . . . as 'Main Street' and as relentlessly realistic as 'Babbitt.' "

Not surprisingly, the psychic costs of living in the twenties were high. Edmund Wilson wrote to his friend John Peale Bishop, "I'm sorry you're feeling exhausted—but come! Somebody's got to survive and write." Almost every literary figure had periods of deep depression and "nervous breakdowns." Scott Fitzgerald had several, complicated by alcoholism. His wife, Zelda, had a number of breakdowns that culminated in her being placed in a sanatorium. Wilson himself entered a sanatorium in 1929 for several months. The poet Louise Bogan had to have special treatment for depression. Edna St. Vincent Millay, Josephine Herbst, and John Herrmann suffered acutely from depression. The poet Hart Crane seemed always on the verge of suicide until after several unsuccessful attempts, he finally succeeded by jumping off a ship while returning from an alcoholic sojourn in Mexico with Peggy Cowley. Nervous breakdowns and suicides were, like nudity, a symptom of the age.

Few suicidal writers and artists went as far as the novelist Vardis Fisher, who proposed forming an organization like Alcoholics Anonymous, "whose membership would proselytize one another on the philosophical advantages of suicide and also promote and publicize painless and speedy methods of taking one's own life." He told Jerre Mangione, "I'll organize the West. You take care of the East. We'll strike a blow for true liberty."

One of the most sensational suicides was that of Ralph Barton, "a gentle, diffident, smallish man," in Burton Rascoe's words, who dressed very formally in pin-striped trousers and a navy blue jacket. He was a gifted caricaturist and lexicographer. Before his suicide he wrote a long and moving letter to the "public" explaining why he found life unsupportable. Hans Stengel, a well-known writer and critic who had been interned during the war as an enemy alien, committed suicide over the loss of the woman he loved. He had a large party in his Greenwich Village apartment and hanged himself in a closet while the party was in progress.

By 1927, Fitzgerald wrote, "contemporaries of mine had begun to disappear into the dark maw of violence. A classmate killed his wife and himself on Long Island, another tumbled 'accidentally' from a skyscraper in Philadelphia, another purposely from a skyscraper in New York. One was killed in a speakeasy in Chicago; another was beaten to death in a speakeasy in New York and crawled home to the Princeton Club to die; still another had his skull crushed by a maniac's axe in an insane asylum where he was confined. These are not catastrophes that I went out of my way to look for—these were my friends. . . ."

The variety of names for the twenties suggests the multiformity of the decade: the Lost Generation (Gertrude Stein's characterization to Hemingway, who placed it at the beginning of *The Sun Also Rises*), the Jazz Age, the Speakeasy Era, the Age of Flaming Youth, among them. It was, paradoxically, an era of terrible disillusionment on the part of the most idealistic young Americans and at the same time the period of our history when youth seized the center of the stage and insisted on its right to speak and act for the larger society of which it was a small but articulate and rebellious part. It was the age in which a literary and intellectual culture defined itself in highly dramatic fashion in opposition to the great mass of ordinary Americans, the booboisie that Henry Mencken delighted in pillorying. It was two Americas, as John Dos Passos expressed it in *The Big Money,* the third volume of his trilogy *U.S.A.* One was literate, knowledgeable, and, above all, emancipated. The other was puritanical (a canard, incidentally, on the original Puritans, who were not notably puritanical), repressed, constipated, fundamentally Protestant, uninformed about Freud, Marx, and other modern thinkers, hostile toward art in all but its most traditional manifestations, obsessed by numerous prejudices, notably racial. It was rural and small-town America, filled with Babbitts and Elmer Gantrys. The phenomenon was a new one in America. Upper-class Americans from the days of James Fenimore Cooper (who expressed his distaste for democracy in a book by that name) had deplored the crudity and vulgarity of the "people" and feared and distrusted the "lower orders," or the "dangerous classes," essentially working-class men and women, and fled, when they could, to Europe. But the emergence of a literary-intellectual class that expressed contempt and derision for a large and essentially middle-class segment of American society was without precedent. Mockery and ridicule are far harder to endure than simple hostility. The other America, the one denominated "bourgeois," was not necessarily capitalist; it was simply culturally benighted.

We have spoken earlier of the shift from the preacherly role of American intellectuals, exemplified by Emerson, the Beechers—Harriet, Catharine, and Henry, most conspicuously—Henry George, William James, Charles Sanders Peirce, Henry Demarest Lloyd, and Washington Gladden, to name a few, to the priestly functions, marked by the assumption that the mass of Americans were incapable of understanding the more recondite sciences, natural and social. These had been delivered into the keeping of the new order of intellectuals, a kind of priesthood, whose function was not to instruct, guide, and inspire their countrymen and women but to preside over and augment the mysteries, the new "sciences." To "popularize" came to mean to cheapen or degrade, to diminish. The "other" America was bourgeois; *épater les bourgeois,* or to prick the middle class, became the favorite sport of the new intellectual class. That was all very well; the bourgeoisie, or the middle class was often an appropriate and irresistible target for well-aimed barbs. But there was a notable lack of compassion or simple regard for human dignity in the sticking and pricking which was certainly not good for the character of the prickers and not surprisingly bitterly resented by the prickees.

For Burton Rascoe and many other men and women of his generation T. S. Eliot's *The Waste Land* and George Gershwin's *Rhapsody in Blue* were the most representative works of the twenties. The major cultural event of the winter of 1924 was the performance of Gershwin's revolutionary piece played by the composer himself on the piano with Paul Whiteman's band in Carnegie Hall. Rascoe was in the top balcony to hear "that tremendously thrilling event." Like *The Waste Land,* "it mixed classico-heroic themes with barrelhouse wails of sorrow with a brooding overtone of lost loveliness."

The first part of *The Waste Land,* "The Burial of the Dead," begins:

> April is the cruelest month, breeding
> Lilacs out of the dead land, mixing
> Memory and desire, stirring
> Dull roots with spring rain.

What are the roots that clutch, what branches grow
Out of this stony rubbish? Son of man,
You cannot say, or guess, for you know only
A heap of broken images, where the sun beats,
And the dead tree gives no shelter, the cricket no
relief,
And the dry stone no sound of water. Only
There is shadow under this red rock. . . .

It ends:

> Datta, Dayadhvam. Damyata
> Shantih shantih shantih

"Give, sympathize, control . . ." and then the last words of the Upanishads, the equivalent of "The Peace which passeth understanding."

# Europe

In Europe, a part of the world many Americans did their best to ignore, things went, generally speaking, from bad to worse. In virtually every country, politics degenerated into responses to the Soviet Union. Liberals and radicals looked to Moscow for inspiration and, more specifically, policy directives; the actions of royalists, capitalists, and assorted parties of the right were largely dictated by the menace of bolshevism.

When Jane Addams visited Europe at the end of the war, she was struck by the difference in atmosphere between the present and her visit in 1885, almost thirty-five years earlier. Nationalism had then, too, been very much in evidence, but it had been a nationalism marked, in her recollection, "by a burning humanitarianism." The unification of Germany under Bismarck and of Italy under the spirit of Mazzini were felt to anticipate larger unities, to anticipate the emergence of a genuine European community. It had been "generous and inclusive, stressing likenesses"; now it appeared greedy, dogmatic, and ruthless, seeking to punish the losers mercilessly, "insisting upon historical prerogatives quite independent of the popular will."

Addams was especially troubled by the vindictiveness of Europeans toward the Germans. In Rotterdam she encountered hundreds of German families from all over the world, driven from their homes merely because "they belonged to the outlaw nation. . . . They told of prohibition of language, of the forced sale of real estate, of the confiscation of business, of the expulsion from university faculties and the alienation of old friends." Their stories seemed of another age; they summoned up images of the Inquisition, of the expulsion of the Jews from Spain, of the massacre and banishing of the Huguenots from France. It was impossible for Jane Addams (and, of course, many others) to reconcile the spirit that she observed in a postwar Europe that was busily dividing up the spoils of war with her dreams of a true world community, her visions of universal brotherhood and peace. But she would not, could not cease to hope. If a hypothetical council were appointed to examine the causes of the war, she wrote, it might well discover that just as the greatest religious war had come at the "very moment when men were deciding that they no longer cared intensely for the theological creeds for which they had been fighting, so this devastating war [the World War] may have come at a similar moment in regard to national dogmas."

Fascists and Communists were rioting in Italy, pushing impotent moderate governments to the wall. Despite diplomatic successes in Paris, by means of which Eleutherios Venizelos had doubled the size of Greece, a wave of royalist sentiment brought King Constantine, brother-in-law of the kaiser, to power in 1920. "This political turnabout," Hamilton Fish Armstrong wrote, "was only one in the long series of Greek vacillations between love and hatred of the monarchy, devotion to and repudiation of the republic; always the split in personality has been and is there, deep and seemingly uncurable." In addition, Greece was involved in a hopeless war with Turkey in Asia Minor. In Turkey Mustafa Kemal and the new generation of Turkish nationalists were preparing to take over such remnants of the old Ottoman Empire as were not already in their control. In Hungary Count Stephen Bethlen, the prime minister, was, in Armstrong's words, "endeavoring to restrain the partisans of the Hapsburgs, curb the 'Awakening Magyars,' limit anti-Semitism and prevent these and other national excesses from embroiling the country with its neighbors."

In Yugoslavia King Alexander, a personal friend of Armstrong's, was trying to fight off the Italian Fascists in Fiume and Albania. The nation seemed to have a reasonable prospect of surviving the tension between the Croats and Serbs. The so-called Little Entente between Czechoslovakia and Rumania gave both those countries an important measure of security by holding Hungary's expansionist tendencies in check. Calls for an anschluss between Germany and Austria had been suppressed.

Only in Bulgaria did the Communists seem a serious threat. There Alexander Stamboliski, the head of the Peasant Party—also called the Agrarian Party—became premier. He broke up the great estates, levied a heavy income tax, distributed land to the peasants, shut down the opposition press, and closed the university. After four years of repressive rule he was overthrown by an alliance of Macedonians and army officers and shot. In a five-year period five of his Cabinet members were shot—"in bed, in prison, in the street or under convoy"— as were twenty-eight deputies. The number of individuals killed by the police or terrorist bands was never calculated. One of the most unsettling elements was the Internal Macedonian Revolutionary Organization, rival factions of which were constantly engaged in political assassinations. One Macedonian leader admitted to Hamilton Fish Armstrong that his faction "had assassinated Protoguerov [a rival for control of the IMRO], who in turn had helped assassinate Todor Alexandrov, who in turn had been implicated in the murder of Stambuliski. Murder was a Macedonian speciality. . . ." An IMRO leader asked plaintively of Armstrong: "Who can one trust now? One understands assassination, but not of one's colleagues."

Armstrong was especially impressed by Bishop Nicholai of the Orthodox see of Ochrida in Serbian Macedonia. "Nations die," he told Armstrong, "from either too much prosperity or too much poverty." If America did not "add introspection and self-examination to giving and acting, prosperity can be her undoing. With prosperity, however, and with a soul to animate it, she can do everything." Africa, the bishop declared, represented "emotion, heart; Asia, thought, mind; Europe, will, action. Only America could synthesize the three." Instead, the bishop told Armstrong, the United States was looking for some way to evade its responsibilities in the world. It was looking backward to an age of innocence and isolation. He warned of the powers of communism. There was "only one organized system, living and working by day and night for its ends. . . . At the moment the chief propaganda argument of the Communists is that they are the only peacemakers, the only idealists, the only real workers, the only ones who are willing to go to all lengths in order not to see the world drift back to its old standards and habits." The League of Nations was powerless. There should be formed a "World Construction Committee," in which the

United States would play a central role. This committee should "send out (as America has herself sent out, though on an inadequate scale in view of the immense undertaking) engineers, doctors, financiers and builders to bring water to lands where no water is, to bring health to lands ravaged by disease, to build up where all has been torn down, or where nothing worth building has ever been built. There is hardly a part of the world but has been exploited and crippled and is now reaching a stage of desperation and chronic dissatisfaction—Poland, Albania, Calabria, Armenia, China, Russia, Austria, Persia, Ireland, Senegal, Palestine, and the Congo, to mention just the first that come to mind." The bishop called for the "best thought of the world" to try to cure "these festering sore spots." He pointed to the contributions of Americans in fighting hunger and disease during and immediately following the war as a model of intelligent and disinterested action. The United States must, by such measures, assume the moral leadership of the world.

Austria was one of the trouble spots of Europe. It wanted and needed, from an economic point of view, a union of some kind with Germany, but France was obdurate. In Armstrong's words, "The war had left Austria in even more desperate straits than Hungary. By the time the League of Nations sent its rescue team to Vienna, late in 1922, the country was in collapse, helpless, . . . doubtful about even the wish to survive. Bereft of its empire, it lay like an exhausted tadpole in a dried-up marsh: Vienna an enormous hungry head, the rest a straggling tail of liabilities." The Austrian foreign minister, Alfred Grünberger, declared: "The first objective was simply to live. We have lived. The second was to see how Austria could accommodate herself to the peace treaties, not simply in order to continue living but to do so on a basis beneficial to both ourselves and our neighbors. We are now trying to find that basis."

Vienna was a kind of socialist dream come true. Its working-class housing—the Karl Marx apartments—was a model of advanced planning. With its clean modern lines and comfortable interiors, it offered a dazzling prospect of the future. There was free public education, and health and old-age benefits were the most liberal in the world. Many Europeans of a conservative bent considered "Red Vienna" indistinguishable from Soviet Russia, although the city gave more objective observers an intimation of what non-Marxist socialism might achieve (perhaps that was why it was considered a particular menace). The socialists, convinced that although they held power in Vienna, they could never gain power in the "tail" of Austria, the conservative rural areas and small towns, began playing the anschluss game, hoping to join with the German trade unionists to consolidate their power. The League of Nations, having helped Austria recover from the war, was reluctant to turn it loose on its own. Some of the League's principal officers feared the power of the socialists. The League's financial controller was said to have declared: "Until the socialist fortress of Vienna is subdued, Austria's finances will not be secure."

Hungary was Austria's enemy; the Hungarians feared contamination from Austria's socialist trade unions. Czechoslovakia was opposed to anschluss because that would leave it even more vulnerable to Germany.

In October, 1922, in the midst of these manifold problems, the Italian Fascisti, led by the ex-journalist and socialist Benito Mussolini, began seizing control of Italian cities. Two days later King Victor Emmanuel invited Mussolini to come to Rome to form a new ministry. Mussolini "insisted," according to a *New York Times* report, "on the highly patriotic aims of the Fascisti party, who, he declared, had no intention of overthrowing the institutions of Italy or the monarchal regime, only wishing to cleanse Italian public life and infuse a new spirit. . . . The King was much moved. . . . The announcement that Mussolini had been officially entrusted with the formation of a Cabinet immediately caused all agitation to subside." The next day the Fascisti entered Rome in a scene of wild excitement. Mussolini, the *Times* reported, was greeted with "delirious enthusiasm." He promptly gave a hint of things to come by bombarding and seizing the Greek island of Corfu. The Greeks appealed in vain to the League of Nations. The occupation of Corfu by the Italians was followed by the seizure of two more Greek islands, Paxos and Antipaxos.

In the words of Hamilton Fish Armstrong, "Mussolini dismissed recalcitrant officials, ousted legally-minded judges, suppressed opposition papers and expelled independent-minded professors from the universities." In June a Socialist deputy in Parliament, Giacomo Matteotti, was assassinated on the orders of Fascist officials whose defalcations he had discovered. The non-Fascist deputies withdrew from Parliament and became known as the Aventine Opposition, a reference to the Roman plebs who had withdrawn to the Aventine Hill 492 A.D. to call attention to the abuses of the ruling party.

Mussolini, after a period of panic, resorted once more to acts of violence to silence his adversaries. The royal coat of arms was replaced on public buildings by the Fascist bundle of rods and ax. That act marked the end of constitutional government in Italy for years to come and made Mussolini the first successful postwar dictator. When Armstrong visited Count Carlo Sforza, heir of one of the great families of Italy, the count talked freely "off the record." He told Armstrong: "You are being told to count the beggars in the street and see how much fewer there are. You are being told that garbage is removed promptly instead of being left in the cellars. But what is the use of having garbage removed if our souls die? Mussolini's 'order' is the 'order' the Prussian military gave Germany before the war. I didn't like it in 1914, and neither did the Italian people. They don't like it now, and neither do I." The "old political class"was impotent, according to Sforza, and "our political character is debased." Out of 100 friends of Sforza's own class, "seventy-five of them if I meet them individually will wring my hand, whisper all they think of the regime. But will they join in a movement to put their convictions at work? Each can find 300,000 reasons not to go into open opposition—Mussolini's 300,000 armed ruffians."

Sforza's hopes rested with the Pope and the army. Of the latter he said, "Do you suppose it doesn't feel a professional jealousy when it sees these bands of boys and adventurers strutting around?" Other anti-Mussolini strongpoints were the Masons and the Socialists. But Sforza ended his conversation with Armstrong by emphasizing Mussolini's strength. The forces opposed to him were scattered and lacking in leadership. The outcome was highly uncertain; the odds clearly favored Mussolini.

The famous Italian professor of history at the University of Florence Gaetano Salvemini was arrested for refusing to give the Fascist salute at the start of his classes. When he was released, he left for London; some of his less fortunate colleagues were murdered by Fascist toughs.

The United States' reaction to Mussolini's seizure of power was varied. To those Americans of an older generation who had been strong nationalists of the Herbert Croly stripe and who believed in government social and economic planning, Mussolini appeared a "progressive" politician. Sam McClure, the editor of *McClure's Magazine,* the virtual inventor of the turn-of-the-century exposé journalism, was captivated by the promise of the Italian dictator's "corporate state." Ida Tarbell went to report on the Italian leader, although the State Department considered her a "pretty red radical" who could not be trusted to make a fair report. But Tarbell shared her old editor's enthusiasm. It must be said that there was a strong element of anti-Italian prejudice in many such favorable assessments of the dictator. Italians were considered by most upper-class Americans a violent, passionate, largely ungovernable people with little notion of or capacity for democratic government. Anyone who could impose order on that turbulent nation must, it was thought, be something of a genius. This attitude was reflected in an editorial in the *Washington Post*. "Mussolini's dictatorship evidently appeals to the Italian people," the *Post* noted. They needed a leader, and having found him, they gladly conferred power upon him. If he continued his policy of "order, discipline and work," while "avoiding imperialistic adventures, Italy doubtless will find full and profitable employment within its proper field [presumably that of a third-rate, rather comic opera-like power]." The editor of *Nation's Business* acclaimed Mussolini "as a fine type of business executive. He cuts through. No idle words. Not too few, not too many, just enough. . . . Not fine-spoken theories; not plans . . . things done! And this is your successful American executive."

Lincoln Steffens, loyal as he remained to causes of the left, found the "Scarface Mussolini" appealing for many of the same reasons that had attracted him to the big-city bosses. The journalist Anne O'Hare McCormick wrote: "A nation [the United States] that thrilled to the Vigilantes and the Rough Riders rises to Mussolini and his Black Shirt army."

Charles Beard, whose *An Economic Interpretation of the Constitution,* a work that debunked the Founding Fathers by suggesting that they were less interested in exalted principles of government than in drafting a document to protect their property interests, made him the unofficial historian of the left, was equally enamored of Mussolini. "Beyond question, an amazing experiment is being made here," he reported from Italy in 1929 for the *New Republic,* "an experiment in reconciling individualism and socialism, politics and technology. It would be a mistake to allow feelings aroused by contemplating the harsh deeds and extravagant assertions that have [accompanied] the Fascist process (as all other immense historical changes) to obscure the potentialities and the lessons of the adventure—no, not adventure, but destiny ridden without any saddle and bridle. . . ."

Sinclair Lewis had no illusions about the dictator. To Lewis he was "a flabby hard-jawed, mad-eyed fanatic." And both Scott Fitzgerald and Ernest Hemingway were among the Italian dictator's earliest and most vigorous critics (poets seemed more apt to like him than novelists, although T. S. Eliot would have none of him). Hemingway called him the "biggest bluff in Europe." His photographs revealed the weakness of his mouth. "Study his gift for developing small ideas into great words," Hemingway advised. Herbert Croly extolled his "spiritual" qualities. *Fortune* magazine put out an issue concerned entirely with Mussolini's efforts to create a "new" Italy, and the *Saturday Evening Post* was enthusiastic. The *New York World* was one of the few dissenters; Lippmann was an outspoken critic. As early as 1925 he wrote: "We do not trust Mussolini because we regard his regime as the supreme menace to the peace of Europe." Undoubtedly Lippmann was influenced by his friend Hamilton Fish Armstrong, who, as editor of *Foreign Affairs*, traveled frequently in Europe and was well aware of Mussolini's ambitions in regard to both Yugoslavia and Albania. Many Europeans (and Americans) suppressed their misgivings about Mussolini by taking the line that he had saved Italy from bolshevism. That, apparently, was sufficient justification for any villainy. Everywhere in Europe British policy was perceived as, in practical fact, supporting Mussolini. When Il Duce justified his intrusions into the affairs of Albania by a long list of fabrications that the Yugoslavian delegates wished to refute, the British prevailed on them to refrain.

Lord Tyrrell, the British ambassador to France in the early 1930s, recalled a conversation with Mussolini during which the Italian dictator asked what the English thought of him. Tyrrell had replied, "They admire what you have done to make Italians orderly and washed and ready to pay taxes, but they think that in foreign policy you talk too much like the Kaiser." Mussolini replied: "Oh, it is all for home consumption. If I were a French leader I couldn't say those things, because when the French get excited they act. But Italian excitement is always very restrained."

When Armstrong visited Italy in 1927, he talked to Professor M. Ruini, an anti-Fascist who had been minister of industry in the pre-Fascist era. "We are dead men," Ruini told Armstrong, "or at best living in the catacombs. We can only exist, think, study history, and prepare to meet fresh dangers. And hope? Yes, in Italy everything is possible." If unemployment continued to grow, Ruini predicted, Mussolini would have only two alternatives: to start a military venture to distract the public and acquire new possessions or to swing sharply to the left. "Mussolini is a man of ideas and inspiration," Ruini added. "Principles mean nothing to him. His objective is to retain power. If he feels unable to wage a foreign war your American conservatives who have applauded his materialism and listened complacently to his bellicose tirades may find themselves uncomfortably arm-in-arm with a protagonist of the aroused proletariat."

The Italian-American community was deeply divided over the issue of Mussolini and Fascism. Many immigrant Italians were enthusiastic supporters of the proclaimer of Rome's restored glory, but there had been a strong radical socialist and anarchist tradition among Italians who came to the United States in the last decade of the nineteenth century and the first decades of the twentieth. Arturo Giovannitti and Carlo Tresca were only the most noted of Italian radicals. In the spring of 1923 the Anti-Fascist Alliance of North America was founded, primarily by the Amalgamated Clothing Workers' Union, with Giovannitti at its head. *Il Nuovo Mondo,* an influential Italian newspaper with a circulation of some 30,000 published in New York, also took a strong anti-Fascist line, as, needless to say, did Carlo Tresca.

Germany was, of course, the critical patient in the hospital of European nations. The notion that the strongest and most enterprising nation in Europe could be turned into a permanent invalid was the assumption underlying the Versailles Treaty. Most of the mischief on the Continent was related to this dismal error. Josephine Herbst was in Germany in 1921 in the period of wild inflation. Stories were told of a woman who had sold her furniture to raise enough money to buy a postage stamp to send a letter to American relatives, of a scholar who had sold his library for sufficient food for his family for a few days. The liberal democrats and socialists, stirred by dreams of freedom and democracy, tried to deal with Prussian Junkers, aristocrats, devotees of the deposed kaiser, and militant Communists dedicated to the Bolsheviks. Frazier Hunt was troubled by the nation's air of "false gaiety" and decadence. "The inevitable flock of international carrion vultures were scattering their money about the hotels and cafés. In a most tragic way they were aided and abetted by naïve men and women who felt that the jig was up, and that they may as well dance before they faced starvation and oblivion. It was the spirit of the soldier on leave from the front."

One of the most blood-chilling developments was the appearance of terrorist gangs of young German aristocrats who revived ancient pagan blood rituals and specialized in political murders. They had come out of the war, in Armstrong's words, "with nothing to do—no work, no play, no culture, no faith, no history. . . ." They seemed com-

pounded of "ignorance, dilettantism, hardness, terrorism, heroism."
The "young barbarians were taking charge." A liberal German newspaper editor declared: "It is the Middle Ages in the twentieth century."
The strength of the feelings of even moderate German leaders can be
deduced from the fact that when the Woodrow Wilson Foundation
proposed to give an award to Gustav Stresemann, the liberal German
foreign minister who had been active in pushing for Germany's membership in the League of Nations, Stresemann refused the award. He
declared that he would never accept an honor from any American
foundation, especially one bearing the hated name of Woodrow Wilson, who had betrayed Germany by not adhering to the Fourteen
Points on the basis of which Germany had surrendered to the Allied
armies.

The bar of the Adlon Hotel in Berlin was the center of an international set of journalists, writers, artists, and social hangers-on. The
Dadaists and Surrealists were probing the subconscious; the German
Expressionists were producing their vivid and disturbing canvases. Edna
Ferber, the American novelist, accompanied by her mother and squired
by Alexander Woollcott, held court at the Adlon. Sinclair Lewis appeared with Dorothy Thompson, a brilliant young American journalist.
Sigrid and Mamma Schultz, American émigrés, established an American salon in their Berlin studio, where George Seldes, correspondent
for the *Chicago Tribune,* reigned. Floyd Gibbons, the most famous of
the American war correspondents, was often there, as was Frazier
Hunt.

Hunt heard from his German friend Karl von Weigand of a "rising figure" in German politics, an ex-corporal who called himself a
National Socialist. The phrase had an attractive ring, suggesting socialism and patriotism in some combination. Hunt traveled to Munich
to meet a young man with "burning hazel eyes, and straight brown
hair parted on one side, with a stern lock draped over a broad forehead;
his cheeks were pink," Hunt noted, "and there was about him a feeling
of shyness and uncertainty." A young man with him said, "This is Herr
Adolf Hitler." Hitler was dressed like "a Midwestern bridegroom" in
a plain black suit with a lavender tie and clumsy black army shoes. He
made his views known at once. "The Jews forced Germany's surrender," he announced. "They brought us this impotent German Republic.
They dominated both the Russian and German Communist parties.
They are to blame for much of our sorrow and disgrace. They must
go." As for the Treaty of Versailles, the National Socialist stood "squarely

against it. It is making slaves of the German people. We must have back our colonies and our beloved Rhineland. That which was stolen from us must be returned. . . . We cannot pay the indemnities. Our children and their children will starve trying to do it. . . . Germany must break the chains of the Treaty. We must have our own army. We must again take our place as an equal among the nations of the world. We must crush Bolshevism and check Soviet Russia. Our future lies to the east."

The German people, Hitler declared, were tired and disillusioned. They yearned for strong leadership. "We National Socialist . . . are ready to take over the leadership when the right moment comes. . . ."

"Ready for just what?" Hunt asked.

"Ready to crush the Communists and take over the dictatorship of the country." When did Hitler anticipate such a crisis? It would come, he replied, when the Communists next tried to seize power. Only the National Socialists had the power to check them, In Armstrong's words, "The middle and lower classes were in despair; they were turning away from reason and more and more listening to Hitler." Paul Scheffer, a German newspaper correspondent in the United States, told Armstrong that he had heard Hitler speak in Hamburg to "thousands of well-behaved but dispirited middle-class persons." Hitler had declared: "Some say we should work for a rapprochement with France, some with England, some even that we should draw closer to Russia. None of these propositions means anything so long as there is no 'We.' The first task is to create a German 'We.'" The words were greeted with prolonged applause.

The year 1923 began with French troops entering Essen and seizing the Ruhr on the ground that Germany had reneged on the agreed-upon reparations. Some 1,200 American soldiers, who had been part of the Allied occupation force since the end of the war, found that with the French seizure of the area their time of high living was over. In the words of a newspaper dispatch, "A terse cable from Washington tumbled 1,200 of the snappiest, happiest soldiers . . . off the top of the world today." They had been living like kings on salaries of 3,000,000 marks a year paid by their reluctant German hosts.

The occupation set off rioting in a number of German cities, frequently occasioned by efforts of the German Communists to seize power in the crisis brought on by the French occupation. The air was filled with predictions that "war and revolution" must follow the widespread disorders. At Aix-la-Chapelle, a "Rhineland Republic" was proclaimed on October 22, 1923. Separatists had seized public buildings during the night and proclaimed the Rhineland's independence of both Germany and France. In America the United German Societies called on the 7,500,000 Americans of German descent to come to the aid of the "crumbling German Reich" before the republic was "overwhelmed in the raging seas of internal troubles and engulfed by the cruel French bayonets which menaced the Ruhr and threatened the Rhineland."

General Erich Ludendorff assumed the role of a military dictator in Bavaria and announced that Bavaria would no longer accept instructions from Berlin. Through much of the month of November, 1923, Germany was in turmoil. The word spread that a putsch had been started in a Munich beer hall by Hitler. "Armed Hitlerites," the *New York Times* reported, "occupy the principal squares." Rumors spread that the deposed kaiser, in exile, had procured a passport and that the Hitlerites intended to restore him to the throne. Woodrow Wilson, weak and ailing, roused himself to denounce the action of the French, and Mussolini declared that Italy could not approve "any further occupation of territory" by France. "Germany may be an integral part of Europe tomorrow," he added. Britain also expressed its opposition to further French incursions.

Meanwhile, it turned out that Hitler's putsch was premature. He and his followers were dispersed by the police, and he was arrested and sentenced to five years in prison. It seemed the end of the young Austrian house painter and the National Socialists, but Hitler took the opportunity provided by his relatively brief incarceration (he was pardoned after serving fewer than two years) to write one of the most fateful books in history, *Mein Kampf*, spelling out in detail his plans for restoring the greatness of Germany.

When Hutchins Hapgood visited Germany, wild inflation that had reduced the country to a kind of terrible collective anxiety and the French invasion of the Ruhr Valley had awakened an angry patriotic response. But Hapgood was struck by the Germans' openness to fresh ideas and new visions, especially in the arts and in architecture. The old university town of Freiburg was especially attractive to Hapgood. "The churches," Hapgood noted, "which before the War had been visited mainly by women, were now filled with men; and the university reflected a freshened theological intensity." A group of young philosopher-theologians that included Paul Tillich, Karl Barth, and Eugen Rosenstock-Huessy had formed the Patmos Group to search out new directions in religion. Rosenstock-Huessy, a veteran of the war and a former *Privatdozent* at the University of Heidelberg, was busy organizing work camps to bring together workers, theologians, intellectuals, and businessmen to make plans for the reconstruction of Germany. The men and women who gathered in the camps alternated between useful labor and serious discussion. People spoke their minds in public on touchy political issues. Hapgood attended a radical political meeting expecting "to see the police arrest the speakers, accustomed as I was to such happenings in America," but they spoke without interruption.

It seemed to Hapgood in retrospect that the history of Germany might have been very different if the Allies had discovered some compassion, some broader vision than simply the impulse to punish the defeated enemy, measures such as "giving Germany a colonial outlet and enabling her to pay her debt through commerce alone and encouraging the humane internal governments. In other words a friendly rather than a hostile attitude. . . ."

The year 1924 in Europe seemed especially momentous to Hamilton Fish Armstrong. It marked the end of the attempts of France to exact reparations from Germany by force. There was support in Great Britain for modification of the demands on Germany and an appeal by that country to the United States to reach some agreement on the reduction of British war debts to America. In April the Dawes committee urged that the French evacuate the Ruhr in order to increase German productivity and thereby help restore German credit and, as a corollary, the economic well-being of Europe. Even Henri Poincaré, the French prime minister, who had come to power as an advocate of draconian measures against Germany, was impressed by the logic of the Dawes committee report, but while he hesitated, his ministry fell and Georges Herriot succeeded him. (In the next six years a series of encouraging steps followed. The Locarno Pact was agreed to, Germany was admitted to the League, and the Kellogg-Briand Pact "outlawed" war.)

But 1924 was also the year Mussolini strengthened his grip on the Italian state. Following riots and disorders, Il Duce secured from the king and Parliament a temporary grant of dictatorial powers to restore order. He used his powers to force through an electoral law that gave him some 60 percent of the seats in Parliament. Gangs of Fascist toughs—the *Squadristi*—suppressed the Communists, Socialists, and trade unionists, all bitterly divided. Italian industrialists supported the "strong man," and those who resisted were bullied into silence.

The epoch that the British and French and what remained of the

European aristocracy were trying to perpetuate was described by Harold Macmillan, the British politician, as "a period, highly cultivated and civilized . . . when international society was indeed an agreeable system for those who by birth, or talents formed an international governing class with common ties, interests, pleasures and traditions." It was true, moreover, that this "international class" which found life so pleasant was based on the exploitation of its own working class and of colonial people the world over.

The European nations, Walter Lippmann wrote, were content to invoke the Versailles Treaty as though it were some kind of magic formula that would ward off evil. They showed "neither the will to defend it with force nor the wisdom to save it by concessions. In a world of rebellious great powers they have tried to combine the advantages of imperialism with the conveniences of pacifism."

In the voting for the president of Germany in 1925 neither of the leading candidates received enough votes to win. A second poll was held on April 27. The Centrist Party had joined with the Democrats and the Social Democrats to nominate the Centrist leader, a former chancellor, Wilhelm Marx. The Nationalists and the People's Party had united on Field Marshal Paul von Hindenburg, then seventy-seven years old. The Nazis were not in evidence. Hitler had served thirteen months in prison for treason and been forbidden to deliver his demagogic harangues. The Ruhr was in the process of being evacuated by France, and the Dawes Plan for reducing reparations was having a beneficial effect on the German economy. The Communists voted for their candidate Ernst Thälmann. Hindenburg, who was presented to the voters as a link with the best of the old Germany, won by 1,000,000 votes. Many Germans, however, deplored the exploitation of Hindenburg by the Nationalists. The old general proved faithful to the ideals of the republic until he lapsed into senility. It was Hamilton Fish Armstrong's conviction that if Wilhelm Marx had won the election, as he doubtless would have had not Hindenburg been pushed forward, perhaps Marx "with the support of the great moderate and centrist parties would have set the course of German history on different lines. . . ." The "perhaps" was, Armstrong reflected, "enough to give the date tragic significance."

The year 1926 was marked by a bitter general strike in Great Britain that raised the specter of revolution. British credit became dangerously extended as that nation sought exports from the Continent. William Bullitt reported to Colonel House that a group of British

Conservatives that included Lord Max Beaverbrook, the great news-paper tycoon, and Winston Churchill were arguing for closer ties with Japan, with the expectation that when Ramsay MacDonald's Labor government fell and they took over, they would be in a position to cooperate with Japan—"the Japanese to do the shooting in China," Bullitt wrote, "the English to do the shooting in India." The degree of cynical calculation involved in such a course was certainly not in-compatible with the British policy in general. Moreover, as far as the preservation of its imperial interests was concerned, the British made no pretense of behaving honorably. Gentlemen at home, they were toughs abroad.

# The South in the Twenties

The dramatic changes that we have attended to in the opening chapters of this volume were experienced most acutely in the northeastern corner of the country, specifically in New York City, in Philadelphia, and, to a lesser extent, in Boston. The West Coast, most notably Los Angeles, was also strongly affected; the Midwest, of which Chicago was the capital in this era, and the South hardly at all. The South, still cherishing the "Lost Cause," stewed in the bitter brew of defeat and poverty.

The antebellum South had prided itself on being the same yesterday, today, and forever. After the war, men like Henry Grady appealed for a New South, a South of "scientific" farms, bustling cities, and burgeoning industry, but nothing had turned out as had been hoped. Mill towns were built, but wages were low, and conditions of labor appallingly bad. Mines were dug, and coal and iron produced in substantial quantities, but they, too, seemed to breed poverty and despair rather than prosperity. In Louisiana and western Mississippi, oil was struck, but it served primarily to enrich strangers and a few fortunate Southern entrepreneurs. If the word "feudal" had a meaning, the South was feudal. Emigration from the South for both blacks and whites was constant. Those who left were the most enterprising or the most desperate. By 1920 almost 3,000,000 Southerners were living elsewhere.

Underlying everything, exacerbating all problems, was the issue of race: white against black. The terrible legacy of slavery was omnipresent. Fear haunted the dreams of blacks and whites alike. The most enlightened whites constantly professed their love and understanding of blacks *in their place;* the less enlightened did not dissemble their hatred. They joined the nearest Klan chapter, and when the opportunity presented itself, they lynched black men and women *to remind other blacks of their place.* In Northampton County, Virginia, it was as though Nat Turner's uprising had happened a few days before. Whites living in the vicinity continually referred to it. "White folk'll move to town when we old heads is gone," an elderly farmer told one interviewer; "they won't be no more white churches and schools. The country will be turned over to the niggers. I don't know what'll happen then—another Nat Turner risin', I reckon." A white woman recalled the rumor of a black "risin' ": "Most of our neighbors took quilts and blankets and spent several nights in the thickets, 'fraid to stay at home. . . . I remember plannin' if we heard the niggers comin' we'd run hide in my butter-bean vines; they was real thick that year. . . . Some folks is so scared o' ha'nts and ghosts, but it's the livin' I fear, niggers and such."

After the World War a kind of panic swept the South. The returning black soldiers, many of them outspokenly opposed to the racial practices of the region, were seen as a special menace. Word spread through white communities that "radical Negro organizations . . . are organizing in secret meetings and arming themselves." John Hope, a college-educated young black, returning to his home in Georgia after serving overseas, found "colored soldiers and their families . . . being driven from their homes because of the hysterical fears of their white neighbors." Some seventy blacks were lynched in the first year after the war. The *Shreveport Times* announced: "We venture to say that fully ninety per cent of all race troubles in the South are the result of the Negro forgetting his place. . . . If the black man will stay where he belongs, act like a Negro should act, work like a Negro should work, talk like a Negro should talk . . . there will be very few riots, fights or clashes." The newspaper told black leaders that instead of forming "societies" and "unions," they should foster education that will "impress upon [the Negro] the NECESSITY of keeping his place." Senator J. K. Vardaman of Mississippi declared in the same spirit, "The way to control the nigger is to whip him when he does not obey without it, and another is never to pay him more wages than is actually necessary to buy food and clothing." Recalling the era, Hosea Hudson, a black union organizer, noted, "This was also when the young Negroes were coming back from the war and the white hoodlums was whipping them up." He heard they were after him but were afraid to tackle him head-on. "I was pretty fiery back in those days. I didn't take nothing." But he knew it was time for him to move on.

Fear of blacks combined with fear of Communists. The notion of "black Reds" was clearly terrifying to white Southerners. It was the conjunction of two nightmares. Fear of blacks and blackness was deeply rooted in slavery days. Mary Chesnut had written of the terror that she and her family felt of being murdered in their beds. Rumors of a black uprising had been enough to drive whites to the edge of hysteria. Similarly, the fear of foreign influences and foreign ideas had been in the consciousness of Americans since the early days of the Republic, and the endless stream of immigrants had fed those fears—fears of Catholics, first and most terrifying, and then later fears of anarchists and, long before the Russian Revolution, fears of communists with a small *c*, of the black international and the Red international, of Jews and Italians, Poles, Slavs, Chinese. The fear of foreigners and for-eignness clearly lay at the heart of the country's massive and pervasive isolationism. Now that fear took on a more concrete, tangible form, the form of Soviet Russia, a great, crude Communist bear ready to devour the world.

What the South had uniquely was a view of the human condition that, however retrograde in certain respects, constituted a coherent and stubbornly enduring whole. No rival region could make that claim. Perhaps the Midwest, with its devotion to small-town virtues, came closest. New England was as spiritually barren as its flinty acres, a kind of museum of its ancient virtues, withdrawn and passionless. The Rocky Mountain West still cherished that part of the Southern ethic that had gone West with the cowboys—guns and violence and honor. It ran second to the South in lynchings, and it added Indians and Mexicans to the breeds "outside the law."

To the South, the North seemed like Sodom and Gomorrah. Every form of modern wantonness flourished there. New York City was the capital of wickedness, Babylon-on-the-Hudson; Yankees were a fro-ward and faithless people, alternately patronizing and admonishing the South. Northern capitalists pillaged the South, and Northern intellectuals ridiculed it; the South felt itself an exploited colony of the North, which was close to the truth. The North abounded in heresies—Darwinism, communism, and other ingenious forms of atheism. It scorned tradition, was contemptuous of religion, bowed down before Mammon, and swarmed with hordes of aliens.

Gerald Johnson wrote: "We have our own methods of handling the Negro and they are sometimes rather too summary; but we at least admit that he is a human being, and the cold ferocity with which the North oppresses, tortures, and not infrequently butchers him sickens the South. We know the Negro. We are honestly fond of him. We know that as a race he is incapable of exercising wisely all the functions of citizenship, but we also know that under firm, but just, control he makes an honest, peaceable and efficient workman. . . . On the Negro question the North is insane."

It seemed clear to W. J. Cash, the relatively emancipated author of *The Mind of the South,* that "the general dissemination of the modern ideology—often by piecemeal and at third hand—with its predominant emphasis on biology and mechanistic philosophy and its skepticism about everything which has not been rigidly established, certainly had its effect. . . ." In the North the foolish took it as "*carte blanche* for the free exercise of their appetites. And on even the best the immediate effect of almost sudden contact with it was apt to be the collapse of old standards without the creation of adequate new ones." The consequences were, in Cash's opinion, observable everywhere. "But it was in the colleges and universities, precisely where the modern mind most flourished, that it reached its greatest development, or at least that it was most plainly in view. Swinish drunkenness, eternal and blatant concern with the theme of sex, and promiscuity in one degree or another flourished—not so extravagantly as rumor had it, surely, but still to such an extent that it was impossible to be blind to it." To Cash the old Southern habit "of high and noble affirmation," of veneration for "the way handed down by the fathers, tested by experience, and hallowed by the blood of the Confederate dead," had a tendency "to emerge in form of terror and anger. . . ." The South was dismayed, again in Cash's words, at the "strange new ideas and faith and systems . . . sweeping through the Western lands, . . . all the old ideas and faiths and systems were under attack, in danger, crumbling or even vanishing in places. Everywhere there was doubt and change and chaos and flux and violence." Russia was the symbol of it all, of "godless and propertyless and coldly murderous revolution . . . [T]he common people wholly, and even upper-rank Southerners largely, lumped all aliens indiscriminately together as carriers of the Communist seed."

When Jerre Mangione toured the South as a member of the Farm Security Administration, Southerners displayed such hostility at the mention of his Italian name that his traveling companions renamed him Smith for the duration.

Politics was the mother's milk of the white South, and political oratory its folk literature. Sweating, haranguing, reviewing the ancient inventory of wrongs inflicted by "them" on "us," the Southern politician was a cross between a comic actor and a therapist. And while he performed his ritual acts, the vested interests—the coal mine owners in Alabama; the lumber interests in Georgia; the oil companies in Arkansas, Texas, and Louisiana; the textile mills' owners in North Carolina; the railroads everywhere—strengthened their hold on the Southern states, most commonly in the name of the "New South," a South industrialized with the helpful cooperation of the North, a South docile and obedient to the iron hand its politicians publicly deplored.

In 1924 one of the most reactionary of Southern politicians, Coleman Blease, defeated the popular and able James F. Byrnes for the Senate seat in South Carolina. A millowner conceded to Byrnes that Blease was a demagogue, "but all he ever gets the hands excited about is liquor and niggers. Well, we'll drink the liquor and take care of the niggers. Coley will keep the hands quiet."

The main feature of the political speech was the story. No short story was tolerated. The story, designed to illustrate an often rather elusive point, was a long, carefully crafted work of oratorical art with a beginning, a middle, and a punchline ending. The crowd, which had usually heard it numerous times before, listened as raptly as the audience at a performance of Shakespeare's *Hamlet* or the Japanese at a classic No play and roared with laughter at the familiar ending. "Old Hugh never told that 'un better," a gallused listener would say appreciatively.

Alben Barkley of Kentucky was the prototype of the Southern Senator, expansive, eloquent in the old-fashioned spread-eagle style dear to the hearts of Southern voters, and a skillful "fixer" to whom one went when important legislation was bogged down or locked up in committee. He was famous for his "stories," many of them demeaning to blacks. William Douglas remembered one of Barkley's favorites about a black man who tried to register to vote in a Southern

*[handwritten margin note: ANTI-BLACK JOKE BY ALBAN BARKLEY]*

town. The registrar, looking at his application, asked him to quote the First Amendment. The black man shook his head. "Recite the Fourteenth Amendment." Again a shake of the head. "What is a bill of attainder?" Another negative response. "Tell me, nigger, don't you know anything?"

"One thing."

"What is that?"

"No nigger is going to vote in the next election." (Laughter.)

"Nigger baiting" was a standard feature of Southern political oratory. "Nigger baiting" was a fixed formula that required the affirmation that "This is a white man's country, by God, and no nigger is going to tell us what to do." It required a reference to the sacredness of Southern womanhood and what would happen to any black man who defiled it by look or gesture or, even more unthinkable, by act. It included favorable mention of "good niggers" who knew their place. It might very well include an illustrative story about "good niggers" and "bad niggers," intended to demonstrate the speaker's affection for the former variety, usually an "Uncle" somebody, Uncle Ned or Uncle Billy or Uncle Tom. When a black minister stepped forward at the Democratic Convention in 1936 to give the invocation, Senator "Cotton Ed" Smith of South Carolina rose and stalked indignantly from the convention hall. When he ran for reelection in 1938, he made a special point of his walkout: "[When a] slew-footed, blue-gummed, kinky-headed Senegambian . . . started praying . . . I started walking, and as I . . . walked . . . it seemed to me that old John Calhoun leaned down from his mansion in the sky and whispered . . . you did right, Ed."

Long before the Civil War the South had formed the cult of sacred Southern womanhood. It survived the war not only intact but reinforced by inevitable stories of feminine heroism in the face of the Yankee invaders. The cult had deep psychological and political roots. In *Stars Fell on Alabama* Carl Carmer describes a University of Alabama fraternity ritual carried out at the chapter's dances: "The lights were turned out and a procession of young men carrying torches enters the room. Four carry a long cake of ice. The leader mounts a table and proposes a toast in water: 'To Woman, lovely woman of the Southland, as pure and chaste as this sparkling water, as cold as this gleaming ice, we lift this cup and we pledge our hearts and our lives to the protection of her virtue and chastity.' "

The "purity of Southern womanhood" served a dual purpose: It was a bulwark against atheistic communism and an unvarying symbol of the determination of white males to keep blacks in their place. Behind every lynching were profound sexual anxieties but, equally potent, a bloody challenge to the spirit of the new age.

All the moonshine about the sacredness of Southern womanhood did not keep Southern males, especially those at the bottom of the pile, from tyrannizing and abusing their wives. One farm wife told an interviewer that her husband "keeps his jug of liquor in the kitchen and drinks when he pleases. If he wants to beat me or the children he does, and that's all there is to it. He ain't got no mercy on nothing but mules and dogs." The same was true in many black families. The casual promiscuity of black males was taken for granted, and brutalized by the society they lived in, they not uncommonly brutalized their wives and children in turn.

Despite the textile mills, the coal mines, and oil refineries of the New South, the region remained essentially and profoundly agricultural. It was a two-crop economy—tobacco in the upper South and cotton in the lower.

"Backer" raising was a more complex activity than that of cotton. In Smithfield, North Carolina, the Carson family were tobacco farmers. Frances Carson, the wife of Ransome, told Mary Hicks and Edwin Massingill, interviewers for the Federal Writers' Project, that she was "tired enough to die." The respite during a day of putting up the tobacco leaves in a barn for curing was an hour "to let the mules rest. Thank God, we've got the mules to work," she said, "or Ransome would work me to death. . . . I hadn't ought to be so tired. I've worked like this all my life. Papa was a farmer and he made us work so hard that we didn't go to school half the time. We had to stay at home in the fall and grade 'backer and pick cotton, and in the spring we had to stay out to plant it."

She had never gotten out of the fifth grade; her brothers and sister had not gotten that far. "I'll tell you what's so," she added, "tenant farming ain't no pleasure at all. . . . We make mighty little after working ourselves near 'bout to death and we move just about every year, I've heard folks say that there was good landlords and bad ones. I ain't never seen neither one. They're all alike, looking for every cent they can, and landlords was born without hearts." She had married Ransome when she was sixteen "and didn't care a snap that he drunk and fought and had been in jail a time or two. I thought he'd stop it when I married him, but he got worse."

Tobacco was in Lee Hughes's blood. "I love to fool with it and get the gum on my hands and clothes. I love to sell it and I love to chew it and smoke it," he told Mary Hicks. He looked glumly at his tobacco field. "Guess the worms'll eat it in spite of all we can do. We've been worming and suckering since early May and we can't seem to make much headway over the worms. We don't make nothing—but we still stick to tobacco and cotton." He and his wife and children were up before daylight, "winter and summer, and by the time it's light enough to see we're out at work. We fix our plant beds for tobacco in January, and February we plant the seed and cover it with canvas to keep out the cold. We have to pull the weeds about twice or three times before the plants are big enough to set out. While the plants are coming up we break up the land, put a ton of fertilizer to the acre and run rows." The plants were set out as soon as the last freeze was over. "Then the war starts. If it's too dry we have to water the plants after we set them out, and then it's sucker, worm, plow, and chop until the latter part of June when the lugs get yellow. We barn them first, and by the time they're cured the body leaves are ripe and we barn and cure again. . . . We're mighty glad when the last barn is killed out, but the work ain't over yet. The tobacco's still to grade, tie, and carry to market. That means work in the packhouse ten hours a day and sometimes by lantern light." Hughes and his wife regretted that their oldest son hated tobacco and had no desire to take over the farm, giving as a reason the "number of times we'd whipped him with tobacco sticks." It didn't help to tell him that "mighty near every farmer in North Carolina had been whipped with tobacco sticks and had whipped their younguns . . . too."

On Carson's tobacco farm the younger children in the family were left to shift for themselves while their mother and aunts worked long days in the curing sheds. "I left [my baby]," Frances Carson told an interviewer, "in the yard once but it eat sand, chicken manure, and strings, so I decided to leave her in the house and take a chance of her eating buttons. If I left the backer [tobacco] every hour or two . . . Ransome would raise the devil." She tied the baby to a table leg in the house while she worked.

The Jeffcoats, living for the time being at McDuffie's Baptist Chapel, near Chapel Hill, were typical of poor white tenant farmers, constantly on the move. In twenty-seven years of marriage Jim Jeffcoat and his wife had been tenants on seven different farms. They could neither read nor write, and none of their eight grandparents had been able to either. "Book larnin' never come easy in our families," Mrs. Jeffcoat told an interviewer, "but all of our menfolks and some of our womenfolks has been good at machinery and tools of every kind." Her father-in-law had run "an old-timey gin," and it was said of him, "Give old Bob a nail, a piece of wire and pair of pliers and he'll fix anything." The problem was that the gin broke down so often farmers didn't want to wait for old Bob to display his ingenuity; he lost business. "If I could only read and figure and buy some new machinery or purchase new parts for what I do own, I could make money hand over fiss," he often declared. The Jeffcoats had few worldly possessions to haul with them from place to place—"three old wooden double beds covered with ragged quilts. I used to have sheets and pillowcases for every bed, but I can't afford them anymore. . . . The dresser and that settee look like they might have come out of Noah's Ark," Mrs. Jeffcoat added. Tenant farmers or sharecroppers all their lives, the Jeffcoats had nothing to show for their labors. "We have never owned a horse or a mule or a cow, or any tools or anything to ride in. Of course we ain't never owned a house, and we never will. The houses we've lived in ain't worth owning," Mrs. Jeffcoat declared.

Attitudes toward the soil differed widely in the South, needless to say. One farm wife in Big Ivy, Tennessee, whose husband was crippled, told a Federal Writers' Project interviewer, "Nothing on this living earth I'd rather do than get out and hoe a patch of cotton in good weather. These days I ain't got that patch and no hoe to work it if I did have. Here I set, day in and day out, looking after my poor man Patey and hoping somebody will come by that I can pass a chat with."

Big Ivy was an exclusively white town; no black dared show his face. Another farm wife told an interviewer, "Cotton is the most thing they raise around here. Generally always farmers will put in a field of corn and a vegetable patch and some raise a few hogs and chickens, but cows is pretty few and milk and beef meat is scarce. Cotton is the standby and always will be, seems like. Now, every place I've ever heard of before, cotton and niggers just naturally grow together."

Throughout the 1920s the boll weevil decimated the Southern cotton crops, and thousands of small farmers and tenants were driven off the land. From 1920 to 1927 the average annual return per acre on cotton farms was around $29; in 1919 it had been more than $60. But in the long run foreign competition was a greater threat to Southern cotton than the boll weevil. Foreign production tripled in the period from 1920 to 1937. In 1929 the Southern cotton crop was 15,000,000 bales while the foreign crop totaled some 11,500,000. The price of cotton dropped from twenty cents a pound to twelve, and a year later it fell further to eight. Many planters abandoned their farms or left them in the hands of tenants to make out as best they could. In 1900 some 36 percent of white farmers in the South were tenants or share-croppers. By 1930 the percentage had gone up to 45 percent.

In sharp contrast with other sections of the country, where small farms were consolidated into larger ones, often by farm corporations, Southern farms grew smaller. By 1930 almost 80 percent of all South-ern farms were less than 100 acres; 1 percent were larger than 500. While the per acre value of Southern farmland increased, the value of the crop produced on that land declined, placing the farmer in an impossible squeeze. In addition, Southern farmlands were so poor that the region's bill for fertilizers was almost double that of other farming regions.

Besides cotton and tobacco, Southern farmers produced soybeans, hay, pulpwood, turpentine, and feed. The motive power on Southern farms was the mule, the totemic animal of the South. "A good pair of mules is just about as good assets as a farmer can have when he wants to arrange a small loan," a horse trader in Raleigh, North Carolina, told an interviewer. The man who owned a mule or, better, two mules was on the way to being an independent entrepreneur. He could "hire out," borrow money, or otherwise improve his status. Hogs were close behind. The mule pulled a plow or a wagon or served for riding to town. The hog, in a dozen forms—ham, bacon, sausage, fatback, pork chops, chitterlings, pigs' feet—was food. Everything was utilized, it was said, but the squeal.

Next to the hog came the catfish and, less commonly, bass from the innumerable ponds and rivers and creeks. For many farm families catfish were the margin of survival. Corn was the other essential ele-ment—corn cakes, corn bread, corn pone, grits—corn in as many forms as hog meat.

A phenomenon not confined to the South but characteristic of it was the farm run by several women. Usually they were sisters, one a spinster lady and the other often a widow. On the Virginia frontier in the 1740s William Byrd had encountered women who ran farms, slaughtered beef and hogs, and shot game. Southern women were a tough-grained breed, doubtless made so by the necessity of putting up, generation after generation, with domineering but often inept hus-bands who loathed work and demanded deference. Gertha Couric, working for the Federal Writers' Project, interviewed two of that tribe in rural Alabama. Mrs. Dora Healy and Miss Annie Franklin, both in their late sixties, had been "right here on the farm since 1881." Dora's husband had died after a year of marriage, and she had come to help her unmarried sister run their father's farm. They kept a classic Southern table; Couric was invited for lunch to a groaning board, "snowy white cloth and napkins with old-fashioned china." The table held "platters of sliced turkey, country ham, fried chicken, and sausage . . . turnip greens, peas, stewed tomatoes, pickles, brandy peaches, jelly, cornbread and hot biscuit, coffee, buttermilk, fruit cake, and cocoanut cake." Miss Annie told her proudly: "We don't have to buy a thing, except a little flour, coffee, sugar, and kerosene now and then. Everything is raised right here on the farm." They were remarkably ingenious women. They sold cedar posts and timber. They raised cotton but barely broke even on it. They had 100 hens and sold the eggs for thirty-five cents a dozen. They raised, in addition to cotton, corn, peanuts, velvet beans, sugarcane, and potatoes, and kept a vegetable garden. They canned the vegetables for winter use, 300 quarts in neat rows, along with jelly and preserves and marmalade. Peach and pear, crab apple and pecan trees were abundant, and they made blackberry, elderberry, and scuppernong wine. "We don't waste nothing; save all of our leaves even. Leaf mould is one of the best fertilizers," Miss Annie told her guest. The farm was rich in game. Annie was the hunter. Dora would hear her gun "early in the morning, *pop, pop,* at first light—that's when the birds start coming in—and in no time she would come in with enough to last several days." Annie was the hunter, but Dora could beat her fishing. She usually fished Sunday. "That's when I see God most. Setting on the bank, it's so beautiful down there. In the spring time—that's my favorite time of the year—the wood violets, the lilies, the honeysuckle, yellow jasmine, and dogwood are all blooming at the same time. It smells like heaven." Annie, the hunter, preferred the fall, when the game was plentiful. Annie cursed a black man whom she suspected of stealing money from them. She apologized to Gertha Couric. "But you got to cuss if you run a farm." The preacher knew she cussed. Dora "didn't cuss but she liked a drink better."

"There you go," Dora replied, "don't you like a little toddy too?"

" 'Course I do; it hopes me up; but I don't take but one and you take two." She explained to Couric, ". . . honey, we takes a little toddy in the winter and a little mint julep in the summer. As Pa used to say, 'a little for the stomach's sake.' "

Often the landlords were little better off than their tenants. In addition, they felt greatly put upon. A typical landlord complaint was that few sharecroppers were "thrifty and saving." In the words of a landlord in Seaboard, North Carolina, "The white ones as a rule ain't no better than the niggers. They're usually the slums of the world. I had one white family a few years ago that sickened me on white labor. They come to me from one of the southern counties, a big family of about twelve, as destitute as I ever saw anybody. They was literally naked. The whole town through different organizations begun to take them clothes, bed cover, furniture.... While the men worked smart, I didn't like their attitude; after the new wore off, they wanted to figure their way through.... Some of them was always sick; three of the children was down at one time with colitis, with the old lady in bed with a broken leg. The baby died, and I had to furnish the plot for its grave and its burial expenses.... If 'twasn't for we landlords, what in God's world would become of this shiftless crowd?"

He complained bitterly that he was going deeper in debt every year. It took him, he told an interviewer, $4,000 to produce a cotton crop for which he could get only $3,500. He had borrowed $2,000 from the bank to run his farm. The value of the land had declined by a half, and his tenants were a constant burden. They often departed without notice, taking with them everything that wasn't nailed down. Sometimes they burned up the outhouse for firewood or tore down a perfectly decent shed. One family had demolished the better part of a kitchen for "lightwood kindling." Another tenant family blackened the walls of their cabin with fires and had "drunk whiskey and fired shotguns all day Sunday," leaving the walls riddled with pellets. "Sometimes," he continued, "they worry us with an old cow or hogs, letting them get into our corn or cotton and do a lot of damage.... We fork over the money, and it's throwed away for gas or whiskey or something trifling. As soon as one has a little prosperity he's likely to want to leave, try somebody else." Many tenants stole, the landlord declared. "Not only does the sharecropper get corn out of our barn, but cotton out of our fields. He picks sackful after sackful, throws them in a ditch or in the woods, and at night collects them to sell." A cousin had found 1,400 pounds in the loft of a tenant's house.

The attitude of poor whites to blacks was described vividly by the wife of one of them. Her husband's grandfather had told of how he used to work for white farmers for wages and "didn't mind that until slaves were hired from the plantation to work beside him. This made him look down on work, and wuz tempted to steal rather than git down on a level with the niggers. The thing that made him boil wuz the fact that slaves instead of looking up to him called him 'pore white trash.' " When the Civil War broke out, he had been one of the first to volunteer. "I'd rather git killed than have all those niggers freed and claimin' they's as good as I is." People didn't call him "pore white" anymore, he added. "But Jim still believes that people are thinkin' it. . . . I believe that's one reason Jim drinks so much. The only time he forgets that he came from pore folks is when he gits drunk. Boy! He's rollin' in clover then."

Jerre Mangione was dismayed at the poverty he saw in the South. "Every variety of erosion afflicted [the farm families he saw]; poor housing, inadequate food, bad health, and chronic despair. Not since the slums of Sicily and Genoa had I beheld such overwhelming poverty. But here, without the presence of Italian bravura, it seemed to me to be far more abject. The houses were rickety shacks with leaking roofs and gaps in the walls that let in rain and wind. Some had no windows and doors, no running water, no indoor toilets. Large families were jammed into two- or three-room shacks. Among them was a family of thirteen children and only three beds. The youngest of the children, thin and pale, grouped themselves around the mother like a gang of hungry suckling puppies. The same family kept a cow in a pen that fitted as snugly as a glove, but the cow was too emaciated to give milk."

Mangione discovered that "one of the standard procedures among southern men for achieving some degree of cordiality with strangers was to urinate together. As soon as introductions had been made, someone in the group would unbutton his fly and take out his penis, and the others would immediately follow suit."

The typical hand in a Southern textile mill had already experienced defeat. He or she had been driven from the land by failure to make it as a tenant farmer or sharecropper. Writing of the Southern cotton millworker, W. J. Cash noted, "At the very time when his pay was being cut to about half of what he had come to count on in war times, the physical and social gulf which . . . was already opening appreciably by 1914, was now widening again, and more signally and rapidly." Along with the widening economic gulf went growing social distinctions. The Southern plantation "master" or millowner had always prided himself on his friendly paternal relations with his slaves or his workers, his "people." Now he was seldom to be seen. He lived in a city or a suburb, and the older social cohesiveness that had mitigated the class system broke down. "Most of the old barons were dead or dying," Cash wrote, "and when they weren't, were usually so engrossed in golf at the country club or in the mania for speculating in land values or stocks that they had no time left for the practice of their ancient amiable habits."

In 1930 the cotton millworkers in the South numbered some 400,000, or about a fifth of the factory workers of the region. The small farmers, the sharecroppers, and the tenants outnumbered industrial workers by a margin of two to one.

Not only did the millowners own the mills, but they in effect owned the towns that grew up around the mills. They commonly owned the houses their workers lived in, and they usually encouraged churchgoing by contributing to the building costs and the preachers' salaries, provided that the churches were built on company property. Such generosity was a strong deterrent to rocking the boat.

In Knoxville, Tennessee, Calvin and Lola Simons told Dean Newman, another Federal Writers' Project interviewer, that they had "come from the mountains, for Calvin know'd he could make a living some way or another about town doing odd jobs. We fared on down to Knoxville. Our times has not been easy there," Lola Simons said. "We was both born poor. Lived poor all our lives." In town they rented a two-room house and had, for the first time in their lives, a sink with running water, a luxury. "We's had more butter and milk and meat and eggs here in town than we ever see on that farm. Farm living is plain slaving from one month to the next, from morning to night. And they's nothing left to show for the hard work you do."

Older millworkers looked back to better days when most millowners practiced a kind of benevolent paternalism in the tradition of the kindly plantation owners. A retired millworker in Athens, Georgia, told Sadie Hornsby that his whole family had worked in the cotton mill. His grandmother had kept their two-room house while his grandfather, mother, two uncles, and three aunts worked in the mill "and did real well. To make a good textile worker you had to start young, say around the age of eight." Mr. Bloomfield, the president of the Athens Manufacturing Company, was "a devoutly religious man, and was good to the people that worked for him." They lived in his "mill village," and every "man, woman and child among them simply worshipped him." The mill hands were paid every four weeks, and once a week they were sent "meat, meal, and flour," distributed from a two-mule wagon. "He visited every house and knew every man, woman and child that lived in his village by their first names." In watermelon season the mill closed down "to give us the opportunity to enjoy eating watermelons. During the rest spell," he recalled, "hands were allowed to get food from the company store and pay for it when they returned to work. . . . When a father or mother, or an older sister or brother were sick, a younger one was sent to hold the place until the absent one returned . . . many a child has started to work when they weren't no larger than this dog." There were no strikes, and those lucky enough to work for Bloomfield felt themselves blessed. The foreman, Thomas Beal, took "us boys out on fishing trips at his own expense," the old mill hand recalled. But the times had changed. The mill was now owned by absentee owners. There were many more looms. The stretch-out and piecework rates had been established. When piecework was introduced, many workers quit. "Said they would rather starve first."

While the millworker referred nostalgically to the days when Bloomfield owned the mill, he emphasized that working conditions had improved greatly. "In my young days," he recalled, "the life of a mill worker wasn't very long. The close confinement, long hours, lint and dust that they had to breathe, all worked together to shorten their lives. Most everybody had a cough. I've had this cough ever since I can remember. Men and women all had sallow complexions, and the younger folks didn't have any color in their cheeks. The mills of those days didn't have any way of controlling the dust and lint, and the air we breathed was dry and stale."

Labor unions were considered Red by most Southerners. The Virginia Senator John Sharp Williams called unions a "conspiracy to commit murder." Another Southern politician spoke of that "unholy foreign-born, un-American, despotic thing *known as labor unionism.*" In Grover, North Carolina, a local of the United Textile Workers' Union gave up its charter on the ground that its members had decided that "unions were incompatible with Christianity."

James Edmonds had given up farming for the job of a mill hand in Rudd, North Carolina. The stretchout (actually a form of speedup) was introduced in the Cone Mills in 1925, and Edmonds raised his voice, as he put it to Ida Moore, "against what I think is one of the most inhuman things that ever hit any industry. Hundreds of folks go to jail every year and spend the best part of their lives there for doing things not half as harmful to their fellow man as the stretch-out." The notion was that the looms ran faster and made better cloth if the weaving room was kept at a temperature of more than 100 degrees.

"You see, Lady," Edmonds said, "I had seen women, one of my own daughters, going all day long in that unbearable heat with their clothes stuck to their bodies like they had been dipped in a pool of water. Going up and down their alleys weeping, working all day long." With the speedup every fourth weaver lost his or her job. It seemed to Edmonds that "I could look out there in the years and see the awful misery ahead for working people. Thousands throwed out of jobs and the rest drove like machines till they died before their life was half over. When they was gone there'd be plenty others to take their place, young folks with hopes for living to be ground out of them until they had no life left, just to feed the selfishness and greed of the people in power." When Edmonds protested the stretch-out, the general manager, his face flushed with anger, told him to go back to work or go home. Edmonds said, "Mr. Gordon, there's no cause to be excited, because we're not after violence unless it's forced on us. We stand before you unarmed except with a awful determination to have adjustments made in our work so's we'll again feel like free humans living in a free country. We mean to stand here, though, in this mill yard until a promise of adjustments is made. Every man, woman, and child is pledged to defend his job at the cost of his life. We hate violence but we hate slavery worse. To work under the stretch-out system is the same as committing suicide, and we've made up our minds not to do it. . . . It's your time to speak." The company backed down briefly, but the speedup went on, directed by Northern efficiency engineers, and when the agitation died down, Edmonds and all the members of his family employed in the mill were fired.

Back on a farm, James Edmonds gave all his spare time to organizing the workers at the Cone Mills. When he had signed up most of them, Cone started an all-out assault on the union. The millworkers were told they must sign a paper rejecting the union or lose their jobs. Edmonds's son, Henry, who had a wife and two small children, was among those who capitulated. "There was seventy families in all that wouldn't disclaim the union," Edmonds told Ida Moore. "They stayed in their houses until the law come and throwed their things out on the street." The attitude was: "You'll do what we tell you, you'll shut your mind up and let us think for you, or we'll starve you to death." With that attitude among employers, Edmonds thought, it was "foolish to set back and say that nothing could happen in our country to bring on a revolution. I had a belief that's the strongest kind of religion, and

I was called on to pay the price for it. They almost starved me out, but they didn't change my way of thinking. I'm still certain I took the right road. . . . Peace inside is worth a whole lot to man."

By the end of the 1920s many mills had closed down. Molly Sharp, who had started working in a Greensboro cotton mill at the age of fifteen, told Ida Moore that she and her husband "fed from two or three people a day that was passin' through . . . , people that had been throwed out of their jobs and sometimes their homes. One day," she recalled, "there come a crowd of six men, six jobless men. That was the day the whole family cried. We took them in and fed them, they could hardly talk, only one man kept saying, 'I've got a Christian wife at home and three babies. I've got nothing to give them. They seems to be no sort of job in the land for me.' " Molly's daughter, Annie, who also worked in the mill, joined in with the story of one jobless man who prayed before he sat down to the table. "This is what he said, 'God in Heaven, it's good to be settin' at a table and eatin' victuals agin. I got no work and I'm agettin' old. The mills done with me. I'm weary and footsore, Lord, and I'm not knowin' where on the face of the earth I ought to go. I'd like yore guidance, God, and I'll try to listen.' . . . He ate his meal while the tears streamed down in his plate."

Southern blacks experienced the physical hardships, the poverty, the hunger, and the malnutrition common to Southern whites. In addition, they endured relentless oppression. "I don't mind workin' hard," Mary Matthews told an interviewer; "I 'spects that. But it is hard, after you done de best you can, to be cussed at and talked to like a dog. Aaron killed hisself a-workin' for Mr. Jones. . . . I spent de best years o' my life on de Jones farm, and what has we got to show for it? Nothin'—nothin' but younguns!"

A black husband and wife in Holly Grove, Arkansas, told interviewers, in answer to the question of how they farmed, "Well, dey's sev'ul diff'unt ways. Dare is de cash rentuh, but we has always share-cropped, on a third and a four—he furnish de house and de land en credicks you enough to live on, en den you settles at de end of de year. In de cotton we gives him a fourth, in the cawn he gits a third. . . . Anyhow, when you raise four bales of cotton de landlord gits one en you git three. . . ." The rations provided by the landlord before the crops came in were meager—flour, meal, lard, molasses, or a little sugar. "Meat? Whoooo! We didn't git no meat, but we'd ketch a mess of fish now en den, en de nex' year we had ouah own meat."

The most humble channels of advancement were closed to blacks.

Black parents in Holly Grove boasted to an interviewer that their son could do anything in the line of repairing or driving a tractor. He had learned it all from a book but had no opportunity to use the knowledge. "You see, dey doan use no colored mechanics hyar in Holly Grove, en I guess he *could* go off somewhare, but I doan speck he will." The cost of items at the landlord's store was roughly double the cost in town— "a dime foh a nickel bah of soap." But there was no credit in the town stores; the landlord gave credit. "De landlord is de landlord, de politicians is landlord, de judge is landlord, de shurf [sheriff] is landlord, everybody is de landlord, en we ain't got nothin'."

When Mary Matthews questioned items charged to her and her husband by their landlord, a Mr. Jones, he cursed her, "said I didn't have no sense, I was a fool, and to move out. He said nobody should keep no dam' books on his place, and if we didn't like it, Goddam' it, git out!" Her husband added, "He charged us wid stuff we didn't know 'twas for an wouldn't explain nothin'. . . . If I had justice, we'd be living on a farm o' our own right now. I'll tell you one thing: hell's gettin' het up right now for some folks."

Uncle Charles Holcomb's grandfather tried to teach him a lesson about his relationships with white folks when he was still a child. They went fishing, and Holcomb's grandfather caught "a big fat catfish and jist played with him for a long time. He pointed to de fish and tol' me to watch him. Den he lifted de fish outen de water and dat fish kicked and thrashed sumpthin' turrible. Den he lowered de line and let de fish back in de water. When he did dat de fish jist swum around as easy as you please." His grandfather repeated the process. Finally, when the fish was dead, his grandfather pointed out the moral. "Son," he said, "a catfish is a lot like a nigger. As long as he is in his mudhole he is all right, but when he gits out he is in for a passel o' trouble. You 'member dat, and you won't have no trouble wid [white] folks when you grow up." When Holcomb's landlord cheated on his tobacco money, he forgot his grandfather's advice and beat him badly. The result was a year of labor on the county roads while his wife and children made out as best they could.

With great sacrifices, Charlie Holcomb and his wife sent their bright young son, Willie, to the Agricultural and Technical College of North Carolina. Back home Willie got in an argument with a white man at the cotton warehouse and was beaten to death. With his dead son in his arms, Holcomb recalled his grandfather's demonstration with the catfish. His son "had stepped outen his place when he got dat eddycation. If I'd kept him here on de farm he woulda been all right. Niggers has got to l'arn dat dey ain't lik white folks, and never will be, and no amount o' eddycation can make 'em be, and dat when dey gits outen dere place dere is gonna be trouble. . . . White man didn't Jim Crow de nigger—it was God Jim Crowed 'im, back yonder when Ham laughed at pore old Noah for gettin' drunk. . . . God made a nigger like a mule to be close to nature and git his livin' by de sweat o' his brow like the Good Book says. And when a nigger is workin' and feelin' de strength o' his muscles and de good hot sun in his face he is happy. Long as he has plenty o' cornpone and pot likker to wash it down wid, he don't need nothin' else."

Ned Coad had vivid memories of how cruelly blacks were abused and exploited. Whites, he told Theodore Rosengarten, would "over-power you every way, meet colored folks on the road, young colored boys when I was a boy, beat 'em up, whip 'em up, make 'em get in the field and go to work. I knowed too darn well they weren't payin' 'em nothin' hardly. . . . These people in this country . . . done that—called it vagrancy. It was just like slavery. God knows it weren't a bit of difference. In place of ever changin' and gettin' better, it was gettin' worser and worser as I come up in this world."

Avis Briar's uncle was born in Mississippi. "He told us," she recalled, "that he and four other boys were swimming and some white men came and shot at them and wouldn't let them get out of the water. They hit two of the black boys and one of them almost drowned because those white men wouldn't let them get out of the water."

Grant Smith, who grew up in rural Georgia, had an indifferent education, "dictated by the whims and agricultural needs of the whites who controlled our schools. They closed our wretched schools whenever it suited their purposes. . . ." Smith spoke bitterly about his Southern childhood and the miserable conditions in which his family lived: "It was staying in that sinkhole which ruined all of us; I mean, it decayed our brains before we even knew we *had* brains! It reduced us to polite, hypocritical opossums. The whites fed on us and we fed on each other! . . . For me the air was filled with the spirits of dead people and animals. . . . To me, my past is almost all bad. In many ways I was more of a slave than my black ancestors. At least they knew they were slaves, and it was only their physical bodies and actions that their enemies could try to control. They helped each other and they were merciless to their enemies. . . ." After slavery was ended, whites began to manipulate the minds of black people to try to convince them that they were inherently inferior human beings. That was the most grievous slavery of all. When Grant Smith's aunt Velma came North, she was obsessed by the fear of being arrested. "She would not take a chance on eating in a restaurant if she saw any white people around. So she got very weak during job hunting. . . . Fear was always with us, so much so that we took it for granted. It made clever people seem dull and stupid."

Hosea Hudson told of an episode that occurred in Smithfield, Alabama, in which a white man accused a fifteen-year-old black boy who was acting as baby-sitter in his wife's absence of raping his eight-year-old daughter. The boy was tried at once and sentenced to be executed. During his trial a note was passed to the judge, who then ordered the boy removed from the courtroom. It turned out that the note was from the girl's father, informing the judge that he wished to shoot the boy himself. As a deputy took the boy from the courthouse, the father shot and killed him. The boy's mother in the courtroom, hearing the shot, cried, "Oh, Lord, is they killing my child?" The judge refused to allow anyone to leave the courtroom until a bailiff whispered to him that the boy's body had been removed and the blood on the courthouse steps mopped up.

In a suburb of Birmingham a black man, "a kind of well-dressed young fellow," entered a drugstore to buy a package of cigarettes. The cigarettes cost fifteen cents, and the man gave the proprietor of the store, a man named Warden, twenty-five cents. When he asked for his change, the proprietor of the store insisted that he had given it to him. There was a heated exchange of words, and the black threw the cigarettes onto the counter and asked for fifteen cents back. The proprietor gave him fifteen cents and, as the customer turned to leave, shot him in the back with a pistol. He was hospitalized but recovered. Black leaders in Birmingham were determined to have Warden indicted and tried for the shooting, but when the young man's sister asked the police what action they planned to take, a policeman replied, "We ain't doing nothing about it. Who is that nigger out'n there who insulted that white man in that drugstore? . . . He oughta killed the so-and-so." When Hosea Hudson and other Communist Party members raised money for a lawyer and tried to secure a conviction, they found that the hospital would not release the records that showed where the man had been struck by the bullet. The judge dismissed the case.

One of the most flagrant cases of police "crime" was recounted by Hudson to Nell Painter. Collegeville, near Birmingham, was run by a man called Police Dukes. Even the churches in the town could not have social meetings without permission from Dukes. A young black man named Eddie Powell was a thorn in Dukes's side because of his persistence in raising questions about arbitrary, warrantless arrests of blacks and the beating by the police of blacks suspected of radical inclinations. Dukes sent a black "stool pigeon" named Fat Harsh with two henchmen to kill Powell. In their zeal they killed two of Powell's brothers as well. That was more than Dukes had intended. Hudson and Mack Coad began a campaign to get the murderers indicted. They flooded city hall with postcards protesting the killings and demanding punishment for the guilty ones. A seer and "card reader," Miss Lena, told Hudson that Dukes had come to her in great distress. "Boy," she asked Hudson, "what is you all doing? . . . You know you done near about run Dukes crazy . . . he come here crying, said he didn't tell Fat Harsh to go there and kill all the brothers. He told him to kill Eddie." Organized protests in the black community forced the resignation of Dukes.

Few black women that the anthropologist John Langston Gwaltney talked with had not been the victims of sexual aggression by white men. Nancy White was a sharp-tongued old woman who had been born in Tennessee and worked hard all her life. "White men were always messing with black girls," she told Gwaltney. "Sometimes a black woman would have to move someplace away from there just so some white man or boy couldn't get his hands on her. . . . I saw these things happen and they happened to me. One of my best girl friends got sick from the falling-out sickness and the doctor that was supposed to cure her gave her a baby. He was a devil when it came to that kind of carrying on." Nancy White was especially critical of the relationship between white men and women. Her mother had told her "that the black woman is the white man's mule and the white woman is his dog . . . we do the heavy work and get beat whether we do it well or not. But the white woman is closer to the master and he pats them on the head and lets them sleep in the house, but he ain' gon' treat either one like he was dealing with a person." The middle- or upper-class white woman who relied on her husband for support surrendered her own independence, White declared. As the source of the family's income her husband could "pocketbook her to death" and tyrannize over her. In black families wives as well as husbands had to work, and the wife sometimes earned more than the husband. White made clear to her three husbands that she would not be struck or beaten "because I do not need a man to feed myself." When her first husband tried to dominate her as though she were a child, in her words, she told him, "If you gon' treat me like I was old enough to *have* children, you cannot treat me like I *was* a child myself! Now that's it." Her husband, James Tucker, was a "fine man" and a hard worker, but when he struck her, she left him without a word. "I have not seen him since and I don't want to see him," she told Gwaltney.

Having spent her life working for white families, Nancy White had wondered at the indignities that white wives put up with. One woman was well aware that her husband was doing his best to seduce White but tolerated it. What such wives should have done, in White's view, was "fire these worthless white boy-men they married to and get out here and get it [earn their living] just like we have to do. But laziness and all that trash them white men talk to them keeps them running along beside these no-good men of theirs just like little yard dogs. Now, that won't work with black woman," she announced, "because black men don't have any more than we do. . . . [W]hat I'm trying to say is that there is a very few black women that their husbands can pocketbook to death because we can do for ourselves and will do so in a minute." Nancy White's argument is strikingly like that of Charlotte Perkins Gilman in her *Women and Economics*. Gilman wrote that the feeder became the environment of the fed and that women could break out of their subordination to men only when they earned their own living.

To Nancy White, black men were as adept at "all that moonlight boogie-joogie" as whites. She had learned the painful way. She had listened, too, "and before a hoecake could make a crust," she'd had two children.

While many white farmers slipped into tenancy as the result of poor soil, poor farming methods, and the pernicious boll weevil, a number of blacks, men like Ned Coad, rose from sharecropping and tenancy to ownership of farms in their own right. In 1930, W. J. Cash tells us, some 21 percent of black farmers owned their own farms.

Coad's father remembered when the vote was taken away from him. "As I growed to knowledge," he told Theodore Rosengarten, "I thought it was as bad a thing as ever happened—disfranchise the nigger. Tellin' him he didn't have a right to his thoughts. He just weren't counted to be no more than a dog." Coad grew up and took to farming. Through shrewdness and hard work he was able to establish himself as a farmer, owning his own farm, heavily mortgaged though it was; he had two mules and a cow, pigs, and chickens and was rated prosperous among his neighbors.

In Durham, North Carolina, blacks built up a substantial insurance company. Black burial societies were another important black business, and morticians were members of black society. Prosperous urban blacks displayed their wealth by driving expensive limousines, living in handsome homes, and wearing flashy clothes; it was a common experience for blacks who drove handsome cars to have the car bodies scratched and defaced by jealous whites.

Cash gives an account of one of the most common and curious black-white contacts in the South. With the suppression in many Southern cities of red-light districts, Southern hotels became "public stews," the common haunts of prostitutes. Black bellboys "acquired a virtual monopoly of the trade of pander and pimp, and demanded and secured from the white prostitutes that they serve, all the traditional prerogatives of the pimp, including not only a large share of their earnings but also and above all the right of sexual intercourse. . . . The result was a horde of raffish blacks, full of secret, contemptuous knowledge of the split in the psyche of the shame-faced Southern whites and their hedonistic practices—scarcely troubling to hide their grinning contempt for their clients under the thinnest veil of subservient politeness and, in the case of the bell boys, hugging to themselves with cackling joy their knowledge of the white man's women."

The main consolation of both blacks and whites was some form of Protestant Christianity. In "Big Ivy," Tennessee, there were "just two peculiar men . . . when it comes to religion," a white farm wife declared. "One don't believe in nothing and the other one he's a Jehovah Witness man. The rest of us is Baptist, Missionary and Primitive Hard-Shell Baptist. Missionaries go to Shady Grove Church and the Hard-Shells to Pilgrim Glory." Big Ivy contained mostly children and old people. The young men and women had gone to town "because they want to be at the county seat where things is stirring. Gone everywhere and anywhere to get away from farming life. Young folks this day and generation can't seem to abide the hard scuffling ways to have to get by on a farm, even with the government paying good money to help out." Occasionally there was a sensational murder trial at Poplin that provided some diversion. Otherwise there was little for old people to do but "set."

Blacks were sustained by their faith in another, better world. "When we gits up before dat golden throne," the wife of a black sharecropper in Dillon, South Carolina, told an interviewer, "de Lawd gwine to say to Mister Stores: 'Stores, yo' ain't treated people right, nawsuh, dat yo' sho' ain't!' An' de Lawd gwine call St. Peter an' tell him to throw Mister Stores in de bottomless pit! . . . Yassuh! . . . [D]ey's gwine to be a scatterin' er blacks an' whites up dere near de throne. Heaben gwine to be full er dem dat's kept de law of de Lawd, an' hell gwine to be packed to overflowin' wid dem dat *ain't,* yassuh, dat hit sho' is! . . . Thank Gawd, dere won't be no landlawds up dere before Jesus's seat, an' dat's what will meck hit heaben!"

What may well have stuck in white craws was the sense that despite their terrible hardships and oppression, blacks had the gift to infuse life, wretched as it might be, with a kind of joy. When Charlie Holcomb was a young tobacco sharecropper, he and his family and friends "always did have a grand time durin' the curin', as we have ter stay wid de fire all de time 'till de 'baccer was done. Most o' de time some o' de neighbors would come over and bring a fiddle or a guitar and we would sing and dance and hav' de biggest kind o' time."

When all was said and done, the ultimate horror experienced directly or indirectly by every black Southerner was the ancient custom of lynching. Out of the total of 3,397 blacks lynched between 1882 and 1938, only 181 were lynched outside the Southern states, Missouri, Maryland, and West Virginia included. In 26 percent of the known lynchings committed between 1882 and 1946, the lynched person was accused only of some minor offense or of no crime at all. Even so, the figures were deceptive. One of the ways in which lynchings were avoided was by assurance to the prospective lynchers that the law should be allowed "to take its course." That course was often foreordained: a hasty trial with little regard for the rights of the accused or the evidence followed by the execution of the defendants. In fact, it was said that no Southern jury had ever acquitted a black man accused of rape by a white woman. In the South Carolina senatorial campaign of 1930 Coleman Blease defended lynching vehemently. "Whenever the Constitution comes between me and the virtue of the white women of the South, I say to hell with the Constitution."

Anthony Crawford was a prosperous farmer who owned "427 acres of the prettiest cotton land in the county" of Abbeville, South Carolina. He had twelve sons and four daughters. He had had a school for black children built on his farm and paid the teacher's salary. He was secretary of the African Methodist Episcopal Church and the head of the Black Masons in the state. During the cotton-picking season Crawford got into an argument about the price of cotton. He cursed a group of whites for trying to cheat him. A mob formed, swearing to kill him for swearing at a white man. When the mob arrived at his house, Crawford swung a sledgehammer at the first man who tried to lay hands on him and crushed the man's skull. He was knifed and shot, and "two hundred white men kicked him into unconsciousness and continued for forty-five minutes to beat and mutilate his body." The next day the whites of Abbeville met and passed a resolution that every member of the Crawford family (nine of his children lived near his farm) must leave the county within two weeks. They then ordered all black businesses in Abbeville shut down. Gos Roman, the blacksmith, refused, and a white man helped him guard his shop. One of those warned out was Alfred Ellison, who walked down the town's street, telling the whites he encountered, "If you're going to kill me, you'll have to kill me right here because I am not leaving. This is where I have my family, my farm, my friends; and I don't plan to leave." But Ellison did leave for Oklahoma, where his son, Ralph, was born.

After Crawford's lynching a white man was reported to have said, "I reckon the crowd wouldn't have been so bloodthirsty only it's been three years since they had any fun with the niggers and it seems as if they just have to have a lynching every so often." A local newspaper editor suggested the real motive behind the lynching was Crawford's prosperity. He was considerably better off than most of the white farmers in the county, and "property ownership always makes the Negro more assertive, more independent, and the poor whites can't stand that. There is an element of jealousy that enters wherever they see a 'nigger' forge ahead of them and they lay for a chance to get him."

In Adamsville, Alabama, a black named Will McBride, sixty years old, "was taken from bed by a mob and beaten to death. He had been arrested on a charge of assault but it had been dismissed by the judge. Some school children had become frightened at seeing him walk along the road."

A. Philip Randolph recalled his mother's sitting up all night in their home in Jacksonville, Florida, with a rifle in her lap to protect her two sons against marauding whites while his father posted himself with other blacks at the jail to keep whites from lynching a black prisoner.

Upper-class whites professed to be horrified by lynchings, which they often blamed on uneducated poor whites, but it is clear that all classes of whites in the South were co-conspirators. Time after time prominent citizens of a community or a city—lawyers and preachers and almost invariably policemen and law officers, including judges— were noted in lynch mobs. Newspaper editors were perhaps the worst offenders, writing editorials of the most inflammatory kind, lurid invitations to violence. It was Jessie Daniel Ames's conclusion that more than 50 percent of the lynchings in the Deep South were encouraged or led by "prominent people" in the respective communities where the lynchings took place.

Volumes have been written on the psychological roots of lynching. Most begin with the reminder that lynching is, after all, a grand old American custom, named after Captain Charles Lynch, who is credited with inventing the practice. Where there were few blacks to lynch, whites lynched each other. But the lynching of black Americans, as we have had ample occasion to observe, had quite different roots. Clearly lynching was a means of oppressing and dominating a class of people. Every lynching of a black man or, less frequently, a woman was intended as instruction for other blacks on their powerless and degraded state. The South did its best to give the impression that lynching was the only way to prevent "black beasts" from raping white women, although it was demonstrated repeatedly that in only a quarter or so of such lynchings was it even alleged that rape had been involved. A black man could be lynched for allegedly *looking* at a white woman in a way that seemed objectionable to her, and as we have seen time and again, hundreds of blacks were lynched for "insulting" a white man— that is to say, questioning anything a white man said or did. Jacquelyn Dowd Hall, in her biography of Jessie Daniel Ames, makes the point that the lynching of blacks on the ground that lynchings were necessary to preserve the chastity of white women was also a way of keeping white women in a position of subordination and dependence. They were weak, frail creatures in constant danger of suffering the fate "far worse than death."

John Templeton Graves, a liberal Southern journalist, warned Atlanta blacks: "No law of God or man can hold back the vengeance of our white men upon such a criminal [a rapist]. . . . We will hang two, three, or four of the Negroes nearest to the crime until the crime is no longer done or feared in all this Southern land we inhabit and love."

A typical letter to the Georgetown, Texas, newspaper declared:

"God will burn . . . the Big African Brute in Hot Hell for molesting our God-like pure snowwhite angelic American Women."

Finally, there was simple, unvarnished fear: fear of darkness, of blackness, of the secret, unknowable life of blacks. It was an ancient pathology. It is also common to fear those we have wronged. Thomas Jefferson was one of the first Americans to articulate that wrong and that fear. The fear of black insurrection, he wrote a correspondent, "awakened and filled me with terror." On another occasion he wrote that "in the gloomiest moments of the revolutionary war, I never had any apprehensions equal to what I feel from this source." Even John Adams confessed, "I have been so terrified with this Phenomenon that I constantly said . . . to the Southern Gentlemen, I cannot comprehend this object. . . ." Jefferson's nephews murdered a slave for breaking a teacup and mutilated his body. Jefferson could never bring himself to speak of the episode.

The murderers of Charles Caldwell, who danced around his corpse all night, drinking and shrieking like Indians, were obviously trying to exorcise their fear of blacks.

In the South blacks were almost invariably tortured and mutilated as part of the lynching ritual. It was the performance of these obscene rituals that revealed so clearly what the lynchings were really about. W. E. B. Du Bois was launched on his career of political action when he saw the knuckles of Sam Hose, a black farmer who had been lynched, displayed in a grocery store window in Atlanta. It came to him as a revelation that in such a world the scientific objectivity that he had been taught at Harvard was wildly irrelevant.

There were repeated efforts to pass Federal legislation outlawing lynching. Leonidas Carstarphen Dyer, a Congressman from St. Louis with a large black constituency, introduced an antilynching bill into the House in 1918. It died there, but three years later he revived it and solicited the support of James Weldon Johnson and the National Association for the Advancement of Colored People (NAACP) in lobbying for its passage. The NAACP, which had first attempted to prevail on specific states to pass antilynching laws, discovered that even when such laws were passed, they had no effect. It thereupon turned its attention to Federal legislation. For months Dyer and Johnson worked to line up support for the bill among Northern Republicans and big-city Democrats who had black constituents.

The bitterness of the debate in the House revealed the depth of feeling on the part of Southern Congressmen. Thomas Sisson from

Mississippi declared that "as long as rape continues, lynching will continue. . . . We are going to protect our girls and womenfolk from these black brutes. When these black fiends keep their hands off the throats of the women of the South the lynching will stop, and it is never going to stop until that crime stops. [Applause]."

Henry Cooper, a Wisconsin Congressman, replied that it was the first time he had "heard mob law openly advocated in the Congress of the U.S." (Applause on the floor and in the gallery.) Sisson answered, "I never advocated mob law. Does the gentleman advocate rape?"

Cooper: "Oh, that is simply silly."

At the end of the exchange blacks in the gallery rose and cheered the Wisconsin congressman. On a roll-call vote there were 230 ayes and 119 nays, with 74 not voting. Only eight Democrats voted for Dyer's bill. The outcome was, in large part, a consequence of James Weldon Johnson's indefatigable lobbying efforts, but he found the going far heavier in the Senate. There the Southerners made clear their determination to filibuster the bill to death.

Throughout the 1920s the liberal elements in the South, always a beleaguered minority, bestirred themselves. The Southern Sociological Congress pressed for scholarly studies of the racial problems of the South, as did the University Commission on Southern Race Questions. Together they formed the Commission on Interracial Cooperation (CIC) and chose a young Methodist minister named Will Alexander to head it. Aided by Northern philanthropic foundations like the Julius Rosenwald Foundation and the Phelps Stokes Fund, the CIC directed its attention to such relatively low-voltage issues as improved housing, better education, and legal justice.

W. E. B. Du Bois hailed the CIC as an outgrowth of the NAACP and an indication that the South was at last ready "to attempt its own internal reform. To be effective, it must attract real black men who dare to look you in the eye and speak truth and who refuse to fawn and lie." Blacks were, in fact, slow to join, but by 1924 the CIC had twenty-two black members, among them Robert Russa Moton, president of Tuskegee; Bishop R. E. Jones, one of the most prominent black leaders in the South; and John Hope, president of Morehouse College. Mary White Ovington, mainstay of the NAACP, endorsed the CIC and described Alexander as "a humane, fair-minded man, without cant and without prejudice." Women were initially excluded on the ground that bringing white women into meetings with black men would foster "social intermingling" and eventually intermarriage. The men debated whether women would be a "Hindenburg" line of reaction or "wild-eyed fanatics" for reform.

The greatest promise for improved relations between the races in the South was an initially hesitant relationship between black and white churchwomen. Methodist churchwomen had a record of concern for racial issues. As early as 1914 Lily Hardy Hammond, the director of the Methodist Women's Bureau of Social Service, made an analysis of racial relations that strongly condemned lynching. Among the black women of the South Lucy Craft Laney was an outspoken opponent of racial barriers. Laney had graduated from the first class of Atlanta University, and in 1886 she opened the Haines Normal and Industrial Institute in Augusta, Georgia. Her most famous student was Mary McLeod Bethune, one of seventeen children born of slave parents. Bethune founded the Bethune-Cookman College at Daytona Beach, Florida, in 1904. She was also founder of the National Council of Negro Women. Janie Porter Barrett and Charlotte Hawkins Brown were two other black women who had been inspired by Lucy Laney. The Locust Street Social Settlement in Hampton, Virginia, was founded by Barrett, as was the Virginia Industrial School for Colored Girls. Brown started the Palmer Memorial Institute in Sedalia, North Carolina.

The Young Women's Christian Association was also a rallying point for women dedicated to racial reform. In 1920 the national organization issued the "Social Creed of the Churches," which called for collective bargaining, the right to organize unions, and "economic justice" for blacks and whites alike. Eva Bowles, the first black field secretary of the YWCA, had established "recreational and industrial centers" in forty-five communities by the end of 1919. There were 86 paid black workers and 12,000 members.

Lugenia Hope, who served during the war as special war work secretary and was active in the YWCA, pressed the national head-quarters to integrate all black and white Y members. "Northern women thought they knew more about it than Southern women—Colored women believed they knew more than both and that's why they wanted to represent themselves," she wrote.

When the National Association of Colored Women met at Tuskegee Institute in the summer of 1920, two white women, Carrie Parks Johnson and Sara Estelle Haskin, both active in the Missionary Council of the Methodist Church, were invited to attend. The experience was a revelation to the white women. "I had a new world opened to me, a world I had never conceived before," Carrie Johnson wrote. Social uneasiness characterized the meeting. The white women, who had never encountered black women except as domestic servants or subordinates, found themselves treated as equals. That was disconcerting enough, but they also sensed a strong current of hostility. Expecting to be featured and deferred to, they found themselves rather awed spectators. "Only after an hour spent in the reading of God's word and in prayer, face to face on the platform of Jesus Christ," Johnson wrote, "did these white women and black women come to a liberty and frankness that made possible a discussion."

Lugenia Hope challenged the white visitors: "We can achieve nothing today unless you . . . who have met us are willing to help us find a place in American life where we can be unashamed and unafraid." Mary McCrorey, one of the white women present, wrote later that "the spirit of that meeting will last me through the remainder of my life." She saw in "the hearts of those Negro women . . . all the aspirations for their homes and their children that I have for mine."

"My heart broke," Carrie Johnson wrote, "and I have been trying to pass the story on to the women of my race." She and Sara Haskin told Will Alexander that "the men might as well hang their harps on a willow tree, as to try to settle the race problem in the South without the aid of the Southern white woman. . . . While we have thought we were doing the best we could, a race has grown up in our very midst that we do not know. We know the cook in the kitchen, we know the maid in the house, we know the man in the yard, we know the criminal in the daily papers, we know the worst there is to know—but the masses of the best people of my race do not know the best of the Negro race."

A few months later Will Alexander prevailed on the executive committee of the Commission on Interracial Cooperation to call a conference of Southern churchwomen, women's club members, and YWCA leaders in Memphis, Tennessee. Ninety-one women gathered to discuss "important problems," which were understood to be racial in nature. They were told that they had been invited to hear black women speak of their views on the racial issue in the South. Margaret Washington, the widow of Booker T. Washington, who had graduated from Fisk University and been dean of the Woman's Department at Tuskegee, was the first speaker. The next day Elizabeth Ross Haynes, also a graduate of Fisk and the first black YWCA national secretary, addressed the conference. Haynes had written widely on the problems of black women and had served during the war in the Women's Bureau of the Department of Labor. She spoke of Sojourner Truth and her role as both an abolitionist and champion of women's rights.

Charlotte Hawkins Brown had been born in Henderson, North Carolina, in 1882 and reared in Massachusetts, where, through the good offices of Alice Freeman Palmer, the president of Wellesley College, she received a college education. She had come, she told the delegates, to bring "the message which the Lord had given me." She declared: "The Negro women of the South lay everything that happens to the members of her race at the door of the Southern white women.... We all feel that you control your men ... [and] so far as lynching is concerned ... if the white woman would take hold of the situation that lynching would be stopped." As for the argument that lynching was necessary to protect "the chastity of white women ... I want to say to you, when I read in the paper where a colored man has insulted a white woman, just multiply that by one thousand and you have some idea of the number of colored women insulted by white men." Her special target was the white notion that blacks were inherently promiscuous. "I know that if you are Christian women, ... in the final analysis you are going to have to reach out for the same hand that I am reaching out for but I know that the dear Lord will not receive you if you are crushing me beneath your feet."

When Brown finished speaking, the women rose spontaneously and began to sing a hymn of Christian fellowship. To Charlotte Brown the meeting was "the greatest step forward ... taken since emancipation." Many of the white women present dated their own commitment to the cause of Southern blacks from that moment.

Despite such exalted moments, black women had to put up with a good deal from their white "sisters." Mrs. T. W. Bickett, chair of the Interracial Woman's Committee and wife of the governor of North Carolina, introduced Charlotte Brown by saying, "I cannot say anymore, Mrs. Brown, for your race today ... than that you are as fine as was my Negro mammy." Another black woman was invited to speak to a group of white Baptist women about the "work of the niggers" and told to enter the hall by the rear door.

In bustling, booming, hedonistic America the South was an anomaly. The ancient tragedy of slavery pervaded it. Time (and progress) seemed to have passed it by. Yet it was the custodian of a great tradition.

# 5

# Coolidge's Election, 1924

When the Republican Convention of 1920 had been stampeded for Calvin Coolidge as Vice-President, the newsmen sitting in the press section had "laughed heartily, thinking it a great joke," Oswald Garrison Villard recalled. Robert O'Brien, a reporter for the *Boston Herald* and a man who knew the new vice-presidential candidate well, was not amused. "I have known all our public men since Grover Cleveland," he told Villard. "This is the worst man I ever knew in politics." O'Brien then turned to a Quaker friend and said, "I will bet thee a dinner that Harding will die and Coolidge become President." Villard did not note whether the bet had been taken or the meal delivered when Coolidge took the reins of office in the summer of 1923.

Henry Mencken's obituary for Warren G. Harding was hard to gainsay: "No great and alarming Cause issued from his fancy. He invented no new and superior Bugaboo. Only once did he ever say anything that attracted attention, and then, I fear, he was laughed at. No one hated him, and no one worshipped him. Even the plain people, I believe, like to find something brilliant in their heroes. Dr. Harding was simply an amiable hand-shaker, a worthy fellow in his Sunday clothes, an estimable noble of the Mystic Shrine."

Calvin Coolidge was sworn in as President of the United States by his father, John Coolidge, a colonel in the state militia, lawyer, and notary public. The oath of office was administered in the senior Coolidge's office-living room.

Calvin Coolidge was born on July 4, 1872, at Plymouth, Vermont. In William Allen White's words, Vermont had "remained calm and sweet and lovely, like the interior of some cool museum preserving colonial life." Five generations of Coolidges were buried in the town cemetery. As a child Coolidge did not care for play. He was quiet and serious. He knew his Bible and the lore of the farm on which he was reared. Vermont was in his blood. "Vermont is my birthright," he wrote years later. "People are happy and content. They belong to themselves, live within their income, and fear no man." That had once been enough to carry a man through the world. Coolidge still believed it sufficient.

In 1890, after a classic New England schooling at an academy in the town of Ludlow, Calvin Coolidge attended Amherst College, where he rubbed elbows with the sons of the New England upper-middle class. There he fell under the spell of Professor Charles Garman, whose students looked upon him "as a man who walked with God. His course was a demonstration of the existence of a personal God, of our power to know Him, of the Divine Eminence and of the complete dependence upon Him as Creator and Father," Coolidge wrote in his *Autobiography*.

The future president was cautious, thrifty, pious, silent, and doggedly ambitious. His "casual aspect was that of a dumb, starved, suppressed young Yankee struggling against an inferiority complex," in White's words. After graduating from Amherst, Coolidge practiced law and began a slow ascent up the ladder of Massachusetts politics, keeping always in mind the revered Garman's observation: "One of the greatest mysteries of the world is the success that lies in conscientious work." Coolidge's principal literary passion was the Italian Renaissance poet Dante. He translated much of Dante from the original Italian.

Taken under the wing of Winthrop Murray Crane, one of the most powerful political figures in the state, Coolidge served in the legislature, then as lieutenant governor, and finally as governor. As we have seen, his handling of the Boston police strike brought him national attention and made him the running mate of Harding, a man no better qualified to be President than Coolidge was to be Vice-President.

Coolidge had two years of Harding's ill-fated term to complete before he had to run on his own or retire to Massachusetts. He soon made it clear that he intended to have his own term of office. Except to those enthusiasts in the Republican Party who had engineered his nomination as Vice-President, Coolidge was one of the more obscure holders of that traditionally obscure office. Few people knew what he thought or what he was like. One of his more ambitious literary efforts as Vice-President had been an article published in 1921 entitled "Are the Reds Stalking Our College Women?" The answer, not surprisingly, was yes.

Coolidge's presidency was one of the most startling incongruities of the age. The new President was the archetypal Puritan in a time when Puritanism had become a code word for everything repressive and archaic in American life. The larger society was, characteristically, difficult to define, but certainly its most conspicuous public mode was that of abandoned hedonism, especially among the generation that had come to its majority during the war years. William Allen White entitled his biography of Coolidge *Puritan in Babylon.* The new President was a classic naysayer in an age when almost anything went. To Waldo Frank his glum face announced, "The Nays have it"; it was a continuing negation of life and joy. Reporters sought access to the new President and came away baffled and frustrated. He had nothing to say. To White, Coolidge with his "curious shell of sardonic silence" seemed "one of the most curious human problems" that he had ever encountered as a reporter.

When Frazier Hunt went to the White House for lunch as a preliminary to an "interview" with Coolidge, everything was simple and homely, including the food—liver and bacon—and the conversation—largely monosyllabic. Once the President asked Mrs. Coolidge, "What was that state that had such tall corn?" She replied that it was Iowa. In the interview itself the President said little, although "now and then a dry and somewhat frostbitten phrase would slip out." The Coolidges invited Hunt to go to a baseball game. During the nine innings Coolidge's only remark was to ask his wife, "What time is it?"

"Four twenty-four," Mrs. Coolidge replied.

The journalist Gamaliel Bradford wrote of the "contrast between the mad, hurrying, chattering, extravagant, self-indulgent harlotry of twentieth-century America and the grave, silent, stern, narrow, uncomprehending New England Puritanism of Calvin Coolidge." Frank Kent, columnist for the *Baltimore Sun,* noted Coolidge's "neat little one cylinder intellect. . . . What he says is mostly non-committal, neutral, evasive . . . [t]he weak and watery utterances of a passive and pallid little man, torn by indecision and doubt. . . . It has been literally amazing that a man could be so long, so consistently and so unqualifiedly dull." At the other extreme the mayor of Springfield, Massachusetts, expressed the conviction "that Calvin Coolidge became President in accordance with a divine plan and that he should be maintained in office in order that the plan may be carried through."

The curious paradox was that while literary figures, journalists and writers and intellectuals, generally found him a symbol of everything they deplored in America and delighted in making him the target of their gibes, the public, the voters, discovered an odd affection for a President singularly lacking in attractive qualities. Perhaps his stubborn commonplaceness appealed to them. He tried to sit on the front porch of the White House in a rocking chair as he had done in his house in Northampton, but crowds collected, and he was forced to abandon that classic small-town diversion. Sometimes he simply sat at an upstairs window facing Lafayette Park and counted the automobiles that went past.

When James Derieux and his wife visited Coolidge during his last days in the White House, Mrs. Derieux asked the President what had worried him most of all during his tenure in the executive mansion. "The White House hams," he replied; "they would always bring a big one to the table. Mrs. Coolidge would always have a slice and I would have one. The butler would take it away and what happened to it afterward I could never find out." Then he added, "almost wistfully, 'I like the ham that comes from near the bone.'" Like a thrifty housewife, the President spent much time in the kitchen, the pantry, and the storerooms of the White House, possibly trying to find out what had happened to the missing hams.

He had an unhappy genius for permitting himself to be cozened by news photographers into bizarre iconographies. Visiting an Indian tribe, he was photographed wearing a headdress of eagle feathers. From beneath that savage bower peered out the glum Yankee face, which was antithetical in spirit to everything Indian. On another occasion he played cowboy in a ten-gallon hat and chaps. Gamaliel Bradford described the "garish cowboy rig and in the midst of it the chilly Vermont countenance wondering painfully, wearily what it was all about."

The presidential election year of 1924 was overshadowed by the revelations of the scandals of the Harding administration. There was evidence of corruption in the departments of Justice, Interior, and Navy, the Veterans Bureau, and the Office of the Alien Property Custodian. Colonel Charles R. Forbes, who had headed the Veterans Bureau, was indicted for conspiracy, fraud, and bribery and sentenced to two years in a Federal penitentiary. The most sensational disclosures concerned the administration of the Federal oil reserves at Teapot Dome, Wyoming, and Elk Hills, California, under the administration of Albert Fall, Harding's secretary of the interior. Fall had secretly leased the Teapot Dome lands to Harry Sinclair and the California fields to Edward Doheny. Senator Thomas Walsh of Montana discovered that Doheny had "lent" Fall $100,000 without interest or collateral.

Attorney General Harry M. Daugherty, working in collusion with the "Ohio gang," had accepted bribes for ignoring violations of Prohibition statutes. Poor Harding was safely underground, but the Democrats and the Independent Progressive Party took hope from the extent of the scandals and from Coolidge's reluctance to force Daugherty to resign. The fact was that in the atmosphere of the times, while the lurid accounts of public defalcations made newspaper headlines, they seem to have had little effect on the way people voted.

As the election of 1924 approached, Henry Mencken predicted that only two political types would be available: "first, unconscionable demagogues of the Roosevelt kidney, eager to embrace any buncombe that will enflame the proletariat, and, secondly, inarticulate vacuums of the Harding-Coolidge type, too poor in ideas to be capable of arousing any serious opposition."

One of the notable events of the Republican Convention, which met at Cleveland on June 10, was the quiet but firm deposition of Henry Cabot Lodge as the leader of the New England Republicans. It was Lodge who had rejected Coolidge as Harding's running mate four years earlier, dismissing the Vermonter snobbishly (and incorrectly) as a man who lived in a semidetached house. A supporter warned Lodge that the Coolidge men "intend to stick an elbow into your ribs at every turning. . . . They will permit you to have no position in the convention except that as a delegate from Massachusetts." At the convention Lodge was described by the journalist John Owens as being "in a state of ornate petrification." The Republican platform called for reduced taxes and government spending, high tariffs, the limitation of armaments, and United States cooperation in arms reduction and the World Court.

To no one's surprise, Coolidge was his party's nominee for President while Charles Dawes beat out Herbert Hoover for second place on the Republican ticket.

When the Democrats gathered on June 24, 1924, at Madison Square Garden during a withering heat wave, the party was at a low ebb. It was torn by regional divisions, most strikingly the ancient one that went back to the days of Jefferson and the formation of the party: the inherent tension between the industrial cities of the North, with their large ethnic and Catholic constituencies, and the rural South. The North was relatively liberal and predominantly wet; the South was conservative, Protestant, dry, and home to the Klan (as, to be sure, was the Midwest). In addition, the party had suffered a devastating defeat four years earlier and was still burdened with the overwhelmingly negative reaction to the Versailles Treaty.

The leading Democratic candidates were William McAdoo and Governor Alfred E. Smith of New York in that order. McAdoo had been urged by his supporters to refuse to consent to the convention's meeting in New York City, Al Smith's home ground. Assured by the editors of the city's Democratic papers that he would be treated fairly, McAdoo had suppressed his misgivings and accepted New York as the convention site. The journalist-historian Claude Bowers described the front-running McAdoo as "Tall, thin, graceful in bearing, . . . youthful in spirit and manner. . . . His deep-set eyes, sometimes quizzical, thoughtful and humorous, sometimes sad, suggested those of Lincoln." It was soon clear that powerful forces were opposed to McAdoo. His candidacy was badly compromised by the support of the Texas leader of the Ku Klux Klan and by the rumor that McAdoo was the Klan's candidate. Even the hint was enough to rouse Irish Catholic fears.

Popular as Al Smith was, the received political wisdom was that his Catholicism, his "wetness," and his image as a big-city boss would make him unacceptable to the mass of the voters in the South and Middle West, who were both anti-Catholic and pro-Prohibition. But Smith, with that touching optimism characteristic of politicians, determined to have a go at it.

The delegates had hardly sunk damply into their seats in the humid hall when the first dangerous fissure appeared. It was over a proposed plank in the platform denouncing the Ku Klux Klan. William Jennings Bryan, who had moved to Florida, represented that state on the platform committee. He insisted on a plank that would provide for stricter enforcement of Prohibition, and he opposed any specific indictment of the Ku Klux Klan on the ground that such a plank would lose many Southern votes (interestingly enough, the Klan issue had far more to do with Catholics than with blacks; not enough blacks voted to constitute a serious political issue). The Klan plank divided the platform committee. Bainbridge Colby led the fight by a minority of the committee on resolutions to denounce the Klan by name. Bryan replied for the majority, urging that the Democrats content themselves with a general statement supporting religious liberty and toleration. As Bryan tried to speak, he was greeted by a chorus of boos and jeers. Bryan praised the Catholic Church "as an institution that had withstood the assaults of centuries and did not depend for life on a resolution of a political convention. . . ." Josephus Daniels, a member of the resolutions committee, had voted for naming the Klan, but he could not bring himself to speak out against his old leader and friend. "Every delegate of Catholic faith," Henry Stoddard wrote, "has been made to feel that a plank inferentially against the Klan without naming it is directed against his religion." On the floor the "no name" plank carried by one vote.

The most dramatic event of the 1924 Democratic Convention was the reappearance of Franklin Roosevelt. Since his brilliant debut on the national political scene four years earlier, when he had been the running mate of James Cox on the Democratic ticket, Roosevelt had suffered the devastating polio attack which, it was generally assumed, had to mark an end to one of the most promising careers in America's political history. From the point of view of Roosevelt's physical rehabilitation, the Democratic Convention came too soon. He had barely started the exercises in the therapeutic waters of Warm Springs which, he was convinced, would restore the use of his legs. But the rumors that he was a hopeless cripple were so persistent that both Roosevelt and Louis Howe agreed that it was essential that he not only appear at the convention but play a prominent role. That role, it was decided, should be as nominator of Al Smith as the Democratic candidate in the upcoming election. Roosevelt's appearance before the party faithful would demonstrate that he had overcome the terrible disease that had struck him. It was also his opportunity to state his view of his party's principles and in effect to assert, even at the moment of nominating his chief rival, his ability to become his party's leader.

Any hope that Roosevelt had of being a spokesman of party principles was vetoed by Smith, who was obviously wary of having Roosevelt make too much political hay with *his* nomination. He wanted Roosevelt's speech to be limited to the conventional praise of the nominee plus harmless generalities.

Not wishing to be seen in a wheelchair, Roosevelt came early to Madison Square Garden every day, before the delegates arrived, and made his way laboriously, with crutches, to his seat in the New York delegation.

Now, the time to nominate Smith at hand, Roosevelt came slowly to the platform, perspiring heavily and gripping the arm of his son James so hard it ached. The delegates were caught up by the sight and began cheering wildly. Roosevelt grasped the rostrum, abandoned his crutches to his son, and gave the grin that was by now almost as famous as his cousin's. When the cheering subsided, Roosevelt's magic "singing" voice rang through the hall: "You equally who come from the great cities of the East and from the plains and hills of the West, from the slopes of the Pacific and from the homes and fields of the Southland, I ask you in all seriousness . . . to keep first in your hearts and minds the words of Abraham Lincoln—'With malice toward none, and charity for all.' " Roosevelt then offered the ritual praise for the nominee, a man who "has power to strike at every error and wrongdoing that makes his adversaries quail before him. He has a personality that carries to every hearer not only the sincerity but the righteousness of what he says. He is the 'Happy Warrior' of the political battlefield. . . ."

At the end of Roosevelt's nominating speech a demonstration began, led by young men and boys, "endlessly parading up and down the aisles with a band, shouting hoarsely, and to this horrid confusion mechanical devices contributed. . . . Sirens from the fire department had been put to work in the hall." Senator Thomas Walsh, chairman of the convention, tried in vain to bring about a degree of order and then declared that he would entertain a motion to move the convention to another city—all to no avail. Claude Bowers described the "mob" as a body "determined to rule or ruin." The anti-Smith forces responded in kind, and the scene bordered on outright riot. It was more than an hour before order was restored.

In the balloting that followed the nomination of McAdoo, neither McAdoo nor Smith was able to make any substantial inroads on the other's delegates. The deadlock seemed hopeless. After thirty-eight ballots no candidate had emerged as a front-runner. Williams Jennings Bryan got the floor amid jeers mixed with applause. When he reminded the delegates that this was probably his last convention, there was a round of somewhat ambiguous applause. Bryan, always the master of himself, responded, "Don't applaud, I may change my mind." (Laughter, applause, and cheers.) Finally, after mentioning a dozen obscure Democratic hopefuls, Bryan indicated his support for William McAdoo. The minutes of the convention note "applause, and boos, considerable disorder on the floor and in the gallery." There were cries of "Oil, oil" from the floor, referring to McAdoo's relationship with Edward Doheny. There were other cries: "Who's paying for this?" "Come off, come off." A New Jersey delegate rose and shouted: "The same old 'Dollar Bill,' the same old 'Dollar Bill,' " a reference to Bryan's large personal fortune. Still, the delegates held fast. Will Rogers wrote: "This thing has got to come to an end. New York invited you people here as guests, not to live." A refrain that began each of the interminable roll calls—"Alabama casts twenty-four votes for Oscar Underwood"—was carried to the nation by radio and became an instant national joke.

A discouraged McAdoo told Claude Bowers that it was Underwood who had tarred him with the Klan brush, but he resisted pressure to renounce support of the Klan. "Why isn't Smith asked to state where he stands?" he asked Bowers. Bowers might have replied that Smith as a Catholic was above suspicion.

With the delegates still deadlocked, McAdoo drew Bowers into a small, dimly lit room and told him that "attempts were being made to seduce his delegates with gin and whiskey"; as a veteran of numerous conventions McAdoo should not have been surprised at such tactics, which were as old as party conventions. Bowers himself was committed to an all-out effort to secure the nomination for his Indiana friend Senator Samuel Ralston. McAdoo, determined to do all in his power to prevent Smith from getting the nomination, agreed to release his delegates to Ralston, which would have given the Hoosier politician some 600 votes and presumably swung the convention to him. But Ralston, at that point, changed his mind and withdrew his name. His health, he felt, was too bad.

As the deadlock continued, the name of Roosevelt began to be heard more and more frequently among the delegates as the only person who could break the deadlock and carry the convention. In the words of a *New York Herald Tribune* reporter, "From the time Roosevelt made his speech in nomination of Smith . . . he has been easily the foremost figure on floor or platform. . . . Without the slightest intention or desire to do anything of the sort, he has done for himself what he could not do for his candidate." The reporter was naïve. Roosevelt and Howe knew very well what he had done, and they displayed their political astuteness and sense of timing by not yielding to the temptation to pick up a nomination that lay there for the taking, so to speak. The presidency is such an alluring prize that to refrain from reaching out to grasp the nomination for the office, however great the odds against ultimate victory may appear, requires considerable forbearance and calculation. Life is so full of contingencies that anyone with some experience of the world is bound to reflect that an opportunity passed up may not come again. But Roosevelt and Howe were, by now, old hands. They had a plan for inhabiting the White House and refused to allow themselves to be hurried or diverted. The *New York Evening World* noted shrewdly: "No matter whether Governor Smith wins or loses, Franklin D. Roosevelt stands out as the real hero of the Democratic Convention of 1924. Adversity has lifted him above the bickering, the religious bigotry, conflicting personal ambitions and petty sectional prejudices. It has made him the one leader commanding the respect and admiration of delegations from all sections of the land."

On the ninety-third ballot Smith had 355½ votes to McAdoo's 314, both far short of the 732 needed for the nomination. Roosevelt made his way once more to the rostrum to announce that Smith was ready, for the sake of party unity, which now seemed shattered beyond repair, to withdraw if McAdoo would do the same, thus leaving the way open for a compromise candidate, John W. Davis. So the party of the people ended up with a wealthy Wall Street lawyer of the House of Morgan as its presidential candidate and Charles Bryan, brother of William Jennings, as his running mate.

In Bowers's opinion the Democrats had destroyed themselves publicly by their prolonged and bitter wrangling: "The contest has become disreputable." Theodore Dreiser, a disillusioned witness, said to Bowers, "My God, is this the meaning of democracy?" When Bowers saw Bryan that night, still fanning himself with a palm-leaf fan, he looked exhausted. "He made a tragic figure. He who in the darkest days had rehabilitated and galvanized a great party bordering on collapse and had made possible the nomination of Wilson . . . walked alone, almost ignored."

Walter Lippmann had, somewhat excessively, called Smith the hope of "millions of half-enfranchised Americans . . . making their first bid for power." He credited the *World* with defeating McAdoo and wrote to Bernard Berenson, "The *World* led the fight against him, and it was the hardest, bitterest, most successful battle I've ever been [in].

We exposed his record, rallied the whole bloc of northern and eastern delegates against him, and after 103 ballots he broke down entirely."

Lippmann was determined to find good in the compromise candidate, John W. Davis, corporate lawyer and a man of thoroughly conservative bent. He described him as a man of "far more sheer ability than Wilson, a much richer experience in both industrial and diplomatic affairs, and . . . a man of finer grain."

The choice between Coolidge and Davis seemed to many liberals, not to mention radicals, no choice at all. Coolidge was a colorless nonentity, who was nonetheless adored by many of his countrymen and especially revered by such champions of capital as Henry Stoddard, who, it may be recalled, compared him to Lincoln. Davis, on the other hand, was an associate of the House of Morgan, a wealthy attorney, who as chairman of the American Bar Association not only had refused to speak out against Palmer's suppression of civil rights but had given such activities his tacit support. Felix Frankfurter reminded Walter Lippmann, who gave Davis his endorsement in the *World,* that Davis had returned from his ambassadorship in England "with great prestige at a time when the 'Red hysteria' and all the nonsense about 'Radicals' was in full swing. From that day to this, never a peep from Davis!" If Lippmann would take the trouble to read Davis's presidential address before the bar association in 1923, he would find "a regular stand-pat, hard-boiled enunciation of all the conventional bunkum in regard to the criticism of the courts, and all the conventional sophistication in defense of the invalidation by the courts of social legislation . . . if the *World* deems John W. Davis a liberal or a 'progressive,' then I wonder what its tests of liberalism or progressivism are." It was far from clear, in Frankfurter's opinion, that the Democratic Party's "liberal" period under the sway of Wilson was any more than a passing flirtation. It was still wedded to the Solid South, and the Solid South with its ingrained racism, was, to Frankfurter, "the greatest immoral factor of American politics." The only alternative, it soon became clear, was the Independent Progressive Party.

In 1922 an alliance of Progressives had called a Conference for Progressive Political Action. The backbone of the conference was fifteen railroad brotherhoods (unions), whose primary loyalty was to William McAdoo. (As head of the wartime railroad system McAdoo had proved a friend of the unions, raising wages and increasing benefits.) Faced with the postwar reaction against unions on the part of the railroads, the conference fought to maintain its gains. At a meeting which included Socialists, Farmer-Laborites, and members of the Committee of Forty-eight, delegates voted not to try to form a third party but to support the older parties.

When both Democrats and Republicans chose conservative candidates, the Conference for Progressive Political Action called its own convention for July 4 in Cleveland. It was one of those classic gatherings of enthusiasts from the margins of American political life. General Jacob Coxey, who had led the "army" of unemployed workers and discontented farmers on its march to Washington in 1893, was there. There were socialists from the garment workers' unions—the International Ladies' Garment Workers and the Amalgamated Clothing Workers. W. T. Raleigh, the patent medicine tycoon and bankroller of left-wing causes, was present. There were union leaders by the score, Bryanites and Populists, vegetarians and temperance men.

The conference met amid a fervor that recalled the Bull Moose Convention in 1912. There were many veterans of that convention among them. The old Socialists William English Walling and Charles Edward Russell, two of the founders of the NAACP, were much in evidence, as were Amos Pinchot, Arthur Garfield Hays, and Frederic Howe, in addition to representatives of the railroad brotherhood, the Farmer-Laborites of Wisconsin, and the American Federation of Labor. It was as though all the buried hopes and defeated dreams of a generation of political have-nots rallied for one more battle against Wall Street and the Eastern capitalists. A conscious effort was made to exclude Communists, but William Z. Foster, Charles Hathaway, Alfred Knutson, and Joseph Manley, Foster's son-in-law, all were present as members of the Farmer-Labor executive committee. William Pickens, a field secretary of the NAACP, represented that association. He found to his dismay that the conference, tantalized by the hope of victory, illusory as it might be, was almost as leary of taking a strong stand on any racial issue as the Democratic Convention. There was an effort by the conference's manager to prevent Pickens from even addressing the delegates, but pressure from Russell and Walling, as well as others, forced the leaders to give him his inning. He was greeted with enthusiastic applause when he listed the concerns of black Americans—the Klan; lynching; protection of the voting rights of blacks; freedom for the Philippines, Haiti, Santo Domingo, and Nicaragua—but none of these issues found their way into the party's platform. Angry over the refusal of La Follette and the "new" Progressives to take a stand on black issues, black leaders refused to endorse the new party—with the conspicuous exception of Pickens.

The delegates settled on old and ailing Bob La Follette as their candidate under the name of the Independent Progressive Party, with Burton K. Wheeler as his running mate. Bob La Follette thus made his final political appearance as the ghost of progressivism. He called for government ownership of the railroads and hydroelectric power. Congress, he declared, should be able to override Supreme Court decisions. These were the ancient battle cries of the Progressives, making a last, despairing bid for political power. The aging warriors of that great crusade rallied to his banner. Helen Keller, friend of Emma Goldman and advocate of revolution, joined a notable company that included Congressman Fiorello La Guardia, Jane Addams, John Dewey, the Pinchots, Oswald Garrison Villard, and Harold Ickes—"the forces that are struggling and groping for a dream," Felix Frankfurter wrote to Lippmann.

As for the other presidential candidates, the Commonwealth Land Party, formerly the Single Tax Party, had nominated W. J. Wallace for President in February. The Socialist Labor Party, gathering in New York in May, had nominated Frank Johns of Oregon for President. The American Party Convention chose as its leader Judge Gilbert O. Nations. The Prohibition Party held its convention in Columbus, Ohio, and nominated Herman Faris.

Like Frazier Hunt, Frederic Howe, Hutchins Hapgood, and so many reformers who had experienced their glory days in the decade before the outbreak of the European war, Felix Frankfurter deplored the materialism of the times. It was demoralizing to the "lads" in his law classes at Harvard. It was deeply troubling that "at a time when we need the discouragement of material ambitions and the instilling of spiritual concerns that really matter," he wrote Learned Hand, "and out of which alone will come the atmosphere of faith and understanding and confidence in one another, indispensable for the solutions of our greatest problems, that we should reward with the Presidency one [Davis] to whom big money was the big thing. . . ."

Frankfurter's solution was to vote for La Follette. He alone, Frankfurter wrote in a public statement, "represents a determined effort to secure adequate attention for the great interests of the workers and of agriculture in those economic and social compromises which, in the last analysis, underlie all national action." To those who, like Lippmann, pointed to the futility of third parties in light of their history, Frank-furter replied, "If the clarification of American politics through the formation of a new party is required to make our politics more honest and more real, then all the talk of 'throwing one's vote away' is cowardly philosophy of the bandwagon."

Touring with La Follette in 1924, Frederic Howe was persuaded by the large and enthusiastic crowds that "Fighting Bob" had, at last, a fighting chance.

The Republicans did their best to discredit La Follette, calling him a tool of the Soviet Union. Calvin Coolidge so far broke his silence as to announce that the question before the country was "whether America will allow itself to be degraded into a communistic or socialistic state of whether it will remain America." To Lippmann, La Follette's candidacy was a disaster. He had "united the conservatives and divided the progressives . . . paralyzed the liberals and revivified the reactionaries . . . muddled every issue, dragged a red herring across every trail, and done his complete and most effective best to insure the re-election of Coolidge." The Wisconsin Senator was "violently nationalistic and centralizing," an "illogical mixture of the individualism of 1890 . . . and pre-war Socialism." The "new" Lippmann announced that the real issues were the "decentralization of the federal political power and the reduction of government at Washington. . . ."

Coolidge won one of the most lopsided popular votes in our history, 15,725,016 to Davis's 8,385,586. La Follette's 4,822,856 votes were pitifully small by comparison. The electoral college vote was closer—382 to 136—primarily because the Solid South stuck with the Democratic candidate. Significantly, La Follette won more votes than Davis in seventeen Western states; it was dramatic testimony to the power of old memories. It seemed to Democrats in many of the states west of the Mississippi that in nominating Davis, the party had finally and completely capitulated to Wall Street.

Faris, the Prohibition candidate, received 57,551 votes. Johns, candidate of the Socialist Labor Party, polled 38,958 votes, 5,000 more than the Communists. Judge Nations of the American Party received 23,867 votes.

"The people," a dazzled Henry Stoddard wrote, "see in Coolidge the fine simplicities, the sturdy patriotism, the firm unpretentious character, the spirit of New England; they have faith in him beyond any they have shown in any other President of my time." There was, to be sure, adulation for Theodore Roosevelt, but the American people,

Stoddard maintained, "has a different kind of faith in Coolidge." His was "a period of world-healing, of restoration—of an effort toward what Harding called normalcy. Vision clear, judgment cool, course always marked straight ahead toward a fixed purpose." The enthusiastic Stoddard added that "he inspires a deep nation-wide confidence that all will go well with the country while he is in the White House."

Coolidge's inaugural address was vintage Coolidge, indeed vintage America. He concluded: "Here stands our country, an example of tranquillity abroad. Here stands its government, aware of its might but obedient to its conscience. Here it will continue to stand, seeking peace and prosperity, solicitous for the welfare of the wage-earner, prompting enterprise, developing waterways and natural resources, attentive to the intuitive counsel of womanhood, encouraging education, desiring the advancement of religion, supporting the cause of justice and honor among the nations. . . . No ambition, no temptation, lures her to the thought of foreign dominions. The legions which she sends forth are armed, not with the sword but with the cross."

In his comment on the address William Allen White noted how well it summarized the man giving it, a man "full of good will, a man not without an eye to the political main chance, a man . . . shrewdly eloquent about accepted beliefs, never raising debatable issues, a good man honestly proclaiming his faith in a moral government of the universe."

Coolidge's domestic program for his first elected term as President was a modest one. He stressed "rigid economy in public expenditures," recommended a labor conciliation board to resolve labor disputes, and supported the principle of collective bargaining. His foreign policy objectives were bolder. He urged that the United States join the World Court and called for disarmament talks looking toward "outlawing war" as a means of settling international conflicts.

Al Smith won the New York gubernatorial race in 1924 against Colonel Theodore Roosevelt, son of the original, by a large margin. Eleanor Roosevelt campaigned vigorously and somewhat unfairly against her cousin; she followed poor Ted around the state in a car with a giant teapot mounted on the roof, the unfair implication being that Colonel Roosevelt, as assistant secretary of the navy under Harding, had been involved in the Teapot Dome oil scandal. Franklin Roosevelt had no appetite for campaigning in behalf of Davis, a man who, in his opinion, represented the most reactionary elements in the Democratic Party. Not wishing to be identified with his party's presidential candidate, he begged off on the ground of ill health. He was convinced that there was no hope for the Democrats "until the Republicans had led us into a serious period of depression and unemployment. . . . As much as we Democrats may be the party of honesty and progress the people will not turn out the Republicans while wages are good and the markets are booming," he noted.

Shortly after Coolidge's reelection he suffered a major defeat at the hands of the Progressives, who remained strong in Congress and who, with the support of the more liberal Democrats, were still able to make their weight felt on occasion. When Coolidge tried to appoint Charles Warren, a Detroit corporation lawyer whose record was clouded by dubious dealings in sugar, as attorney general in place of Harry Daugherty, the Progressives, led by La Follette and William Borah, blocked the nomination. Turned back once, Coolidge submitted Warren's name again to the Senate with the approval of the *New York Times*, which declaimed that "at least the middle west was going to find out that the President was not lacking in the elemental force necessary to maintain party leadership." Finally he was forced to bow to the will of the Senate; the name of Harlan Stone was submitted and quickly approved. Stone at once announced a new policy. "The bureau of investigation," he declared, "is not concerned with political or other opinions of individuals. It is concerned only with their conduct and then only such conduct as is forbidden by the laws of the United States. When a police system passes beyond these limits, it is dangerous to the proper administration of justice and to human liberty, which it should be our first concern to cherish."

# 6

# The Sacco-Vanzetti Case

In 1927 the Sacco-Vanzetti case, which had smoldered since the arrest of the two Italian anarchists in 1920, rushed to its denouement. One of the historians of the trial, Louis Joughin, divides it into five periods. The first was that of the crime itself, the holdup and murders in South Braintree, Massachustts, of two payroll guards. The second, which extended from May 6, 1920, to July of the following year, covered the indictment, trial, and conviction of Nicola Sacco and Bartolomeo Vanzetti for the crime. The third period, from July, 1921, to October, 1924, was the period during which the motion for a new trial was examined and denied and five additional motions, based on new evidence, were rejected. The fourth period, which lasted some two and a half years, was taken up with the preparation and subsequent denial of appeals as well as renewed application for a retrial based on the confession of a convicted murderer. The fifth and final period lasted from April, 1927, to August 23 of the same year, when the two men were executed.

Vanzetti was also convicted of another crime: an attempted holdup in December, 1919, of the payroll of the L. O. White Shoe Company in Bridgewater, Massachusetts. Shots were exchanged between the guards and two holdup men, who fled from the scene in a getaway car. Some four months later, when the payroll of the Slater and Morrill shoe manufacturing company in South Braintree was being carried from the company's office to the main factory building some 200 yards away by the paymaster and a guard, they were shot and killed by two men leaning against a nearby fence, who seized the boxes containing the payroll, jumped into an automobile waiting nearby with several men in it, and fled.

Twenty days after the robbery and murders Sacco and Vanzetti were arrested. Both men were carrying guns. Vanzetti had a loaded revolver and four shotgun shells, and Sacco had a pistol with twenty-three cartridges. Their excuse for carrying the guns was that they were afraid of being attacked while distributing radical literature. Vanzetti also claimed that as a fish peddler he carried money on his person and was afraid of being robbed. Both men confessed to being anarchists and gave confused and contradictory accounts of their whereabouts at the time of the initial attempted robbery and of the murders four months later. There was, in the opinion of the district attorney, sufficient evidence connecting Vanzetti to the abortive Bridgewater robbery attempt to justify trying him separately. He was linked to the stolen getaway car and identified by eight or nine witnesses, all of them Italians, as the man carrying the shotgun at the attempted holdup. After Vanzetti's conviction he and Sacco were tried for the murder of the two guards at South Braintree. Judge Webster Thayer presided over the trial. An expert witness for the prosecution testified that the bullet that killed the guard bore markings which indicated that it had been fired from the gun found on Sacco at the time of his arrest. A defense witness questioned the validity of the identification, but the jury was obviously impressed.

While Judge Thayer showed evidence of bias against the defendants both in court and, reportedly, out, the evidence presented at the first trial seems sufficient to have justified a verdict of guilty. Neither Sacco nor Vanzetti helped his own cause by proclaiming his anarchist principles at every opportunity. The jury, in any event, found the defendants guilty, and Judge Thayer sentenced them to death by electrocution.

When Thayer asked Vanzetti if he had anything to say before he passed sentence, Vanzetti replied: "This is what I say: I would not wish to a dog or to a snake, to the most low or misfortunate creature on earth—I would not wish to any of them what I have had to suffer for things that I am not guilty of. But my conviction is that I have suffered for things that I am guilty of. I am suffering because I am a radical and indeed I am a radical; I have suffered because I was an Italian, and indeed I am an Italian; I have suffered more for my family and my beloved than for myself; but I am so convinced to be right that if you could execute me two time, and if I could be reborn two others times, I would live again to do what I have done already.

"I have finished. Thank you."

Even before the trial and conviction of the two men there had been widespread expressions of sympathy for them and assertions that they were being prosecuted primarily because they were radical immigrants. Their conviction and their death sentences strengthened that conviction in radical and liberal circles already alarmed by the repressive atmosphere in the country.

Although as anarchists Sacco and Vanzetti were the avowed enemies of the Communists, the Communists rushed forward to help organize their defense. Money was raised through the Workers Defense Conference of New England and the Workers Defense Union of New York, both Communist-front organizations.

Soon other groups were formed, some socialist or anarchist "fronts," others started by liberals or radicals of one denomination or another. Gradually a network of organizations dedicated to freeing the two men was established. Radicals and liberals in various foreign countries took up the cause as well. Not long after the conviction of the two men the *New York Times* had predicted, "All over Europe, apparently, the various congeries of the Bolsheviki are going to howl against a fictitious injustice." The prediction proved accurate. When 20,000 protesters met at the Salle Wagram in Paris to protest the conviction, 20 persons were injured by a bomb explosion.

Secretary of State Charles Evans Hughes, well aware of the potentially explosive character of the Sacco-Vanzetti affair, sent a circular telegram to all United States diplomats, reviewing the facts of the case in detail and concluding that "the trial throughout was conducted in accord with the high traditions of the Massachusetts courts."

Guilty or innocent, the two men were appealing figures. Nicola Sacco was born in 1891 in Torremaggiore in southern Italy of a prosperous farm family. He came to the United States in 1908 and soon began to work in shoe factories, where he became a highly skilled worker, making as much as $80 a week. He married a beautiful young woman and had a small house with a lovingly tended garden and $1,500 in the bank at the time of his arrest. He had also thrown himself ardently into the cause of anarchism and become a leader in union activities, in strikes and protests along with his friend Bartolomeo Vanzetti. When the United States entered the war, Sacco and Vanzetti, like all orthodox anarchists, opposed our participation in the conflict; they headed for Mexico with some 100 fellow pacifists. At the end of the war the two men came back to Boston and resumed their activities as anarchists. Sacco returned to the shoe factory, and the more improvident Vanzetti became a fish peddler.

Bartolomeo Vanzetti, three years older than Sacco, was born in the town of Villafalletto in northern Italy. When he was in his early teens, he was apprenticed as a pastry cook. After his mother's death he emigrated to the United States in the same year as Sacco, 1908. His immigrant experience in America was more typical than Sacco's. He drifted from job to job, working often as a day laborer and sometimes as a dishwasher or pastry cook. More of an intellectual than Sacco, he read such anarchist writers as Prince Piotr Kropotkin and Enrico Malatesta as well as Karl Marx, Giuseppe Mazzini, Ernest Renan, Charles Darwin, Herbert Spencer, Leo Tolstoy, and Emile Zola. Vanzetti had no family. Sacco and his young wife had a son, Dante, and a daughter, born after Sacco's imprisonment. Katherine Anne Porter could not forget the face of "small, slender Mrs. Sacco with her fine copper-colored hair and dark brown, soft, dazed eyes," or Vanzetti's sister, Luigia, imported from Italy, "the gaunt, striding figure of a middle-aged plain woman who looked more like a prisoner herself than the leader of a public protest."

Urged on by covert Communists, Italian-Americans contributed over the years almost a third of a defense fund that eventually ran into the hundreds of thousands of dollars. Aldino Felicani, a radical Italian newspaper editor (his paper was named *Agitazione*), was treasurer of the Sacco-Vanzetti Defense Committee. In that capacity he took in and expended something in excess of $360,000. His coadjutor was a wealthy young newspaperman, Gardner Jackson, who served as secretary of the committee and put out its *Official Bulletin,* keeping thousands of supporters informed of the progress of petitions for new trials and appeals. In addition, the committee turned out a flood of pamphlets: *The Story of the Sacco-Vanzetti Case, Including an Analysis of the Trial; Victory Is in Sight; The Fight Continues: The Story of a Proletarian Life.* Works in Italian and in Yiddish were also published; indeed, not a year passed from the time the two men were convicted until they were executed, almost seven years later, without the appearance of a number of books and pamphlets dealing with the case.

Carlo Tresca, a hero of the abortive Paterson strike in 1912, hastened to the defense of Sacco and Vanzetti. Picnics, plays, concerts, and sporting events were put on to raise money. Labor unions, especially those with Italians as members, were appealed to, and some sixty-four locals from as far away as Texas and California made contributions. The American Federation of Labor, despite its deep-seated conservatism, voted in 1922 to join in the call for a new trial and two years later called Sacco and Vanzetti "victims of race and national prejudice and class hatred."

In May, 1926, 15,000 members of the Communist-dominated New York furriers' union met in Madison Square Garden in an impressive demonstration of support for the two men. Sacco's wife and Vanzetti's sister "faced the raging crowd . . . who rose at them in savage sympathy," Katherine Anne Porter wrote, "shouting, tears pouring down their faces, shaking their fists and calling childish phrases, their promises of revenge. . . ." Luigia Vanzetti "was led away like a corpse walking. The crowd roared and cursed and wept and threatened. It was the most awesome, the most bitter scene I had ever witnessed."

Support for Sacco and Vanzetti was not limited to Italians. Many Southern European immigrants identified with the two men. The historian John Dizikes recalls that his father, a Greek immigrant, believed to his dying day that Sacco and Vanzetti were the victims of a system hostile to immigrants.

In the spring of 1924 the Sacco-Vanzetti New Trial League was formed, headed by Elizabeth Glendower Evans. Evans, who headed the League for Democratic Control, was only the latest of a notable line of Boston ladies committed heart and soul to preventing injustice and improving the world. Julia Ward Howe was her spiritual godmother. Evans recruited such notable liberals as Mrs. Louis Brandeis and Samuel Eliot Morison and such conservatives as Henry L. Mencken. Endorsing the cause of Italian anarchists was not at all Mencken's cup of tea.

Eugene V. Debs, who had served so many years in various prisons, wrote to Sacco, referring to him and his fellow anarchist as "two absolutely innocent and shamefully persecuted workingmen . . . framed and doomed from the start." Debs called for a "thousand protest meetings . . . a million letters of indignation and resentment." The old passion flared up in Debs's cry for all those who "hold sacred the cause of labor and the cause of truth and justice and all things of good report" to rally to the defense of the two men, "your brothers and mine, innocent as we are," who must not be "foully murdered to glut the vengeance of a gang of plutocratic slave drivers."

Here and there men whose credentials as enemies of injustice were unimpeachable refused to join in the cry that Sacco and Vanzetti were the victims of judicial lynching. Moorfield Storey had been secretary to Charles Sumner and, throughout a long and distinguished career as a lawyer, a resolute fighter for the rights of labor, for peace, against the draft in the World War, and in other good causes beyond counting. He publicly endorsed the conduct of the prosecution, though it cost him old and valued friends. Herbert Croly angered his younger editors by refusing to take the line that the Sacco-Vanzetti case was evidence of class conflict in the United States.

Eugene Lyons, the journalist, who had committed himself wholeheartedly to socialism in the aftermath of the Palmer raids, was on assignment in Italy and did his best to arouse the Italian press. Alhough Lyons knew no more of the facts of the Sacco-Vanzetti case than he could read in the newspaper, he wrote "Another Frame-Up Exposed," which was published in the magazine of the International Workers in the Amalgamated Food Industries. The trial was not a simple "frame-up" (as he had claimed immediately after it was over); it was "a far more terrible conspiracy. . . . It was a frame-up implicit in the social structure. It was the perfect example of the functioning of class justice. . . ."

"World opinion" joined in excoriating Massachusetts—i.e., "capitalist"—justice.

In the fall of 1921 Anatole France, the most famous French man of letters, published an address to the "People of the United States . . .":

"Listen to the appeal of an old man of the old world who is not a foreigner, for he is a fellow citizen of all mankind.

"In one of your states, two men, Sacco and Vanzetti, have been convicted for a crime of opinion.

"It is horrible to think that human beings should pay with their lives for the exercise of that most sacred right which, no matter what party we belong to, we must all defend.

"Don't let this most iniquitous sentence be carried out. . . .

"You are a great people. You ought to be a just people. There are crowds of intelligent men among you, men who think. I prefer to appeal to them. . . .

"Save Sacco and Vanzetti.

"Save them for your honor, for the honor of your children, and for generations unborn."

France's "letter" is a remarkable document, most notable perhaps for its dogged assumption that Sacco and Vanzetti were to be executed for no other reason than that they were anarchists. Two men had been shot and killed in the commission of a brutal crime; some person or persons had carried out that crime. It was that crime for which Sacco and Vanzetti, on the basis of a substantial, if perhaps not conclusive, amount of evidence had been convicted. To maintain that their nationality and their political opinions had prejudiced the case against them was an understandable and, under the circumstances, natural reaction. But simply to state as a fact that they were to be electrocuted because of their political opinions was hardly a contribution to truth *or* justice.

In the summer of 1926 the president of the German Parliament, the Reichstag, made a personal plea for Sacco and Vanzetti. Mussolini also wrote to Governor Alvin Fuller of Massachusetts asking for clemency. Protests came as well from England, where Labor Members of Parliament signed a letter of protest and sent contributions to the defense fund. One hundred members of the Paris bar signed a letter calling for a new trial for Sacco and Vanzetti, and when Governor Fuller visited France in 1926, death threats resulted in his being heavily guarded.

Senator William Borah took advantage of the opportunity provided by an inquiring reporter to express his opinion of foreign interference in the Sacco-Vanzetti matter. He was on the side of fairness to the defendants, he declared. "But it would be a national humiliation, a shameless, cowardly compromise of national courage, to pay the slightest attention to foreign protests or mob protests at home."

In their Charlestown, Massachusetts, jail, Sacco and Vanzetti were allowed broad privileges. As the months passed, they received a constant stream of visitors, many bringing gifts of food, books, and magazines. They were able to follow closely their various hearings and appeals. Volunteers gave them English lessons, and Vanzetti developed a wide correspondence, his letters growing more "literary" and philosophical as he gained a better mastery of English. One of his principal correspondents was Alice Blackwell, daughter of Lucy Stone and Henry Blackwell, pioneers in the women's rights movement.

Among Vanzetti's readings were the *Meditations of Marcus Aurelius,* Feodor Dostoyevsky's *Letters,* and Leo Tolstoy's *Resurrection.* All such matters were faithfully broadcast by the Defense Committee. Vanzetti was given Charles and Mary Beard's *The Rise of American Civilization,* and he noted that he found little in it "of the instinctive and intuitive aspirations of the poor, of the hardly articulated but incommensurable souls of the humbles. . . ." That was, of course, what made Vanzetti so irresistible to intellectuals and reformers. He seemed able to articulate the "incommensurable souls of the humbles" and in doing so, he gave wings to the faith that the "humbles," in the form of the workers, would redeem the world. He had a gift for aphorisms; he wrote: "Nothing is worse than false belief of self-goodness or greatness. It is that which permitted Nero to kill his mother without remorse." His letters were filled with reflections on history, on nature and humanity. "The dearest manifestation of Nature to me is mankind," he wrote in one letter, "with his miseries and proudness, his glories and his shames, his smallness and his grandeur." In 1924 he wrote gloomily: "Mankind want not, cannot understand us. It is too villain, too tartuffe, too traviated, too coward. We climb our calvary under our cross—but indeed, to madness, the ignominious tragedy of our crucifisers, peoples and tyrents, made us laugh at our worst moment by its terrible and stupid immensity. . . . We go to hell, but with many in company. We witnessing the end of a world with Christ and Socrates for teachers."

To many readers of Vanzetti's letters it was simply inconceivable that a man who could express such noble thoughts so eloquently could have committed a brutal crime. A special treasure was his widely published description of Sacco's character to Judge Thayer: "Sacco is a heart, a faith, a character, a man; a man lover of nature and mankind. A man who gave all, who sacrifice all to the cause of Liberty and to his love for mankind; money, rest, mundain ambitions, his own wife, his children, himself and his own life. . . .

"Oh, yes, I may be more witfull, as some have put it, I am a better babbler than he is, but many, many times in hearing his heartful voice ringing a faith sublime, in considering his supreme sacrifice, remembering his heroism I felt small small at the presence of his greatness and found myself compelled to fight back from my eyes the tears, and quanch my heart trobling to my throat not to weep before him—this man called thief and assassin and doomed. But Sacco's name will live in the hearts of the people and in their gratitude when Katzmann's and your bones will be dispersed by time, when your name, his name, your laws, institutions, and your false god are but a deem rememoring of a cursed past in which man was wolf to man. . . ."

Vanzetti was, of course, right. His encomium to Sacco was one of the most moving tributes of one friend to another in history. It was soon anthologized and rang in the halls of academe. It was the more marvelous because it was spoken by a self-educated *worker*. The socialists, the anarchists, the Communists, and many of the Progressives pinned their hopes on the wisdom and the innate nobility of the "worker." But most workers were distressingly mundane. They were far less interested in the class struggle than in better wages and shorter hours. In Vanzetti they had a bona fide worker who was eloquent beyond their wildest dreams, who had read Marx and Darwin and Kropotkin and, with some nudging, Jefferson and Lincoln and spoke in their cadences. But none of this, of course, bore directly on the issue of the guilt or innocence of the two friends. Josephine Herbst suspected that many intellectuals succumbed to the news that Vanzetti was reading Dante's *Vita Nuova*. "Did the seashells Vanzetti liked to hold in his hands call to some?" she wondered.

The attitude of the two men toward Vladimir Lenin was expressed by Vanzetti when he heard the news of the Russian leader's death. "I am convinced that unintentionally he has ruined the Russian Revolution," Vanzetti wrote. "He has imprisoned and killed many of my comrades. And yet, he has suffered much, toiled heroically for what he believed to be the good and the truth and I felt my eyes filled with tears in reading of his passing and his funeral."

Both men felt keenly their anomalous position; convicted murderers, they were also political prisoners. Committed to class warfare and bitterly opposed to communism, they found that their staunchest champions were members of the haute bourgeoisie, their sworn enemies, and the Communists, equally obnoxious. The conflict was evident in Sacco's letters to two of his most ardent upper-class supporters, Gardner Jackson and Mrs. Leon Henderson. "Although . . . we are of one heart," he wrote Jackson, "unfortunately we represent two opposite class." And to Mrs. Henderson he wrote in a similar vein: "it is not for discredit or to ignore you, Mrs. Evans and other human generosity work, which I sincerely believe that is a noble one and I am respectful; but it is the warm sincere voice of an unrest heart beat and a free soul that loved and lived amongst the workers class all his life. . . ."

One of the most important recruits to the Sacco-Vanzetti cause was Felix Frankfurter. His involvement came initially through his wife, Marion. Her sense of the injustice aroused Frankfurter's own interest. He read the transcript of the original trial and was appalled at the numerous instances of improper procedure. Convinced that the two anarchists had not received a fair trial, Frankfurter threw himself into the case with characteristic enthusiasm. His principal opponent was A. Lawrence Lowell, president of Harvard and a man with whom Frankfurter had already clashed over the proposal for a "Jewish quota" at Harvard, a scheme of Lowell's that provoked a furious response from Frankfurter. Somehow the question of the guilt or innocence of the two Italian immigrants became involved with the moral authority of Harvard.

When Frankfurter cast his lot with Sacco and Vanzetti, some of his more orthodox friends refused to speak to him. A distinguished alumnus of the Harvard Law School, Dean John H. Wigmore of the Northwestern University Law School, entered the lists against him. To Wigmore's defense of the Massachusetts court, Frankfurter replied: "I can say without fear of contradiction that Dean Wigmore could not have read the record, could not have read with care the opinion of Judge Thayer, on which his own article is largely based, could not even have examined my little book [a reference to Frankfurter's dissection of the trial record]. . . ." Lowell was said to have lamented: "Wigmore is a fool! Wigmore is a fool! He should have known that Frankfurter is shrewd enough to be accurate."

William Howard Taft wrote to the president of Yale urging him to muzzle Robert Hutchins and other members of the Yale Law School faculty who were meddling in the Sacco-Vanzetti case. Felix Frankfurter, Taft added, "seems to be in touch with every Bolshevist, Communist movement in the country."

As the agonizing affair dragged on, men and women of liberal persuasion like Moorfield Storey, who had remained above the battle, largely on the ground that the legal record did not support the charge that Sacco and Vanzetti had not received a fair trial, joined in the call for a new trial; a retrial, they believed, would at least moderate the suspicion and hostility of liberals and radicals in the United States and Europe as well.

Only a handful of those passionately involved in the fight for the lives of the two men could be expected to work their way through the mass of legal material and then reach an impartial judgment based upon it. All the rest believed what they were told, which in the radical press was that the two men were victims of a capitalist conspiracy. The chief editorial writer of the *Boston Herald,* F. Lauriston Bullard, spoke for this "party" when he wrote; "In our opinion Nicola Sacco and Bartolomeo Vanzetti ought not to be executed on the warrant of the verdict returned by a jury on July 14, 1921. We do not know whether the men are guilty or not. We have no sympathy with the half-baked views which they profess. But as the months have merged into years and great debate over this case has continued, our doubts have solidified into convictions, and reluctantly we found ourselves compelled to reverse our original judgment." Bullard went on to argue: "If on a new trial the defendants shall again be found guilty we shall be infinitely better off than if we proceed to execution on the basis of the trial already held; the shadow of a doubt, which abides in the minds of large numbers of patient investigators of this whole case, will have been removed." Other newspapers, including the *Baltimore Sun* and the *Washington News,* joined in the call for a new trial. Even the highly conservative Massachusetts State Council of the Knights of Columbus, while abjuring the "false doctrines and deductions of atheism, communism and similar sophistries," called on Governor Fuller to be sure that "no human life will be taken without the fullest examination the law permits into the guilt of those accused."

On Sunday, April 10, 1927, newspaper headlines all over the country announced that Judge Thayer had confirmed the death sentences of Sacco and Vanzetti. Sacco had leaped to his feet and denounced the court. "We fraternize the people with books, with literature," he exclaimed in his broken English, "you tyrannize and kill them. . . . I know the sentence will be of two classes, that oppressed class and the rich class, and that they will always be in collusion. That is why I am here on this bench for being of the oppressed class. You are the oppressors." Vanzetti followed Sacco. "I am innocent of these two crimes [referring to his conviction for the earlier abortive robbery]," he declared, "but that is not all I wanted to say. Not only am I innocent of them, not only in all my life I have never stole, never killed, never spilled blood, but I have struggled all my life since I began to reason, to eliminate crime from the earth." Vanzetti mentioned that Debs had expressed his conviction of their innocence. "And not only he but every man of understanding in the world, not only in this country, but in other countries, the flower of mankind, the greatest thinkers of Europe have pleaded in our favor."

When the United States Supreme Court refused to accept the case, attention turned to Governor Fuller, who was urged by supporters of the two immigrants to commute the death penalty. Fuller's response was to appoint a three-man commission to review the case and make recommendations. The commission was made up of Samuel Stratton, president of the Massachusetts Institute of Technology; Robert Grant, an elderly novelist; and A. Lawrence Lowell, president of Harvard University, and by virtue of that fact alone a powerful weight in the affairs of the commonwealth. It was not, on the whole, an impressive trio. Stratton, it seems, had little to say in the committee meetings and, independent of his office, was not a forceful or distinguished figure. Lowell, who had done his best to block the appointment of Brandeis to the Supreme Court during Wilson's administration, was, as noted, the avowed enemy of Felix Frankfurter, whose activities on behalf of Sacco and Vanzetti he resented. John Dos Passos wrote an open letter to Lowell: "It is upon men of your class and position that will rest the inevitable decision as to whether the coming struggle for the reorganization of society shall be bloodless and fertile or inconceivably bloody and destructive."

A liberal member of the Harvard Corporation, John F. Moors, greeted the news of Lowell's appointment with the not intentionally ironic words "Now we can sleep nights, in the thought that a president of Harvard is on the committee."

When the committee supported the jury's verdict, Moors spoke in a somewhat different vein, declaring that Lowell "was incapable of seeing that two wops could be right and the Yankee judiciary could be wrong." He told Harold Laski that Lowell's "loyalty to his class transcended his ideas of logic and justice." When Lippmann wrote an editorial in the *World* praising the commission for its fairness, an angry Frankfurter rushed down to New York to remonstrate with his friend, arguing that the commission could not have read the record of the trial.

"It is not every prisoner who has a president of Harvard University throw the switch for him," Heywood Broun wrote. Sacco and Vanzetti should "take unction to their souls that they will die at the hands of men in dinner coats or academic gowns." To Broun their execution would be "legalized murder conducted under academic auspices and prestige." He severed his relationship with the *New York World* when it refused to print one of his columns on the Sacco-Vanzetti case on the ground that it was inaccurate and inflammatory.

Graham Wallas wrote to Walter Lippmann from England: "I am sorry for Lowell, whom I believe I know rather well. He is public-spirited, with a vast amount of administrative drive, but if one goes for a long walk with him one finds him a little stupid. He will suffer horribly over the Sacco-Vanzetti business." Lippmann himself confessed to Learned Hand: "I have not been so troubled about anything since 1919 . . . when against what I really believe was my own deepest and best feeling, I let irritation against Wilson push me into intransigent opposition to the Treaty." Lippmann added a revealing sentence when he wrote that his judgment had been affected by "the atmosphere of horror and the very real danger of Red violence followed by White violence." Just what the character of the "Red violence" might have been Lippmann did not discuss, but the phrase suggests that he believed that the Communist Party and its sympathizers did in fact represent a genuine menace to American democracy. If Lippmann, who prided himself, above all, on his detachment and objectivity in regard to the American political scene, could seriously entertain such a notion, it is no wonder that millions of less informed and sophisticated fellow citizens could subscribe to them, and it reinforces the argument that the Sacco-Vanzetti case was profoundly affected by something close to panic on the part of the "ruling class" in the United States.

Once more Governor Fuller was appealed to. "Everywhere there is doubt so deep, so persuasive, so unsettling that it cannot be ignored," Frankfurter wrote. It could not be said that Fuller did not take his responsibility in this case seriously; he twice visited Vanzetti in prison.

At last things rushed to a conclusion. On August 3 Fuller announced that he had rejected the call for clemency. Four days later the advisory commission report was published to a storm of denunciation. On August 10, forty minutes before the two men were to be electrocuted, a stay was granted until August 22 in order to allow for last-minute legal moves by the defense. The Kremlin announced after the stay of execution: "The mighty roar of protest from the Soviet Union, together with the voice of the working classes the world over, forced even the plutocratic American bourgeoisie to hesitate and manoeuvre."

In the last days before the executions the Defense Committee decided to keep vigil at the Charlestown jail, hoping against hope to persuade Fuller to pardon the two men. Poets, writers, intellectuals, and radicals poured into Boston, where most of them were organized by Communist Party members for picketing. Edna St. Vincent Millay, small and frail, marched with Katherine Anne Porter. John Dos Passos, with Portuguese blood in his veins, marched with Paxton Hibben and Lewis Mumford; socialites and factory girls rubbed elbows. Socialists, anarchists, Communists of all denominations joined hands with progressive Republicans and liberal Democrats. It was like a gathering of the clan. There were old Wobblies and young anarchists, municipal reformers and labor leaders, seasoned battlers and excited novices, veterans of uncounted battles for social justice, for unions, for the single tax, for the League of Nations. Differences were forgotten or suppressed in the common cause. For many of those who came to Boston in body or in spirit, it would remain the most agonizing and profoundly remembered event of their lives. Fifty years later Katherine Anne Porter, a woman in her eighties, wrote a poignant memoir of the moment entitled *The Never-Ending Wrong,* which managed in a few pages to capture the essence of the experience. She was thirty-seven years old at the time and "knew a good deal about the evils and abuses and cruelties of the world; I had known victims of injustice, of crime, I was not ignorant of history, nor of literature." She had witnessed a revolution in Mexico, but nothing had prepared her for the emotions she felt as time wound down for the two Italians. She described herself as being, at the time of the Sacco-Vanzetti case, "a sympathizer with the new (to me) doctrines brought out of Russia from 1919 to 1920 onward by enthusiastic, sentimental, misguided men and women who were looking for a New Religion of Humanity, as one of them expressed it. . . . We were as miscellaneous, improbable, almost entirely unassorted a gathering of people to one place in one cause as ever happened in this country . . . pure exotics transplanted from the never-never land of the theoretically classless society . . ." Porter wrote.

Everywhere the organizing abilities and the remorseless dedication of the Communists were apparent. Porter was in a group of protesters headed by a "grim little woman" named Rosa Baron, who horrified Porter by replying to her expression of hope that Sacco and Vanzetti might still be pardoned, "Alive—what for? They are no earthly use to us alive." And when Baron's younger brother protested one of her decrees, she warned him that she would report him to the committee of the party if he dared dispute her orders in front of others. "The air," Porter wrote, "was stiff with cold, mindless, irrational compliance with orders from 'higher up.' The whole atmosphere was rank with intrigue and deceit. . . ." She noted: " 'Morality' was a word along with 'charitable' and 'humanitarian' and 'liberal' that brought smiles of contempt to the lips of the true believers in Marxist dogma."

John Dos Passos belonged to the "New York gang," which was resented by the "Boston gang" for invading its territory. The two groups were quite different in composition and temperament. The Bostonians were mostly upper-class liberal reformers of old family. The New Yorkers were radical literary types. There were inevitable clashes and misunderstandings. Powers Hapgood, nephew of Hutchins and Socialist candidate for governor of Indiana, was among those arrested during the protests. Elinor Wylie was another "literary" picket. Married to the poet William Rose Benét, she had won the Pulitzer Prize for her poetry. Fragile and elegant, she had come to Boston with thousands of others to walk in the picket line, "crowded, anxious and slow-moving," Porter wrote. On the picket line were Lola Ridge, Paxton Hibben, Michael Gold, William Gropper, the cartoonist for the *New Masses,* and Grace Lumpkin, all ardent Communists.

There were, of course, counterdemonstrators, many of them Irish workingmen, who hooted at the pickets, called out obscenities, and reviled the condemned men. Katherine Anne Porter and the policeman who was escorting her to the paddy wagon were showered with stones and sticks, mixed with flowers from more sympathetic onlookers.

Every day Katherine Anne Porter was arrested by the same polite, embarrassed, and rather bewildered Irish cop. He belonged to the so-called Pink Tea Squad, members of which wore white gloves and were "well instructed that in no circumstance were they to forget themselves and whack a lady with their truncheons, no matter how far she forgot herself in rudeness and contrariety." One day it was a time before she saw "her" policeman. "You're late," she said.

When Porter and her fellow picketers were arrested, Edward James, whom Porter identified as William James's nephew, appeared to bail them out. James had given a speech in Lawrence, Massachusetts, at the end of May, in which he declared defiantly, "Mr. Fuller will not give in to us, and we will not give in to him. What happens when you have a situation of this kind? Something breaks. Either we break the government or the government breaks us. You may say that means revolution. I don't care what it means. I face facts as they are. I see aggression in the court-house, in the state-house, in the city-hall. I fight aggression." Porter described James as "a thin, stiff, parchment roll of a man . . . immaculately turned out in tones of expensive-looking gray from head to foot, to match his gray pointed beard and his severe pale gray eyes with irritable points of light in them." He was accompanied everywhere by "a dark young Portuguese boy," the "picture of exuberance, with his oily, swarthy skin, his thick glistening black hair, the soft corners of his full red mouth always a little moist." He confided to Porter in his childish voice, "Mr. James and I . . . we have our own little organization. I'm Mr. James' secretary and we are perfectly independent. . . . Mr. James and me, we've been working on this *for* years!"

"Now and then," Katherine Anne Porter wrote, Florence "Daisy" Harriman "floated [into picket headquarters,] in all white, horsehaired lace garden hats and pink or maybe blue chiffon frocks, on her way to or from some social afternoon festivity." Porter confided to Harriman: "I sometimes wonder what we are doing really. The whole thing is losing shape in my mind, but I can only hope we may learn something we need to know—that something good will come of this." Daisy Harriman's "broad, healthy face smiled reassuringly from under its flowering shade. Intoxicating perfume waved from her spread handkerchief when she dried her forehead. 'What good?—Oh, they'll forget all about it. Most of them are just here for the excitement. They really don't know what's going on. . . .' "

All over the country and all over the world there were demonstrations and protests as the day appointed for the execution approached. There was an outbreak of bombings. A bomb went off in the basement of a Philadelphia church, and another at the home of the mayor of Baltimore. Two were detonated in the New York subway. The press fanned anxiety that the execution would be accompanied by terrorist acts. Marines were stationed at strategic points in Washington—at the White House and the Capitol—and the Washington Monument was closed. The Boston police was heavily armed, and the state guard placed on the alert. In Sacramento, California, the roof of the new State Theater was blown off by a powerful bomb. On August 15 a bomb in Dedham, Massachusetts, destroyed half the home of one of the jurors and narrowly missed seriously injuring members of his family. At a picnic-demonstration in Cheswick, Pennsylvania, state troopers fought off an angry crowd that included women and children. A number of people were injured, and a policeman was killed.

In the last days Vanzetti imagined that "all the nations of the world" were mobilizing to free him and Sacco. They were advancing up the Rio Grande, he believed, and across the Panama Canal. He sent instructions to the Defense Committee to keep him informed of "each move."

Before the execution Carolyn Goodenough wrote:

> So live or die, brave men, in peace!
> A world will welcome your release;
> Or, if you die, mankind will say,
> "Two martyrs' crowns were won today."

As the hour set for the execution of the two men approached, many of the men and women who had fought so long and hard to save their lives began a vigil. Some knelt and prayed in the cold gray streets of Charlestown. Others huddled together and sang softly. Felix and Marion Frankfurter roamed aimlessly about the streets of Boston.

Vanzetti "fasted, kept his silence, and went to his death with his fellow, a sacrifice to his faith," in Porter's words. As he was being strapped into the electric chair, he said, "I wish to tell you that I am an innocent man of any crime but sometimes some sin. I wish to forgive *some* people for what they are now doing to me." Porter wrote: "They both spoke nobly at the end; they kept faith with their vows for each other. They left a great heritage of love, devotion, faith and courage— all done with the sure intention that holy anarchy should be glorified through their sacrifice and that the time would come that no human being should be humiliated or made abject."

Katherine Anne Porter was "one of the many hundreds who stood in anxious vigil watching the light in the prison tower. . . ." People crowded in the open area around the prison. The Boston mounted police, armed with clubs, tear gas, and guns, "galloped about bearing down on anybody who ventured out beyond the edge of the crowd and then pulling their horses up short violently so that they reared and their fore-hoofs beat the air over a human head. . . . This was not a mob, however. It was a silent, intent assembly of citizens—of anxious people come to bear witness and to protest against the terrible wrong about to be committed, not only against the two men about to die, but against all of us, against our common humanity and our shared will to avert what we believed to be not merely a failure in the use of the instrument of the law, an injustice committed through mere human weakness and misunderstanding, but a blindly arrogant, self-righteous determination not to be moved by any arguments, the obstinate as- sumption of the infallibility of a handful of men intoxicated with the vanity of power and gone mad with wounded self-importance . . . it was a moment of strange heartbreak . . . a night for perpetual remembrance and mourning."

When Marion Frankfurter heard over a radio that Sacco and Vanzetti had been executed, she fainted. Many others wept. So it was across the land, across the world. Porter wrote: "In small groups, subdued people began to scatter, in a sound of voices that was deep, mournful, vast, and wavering. They walked slowly toward the center of Boston. Life felt very grubby and mean, as if we are all of us soiled and disgraced and would never in this world live it down." She and a small party of her friends gathered in someone's hotel room, and one man said, "Damn it, I'm through. I'd like to leave this country!" Someone asked, "Where would you go?" Half a dozen voices called out "as one, 'Russia!' " Porter recalled: "Some of the mourners were children of the oldest governing families and the founders of this nation, and an astonishing number were children of country preachers or teachers or doctors—'the salt of the earth'—besides the first-born generation of emigrants who had braved the escape . . . the awful exile, to reach this land. . . ." They drank, they sang revolutionary songs and sentimental songs, and one woman tried to leap from the hotel window but was restrained. When Katherine Anne Porter began to sing, defiantly, "The Battle Hymn of the Republic," the others "flinched, and . . . the faces turned sour, frowning." She had touched a forbidden note. Once the would-be suicide had been put to bed, "the rest of us," Porter wrote, "sat up nearly all night, with nothing to say, nothing to do, brought to a blank pause, keeping a vigil with the dead in the first lonely long night of death. . . . I have never felt such a weight of pure bitterness, helpless anger in utter defeat, outraged love and hope, as hung over us all in that room. . . . A darkness of shame, too, settled down with us. . . ."

Josephine Herbst and her husband, John Herrmann, were on a sailing vacation in Maine. They went to a dockside Italian restaurant crowded with truck drivers and fishermen. There they heard the news of the executions over the radio. The proprietor's face was "tense but calm. . . . He spoke in a quiet voice, confidentially, 'Electricity. Is that what it's for? Is that the thing to do? Seven years they waited. Not bad men. No, *good* men.' "

Herbst wrote: "On the early morning of August 23, 1927 . . . we walked out on the foggy streets, feeling very cold in our sweaters and reached out to take one another's hand for the walk back to the hotel. Without saying a word, we both felt it and knew that we felt it; a kind of shuddering premonition of a world to come. But what it was to be, we could never have foreseen. . . . So far as I am concerned, what had been the twenties ended that night." Three years later they were to cast their lot with the Communist Party as the only stop to chaos.

The day after the executions the protesters who had been arrested during the picketing were arraigned in court, John Dos Passos, Katherine Anne Porter, Lola Ridge, and Edna St. Vincent Millay among them. Their attorney was Arthur Garfield Hays. The judge was "a little gray old man with pointed whiskers and the face of a smart, conspiratorial chipmunk," in Porter's words. The pickets were found guilty of "loitering and obstructing traffic" and fined $5 each. "A busy, abstracted woman wearing pinch-nose spectacles" gave each of the defendants $5 to pay their fines, along with railroad tickets. Porter was told severely, "Go straight to the station and take the next train." Learned Hand reported meeting Felix Frankfurter the next day and found him "like a mad man . . . really beside himself." When Frankfurter learned that his friend Gardner Jackson was planning to publish the letters of Sacco and Vanzetti, written from prison, he asked him if his wife could help with the project. Since the execution she had been under the care of a psychiatrist, and working on the letters might be an ideal therapy for her.

"It is fifty years, very long ones, since Sacco and Vanzetti were put to death in Boston," Katherine Anne Porter wrote in 1977 in her account of the case, "accused and convicted of a bitter crime, of which, it is still claimed, they may or may not have been guilty. I did not know then and I still do not know whether they were guilty. . . ." She suspected that Sacco was guilty and Vanzetti had allied himself with his friend in anarchist solidarity. "Yet no matter what, it was a terrible miscarriage of justice; it was a most reprehensible abuse of legal power, in their attempt to prove that the law is something to be inflicted—not enforced—and that it is above the judgment of the people." To her the case "which began so obscurely . . . ended as one of the important turning points in the history of this country. . . ." It was the "symptom of a change so deep and so sinister in the whole point of view and direction of this people as a nation that I for one am not competent to analyze it. I only know what happened by what has happened to us since, by remembering what we were, or what many of us believed we were before. We were most certainly then of a different cast of mind and feeling than we are now, or such a thing as the Sacco-Vanzetti protest could never have been brought about by any means."

There were widespread demonstrations in most European countries. The American Embassy was besieged in London. A large hostile crowd gathered at the League of Nations Palace in Geneva. In Paris twenty police were injured in riots. There were riots in Lyons. Barricades were erected in Cherbourg, where police and demonstrators clashed. The French novelist Romain Rolland outdid his compatriot Anatole France in his indictment of America. "I am not an American," he wrote, "but I love America. And I accuse of high treason against America the men who have soiled her with this judicial crime before the eyes of the world. Their abominable parody on justice has destroyed the most sacred right of humanity." The Italians were, if possible, more florid. The Italian paper *Corriere della Sera* observed that "the gloomy puritan resoluteness and crusading of the first immigrants in the Mayflower has degenerated into a squalid and obtuse fanaticism of legality." The respected leftist British journal the *New Statesman* called the execution of Sacco and Vanzetti "the most obvious and indefensible miscarriage of justice that has ever occurred in any modern civilized country."

In the aftermath of the execution John Dewey wrote in the *New Republic:* "The issue [of guilt or innocence] is now merged in the larger one, that of our methods of insuring justice, one which in turn is merged in the comprehensive issue of the tone and temper of American public opinion and sentiment, as they affect judgment and action in any social question wherein racial division and class interests are involved." Walter Lippmann poured out his misgivings to Learned Hand. While he believed the men might well have been guilty, he agreed that the evidence was "insufficient," that the "trial was almost certainly conducted in a prejudiced atmosphere," and that Governor Fuller "was infected with the psychology of class conflict." For the defenders of the status quo, Sacco and Vanzetti clearly symbolized the disposition of the "dangerous classes" to challenge their masters. It followed that the punishment of the two men was necessary for political and psychological reasons if not to satisfy the requirements of justice. Their execution could be expected to be a salutary lesson to those of their class who might be so deluded as to believe they could topple their betters into the proletarian dust.

The fact that what Lippmann and many of his friends in the business world had most feared—a popular uprising—had not happened proved to Lippmann that the "stability of this society is beyond anything we had imagined for it was subjected to a strain which I thought ominous." Or, it could be said, that their fears were vastly exaggerated, if not groundless. As Lippmann put it, "our conservative classes . . . sit upon the rock of Gibraltar and behave as if they were upon a raft at sea." But of course Lippmann, too, had behaved as though he felt himself upon a raft tossed by the turbulence of the angry masses.

The brilliant young critic and teacher Robert Morss Lovett spoke for many of his class and generation when he declared the executions "forced me to accept a doctrine which I had repudiated as partisan tactics—the class war."

His friend and fellow-teacher Granville Hicks noted that the Sacco-Vanzetti case "crushed my faith in liberalism," and discussions with a Communist friend enabled him, in his own words, "to break through the fog of self-delusion and confusion" and become a member of the party.

Perhaps the most accurate measure of the psychological impact of the Sacco-Vanzetti case on the intellectual class was to be found in the expressive arts—in poetry, literature, drama, and painting. The indefatigable Louis Joughin unearthed 147 poems on the Sacco-Vanzetti case. Not surprisingly, the most commonly evoked image by poets was of Christ crucified. E. Merrill Root in "Eucharist" wrote:

> Not by the grape or wheaten bread
> Can we partake the Eucharist:
> Communion is to give to God
> Our blood and bodies, like the Christ.

Root called on nature to

> Crush man, the angel with the maggot's brain:
> Crush man, the idiot ape, the spawn of Cain!

Malcolm Cowley, not notably pious, wrote:

> March on, O dago Christs, whilst we
> march on to spread your name abroad
> like ashes in the winds of God.

Lucia Trent, in her poem "To Sacco and Vanzetti, by a Rebel of Anglo-Saxon Descent," wrote:

> How in God's name can we lose faith today
> With men like you to forge a rebel's way!

Edna St. Vincent Millay's best-known Sacco and Vanzetti poem is "Justice Denied in Massachusetts" with its famous line: "Evil does overwhelm / The larkspur and the corn. . . ." Several years later Millay wrote "Two Sonnets in Memory."

By 1928 Lucia Trent and Ralph Cheyny were able to publish an anthology of poems about Sacco and Vanzetti. But it was perhaps Lola Ridge, whom Katherine Anne Porter would always remember standing pale and defiant before the flashing hooves of a Boston mounted policeman's large horse, who wrote most passionately and continuously about the trial and execution, beginning with "Two in the Death House" and ending some seven years later with "Three Men Die," about two Christs and a thief.

> . . . old myth
> Renews its tenure of the blood
> Recurrently; in a new way
> Reforms about its ancient pith
> With all the old accessories.

Maxwell Anderson wrote two plays, the first with Harold Hickerson, *Gods of the Lightning* in 1928 and, seven years later, the blank verse drama *Winterset,* which drew directly on the Sacco-Vanzetti case.

The young artist Ben Shahn did a series of twenty-three powerful paintings on the theme of the Sacco-Vanzetti case in 1932.

The case appeared in one form or another in Nathan Asch's *Pay Day,* James Farrell's *Bernard Clare,* Bernard De Voto's *We Accept with Pleasure,* and, most strikingly, in *The Big Money,* final volume of John Dos Passos's trilogy *U.S.A.*

The heroine of Upton Sinclair's *Boston* is Cornelia Thornwell, who, after the death of her wealthy, socially prominent husband, leaves her children to squabble over the estate and goes off to work in the bailing room of a cordage factory and live with a poor Italian family. There she meets Bartolomeo Vanzetti, and they become fast friends. Later, traveling in Europe, she reads of his arrest for robbery and murder and returns home to fight for his freedom. Sinclair ends the novel with reflections on Boston, which had rejected "the advice of the shrewd old Frenchman [Anatole France] and made two martyrs. Mystic beings with supernatural virtues, destined to become a legend; to expand like the genii released from the bottle, until they spread over the sky, completely overshadowing the city and its fame. No more would Boston be the place of the tea-party and the battle of Bunker Hill; Boston would be the place where Sacco and Vanzetti were put to death! . . ."

Sinclair's last lines were from the prophet Isaiah: "And they shall build houses, and inhabit them; and they shall plant vineyards, and eat the fruit of them. They shall not build, and another inhabit; they shall not plant, and another eat: for as the days of a tree are the days of my people, and mine elect shall long enjoy the works of their hands."

Upton Sinclair's title was an appropriate one. It was Boston itself that was, in a sense, on trial as much as Sacco and Vanzetti—Boston and Massachusetts and New England as well. Even that dour New Englander Calvinistic Calvin, the President of the United States, was on trial. It is not recorded that he broke his famous silence in regard to the Sacco-Vanzetti case; it might be said that his expression covered it. Boston Puritanism was a down-at-the heels, halfhearted Puritanism, to be sure, but Puritanism nonetheless. Puritanism meant repression, and every enlightened modern person knew that repression was what was wrong with America. Boston symbolized the old repressive order, and that order had mustered all its reserves to beat back the alien forces that had risen to challenge it: Jews and intellectuals; Communists, socialists, anarchists; short-haired women and long-haired men, including a number of defectors from its own ranks. And the old order had done this with an eerie, if inadvertent, evocation of names. The trial judge was named both Thayer and Webster, two of the most notable names in the gallery of New England's greats, and the chairman of the special committee set up by Governor Fuller to review the entire proceedings was, with marvelous appropriateness, A. Lawrence Lowell, president of Harvard and head of the famous clan that rivaled or outdid the Adamses. The names of two of New England's most malodorous mill towns—Lawrence and Lowell—were contained in the name of the president of Harvard as well as that of one of its most illustrious poets and critics, James Russell Lowell.

So, among many other things that had nothing directly to do with the guilt or innocence of the Italian anarchists, the trial marked the passing of the old order of New England, the classic representative of which occupied the White House.

The formative experience of John Dos Passos's mature years was undeniably the Sacco-Vanzetti case. His identification with Sacco and Vanzetti may well have been related to his feelings about his Portuguese ancestry. The critic Alfred Kazin has written, "For many writers the Sacco-Vanzetti case was at most a shock to their acquiescent liberalism or indifference; for Dos Passos it provided immediately the catalyst that made *U.S.A.* possible." Kazin clearly refers to the concluding volume, *The Big Money,* since the first two volumes, *The 42d Parallel* and *1919,* had already been published.

In *The Big Money* the narrator is walking through Plymouth, thinking of the earliest settlers. Later he reflects, "how can I make them feel how our fathers our uncles haters of oppression came to this coast how say Don't let them scare you how make them feel who are your oppressors America

"rebuild the ruined words worn slimy in the mouths of lawyers district attorneys college presidents judges without the old words the immigrants haters of oppression brought to Plymouth how can you know who are your betrayers America

"or that this fishpeddler you have in Charlestown Jail is one of your founders Massachusetts?

"they have clubbed us off the streets they are stronger they are rich they hire and fire the politicians the newspaper editors the old judges the small men with reputations the college-presidents the wardheelers (listen businessmen colleges presidents judges America will not forget her betrayers) they hire the men with guns the uniforms the policecars the patrolwagons

"all right you have won you will kill the brave men our friends tonight

"there is nothing left to do we are beaten . . .

"America our nation has been beaten by strangers who have turned our language inside out who have taken the clean words our fathers spoke and made them slimy and foul . . .

"they have built the electricchair and hired the executioner to throw the switch

"all right we are two nations . . . . . .

"they have won why aint they scared to be seen on the streets? on the streets you see only the downcast faces of the beaten the streets belong to the beaten nation . .

"we stand defeated America."

We come, finally, to the question of the meaning or significance of the most famous trial in our history (its only serious rival is the trial of the Haymarket anarchists). Under certain circumstances political or legal issues get "out of hand." The facts, in such instances, become far less important than the symbolic significance attached to what are often peripheral matters. Once this process has gained momentum, it is almost impossible to reverse. Emotions such as fear, hatred, loyalty, conformity—not necessarily to public opinion in general but to the opinion of the circle to which individuals look for friendship—engulf and bury beyond retrieval the facts themselves. Moreover, the clouds of suspicion, prejudice, and passion are not easily dissipated; they linger on for decades and even generations, long after most of the principals are dead. The case of Captain Dreyfus in France was such a case; the journalist Georges Clemenceau built on his defense of Dreyfus the political career that made him prime minister of France during the World War. The Sacco-Vanzetti case was another. To Edmund Wilson it "revealed the whole anatomy of American life, with all its classes, professions, and points of view, and all their relations, and it raised almost every fundamental question of our political and social system. It did this, furthermore," he wrote to John Peale Bishop, "in an unexpectedly dramatic fashion." It was Dos Passos who had pointed out that "during the last days before the executions, as if, by some fairy-tale spell, all the different kinds of Americans, eminent and obscure, had suddenly, in a short burst of intensified life, been compelled to reveal their true characters in a heightened exaggerated form."

There were, it might be said, several categories of people who took up the cause of Sacco and Vanzetti with widely varying degrees of fervor. There were, first of all, those who believed, without any particular attention to the evidence, that the men were innocent because they had a strong, one might say, almost doctrinal sympathy with their declared aims: to create a more just and humane society, distinguished by brotherhood rather than greed. These supporters were in general of what we might call a Manichaean turn of mind. That is to say, for them the world was divided into mutually exclusive good and evil. They could not imagine that the "good" might be tainted with "evil" or that idealists might use criminal methods to achieve their noble ideals, although there was a mass of evidence to the contrary, going back to Alexander Berkman's attempt to perform an attentat, or assassination, on the person of Henry Frick at the time of the Homestead strike. An American President—William McKinley—and numerous public officials in Europe, including Sadi Carnot, the president of the

Third French Republic, had been assassinated by anarchists. It was a central tenet of at least one branch of anarchism that virtually any crime on behalf of the people and against the tyranny of the state was justified. So there was nothing inherently incongruous or improbable about the guilt of Sacco and Vanzetti. Whether or not they murdered the payroll guards, it was an act in no way inconsistent with the principles and practices of anarchism.

Another category had doubts about the guilt or innocence of the condemned men. They considered it by no means inconceivable that they were guilty as charged. But these supporters felt that there were numerous irregularities in the trial and in the rejection of the various appeals entered by the lawyers of the accused in their efforts to secure a new trial. They were especially aware of the hostility toward the men as immigrants, "dagos" or "wops," with radical political views. They felt that any question of a doubt should be removed before the men were executed. There were many Italians, devout Catholics and by no means anarchists, who aligned themselves with their countrymen because they themselves had suffered so severely from discrimination that they were instantly prepared to believe that Sacco and Vanzetti were to be killed *primarily because they were Italians.*

There were the opponents of capital punishment to whom it was a matter more or less of indifference whether Sacco and Vanzetti were guilty. They were simply opposed to capital punishment per se.

There were those kindhearted individuals and groups that were distressed by suffering. They heard a great clamor for the prisoners; they read their brave and touching letters and the accounts of sympathetic journalists. They drifted into the protest headquarters, where Katherine Anne Porter was often on "kitchen police," typing letters and mailing appeals for funds, "in their smart thin frocks, stylish hats, and their indefinable air of eager sweetness and light, bringing the money they had collected in the endless, wittily devious ways of women's organizations."

Finally, there was the Communist Party, which was determined to use the case to further the cause of world revolution. The Communists were indefatigable and untiring. When interest in the case flagged during the long years of appeal, they worked to revive it. When it revived, they worked to exploit it. It would perhaps be comforting to give them the credit (or blame) for the greater part of the agitation, but it would be a serious mistake to do so. They were successful only to the degree that they tapped into a great reservoir of liberal opinion.

The fact is that the case marked a kind of gathering of liberal and radical spirit to take up the fight once more. The Sacco-Vanzetti case was not the end of some halcyon era when justice was evenhanded and democracy everywhere in the ascendancy. It marked not a "deep . . . and sinister" change in the "direction of this people as a nation" but a revival of the radical spirit that had been evident in the last decade of the nineteenth century and the first decade and a half of the twentieth (to the outbreak of the European war). The Communists were its principal beneficiaries, since it moved the intellectual class and the middle- and upper-class reformers strongly to the left. It prepared, in a sense, the ideological ground for the coming of the Great Depression. It was interpreted to mean just what the Communists insisted that it meant: Justice, compassion, and social change could not be achieved through the "system." The system was firmly in the hands of the enemy; if there was to be change, it must be wrested from those who held power. It was, to be sure, a thin reed on which to hang such a weighty proposition, and as the Communists liked to say, the "objective reality" appears to be something rather different.

Vanzetti wrote that had it not been for "these things," he might have lived out his life talking at street corners to scorning men. He might have died unknown, a failure. "Now we are not a failure. This is our triumph. Never in our full life could we hope to do such work for tolerance, for justice, for man's understanding of man as we do now by accident. Our words—our lives—our pains—nothing! The taking of our lives—lives of a good shoemaker and a poor fish peddler—all! The last moment belongs to us—that agony is our triumph."

That, in a profound sense, was what made their story so moving. Whatever they had done (or not done), they had, by the dignity and resolution with which they met their fate, elevated their "case" to the realm of tragedy and myth, and that was what their most unselfish advocates at *their* best knew to be true. In the crassness and materialism of a degenerate age two most unlikely heroes had emerged. The world projected onto them the world's multifarious dreams and hopes and fears and hatreds and made of them what it wished: criminal anarchists or modern-day secular saints of the "New Religion of Humanism." Reflecting for the thousandth time on the meaning of the case, the cause, Katherine Anne Porter remembered reading the memoirs of the oracle of the anarchists Prince Kropotkin and Emma Goldman's account of her early life and how "it was a most marvelous thing to have two splendid, courageous, really noble human beings speaking together, telling the same tale. It was like a duet of two great voices telling a tragic story. I believed in both of them at once." Although life taught her (and them) better, that fact had not, she wrote, "changed my love for them or my lifelong sympathy for the cause to which they devoted their lives—to ameliorate the anguish that human beings inflict on each other—the never-ending wrong, forever incurable."

At the end of his exhaustive and exhausting compilation of material relating to the Sacco-Vanzetti case, Louis Joughin writes: "Did Sacco and Vanzetti kill Parmenter and Berardelli? No answer can be made." A more recent and equally exhaustive review of the record brings its author close to conviction that they did kill the paymaster and the guard. Katherine Anne Porter suspected that Sacco was probably guilty and Vanzetti innocent. The response in America and around the world to their story is far more important than the simple fact of their guilt or innocence. Certainly in one sense they were innocent beyond peradventure of a doubt—that is to say, in the ideas they espoused, ideas that, means aside (which, of course, they never are), were noble and inspiring ones. In that, they were innocent. In the sublime confidence that the purity of their ideals and the nobility of Vanzetti's expression of them excluded the possibility of their guilt, the tens of thousands of Americans who gave their hearts and hopes to the two men were as innocent as the accused. The affair, the case, call it what one will, marked a watershed in our history in another way. Although it seemed to mark the triumph of the old repressive order (or, in Dos Passos's words, the triumph of the "strangers," whoever *they* were), it actually marked the passing of that order, though that would not be immediately apparent.

And then, not finally, because there seems to be no "finally" for Sacco and Vanzetti, there is the matter of the translation by many writers, poets, artists, as well as by Vanzetti himself of the episode into traditional Christian terms: Gethsemane; Golgotha; crucifixion; the bearing of the cross; Christ's agony; the passion; Christ and the thieves; the Eucharist; life beyond the grave. It is as though secular America needed desperately, in a time of confusion and distress, to retrieve those inexhaustible symbols of suffering and hope; as though the tragic drama of the two condemned men could be endured only if it were placed in the context of an earlier tragedy and a greater promise.

Historians (especially the brand known as psychohistorians) and political philosophers will continue to puzzle over the meaning of the Sacco-Vanzetti case for generations to come. It belongs to that small category of events of which one can say with some confidence that they have changed the course of our history. Whatever it meant, who was guilty or not guilty, nothing would ever be quite as it had been before. In that sense it had a psychological effect on a large number of Americans comparable to the World War.

Perhaps the last word should be Vanzetti's. He wrote to Alice Blackwell expressing gratitude to her and to the "people of the world, the laborers (I mean workers) and the greatest minds and hearts. . . ." Such efforts proved "beyond any possible doubt that a new conception of justice is planing its way in the soul of mankind: a justice centered on man as man. For as I have already said, you, they are doing for us what once could only have been done for saints and kings. This is real progress."

# 7

# Lindbergh

Charles Augustus Lindbergh was born in Detroit, Michigan, in 1902. From the moment of his birth all the ingredients of a classic American myth were there. Augustus Lindbergh, his grandfather, had been a reformer, a champion of the rights of women, and an important figure in Swedish politics. He had been forced (or encouraged) to emigrate to the United States in the 1860s. Lindbergh's father had been a leading Progressive in the state, a five-time Congressman who had sacrificed his political career by standing fast with La Follette in his opposition to the entry of the United States into the war. His mother, Evangeline Lodge Land Lindbergh, was a graduate of the University of Michigan with an M.A. in chemistry from Columbia University. She had been a high school chemistry teacher before she met and married Charles's father and made her home at Little Falls on the west bank of the Mississippi River. Charles's father was as handsome as any movie star, and his mother "as pretty as a picture." He took after his mother, friends said.

Charles, or Slim, as his friends called him when he had gotten his first quick growth, had the archetypal small-town Midwestern boyhood celebrated by dozens of the products of such towns from Sherwood Anderson and Booth Tarkington to Floyd Dell and Carl Sandburg.

He loved machines from his earliest days, tinkering with old engines and dreaming of flying. "Guns played a big part in the values of my boyhood," he wrote. "The soldiers' guns had saved my grandfather's homestead farm. On that farm, my father's guns had kept the family supplied with deer meat and game birds. . . . At the age of six I was given a twenty-two caliber rifle. I owned a twelve-gauge shotgun before I was old and strong enough to hold it steadily to my shoulder." There was an edge of reckless daring in the young Lindbergh's romance with guns. He and his friends delighted in shooting twenty-five-cent pieces out of each other's fingers at a range of fifty feet, a kind of modified Russian roulette.

Lindbergh's maternal grandfather, Charles H. Land, was a successful dentist in Detroit. Dedicated to improving the American smile, he prided himself on being known as the "father of porcelain dental art." He was both an artist and a scientist; in his home laboratory his fascinated grandson watched him make porcelain teeth in his ceramic kiln. He was famous for his gold inlays and porcelain caps.

Lindbergh's father's political career, which was at its height during the boy's adolescent years, resulted in frequent trips between Washington and Little Falls as well as constant campaigning. In consequence, Lindbergh never attended a full year of school in one place before he entered the University of Wisconsin. He discovered that the university had little to hold him. His motorcycle, his gun, the open fields, and, above all, the sky drew him away from academic pursuits. It had been fewer than twenty years since the Wright brothers had flown their crude plane at Kitty Hawk, but the country was swarming with ardent young men and their flying machines. Their stunts were a feature of every county fair. The more daring spectators could take a thrilling ride for $5. Wing walking and parachute jumps were popular attractions.

Halfway through his sophomore year at Wisconsin Lindbergh informed his dismayed parents that he was dropping out of college to enroll as a flying student with the Nebraska Aircraft Corporation at Lincoln. A few weeks later he had his first flight with Otto Timm. Shortly thereafter he began instruction with I. O. Biffle, and by the end of May, after some eight hours of flying instruction, he was pronounced ready to solo. Before he could take that step, however, the plane in which he was learning to fly was sold out from under him by the Nebraska Aircraft Corporation to a young aviator who planned to go barnstorming around the state at county fairs. Lindbergh went with him and was soon wing walking. After a stint back in Lincoln working at the Standard Aircraft factory, he received an invitation to another barnstorming expedition, this time in Kansas and Colorado. He was to do the parachute jumping and "a little wingwalking." In the fall it was barnstorming once again with a wheat rancher who owned a plane, this time through Wyoming and Montana.

Barnstorming in other people's planes was all very well for a start, but Lindbergh longed to own his own plane. He found the opportunity in Americus, Georgia, where the government was auctioning off surplus planes from the World War. Lindbergh bought one of the Jennies, an army training plane with a new Curtiss OX-5 engine, for $500. When he bought it, he had never soloed because he had not had the money to post a bond for a plane to solo in. Moreover he had never flown a Jenny. A friendly pilot gave him a half hour or so of instruction, and that evening Lindbergh flew his plane, alone in the air for the first time in an unfamiliar aircraft.

After a week of practice flights around Americus Lindbergh rolled up his clothes and "a few spare parts" in his blanket and took off on his first cross-country flight. In flying cross-country, pilots, aided by often rather rudimentary maps, headed from one small flying field to another, flying generally as far as their gas would take them on a single hop. Frequently they were forced by bad weather, engine trouble, or faulty navigation to land in the nearest available field. On several occasions Lindbergh had to make emergency landings; twice, when he ran out of fuel, he was able to flag down a gasoline truck and fill his tank. Lindbergh's goal was Minnesota, and his plan was to barnstorm on his own around that state and in the Rocky Mountain region. En route, he stopped frequently to make much-needed money by carrying passengers aloft on joyrides.

Lindbergh's father had objected strenuously to his flying career, but his mother, after overcoming her initial fears, had given him her support. Now he returned to Little Falls in his Jenny, picked up his mother, and barnstormed with her in the southern part of the state. He found stiff competition in the barnstorming field, and so in January, 1924, he took the entrance examinations for training as an Army Air Service flying cadet. A few weeks later he received word from the War Department to report to Brooks Field in San Antonio, Texas, to begin his training. The army, which had been cut after the war to a skeleton force, had little use for pilots. The course of instruction was correspondingly difficult; out of the 104 young men in Lindbergh's class, only 18 survived the rigorous training. Lindbergh graduated at the head of the survivors, received the precious wings, and was commissioned a second lieutenant in the Air Service Reserve Corps. His father died that same year at the age of sixty-five.

In the months following his graduation, Lindbergh barnstormed, did some wing walking, worked in a "flying circus" doing formation flying at county fairs, and in April began flying U.S. mail between St. Louis and Chicago. During his months as a mail pilot Lindbergh was forced to make two emergency jumps.

In 1919 Raymond Orteig, a New York financier, had established a prize of $25,000 for the first successful flight from New York to Paris. Orteig's prize had immediately attracted attention to the problems of transatlantic flight, but the initial plans of various pilots and their backers all involved large, three-engine planes with a pilot and pilot-navigator for relief during the long flight.

The idea of trying for the prize hit Lindbergh one night in the fall of 1926 when he was flying his mail route. The thought struck him that with the new radial air-cooled engines and lighter aluminum construction it would be possible to reach Paris in a single-engine plane with a substantial reserve of fuel. The new monoplanes could carry more weight than the biplanes that they were rapidly replacing; a single engine had less resistance to the flow of air; moreover, with a trimotor plane, Lindbergh realized, there was three times the chance of engine failure. If one engine failed in the early part of the flight, the attempt would have to be abandoned.

He found financial backers among young St. Louis business and professional men interested in aviation and anxious to promote their city. His plane would be named *The Spirit of St. Louis*. With $25,000 pledged, Lindbergh on February 28, 1927, ordered a plane built to his specifications by the Ryan Airlines in San Diego, California. It was to have a Wright Whirlwind 200-horsepower radial air-cooled engine and Pioneer navigating instruments. Lindbergh headed for San Diego to supervise the construction of the plane. In an effort to save every ounce of weight possible, the order for the plane had been preceded by weeks of careful calculations of such technical details as the rate of climb with specific weights of gasoline. "Day and night, seven days a week," Lindbergh wrote in *We*, "the structure grew from a few lengths of steel tubing to one of the most efficient planes that has ever taken the air." Ryan's engineers, catching the spirit of the venture, sometimes worked twenty-four hours at a time.

Lindbergh had learned a verse in school that became a guide for him:

> In elder days of Art,
>   Builders wrought with greatest care
> Each minute and unseen part;
>   For the Gods see everywhere.

Much of Lindbergh's time in those hectic weeks was spent mapping out a flight route which would take him in a partial great circle over New England, Newfoundland, and Greenland to a final cross-water flight to the coast of Ireland. By being his own navigator, Lindbergh calculated that he could carry enough extra gasoline for 300 miles' additional range. He weighed his equipment by ounces. Every pound meant another quart or so of gasoline. He would carry five tins of concentrated army rations, two canteens of water, an Armburst cup which condensed breath into water, two lightweight flashlights, a ball of string and a ball of cord, a hunting knife, flares, a needle, an inflatable raft and pump, a hacksaw blade. He carried no parachute. It would add twenty pounds to the weight of the plane, "a third of an hour's fuel . . . and it would be useless over the ocean. . . . It would be better to stay with the plane even if it crashed."

Sixty days after Lindbergh had placed the order for his plane, it was assembled and finished in its hangar, and he gave *The Spirit of St. Louis* its first test flight. "The actual performance," he wrote proudly, "was above the theoretical. The plane was off the ground in six and one-eighth seconds, or in 165 feet, carrying over 400 lbs in extra gas tanks and equipment." On the flight itself it would have to carry 300 gallons for a total weight of some 5,000 pounds. A series of careful tests beginning on April 28 at San Diego convinced Lindbergh that his plane had the capacity to perform its mission. Now every hour was precious.

There were three or four other efforts already under way when Lindbergh began his race to be the first to cross the Atlantic. The most serious rivals were Richard Byrd, the world-renowned adventurer and flier, and Clarence Chamberlin who, flying a Bellanca trimotor plane, had recently broken the world record for hours aloft. The pressure was relieved somewhat when Chamberlin's Bellanca, the *Columbia*, suffered injuries to its landing gear on April 24. Another serious rival was Lieutenant Commander Noel Davis, who planned to make the transatlantic flight in June in a three-engine biplane carrying fuel for fifty-four hours of flying time. He was backed by the American Legion, and his plane was so named.

Commander Richard Byrd's backer was the wealthy sportsman and department store heir Rodman Wanamaker. Wanamaker had put up $100,000 to underwrite Byrd's "huge three-engined Fokker monoplane." The plane, under construction, was expected to be ready in May and the *New York Times* reported that "on the European side of the ocean, it is understood that transatlantic planes are being constructed in France, England, and Italy."

On April 10, 1927, *New York Times* headlines exclaimed: "Two Famous Navy Fliers Preparing for Dashes Across the Atlantic Next Month Both to Report by Wireless to the *Times*." Byrd was to be accompanied by two aides—"Crack Navy Pilots to Man Both Planes"— the paper announced.

On May 9, with the weather in San Diego good and reports of clearing over the Rockies, Lindbergh took off for St. Louis. Fourteen hours and twenty-five minutes later he landed at Lambert Field, the first leg of his journey complete. The next morning he headed for New York and nine hours later put *The Spirit of St. Louis* down at Curtiss Field, Long Island.

Now a period of anxious waiting began. The weather reports, which Lindbergh consulted every few hours, indicated storms over the Atlantic. He and his rivals had to wait for the weather to clear. Lindbergh passed the time as best he could, checking and rechecking his plane, his equipment, and his navigational calculations. On the morning of May 19, with a light rain falling, he visited the Wright plant at Paterson, New Jersey, and later made plans to attend the theater, but at six o'clock he received a call from the New York Weather Bureau. A high-pressure area had developed over the North Atlantic. For a few days at least the North Atlantic would be clear of storms and turbulence. Lindbergh went at once to Curtiss Field to supervise the final preparations for the flight. The plane was to be towed the short distance from Curtiss Field to Roosevelt Field, which had a longer runway. Lindbergh then went to his hotel to try to get a few hours of precious sleep. The effort proved futile. He was interrupted by a visit from a friend. Without a full night's rest he would have to remain awake at the controls for some thirty-six hours more.

Before dawn Lindbergh was back at the field for a final check of the plane. Then, helmeted and buckled in, he peered out of the cockpit windows "through the idling blades of the propeller, over the runway's wet and glistening surface. I study the telephone wires at its end, and the shallow pool of water through which my wheels must pass," he wrote. " . . . Wind, weather, power, load—how many times have I balanced these elements in my mind, barnstorming from some farmer's cow pasture in the Middle West! . . . No plane ever took off so heavily loaded. . . . " As Lindbergh advanced the throttle, the little plane began to lumber down the soggy runway. The plane was slow to pick up speed; Lindbergh watched his instruments anxiously. Finally it began to roll, and with 2,000 feet of runway left, it had almost reached flying speed. He took the plane a few feet off the ground and then let it drop back. A pool of water slowed him, but a few seconds later he was airborne. He cleared the telephone wires at the end of the runway by twenty feet.

Especially captivating was Lindbergh's unselfconscious reference to himself and *The Spirit of St. Louis* as "we," which became the title of the instant book he produced three weeks after his flight. The notion of the unity of man and machine was particularly enchanting to a generation still infatuated with the marvels of flying and, indeed, of driving as well. In his more formal autobiography, *The Spirit of St. Louis*, Lindbergh later referred constantly to the subtle and instinctive interaction between him and his plane. *The Spirit of St. Louis*, once in the air, was "no longer an unruly mechanical device, as it was during the take-off . . . ; rather, it seems to form an extension of my own body, ready to follow my wish as the hand follows the mind's desire— instinctively, without commanding." When the plane encountered turbulence, Lindbergh felt the structure's strain "in my shoulders—in my body—in my mind. . . . " The plane was an animated, responding creature, as vibrant and alive as its pilot. When he decided in flight not to open the windows, thereby increasing the streamline of his plane and saving a few gallons of gas, he described that as a gift of the plane to him. "I'm taking a favor from my plane. It makes *The Spirit of St. Louis* seem more like a living partner in adventure than a machine of cloth and steel."

Carefully, meticulously, Lindbergh kept a log of each hour: wind velocity; direction; "true course"; variation; magnetic course; deviation; compass course; drift angle; compass heading; ceiling; visibility; altitude; airspeed; tachometer; oil; temperature and pressure; gas mixture. Often he flew a few feet above the crests of the waves in a kind of pocket of air at a cruising speed of 100 miles per hour. It occurred to him as he skimmed the waves that *The Spirit of St. Louis* was like a butterfly blown out to sea. As a child he had watched butterflies blown over the Mississippi River, "dancing up and down above the water, as I am dancing now. . . . But a touch of wing to water, and they were down forever, just as my plane would be. . . . Why, I used to wonder, did they ever leave the safety of the land? But why have I? How similar my position has become."

Another major theme of Lindbergh's imaginative reconstruction of his flight was the advantage he enjoyed, the "freedom" as he expressed it, of being on his own, a single individual joined with his beloved machine to fight nature. "My movements were not restricted by someone else's temperament, health, or knowledge. My decisions aren't weighted by responsibility for another's life. When I learned . . . that the weather was improving, I had no one to consult. . . . Now, I can go on or turn back according to the unhampered dictates of my mind and senses." Lindbergh's father had told him that when he could make his own unguided decisions, he would be "a full boy." The words came back to him on the first exultant moments of his flight. "I'm a full boy—independent—alone."

The profoundly American book that *The Spirit of St. Louis* demands to be compared to is Richard Henry Dana's *Two Years Before the Mast.* Like Lindbergh's autobiography, it is the story of a young man's great adventure. Dana was the scion of a famous and prosperous Boston family. The sailing vessel that carried him to the California coast and back was the greatest achievement of a pretechnological society. On it, sailors had to move as one in their intricate dance with the sails in a single magnificent choreography, each dependent on the other's grace and skill. For Lindbergh, the source of power was a single machine, beautiful and complex beyond one man's making yet giving him inconceivable power over the natural world. So in the midst of an almost excessively interrelated, interdependent society, one man exerted his lonely, independent will, a pioneer in the limitless sky.

Lindbergh considered flying over St. John's, Newfoundland, so that word might be broadcast that he was well on his way and safe. It would be a comfort to his mother. "But the principles I laid down for this flight involve no waste, no luxuries, no following of shore lines." The disciplined will, traveling light, no "waste, no luxuries."

The most harrowing moments of the flight, moments that Lindbergh re-creates with great skill in *The Spirit of St. Louis,* had to do with his desperate struggle with sleep; it takes on the proportions of legend. "Sleeping is winning. My whole body argues dully that nothing, nothing life can attain, is quite so desirable as sleep. My mind is losing resolution and control." The trying time for all pilots flying long hours during the night comes at dawn, when all the body's functions seem to decline. Lindbergh hallucinates. He sees "a great black mass ahead—It *necks out toward the route my compass points for me*—Its ears stick up—its jaws gape wide—It's a cloud—or—maybe it's not a cloud—It could be a dragon, or a tiger—I could imagine it into anything at all—What's that whitish object, moving just beyond the window of my room—I push my goggles up to see more clearly—No, they're bedsheets I'm peeking out between—I'm in the nursery of my Minnesota home, and I'm afraid of the dark!"

At last the flight neared its end. Lindbergh picked up the Irish coast, passing a number of offshore steamers, and then was over southern England, looking down at countryside with its farms, "extremely small and unusually neat and tidy," compared to the great sprawling farms of his own Middle West. Then came the Channel and Cherbourg. By this time most of the world within reach of the wireless telegraph knew that a young American was winging his way across the Atlantic. Lindbergh, well aware of the advantages of publicity, had been at pains to notify reporters of his takeoff. Photographers had been present in reassuring numbers at Roosevelt Field. The news had been flashed around the world and had already caught its fancy, the more so when the story was accompanied by photographs of a face of startling purity and innocence and, above all, *youthfulness*. The pilot was twenty-five, young enough, to be sure, but the untouched face could have been that of a sixteen-year-old off on a lark; it suggested the innocence of original creation. That its owner was a man of remarkable skill, singleness of purpose, and maturity, a prodigy of judgment, a genius of a kind was not apparent. It was enough that he was *young* and *alone*, with a *single engine* to carry him over the vast waters of the Atlantic.

When the first ships to spot *The Spirit of St. Louis* wired the news that he had been sighted off the shores of Ireland, a kind of collective insanity seized the world. Since he was headed for Paris, it seized the French first. Thousands of them rushed for Le Bourget Field on the outskirts of Paris. It was dark when his tiny plane circled the Eiffel Tower at the height of some 4,000 feet with the lights of Paris below and hundreds of thousands of Frenchmen straining to see the lights of his plane. Circling lower, he could make out the long line of hangars that marked the boundaries of the field. To his surprise the roads leading to the airport appeared to be jammed with cars, their headlights making a continuous row of light.

He circled around into the wind, landed, and started to taxi back toward the hangars, but the entire field was filled with thousands of people running toward the plane. Lindbergh's first thought was for its safety. He tried to organize some of the crowd into an improvised picket line around the plane, but in the noise and wild confusion it was impossible. He felt "parts of the ship" begin "to crack under the pressure of the multitude. . . . " When he tried to climb out of the plane, he found himself borne aloft by dozens of eager hands. For almost a half hour his ecstatic bearers carried him about like a banner, his feet never touching the ground. Some French Army pilots came to his rescue. One of them ingeniously snatched his helmet from his head and placed it on a tall, thin blond Frenchman, and an American correspondent called out, "Here is Lindbergh." The crowd swung about and moved in the direction of the imposter, while Lindbergh escaped into a hangar. The plane was meanwhile rescued by soldiers, and Lindbergh was escorted to Ambassador Myron Herrick, who whisked him away to the ambassadorial residence with reporters trailing in his wake.

Lindbergh's arrival was given a heightened drama by the fact that two famous French aviators, Charles Nungesser and François Coli, had taken off a few days earlier and disappeared over the Atlantic. The French, who love heroes, lost their heads completely over the young American. In doing so, they gave a taste of what was to come. Relations with France had been difficult since Versailles, and quarrels over disarmament, war debts, and other matters had placed additional strains on the ancient friendship between the two countries. To Ambassador Herrick, Lindbergh appeared to be quite literally heaven-sent. He did not hesitate to suggest as much, comparing the American flier to Joan of Arc, Lafayette, and the shepherd boy David, who slew Goliath. "I am not a religious man," he declared in his official welcome to Lindbergh, "but I believe there are certain things that happen in life which can only be described as the intervention of a Divine Act." Lindbergh had brought the French the "spirit of America in a manner in which it could never be brought in a diplomatic sack."

After a good night's sleep the hero arose, went out to Le Bourget to check on the condition of *The Spirit of St. Louis*, and there accepted the invitation of French military pilots to fly a black Nieuport. To the delight of the French fliers "as well as the populace," an American newsman wrote, "he went aloft and began stunting with a skill and ease that stamped him once and for all an expert."

Everywhere his freshness, his natural charm, his tact and graciousness were acclaimed. He expressed repeatedly his admiration for Nungesser and Coli and his gratitude to the French people for their generous reception: Lafayette was evoked a hundred times. Lindbergh lunched at the Ministry of War and was received by the senators at the Luxembourg Palace. He attended a gala performance at the Champs Élysées Théâtre, his every word and expression carefully recorded and declared perfect. Honors, medals, ribbons, decorations of every kind were bestowed on him. Leaving for Brussels, he circled the Eiffel Tower and dropped a note of thanks and good-bye in the Place de la Concorde on his way out of town. In Belgium, where King Albert and Queen Elisabeth received him in the manner reserved for heads of state, Burgomaster Adolphe Max, mayor of Brussels, made a welcoming speech in English. Again divine favor was implied. Since the flight appeared to be "beyond human forces, the victory was really a victory of humanity. . . . In your glory there is glory for all men. An apparently impossible task loomed before you. You surmounted it. . . . You must have heard many times during these five days that in crossing the ocean with your 'Spirit of St. Louis' you have done more than all the diplomats to bring closer together the different peoples. . . . In you the symbol of daring and courage is impossible not to admire. . . . I salute you, dear Captain Lindbergh, a noble son of your great nation which at an hour when civilization was in danger came to its help and with us conquered."

Lindbergh replied, thanking his hosts for their hospitality and praising the progress that the Belgians had made in aviation. Lindbergh then flew on to London, where word came that President Coolidge was sending the U.S. Navy flagship *Memphis* to bring him and *The Spirit of St. Louis* home.

The allegedly phlegmatic British bid fair to outdo their cross-Channel neighbors in effusiveness. A huge crowd awaited Lindbergh at the airport, and another surrounded the American Embassy for blocks. Again there were endless official ceremonies. Lindbergh joined Ambassador Alanson B. Houghton in a procession to Westminster Abbey to lay a wreath on the tomb of Britain's Unknown Soldier. King George V chatted with him about his flight and gave him the Royal Air Force Cross, only once before awarded to an American. He met Queen Mary and the Prince of Wales and visited Prime Minister Stanley

Baldwin at 10 Downing Street. Sir Samuel Hoare described the advances in aviation suggested by Lindbergh's flight and ended a luncheon address before the Air Council by declaring, "I ask you to drink to his health as a young man who embodies the spirit of adventure and lights up the world with a flash of courage and daring, and, I am glad to say, of success."

Every act, every gesture of the hero seemed to bring forth new waves of ecstasy. He telephoned his mother in Detroit. *"His mother,"* the correspondent Fitzhugh Green wrote, "the world rolled the two words around its collective tongue as might a wine connoisseur his nectar."

Finally it was time to return home to an America impatient to outdo all other receptions of the hero. "It is probable," Green wrote, "that when Lindbergh reached America he got the greatest welcome any man in history ever received; certainly the greatest when judged by numbers. . . . " As the *Memphis* steamed up Chesapeake Bay, four destroyers, two army blimps, and forty airplanes representing the army, the navy, and the Marine Corps convoyed it.

The next day, June 11, was hot and clear; crowds began gathering at street corners in the morning. "Every roof top, window, old ship, wharf and factory floor was filled with those who simply had to see Lindbergh come home," Green wrote. "Factory whistles, automobiles, church bells and fire sirens all joined the pandemonium." Fifty pursuit planes as well as flights of bombers flew in formation over Washington. The huge dirigible USS *Los Angeles* hovered above the *Memphis*. The firing of salutes began from the warships. At the gangplank in the navy yard were the secretaries of the navy and the army, Charles Evans Hughes, a host of other dignitaries, and Commander Richard E. Byrd, who had flown to the North Pole and had hoped to make the first transatlantic crossing. Evangeline Lindbergh was also there to greet her son. When she was conducted aboard to greet him prior to the official hoopla, "a new burst of cheering went up; but many wept—: they knew not just why," Green reported. The meeting took place in one of the ship's cabins; they shook hands. They appeared together amid renewed cheers. "It was a nice touch," Green noted. " . . . And it somehow symbolized a great deal of what was being felt and said that hot morning. . . . "

A procession formed for the trip to the Washington Monument, where the President and Mrs. Coolidge were awaiting the hero. As Lindbergh passed the packed rows of sidewalk spectators, many observers felt a reverential mood, a kind of religious spirit. Some people wept; others stood transfixed, without expression as if the moment were somehow too awesome to comprehend, a historic moment somehow encapsulating ages. "Ranged about the President were the ambassadors of many foreign countries, members of the diplomatic corps with their wives and daughters, and nearly all the high officials of the government," Green wrote. The President, his normally glum countenance bearing an unfamiliar expression of cordiality, came forward to shake the hero's hand. When the applause had died down, the President began to speak. He reviewed the achievments of American aviators. The greatest challenge that had remained was a flight from America to Europe. "Others were speeding their preparations to make the trial, but it remained for an unknown youth to attempt the elements and win. It is the same story of valor and victory by a son of the people that shines through every page of American history," Coolidge declared, rising to what were for him unprecedented heights of eloquence. The President then went on to praise the Lindbergh family, his father, who had served in Congress "several [sixteen] years" and about whose radical politics the less said the better, and his mother, "who dowered her son with her own modesty and charm."

The President noted that as a reserve officer in the Army Flying Service Corps, Lindbergh had joined the 110th Observation Squadron of the Missouri national guard and that his superior officers had reported that he was "intelligent," "industrious," "energetic," "dependable," "purposeful," "alert," "quick of reaction," "serious," "deliberate," "stable," "efficient," "frank," "modest," "congenial," "a man of good moral habits and regular in his business transactions"—all the things a fine young American should be. "On a morning just three weeks ago yesterday," the President continued, "this wholesome, earnest, fearless, courageous product of America rose into the air from Long Island. . . . It was no haphazard adventure . . . driven by an unconquerable will and inspired by the imagination and spirit of his Viking ancestors, this reserve officer set wing across the dangerous stretches of the North Atlantic." The plane, his "ship," as Lindbergh preferred to call it, was a "silent partner" that represented "American genius and industry." The President welcomed Lindbergh, "a Colonel of the United States Officers' Reserve Corps, an illustrious citizen of our Republic, a conqueror of the air. . . . " Coolidge then bestowed the Distinguished Flying Cross on the young hero. Pandemonium.

The hero responded briefly and modestly. He had had the good fortune to be the instrument of good feeling between the "people of

France" and the "people of America. . . . I thank you." It was over. The few brief sentences to the listening crowd in its infatuation with the hero sounded like the greatest eloquence. "The final touch of the miracle [of Lindbergh's brief response]," Fitzhugh Green wrote, "was that this speech was extemporaneous. Just as when Lincoln finished his Gettysburg address his listeners sat stunned at the very brevity of it, so there was a curious silence immediately following Lindbergh's utterance . . . [and then] men and women clapped until their palms were numb. Again many wept." A radio announcer "broke down and sobbed."

There was, of course, more to come: dinner at the White House with the Cabinet, Lindbergh on Mrs. Coolidge's right. Lindbergh's "eyes were clear, his smile quick; like a practiced diplomat he eluded entangling discussions; and he had a ready reply for every intelligent inquiry put to him within his range of knowledge or experience."

At the National Press Club the orator of the day gave free rein to his tongue: "The whole world was carried off its feet by an accomplishment so daring, so masterful in execution, so superb in achievement, by the picture presented of that onrushing chariot of dauntless youth, flashing across the uncharted heavens straight through the storm's barrage. . . . He personified, to a Europe amazed at the revelation, the real spirit of America. . . . It brought to the peoples of the world a new realization that clean living, clean thinking, fair play and sportsmanship, modesty of speech and manner, faith in a mother's prayers . . . are still potent as fundamentals of success."

The postmaster general of the United States then stepped forward to present Lindbergh with the first airmail stamp of an issue dedicated to him and *The Spirit of St. Louis*, to "We," the first time a living person had been so honored. Before he left Washington, there was a final ceremony presided over by Charles Evans Hughes. Presented with the Cross of Honor, Lindbergh replied that credit for his flight should go not to him alone "but to American science and genius which had given years of study to the advancement of aeronautics. . . . It was the culmination of twenty years of aeronautical research and the assembling together of all that was practicable and best in American aviation. It represented American industry."

Finally it was on to New York for the greatest show on earth, the ticker tape parade down Fifth Avenue, already an established American folkway. The police estimated that between 3,000,000 and 4,500,000 people lined the sidewalks from the Battery to Central Park to hail the hero. Claude Bowers, columnist for the *World*, witnessed the spectacle from the window of his office. New York had never seen anything like it. Windows were packed with spectators, men and women lined the parapets of buildings, and a military band played in anticipation of Lindbergh's appearance. "And then the hero came. Mounted police surrounded his car, and the crowd roared its enthusiasm when the bareheaded youth, serious and clearly astonished, alighted and ascended the steps of the City Hall to receive Mayor Jimmy Walker's greeting." Walker, the cynical and wicked mayor of what many people considered the world's greatest metropolis, officially greeted Lindbergh. The young pilot had given the world a new pronoun, "the aeronautical 'we' . . . a flying pronoun." In a city of immigrants the mayor welcomed Lindbergh as "another son of an immigrant." Nor did he neglect the standard tribute to motherhood: "sitting side by side with your glorious mother."

When the mayor was through, Governor Alfred E. Smith was waiting in the wings for his moment of reflected glory on another reviewing stand. Again there were speeches while a skywriter wrote "Hail Lindy" in smoky letters. That night there was a party at the Long Island estate of Clarence Mackay, head of the Postal Telegraph Cable Company. "Eight of New York's most prominent people attended the dinner which was kingly in its appointments," Green noted.

The final and fullest encomium was still to come. It was as though words could hardly serve to convey the nation's ecstasy. The city of New York gave a dinner for 4,000, yes, 4,000, guests at the Hotel Commodore. Charles Evans Hughes, Republican presidential candidate in 1916, who had lost to Woodrow Wilson by the margin of California, twice secretary of state and a justice of the Supreme Court, safe to say the nation's most distinguished elder statesman, presided. Hughes recapitulated the themes that had emerged as the most compelling ones: "When a young man, slim and silent," telephoning "his greetings to his mother in Detroit," is praised by the President of the United States and given honors "which are but a faint reflection of the affection and esteem cherished in the hearts of the countrymen of the West who distinguished America by that flight, then indeed is the day that hath no bother; then is the most marvelous day that this old earth has ever known." Ships were measured by their displacement. "Colonel Lindbergh has displaced everything. His displacement is beyond all calculation. He fills all our thoughts. . . . For the time being he has lifted us into the freer and upper air that is his home. He has displaced everything that is petty; that is sordid; that is vulgar. What is money in the presence of Charles A. Lindbergh? . . . This is the happiest day, the happiest day of all days for America, and as one mind she is now intent upon the noblest and the best. America is picturing to herself youth with the highest aims, with courage unsurpassed; science victorious. Last and not least, motherhood with her loveliest crown. . . . What a wonderful thing it is to live in a time when science and character join hands to lift up humanity with a vision of its own dignity.

"There is again revealed to us, with a startling suddenness, the inexhaustible resources of our national wealth. From an unspoiled home, with its traditions of industry, of frugality and honor, steps swiftly into our gaze this young man, showing us the unmeasured treasures in our minds of American character.

"America is fortunate in her heroes; her soul feeds upon their deeds; her imagination revels in their achievements. There are those who would rob them of something of their lustre, but no one can debunk Lindbergh, for there is no bunk about him. He represents to us, fellow-Americans, all that we wish—a young American at his best."

If we grant without hesitation that Lindbergh's achievement was extraordinary and, moreover, that he had an "angelic" presence and was most of the things people said of him, his feat was not really all *that* remarkable. The acclaim *was* excessive. The times had been difficult and demoralizing ones, as we have had more than one occasion to note. Many thoughtful Americans despaired of the future of the Republic. Many of the nation's best spirits had sought refuge abroad. Individuals who dared question the status quo were denounced as radicals, Reds, traitors. If those so accused were alien immigrants, they were deported without ceremony or without due process of law. Morals were in disarray, and the behavior of the nation's youth was a source of anxiety to the older generation: bathtub gin and bootleg liquor; short skirts on promiscuous young women; coonskin coats and pocket flasks and illicit love in rumble seats. Wild speculations and sudden riches. Gangsters running Chicago. A libertine mayor of the nations's greatest city. Crippling racial prejudices, the Ku Klux Klan. A feeling, amid all the high life, that things were not right, that America, with the World War and the divisions in American society that it revealed or created, had lost its way. That the patient was ailing there was little doubt. Although millions of Americans had suppressed their misgivings and decided to "stay cool with Coolidge," there were millions more who lived in considerable anguish of spirit. Leaders were in disrepute; politicians, alive and dead, had come under severely critical scrutiny. It was the age, as Charles Evans Hughes suggested, of "debunking," of cynicism, of the loss of illusion and the loss of innocence. Pundits were declaring that the nation was old and sunk in dissipation. But here suddenly was a genuine, apparently undebunkable hero, sent, Ambassador Herrick suggested, by the Divine Power for the redemption of a fallen world. About him clustered congeries of old hopes and old faiths. If fallen America could still produce a Lindbergh out of the lumber of old dreams and illusions, then things might not, could not, be so bad after all.

In Scott Fitzgerald's words, "something bright and alien flashed across the sky. A young Minnesotan who seemed to have nothing to do with his generation did an heroic thing, and for a moment people set down their glasses in country clubs and speakeasies and thought of their old best dreams. Maybe there was a way out by flying, maybe our restless blood could find frontiers in the illimitable air. But by that time we were all pretty well committed; and the Jazz Age continued; we would all have one more."

Looking back many years later, Malcolm Cowley reflected that Americans of the twenties suffered from a lack of challenges, of heroic tasks and obstacles to be overcome. That, he felt, was why Lindbergh had become such a hero. He had created a daring task and then accomplished it, thereby reviving the image of the brave and ingenious pioneer, the fearless individual who triumphs over both machine and nature.

There is no use quarreling over the somewhat insane response of Americans of all classes and degrees of sophistication; excessive as it may have been, it is still one of those immutable historical facts that the historian in a later time may circle in endless perplexity. We have stated as a simple law that when the response to a particular event far exceeds the stimulus or the provocation, something more is going on than meets the eye. Certainly that was true of Lindbergh's spectacular flight across the Atlantic.

It was not long after the moment of euphoria that the knowledge of wickedness and sin crowded in on the hero and on the nation that adored him so touchingly and so unreservedly.

President Coolidge, prompted by Walter Lippmann, sent his Amherst schoolmate wealthy, able Dwight Morrow to Mexico to negotiate the extremely delicate issue of that nation's treatment of the Catholic Church and related matters. Morrow took with him his brilliant young daughter, Anne, a recent graduate of Smith College. Lindbergh was dispatched on a goodwill flight to Mexico to help create an atmosphere favorable to the negotiations. He sat beside Anne Morrow at an ambassadorial function. He was tall and blond and somewhat shy. She was small, intense, "poetic," a member in good standing of the Eastern upper class; he was indubitably Midwestern. They fell in love, of course, and were married. She learned to fly and became his companion on his constant aerial journeys about the world. Then their first child, Charles A. Lindbergh, Jr., was stolen from his crib in their Hopewell, New Jersey, home in the spring of 1932 by a deranged carpenter named Bruno Hauptmann, and the dream turned into a nightmare. It was not simply the tragic loss of the child but the circus created by the American press around the kidnapping, the discovery of the child's body, the arrest, trial, and execution of Hauptmann that so profoundly disillusioned Lindbergh. Heretofore he had experienced the press as a relatively benign "estate," eager to be an instrument of his missionary zeal for the advancement of aviation or, indeed, whatever he had on his mind. It had often been a nuisance, but it had never revealed, at least to him, its awesome power to humiliate and degrade. It was, it turned out, too much to bear. The Lindberghs fled to England and rented the picturesque estate of Harold Nicolson, the British diplomat who had been such a conspicuous figure at the Versailles Treaty making. Then they bought, rather symbolically, an island off the French coast as an ultimate refuge. They had five more children, three boys and two girls. Lindbergh, as a classic American tinkerer-inventor, worked with his friend Alexis Carrel on an artificial heart, dabbled in mysticism, and flew and flew around and about the world, to India, to China, to South American nations. Only in the air were he and his wife ever truly free; they soared like birds over the disorderly world. One feels that he was forever troubled by the problem of the "second act" (apropos of the comment that there are no "second acts" in America). If, at the age of twenty-five, you have done what your contemporaries acclaim, however excessively, as the greatest human achievement, what do you do at thirty or forty or fifty?

It is, on a certain level, an unsolvable problem, a classic American tragedy. But with the very considerable help of his remarkable wife he—they—managed it reasonably well. Although, as we shall see, Lindbergh was destined to fall into disrepute, he kept his balance and his sanity, no inconsiderable accomplishment, and twenty-five years after his famous flight wrote a great and enduring book about it, *The Spirit of St. Louis.*

# 8

# 1927

There are certain years in American history that seem almost too packed with significant events (or disasters) to account for well. Most such years—1819, 1837, 1854, 1876–77, 1892—have been years of serious or devastating depression. Others, such as 1912 and 1917 have been significant turning points of one kind or another. A remarkable year in which man-made events competed with natural disasters for public attention was 1927. It was the year the Sacco-Vanzetti case culminated in their deaths in the electric chair at Charlestown prison; it was the year a daring young pilot flew alone across the Atlantic Ocean; it was the year of one of the longest and bloodiest series of strikes in the war surrounding capital and labor. But it was events halfway around the world that were most dramatic. In China, Communists attacked government forces. "Foreign Buildings Are Stormed by Mob of Frenzied Coolies," the *New York Times* informed its readers. Women and children were being evacuated in Hankow. The revolt quickly spread to Shanghai, where American marines landed to protect U.S. diplomatic personnel and U.S. nationals, and then to Nanking. Alarm bells rang in world capitals at the threat that the vast nation of China might join Russia in the Communist ranks. In Moscow, it was reported, there were wild celebrations. Tens of thousands of Russians turned out to march and sing revolutionary songs at the news that China was aflame with revolutionary zeal.

Hankow appeared to be the center of revolutionary activity. There a Russian, Mikhail Borodin, held power. One of his principal aides was a young American woman, a graduate of the University of Illinois, named Rayna Prohme. This odd arrangement was the result of an agreement reached in 1923 between Sun Yat-sen, the "George Washington" of the initial phases of the Chinese Revolution, and the Russians, who agreed to supply him with armaments, political advisers, and even soldiers if needed.

Sun Yat-sen's ties to the United States had been close. John Dewey had been one of his inspirations; that odd soldier of fortune Homer Lea had been a general in his army; Sun had visited America to raise money to finance his armies, and his wife, Soong Ching-ling, was a graduate of the Wesleyan College for Women at Macon, Georgia. Soong Ching-ling, in the words of journalist Vincent Sheean, "travelled with Sun Yat-sen, acted as his secretary, participated with him in mass meetings and party councils, public triumphs and secret flights. She learned to share his passion against injustice of every kind" and to share his dream of "Democracy, Nationalism, Social Welfare."

Sun Yat-sen died a year after his agreement with the Soviets, but his armies, "advised" and in some cases commanded by Russian officers, swept up the Yangtze to Hankow, Nanking and Shanghai. A rift was already evident in the Kuomintang between Chiang Kai-shek, whose loyalties were to the middle-class business interests, and those Chinese who were determined to carry the revolution through to what they believed was its proper Marxist conclusion. Hankow became the center of left-wing opposition to Chiang Kai-shek, who was based at Nanking.

When Sheean arrived in Hankow in 1927, the city was crowded with delegations from Europe, Asia, and America who had come to witness what they believed to be the final stages of the Chinese Revolution. In Sheean's words, "Communists everywhere regarded Hankow as not only the most conspicuous success of revolutionary technique since 1917, but as the test case; if its success could be extended and made permanent, the victory of the international (Trotskyist) tendency was assured; but if Hankow failed, the militant world-revolutionists failed as well, and even in Russia the future became obscure." Well-known Communists from around the world were seen everywhere. Sheean noted the "beautiful carved-oak head of Manabendra Nath

Roy," head of the Far Eastern section of the Comintern. "When I saw agitators," he wrote, "they were . . . talking—talking, talking, talking, as only theoretical Communists can talk when they see under their eyes the materials for the manipulation of history. . . . Other immediate visible phenomena: frequent strikes, mass meetings and demonstrations. . . ."

Madame Sun Yat-sen was the most famous figure in the city, but Rayna Prohme bid fair to rival her. "Red-headed gal, spitfire, mad as a hatter, complete Bolshevik. Works for Borodin," Sheean was told. He interviewed her and fell for the "Wildest Bolshevik in town." While Sheean and Prohme fell more and more deeply in love, Rayna's husband, Bill Prohme, seemed sullen and unhappy. "His violent revolutionary enthusiasm resented my bourgeois lethargy," Sheean wrote, "my innumerable changes of white silk clothes, my Scotch whisky and Egyptian cigarettes," not to say his attentions to his wife.

"Hankow . . . " Vincent Sheean wrote, "was a marvellous revolutionary spectacle, in which the courage and devotion of the Chinese agitators, the skill of the Russians, the high hopes and frenzied determination of the workers, and the individual splendour of characters like Sun Yat-sen, Borodin and Rayna Prohme, combined to give me a glimpse into a new world." The self-consciously cynical and worldly Sheean felt himself drawn closer and closer to the Communists, partly by his love for Rayna Prohme, partly by the courage and fortitude of the Chinese revolutionaries.

Everyone waited for the decisive uprising. But although the European press referred to the "Communist experiment at Hankow," Borodin was unable to create the revolution everyone was waiting for. Meanwhile, Chiang Kai-shek strengthened his own position at Nanking, conferring with representatives of Standard Oil and other companies with large investments in China.

The news from China was followed a few weeks later by Communist uprisings in Vienna. "Austria may become a Soviet Republic before the day is out," a *New York Times* correspondent wired. Some 100 people had been killed, and 500 wounded, the paper announced. The Palace of Justice had been set on fire by angry workers, and fierce fighting raged around the House of Parliament. It seemed to those who hoped, as well as to those who feared, that the last phase of the world revolution had begun its inexorable course, the conclusion of which good Marxists considered as certain as the laws of nature. Even the disbelief of skeptics was shaken: the "right" moved farther right;

the "left" moved left. But when Chiang denounced the Hankow government as a foreign imposition and carried twenty-one of the thirty-three members of the Central Executive Committee of the Kuomintang with him, the days of revolution, so confidently anticipated, were numbered. The problem of those who had come to witness the triumph of the revolution turned out to be how to escape from the beleaguered city. Borodin told Sheean, "When I am forced to go, I shall go. But do not suppose that the Chinese revolution is ending or that it has failed in any but the most temporary sense. It will go underground. It will become an illegal movement, suppressed by counter-revolution and beaten down by reaction and imperialism; but it has learned how to organize, how to struggle. Sooner or later, a year, two years, five years from now, it will rise to the surface again. It may be defeated a dozen times, but in the end it must conquer. The revolutionary impulse is profound in China. . . . What has happened here will not be forgotten."

In Austria, too, the uprising of the Vienna workers was bloodily suppressed, and that country turned to a "strong man" of the right.

Vincent Sheean, Rayna Prohme, Borodin, and Madame Sun Yat-sen escaped from the besieged Hankow by various routes to rendezvous in Moscow, where the Russians were preparing to celebrate the tenth anniversary of the revolution. Rayna Prohme had, in the course of her flight, discarded her husband, Bill. Because of her services to the Comintern, she and Sheean had a privileged place at the celebration, in the ranks underneath the walls of the Kremlin, not far from Lenin's tomb. "The enormous square was filled with marching people," Sheean wrote. "Crowded, disciplined, innumerable, they came into the square under the arch of the Iberian Virgin and rolled across it to the Cathedral of St. Basil. . . . For half a day the delegations from all parts of European and Asiatic Russia had been riding or marching through the square, and there were still scores of thousands to come. . . . In a high box near to the tomb of Lenin the Russian Communist leaders stood and received the cheers of the uncountable crowd."

Sheean could not suppress the thought that Leon Trotsky, the "revolutionary genius who had directed the events of November 17, 1917, was now muzzled and locked away; that with him a whole phalanx of Communist intellectuals, some of the best writers and speakers in the party, were suppressed or about to be suppressed; that the world revolution was abandoned and the actual dictatorship of Russia lodged, not in the proletariat or even in the Russian Communist party, but in a tiny group called the Political Bureau. . . . There were too many rumours afloat, too many dark stories and desperate suppositions. . . . [Leo] Kamenev had been exiled; Trotsky had been killed; Trotsky had not been killed. . . . The Komintern had been reorganized, or was going to be reorganized . . . ; there was going to be a further retreat toward Capitalism. . . . "

Sheean attempted to persuade Rayna Prohme not to enter the Soviet underground espionage network. To do so, he argued, would mean her virtual disappearance from the world "aboveground" and any hope of marriage or happiness for them. It proved a one-sided contest. "Rayna's individual impulses had been by now, so subjugated and harmonized by her intelligence that the conflict was over," Sheean wrote; "she was unified, integrated, and burned with a pure white flame. She was prepared for any sacrifice up to and including death itself; petty questions (among which she included her personal destiny) could not disturb her any more. It was a marvelously pure flame. . . . Nothing else I have ever seen gave the same light and heat." In another age it would have been to a convent that her lover was surrendering his beloved. But Rayna Prohme was stricken with a mysterious illness, which Sheean implies may have resulted from the conflict between her love for him and her duty to the Communist Party. She died in Moscow with a grieving Sheean at her bedside, convinced, by her death, that "personal history" no longer mattered.

It was principally in the realm of foreign policy that Calvin Coolidge showed some signs of life. As Harding's secretary of state Charles Evans Hughes had managed to extricate the marines from Nicaragua (they had occupied that country from 1912 to 1925), but Coolidge sent them back. On January 10, 1927, the President delivered a special message to Congress. The marines had been ordered to return to Nicaragua to secure the dominance of the American-backed "president," Adolfo Díaz. The Bolsheviks were trying to take over Latin America, Coolidge told Congress, using Nicaragua and Mexico as bases. The United States could not "fail to view with deep concern any serious threat to stability . . . in Nicaragua . . . especially if such state of affairs is contributed to or brought about by outside influences or by any foreign power."

Hughes's successor, Frank Kellogg, delivered a white paper to the Senate Foreign Relations Committee two days later describing "Bolshevik Aims and Policies in Mexico and Latin America." According to this document, Mexico was the Bolshevik command post in the Western Hemisphere.

A number of Congressmen and Senators ridiculed the Coolidge-Kellogg maneuver, and the *Baltimore Sun* described Kellogg's white paper as "utterly indecent intellectual exposure. . . . Such drivel, offered by a Cabinet officer in charge of foreign relations . . . is, we believe, without previous example in the history of this country." Alabama Congressman George Huddleston described it as "an expression of imperialism, with all its most extreme implications," and William Borah, always on the alert for American intervention in the affairs of other countries, defined the President's policy as based on "mahogany and oil." Walter Lippmann wrote that Coolidge's actions made it clear that Nicaragua was "not an independent republic, that its government is the creature of the State Department, that the management of its finances and direction of its domestic and foreign affairs is determined not in Nicaragua but in Wall Street. . . . We continue to think of ourselves as a kind of great, peaceable Switzerland, whereas we are in fact a great, expanding world power. . . . Our imperialism is more or less unconscious."

Mexico—the command post of Communist subversion in the Americas, according to Kellogg and Coolidge—had been at sword's point with the United States since assumption of power in that country by Plutarco Calles in 1924. The Mexican writer Octavio Paz wrote of "poor Mexico, so far from God, so close to the United States." As they had in the revolutionary upheavals earlier in the century, the American oil companies with large investments in Mexico, and the Catholic Church, indignant at the appropriation of church properties, the expulsion of foreign priests (including a number of Americans), and the closing of parochial schools, clamored for military intervention by the United States. A particular sore point was the fact that the Mexican president, Calles, insisted that American oil companies with their vast holdings in Mexico accept fifty-year leases instead of outright ownership of Mexican wells—a reasonable enough proposition, it would seem, but one that was bitterly opposed by the oil companies, which looked on Mexico as a kind of fief. To Kellogg's cries of Communist infiltration in Mexico, Walter Lippmann replied contemptuously that bolshevism had nothing to do with the unrest in that nation. It came from the "desire to assert the national independence and dignity of an inferior race" (Lippmann might more tactfully have written "by a people that had been *treated* as an inferior race"). Nothing could be more prejudicial to the long-term relationship of the peoples of North America and South America than the "realization in Latin America that the United States had adopted a policy, conceived in the spirit of Metternich, which would attempt to guarantee vested rights against social progress as the Latin American peoples conceive it." He suggested to a business friend that he and his associates might "gain more by attempting to work with this growing nationalist movement, by winning the confidence of its leaders, and trying to persuade them that you are not their enemies."

Walter Lippmann and the *World* became the rallying point for anti-interventionists. Lippmann saw it as his task to persuade the business community, with the assistance of liberal financiers like Thomas Lamont and Dwight Morrow, both, incidentally, Morgan partners, that military intervention would be not only contrary to the best interests of the United States in Latin America but, more important to them, contrary to their own interests. In advancing this argument, he was assisted substantially by the fact that the bankers, as opposed to the oil interests, did not want intervention, on the practical grounds that it would imperil the investments of the holders of Mexican bonds.

An indignant Coolidge demanded that all reporters clear their stories on Mexico with the State Department before printing them. What Coolidge wished, in Lippmann's words, was "a reptile press" printing only what those in power wished to have printed. In other countries that was called dictatorship or tyranny. In the face of growing opposition Coolidge, perhaps mindful of his campaign slogan "Keep cool with Coolidge," appointed Henry Stimson a special mediator in the spring of 1927 and, as we have seen, appointed his Amherst classmate Dwight Morrow ambassador to Mexico. The appointment of Morrow was attacked promptly as evidence that the delicate matter of diplomacy with Mexico had been placed in the hands of the House of Morgan.

While the Senate was still arguing over Morrow's appointment, the latter left for his post. He embraced Calles with almost Latin effusiveness. Morrow was successful in his pursuit of an agreement with Calles on the oil issue, an achievement hailed by Morrow's friend Lippmann as "one of the most brilliant exploits in American diplomacy."

The matter of the relations between the revolutionary government and the Catholic Church proved more complicated. The most difficult issue to resolve was the determination of the government to "register"—that is to say, approve of—foreign priests. The clergy responded to the government's restrictions by going on a religious strike, refusing to carry out their parish duties until the government relented. Lippmann recruited Catholic friends in the United States to assist in the negotations and himself entered into the discussions by going to Havana, ostensibly to cover the Sixth International Conference of American States for the *World* but actually to meet secretly with a delegation of Mexican bishops. Further secret negotiations followed between representatives of the Catholic hierarchy of the United States and Calles. The Mexican government assured the priests and bishops that it had no intention of trying to "destroy the identity of the Church," but it was a year before the parish churches reopened.

Coolidge continued the occupation of Haiti and landed marines in Honduras in 1924. American troops also intervened in Panama to quell riots in 1925. The Nicaraguan operation was particularly offensive to South Americans sensitive to Yankee imperialism. The liberal leader Agustino Sandino, was routed with the complicity of the United States, and the conservative Adolfo Díaz became president.

With Coolidge's encouragement Frank Kellogg joined with French Foreign Minister Aristide Briand to draft a treaty, to be signed by all the world powers, outlawing war. Known formally as the Pact of Paris, the Kellogg-Briand Pact condemned "recourse to war for the solution of international controversies, and [the signatories] renounce[d] it as an instrument of national policy in their relations with one another." Conflicts between the signatories would, in the future, be settled wholly "by pacific means." On the other hand, each nation that was party to the pact reserved the unqualified right of self-defense. Senator Borah, defending the pact in the Senate, countered the charge that since the signers of the pact were left free to decide what constituted "self-defense," the agreement could not prevent war. Borah took the rather ingenious line that its purpose was less to prevent war than to "organize peace." Under Hiram Johnson's somewhat incredulous questioning, Borah conceded that "when the treaty is broken the United States is absolutely free. It is just as free to choose its course as if the treaty had never been written. . . . " Claude Swanson returned to what seemed to him the excessively large loophole which exempted wars of self-defense from the treaty. "It should be noted," Swanson declared, "that this question of self-defense is not limited to territory, but includes anything that any nation may determine is vital for its protection and self-defense. . . . It practically excludes from the operations of this treaty almost any war that has occurred in the last century." Nonetheless,

Swanson concluded, surprisingly, that although the treaty was a "mere gesture," it was "a gesture of peace, not hostility, of good will and conciliation. . . . It permits but it does not approve war. It is a noble gesture or declaration for world peace and as such I shall support it."

The Kellogg-Briand Pact was signed by fifteen nations initially and by sixty-three subsequently. The signing was hailed as marking "a new date in the history of mankind." From the day it was first proposed, William Allen White wrote, "until the treaty was ratified in Paris, in August, 1928, it was an American treaty. The Kellogg tactics, the Kellogg energy and America's prestige framed it, took world leadership for whatever it was worth, convinced mankind that the outlawry of war at least was a realizable ideal."

Cynical Elihu Root, who had served as secretary of state under Theodore Roosevelt, was contemptuous of the pact. It contained nothing more than the "vague fantasies of inexperienced persons," he told Hamilton Fish Armstrong. "We are powerful, arrogant and bad-mannered," the old politician declared. "Our attitude is that we do not need friends. We feel that we can stand outside all international organizations and that our prosperity is such that it cannot be touched by external events. We are profoundly mistaken."

In the United States one of the by-products of the era's mania for speculation—the Florida real estate boom—burst. Burton Rascoe traced the boom back to the 1890s when a certain Bingham bought 3,000 feet of oceanfront property near Palm Beach for $4.65 per front foot. In 1917 Paris Singer, a land speculator, bought part of Bingham's land at $90 per front foot. In the early 1920s the Reverend Solomon Merrick brought his ailing wife to Florida for her health. He established himself on 160 acres of land near Miami and started a fruit farm which he called Coral Gables. He prospered to the point where he was able to send his son, George, to Columbia University. Like any ambitious American youth, George Merrick aspired to become a writer and seemed well on his way to success when he won a short-story contest sponsored by the *New York Herald*. His budding literary career was interrupted when, because of his father's death, he was called back to Florida. There he became obsessed with the notion of turning the swamps and marshes adjacent to the farm into a paradisaical land. He enlisted the interest of William Randolph Hearst's journalistic star, Arthur Brisbane, who came from a line of utopian dreamers; *his* father, Albert Brisbane, had been a follower of the French utopian Charles Fourier. Arthur Brisbane invested heavily in Florida real estate and shamelessly promoted Merrick's vision in his newspaper columns. Wilson Mizner, one of the most exotic figures of the era and the lover of writer Anita Loos, and his brother, Addison, an architect and an eccentric in his own right, also plunged in, bringing with them a host of their film world friends and numerous connections from the New York literary and financial realm. The "land rush" was on, one of the most spectacular since the gold rush days. In Rascoe's words, "In cities and towns men sold out their small shops, disposed of their homes, quit their jobs; on western prairies and New England hillsides families gave up their holdings; waiters, clerks, salesmen, writers, lawyers, mechanics, medicine men— all fevered by dreams of easy wealth—formed an astounding caval- cade of teams, trains and motorcars, dribbling from all parts of the Union. . . . Sanity fled the scene. . . . " The father of the writer of this work chartered a private railroad car, stocked with whiskey and com- pliant females, to carry prospective investors in *his* prospective paradise to Florida. The speculative mania was not, of course, confined to the Coral Gables area. The Palm Beach land that Paris Singer had paid $90 per foot for in 1917 was sold to Horace Dodge, of the Dodge car fortune, for $888 per front foot in 1924, and a year later he resold it for $3,300 per front foot.

Then the boom burst. Florida banks that had made loans on the inflated real estate values went bust, and an estimated 60 percent of the later arrivals lost their homes.

Among the other notable events of 1927 was Henry Ford's de- cision to abandon the Model T. For almost twenty years it had been the wonder of the world, the cheapest and most reliable method of conveyance ever devised, the mule aside. Times had changed; Amer- icans wanted more luxurious and better-appointed, if less reliable, cars in a variety of colors and finishes. Chevrolet, more responsive to the times, had crept up on Ford and then, finally and unthinkably, ex- ceeded it in sales. With the greatest reluctance Ford agreed to retool for a more up-to-date model, the Model A. From June to December, 1927, the Ford Motor Company was out of production while the great Ford plant changed over to the new model.

While the events herein related transpired, the President of the United States, the great naysayer, preserved, for the most part, his by now famous taciturnity. He counted apples and cars, prowled about the White House looking for elusive hams, took his afternoon naps, "moved about his squirrel cage routine," William Allen White wrote.

On only one issue did he display any hint of passion: the boom in stock market speculation, *his* boom, the Coolidge boom, as it was coming to be called. Some economic historians have dated the beginning of the Coolidge boom from July, 1926, when General Motors replaced United States Steel as the "market leader." Within a month its stock rose from 146 to 189. Thomas Cochran, a Morgan partner, incautiously expressed the opinion to a reporter of the *Wall Street Journal* that General Motors was undervalued. It would, he believed, rise 100 more points before the year was out. When Cochran's views were quoted in the *Journal*, the stock at once began a dizzy ascent, triggering a wild burst of speculation which did not end until September, 1929, when General Motors reached 396½.

Whenever the market faltered, the President spoke some reassuring, patently false words of encouragement and it soared again. He had done his best, the *New York Times* noted exultantly in the fall of 1927, to convert "an aimless, colorless stock market into a lively buoyant affair." His cheerful prognostications "dispelled much of the pessimism that recent reports of reduced industrial and commercial activity had created."

The business of America was business. Under the benign neglect of Republican Presidents there was every reason to believe that business would boom perpetually. To Coolidge's mind the responsiblity of the nation's chief executive was to ensure that no one interfered with, troubled, or harassed the agents of the nation's prosperity, the businessmen. Tycoons came and went in the White House, confident of a genial, if not exactly a warm, welcome. An impudent reporter asked Coolidge, "Why is it that your White House guests are limited to men of business?" The reporter then reeled off a list of visitors such as Harvey Firestone, E. T. Stotesbury, J. P. Morgan, and A. P. Giannini, head of the Bank of America, who were White House regulars. "Why don't you have artists, musicians, actors, poets around the White House as Wilson and Roosevelt did, and sometimes Taft and Harding?"

The President's response: "I knew a poet once when I was at Amherst; class poet, name of Smith." Pause. "Never heard of him since." It was supposed to be a Coolidge type of joke, but it was truer to the President's convictions (and doubtless those of the great majority of his countrymen) than he perhaps intended. In the United States money counted, money and fame, and they were usually synonymous.

As the boom continued, a disillusioned Edmund Wilson wrote: "With a business man's President in the White House who kept telling us . . . that the system was perfectly sound . . . we wondered about the survival of republican American institutions; and we became more and more impressed by the achievement of the Soviet Union."

The wild outbreak of speculation in the stock market, extravagant and eventually destructive as it was, was based on a booming economy in every area but agriculture. Electrical cooking and heating appliances increased 200-fold in American homes in the period from 1919 to 1929, and a third of all households had radios. The number of telephones also increased greatly. There was an explosive growth in the domestic use of electricity, and the expectation was that before long all but the most isolated rural communities would be electrified.

Fifty percent of the power provided to run the industries of America was purchased from private power companies, which held the nation in thrall through their control of the energy that made the country's machines run and the householder's appliances work. Never was the axiom that absolute power corrupts more dramatically illustrated than in the vast fortunes created by utility holding companies, most of which were a law unto themselves. For fifty years or more critics of American capitalism had deplored the fact that giant corporations exploited the natural resources of the country—the coal and copper and iron mines, the timber and the "highways," as Brooks Adams called the railroads—for private gain. These should be the nation's common wealth, the reformers and socialists argued, and they should be used (and preserved) for the nation.

In the words of William Allen White, "the incomes from the financing companies, banks, trust companies, insurance companies, brokers, speculators . . . more than doubled in number while Coolidge was in the White House . . . [and] those who were making the mergers, amalgamations, the combinations of industry were taking an increasing toll from the national income as a reward for their services."

Most impressive perhaps was the fact that the productivity of the average American worker was growing at an amazing pace. In the period from 1919 to 1927 it had increased almost 43 percent, or $3\frac{3}{8}$ percent a year, well in excess of any other nation. Every $5\frac{1}{2}$ persons in the land owned an automobile, almost one to a family. That fact, which seems commonplace now when 90 percent of all adult Americans own a car and 50 percent of all families own two, was nonetheless a revolution of very considerable proportions. It is probably safe to say that there has never been and will never be a primarily economic revolution in a land where virtually everyone owns an automobile; that at least was the conviction of Karl Radek, the Bolshevik theoretician. As the statistics suggest, it was not merely middle- and lower-middle-class Americans who owned cars. The poor owned them as well. They were the nation's most cherished symbol of progress, of prosperity, of "keeping ahead," of the promise of American life. Americans schemed and plotted, saved and, if necessary, stole money to buy a car even if they could not afford to buy the gas to run it. Not only did ownership of even the most dilapidated car bestow a degree of status, but it meant mobility, the ability to escape, so precious to Americans. Those who could not afford to take their cars to mechanics became practical automobile geniuses themselves; junkyards became their temples, sacred places where an essential and illusive part could be tracked down and purchased for a few cents. Junkyards were not so much the burial grounds of decrepit vehicles past their prime as inventories of organs for the living vehicle.

While farm productivity increased rapidly during the twenties—27 percent—farm income generally fell. It was a discontinuity fraught with peril for the nation's economy. There were a number of other danger signs. In addition to the depressed state of the nation's farmers, the international monetary system, if it could be called a system, was in disarray. Four international bank governors met in New York in July, 1927, to try to resolve the world's economic difficulties. Governor Montagu Norman represented the Bank of England, Professor Charles Rist the Bank of France, Dr. Hjalmar Schacht the German Reichsbank, and Benjamin Strong the Federal Reserve Bank of New York. D. R. Crissinger of the Federal Reserve Board also attended. An effort by Rist to check the worldwide expansion of credit failed. On the contrary, the decision was made to have the Federal Reserve Board adopt a more liberal credit policy.

Such warning signals were ignored by speculators in the stock market. Banks made loans not to businesses interested in expansion and modernization but to brokerage houses and speculators which used the money to buy inflated stocks. The Federal Reserve Board made halfhearted efforts to dampen the speculative mania, but President Coolidge, whose Yankee caution should have been emitting danger signals weekly, announced that he was confident that 1927 would be a year of "continued healthy business activity and prosperity," and Andrew Mellon, who was praised by his supporters as "the greatest Secretary of the Treasury since Alexander Hamilton" but was a simpleminded optimist at best, reinforced the President's cheery announcement by declaring, "While the saturation point may have been reached in some cities [in regard to excessive unoccupied office space, etc.] that condition was not reached in others." Again the market surged upward, wafted by hot air. The House of Morgan was already feeling the effects of defaulted loans, foreign and domestic, but J.P. subscribed to the venerable doctrine that investor confidence was paramount and joined in the chorus of reassurances. By the middle of the summer of 1927 the average of the leading industrials had reached 217 from 171 in January. What the market was doing was, partly through manipulation and partly through the naïve optimism of investors, successfully concealing the true state of the American economy.

A number of economists pointed out the dangerously uneven nature of the boom, which was profiting the few at the expense of the many. It was well known that Herbert Hoover was deeply disturbed at the condition of the stock market and the continuing emphasis on cheap money; such views damaged his reputation among the great financial interests and dimmed his presidential prospects. Chief Justice Taft wrote to Associate Justice George Sutherland, expressing his alarm over the effort of the Democrats and "radicals" in Congress to block the reduction of income taxes in the higher brackets. It was, in his view, simply an effort to "get even with the wealthy and prosperous. . . . When the whole business community is against the Democratic party," he added, "it cannot win." The country was fortunate to have a President who was "not disposed to interfere in any way with the even flow of events" and was committed to allowing "the people to work out for themselves the prosperity they deserved." The implications were plain enough. The United States, because of special virtues of its citizens, "deserved" prosperity. Equally important, the financiers and speculators who made great killings in the stock market or through various holding companies or pyramided investments deserved their riches, just as the desperately poor Southern or Midwestern farmer or the underpaid industrial worker received under the American system what he or she "deserved."

Those of less sanguine temperament fretted over the fact that brokers' loans to speculators in the stock market had risen to almost $4,000,000,000 by early January, 1928. But once more the President poured the oil of his unction on the troubled financial waters. Once more a *New York Times* insider reported that the President "believes that the increase represents a natural expansion of business in the securities market and sees nothing unfavorable in it."

For William Allen White the diamonds of South Africa's Kimberley mines and the riches from the "gold veins on the Rand," produced by the "degradation of the blacks and . . . the bestial cruelty of the whites," symbolized the spirit of the times, "a delirium of triumphant money lust . . . well refined of the filth, fumes and dust that caked the blood in men's veins. . . . From every corner of the earth . . . the unfettered industrial system was grinding out the raw materials for wealth, crushing men's bones, parching their blood, following them in a perpetual orgy of chicane and debauchery. . . . The Puritan in the White House . . . gave his pious blessing to the devil's dance. . . . Coolidge was business, big business, little business, the magnified horsetrade which is American commerce." White wrote: "The Coolidge boom was ordained by the American democracy. It came out of the people. It was woven inextricably into the lives of the people. It was their conscious purpose, their highest vision. In the bull market of the Coolidge era, democracy was having its will and going mad in its appointed way." Calvin Coolidge, with his stage Yankee mannerisms, seemed destined by fate to preside over the strange scene. "The people took his very tenuous qualities, his curt manner, his drawling Vermont *patois* by which he was able to make three syllables out of the word cow, his lank body, his parsimony of word and deed, his obvious emotional repression, the glints of his sentimentality which they saw fleetingly at times, and piecing all these together they made a man, a little man to be sure, but one of their kind, a hero in fact . . . a sort of midget Yankee Paul Bunyan. . . . " To a nation far gone in an eat-drink-and-be-merry hedonism, Coolidge was a reassuring symbol of classic American values more honored in the breach than the observance. Again in the words of White's disillusioned Midwestern progressivism, "A world gone gaudy, even morally bawdy in its Babylonian excesses . . . a sin-sick world in the nature of things would erect this pallid shrunken image of its lost ideals and bow down before it in subconscious repentance for its iniquities."

Coolidge had difficulty keeping Cabinet members. Charles Evans Hughes, appointed secretary of state by Harding, resigned and was replaced by the amiable but far less capable Frank Kellogg. Hamilton Fish Armstrong wrote of Kellogg: "He was in every respect a nice and sincere person, but beyond his depth in dealing with great affairs." His general air of uneasy apprehension led to his being called Nervous Nelly by his associates and subordinates.

Coolidge had three successive secretaries of agriculture, Henry

C. Wallace, Howard M. Gore, and William M. Jardine, an accurate measure of his indifference to farm problems. Herbert Hoover, secretary of commerce, and Andrew Mellon, secretary of the treasury, remained in Coolidge's Cabinet throughout his tenure as President. Mellon was by far the most influential Cabinet member, so much so that it was suggested that the administration be known as the reign of Coolidge and Mellon.

There was little love lost between Coolidge and Hoover, whom he had inherited from Harding. Coolidge knew that many members of his Cabinet thought Hoover an abler man than the President. Coolidge was also aware of Hoover's ambition to be his successor, and while he did not interfere with his secretary's efforts to promote voluntary cooperation between government and business, he plainly considered it meddling. Hoover was to a degree identified, at least in Coolidge's mind, with the Progressive wing of the Republican Party, men regarded by the President as little better than socialists or Populists. Coolidge was indignant when the Progressives succeeded in steering the McNary-Haugen bill through Congress. The principal feature of the bill was the so-called ratio price, the price at which an item on a list of enumerated farm products failed to return to the farmers an amount sufficient to cover the costs of production and an appropriate profit. At this point the government, under the terms of the bill, was required to buy the crop in question at the ratio price and, if necessary, to store it until the price rose or sell it on the international market at whatever price it would bring. The bill covered wheat, flour, rice, corn, wool, cattle, sheep, and hogs, and food products derived from cattle, sheep, and hogs.

Hoover favored the McNary-Haugen bill, primarily on the grounds that something had to be done for the relief of farmers and that the bill would at least remove the farm issue from the upcoming presidential election. When Coolidge was urged to support the bill for Hoover's sake, he replied shortly, "That man has offered me unsolicited advice for six years, all of it bad."

On vacation in the Black Hills in the summer of 1927 Coolidge, devastated by the death of his son from a foot infection and apparently irritated with his wife for taking a long, unauthorized walk that day and thereby delaying lunch, announced that he did not choose to run for reelection in 1928. There was the merest hint in his announcement that he would be susceptible to popular demand; he certainly did nothing to encourage the candidacy of the man who seemed to many his logical successor, Hoover. In White's words, "Mr. Hoover received no blessing [when he visited the President at his Black Hills summer retreat] save one of those conspicuous fanfares of silence with which Coolidge sometimes proclaimed his cryptic maledictions."

The publisher Henry Stoddard, devoted follower of Theodore Roosevelt and Calvin Coolidge, was putting the finishing touches on his memoirs in August, 1927—"a perfect summer afternoon, the country calm, serene and properous"—when the startling but thrilling words issued "out of Dakota's Black Hills . . . like a rifle shot—sharp, clear, direct at the target: 'I do not choose to run for President in 1928.' " To an astonished Stoddard it seemed of a piece with the President's noble and self-renouncing character. "No fanfare of trumpets" but the simple decision of a great man to embrace once more "the life of a plain citizen of the republic." Stoddard's only regret was that he himself had not been present at "one of the most historic events in American history. The thrill of playing a part in such a scene would last a lifetime . . . .

"It has been the good fortune of our people," Stoddard wrote, in a final burst of enthusiasm, "that in times of crisis they have had at the head of their government the man suited to the task beyond any other man then known to them. Calvin Coolidge is in that class of Presidents. Not quite a Lincoln but far above the common run." Under Coolidge's benign rule, the "frenzied finance" of the McKinley days had been avoided. American prosperity was sound. "Business men," Stoddard wrote, "have kept their heads and wage-earners have put their savings into banks, into home ownership or securities to an amazing amount. To no one person so much as to Calvin Coolidge is this due; by example not by preaching [a slap at Wilson] he has persuaded a whole nation to his habit."

Posterity has hardly sustained Stoddard's evaluation of Harding's successor, but his sentiments are nonetheless of more than passing interest as a specimen of the American mind in the aftermath of the war. Perhaps two vigorous Presidents in a row or, more accurately, twenty years of political storm and stress are all that a democratic society can tolerate. The qualities that endeared Coolidge to many Americans were clearly the polar opposites of those displayed by his predecessors (Taft and Harding, of course, excluded). Coolidge was, apparently, a decent enough man whose mind was furnished by a benumbing inventory of clichés, which he fortunately doled out with a parsimony characteristic of his Vermont origins. There is no indication of the "vision clear" that Stoddard admired or, indeed, the "fixed purpose," other than to let big business run the country as it pleased without restraint from government.

The most spectacular sporting event of the era was the Dempsey-Tunney rematch on September 23, 1927. The fight was held in Chicago. Some 150,000 spectators attended what was hailed as the "greatest ring spectacle of all time." In the seventh round Jack Dempsey knocked his opponent to the mat, but instead of going to a neutral corner, Dempsey stood over Gene Tunney, waiting for him to rise so that he could renew the assault. The referee delayed the count until he had guided Dempsey to the corner of the ring. The interruption gave the dazed Tunney some fifteen seconds to recover his senses before the fight resumed. Dempsey and his supporters insisted that if the referee had begun his count at the moment Tunney hit the mat, he could not have regained his feet in time to have continued the fight. The revived Tunney won by decision.

Nature's contribution to the year's chronology of major events was one of the worst floods in our history, a terrible storm that broke the Mississippi River levees and inundated the land, resulting in the loss of hundreds of lives and uncountable millions in property. "The 1927 flood," William Alexander Percy wrote, "was a torrent ten feet deep the size of Rhode Island. It was thirty-six hours coming and four months going; it was deep enough to drown a man, swift enough to upset a boat, and lasting enough to cancel a crop year.... The south Delta [of the Mississippi] became seventy-five hundred square miles of mill-race in which a hundred and twenty-five thousand human beings and one hundred thousand animals squirmed and bobbed." Thousands of people fled Greenville, Mississippi, in the path of the flood. People made for such high ground as there was and those trapped in their homes climbed to the second floors or to the ridges of their roofs. Herbert Hoover was put in charge of a relief operation that recalled the days of the German invasion of Belgium. The 1927 flood covered 20,000 square miles, drove 300,000 people from their homes, and resulted in some 250 deaths as well as in a number of memorable "blues."

In September, a tornado raced through St. Louis, killing 69 people, injuring hundreds, and causing an estimated $75,000,000 in damages.

# 9

# The Left

A basic assumption of this work is that some of the most essential aspects of our past cannot be understood without close attention to the radicals and reformers who have played such a critically important role in American history. The 1920s saw that spirit at perhaps its lowest ebb. To William Allen White the twenties were the "slough of reaction." He thought it a mistake even to try to pass social legislation. Its inevitable defeat discredited reform itself. Yet even during the lean years a few hardy spirits tended the flickering fires of radical change. While the once-flourishing Socialist Party dwindled to a handful, the Communists under a series of names (constant only in their devotion to Moscow and the Communist International, or Comintern) grew slowly but surely, confident that the party under whatever title bore the seeds of the future.

The Russian Revolution had presented American Socialists with a dilemma. Should the party continue its traditional meliorism, working for the peaceful and democratic achievement of socialism in the United States by education and persuasion, or should it cast its lot with the Communist International and work for an early and, if Russia was a model, bloody and violent revolution? The left wing of the Socialist Party, unable to capture the party machinery, broke off in the fall of

1919 to form the Communist Labor Party. John Reed was one of the leaders in the defection and in the organization of the new party. The Communist Labor Party affirmed its loyalty to the Third International.

Another group of dissidents, also loyal to the Comintern, went its own way. In 1924 the Comintern ordered the two groups to unify as the Workers' Party. It has been estimated that the membership of the combined organizations was between 25,000 and 30,000, but the harassments of Attorney General A. Mitchell Palmer and, perhaps more important, the disastrous failures of a series of strikes sharply reduced its numbers.

In addition to challenging the Socialists, the Russian Revolution brought about a redefinition of radicalism. Anarchism virtually disappeared. Those former anarchists who could swallow the Bolsheviks became members of the Workers' Party which, increasingly, became an adjunct of the Soviet dictatorship. Those who put their faith in the achievement of a socialist or socialized democracy were viewed by the Communist hard-liners as sentimental liberals unfit for the strenuous duties of revolution. Other old-line radicals backed and filled, leaning alternately toward the Communists and toward "political democracy," an impulse without a party.

American interest in the Soviet Union extended, of course, far beyond the Workers' Party and its fellow travelers. The movement in the United States to recognize Soviet Russia was made up of oddly assorted elements. When Felix Frankfurter presided over a meeting at Faneuil Hall in Boston, the famous cradle of American liberty, to urge recognition of the Soviet Union, Senator Borah, a leading isolationist and enemy of the League of Nations, was the featured speaker.

In 1919 the American Communists had attracted 10,000 friends of the Soviet Union to Madison Square Garden in New York City to celebrate the twelfth anniversary of the beginning of the revolution in 1907. William Weinstone, the principal speaker, declared that "events since the . . . revolution . . . have shown that workers can build socialist industry besides administering the state." Otto Hall, a black party official, called special attention to the fact that some 106 ethnic groups lived in harmony in Russia. "This shows," he said, "that the cause of race division and exploitation of the Negro is not color but the capitalist system."

In 1921 Lenin announced the New Economic Policy, which was, in effect, an effort to rebuild the shattered Soviet economy, and the Comintern declared a policy of a "united front of the left," under which the party would work with all leftist organizations in an effort to broaden its base. The man sent to deliver this message to the American Communists was John Pepper, né Joseph Pogony, a Hungarian journalist who had been commissar for war in Béla Kun's brief Bolshevik government. In the United States he cloaked himself in the authority of the Kremlin. It was the wish of the Comintern, he assured the American comrades, that the party should promote unity with all labor and working class organizations. Jay Lovestone, Ben Gitlow, and the secretary of the party, Charles Rutherberg, all subscribed to Pepper's line. Having recently denounced the Nonpartisan League and the Farmer-Labor Party, they now proposed an alliance. The Farmer-Labor Party itself was a hodgepodge of the right and left, single taxers, Irish nationalists, the remnants of the old Progressives. It was the hope of the Farmer-Labor Party to persuade Bob La Follette to be its candidate for President in 1920. While the party's eventual candidate, Parley P. Christensen, got only a handful of votes, Farmer-Labor candidates did well in Minnesota, Washington, South Dakota, and Nebraska.

The initial phase of the postwar Communists was "Americanization." In Steve Nelson's opinion it was primarily the foreign-born workers, many of whom felt a strong identification with Russia, who kept the party alive during the twenties. In that era the construction of a new hydroelectric plant in Russia was "considered big news." Nelson noted that "the language branch was the standard form of party structure. . . . There might be a Lithuanian branch on the South Side of Chicago, a Jewish branch on the North Side, and a Croatian or Greek branch on the West Side. A citywide Central Committee that coordinated activities carried on its business in English. . . . Of a membership of some seventeen thousand, fewer than two thousand were involved in English-speaking groups, and it was seen as imperative to get beyond the language barrier." The language branches were thus abolished in favor of "neighborhood and shop branches," but the foreign-language newspapers continued to be printed.

Members with foreign-sounding names were ordered to "Americanize" them. Stiepan Mesaroš was a Croatian coal miner in the anthracite coalfields of Pennsylvania. His base was Minersville, where the "Lithuanian Communists" were militant union members with a long tradition of radicalism. He was a member of the Young Workers League, a Communist youth organization, and when the order came to Americanize the party and its auxiliaries, Mesaroš changed his name to Steve

Nelson. Many immigrants, unwilling or unable to make the transition, dropped out. Their ethnic identities were stronger than their identifications with the Communist Party. Classes in American history and politics were organized to enable those who remained "to sink roots outside our subcultures of immigrant radicalism."

In Nelson's efforts to unionize the anthracite coalfields, he often found party dogma an obstacle. Many old-line radicals took the position "Things are gonna get worse, and I hope they do. We'll see what happens to these smart alecks when they're laid off. Wait till they starve. Wait till they're fired and their bellies reach their backbones. Then they'll do something." Capitalism was, after all, scheduled to collapse. Why waste time organizing workers when they would soon be recruited for revolutionary cadres? There were no unions in Soviet Russia.

Since organizations are made up of individuals, it might be well to consider some of those who were active members of the Workers' Party in the 1920s. Benjamin Gitlow was a second-generation American whose father, driven out of Russia, had worked in a shirt factory in New York. Gitlow's father and mother both were ardent Socialists (his mother was known in Socialist circles as Ma or Mother Gitlow). A star athlete in high school, Gitlow joined the Socialist Party at the age of sixteen, went to work shortly thereafter, and soon became a Socialist Party organizer. At the outbreak of the Russian Revolution Gitlow was a Socialist member of the New York legislature. He soon became an ardent Communist, and when he was arrested, Clarence Darrow defended him. Gitlow did nothing to help his case when in court he denounced the United States as a "capitalist dictatorship" and called for its overthrow. For his radical ideas and his boldness in proclaiming them, he was sentenced to five to ten years at hard labor. An instant hero to the left, he was pardoned after three years by Al Smith and thereafter became the leading figure in the American Communist Party in its various permutations. He led the Passaic textile workers' strike and edited the party newspaper for several years. When Whittaker Chambers entered the party, Gitlow was the first old-line Communist he met. A "big, rather soft-looking, very pallid man [he was just out of jail] with a pleasant, brooding somewhat sad face," Chambers wrote. After a trip to Russia in 1927 at Stalin's invitation, Gitlow became the first American member of the Comintern and was subsequently elected to the Presidium, the inner circle of Comintern leadership.

An important recruit to the party was a young woman with a

background as different as could well be imagined from that of Steve Nelson or Benjamin Gitlow. Anna Louise Strong had been born in Friend, Nebraska, in 1885, and had graduated from Oberlin College. She was the first woman to be awarded a doctorate from the University of Chicago. Her dissertation was on "The Psychology of Prayer," a thoroughly modern topic. In 1922 she traveled to Russia with a Quaker famine relief mission. In the struggle of the Russian people she saw a power consistent with her own deep religious convictions. "This power, I saw rather mystically," she wrote, "as a Common Consciousness coming into being to plan the future of mankind." She became editor of *Moscow News*, a journal devoted to enlisting American engineers and specialists to help develop Russian industry and agriculture, and in 1932 she married a Russian agronomist, Joel Shubin. The journalist Eugene Lyons recalled "days when she sat in my office, on returning from a trip outside Moscow, in a condition near spiritual collapse . . . the poor blundering revolution needed her mothering and understanding. . . . Her whole emotional life was invested in this Russia."

William Z. Foster was born in the Philadelphia slums in 1881. His Irish parents were devout Catholics; his mother gave birth to twenty-three children, only five of whom survived to maturity. His neighborhood was known as Skitereen. There the Bulldogs fought rival gangs and joined gleefully in the bitter Philadelphia streetcar strike of 1895.

Foster's formal education stopped when he was ten years old and he took a job as a typefounder. An avid reader, he devoured every book he could get his hands on from Tom Paine's *Age of Reason* to the works of Herbert Spencer. There was "very little, if any, religion left in me," Foster wrote. "All I needed for a completely materialist outlook on life were the works of Marx and Engels. . . . "

Attracted to populism and subsequently to William Jennings Bryan, Foster became a member of Daniel De Leon's Socialist Labor Party, a Wobbly, and, after the World War, the leader of the abortive steelworkers' strike in 1919, which drove many strikers, Foster among them, into the Workers' Party.

Irwin Granich joined the party under the name Mike Gold. He prided himself on his proletarian background. A friend wrote, "He affected dirty shirts, a big, black uncleaned Stetson with the brim of a sombrero; smoked stinking, twisted Italian three-cent cigars, and spat frequently and vigorously on the floor—whether the floor was covered by an expensive carpet in a rich aesthete's studio or on the bare wooden floor of [his] small office."

As editor of the *New Masses* Gold was one of the best-known journalists of the left. In May, 1922, he visited the Pennsylvania coal-fields during a strike. His account, published in the *Liberator*, was one of the most eloquent examples of what we might call "romantic radical labor prose." After attending a meeting of the Central Labor Union in Pittsburgh and then adjourning to a bar decorated with the hammer and sickle, Gold traveled to Brownsville, Pennsylvania, where, he wrote, "for the past thirty years [Henry] Frick and his fellow-Christians had seen that no union got a foothold here, using the blacklist, the blackjack, the assassin's revolver and other New Testament methods of persuasion. . . . There had been no union here since Frick and his comrades in Christ had shot the Knights of Labor out of existence in 1894." Now a "miracle" had happened, a non-Christian one, to be sure. "There had been a wonderful spontaneous movement of the masses; 28,000 miners [in the Brownsville area] . . . , and as many more in the Connellsville area, had joined the union. . . . " Three big steel companies had already been forced to close down, and the capitalist assumption that the power of labor had been broken once for all "was proven false as the complexion of a chorus girl, or the heart of a Wilson liberal; it was as dead as . . . Pharaoh's scented, mouldy mummy." The miners were gathered in the streets of Brownsville, "big, brawny, self-contained men, of all of the races in the world, and they stood about on the sidewalks in the yellow sunlight of the warm spring afternoon, smoking, chewing, and talking in quiet tones of the strike. . . . Something great was happening." Everywhere Gold heard stories of courage and resolution against the intimidating tactics of the mineowners. Such stories were the "reasons why thousands of Fourth of July speeches by corporation-owned congressmen, tons of Americanization literature written by lecherous, booze-soaked press-agents and paid for by murderous bosses, miles of editorials by prostitute newspapermen and oceans of oily lies flowing from the ministerial sewers can never divert Labor from the path on which its feet have been set by history."

John Brophy, president of District No. 2 of the United Mine Workers, a Communist and a bitter opponent of John L. Lewis's reactionary leadership, addressed the Brownsville miners, urging them to avoid violence and promising them the support of the UMW. "Don't let racial differences stand in your way," he admonished them. "Labor is a nation all its own, inside the other nation . . . we keep the works going; we've got the real power."

The experience with the striking miners had a religious quality for Gold. On the way back to Pittsburgh one of the young women volunteer organizers, Peggy Delbarre, who was driving, "laughed and sang. The dark masses of trees fled past like defeated ghosts. We caught the glimpse of immense bouquets of peach and cherry blossoms in the gloom. It was great to be moving, to be alive. We were going somewhere. This miners' strike would be won, and other strikes for greater ends would be won. Some day the miners would sit in the congress of workers that ruled America. Some day the men who were near to the sources of life, the men who were brave enough to make steel and mine coal, would be building a new civilization in America, a new art and culture, a new society. It would be a brave culture, a heroic culture for strong men and women, a culture near to the sources of life. It would move along in beauty under the stars, it would laugh and sing."

If Mike Gold was the prototype of the romantic intellectual drawn to the party, Whittaker Chambers was typical of the young men who turned to the party because of their own emotional needs as well as dismay over the inequities of capitalism. Chambers's youth had been a tale of psychological horrors. "Mine was a dry birth," he wrote in *Witness*. He weighed twelve pounds and "had to be taken with instruments." After the "frightful delivery" his mother almost died of a torn artery. Chambers's father was a moody and brutal man; his brother, an alcoholic who committed suicide. His brother's death drove Chambers himself to the verge of suicide. A year later he wrote in the bleak graveyard where his brother was buried:

> My brother lies in the cold earth,
> A cold rain is overhead.
> My brother lies in the cold earth,
> A sheet of ice is over his head.
>
> The cold earth holds him round;
> A sheet of ice is over his face.
> My brother has no more
> The cold rain to face.

In his book Chambers described his conversion to Communism. He had asked himself if he could go on living in a world that seemed devoid of decency and humanity. If one decided to live in such a world, communism seemed the only haven. "It was not an attractive answer," Chambers wrote, "just as the Communist Party was not an attractive party. Neither was the problem which had called it forth, and which it proposed to solve, attractive. But it had one ultimate appeal. In place of desperation, it set the word: hope." To Chambers it was "a choice against death and for life." He wished "only the privilege of serving humbly and selflessly that force which from death could evoke life, that might save, as I then supposed, what was savable in a society that had lost the will to save itself."

He was willing to accept communism on its own terms, "to follow the logic of its course wherever it might lead me, and to suffer the penalties without which nothing in life can be achieved. For it offered me what nothing else in the dying world had the power to offer at the same intensity—faith and a vision, something for which to live and something for which to die." It stirred in him "those things which have always stirred what is best in men—courage, poverty, self-sacrifice, discipline, intelligence, my life, and, at need, my death."

It was later important to Chambers that he had joined the Communist Party (or Workers') in 1925, some five years ahead of the rest of the intellectual pack. He thus had signed on before the crisis of capitalism had become a fact; he had joined at the moment when capitalism seemed triumphant and only the more discerning could perceive the decay beneath the glittering surface. He had joined when the issue was a simple moral one—America was a sick and dying society—when there was in practical fact no Communist Party. It had "just come up from the underground" and called itself the Workers' Party.

Harold "Hal" Ware was the son of Ella Reeve, the famous radical known as Mother Bloor. Ware had been an ally of John Reed's in forming the Communist Labor Party and had done some gentlemanly farming as a member of a single tax colony at Arden, Delaware. A scholar and an intellectual, he was a Debs-like figure, mild of manner but with a charisma that won the devotion of many of those who were associated with him throughout a lifetime of party activity. Whittaker Chambers described him as constantly attired in a carefully-pressed brown suit with a fedora hat at a jaunty angle. He seemed to Chambers a combination of a "progressive county agent or a professor at an agricultural college" and a racetrack addict about to leave for the track at Pimlico.

After the Arden experience Ware entered a program in agriculture at Pennsylvania State College and then set himself up as a scientific dairy farmer in Westchester County, New York. When Lenin chided the American Communists for not paying sufficient attention to the needs of farmers, Ware became a migratory worker, making himself an expert on farm issues in various parts of the country. The party made him national agrarian organizer. He bought a Ford van, recruited young Marxist "teachers," and dispatched them through various farm states. The traveling school would spend three or four weeks in each area, training local leaders in the tactics of political action. Places where the party already had connections were generally chosen. But the party failed to provide funds, and the disheartened Ware, concerned at reports of famine in Russia, decided to try his notions of scientific farming there. From the American Federated Russian Famine Relief Committee he secured a grant of $75,000, with which he bought machine tools and twenty tractors for export to the Soviet Union. Having recruited nine tractor drivers, Ware arrived in Russia with his crew and went to work to improve the production of a 15,000-acre state farm at Perm Oblast. One of Harold Ware's colleagues in the Russia tractor mission was Otto Anstrom, a war veteran and farmer from North Dakota. Another upper-class activist was Jerry Ingersoll, who was a graduate of Amherst College and whose father was president of the borough of the Bronx. Ware also recruited Lem Harris. Tall and wiry, balding with rimless glasses, Harris bore a striking resemblance to Ware. Both men looked more like college professors than radical agitators. Harris had graduated from Harvard and, attracted by rural life, had worked on a Quaker dairy farm in Bucks County, Pennsylvania. Roger Baldwin, conscientious objector and fellow Harvard graduate, had introduced him to Ware. After several years at Perm Oblast, Ware and his group transferred their activities to the Caucasus, where they set up a model mechanized farm. Through the decade of the twenties Ware played an important role in the modernization of Soviet agriculture. Two years in Russia made Lem Harris a confirmed Communist. His wealthy father disowned him, but Harris persevered and, despite the handicap of his Harvard antecedents, became a highly effective money raiser (from prosperous liberals) and farm organizer.

The basic goal of the American Communist Party, on instruction from Moscow, was the organization of industrial workers into Communist-dominated unions. The greatest allocation of party funds and human resources went into this largely abortive effort. Part of the problem was that the aim of the party was not so much to win higher wages and better working conditions as to educate the workers to the true nature of capitalism and thereby win their allegiance to the Communist Party. For the latter purpose, failure to improve workers' lives might serve better than victory. The important thing was that Communist-led strikes be bitter, bloody, and highly publicized.

Throughout the twenties the Communists inspired a series of strikes that were, for the most part, unsuccessful: the Passaic, New Jersey, textile workers' strike in 1925 and 1926; the New York furriers' strike of 1926; the Gastonia, North Carolina, and New Bedford, Massachusetts, textile strikes.

Benjamin Gitlow, who was intimately involved in the Passaic strike, gave a vivid account of Communist tactics. The decision to call a strike was made when the party leaders calculated that they had signed up 10 percent of the workers in the Communist-dominated union. When word of a prospective wage cut leaked out in the Passaic mills, the Communists called a meeting to urge workers to join the party. Shills were posted around the hall where the meeting was held with instructions to come forward with their dollar bills. "The Party committee," Gitlow wrote, " . . . had before it floor plans of the large textile mills to be struck, plans which indicated where the switches were which controlled the power, and all other vital information. Like commando officers directing a raid, the Party planned each step, designating who was to shut off the power, how the riotous marches through the mills were to be conducted, who was to lead them. . . . " Once the strike had begun, they "staged militant and picturesque picket demonstrations. Helmets, overseas hats and uniforms of World War I were bought up in large quantities. The strikers and the captains of the picket line who were communists were dressed up in these. They staged huge picket demonstrations behind large American flags led by men who masqueraded as veterans." The party wanted, above all else, newspaper headlines, Gitlow wrote, so that "what was happening in Passaic" would "reach Moscow . . . in order to enhance the prestige of the American communist leadership. . . . Disorder, on order, broke out. The picture tabloids and other newspapers were duly informed in advance to be on hand. . . . " According to Gitlow, the party produced an attractive female reporter "who obliged the male reporters in more ways than one." An organization to raise money from sympathetic liberals to support the strikers was created. Even schoolchildren were organized into a Junior Young Communist League and persuaded to go out on a sympathy strike. When scabs were brought in to break the strike, the party leaders sent to Pittsburgh for a Russian expert on irritant gas bombs; he was asked to come to Passaic and drive the scabs out of the plants with tear gas and nauseating gas. The tactics were successful.

The most violent struggle for the control of unions took place in the needleworkers' trade, a war which Gitlow called "the bloodiest and costliest internal war in labor history." Certainly no holds were barred on the Communist side. Virtually every legal and illegal weapon was used in an effort to take over the unions in the dress and clothing industries. The Communist excuse for such tactics was that the union leaders had grown complacent and were indifferent to the needs of the workers. They pointed for confirmation to the drastic decline in union membership. They saw their role as that of injecting a new militancy in the entire American labor movement, starting with the needle trades, which had a long tradition of radical union activity.

The most notable Communist success came in the International Fur Workers' Union, whose chairman, Ben Gold, was a Communist. Gitlow, not, to be sure, the most reliable witness, estimated that the party spent more than $3,000,000 in the furriers' strike, the greater part of which went to pay lawyers' fees and to "buy" a climate of opinion favorable to the strikers.

John L. Lewis termed the opposition to him in the United Mine Workers' union "the first step in the realization of a thoroughly organized program of the agencies and forces behind the Communist International at Moscow for the conquest of the American continent." At the AFL convention in 1926 Lewis pointed to William Foster, sitting in the balcony, and denounced him as "the Archprince of communism in the United States."

When George Voyez, a "rank-and-file miner" with a record of Communist associations, ran against Lewis in 1924, he received 66,000 votes to 136,000 for Lewis. Certainly many of Voyez's votes were more anti-Lewis than pro-Communist, but they also suggested a large and militant "left wing" in the union that refused to be frightened by the Communist specter.

The parent organization of the party, under whose auspices the efforts to take over established unions proceeded, was the rather ironically titled Trade Union Educational League, in which Voyez figured prominently. It produced a vast amount of disunity, as union leaders fought desperately to repel the takeover efforts of the Communists.

The most extensive, prolonged, and bloody strike led by the Communists occurred in the cotton mills of North Carolina. In March and April, 1929, strikes broke out in Greenville, South Carolina, Marion and Gastonia, North Carolina, and Elizabethtown, Tennessee. Most were spontaneous walkouts. At Gastonia, Fred Beal and George Pershing, both seasoned Communist union organizers, joined with the National Textile Workers' Union, a Communist organization, to direct the strike. There were murderous incidents from the first. A woman striker was killed on her way to a meeting when men in an automobile fired into her truck. In Marion sheriff's deputies fired on a group of strikers who were fleeing from tear gas. Twenty-one men and women were hit in their backs and six died of their wounds.

When the Gastonia police chief, O. F. Aderholt, was killed trying to break up a strike meeting, Fred Beal and six other strike leaders were arrested and charged with "conspiracy to murder," although no evidence was produced linking them in any way with Aderholt's death. There were indications that he had been inadvertently shot by one of his own officers, but the strikers were nonetheless convicted and given sentences of from five to twenty years in prison.

Another crippling factor was that the workers in some 100 cotton mills in the Gastonia area refused to give aid or comfort to the Gastonia strikers, taking the line that they had been led astray by Yankee Communists. In the words of W. J. Cash, Gastonia served "to fix solidly in the minds of the great mass of Southerners the equation: labor unions + strikers = Communists + atheism + social equality with the Negro—and so served to join to the formidable list of Southern sentiments already drawn up against the strikers the great central one of racial feeling and purpose. . . . "

Although the Gastonia strike was broken, it was an ideal strike from the Communist point of view. The attendant violence and the wide publicity given to it further helped radicalize Americans concerned with the issues of social justice. Its impact may be gauged by the progeny of proletarian novels it spawned. Mary Heaton Vorse wrote *Strike* and Grace Lumpkin *To Make My Bread*. Also based on the strike were *The Gathering Storm* by Myra Page and *Call Home the Heart* by Fielding Burke.

Sherwood Anderson, living in Danville, Virginia, became involved in the textile workers' strike in that town. The work of the strike leaders seemed to Anderson heartbreakingly difficult, "always going about to little halls, seeing people such as I saw at Danville, people struggling for some right to live. You feel them almost inevitably doomed to defeat just now. It gets you.

"There they are. They crowd into the little halls. They cheer you when you come in. . . . There is hope, love, expectation in the eyes of the people. . . . They so believe in you, or in someone like you, some talker, some writer, some leader, some poet who is to come and make what they want understood to their boss, to all bosses.

"Well, you do nothing. You say a few words. You go away. You go back to your hotel. . . . It is a pretty heart-breaking matter—this situation of most industrial workers in America." The American Communists devoted a considerable part of their energies to that segment of society with the strongest tradition of radicalism, the farmers. The farm and farmers fitted awkwardly into party doctrine despite Lenin's strong interest in the often desperate situation of the American farmer. Part of the trouble lay in deciding whether the American farmer was a "capitalist" or a "worker." If the farmer was a worker, what were his hired hands or his tenants? Did a farmer who was a tenant cease, in some way, to be a farmer? Was he then a worker? From the days of Shays's rebellion in post-Revolutionary War Massachusetts down to the Farmers' Alliances and, finally, the Populist Party, farmers had been inveighing against bankers, capitalists, and Wall Street. The Progressive Party had its roots in Midwestern farm discontent. The Socialist Party had recruited tens of thousands of farm members in Oklahoma, Nebraska, and the Dakotas, and the Nonpartisan League was a rallying point for rural radicalism. Yet in Communist doctrine the farmers had one fatal flaw: They were entirely devoid of the proper "class consciousness"; that is to say, they were stubbornly unwilling to think of themselves as members of the lower class or working class or proletariat.

Not surprisingly, the farm states most responsive to the Communists were those with a long tradition of Populist-Progressive politics. In the words of Lowell Dyson, historian of the Communist Party's efforts to recruit American farmers, "In Montana and the Dakotas a thoughtful and articulate minority of farmers had moved successively from the prewar Socialist party, to the Nonpartisan League, and into the Communist Party in the early 1920s." There were party units in Minot, Fargo, Bismarck, Williston, and four other North Dakota towns. Richard F. Pettigrew, former South Dakota Senator, was a friend and supporter. Sheridan County, Montana, was that state's radical stronghold. It was there that Charles E. Taylor edited the "Red" *Producers News*. In the years between 1920 and 1924 Communists won local offices in a series of elections, and the *Daily Worker* was widely read. Taylor, a huge man with an obsession about the right to fly the red flag of revolution (hence his nickname Red Flag Charlie), was elected to the Montana State Senate in 1922.

The leader of the Nonpartisan League in South Dakota was grizzled ex-Senator Pettigrew. Two of Pettigrew's coadjutors were Tom Ayres, a rancher and friend of William Jennings Bryan, formerly a professor of speech who had been sacked for pacifism during the war, and the handsome Alice Lorraine Daly. Both were active Farmer-Laborites. Vieno Severi Alanne, who had been Lenin's roommate at one time, was a candidate for governor of Wisconsin in 1924. He had participated in the Communist takeover of the Farmer-Labor Convention in Chicago.

Another important Communist farm leader was Alfred Knutson. Born in Norway in 1880, Knutson had come to the United States at the age of nineteen. Alternating work and study, he was graduated from the University of South Dakota at the age of thirty-two and took up the occupation of a carpenter in Williams County, North Dakota. In Dyson's words, "The western Dakotas were a radical hotbed, and [Knutson] soon abandoned his Lutheran faith and embraced Marxism." From the Socialist Party he moved on to Townley's Nonpartisan League and then to the Communist Party, where he found an ally in Charles Taylor. Knutson started the United Farmers Educational League and began publishing, under its name, a monthly paper called the *United Farmer*. The league was yet another front, modeled on the Trade Union Educational League. The head of the Farmers National Committee for Action, also a party front, was Lem Harris, Harold Ware's coadjutor in the tractors for Russia project.

When Lenin died in January, 1924, of a cerebral hemorrhage, a wave of mourning bordering on hysteria swept the Soviet state. His death left the question of succession in the air. Trotsky, ill, was reported to have left Moscow, and Karl Radek, one of Lenin's closest associates, was said to be in disfavor with the Supreme Soviet. A fierce struggle for succession followed. Trotsky represented that faction of the party in Russia that believed that it was essential to work for immediate world revolution because the Russian Revolution itself could not be sustained in a sea of hostile capitalisms. The "Old Bolsheviks," led by Joseph Stalin, Nikolai Bukharin, Grigori Zinoviev, and Leo Kamenev, took the line that communism must be consolidated in Russia, that capitalism was not yet ready to perish from its own internal inconsistencies, and that, in consequence, some patience was required. At the Comintern meeting these and other issues, domestic and international, were hotly debated. The American party leaders were instructed to support Bob La Follette in American presidential elections if La Follette would agree to place the direction of his campaign in the hands of the Communist-directed Farmer-Labor Party.

The chairman of the Farmer-Labor Convention was Charles Parker, and Alice Lorraine Daly was chosen as secretary, but William Foster dominated the sessions. When La Follette's name was put in nomination, Ben Gitlow denounced La Follette. Foster then rose, as instructed, to propose that the convention support La Follette if he agreed to place his campaign in the hands of the Farmer-Labor Party. At this point W. J. Taylor of Nebraska, an old war-horse of the Non-partisan League, gave vent to his feelings. "If I were La Follette, I wouldn't want your endorsement," he declared. " . . . This is no farm-labor convention. It is a meeting of Communists, and when you call it anything else you disguise its real character. Foster and Rutherberg are the real bosses here, and you know it." Well aware of the situation, La Follette rejected the Farmer-Labor endorsement.

The Communists appeared on the ballot in a dozen or so states in 1924 under the name of the Workers' Party and garnered some 33,000 votes, but the party remained in a state of suspended animation while the Trotsky-Stalin battle for Lenin's succession continued in Russia. Zinoviev, as one of the party's leading theoreticians, led the fight for "socialism in one state"—Russia—while Trotsky lost ground, being removed as war commissar in January, 1925. Stalin, meanwhile, consolidated his own political power. Bukharin increasingly challenged Zinoviev's prominence, arguing that the work of building revolutionary cadres in other countries was bound to be a long, slow process. Even in Russia much remained to be done, especially among the peasants.

In the United States Charles Rutherberg and Jay Lovestone were quick to sense the way the party winds were blowing. They found an ally in Alfred Knutson, who had toured through Russian farming areas in the spring of 1925 and had returned to America thoroughly committed to Bukharin's policies. At the Fourth Convention of the Workers' Party in the United States in 1925, a mysterious messenger appeared with word from the Comintern which ordered the party to put Lovestone and Rutherberg at its head. With Foster thus summarily deposed, Lovestone headed the party for the next three and a half years.

Undoubtedly the most successful Marxist farm organization was the Cooperative Central Exchange set up by Finnish farmers. The process of the radicalization of the Finns is simply described. Most of the Finnish immigrants found work initially in the mines. When they attempted to form unions to protest the egregious conditions under which they worked, they were not only fired but blacklisted so they could not get jobs in any mines in the region. Many turned of necessity to farming, with a profound hostility to the economic system that had victimized them. Starting out as the brainchild of a physician named J. P. Warbasse, the exchange fell increasingly under the control of its most radical members, finally declaring itself in 1926 to be "primarily a working class movement against the present system based on profit." Claiming 25,000 members and grossing more than $6,000,000 in 1929, the Cooperative Central Exchange placed on its packaged goods the hammer and sickle and underwrote a camp for Young Communist League members in Superior, Wisconsin, where they were addressed by, among other prominent Communists, Mother Bloor, back from Moscow.

Since virtually all the important officers of the Cooperative Central Exchange were Communists, the exchange was an appealing target for the party, which anticipated some of the exchange profits flowing into its coffers. But when William Foster and the party tried to move in, they encountered strong resistance. The party thereupon began its own cooperative, the Cooperative Unity Alliance, and there ensued a struggle between the two organizations that ended in the defeat of the Cooperative Unity Alliance and the movement of the Cooperative Central Exchange toward political neutrality. In 1931 it removed the hammer and sickle from its products and replaced it with the conventional twin pines of an orthodox cooperative.

While the more moderate farm leaders tried to unite the constantly shifting coalitions of farm groups and steer them on a course only slightly to the left of center, things repeatedly got out of hand when farmers actually met in the conventions and conferences that were constantly being called. On those occasions any fiery orator could call up ancient passions. The mention of Wall Street would evoke howls of anger and derision; the promise to nationalize the railroads and mines, a storm of cheers. An air of fantasy hung over all such deliberations. Conventions were less political meetings than therapeutic sessions, dominated by the most radical elements. The Communists talked a language the farmers loved to hear; it was definitely their kind of rhetoric. For the sober morning-after consequences they had little regard. The result was that everyone was deluded. Those Communists like John Pepper who were committed to the Leninist view that farmers were the most radical segment of American society and should be in the forefront of the revolution suffered crushing disillusionment at the inability of farmers to hold fast to any form of enduring political organization. The farmers, for their part, were repeatedly disenchanted by what appeared to them the devious (or, more accurately, party-serving) and self-serving maneuvers of their Communist allies. What it all demonstrated was that radical as the farmers undoubtedly were, they were distinguished by a kind of individualistic anarchism incapable of coping with the real political world. The Communist Party, thoroughly committed to what we might call delusional politics, met its match in the farmers of the Dakotas, Nebraska, Iowa, Wisconsin, Minnesota, Montana, and Washington.

The most notable accomplishment of the Communist Party was undoubtedly its work with black Americans. The Sixth Comintern Congress, which met in Moscow in 1928, laid down the "party line" on blacks for the American Communist Party to follow. A thirty-two-member Negro Commission, which contained seven Americans, decided that American blacks must secede from the United States and establish "a Negro republic in the Black Belt" of the South. The idea was attributed to Otto Kuusinen, a member of Stalin's "think tank." It showed the influence of Marcus Garvey and other "black nationalists" who had argued for a separate black state in the United States, but it had astonishingly little relation to the realities of American life or the desires of the vast majority of the nation's blacks, whose ambitions went no further than to be treated in every respect as citizens of the United States.

In line with its campaign to attract blacks to the party, the Communists made a well-publicized drive to eject all members who had "petty bourgeois" racist attitudes. August Yokinen, a Finnish immigrant who was alleged to have made racial slurs to blacks at a dance sponsored by the party, was called before a meeting of 1,500 party members at which a "jury" of 14 "workers" voted to expel him. The "trial" reaped a harvest of favorable comment from black newspapers and served the intended purpose of dramatizing the party's stand on the race issue. It was the opinion of Earl Browder that Yokinen's trial "can be taken as marking the sharp turn which the Party began toward the struggle in specific concrete issues."

The consequences of the Comintern policy were also evident at the party's Sixth National Convention in March, 1929, when five black Communists, including Cyril Briggs, who was made head of the Negro Department, were elected to the party's Central Committee. At Briggs's suggestion the party designated May 10 to 17, 1929, as National Negro Week, a period to be spent in lectures and discussions of black problems and active agitation against Jim Crow laws.

In fact, the party had paid special attention to the recruitment of blacks since the early twenties. Many of the prominent figures in the Harlem Renaissance were either Communists or closely identified with the party. Claude McKay had warned white radicals that, "the problem of the darker races is a rigid test of Radicalism. To some radicals it might seem more terrible to face than the barricades." What was needed was a "revolutionary attitude towards Negroes different from the sympathetic interest of bourgeois philanthropists and capitalist politicians."

The principal Communist-front organization for the recruitment of blacks was the American Negro Labor Congress, which met in Chicago in the fall of 1925 with a few hundred black delegates and was hailed as "an unprecedented mass organization." While the "black masses" showed little interest in communism, the party recruited a number of able black intellectuals. Four of the first five prominent black Communists in Harlem were West Indians. Cyril Briggs had been born on the island of Nevis, moved to New York as a young man, and been editor of the black *Amsterdam News*, one of the oldest and most influential black newspapers. His opposition to America's entry into the war had resulted in his being fired, and in 1918 he had founded the *Crusader*, a magazine "dedicated . . . to a renaissance of Negro power and culture throughout the world." A year later he organized the African Blood Brotherhood for African Liberation and Redemption.

Briggs, a tall, handsome man, light in complexion, believed that blacks could never achieve equality in white America. He was an ardent black nationalist and a cautious supporter of Marcus Garvey. "The ultimate, equitable, peaceful solution of this country's race problem is by all signs . . . a chimera and an idle dream. . . . Thus it is that Glory and Necessity both call us to the mother land to work out a proud and glorious future for the African race," he wrote. A year or so later Briggs began to urge blacks to form "alliances with the liberal and radical forces of the country and of the world." Impressed by the antiracist policies of the Soviet Union, he took the line that blacks might indeed achieve equality with whites the world over when capitalism had been overthrown. "Just as the Negro in the United States can never hope to win equal rights with his white neighbors until Africa is liberated and a strong Negro state (or states) created on that continent," he wrote, "so too we can never liberate Africa until the American Section of the Negro race is made strong enough to play the part for a free Africa that the Irish in America now play for a free Ireland. Every Negro in the United States should use his vote, and use it fearlessly and intelligently, to strengthen the radical movement and thus create a deeper schism within the white race in America. . . . "

Briggs's closest friend and associate was another West Indian, Richard B. Moore. Born in Barbados, Moore was a fiery public speaker (whereas Briggs had a speech impediment). Like Briggs, Moore was very light in color. He was also something of a bibliophile and a student of black history. The editor of Garvey's *Negro World*, another West Indian named W. A. Domingo, was a friend of Briggs and Moore. When Garvey forced Domingo to resign as editor of the *Negro World* because of the latter's "Socialist" ideas, Domingo joined Moore and Briggs in signing up with the Communist Party.

James Ford had been an outstanding athlete at Fisk University. In the words of the *Amsterdam News*, "Nobody at Fisk University in the years before the World War ever dreamed that 'Rabbit Ford,' the fleet-footed athlete, would become other than what Fisk expected of her sons—a loyal respectable citizen, a school teacher, a doctor, or a lawyer, or perhaps a 'race leader.' A model student, ambitious, hardworking, steady, a baseball and football star, a leader in the YMCA and other student activities, James W. Ford was the kind of Fisk man that the faculty was proud of, the kind for lower classmen to emulate. He had that Fisk spirit."

Ford had been in the Signal Corps during the World War, and the segregated treatment of black soldiers had deeply offended him. When he returned to the United States, he found that even though he was an outstanding graduate of one of the best black colleges in the United States and an army veteran, the only job he could find was that of a worker in the Chicago post office. His rise in the party was rapid. By 1930 he was head of the Negro Department of the Trade Union Unity League and two years later the party's vice-presidential candidate.

A party member and business manager of the *Harlem Liberator*, Merrill Work had grown up in Nashville, Tennessee, where his father was a professor of music at Fisk University and famous as the conductor of the Fisk Jubilee Singers, who had been raising money for the university since Reconstruction days. Work, like Ford, had been an outstanding athlete and student at Fisk and gone on to become a social worker and director of a settlement house for the Brooklyn Urban League. Increasingly alienated by what he perceived as racist attitudes even among his fellow white social workers, Work, who was married to a white woman, gravitated toward the Communist Party.

William Patterson, a young black lawyer who was a close friend of Paul Robeson's, was recruited for the party by Richard Moore. Patterson took an active part in the movement to save the lives of Sacco and Vanzetti; soon afterward he was sent to Russia for training as a prospective party leader. During his stay in Moscow he married a Russian woman.

Another important black Communist leader was Abner Berry. Berry came from a theatrical family; his brothers were popular tap dancers. Berry had worked among black sharecroppers in Texas and Missouri, where his life had often been in danger. His tact and good humor won him a special role as peacemaker and conciliator in party infighting. One of his tasks was to encourage the mixing of whites and blacks in Harlem meetings. He found it an uphill job. The fact was that blacks "wanted to be together. They didn't mind on occasion being integrated, but in general they wanted to be involved in something they could call their own, something they organized and led . . . [and] they had some things they wanted to discuss by themselves, for themselves." Beyond that, the presence of whites in even quasi-social events made ordinary blacks uncomfortable.

Harry Haywood was a black Communist from the Middle West who quickly achieved a position of importance in the party. On the eve of the Sixth World Congress, Haywood, suppressing his misgivings, went along with a resolution which declared that American blacks were in fact an oppressed nation and as such should have the right to form their own country in that portion of the South—the Black Belt, so called—where they outnumbered whites. American blacks on the Comintern's Negro Commission, among them Otto Hall from Chicago, James Ford, and Harold Williams, a West Indian seaman, all were skeptical about the "Black Nation" approach. On the other hand, the Sixth Congress of the Comintern spoke out unequivocally on the status of American blacks. The party in the United States must "consider the struggle on behalf of the Negro masses . . . as one of its major tasks." It was charged with "training a cadre of Negro comrades as leaders. . . . White comrades must be especially trained for work among Negroes," and "the Negro problem must be part and parcel of all and every campaign conducted by the Party." White party members who showed signs of "white chauvinism" must be called to account in an effort "to stamp out all forms of antagonism, or even indifference among our white comrades toward the Negro work."

Louise Thompson's decision to join the Communist Party was, in part at least, the result of her "distaste [for] and hatred of white philanthropy. . . . When I was being interviewed for jobs by white organizations devoted to black advancement, people took all kinds of liberties with me, inquiring about the most personal details of my behavior, what I ate, when I went to the bathroom."

In addition to Louise Thompson, the party enlisted a number of able black women. Audley Moore had been born in Louisiana, and after a period as an enthusiastic Garveyite in New Orleans she had moved to New York and been drawn to the Communist Party. She was a large light-skinned woman with a natural eloquence that soon made her one of the most prominent leaders in Harlem. Bonita Williams was a West Indian whose family's means had enabled her to get a college education. Her special assignment was to organize black housewives for protests against price gouging by Harlem merchants, the great majority of whom were white. Maude White, an organizer for the Communist Party's Needle Trades Industrial Union, was sent to Russia by the party to receive special training.

Mark Naison points out that the "most significant Party presence came in the schools [of Harlem] . . . where white Communist schoolteachers maintained close working relationships with black teachers, parents and community leaders." Alice Citron, a brilliant Jew, came from a background of union activism. She headed the party's teacher branches in Harlem and made it her special mission in life to encourage and demonstrate the talents of her black students. "She wrote plays for her classes dramatizing themes from black history, took them on field trips and invited them to her home, compiled bibliographies on black history for other teachers in the system, and joined black teachers in agitating for the celebration of Negro History Week in the city school system," Naison wrote. A Harlem minister told Naison that the Communist teachers who had been kicked out of the school system in the post-World War I era "were much more dedicated to teaching black children the way out of the crucible of American life than the teachers we have now. When they left Harlem became a worse place. . . . You didn't have these reading problems like you have today. These people were dedicated to their craft" and, above all, it may be added, to their students.

Meanwhile, in Russia Stalin was winning the protracted contest with Trotsky. Trotsky, Kamenev, and Zinoviev had given ground to Stalin-Bukharin, and at the Fifteenth Congress of the Communist Party in 1927 Stalin took firm control. Trotsky and eighty-six other members of the original Bolshevik faction under Lenin were expelled from the party and banished from Russia.

Stalin reversed the policies associated with his ally Bukharin, denouncing them as reactionary and defeatist. The party worldwide must rid its ranks of bourgeois elements, disavow cooperation with other liberal and radical movements, and prepare the cadres of the revolution. Capitalism, far from being in the period of stabilization that Bukharin had described, was on the verge of collapse as an international economic system. Stalin also announced the first Five-Year Plan to stimulate industrial growth and extend the collective farm system, a move that was to be stubbornly resisted by millions of peasants.

When the Sixth World Congress of the Communist International (Comintern) met in Moscow from the middle of July to September, the new line was laid down explicitly for the delegates by Stalin. A careful reading of Marxist-Leninist doctrine made it clear, Stalin announced, that capitalism had entered its third (and final) period. This revelation was hailed with enthusiasm by the delegates, delighted to know that the triumph of international communism, always considered inevitable by the faithful, was now actually in sight, an event that could be confidently anticipated within a few years.

Stalin also made clear his determination to subordinate *all* foreign branches of the party to his will. When Jay Lovestone and Benjamin Gitlow insisted that special conditions in the United States made it essential that the American branch of the party be independent of the dictates of Moscow, a series of speakers denounced the Americans as "Right deviators," "gross intriguers," and "slanderers of the Russian Communist Party." The American delegation was then instructed to sign Stalin's diatribe. When Lovestone and Gitlow refused, Stalin himself appeared to castigate the rebels. "Now the question arises: do the members of the American delegation, as communists, as Leninists, consider themselves entitled not to submit to the decision of the Executive Committee of the Comintern on the American question?"

The Comintern then adopted "The Address to the American Party." The only dissenting vote was that of Gitlow.

Lovestone and Gitlow returned to the United States determined to fight against Stalin's domination of the American party. They appeared firmly in control when the delegates gathered in Chicago in 1929 for the party's annual convention, but a telegram from Stalin burst upon the convention like a bombshell. Lovestone and Gitlow were deposed and ordered to report to Moscow. They returned to the United States disgraced and were expelled for "rightist" heresies. They took a number of party members with them and formed what they called, with more wishful thinking than accuracy, the Communist Party (Majority Group). William Foster, Robert Minor, and Will Weinstone were designated as the party's interim directors, and some months later Earl Browder was chosen by Stalin as general secretary of the party. Lovestone was described by Charles Taylor, a former supporter, as "spokesman for the pseudo-intellectuals, dentists, chiropractors, naturopaths, social workers, liberal cloak and suit merchants and small business men."

It was Steve Nelson's estimate that although not more than 1,000 members left the party with Lovestone, "a fair number of others threw up their hands in despair and took a walk. . . . But most members, either because they were in disagreement with Lovestone or found bucking the Comintern's decision too difficult, remained in the Party," Nelson wrote. His lifelong friend and countryman Joe Jursak cast his lot with Lovestone, as did Jursak's wife. Jursak was a devoted disciple of Bukharin, "an idol of young Communists everywhere because he wrote popular understandable pieces like the *ABC of Communism*."

In the United States fighting between the various party factions was carried to the streets. "The streets are ours" was one of the party slogans. Indeed, it may have been that there were more cracked heads and bruised bodies inflicted by the Trotskyites and Stalinists on each other, at least in such cities as New York and Chicago, than by the police on either. Benjamin Gitlow, in his history of communism in the United States, recounts a typical episode of Communists against Communists. When a Trotskyite street orator set up his portable platform in the Union Square area of New York to address passersby, Communist Party members attacked him. Gitlow's account: "The communists surrounded the platform of the so-called intruders as the communist gangsters pulled out their pocket-knives, cudgels and iron pipes." They began heckling the speaker and trying to overturn his platform, "while women communists, close to the platform, screamed and spat upon the speaker." Finally, with the Trotskyite routed, "the literature of the intruders was torn up and scattered . . . the communists cheered, sang the *Internationale* with raised fists and conducted a meeting of their own."

But the Trotskyites recruited from sympathetic unions "a strong-arm squad" of their own, and "when the unsuspecting communists came [to a street meeting] they got the beating of their lives and re-treated."

At the funeral in New York of two "ordinary workers" killed in the fighting between Trotskyites and Communists (each blamed the other for the deaths; Gitlow accused the Communists of deliberately killing the men in order to make martyrs of them), some 20,000 Com-munists turned out to march through the streets of the Lower East Side to Union Square. With clenched fists held aloft, they chanted, "Death to the Trotskyites. Death to all renegades."

In the bitter political infighting, Charles Edward Russell wrote, "Life-long champions of the weary and heavy-laden" were denounced as " 'has-beens and Social-Fascists.' " Sidney Hillman, veteran of a hundred bitter battles in the clothing industry, was called a "Mis-leader of Labor" and a counterrevolutionist. "Old friends and comrades as-sailed one another's character and bloodied one another's noses over policies and tactics the correctness of which only trial and error can prove or disprove. Wings over Union Square. Right wings, left wings and winglets of wings, and most of them attached to dead birds," in the words of a disillusioned Oscar Ameringer. "The rattle, gabble, prattle" of the "Trotskyites, Gitlowites and Lovestoneites, Socialist Party members, Old Guards and Militants, fighting over the soul of radical labor" echoed "throughout the whole rocking structure," which, in-deed, seemed in the process of disintegration. The only question was what faction would fall heir to the ruins. "The war between the sects of irate upheavers" was "far more savage than that between capital and labor. . . . Old labor unions reared in sacrifice, agony and blood," Ameringer added, "are torn asunder for the sake of fine-spun and impossible theories."

Since the Communist Party under whatever name figures so prominently in this era, it may be well to take note of its method of organization. The basic group in the party was the unit. Units were of two types: the shop unit, made up of all the Communists in a particular factory or office, and the street unit, organized on the basis of a particular area. A number of units formed a section, and sections a district. Above the districts was the Central Committee of the party, made up, in part, of the district leaders. The headquarters of the Communist Party of the United States (CPUSA) were at 50 East Thirteenth Street, New York City. In the same building was the Workers' Bookshop, patronized, needless to say, primarily by writers and intellectuals, and the offices of the *Daily Worker*.

The party was a political, social, and quasi-religious organization that claimed authority over every aspect of its members' lives. One of the features of party life that new members often found difficult was what was known as Bolshevik self-criticism, sessions in which members criticized each other's (and their own) shortcomings unmercifully. It was a rite of group confession and expiation common to almost all religions and cults. Elizabeth Bentley, experiencing it for the first time, was impressed by the apparent sincerity with which the members of her group embraced self-criticism. In the third period trials for unorthodoxy multiplied alarmingly. Such trials were inquisitions that few party members escaped. An injudicious sntence or paragraph in a speech or article that was judged to smack of unorthodoxy might, unless it was followed by a prompt recantation, result in a hearing before members of the culprit's unit with several higher officials present. The "deviationist" was mercilessly grilled until he or she confessed the error of his or her ways and promised to do better. Such proceedings recalled the trials by congregations of sinners in Puritan New England.

The CPUSA had, in addition to innumerable affiliated bodies, or fronts, its own educational institutions, vacation spots, doctors and lawyers, and perhaps most important of all, philanthropists. Commonwealth College was a labor college organized in 1924 with Communist sponsorship. Lucien Koch, the director, was closely allied to the party, and there were a number of Communists among the faculty and student body. The party ran a training center in New York for members with leadership potential, and it also sent promising members to Moscow for advanced training at the Lenin School. Steve Nelson was among a group of young party members chosen to attend the Lenin School in Moscow. His was the third group to go from the United States. There were fifteen members of whom six were blacks. There was a steelworker from New York, a shipyard worker from Baltimore, and two women from the "Cleveland and New York needle trades."

Mack Coad, who was forty-two, was barely literate. Nelson helped him with his reading and notetaking.

The Lenin School was run by a woman historian known simply as Krisanova, who was assisted by a faculty of European intellectuals. The school was located across the street from the British Embassy in a handsome old house thoroughly modernized with steam heat and modern plumbing. Nearby was the Sun Yat-sen University for students from colonial countries, where courses were taught in the native languages of the students. Some 500 foreign students attended the Lenin School; they were divided into language sections—German, French, Italian, Spanish, and English. The school offered two programs, one for a year and the other for three years. Nelson and his fellow students studied political economy, the origins of capitalism, and Lenin's writings. There were frequent lectures by veterans of various revolutionary movements, including an old man who had been a drummer boy in the Paris Commune of 1871. Another speaker was a veteran of Béla Kun's abortive Hungarian Revolution in the aftermath of the World War. The school's cafeteria offered "a very simple fare," Nelson wrote with restraint: potatoes, cabbage, fish, and black bread. The most valuable part of the experience for Nelson was the friendships he formed with Welsh, Scottish, Irish, English, and Australian students, some of whom he met again during the Spanish Civil War. Most important of all, "they really made me feel part of a movement in which solidarity on a global scale was more than an abstraction."

Americans chosen to study at the Lenin School received, in addition to their boat and train fare and living quarters in Moscow, $50 a month for the support of their wives and an extra $25 for each child. In Ben Gitlow's words, "The students also got free laundry service and were provided with free entertainment and travel. The theater, opera and concert halls were for the students to enjoy as they saw fit." The Karl Marx and Lenin Institute, with the world's greatest library of revolutionary literature, was available to students. The library had been collected by one of Russia's most noted Marxist scholars who a few years later fell before a Soviet firing squad charged with being a "fascist traitor."

The party's principal organs in America were the *New Masses* (for the intellectuals) and the *Daily Worker*, the party's newspaper. The *New Masses*, revived by Max Eastman as the successor to the *Masses*, served as a direct line to the Communist Party itself, though few of its editors and contributors were members of the party. As late as 1926 it carried

on its masthead the names of a number of the nation's literary stars—
Carl Sandburg, Eugene O'Neill, John Dos Passos, Upton Sinclair, Louis
Untermeyer, Edmund Wilson, Claude McKay, and Jean Toomer.

Typical of the rhetoric of the *Daily Worker* was the statement that
the "toiling masses, white and black, [will] continue to build the united
front to rescue these working-class children from the bloody claws of
the murderous ruling class." Malcolm Cowley listed the favorite vituperative vocabulary of the *Daily Worker* and other publications of the
left: "bloated," "cancerous," "chancres," "diseased," "gorged with,"
"maggots," "pus," "putrefying," "rotten flesh," "syphilis," and "vomit."

The result of all this was an enclosed universe where everyone
spoke the same lingo and, in the main, thought the same thoughts; it
was sealed off from the outside world. Only so could its beleaguered
members endure the suspicion and hostility of that outside world.

Viewed in its broader philosophical connotations, the Communist
Party "movement" might be seen as the residuary legatee of Enlightenment, with its faith in science and reason, and social Darwinism
(which, in turn, had absorbed Enlightenment rationalism). The Enlightenment, with its belief in human perfectibility and an end to suffering, poverty, and war through the use of reason, had prepared the
ground for social Darwinism. The religion of science, against which
William James and Charles Sanders Peirce had contended in vain, was
also an important ingredient: Progress was in the very material substance of the world. Put another way, man and his social institutions
were "evolutionary," were evolving from lower to higher and better
forms. Marx's dialectical materialism was simply an adaptation (or a
variation) of this theme. Above all, it was a faith. In the words of Edna
St. Vincent Millay, "if one could not be a Christian, one had to be a
Communist."

The Communist Party and its affiliates and sympathizers did not
exhaust the left. There was, of course, the wholly commendable Norman Thomas, leader of the Socialists, a mild, generous, intelligent man
of goodwill, ill suited for the violent ideological wars of the era. There
were also men like Frederic Howe, Charles Edward Russell, Lincoln
Steffens, and Oscar Ameringer whose radical credentials were unassailable but who represented an older generation.

One of the most appealing figures of the non-Communist left was
a tall, thin preacher turned Marxist named A. J. Muste. Muste had
been born in Holland and reared in Grand Rapids, Michigan, where
he was an outstanding athlete—a basketball star and a baseball player—

and class valedictorian. His parents were members of the Dutch Reformed Church, and Muste was ordained a minister in that church at the age of twenty-four. When he attended a lecture of William James at New York University, he found himself strongly inclined to James's way of thinking about the world, an inclination strengthened by John Dewey's friendship. First a Congregational minister with a church in Boston, Muste moved on to the Society of Friends. As a Quaker, he helped raise money for the relief of striking textile workers in Lawrence, Massachusetts, and, in the process, found himself the leader of the strike. When the strikers won, Muste was elected head of the Amalgamated Textile Workers of America. The union disintegrated in the hard times of 1921, and Muste became a kind of itinerant "labor minister without portfolio," working with various union leaders to train organizers and broaden the education of union officials. One important result was the Brookwood Labor College in Katonah, New York, which was underwritten eventually by thirteen national unions. Many of the most effective union organizers in the country were trained at Brookwood College.

"The Brookwoodites," Edmund Wilson wrote, "are quite unlike the Communists and superficially rather like Red Cross workers or young radical professors, but, without being particularly militant, they seem to have a good deal of backbone." One of Brookwood College's extracurricular activities was the producing of one-act plays on social issues, most particularly pacifism, to tour the country on the Chautauqua circuit.

Muste wrote of Brookwood that "It was influenced by Marxist thought but was not Marxist. The faculty members were chosen for their competence as scholars and teachers." The Communist Young Workers League warned against Brookwood. It was, they told its members, "no more Communist than the executive board of the A.F. of L. itself. . . . "

Brookwood Labor College was commonly taken to be a dangerously subversive institution. Sophie Goodavich, who was to marry Victor Reuther, was working in the bakery department of the Braintree, Massachusetts, A&P when she got word that she had been accepted as a student at Brookwood. Her supervisor was horrified. "Why, that's a Communist school," he declared.

"Who are Communists?" Goodavich asked.

"Well, if you have a wife and your friend has no wife, you share your wife with him."

Sophie Goodavich looked uncomprehending.

"Look, if you have a toothbrush," the supervisor continued, "and your neighbor doesn't, you must share it with him." Before she left for Brookwood, Goodavich bought several toothbrushes to be prepared for such an eventuality.

Sympathetic to the aims of the Communist Party and a supporter of Soviet Russia, Muste was nonetheless dismayed at the factional infighting that characterized the party and at its slavish adherence to the "line" that emanated from Moscow. In May, 1929, he assembled 151 delegates from thirty-one cities to found the Conference for Progressive Labor Action with the specific purpose of trying to reform the reactionary AFL. The delegates called for the formation of a labor party, "a complete system of social insurance against the hazards of unemployment, sickness and old age" and "an end to imperialism, militarism and war." It was Muste's dream to form a "truly American radical party, independent of both the socialists and the communists," somewhat along the lines of the Populist Party. It soon became evident that the Trotskyite intention was to take over the American Workers' Party. Muste visited Trotsky in exile in Norway, and returning home by way of the Cathedral of Notre Dame in Paris, he experienced a revelation of the power of Christ's love and abandoned Marxism altogether, becoming a pacifist. For the rest of a long life Muste's energies were to be devoted to the causes of labor and pacifism.

# 10

# Black Americans

The constant migration of Southern blacks to Northern industrial cities had vast consequences for blacks and whites alike. This redistribution of population was unique in American history. Tides of immigrants had poured into American cities in the decades following the Civil War and in the early years of the twentieth century. But they had by and large stayed where they first arrived or gradually distributed themselves westward. Some Southern blacks had gone North each year since the early days of the Republic, some as free blacks, many as escaping slaves, but the great tide of black migration occurred during the two world wars. The lure of somewhat greater freedom and steady wages instead of the uncertain fortunes of the sharecropper proved an irresistible attraction to millions of blacks from every state below the Mason-Dixon Line. The great majority went by what we might call family increments, a son or daughter first and then siblings and parents and cousins and aunts.

The migrants were, in fact, less migrants than coresidents, men and women with what might be called dual citizenship, citizenship in some small Southern town, where they knew and loved the earth and its forms and fruits, and citizenship in some cold, strange Northern city. In the cities the new arrivals found their way to those streets and blocks where friends and relatives were already established. They were taken in and helped through the difficult process of adjustment. The ways of Southern small-town and farming blacks were as different from the ways of city blacks as the ways of members of the same race and nationality could be. So there was, inevitably, homesickness and a continuous movement between the old home and the new home.

The black upper class and middle class, long in the city, looked down on the poor blacks and on the rural blacks, who were often illiterate and superstitious, with country manners and country ways. Like the prosperous German Jews who viewed the arrival of the poor (and alien) Russian Jews with alarm, the black upper class fretted that the new arrivals, by reinforcing white stereotypes of blacks, would make its own position more precarious. The rural and small-town blacks in turn felt threatened by the involvement of poor urban blacks in crime and drugs and, during Prohibition, bootleg liquor. Yet somehow the cities became crucibles in which a distinctive black culture took form. Music was the heart and soul of it, although the black music of the city was a far cry from the music, largely spirituals, of the black South. Jazz was initially a word for sexual intercourse; the music called jazz had its origins in New Orleans whorehouses and the houses of Nashville and St. Louis. Spirituals were what the name implied, songs having to do with the spirit, with grieving and suffering and death and endurance: "Nobody knows the trouble I've seen, glory, hallelujah." The spirituals were from slave days, from the rich soil of the South and the dark, secret lives of Southern blacks. Jazz, on the other hand, was city music, dangerously suggestive—the devil's music to pious black Baptists translated to Chicago or New York or Baltimore, who dreaded seeing their children slip away into that compelling underworld of hustlers, pimps, prostitutes, jazz musicians, petty criminals, agents of the "man." So there were as many black worlds as white worlds and, perhaps even more tensions and anxieties, more desperate struggles to preserve respectability and protect the family.

Migrating blacks took their churches with them or found a home in a familiar denomination. The importance of the churches in the social and emotional life of blacks who had migrated from rural areas of the South cannot be overstated. Richard Wright, the black novelist, wrote: "Many of the religious symbols appealed to my sensibilities and I responded to the dramatic vision of life held by the church, feeling that to live day by day with death as one's sole thought was to be so compassionately sensitive toward all life as to view all men as slowly dying, and the trembling sense of fate that welled up, sweet and melancholy, from the hymns blended with the sense of fate that I had already caught from life."

In addition, black messiahs claiming at least semidivine powers appeared in some cities to create new religions that seemed especially adapted to the needs of urban blacks. In New York City Father Divine had a large following of "children" who took such names as Glorious Illumination, Heavenly Dove, and Pleasing Joy. Celibacy was a rule. Father Divine's flock refused any form of welfare and lived in one of the dozen or so "Heavens" in Harlem, where a nourishing meal could be had for fifteen cents. "The real God," Father Divine declared, "is the God that feeds us." Jerre Mangione went with a friend, Robert Ballou, to a "Heaven" where several hundred "angels" ate fried chicken and testified to the power of the Lord in their lives. When a young woman in an ecstatic trance danced on a table covered with plates and dishes, the meeting grew wilder and wilder. The "angels," Mangione reported, "screamed and groaned and rolled on the floor while their God went on orating. . . ." Only when he stopped did the worshipers subside. The scene was reminiscent of a frontier revival meeting raised to a somewhat higher degree.

In Philadelphia Prophet Cherry organized the Church of the Living God. Without formal education, he taught himself Yiddish and Hebrew and told his congregation that Christ was black. During a sermon he would hold up a picture of a white Jesus "and scream to his followers: 'Who in the hell is this? Nobody knows. They say it's Jesus, but it's a damn lie.' "

The black churches were the primary socializing institutions of the Northern cities. Members of a congregation from the African Methodist Episcopal Church of Salem, South Carolina, felt immediately at home in the African Methodist Episcopal Church of Philadelphia. So pervasive was their influence that the churches constituted communities within the larger black community, or to put it another way, those blacks who were not members of some black congregation were by that fact a distinctive minority, regarded with suspicion and often hostility by the faithful. They were apt to be "bad niggers."

Marcus Garvey continued to be a power in black America. The poet Claude McKay defended him against the criticism of the black "intelligentsia," who scorned his "spectacular antics—words big with bombast, colorful robes, Anglo-Saxon titles of nobility (Sir William Ferris, K.C.O.N., for instance, his editor, and Lady Henrietta Vinton

Davis, his international organizer), his steam-roller-like mass meetings and parades and lamentable business ventures— . . ." But the Black Star (Steamship) Line had "an electrifying effect upon all the Negro peoples of the world—even the black intelligentsia. . . . The movement for African redemption had taken definite form in the minds of Western Negroes, and the respectable Negro uplift organizations were shaken up to realize the significance of 'Back to Africa.' . . . No intelligent Negro dared deny the almost miraculous effect and the world-wide breadth and sweep of Garvey's propaganda methods." At the same time, McKay added, "those who think broadly on social conditions" were "amazed at Garvey's ignorance and his intolerance of social ideas."

Hubert H. Harrison, a black writer and editor, tried to form an alliance with Garvey, whose *Negro World* had a large circulation among blacks in all sections of the country. It was also McKay's hope to move Garvey in the direction of black socialism. But he spurned their efforts, insisting that the "fundamental issue" was "the appeal of race to race . . . of clan to clan . . . of tribe to tribe."

When Garvey was arrested for fraud and misuse of funds in the spring of 1922 "after five years of stupendous vaudeville," McKay wrote he could take comfort in the thought that he "was the biggest popularizer of the Negro problem, especially among the Negroes, since *Uncle Tom's Cabin*. He attained the sublime. During the last days he waxed more falsely eloquent in his tall talks on the Negro Conquest of Africa, and when the clansmen yelled their approval and clamored for more, in his gorgeous robes, he lifted his hands to the low ceiling in a weird pose, his huge ugly bulk cowing the crowd and told how the mysteries of African magic had been revealed to him and how he would use them to put the white man into confusion and drive him out of Africa." (Garvey considered Ku Klux Klansmen his allies in that they, too, wanted American blacks to return to Africa.)

Besides the church, the two principal black urban institutions were probably the barbershop and the beauty parlor. The writer Ralph Ellison noted that there was "no place like a Negro barbershop for hearing what Negroes really think. There is more unselfconscious affirmation to be found there on a Saturday than you can find in a Negro college in a month. . . ." Black beauty parlors became the organizational centers for black women committed to the fight for justice in white America. Hair was a major obsession of black men and women alike. The quality and texture of black hair were only less obsessional than skin color. The methods of straightening hair were numerous. Fortunes were made from the concoction of creams and unguents guaranteed to straighten hair. Hairdressers were, in consequence, women with high status in the black community. In all major cities with large populations, and many smaller towns and cities, black hairdressers were part of the black elite, a handful of professional and semiprofessional blacks, including doctors, lawyers, teachers, storekeepers. Madame C. J. Walker made a fortune in Indianapolis by manufacturing beauty aids for black women, skin creams, "whiteners," and hair-straightening preparations prominent among them. Indeed, she was credited with being the first American woman to become a millionaire by her own efforts. Moving to Harlem, Walker and her daughter, A'Lelia, became leaders in black society. The Walker town house at 110 West 136th Street was called the Dark Tower.

As Southern blacks migrated west, often to the Pacific coast, they encountered a rising tide of prejudice. The West had been relatively little affected by racial prejudice. Horace Cayton's grandfather was Hiram R. Revels, who, in 1870, became the first black man to sit in the United States Senate as Senator from Mississippi. Cayton grew up in Seattle in a large two-story house in the most prosperous section of the city. His father and mother were graduates of Alcorn College in Mississippi. His father was the editor of the most successful newspaper in Seattle, and the Caytons' neighbors all were white. "As a newspaper editor and publisher," Cayton wrote, "my father was known and respected in the community, and though we were not warm social friends, our neighbors were pleasant and respectful." But all this changed during the period when Horace Cayton was growing up. As more and more poor blacks found their way to Seattle, signs of white prejudice grew year by year until Cayton's father found himself forced to take a position in support of the new arrivals. His paper became a black newspaper rather than a paper for the whole city, and as his white subscribers and advertisers fell away, he was forced to sell his paper and take a far more humble job.

One by one the bars of prejudice were erected in Seattle. Restaurants that had served blacks without question now began to turn them away. Young Cayton, in his early teens, began to make "pilgrimages to restaurants I had heard would not serve Negroes and tried to force them to serve me." When he was told by a theater manager that he would have to sit in the balcony because he was black, Cayton refused, and the manager had him arrested. After he was freed with a warning, he was told by his father, "When I first came out to this territory, a man was as good as his word. I went out in man-to-man competition and was successful. I provided a good home for my family. I had high hopes. . . . But now the South has overtaken us, and freedom is only in name—not in fact. I'm defeated; you may not know that, but I seldom forget it, even at home. I have given up any hope of ultimate freedom for myself. It may not even come for you children, but for this I want you to fight all your life. America may not offer much but it is the only country we have or ever will have."

Cayton's father blamed himself for not having prepared his children for the facts of racial prejudice. "But it was a mistake that was easy to make in those days, because neither [your mother nor I] ever dreamed that the insanity of the South could catch up with us out here. It's defeated me, but you must prepare yourself to go on fighting."

When Booker T. Washington visited Seattle, it was natural that he should stay with the Caytons, but Horace remembered an unpleasant quarrel between his father and the black leader over Washington's doctrine of accommodation.

Cayton graduated from high school and after completing college made his way to Chicago to do graduate work at the university. To him the world of black Chicago was a revelation. "Never had I seen so many Negroes," he wrote; "it came almost as a shock to see so many dark faces. . . . I felt I was finally entering the mainstream of Negro life. There was much that was similar, as well as many things in contrast, to the Mississippi from which my parents had escaped."

Philadelphia, New York, and Chicago were the major centers of black life north of the Mason-Dixon Line. Allen Ballard, professor of political science at New York University, has told the story of the migration of his own family from Greenwood, South Carolina, to Philadelphia. Long after the family had moved North, Greenwood remained home, and Greenwood ways persisted. Ballard's "sweet and loving grandmother from South Carolina used to sing softly, 'Glory, Glory, Hallelujah, when I lay my burden down,'" and tell him of Greenwood and the South. The stories were alluring and frightening. "Since my childhood," he wrote, "South Carolina has meant fear and darkness." His father resented any reference to the South and rebuked Ballard for singing Southern chain gang songs. Somehow they were associated in Allen's mind as a boy with thunder and lightning. His grandfather would say, "The Lord is in his Holy Temple, let all the earth be silent before him."

In the words of Allen Ballard, "The Old Philadelphia [black] families, by and large, reacted to the 1917–23 migration with shock and disbelief, fearing that they would lose all the gains they thought they had made in integrating themselves into the Philadelphia community." The black elite of the city worked for whites as butlers, caterers, headwaiters, and chauffeurs, with some black professionals. While they looked down on the "field Negroes," they were, in turn, viewed with a degree of contempt by the new arrivals because of their dependence on wealthy whites as well as for their superior airs. One black migrant from Greenwood who became a successful businessman told Allen Ballard, "We really washed out the supposed intellectual superiority of the Northern Negroes, just washed them away. And I can see the waves coming in now; I can see myself in that wave; I can see my brother in that wave; and our kids and my sister's kids. . . . All our brainy kids grew out of the field Negroes." Not having access to white-dependent jobs, "they had to make it. And they became more versatile, smarter, more competitive, tougher. . . . They were dark and brown, and could not lay claim to the kind of life that these people [the Old Philadelphians] had here." While the Old Philadelphians "sat back and laughed at the crudities" of the newcomers, in the words of one of their number, "these people took over the important places. . . . "

In Philadelphia the population density in white sections averaged 28.2 people per acre; in the black sections it was 111 per acre, with some sections running as high as 170 per acre. The death rate from tuberculosis was four times as high as it was for whites. Churches sponsored black building and loan associations to help blacks to buy their own homes.

There were numerous black organizations and savings clubs: the Royal Lion of Judah Savings Club, the Mae West Follies Girls' Savings Club and the Twenty Virgins' Savings Club, the Public Waiters Association, the O. V. Catto Lodge of the Elks Club. Sam Evans, who had been born in Florida and had seen ten lynchings before he was ten, came to Philadelphia in 1917 and organized Youth City to work with young blacks caught in the cycle of "poverty, broken homes, vice, habitual corner lounging and crime."

Blacks were shut out of most jobs in shipping and construction. In 1930, 260 factories in Philadelphia employed 43,000 workers, but less than 1 percent were young blacks, who made up 15 percent of the city's population. Of those black women who were employed, the great majority worked as domestics. Overall, 44 percent of blacks were unemployed. One woman told Allen Ballard, "I worked for a family as a laundress for thirty-five years. I worked for mother and daughter. I worked the hard way. Wasn't no machines. You had to do everything with your hands. My hands were getting bad. And I washed, put the clothes in a tub, walked up the hill, and put them on the line, then go back. Then my legs commence to give out. It's no wonder I have no legs cause I wore them out working."

The black slum section of Philadelphia was vividly described by the black novelist William Gardner Smith, who had grown up there: "Part of the sidewalk space [was] occupied by stands piled high with vegetables. Restaurants, beer gardens, pawn shops, jewelry stores, and an intermittent voodoo den, in the windows of which the herb doctor display[ed] his fantastic roots, concoctions, and weird symbols, with sometime a live snake undulating its coils in the midst."

Smith remembered South Philadelphia and his own "little house on the tiny street with much dirt and horse manure and the house with four rooms and a toilet outside in the back yard and the dirty little children that ran outside the house all day and half the night playing games and writing dirty names on the wall . . . homes packed so tightly together that they were no homes but shelters from the rain and wind. . . . With big cracks in the plaster and the paper sagging and spotting in the ceiling from the rain that leaked through the roof. . . . With the little bed bugs that you could not get rid of though you sprayed day after day . . . walls so dirty that you walked in the halls straight and with your shoulders pulled in so that you would not touch the walls." In the poorest black districts there were no libraries, no recreation centers, but rather "ignorance, dirt, overcrowding, disease, sloth, wine, drunkenness, corruption of youth. . . ." Many of those who left towns like Greenwood for Philadelphia found the adjustment to city living too demanding; they died of alcoholism. "You could see them lying on the streets, just like dogs lying in the shade," one older Philadelphian recalled.

The great black preacher of Philadelphia was the Reverend Charles A. Tindley. He had been born a slave on Maryland's Eastern Shore. From a job as hod carrier and janitor he went on to become the pastor of what was, at one time, the largest black congregation in the United States. Music, specifically spirituals, was his passion. "All he had to do was walk into the church," one man recalled, "and the people would start applauding. Never saw anything like it in my life." Ballard calls him the "catalyst for the creation of modern Black gospel music."

Tindley's "I'll Overcome Someday" was the inspiration for "We Shall Overcome." Among his other compositions were the gospel songs "Stand by Me," "The Storm Is Passing Over," and "We'll Understand It Better Bye and Bye." Largely as a result of Tindley's influence, Philadelphia by the 1920s had become the center of black church music, with the Clara Ward Singers from the Ebenezer Baptist Church, Sister Rosetta Tharpe, and the Dixie Hummingbirds among the most popular performers. Dizzy Gillespie migrated from Cheraw, South Carolina, to Philadelphia and bought his first trumpet there; Bessie Smith was married by the Reverend Mr. Tindley. Billie Holiday and Billy Eckstine were part of the black musical scene in Philadelphia at one time, and Pearl Bailey, born in Virginia, became, like Ethel Waters, a Philadelphia girl.

In Allen Ballard's words, "there was dirt, unemployment, sickness, and death all around our community. Yet, through it all, and out of the very depths of human degradation, came a triumphant sense of certitude about the Southern Blacks' ability to survive the city, as they had surmounted oppression. . . . The Black nationalism of the Old Philadelphia intelligentsia was refined and shaped by contact with the Black masses." In that process, black churches played a decisive role.

Chicago, by the outbreak of the World War, already had a long and dismal history of racial conflict. The influx of more Southern blacks simply heightened the tensions in that city. A classic split occurred between the older black politicians, who brokered power between the black voters and the white politicians and received a share of jobs and graft in return, and the young rebels, or New Negroes, whose hero was W. E. B. Du Bois. The journal of the New Negroes was the *Whip,* which attacked the "big-fake politicians who for a 'mess of pottage' . . . preached submissiveness to the black masses." The Wabash Avenue YMCA was their headquarters, a "segregated, Jim Crow institution" for "all the black Blue Stockings or better styled cod fish aristocracy of the race." They insisted that "Pacifism and patience" were "not the medicine for all racial ailments. . . . This is no time for pussy-footing and watchful waiting, but for intelligent concerted attack on existing evils with all necessary methods." The New Negroes would no longer accept half a loaf. Their program called for an "end to Jim Crow, preferably by legislation [but] if not, through more drastic means."

Chicago blacks prided themselves on their interest in black culture. The Race Relations Committee of the Chicago Women's Club arranged a week of exhibits of the art and music of black people at the Art Institute. Plays were produced "concerning colored people which portrayed something of that inner life upon which the kinship of the races is founded," Jane Addams wrote, with "recitals and lectures by well known artists, poets, and scholars." Modest as they were, the events and exhibits suggested poignantly to Addams "what has been and is being lost by the denial of free expression on the part of the Negro. . . ." It was a matter that weighed heavily on her conscience. "Because we are no longer stirred as the Abolitionists were," she wrote, "to remove the fetters, to prevent cruelty, to lead the humblest to the banquet of civilization, we have allowed ourselves to become indifferent to the gravest situation in our American life. The Abolitionists grappled with an evil intrenched since the beginning of recorded history. . . . To continually suspect, suppress or fear any large group in a community must finally result in a loss of enthusiasm for that type of government which gives free play to the self-development of a majority of its citizens. It means an enormous loss of capacity to the nation when great ranges of human life are hedged about with antagonism. We forget that whatever is spontaneous in a people, in an individual, a class or a nation, is always a source of life," she added.

The University of Chicago was, in its heyday, a center of radical ferment and the "new sociology" of Robert Park and his colleagues. Horace Cayton took as his field of study the lives of Chicago's blacks (the notion that as a black he would be too biased to report objectively had not yet become as persuasive as it was to be). "The huge South Side black belt fascinated, frightened, and haunted me with its crime, disease, local color and vitality," he wrote. "I eagerly responded to its jazz and rocking gospel music. No one really knew the why and wherefores of this isolated island of color where people died from tuberculosis seven times faster than did whites, a seat of grinding poverty which still had a verve and vitality that white people secretly envied."

Underlying the culture of every black ghetto were the "numbers." Catalan, a West Indian, controlled the Harlem numbers game for years until he was succeeded by a Cuban named Messalino, who drove around Harlem in a chauffeured limousine. In Claude McKay's words, "He expanded the game, exciting community interest and making all Harlem numbers-minded. He was the first of the dazzling line of numbers' kings. . . ."

Prohibition gave an added stimulus to the numbers game—many black bootleggers began as adjuncts to the numbers—and soon white gangsters began to muscle in. Dutch Schultz was the most prominent, but even he found it almost impossible to penetrate the black world; whites, however disreputable their credentials, were simply excluded. Perhaps the numbers were the only public betting scheme where the bettor could wager as little as a penny. "Runners" went from house to house, store to store, in the black neighborhoods of large cities, taking bets, usually in pennies, on the "number." The number was, for a time, the last three digits of the day's stock transactions and thus available to anyone who bought a paper. The runners were presided over by collectors, who took in the receipts from the black districts of the various cities and supervised the paying off of those with the winning numbers. It was more than a game; it was the ruling obsession of a large part of the black population of cities like Chicago, Baltimore, and Philadelphia, and it generated enormous profits for those involved. The odds were high. For instance, a penny might return $5, twenty-five cents $50. Around the numbers an extensive industry developed: Fortune-tellers thrived on selling lucky numbers; innumerable books interpreted dreams into numbers. "Got a good number?" was a common greeting. Typically, numbers were played in combination—617, 167, 716, 671, 176—with a few cents on each number. When Caspar Holstein, Messalino's successor, was kidnapped in 1928 and held for $50,000 ransom, the outside world became aware of the game. Holstein was a high roller and, according to McKay, the only black philanthropist who gave generously to black colleges and churches as well as to needy individuals. He also helped promising young black writers and artists.

Whatever the rival claims of Philadelphia or Chicago, New York City was the capital of black America, indeed, the capital of the black Caribbean as well. By 1930 only 21.2 percent of Manhattan's black population had been born in the city; 49 percent had been born in the South, the rest in the West Indies or in other regions of the United States. It was in New York that what came to be known as the Harlem Renaissance manifested itself. A precondition of the Renaissance was that a black culture, typified but by no means limited to Harlem or New York, had taken form there. The other precondition was a keen interest on the part of the white intellectual class, which was in the process of defining itself, in black culture. Lower-class blacks at least seemed to be free of the inhibitions and repressions which the white creators of the new consciousness so deplored. The abolitionists had cherished the dream that the emancipated slaves would, by their intensely expressive spirit, their "soul," redeem white Americans from the aridity of their affective life. Harriet Beecher Stowe had written in *Uncle Tom's Cabin* that the time must come when God, having tried all the other races of the world and found them wanting, would come to black Africa, and life would "awake there with a gorgeousness and splendor of which our cold western tribes have faintly conceived." That continent and its people would then be revealed as "the highest and noblest which He will set up . . . and the last shall be first and the first shall be last." Stowe was, to be sure, talking about Africans, not American blacks, but the theme of the redemption of white America by black Americans was evident through much of the writing of both black and white abolitionists. In the 1920s it once again became a major theme for the new intellectual class.

W. E. B. Du Bois, as editor of the *Crisis,* the magazine of the National Association for the Advancement of Colored People, stood ready to encourage black writers. Liberal and radical journals like the *New Republic* and the *New Masses* were also anxious to publish the work of black poets, short-story writers, and essayists. Alain Locke, professor of literature at Howard University, a graduate of Harvard, and the first black Rhodes Scholar, wrote a book entitled *The New Negro.* In the Introduction he called on black writers and intellectuals to join forces to create a genuinely black literature. "The younger generation [of blacks]," Locke wrote, "is vibrant with a new psychology . . . the new spirit is awake in the masses, and under the very eyes of the professional observers is transforming what has been a perennial problem into the progressive phase of contemporary Negro life." Although *The New Negro* did not appear until 1925, when what was later identified as the Harlem Renaissance was already well under way, Locke's book became a kind of manifesto for the movement.

One of the most remarkable of the older generation of black leaders, a link between Booker T. Washington and W. E. B. Du Bois and the younger figures of the Harlem Renaissance, was James William (later Weldon) Johnson. Johnson was born in Jacksonville, Florida, of parents who represented the more prosperous and well educated of that city's black population. Johnson's father was a headwaiter at one of Jacksonville's best restaurants and by that fact a member, with teachers, ministers, lawyers, and doctors, of the town's black elite. Jacksonville, Johnson recalled, "was known far and wide as a good town for blacks." Johnson's mother had been born in Nassau in the Bahamas of a father part French and part Haitian. *Her* mother was the daughter of a white planter and an African woman who had come to the Americas on a slave ship. After her marriage Helen Johnson taught in the Stanton School, the city's largest black grammar school. James William, the Johnsons' second child, was born in 1871.

In Jacksonville, in the 1870s before the rise of white reaction, there were blacks on the police force. Black barbers virtually monopolized the cutting of hair. There were black carpenters and masons and black stalls in the city's market. A black volunteer fire department and a black band participated in public ceremonies. Johnson's ambitions as a boy varied from wanting to play drums in a marching band to attending West Point or becoming governor of the state. He toyed with the idea of becoming a lawyer or a doctor. His parents encouraged his interest in music, and the Baptist Church encouraged his piety. He did well in school and was admitted to Atlanta University, which, along with Fisk, ranked as one of the best black institutions of higher education in the South. In an interval in his college career Johnson found a job with a white physician in Jacksonville, Dr. Thomas Osmund Summers, a freethinker and something of a radical, who was impressed by Johnson's quick intelligence and his ability to read Latin. Summers became the mentor of his bright young assistant, encouraging him to read Thomas Paine and Robert Ingersoll and opening his large library to him.

Johnson's acquaintance with the world outside Jacksonville was considerably extended by his job at the Chicago World's Columbian Exposition as a "chair boy," pushing visitors around the fairgrounds in wheelchairs. During his summer at the fair Johnson became a friend of Paul Laurence Dunbar, the young black poet who had been befriended by James Whitcomb Riley and whose dialect poems about Southern Blacks were enjoying a vogue.

After Johnson was graduated from Atlanta University, he passed up a scholarship to study medicine at the Harvard Medical School to take the job of principal of the Stanton School, which he had attended and where his mother had taught. His most serious problem came when he received permission from the white superintendent of schools to visit classes at the largest white school in Jacksonville. Outraged parents at the white school demanded that he be fired for crossing the color line, but the incident blew over. In addition to his duties as school principal, he edited a black newspaper, the *Daily American,* and studied law. The paper failed, but Johnson passed the bar examination and while continuing as principal at Stanton, became the first black lawyer in Duval County. He took as his law partner Douglas Wetmore, a fellow

student at Atlanta who had been expelled for drinking and had subsequently gone to law school at the University of Michigan. Very light
in complexion, Wetmore realized after a few weeks that the Michigan
students assumed he was white; it was his first experience with "passing."

Increasingly Johnson devoted time to writing poems and songs,
collaborating with his brother J. Rosamond, who was an excellent musician. In February, 1900, the two young men composed a song in
honor of Lincoln's birthday:

> Lift every voice and sing
> Till earth and heaven ring,
> Ring with the harmonies of Liberty.
> Let our rejoicing rise
> High as the listening skies,
> Let it resound loud as the rolling sea.
> Sing a song of the faith that the dark past has taught us.
> Sing a song full of the hope that the present has brought us.
> Face the rising sun of our new day begun,
> Let us march on till victory is won.

Two more stanzas followed, the last of which began: "God of our
weary years,/ God of our silent tears,/ . . .May we forever stand./ True
to our God,/ True to our native land." Five hundred of the black
children of Jacksonville sang the song on Lincoln's Birthday. Other
black organizations picked it up, and before long it was being referred
to as the Negro national anthem. It marked the beginning of Johnson's
career as a songwriter. Encouraged by the success of "Lift Every Voice
and Sing," Johnson resigned as school principal, and he and his brother
traveled to New York, where they met a number of black performers
including the songwriter Robert "Bob" Cole. Cole and the Johnson
brothers wrote "Louisiana Lize": "I love her so; she's just as sweet as
'lasses candy. . . ." Soon Cole and the Johnsons were the most successful
team of songwriters in the country. One hit followed another. Most
were "race" songs, somewhat in the spirit of Dunbar's poems, depicting
blacks as happy-go-lucky "coons" and "darkies." (Dunbar, before his
early death in 1906, collaborated on several such songs adapted from
his poems.) One musical show, written by a black writer and starring
black performers, featured a song called "No Coon Can Come Too
Black for Me." One of their hits was entitled "The Maiden with the
Dreamy Eyes," but their most famous, perhaps, was "Under the Bamboo Tree," which ran:

If you lak-a-me, I lak-a-you;
and we lak-a-both the same,
I lak-a-say, this very day,
I lak-a-change your name;
'Cause I love-a-you and love-a-true
And if you-a-love-a-me,
One live as two, two live as one,
Under the bamboo tree.

Johnson blossomed as a Broadway dandy, sporting a goatee and "attired in garments rich and almost rare, tailored with the sartorial effect obtained only in New York," according to the *New York Age*. Ironically, Johnson's most successful poem, entitled "The Creation" with the subtitle "A Negro Sermon" and published in the *Freeman* in 1920, served primarily to inspire a white playwright, Paul Green, to write the hit play *Green Pastures*. "The Creation" began:

And God stepped out on space,
And He looked around and said,
"I'm lonely—
I'll make me a world."

God appeared in the guise of a black preacher.

In addition to his musical activities, Johnson sought to widen his literary horizons and prepare himself for a serious career as a writer. He enrolled at Columbia, where, in Professor Brander Matthews he found an encouraging and sympathetic mentor. Balanced between show business and the literary world (he collaborated on the highly successful musical *The Shoo-fly Regiment* and started a novel), Johnson found himself launched on a surprising new career as a diplomat. Charley Anderson, the city's most prominent black Republican, was looking for a qualified black to push for a government post in Theodore Roosevelt's second term of office. Johnson seemed to him an ideal candidate, and he set about promoting him for a consular job. After he had been approved by Booker T. Washington, who wished to assure himself that Johnson was not allied with the Du Bois faction, Johnson was appointed American consul at Puerto Cabello, Venezuela. The fact that Johnson spoke Spanish fluently was also in his favor. Two years later he was transferred to Corinto, Nicaragua, a Class VII post, two notches above Puerto Cabello. Johnson was consul in 1912, when a rebellion broke out in Nicaragua against President Díaz. The United States threw its support to Díaz in the form of 2,400 marines and sailors. With the election of a Democratic President, Woodrow Wilson, the future of Republican officeholders, white or black, became uncertain, and Johnson decided to resign from his Foreign Service post. His novel *The Autobiography of an Ex-Colored Man*, the story of a light-colored "black" who passed into the white world, was published in 1912. Praised by the editor of *Crisis*, Jessie Fauset, it was one of the important precursors of the Harlem Renaissance. It took its place in the line of black narratives that extended from Frederick Douglass's autobiography, first published in 1845, to Booker T. Washington's *Up from Slavery*. As we have seen, the subject of miscegenation was not new. Charles Chestnutt, a black author, had used it in many of his short stories, and Herbert Croly's mother had made it the subject of a highly successful novel.

Looking back, James Weldon Johnson wrote of his "effort to arouse and deepen the Negro's imagination, to awaken him to pride in the things he had done best . . . to put him firmly on the ground he was sure of; to call forth more fully his *native* gifts, and to lessen his feeling that the gifts of others counted most; to build unified ideas and ideals on his own rock bottom foundation."

The publication of *The Autobiography of an Ex-Colored Man* was followed in 1913 with a poem entitled "Fifty Years," written for the fiftieth anniversary of the Emancipation Proclamation. Like "Lift Your Voices in Song," which had launched the Johnson brothers on their career as songwriters, "Fifty Years" helped open up the next phase of Johnson's life. It began:

> O brothers mine, to-day we stand
>   Where half a century sweeps our ken,
> Since God, through Lincoln's steady hand,
>   Struck off your bonds and made us men.
>
> Just fifty years—a winter's day—
>   As runs the history of the race;
> Yet, as we look back o'er the way,
>   How distant seems our starting place!

After verses describing the arrival of slaves from Africa, the poem continues:

> A part of His unknown design,
>   We've lived within a mighty age;

And we have helped to write a line
  On history's most wondrous page
* * * * *
This land is ours by right of birth,
  This land is ours by right of toil;
We helped to turn its virgin earth,
  Our sweat is in its fruitful soil.
* * * * *
Then should we speak but servile words,
  Or shall we hang our heads in shame?
Stand back of new-come foreign hordes,
  And fear our heritage to claim?

No! stand erect and without fear,
  And for our foes let this suffice—
We've bought a rightful sonship here,
  And we have more than paid the price. . . .

Johnson cut from his original version sixteen stanzas describing the wrongs suffered by black Americans, ending with a warning that if blacks sank beneath the burdens imposed on them by white Americans, they would pull down the proud white civilization that denied them their humanity. Johnson's friend and teacher Brander Matthews sent a copy to Theodore Roosevelt, who wrote that it was "corking." It was praised everywhere as a brilliant evocation of the black ethos. Booker T. Washington lauded it, and Du Bois also commended it warmly. Charles Chestnutt, the pioneer black author, called it the "finest thing I have ever read on the subject. . . ." It was widely reprinted and anthologized, read from the pulpits of black churches, and committed to memory by black schoolchildren. Johnson changed his middle name from William to Weldon as more suitable for a writer. It was as James Weldon Johnson that he took over as director of the editorial page of the *New York Age*, founded thirty years before by the great black newspaper publisher T. Thomas Fortune. Although the *Age* was in the Booker T. Washington camp (Washington had secretly put up the money to buy the paper), Johnson's editorials appealed to a wide segment of the black community and to those whites who were active in fighting racial discrimination. Oswald Garrison Villard, one of the founders of the NAACP, complimented Johnson for "doing the best newspaper writing of any colored man in the country."

As discrimination against blacks increased—the New York state legislature was considering a ban on interracial marriages, and the

State Boxing Commission refused to allow bouts between black and white pugilists—Johnson, like most prominent blacks, grew more and more militant. Blacks, he was convinced, must force the issue of discrimination or simply lapse into a permanently servile condition.

When Anthony Crawford, a respected and prosperous black in Abbeville, South Carolina, was lynched for insulting a white man, Johnson wrote, "No colored man in the country, no matter how successful and prosperous is really free and independent or even safe, so long as the humblest and most ignorant Negro may be deprived of his rights and oppressed simply because he is a Negro."

In *Negro Americans, What Now?* Johnson spelled out his creed: "I will not allow one prejudiced person or one hundred million to blight my life. I will not let prejudice or any one of its attendant humiliations and injustices bear me down to spiritual defeat. My inner life is mine, and I shall defend and maintain its integrity against all the powers of hell."

One of the first voices of the New Negro movement was that of Claude McKay, born Festus Claudius McKay in 1889 in Sunny Ville, Jamaica, of a farm family. McKay's parents were leaders in the local Baptist church and were determined that he should receive a proper education and make his way up in the world. Since there was no adequate schooling in Sunny Ville, Claude, as he was called, lived with his older brother, Uriah Theophilus, in Kingston while he completed grammar school. He then became a constable in that town's police force. He had started to write poetry while still in school, and in Kingston he found a patron in Walter Jekyll, a young Englishman who urged him to write in the dialect of the island rather than in the style of the English poets whom McKay admired. Jekyll also introduced McKay to "Buddha, Schopenhauer and Goethe, Carlyle and Browning, Wilde, Carpenter, Whitman, Hugo, Verlaine, Baudelaire, Shaw. . . ."

Dissatisfied with his job, which proved a barrier between him and most Kingston blacks, McKay decided to make his career as an agricultural adviser to Jamaican farmers, the great majority of whom were black. He enrolled in Tuskegee to study agronomy, but he was completely unprepared for the racial attitudes he discovered in the South. In McKay's words, he arrived in America "to find here strong white men, splendid types, of better physique than any I had ever seen, exhibiting the most primitive animal hatred toward their weaker black brothers. In the South daily murders of a nature most hideous and revolting, in the North silent acquiescence, deep hate, half-hidden under a Puritan respectability . . . flaming up into an occasional lynching—this ugly raw sore in the body of a great nation." After six months at Tuskegee he fled to the somewhat less repressive atmosphere of Kansas State College in Manhattan, Kansas. From there, in 1914, McKay made his way to New York City, where an attempt to go into the restaurant business ended in failure. He thereupon decided to become a poet and for the next five years took whatever casual jobs he could find, among them stevedore, railroad porter, and dining car waiter on the Pennsylvania Railroad, while turning out a steady stream of poems and becoming more and more involved in radical politics. By the end of the war he considered himself a Communist. He wrote:

> My ear is tuned unto new voices shrieking
> Their jarring notes of life-exalting strife;
> My soul soars singing, with flame-forces seeking
> The grandest purpose, the noblest path of life;
> Where scarlet pennants blaze like tongues of fire
> There—where high passion swells—is my heart's desire.

Waldo Frank, one of the editors of the *Seven Arts* magazine, published two of McKay's sonnets in 1917. Attracted to the *Masses*, then edited by Floyd Dell, John Reed, and Max Eastman, McKay became a regular contributor to that magazine after it had been suppressed and revived as the *Liberator*. In Eastman, McKay found a friend and mentor. He wrote Eastman in 1919 shortly after they met, "I was glad to see how you live—so unaffectedly free—not striving to be like the masses like some radicals, but just yourself. I *love* your life—more than your poetry, more than your personality."

By 1920 the *Liberator* had established itself as the premier radical literary journal, carrying the work of Helen Keller, John Dos Passos, Edmund Wilson, Elinor Wylie, and Carl Sandburg. McKay's "If We Must Die," published in the *Liberator,* was taken as a kind of proclamation by radical black intellectuals:

> If we must die, let it not be like hogs
> Hunted and penned in an inglorious spot,
> While round us bark the mad and hungry dogs,
> Making their mock at our accursed lot.
> If we must die, O let us nobly die,
> So that our precious blood may not be shed
> In vain; then even the monsters we defy

Shall be constrained to honor us though dead!
O Kinsmen! we must meet the common foe!
Though far outnumbered let us show us brave,
And for their thousand blows deal one deathblow!
What though before us lies the open grave?
Like men we'll face the murderous, cowardly pack,
Pressed to the wall, dying, but fighting back!

"The White City," which appeared two years later, expressed the same fierce passions:

I will not toy with it nor bend an inch.
Deep in the secret chambers of my heart
I muse my life-long hate, and without flinch
I bear it nobly as I live my part. . . .

Both poems satisfied in every respect the canons of revolutionary art and delighted the ideologues of the Communist Party. McKay was soon a celebrity. He was especially scornful of "the convention-ridden and head-ossified Negro intelligentsia who censure colored actors for portraying the inimitable comic characteristics of Negro life, because they make white people laugh! . . . Negro art, these critics declare, must be dignified and respectable like the Anglo-Saxon's before it can be good. The Negro must get the warmth, color and laughter out of his blood, else the white man will sneer at him and treat him with contumely. Happily the Negro retains his joy of living in the teeth of such criticism. . . . " McKay wrote: "Cherish your strength, my strong black brother. Be not dismayed because the struggle is hard and long. O, my warm, wonderful race. The fight is longer than a span of life; the test is great. Gird your loins; sharpen your tools! Time is on our side. Carry on the organizing and conserving of your forces, my dear brother, grim with determination, for a great purpose—for the Day!"

In 1922 McKay published his fourth book of poetry, *Harlem Shadows*. James Weldon Johnson hailed it in the pages of the *New York Age*, writing that McKay "is a real poet and a great poet. . . .No Negro has sung more beautifully of his race than McKay and no poet has ever equalled the power with which he expressed the bitterness that so often rises in the heart of the race. . . . "

When McKay became an editor of the *Liberator* with Mike Gold, they soon found themselves at odds. In McKay's words, "Gold's idea of the *Liberator* was that it should become a popular proletarian magazine, printing doggerels from lumberjacks and stevedores and true revelations from chambermaids." McKay argued that it should be good as well as proletarian. In Joseph Freeman's words, "Claude McKay's warm sensuous . . . heart swam in thoughtlessness; he was aggressively antirational on the principle that art comes exclusively from the emotions. . . ."

Invited to review a Theatre Guild play as an editor of the *Liberator*, McKay was "shunted" into the balcony. It evoked one of his bitterest outbursts: "Poor, painful black face, intruding into the holy places of the whites. How like a specter you haunt the pale devils! Always at their elbow, always peering darkly through the window, giving them no rest, no peace! How apologetic and uneasy they are, yes, even the best of them, poor devils, when you force an entrance, blackface, facetiously, incorrigibly smiling or disturbingly composed. Shock them out of their complacency, blackface, make them uncomfortable, make them unhappy! Give them no peace, no rest. How can they bear your presence, blackface, great, unappeasable ghost of Western civilization."

After less than a year on the staff of the *Liberator* McKay resigned and headed for the headquarters of the world revolution which he was constantly proclaiming—Russia. He wished, he wrote, to "escape from the pit of sex and poverty, from domestic death, from the cul-de-sac of self-pity, from the hot syncopated fascination of Harlem, from the suffocating ghetto of color-consciousness."

Crystal Eastman, Max Eastman's sister, helped raise money for McKay's expedition. He arrived in Moscow in November, 1922, on the eve of the Fourth Congress of the Third International. The American Communist delegation objected to his unannounced and unofficial appearance. The delegation was split over the issue of whether the American party should be underground. When Rose Pastor Stokes sounded out McKay on the question, he declared that he saw no need for the party to go underground, thus putting himself in the middle of the dispute. He was apparently rescued by Sen Katayama, a Japanese Communist who had attended Fisk University in Nashville and was aware, as few European party functionaries were, of the practical realities of black America. Through Katayama's influence, McKay was invited to speak to the delegates. It was a remarkable moment for the young black American.

"Comrades," he declared, "I feel that I would rather face a lynching stake in civilized America than to try to make a speech before the most intellectual and critical audience in the world. I belong to a race of creators but my public speaking has been so bad that I have been told by my own people that I should never try to make speeches, but stick to writing, and laughing." In the United States members of the party had to overcome their own evidences of racial discrimination, "and this is the greatest difficulty . . . the fact that they first have got to emancipate themselves from the ideas they entertain toward the Negroes before they can be able to reach the Negroes with any kind of radical propaganda." McKay also cautioned against the disposition of the party in the United States to send "black comrades into the South" as party organizers. "They generally won't be able to get out again—they will be lynched and burned at the stake."

McKay's visit turned into a triumphal tour. The Moscow press printed long articles about the plight of blacks in America. Russian poets wrote poems about blacks. "Soon I was in demand everywhere," McKay wrote, "—at the lectures of poets and journalists, the meeting of soldiers and factory workers. . . . I was welcomed as a symbol, as a member of the great American Negro group—kin to the unhappy black slaves of European Imperialism in Africa. . . . [M]y days in Russia were a progression of affectionate enthusiasm of the people toward me. . . . At every meeting I was received with boisterous acclaim, mobbed with friendly demonstrations. . . . Those Russian days remain the most memorable of my life. . . . Never in my life did I feel prouder of being an African, a black, and no mistake about it. . . . From Moscow to Petrograd and from Petrograd to Moscow I went triumphantly from surprise to surprise, extravagantly feted on every side. . . . I was like a black ikon in the flesh. . . . I was the first Negro to arrive in Russia since the revolution [not quite accurate] and perhaps I was generally regarded as an omen of good luck." With his arching eyebrows and constant grin, McKay looked like a black Pan.

From Russia he traveled to Germany and then to Paris. In Toulon, in the south of France, he completed his first novel with the prospective title of *Color Scheme.* He wrote to Arthur A. Schomburg, who was collecting literature on American blacks, "I make my Negro characters yarn and backbite and fuck like people the world over."

When Louise Bryant Reed Bullitt, John Reed's widow, now married to William Bullitt, met McKay in southern France, she took a group of his short stories with the intention of finding an American publisher for his work. They were submitted to Harper Brothers, which suggested that they be woven into a novel. The result was *Home to*

*Harlem,* published in 1927 at the high tide of the Harlem Renaissance.

The central portion of *Home to Harlem* draws on McKay's experience as a Pullman dining car waiter. Ray, the narrator, a Haitian by birth, encounters Jake when they both work in the same dining car. Awake in the filthy, bedbug-ridden barracks where black cooks and waiters sleep between runs, Ray looks with distaste on the black men snoring around him. "These men claimed kinship with him. They were black like him. Man and nature had put them in the same race. He ought to love them and feel for them (if they felt anything). He ought to if he had a shade of social morality in him. They were all chain-ganged together and he was counted as one. Yet he loathed every soul in the great barrack-room, except Jake. Race. . . . Why should he have to love a race? Races and nations were things like skunks, whose smell poisoned the air of life. Yet civilized mankind reposed its faith and future in their ancient silted channels. Great races and big nations! There must be something mighty inspiring in being the citizen of a great strong nation. To be a white citizen of a nation that can say bold challenging things like a strong man. . . . Something a black man could never feel or quite understand."

McKay was fascinated by the shades comprehended by the word "Negro" or "black." In *Home* he ran through them as a kind of litany: "Brown girls rouged and painted like dark pansies. Brown flesh draped in soft colorful clothes. . . . She was brown, but she had tinted her leaf-like face to a ravishing chestnut. . . . Aunt Hattie was weather-beaten dark-brown cherry-faced. . . . The cabaret singer, a shiny coffee-colored girl in a green frock . . . chocolate, chestnut, coffee, ebony, cream, yellow, everybody was teased up to a point of excitement. . . . A potato-yellow man and a dull-black . . . a tall, thin, shiny black man. . . . The copper-hued lady . . . two cocoa-brown girls . . . a crust-yellow girl in Petersburg. . . . Ancient black life rooted upon its base with all its fascinating new layers of brown, low-brown, high-brown, nut-brown, lemon, maroon, olive, mauve, gold. Yellow balancing between black and white. Black reaching out beyond yellow. Almost-white on the brink of a change. Sucked back down into the current of black by the terribly sweet rhythm of black blood. . . . "

Jake was the "natural nigger," the uninhibited, joyful, sensuous man. McKay contrasts Jake with Ray, a black intellectual tormented by self-consciousness and bewildered by the conflicts within him about his relationship to ordinary black ghetto life and the lure of the white world. Ray is obviously McKay. He appears again in a subsequent

McKay novel, *Banjo*. In the latter work Ray reflects: "At college in America and among the Negro intelligentsia . . . he has never experienced any of the simple, natural warmth of a people believing in themselves, such as he had felt among the rugged poor and socially backward blacks of his island home [Jamaica]. . . . Only when he got down among the black and brown working boys and girls of the country did he find something of that raw unconscious and the-devil-with-them pride in being a Negro that was his own natural birthright. . . . Among them was never any of the hopeless, enervating talk of the chances of passing white. . . . Close association with the Jakes and Banjoes had been like participating in a common primitive birthright. . . . He loved their natural gusto for living down the past and lifting their kinky heads out of the hot, suffocating ashes, the shadow, the terror of real sorrow to go on gaily grinning in the present."

Although *Home to Harlem* was harshly criticized by the black press and, more woundingly, by Du Bois, James Weldon Johnson hailed it as "the finest thing 'we've' yet done. . . ." It should "give a second youth to the Negro Vogue." Johnson wrote McKay that while he sympathized with middle-class blacks caught "between the devil of Cracker prejudice and the deep sea of white condescension," he believed that the writer must follow where his own search for truth led him. Black writers "must leave the real appreciation of what we are doing to the emancipated Negro intelligentsia of the future while we are sardonically aware that only the intelligentsia of the 'superior race' is developed enough to afford artistic truths," certainly a bitter reflection.

Another enthusiastic reader was Langston Hughes. "Just finished Claude's *Home to Harlem* and am wild about it," he wrote to his patron Alain Locke. "It ought to be named *Nigger Hell* but I guess the colored papers will have even greater spasms than before. It is the best low-life novel I've ever read. . . . Up till now, it strikes me that *Home to Harlem* must be the flower of the Negro Renaissance—even if it is no lovely lilly."

If Claude McKay was the prophet of the Harlem Renaissance, James Mercer Langston Hughes was his heir apparent. Called Langston, Hughes was born in Joplin, Missouri, in 1902. Hughes's father was a lawyer whose parents had been slaves. Both his male grandparents were white, and his grandmothers black. His mother's paternal grandfather was a wealthy white planter, and her grandmother was his half-Indian, half-white mistress and housekeeper. Their oldest son, Charles Howard Langston, attended Oberlin College for two years, then taught school and became an active abolitionist, declaring, "I have long since adopted as my God, the freedom of the colored people of the United States, and my religion to do anything that will effect that object. . . . "

One of the young blacks who joined John Brown in the attack on Harpers Ferry was Lewis Sheridan Leary, who was killed in the fighting that followed. Charles Howard Langston married his widow, Mary, one of the first black women to attend Oberlin College. After they had moved to Lawrence, Kansas, their first child was born and named Nathaniel Turner Langston. Their second child, Carolyn, or Carrie, was Langston Hughes's mother. She married Charles Howard Hughes, who was active in civic affairs in that traditionally abolitionist town, being a Republican nominee for the state legislature. Carrie's uncle John Mercer Langston was a lawyer, a college administrator, and served a term as Republican Congressman from Virginia. He was widely recognized as one of the most prominent black leaders of his generation, and the largely black town of Langston, Oklahoma, was named for him.

Langston Hughes's father left for Mexico soon after Langston's birth, abandoning his wife and two sons to seek his fortune in the town of Toluca, where he was successful in amassing a modest fortune. It was, however, a hard, hand-to-mouth existence for Carrie Hughes and her two sons. While his mother sought work wherever she could find it, Hughes lived with his grandmother Mary Langston. With a family tradition of interest in cultural and literary matters, young Hughes read widely.

When his mother married a chef named Homer Clark, Langston went to live with his mother and stepfather in Lincoln, Illinois. In high school he was elected class poet. Paul Laurence Dunbar was his model, and he soon added Walt Whitman and Carl Sandburg to those poets whose work consciously influenced him. The Sandburg influence was evident in one of his first poems written while he was a student at Central High School in Cleveland, Ohio, where Homer Clark had gone to find work.

> The Mills
> That grind and grind
> That grind out steel
> And grind away the lives
> Of men—
> In the sunset their stacks

Are great black silhouettes
Against the sky.
In the dawn
They belch red fire.
The mills—
Grinding new steel,
Old men.

While he was still in high school, Hughes began to attend a Presbyterian settlement house, the Neighborhood Association, later called Karamu House, organized and run by Russell and Rowena Jelliffe, graduates of Oberlin, as a center for the arts and crafts. They produced plays as well, and Hughes had his first experience as a playwright and actor with the Jelliffes. It was at Central High that his interest in Marxism was aroused. "The daily papers," he wrote later, "pictured the Bolsheviki as the greatest devils on earth, but I didn't see how they could be that bad if they had done away with race hatred and landlords—two evils that I knew well at first hand." He read John Reed's *Ten Days That Shook the World,* the story of the opening phases of the Russian Revolution, and was much moved by it. He also read Theodore Dreiser and dipped into Arthur Schopenhauer and Friedrich Nietzsche with the encouragement of teachers who took an interest in the precocious young black. He read Guy de Maupassant in French and gave his heart to D. H. Lawrence.

When he visited his father in Toluca, Mexico, the elder Hughes, rich but miserly, had been living there for fifteen years. During his stay in Mexico Langston Hughes began the study of Spanish and of Spanish and Latin American writers. His father wanted him to study in Switzerland or Germany with the idea of becoming a mining engineer in Mexico, which he insisted was the only country where a black could live with some decency and self-respect, but Hughes was already strongly inclined to a literary career. His father finally agreed reluctantly to underwrite his college education at Columbia. While he was in Mexico, Hughes wrote a number of poems, most of which were published in *Crisis.*

When Hughes arrived in New York in the fall of 1921, Harlem was already being called the "Negro capital of the world." An estimated 77,000 blacks, most of them from the South and many from the Caribbean islands, lived in the area between Fifth and Eighth avenues and 130th to 145th Street. "It was Harlem's Golden Era," Hughes wrote; "I was nineteen when I first came up out of the Lenox Avenue sub-

way . . . and looked around in the happy sunlight to see if I saw Duke
Ellington . . . or Bessie Smith passing by, or Bojangles Robinson in
front of the Lincoln Theatre, or maybe Paul Robeson or Bert Williams
walking down the avenue." He also hoped to see "some of the famous
colored writers, and editors whose names were known around the
country, men like Claude McKay and James Weldon Johnson. The city
within a city seemed to crackle with creative energy and excitement.
Jazz had become the national music and the Cotton Club, Barron's,
Leroy's and Small's nightclubs were the rage, invaded by tuxedo-clad
and expensively-gowned whites. Harlem was on everyone's list of places
to go. Black entertainers were the rage. The New York Public Library
had established the Schomburg Collection of Negro Literature and
History. But all was not as it seemed. Harlem was inhabited by blacks
but owned by whites. Most of the theatres and nightclubs were owned
by whites as were the stores and businesses of Harlem."

White intellectuals acted as patrons and, to a degree, exploiters
of promising young black writers and artists. The Carl Van Vechtens
made their comfortable apartment a center for black writers. Taylor
Gordon, the partner of J. Rosamond Johnson, described Carl Van
Vechten as "dressed in a long green lounging gown. The soft collar
of his white shirt was standing wide open and his white hair stood up
like a music-master's over his large red forehead." His piercing blue
eyes took Gordon's breath away. The actress Fania Marinoff, Van
Vechten's wife, appeared in a Japanese robe, "a bewitching creature
five feet six, exquisite figure, dark eyes, fascinating face with a head
full of jet black hair and keen feet!"

Muriel Draper's salon rivaled the Van Vechtens'; her emphasis
was on music. "Having the great wisdom of many and being a marvelous writer," Gordon wrote, "is not enough for her. She knows how
to drape her shapely figure in all materials—window curtains, silk
bedspreads, satins, Spanish shawls—so that no matter where or how
big the party may be people always ask, Who is that woman?"

As we have noted, the Harlem Renaissance depended in large
part on the sympathy and sponsorship of the new white intellectual
class. Langston Hughes wrote: "We younger Negro artists who create
now intend to express our individual dark-skinned selves without fear
or shame. If white people are pleased we are glad. If they are not, it
doesn't matter. . . . If colored people are pleased we are glad. If they
are not, their displeasure doesn't matter either." Brave as this declaration of artistic independence was, it was only provisionally true. A

writer without readers is only half a writer. Hughes was as dependent on the response of his readers, black and white, as any author must be.

His principal patron was a wealthy widow named Charlotte Mason, whose hobby was the sponsoring of black writers. Alain Locke, the discoverer of the New Negro, had been one of her earlier beneficiaries. Mason not only gave money to those black writers who might be said to have constituted her stable but also prescribed what they should read and how they should write in order to express properly what she perceived to be their true selves, and she required them to submit all their work to her for criticism and to write to her every day, addressing her as "Godmother." Mason believed that "primitive peoples," blacks and Indians, were more "spiritual" than "civilized" or posttribal people. In Hughes's words, "Concerning Negroes, she felt that they were America's great link with the primitive . . . that there was mystery and mysticism and spontaneous harmony in their souls . . . and that we had a deep well of the spirit within us and that we should keep it pure and deep." For Hughes's twenty-sixth birthday, she gave him Sandburg's *Lincoln*. Hughes wrote Locke: "She has her victrola now and a great collection of records, all of Paul Robeson, I believe, and almost all the best blues. She loves the 'Soft Pedal' and even the 'Yellow Dog.' And they sound marvelous on her machine." Hughes wrote of her: "No one else had ever been so thoughtful of me or so interested in the things I wanted to do, or so kind and generous toward me."

But such attentions could be suffocating as well as encouraging. It was apparently with Charlotte Mason in mind that Langston Hughes wrote a poem entitled "Poet to Patron":

> What right has anyone to say
> That I
> Must throw out pieces of my heart
> For pay?
>
> For bread that helps to make
> My heart beat true,
> I must sell myself
> To you?
>
> A factory shift's better,
> A week's meager pay,
> Than a perfumed note asking
> *What poems today?*

In New York Hughes wrote and published a number of poems: "Negro," "My People," "Mother to Son." "Negro" became one of the best known of his poems:

> I am a Negro
> Black as the night is black,
> Black like the depths of my Africa.
>
> I've been a slave:
> Caesar told me to keep his door-steps clean.
> I brushed the boots of Washington.
>
> I've been a worker:
> Under my hands the pyramids arose.
> I made mortar for the Woolworth Building.
>
> I've been a singer
> All the way from Africa to Georgia
> I carried my sorrow songs.
> I made ragtime . . .

The poem expressed the artistic dilemma of the American black writer. Hughes was far from "black" in complexion. With almost as many white forebears as black, he was light brown. He had never been to Africa, and when he went, he found that Africans considered him a white man. Neither he nor any member of his family had been, in the strictest sense of the word, a "worker." Most of them had been college-educated when relatively few Americans of either race attended college.

Unhappy at Columbia and determined to see the world, Hughes signed on the *SS Malone* as a messboy and sailed for Africa. When he reached that continent, he was surprised to find that many self-conscious, educated blacks proclaimed themselves followers of Marcus Garvey. Africans, he wrote, "looked at my copper-brown skin and straight black hair, . . . except a little curly—and they said: 'You—white man'."

From Africa Hughes found his way to Paris, which was even more preoccupied with things black than America. Montmartre was the Harlem of Paris. Picasso and other French artists were enamored of African sculpture. The city was full of jazz clubs with black singers like Josephine Baker, Bricktop (Ada Smith), and Mabs Moberly. A black jazz musician told Hughes, "Less you can play or tap dance, you'd just as well go home." Hughes found a job as a doorman at a Montmartre nightclub and then as a dishwasher at Le Grand Duc on the Rue Pigalle. Free from the discrimination that he had experienced in the United States, the months in Paris in a classic French garret were happy ones for Hughes. Alain Locke joined him and introduced him to the cultural riches of the city and to literary figures like Paul Guillaume, who had an outstanding collection of African art.

Italy was next on Hughes's itinerary. He continued to write and sent Locke what became one of his best-known poems, "I, Too":

> I, too, sing America
>
> I am the darker brother.
> They send me to eat in the kitchen
> When the company comes,
> But I laugh,
> And eat well,
> And grow strong.
>
> Tomorrow,
> I'll sit at the table
> When the company comes.
> Nobody'll dare
> Say to me,
> "Eat in the kitchen,"
> Then.
> Besides,
> They'll see how beautiful I am
> And be ashamed—
>
> I, too, am America.

Back in the United States, Hughes decided to abandon Columbia for a black college or university. In trying to save money to enroll at Lincoln University, he got a job as a busboy at the Wardman Park Hotel in Washington, D.C., where, needless to say, no blacks were admitted as guests. While he was there, Vachel Lindsay came to give a poetry reading. The author of "The Congo" and "General Booth Enters Heaven" was at the height of his popularity. Hughes, too diffident to introduce himself to the poet (and not allowed to attend his reading), placed some of his poems beside Lindsay's plate with a note. Lindsay, impressed, read several of them that evening and praised their author, who, he revealed, was a black busboy at the hotel. Hughes immediately became a minor celebrity as newspaper reporters swarmed around to write of the busboy-poet. It was an ironic episode. Hughes, then twenty-four, had spent two years at Columbia University and had been widely published not simply in black literary journals but in such respected "white" magazines as the *Nation,* the *New Republic,* and *Vanity Fair.*

When he enrlled at Lincoln, Hughes was already a highly regarded member of the Harlem Renaissance. He found himself in demand for poetry readings at college campuses, schools, and churches. It was a way of augmenting his modest income; he soon began to read to blues and jazz accompaniments.

"The Weary Blues" began:

> Droning a drowsy syncopated tune,
> Rocking back and forth to a mellow croon,
>     I heard a Negro play.
> Down on Lenox Avenue the other night
> By the pale dull pallor of an old gas light
>     He did a lazy sway . . .
>     He did a lazy sway . . .
> To the tune of those Weary Blues
> With his ebony hands on each ivory key
> He made that poor piano moan with melody.
>     O Blues!

Langston Hughes was one of the first black writers to use jazz and blues themes and tempos in his poetry. "Motto" had the same blues theme:

> I play it cool
> And dig all jive—
> That's the reason
> I stay alive
>
> My motto,
> As I live and learn
> Is
> Dig and be dug
> In return.

Another blues poem of Hughes's was "Minstrel Man":

> Because my mouth
> Is wide with laughter
> And my throat is deep with song,
> You do not think
> I suffer after
> I have held my pain
> So long
>
> Because my mouth
> Is wide with laughter
> You do not hear
> My inner cry.
> Because my feet
> Are gay with dancing
> You do not know
> I die.

Hughes's enthusiasm for blues music led to his collaboration with W. C. Handy on "Golden Brown Blues." Hughes wrote: "The folk blues are pictures of the life from which they come, the life of the levees, of the back alleys, of dissolute streets, the red light districts and the cabarets of those with not even a God to look at. They are a long ways removed from the expectancy and faith of the Spirituals. Their hopeless weariness mixed with absurdly incongruous laughter makes them the most interesting folk songs I have ever heard. Blues are sad songs to the most despondent rhythms in the world. . . . "

While his poetry grew increasingly political (over the protests of his friend Arna Bontemps), it retained its strong "racial" emphasis as in "Flight":

> Plant your toes in the cool swamp mud;
> Step and leave no track.
> Hurry, sweating runner!
> The hounds are at your back.
> No, I didn't touch her.
> White flesh ain't for me.
> Hurry! Black boy, hurry!
> Or they'll swing you to a tree!

For Hughes the shift from "race" poetry to political poetry was signaled by his poem "Merry Christmas," which accompanied an open letter headed "Greeting to the Soviet Workers." The poem ended:

> While Holy steel that makes us strong
> Spits forth a mighty Yuletide song:

SHOOT Merry Christmas everywhere!
Let Merry Christmas GAS the air!

In addition to James Weldon Johnson (really a precursor of the Harlem Renaissance), Claude McKay, and Langston Hughes, there were dozens of other men and women associated with the movement. Rudolph Fisher was one of the more striking figures. A physician, novelist, and short-story writer, Fisher was as famous for his wit as for his skill as a doctor. In his words, "Roland Hayes and Paul Robeson, Jean Toomer and Walter White, Charles Gilpin and Florence Mills— 'Green Thursday,' 'Porgy,' 'In Abraham's Bosom'—Negro spirituals— the startling New African groups proposed for the Metropolitan Museum of Art; Negro stock is going up, and everybody's buying." Hughes wrote of Fisher that he was the "wittiest of these New Negroes of Harlem, whose tongue was flavored with the sharpest and saltiest humor. . . . I used to wish I could talk like Rudolph Fisher. Besides being a good writer, he was an excellent singer, and had sung with Paul Robeson during their college days."

Nathan Eugene "Jean" Toomer, was the author of *Cane,* a book of prose and verse. Toomer's second marriage was to a white woman, Marjorie Content, the wealthy daughter of a New York stockbroker. In addition to "crossing over," Jean Toomer became a devoted follower of Georges Gurdjieff, one of the first modern gurus, who established the Institute for the Harmonious Development of Man at Fontainebleau.

Hubert Harrison was a familiar Harlem figure, toting his stepladder about and mounting it to harangue any listeners he could attract on the advantages of socialism. Harrison had been born in the Virgin Islands and grew up in Harlem. He founded a series of short-lived black magazines and served, for a time, as editor of Marcus Garvey's *Negro World.* To young Henry Miller, Harrison was a "soapbox orator without peer. . . . There was no one in those days . . . who could hold a candle to Hubert Harrison. With a few well-directed words he had the ability to demolish any opponent." Miller admired "the wonderful way he smiled, his easy assurance, the great sculptured head which he carried on his shoulders like a lion . . . he was a man who electrified one by his mere presence. Beside him . . . other speakers, the white ones, looked like pygmies, not only physically but culturally, spiritually."

One of the most exotic figures of the Harlem Renaissance was

Taylor Gordon, whose autobiography, *Born to Be,* published in 1929 and illustrated by the artist Miguel Covarrubias, was one of the literary events of the season. Gordon was born in 1893 in White Sulphur Springs, Montana. His father cooked for mining companies, and his mother took in washing. Young Gordon had a kind of classic small-town Western boyhood. Since his was the only black family in town, he was hardly conscious of racial prejudice. He was an outstanding athlete and hustled and ran errands for the prostitutes who provided services for the miners who crowded the town on Saturday nights. He also became a skilled mechanic. The famous circus entrepreneur John Ringling owned substantial portions of Montana adjacent to White Sulphur Springs. He met Gordon there and engaged him to be his chauffeur. After several years with Ringling, Gordon tried making it on his own, working as a railroad porter, a doorman at a theater, and various odd jobs, returning eventually to Florida to work as a cook and handyman on Ringling's private Pullman car and finally finding a career as a singer with Rosamond Johnson, James Weldon Johnson's brother. Gordon and Johnson performed in concert throughout the United States and then traveled through England and Europe, giving concerts. In England the two black men were lionized. The tall, handsome Gordon with his "cowboy" background was a special favorite. He met John Galsworthy, Somerset Maugham, Lady Astor, and dozens of other notables, literary and social.

Gordon was the epitome of the elegant, cultivated Harlem black doted on by liberal whites. A natty dresser with a style all his own, he was befriended by Carl Van Vechten, who both encouraged his singing career and urged him to write a book about his adventures on the way from White Sulphur Springs to Harlem. Van Vechten described Taylor as a "lanky six-feet, falsetto voice, molasses laugh, and . . . a brain that functions and an eye that can see." It was Van Vechten who introduced Gordon to Muriel Draper. Draper, like Van Vechten, was always on the lookout for promising black artists—writers and musicians—to take under her wing. She encouraged Gordon to write his autobiography and became, in effect, his editor, helping him with his book, *Born to Be,* most of which he wrote in A'Lelia Walker's Dark Tower. In *Born to Be* Taylor Gordon thanked Draper, "broad-minded caucasian . . . who published the books that kept me from committing suicide when I was in love, and believed my people had always been the inferior race, a band of slaves. That particular infatuation started me reading everything I could get my hands on, and was the cause that lifted high the dark shadows on my life before me. . . . I paid many a sleepless night for my admission into light."

Another important literary figure was Arna Bontemps, who had been born in Louisiana and reared in California, where he had graduated from Pacific Union College. Bontemps was described by Horace Cayton as "extremely good-looking, a beautiful brown color, [with] long wavy hair." Like Hughes, he had just begun to be published in *Crisis*, and he and Hughes became fast friends and, in time, collaborators. One of Bontemps's best-known poems was entitled "A Black Man Talks of Reaping":

> I have sown beside all waters in my day.
> I planted deep, within my heart the fear
> that wind or fowl would take the grain away.
> I planted safe against this stark, lean year.
>
> I scattered seed enough to plant the land
> in rows from Canada to Mexico
> but for my reaping only what the hand
> can hold at once is all that I can show
>
> Yet what I sowed and what the orchard yields
> my brother's sons are gathering stalk and root;
> small wonder then my children glean in field
> they have not sown, and feed on bitter fruit.

Wallace Thurman had been born to prosperous black parents in Salt Lake City, and after graduating from the University of Southern California, he had come to New York and entered at once into the literary life of Harlem. He presided over a black salon at 267 West 136th Street, where black and white writers and artists gathered. The building had been bought by a black businesswoman named Iolanthe Sydney, who turned it into apartments for writers and artists. Thurman was a homosexual, and several of his lovers had been white writers, a fact of which he seemed excessively proud. One of his friends, Bruce Nugent, said of him: "Wallie had a fascination for people that only the devil could have—an almost diabolical power." Hughes was the opposite, for "he couldn't touch anyone without making them better. He brought out the good in every one . . . he was not corrupted." Thurman was the editor of two literary journals that published primarily the work of black writers, the *Messenger* and *Harlem*. He published a number of Hughes's poems and his first short story.

Countee Cullen, a protégé of Alain Locke's, was much influenced by Keats and felt that Hughes was too preoccupied with racial and political themes. Cullen married W. E. B. Du Bois's daughter, Yolande, in one of Harlem's premier social events. It turned out to be a brief alliance.

A well-known Cullen poem was "Yet Do I Marvel":

> I doubt not God is good, well-meaning, Kind.
> And did He stoop to quibble could tell why
> The little buried mole continues blind,
> Why flesh that mirrors Him must some day die,
> Makes plain the reason tortured Tantalus
> Is baited by the fickle fruit, declare
> If merely brute caprice dooms Sisyphus
> To struggle up a never-ending stair.
> Inscrutable His ways are, and immune
> To catechism by a mind too strewn
> With petty cares to slightly understand
> What awful brain compels His awful hand.
> Yet do I marvel at this curious thing:
> To make a poet black, and bid him sing!

Charles Spurgeon Johnson was one of the three people, in Hughes's opinion, who, with Jessie Fauset, an editor of *Crisis*, and Alain Locke, "mid-wifed the so-called New Negro literature into being." As the editor of the magazine *Opportunity* Charles Johnson encouraged black talent wherever he found it.

Fenton Johnson, born in Chicago in 1888 to a prosperous black family and educated at the University of Chicago, published his first poem in 1914, six years before the Harlem Renaissance, and edited several small poetry magazines. One of his best-known poems was "Tired":

> I am tired of work; I am tired of building up
>   somebody else's civilization
> Let us take a rest, M'Lissy Jane.
>
> I will go down to the Last Chance Saloon, Drink a gallon
>   or two of gin, shoot a game or two of dice and sleep
>   the rest of the night on one of Mike's barrels.
> You will let the old shanty go to rot, the white people's
>   clothes turn to dust, the Calvary Baptist Church sink
>   to the bottomless pit.

You will spend your days forgetting you married me and your
    nights hunting the warm gin Mike's serves the ladies
    in the rear of the Last Chance Saloon.

Throw the children into the river; civilization has given us
    too many. It is better to die than to grow up and find
    that you are colored.

Pluck the stars out of the heavens. The stars mark our
    destiny. The stars marked my destiny.

I am tired of civilization.

Many gifted black women were involved in the Harlem Renaissance. Zora Neale Hurston and Gwendolyn Bennett were among the black women writers who contributed to Wallace Thurman's *Messenger* and *Harlem*. The two women undertook to start a literary journal of their own with the title *Fire!!* Hurston had studied at Howard and at Barnard and been a student of Franz Boas in graduate school. "Blind guitar players, conjur men, and former slaves were her quarry, small town jooks and plantation churches her haunts," Langston Hughes wrote. She was, he added, "a perfect book of entertainment in herself." Like Alain Locke and Langston Hughes, Zora Neale Hurston was a protégé of Charlotte Mason's. Hurston addressed her "Godmother" in terms of mock humility, referring to herself as "Godmother's primitive child" and "dumb darkey," and "loving pickaninny." She wrote: "There was and is a psychic bond between us. She could read my mind, not only when I was in her presence, but thousands of miles away." She wrote to Mason: "I am meeting you at the altar place and I am acquiescent."

Jessie Redmon Fauset was born in Philadelphia in 1882. A Phi Beta Kappa graduate of Cornell, she wrote four novels. The best known, a novel of middle-class black life, was titled *There Is Confusion*. McKay wrote: "[A]ll the radicals like her, although in her social viewpoint she was away over on the other side of the fence." She was, in fact, an OP, or Old Philadelphian, a member of a family that prided itself on its background and social position in the black community as much as did any of the city's white aristocrats.

One of the most influential members of the Harlem literary (and increasingly political) group was Louise Thompson, who was graduated from the University of California at Berkeley in 1923, having majored in economics and business and minored in Spanish. Although she was light enough to pass as a white, she found the doors of white businesses closed to her. She went on to do graduate work at the University of Chicago and then taught briefly in a black college at Pine Bluff, Arkansas, and at the Hampton Institute before coming to Harlem in 1928. She was striking looking, and her arrival caused a stir in the rather ingrown community of black literati.

Louise Thompson's apartment was an intellectual center for black artists and intellectuals. Paul Robeson, Langston Hughes, young Ralph Ellison, Richard Wright, and Hughes's friend Jacques Romain, the Haitian poet, were often members of intellectual "jam sessions, long discussions" of such writers as Marcel Proust, James Joyce, Fyodor Dostoyevski, and André Gide.

Louis Thompson and Augusta Savage started Vanguard, an organization designed to educate upper-class Harlemites to "new and progressive" trends in the arts. Vanguard sponsored dance and theater groups, musical programs, and political forums, as well as Marxist study groups.

Margaret Bonds was a gifted black pianist and composer who had appeared with the Chicago Symphony. She became a friend of Langston Hughes and wrote the music for his poem "The Negro Speaks of Rivers," for Marian Anderson to sing.

Black women felt that they suffered both from white prejudice and from the sexual arrogance and domineering attitudes of black males. Nannie H. Burroughs, a leader of black women, wrote: "The Negro woman 'totes' more water; grows more corn; picks more cotton; washes more clothes; cooks more meals; nurses more babies; mammies more Nordics; supports more churches; does more race uplifting; serves as mud-sills for more climbers; takes more punishment; does more forgiving; gets less protection and appreciation, than do the women in any other civilized group in the world. She has been the economic and social slave of mankind."

Harlem had, of course, a strong attraction for whites. They poured into Harlem night spots such as the Cotton Club, where black patrons were barred, to watch black entertainers, and they also haunted "black and white" nightclubs, where the races mixed daringly. "Thousands of whites came to Harlem night after night," Langston Hughes wrote, "thinking the Negroes loved to have them there, and firmly believing that all Harlemites left their houses at sundown to sing and dance in cabarets, because most of the whites saw nothing but the cabarets, not the houses." It was, in fact, part of the spirit that fostered the Harlem Renaissance itself. Blacks were in style. In the words of Langston Hughes, "Some Harlemites thought the millennium had come" with the Harlem Renaissance. "They thought the race problem had been solved through Art. . . . I don't know what made any Negroes think that—except they were mostly intellectuals doing the thinking. The ordinary Negroes hadn't heard of the Negro Renaissance." Hughes had had "a swell time while it lasted. But I thought it wouldn't last long . . . [for] how could a large and enthusiastic number of people be crazy about Negroes forever?"

There was, indeed, a consuming fad for things black—for black poems, black novels, black plays, black life. In part it was a hunger for information about an exotic side of American life. It couldn't last forever, and it wasn't the millennium, but it had a strong and enduring impact on the consciousness first of black leaders and intellectuals and then their white counterparts.

Hughes wrote in his autobiography, *The Big Sea,* "It was a period when, at almost every Harlem upper-crust dance or party, one would be introduced to various distinguished white celebrities there as guests. It was a period when almost any Harlem Negro of any social importance at all would be likely to say casually: 'As I was remarking to Heywood,' meaning Heywood Broun. Or: 'As I said to George,' referring to George Gershwin. It was a period when local and visiting royalty were not at all uncommon in Harlem. And when the parties of A'Lelia Walker, the Negro heiress, were filled with guests whose names would turn any Nordic social climber green with envy. It was a period when Harold Jackman, a handsome young Harlem school teacher of modest means, calmly announced one day that he was sailing for the Riviera for a fortnight to attend Princess Murat's yachting party. It was a period when Charleston preachers opened up shouting churches as sideshows for white tourists. . . . It was a period when every season there was at least one hit play on Broadway acted by a Negro cast. And when books by Negro authors were being published with much greater frequency and much more publicity than ever before or since in history. It was a period when white writers wrote about Negroes more successfully (commercially speaking) than Negroes did about themselves. . . . It was the period when the Negro was in vogue." W. E. B. Du Bois wrote in the *Crisis,* that "in the dull brain of white America, it is beginning to become clearly evident that the most virile future force in this land, certainly in art, probably in economics and possibly in science, is the Negro."

But there was also, as Hughes noted, a negative side to white attentions. "One of the great difficulties about being a member of a minority race," he wrote, "is that so many kindhearted, well-meaning bores gather around to help you. Usually, to tell the truth, they have nothing to help with, except their company—which is often appallingly dull." Hughes described a black social worker named Caleb Johnson, "who was always dragging around with him some non-descript white person or two, inviting them to dinner, showing them Harlem, ending up at the Savoy—much to the displeasure of whatever friends of his might be out that evening for fun, not sociology. . . . We literary ones in those days considered ourselves too broad-minded to be bothered with questions of color. We liked people of any race who smoked incessantly, drank liberally, wore complexion and morality as loose garments, and made fun of anyone who didn't do likewise. We snubbed and high-hatted any Negro or white luckless enough not to understand Gertrude Stein, Man Ray . . . Jean Toomer, or George Antheil."

The issue of the relationship between black men and white women remained an awkward one. When Bertrand Russell came to the United States, he expressed a desire to see something of the famous night life of Harlem. Tommy Smith, Horace Liveright's "editorial chief," gave a party for Russell and invited Sherwood Anderson and two black women, graduates of Bryn Mawr or Smith, "from the very upper crust of Harlem's social and intellectual set." Anderson noted: "They were also very beautiful . . . both slender and tall, both with rich high brown skins and both beautifully clad." They—Russell and Anderson, Smith and the two black women—dined and then went to a cabaret, "a brown and white place." Smith and Russell danced, but only with other white women. Anderson danced with the black women, who danced "wonderfully," and then endured the reproaches of Russell, who told him, "It isn't done, old chap."

Horace Cayton, whose first wife was white, found increasing difficulty in establishing close and affectionate relationships with men and women of his own race. Restless and unhappy, he decided to undergo a classic Freudian analysis with a white woman doctor. The analysis lasted five years, and its crucial point came when Cayton confessed, "Yes—I hate white people. Not all of them, but the idea of white people as a group. I hate them for what they have done to me, to my parents, to my people. I do hate them but I never realized it before." His analysis led him to consider the possibility that fear was also involved. Cayton jumped at that formulation, a cycle of fear-hate-fear.

Richard Wright told Jerre Mangione that he would never consider marrying a white woman. Yet several years after his first marriage to a black woman had ended in divorce, Wright married a Jewish woman. Mangione speculated that *Native Son* and his short stories had allowed Wright to expend his hatred of whites and accept the fact that certain whites could be friends or, in his marriage, lovers.

Middle-class black women, with their "bourgeois" notions of family life and strict sexual morality, were perceived by many black bohemians as a threat to their free and uninhibited (and highly mobile) way of life. Lower-class black women were apt to be *too* uninhibited, and more important, they lacked the intellectual interests that would make them compatible. There were fewer educated black women than black men. Women like Louise Thompson were friends, colleagues, and occasionally mistresses or wives successively to half a dozen black males. It was almost as though they had to be shared, as though there were not enough to go around. Finally, there was the fact that the intense nature, the almost hothouse atmosphere of the Harlem Renaissance, taking the phrase in its broadest connotations, encouraged close intellectual and emotional ties between men.

Despite his homosexual inclinations, Langston Hughes, who was very attractive to women, had intensely romantic affairs with a famous Russian dancer, a Chinese actress and singer, and, when he was in his fifties, a beautiful black graduate student at the University of Chicago. Walter White married a white woman. The very fact that sexual relations between black men and white women—though not, of course, the other way, white men and black women—had so long been taboo and indeed still were taboo for whites outside the more advanced intellectual circles may have been an incentive to blacks seeking emancipation from white prejudices. At the lower end of the social scale in both North and South sexual relations between black men and white women were common.

Cynics might question whether white writers, playwrights, and librettists for Broadway musicals did not profit more from the Harlem Renaissance than blacks. Out of more than a dozen plays on Broadway with black themes during the period of the Harlem Renaissance, roughly from 1919 to the crash in 1929, only three were by black playwrights. Dorothy and DuBose Heyward and Marc Connelly were white writers who had Broadway hits with *Porgy* and *Green Pastures,* respectively.

Eugene O'Neill was especially sensitive to the new currents of black expression. Between 1916 and 1924 he wrote three plays with "black" themes: *The Dreamy Kid, The Emperor Jones,* and *All God's Chillun.* They all were manifestations of the major theme of the new consciousness—the primacy of the passional and instinctive over the rational and intellectual, in Freudian terms the struggle of the id against the policemanlike ego.

In 1923 another white author, Waldo Frank, checked in with the by now almost obligatory "Negro" novel, *Holiday.* The central theme is the expressive, uninhibited life of Southern blacks in the little town of Nazareth, as contrasted with the rigid and repressive mores of the local whites, symbolized by Judge Hade (as perhaps in Hades?). John Cloud is a handsome young black man in love with Mary Cartier, but Judge Hade's daughter, Virginia, who is drawn irresistibly to Cloud, brings on tragedy. His hesitant responses to Virginia are interpreted by whites as sexual aggressiveness on Cloud's part, and he is lynched.

Sherwood Anderson wrote a "black" novel, *Tar,* and the genteel South Carolinian Julia Peterkin wrote three novels about Southern blacks, *Green Thursday, Black April,* and *Scarlet Sister Mary,* the latter two of which were best-sellers.

Carl Van Vechten's novel *Nigger Heaven,* published in 1926, was an instant hit and made his literary reputation. Langston Hughes wrote, perhaps a little enviously, that "colored people can't help but like it. It sounds as if it were written by a NAACP official or Jessie Fauset. But it's good." The book was attacked by many black reviewers as an exploitation of their race, but James Weldon Johnson praised it, as did Wallace Thurman and Charles S. Johnson. Hughes assured Van Vechten that "more Negroes bought it than ever purchased a book by a Negro author."

All black writers had a major problem to deal with in their relationship to white writers, whose sponsorship and encouragement they needed (they also badly needed white readers since there were not enough sophisticated black readers to constitute a market for the poems, short stories, plays, and essays of black authors). The price they paid for their relationship to white writers and patrons was that they were constantly being advised about what black themes would be most appealing to white readers. Within their own ranks they had to confront the meaning of being a "black." (The prevailing word in that era was "Negro," which had only recently replaced "colored" in the use of blacks themselves.) Not surprisingly, they often changed their minds. Countee Cullen for a time insisted that he was a *writer,* a poet specifically, who happened to be black. Langston Hughes through most of his literary career insisted that he was a *black* writer. If black writers wrote about "low-down" blacks, black pimps and hustlers, the jazzmen and women singers, the tenant farmers or the desperately marginal poor blacks of the big-city ghettos, they were accused by middle-class blacks of pandering to and reinforcing white stereotypes of blacks as lazy, tap-dancing, happy-go-lucky, promiscuous types. Since the Civil War middle- and upper-class blacks had struggled desperately to gain respectability and win white acceptance. To see the qualities of lower-class blacks that they deplored in a sense celebrated by black writers was unsettling to them. The emphasis of black writers like Hughes and Claude McKay (and white writers like Carl Van Vechten) on black sexuality was especially unnerving to upper-class blacks, most of whom were as puritanical in their sexual code as their white counterparts. Of all the psychological tensions between blacks and whites, none was more persistent or severe than those revolving around sex. In the South it was symbolized in horrifying form by the lynching of alleged rapists; rape, as we have seen, could consist of speaking to a white woman in any but a humble and subservient tone of voice. The irony in all this was that the black writers, almost without exception, were themselves members of the black middle or, more commonly, upper class, often college-educated men and women with strong family traditions of education and cultivation.

Not only was there a color barrier for promising black writers to contend with, but there was an education barrier. There was little incentive for blacks with strong intellectual interests to go to college; only too often jobs as redcaps, waiters, and Pullman porters awaited them. At the same time, when jobs for which they were suited by experience and intelligence turned up, blacks who had not gone to college found that fact cited as the reason for not hiring them. Claude McKay wrote to Max Eastman toward the end of his life when he was still searching desperately for employment, "You should be aware that the chief reason why I have not had an opportunity equal to my intellectual attainments is simply because I have no close academic associates nor college degree, and also I am a Negro. My racial group is even more than the white, narrow and hidebound about college qualifications. I know many persons in it who are not very capable, but have good jobs because they are graduates of Harvard, Yale, and Columbia." When white library officials offered Arthur Schomburg, the great black bibliophile, a job as curator of his own collection, black academics, led by W. E. B. Du Bois, protested on the ground that Schomburg did not have a college degree.

From one perspective the Harlem Renaissance was a by-product of the new consciousness, which is not to denigrate the importance of the movement or the talent of the able and courageous company of men and women who created it and made an important contribution to the literature of the period. Because it was so racially and politically oriented, it performed a deep and essential service in the creation of a "black" consciousness which, if in certain specific ways a component of the new consciousness, was certainly distinguishable from it and was as important in the emancipation of black people as any set of statutes or judicial decisions. As long as white people defined black people, as long as the interpretation of what it was to be black in white America remained in the hands of white Americans, blacks could not fully claim their own souls. The only people who could change white perceptions of blacks were blacks themselves. To do so required a struggle as dramatic in its own way as any in the political arena. The black middle and upper classes had to identify themselves, body and soul, with the oppressed blacks of the cities and the black sharecroppers of the South. The racial solidarity that had existed before the Civil War and that had, in a large degree, disintegrated after the war had to be reestablished.

Finally, there was the fact that the mind was the one territory where white prejudice could not constrain or bar the way. "I learned very early," Ralph Ellison wrote, "that in the realm of imagination all people and their ambitions and interests could meet." He wrote of his years at Tuskegee Institute: "In Macon County, Alabama, I read Marx, Freud, T. S. Eliot, Pound, Gertrude Stein and Hemingway. Books which seldom, if ever, mentioned Negroes were to release me from whatever 'segregated' idea I might have had of my human possibilities. I was freed not by propagandists . . . but by composers, novelists, and poets who spoke to me of more interesting and freer ways of life." For young blacks, reading great literature, or simply diverse literature, had a far greater potency than it did for their white counterparts. Despite, in Ellison's words, the "surreal incongruity of . . . our projections," he and his friends could become "Gamblers and scholars, jazz musicians and scientists, Negro cowboys and soldiers from the Spanish-American and First World Wars, movie stars and stunt men, figures from the

Italian Renaissance and literature. . . ." Such images were often "combined with the special virtues of some local bootlegger, the eloquence of some Negro preacher, the strength and grace of some local athlete . . . the elegance in dress and manner of some headwaiter or local doorman." It was the passion of Ellison and his companions "to make any-everything of quality *Negro American*; to appropriate it, possess it, re-create it in our own group and individual images." They knew intuitively that there was a black "style" apparent "in jazzmen and prize fighters, ballplayers and tap dancers; in gesture, inflection, intonation, timbre and phrasing. Indeed, in all those nuances of expression and attitudes which reveal a culture." They had only the dimmest notion of the price which had been paid for that style, but they "recognized within it an affirmation of life beyond all question of our difficulties as Negroes."

In the 1920s and 1930s black writers, jazz musicians, and ministers of the more affluent black big-city churches were the most cosmopolitan Americans of their generation. One way or another most of them managed to travel widely and were treated with hospitality and even lionized by the artists and radical intellectuals in most of the countries they visited. This was, of course, especially true in the Soviet Union. Indeed, American blacks could be said to have had a kind of dual citizenship: that of the United States, where they were the constant victims of discrimination, and a kind of world citizenship. They wrote and talked constantly of the brotherhood of the colored peoples of the world as part of the anticipated world socialist order. They experienced an exhilarating feeling of freedom when they stepped onto foreign soil. Langston Hughes told of encountering hostility from a hotel manager in London when he tried to register. When the manager discovered Hughes was an American black instead of an Indian, he was profuse in his apologies.

Hughes was, of course, one of the most widely traveled writers of his day. He visited Mexico, Cuba, and other Latin American countries and was lionized in Paris. Carmel, California, where he stayed with Lincoln Steffens and Ella Winter, was a kind of second home. In Paris, at a writer's conference, Hughes met Stephen Spender, W. H. Auden, and John Strachey from England, Pablo Neruda from Chile, Ilya Ehrenburg from Russia, and André Malraux. Paris, as we have noted, was full of black singers and jazz musicians. With Nancy Cunard, Hughes visited the nightclub where his old friend Bricktop was singing. Cunard called Hughes the "travelling star of coloured America, the leader of the younger intellectuals," and she and Neruda published his poem "Song of Spain," as one of a series with the English title of "The Poets of the World Defend the Spanish People." Hughes wrote: "Nancy Cunard was kind and good and catholic and cosmopolitan and sophisticated and simple all at the same time and a poet of no mean abilities and an appreciator of the rare and the offbeat from jazz to ivory bracelets and witch doctors to Cocteau. . . ." But Hughes could not convert her to chitterlings.

Hughes established strong ties with Cuban and Haitian poets, translating some of the Cubans' poems into English for the *New Masses* and the *Nation*. The American domination of Haiti was a revelation to Hughes, who wrote, "Ashore, you are likely to soon run into groups of marines in the little cafes, talking in 'Cracker' accents and drinking in the usual boisterous American way. . . . And if you read the Haitian newspaper, you will soon realize from the heated complaints there, that even in the Chamber of Deputies, the strings of government are pulled by white politicians in far-off Washington—and that the American marines are kept in the country through an illegal treaty thrust upon Haiti by force. . . ."

Because the Communists made equality for colored peoples the world over a central credo, the Soviet Union was a mecca for American blacks. Hughes, who visited Russia a number of times, reported that there were among the "permanent foreign working residents of Moscow, perhaps two dozen Negroes . . . and colored people mix so thoroughly in the life of the big capital, that you cannot find them merely by seeking out their color." Like McKay before him, Hughes was treated as a celebrity. A Russian journalist described him as "a revolutionary poet who uses his writing as a weapon in the struggle against capitalism, for the emancipation of toiling Negroes and toiling humanity in all countries." Hughes wrote that Moscow was the "only place I've ever made enough to live from writing. Poets and writers in the Soviet Union are highly regarded and paid awfully well as a class, I judge, the best cared for literary people in the world." In Moscow he met the French poet Louis Aragon, for years Nancy Cunard's lover and now married to an ardent Russian Communist, Elsa Triolet. He also got to know Karl Radek and other "theoreticians" high in Soviet circles.

Claude McKay's decade abroad included visits to Germany, Russia, Spain, and North Africa, but most of his time was spent in southern France. Horace Cayton, like other American blacks, walked the streets of Paris with a feeling of happiness and freedom that he had never felt in the United States. For many American blacks the absence of sexual taboos was one of the most striking facts, but for Cayton the experience of having his hair cut by a white barber in Paris was the most emotional experience of all. It was the "last racial taboo I had to break and in many ways the most difficult," he wrote.

Cosmopolitan world travelers though they were, alienated as they were from white America, black writers and intellectuals discovered, usually to their surprise, that they were also profoundly American. Like Hughes, Horace Cayton was taken up by Nancy Cunard. Cunard, living with the black jazz musician Henry Crowder, lectured to Cayton on black art and black sensibility. She took him to a "circus," a sexual performance involving men, women, and animals, and then upbraided him for not asserting that he hated America. Wasn't he loyal to his own people? she asked. Offended by her manner, Cayton replied, "I don't need any white person to tell me how to act. . . . I'm not trying to justify racial practices in the United States. But I don't hate all of America."

When Cunard took Cayton to her apartment, apparently with the intention of seducing him, he discovered her remarkable collection of books on blacks, many in foreign languages, and her collection of African art. She was compiling an anthology of "Negro writings and writings about Negroes from contributors around the world." It was the most complete collection that Cayton had ever seen. Why had she done it? Cayton asked. "I did it, my dear," Cunard replied, "because your people, the black people, shall inherit the earth. Since I have come to know Negroes I have turned my back on my own people. They seem pale, and their white bodies make me a little ill. I love Negroes. I am going to devote my life to making up for what the white people of the world have done to them."

Cunard resumed her attack on the United States, urging Cayton to move to Paris. "America is crude, brutal, uncivilized. I've helped musicians to become established in Paris; I would help you." When Cayton refused to make love to her, she challenged him: "You are afraid, afraid of white women. I should have realized that. But you aren't from the South! What has America done to your manhood?" Cayton, furious, reflected as he walked home that he would never understand white people—nor why he was unalterably American.

Although A. Philip Randolph was not a prominent figure in the Harlem Renaissance, he became a power in the black community. Randolph was the second son of an African Methodist Episcopal minister.

He was born in Crescent City, Florida, in 1889 and grew up in Jacksonville. His older brother, James, and his mother encouraged him to set his sights on a higher education. At the age of twenty-two Randolph left Jacksonville to pursue a career as an actor in New York. He found the opportunities for a black actor limited, to say the least, and for six years he lived a hand-to-mouth existence, taking a succession of menial jobs, attending classes at the City College of New York, and occasionally lecturing on black history at the Rand School of Economics, established by George Herron's patroness Carrie Rand to spread the doctrines of Christian socialism. He read Marx and Lenin, joined the Socialist Party, and married a beauty shop operator, Lucille Green, five years older than he. Lucille Green had been a schoolteacher and was a member of the city's black upper class. Her flourishing beauty shop provided a major part of the Randolphs' income. In the same period Randolph found a close friend in Chandler Owen, a student in sociology at Columbia, whose studies had been made possible by a grant from the National League on Urban Conditions Among Negroes, later the National Urban League. The two young men found positions editing the *Hotel Messenger,* a journal of the headwaiters' union. When Randolph and Owen exposed corrupt practices in the union, they were fired, but they scraped together funds to start their own journal, which they titled the *Messenger* and which hewed out a progressive line for black readers. Its banner proclaimed it "The Only Radical Negro Magazine in America."

Owen and Randolph opposed the entry of the United States into the war in 1917 and thereby made themselves the target of Red-hunting Attorney General A. Mitchell Palmer, who called Randolph the "most dangerous Negro in America," a flattering appellation for the twenty-eight-year-old. J. Edgar Hoover, a special assistant to the attorney general, conducted the investigation. Palmer was unable to squelch the *Messenger,* and Randolph continued to turn out editorials denouncing such consequences of racial prejudice as lynching and job discrimination, advising blacks to arm themselves as protection against white harassment. Among his targets was the grand panjandrum of American labor Samuel Gompers, whom Randolph attacked as the "Chief Strike Breaker" in the country. But Randolph's job as an editor of the *Messenger* was insufficient outlet for his remarkable energies. In 1919 the *Messenger* took up the cause of the National Brotherhood of Workers in America, an organization which Randolph helped found;

its goal was the federation of all black unions and the unionization of all black workers. When the national brotherhood expired, Owen and Randolph launched the National Association for the Promotion of Trade Unionism Among Negroes, with Owen as president. Frankly socialistic, the association drew the support of white radicals, although the NAACP kept its distance. The association was supplemented by the Friends of Negro Freedom, with Randolph as president. Having declared themselves socialists, Owen and Randolph began to direct their attention to the specific problems of blacks.

One of the important chapters of black history concerns the efforts of Randolph and Owen to organize the Pullman porters. Porters were among the elite of the black community; their only rivals for prestige were black headwaiters, caterers, teachers, and other black professionals. While their duties were menial—making beds in the Pullman cars, shining shoes, and attending to the comforts of Pullman passengers—they were relatively well paid, and their uniforms and their visibility as well as their mobility made them the object of admiration and envy. Moreover, jobs as Pullman porters were often the only jobs that college-educated blacks could get. Claude McKay worked for a time as a Pullman porter, and porters are the heroes of *Home to Harlem*. Langston Hughes was another black intellectual and college graduate who was glad to get a job as a porter. After a disastrous train wreck a dead porter was identified by his Phi Beta Kappa key as Theodore Seldon, a graduate of Dartmouth College, class of 1922.

The Pullman Company generally followed the policy of hiring Southern blacks on the ground that they had already accommodated themselves to serving white people. By 1920 the company employed more than 10,000 porters. One prominent black leader who had worked as a porter was Perry Howard, Republican national committeeman from Mississippi. Despite the status attached to the job of sleeping car porter, porters were grossly underpaid in comparison to unionized white railroad workers such as conductors and trainmen, and worked under demanding conditions.

A black socialist named Frank Crosswaith founded the Trade Union Committee of Organizing Negro Workers in 1925, and a few months later a group of Pullman porters formed the Brotherhood of Sleeping Car Porters. The acknowledged leader of the porters was Ashley L. Totten, who invited Randolph to address the Pullman Porters' Athletic Association. The eloquent and outspoken Randolph, a firm believer in unions for blacks, evoked such an enthusiastic response from his audience that one of his listeners urged him to try to organize the porters.

In 1925, when the Pullman porters made Randolph their leader, his principal claim to fame was his record as one of the editors of a radical black journal and the cofounder of a series of relatively short-lived organizations devoted to the unionizing of black workers. The fact that he had never worked as a Pullman porter and was unfamiliar with their problems at first hand, that he was unabashedly a radical intellectual and something of a dandy provided his opponents with a convenient stick to beat him with but counted for little against his charm, his eloquence, and his ability to win the confidence and affection of those with whom he worked. (Being a natty dresser had never been detrimental to a black leader, as the career of W. E. B. Du Bois demonstrated.) In his long service to the union Randolph revealed an unexpected tenacity. The history of the union from the time that Randolph assumed leadership in 1925 until the day twelve years later, when the Pullman Company finally agreed to recognize the union was one of devastating defeats and setbacks, followed by modest recoveries whereby the patient was barely kept alive.

The Garland Fund, the *Jewish Daily Forward,* the International Pocketbook Makers, and Sidney Hillman's Amalgamated Clothing Workers all contributed to the Brotherhood of Sleeping Car Porters. The addition of Frank Crosswaith, an experienced union organizer and, above all, the dedicated Milton Webster, a friend and ally of Randolph's, helped keep the brotherhood alive. On the West Coast, C. L. Dellums, a resident of Oakland, California, was a valuable addition to the union's staff. Randolph assembled as union leaders and organizers a band of young men distinguished for intelligence, dedication, good looks, and sharp dressing. It is safe to say that no comparable band of white or black union leaders could match them in masculine pulchritude. What role their good looks played in the history of the union cannot be well calculated, but it may well have been of some considerable consequence.

In any event, Randolph soon realized that his own role as a black leader was inextricably intertwined with his Pullman porters. If they went down to final defeat, his own career would suffer grievously. The issue was not simply the organization of a black union. As the most prominent, visible, and "high-status" black occupation in the country, black professionals aside, the sleeping car porters had a great symbolic importance. It had been said time and again that blacks could not be organized effectively into stable unions. If not the porters, then who? In addition, as long as the union was still breathing, it provided Randolph with a position of great prestige in the black community. It opened doors in the white world that would otherwise have been closed to him, a world that provided desperately needed grants and stipends. It gave his statements in the *Messenger* a weight that they would not otherwise have had. Not least in importance it gave Randolph a voice in the American Federation of Labor which, hostile or indifferent to the problems of black workers, was forced reluctantly to allow him to use its conventions as a platform to press his charges that the AFL treated blacks in the shabbiest fashion. He was the lone champion of black workers, speaking angrily in his "Harvard-accented voice."

At the AFL convention in San Francisco in 1934 the San Francisco-Alameda County branches of the NAACP picketed the meeting hall, protesting the color bar in unions. Brushed aside by William Green, Randolph took up the fight against union discrimination on the floor of the convention. Racist unions, Randolph insisted, should be expelled from the AFL. John L. Lewis and David Dubinsky spoke in support of Randolph's resolution, but it was buried in parliamentary maneuvers. The only positive result was an agreement to appoint a committee to study the question. The NAACP, responding to pressure from Abram Harris, asked Charles Houston, the young black dean of the Howard University Law School, to represent the Brotherhood of Sleeping Car Porters before the AFL's so-called Committee of Five on Negro Discrimination. The committee reported to the Executive Council that widespread racial discrimination did indeed exist in many AFL affiliates. The Council thereupon rewrote the report, in essence adopting the racist views of the committee's one dissenter, George M. Harrison, president of the Brotherhood of Railway Clerks. The final strategy of the AFL executive council was to bury the report under a pile of empty generalizations about the federation's lack of prejudice. Beyond that it tried to obliterate the Brotherhood of Sleeping Car Porters, and the troublesome Randolph with it, by ordering that it be absorbed by the white Order of Sleeping Car Conductors. This move Randolph and the brotherhood rejected, and finally, on July 1, 1935, the Pullman Company and the National Labor Relations Board certified the Brotherhood of Sleeping Car Porters. In the words of the historian of the union's fight for recognition as the legitimate representative of the porters, "Thus ended one of the longest continuous struggles for recognition in the annals of American trade unionism." But two more years passed before the Pullman Company finally signed a union contract with the brotherhood. Ironically, the union was recognized at the moment when competition from buses and airplanes was cutting heavily into railroad travel and the number of porters was declining; the great days of the Pullman car, the luxurious sleepers, and the elegant diners were almost over.

Writing of the struggle, Randolph noted that "hundreds of men lost their jobs. . . . Leaders of the movement like Ashley Totten, Milton P. Webster, Bennie Smith . . . and C. L. Dellums lost their homes and underwent severe privations to put the union over. Totten was nearly murdered by thugs in Kansas City and Smith was threatened with a lynching and driven out of Jacksonville, Florida. These men were former porters, all. None of them received any pay over half the life of the Brotherhood."

The problem of the black intellectual was that many blacks had created an endurable world of their own which accepted white prejudice and all its consequent cruelties as a permanent and intractable fact. To challenge that vast and monolithic structure meant to expose oneself to wounds and dangers, physical and psychological, that were almost too much to contemplate, let alone to bear. The radical black intellectual thus initially encountered strong resistance from those of his own race whom he wished to stir to action; that passivity was almost as great an obstacle to surmount as white prejudice. They were indeed the opposite sides of the same coin. The men and women of the Harlem Renaissance and men like A. Philip Randolph helped rouse that passivity to active involvement.

# 11

## Election of 1928

As the presidential election of 1928 approached, Herbert Hoover was clearly the front-runner for the Republican nomination, which was assumed, in boom times, to mean the presidency.

The Socialist Party met in the early spring and dutifully nominated Norman Thomas for President and James H. Maurer of Pennsylvania for Vice-President. The Workers' Party (the Communists) met in May and nominated William Z. Foster for President and Benjamin Gitlow for Vice-President.

At the Republican Convention in Kansas City Vice-President Charles Dawes had supporters, as did Frank Lowden, ex-governor of Illinois, but it proved to be no contest. Hoover won the nomination with 837 votes out of 1,084 on the first ballot, and Senator Charles Curtis of Kansas was nominated for Vice-President. The Republican platform contained few surprises. It reasserted its support of Prohibition, high protective tariffs, and the Coolidge foreign policy (whatever that was). Having been attacked vigorously by the Democrats for the President's intrusion in Nicaragua, the Republican platform asserted piously that it was "engaged in cooperation with the government of that country upon the task of assisting to restore and maintain peace, order and stability, and in no way infringe upon her sovereign rights." The U.S.

marines in that country were there to protect American lives and property and "to insure a fair and free election. Our policy absolutely repudiates any idea of conquest or exploitation. . . . "

While the Republican Party repudiated the long-fought-over McNary-Haugen bill, it paid lip service to the farm problem by calling for a Federal farm board "authorized to promote the establishment of a farm marketing system and of farmer owned and controlled stabilization corporations . . . to prevent and control surpluses. . . . "

In a brief reply to the formal notification of his nomination, Hoover expressed his determination to "assure national defense, maintain economy in the administration of government, protect American workmen, farmers, and business men alike from competition arising out of lower standards of living abroad [in other words, to support high tariffs], foster individual initiative, insure stability of business and employment, promote foreign commerce, and develop our natural resources," all unremarkable enough. But Hoover went on to stress that in his view the problems facing the country were "more than economic. In a profound sense they are moral and spiritual. . . . Shall the world have peace? Shall prosperity in this nation be more thoroughly distributed? Shall we build steadily toward the idea of equal opportunity to all our people?" Government was more than mere administration, he added; "it is power for leadership and co-operation with the forces of business and cultural life in city, town, and countryside." The presidency was the "inspiring symbol of all that is highest in America's purposes and ideals." It was, above all, with the family that the nation's future rested, Hoover said. "That is the sanctuary of our loftiest ideals, the source of the spiritual energy of our people. . . . Racial progress marches upon the feet of healthy and instructed children. There should be no child in America that is not born and does not live under sound conditions of health; that does not have full opportunity of education from the beginning to the end of our institutions; that is not free from injurious labor; that does not have every stimulation to accomplish the fullest of its capacities."

The fact that Hoover's sentiments were impeccably liberal was emphasized in the introduction to an edition of his speeches published in 1928 by his alma mater, Stanford University. The president of the university, Ray Lyman Wilbur, noted that they were the "measured statements of a new liberalism facing new conditions with courage and with confidence in the individual to act wisely for himself and for his neighbor." Herbert Hoover was indeed close to Walter Lippmann's ideal of the cool, efficient expert. Lippmann described the Great Engineer as "a reformer who is probably more vividly conscious of the defects of American capitalism than any man in public life today." Lippmann was confident that if elected, Hoover would do his best to "purify capitalism of its predatoriness, its commercialism, its waste, and its squalor, and infuse it with a very large measure of democratic consent under highly trained professional leadership"—in essence Lippmann's own prescription for the ills that beset America.

"No one loved Hoover," Rexford Tugwell wrote (that, indeed, was his tragedy), "but everyone—or nearly everyone—respected him. He was not a toady to business . . . he was more its best representative, its better embodiment. He was an administrator of note as well as a humanitarian—of a cold and withdrawn sort, perhaps, but with enormous prestige."

Hoover's formal speech of acceptance, delivered on August 11, 1928, was the first acceptance speech broadcast by radio. In it he stressed the same themes that he had touched on in his letter of reply to his nomination. The problems that faced the nation were the "problems of progress. New and gigantic forces have come into our national life," he told his millions of listeners. Through science and invention there had come "to each of us wider relationships, more neighbors, more leisure, broader vision, higher ambitions, greater problems." He described the nation's condition at the beginning of the Harding administration: "Agriculture was prostrated; land was unsalable; commerce and industry were stagnated; our foreign trade ebbed away; five millions of unemployed walked the streets. Discontent and agitation against our democracy were rampant. Fear for the future haunted every heart." But the Republicans had changed all that. Under their wise and restrained administration a better day had dawned. Taxes had declined along with the national debt. Foreign trade had flourished and, most important, the nation's "faith in the future" had been restored. More than 3,500,000 "new and better homes" had been built, and 9,000,000 had been equipped with electricity. There were millions more telephones and automobiles in the nation. Wages and purchasing power had increased. "Unemployment in the sense of distress is widely disappearing." The population of the country had grown 8 percent, but 11 percent more children were in grade schools, and 66 percent more were in high schools. In colleges and universities the percentage of increase in enrollment was even higher—75 percent. The proudest achievement of the Republicans had been the virtual elimination of poverty. "By poverty," Hoover declared, "I mean the grinding by undernourishment, cold, and ignorance, and fear of old age of those who have the will to work. We in America today are nearer to the final triumph over poverty than ever before in the history of any land. . . . We have not yet reached the goal, but, given a chance to go forward with the policies of the last eight years, we shall soon, with the help of God, be in sight of the day when poverty will be banished from this nation."

Hoover confessed that the "most urgent economic problem in our nation . . .is in agriculture. It must be solved if we are to bring prosperity and contentment to one-third of our people directly and to all of our people indirectly. We have pledged ourselves to find a solution. . . . Farming is and must continue to be an individualistic business of small units and independent ownership. The farm is more than a business; it is a state of living. We do not wish it converted into a mass-production machine." In striving to solve the problems of the farmers, expense must be no obstacle. Several hundred million dollars might be needed for various projects designed to assist the individual farmer. It must be expended without hesitation.

Hoover was especially proud of his achievements as secretary of commerce under two Republican administrations in bringing about cooperation between government and business. He had made it a practice to call together all those interested in the problems of a particular industry—manufacturers, distributors, workers, and consumers—to develop, over a period of time, plans for mutual benefit. Waste had been eliminated, abuses corrected, costs of production lowered, and employment made more stable, all "without interference or regulation by the government." The government's role must be strictly limited to that of an initiator and helpful friend to all parties. What had worked so well with industry, Hoover suggested, should work for farmers.

Finally, the government must undertake a vast program, running into the billions of dollars, to "co-ordinate transportation with flood control, the development of hydro-electric power and of irrigation . . . the largest engineering construction ever undertaken by any government." It would involve "three times the expenditure laid out upon the Panama Canal."

The last eight years of "magnificent progress" had proved the "fundamental correctness of our economic system." It must be credited to "our magnificent educational system . . . the hard-working character of our people . . . , the capacity of farsighted leadership in industry, the ingenuity, the daring of the pioneers of new inventions, in the abolition of the saloon, and the wisdom of our national [Republican] policies." All these splendid accomplishments rested, in the final analysis, upon the faith of the American people in the "integrity of business men. . . . Our whole system would break down in a day if there was not a high sense of moral responsibility in our business world." He paused in his unstinting praise of the nation's progress to lay a couple of licks on "socialism," which, above all else, contradicted the precious American tradition of individualism.

Governor Al Smith was as much a front-runner among the Democrats as Hoover among the Republicans. The only Democrat in a position to challenge Smith was Franklin Delano Roosevelt, but Howe and Roosevelt were of one mind in preparing to sit this election out. While Eleanor and Franklin Roosevelt announced their early support for a Smith candidacy and Roosevelt worked hard for his fellow New Yorker in the South, where the greatest opposition lay, he was not entirely disinterested. He told Josephus Daniels, "I am doubtful whether any Democrat can win in 1928." Since Smith was eager to have another try, Roosevelt was delighted to assist. If Smith had been reluctant or unwilling to run, it would have been difficult for Roosevelt to refuse the party's draft. If Smith were to win the nomination and lose the election, the way would be cleared for Roosevelt's own candidacy four years later.

Howe's timetable called for Roosevelt to run for President in 1932 or perhaps 1936 if the country was still booming in 1932. When Roosevelt was urged in 1926 to run for the Senate from New York State, he had replied: "There are two good reasons why I can't run for the Senate. The first is that my legs are coming back in such fine shape that if I devote another two years to them I shall be on my feet again without my braces. The 2nd is that I am temperamentally unfitted to be a member of that uninteresting body known as the United States Senate. I like administrative or executive work. . . ." Perhaps a more basic reason was that being a Senator would have inevitably involved him in controversial political issues that might have damaged his chance to be President.

Al Smith was one of the century's most appealing political figures. In 1926 he had won an unprecedented fourth term as governor of New York. Although he projected a classic Irish image, he was actually a mix of English, Irish, German, and Italian—one quarter each. Two women, Belle Moskowitz and Frances Perkins, were his mentors. As a member of the Factory Investigating Commission Perkins induced Smith to observe the conditions of working people at first hand while he was still a state legislator. Deeply affected by what he had seen, Smith said to her: "The industries of this state can surely afford to put their premises into conditions that won't burn people br poison them or give them industrial diseases or cut off their hands or put out their eyes. And it can afford, too, to make their hours of work civilized so that they can stay home nights. And if that means raising the wages then I think they've got to do that. I don't think it's right to let this kind of thing go on unchecked." In the era of "normalcy" after the war, Smith had been one of the few governors to fight for social legislation. An old Tammany man explained Smith's obsession by saying, "He read a book." The "book" was Frances Perkins.

Perkins, who worked closely with Smith through his terms as governor, believed his capacity for leadership stemmed from "his capacity to love, to love personally and to extend that personal love which he had for individuals and his family to embrace thousands of other people whom he could actually feel to be his brothers and sisters and to feel with them and for them and sense how their backs ached and their feet ached. And then he had the capacity to translate into practical action this love of his fellows. This would never seem to him or to anyone else a pious pose."

To Eleanor Roosevelt the key to Al Smith was that as a self-made man who gloried in "his success in overcoming difficulties," he felt a kind of contempt for those who, like Franklin Roosevelt, had been born with the proverbial silver spoons in their mouths and admired inordinately those who had achieved material success through their own efforts. He wore expensive tailor-made suits and ate gourmet foods; they were tangible marks of his rise in the world. The Roosevelts, on the other hand, seemed indifferent to what they put into their mouths; scrambled eggs were preferred to oysters Rockefeller. Roosevelt boasted of buying shirts for $1.50 and never had more than two pairs of well-worn shoes.

Eleanor Roosevelt admired Smith's "extraordinary flair for government and his phenomenal memory." She "believed in him and considered him a great man in many ways" and worked cheerfully and wholeheartedly for his election. And she was among those who credited Belle Moskowitz with much of the "humanitarian" legislation that Smith got credit for. Moskowitz, according to Herbert Bayard Swope, played a major role in keeping Smith on the liberal path until 1928.

Skillful as he was in managing Tammany Hall and big-city politicians, Smith was woefully inept in his dealings with Southerners and rural politicos from the Midwest. It was said that he received a delegation of Kansas Democrats "in a swallowtail coat [he had been to the christening of a friend's daughter], a silk hat at a rakish angle and with the usual cigar in his mouth . . . 'Hello, boys,' said Smith. . . . 'Glad to see you. Y'know, the other day some boys were in from Wisconsin and I learned somethin'. I always thought Wisconsin was on this side of the lake. It's on the other side. Glad to know it. Glad to know more about the place where the good beer comes from.' " Kansas was a dry state; it was, in any event, not precisely the tone that would be encouraging to Midwesterners, to whom Tammany Hall was hardly less objectionable than Wall Street.

When the Democrats met in Houston in July, the atmosphere in that Texas city was a strange one. Northern Democrats, with their liberal notions, their big city Catholic immigrant voters, and their talk of governmental initiatives, were, in the view of many Southern Democrats, agents of the devil and traitors to the true principles of the party. Bishop James Cannon, head of the Southern Methodist Episcopal Church, insisted that "no subject of the Pope" should be permitted to occupy the White House. The United States would then be run from Rome. Rumors circulated that Smith had had illicit affairs with nuns and that he was an alcoholic. The Klan, in decline, bestirred itself and summoned up the old demons of race and bigotry. Smith, under such attacks, grew testy and secretive, relying on his own circle of Tammany politicians and sounding increasingly defensive as he began to sense that the nomination he had worked so long and hard for might prove worthless.

Claude Bowers, who had done so much to resurrect Thomas Jefferson's reputation, was the keynote speaker. Bowers stressed the difference between the Republicans and Democrats in terms of basic political philosophy rather than simply in terms of specific issues. "The issues," he told the steaming delegates, "are as fundamental as they were when Jefferson and Hamilton crossed swords more than a century ago. . . . Now, Hamilton believed in the rule of the aristocracy of money, and Jefferson in the democracy of men.

"Hamilton believed that governments are created for the domination of the masses and Jefferson that they are created for the service of the people. . . .

"Just put a pin in this: There is not a major evil of which the American people are complaining now that is not due to the triumph of the Hamiltonian conception of the state."

If that was dubious history, it was good politics. Bowers went on to argue that the Republican Party was the party of Alexander Hamilton, irrevocably committed to the welfare of the rich and powerful, while the Democrats were the party of the people, committed to the well-being of all the citizens of the Republic but especially to the downtrodden and dispossessed. Having placed Jefferson securely in the Democratic firmament, Bowers also claimed Lincoln: "You cannot believe with Lincoln in a government 'of the people, by the people and for the people' and with Hamilton in a government of the wealthy, by the powerful and for the privileged.

"There are Lincoln Republicans and Hamilton Republicans, and never the twain shall meet until you find some way to ride two horses going in opposite directions at the same time."

When Bowers paid a warm tribute to Woodrow Wilson, the delegates startled him by rising to their feet in a spontaneous outburst of emotion. And when Bowers declared, "We do demand that privilege take its hand out of the farmer's pockets and off the farmer's throat," the delegates from the farm states "sprang up cheering, and . . . started a march around the hall." The other delegates joined, and Bowers's address was interrupted for twenty minutes.

The response of the press was mixed. Many editorial writers denounced Bowers for introducing a divisive note into American politics by encouraging class prejudices and turning the poor against the well-to-do. The speech marked a significant moment in twentieth-century politics. Increasingly, to the disapproval of editors of a conservative turn like Walter Lippmann, now editor of the *New York World*, Democratic orators stressed the view that the Republican Party was the party of Hamilton and privilege and the Democratic Party the party of Jefferson and the people.

The Democratic platform called for a farm program that would be based on the principle that "farm relief must rest on the basis of an economic equality of agriculture with other industries." The platform pledged to enforce Prohibition and support the principle of collective bargaining, as well as the abolition of the injunction in labor disputes "except upon proof of threatened irreparable injury," a substantial loophole, to be sure. The platform also called, as it had for years, for independence for the Philippines. It affirmed the principle of "Non-interference with the elections or other internal political affairs of any foreign nation," including, specifically, Mexico, Nicaragua, and all other Latin American nations. "Interference in the purely internal affairs of Latin-American countries must cease," as well as "agreements with a foreign government . . . for the protection of such government against revolution or foreign attack," except when such actions had been agreed to by the Senate "as provided in the Constitution of the United States. . . ." The Republicans were condemned "for carrying out such an unratified agreement that requires us to use our armed forces in Nicaragua."

Roosevelt was Smith's floor manager and once more put the governor's name in nomination. His speech was broadcast by radio and skillfully adapted to the new medium. America, he declared, in what would in time become the nation's most familiar voice, needed a leader "who grasps and understands not only the large affairs of business and government, but in equal degree the aspirations of the individual, the farmer, the wage-earner. . . ."

Despite the hostility of most Southern delegates, Smith was nominated on the first ballot, with Senator Joseph Robinson of Arkansas as his running mate. In his acceptance speech Smith stressed his liberal accomplishments as governor of New York. "Under my leadership," he declared, "the State of New York provided a forty-eight-hour week for women. It prohibited night work of women in industrial establishments. It prohibited the employment of women in dangerous occupations. It required restrooms in factories and mercantile buildings, and made many contributions by law to the health and comfort of women in industry." Listening to him, Frances Perkins realized that such accomplishments meant little to middle-class housewives, farm women, and the great majority of men. A Maine farmer, in response to her praise of Smith, replied, "Never heard of him. What happens in New York don't make any difference down here."

In the opinion of many experienced political observers, Walter Lippmann did irreparable damage to Smith's candidacy by prevailing on him to issue a public statement calling for repeal of the Eighteenth Amendment. Smith sent a telegram to the Democrats meeting in Houston stating that he was convinced that Prohibition was "entirely unsatisfactory to the great mass of our people." Roosevelt wrote a friend: "It was the *World* which literally drove Al Smith into sending that fool telegram after the Houston convention telling how wet he was. Al had every wet vote in the country, but he needed a good many millions of the middle-of-the-road votes to elect him President. . . . If Walter [Lippmann] would stick to the fundamentals, fewer people would feel that the *World* first blows hot and then cold."

Prohibition promptly became a central issue in the campaign; Catholicism was the sub rosa issue. William Allen White doubted if "any subsequent generation" would be able to understand the moral fervor and visionary hopes of the prohibitionists, the faith that Prohibition would "abolish alcoholism, and that it would be a tremendous step forward in human happiness."

Smith put tremendous pressure on Roosevelt to run for governor of New York. Roosevelt's popularity with upstate and rural voters would, the Smith strategists believed, turn out voters for whom Smith had little appeal and improve his chances of carrying the state. Roosevelt, for his part, was anxious to avoid running for governor. He wanted to be free to lay the groundwork for his own presidential candidacy in 1932. When he took refuge in Warm Springs, Georgia, and failed to return telephone calls, John J. Raskob, one of Smith's wealthiest backers, offered to help Roosevelt finance the development of Warm Springs into a high-class resort if he would run for governor. Smith himself pleaded with him to enter the gubernatorial race. "Frank, I told you I wasn't going to put this on a personal basis, but I've got to," Smith said. When Roosevelt continued to resist, Smith asked: "If those fellows [delegates to the Democratic State Convention which was meeting to nominate, among other state officers, a gubernatorial candidate] nominate you tomorrow and adjourn, will you refuse to run?" When Roosevelt equivocated, Smith took his response as the equivalent of acquiescence. The next day Roosevelt was nominated by acclamation by the Democratic delegates. Smith had forced Roosevelt's hand and upset Howe's schedule.

Despite his reluctance, Roosevelt campaigned with characteristic thoroughness and panache. By train and car he covered some 1,300 miles, giving as many as fifty speeches a day in a period of three weeks, many of them to a few dozen people at a small-town train station or town square; he wore out reporters and staff alike. In the towns and cities where he was scheduled to give talks in halls, he often had to be carried to the podium. In the words of Frances Perkins, he had "accepted the ultimate humiliation which comes from being helped physically. He had accepted it smiling. He came up over that perilous, uncomfortable, and humilating 'entrance'," she wrote of one such scene, "and his manner was pleasant, courteous, enthusiastic. He got up in his braces, adjusted them, straightened himself, smoothed his hair, linked his arm in his son Jim's, walked out on the platform as if this was nothing unusual. . . . I don't recall the speech at all. For me and for others who saw that episode his speech was less important than his courage." Since Roosevelt's Republican opponent was a popular liberal Jew, Albert Ottinger, the first of his religious group to run for high elective office in the state, Smith had persuaded Herbert Lehman, also a Jew, to run for lieutenant governor on the Democratic ticket.

As the campaign progressed, William Allen White aroused Lippmann's indignation by writing editorials that charged Governor Smith with vetoing bills that were designed to check gambling and prostitution because of Tammany pressure. White was the voice of small-town Midwestern progressivism, now, in the view of Lippmann and other big-city journalists, turned sour and reactionary. "White surely is about the best thing that the Middle West and the small town in the Buick-radio age has produced," Lippmann wrote to Herbert Croly. "And judged by any standard of civilized liberalism, it's a pretty weedy flower." White had conveyed the impression that he felt as though defeating Smith were the "equivalent of heaving a stray cat out of the parlor. Intellectually he's able to comprehend, of course, that Smith is a real person, representing real things, but emotionally he's no more able to comprehend the things you and I feel than he would if we suddenly announced that we'd embraced Buddhism." Ironically, Croly had embraced his own modified form of Protestant Christianity, which had caused more uncomprehending astonishment among his friends than if he had embraced Buddhism, which was, in fact, quite fashionable.

The ranks of liberals were split on the Smith candidacy. The fact that he was a Roman Catholic was almost as difficult for many liberal Democrats to swallow as it was for Southern Baptists, though for very different reasons. Liberal intellectuals like Newton D. Baker were distrustful of anyone with strong religious convictions; they were most distrustful of Catholics, who, they believed, were basically reactionary in their politics and hopelessly warped in their thinking by virtue of their commitment to the tenets of their religion. The Southern Baptists adhered to the ancient conviction that the Pope was the Antichrist, the earthly agent of the devil, whose evident intention was to rule the United States. Baker wrote to Lippmann that he would vote reluctantly for Smith to help "kill religious prejudice."

Smith appealed to Lippmann as a representative of the immigrants who were seeking their proper place in American life against the "older American civilization of town and country which dreads and will resist him." That "civilization of town and country" was made up, in large part, of that doggedly Protestant "booboisie" that Henry Mencken and the *American Mercury* never ceased ridiculing as figures of prejudice, repression, and provincialism; it was the "civilization" from which so many young men and women had fled as though from prison to the larger, more tolerant, and inviting life of the cities. Those who remained behind, defending their archaic "household gods," were convinced that they were waging a desperate war for the soul of America against the armies of Satan, recruited in the cities. The cities were the conspicuous enemies of Prohibition. Prohibition was the final measure of orthodoxy for many small towns of the South and Middle West.

It must be said that Lippmann, who acted as Smith's adviser on foreign policy issues, grew increasingly disenchanted with his candidate. "The plain truth is that he [Smith] did practically nothing, except on prohibition, and in a somewhat amateurish way on farm relief, until he had been nominated," he complained to Newton Baker. "His heart is all right, his character is all right, his head is all right, but his equipment is deplorable."

Everywhere the Catholic issue rose to plague the Democrats. In the South Frances Perkins, campaigning for Smith, encountered the full force of anti-Catholicism. She was informed repeatedly that land had already been bought for the Pope so that he could take up residence in the United States as soon as Smith was elected. Stories circulated that Smith's wife, Katie, was a drunkard. Claude Bowers told of a man, a Civil War veteran, it was said, who was paid by the Republicans in a small Delaware town to stand on a street corner and engage young men in conversation, warning them against Al Smith and popery. A young friend of Bowers, Frank Oliver, was introduced to the old man as someone who was thinking of voting for Smith. "If this man Smith is elected," Oliver was told, "the Pope is goin' to come over here with all his wives and concubines and live in the White House and run the country. Y'may not have noticed that Catholics in droves are goin' into the Army, for if Smith is elected, they're goin' to take over the country and make the Pope President."

"Well," said Oliver, falling in with the line, "I won't stand for that."

The Ku Klux Klan lined the railroad tracks into Oklahoma City with flaming crosses when Smith was scheduled to speak. At Independence, Missouri, anti-Smith toughs prevented people from entering the hall where Frances Perkins was scheduled to speak. Even the presence of Harry Hawes, a Missouri Senator, failed to placate the crowd, but the hall was finally filled after the intervention of the sheriff. The speakers for Smith were loudly booed, and the meeting broke up in scuffles and fistfights. One of the organizers of the meeting was a young Democrat named Harry Truman.

Mrs. Champ Clark told Bowers about her attempt during the campaign to make a speech in behalf of Smith in a small Midwestern town. She was not allowed to speak, and when Mrs. Clark asked her reluctant hostess why she and her husband, although "Demmycrats," were so opposed to Smith, "she brought her clenched fist down on the table with a resounding whack," and declared, "They brung in sprinklin'!" The woman and her husband and most of their neighbors were total-immersion Baptists. To them "sprinklin' " was worse than adultery.

A disillusioned Eleanor Roosevelt wrote: "I think by nature I am a fairly liberal person, without intense prejudice, but if I needed anything to show me what prejudice can do to the intelligence of human beings, that campaign was the best lesson I could have had."

For his part, Hoover stressed the "Republican prosperity" and promised to extend it to include "a chicken in every pot and a car in every garage." Beyond that he stuck to such tried-and-true themes as the primacy of the family. In his birthplace—West Branch, Iowa—Hoover praised the family as the "unit of American life . . . the sanctuary of moral inspiration and of American spirit." The United States was not so much a nation of 110,000,000 people as it was "a nation of 23,000,000 families living in 23,000,000 homes."

Hoover also pledged himself to measures designed "to mitigate the violence of the so-called business cycle. That is, the recurrent periods of boom and false hope, waste and extravagance, followed by hard times, with hideous unemployment, decreasing wages, bankruptcy on business, and ruinous prices to the farmers." Cooperation "with industry and banking and public officials" had already greatly lessened the danger of such disasters. Another important measure to help cope with such depressions in normal business activity might be "public works, including the development of water resources, public roads, and the construction of public buildings." He was committed to "voluntarism," or, as he liked to call it, "spiritual individualism." He wrote: "The vast multiplication of voluntary organizations for altruistic purposes are themselves proof of the ferment of spirituality, service, and mutual responsibility. These associations for advancement of public welfare . . . represent something moving at a far greater depth than 'joining.' They represent the widespread aspiration for mutual advancement, self-expression, and neighborly helpfulness." Hoover praised such organizations as "chambers of commerce, trade associations, labor unions, bankers, farmers, propaganda associations, and what not." As secretary of commerce he had demonstrated a strong disposition to intrude into State Department territory since he saw his job as that of advancing American trading interests overseas. At the same time he resisted all efforts to involve the government directly in the solution of economic problems, most notably the attempt of Henry Wallace and the farm bloc Republicans to prevail on the government to take a leading role in trying to cope with what amounted to a continuing farm depression in the midst of the Coolidge boom.

Hoover's final Eastern campaign appearance was at Madison Square Garden in New York, where he returned to the theme of the relationship of government to business. "Even if governmental conduct of business could give us more efficiency instead of less efficiency," he declared, "the fundamental objection to it would remain unaltered and unabated. It would destroy political equality. It would increase rather than decrease abuse and corruption. . . . It would undermine the development of leadership. It would cramp and cripple the mental and spiritual energies of our people. It would extinguish equality and opportunity. It would dry up the spirit of liberty and progress."

The modern reader of Herbert Hoover's campaign addresses will be impressed by a number of things: the "liberality" of his sentiments as well as their sentimentality; his vision of a great scheme of public works—roads and dams, canals and irrigation projects—to benefit first the farmer and then the rest of Americans; his plea for cooperation between the often competing segments of the marketplace; and, perhaps above all, the disparity between his roseate description of the state of the nation and the perceptions of the "other America," the America of the radical intellectuals, of working-class men and women, of sharecroppers in the South and hardscrabble farmers on marginal land that was already beginning to be blown out from under them in the first intimations of a dust bowl. Certainly we cannot fault Hoover for indulging in the famous "pointing with pride" that is the stock-in-trade of all politicians speaking for a party in power. Hoover's statistics were, for the most part, true and significant even if they were only half, or perhaps less than half, the story. Numerous of his predecessors had taken as great or greater liberties with the complex and often disheartening truth. There was, in practical fact, little in his public utterances to suggest that he would be unable to cope with the disaster that was rushing down upon him and a good deal to indicate that he might be just the man, except for one thing: his repeated stress on the notion that the government must not intervene directly in the realm reserved for business enterprise. If government once took a hand there, calamities, beside which the plagues Jehovah imposed on Egypt would pale, must descend upon the nation.

"The campaign of 1928," Claude Bowers thought, "was the most disgraceful and threatening in our history up until that time. At some periods, happily wide apart, waves of religious and racial intolerance had swept the country, but never had there been anything so widespread and sinister in its implications. It came so suddenly and was so incredible. . . . The nomination of Smith, a Catholic, only added fuel to the flame. . . . [T]here is not a scintilla of doubt that the Republican managers expected to profit from the bigotry and gave discreet encouragement to its growth."

If the voters liked Herbert Hoover's sentiments, they liked the Coolidge boom even more. They had no intention of rocking the boat. The election was a triumph for the friends of business and a crushing defeat for Al Smith. Smith got no votes in four Southern states, and Hoover won in a landslide. His popular margin was one of the largest in the country's history, more than 6,000,000 votes—21,392,190 to 15,016,443—and 444 electoral votes to 87. Outside the Solid South Smith carried only Rhode Island and Massachusetts. Hoover carried New York by almost 100,000 votes, and for a time it looked as though Roosevelt, too, had gone down in the debacle. Upstate returns came in slowly, and Roosevelt's staff suspected fraud. His staff began calling local sheriffs, threatening legal action unless the vote count was speeded up, and by morning it was evident that Roosevelt had squeaked into office by a margin of some 25,000 votes out of 4,250,000. Roosevelt promptly called himself the "one half of one percent Governor." More important, he was one of the few prominent Democrats to survive the Republican sweep.

If there was ever a child of fortune, it was Franklin Delano Roosevelt. He had done his best to avoid running for governor of New York State as Al Smith's successor. Out of the debacle of the Democrats, he had emerged a survivor, far stronger in party circles than before.

Another clear gain for Roosevelt was that he assembled a staff of experienced politicians and aides whose collective experience would prove a valuable asset to him in the White House. The best known was James Farley, secretary of the State Democratic Committee. Edward J. Flynn was the Democratic chieftain of the Bronx. Henry Morgenthau, Jr., was a wealthy Jewish financier with political instincts as shrewd as Bernard Baruch's. Another important recruit was Samuel I. Rosenman, a lawyer who had served a term in the state legislature and was adept at summarizing complex issues; his primary function was that of a speech writer. Al Smith was made manager of the Empire State Building project. Increasingly, his life was absorbed by John Raskob and his circle of financiers and tycoons, and Smith, always inherently conservative, drifted farther and farther to the right.

Irwin "Ike" Hoover, the head usher of the White House, who had no liking for Coolidge, reported that after the Republican Convention a deeply disappointed President departed for his summer camp in Wisconsin "a nervous wreck. He could not eat or sleep with satisfaction and as compared with his former self was helpless for at least ten or twelve days after his arrival." It was Ike Hoover's conviction that the President was bitterly disappointed, first, not to be nominated himself and, second, to see the nomination go to Herbert Hoover. "He never fully recovered from the shock, and a shock it was," Ike Hoover wrote.

While Herbert Hoover waited to take over the reins of office, the signs of economic trouble multiplied. Roy Young, governor of the Federal Reserve Board, in an address to the Indiana Bankers Association in the fall of 1928, declared, "Many people in America seem to be more concerned about the present situation than the Federal Reserve system is. If unsound credit practices have developed, these practices will in time correct themselves. . . ." It was February, 1929, before the board undertook to check the use of credit for speculative purposes, but the frantic speculation continued. Perhaps to excuse his own speculations, Burton Rascoe wrote: "The world seemed to have gone mad in a hectic frenzy of speculation and wild extravagance and I was interested in the phenomenon, especially since nearly all the other values of life had been engulfed by it. To retreat from it was to retreat from life itself."

According to Claude Bowers, "Every semblance of control over the misuse of wealth and corporate power had been withdrawn, and robust individualism was paying enormous dividends to a few. . . . Half the people I knew, living in a fool's paradise, were joyously anticipating

riches through the magic of the stock market, which had become literally a gambling den. . . . Riding in the subway to Park Row [the offices
of the *World*] each morning, I observed the girl stenographers crowding
the cars, who had previously preferred the highly spiced tabloids with
their lurid tales of scandals and crimes, had suddenly become sober
and intellectual in their taste: the tabloid had given way to the New
York *Times*." Bowers noted that their attention was fixed on the financial section of that austere paper.

Of the orgy of speculation, Oswald Garrison Villard wrote that
to try to call attention to its inevitable consequences "was crying in vain
from the housetops. Nobody wanted anything but to be left alone to
make money. Nobody was interested in the fact that, in the midst of
unheard-of luxury and unprecedented fortunes, vast numbers of
Americans were not only living at or below the subsistence level but
were steadily sinking in the economic scale; that millions upon millions
of Americans in the South were worse housed and fed than any peasants in Europe. Harding, Coolidge, and Hoover, one after the other,
mouthed the sickening old lies about the high American standard of
living and prided themselves that we were so far ahead of the rest of
the world." So calamity gathered, soon to fall on the unsuspecting head
of the new President.

The bellwether of public opinion, Walter Lippmann, announced
the imminent demise of the unbuttoned spirit of the twenties in his
book *A Preface to Morals*. It seemed to Lippmann that the country was
in a hopeless muddle as far as moral standards were concerned. On
the one hand, there were the defenders of tradition wringing their
hands over the moral decay of the nation and prophesying doom and
disaster—God's judgment on a froward and stiff-necked people. On
the other hand, there was a growing suspicion even in the more advanced circles of what Lippmann called "modernity" that satisfying the
lusts and passions of the human animal was not an entirely sufficient
guide for a happy life. Lippmann insisted that what he called the
"religion of the spirit" must prevail. Although it was not entirely clear
what the "religion of the spirit" was, he suggested that a new type of
moralist was necessary. This moralist must in effect rediscover the
requirements of the good life and express them in a way congenial to
the new consciousness. His job was "not to exhort men to be good but
to elucidate what the good is. . . . The acids of modernity are dissolving
the usages and the sanctions to which men once habitually conformed.
It is therefore impossible for the moralist to command. He can only

persuade." He or she can do little more than indicate "which experience . . . is desirable among the choices that are possible and necessary." The "established codes" were no longer relevant. "A religion which rests upon particular conclusions in astronomy, biology, and history may be fatally injured by the discovery of new truths. But the religion of the spirit does not depend upon creeds and cosmologies. . . . It is concerned not with the organization of matter, but with the quality of human desire."

The problem was, of course, that the class to which Lippmann was appealing to create a morality based on "religion of the spirit," a morality appropriate to the new age, was the very class that, having overthrown the old consciousness, was most adrift and in need of moral signposts. The mass of the citizens clung stubbornly (indeed, one suspects desperately) to those traditional dogmas and doctrines which, in Lippmann's eyes, were hopelessly discredited. As it happened, the Great Depression solved Lippmann's dilemma, at least for the moment, and in a fashion that he thoroughly disapproved of. Most of the class to whom he addressed *A Preface to Morals* became, in the brief space of a year or two, believers not in the "religion of the spirit" but in the religion of dialectical materialism; they became Marxists of one kind or another or one degree or another and, in doing so, adopted a morality, or, as some skeptics thought, an immorality, quite as comprehensive and as rigid as any propounded by a Baptist fundamentalist in rural Georgia.

Waldo Frank, who kept discovering and rediscovering America, published *The Re-Discovery of America* in 1929. It was dedicated to Herbert Croly, "Whose 'Promise of American Life,' laid the foundation in modern, real terms, for the view of America as a democratic nation led by an aristocracy of spirit. . . ." Like Lippmann, Frank was sympathetic to the traditional religions. It was preeminently the great religions which conveyed an essential "sense of the Whole," which offered coherent unifying visions of the world. Modern man had lost all feeling for the "Whole," for an ordered cosmos. But what Frank called the "American Jungle" was rich in the promise of a new integration. Frank appealed to "mystic America," to the America of Whitman and Melville, an America of irrepressible dreams, finally to "the symphonic nation," in which individuality was preserved and strengthened by a harmoniousness, by the recognition by "groups" that they were integral parts of the Whole. In addition, Americans must recognize that in Russia "a race of genius rises from [a] base of servitude" and must be regarded with patience. However sunk in violence Russia seemed, the Russian was "still human . . . [and] is working at a *method* to bring about what men have always professed. And this is holy work; this is a Cause and a soil for those who need a concrete thing to work for." The United States must not threaten the "peace of the high experiment in Russia. . . ."

# 12

## Hoover and the Depression

In Frazier Hunt's words, Calvin Coolidge "played a shabby trick" on his successor, for "he had handed him the toy balloon of inflated prosperity . . . and then hurried up to Massachusetts and hidden in the woodshed."

Herbert Hoover was intelligent, experienced, humane, the best product of what we have referred to as the old consciousness. He was, in practical fact, one of the best known and most admired men in the world: the Great Engineer, the Great Humanitarian. His liberal credentials were unimpeachable. Franklin Roosevelt had counted himself among Hoover's admirers. In 1920 Roosevelt had written to Hugh Gibson, a friend and then ambassador to Poland: "I had some nice talks with Herbert Hoover before he went West for Christmas. He is certainly a wonder, and I wish we could make him President of the United States. There could not be a better one."

Hoover was certainly not devoid of imagination. His bold plan for having the Federal government spend billions of dollars to control floods and generate electrical power was a startling innovation and led many in his own party to grumble about the socialist tendencies of the President-elect. "Order was imposed on chaos everywhere he went because of his integrity, his single-mindedness, and his administrative genius," Rexford Guy Tugwell wrote. "He was a self-made man, a millionaire by his mid-thirties, and proud that he had never sought a job after he was twenty-one. His skill was so readily recognized, eagerly sought after and generously rewarded. At the outbreak of World War I he had offices in San Francisco, New York, London, Petrograd and Paris. . . ." Until the time he became President, Tugwell added, "there was . . . never a backward step, a check, a humiliation, or a disappointment in his whole life. . . ."

With all that there was some essential sentiment missing, something cold and distant locked away in a remote chamber of his heart. He was stiff as his collars. Like Coolidge, he had all the proverbial rectitude of the Puritan. Like Coolidge, he could not bring himself to be polite and gracious to the White House staff. He experienced difficulty in saying good morning, or in engaging in any of the small amenities of daily life. Graciousness was simply beyond him.

Again like Coolidge, Hoover unselfconsciously provided the nation with a classic icon. He loved trout fishing (which was certainly in his favor), but he went trout fishing (at least allowed himself to be photographed trout fishing) in a business suit with the unvarying stiff collar, tie, vest, and felt fedora; wading boots were his only concession to his environment. The image somehow belonged with that of Coolidge in an Indian war bonnet or a cowboy outfit. It seemed to say, "I am not really at home in the world; I wear my clothes like a suit of armor; even in the middle of a stream I cannot unbend."

When he and Mrs. Hoover were ensconced in the White House, the usual train of journalists made its way there to report on the new President's foibles. Among them was Frazier Hunt. In distinct contrast with his lunch with the Coolidges six years earlier, the meal was a sumptuous one. Hoover was an intelligent and articulate man who talked knowingly of the "new age of Machinery, of distribution and standardization," of the spread of economic democracy whereby all Americans shared comforts and conveniences that were once available only to the rich. Only when Hunt brought up the subject of Russia did he find his host's mind firmly closed. "He would have nothing to do with a country that repudiated her debts, governed by a dictatorship and confiscated all personal property," he told Hunt. "He spoke bitterly and uncompromisingly," Hunt added.

It was not until Hunt got him on the subject of elementary education and improved health facilities for children that the President thawed out. He had called a Child Health Conference to consider the problem. Crime was increasing at an alarming rate. It could be combated, in Hoover's view, only by a "charter for children." He had had a survey made of the criminal population of the large cities. The great majority were foreign-born—67 percent had come from southern Italy; 12 percent were from Poland and Eastern Europe—while 11 percent were blacks. A "new generation of children—healthy, trained, and mentally inspired—would go a long way," the President said enthusiastically, "toward solving all of this." The criminal class came largely from ghetto slums. "If the character, quality, and health of these children were watched and nurtured, a criminal type would not develop. . . . City children must not be denied grass and flowers, fields and streams—all the imaginative surroundings that are a part of nature. . . . Ten years will see the start of this new generation. We can move swiftly after that," Hoover concluded. Reflecting later on the interview, Hunt wrote: "No man ever sat in the White House with a finer heart or a broader general knowledge . . . but he could not shake himself free from the ancient theory that private property and capital, the rewards of the sweat of one's brow were sacred beyond all else. So it was that he could not get himself around to placing hungry mouths and human rights above property rights."

Through the last months of 1928 and into the new year the Coolidge boom went on despite accumulating signs of trouble. Stories circulated constantly of scrubwomen and secretaries who had made fortunes and rode to work in chauffeured limousines. In the words of Vincent Sheean, "Everybody speculated, everybody believed 'propserity' was eternal, and nobody I knew seemed to think that free speculation with the produce of a nation's labour was criminal." Sheean had "some terrible moments over that question because Wall Street in 1928 and 1929 made me feel very indignant, and I could seldom keep still about it if the subject arose." One night at a party with friends Sheean expressed his conviction that "a crash was inevitable, and it would disclose what had been going on underneath the speculative inflation, a true crisis of overproduction in the Marxian sense, and that this must be followed by wide unemployment and terrible suffering." The reaction of the other guests was that Sheean had made "a rude Bolshevistic attack" on them. To him "The greatest curiosity of the time was the failure of educated people to speak out on the question of Wall Street. Thousands of people must have known that a speculative boom of such dimensions would be followed by a terrible crash, and yet, in a country strewn with colleges and universities, nobody spoke up loudly." The fact was that "a whole crop of professors . . . proclaimed . . . that the 'prosperity' of 1928 had definitely disproved the 'theories of Karl Marx.' " Except for Dorothy Thompson and Sinclair Lewis, Sheean could not recall a single acquaintance who "perceived the inevitability of the crash."

Meantime, danger signals multiplied. Freight car loadings, considered a prime economic indicator, were down, unemployment was increasing, and the farm economy labored on in a predepression depression of its own. Abroad, Great Britain struggled desperately to remain solvent, the German banking system was in crisis, and France pursued policies that were unpredictable and often mischievous.

While doubts such as Sheean expressed were relatively rare, many Americans were uneasy about the effect of the boom on the American character. Edmund Wilson expressed his doubts to Allen Tate in May, 1929, a few months after Hoover's inauguration. He distrusted both the champion of the status quo, who "seems to have no hope or faith in the future, and the American social revolutionaries who look forward to a clean sweep of American bourgeois civilization. . . . I think it is true . . . that the only thing possible in the present situation is for the individual to save his own integrity. As a matter of fact," Wilson added, "this has always been true in America—in the North at least—but I begin to wonder whether the time has not arrived for the intellectuals, etc., to identify themselves a little more with the general life of the country. This is pretty difficult, God knows, and it may be that the United States will develop into a great imperialistic power with all its artists, critics, and philosophers as ineffective and as easily extinguished as the German ones were in 1914."

As the stock market rose higher and higher, investors made hundreds of thousands of dollars on paper. Burton Rascoe's Montgomery Ward stock, the virtual gift of his benefactor Herbert Collins, reached 447 in early October. On Wednesday, October 23, in the space of five hours, stock prices dropped so rapidly that an estimated $5,000,000,000 was lost. By eleven the next morning all the banks in New York City were in danger of collapse. The market continued its decline, with the small investors and those who had bought on margin provided by their brokers being wiped out.

To meet the crisis, six of the city's leading banks pledged $40,000,000 each. The purpose was to "fill the air pockets"—in other words, to buy stock which was being offered and for which nothing was being bid. Some $100,000,000 was spent on the Thursday following the market's collapse. Richard Whitney, perhaps the most prominent of the New York bankers, won wide praise for bidding $205 for 25,000 shares of United States Steel on Thursday, October 24, in what was believed to have been a courageous effort to check the general market decline. He and his fellows were referred to by the press as the "Saviors of the Market." Lippmann wrote to Bernard Berenson: "The most exhilarating thing I have seen is the courage and quiet unselfishness of some of the big bankers who have really done extraordinary things."

The encomiums proved premature. What the bankers in effect had done was to force the market up temporarily, sell their own securities, get out of the market, and allow it to drop to the cost of those who had remained in, or gone back in, confident that the bankers and brokers would, between them, check the decline. They did not and could not; the long slide into the nation's severest economic crisis had begun. It was barely eight months since Herbert Hoover had taken office.

The third day after the crash Claude Bowers attended a dinner at Bernard Baruch's for Winston Churchill. It was a plutocratic evening with John W. Davis, Charles Schwab, head of U.S. Steel, Gerard Swope of General Electric (and brother of the journalist Herbert Bayard Swope), and Charles Mitchell, head of the National City Bank. Former Senator Simon Guggenheim was present, along with Cyrus Curtis, owner of the *Saturday Evening Post* and the *New York Evening Post*. Among those titans of the financial and industrial world, Bowers sensed a feeling of panic and confusion. The conversation carefully avoided any reference to the collapse of the stock market, and the atmosphere, to Bowers, was one of "abnormal gaiety." As the star of the evening Churchill gave a brief talk "with numerous little whimsical touches." He made no mention of the crash and talked of the importance of cordial Anglo-American relations.

Appropriate metaphors for the crash are not hard to find: A house of cards came tumbling down, unemployment snowballed, banks and factories closed, and soon millions of Americans were walking the streets in search of nonexistent jobs. "May we not well fear," Edmund Wilson wrote at the end of 1929, "that what this year has broken down is not simply the machinery of representative government, but the capitalist system itself?—and that, even with the best will in the world, it may be impossible for capitalism to guarantee not merely social justice but even security and order." The thought occurred to many others.

Faced with a nationwide disaster, the Republicans reacted like

Pavlov's dog. For sixty years the party had made high tariffs the response to every crisis. Now it must be high tariffs once more; the Hawley-Smoot tariff bill was presented to Congress. In May, 1930, when Congress began consideration of the bill (1028), members of the American Economic Association, most of them college and university professors of conservative persuasion, urged Congress not to pass the bill (it seems safe to say that so many economists had never before or since agreed on any issue) and Hoover to veto it if Congress did such a foolish and destructive thing. The economists pointed out that European nations that owed money to the United States would not be able to pay on their loans if imports were cut back by high tariffs. Increased tariffs would inevitably cause a drop in American exports as well, thus deepening the crisis.

The warnings of the experts were ignored. Congress passed the Hawley-Smoot tariff, which set the highest rates in American history. With no rational notion of what to do, Congress did the most destructive thing it could have done. The bill was signed into law by Hoover on June 16, and the stock market took an immediate plunge (it didn't, to be sure, have far to go).

European nations responded by raising their tariffs. Trade between the United States and European nations, already faltering, came to a virtual standstill. Unable to earn favorable trade balances, various European nations repudiated millions of dollars in World War debts. A dismayed Walter Lippmann wrote in the *World*: "He [Hoover] gave up the leadership of his party. He let his personal authority be flouted. He accepted a wretched and mischievous product of stupidity and greed." Lippmann complained to Frankfurter that Hoover had "no resiliency. And if things continue to break badly for him, I think the chances are against his being able to avoid a breakdown." Yet Lippmann was plainly of two minds. He wrote Herbert Croly: "Hoover's had a wretched first year. Everything he touches seems to sour on him. And yet I cannot bring myself to condemn him completely. For underneath all his failures, there is a disposition in his administration to rely on intelligence to a greater degree than at any time, I suppose, since Roosevelt." Hoover, Lippmann believed, had been the victim of bad luck and of "a temperamental weakness in dealing with irrational political matters. . . ."

Prodded by the economists, Congress amended the Hawley-Smoot Act. Out of 3,300 duties, 11 were changed, 3 raised, and 8 lowered. Among those lowered were "hats, bonnets and hoods of straw, chip, paper, grass, palm-leaf, willow, osier, rattan, real horsehair, cuba bark, ramie, or manila hemp, wholly or partly manufactured, *if sewed.*" No improvement in the economy was noted.

Adding to the nation's distress in 1930 was a devastating drought, which seized the South from Virginia to Oklahoma as well as portions of Pennsylvania and Ohio. Malcolm Cowley, driving through the drought-stricken countryside, saw "the gaunt ribs of the cattle . . . [and] the fields that had the uniform color of old straw matting." At a general store where he stopped to buy cigarettes, the storekeeper couldn't change a $5 bill. "Three farms, along with their stock, implements, and household furnishings, were being advertised for sale in handbills tacked to the wall." In Tennessee the corn and hay crops had been ruined, and there was no feed for the cattle. In the Shenandoah Valley of Virginia an old man told him that fodder "hadn't been so scarce since Sheridan laid waste the valley" during the Civil War.

The sharecroppers and tenant farmers of Kentucky, Mississippi, and Arkansas, near the poverty line even in the good times, were faced with starvation, but Congress, with Hoover's guidance, was willing to lend money only "for the purpose of seed and feed for animals." Money for hungry people would turn them into mendacious parasites, the President thought. The Red Cross did its best, but its best was much too little: $5,000,000 for seven drought-ravaged states. Applicants for food had to fill out forms and endure a grilling to be sure that their need was really desperate.

At England, Arkansas, a band of 500 farmers armed with shotguns and rifles asked a Red Cross administrator for food. When he told them that he had no more requisition blanks, they invaded the town's stores, and the alarmed merchants gave them $900 worth of groceries. The episode, encouraged by the Communists as an example of "direct action," attracted nationwide attention and, in the main, sympathy. "Paul Revere just woke up Concord. Those birds woke up America," Will Rogers wrote in his column.

While people went hungry in New York City, Long Island potatoes rotted in the fields because at the price of twenty-four cents a bushel it did not pay to pick them. In many cities subsistence gardens were started on vacant lots. Gary, Indiana, counted 20,000 such gardens. When farm tractors broke down or farmers could no longer afford gas, mules were once more used for plowing. In many rural areas systems of barter appeared, and even in cities people exchanged labor.

In Minneapolis a Methodist minister developed an elaborate system whereby machines in closed factories were used by individuals to make tools and utensils for exchange. Teams of unemployed men cut wood to trade for canned goods. Tenino, Washington, a lumbering town, issued $5,000 in "wooden money," covered by the assets of the town's failed bank. Gold mining was resumed in many spots throughout the Sierra Nevada, and bootlegging provided a precarious livelihood for hundreds of thousands of otherwise law-abiding citizens.

Millions of Americans took to the road or the rails, drifting from town to town, looking for odd jobs or handouts. In 1929 the Missouri Pacific Railroad reported that its brakemen and yard police had rousted out 13,745 transients. Two years later the number had risen to 186,028. The Southern Pacific counted 416,915 in a period from September, 1931, through April, 1932. Hundreds of thousands more never registered as statistics. Finally the railroads stopped trying to eject the migrants. In the summer it was estimated that more than 1,000,000 Americans rode the rods, a hazardous way of traveling under the best of circumstances. Sometimes whole families—father, wife, and a child or two—would go hoboing, especially in the picking seasons of California and the Northwest. Every large city had half a dozen or more Hoovervilles, shantytowns fashioned out of old crates and cartons patched together to provide a modicum of privacy and protection from the elements. It was estimated that 1,000,000 Americans lived in Hoovervilles by the end of 1933.

"Everybody in America was looking for work . . ." Langston Hughes wrote, "everybody moving from one place to another in search of a job. People who lived in the West were hoboing on trains to the east . . . sometimes they wouldn't go any further than Reno, whichever way they were going, and none of them had any money, they'd build these big fires near the railroad tracks . . . and they'd just live collected around those fires until they could make enough money at odd jobs to move further on their way." Meantime, they lived in "makeshift houses made out of boxes of tin and old pieces of wood and canvas." Hughes wrote a short story about a family of such migrants, entitled "On the Road."

Oscar Ameringer and a friend stood on a knoll in Oregon overlooking the Columbia River and observed a pall of smoke hanging over the valley. Ameringer's companion explained that the fires had been burning all summer and fall; the government paid fifty cents an hour for fighting fires, and since that was the only way for unemployed loggers to make a living, the fires were not allowed to die out. In the Oregon apple orchards the ground was covered with rotting apples. It cost forty cents to pick, pack, and ship a crate of apples, and the market price was less than thirty cents. In the same spirit ewes were killed by sheep ranchers who could not afford to feed them or find buyers for their wool or meat. Below the window of his hotel in Los Angeles, Ameringer saw children quarreling over the refuse of garbage cans. "Highway 66, crawling over the staked plains toward the land of promise," he wrote, "is . . . covered with hitchhikers, forlorn jalopies, devastated trucks, and here and there remnants of a covered wagon, bearing the army of refugees from the marching desert."

At an auto park a few hundred miles farther east a rancher approached Ameringer. "You don't know me from Adam's off ox," he announced. "But I know you. I used to hear you make Socialist speeches down in the Comanche pasture after the opening. I always took you for a damn fool preaching dividing up and social revolution. This country was good enough for me and if the Dutchman didn't like it, why in the hell don't he go back where he came from. Anybody, I says to myself, *anybody* can get ahead in this country if he knows his business, works hard and saves his money. I came to the Territory with nothing but a saddle and a horse to my name. I could barely make out a check and read print. But I worked hard and saved my money . . . and that's how come I got a little bunch of cows of my own together, leased a good pasture, and finally bought a section of grass land. By the time the big war came I owned over a thousand white-faced steers. . . ." When the crash came and beef dropped to four cents a pound, he could no longer borrow money on his land and herd or sell his cattle. First the bank took his breeding stock, and then the insurance company, which held a mortgage on his land, foreclosed. "Now I'm cleaned out," the rancher told Ameringer, "and by God I won't stand for it. I've played the game according to the rules. I knew cows, I saved my money. . . . I didn't booze, gamble or run around with whores, and still I'm cleaned out and by God, I won't stand for it."

What did he intend to do? Ameringer asked.

"Do?" the enraged cattleman replied. "That's what I want to talk to you about. What we've got to do is have this here revolution you used to preach about." The rancher's plan was to destroy the bridges over the Mississippi, cutting the East off from the food-producing West, "until those damned Eastern high-binders are starved to death."

In Arkansas Ameringer picked up a hitchhiking family. The wife had a dead chicken under her coat; she had found it on the road. "They promised me a chicken in the pot, and now I got mine," she told Ameringer. As Ameringer summarized the plight of Americans, "The farmers are being pauperized by the poverty of the industrial populations and the industrial populations are being pauperized by the poverty of the farmers. Neither has the money to buy the produce of the other; hence we have overproduction and underconsumption at the same time in the same country."

Tennessee was a land of desolation. In Chattanooga Ameringer found "more closed banks and stores, cold factory stacks, bigger and better bread lines. On the road eastward more hitchhikers, tin lizzies, atavistic covered wagons, fear-stricken men, women, and children, whole families fleeing in every direction, as if pursued by unknown foes." There was security nowhere to be found, "for neither high nor low, bishop, banker or begger man," Ameringer wrote. "Brokers, bank clerks, counter jumpers, A.B.'s, M.D.'s, Ph.D.'s, D.D.'s, shoveling snow in the lowly company of bricklayers, 'cellists, hod carriers, oboeists, garment workers, concert masters, stevedores, dramatists, and dock wallopers. A nightmare of want, woe and despair. . . . Learned clowns in caps and gowns uttering scholarly nonsense about the mysteries of the 'businesscycle,' assuring a gasping world that what goes up must come down (but how about that which is down going up?), explaining the changed behavior of the stock market registering all down and no up. Economic morons in top hats and pince-nez uttering prophecies concerning the temporariness of the temporary business depression . . . and predicting that Dame Prosperity was lurking just around the corner."

The major difference between the farmers and other segments of American society was that the farmers had been in a depression of their own for five years or more before they were joined by the rest of the nation. They had already attended to the siren song of the Marxist chorus. The Comintern theorists had declared that although "agrarian revolution is petty bourgeois inherently . . . it is none the less of extreme importance to the revolutionary proletariat." The organization of "committees of action" to prevent foreclosures and dispossessions were tactics that were recommended and promptly adopted.

Organizations sprang up like mushrooms simply to stop farm foreclosures; among them were the Modern '76ers, the Loyal Order of Picketeers, and the Farm Relief League. The most effective farm organization proved to be Milo Reno's Farmers Holiday Association.

The word "holiday" was borrowed from the notion of a bank holiday. When the prices paid to farmers for their produce fell below the cost of production, the farmers, Reno argued, should call a holiday and cease to sell their produce. In Boone County, Iowa, on February 19, 1932, some 1,000 farmers met at Reno's invitation, to form the first chapter of the Farmers Holiday Association. Three months later some 2,000 men and women met in Des Moines to launch the National Farmers Holiday Association. Its members pledged to withhold their produce from the market whenever the price fell below the established cost of production.

One of the ideas put forth by Reno and his Farmers Holiday group was that of "councils of defense" to forestall foreclosures of farms. Each council was made up of between five and eleven members whose responsibility it was to rally farmers whenever a farm in the vicinity was about to go on the auction block to satisfy a judgment against it for unpaid debts. The councils began by trying to arrange terms between the mortgage holder and the mortgagor when the mortgagor wished to retain his property. In cases where the mortgagor was willing to give up possession the council would try to ensure that he got a proper return for his possessions, so that the mortgage holder would not profit beyond the actual value of the mortgage.

More effective in the long run than the councils was the growing determination of the farmers not to let their lands and their neighbors' lands pass under the auctioneer's hammer. In Reno's words, "The truth is, that the farmers are carrying too many ropes under their coats for to continue foreclosures in the state of Iowa." Farmers would gather at a farm to be auctioned and prevent bidding, or simply bid a few cents for a horse or cow until all of a farmer's possessions had been auctioned off for a few dollars and then returned to him.

In August, 1932, dairymen around Sioux City, Iowa, most of them members of Milo Reno's Farmers Holiday, declared a general farm strike, and a few days later picket lines were organized on all the major roads leading into the city. All produce except moonshine was stopped. When truckers tried to run the picket lines, violence followed. Nail-studded planks were laid across the roads. By the middle of the month it was estimated that 1,500 pickets were scattered along the roads leading to Sioux City. The result was an 80 percent increase in the price of milk. In the city Frazier Hunt met Will Daniel, who had organized the milk picket lines. "We can get five hundred men together in any spot in a couple of hours," Daniel told Hunt. "And we're no longer afraid of even the state militia. Say, they're our own people." If justice weren't done, he declared, there would be a revolution. What kind of revolution? Hunt asked. "I ain't got imagination enough to know," Daniel replied. "I suppose we'd be foolish if we started anything away from home; you know a rooster can fight best on his own dung-hill. Maybe we'll just sit around under a tree with a shotgun in our lap and wait. Anyway, they're not going to keep on putting us off our land. . . . The East has got to play fair with us. They got to help somebody else besides bankers and railroads and such, or we'll figure out something ourselves."

Encouraged by the success of the Sioux City strike, Farmers Holiday members around Council Bluffs initiated a strike there. When the sheriff arrested 55 pickets, 1,000 or so furious farmers marched on the courthouse. The state capital, Des Moines, was also picketed. A conference of farm state governors was proposed by Floyd Olson, the Farmer-Labor governor of Minnesota. His solution was for national guard troops in the affected states to enforce a commodity embargo until prices rose to the cost of production formula of the Farmers Holiday.

Meantime, vigilante groups of businessmen and processors made a night attack on a Farmers Holiday meeting near Cherokee, Iowa, wounding fourteen people, some seriously.

The Communist-edited *Producers News* sacrificed much of its credibility among farmers by attacking the strikers and criticizing Farmers Holiday, but Mother Bloor and her son, Harold Ware, repaired some of the damage by drawing up and publicizing a list of farm demands that was printed in Lem Harris's Communist *Farm News Letters*. Included was the demand for a moratorium on all taxes, debts, and mortgages. The right to picket "against the food trusts and middlemen who rob both producer and consumer" was also asserted, as was the right to continue the strike until farmers received "more than the accepted local cost of production from the middlemen." The statement ended with a call for a Farmers National Emergency Relief Conference to meet in Washington in December "to present our demands to Congress and to the Nation."

John Bosch, president of the Farmers Holiday Association in Minnesota, told a governors' conference in Washington: "The very foundations of government are trembling. . . . [O]ur homes must be saved or there will be a revolution." The farm state governors rejected producer strikes as a solution to depressed prices and approved a series of mild resolutions calling for more farm loans at lower interest rates.

Following the governors' conference the attention of farmers switched from the cost of production issue to demands that there be no evictions for farmers delinquent in taxes, loans, and mortgage payments. Plans were made for the protest meeting in Washington, and in the first week of December old trucks and jalopies, packed with Midwestern farmers, began rolling into the capital. Along the way the farmers had received food and lodging from the Salvation Army and church groups as well as from unions and the Communist-inspired Unemployed Councils.

Among the 250 delegates convened on December 7 were 6 black sharecroppers, a sure sign of Communist influence at the conference. Much of the conference was taken up with a somber recital of the depressed conditions in various rural areas, a grim tale of poverty and desperation. Like other observers, Malcolm Cowley was moved by the obvious sincerity of the "huge men in overalls with bright-red faces and yellow hair." The conferees called for the allocation by Congress of some $500,000,000 for farm relief, coupled with purchases by the government of food for the urban unemployed to be paid for at cost of production prices. They also rejected the idea of legislation that was designed to raise farm prices by limiting production and called for a moratorium on mortgages, interest, taxes, and rents for formerly successful farmers and a cancellation of such indebtedness for marginal farmers. Finally, they demanded no evictions.

There were twelve other resolutions, including calls for recognition of the Soviet Union, approval of the veterans' bonus, and withdrawal of American soldiers from Latin America. The conferees voted to "consolidate their power and in a friendly alliance with the workers, fight against Wall Street and the middlemen for the safety of their homes and livelihood." Lem Harris, an active Communist, was elected secretary of the radical wing of the convention, which called itself the Farmers National Committee for Action and undertook to publish the *Farmers National Weekly*.

John Bosch pushed for a union of the Farmers Holiday Association, the Farmers' Union—largely Communist-dominated—the Sharecroppers' Union, under Communist control, and the Southern Tenant Farmers Union, a non-Communist union. Bosch spoke for many old-line radical farmers when he told the delegates at a Wisconsin convention of the Farmers Holiday Association, "If I have to choose between a stalwart, rock-ribbed Republican or a Democrat and a Communist, I would choose a Communist. In Minnesota we don't make an issue of Communism." In that spirit Bosch worked closely with Lem Harris and his wife, Kay. In Nebraska, in the bitter winter of 1933, the Communists organized a march on the state capitol to demand that the legislature pass a moratorium on farm debts; 4,000 farmers joined in the demonstration. In Plymouth, Cerro Gordo County, Iowa, angry farmers repeatedly blocked the eviction of a poor farm family, the Durands, from their land. On April 27 at Primghar, in O'Brien County, Iowa, some 600 farmers were met by a sheriff, determined to carry out a foreclosure sale, and a number of hastily deputized men armed with ax handles. In the scuffle that ensued a number of farmers were badly battered. A group of farmers turned up at the county courthouse, dragged the district court judge from his chair, put a rope around his neck, and threatened to hang him unless he promised not to issue any further eviction notices. When state officers in Crawford County were beaten and put to flight, the governor placed the three counties under martial law, and national guardsmen began rounding up farmers who had participated in the antiforeclosure actions. Although there was no evidence that Communists were involved, the embattled farmers appealed to Harold Ware and his mother, Mother Bloor, in Sioux City for arms and ammunition to defend themselves and their farms. As the reaction to farm violence grew, Harry Lux, a party organizer in Michigan, was arrested along with five other United Farmers' League members, and all were charged with criminal syndicalism.

Statistics on the state of the economy seemed endless. Collecting them became a hobby. There were 5,000,000 unemployed in the spring of 1930, 10,000,000 a year later, 15,000,000 in 1932—approximately a third of the nation's labor force. Four-fifths of the steel mills had shut down. Farm income fell to a third of what it had been in 1929. Cotton, which in good years sold for thirty cents a pound, was down to six cents.

Lewis Corey, originally Louis Friana, a longtime functionary of the Communist Party, argued that the most significant fact of the Depression was that the fancied security of the middle class was finally destroyed. "The earnings, employment and privileges of lower-salaried employees . . . were mercilessly slashed, almost as mercilessly as among the workers. . . . Unemployment among technicians was catastrophic; it included 50 per cent of the pharmacists; 65 per cent of the engineers, especially civil engineers, and 90 per cent of the architects and draftsmen. . . . By 1934 over 200,000 teachers were unemployed. . . ."

People reacted differently to the loss of their jobs (or the inability to find jobs in the first place) according to class and age. Perhaps those who suffered the most were middle-aged white-collar workers, men and women, who had played the game according to the rules, who had enjoyed at least a moderate degree of success, who felt secure in their jobs and careers; decent, competent, hardworking Americans for whom a degree of economic security was life's principal desideratum. They were individuals who had comfortable, heavily mortgaged homes and cars, married men with children and the typical ambitions for them: that they would better themselves, go to college, mount to the ranks of professionals as doctors, lawyers, or teachers. In one dismal year, 1933–34, 5,680 college teachers and two-thirds of the 15,000 members of the American Federation of Musicians were out of work. Even physicians felt the pinch as their incomes dropped by more than 40 percent.

A man named Langlan Peinz, charged with vagrancy in a Brooklyn court in May, 1932, told the judge that he had graduated from the University of Colorado, worked as a civil engineer in China, Panama, and Venezuela. At the age of forty-four he had been unable to find work, and for more than a month he had been sleeping on a cot in a vacant lot near Flatbush Avenue. Of 455 experienced chemists registered for employment at a relief agency, 109 were destitute, 130 others were in need, and the remaining had funds to last only a few months.

Finally, there were all the boys and young men who had never had jobs at all and to whom it seemed that they might never have one. They were the most combustible revolutionary segment of society. Condemned to live at home, often with financially pinched and unhappy parents, or to hit the road in desperate searches for jobs, however menial or temporary, they gave up the hopes and expectations that were common to youth in every generation and sought instead simple survival. The dream of being a doctor or an engineer, a teacher or a professor was difficult, indeed often impossible, to sustain. It was for them that Alfred Hayes wrote his poem "In a Coffee Pot." Starting out as a Hearst reporter, Hayes had worked as a process server, waiter, delivery boy, and bootlegger. He had hoboed, worked as a hired man on a farm, and searched in vain for a decent job:

> You'll find us there before the office opens
> Crowding the vestibule before the day begins. . . .
> . . . . . . . . . . . . . . . . . . . . . . . . . . . . . . . . . . .
> These mornings always find us waiting there

Each one of us has shined his broken shoes
Has brushed his coat and combed his careful hair
Dance hall boys pool parlor kids wise guys
The earnest son the college grad all, all
Each hides the question twitching in his eyes
And smokes and spits and leans against the wall.

Sidney Lens was a New York Jew, the son of immigrant parents, who attended De Witt Clinton High School, loved baseball, and shot pool with a gang of young friends. Despite his mother's pleas that he go to college, Lens got a job in a fountain pen factory, from which he graduated to a runner on Wall Street. Fired after the stock market crash, young Lens occupied himself by reading Marx and Engels. Unable to find work and living at home with his parents, he "developed a feeling of worthlessness—and loneliness; I began to think of myself as a freak and misfit," he wrote, "particularly when I confronted my mother each evening with the bleak news, and watched those questioning eyes accuse me of not looking hard enough. . . ."

Burton Rascoe, the journalist and critic, had grown up on an Oklahoma farm. When he lost his job with the *Chicago Tribune*, he and his wife and young son returned to his father's farm, where Rascoe patched together out of old army tents a surprisingly commodious and comfortable "house."

In Monterey, on California's beautiful coastline, life was better than it would ever be again for John Steinbeck. There was, he wrote, "a fairly large group of us poor kids, all living alike. We pooled our troubles, our money when we had some, our inventiveness and our pleasures. I remember it as a warm and friendly time. . . . Given the sea and the gardens, we did pretty well with a minimum of theft. . . . Farmers and orchardists in the nearby countryside couldn't sell their crops. They gave us all the fruit and truck we could carry home. . . . For entertainment we had the public library, endless talk, long walks, any number of games. We played music, sang and made love. It was not easy to write when no one was interested in reading or publishing what you had written. But I do remember it as a time of warmth and mutual caring," Steinbeck wrote. "Everyone shared bad fortune as well as good."

Engaging as Steinbeck's picture of the Depression in Monterey Bay is, the story was quite different in most other places.

Working-class men and women (wives and daughters made up a much larger portion of the work force because their earning power was desperately needed; they could afford no middle-class scruples about being "working wives") were well acquainted with insecurity, with lost jobs, with illness and crippling industrial accidents, with tedious and arduous labors that made them old before their time. They were used to hard expedients, to making do, to sharing what little they had with friends and relatives. They had always suffered first and most severely and were often able to survive better psychologically than those above them in the social and economic scale. Hunger was familiar to them; hardship, their way of life.

Those at the top had farthest to fall. Often they could not endure the material loss; it seemed to them far worse than the familiar human disasters: illness; the death of loved ones; the pain of separation; the loss of faith. Many of them jumped from the tall buildings that symbolized how high they had risen above their fellow citizens; they put revolvers to their heads and blew out their brains; they jumped into the ocean from luxury liners at sea; where there was an available ocean and a pier, they often jumped off the pier. In Santa Monica, California, so many "busted" capitalists used the municipal pier as a jumping-off place that the captain of the Santa Monica lifeguards stationed a special watcher to forestall or rescue the despairing jumpers. In San Francisco the Golden Gate Bridge when completed provided the most dramatic exit of all. A grim joke circulated. Hotel clerks, it was said, routinely asked guests requesting a room, "Do you want it for sleeping or jumping?"

Searching for some positive consequence of the Depression, Edmund Wilson expressed the feelings of many of his fellow writers and journalists in his "Appeal to Progressives." The Depression might mean the end of the "success ethic" in America. "The Buicks and Cadillacs, the bad gin and scotch, the radio concerts interrupted by advertising talks, the golf and bridge of the suburban household, which the bond salesman can get for his money, can hardly compensate him for daily work of a kind in which it is utterly impossible to imagine a normal human being taking satisfaction or pride—and the bond salesman is the type of the whole urban office class. The brokers and bankers who are shooting themselves and jumping out of windows have been disheartened by the precariousness of their profession—but would they be killing themselves if they loved it? Who today, in fact, in the United States, can really love our meaningless life?" Wilson asked. The nation had fallen into an "abyss of starvation and bankruptcy . . . with no sign of any political leadership which will be able to pull us out. . . ." Liberalism seemed "to have little to offer beyond a discreet recommendation of public ownership of water power and certain other public utilities, a cordial feeling that labor ought to organize in a non-revolutionary way and a protest, invariably ineffective, against a few of the more obviously atrocious of the jailings, beatings-up and murders with which the industrialists have been trying to keep the working class docile." Wilson dared hope that "the whole money-making and spending psychology" has played itself out "and that Americans would be willing now for the first time to put their idealism and their genius for organization behind a radical social experiment. . . . After all, the Communist project has almost all the qualities that Americans glorify—the extreme of efficiency and economy combined with the ideal of a herculean feat to be accomplished by action in an atmosphere of enthusiastic boosting—like a Liberty Loan drive—the idea of putting over something big in five years [an obvious reference, for the knowledgeable, to the Russian Five-Year Plan]." Americans must "take communism away from the Communists . . ." Wilson concluded.

Mauritz A. Hallgren, a left-leaning journalist, traveled around the country talking with thousands of jobless workers. "I found them," he wrote, "increasingly sympathetic with activities of the Communist Party, at least to the extent that those activities dealt with their own immediate problems. In large cities like Chicago and New York the Communists experienced no difficulties at all in persuading entire neighborhoods to take part in demonstrations against evictions and relief cuts. Yet a vast majority of the unemployed with whom I talked," Hallgren added, "were utterly cold to communism as a way of life."

Apples became a symbol of the Depression when an officer of the International Apple Shippers Association, faced with a glut of apples, got the notion of providing the unemployed with apples on credit to sell on street corners. Soon there were 6,000 apple sellers in New York City alone. Sarah Boutelle recalls that the horror of the Depression hit her fully for the first time when a handsome, well-dressed man approached the taxi she was riding in in New York City to sell her an apple. Panhandling was routine. The writer and editor Orrick Johns bet a friend that a well-dressed panhandler would collect more money in an hour than a panhandler whose ragged clothes proclaimed his poverty. The experiment was tried. Johns dressed in evening clothes with a top hat and cane; a friend dressed "to look hungry and pathetic." The experiment was tried in Washington Square. Johns collected $2 and his friend fifteen cents.

The Depression tune was "Brother, Can You Spare a Dime?" A typical verse went:

> Once I built a railroad, made it run,
> Made it race against time,
> Once I built a railroad, now it's done.
> Brother, can you spare a dime?

One account of Hoover's economic theories ran: "First feed oats to the horses, and in time there will be enough manure to keep the chickens busy." Hardly less bizarre was the plan of John B. Nichols, head of the Oklahoma Gas Utilities Company, who proposed having all food left on plates in restaurants scraped into five-gallon containers to be passed out to the unemployed who could qualify for it by chopping wood contributed by farmers (it was not clear what the farmers were going to do for wood, or for food, either, for that matter). "We expect a little trouble now and then from those who are not worthy of the support of the citizens," Nichols added, "but we must contend with such cases in order to take care of those who are worthy."

Many of the unemployed displayed characteristic American ingenuity in helping each other. Block aid was a common practice in Harlem, whereby the residents of a particular block were solicited each week for contributions for the most destitute on it. Often more direct action was taken. Horace Cayton, sitting in a restaurant window in Harlem, saw blacks marching three abreast along the street. He was impressed by "their serious and determined faces and their extreme poverty." Curious, he joined the procession, which extended for several blocks. When he inquired about the purpose of the march, he was told that the marchers were on their way to put a woman who had been evicted for nonpayment of rent back in her apartment. When they arrived, her meager possessions had been returned to the apartment. Surrounded by the crowd, she "was intermittently crying and loudly thanking God." The group moved on to another eviction several blocks away. There police had arrived; the crowd swarmed around their cars. The police jumped out and ordered the crowd to disperse. When no one moved, an officer drew his pistol and pointed it at the crowd. A young black stepped forward and said, "You can't shoot all of us so you might as well shoot me. I'd just as soon die now as any time. All we want to see is that these people get back into their homes. We have no money, no jobs, sometimes no food. We've got to live someplace." The officer and the crowd confronted each other silently. "No threats, no murmurs, no disorder," Cayton reported; "they just looked at him. There he stood surrounded by a crowd of dirty, ragged Negroes, a sea of dark eyes watching him. He replaced his gun in its holster. . . . An old, wild-eyed haglike woman mounted a soapbox and began to harangue the crowd about food and jobs. While she talked more police cars arrived; much of the crowd dispersed and policemen attacked those who remained with their night sticks, pulling the old woman off her improvised podium and striking out at her auditors." It was Cayton's first experience with the Unemployed Councils which sprang up in every major city and were soon firmly in the grip of the Communists.

It became standard practice in Birmingham, Alabama, for men whose families were in desperate need of coal for heating and cooking to climb aboard coal trains that slowed down in the railroad yards on the outskirts of the city and then throw off lumps of coal to friends waiting along the track as the train passed through black neighborhoods. Hosea Hudson remembered picking up a lump so heavy he could hardly carry it. He estimated its weight at more than 100 pounds. Such prizes were rare; lumps the size of a fist or a football were more common. Coke, which burned longer and hotter than coal, was especially prized.

More than 150 barter associations were formed in twenty-nine states where people exchanged products or service. A barter association in California counted some 200,000 members.

The only thing that boomed during the Depression was libraries. In Muncie, Indiana, Helen and Robert Lynd's Middletown, the circulation of books rose 145 percent between 1929 and 1933. "Big things were happening that were upsetting us, our business and a lot of our ideas and we wanted to try to understand them," a businessman told the Lynds. "I waked up to the fact that my business was in immediate danger. We small businessmen began to see that we had to save our own necks. And so we stopped trying to understand the big issues and kind of lost touch with them." Now they were busy reading and trying to puzzle out the causes of the economic disaster that had overtaken the country.

Some people saw a sign of hope in the election of Philip La Follette, son of "Fighting Bob" and brother of Robert, as governor of Wisconsin in 1930. When La Follette delivered his initial address as governor to the legislature, he began by recalling Frederick Jackson Turner's essay on the role of the frontier. The physical frontier had passed; the task of the Progressive Party in Wisconsin was "to find a new equivalent for the old opportunities offered by the frontier. As we look back upon this movement, we see it as an attempt to re-create the equality of opportunity that has been lost sight of in the society that was arising." Abroad in the world there were two conflicting theories about the planet's future. One argued that the "role of the individual is ended; that a bankrupt social system must inevitably pass into the receivership of a class dictatorship to be discharged in an unspecified Utopia." The other line was that democracy had proved a failure; a "superior man . . . must be given absolute power; representative institutions are corrupt and time-wasting. . . . Today the average citizen feels lost and friendless in a complicated world. . . . It is by no means clear that the American experiment of self-government will succeed. We must be prepared for genuine, profound readjustments, not merely of institutions but of mental habits, if it does."

La Follette's central theme was the creation of "machinery by the state that would enable business to govern itself." This program he called "collective individualism." The notion was that the legislators should decide on an appropriate policy for private business to follow. Then, instead of simply imposing the plan, business itself should be invited to participate in the detailed planning so that its own interests were properly represented and so that it became a partner in carrying it out. In addition, La Follette called for the government to take the lead in urban and regional planning, again involving businessmen and individuals in the process. The historian Charles Beard wrote of La Follette's address, "In all the history of American public documents there has not appeared a more important or more reasoned state paper," and Felix Frankfurter wrote him: "Your message . . . is the most heartening state paper that has come out of the Depression. . . . I have only one regret, that your pioneer Father and your dead Mother are not here to glory in your leadership."

Claude McKay was indignant that Heywood Broun, Max Lerner, "and the scribes of the *Daily Worker* and the *New Masses*" attacked La Follette as a Fascist when he issued "his extraordinary progressive manifesto." (It might be said parenthetically that La Follette was an admirer of Mussolini and had a portrait of the Italian dictator in the executive office.)

La Follette's legislative program in Wisconsin was rivaled only by that of Franklin Roosevelt in New York State. Wisconsin enacted a statewide old-age pension system, passed a labor code that protected the rights of workers in disputes with their employers, revised the state's workmen's compensation law, and took initial steps toward state involvement in public power. Much of the legislation was the product of the system of legislative research that Bob La Follette had established thirty years earlier, using the resources of the University of Wisconsin.

The midterm congressional elections of 1930 marked substantial gains for the Democrats. Perhaps the most notable addition in the Senate was Edward Costigan of Colorado, who promptly formed an alliance with Robert E. Wagner of New York, and Robert La Follette, Jr., of Wisconsin.

Wagner, an Al Smith appointee to the New York State Supreme Court, had been persuaded by the Smith forces to run for the Senate in order to improve Smith's chances of being reelected governor of New York in 1926. Claude Bowers, one of Wagner's early supporters, wrote: "His strength and character were in his then thin brown face lighted by intelligent gray-blue eyes. He mingled dignity with an air of familiarity. . . . His voice was warm and honest, and he talked with fluency and force . . . [and he] had an innate sympathy with the working masses, then all too rare." Wagner was a German immigrant whose parents had brought him to the United States at the age of nine. He was the youngest of six children and the only one who went to school; the others worked. His parents were among those immigrants who returned to their native lands, defeated by the effort to make a living in America. When a reporter, on one occasion, pointed to him as an example of the fact that immigrants could succeed in the United States, an angry Wagner replied, "I came through it, yes. But that was luck, luck, luck! Think of the others!"

A columnist wrote of him: "He is a widower, lives in the most exclusive hotel in Washington, and is active socially. He is immaculately groomed at all times, is short—a bit rotund—has iron gray hair and is in perpetual good humor." But as far as his role as Senator was concerned, he was all business. "Wagner," the reporter complained, "does not put on a good show." His basic credo was that "there can no more be democratic self-government in industry without workers participating therein than there could be a democratic government in politics without workers having the right to vote. . . . That is why the right to bargain collectively is at the bottom of social justice for the worker as well as the sensible conduct of business affairs. The denial or observance of this right means the difference between despotism and democracy."

Wagner joined with Costigan to introduce legislation calling for the appropriation of $1,000,000,000, an enormous sum at that time, for Federal public works and "employment services." Congress passed the bill in 1931, and Hoover vetoed it with a little sermon on the importance of self-reliance and the wickedness of government assistance. Wagner's bill to establish a system of unemployment insurance was also defeated. La Follette and Costigan thereupon drafted a bill calling for Federal grants to the states for relief of the unemployed; it, too, was rejected. A Senator from Oklahoma spoke for a majority of his fellow legislators when he declared that it would mark the "beginning of the dole. . . . Of all the diseases known to pathology, the passion for a pension such as this is the most debilitating."

The President, meanwhile, was not inactive. Home loan banks were established, backed by Federal funds to try to prevent foreclosures. Some public works projects were initiated to give work to the unemployed. Hoover also committed the government to supplement relief payments when states and municipalities could no longer carry the burden. At the same time he did his best to negate the effect of these modest measures by timidity and by constantly bemoaning the effect on the American psyche of assistance—relief—to desperate people. It was Hoover's conviction that, in Rexford Tugwell's words, "the depression was an after effect of the dislocations remaining from the war; it had begun in Europe and spread to America; it was not a particularly serious matter because foreigners bought only a small percentage of American production; it would soon be over; minor precautions would be needed but no federal unemployment relief, for instance, was needed."

Hoover insisted that private charity could best care for the needy. The giving of charity was good for the character of the giver. "A voluntary deed by a man impressed with the sense of responsibility and the brotherhood of man is infinitely more precious to our National ideals and National spirit than a thousandfold poured from the Treasury of the Government under compulsion of law," he declared. By the same token, "the distress of the wheat farmers is the distress that inheres in over-production. . . . Artificial price fixing or subsidies from the government would stimulate production and aggravate the evil we are asked to cure. . . . The economic hurt of over-production is self healing. . . . Nature when given a chance corrects a lopsided economic situation." The Republican Party could not "approve of governmental subsidies to overbuilt industries." The comparison of farm production to "overbuilt industries" showed how far Hoover was from understanding or sympathizing with the farmers' plight. When a delegation came to him in June, 1930, to plead for a Federal program of public works for the unemployed, the President told them, "Gentlemen, you have come sixty days too late. The Depression is over."

In October, 1930, when the economy continued in desperate straits, Hoover set up the Committee for Unemployment Relief, headed by Walter Gifford of American Telephone and Telegraph. The principal task of the committee was to raise $175,000,000 by putting on sporting events and theater benefits. Although Gifford called the committee's work "a great spiritual experience," only $100,000,000 was raised before it disbanded. Perhaps Hoover's most bizarre remedy for the Depression was his suggestion "Perhaps what this country needs is a great poem. Something to lift people out of fear and selfishness. Sometimes a great poem can do more than legislation. . . ."

Congress passed legislation establishing the Reconstruction Finance Corporation, which provided government loans to corporations, specifically banks and railroads, as a stimulus to the national economy and to help create jobs. The RFC was given some $500,000,000 and authority to borrow $2,000,000 more for loans; Charles Dawes was appointed to head the new agency. Within six months it had made loans to some 5,000 financial institutions, among them life insurance companies and farm credit corporations. Under the Glass-Steagall Act, passed a few weeks later, the Federal Reserve Board was authorized to make another $750,000,000 available out of the government gold supply to support the currency.

The Federal Home Loan Bank Act was proposed by Hoover and passed in July. It provided for a five-man board and established a number of discount banks for home mortgages. The purpose was to reduce foreclosures and stimulate construction of new homes, but the money was made available only to banks, savings and loan institutions, and insurance companies. It was little comfort to desperate farmers and men and women without jobs.

The hard times were felt in Europe as acutely as in the United States. In the election of September, 1930, the Nazi Party received eight times as many votes as it had two years earlier.

Austria and Germany entered into a customs union to encourage free trade between the two nations. France took the line at once that the agreement was tantamount to a union between the two nations in defiance of the Versailles Treaty, and when the Kreditanstalt in Vienna in May, 1931, was faced with collapse, France refused to join the United States and Great Britain in an effort to salvage the bank. Two months later the Darmstädter National Bank in Germany collapsed, and Chancellor Brüning declared a bank holiday. His policies were much the same as Hoover's: governmental economy and retrenchment.

Hoover responded to the failure of the Darmstädter und National bank by a moratorium on reparations payments and debts among allies. There was a run on the Bank of England in September, and Britain was forced off the gold standard. The economy of the entire Western world felt the shock. A run on the dollar followed. In the United States more than 1,000 banks went belly up during the last three months of 1931.

The Nazis reveled in the opportunity that the economic chaos presented to them. "Never in my life have I been as well disposed and inwardly contented as in these days," Adolf Hitler announced in his party's newspaper. When Langston Hughes passed through Berlin on the way to his exotic film venture in Russia, it seemed to him "a wretched city. . . . The streets . . . teemed with prostitutes, pimps, panderers and vendors of dirty pictures. Some of the young men in our group got acquainted for the first time with . . . 'perversions.' "

In Hamburg, a year later, on his way to the Lenin School, Steve Nelson saw squads of Nazis in parliamentary dress, some with weapons, strutting and posturing. There were constant skirmishes in front of the headquarters of leftist organizations. "I felt that I was in some kind of a madhouse," Nelson wrote. Germans taunted Nelson and Mack Coad, a black man, calling out "Monkey" and "Go back to Africa."

In the Far East the Japanese Army had become virtually autonomous. After capturing Mukden and Dairen, it had undertaken the "rape of Manchuria." When the Japanese premier, Ki Inukai, ordered the army home from its orgy of pillage, the seventy-seven-year-old premier was murdered by a band of young naval officers. The assassins had met first at a Shinto shrine sacred to the dead warriors of Japan and then had gone to the shrine of the forty-seven *ronin*, where a band of samurai warriors had committed seppuku after avenging an insult to their feudal lord.

The minister of war, Sadao Araki, the virtual ruler of Japan and the architect of its imperial expansion, told Frazier Hunt that Japan had assimilated too many ideas from the West. It must now retrieve its own culture, the warrior culture of feudal Japan. "If we fail to do this," Araki declared, "Japan fails. There is no time for talk; we must act before it is too late. We must purify our national life and build a new Japan."

When Japan invaded Manchuria in October, 1931, Walter Lippmann wrote to his friend Russell Leffingwell that it would be an "absolute disaster" if the League of Nations failed to take strong action. Secretary of State Henry Stimson informed Japan *and* China that the United States would not recognize any treaty or accord that was in direct or indirect conflict with John Hay's Open Door policy or that was in violation of the Kellogg-Briand Pact.

The League's solution, if it could be called that, was to propose that Manchuria be recognized as "an autonomous state" under Chinese sovereignty but Japanese control, surely one of the oddest notions in the history of international diplomacy. Japan was dissatisfied with even such a mild rebuff and withdrew from the League.

Hamilton Fish Armstrong found that everyone in Washington "agreed that Europe was in a mess and that France was responsible. . . . Ogden Mills [secretary of the treasury], in a bellicose and rah-rah mood, thumped on his desk as he related Europe's stupidities, failures and iniquities and emphasized that the United States had best leave Europe out of its calculations for the next generation or so." The secretary declared the French the "most stupid and obstructionist people in the world. They were responsible for the failure of the Hoover moratorium last year. It was their last chance to get American cooperation. We will never again take the initiative to help save Europe. If anything was needed after that experience to give a measure of the puny people who are running Europe, it was supplied the other day in London when they couldn't agree on measures to save the miserable little Danube states which had been established by the insane people at the Paris Peace Conference and allowed to set up insane tariff barriers." When Armstrong replied that it hardly behooved the United States to criticize other nations for raising tariff barriers, Mills said curtly that American tariffs were "traditional," as though that excused them. He thanked God for them; Europe was "done for and deserved to be."

Amid such international and domestic disarray, Russia seemed to an increasing number of Americans a beacon of hope. When Frazier Hunt returned to Russia, he had, he noted, "lost much of my initial passionate enthusiasm for this magnificent experiment." He had become too much absorbed "by the easy flow of life." His most illuminating talk was with Madame Aleksandra Kollontai, the first woman ambassador of the Soviet Union—ambassador to Mexico. America, she told him, had had an enormous influence on Russia. "You never hear the name of any other country but America spoken here. When a boy is dressed up his friends tell him he is 'dressed like an American.' America is always the point of comparison. Our people like Americans. We do not mistrust you. We know deep down that in your hearts you do not wish us ill." All revolutions, Kollontai told Hunt, had their own individual characteristics and trajectories. The French Revolution had little similarity to that original revolution, the American Revolution. The Russian and Mexican revolutions, by the same token, had nothing in common. "And the Chinese revolution will be unlike either. China will have her great upheaval when her people get ready for it—and they will have it in their own way. It is silly to think that a handful of Russian advisers can prepare the minds of four hundred million Chinese for any great change. They have to do that themselves."

Hunt was impressed with a school where young men and women, many of them from peasant families, were learning to be factory foremen and supervisors. They were full of zeal for the new order. Black leather coats and high boots were the uniforms of the new bureaucrats, most of whom were conspicuously young. "They were the new men of the new Russia . . . [and] the result of twelve years of intense preaching and propaganda; and of three previous years of war and starvation. They were hard, unsympathetic, determined . . . [and] turned into steel by the fires of revolution." They had had it drilled into them that they were the "chosen people of tomorrow's world. They alone were wise and right." The result was an arrogance that was matched only by their ignorance of the world outside the Soviet Union. To Hunt's Western eye, everything was "slipshod, inefficient, and very dirty. But behind and underneath it was something fine and gallant. With pathetic bravery," Hunt wrote, "these people were trying suddenly to transform a backward agriculture into a modern, efficient industrial system." Everywhere he heard the slogan "America is our goal." In Hunt's words, "they believe that to date America has built the finest civilization in the world, but they believe the Soviet Union can build a paradise, and that they can surpass America. Once they build their new life they think the rest of the world will revolt and build a culture like theirs." To Hunt it seemed evident that Russia and the United States were the "two great imaginative nations of the world. . . . Both countries had power, will, energy, imagination, and good hearts. Each had unlimited lands, vast resources, sturdy peoples, mighty dreams." They had entered into a contest to see which "could do most for common man—could first do away with poverty, disease, ignorance, intolerance."

The slowest and, in the long run, most important consequence of the continuing Depression was the nation's gradual disenchantment with business leadership. As Claude Bowers put it, "The long depression, with millions dependent on charity for life, had the result of disillusioning the average American about the superhuman wisdom of the great financiers. Most Americans until then had kept a childlike faith in the capacity of the bankers and great industrialists to do anything they wished. For some months it was pathetic to see how many clung to the illusion." Hoover inadvertently contributed to that disillusionment by summoning the great tycoons to the White House, where it became increasingly evident they were as bankrupt of ideas and as demoralized as the President himself.

Lincoln Steffens, who had returned to the United States with his family in the midst of the boom and been struck by the apparent vitality of capitalism, not surprisingly had second thoughts. In his words, it was "a hard-boiled business perception that mass production and mass distribution required mass prosperity, not individual riches—not a few, not even a lot, of rich people, but the general distribution of wealth in the form of wages, salaries, and earnings among men and women who are both workers and consumers." But business, out of greed, had ignored that "perception." Steffens was ready to concede that "big business had won in the long struggle which we muckrakers had reported only the superficial evils of; we and the liberals, progressives, and reformers had been beaten. The process of corruption had culminated in the comfortable establishment of the big bribers in power." The symbol of the victory of the "big bribers" to Steffens was their summoning to the White House by Hoover. The President thereby recognized officially, so to speak, that big business ran the country. Now there was no longer the need to pretend that the "people" were in the driver's seat. To Steffens, veteran of so many campaigns against the alliance of business and politics, it seemed the most significant moment in his lifetime. Business had absorbed government. Hoover affirmed the "ownership and management by business men of all business, including land and natural resources, transportation, power, light. Good business is all the good we need. Politics was the only evil." Hoover was contemptuous of traditional politicians. He was an engineer, at heart neither a Democrat nor a Republican. "I can assert,"

Steffens wrote, "that everybody was for business; even the Democrats, who voted for Smith, were for good business. . . ."

The election of 1928 was "an economic election which sent to the White House Herbert Hoover to do what he is trying to do: to represent business openly, as Coolidge and other presidents had covertly. . . . The Harding way was the old, the politician's way. The Coolidge way was the new American, the old English, the respectable, businesslike way of representing business, and that Hoover personified. No need of bribing him, no excuse for any graft in the White House. Bribery and corruption were over. President Hoover, like Coolidge, honestly believed that government should favor big business, without price. . . . The engineer President was bringing to the throne, formally and publicly, the potential heads of our two actual governments: the industrial government and the political government; the government which fixes the people's wages, working-hours and conditions and therefore governs their lives in the shop and in the kitchen, and the political government which manages them socially. . . . A victory. A marriage. One can't sneer any more that Washington is the kept woman of Wall Street. They are man and wife, and that changes everything; it makes the old wrong right. It makes Washington a decent woman."

But, as became increasingly evident, it did nothing to remedy the disasters of the Depression. The newly married couple—business and politics—seemed to be on the way to the poorhouse or, some thought, to revolution. "I went to New York," Steffens wrote, "to hear the semi-scientific captains of industry say in words and facial expressions that they did not know what had happened or what was to be done about it. They did not understand their own experiment. Then—not until then—did I give up—and turned to see what else there was." In another letter he wrote, "Nobody in the world *proposes* anything basic and real except the Communists." Steffens declared: "I am not a Communist, I merely think that the next order of society will be socialist and that the Communists will bring it in and lead it."

The principal beneficiary of the debacle of Black Monday and the subsequent slide into the depths of the nation's worst depression was, of course, the Communist Party. The worldwide economic collapse was an almost letter-perfect fulfillment of Marx's predictions about the inevitable breakdown of capitalism essentially caused by its inherent contradictions. Stalin, interpreting Marx, had predicted in 1928, at the time of the enunciation of the third period, that the collapse of capitalism was imminent. A little more than a year later capitalism had obligingly collapsed. What could be more scientific! For millions of "leftists" the world around, the fulfillment of Stalin's prediction was the conclusive proof of the scientific character of "dialectical materialism." The present Communist leader, William Foster, gave an account of the crisis that was hard to disagree with: "Millions of workers must go hungry because there is too much wheat. Millions of workers must go without clothes because the warehouses are full to overflowing with everything that is needed. Millions of workers must freeze because there is too much coal. This is the logic of the capitalist system." What was less noted (although it could not be wholly ignored) was that Stalin negated much of the effectiveness of his prediction by what, in retrospect, appeared a serious strategic error: the "separate course" for communism, in which cooperation with all "bourgeois" or "reformist" organizations was forbidden.

Not surprisingly, the Communists were most successful with the unemployed. When Steve Nelson moved to Chicago to do organizing work for the party, a fellow carpenter told him, "You might as well store the toolbox away. Save yourself the trouble of looking around. There's not a job in the city." Nelson wrote: "Unemployment hung over the city like a storm cloud. . . . Workers lined up in front of factories and mills in spite of signs 'No Help Wanted.' Standing around the lines you could feel a desperate mood. No one knew where the next dollar for food or rent would come from. . . ."

Although the third period dogma forbade cooperation with liberals and radicals, non-Communist "social-Fascist" organizations, the party often skirted or evaded the prohibition by its use of fronts, which, while not carrying the party designation, were in effect controlled by it. The fronts seemed endless. Josephine Herbst had her name on the letterheads of several dozen: the Prisoners Relief Fund, the National Committee for the Defense of Political Prisoners, the League of Women Shoppers, the League of American Writers, the Anti-Fascist Literature Committee, Frontier Films, and a number of others. The most successful front was the so-called Unemployed Councils.

When Steve Nelson and his wife, Margaret, began organizing Unemployed Councils in the Pennsylvania coalfields, they were astonished at the response. Seventy people crowded into the poolroom that served as a meeting hall. "Just being together with others facing similar problems made people willing to voice their grievances," Nelson noted. "One woman was suffering from diabetes and had no money for medicine. Others had little or no food, and right in the middle of the anthracite coalfields, people were often short of heating fuel. The neighborhood kids walked the railroad tracks searching for stray lumps of coal, and they often boarded the freight cars to push a few lumps off."

For all its "ugliness and poverty," Nelson wrote, "Margaret and I loved the anthracite fields. It was the first place where we actually felt at home. Even though we seldom had a nickel between us, we could feel that we were sharing what we had with others and we counted on them to share with us. Margaret spent a lot of her time bailing me out of jail, but we never felt defeated or isolated, I could always rely on the support of a group of comrades who were as dedicated to one another as to the movement itself." It was a feeling that remained with the Nelsons throughout their lives together, long after the clamor of battle was only a memory.

Hosea Hudson, the black Communist, organized "unemployed block committees" in the various black sections of Birmingham, Alabama. The principal task of a block committee was to assist people on welfare who were having difficulties with the state or municipal agencies responsible for distributing welfare. In Hudson's words, "We didn't wait for people to come to get us when they didn't get their grocery order or their coal order from welfare. We would go around to see what the conditions was." A representative of the block committee or, in more serious cases, of the Central Unemployed Council would visit the welfare office in support of an individual or a family entangled in some bureaucratic web or simply to have a new regulation or policy explained and spread the word to the community of unemployed. According to Hudson, unemployment relief was the most important issue for blacks. It was a matter not only of food but of fuel and, above all, of rent or mortgage payments. Hudson and his fellow party members helped organize demonstrations and protests on a wide variety of issues, but aside from lynchings, few were as potent as the issue of preventing evictions. The principal deterrent to eviction was the fact that an abandoned house was soon dismantled for fuel. It happened most commonly at night. Within a few weeks an abandoned house was often reduced to a chimney. Landlords who tried to evict tenants or banks that threatened to foreclose were reminded that their houses might not long survive. "When they'd put a family out, the people's like eating them up, just like a fire, eating them up," in Hudson's words.

Wyndham Mortimer testified that he was attracted to the Communist Party by one of its most successful fronts, the Small Home and

Landowners League, formed to prevent people behind on their rents or mortgage payments from being evicted. "I attended their meetings and joined their association," Mortimer wrote. ". . . I was not so much interested in the labels the newspapers attached to the organization as to the work they were doing: saving people's homes. . . . A moratorium on mortgage payments was eventually established, and thousands of little people's homes were saved largely through the leadership of the Communist Party and organizations it influenced. I became very active in this movement, and worked with the Communists in organizing picket lines, demonstrations and other activities. In fact, the only effective struggles against unemployment and evictions were those organized by the Communist Party." In Cleveland the Small Home Owners League counted some 20,000 members.

The cry of "Reds" directed at the Unemployed Councils often backfired. Steve Nelson recalled that people started answering, "So what? Even if they are Communists, they are trying to help us help ourselves and no one else is doing that." That response was especially common among blacks.

The National Unemployed Council led demonstrations and hunger marches in cities across the country. These were, in essence, Communist-organized events that helped dramatize the desperate situation of the unemployed. They were in practical fact the most effective measures undertaken during the Depression. It would not be far off the mark to call them guerrilla theater on a national scale.

March 6, 1930, had been set by the Comintern as the date for demonstrations by the unemployed in industrial nations around the world. Two weeks before the demonstrations Steve Nelson summoned the heads of the Chicago Unemployed Councils and other radical activists to a planning session at Machinists' Hall. About 600 men and women attended. As they left the meeting, a dozen paddy wagons drove up. Those who had attended were forced to pass through police lines and be searched, and 113 were pushed into the paddy wagons. At the police station members of the police force's "Red Squad" winnowed the group further, keeping 14, Steve Nelson among them, as "masterminds" of the "Red Conspiracy." They all were systematically beaten. A detective named Miller singled out Nelson for his attentions. Taking off his glasses and wristwatch, Miller put on a pair of canvas gloves and took out a pearl-handled blackjack. Starting with Nelson's head, the detective beat him all over his body. When he fell out of the chair semiconscious, Miller kicked him as hard as he could in the ribs. The others fared as badly or worse. One man was ruptured. B. D. Amos, a black, had all his front teeth knocked out. Two weeks later Nelson marched with 75,000 other Chicago unemployed; over the nation more than 1,000,000 men and women turned out to demonstrate for relief funds and unemployment insurance. By this time the beating of Nelson and his friends had become something of a national scandal. When they came to trial before a jury made up largely of workingmen, some of whom were themselves unemployed, they all were acquitted of criminal conspiracy.

In Chicago and many other cities a systematic policy of police harassment was directed against street corner speakers, against radicals, protesters, and the Unemployed Councils. In the spring of 1930 Steve Nelson estimated that more than 100 political activists were in Chicago jails, but with the support of the International Labor Defense all of them were freed.

In New York City in 1930 the Communist Party called for a May Day mass meeting of the unemployed at Union Square. With the square ringed by police, many of them mounted, a scuffle broke out and soon flared into wild fighting, with police clubs raining down on the skulls of the demonstrators. Again hundreds were injured, some seriously, and Robert Minor was arrested and given a prison sentence for speech tending to produce riot.

Wyndham Mortimer recalled that demonstrations of 10,000 people in the Cleveland Public Square were not uncommon. During one of them a farmer arrived with a truckful of strawberries which, in desperation, he offered to sell for four cents a box. There were no buyers; everyone was too poor. The farmer gave his strawberries away, asking only that the boxes be returned.

By the fall of 1931 virtually every large city had an Unemployed Council. Anxious to exploit the popularity of the councils, the Communist Party organized a National Hunger March to be made up primarily of Unemployed Council members from various cities. It was to converge on Washington early in December to present a petition for unemployment relief to Congress. According to Benjamin Gitlow, the Comintern put $100,000 into organizing the hunger march, a sum that grew to $200,000 before the march was over. Much of the money was spent to hire trucks and buses to carry the demonstrators to Washington. Among the sponsors of the march were the Young Communist League; the Young Pioneers; the Trade Union Unity League (a Communist-front group); the International Workers Order;

the League for the Defense of the Foreign Born; the Workers Ex-Servicemen's League; the United Council of Working Class Women; various social and fraternal organizations, church, school, and college groups; and, of course, the Unemployed Councils.

Malcolm Cowley and Robert Cantwell drove to Washington to cover the march. They joined one column as it passed through a town in Virginia some thirty miles from the capital. It was made up of old trucks and buses. Outside Washington, police separated the ragged cavalcade from the regular traffic and directed it into a kind of trap—a long stretch of highway with steep embankments on each side. When most of the vehicles of the march were strung along that particular stretch of road, both ends were closed by police with machine guns. Other police armed with tear gas and a new nauseating gas patrolled the line while police officials communicated with headquarters by field telephones. Army planes circled above. Rumors had circulated that the marchers planned to seize the city and place Congress under siege. Since it was evident that the marchers were unarmed (about a third were women), it was reported that one van contained machine guns and rifles. When a truck came out of Washington with hot soup and coffee, the police stopped it. Although it was December, the chilled men and women were not allowed to start fires. When nightfall came, the little army made itself as comfortable as it could.

Cowley and Cantwell spent the night in Washington, and when they returned the next morning to what Cowley called the "detention camp," they discovered that the police had been trying to provoke an "incident" that would justify the use of tear gas. "They bullied and cursed the marchers in the hope of meeting resistance," Cowley wrote. Food had finally been allowed to reach the caravan, but there were no latrines or running water, and if a woman went into the bushes, she would be surrounded by mocking police. When one column of trucks approached a barricade, Cowley heard a policeman shout, "Come on, you yellow bastards. Try and break through." Stories of the treatment of the protesters appeared in Washington newspapers, and angry Congressmen of progressive persuasion demanded that the "army" of unemployed be permitted to enter the city and present its petition to Congress. Those who were not too ill or weary from their detention did finally "march" to Capitol Hill. Congress received their "demands" but, not surprisingly, adjourned without taking any action.

State capitols were favorite sites for demonstrations when legislatures were in session. A typical such demonstration was that at Harrisburg, the capital of Pennsylvania, in 1932. Gifford Pinchot, father of the American conservation movement, was governor of the state. When the various contingents, totaling about 7,000 men and women, arrived at the outskirts of Harrisburg, they were met by a large force of state troopers, who informed them that Governor Pinchot forbade their entering the city. The "marchers," most of whom were in battered trucks and old Fords, had nowhere to make camp. A hospitable Moravian farmer made his large barns and ample fields available, and the next day Pinchot allowed the protesters to enter the state capital. They marched twenty abreast for eight blocks, carrying banners which declared, "We Demand Unemployment Insurance!" "We Demand Relief!" "We Demand Assistance to the Needy!" "Moratorium for Farmers!" State legislators, always susceptible to voters, mingled with the marchers on the capitol grounds, assuring them of their sympathy and concern. Pinchot offered them the state grounds for their encampment until they had had time to present their demands to the legislature. The marchers wanted four speakers to address the legislature; the governor replied that he would allow one. But three others slipped down ropes from the balcony and were granted permission to speak.

The May Day parade in 1932 in New York City was an unusually large one: The *Daily Worker* reported more than 100,000 marchers; the *New York Times*, 35,000. Malcolm Cowley was one of the marchers, along with a number of writers from the National Council for the Defense of Political Prisoners. He marched with John Herrmann and the members of the John Reed Club and a delegation from the *New Masses*. A large group of college students was in the parade, chanting, "We confess communism." Heavy rain hardly dampened the mood of the marchers, which was jubilant and "revolutionary" but orderly.

Benjamin Gitlow points out that while the Communist Party polled only 103,000 votes in 1932, it was successful in organizing 4,000,000 unemployed workers. Gitlow estimated that of the more than 100,000 marchers who turned out for May Day parades in New York City during the midyears of the 1930s, fewer than 10,000 were party members. The rest of those who marched and sang, who carried banners and displayed revolutionary slogans were Communist sympathizers. It seemed to them that communism was the next stage in American history, and they were anxious to abet it, if not zealous enough to join the party itself.

# 13

## The Democratic Convention

As the presidential election of 1932 approached, talk of revolution was common. In Mississippi Senator Theodore Bilbo, the embodiment of reactionary politics, declared late in 1931, "Folks are getting restless. Communism is gaining a foothold. Right here in Mississippi some people are about ready to lead a mob. In fact, I'm getting a little pink myself." In the spring of 1932 Edward F. McGrady, a conservative old-line AFL officer, told a Senate committee, "I say to you gentlemen, advisedly, that if something is not done and starvation is going to continue, the doors of revolt in this country are going to be thrown open." Hamilton Fish, Franklin Roosevelt's Dutchess County neighbor, declared that if the "existing system" could not provide security for Americans, "the people will change the system. Make no mistake about that." The labor journalist Benjamin Stolberg wrote in the summer of 1932: "From Union Square to Park Avenue, New York is full of crazy talk about the 'coming revolution.'" He then went ahead in a jocular spirit to list his choices for commissars under the revolutionary regime.

There was also much talk of the need for a "strong leader." Senator David A. Reed of Pennsylvania declared, "I do not often envy other people their government but I say that if this country ever needed a Mussolini, it needs one now." Al Smith asked, "What does a democ-

317

racy do in war? It becomes a tyrant, a despot, a real monarch. In the World War we took our constitution, wrapped it up and laid it on the shelf and left it there until it was over." The clear implication was that the time had arrived for similar measures.

Felix Frankfurter wrote to Walter Lippmann in April 1932: "Mine being a pragmatic temperament, all my scepticism and discontent with the present order and tendencies have not carried me over to a new comprehensive scheme of society, whether socialism or communism. Or, perhaps ten years in government, and as many more of intensive study of its problems, have made me also sceptical of any full-blown new scheme and left me most conscious of the extraordinary difficulties of the problems of the Great Society." Frankfurter feared that a consequence of the Depression would be that "a greater percentage of the wealth of the country will have been found to have come into the control of even a smaller percentage of the population than was the case before the depression." If that turned out to be true, it would be difficult to prevent "a sudden and drastic break with the past. . . ." The result would be that the hopes of gradualists like himself that "successive, although large, modifications may slowly evolve out of this profit-making society [would be] reduced to a house of cards."

Claude Bowers, looking back on those perilous days from the relative calm of the 1950s, wrote: "In sober truth we were on the verge of revolution." Political parties and movements sprang up like mushrooms: Labor, Socialist Labor, Farm-Labor, Farmer-Labor, Progressive, Independent Liberty, Independent Republicans, Farmer, Independence, Single Tax, Law Preservation, Enforcement Allies, American, National Jobless, Populist, and People's. Colonel House, Woodrow Wilson's mentor, was convinced that "a social overturn" was coming in the United States. He pledged Hamilton Fish Armstrong to absolute secrecy and then told him that William McAdoo had informed him a few days earlier that anticipating the collapse of both the old parties, he was preparing with Senator Bob La Follette and other "progressives" to start a new party. House did not take the report lightly; McAdoo was a man of "great drive, courage and intellectual power."

That Hoover would be the candidate of the Republican Party in 1932 was a foregone conclusion. The leading Democratic candidate was the governor of New York, Franklin Delano Roosevelt. To Roosevelt and Louis Howe there was no question that the time was ripe for Roosevelt's candidacy. Roosevelt had expressed doubt that a Democrat could win the office until a Republican had led the country into a depression. That had happened far more extremely, indeed, than Roosevelt could have imagined.

The groundwork for Roosevelt's campaign had been laid with great care over the past twelve years (it would not be farfetched to say twenty-two if we take account of the fact that he was spoken of as a prospective President from the time of his first entry into politics as a New York legislator). Roosevelt had served a dutiful apprenticeship: vice-presidential candidate on the Cox ticket in 1920; loyal supporter of Al Smith in the preconvention period in 1924, when the nomination went to John W. Davis; nominator of Smith again in 1928, when Smith won his party's nomination, and, more important, a reluctant candidate for governor of New York in order to strengthen Smith's ticket; and then a highly visible and very successful governor of the nation's largest state. On January 30, 1932, he would be fifty years old. Roosevelt and Louis Howe decided to make his candidacy official by entering his name in the North Dakota primary. James Farley had that state's nine delegates already lined up for Roosevelt. Smith had given repeated assurances to the Roosevelt camp that he had no further political ambitions. He had lost heavily in the stock market, he told Ed Flynn, and had to recoup his own fortunes. But political office is like a fatal disease, generally incurable. Al Smith had terminal politics in his blood. To Roosevelt's surprise, he declared soon after Roosevelt's announcement that he, too, would be a candidate for his party's nomination.

Colonel House's explanation of Smith's change of mind was that as a down-to-earth, lower-middle-class Tammany politician he simply could not take Roosevelt, the politician, seriously. To Smith Roosevelt was a gentleman playing at politics for want of something better to do, to entertain himself. "Smith looks on Roosevelt as a sort of Boy Scout," House told Hamilton Fish Armstrong; "doesn't really think of him as an equal."

When Clark Howell, publisher of the *Atlanta Constitution*, asked Smith if he would support Roosevelt if he became the Democratic nominee in the coming presidential election, Smith was evasive. "He has always been kind to me and my family," Smith said, "and has gone out of his way to be agreeable to us at the Mansion at Albany but [stamping his foot] do you know, by God, that he has never consulted me about a damn thing since he has been Governor? He has taken bad advice and from sources not friendly to me. He has ignored me!" Al Smith would not have been human if he had not had bitter reflections on having been his party's candidate in what had turned out to be a hopeless race. The principal beneficiary of his defeat had been Roosevelt.

Although Roosevelt may have appeared the inevitable candidate, he and Howe were acutely aware of the dangers facing a front-runner in any presidential nominating convention. All prospective rivals are ready to make common cause in opposing him. For a Democrat front-runner the problem was made additionally hazardous by virtue of the fact that a two-thirds majority vote was necessary for nomination. This requirement had been the downfall of one front-runner after another, the most recent victim having been William McAdoo in 1924. In addition to those party leaders who coveted the nomination for themselves, Roosevelt had enemies in the conservative wing of the party, men and women who considered him much too radical to be the party's standard-bearer. It was, in consequence, necessary to proceed with the greatest caution, keeping a careful eye out for all potential booby traps, the most dangerous of which may well have been Tammany Hall.

Among those elder statesmen of the party whose advice and support Roosevelt sought were Colonel House and Roosevelt's old boss Josephus Daniels. The fact was that Roosevelt's ties to Wilson's administration were strong. It was his conviction that the last Democratic President had initiated a program of reform that must be revived for the good of the nation. The war and its dismal aftermath had all but obliterated the memory of the New Freedom from the minds of the American electorate, but to Roosevelt it was an incomplete agenda that was never far from his thoughts. House was the closest living link to the Wilson administration. Despite Wilson's rejection of him, House had preserved his affection and admiration for the strange man whom he had served faithfully. Almost a year before the Democratic presidential convention Roosevelt sought House out. He would, he told him, like House and Owen D. Young, another relic of the Wilson days, to act as his confidential advisers. Approaching House at all represented a risk for Roosevelt. House was identified in the popular mind with the Versailles Treaty and the League of Nations—with internationalism in general—and was thus a red flag to isolationists in the Republican Party and in the Democratic Party as well. He was particularly obnoxious to the old Progressive-isolationists like William Borah and Hiram Johnson, men of otherwise liberal persuasion who were, for the most part, favorably inclined toward Roosevelt. House, plainly pleased to be consulted, consented to act as an adviser but warned against Young. Young's advice on political matters, House declared, "couldn't be of any conceivable use to Roosevelt." Roosevelt told Louis Howe of his session with House, and Howe, apparently jealous of the threat to his role as Roosevelt's closest counselor, tipped off a reporter for the *Herald Tribune*. The Howe leak brought the prospective role of House out into the open; after that the contacts were infrequent. For Roosevelt the seeking out of House had been in the nature of an apostolic succession; it symbolized Roosevelt's place in a Democratic line of descent that, for him at least, began with Thomas Jefferson and continued down through Woodrow Wilson.

House, perhaps piqued when Roosevelt failed to consult him, gave Hamilton Fish Armstrong a rather unflattering estimate of Roosevelt. "Between you and me and the angels," he did not consider him a great man or even the best man available for President. House preferred Newton D. Baker, an important participant in the Wilson administration. But House agreed that Roosevelt was "honest and able, that he was the most available candidate and the one that stood the best chance of being elected if nominated." Roosevelt was strong in those states where Wilson had been strong, and the progressive wing of the Democratic Party supported him. "I would very much like to see Baker President," House told Armstrong, "but it would be much harder to elect him than to elect Roosevelt, and I don't at all agree with the people who say any Democrat can be elected this year." Then he added, "The only Democrat in sight for the nomination that I think definitely could *not* be elected is Smith." If Roosevelt were elected President and chose Baker as his secretary of state, House believed, "we would get just as much of what you and I want . . . as we would with Baker as President; and the first is much easier to get than the second." What "you and I" wanted was an enlightened foreign policy in which the United States would abandon its isolationism and play a responsible role in trying to prevent the outbreak of another European war.

On April 7, 1932, Roosevelt gave a radio speech as a spokesman for the Democratic National Committee in which he staked out the grounds on which he intended to run. He attacked what was later termed the "trickle-down" proposals of the Republicans and called for a program "that builds from the bottom up and not from the top down, that puts the faith once more in the forgotten man at the bottom of the economic pyramid." Raymond Moley, who wrote the speech, had picked up the phrase "forgotten man" from William Graham Sumner, who was referring to the middle-class taxpayer who, he felt, bore a disproportionate burden in society. Roosevelt's talk, widely rebroadcast, came to be known as the "forgotten man" speech. It made a deep impression in the farm areas of the Middle West, but it angered conservatives in the Democratic Party. Al Smith declared, "I will take off my coat and fight to the end against any candidate who persists in any demagogic appeal to the working people of this country to destroy themselves by setting class against class, and rich against poor."

A month later Roosevelt further alarmed the conservatives. At Warm Springs several reporters assigned to the leading candidate for the Democratic nomination chided him for not being bold enough in his public pronouncements. When Roosevelt challenged them to produce a speech that would meet their requirements, Ernest Lindley, a reporter for the *New York Herald Tribune*, offered to produce such a document.

The ideas and much of the language of Lindley were incorporated in a speech Roosevelt gave several weeks later at Oglethorpe University in Atlanta. "The country needs and, unless I mistake its temper, the country demands bold, persistent experimentation. It is common sense to take a method and try it," Roosevelt declared. "If it fails, admit it frankly and try another. But above all, try something. The millions who are in want will not stand by silently forever while the things to satisfy their needs are within easy reach."

Roosevelt called on his listeners to look back at the "history of our industrial advance." One could not do so without being struck "with its haphazardness, the gigantic waste with which it has been accomplished, the superfluous duplication of productive facilities, the continual scrapping of still useful equipment, the tremendous mortality in industrial and commercial undertakings, the thousands of dead-end trails into which enterprise has been lured, the profligate waste of natural resources." Much of the waste and misuse of the nation's material wealth had been the "inevitable by-product of progress in a society which values individual endeavor. . . . But much of it . . . could have been prevented by greater foresight and planning." The fact was that "such controlling and directive forces" had been developed by special-interest groups whose "interests . . . do not coincide with the interests of the Nation as a whole. . . . [A]rea after area has been preempted altogether by the great corporations," Roosevelt declared, "and even in the fields which still have no great concerns the small man starts under a handicap." A recent study had revealed that the nation's economic life was dominated by "some six hundred and odd corporations, who controlled two-thirds of American industry . . .

[and] it appeared that, if the process of concentration goes on at the same rate, at the end of another century we shall have all American industry controlled by a dozen corporations and run by perhaps a hundred men." Roosevelt rejected emphatically the idea that under the banner of the "sacred word" "individualism," "a few powerful interests should be permitted to make industrial fodder of the lives of half the population of the United States."

The speech, which bore the imprint of the Rexford Tugwell "collectivist" faction in what was already being called Roosevelt's Brain Trust, charmed Senator Huey Long. He quoted it with warm approval in *Every Man a King*. That was indeed what Long had been saying for ten years or more in Louisiana. "I drank of the fountain of a new life," he wrote, "as I saw, heard and read of his expounding the principles which had guided my activities throughout my public career. To my heart, such pronouncements were relighting the lamp of 'America's dream.'"

The fact that Roosevelt responded to the challenge of a party of newsmen and then incorporated their handiwork in a public address tells as much about him as any single episode from this period of his life. His supreme self-confidence freed him to gather ideas wherever he found them without fear of seeming imitative or dependent on the judgment of others. The speech alarmed, among others, Louis Howe, who warned him that many influential Democrats, among them some of the party's leading financial backers, already suspected him of being a dangerous radical. Such talk might be acceptable once he had won the nomination, but before that it could only cost him precious votes among the delegates. The fact that Roosevelt subsequently muted his calls for change and experimentation and, even after his nomination, spoke more in generalities than particulars, helped contribute to the impression that the New Deal was, in a manner of speaking, thought up on the spot once he had become President. The truth was far different. Roosevelt's own basic political philosophy and, perhaps even more important, the moral imperatives that moved him were deeply rooted in his education, his family tradition, his own thinking and reading, and, above all, those brilliant and interminable conversations over which he presided with such skill and assurance.

Nor was it the fact that timidity or even the desire not to alarm any substantial segment of the voting public inclined Roosevelt to talk more about general principles than about practices. With his questing, restless mind, he wished to remain free to shift his ground, to change direction, or to improvise as the occasion required or offered. Even more important, he believed it was his mission to educate the electorate, to wean or woo it from restrictive, obsolete, or irrelevant notions, to prepare it psychologically and intellectually for the specific measures that must be enacted. He needed, above all, the support of that mysterious element called a climate of opinion if he was to have a relatively free hand to develop an effective legislative program. His enemies were not conservative Republicans or Southern Democrats but outmoded ideas, inhibiting political shibboleths.

The first national convention in 1932 was that of the Socialist Labor Party, which held its convention in New York in April and nominated Verne L. Reynolds for President and J. W. Aiken from Massachusetts as Vice-President. The Socialist Party, meeting at Milwaukee, the city most closely identified with it, nominated Norman Thomas for President and James H. Maurer of Pennsylvania for Vice-President. At the end of May the Communist Party held its convention in New York City in an euphoric atmosphere. Despite the bitter factional quarrels occasioned by Stalin's third period dogma, the party had grown rapidly. William Foster, who had demonstrated a notable capacity for adapting himself to Moscow's line, was once more the party's presidential candidate, but Benjamin Gitlow, vice-presidential candidate in 1928, was conspicuous by his absence. He had been expelled for his Trotskyite heresies and replaced by James Ford, the first black vice-presidential candidate. The party's platform contained six planks. It urged that "unemployment and Social Insurance" be paid by the state and the employers for all workers, that there be emergency relief for farmers without restriction, and that poor farmers be exempt from taxes and forced collection of rents or debts. Perhaps the most controversial and impractical plank called for the establishment of a Black Belt black state. This, of course, was a reflection of Comintern policy. Another plank denounced all forms of suppression of the right of workers to organize. Finally, the sixth plank opposed "imperialist wars" and called for the defense of the Chinese and of the Soviet Union.

The Prohibition Party, well aware that Prohibition was under attack, convened in Indianapolis and nominated William Upshaw of Georgia as its Presidential candidate.

On July 9 the Farmer-Labor Party National Committee met at Omaha and nominated old Jacob Coxey, who had led the "army" of unemployed to Washington to seek relief during the depression of the mid-nineties. In August the Liberty Party Convention met in St. Louis and nominated another ancient relic as their candidate for the presidency. William H. Harvey had attracted national attention in the year of Coxey's Army with his bimetallist journal *Coin's Financial School*, which had become the bible of the unlimited coinage of silver faction.

The Republican Convention was held in Chicago on June 14. At the Blackstone Hotel Claude Bowers found Nicholas Murray Butler, "looking tired and discouraged" but prepared to fight for the inclusion of a plank in the Republican platform calling for repeal of the Eighteenth Amendment. Indeed, Prohibition was the only issue that roused the dispirited delegates from their lethargy. When the Prohibition issue was presented to the delegates by James Garfield, "old, austere in appearance," they stirred into fierce emotion. Garfield opposed repeal. "The youth of today knows nothing of the taste of liquor," he declared. At that pious hope the galleries burst into shouts of laughter mingled with boos. Ogden Mills followed Garfield, "arrogant, with his small, cold supercilious eyes," Bowers wrote, and made the best speech of the session. But the old passions flared forth; the Republican Party had invested too many years of conflict and too many hopes in Prohibition. The small-town delegates from the Middle West remained true to the cause. The plank calling for repeal of the Eighteenth Amendment lost by some 200 votes. The Republican platform called for reduction in government spending, a balanced budget, further restrictions on immigration, modifications in the Volstead Act (Prohibition), continued high tariffs, an international monetary conference, and veterans' pensions for service-connected disabilities. The demonstration for Hoover when he was nominated was without enthusiasm. The band lent the gathering an eerie air by playing "California, here I come, right back where I started from. . . ."

As the date set for the Democratic Convention approached, Roosevelt's nomination seemed increasingly uncertain. In seven Democratic primaries during the spring, Roosevelt had won four, and Smith two. California, always unpredictable, had gone for the Texan John Nance Garner. In Massachusetts, with a large Catholic and Irish vote, Smith defeated Roosevelt in the primaries by a three to one margin. Roosevelt also suffered a setback in his home state, where Smith, with the all-out support of Tammany Hall, took two-thirds of New York's delegates.

In the aftermath of the Massachusetts setback the announcement by Huey Long of his support for Roosevelt gave new momentum to

Roosevelt's drive for the nomination. As Long put it, "Governor Roosevelt . . . all the time, day by day, made commitments exactly consistent with my belief and understanding of correct government." George Norris and Burton K. Wheeler, old Progressives, helped play a part in converting Long to Roosevelt. "They were the boldest, most courageous men I had ever met," Long wrote. Long's preconvention efforts to lure Alfalfa Bill Murray of Oklahoma into the Roosevelt camp proved unsuccessful.

Besides Al Smith, Roosevelt's rivals for the nomination were John Garner of Texas, John W. Davis, still ambitious for the presidency, and James Cox. Diminutive Newton D. Baker hovered in the wings, and handsome governor Albert Ritchie of Maryland was a dark horse. As Claude Bowers put it, "it was the field against Roosevelt."

Lippmann's candidate was Baker. With perhaps a bit more than the common human propensity for believing what he wished to believe to be true, Lippmann assured Baker that pro-Baker sentiment in the party had "passed the phase of individual admiration and assumed the proportions of what politicians call groundswell." Although the ground swell was not visible to the naked eye of experienced politicians, Baker did his best to augment it by renouncing one of the lodestars of his political career: support for the League of Nations. Pressing Baker to become an active candidate for the Democratic nomination, Lippmann stressed the importance of blocking Roosevelt's bid. The squire of Hyde Park "just doesn't happen to have a very good mind," he wrote. He "never really comes to grips with a problem of any large dimensions." For Roosevelt "the controlling element in almost every case is political advantage. . . . He has never thought much, or understood much, about the great subjects which must concern the next President." He was, finally, a "kind of amiable boy scout."

Oswald Garrison Villard, who had once hailed Roosevelt as the most promising young politician in the country, had similar misgivings. If the Democratic nomination were to go to an individual of "proved boldness in grasping issues and problems or courage and originality in finding solutions," it certainly would not go to Roosevelt.

Increasingly alarmed by Roosevelt's lead over his rivals, Lippmann finally attacked him in his column. He was, Lippmann declared, "a highly impressionable person without a firm grasp of public affairs and without very strong convictions. . . . He is an amiable man with many philanthropic impulses, but he is not the dangerous enemy of anything . . . a pleasant man who, without any important qualifications for the office, would very much like to be President." In later years, when Lippmann was confronted with the column, he insisted: "I will maintain to my dying day that [column] was true of the Franklin Roosevelt of 1932." If so, Roosevelt's change in character in a period of some six months was one of the most remarkable transformations in all history, perhaps exceeded only by the conversion of St. Paul on the road to Damascus. Lippmann's assessment of Roosevelt in that election year is of interest primarily because it contributed to the theory that Roosevelt was a kind of political playboy whose achievements as President had little relation to his earlier career.

As the convention date drew closer, the mood of the Democrats, shut out of the presidency for twelve long years, grew mildly euphoric. At least for Democrats the Depression had a silver lining. But to many Americans there seemed little to choose between the two parties. The journalist Walter Duranty told the guests at a dinner given in his honor that the "country was broke and whoever was elected President couldn't do much about it."

Al Smith arrived in Chicago in an ebullient mood, fortified by his primary victories in Massachusetts and New York. He announced he came to "write an honest, concise, clear platform and nominate me." Senator Alben Barkley of Kentucky in a gleaming white linen suit, opened the convention with an old-fashioned stem-winding oration that placed the blame for the Depression squarely on the shoulders of the Republicans. When he called for the repeal of Prohibition, the wilting delegates, doubtless stirred by the thought of a refreshing beer, broke forth with startling fervor. The pipe organ began to play "Happy Days Are Here Again," and Barkley's speech was interrupted for almost fifteen minutes.

The next day there were crucial votes on seating disputed Southern delegates and on the permanent chairman of the convention.

Huey Long claimed credit for frustrating the plans of the anti-Roosevelt forces who, according to Long, had struck a bargain whereby Barkley, a pro-Roosevelt delegate, would be temporary chairman of the convention and Jouett Shouse, director of the Democratic National Committee and a Smith supporter, would be permanent chairman. The agreement seemed to Long fraught with peril for the Roosevelt candidacy. His fears were strengthened by Senator John S. Cohen of Georgia, who said, "Why, this thing trades our man out of the nomination. You know the fight that we are going to have there if we ever get across. The most trivial of rulings from the chair against us will blow us out of the water."

The agreement finally hammered out by the Roosevelt camp was that John Jacob Raskob, known to be an immovable backer of Al Smith, would be temporary chairman and Senator Thomas Walsh of Montana permanent chairman.

Roosevelt's headquarters at the Congress Hotel were under the direction of Louis Howe. Howe seemed never to sleep; he napped when he could, and as far as Raymond Moley, the Columbia professor and brain truster, could tell, he never had his clothes off for a week. While Jim Farley managed things for Roosevelt on the floor of the convention, Howe kept in constant contact both with Roosevelt at Hyde Park and with Farley. In Moley's words, "This wizened, gnarled little Nibelung had watched his Siegfried grow to hero's size and now he lived in an agony of apprehension that 'someone' . . . would smash all his well-laid plans . . . would give Franklin bad advice or let his impulses run away with him."

Alfalfa Bill Murray, Oklahoma's favorite son candidate, stood in the door of his deserted headquarters in his shirt sleeves. One gallus held up his trousers, and his shirt was collarless. Another prominent delegate was Ruth Bryan Owen, daughter of William Jennings Bryan; she had served a term in Congress but had been recently defeated. Bryan's son, William, Jr., was also present. He sought out Huey Long and, expressing his admiration, gave him a gold fountain pen which had been given to his father by the schoolchildren of Mexico. Long was delighted; he considered himself Bryan's heir. Florence Harriman, by now a kind of dowager empress of the Democratic Party, was very much in evidence. Hamilton Armstrong followed in her wake as she visited the headquarters of the various candidates.

Apprehensive over the efforts of the Al Smith cabal to deny Roosevelt the nomination, the Roosevelt forces toyed with the idea of trying to have the rule requiring the votes of two-thirds majority of the delegates for nomination changed to a simple majority (this was also apparently Huey Long's notion), but the scheme backfired, and the hostility the effort evoked seemed for a moment about to overwhelm the Roosevelt camp. Al Smith and his chief lieutenant, Belle Moskowitz, radiated confidence; Smith was sure that the Roosevelt forces, in trying to change the two-thirds rule, had delivered the convention into his hands.

Huey Long, the Louisiana "Kingfish," was scheduled to address the convention. Liberal Democrats viewed Long as a crude, red-necked Southern hillbilly, and there was concern that with the convention speeches transmitted by radio to an audience of millions, Long would "mutilate the English language, tear a passion to tatters, make a vulgar exhibition and humiliate the party," in Claude Bowers's words. To the astonishment of the Northern delegates, Long spoke "rapidly in excellent English and with closely knit logic . . . [and] made one of the strongest and most dignified speeches of the convention." Bowers wrote an editorial for his paper the next day praising the speech, and Long, summoning him, declared, "As a rule I don't care a damn what any crooked newspaperman says about me, because they're mostly goddam liars, but you gave me a square deal and I want to thank you for it." When a pleased Bowers commented to Jack Garner that Long had "charm," Garner replied, "Too damn much charm. He has more charm than any man in the Senate, and that's what makes him dangerous." In Bowers's considered opinion, Long had "a superabundance of natural ability, in which rare cunning played a part."

Roosevelt wanted Claude Bowers, the biographer of Jefferson, to nominate him, but Bowers worked for William Randolph Hearst and apparently did not wish to offend his boss, so delegate John Mack, who had launched Roosevelt's political career in Dutchess County twenty years earlier, was given the honor. The question of what tune the organ should play at the conclusion of the nominating speech became a crucial issue. Al Smith's theme song was "The Sidewalks of New York." Roosevelt always favored "Anchors Aweigh," but Howe and others objected that the tune was too draggy, that something more upbeat was needed. "Happy Days Are Here Again" was the choice of Lela Stiles, one of Roosevelt's campaign workers. She began to sing the melody for Howe while dancing around the room. Howe approved "Happy Days," and the order was relayed to the organist at the auditorium.

Mack's speech was a pedestrian one, but as soon as he had finished, Roosevelt's followers poured onto the floor and put on a respectable demonstration for their candidate.

When Al Smith was nominated, pandemonium broke out. Chicago's Mayor Anton Cermak, a Smith supporter, had packed the galleries with his minions, all under instruction to raise the rafters for the Happy Warrior.

Eight other candidates had to be put in nomination, and while this ritual was carried out to its exhausting end, Roosevelt, his wife, and his mother sat in the Executive Mansion at Albany, listening over the radio. Sam Rosenman was present, working intermittently on Roosevelt's acceptance speech, while the governor, in shirt sleeves, chain-smoked and listened to the interminable oratory, "nodding approval of some parts, shaking his head in disapproval of others, laughing aloud when the eloquence became a bit too 'spread-eagle' in tone." Eleanor Roosevelt sent coffee to reporters who had set up shop in the garage and scrambled eggs for them.

Huey Long called up with advice. He introduced himself to Roosevelt as the Kingfish and advised him to announce that he would pay the soldiers' bonus as soon as he became President. That would assure him the nomination. But Roosevelt, who believed in at least one article of the old faith—balanced budgets—refused, and Long told him, "You are a gone goose."

The first roll call came at four-thirty in the morning of July 1. Some delegates slept on chairs pushed together and woke only to vote. When the votes were tallied, Roosevelt had a substantial lead: $666\frac{1}{4}$ votes to $201\frac{3}{4}$ for Smith. Garner had $90\frac{1}{4}$, Harry Byrd of Virginia, 25; and Ritchie, 21. Roosevelt was 104 votes short of the magic two-thirds needed for nomination. Determined not to give Smith and the stop Roosevelt forces a chance to regroup, Walsh called for a second ballot, while Farley and the principal Roosevelt staff members canvassed the various delegations for additional votes. Farley pried 11 more from Tom Pendergast, the boss of Kansas City and head of the Missouri delegation, bringing Roosevelt's total to $677\frac{3}{4}$. It was essential at this point that each successive ballot show some gain or at least Roosevelt holding his own. Since he had shown only a modest advance on the second ballot, the anti-Roosevelt forces pressed for a third ballot, hoping that it would reveal that the tide had turned. The pro-Roosevelt forces, on the other hand, now wished for an adjournment to give them time to negotiate with Garner, who clearly held the key to Roosevelt's nomination.

The Arkansas delegation had shown signs of defecting, but Huey Long held them in line with the threat to destroy them politically if they switched to Smith. McAdoo, who, with Hearst, controlled California, had old scores to settle. Cermak resisted pressure from Farley to take Illinois into the Roosevelt camp. Gloom invaded the Executive Mansion at Albany as the roll call began on the third ballot. This time Roosevelt picked up another 5 votes; the worst had been avoided. Equally important, Smith dropped to $190\frac{1}{4}$, while Garner rose to

$101\frac{1}{4}$ and Baker appeared for the first time with $8\frac{1}{2}$. At 9:15 A.M. Walsh adjourned the convention, and the exhausted delegates scattered to wash and shave and catch a few hours of sleep before reassembling.

The intervening hours were important ones for the Roosevelt forces. Word came that various delegates who had voted for Roosevelt on the first three ballots were weakening. The general opinion, expressed in the press and in hotel corridors, was that if Roosevelt failed to get his two-thirds (he was still 87 votes short) on the fourth ballot, the convention would swing to Baker. Moley found Howe's room "full of hell and desperation." It was rumored that Louisiana, Minnesota, and Mississippi were prepared to abandon Roosevelt.

No tactics were considered too disreputable to be employed to pry a delegate loose from his allegiance. Threats, bribery, physical intimidation—all were familiar weapons in a merciless game. "The nervous strain during this period of suspense was very close to the limit of physical endurance," Farley wrote. "I was working eighteen or nineteen hours a day, conversing with hundreds of people, constantly consulting with other leaders, receiving reports from every delegation, and meeting at least twice daily with several hundred newspapermen. I ate my meals, usually consisting of sandwiches and milk, off a tray, and slept a few hours just before dawn if the opportunity offered. To add to my burden, I was besieged on all sides for convention tickets. . . ." Howe's asthma was aggravated by the heat. A secretary, seeing him lying on the couch, pale as death and breathing laboriously, was afraid he was dying. "Hell," said a reporter who knew him, "Louis Howe has come this far alive, and you damn well know he isn't going to die until he sees Franklin Roosevelt nominated for President."

All the anguish and uncertainty could, of course, have been avoided, and Roosevelt's nomination assured, if Al Smith had thrown his support to the man who had loyally supported him four years earlier. But Smith, with consuming bitterness in his heart, refused to budge. He appeared to be willing to tear the party apart and imperil its chance of success in the presidential election rather than see his rival get the nomination.

In a frantic effort to line up the necessary two-thirds before the fourth ballot, negotiations were started with various other candidates. The California and Texas delegations, pledged to Garner, seemed to be the keys. Jim Farley approached Garner's floor manager, Texas Congressman Sam Rayburn, to appeal for Garner's help. Garner's brand of Southern populism was much closer to the philosophy of Franklin Roosevelt than to the Smith-Raskob wing of the party or to that of Newton Baker. Garner was also well aware that a failure by Roosevelt to take the nomination on the fourth ballot might result in things becoming unraveled. He refused to accept a call from the Smith forces and agreed to release the California and Texas delegates. "Hell, I'll do anything to see the Democrats win one more national election," he was reported to have said. Farley's negotiations re the Californians had been with McAdoo. When it turned out that McAdoo could not control the delegation, an apprehensive Farley approached the mercurial Hearst. If Hearst had no love for Roosevelt, he loved Al Smith less. He delivered the Californians. The Texans balked, however. They demanded a quid pro quo. Roosevelt would have to accept Garner as Vice-President. In Garner's view the vice-presidency was not worth "a pitcher of warm piss." He would have to step down from his powerful position as speaker of the House. Reluctantly he consented. The task was completed. An elated Farley rushed off to inform Howe, who gave his approval. "He had labored for years for just such a moment," Farley wrote in recollection, "yet his face failed to change expression or betray the slightest sign of emotion." Howe, determined to take no chances, conferred with Harry Byrd to find his price for the Virginian's delegates. Byrd wanted to be Senator from Virginia, which already had two well-entrenched Senators, the popular and very senior Carter Glass and Claude Swanson. Howe promptly committed Roosevelt to appointing either Glass or Swanson to the Cabinet to make room for Byrd.

Rumors of a deal to break the deadlock spread. The convention stirred to life. As the fourth ballot began, the auditorium was filled with a sense of expectancy. The A's held fast for Roosevelt. California came next. McAdoo, the veteran of many political wars, the man who eight years earlier had been deadlocked with Al Smith through some ninety ballots, was greeted by jeers and catcalls when he went to the rostrum to announce the California shift to Roosevelt. When the booing of Smith's supporters died down, McAdoo announced: "California came here to nominate a President. She did not come here to deadlock this convention. California casts forty-four votes for Roosevelt!" Claude Bowers, standing beside John W. Davis, heard him murmur, "What a pity." Mayor Cermak of Chicago got the microphone to announce that Illinois's fifty-eight delegates had switched to Roosevelt. One after another the candidates threw their support to the man it was now clear would be the party's nominee. It was the moment to close ranks in a symbolic gesture of party unity. But Smith held out, clutching his votes like a drowning man, implacable, irreconcilable, the Unhappy Warrior.

There was elation at Albany, where friends and relatives poured into the Executive Mansion to congratulate the man who most assumed must be the next President of the United States. Custom decreed that a committee of distinguished politicians travel to the candidate's residence to inform him officially of his nomination. Theodore Roosevelt had defied that tradition by going to Chicago in 1912 to accept the nomination of the Bull Moosers. His cousin decided to emulate him. He sent word that he and his wife would fly to Chicago, where he would deliver his acceptance speech. Considering his physical disability and the relative novelty of air travel, it was a highly dramatic gesture. The acceptance speech was read to Howe over the phone. He had it transcribed by a secretary and proceeded to rewrite it, declaring that it was inadequate to the occasion. The flight, nine hours in a Ford trimotor, turned out to be a hazardous and exhausting one, with high winds that necessitated two stops for refueling, but Roosevelt appeared undaunted. On the flight, Eleanor Roosevelt, Marguerite "Missy" LeHand, and Sam Rosenman huddled under blankets in the cabin while Roosevelt went over and over his acceptance speech, written in longhand on a yellow pad.

When he appeared at the auditorium after having driven through the streets of Chicago, crammed with cheering throngs, he was greeted by a storm of applause. In addition to the thousands seated around him, it was estimated that 10,000,000 Americans were gathered at their radios. Roosevelt struck the note of innovation in his opening sentences. "I have started out on the tasks that lie ahead," he declared, "by breaking the absurd tradition that the candidate should remain in professional ignorance of what happened for weeks until he is formally notified of that event many weeks later. You have nominated me and I know it, and I am here to thank you for the honor. Let it also be symbolic that in doing so I broke traditions. Let it from now on be the task of our Party to break foolish traditions." The one tradition that he would honor was that the Democratic Party was the party "of real promise, of real justice, of real equality for all our citizens." He was committed to preventing an outburst of "wild radicalism" by putting forward "a workable program of reconstruction. . . . What do the American people want more than anything else? To my mind they want two things: work, with all the moral and spiritual values that go with it; and work with a reasonable measure of security—security for themselves, and for their wives and children. Work and security— these are more than words. They are more than facts. They are the spiritual values, the true goal toward which our efforts of reconstruction should lead."

Roosevelt was a champion of balanced budgets. It was not clear how he was going to balance the budget in a government already in debt while at the same time providing jobs through public works. His prescription for abolishing "useless offices" and eliminating "unnecessary functions of Government" must have seemed even to Roosevelt and his advisers contradictory in the extreme, but if he had doubts, he suppressed them, and so did his listeners. He ended his speech with a ringing eloquence that recalled to some the last passages of Lincoln's first inaugural. "I pledge you, I pledge myself, to a new deal for the American people. Let all of us here assembled constitute ourselves prophets of a new order of competence and courage. This is more than a political campaign; it is a call to arms. [Here one thought of Cousin Theodore, calling on the Progressives to join him at Armageddon to fight for the Lord.] Give me your help, not to win votes alone, but to win in this crusade to restore America to its own greatness."

Rollin Kirby, the cartoonist of the *New York World*, drew a cartoon that showed a farmer looking up as an airplane flew over with "New Deal" painted on its wings. It was the latest political "new." There had been Theodore Roosevelt's New Nationalism, Wilson's New Freedom, and now the New Deal.

The Democratic platform called for reduced government spending and a balanced budget, a tariff for revenue only, old-age and unemployment insurance on a state basis, repeal of Prohibition, and "every constitutional measure that will aid the farmer to receive for basic farm commodities prices in excess of the cost of production." It also called for regulation of holding companies and of the securities market.

Liberal and radical "opinion makers" were almost unanimous in their doubts about Roosevelt's qualification to be President. "People," Raymond Moley wrote with obvious reference to Walter Lippmann, "who were merely 'intellectual' were almost unanimous on the subject of Roosevelt's inadequacy in the spring of 1932: he was a 'weakling,' they said, an 'opportunist,' 'an amiable gentleman who wants to be President.' " A newspaper friend of Moley in the Midwest wrote: "waddya mean—'progressive'? The guy doesn't seem to have any stuff."

Intellectuals especially like things laid out plainly and logically. They have a checklist of orthodoxies as detailed and specific as their conservative counterparts, and they were put off by what they considered Roosevelt's refusal to subscribe publicly to their tenets. Elmer Davis, a journalist who was about to undertake a new career as a radio news commentator, wrote of a particular speech: "You could not quarrel with a single one of his generalities; you seldom can. But what they mean (if anything) is known only to Franklin Roosevelt and God." Henry Mencken called him "Roosevelt Minor." The famous liberal rabbi Stephen Wise warned Felix Frankfurter: "There is no basic stuff in the man. There are no deep-seated convictions. He is a tremendously agreeable and attractive person, but there is no bedrock in him. He is all clay and no granite."

Frankfurter shared some of his friend Lippmann's reservations about Roosevelt:"I know his limitations," he wrote. "Most of them derive, I believe, from lack of an incisive intellect and a kind of optimism that sometimes makes him timid, as well as an ambition that leads to compromises with which we were familiar with Theodore Roosevelt and Wilson. But on the whole he has been a very good Governor."

The "far left"—the large and small C communists—were even less impressed. Heywood Broun called Roosevelt the "corkscrew candidate of a convoluting convention." Paul Douglas, University of Chicago professor of economics, announced a plague on both Hoover and Roosevelt and looked forward to the collapse of the Democratic Party and the formation of a new liberal coalition. John Dewey joined Reinhold Niebuhr, the leading liberal theologian in the country, and Elmer Davis in declaring his support for Norman Thomas, and many liberals followed suit. Lewis Mumford, the influential critic and student of cities, expressed his intention of voting for the Communist Party's candidate to dramatize his conviction that "our present crisis calls for a complete and drastic reorientation." In the words of the critic Alfred Kazin, left-wing intellectuals considered Roosevelt a "wily, slippery confidence man unable for long to satisfy 'people of principle.' "

Needless to say, that was not everyone's point of view. The journalist George Creel described Roosevelt's nomination as a draft of "clean air . . . through a sick room." When Creel talked to Roosevelt shortly after his nomination, he was more impressed than ever. The "debacle of 1929," Roosevelt told him, "was no mere financial panic, but the *end of an era*." The old order, as Roosevelt called it, had been based on an agricultural society. "Rugged individualism and unrestricted competition were the rules of the day because there was no great need of cooperation, and very little opportunity for it." But times had changed. "Free and helpful competition" had been replaced by "wolfish competition," with all its attendant evils. The new order involved interdependence. "No longer were there vacant lands or frontiers offering the promise of escape. No longer was the head of a family able to care for his women and shelter his elders. Age had become a thing of terror just as involuntary idleness had become a thing of despair. The new economic order, recognizing these changes, was compelled by common sense and every instinct of self-preservation. A government that could not care for its old and sick, that could not provide work for the strong, that fed its young into the hopper of industry, and that let the black shadow of insecurity rest on every home was not a government that could endure or should endure. . . . Unless great unitary systems, such as mining, milling, manufacture, and agriculture, were brought under one central policy control, instead of being left to the favoritism or prejudice of forty-eight different states, how could anarchy be avoided . . . ? What," Roosevelt asked, "was more plain than that all business had come to be vested with a public use, and that business unable to make a fair return except by child labor, long hours, dogs' wages, lying and cheating was not a business that the country wanted?"

Roosevelt believed, as Creel paraphrased him, in "the right of workers to organize and bargain collectively; a drive against monopoly; the development of our natural resources; a far-flung social-security program; the protection of bank deposits; a federal works program to fill the valleys of unemployment; soil conservation; taxation based on ability to pay. . . . A new order . . . that would raise consumption to a level with our highest possible production; an order that would banish the terrors of present-day existence, so that a man might go to bed at night without fearing that the morrow would drag him down from security to despair; an order that would make for true individualism by restoring and safeguarding independence and self-respect." To an excited George Creel it seemed that there had truly dawned a new day, one that he and his fellow progressives had almost abandoned hope for, at least under the existing "system."

The most dramatic and, for many Americans, troubling event of the summer of 1932 was the appearance in the nation's capital of a ragged army of men, women, and children. On May 29 an advance guard of some 1,000 veterans arrived in Washington. The men, unemployed, had come to claim a bonus for service in the World War thirteen years ahead of its promised date in 1945. The leader of the veterans' army was Walter W. Waters from Portland, Oregon. Word of its march had flashed across the nation when several hundred of the Bonus Expeditionary Force, as the veterans called themselves, encountered their first obstacle. In East St. Louis, when they tried to board empty boxcars, railroad officials established a special guard to prevent the "marchers" from riding the rails. The marchers, in retaliation, soaped the rails, uncoupled freight cars, and otherwise disrupted normal railroad operations. The police were called in, and scuffles took place between them and the veterans. The veterans, without locomotion, were trucked out of town. As had been the case of the members of Coxey's Army forty years earlier, sympathetic townspeople along their route gave what they could out of their own meager supplies.

As they moved east, the veterans picked up recruits. By the time they reached Washington they numbered in the hundreds, with more arriving each day until by mid-July there were between 10,000 and 20,000 men, women, and children living on the "flats" beside the Anacostia River in improvised shacks. John Dos Passos, at work on *The Big Money*, wrote of the "same goulash of faces and accents" that he had known during the war. Then they all had been young. "Now we are getting on into middle life, sunken eyes, hollow cheeks off breadlines, pale-looking, knotted hands of men who've worked hard with them, and then for a long time have not worked."

The army was like an assemblage of ghosts of the past. "General" Jacob S. Coxey, leader of another raggle-taggle army in the terrible depression year of 1893, was one of those ghosts. He was, as we have noted, the presidential candidate of what was left of the Farmer-Labor Party. Father James R. Cox of Pittsburgh had founded the Jobless Party and announced himself its candidate for President. Father Charles Coughlin, the "radio priest," traveled from Royal Oak, Michigan, gave the army $5,000 and in a fiery speech asked for its support. The veterans soon had their own songs and games and social institutions. They sang:

> Mellon pulled the whistle,
> Hoover rang the bell,

> Wall Street gave the signal,
> And the country went to hell.

The Washington chief of police was Pelham Glassford, who had served as a brigadier general in 1918. As an "old soldier" he had the enlightened and sympathetic attitude that the Bonus Marchers were campers rather than tramps or revolutionaries and that his job was to help them as much as he could by finding food and supplies for them. He had an easy, bantering way about him that gave the veterans a feeling that he understood their plight. Waters announced that there were 23,000 veterans camped at nineteen sites around the city. Some had moved into abandoned buildings and were rather casual in their treatment of the properties. After Congress had adjourned without taking action on their demand for an early payment of the bonuses, the mood of the "army" grew increasingly surly. Thefts and petty crimes were increasingly attributed to the veterans, and the permanent residents of the city living in areas adjacent to the odorous and unsanitary camps were insistent that something be done to relieve them of their unwelcome neighbors. The administration or, more specifically, the President seemed paralyzed by indecision. For members of the Communist Party, the march provided an irresistible opportunity for propaganda; it was a living daily demonstration of the breakdown and the inhumanity of capitalism. Nothing like this, they declared, could happen in Soviet Russia. There everyone had a job. Under the guise of the Workers' Ex-Servicemen League, they moved in on the camps and did their best to recruit members for the Communist Party of the United States. Their efforts met with little success, but their presence further alarmed the administration. Secretary of War Patrick Hurley and Army Chief of Staff Douglas MacArthur had a solution that they pressed on the President. In the name of "law and order" the army must be routed out of its improvised and illegally occupied quarters and its members scattered to make their way back to their homes, if they had any, as best they could. The operation was prepared with all the care of a military campaign.

The tension was further increased when John Pace, a Detroit radical, persuaded several hundred veterans to picket the White House. When police were brought in on July 28 to evict men who had occupied abandoned buildings, the men responded by barricading themselves and throwing bricks and stones. The police fired on the veterans, and two were killed and several others injured. The police then called for support from the soldiers, and Hoover ordered the secretary of war to oust the recalcitrant men. Regular army cavalry troops with tanks and tear gas were called out in the charge of General MacArthur, Major Dwight Eisenhower, and Captain George Patton. The veterans, assuming the soldiers were coming to protect them against the police, greeted their arrival with cheers. But the cavalrymen drew their sabers and rode into the crowd, which included women and children who had gathered to watch the eviction. Tear gas was also used, and clouds of choking gas added to the disorder of the scene as veterans and spectators alike ran for their lives. The troops then moved across the bridge to the remnants of the Bonus Marchers' encampment and set the shacks and tents on fire. Those who resisted were arrested and often roughly handled. Pictures of the "Battle of Washington," with men, women, and children fleeing before the soldiers like refugees before an invading army, were splashed across the newspapers of the country along with blaring headlines and sensational accounts of the desperate state of the scattered army.

"After months of patient indulgence," President Hoover's proclamation read, "the government met overt lawlessness as it always must be met if the cherished processes of self-government are to be preserved."

To those disposed to believe that the government of the United States was moving rapidly in the direction of Mussolini's Italy, the President's pious announcement and the actions of the soldiers seemed vivid confirmation. The scattered and demoralized veterans were gathered up in army trucks and transported north and west out of the city. Mayor Edward McCloskey of Johnstown, Pennsylvnia, an industrial city well acquainted with hardship, offered them a temporary haven, but the solid citizens of the town raised the alarm. The city's leading newspaper warned that there was "certain to be a mixture of undesirables—thieves, plug-uglies, degenerates. . . . The community must protect itself from the criminal fringe of the invaders." The editor of the paper called for booster clubs and community organizations of every kind to get together "to protect property, women and possibly life. It is no time for half-way measures. . . ."

Malcolm Cowley, reading of the exodus, drove to a highway intersection and watched as truck after truck, fifty in all, rolled by, each filled with twenty or so men and watched coldly by state troopers standing beside their motorcycles, presumably on the lookout for thieves and degenerates. "The men in the trucks were kneeling, standing with their hands on each other's shoulders, or clinging unsteadily to the sideboards," Cowley wrote; "they had no room to sit down. Behind each truck rode a trooper." A woman standing near Cowley showed evident distress at the "contrast between the hatless, coatless, unshaven veterans, all looking half-starved—most of them hadn't eaten or slept for thirty-six hours—and the sleekly uniformed, well-nourished troopers who were herding them past their destination."

When they finally reached a spot chosen as a campsite, Cowley circulated among the angry and exhausted men. One veteran, who had won three medals for his service and spent five years in a government hospital recovering from wounds he received fighting in France, told Cowley, "If they gave me a job, I wouldn't care about the bonus." Another man, his face streaked with tears, declared, "I used to be a hundred-percenter but now I'm a Red radical. . . . Now I don't ever want to see a flag again. Give me a gun and I'll go back to Washington." Another called out, "You know what this means?" and another shouted, "This means revolution."

When Rexford Tugwell visited Roosevelt at Hyde Park early the day after the "battle," he found him in bed looking at a page of pictures in the *New York Times*. In Tugwell's words, "he pointed to soldiers stamping through smoking debris, hauling resisters, still weeping from tear gas, through the wreckage to police wagons; women and children, incredibly disheveled and weary, waiting for some sort of rescue." Roosevelt then launched on an analysis of Hoover and his career: his accomplishments as head of the Allied relief effort for Belgium in 1916; his considerable achievements as Harding's and then Coolidge's secretary of commerce—and Roosevelt's own high opinion of him in 1920 when he considered him "a wonder." Now the incident of the Bonus Army had revealed him to the country as a weak and inept leader. If he had had any chance of being reelected, Roosevelt said, it was gone with the Bonus Army.

What would Roosevelt have done? Tugwell asked. Hoover should have invited the leaders into the White House to discuss, in a helpful and sympathetic spirit, the plight of the veterans and what might be done. Anything was better than the sight of U.S. soldiers attacking veterans of the war.

Sherwood Anderson was one of a group of writers asked to go to Washington to protest to President Hoover. To Anderson it was all "a sad mistake." If Hoover had had more courage, he could have gone and talked to the men. When Anderson arrived at the train station in

New York to join what he had been assured would be a company of America's most respected writers accompanied by newspapermen and photographers, there were only two writers there, Elliot Cohen and Waldo Frank. In Philadelphia a black writer joined them. Arriving in Washington, they went to the White House. No, they could not talk to the President. He was having a birthday party. Instead, they got a pretentious press secretary, who lectured to them "as a fellow-craftsman." Frank, in his quiet way, insisted on speaking. "He began to say that we were there as representatives of the writers and artists of America. . . ." That seemed a bit presumptuous to Anderson. In any event it served no purpose so far as he could see. The others went back to New York, and Anderson returned to his hotel room to write an open letter to the President. He had come to Washington to protest the treatment of the Bonus Army. He wrote: "With me it is like this: I am intensely interested in the lives of the common everyday people, laborers, mill hands, soldiers, stenographers or whatever they may be." He had been observing "at first hand the condition of men out of work in America. I have been walking about with them, talking with them, sitting with them. To me, although they are men and women out of work, they remain fellow-Americans. I have been seeing things with my own eyes: men who are heads of families creeping through the streets of American cities eating from garbage cans; men turned out of houses and sleeping week after week on park benches . . . in mud under bridges. The great majority of these men are eager enough to work. Our streets are filled with beggars, with men new to the art of begging.

"I came to you with the other writers because I was ashamed not to come. . . . What I am trying to say to you is that men like me do not want to be radicals. I am, myself, a story teller, I would like to give all my time and thought and energy to story telling. I can't." It seemed to Anderson that rich and successful men got "horribly separated from actuality." The Bonus Marchers "demanded so little from their government, after all the things that had been promised to them, that the situation was laughable." Yet when the writers came to protest and to ask for the government's sympathy and help for the unfortunate, the President refused to see them. From the attitude of politicians and journalists, "you would have thought that the soldiers and police were unarmed rather than these distraught, puzzled men out of work—the same men who but so short a time ago were our national heroes."

# 14

## Roosevelt Prior to the Campaign of 1932

We are already well acquainted with the man whom the Democrats, after some bitter infighting, chose as their presidential candidate. He had served in Woodrow Wilson's administration as assistant secretary of the navy and had run for Vice-President on the ill-fated Democratic ticket of 1920. He had subsequently been stricken by polio and made a dramatic appearance at the Democratic Convention of 1928 to nominate Al Smith as the party's standard-bearer. Smith had subsequently prevailed upon a reluctant Roosevelt to become a candidate for governor of New York in order to improve Smith's chances in that state. We must now take a longer look at the man who, it was generally agreed in 1932, would be the nation's next President.

Franklin Delano Roosevelt was by birthright a member of the old aristocracy of the Hudson River valley, which traced its ancestry in most instances back to the Dutch patroons of colonial New York. The training, the education, and the careers of the members of his class were very carefully prescribed: the appropriate schools and colleges, the appropriate religion, and the appropriate ideas and behavior.

For the Roosevelts, Groton was the appropriate school. There young Franklin Roosevelt, slight and short, had trouble "fitting in." While he was a student, Franklin heard his already well-known cousin

Theodore, assistant secretary of the navy, give the boys "a splendid talk on his adventures when he was on the [New York] Police Board. . . . He kept the whole room in an uproar for over an hour, by telling us killing stories about policemen and their doings in New York," Franklin reported to his parents. Franklin visited Sagamore Hill with numerous other cousins and went on breakneck hikes led by the inexhaustible Theodore. Picnics, overnight camping expeditions, and ghost stories were a special delight.

At Groton Roosevelt came under the benign and well-nigh irresistible influence of the famous Endicott Peabody, the very embodiment of upper-class Eastern muscular Christianity. Peabody viewed his young charges as the future leaders of the nation (many of its graduates already were), marked, by virtue of their presence at Groton, as being among the anointed of the Lord. Their privileged status meant, at least to Peabody, that they were under a heavy charge to uplift and enlighten the less fortunate, the sturdy old doctrine of noblesse oblige: Social privileges meant social responsibilities. It was, quite clearly, the code of the gentleman (and the gentlewoman as well). It meant being a "good sport," "playing the game," "hitting the line hard," not fudging or lying or being "yellow." It meant thinking exalted thoughts and being, above all, "clean in mind and body." And it meant a self-assurance that often graded off into self-complacency or, worse, arrogance, a kindly but patronizing attitude toward one's inferiors, the members of the great middle class, Midwesterners, people who were "common." At Groton Roosevelt, a lifelong Episcopalian (the religion of the upper class), belonged to the Missionary Society, a group of specially pious students who held services in nearby towns (one wonders what those rural Yankees thought of the young gentlemen with their upper-class accents). He was counselor one summer at the St. Andrews Boys Club on Squam Lake in New Hampshire. At Groton he helped look after an eighty-four-year-old black woman living near the school whose deceased husband had been a drummer in the Union Army. Roosevelt and another student in the Missionary Society were assigned to keep her supplied with coal and water from her well. "It will be very pleasant," he wrote his mother, "as she is a dear old thing, and it will be a good occupation for us."

Despite an inclination for the Naval Academy, Roosevelt passed dutifully on from Groton to Harvard, armed with the Latin Prize, an edition of Shakespeare in forty volumes. Headmaster Peabody declared that he "has been a thoroughly faithful scholar & most satisfactory member of the school throughout his course. I part with Franklin with reluctance." Years later Peabody wrote to an angry Grotonian who belonged to that considerable company who felt that Roosevelt had "betrayed his class": "He was at Groton for four years and as far as I can remember there was no suspicion of untruthfulness or insincerity during his entire course; nor did I hear of anything against his reputation at the University."

Endicott Peabody's observation is worth noting. Harvard was, in many ways, a continuation of Groton. Since most of the Groton boys went on to Harvard (some, of course, went to Yale, and a few to Princeton), established friendships continued. Groton students joined the clubs that those who preceded them had joined, that their friends joined, and that, not infrequently, their fathers had been members of. They made, to be sure, new friends from Exeter and Andover, young men of the same class, with the same antecedents and accents and style of dressing.

There was, for example, a "Groton table" at the eating house to which Roosevelt belonged. Like Theodore, Franklin had a horse and buggy and participated enthusiastically in the social life of Boston. The fact was that he did everything "enthusiastically," from his schoolwork and his social activities to his many extracurricular involvements, the principal one being on the *Harvard Crimson*, the college newspaper. Although he worked when it suited him, he discovered, as many undergraduates before and since, that the extracurricular life of the university was often more stimulating than the curricular. He dropped out of Josiah Royce's philosophy class after three weeks and applied himself only fitfully to his economics "major." The one subject that had a strong attraction for him was American history, especially the history of the Roosevelt family. Endicott Peabody's influence was evident in his reflection that the "One reason—perhaps the chief—of the virility of the Roosevelts is this very democratic spirit. They have never felt that because they were born in a good position they could put their hands in their pockets and succeed. They have felt, rather, that being born in a good position, there is no excuse for them if they did not do their duty by the community."

As a member of the Harvard Republican Club Roosevelt worked for the election of the ticket of William McKinley and Theodore Roosevelt in 1900.

The more venturesome Harvard students met young men not of their class, especially in the more violent sports where skill and muscle mattered more than breeding. A few became friends with some of the brilliant young Jews, students like Felix Frankfurter or Walter Lippmann. Although Franklin Roosevelt was, in most respects, a thoroughly conventional representative of his class (and family), he was more enterprising than most in his friendships. He demonstrated a combination of charm and energy that called to mind his famous cousin. In addition, he was far handsomer than Teddy. He looked like the illustrations in popular novels and short stories by Howard Chandler Christy: tall, slender, square-jawed, blue-eyed, dark-haired, impeccably dressed, gracious and easy in manner.

The most prestigious of the undergraduate clubs was Porcellian. Roosevelt assumed that he would be elected, and when he was passed over and had to settle for the less desired Fly, he wrote of his setback as "the greatest disappointment he ever had." Roosevelt's biographers have indulged in considerable speculation about why, indeed, he was rebuffed by the members of Porcellian, thereby giving the episode as much prominence as it had in Roosevelt's own psychic life. One of the explanations that has been offered was that his being passed over was the result of a scandal involving his cousin Taddy, who ran off with a well-known prostitute from a Boston bawdy house. Another is that despite his easygoing charm he had a certain aloofness and reserve that put people off.

Theodore Roosevelt's father had died while Teddy was still an undergraduate at Harvard, and that death had been devastating to him. The rest of his life had been dominated by the determination to be worthy of his dead father. The same thing happened to Franklin Roosevelt; his father died while he was still a freshman. He, too, had been deeply attached to his father, whose temperament was much like that of Theodore's father. But Sara Delano Roosevelt had always been the dominant parent, and Franklin's solicitude for her helped assuage his grief at his father's death.

The most important event of Roosevelt's Harvard years was his cousin's succession to the White House upon McKinley's assassination. His admiration for his cousin increased if possible. Already strongly drawn to politics, he was delighted by his access to the holder of the highest office in the land. At a Christmas party given by Theodore Roosevelt's younger sister, Corinne Roosevelt Robinson, for the multitudinous Roosevelt relatives, Franklin met another cousin, Eleanor Roosevelt, a tall, graceful, serious girl with prominent teeth. She was a wallflower, grateful when the handsome young Franklin asked her to dance. Not long afterward he remarked to his mother, "Cousin Eleanor has a very good mind."

A recent biographer of Roosevelt, Nathan Miller, suggests that Franklin and Eleanor were drawn to each other by a shyness and insecurity common to each of them. The argument is more plausible if applied to Eleanor. The ugly duckling daughter of a famous beauty, she experienced a childhood, she wrote later, full of corrosive anxieties—"fear of being scolded, afraid that other people would not like me"—and, above all, the consciousness of having somehow failed by being the rather homely daughter of a beautiful mother. That she should have succumbed readily to her handsome, dashing cousin was hardly surprising. What was somewhat more surprising was that Roosevelt, attractive to women and, in turn, highly susceptible, should have been so drawn to Eleanor. Since the first Charles Francis Adams had congratulated himself on having no "voluptuous feelings" toward his fiancée, Abigail Brooks, sexual attraction had had little to do with most upper-class alliances. A degree of compatibility was certainly desirable; even more important were social position and financial resources. "Love" between young males and females of the upper class was more inclined toward the platonic than the erotic; thus the question of strong physical attraction was nugatory, more apt, as we have seen, to be a source of anxiety than a reason for matrimony. A well-brought-up young man of Roosevelt's social milieu looked for moral and intellectual congeniality in a prospective mate rather than a pretty face or beguiling figure (Eleanor's figure was, in fact, her strongest point, physically speaking).

Eleanor Roosevelt adored her rather inept father, Elliott, an alcoholic, whose most appealing quality was his devotion to his oldest child and only daughter. She reciprocated in one of those classic father-daughter relationships we have encountered often in the course of this history. "He dominated my life as long as he lived," she wrote later, "and was the love of my life for many years after he died." She lived, after her father's death, "in a dream world in which I was the heroine and my father the hero." In the words of her cousin Alice Roosevelt, "She was full of duty, never very gay, a frightful bore for more frivolous people like ourselves." Edith and Theodore Roosevelt were generous with their love for their niece. "Poor little soul, she is very plain. Her mouth and teeth have no future," Edith Roosevelt wrote a friend. "But the ugly duckling may turn out to be a swan."

The most formative experience of Eleanor Roosevelt's young life had been three years' attendance at an English boarding school at Wimbledon, England, run by a remarkable Frenchwoman, Mlle. Marie Souvestre. The British socialist Beatrice Webb praised Souvestre's "veracity, undeviating directness of intelligence, faithfulness and warmth of affection. . . ." The three years at Souvestre's school were the happiest of Eleanor's life. Souvestre saw in her shy and somewhat wounded American pupil a rare spirit. "She is full of sympathy for all those who live with her and shows an intelligent interest in everything she comes in contact with," Souvestre wrote. Eleanor, ungainly but strong and supple, made the field hockey team, an achievement which she recalled as "one of the proudest moments of my life." A schoolmate described her as "a tall, slim, elegant young girl who was so much more intelligent than all the others." Souvestre's radical ideas—she was a freethinker and a pacifist—proved a strong stimulus to Eleanor's natural bent for independence and helped lay the foundation for her liberal view of the world.

Back in the United States to "come out," Eleanor felt once more awkward and out of place—too tall and too homely to fit in with her set. "By no stretch of the imagination could I fool myself into thinking I was a popular debutante." She did her best with a cruel and archaic system, but her unhappiness was compounded by family problems, an alcoholic uncle and a hysterical aunt living in the family home at Tivoli. Like many young women of her class, she found an outlet for her energies in the Junior League, on behalf of which she taught dancing to ghetto children on the Lower East Side.

Souvestre wrote to her after her return to the United States, addressing her as "My dear little girl" and urging her to "bear in mind that there are more quiet and enviable joys than to be among the most sought-after women at a ball . . . and various fashionable affairs. . . . A thousand and a thousand tendernesses to my Totty whom I shall always love." In another letter she wrote of the "immense emptiness" she had left behind "for all those who knew and loved you." That the relationship between Eleanor Roosevelt and Marie Souvestre was far closer than that which commonly exists between teacher and student is evident from the Gallic ardor of Souvestre's letters to her "Totty," letters in which she expressed her distress at the thought that the parties and pleasures and "flirtations" which were a necessary part of Eleanor's life and "coming out" would "estrange" her "from all that I knew you to be."

Franklin Roosevelt as a senior at Harvard resumed his courtship of Eleanor and in the fall of 1903 asked her to marry him. When her aunt asked her if she was in love, she replied affirmatively. Later she wrote, "It was years . . . before I understood what being in love was or what loving really means." The engagement, an early one by the standards of the day (Roosevelt was just twenty-one), came as a blow to Sara Delano Roosevelt, who, in the classic fashion of the overprotective mother, doted on her son. Writing her of his engagement, Roosevelt declared, "And for you, dear Mummy, you know that nothing can ever change what we have always been & always will be to each other—only now you have two children to love & to love you. . . ." Once she had become resigned to the inevitable—and it was not without a struggle—Sara simply took over the domestic lives of "her children." She chose their house, furnished it, hired the servants, and in other small and large ways made her presence felt.

Uncle Ted, still reveling in his unexpected ascension to the presidency, was an enthusiastic supporter of the union. He heard the news with "great rejoicing," he wrote Franklin. "I am as fond of Eleanor as if she were my daughter; and I like you, and trust you, and believe in you. . . . May good fortune attend you both, ever." He would certainly come to the wedding and, since Eleanor's father was dead, give the bride away.

The engagement, as again was usual in that class and era, was projected as a long one. Since any sense of sexual urgency was absent or suppressed, engagements lasting a year or two were not uncommon. Indeed, a hasty marriage might raise the suspicion that it was the unfortunate result of a breach of the code: that the bride was pregnant. Since sex and more specifically sexual intercourse were generally viewed as a "bad" thing, enjoyed with mistresses (as had been the case with Charles Francis Adams), in brothels, with maids, or with "bad"—generally speaking lower-class—women, it was not closely identified with "good"—i.e., upper-class—girls, although, to be sure, some of them were "bad" and the objects of gossip and scandal. In any event, it seems clear (and normal) that sexual attraction was not a major element in the relationship of Franklin and Eleanor. Franklin entered the Columbia Law School in order to be near Eleanor, and they spent much time together, taking long walks, talking of the things that mutually interested them, dancing (Eleanor was a graceful dancer, and Franklin loved to dance), going to the theater, and in the spring of 1905, when they had been engaged a year and a half, attending Uncle Ted's inauguration for his second term in Washington. They were married a few months later, on St. Patrick's Day, by—who else?—the Reverend Endicott Peabody, Franklin's headmaster from Groton days.

The President of the United States, as he had promised, gave away the bride, who was several inches taller than he, and after the wedding exclaimed, "Well, Franklin, there's nothing like keeping the name in the family." After the first year of law school was over, the bride and groom took a delayed three-month honeymoon in Europe. From London Eleanor wrote to reassure her bereft mother-in-law: "You are always just the sweetest, dearest Mama . . . and I shall look forward to our next long evening together, when I shall want to be kissed all the time." It should be said, parenthetically, that a great deal of kissing went on among the members of upper-class families.

When the newlyweds returned to New York, they were ensconced in a house rented for them by the senior Mrs. Roosevelt and staffed by three servants chosen by her. As children began to arrive in rapid succession (the first Franklin, Jr., died of the flu while still an infant), Sara Roosevelt even hired the British nannies or nurses who looked after them, as was, again, the custom in upper-class families. To be without a nanny in a well-appointed household was almost as bad as being without a cook.

Roosevelt soon found that he had little interest in or aptitude for the law; politics was what drew him like a magnet, and his Republican cousin was his inspiration. In his political ambitions his name was both an asset and a handicap. It was an undoubted asset in that it opened doors that would have been closed to anyone without that magic appellation; it was a liability in that there was, at least at the beginning of his political career, the widespread suspicion that the younger Roosevelt was an attractive lightweight trading on the family name. But the fact was that from the first instant he showed, if anything, keener political instincts than his cousin. In 1910 he responded eagerly to the suggestion from the political boss of Dutchess County that he run for the State Assembly. His assembly district was predominantly rural and Republican. Roosevelt was a Democrat, and few Democrats had won office over the years, but Roosevelt was undaunted. He gave his first political address at a rally in Poughkeepsie in the summer of 1910. "On that joyous occasion of clams and sauerkraut and real beer I made my first speech . . ." he wrote. The democratic impulse of the Roosevelts that he had celebrated in his college paper he expressed now by urging everyone to call him Franklin. On one point he plainly outdid his famous cousin. Theodore's voice was high-pitched, rising to a kind of falsetto when he was excited; Franklin's was a powerful and melli-fluous tenor (he loved to sing) with, to be sure, strong upper-class accents.

Delighted with his first modest venture into politics, Roosevelt was downcast to learn that the Democratic incumbent who had planned to run for a seat in the State Senate had changed his mind. The Demo-cratic machine would support the incumbent for reelection to the As-sembly. Roosevelt's only hope, and that a slim one, was to run instead for the State Senate seat in a district in which no Democrat had been elected since the Civil War.

Sara Roosevelt tried to persuade her son not to mix in the "messy business of politics." Eleanor dutifully acquiesced, writing later, "It never occurred to me that I had any part to play." Having secured from the district's Democrats what was generally assumed to be a worth-less nomination for the Senate seat, Roosevelt, sounding like a can-didate for the U.S. presidency, declared: "I accept this nomination with absolute independence. I am pledged to no man; I am influenced by no specific interests; and so I shall remain. . . . In the coming cam-paign, I need not tell you that I do not intend to stand still. We are going to have a very strenuous month."

One of Roosevelt's political counselors at the beginning of his career gave him a list of don'ts: "Don't be seen smoking cigarettes in public. Don't wear white clothes. Don't wear yellow shoes." Observing his counselor's admonitions, renting a red Maxwell and festooning it with flags, Roosevelt covered his entire district village by village, making as many as ten talks a day to what were seldom more than a handful of farmers or townspeople. "When we met a horse or a team—and that was about every half mile or so—we had to stop, not only the car but the engine as well," Roosevelt wrote later. He attacked the Payne-Aldrich Tariff, unpopular with farmers, and denounced "Bossism." More important, Roosevelt found an abundant source of campaign material in Herbert Croly's *The Promise of American Life*. Croly's book severely criticized the notion that "progress" was somehow an inevitable or divinely appointed aspect of American history and argued that the abuses and injustices so evident in the larger society were the results of a shallow optimism and the absence of intelligent planning. The enemy was the ancient doctrine of states' rights, which inhibited all truly national efforts to deal with national problems. Ironically, Croly's book had been written in the aftermath of Teddy Roosevelt's "pro-gressive nationalism," which, in Croly's view, offered the only rational approach to solving the nation's problems. A book that had been written to extend and ratify the policies of the first Roosevelt became an inspiration for the second.

The Republican Party in New York was badly split between the Theodore Roosevelt Progressives and the old guard: the Insurgents and the Stalwarts. Franklin Roosevelt's cause was helped materially when Charles Evans Hughes and the Progressive Republicans endorsed his candidacy. To the surprise of virtually everyone, Roosevelt, riding a strong Democratic tide, carried his district by a comfortable margin (many voters persisted in believing he was Theodore's son).

The *New York Times* wrote a few months after Roosevelt had taken his seat in the State Senate that he had immediately gained the "limelight."

The *Times* reported: "Those who looked closely . . . saw a young man with the finely chiseled face of a Roman patrician, only with a ruddier glow of health upon it. . . . Senator Roosevelt is less than thirty. He is tall and lithe. With his handsome face and his form of supple strength he could make a fortune on the stage and set the matinee girl's heart throbbing with subtle and happy emotion."

A reporter for the *New York Post* was even more enthusiastic. In addition to Roosevelt's ability to lay out the liberal position skillfully, his "physical impression leaves nothing to be asked—the figure of an idealized college football player, almost the Post type in public life . . . making clean, direct . . . gestures; always with a smile ready to share. . . . He speaks with a strong, clear voice, with a tenor note in it which rings—sings, one is tempted to say—in key with [an] intangible, utterly charming and surely vote-winning quality." In distant Ohio the *Cleveland Plain Dealer* noted: "Theodore Roosevelt as a young man merely took advantage of all opportunities to keep himself in the public eye, and to strengthen the impression that he was a fighter. . . . Franklin D. Roosevelt is beginning his public career fully as auspiciously. If none of the Colonel's sons turns out to be fit objects for public adoration, may not it be possible that this rising star continue the Roosevelt dynasty?"

Another politician who took note of Roosevelt's increasing prominence in Democratic circles was the newly elected governor of New Jersey. Woodrow Wilson told Joseph Guffey, a powerful Pennsylvania Democrat, "The young man just elected as state senator from a safe Republican district in New York will bear watching. His name is Roosevelt."

Guffey replied that he thought all Roosevelts were Republicans.

"No, Guffey," Wilson replied, "this one comes from the Democratic branch of the family, and he is the handsomest young giant I have ever seen." Wilson and Roosevelt had had a talk, and Roosevelt reported that the former Princeton president was determined "to remedy conditions which the American people will no longer tolerate." He was "keenly alive to the social and industrial welfare of the great body of workers," and could be counted on to work for "better conditions of life for people of all kinds."

Two years later, at the Democratic Convention in 1912, Roosevelt did his bit to halt the Champ Clark bandwagon. Discovering that the Clark forces had instructed the doorman to admit only those nondelegates wearing Clark badges, Roosevelt turned up similar badges for Wilson's forces and hustled them into the convention hall, where they chanted, "We want Wilson," to counterbalance the shouts of "We want Clark."

Not everyone fell under Roosevelt's spell. The clerk of the New York Senate, Patrick "Packy" McCabe, called him one of the "snobs in our party . . . political accidents . . . fops and cads who come as near being political leaders as a green pea does to a circus tent." Frances Perkins was equally unimpressed. "He had a youthful lack of humility, a streak of self-righteousness, and a deafness to the hopes, fears, and aspirations which are the common lot," she wrote.

As a state legislator Roosevelt gave special attention to the state's forests and parks. He was attracted by the idea of moving farm families off marginal, unproductive land and resettling them on more fertile valley acres. The land they had left could then be reclaimed to forest.

The most important consequence of Roosevelt's tenure in the New York Senate was his friendship with a diminutive political reporter named Louis Howe. It seems safe to say that there has been no odder alliance in the nation's political history. Scruffy, a chain-smoker (as was Roosevelt), with a hacking cough and a face that was like a map of the political wars he had survived, he was, in his own way, as ambitious as Roosevelt. But like the wizard in a fairy tale, he knew that he must find a handsome young prince whose counselor he might be if he were to realize his ambition to find a place among the mighty of the land. Roosevelt appeared to Howe as the answer to his prayers. He told Roosevelt's son James years later that soon after they had met, he became determined to make the young politician President of the United States. "We hit the timetable right on the button," he declared. "He

[Roosevelt] didn't know the details. No one did. I've never talked about it. But I worked out in my mind when the right times to make our moves might be, and we made them at those times and we were successful."

Born in 1871, Howe was the son of a former captain in the Union Army who was a successful real estate speculator until he lost everything he owned in the Panic of 1873. Howe grew up in Saratoga, New York. "I am one of the four ugliest men, if what is left of me can be dignified by the name of man, in the State of New York," Howe said of himself. "I am wizened in the Dickens manner. . . . Children take one look at me on the street and run." Roosevelt, for his part, recognized Howe's remarkable political instincts as complementary to his own. He responded to Howe's exuberant spirits, which had survived misfortune unimpaired, and to his wicked gift of mockery. Eleanor Roosevelt, on the other hand, considered Howe, in his soiled clothes, to which the scent of stale tobacco clung tenaciously, a disaster and resented his hold on her husband's affections.

Roosevelt had done his best to help secure the Democratic nomination for Wilson in 1912. He was equally indefatigable in his efforts during the presidential campaign. His reward was the post his cousin Theodore had held in the first McKinley administration, assistant secretary of the navy. He had been married eight years and been "in politics" for three. Howe was right on schedule. "I am baptized, confirmed, sworn in, vaccinated—and somewhat at sea," Roosevelt wrote his mother from Washington.

The seven and a half years that Roosevelt spent as assistant secretary of the navy were critically important years in his development. A newspaperman described the new assistant secretary as "friendly as a pup. . . ." Roosevelt had his cousin's genuine interest in people and his skill in ingratiating himself without loss of dignity. He soon made friends of that portion of the press corps with whom he had most frequent contact. More important, he threw himself into his job with unflagging enthusiasm, making personal tours of inspection where no high official of the Navy Department had ever gone before and talking to sailors, officers, and shipyard workers with the cheery informality that had become his trademark. He also proved to be a thorough and able administrator with a prodigious memory and a passion for all the more recondite details of the navy. He obviously relished the more formal aspects of navy life—the ceremonies, the drills and naval exercises, and the seventeen-gun salutes he received when he made his tours of ships of the fleet. His relations with his boss, Josephus Daniels, Wilson's pacifist, teetotaling secretary of the navy, were amicable (Roosevelt called Daniels the "funniest-looking hill-billy I had ever seen"). Daniels, for his part, was puzzled by the frequent presence of Louis Howe, whom he described as "one of the strangest men I have ever met and one of the smartest. . . . He would have sidetracked both President Wilson and me to get Franklin Roosevelt to the White House," he added.

Soon after Roosevelt had taken up his duties as assistant secretary, he and Daniels were photographed on the portico of the State, War, and Navy Building. When Daniels saw the photograph, he asked Roosevelt why he was "grinning from ear to ear," and when a somewhat disconcerted Roosevelt replied that he was trying to present a pleasant appearance, Daniels remarked, "We are both looking down on the White House and you are saying to yourself, being a New Yorker, 'Some day I will be living in that house'—while I, being from the South, know I must be satisfied with no such ambition." A lot of history and a good deal of heartache were contained in the North Carolinian's observation.

Different as they were in background and outlook, the Southern hillbilly and the New York aristocrat became fast friends; both men were political to their fingertips, and they shared a common devotion to the navy. Newton Baker, Garrison's successor as secretary of war, observed to Frances Perkins, "Young Roosevelt is very promising but I should think he'd wear himself out in the promiscuous and extended contacts he maintains with people. . . . But as I have observed him, he seems to clarify his ideas and teach himself as he goes along by that very conversational method." William Phillips, third assistant secretary of state and a close friend of Roosevelt's, described him as "likeable, attentive but not a heavyweight, brilliant but not particularly steady in his views. . . . He was always amusing, always the life of any party, but he did not seem fully mature." Phillips also commented on Roosevelt's "tremendous vitality." It reminded people of his cousin the Colonel.

To his children Franklin Roosevelt, like Theodore Roosevelt's father and like Theodore himself, was an ideal father, never too busy to stop for a romp with them. James, the eldest son, named after Franklin's father, thought him the "handsomest, strongest, most glamorous, vigorous, physical father in the world."

But all was not as well as it seemed. Despite a series of children, Roosevelt, with his strong masculinity and almost animal energy, apparently found Eleanor, like any properly brought-up young woman of her class, an indifferent sexual partner, as inhibited in such matters as she was supposed to be. Eleanor Roosevelt's social secretary was a strikingly handsome young woman of twenty-three named Lucy Page Mercer. She was a member of both the Page and Carroll families of Virginia and Maryland.

In 1919, while her husband was recovering from pneumonia, Eleanor Roosevelt, gathering up some of her husband's personal belongings, discovered love letters from her former social secretary to her husband. "The bottom dropped out of my own particular world," she told her biographer Joseph Lash. "I faced myself, my surroundings, my world, honestly for the first time." Her old self-doubts rushed back. Bitterly offended, she proposed a divorce. Roosevelt could not, in any event, have married Lucy Mercer, who, as a devout Catholic, could not have married a divorced man. In addition, the scandal would have ended his political aspirations. According to the Roosevelts' daughter, Anna, her father "voluntarily promised to end any 'romantic relationship' and seemed to have realized how much pain he had given her."

The episode marked a turning point in Eleanor Roosevelt's life. According to her son Elliott, "she was bound and determined that she would have nothing to do with my father physically even though he was quite abject in seeking to rehabilitate himself in her eyes. . . . Through the entire rest of their lives, they never did have a husband-and-wife relationship." Instead, they had, in Elliott's phrase, a "partnership arrangement. This partnership was to last all the way through their lives; it became a very close and very intimate partnership of great affection—never in a physical sense, but in a tremendously mental sense. . . ." That kind of punishment of an erring spouse—the denial of sexual "favors"—was common to upper-class marriages of the time. One suspects that it was often imposed with a sense of relief on the part of wives whose distaste for the physical side of marriage had helped drive their husbands into alien beds.

In the period after the revelation of the Lucy Mercer affair, Eleanor Roosevelt's favorite choral music became Marian Anderson singing the aria from Handel's *Messiah*: "He is despised and rejected of men/ A man of sorrows/ And acquainted with grief."

Another consequence of her discovery of the liaison was a deep affection between Eleanor Roosevelt and Louis Howe. Anna Roosevelt came into her mother's room on one occasion and saw her sitting at Howe's feet as he stroked her hair. Eleanor Roosevelt's own public career began, in a sense, with her discovery of her husband's infidelity. She took courses in typing and shorthand and involved herself in a variety of causes, most prominently perhaps the work of the League of Women Voters.

Essential to Roosevelt through the years of his developing political career was the family residence at Hyde Park. It was there that he was most at home, most comfortable, most relaxed, playing indefatigably his treasured role as gentleman farmer. Hyde Park was rather like an English estate with its gardens and orchards, meadows and woodlot. And it had a staff almost as large as that required for an English manor house: a cook, maid, personal maid, waitress, butler, houseman, coachman, chauffeur, laundress, several gardeners and their assistants, and, not infrequently, a governess or tutor. When the boys were growing up, Hyde Park, in Rexford Tugwell's words, was "a kind of adolescent bedlam." The boys and Anna engaged in noisy debates and "challenged their father in every issue." He encouraged their outspokenness. "In summer and holidays, the children were at home," Frances Perkins wrote. "There were boys rushing all over the place, riding ponies, practicing hurdle jumps, swinging baseball bats and tennis rackets, filling the air with their shouting. Large companies would sit down to lunch. The windows would be open, with a pleasant breeze blowing in from the Hudson River. Roosevelt would be at the head of the table, talking to everybody, bantering with his children, teasing them and they him. The youngsters would tell preposterous stories to dignified visitors to see if they could get away with them, and would burst into gales of laughter regardless of whether the visitor fell for the story or saw through it. Roosevelt played with his children as though he were one of them."

Tugwell was especially perceptive about Roosevelt's "impulse to build and change and improve." It was evident everywhere at Hyde Park, where he was constantly adding to the house, reforesting his land, and planting experimental crops of trees. In Tugwell's opinion, Roosevelt consciously made Hyde Park a projection of his own spirit—spacious, accommodating, comfortable, practical, not at all grand like so many of the mansions of his wealthy neighbors along the Hudson. It was as though he wished to demonstrate, in the contrast between his *relatively* simple style of living and the lavishness of such estates as that of Frederick Vanderbilt, north of Hyde Park, with its vulgar ostentation, "the moral bankruptcy of the class he had 'deserted.'"

In his interminable building and endless experimentation with growing things, Roosevelt bore an almost eerie resemblance to his hero, Thomas Jefferson. In much the same spirit that Jefferson had made Monticello a remarkable projection of *his* mind and temperament, Roosevelt fashioned Springwood (the name of the actual house) in his. He may also have had "Uncle Ted's" Sagamore Hill in mind. That, too, was a kind of concretization or material representation of the earlier Roosevelt.

When Roosevelt was first stricken with polio, in August, 1921, doctors were at a loss to identify the illness, which left him completely paralyzed. Roosevelt felt, he told Frances Perkins later, "utter despair . . . fearing God had abandoned him." Finally, the disease was correctly diagnosed, but no one realized at first the severity of the attack on Roosevelt's system. Later it seemed not only that he would never walk but that he might never even be able to sit up again.

Slowly, by relentless efforts of the will, he began, to the surprise of his doctors, to regain some movement, first in his arms and shoulders, then in his back. "He has such courage, such ambition, and yet at the same time such an extraordinarily sensitive emotional mechanism," his doctor, George Draper, wrote, "that it will take all the skill he can muster to lead him successfully to a recognition of what he really faces without crushing him." By October he was able to struggle into a wheelchair, and four months later he strapped himself into the cruel steel and leather braces which weighed seven pounds apiece and were to be his constant companions the rest of his life. With crutches and his leg braces locked at the knee he was able to move, painfully and precariously.

Draper, a schoolmate and friend of Roosevelt's, played a crucial role, according to William O. Douglas, in encouraging Roosevelt to continue his political career. "Why are your legs important in speechmaking?" he would ask Roosevelt. "It's your heart and your mind that are important in politics, not your feet." Douglas wrote: "My own experience with polio put me on FDR's wave length, and he was my hero long before I met him." As an orthodox Freudian Draper saw Roosevelt's mother as his opponent. Sara Roosevelt wished to see her crippled son propped up on the porch at Hyde Park, attended faithfully by her and the servants and thus, in Freudian terms, restored to her as her "helpless and obedient child once more." Draper set out, as he saw it, to free the wounded statesman from his bondage to the overprotective mother. The issue of Roosevelt's recovery was translated into classic Oedipal terms; Draper believed Roosevelt, even before the polio attack, was too dependent on his mother.

Draper suggested water therapy, which proved so successful that Roosevelt decided to try the hot baths at a run-down resort at Warm Springs, Georgia. He loved the water, and for a time he harbored the hope that he might regain the use of his legs, but the hope proved vain. What he did recover were his spirits and zest for life.

In the spring of 1926 Roosevelt, with the help of a generous gift from John J. Raskob, purchased Warm Springs with the intention of making it a center for the treatment of polio victims. "I undertook to be doctor and physiotherapist, all rolled into one," Roosevelt recalled of the patients who came for treatment. "I taught them all at least to play around in the water." He gave special attention to "two, quite large ladies." Tugwell wrote: "The student [of Roosevelt] can hardly escape the obvious inference that he was following in the Master's way by ministering to the halt and the lame, the ill and the heavily burdened."

Roosevelt bought a run-down farm, Pine Ridge, near Warm Springs, and, establishing a tenant, Otis Moore, on the farm, undertook its rehabilitation. One of the main attractions of Warm Springs was his talks with Moore about the progress of the farm, new crops to plant, and new techniques to try. As Moore told Tugwell years later, "That was the whole idea from the start—not to make money, but to show the people. . . ." There were rabbits and pigs, thirty or forty of them, as well, of course, as chickens. Roosevelt hoped to improve the scrawny cattle in the region by offering to breed his prize bull to the cows of farmers in the area.

Warm Springs never had a strong appeal to Eleanor Roosevelt. She saw there how "hard and poor and ugly" the life of many Southerners was, so different from the romantic tales of plantation life that had been passed down from her paternal grandmother, Mrs. Theodore Roosevelt, Sr.

Roosevelt's illness, it is commonly said, turned him from a rather self-centered, self-indulgent man into a much deeper and stronger person. Not only was that the line taken by Stephen Early, his longtime press secretary, but it was stated by Eleanor Roosevelt in her autobiography, *This I Remember*, in which she wrote that his illness "proved a blessing in disguise; for it gave him strength and courage he had not had before. He had to think out the fundamentals of living and learn the greatest of all lessons—infinite patience and never-ending persistence." Certainly Roosevelt responded, with the aid of George Draper and Louis Howe, to his illness and above all, to the crippling of his lithe and powerful body, with a remarkable demonstration of will-power. Howe wrote: "Suddenly, there he was flat on his back, with nothing to do but think. . . . His thoughts expanded, his horizon widened. He began to see the other fellow's point of view. He thought of others who were ill and afflicted and in want. He dwelt on many things which had not bothered him much before. Lying there, he grew bigger day by day."

His illness deepened and strengthened Roosevelt's essential character, but that it somehow transformed him is as incorrect as the Lippmann thesis that the responsibilities of the presidency changed him virtually overnight from a lightweight into a heavyweight. That he was frivolous or lacking in determined idealism and well-thought-out political goals *before* his illness and emerged as the commanding figure known to history only *after* it is not supported by the evidence. "It is a mistake," Rex Tugwell wrote, "to think that his exprience with polio revolutionized his character or his intentions. . . . It was equally wrong to assume that it had no effect at all." It made him, in Tugwell's phrase, "more deeply experienced."

In the difficult years of Roosevelt's convalescence, as his strength came back slowly and then, more dishearteningly, as it became clear that he would never walk again, the rehabilitation of the Warm Springs farm and the conservation work at Hyde Park became increasingly important to him. But, Tugwell noted, "all this was not his real business on this earth. There was no hour when he did not know that this was so, no hour when he did not govern himself appropriately for participation in public affairs. In his most relaxed moments—organizing miniature sailboat regattas on the Hudson, for which he carved out the hulls and contrived the rigs himself, or presiding over ceremonial occasions among the patients at Warm Springs—what he said and what he did was entirely congruous with a larger destiny. . . . It must have occurred to him," Tugwell wrote, "that he could be mistaken and that at some point he might be deserted by the Providence guiding his career." But if that was the case, no one around him "was ever able to recall in him anything but confidence and serenity. He was steadily, almost gaily, going forward to his destiny. If that required of him the overcoming by almost superhuman persistence and cruel effort the trial put upon him by one of the most terrible of diseases, that was an ordeal he must come through."

Eleanor Roosevelt developed her own life at Hyde Park. Nancy Cook and Marion Dickerman were two emancipated young women who became her close friends and helped draw her into active participation in Democratic Party politics. In 1927 Eleanor Roosevelt, Cook, and Dickerman bought the Todhunter School from its English founder, and Eleanor taught courses in American history and British and American literature and current events for two and a half days a week.

At a Hyde Park brook called Val-Kill, where the Roosevelts went to picnic in the days of his recovery from polio, Eleanor decided to join forces with Cook and Dickerman to build, with her husband's help and encouragement, a cottage which was to be the home of a cottage industry to make by hand fine reproductions of early American furniture. The idea was to employ members of local farm families who needed cash salaries to help them get by on their small farms. The Roosevelts saw the sons of farmers they knew leaving their fathers' farms because the work was hard and the returns meager; they decided to try to do something to arrest that tendency.

Although Eleanor Roosevelt put most of the fees she made from lecturing and writing into the "factory," and some of her inheritance besides, it failed to thrive. "We found," she wrote, "that as soon as a young man learned a trade in which he could make more money than he could on a farm he did not care enough about farm life to want to give up for a summer the good wages and regular hours he enjoyed in his trade." It was a disillusioning experience for Nancy Cook and the Roosevelts, and it was years and many dollars before they reluctantly reached the conclusion that for most young people the small family farm could not compete with the attractions of city life and regular wages.

Rexford Tugwell equated Roosevelt's recovery from polio with his determination to be the instrument of the nation's recovery from the illness of the Depression. The "inner convictions making Roosevelt the instrument of his nation's return to health were very deep," Tugwell wrote years later, "and they were his own, so determined and so full fed, so ardently and with such artfulness fought for, that they can only have been an extension of his own nature, at last come to full maturity through suffering, contemplation, and conviction—not created by those experiences but ripened by them." Equally important, in Tugwell's view, was Roosevelt's "deep religious faith assumed by most contemporary commentators to be no more than the nominal affiliation any politician would maintain. . . . The Roosevelt religion was consistent with gaiety and intellectual freedom; but it was nevertheless deeply held."

# Roosevelt's Philosophy

I t is important, before an evaluation of Roosevelt's critically important apprenticeship as governor, to consider the formation of the ideas that shaped his political career.

In the years prior to his presidency Roosevelt's intellectual world was growing and expanding. History was his special delight. It was both entertainment and serious study. A neighbor, Olin Dows, remembered his keen interest in history: "His conversation was full of personal and historical reminiscences, as well as facts and stories about local history. . . . He talked about Jefferson as if the third President had been one of his grandfathers. He felt the past of the United States . . . as if it were his own immediate past." The poet Archibald MacLeish testified to the same effect. Roosevelt, he wrote, "approached the culture of Americans as he approached their political life and their social and economic institutions, as an historian, or, rather, as a political leader whose intellectual preoccupation was history." MacLeish added, "[T]he sense of history in a political leader is a sense of the past as the past has meaning for the future. The sense of posterity is a presence in the earth. And to any man who feels it, learning and the arts are continuing realities."

Roosevelt went back to the constitutional "sources": Madison's records of the debates in the Federal Convention and Jonathan Elliot's volumes on the state-by-state debates on ratification. Among the Founding Fathers he chose an unlikely mentor: Thomas Jefferson, long in bad repute among liberal thinkers. Herbert Croly, for one, had deplored Jefferson's influence on American history and Cousin Ted considered him a villain pure and simple.

Roosevelt's coadjutor in the rehabilitation of Jefferson was the journalist Claude Bowers. In 1924 Bowers began a book with the prospective title *Jefferson and Hamilton*. It was less a historical study than a modern morality play with Hamilton cast as the villain and Jefferson as the hero. The book was significant for a number of reasons. In the recasting of the public image of the Democrats as the party of progress and reform and the Republican party as the party of the "interests," the party of reaction and preservation of the status quo, it was important to evoke symbolic figures from among the Founding Fathers and claim them as progenitors. Jefferson had been under a cloud in the minds of the reformers ever since the Civil War because he had formulated the mischievous doctrine of states' rights, under the banner of which the South had seceded. Conversely, Hamilton, the champion of nationalism, the brilliant financier and the loyal aide to Washington, had been held up as hero and model. Now the picture was reversed, at least by the Democrats. Franklin Roosevelt fastened on Jefferson as the appropriate "father" of a revitalized and modernized democracy. It was not Jefferson the slaveholder, Jefferson the enemy of centralized government and the philosopher of states' rights that Roosevelt summoned up but Jefferson the friend of the people, the believer in democracy, the defender of free speech. It symbolized the beginning of a profound shift. In Bowers's words, for generations Americans had been presented with a Jefferson who "was a liar and a hypocrite, . . . a mere dreamer and atheist without any sound claim to statesmanship."

Bowers was surprised at the enthusiastic reception of *Jefferson and Hamilton*. Senator Borah reviewed it in the *New Republic*. More significantly, Franklin Roosevelt wrote a glowing review for the *Evening World*, the only book review, according to Bowers, that Roosevelt ever wrote. "Jefferson," Roosevelt noted, "brought the government back to the hands of the average voter. . . . I have a breathless feeling . . . as I wonder, if, a century and a quarter later, the same contending forces are not again mobilizing. Hamiltons we have today. Is a Jefferson on the horizon?" America had, in the 1920s, "side by side an old political order fashioned by a pastoral civilization and a new social order fashioned by a technical civilization. . . . The two are maladjusted. Their creative interrelation is one of the big tasks ahead of American leadership."

Not only did Roosevelt praise the book and the author, but he made Bowers a kind of unofficial adviser and political aide, drawing on him for help in writing his political speeches and consulting him on political strategy.

A by-product of the rehabilitation of Jefferson was a campaign to rehabilitate Monticello, that beautiful and eccentric structure which told so much of its architect's character and the woeful dilapidation of which corresponded to the eclipse of Jefferson's reputation. It was owned by New York Congressman Jefferson Levy, who consented to sell it to the Thomas Jefferson Memorial Foundation, headed, of course, by Claude Bowers. The foundation solicited the pennies of schoolchildren, bought Monticello, and began the long and expensive task of restoring it. At the ceremony presenting it to the nation as a shrine the president of the University of Virginia spoke of the "gross caricature of [Jefferson] built up by malice and misunderstanding" and now replaced by the true picture of "a calm, courteous, versatile, patient, steadfast, courageous statesman . . . a master in managing men, a robust hater of ignorance, tyranny and intolerance, an apostle of peace and a lover of nature and mankind."

Congress completed the process of deification by creating the Jefferson Centennial Commission in 1926 to plan the observance of the hundredth anniversary of his death. Among the members of the commission were the international bankers and financiers Felix Warburg, Thomas Fortune Ryan (Jefferson mistrusted all bankers), Henry Ford (Jefferson feared the industrialization of America), and Nicholas Longworth, son-in-law of Theodore Roosevelt (who had hated Jefferson with a passion and frequently spoke of him as the worst President in our history). Warburg, a prominent Jew, offered to give $100,000 if a like sum was contributed by a Protestant and a Roman Catholic. All this happened, of course, in the administration of Calvin Coolidge, whose opinion of Jefferson is not recorded.

Franklin Roosevelt valued Jefferson on two counts: his unquestioned devotion to democracy and his importance to the southern wing of the Democratic Party. If Jefferson could be established not simply as a regional hero but as a national one, Roosevelt reasoned, it would help strengthen the often precarious ties of the Northern wing of the party with the Southern.

In addition to Roosevelt's intellectual debt to Jefferson, there was clearly a temperamental affinity. As a country gentleman Roosevelt found it easier to identify with the aristocratic Jefferson than with the hustling and ambitious Hamilton, although Hamilton's brand of nationalism was far closer to Roosevelt's own political philosophy than was Jefferson's devotion to states' rights. Roosevelt also shared his hero's distrust of banks and bankers, of the manipulators of money and credit. Another common characteristic of the two Presidents was their devotion to nature, to the land, and, above all, to the farmer. Jefferson's paeans to the "tillers of the soil," God's favored ones, the yeoman farmers of Virginia, are among his best known and most eloquent utterances; Roosevelt was obsessed with the plight of the farmers and the possible remedies. Besides sharing a rather naïve faith in the farmer as the backbone of the nation, both men were tireless experimental farmers themselves (it was an aspect of their "visionary idealism"), constantly trying new methods and new techniques. Even in their restless building of specific structures and their passion for practical "improvements" they were akin.

Like Roosevelt, Jefferson was a man of great personal charm and remarkable political charisma, whose supporters adored him. Jefferson had the power to draw to him the affections of great numbers of ordinary people as well as the unrelenting hatred of others, primarily the rich and wellborn. Both men, despite their charm and affability, had few close friends and were jealously protective of their inner lives.

Although Jefferson complained frequently that he preferred the quiet retreat of his study to the political arena, his actions belied him. He was one of the most astute politicians in our history, and he clearly reveled in the possession and use of power.

There were, of course, significant differences as well, the principal one being, as we have noted, Roosevelt's deep religious faith, which was an important source of strength to him. Jefferson always professed to be horrified by the grimy world of politics in which he was such an accomplished practitioner; Roosevelt never pretended to be anything but a political being. Jefferson had a strong aesthetic sense, a passionate attachment to particular material things, to paintings, music, sculpture, architecture, a whole sensuous realm to which Roosevelt was insensitive.

In more contemporary times the most important influences on Roosevelt were his cousin Theodore Roosevelt, Louis Brandeis, and Woodrow Wilson. Indeed, it is hard to imagine Franklin Roosevelt's career in the absence of his cousin and precursor Theodore. Their lives provide fascinating parallels and contrasts. First of all, both came from the Eastern upper class. That was perhaps more important than the fact that they were relatives. Not only were they well established members of a class that was as close to an aristocracy as a democratic society allows, but they did not dissemble that fact. Their manner of living, their friends, their clothes, and their accents proclaimed their social status. Moreover, their class was an inseparable part of their personalities, of the assurance with which they faced the world, of their relations with others not of that class. The two men had the same remarkable energy, the same exuberant delight in life, the same far-ranging interests, the same serene faith in the God of their fathers. They both had moral and physical courage in abundance. Harry Hopkins and Raymond Moley were only two among dozens of men and women who spoke of Franklin Roosevelt's "fearlessness," and the same was commonly noted of his cousin. Theodore was, in fact, not only fearless but reckless beyond reasonable bounds and, indeed, slightly mad in his enthusiasms. They both loved to sail. They both had famous smiles; with Theodore Roosevelt it was a voracious grin. They both loved nature; TR loved nature in the raw; FDR loved cultivated nature—farms and gardens. They both loved Groton, Harvard, and the Episcopal Church. TR and Gifford Pinchot invented conservation, both the word and the fact, at least as it applied to the American landscape, and FDR was a tireless advocate of that cause. Both men wanted to be President of the United States and planned and plotted unceasingly to that end. When TR was police commissioner in New York City, a post about as far away from the presidency as one could well get, Lincoln Steffens and Jacob Riis realized that his ultimate ambition was to be President; when they confronted him with their insight, he flew into a rage and denounced them as tempters. It was hard enough to do one's job honestly and intelligently. If, he implied, he allowed himself to think of that office, he would find himself acting in such a way as to advance his career rather than do his job.

From FDR's first appearance on the political stage as a state legislator from Dutchess County, New York, there were those who saw in him a future President, if only because of his magic name. Fortune made TR President: San Juan Hill and Boss Platt's scheme to get him out of New York State and an assassin's bullet. But FDR's progress to the presidency was as measured as the march of the seasons, the result of painstaking planning, interminable campaigning, and enormous energy.

The differences were as intriguing as the similarities. While TR (both men were unique among Presidents up to that time in being known by their initials; no one had ever referred to Washington as GW or Jefferson as TJ) was more "literary" and far more widely read than FDR, the younger Roosevelt had the keener political intelligence and the more certain grasp of American history. TR was, in a sense, the by-product of the passion for reform that characterized the era from about 1890 to the Bull Moose campaign in 1912. By the time FDR became President, the forces of reform had been badly scattered and demoralized. The Wilson Democrats like Newton Baker had become notably conservative and were, in addition, tarred with the brush of Wilsonian "internationalism" and the League and thereby rendered politically impotent. Whereas TR was borne aloft, so to speak, by the rising tide of Progressive sentiment, his cousin had to create a liberal constituency out of whole cloth. TR's political method was bluff and bluster; FDR's was subtle management. In comparing the two Roosevelts, Tugwell quoted Lincoln Steffens's famous observation that the first Roosevelt "thought with his hips"—that is to say, relied on his intuitions. "The latter Roosevelt," Tugwell added, "was in a way, subtler; he had more resources of charm and yet more directness of thought. He used his head, all right, and not his hips, but it was a kind of thinking that I was unable to follow because he had pictures for references I could not always visualize."

A distinction can be made between the first and second Roosevelts' attitude toward "labor" and the disadvantaged members of society generally. As we have noted, the first Roosevelt saw himself as a kind of referee between exploitive capital and aggressive labor. The notion that labor was engaged in an unequal contest with capital and desperately needed the intervention of government to make the contest equal was quite alien to him. His angry fulminations against hyphenated Americans—that is to say, immigrants—showed a moral blind spot. FDR was far more aware of the depth and nature of the nation's inequalities.

Perhaps the most important quality that both men shared was their unabashed pleasure in the game of politics. There were thousands of upper-class reformers, good government men, or goo-goos, as the old pros called them contemptuously, but they lacked the instinct for politics; they were too addicted to the pleasures of their class: sailing and tennis; trips to the Continent; lavish social events. They lacked the stamina that democratic politics requires; they grew bored and inattentive at the endless meetings, caucuses, conclaves, and rallies that are, for better or worse, the essence of American democracy. They disliked the standard, serviceable, run-of-the-mill politician with his lower-middle- or middle-middle-class origins and manners; when they were not simply disenchanted, they were, in a word, patronizing. TR and FDR, on the other hand, were exotic plants in the circle of upper-class reformers. Politics was food and drink to them; they loved its murky air and sly chicanery.

Roosevelt was like his cousin Theodore in his restless activity. Graceful and lithe, he seemed always in motion. "Even when working at a desk, he kept jumping up and walking rapidly about the room," a friend recalled. After his paralysis he never "wholly overcame the motor impulses." The constant movements of his hands and head and even his volubility, Tugwell suggested, had their source in a need for physical activity that was as sharp as hunger.

George Creel, who saw heavily underlined copies of Theodore Roosevelt's speeches on FDR's desk during the latter's presidency, was convinced that the younger man's "love of phrases" came from his cousin. "Quotations from 'Uncle Ted' also figured frequently in his conversation," Creel noted.

Louis Brandeis was another important influence on Roosevelt. The younger man was especially attracted by Brandeis's view of the limited and contingent nature of political change. In Felix Frankfurter's words, Brandeis believed that true virtue was to be found in the "pursuit of enlightened purpose. . . ." Problems were never finally solved; civilization was "a sequence of new tasks." Brandeis insisted on "the extreme difficulty of government and its dependence on sustained interest and effort, on the need for constant alertness to the fact that the introduction of new forces is accompanied by new difficulties." He "disavowed allegiance to any general system of thought or hope." Brandeis declared: "I have no rigid philosophy; I have been too intent on concrete problems of practical justice." Roosevelt told a friend, "I always hate the frame of mind which talks about 'your group' and 'my group' among liberals." He shared Brandeis's suspicion of such alignments; he was "one thousand per cent right in principle. . . ." But Roosevelt stopped short of Brandeis's passion for decentralization; "in certain fields there must be a guiding or restraining hand of government."

Woodrow Wilson was the third important influence on FDR among modern politicians. By Eleanor Roosevelt's testimony, Wilson had "a profound effect" on her husband's "thinking and political philosophy. Franklin admired him greatly, I know," she added, "and believed deeply in his ideas and ideals." By the same token he was well aware that the basis of Wilson's power lay in the eloquence of the writings and, above all, of his speeches. He had learned from Wilson the importance of oratory, of communication, as we would say today, in leading a democratic nation. "There is no question in my mind," Eleanor Roosevelt added, "but that all three of these great men [Theodore Roosevelt, Brandeis, and Wilson] had an effect on Franklin that was evident in his actions both as governor and as president."

As early as 1912, in a talk in Troy, New York, Roosevelt declared himself in favor of a central role on the part of the government in regulating the economy to provide for the common interests of all rather than the special interests of a few. "We are beginning to see that it is necessary for our health and happiness of the whole people of the state that individuals and lumber companies should not go into the wooded areas like the Adirondacks and the Catskills and lumber them off root and branch for the benefit of their own pocket. . . . After all, if I own a farm of a hundred acres and let it lie waste and overgrown, I am just as much a destroyer of the liberty of the community—and by liberty we mean happiness and prosperity—as the strong man who stands idle on the corner, refusing to work, a destroyer of his neighbor's happiness, prosperity and liberty." The speech was an odd jumble of Henry George notions and Edward Bellamy "nationalism." To compare the farm left fallow with "the strong young man who stands idle at the corner" was an odd analogy; certainly it was eccentric to suggest that both were robbing their neighbors of "happiness, prosperity and liberty."

In a speech before the Democratic National Committee in Chicago in May, 1919, that helped establish him as a national figure in the party, Roosevelt took the line that for the first time since the Civil War the two parties had taken on a distinctive character based on fundamental political principles. In rejecting the Progressive wing of its party, the Republican old guard embraced conservatism and reaction. Under the leadership of Wilson the Democratic Party had taken up the banner of a "sane liberalism." The Republican policy, on the other hand, seemed to be directed at lightening the "burden of those unfortunate individuals who have incomes of $1,000,000 a year or more."

A year later at the Democratic Convention Roosevelt staked out his position as leader of the liberal wing of his party. The platform planks that he and Howe drew up called for the national government to use all its powers to remedy inequities, a guarantee of labor's right to organize, a heavier tax on unearned than on earned income, and, perhaps most portentous, "deficit spending by the government in time of depression to create jobs." Indeed, much of the New Deal program was foreshadowed by Roosevelt's platform resolutions, most notably not only the right but the obligation of the Federal government to use its vast powers for the welfare of its citizens, especially the less fortunate. "Every man has a right to life and this means that he has also a right to make a comfortable living," Roosevelt wrote. The function of the Federal government was the "maintenance of a balance, within which every individual may find safety if he wishes it; in which every individual may attain such power as his ability permits. . . ." This had, after all, been the view of the Founding Fathers, expressed most cogently in the tenth *Federalist Paper* by James Madison. In that essay Madison had described the role of the national government as that of preventing any particular segment or interest in the society—whether business, agriculture, creditors, or debtors—from dominating the government and using it to exploit others for its own advantage. Just as the various branches of the Federal government—the executive, legislative, and judicial—should be able to balance one another so that no single branch or combination of branches would predominate, so must the government be used to ensure that all Americans had an equal opportunity to enjoy the fruits of their labor.

To Raymond Moley, the most important aspect of Roosevelt's thought was the conviction that the "government . . . should achieve the subordination of private interests to collective interests. . . ." On the emotional level it was his "profound feeling for the underdog" and his "very keen awareness that political democracy could not exist side by side with economic plutocracy."

Roosevelt was convinced that the age of unchecked or "rugged" individualism was over and that the new order required cooperation, or "concert of interests," involving in greater or lesser degree conscious planning and the creation of agencies and instrumentalities to make such planning possible. Tugwell called it Roosevelt's "holistic or collective thinking," which ran, in Tugwell's words, "concurrently with his older assumptions and understandings." Tugwell and many other "searchers" for Roosevelt (Tugwell's book is called *In Search of Roosevelt*) have assumed that these impulses or inclinations were necessarily incompatible or contradictory, but Roosevelt clearly did not think so. The Protestant ethic of thrift, piety, hard work, and moral principle was in no way incompatible with "holistic . . . thinking." In fact, Roosevelt would doubtless have argued that it was more important than ever, since the guardians were every bit as subject to corruption as those they were assigned to guard, presumably the businessmen.

In an address to the graduating class at Milton Academy in 1926, Roosevelt said: "Unrest in this world of ours is caused as much by those who fear changes as by those who seek revolution; and unrest in any nation or organization, whether it is caused by ultraconservatism or by extreme radicalism, is in the long run a healthy sign. In government, in science, in industry, in the arts, inaction and apathy are the most potent foes."

Roosevelt also formulated a principle that, while first enunciated by the more radical of the Founding Fathers, had received little attention from American political theorists and even less from practicing politicians: "Taxes should and must be levied in proportion to *ability to pay* and in proportion to *benefits received*" (the italics are Roosevelt's). "Wealth," he declared, "does not come from individual effort alone, but through the cooperation of the entire community, from the people in the mass." The proposition is almost identical with Benjamin Franklin's assertion that all wealth earned by the individual is the consequence of the opportunities afforded him by the larger society of which he is a part. From this it followed for Ben Franklin, as it did for FDR, that after the needs of comfortable subsistence had been met, the society had the right to claim as much of the surplus for its own use as necessity dictated. "Superfluous property," Franklin wrote, "is the creature of society." The instinct of the wealthy to "protect their property at the expense of humanity" in all ages was well known. In Franklin's view, this had been invariably the beginning of "a tyranny." Jefferson had gone further. He was so concerned with the tendency of certain individuals and groups in America to take advantage of their fellows that he wished, on the biblical principle, to redistribute land every generation so that large amounts could not be sequestered by individuals, families, or corporations. "The earth is given as a common stock to man to labor and live on. If, for the encouragement of industry, we allow it to be appropriated, we must take care that other employment be permitted to those excluded from appropriation. If we do not, the fundamental right to labor the earth," Jefferson concluded, "returns to the unemployed."

As we have noted on more than one occasion, Gouverneur Morris, one of the most conservative of the delegates to the Constitutional Convention, warned that if the power of the rich to exploit the poor were not curtailed by constitutional safeguards, the rich would in time impose a despotic regime on the country and run it for their own aggrandizement. Roosevelt came to similar conclusions.

In the realm of foreign policy, Roosevelt might best be described as a secret Wilsonian or perhaps as a "closet" internationalist. Hamilton Fish Armstrong, editor of the influential *Foreign Affairs* magazine, was pleased and somewhat surprised to find that Roosevelt, who believed the League of Nations was a dead issue in American politics at least for the time being, was still a firm supporter of the League in principle. He told Armstrong that he believed that the United States, "without entering European politics," in Armstrong's paraphrase of his words, "should cooperate with the League and take an active, hearty and official part in all its proceedings which affected the general good." It was his conviction that "even without full membership we Americans [must] be generous and sporting enough to give the League a far larger share of sympathetic approval and definite help than we have hitherto accorded."

Something needs to be said about Roosevelt's relationship to women and their influence on him. There was, for one thing, a deeply feminine and intuitive side to his character; he had a particular affinity for what seemed to him the qualities of mind and spirit that are associated with the feminine temperament. He had been drawn to Eleanor Roosevelt by her mind and spirit far more than by her body, and it was her mind and spirit that he valued throughout their life together. Grace Tully and Marguerite "Missy" LeHand, his secretaries, were much more than that; they were members of the family, surrogate daughters, valued and beloved. Frances Perkins became in time a kind of alter ego, not a rival but a complement to his wife. His mother was also a persistently powerful figure in his life. He was sentimental and romantic in his attitude toward women as well, a trait of his class. "It is my firm belief," he wrote in 1928, "that had women had an equal share in making the laws in years past, the unspeakable conditions in crowded tenement districts, the neglect of the poor, the unwillingness to spend money for hospitals and sanitariums, the whole underlying cynical attitude towards human life and happiness as compared to material prosperity, which has reached its height under the present Republican administration would never have come about. . . . I have always believed in giving women an equal share in the making of our laws. I have regarded their entry into politics—for they must enter politics if they are to have a voice in our legislative halls—the most noteworthy step toward securing greater happiness and greater prosperity for the individual that we have ever taken."

Roosevelt's study of history and, more basically, his deep historical sense made him acutely conscious of what might be called the "streams" or "tides" of history. "Streams of history are very difficult to create," Roosevelt said to William Douglas. "There is a time and a place for everything." Not long after the stock market crash Roosevelt declared that it was "time for the country to become fairly radical for at least one generation. History shows that where this occurs, occasionally, nations are saved from revolutions." The notion was obviously drawn from Jefferson's famous observation that "a little rebellion now and then" could be counted on to afford relief from accumulated social injustices and thus, he hoped, avoid a French Revolution type of upheaval. Roosevelt told the biographer Emil Ludwig that every civilization creates its own rot. "The radical says: 'Cut it down.' The conservative says: 'Don't touch it.' The liberal compromises: 'Let us prune, so that we lose neither the *old* trunk nor the *new* branches.' " While most Americans (dedicated Communists being perhaps the only exception) viewed the Depression as an unmitigated disaster, *Roosevelt saw it as an opportunity.*

Perhaps the most important single aspect of Roosevelt's temper, character, and political thought was his freedom from clichés and dogmas of either the right or the left (it was, of course, exactly the quality that alarmed intellectuals, most of whom were dogmatists by definition). "We were all ideologists in those days," Malcolm Cowley wrote in his memoirs, "from Hoover on the right to the Trotskyites on the far left—all except Roosevelt, who was the only convinced and happy experimentalist." Tugwell made the same observation. Those engaged in active political life fell into familiar and increasingly deeply worn ruts defined by ancient shibboleths and stereotypes, but Roosevelt, Tugwell decided after considerable observation and reflection, "was most unusual in having escaped much of the grooving so characteristic of other Americans." FDR was stubbornly opposed to being counted "as belonging to any system or committed to any philosophy." Tugwell concluded that "he had objectives and schemes of his own, deeper and wider than we knew. . . ." But Tugwell's immediate and impatient response was often irritation at Roosevelt's "contradictory sympathy with the underprivileged and his frequent excursions into policies favorable to their exploiters."

The story was told of a young reporter asking Roosevelt if he was a communist, capitalist, or socialist. When Roosevelt replied in each instance in the negative, the reporter asked despairingly what his political philosophy was. "Philosophy? Philosophy?" he asked as though the word were unfamiliar. "I am a Christian and a Democrat—that's all." Whether or not the story was apocryphal, it was marvelously apropos. Among other things it demonstrated the President's disposition for "fooling." It implied that he was a simple soul whose view of life and thought was quite adequately comprehended by "Christian" and "Democrat." Yet there was just enough truth in it to compel attention. He was no pragmatist certainly. The test of a policy for him was not whether it worked or not. While he was ready to try a wide variety of solutions to urgent problems, some of them indeed contradictory or at least competitive, the solutions all derived from a clear and firmly held conviction that the duty of government was to be responsive to the needs of its citizens, that hardship and suffering should be mitigated even if that meant straining the law. That was most clearly the Christian part. But Roosevelt also believed that his party was the party of "democracy," and if it was not, it was his intention to make it so. He was saying, in effect, to his youthful inquisitor, "I am free of secular dogmas, and I am deeply rooted in the historical traditions of the party started by Thomas Jefferson as a protest against wealth and privilege."

Eleanor Roosevelt also stressed the importance of her husband's religious convictions. "[T]hroughout the whole of Franklin's career there never was any deviation from his original objective—to help make life better for the average man, woman and child. A thousand and one means were used, difficulties arose, changes took place, but his objective always was the motive for whatever had to be done," she wrote. In difficult or dangerous times "he felt guided by a strength and a wisdom higher than his own, for his religious faith was simple and direct." He had often to "make the ultimate decisions" that "in some cases would have been well-nigh impossible without faith in spiritual guidance." Finally, in her analysis of her husband's character, Eleanor Roosevelt added the observation that she had "never known a man who gave one a greater sense of security. . . . The church services that he always insisted on holding on Inauguration Day, anniversaries and whenever a great crisis impended were the expression of his religious faith. I think this must not be lost sight of in judging his acceptance of responsibility and his belief in his ability to meet whatever crisis had to be met." She recalled that once when she made light of "some spiritualist conversations" with the dead that had been sent to her, Roosevelt had said to her "very simply: 'I think it unwise to say you do not believe in anything when you can't prove it true or untrue. There is so much in the world which is always new in the way of discoveries that it is wiser to say that there may be spiritual things which we are simply unable now to fathom. Therefore I am interested in and have respect for whatever people believe, even if I cannot understand their beliefs or share their experiences.' "

"On the whole," Rexford Tugwell wrote, "it has to be said that by the time he became President, [Roosevelt] had an equipment of traditions, preferences, attitudes and values—as well as an array of talents and a fund of experience—peculiarly suited to the tasks before him. Perhaps as important as any item of his equipment was his immediate reaction to challenge. . . . Then there was the noblesse his father had taught him and which was part of the Christianity he professed. It was wrong to tolerate injustices. With all this he had the politician's indifference to consistency." It was this lack of consistency that made his liberal critics so unhappy. The mind, as long as it is kept undefiled, does not have to engage the real world. It can be as consistent as it pleases and as scornful of the compromises that the world needs to keep on turning.

In the words of Ernest Lindley, one of the shrewdest observers of the New Deal, "Mr. Roosevelt had developed his political philosophy long before the depression began and long before he met any member of his brains trust . . . [and] long before the presidential campaign of 1932 Mr. Roosevelt had emerged as the leading Democratic exponent of a modern liberalism of which the kernel was readiness to use the power of political government to redress the balance of the economic world."

Finally, there was the simple and essential fact that Franklin Roosevelt was a cripple, for whom every step was a test of will and courage. From the offices of the Council of Foreign Affairs, the home of *Foreign Affairs,* next door to Sara Delano Roosevelt's New York house, Hamilton Fish Armstrong and his staff could see Roosevelt arrive to visit his mother. "Our staff used to watch him from the windows," Armstrong wrote, "as he got out of his car, clicking the brace on one leg into place, then the other. Pulling himself erect by his powerful arms, he would then make his way slowly up the inclined boardwalk which covered one side of the steps. He never failed to pause, grin and wave a greeting to the girls in our windows. . . . As always, every move was a test of courage, met as a matter of course with dignity; he simply would not allow bodily disability to defeat his will."

Roosevelt's ideas and personality were so integral to each other that it is often difficult to make a distinction. When Raymond Moley became a member of the so-called Brain Trust in the spring of 1932, he wrote to his sister, Nell, his estimate of Roosevelt: "One thing is sure—that the idea people get from his charming manner—that he is soft or flabby in disposition and character—is far from true. When he wants something a lot he can be formidable—when crossed he is hard, stubborn, resourceful, relentless. I used to think on the basis of casual observation that his amiability was 'lord-of-the-manor'-'good-to-the-peasants' stuff. It isn't that at all. He seems quite naturally warm and friendly—less because he genuinely likes many of the people to whom he is pleasant (although he does like lots of people of all sorts and varieties) than because he just enjoys the pleasant and engaging role, as a charming woman does. . . . He is wholly conscious of his ability to send callers away happy and glowing and in agreement with him and his ideas." The stories about Roosevelt's illness and its effects on him were the "bunk" to Moley. "Nobody in public life since T.R. has been so robust, so buoyantly and blatantly healthy as this fellow. He is full of animal spirits and keeps himself and those around him in a rare good humor with a lot of horseplay. . . ." That aspect of Roosevelt's character seemed to Moley typically small-town. It reminded him of his days as a high-spirited youth in Olmstead Falls, Ohio. Moley was also fascinated by Roosevelt's "gallantry, his political sophistication, his lack of the offensive traits of men who have a bloated sense of personal destiny."

# 16 ❦

# Roosevelt as Governor

It has been noted how single-mindedly and tirelessly Louis Howe and Franklin Roosevelt pursued the goal of the presidency, each step carefully planned as part of a master schedule designed to place Roosevelt in the White House. There is abounding irony in the fact that what was perhaps the most important and essential step was unplanned and taken only with the greatest reluctance: Roosevelt's yielding to Al Smith's importunings that he run for the governorship of New York in 1928 to strengthen Smith's chances of carrying that state. The one action that he tried hardest to avoid proved most essential to the success of his presidency and perhaps to his nomination as the candidate of his party in 1932 as well. As governor of New York Roosevelt assembled the personal staff and advisers and, after the onslaught of the Depression, initiated the programs that would, in essence, become the New Deal. Some attention to his governorship is thus necessary.

Roosevelt took the oath of office as governor of the state of New York thirty years to the day after his cousin Theodore had been sworn in. He took the office in the shadow of the ex-governor, Alfred E. Smith, who still harbored presidential ambitions and plainly intended to remain a, if not "the," power in state politics. Well aware of the awkwardness of his situation, Roosevelt told Frances Perkins, "I've got

377

to be Governor of the State of New York and I have to be it MYSELF," with no guiding hand. He replaced Robert Moses, Smith's secretary of state, who had remarked that Roosevelt would "make a good candidate but a lousy governor" (he made Moses chairman of the State Council of Parks), and although Smith advised him against the appointment of Frances Perkins to head the Department of Labor on the ground that men did not like to work for a woman, Roosevelt appointed her to the job. ". . . Al's a good progressive fellow but I am willing to take more chances. I've got more nerve about women and status in the world than Al has," he said to Perkins, who, according to her own account, replied: "But it was more of a victory for Al to bring himself to appoint a woman, never appointed before when I was unknown [referring to her appointment to the Labor Commission], than it is for you when I have a record as a responsible public officer for more than ten years."

Smith asked Roosevelt to keep Belle Moskowitz on as his personal secretary, but Eleanor Roosevelt advised against it, arguing that able as Moskowitz was—"extremely competent, far-sighted, reliable"—she was determined to run things. "[Y]ou have to decide now," she told her husband, "whether you or Mrs. Moskowitz is going to be governor of this state. If she is your secretary she will run you. It won't hurt you. It won't give you any pain. . . . It's simply that her competence is so much greater than anybody else's that even with Al Smith, as much as she loves him, she ran him in that subtle way." There was also the problem of Louis Howe, who, after all, was Roosevelt's Belle Moskowitz. Roosevelt, anxious as he was to please Smith, decided not to appoint Moskowitz his secretary, and Smith was offended. The rift widened as the months passed. As Eleanor Roosevelt expressed it, "One of Franklin's main qualities, which Governor Smith was apparently unaware of, was that he never assumed any responsibility that he did not intend to carry through." He intended to be governor of New York State, and if that meant treading on his predecessor's toes (or heels) that was unfortunate.

Henry Morgenthau, Jr., was appointed chairman of the Agricultural Advisory Commission. Grace Tully became a kind of super-secretary. Missy LeHand, already a confidential adviser as well as a secretary, played an important role in the administration. The Executive Mansion at Albany became a kind of clubhouse, swarming with relatives, political associates, friends of Eleanor's and advocates of good causes (often synonymous), as well as the children and their schoolmates. Roosevelt was the host, the ringmaster, or master of cermonies, as the case might be, talking his engaging talk, his laughter ringing out, making his odd assortment of guests at home, drawing them out, lending a sympathetic ear, radiating enthusiasm and zest for life. "It was the Roosevelt habit to treat all visitors as honorable," Tugwell recalled. Newspapermen, even state troopers and secretaries came to the afternoon teas that Eleanor Roosevelt served when she was at home.

As governor of New York Roosevelt had, of course, to face the consequences of the Depression in that state. Although he was as devoted as Hoover to the notion of balanced budgets, he was tireless in his efforts *to do something* to relieve the widespread hardship and suffering so evident around him. Frances Perkins remembered that when an economist told Roosevelt that the laws of supply and demand would bring recovery in due course, Roosevelt turned to him with a "gray look of horror on his face" and said, "People aren't cattle, you know!" He told the New York legislature: "The duty of the State toward the citizen is the duty of the servant to its master. The people have created it; the people, by common consent, permit its continual existence. One of these duties of the State is that of caring for those of its citizens who find themselves the victims of such adverse circumstances as make them unable to obtain even the necessities for mere existence without the aid of others. . . . To these unfortunate citizens aid must be extended by government—not as a matter of charity but as a matter of *social duty*." No one should go "unfed, unclothed, or unsheltered." When the resources of a particular state were inadequate to provide relief, "it then becomes the positive duty of the Federal Government to step in to help."

With Roosevelt's urging, the legislature passed the Wicks Act which set up the Temporary Emergency Relief Administration (TERA). New York was thus the first state in the nation to undertake state aid for the relief of the unemployed. Roosevelt named Jesse Isidor Straus, president of the R. H. Macy department store, head of the new agency. Straus agreed, provided he could name his deputy. He decided on William Hudson of the Russell Sage Foundation, an organization dedicated to good works. But there were already many wealthy men in the state who considered Roosevelt a dangerous radical. They persuaded Hudson to refuse the job, and Hudson proposed Harry Hopkins, whom he knew through the charitable activities of the foundation. Hopkins jumped at the chance. When Straus resigned, Hopkins took his place as head of the agency. Hopkins showed at once a remarkable capacity for responding to Roosevelt's ideas. During a dinner conversation Roosevelt mentioned his interest in some sort of a program to put unemployed young men to work on the conservation of the state's forests. Drawing on his experience working with slum youth from the Lower East Side of New York City, Hopkins immediately contacted Henry Morgenthau and devised a plan to put some 10,000 unemployed young men to work in a program of conservation and reforestation. In Morgenthau's words, "We took the gas house gang, the bad boys who were loafing on the streets and getting into trouble, and we put them on the 4 A.M. train that ran up to the Bear Mountain area where they worked all day. Then, because there was no housing for them, we took them back at night." It soon became one of Roosevelt's pet projects; human conservation and the conservation of the state's natural resources were for him an irresistible combination.

Like Windy McPherson's son in Sherwood Anderson's novel of the same name, Harry Hopkins was the son of a harness maker. He was born in 1890 in Sioux City, Iowa, and in many ways his childhood and youth correspond to those of Anderson's. Hopkins was the fifth child of a rather improvident father and a severe, devout mother. The family moved, in search of a modest livelihood, from Sioux City to Kearney, Nebraska, to Council Bluffs, Iowa, to Hastings, Nebraska, to Chicago, and then to Grinnell, Iowa. Hopkins, tall and skinny, was nicknamed High Pockets. He was an able student, active in school affairs. After graduation he attended Grinnell College, where he encountered the Harvard historian and Bull Moose Republican Albert Bushnell Hart, who was at Grinnell on an exchange professorship. Another professor who had a strong influence on Hopkins was Edward Steiner, a Czechoslovakian Jew who had converted to Christianity and become a Congregational minister. He taught "Applied Christianity," which was, in effect, Walter Rauschenbusch's Social Gospel of service and reform. Having graduated from Grinnell, Hopkins, like thousands of other young men with a literary bent before and since, planned to start a newspaper (in Bozeman, Montana), but Professor Steiner persuaded him to take a job as a counselor at a Christian summer camp in Bound Brook, New Jersey. Run by a New York City settlement house called Christadora, it aimed to give poor Jewish children from the Lower East Side a taste of outdoor life. It was a fateful step for Hopkins, who went on from his summer camp job to work at Christadora House with the boys' clubs that it sponsored. He married a fellow worker, Ethel Gross (like Steiner, she was a Jew who had converted to Christianity), and decided on a career as a social worker. Hopkins worked hard for the election of the reform mayor John Purroy Mitchel and found a job in Mitchel's administration as executive secretary of the Board of Child Welfare. In a series of subsequent social service positions with various agencies, public and private, Hopkins acquired the reputation of a poor administrator but a tireless worker in good causes. A friend described him as "an ulcerous type. He was intense, seeming to be in perpetual nervous ferment—a chain smoker and black coffee drinker . . . always careless in appearance." He would appear at work "looking as though he had spent the previous night sleeping in a hayloft. He would wear the same shirt three or four days at a time." By William O. Douglas's description, Hopkins always looked "hungry, overworked and unkempt," with long, thin, nicotine-stained fingers.

As we have already noted, Roosevelt persuaded Frances Perkins to become state labor commissioner. In that role Perkins was especially concerned with those industries in which there was fluctuation or "irregularity" of employment. These were not only seasonal agricultural operations and their attendant industries, such as canning, but such industries as construction and shipbuilding as well. Perkins advocated a widespread system of unemployment insurance so that industries with fluctuating rates of employment would be offset by those in which employment was more constant. She saw it as a major part of her task to educate Roosevelt in the problems of the industrial world. His heart and the better part of his knowledge were with agriculture. Harry Hopkins told Frances Perkins: "The governor doesn't know anything about industries or how they are conducted. He doesn't know what the clothing industry looks like, or the chemical or paper industries. He doesn't know about unemployment or what might be done about it." But he cared, and that turned out to be the most important thing of all.

The educational efforts of Hopkins and Perkins met with a ready response. On June 30, 1930, when he addressed the Governors' Conference in Salt Lake City, Roosevelt urged the establishment of some plan of unemployment insurance, pointing out that without it workingmen and workingwomen bore an unfair burden of financial insecurity, which in times of depression exacerbated the crisis by drying up buying power in the form of wages. "Some form of insurance," he told his fellow governors, "seems to be the only answer." He did not suggest, nor did he have in mind, a Federal program; he was appealing to the individual states. Nonetheless, he sent Perkins to England to report on the way Great Britain handled unemployment compensation through its public employment offices. While Perkins reported that the British did things in a humane but highly casual way that would never work in the United States, she was more convinced than ever by her trip that some comparable system was both practical and essential. Paul Kellogg's *Survey* published her article on "an American plan" of unemployment insurance, one in which, as she put it, "industry should foot the bill."

Two of the qualities of Frances Perkins that appealed most strongly to Roosevelt were her outspokenness and her wry humor. When a reporter asked her if she found it a handicap to be a woman official, she replied, "Only in climbing trees," and when an official of the Hoover administration gave out figures indicating an increase in employment and a rise in business activity, which Perkins knew to be wrong, she called in reporters and told them so, adding that giving out false figures was "cruel and irresponsible." In her indignation she had forgotten to check first with the governor, but when she informed him of her statement, he replied cheerfully, "I think that was bully; just wonderful. How did you have the nerve? I'm glad you didn't ask me, because if you had, I'd probably have told you not to do it. But you've done it now. The blood be on your hands. If you're not right you'll get plenty of punishment from the country."

To those who declared that social legislation impeded business, Perkins replied that a survey conducted by the Merchants' Association indicated that "the industrial progress of New York State between 1925 and 1927 [the height of the Al Smith legislative reforms] . . . has experienced a ratio of acceleration not accorded to any other manufacturing state."

At a luncheon in her honor at the Hotel Astor in New York in 1929 Frances Perkins told an audience made up of business and labor groups that she did not take a very cheerful view of the coming age of automation, "of the great mechanical man who does things automatically and can perform anything that a human being can perform. I confess to chills of horror lest we become like him." She was committed "to the belief that the human race is not destined for that kind of efficiency, but for an efficiency of the spirit and of the mind. If this robot-man can release us from chores like turning of switches—all right, let him release us! But let him release us to be human beings and let us not develop a race who are going to be patterned after him."

To avoid such a fate, it was essential that "capital and labor" together utilize all their intelligence.

Another important addition to Roosevelt's inner circle was James A. Farley, a seasoned Tammany politician. Farley was the son of a brickyard worker who had been killed by a horse's kick. As an ally of Al Smith's, he had risen through the Democratic ranks. Now, giving his allegiance to Roosevelt, he proved an essential link with Democratic city bosses.

In March, 1930, Roosevelt formed a committee on the Stabilization of Industry for the Prevention of Unemployment. The first state agency of its kind, it gave its attention to such industrial measures as shorter working hours, seeking advance orders, and building inventory, all designed to maintain employment. Often the committee encountered strong employer resistance. In the words of a Utica labor leader, "We've got a lot of skunks here among the employers. They think they know everything. They like to see us sweating. They like to see a breadline." Nobody was going to tell them how to run their businesses.

The most enlightened employer was undoubtedly Gerard Swope. In Schenectady his company, General Electric, put into operation a plan under which a discharged employee would, after two weeks, receive for ten weeks a sum based on a percentage of his salary. It was one of the first employer-initiated unemployment insurance plans in the country.

New York governors served two-year terms, so by the spring of 1930 Roosevelt was busy campaigning for a second term. He hit on the idea of using a New York State Barge Canal boat to campaign through the towns strung along the old Erie Canal. It was a characteristic Roosevelt touch. He had been one of the first, perhaps the first, New York politicians to campaign by automobile; now he utilized a canalboat. It attracted wide publicity as well as provided an extremely agreeable method of campaigning. But as with most of Roosevelt's dramatic gestures, the public relations aspect was not allowed to obscure or supersede the practical goals. The crippled governor found eyes in his wife. He commissioned her to visit prisons, insane asylums, and state hospitals along the way and report to him on the conditions that she encountered. When she returned, he questioned her closely. What was the food like? Had she tasted any of it? Was the place clean? "I learned," she wrote, "to notice whether the beds were too close together, and whether they were folded up and put in closets or behind the doors during the day, which would indicate that they filled the corridors at night."

Roosevelt won reelection by 725,000 votes. It was a margin larger than any Al Smith had achieved, and it immediately made him a front-runner for the Democratic nomination for President. Jim Farley declared, "I do not see how Mr. Roosevelt can escape becoming the next presidential nominee of his party, even if no one should raise a finger to bring it about."

Roosevelt lost no time in proposing an amendment to the state constitution which called for a $19,000,000 bond issue to buy up and reforest marginal farmland. Al Smith, apparently looking for an issue to demonstrate his continuing political muscle in the state and angry with Roosevelt for what he perceived as his cavalier attitude toward him, denounced the project. The amendment carried, and Roosevelt remarked to a friend, "What a queer thing that was for Al to fight so bitterly." It was a foretaste of things to come.

The governor's public power policy was, in Raymond Moley's words, based on "the inalienable property right of all the people in the sources of water power [and] the duty of government to see that this power was produced and distributed at the lowest possible cost to the people." He had, in Moley's view, given more attention to this issue than any other. It included the reforestation of land that had been misused and the relief of farmers from excessive interest rates, price fluctuations, and unfair taxation. What concerned him most was the evident disparity between the relative prosperity of city dwellers and the desperately hard life of small farmers. "If the farming population does not have sufficient purchasing power to buy new shoes, new clothes, new automobiles, the manufacturing centers must suffer," he reminded an urban audience.

Despite the rigors of office, playfulness was never far away; in fact, it was omnipresent. Ernest Lindley described a scene on the eve of St. Valentine's Day in the Executive Mansion in Albany. Howe had been "busy all afternoon with cardboard and scissors and paints making a fancifully humorous centerpiece and valentines peculiarly appropriate to each guest. Occasionally a shriek of laughter comes through the curtain [to the dining room, where Howe was at work with the Roosevelt children and Eleanor]. . . . Mrs. Roosevelt slips in, hands [FDR] a piece of paper with a head pasted on it and whispers that he will have to draw the valentine for Howe. He puts aside his correspondence for a second, swiftly sketches an absurd picture of a man in a long nightgown holding a candle. . . . He puts some caption beneath it which makes them both burst into laughter." When a department head "of sober demeanor" appeared, Roosevelt invited him to accompany him upstairs while he dressed for dinner. As they passed the dining room, Roosevelt paused, drew back the curtain, and shouted "triumphantly, 'I've seen it.' Shrieks and moans from within are his reply."

Eleanor Roosevelt's greatest assistance to her husband was in providing access to him to individuals who would not ordinarily have an opportunity to express their views to the governor. She brought to the Executive Mansion young radicals, black activists, middle-rank union leaders, representatives of groups shut out from power, men and women without voices. Two friends from the Women's Trade Union League accompanied her to talk with the President about the problems of workingwomen and union organization. Corporal Earl Miller of the New York State Police became one of Eleanor Roosevelt's closest friends, somewhere between a son, a brother, and a platonic lover. A tall, handsome man and something of an athlete, he taught her how to swim, drive a car, and shoot a revolver.

Almost without exception the odd assortment of people who came to Albany or, on occasion, to Hyde Park, fell under the spell of the famous Roosevelt charm. It was not just that he joked and laughed with them, conveying at the same time a sense of mastery, of confidence and control, but that he seemed genuinely interested in them and in what they had to say, *that he listened*! This was uncommon in a politician. Labor leaders were especially impressed. One told Frances Perkins, "You'd almost think he had participated in some strike or organizing campaign the way he knew and felt about it." A friend arrived for a visit one night as a young man was leaving. "After he had gone," she recalled later, "Franklin told me that he was an East Side Jew, a tailor from New York. Franklin said he had a chance in this way to learn a great deal about the conditions in his life . . . at first hand."

In the last year of his administration Roosevelt, with an eye toward the presidency, formed a group of academic advisers. The fact was that he had "habitually" consulted with experts in various fields in which he contemplated legislative or executive action; now he decided to form a team of advisers, most of them Columbia University professors. They included, besides Raymond Moley and Rexford Guy Tugwell, who was an expert on agricultural economics, Adolf A. Berle, Jr., an authority on corporations and a protégé of Newton D. Baker, and M. L. Wilson, professor of economics at Montana State College. Moley, as the senior member, was given the title of chairman of the "privy council." The whole idea made Louis Howe nervous. He tried to keep its existence a secret, but a reporter from the *New York Times* got on to it and called it Roosevelt's Brain Trust.

In Moley's words, "the process was smooth, unspasmodic, almost inevitable." The requirements for the brain trusters were "Expertness in at least one field, clearheadedness, cool judgment, unfailing humor, exquisite tact, an iron constitution, and the ability to write well. . . ." He was confident that he was well equipped in these respects.

Moley had been born in Berea, Ohio, in 1886. He was the grandson of Hypolite Moley, who had been a bareback rider in a French circus, had immigrated to the United States, and had become a prominent Ohio Democrat. At the age of ten young Raymond heard William Jennings Bryan speak and was stirred "romantically, emotionally." He wept when Bryan was defeated in 1896. The Cleveland reformer Tom Johnson became his hero. Moley attended law school at night in Cleveland and then decided to teach politics. A bout with tuberculosis ended his legal studies and forced him to spend two years in New Mexico and Colorado. He returned to his hometown, served as mayor, and then went on to Columbia to do graduate work in politics. When he had completed his graduate studies, he taught at Western Reserve College, directed a research foundation in Cleveland, and returned to New York to start a department of government at Barnard College. There Moley made himself an expert on criminal justice. As the "aimlessness" of the twenties became more apparent, Moley decided that what the country needed above all else was a practical reformer of the Tom Johnson type and soon afterward that Franklin Roosevelt was the "only hope."

When Roosevelt called on him to help in drafting "a model state parole system," Moley responded enthusiastically. He subsequently served on a commission to improve the administration of justice in New York State, and when Roosevelt invited him to be a member of his "privy council," Moley found the offer irresistible. "I did want to see and know intimately what went on at the heart of politics," he wrote, "for politics had been the absorbing interest of my life."

Moley's long, pale oval face with its dark eyebrows and sardonic expression was arresting, but it did not inspire confidence in those already skeptical about Roosevelt's political ideas. Professorial as Moley was in some respects (he puffed reflectively on an omnipresent pipe), he was too Irish to be entirely at home in that tidy world and was far from being the dangerous radical that newspapers sometimes depicted him as being; he was, in fact, conservative.

Rexford Guy Tugwell, a graduate of the University of Washington and of the Wharton School of Finance and Commerce, had grown up in a prosperous family in Seattle, and his intellect had been formed by such radical thinkers as Scott Nearing, Thorstein Veblen, and Vernon Parrington. Chautauqua had provided a highly congenial environment. Tugwell had visited Soviet Russia and been both attracted and repelled by what he saw there. Not a Communist, he was definitely an apostle of the "new economics." As a young man he had written:

> I am sick of a nation's stenches,
> I am sick of propertied czars . . .
> I shall roll up my sleeves—make America over!

And he had written in the throes of the Depression: "Business will logically be required to disappear. This . . . is literally meant. The essence of business is its venture for profits in an unregulated economy." America could no longer pay the social price for an unregulated economy, in Tugwell's view. Slim, a natty dresser with an unprofessorial elegance, Tugwell was a kind of intellectual loner, a man curiously reticent about his own life but endlessly and perpetually curious about that of Franklin Roosevelt.

Adolf Berle had been an infant prodigy at Harvard College and Law School and, in Raymond Moley's wry phrase, had "continued to be an infant long after he had ceased to be a prodigy," but Moley admired the "toughness of his mind, his quickness, his energy, and his ability to organize material well." Tugwell spoke of Berle as "so slight, so brilliant, and so contentious."

The members of the Brain Trust served without pay because, in Moley's words, they "wanted to avoid the slightest taint of jobship. . . . [We] wanted our independence, our honesty, our interest in ideas to be above the faintest suspicion." What Moley called "economic jam sessions" of the brain trusters took place once or twice a week. When the professors arrived at Albany, they would dine at the Executive Mansion with the governor and then gather around a fire for the discussion of various issues. Roosevelt, Moley recalled, "was a student, a cross-examiner, and a judge. He would listen with rapt attention for a few minutes and then break in with a question whose sharpness was characteristically blurred with an anecdotal introduction or an air of sympathetic agreement with the speaker." As the evening wore on, the "intervals between [the questions] would grow shorter. The questions themselves would become meatier, more informed—the infallible index to the amount he was picking up in the evening's course. By midnight . . . the Governor, scorning further questions, would be making vigorous pronouncements on the subject we had been discussing, waving his cigarette holder to emphasize his points." Tugwell, a friend and disciple of Scott Nearing, who inclined toward a kind of non-Marxist, Fabian socialism (his visit to Russia had convinced Tugwell that the Marxist-Leninist brand of communism had little relevance for the United States), represented the left wing of the professoriate while Moley was, in most matters, well on the right.

Soon the Brain Trust was augmented by Donald Richberg, considered the country's leading labor lawyer. Hugh Johnson, director of the World War draft, became an important member of the trust. Recruited by Bernard Baruch, "he exploded, like an elaborate fireworks display, into a series of enchanting patterns," in Moley's words. "We had a preview of all the color, spirit, and versatility that were later to fix the eyes of the country on him. . . ."

One of Roosevelt's early supporters and advocates was Felix Frankfurter. The men were the same age, and Roosevelt, with his instinct for attaching to himself men of special talent, courted Frankfurter, employing that charm for which he was already famous (and which made Lippmann suspicious of him). Frankfurter, with his equal inclination toward power, was prompt to place himself in Roosevelt's service. Soon after the latter's election as governor Frankfurter wrote: "You have as [Al] Smith has the conception of government which seems to me indispensable to the vitality of a democratic government, namely the realization that the processes of government are essentially educational processes"—in which, he might have added, lawyers are the primary teachers. Roosevelt told Grace Tully, "He [Frankfurter] has a brilliant mind but it clicks so fast it makes my head fairly spin. I find him tremendously interesting and stimulating." Berle expressed "considerable admiration of Felix Frankfurter's public career and an intense personal desire to see him shot." When Max Lowenthal appeared at Roosevelt's strategy sessions as a surrogate for Frankfurter, over Moley's objections, Berle, who had not been a member of Frankfurter's group when he was a student at Harvard, noted in his diary that Lowenthal was "an inflationist . . . in touch with some of the Jewish financiers . . . with no loyalty except to Felix Frankfurter and the particular little group that revolved around him."

Tugwell noted that when Roosevelt "opened up subjects for discussion he was often far along in making up his mind. . . ." He appeared to reach conclusions by a process that the curious Tugwell could not fathom. "Roosevelt was certainly an exaggerated example of nonrational decision-making," he wrote. Moley was profoundly impressed by "the amount of intellectual ransacking that Roosevelt could crowd into one evening. . . . [T]hose darting questions of Roosevelt's were the ticks of the evening's metronome."

The progressives and the brain trusters were at one in suspecting the motives and morals of "business." In their view, government and business had indeed been in a "partnership," a partnership run by and for the benefit of business. The progressives, in the main, took the Brandeis line that it was only by breaking up the great business and corporate combinations and curbing the excesses of the financiers that the nation could be rescued from a ruthless oligarchy. The collectivists, on the other hand, wanted a business-government partnership in which government through planners would clearly be the senior partner and assure that the activities of business were subordinate to the good of the country as a whole.

It is difficult to suppress the suspicion that Roosevelt fell in with the brain trusters and their addition to "holistic" economics, more specifically to a planned and managed economy, less out of conviction than out of a feeling that he needed their help and support in securing the social legislation that was always his principal goal. While he, according to Rexford Tugwell, allowed his "advisers" ("a word which made most of those intended to be included in this class smile somewhat wryly," Tugwell noted) "some latitude, the end result was always unmistakably Roosevelt's."

It would be hard to imagine the New Deal without Roosevelt's novitiate as governor of the state of New York. This was certainly the conviction of one of his closest aides, Samuel Rosenman, who wrote: "In those messages and speeches from 1929 through 1932 you will find proposals for appropriate state actions in the same fields in which he later urged action by Congress: minimum wages and maximum hours, old-age insurance, unemployment relief through public works and other means, unemployment insurance, regulation of public utilities, stricter regulation of the banks and of the use of other people's money."

As governor Roosevelt fought for legislation limiting the power of judges to issue injunctions against striking or picketing. He insisted on an eight-hour day on all public works and put his weight behind a number of other labor reforms. He also started a modest public works program. In Raymond Moley's words, "the difficulty . . . those over forty found in getting jobs seemed particularly vivid in his mind." He pushed through the state legislature a plan of unemployment insurance and old-age pensions.

Roosevelt's views on the role of the Federal government in helping alleviate the suffering caused by the Depression were undoubtedly influenced by the fact that he, as the governor of a large industrial state, had done his best to afford relief for the citizens of New York and had found those efforts inadequate. To him, it thus followed that Congress and the President must assume responsibility for supplementing the efforts of a particular state. Hoover, on the other hand, viewing the problems from the distorting perspective of Washington, was disposed to blame the states for failing to deal with what was, in his opinion, essentially their problem.

Not only did Roosevelt try out his ideas, or develop them, during his two terms as governor of New York, but he did so in a consciously experimental spirit. Eleanor Roosevelt wrote: "It was part of Franklin's political philosophy—and over and over again I heard him expound it—that the great benefit to be derived from having forty-eight states was the possibility of experimenting on a small scale to see how a program worked before trying it out nationally." It was her conviction that Roosevelt got the notion of the forty-eight states as "experimental laboratories" from his study of Brandeis's writings and opinions. Justice Holmes had been another major influence; Roosevelt, along with Walter Lippmann, had been a member of Holmes's circle when he was assistant secretary of the navy in Woodrow Wilson's administration.

In addition to laying out a kind of mini New Deal as governor, Roosevelt built an able and loyal staff and appointed to state offices a number of men and women whom he later took with him to Washington. Dr. Thomas Parran, who was to become an outstanding surgeon general, was commissioner of public health in New York State; Frances Perkins, as has been noted, was labor commissioner; Henry Morgenthau, Jr., was conservation commissioner, and Harry Hopkins was director of the Temporary Emergency Relief Administration.

# 17

# The Campaign of 1932

After the Democratic Convention there was a rough division of labor in the governor's staff: Louis Howe would carry on as principal strategist; Jim Farley would hustle votes and political support on the state level; and Bernard Baruch took charge of the "war chest," soliciting funds from his wealthy Democratic friends to run the campaign, but he did not hesitate to make "generous intellectual contributions," in Moley's words. Already tempered by its experience while Roosevelt was governor, the staff performed its functions with an efficiency that may have been unique in presidential elections. It seemed as though Farley knew every ward heeler and political boss from New York to New Orleans and west to the Pacific coast. Claude Bowers, visiting his native Indianapolis, was confused by the constant references of his political friends to Jim. "Jim" must, Bowers thought, be an important new local politico. It turned out to be Farley.

Raymond Moley presided over research and speech writing. Bowers was recruited for campaign speeches (his editorials in the *World* were unabashedly Democratic), and a number of his addresses were printed up as campaign literature.

In the campaign for the presidency the confident challenger of the incumbent President assumed the role of educator of the American people, much in the spirit of Woodrow Wilson. Roosevelt's goals were clear: to end the economic crisis and, more important, to make America a more just and humane society. It was time, as he had noted earlier, for the country to become "fairly radical," thereby avoiding a full-scale revolution.

While the means of attaining his goals were the topic of endless discussion and debate in the inner circle of Roosevelt's advisers, the ends were clear enough. It was essential to prepare the people, the electorate, for the necessity of radical change and, in doing so, to suggest some of the measures that might be necessary or appropriate. Candidate Roosevelt set about this educational task with characteristic gusto. In his words, "The achievement of good government is . . . a long, slow task. Nothing is more striking than the simple innocence of the men who insist, whenever an objective is present, on the prompt production of a patent scheme guaranteed to produce results. Human endeavor is not so simple as that. Government is the art of formulating policies and using the political technique to attain so much of them as will receive general support; persuading, leading, sacrificing, teaching always, because perhaps the greatest duty of statesmanship is to educate." That was his task.

The activities of the Brain Trust were directed at speech writing, at the formulation of broad policy questions, and at the preparation of specific legislation to be presented to Congress immediately after the inauguration. The most pressing task was the preparation of material for Roosevelt's campaign speeches. The material on specific issues collected by the Brain Trust was turned over to Sam Rosenman to put into more or less final form. Roosevelt warned him not to attack Republicans per se. "There are thousands of people who call themselves Republicans who think as you and I do about government. They are enrolled as Republicans because their families have been Republicans for generations—that's the only reason; and some of them think it *infra dig* to be called a Democrat; the Democrats in their village are not the socially 'nice' people the enrolled Republicans are. So never attack the Republicans or the Republican party—only the Republican *leaders.* Then any Republican voter who hears it will say to himself: 'Well, he doesn't mean me.' "

Among the brain trusters there were sharp differences of opinion on a variety of issues. The task of developing legislation to aid the farmers was assigned to Tugwell, Morgenthau, Henry A. Wallace, and Mordecai Ezekiel, an economist on the Farm Board. A fifth member was M. L. Wilson, the Montana State College professor. Roosevelt's charge was that they should confer with those members of Congress most interested in and knowledgeable about farm matters and with other important farm leaders, the heads of farm organizations, and anyone else who had some notion of what might be done to help get farmers back on their feet.

Tugwell found the younger Morgenthau a difficult person to work with on the Advisory Committee on Agriculture, in part because he was so strongly identified with the Cornell Agricultural College and because of what Tugwell considered his "fierce ambition," which "made him elbow everyone else out of the way when he could." The Cornell people were strongly opposed to Roosevelt's tentative plan for adjusting prices by restricting acreage. The Cornell solution was to bolster prices by manipulating the gold content of the dollar. Morgenthau's aim was to be secretary of agriculture. George Peek, a Baruch "man," was committed to helping the farmer by helping the food processor, using a combination of marketing agreements, the dumping of food abroad, and temporary subsidies. In Tugwell's not unbiased words, Peek "had the millers, meatpackers, and cotton manufacturers actively with him."

Some of the brain trusters (and others in Roosevelt's inner circle of advisers) were high-tariff isolationists. Others (and Roosevelt himself) were low-tariff men and "internationalists." Raymond Moley was among the former; he used the word "internationalist" like an epithet and usually accompanied it with "romantic" and "sentimental." A tug-of-war thus went on in the expanded Brain Trust. The trick was to say enough about international cooperation to appease the Eastern internationalists without alarming the Midwestern isolationists, who, on domestic issues, were "progressive" and thus potentially valuable allies for the program of reform Roosevelt was adumbrating. Roosevelt would often give different groups, with different ideological predispositions, the task of preparing a paper or a speech on the same topic. He followed that course with the tariff issue and got, in consequence, two almost diametrically opposed speeches. When Raymond Moley pointed out their divergence, Roosevelt replied airily to the astonished Moley, "Weave the two together."

Perhaps the most significant division was between the "orthodox progressives" and the "collectivists," who put their faith in government planning. To Rexford Tugwell and Adolf Berle the campaign of 1932 marked a "crisis in American attitudes," a clash between the older, atomistic individualism and the newer impulse toward rational planning. Tugwell and Berle were the "middlemen of collectivism." Tugwell wrote: "We believed that integration was a principle of civilization's advance. We believed in direction." The economist Charles R. Van Hise had coined the determinative phrase "concentration and control."

Tugwell, who was perhaps the most knowledgeable student of the Progressive era among those who were closest to Roosevelt, described the President-elect as having had his ideas "drastically modified" by "orthodox progressivism." It might have been more accurate to say that Roosevelt, having been an orthodox Progressive and having, in the months immediately prior to the Democratic Convention, fallen rather under the influence of the "holistic," "collectivistic," "conjunctural" (to use their own somewhat cloudy terms) thinking expressed by his coterie of Columbia professors, reverted in time to the faith of his earlier days.

Tugwell believed that large industrial units were desirable; they were more efficient than numerous small units of production. He thus opposed trust-busting. Antitrust laws, rigorously enforced, discouraged "any sort of social management" and caused "destructive . . . competition." He wanted a larger role for the Federal government in setting production goals for industry. He proposed to Roosevelt that industry be reorganized somewhat on the model of the Federal Reserve System with an economic council, made up of industry and government representatives, given the responsibility for planning. Tugwell's schemes for imposing some sort of rational order in American industry were denounced as socialistic. Twenty years earlier such suggestions would have received a far more sympathetic hearing. They would have been considered entirely consistent with the nationalism espoused by such theorists as Edward Bellamy, Henry Demarest Lloyd, and Henry George, not to mention Progressives and former Populists. In the 1930s, in the aftermath of the Russian Revolution and the renaissance of capitalism, they were bitterly denounced.

Among the tasks assigned to the Brain Trust was that of considering legislation to extend "the government's regulatory power to prevent abuses (stock-market regulation and the abolition of child labor, for instance) [and] for the development of controls to stimulate and stabilize economic activity," in Moley's words. The members of the trust were convinced that "any attempt to atomize big business must destroy America's greatest contribution to a higher standard of living for the body of its citizens—the development of mass production."

The mere existence of the Brain Trust, commonly considered a group of radical professors, made the Democratic fat cats nervous. Joe Kennedy, whose money most liberals considered badly tainted, was a major contributor to the Democratic campaign chest, as was Vincent Astor. John J. Raskob, a dedicated follower of Al Smith's, contributed generously, as did Baruch and Pierre S. du Pont. They all were conservative businessmen (Raskob and du Pont) and speculators (Baruch and Kennedy). Garner summarized their views: "Tell the Governor that he is the boss and we will follow him to hell if we have to, but if he goes too far with some of these wild-eyed ideas we are going to have the shit kicked out of us."

On the other side of the street Huey Long called Roosevelt and upbraided him for his contacts with conservative Democrats like Newton Baker and Owen Young. Long claimed to have been responsible for Roosevelt's nomination and threatened retribution if the Democratic nominee did not disavow the conservative wing of the party. Roosevelt turned from the phone and said, "It has its funny side but actually Huey Long is one of the two most dangerous men in the United States today. We shall have to do something about him."

The most exciting aspect of the campaign for Roosevelt's inner circle was the whistle-stop campaigning in the candidate's special train. His delight in campaigning was infectious. He communicated the feeling to everyone who accompanied him. The rather staid Moley called it "an unadulterated joy." Roosevelt conveyed a kind of Whitmanesque love of the land itself, the "broad rivers, green forests, waving corn, and undulating wheat; it was crowds of friends, from the half dozen who, seated on a baggage truck, waved to the cheery face at the speeding window to perspiring thousands at a race track or fairground; it was the hands extended in welcome, voices warm with greeting, faces reflecting his smile along the interminable wayside," Moley wrote. Watching her husband, Eleanor Roosevelt learned how "to observe from train windows: he would watch the crops, notice how people dressed, how many cars there were and in what condition, and even look at the wash on the clothes lines."

Roosevelt was dismayed by the conditions that he witnessed as he toured the country. "I have looked into the faces of thousands of Americans," he told the journalist Anne O'Hare McCormick. "They have the frightened look of lost children." They reminded him of the crowds that had greeted Wilson when he arrived in Europe. "Then they were thinking of the war. Perhaps this man, their eyes were saying, can save our children from the horror and terror we have known. Now they were saying: 'We're caught in something we don't understand; perhaps this fellow can help us out.' "

Between September 12 and November 7, Roosevelt and his party traveled some 13,000 miles. The candidate made sixty-seven speeches and sixteen major addresses, not counting back-platform appearances. Between stations the train was crowded with "governors, senators, mayors, obscure county politicians, farmers, miners, mine-owners, tradespeople, local bankers, newspaper owners, reporters, manufacturers, welfare workers. . . ." And Roosevelt reveled in it all. Jim Farley came aboard in Salt Lake City and left the train at Los Angeles. Joe Kennedy was along for much of the trip. Old Jack Cohen, a newspaperman whom Roosevelt liked, had no official responsibilities. The same was true of Breckinridge Long, a friend from the days of the Wilson administration (he had been assistant secretary of state when Roosevelt was assistant secretary of the navy). Both men were, Moley noted, "glorious entertainers . . . smooth, keen-witted, and amiable."

As the presidential train sped along to Bellefontaine, Indianapolis, Jefferson City, Topeka, Goodland, Limon, Denver, Cheyenne, Laramie, Ogden, Pocatello, Butte, Everett, and Portland, with whistle-stops for brief back-platform appearances at numerous other towns, the brain trusters, ensconced in the Roosevelt Hotel in New York City, labored to produce the more important talks and addresses, the principal parts of what would become the New Deal program. It was Moley's contention in later years that a careful reading of the major speeches, stripped of their reassuring (and often eloquent) generalities and deliberate blurrings, would have given the reader a more or less complete résumé of the New Deal. It was all there, fully formed and only waiting the moment of birth. "Hoover and [Ogden] Mills," Moley wrote, "were among the few articulate outsiders who perceived the boldness and coherence of the political and economic proposals that Roosevelt had made, and people weren't much interested in their horrified outcries."

More important than specific proposals was the task of conveying a mood or theme, the theme of the need for boldness and experimentation. For this purpose Roosevelt made extensive use of the radio. Many of his speeches were broadcast nationwide. His voice, with its intimate, almost caressing, comfortably reassuring tone, was, one might say, made for the medium—or the medium for it. Once the Midwest had accustomed itself to the shock of his upper-class Harvardian accent, it proved almost as susceptible as the South and the Far West.

The production of Roosevelt's speeches was a complex and intense task, embodying the suggestions of a dozen or more people. Raymond Moley noted that Roosevelt's critically important speech on farm problems, delivered at Topeka, Kansas, "was the direct product of more than twenty-five people." The "same careful process" that had produced the farm speech was carried forth in six or seven different fields. Newton Baker was drawn in as an adviser on foreign policy matters, as was Colonel House—Colonel Mouse Roosevelt nicknamed him because of his small size and large ears.

One of the most important speeches of the campaign was delivered to the members of the Commonwealth Club in San Francisco. It was, among other things, Roosevelt's major West Coast appearance. The speech was the result of the efforts of Jesse Straus, Moley, and others to set the record straight for close readers and interpreters of the President's often contradictory statements. Roosevelt came to California with all his political senses alerted. He knew that Charles Evans Hughes had lost the campaign of 1916 to Wilson by ignoring Hiram Johnson and embracing the unsavory William H. Crocker. An aging Johnson was still a major factor in California, as was Hearst. Culbert Olson of Los Angeles, the Democratic candidate for governor, and William McAdoo, Woodrow Wilson's son-in-law, who claimed credit for swinging crucial delegates to Roosevelt in Chicago, had to be taken into account. Roosevelt's inclination was to play California extremely coolly. At the last minute he decided to feed the Commonwealth Club some raw meat. A call was made to the headquarters of the Brain Trust at the Roosevelt Hotel, and Adolf Berle wired a draft of a talk entitled "Individualism, Romantic and Realistic." The theme was that Hoover's individualism was romantic and, above all, outdated. It simply provided a screen behind which the exploiters carried on their nefarious activities. "Happily," Roosevelt declared, "the times indicate that to create [a sound and equitable economy] is not only the proper policy of Government, but it is the only line of safety for our economic structures as well. We know, now, that these economic units cannot exist unless prosperity is uniform, that is, unless purchasing power is well distributed throughout every group in the Nation. This is why even the most selfish of corporations for its own interest would be glad to see wages restored and unemployment ended and to bring the Western farmer back to his accustomed level of prosperity.... That is why some enlightened industries themselves endeavor to limit the freedom of action of each man and business group within the industry in the common interest of all; why businessmen everywhere are asking for a form of organization which will bring the scheme of things into balance, even though it may in some measure qualify the freedom of action of individual units."

Despite Roosevelt's emendations, the Brain Trust was delighted with the speech. They considered it both educational to the general public and a commitment by their candidate to pursue what Tugwell called a "Concert of Interests," cooperation between particular industries in establishing, under governmental supervision, fair standards for production, wages, and hours.

To Tugwell the speech marked a critically important "dividing line" in the campaign of 1932. The Brain Trust believed that the Oglethorpe speech had been a retreat from Roosevelt's earlier and more "holistic" approach. By praising "individualism," he appeared to them to be playing the Republican game, trying to "out-Hoover" Hoover. In San Francisco he reaffirmed his belief in a managed economy.

In a subsequent speech Roosevelt declared: "That which seems most important in the long run is the problem of controlling by social planning the creation and distribution of those products which our vast economic machine is capable of yielding. . . . Our basic trouble . . . is an insufficient distribution of buying power, coupled with an oversufficient speculation in production." There was a "vital necessity of planning for definite objectives." That was the true task of leadership: to set forth such objectives and rally public opinion in support of them. But that was as far as Roosevelt was ever to go publicly in the direction of the Tugwell-Moley philosophy. He soon began to hedge his bets, aware of the alarm that such sentiments caused in a business community the cooperation of which he was anxious to enlist.

A few weeks later Tugwell and Moley were surprised and disconcerted when Roosevelt attacked Hoover for interfering too much in the economy. "This is the tragic folly of the past four years," he asserted. Roosevelt was under continual pressure from the conservatives in the Democratic Party to promise large budget cuts. In Pittsburgh, where Sam Rosenman wrote his speech, he came out flatly for a 25 percent cut in the Federal budget, declaring, "I regard reduction in Federal spending as one of the most direct and effective contributions Government can make to business." He frequently denounced Hoover for enlarging the Federal bureaucracy and spending Federal funds too lavishly. It had been, he asserted, "the most reckless and extravagant [administration] . . . that I have been able to discover . . . of any peacetime Government, anywhere, any time." In his promise to cut the budget, he did allow himself an out. He would perform these fiscal miracles, he promised, unless "starvation and dire need on the part of our citizens make necessary the appropriation of additional funds." No speech of Roosevelt's during the campaign became so famous or was so constantly quoted against him by his enemies, who generally overlooked his essential qualifying clause.

When Hearst attacked Roosevelt as an advocate of the League of Nations, the candidate replied with a disavowal of that body. "The League of Nations today is not the League conceived by Woodrow Wilson," Roosevelt wrote. Its function was less to promote world peace than to discuss "strictly European political national difficulties. In these the United States should have no part." While it was true that the record of the League was not one to inspire confidence, it had become for Democrats of liberal persuasion the equivalent of free silver for Democrats of the Bryan era, a kind of standard of liberal orthodoxy. Roosevelt's disavowal of the League, although doubtless popular with the mass of Democrats, deeply offended many of his liberal supporters and convinced some of them that he placed expediency above principle.

In a speech on October 6 Roosevelt spoke of a plan for cooperation within industries to achieve "regularization and planning for balance"—a notion that found its form in the NRA. Three weeks later in Boston he proposed "temporary" work in national forests for the unemployed, along with "public works" and unemployment insurance. By the end of October, in Moley's view, "every important venture from 1933 to the summer of 1935 had been outlined," with the exception of the abandonment of the gold standard and the acceptance of large budget deficits.

Herbert Hoover's principal campaign strategy was to depict his rival as a dangerous radical—little better, in practical fact, than a Communist. All of Roosevelt's proposals had a common denominator. His was "the same philosophy of government which has poisoned all Europe . . . the fumes of the witch's cauldron which boiled in Russia." If the Democrats were elected, "grass will grow in the streets of a hundred cities, a thousand towns; the weeds will overrun the fields of millions of farms. . . ."

Hoover, in Rex Tugwell's view, "was genuinely convinced that consent to the mild measures of reform proposed by his opponent was immoral. It was immoral because there was almost no distinction, in his mind, between federal relief for the unemployed, for instance and Communism."

One important consequence of Hoover and numerous other Republican politicians and publicists calling Roosevelt and the Democrats Communists before they were even in office was that it devalued the word. If the Democrats were Communists, everyone who voted for them must be presumed to be tarred with the same brush. If some 60 percent of the American voters were Communists in the eyes of Republicans and of the President of the United States, communism was suddenly respectable, or the word had lost all meaning. What resulted from such generous application of the word was that both things happened. Once it became clear that even mildly progressive sentiments provoked the charge of communism, a great many people became indifferent to the charge; indeed, it acquired a modest degree of respectability (in some circles, of course, it was almost mandatory to be a large or small *C* communist). If a President of the United States could, in effect, accuse his Democratic rival of being a Communist, how seriously could the charge be taken? The more his enemies proclaimed Franklin Roosevelt a Communist, the more innocuous the term became.

In a campaign of intimidation which recalled the efforts of the business interests to discredit William Jennings Bryan in the election of 1896, "capitalists" went as far as they dared in their attempt to ensure Hoover's reelection. Henry Ford posted a notice in his plants which read: "To prevent times from getting worse and to help them get better, President Hoover must be elected." Ford plant spies and company police attempted to bring direct pressure on individual workers, hinting that those who voted for Roosevelt would be fired. In other plants workers were fired for wearing Roosevelt buttons. The office where Peggy Cowley worked, having already cut everyone's salaries by 50 percent, announced another 10 percent cut on the eve of the election, promising to restore it if the election *"goes the right way"*—in other words, if Hoover was reelected.

One of the stories spread by Roosevelt's enemies was that he suffered not from polio but from syphilis, that he was subject to periods of insanity as a consequence, and that he often had to be restrained by guards.

The principal Republican election strategy was to manipulate the securities exchanges and the money markets to produce at least the temporary appearance of a recovery. In the words of the *New York Times* of July 29, 1932, "a vigorous attempt will be made to advance the security markets and to bring about some measure of business recovery before the election." That, it was hoped, would swing decisive votes to the Republicans.

The left was hardly more responsive to the programs sketched out by the Democratic candidate. The new intellectual class viewed Roosevelt as little more than an apologist for a discredited system. Heywood Broun declared that a Roosevelt speech offered "a meal of parsnips and fine words." He confessed there was "a little chestnut stuffing," but not enough to persuade him to abandon Norman Thomas. The *New Republic* referred to the Democratic candidate as "an untried jockey on a very lame horse [the Democratic Party]." Another phrase had it that Roosevelt was "just the same as Hoover with meringue on top."

While many liberals and radicals gave their political allegiance to Norman Thomas, that support was often lukewarm. John Dos Passos declared, "I think that becoming a Socialist right now would have about the same effect as drinking a bottle of near beer." When Sherwood Anderson was asked about the difference between Communists and Socialists, he replied, "I don't know, I guess the Communists mean it." Fifty-three writers, artists, and assorted intellectuals announced their support for William Z. Foster (whom Theodore Dreiser, one of the fifty-three, described as "a man of sweet disposition") and James Ford. "We believe," their public statement read, "that the only effective way to protest against the chaos, the appalling wastefulness, and the indescribable misery inherent in the present economic system is to vote for the Communist candidates." Having said that much, the fifty-three formed the League of Professional Groups for Foster and Ford. Among those who put their names to the statement were Sherwood Anderson and Lincoln Steffens.

The league's first task was to address the "writers, artists, teachers, physicians, engineers, scientists, and other professional workers of America." Its pamphlet contained a normal quota of leftist rhetoric— e.g., "Fascism . . . is the death rattle of decaying capitalism" and "The Socialists are the third party of capitalism." Matthew Josephson wrote the preamble and Malcolm Cowley contributed the sentences "The United States under capitalism is like a house that is rotting away; the roof leaks, the sills and rafters are crumbling. The Democrats want to paint it pink. The Republicans don't want to paint it, instead they want to raise the rent."

Josephson wrote: "We, too, the intellectual workers are of the oppressed, and until we shake off the servile habit of that oppression we shall build blindly and badly, to the lunatic specifications of ignorance and greed. If we are capable of building a civilization, surely it is time for us to begin; time for us to assert our function, our responsibility; time for us to renew the fact of comradeship with the struggling masses, trapped by the failure of leadership in the blind miseries of a crumbling madhouse."

Meanwhile, around the nation matters went from bad to worse, if that was possible. Walter Lippmann told the graduating class of Columbia that democracy was in trouble. "With no authority above it, without religious, political or moral convictions which control its opinions, it is without coherence or purpose. Democracy of this kind cannot last long; it must, and inevitably it will, give way to some more settled social order."

"There was, as fall came on in 1932," Rex Tugwell wrote, "a kind of hysteria in the air no one could escape; even the buoyant optimism of Roosevelt was diminished by its prevalence. Thrifty families in every locality of rural America were being torn apart from the acres they had cultivated and turned loose in communities where they had no place."

In the final days before the election Jim Farley confidently predicted a sweeping victory. Louis Howe, ever the worrier, fretted. In Chicago Mayor Edward Kelly assured Harold Ickes that 90 percent of the Italian vote, most of the Jewish vote, and virtually all the Catholic vote would go for Roosevelt. It was a significant trinity. The Jewish vote had been predominantly Republican, and while the Italian (and the Catholic vote generally) had been Democratic, most notably in municipal elections, many Italians, Irish, and Poles in Chicago heretofore had shown little interest in national elections. The South seemed "solid" for FDR.

Roosevelt, confident of victory, was relaxed and cheerful. He took time off from campaigning for a cruise along the New England coast in a forty-foot yawl. In his last speech to his Poughkeepsie neighbors on the eve of the election, Roosevelt spoke in much the same spirit that Lincoln had evinced when he said farewell to the citizens of Springfield as he started his long trip to Washington.

Roosevelt reminded the little crowd of friends and neighbors, swollen by reporters, that he had begun his political career there more than twenty years earlier. "I have learned much of what I know of human life and of political affairs in county and city from you, my friends. . . ." He had traveled the country and found everywhere Americans as direct and honest as his Dutchess County neighbors. He recalled the bright moments of the campaign, "the great crowd under the lights before the Capitol at Jefferson City, the patient attention of the Kansans under the hot sun at Topeka, the long day through Wyoming, with the strong, direct kindness of the people who came some of them hundreds of miles, to bid me welcome . . . the stricken but dauntless miners of Butte, the world consciousness of Seattle. . . ." The physical details of the landscape were engraved on his mind as well: "the sunset at McCook, Nebraska, and the strong progressive Farmers," Sioux City and Milwaukee and Chicago, and his friends at Warm Springs. "These people, all of them, these neighbors of each and every state have made one thing clear: they have expressed some hope in the future, confidence that things will be better. I set out to learn, more than to teach [that was not exactly true]. All of you, East and West and North and South, have helped me.

"And you have graciously helped me, too. . . . The great understanding and tolerance of America came out to meet me everywhere; for all this you have my heartfelt gratitude. . . .

"To be the means through which the ideals and the hopes of the American people may find a greater realization calls for the best in any man; I seek to be only the humble emblem of this restoration." With the aid of his fellow citizens, "with your help and your patience and your generous goodwill we can mend the torn fabric of our common life."

Ernest Lindley, closely associated with the new administration, reflected in later years that one of the most remarkable aspects of Roosevelt's campaign was his scrupulous avoidance of the kind of messianic tone that in Lindley's view, the country was anxious to hear. "He promised no utopia," Lindley wrote; "he calmly asserted, that he knew no patent remedies and did not believe in them. . . ." In retrospect that may have been the best measure of his character. He knew that he could promise his own best efforts, but beyond that he was restrained to the point of caution, in part out of a desire to keep his options open, in part out of a basic skepticism about easy solutions to deep-seated social problems.

Howe remained alone in the campaign headquarters on Madison Avenue, professing to doubt a Roosevelt victory even as the early returns indicated a landslide. Finally, when he could no longer doubt the outcome, he telephoned Roosevelt: "Hello, Franklin, I guess I've worked myself out of a job." Roosevelt insisted that he join him, and with Howe, his closest adviser and political confidant for more than twenty years, Roosevelt declared to the press: "There are two people in the United States more than anybody else responsible for this victory. One is my old friend and associate, Colonel Louis McHenry Howe, and the other is that splendid friend, Jim Farley."

Roosevelt's margin of victory was 22,809,638 to 15,758,901 for Hoover—57.4 percent to Hoover's 39.7 and 472 electoral votes to 59. Hoover carried only six states.

After the election results were in, Frankfurter wired Roosevelt: "No predecessor of yours, not even T.R., I believe, brought to the Presidency so extensive and so intimate a knowledge of his countrymen as you have." Oliver Wendell Holmes had his doubts. "As to the election," he wrote Harold Laski, "if I had a vote it would have been for Hoover—without enthusiasm—Roosevelt when I knew him struck me as a good fellow with a rather soft edge, years ago."

Lippmann promptly urged Roosevelt to assume virtually dictatorial powers in dealing with the crisis produced by the Depression. Frankfurter, on the other hand, cautioned the President-elect to work through Congress, using his talents as a politician and the desperate economic situation to herd recalcitrant Congressmen along. Frankfurter assured Lippmann that FDR would never encourage the country to view him as the "Great White Father" who could "pull rabbits out of a hat. . . . By temperament and experience he knows the importance of carrying the consent of the country—as far as may be—along with him, not merely generally and vaguely but by appeal on specific policies." It was a shrewd observation. Roosevelt was not without a touch of the Great White Father inclination, but whether that was true or not, a great majority of his countrymen were disposed to see him in precisely that light. This fact alone enabled Roosevelt to eschew all the trappings and formalities of power. He measured accurately enough the growing affection of his fellow citizens (as well, indeed, as the growing hostility of a minority of them), and he knew how effectively it could be used to advance his policies.

If Franklin Roosevelt was fortune's darling, Herbert Hoover was the stepchild. Edmund Wilson called him the worst President in the history of the Republic, who "walked in darkness," and "an Amoeba with nothing but self-nourishing and self-protective instincts." William Allen White, who had so often urged President Hoover to exercise leadership, wrote a more just epitaph: "He will be known as the greatest innocent bystander in history. But history will also write him down as an earnest, honest, intelligent man, full of courage and patriotism, undaunted to the last."

In 1952 an embittered Hoover, combing over the debacle of his administration, still seeking scapegoats and justifying his actions as President, noted that one of his major goals was "to prevent industrial conflict and social disorder." He was committed to keeping the "dollar ringing true on every counter in the world," and he had tried "to sustain the morale and courage of the people in order that their initiative should remain unimpaired, and to secure from the people themselves every effort for their own salvation." Finally, this all had been done "with 'rigid' adherence to the Constitution." He added: "We have not feared boldly to adopt unprecedented measures to meet the unprecedented violence of the storm." The measures of the New Deal he dismissed as "panaceas and short cuts." If everything that Hoover claimed as important elements of his policy had indeed been so, the fact was that he failed utterly to exert the personal leadership demanded by the crisis.

# 18

## The New Deal Begins

As the result of the strange hiatus in American political life between the presidential election in November and the inauguration of the President four months later, Roosevelt had to sit by while the country under Hoover's discredited leadership—or, perhaps more accurately, nonleadership—foundered in the rising waters of the Depression. The economy reached its lowest point since the crash four years earlier. The months of waiting were winter months, when the lack of adequate clothing, food, shelter, and heat made life grimmer than ever for millions of unemployed Americans. Hungry people demonstrated in New York and Chicago, and unemployed autoworkers in Detroit smashed store windows and overturned cars in rage and frustration. In the nation's capital the unemployed, led by "Reds," paraded in the streets and sang the "Internationale." In Iowa one-third of the farms were technically under foreclosure.

The poet Archibald MacLeish addressed an open letter "To the young men of Wall Street," challenging them to "create an idea of capitalism which men will support with their hope rather than their despair. . . . If you cannot, you and your children and ourselves with you will vanish from the West." Many wealthy people converted their assets into gold and shipped it abroad, causing a serious drain of gold in the early months of 1933. Even Theodore Dreiser put his money in postal savings, while his wife stocked their Westchester home with canned goods. Some of the rich bought farms or ranches in remote areas, far from angry city mobs. Others looked as far away as New Zealand and Australia.

Congress, meanwhile, held interminable and fruitless hearings on the state of the economy and what to do about it. Bernard Baruch, who considered a place in the President's inner councils his by right, prescribed "Balance budgets . . . stop spending money we haven't got. . . . Tax . . . tax everybody for everything."

Tugwell wrote: "There is no doubt in my mind that during the spring of 1933 the Army felt that the time was approaching when it might have to 'take over.' "

Hoover, for his part, took the line then and to the end of his life that the election of Roosevelt had frightened the business community so badly that an incipient recovery had been aborted. "Whether his policies were justified or unjustified," he wrote later, "they immediately caused our business world to stop, wait and listen. The price of commodities and securities immediately began to decline and unemployment increased." When Roosevelt called Hoover on November 17 to arrange for a meeting to discuss possible steps to deal with the deepening crisis, Hoover had a secretary listen in and take down the conversation in shorthand. It became Hoover's policy to do so, and more than 860 pages of transcribed telephone conversations were found in his papers by the historian Frank Freidel.

As far as Roosevelt's relations with Hoover were concerned, they were polite but cool. Hoover attempted to gain Roosevelt's support for his policies, but the President-elect remained noncommittal to both Hoover and the press. Meanwhile, under the direction of Raymond Moley, individuals as various and ill-assorted as Henry A. Wallace, scion of a famous Iowa farm family and editor of a journal started by his father, *Wallaces' Farmer,* and Henry Morgenthau, Jr., worked on the farm bill to be presented to Congress as soon as the new one convened. Proposals were drafted for regulating the stock market and for reorganizing the government to reduce Federal expenditures.

Raymond Moley undertook the time-consuming task of screening prospective Cabinet members. In Moley's words, Roosevelt "considered himself under direct obligations to no man so far as Cabinet appointments were concerned." It distressed Moley that there was "neither a well-defined purpose nor underlying principle in the selection of the Cabinet members."

Among those considered most likely to be named to the Cabinet were Al Smith and Newton D. Baker, who seemed to many observers a sure thing for secretary of state. Governor Albert C. Ritchie of Maryland was another front-runner, as were Owen D. Young, Norman Davis, and Bernard Baruch. But Roosevelt was determined to avoid individuals who were considered representatives of the business community. Moreover, Roosevelt knew he had to woo the Southerners. Since they chaired most of the important congressional committees, he had to have their support to get through the legislation that he considered essential. At the same time he was aware of the fact that, as Tugwell put it, the Southerners "would be most reluctant to swallow the medicine he expected to prescribe." Roosevelt finally settled on three Southerners for his Cabinet. As he had promised Harry Byrd, he offered the post of secretary of the treasury to Senator Carter Glass of Virginia, architect of the Federal Reserve Act and elder statesman of the party. Glass was so eminent in party circles and so closely attached to such monetary reforms as the Federal Reserve that Roosevelt could hardly bypass him. But Glass was a prima donna, strong-willed and innately conservative. Roosevelt was doubtless relieved when he turned down the job. Roosevelt then turned to William Woodin, a Wilsonian Democrat, often described as "faunlike" and "elfin," a charming and witty man and a loyal adherent of Roosevelt. He was head of the American Car and Foundry Company. In the maneuvering over the secretaryship, Louis Howe wired Roosevelt at Warm Springs in his self-devised code: "Prefer a wooden [Woodin] roof to a glass roof over swimming pool."

Roosevelt wanted the old Progressive Senator Thomas Walsh, who had been chairman of the Democratic Convention, as attorney general, but Walsh died two days after Roosevelt's inauguration, and Homer Cummings was appointed in his stead.

Senator Cordell Hull of Tennessee, a handsome, courtly man and a strong internationalist in the Wilson tradition, was offered the post of secretary of state, rather to the alarm of the isolationists. In Moley's opinion, the genial and handsome Hull "personified the philosophical opposition to the New Deal policies." Perhaps it would have been more accurate to say that Hull personified opposition to what Moley thought the New Deal policies *should* be. Arthur Krock wrote unkindly of Hull that he often talked "in cascades of words, rushing murkily over tangles of syntax." The truth was he was not a notably articulate man.

Considering Roosevelt's commitment to farmers and to labor and his passion for conservation, the most important Cabinet positions were those of secretary of agriculture, secretary of labor, and secretary of the interior.

The post of secretary of the interior was offered first to Hiram Johnson and then to Roosevelt's Groton and Harvard friend Bronson Cutting, Senator from Colorado. Moley described Cutting as "a man of deep passions and great daring, but outwardly so taciturn, so inarticulate, that there was none of the easy conversational give and take that characterizes most practical politicians." Cutting, according to Moley, doubted Roosevelt's commitment to progressive causes. He declined, and Roosevelt appointed Harold Ickes.

Harold Ickes was born in Frankstown Township, Pennsylvania (which he described rather ungraciously as "one of the ugliest and most unattractive cities I have ever seen") in 1874, the son of "black" Republicans, Republicans in the abolitionist and reform tradition. His family moved to Chicago while he was in his teens, and Ickes soon found himself involved with Progressive Republican politics. He became the campaign manager for Charles Merriam, a professor of political economy and an enthusiastic reformer, who was running for mayor of Chicago. Although Merriam lost, he threw a scare into the Republican machine. Ickes's next political venture was in Theodore Roosevelt's Bull Moose campaign in 1912. When the United States entered the war, Ickes, prevented from enlisting by a deaf ear, found his way to France as a Red Cross official.

Like many men of his generation, Ickes was profoundly disillusioned by postwar America; with Wilson ailing and the country in a reactionary mood, there seemed little future for reform-minded politicians of either party. Ickes turned to the practice of law, but the prospective candidacy of his friend from the heyday of progressivism Hiram Johnson brought him quickly back into politics. The Republican convention of 1920 completed his disillusionment. "The miserable machinations that went on were stomach-turning," Ickes wrote. "They were poison ivy even to a curmudgeon. A conspiracy was being brewed . . . where an evil candidate [Harding] was to emerge from the witch's cauldron." When a voice vote was called for on the convention floor, Ickes could be heard in the Illinois delegation, shouting no "at the top of his lungs." Indignant at the treatment of Johnson and at the reactionary bent of the Republican old guard, Ickes gave his support to the only promising young liberal politician in sight, Franklin Roosevelt. Eight years later he supported Al Smith, and in 1932 he organized Mid-Western Republicans for Roosevelt. When Roosevelt won, it occurred to Ickes that having, for the first time since 1904, backed a winning presidential candidate, "he would like to go to Washington." He had had a lifelong interest in and sympathy with the Indians. He might wangle an appointment in the new administration as commissioner for Indian affairs. Or why not head of the Department of the Interior? Ickes, never an excessively modest man, traveled to Washington and solicited the backing of Hiram Johnson and Bronson Cutting. They promised, if asked, to support Ickes for the position.

Summoned to New York to confer with the President-elect, Ickes found himself called aside by Roosevelt, who said, "Mr. Ickes, you and I have been speaking the same language for the past twenty years. I am having difficulty finding a Secretary of the Interior. [Roosevelt had also offered the job to George Dern, the governor of Utah, but Dern had refused and taken the office of secretary of war instead.] I want a man who can stand on his own feet. Above all things, I want a man who is honest, and I have about come to the conclusion that the man I want is Harold L. Ickes, of Chicago." Later that day Roosevelt introduced Ickes to Frances Perkins: "I would like to have the Secretary of the Interior meet the Secretary of Labor." Ickes was certainly an appropriate choice for the office. If his wife's description of him as the "most fanatical conservationist of his generation" was perhaps excessive, he shared the President's strong convictions on the subject. What Ickes could not have known, or Roosevelt either for that matter, was that the Department of the Interior would become, along with Agriculture, one of the two most important agencies of the government in the long struggle to lift the country out of the Great Depression. What is indisputable is that Ickes's heart was in the right place, at least from the point of view of those men and women who made up the inner circle of the administration. For Ickes the issues remained simple and straightforward: The rich, the money lords, the powerful industrialists were against the people. As a complement to his old-time reformer's faith, Ickes preserved the flamboyant rhetoric of those days. Capitalists were to him evil, predatory men suspected of wrongdoing, to be watched closely and checked when they strayed. It was Ickes's old-fashioned view that no man "or set of men had a right, for their own purposes, to exploit an irreplaceable national resource; that the interests of the nation were paramount."

Like Gideon Welles, Lincoln's secretary of the navy, and David Houston, Wilson's secretary of agriculture, Ickes kept a journal or diary of his years as secretary of the interior. Extending to more than 100 volumes and some 6,000,000 words, it is a vast compendium of highly biased but often fascinating information on the inner workings of the New Deal. The portrait that Ickes inadvertently paints of himself is not always flattering. The picture that emerges from his rather flat-footed prose is of an inordinately touchy individual whose self-esteem, while high, is precarious—in constant need, as we would say today, of positive reinforcement. Yet of his basic integrity and fundamental goodness there can be little doubt. One of the most engaging aspects of the diaries is their disarming lack of self-consciousness. The writer constantly relays compliments from other politicians, from journalists and friends: He is the ablest member of the Cabinet, the most hard-working, the most loyal, the most outspoken, the best liked, the most admired, the best public speaker; only he can keep the administration on a progressive course—in all of which there was a grain of truth. Ickes was certainly the most colorful Cabinet member. With his bulldog jowls, fiery temper, and gift for invective, he gloried in the nickname the Old Curmudgeon. Appropriately enough, he raised turkeys on a farm in Maryland and often seemed to be as intimidating as an irascible old gobbler. Yet he was generous and thoughtful of his staff, which adored him. He imparted to the rather staid Department of the Interior his own vast energy and unquenchable spirit.

Interior had charge of the public lands and their mineral resources, involving the management of some 165,000,000 acres. Also under its wing were the Geological Survey, started by Charles King, the Bureau of Fisheries, the Bureau of Biological Survey, the bureaus of Reclamation and of Mines, the National Park Service, and the Office of Indian Affairs. Rather illogically, or so at least it seemed to Ickes, the Forestry Service was in the Department of Agriculture. Ickes was convinced it belonged in Interior. He tried tirelessly to wrest it away from Agriculture, but Henry Wallace, apparently egged on by Gifford Pinchot, clung to it doggedly. Under Ickes the Interior Department received substantial new increments of authority with the addition of divisions that supervised coal and petroleum production as well as grazing. The Division of Territories and Island Possessions was added to the department, which also exercised a degree of supervision over Howard University (the black university in nearby Virginia), the Freedmen's Hospital, and the Columbia Institute for the Deaf. With such varied responsibilities it was often referred to as the "Department of Things in General."

For secretary of agriculture, Roosevelt settled on Henry Wallace. Wallace was somewhat of an anomaly among the bright young lawyers and seasoned liberal politicians in Roosevelt's New Deal. He was a true son of the Middle West. In addition to having performed important experiments in developing a hardy hybrid corn, he was steeped in the romantic and mystical tradition of the prairie states. Behind the rather dour and often disheveled exterior was a Sandburg-like lyricism that startled his colleagues whenever it manifested itself. It made him a brother to Sherwood Anderson, who met and liked him—"No swank," Anderson declared. Wallace startled the President on one occasion by describing him to his face as "the flaming one, the one with an ever upward-surging spirit." Uncertain as to how a Cabinet member should dress, Wallace consulted Rexford Tugwell, who, looking at the thoroughly Midwestern cut of Wallace's suit, agreed to go shopping wih him. Wallace, Tugwell reported, "was outfitted with satisfactory completeness, although he admitted to some discomfort." Looking at himself in the mirror, he was hardly recognizable as an Iowa farmer, but there was nothing to be done for his indomitable Midwestern face and hair (his haircut recalled the elder La Follette). Wallace had the charm of innocence and goodness, and it is interesting to note that Frances Perkins, with her totally different background, was strongly drawn to him and his lively and energetic wife, Ilo. In Iowa and much of the Middle West the Wallace family dwelt just below the Almighty.

Daniel Calhoun Roper of South Carolina got the post of secretary of commerce; Claude Swanson of Virginia was named secretary of the navy, and George Dern secretary of the army, as noted.

Finally, there was the Cabinet member who was, in some ways, closest of all to the President, Frances Perkins. Roosevelt had considered Ruth Bryan Owen, daughter of Williams Jennings, for secretary of labor, but he finally settled on Perkins, whom he knew well and trusted, although he knew that her appointment would stir up a tempest in labor circles. Perkins, aware of how controversial her appointment would be, had deep misgivings about accepting. She consulted her friend, Mary "Molly" Dewson, director of the Women's Division of the Democratic National Campaign Committee. Dewson had been superintendent of parole for girls in Massachusetts and then a researcher for the National Consumers' League, where she had worked with Perkins. Dewson overcame her friend's reluctance. The things they both wanted done—minimum wage and maximum hour laws, the abolition of child labor—could be best initiated from the office of the secretary. "You can do it as nobody else can," Dewson insisted. "What's more, you can get on with Roosevelt. He trusts you. He likes you. . . . You owe it to the women. . . . You mustn't say no. Too many people count on what you do. Too much hangs on it." If she refused the job, "it might be generations before another woman would have such an opportunity." When Frances Perkins consulted her parish priest, he told her he believed "it is God's own will." If, indeed, it was a job that God had assigned her, "He will help you to see it through." The thought strengthened her and was a consolation in the often difficult times that lay ahead.

When her appointment was announced, William Green, who had succeeded Samuel Gompers as president of the AFL, objected vociferously: "Labor can never be reconciled to the selection." In addition to being a woman, she was not a member of a union. Perkins replied tactfully that Green was "a man of great integrity, vision and patriotism." If the representatives of organized labor would not come to see her, she would "hasten to see them."

Perkins was born in Boston—in 1880, although she persisted in subtracting two years from her age. The principal influence on her early years was her grandmother Cynthia Otis Perkins, whom Perkins described as "an extremely wise woman—worldly wise as well as spiritually wise," adding, "I am extraordinarily the product of my grandmother." From her mother, who sketched and modeled in clay, Perkins acquired a lifelong interest in art. When she was twelve, her mother took her to shop for a hat. Picking up a tricornered hat of Milan straw, she declared: "My dear, that is your hat. You should always wear a hat something like it. You have a very broad face. . . . The result is you always need to have as much width in your hat as you have in your cheekbones." Tricornered hats became Frances Perkins's trademark throughout her life.

From Worcester Classical High School, where she distinguished herself as a student, Frances Perkins went on to that citadel of high-thinking and unselfish serving Mount Holyoke, still under the command of Miss Woolley; it was an institution that had turned out more missionaries, missionaries' wives, and reform-minded women in general than could well be counted. Among the students of Perkins's generation at Mount Holyoke, two-thirds were to remain unmarried; they had nobler purposes in mind—the kind of Christian service represented by Jane Addams. While she was still in college, Frances Perkins read Jacob Riis's *How the Other Half Lives*. It was one of the formative experiences of her life. Another critically important influence on Perkins was Florence Kelley. Kelley, the daughter of William "Pig Iron" Kelley, a Congressman from Philadelphia for some thirty years, had served four years as chief inspector of factories for Governor John Peter Altgeld of Illinois. She had spent two years with Jane Addams at Hull House and had then gone to New York to develop the National Consumers' League, which had chapters in most industrial states. Young men and women worked under her direction to bring about industrial reforms on the state level. Her principal cause was child labor. Despite repeated setbacks, her courage never flagged. "Despise not the day of small things," Kelley told her followers. To Frances Perkins the "key to her tremendous drive" was her maternal feeling, which "spread over all the children and helpless people of society." Kelley lived and worked, Perkins wrote, "like a missionary, no sacrifice too great, no effort too much." Kelley knew that her work depended on recruiting others to her causes. "She was willing," Perkins wrote, "to go into these far little corners [small New England or Midwestern towns] where a handful of girls were students and tell them about the program . . . for industrial and human and social justice. And that influence which she had over a whole generation was of extreme significance. She took a whole group of young people, formless in their aspirations, and molded their aspirations for social justice into some definite purpose, into a program that had meaning and that had experience and that had practicality back of it."

After a stint of teaching in a girls' school, Frances Perkins became involved with Chicago Commons, a settlement house started by Graham Taylor, a Dutch Reformed clergyman and a professor at the Chicago Theological Seminary. When Taylor introduced her to the conditions of labor in the Chicago garment industry, Perkins was horrified. Some 45,000 men and women, three-fourths of them immigrants, worked for as little as $2.50 a week. "What *is* the trouble?" she asked Taylor's son. "How *can* we cure this? Is it to go on forever, these people being so poor that we have to give out free milk, we have to have free nursing service, the babies die, there's nothing to do on a Sunday afternoon but get drunk? What *can* be done? What *should* be

done?" Graham Taylor's solution was for every workingman and workingwoman to join a union. Then "there would be no need for the
charity societies and settlements."

Perkins's work with the Chicago settlement houses convinced her
that her vocation was not teaching but reform. "I had to do something,"
she wrote, "about unnecessary hazards to life, unnecessary poverty. It
was sort of up to me. This feeling . . . sprang out of a period of great
philosophical confusion which overtakes all young people. One thing
seemed . . . clear. Our Lord had directed all those who thought they
were following His path to visit the widows, the orphans, the fatherless,
the prisoners and so forth. Definitely, the circumstances of the life of
the people of my generation was my business and I ought to do something about it."

The field that she chose was New York City. "There," she wrote
to her alumnae magazine, "I am in the very heart of both theoretical
and practical efforts to socialize the life of the modern city." She became
a close friend and associate of Paul Kellogg, one of the early editors
of the journal of reform *Common Ground* and later of the even more
influential *Survey*. Sinclair Lewis proposed marriage to her, although
Perkins was not sure how sober the proposal was. Soon she had a job
as a lobbyist for the New York City Consumers' League, a local branch,
so to speak, of Florence Kelley's organization. Sanitary regulations for
cellar bakeries became her special field of reform. She also began to
enter actively into political campaigning on the ground that only legislators well disposed to reform would pass the necessary social legislation.

Perkins's job as a lobbyist took her to the state capitol at Albany
to try to push through the legislature a bill limiting the workweek for
women and children to fifty-four hours. There she found an ally in
Al Smith. Smith played an essential part in her political training, giving
her the benefit of his own shrewd knowledge of how things got done.

In 1913, when Frances Perkins was thirty-three, she married a
fellow social worker, Paul Wilson, a man four years her elder. He was
a handsome, intelligent man who shared her zeal for reform and had
served as secretary to New York's reform mayor, John Purroy Mitchel,
but he was often quiet and withdrawn, and before many years he began
to suffer from manic-depressive symptoms. After her marriage Perkins, who was well known in the circles of political reform, decided to
retain her own name professionally. She told a friend that she had
been reluctant to marry: "I hadn't wanted to marry. I liked life better

in single harness, and the older I grew the less likely I was to marry." A young woman usually married the first man she met "who gives her a thrill. That's that. It's over. She accepts the situation." When her friend Josephine Goldmark protested her marriage, Perkins answered, "I thought it better to get it off my mind, because I was always being challenged by someone who thought he should marry me or wanted to recommend the institution. . . . I finally thought, 'I better marry. I know Paul well. I like him. . . . I enjoy his friends and company, and I might as well marry and get it off my mind.' " Goldmark replied: "That's a strange reason for marrying—to get it off your mind." Some of Perkins's classmates from Mount Holyoke and those dedicated spinsters who labored with her in the cause of reform felt rather as though she were a deserter, but they were reassured by her offhand manner and the fact that she kept her maiden name. "My generation,"she wrote later, "was perhaps the first that openly and actively asserted—at least some of us did—the separateness of women and their personal independence in the family relationship. There was always talk about: should a man support his wife, should he give her an allowance, should everything he had be hers, or did she earn her keep as a housewife?"

When Al Smith became governor in 1918 and Belle Moskowitz became his closest adviser, Smith offered Frances Perkins a position on the Industrial Commission. As Perkins recalled their conversation, Smith said, "I've been thinkin' over my situation since the election. Women have got the vote. It's the first time. Women are going to vote from now on. I thought I ought to show some attention to women. I ought to bring women into the political picture of my administration. I thought about you." Perkins's reply was: "I want to talk to Florence Kelley." When Perkins told Kelley of Smith's offer and asked her advice, Kelley's eyes filled with tears. "Glory be to God," she exclaimed. "You don't mean it. I never thought I would live to see the day when someone we had trained, who knew about industrial conditions, cared about women, cared to have things right, would have a chance to be an administrative officer."

Early in her career as a public official Frances Perkins decided that while the politicians she would have to work with and whom she would have to convert to her cause had ambivalent feelings about women in general and especially about women in politics, they all honored motherhood. "It's a primitive and primary attitude," she wrote. It followed that the way to get things done was to "so behave, so dress and so comport yourself that you remind them subconsciously of their mothers." This she set out faithfully to do. The politicians she had to work with "could take justice at the hands of a woman who reminded them of their mothers. . . . I sort of sympathized with them," she added. "Many good and intelligent women do dress in ways that are very attractive and pretty, but don't particularly invite confidence in their common sense, integrity or sense of justice." All her political life she dressed and comported herself like somebody's mother. She loved to dance and enjoyed parties and social life, but she diligently concealed all such impulses from the politicians on whom she depended to achieve her goals.

With her uncompromising hats and poker face Frances Perkins was one of the most important of Roosevelt's inner circle. To the two most aggressively masculine sectors of American society—labor and business—Perkins, with her unmistakably upper-class accent and antecedents, her formidable presence, and, above all, her sex, was as disconcerting as a visitor from another planet. They simply did not know what to make of her. As Robert Moses put it, "The attitude of both labor and employers [toward her] is a good deal like that of habitués of a waterfront saloon toward a visiting lady slummer—grim, polite, and unimpressed."

Frances Perkins and the Wallaces, Henry and Ilo, attended the Anglo-Catholic Church of St. James. It was at the suggestion of her priest there that she began visiting, at least once a month, a community of Episcopal nuns in Catonsville, Maryland, to participate in silent retreats. "I have discovered the rule of silence is one of the most beautiful things in the world," she wrote a friend. "It gives me time for so many, many ideas and occupations. It also preserves me from the temptation of the idle word, the fresh remark, the wisecrack, the angry challenge, the hot-tempered reaction, the argument about nothing, the foolish question, the unnecessary noise of the human clack-clack."

Perkins liked the story of a debate between two charitably inclined individuals about why shoes should be provided for a poor man. One said, "Because his feet are cold"; the other, "For Jesus' sake." The reason for doing things "for Jesus' sake" rather than out of a general disposition to humanitarian reform was, according to Perkins, that the humanitarian impulse would not last. "The poor aren't grateful in the long run, and quarrels come up." There is resentment over ingratitude and lack of understanding. So kindness, compassion, and justice were, finally, "for Jesus' sake," not for the world's. Her favorite scriptural passage came from First Corinthians: ". . . be ye stedfast, unmoveable, always abounding in the work of the Lord, forasmuch as ye know that your labour is not in vain in the Lord."

Undoubtedly the most colorful figure at Cabinet meetings was the Vice-President, John "Cactus Jack" Garner. When William O. Douglas visited him, he found Garner in his shirtsleeves and stocking feet. "Young man, before we start talking we have to strike a blow for liberty," Garner declared, and thereupon poured and handed Douglas the stiffest shot of bourbon he had ever tasted and tossed one off himself. The greatest threats to the nation, Garner told Douglas, were the three Ms—the Morgans, the Mellons, and the Mills (the last referring to Ogden Mills, secretary of the treasury under Hoover).

Garner's political antecedents could be traced back to Southern populism. Garner, Ickes wrote approvingly, "took the position that fifty or sixty men in the United States, through interlocking directorates and holding companies should not be permitted to control the economic life of the nation. He expressed the utmost distrust of these men and told the President that . . . this was the time to put them in their place and keep them there." He doubted the patriotism of such men "when money is concerned."

At the first Cabinet meeting Garner hailed Frances Perkins with a cheerful "Glad to see you, sister." When Garner's wife asked him about the new woman Cabinet member, he replied, "She didn't interrupt. She didn't butt in. She didn't ask any questions. She kept still until the President asked her what she had to say. Then she said it. She said it loud enough so I could hear. She said it plain and distinct. She said it short. When she was through, she stopped. I guess she's all right."

In addition to the Cabinet positions, there were assistant secretaryships to be filled and jobs to be found for Roosevelt's inner circle of advisers, his informal kitchen Cabinet. Howe was made Roosevelt's chief secretary. "Louis can do that job," Roosevelt said, "and still work behind the scenes being the mysterious figure that he loves." Moley was made an assistant secretary of state, but he continued to function as a kind of chief of staff, advising on appointments and writing the initial drafts of Roosevelt's more important speeches. Tugwell found his niche in agriculture. General Hugh Johnson came aboard on the recommendation of Bernard Baruch, whose last-ditch adherence to Smith made him persona only slightly grata with Roosevelt. Baruch, accustomed to the ear of Presidents, was indignant at finding himself frozen out. Johnson was a West Pointer who had served on the War Industries Board with Baruch and become an executive in Baruch's financial empire.

Lewis Douglas, director of the budget, who had given up a seat in Congress from Arizona, was a fiscal conservative. He viewed with alarm, not to say horror, an unbalanced budget.

Another assistant secretary of state was Roosevelt's old friend and schoolmate William "Billy" Phillips, a longtime diplomat and a thoroughgoing snob in the old State Department tradition. Sumner Welles was another member of the upper crust in State, well mannered and well-to-do. Neither Phillips nor Welles, in Raymond Moley's view, "by any stretch of the imagination, knew what the New Deal was all about."

Cordell Hull took little interest in appointments to the State Department and, specifically, to those ambassadorial posts that were typically handed out to wealthy supporters of the winning presidential candidate. He turned over the job to Phillips, whose principal criterion was that the appointees be gentlemen aware of the proper social amenities. This predilection so alarmed Jim Farley that he insisted Phillips consult with Moley. Claude Bowers was a special problem. His irredeemably Midwestern face with its mournful dewlaps put off Phillips (Moley wrote that Bowers's "charming lack of tonishness gave Phillips an attack of horrid misgivings"), but Bowers had performed important services for the Democratic Party and particularly for Roosevelt. Spain seemed a prestigious but undemanding post, so at Moley's insistence, Bowers was shipped off to Spain, where he could presumably write more "progressive" history; within a few years his scholarly reveries were disturbed by a civil war. Mayor James Curley, Boston's notorious boss, laid claim to the ambassadorship to Italy, which gave Phillips another bad turn; Curley was offered Poland but declined.

When Theodore Roosevelt had succeeded to the presidency upon the assassination of McKinley, reformers all over the land, Lincoln Steffens reported, rose in the air and made a beeline for Washington. When Franklin Roosevelt was elected President, the story was repeated. Socialists and Progressives, young Communists, idealists, visionaries, reformers of all kinds and conditions headed for Washington. Grizzled veterans of reform and ruddy-cheeked young college graduates of both sexes, they came by bus, by flivver, by motorcycle, by train; some of them hitchhiked, and some of the more adventuresome caught rides on freight trains. The members of the intellectual class and the seasoned Communists might view the New Deal with skepticism or contempt, but those who still heard the echoes of the trumpet call for Armageddon or had the bright illusions of youth responded by the thousands.

The "city of Washington," Moley wrote, "became a mecca for the old Socialists, single-taxers, utility reformers, Civil Service reformers, and goo-goos of all types, who at last perceived that a new political era was at hand and who took it to be a kind of crusade which the discontented of every kind were invited to join." In addition to the "old Socialists"—men like Oscar Ameringer and Charles Edward Russell—there were "new" Communists and their sympathizers. There were no loyalty oaths or tests of political purity; such things were alien to the spirit of the New Deal. The consequence was that Communists and their allies, along with liberals, Progressives, and other shades of radicals, found jobs in various government agencies. "We stood in the city of Washington on March 4th like a handful of marauders in hostile territory," Moley wrote. The New Deal consisted, in essence, of ten Cabinet officers, two or three under and assistant secretaries, and the staffs of those officials. "Most of us," Moley noted, "were completely ignorant of the detailed workings of the great departments of which we were a part."

Among the old semi- or quasi-socialists was Frederic Howe, who came to see Moley. Moley had been a noncommissioned officer in Tom Johnson's regiment of reformers in Cleveland thirty years earlier; Howe had been a first lieutenant. Moley had read all of Howe's books— "burning, eloquent books. . . . The debt of progressivism to such men could not be forgotten," Moley wrote. As Howe sat in his office, "misty-eyed at the thought of joining a new cause just as twilight began to steal over his lifetime of labor and frustration," Moley reflected that it was not going to be easy to find a useful place for men of such specialized talents. He subsequently found him a job as a "consumer's counsel" in the Agricultural Adjustment Administration, where he "scared the daylights out of businessmen with talk which, after his many years of gentle agitation, came quite naturally to him."

Another battle-scarred warrior was Oscar Ameringer, veteran of the Socialist Party, the Nonpartisan League, and the peace movement. There was, in fact, no more poignant moment in American politics than the rising up of the still-militant remnants of the heyday of progressivism. What made it all even more moving was that many desperately needed jobs. Ben Lindsey, the diminutive reforming judge from Denver who had set up model juvenile courts and fought for reform with George Creel and Josephine Roche until he was disbarred by a conservative State Supreme Court, was another aging hero who applied to come aboard. Before a suitable job could be found for him, he returned to California, to which he had gone after his disbarment in Colorado. There, with the devoted sponsorship of the Mellinkopf family, wealthy liberals, he ran for and won a seat on the State Superior Court.

Josephine Roche, who had served as Woodrow Wilson's liaison with the immigrant communities during the war, was appointed assistant secretary of the treasury.

Thurman Arnold was another exotic among the New Dealers. He had been mayor of Laramie, Wyoming, before he joined the faculty of the Yale Law School. He found his way to Washington with William O. Douglas.

When Felix Frankfurter, a lifelong Republican, enlisted somewhat reluctantly in the Democratic ranks, Harold Laski reported that friends of the Harvard professor had asked him, "Why is he a Democrat . . .?"

"Because he is an aristocrat with an infinite sense of pity," Laski replied.

"Why does he not want to make money?"

"Because most people who have it are vulgar."

"Why doesn't he collect books or pictures?"

"Because he collects people."

At the Harvard Law School Frankfurter had created a school within the school, to the discomfort, if not displeasure, of its formidable dean, Roscoe Pound, who had held sway, unchallenged, for more than a decade. Justice Holmes asked Frankfurter to recommend law clerks to him. Brandeis followed suit. The result was that Frankfurter exercised an extraordinary and unprecedented influence through the brilliant young students whom he dispatched regularly to serve as clerks for Brandeis, Cardozo, and Holmes. James Landis, one of Frankfurter's hottest "hot dogs," as his students were called, was law clerk to Brandeis, as was Dean Acheson. Holmes got Thomas Corcoran, the Hiss brothers, David and Alger, and Mark DeWolfe Howe. Altogether they constituted a kind of critical human mass, bound together by their devotion to Frankfurter and fired by his ideal of service. They were a caste or order, dedicated, young, and vigorous, intoxicated by their proximity to power, anchorites of the law. "Mind in the service of society" was their implicit battle cry. The reformer-journalists—the

Ida Tarbells, Ray Stannard Bakers, Charles Edward Russells—had, for the most part, chosen the cities as the critical battleground of reform. Their accomplishments had been prodigious, but the physical and psychic cost had been high, and the profoundly reactionary tendency of the country—the witch-hunts, Prohibition, the ferocity and ubiquitousness of the Klan, the sanctification of greed, and the suppression of dissent—had profoundly depressed them. The new evangel must be carried on by the young lawyers, men for the most part, often ably assisted by such women as Molly Dewson, young men whose expectations were not so extravagant as those of their elders.

The lawyer-preachers of the new evangel, who learned their catechism at the feet of Pound, Chafee, and Frankfurter, believed that the state, in the ancient meaning of that term, must be reformed before it was swept away by the tempestuous waters of revolution and that the law was the means by which that reformation must be carried out. The most interesting aspect of any society at a particular moment of its history is where its creative energies flow, what class or profession assumes the burden of service and redemption. For the "rising generation" of the thirties it would plainly be the lawyers, first as practitioners and teachers and then as judges, interpreting the law.

Conservative George N. Peek, AAA administrator, called Frankfurter's hot dogs a "plague of young lawyers settled upon Washington. They all claimed to be friends of somebody or other and mostly of Felix Frankfurter. . . . They floated airily into offices, took desks, asked for papers and found no end of things to be busy about. . . ." Like young William O. Douglas, son of the West and professor of law at Yale, they believed in the new doctrine of sociology, in this instance the sociology of the law. Brandeis had blazed the way, and Yale, more than Harvard, had become its ideological center. The new lawyers did not believe that the law was something immutable, carved on stone like the Ten Commandments. They believed that it was the result of a complex historical struggle between rights and needs, between, in the last analysis, the haves and the have-nots. While most traditional expounders of the law seemed concerned primarily with what the law prevented politicians or private individuals from doing, the advocates of the new law believed that it should be responsive, above all, to the urgent needs of a rapidly evolving society. Indeed, they believed that many of the evident ills of that society came from too rigid an interpretation of the law. Harry Hopkins expressed such a view succinctly in addressing a group of aides, saying, "I want to assure you that we are not afraid of exploring anything within the law, and we have a lawyer who will declare anything you want to do legal."

To newspaper attacks on Frankfurter for his resourceful insertions of his students into the various agencies of the New Deal, he replied with characteristic vigor. A government, he wrote Henry Stimson, could never be better than the civil servants and administrators who made it up. What the United States needed was what it had achieved for a brief, glorious moment under an earlier Roosevelt: "highly trained, disinterested government personnel. . . . What this Administration has had to do is to create something like the English civil service over night. And few things have been more shocking to me," Frankfurter added, "than all the silly and partisan and unworthy prattling on the part of many respectable about the 'brains trust.' The term is silly enough, but wickeder is the implication that somehow or other brains, the brains of men who have given their lives to the study of governmental and economic problems, are either dangerous or unworthy of service to the state." The founders of the Republic were certainly a brain trust if there had ever been one. "Disinterested enthusiasm, freedom from imprisoning dogmatism, capacity for fresh insight, unflagging industry, ardor for difficulties—these are qualities that in the main youthful years must supply." The dedicated young man was "freed from the complicated ramifications of private life; . . . diverted by a minimum of vanities and jealousies; . . . more resilient, more cooperative in taking orders. . . ." In addition, "his technical preparation for his work is on the whole much better than the equipment of the generation that preceded him."

In the words of William Douglas, "Washington, D.C. became a young man's and a young woman's town. . . . Some left comfortable outposts where they were paid well to defend the status quo because the excitement of change was in the air and because they felt a responsibility to participate in the revolution. Some wished to escape the treadmill of trivial and repetitive legal work. The sense of freedom, the feeling of power over people and events, the desire for an all-out effort, the excitement of adventure—all these and more made lawyers, sociologists, economists, and political scientists march to the beat of the new drum that was echoing across the land. They poured in from all over the country. . . . They were filled with idealism and fervor. The best of our men and women were available by the thousands. . . . They swarmed the nation's capital, taking any available job. The air was filled with expectation for a great crusade."

Learned Hand called the legions of idealistic young men who flocked to Washington the *Filii Aurorae*, "sons of the dawn." They often worked long into the night, like Paul Kellogg, intoxicated at the prospect of doing "in a year what might otherwise take a generation." Malcolm Cowley wrote: "On evenings free of government business, there were gatherings in Georgetown houses, partly flirtatious or bibulous, partly devoted to games and singing, but mostly conversational, with arguments that continued till the first streaks of light over Capitol Hill." There had not been such days since young men like Gifford and Amos Pinchot entered government like knights in the service of their feudal lord. Those days had, of course, been quite different in spirit. Now there was an apocalyptic tone to the endless discussions that was missing from the earlier era. "All were excited by ideas," Cowley wrote, "and still more excited by the prospect that some of the ideas they had been discussing since 1929 would at last be tested in action." Rexford Tugwell called those early months "the renaissance spring . . . a time of rebirth after a dark age."

Two of the *Filii Aurorae* who merit special notice among Frankfurter's protégés were a young Irishman and a Jew—Thomas G. Corcoran and Benjamin V. Cohen. They were a kind of duo. Tommy Corcoran, with a gift for singing and playing the accordion was, in Frankfurter's word, a "fixer," an expediter, a contact man with Congressmen and bureaucrats. Raymond Moley was annoyed by what he called Corcoran's "ineffable agreeableness, a way of saying 'Sir' two or three times in the course of a five-minute conversation, a whispering deference." On the other hand, he himself was, Moley wrote, Irish enough to recognize the "durable fiber" behind "the slyly superior eyes above the puckering nose and smiling mouth." Corcoran, in Moley's view, was committed to the "class-struggle" view of history. He declared, by Moley's account, "Fighting with a businessman is like fighting with a Polack. You can give no quarter."

Moley was more attracted to Ben Cohen's "sensitiveness, his taste for the solitary, his intense and ingrown spirit, his indifference to his own comfort (not to say his pleasure). . . ." Moley called Cohen "a magnificent legal draftsman," and William Douglas considered him the "best and the most intelligent man in the New Deal. He put the ideas and the philosophy of the period into legislation. . . . [He] above all others most honored the ethical and intellectual ideals for which FDR stood."

A modest effort was made to employ blacks in the various agencies of the government. Frances Perkins appointed Lawrence A. Oxley, a young black from North Carolina and former director of black Unemployment Relief for that state, as her assistant, and she immediately desegregated the dining hall and the public facilities in the Department of Labor.

Harold Ickes had been head of the Chicago chapter of the NAACP, but he could see nothing inappropriate in appointing a white man, Charles Foreman, with an outstanding record in interracial activities, as his special assistant on black problems. Du Bois was only one of the black editors who took Ickes severely to task. It was, in his view, "an outrage" that "through the efforts of some of our best friends" blacks should be "compelled to have our wants and aspirations interpreted by one who does not know them and our ideas and ambitions expressed by a person who cannot understand them."

It must be said for Ickes that when Foreman later took a job with the Public Works Administration (PWA) Power Division, Ickes appointed Robert C. Weaver, a black, to the position. Weaver, a graduate of Harvard, was described, a little condescendingly, by Will Alexander as "a thoroughly emancipated Negro," and another Interior Department administrator, Edwin Embree, called him a "first class administrator with ability to cooperate with associates. . . . Keen scholar, suave manners, tough mind, excellent personality."

An effort was also made to appoint women. More than in any preceding administration, women were appointed to responsible administrative positions in all agencies of the government, especially in the Department of Labor and in the various relief and public works agencies.

With the major administrative positions settled and a number of the ex-brain trusters hard at work on proposed legislation, the President-elect took a cruise through the Caribbean on Vincent Astor's yacht. On February 15 he disembarked in Miami. He rode in an open car to the Bay Front Park, where he was scheduled to give a brief talk. He spoke from the tonneau of his car and then was joined by Anton Cermak, the mayor of Chicago, who had done his best to secure the Democratic nomination for Al Smith. "Just then," Roosevelt told reporters, "I heard what I thought was a firecracker; then several more." The "firecrackers" were pistol shots from an assailant not more than twenty feet from Roosevelt. A woman standing beside the man gripped his arm, thereby doubtless saving Roosevelt from fatal injury or severe wounds. Cermak was hit, and four other people were wounded, one seriously. "I'm all right! I'm all right!" Roosevelt called out. When the driver of the car started to accelerate to get him out of the frightened crowd, Roosevelt, noting that Cermak was bleeding profusely, stopped the driver, overruled the frantic Secret Service men, and ordered Cermak to be placed in the car so that he could be gotten to a hospital. At first Roosevelt could find no pulse. "I don't think he is going to last," he said to the Miami chief of detectives, who was sitting on the rear mudguard. During the trip to the hospital Roosevelt held the injured man in his arms. He waited until Cermak was brought back from the operating table, spoke reassuringly to him, and then visited the others who had been wounded by the assailant. When news of the attempted assassination reached Eleanor Roosevelt in New York, she said, "These things have to be expected." And after a phone conversation with her husband she told reporters, "He's all right. He's not the least bit excited." The man who had tried to kill him was an undersize Italian immigrant named Giuseppe Zangara, who told police he had no special animus toward Roosevelt. "I hate all Presidents," he declared, "no matter from what country they come, and I hate all officials and everybody who is rich."

Roosevelt seemed unmoved by his narrow brush with death. Back on the Astor yacht he was his usual cheerful self, "easy, confident, poised, to all appearances unmoved," Raymond Moley noted; a Secret Service agent who glanced into his bedroom later saw him in a sound, untroubled slumber. His escape unscathed lent a kind of aura of invincibility to the President-to-be. "There *is* a star," Missy LeHand said to Rexford Tugwell.

Meanwhile, the financial crisis grew more and more acute. Three weeks before the inauguration runs on Detroit banks led the governor of Michigan to declare an eight-day bank moratorium. The runs were not confined to Michigan. Between February 1 and 15 the withdrawal of gold and currency grew from $5,000,000 to $15,000,000 a day nationwide. Five thousand banks had failed in the period since the great crash. A number of states had declared bank holidays or limited withdrawals. In Louisiana Huey Long's governor, O. K. Allen, proclaimed a bank holiday "in commemoration of the sixteenth anniversary of the severance of diplomatic relations between the United States and Germany." Boston could not pay the police. Chicago had no money to pay its schoolteachers. It was estimated that one-third of the nation's work force was unemployed. "Until February," Tugwell wrote, "the sickness had been kept fairly far from the centers of finance by one means or another, but it was now reaching those well-guarded citadels, the metropolitan banks."

To recapture in a period of prosperity and well-being for most Americans the atmosphere of anxiety and dread that prevailed in the early weeks of 1933 is impossible. Even Tugwell, whose literary skills were considerable, concluded his account of the manifold ills besetting the nation with the words "Those who lived through that time and had some responsibility will always recall the narrowness of the escape from chaos."

Two weeks before the inaugural Hoover handwrote a letter to Roosevelt, declaring that in his considered opinion, the country was on the brink of financial chaos and that only a joint declaration by the outgoing and incoming Presidents could restore confidence. The letter from Hoover brought home to Raymond Moley more vividly than anything that had happened to that point the "shock of . . . reality." After the letter had been read, he looked at Roosevelt to see his reaction "in his face or manner." But there was nothing but "pleasant bantering with those who sat at the table with him. . . ." Moley thought, as he had thought at the time of the assassination attempt, that "this can't go on. . . . This is just for show." But there was no reaction of alarm or dismay then or later, when Roosevelt was alone with three or four of his closest advisers. As Moley described the situation, "Capital was fleeing the country. Hoarding was reaching unbearably high levels. The dollar was wobbling on the foreign exchanges as gold poured out."

Hoover's appeal was that Roosevelt give "prompt assurance that there will be no tampering or inflation of the currency; that the budget will be unquestionably balanced [as Hoover had not done]; that the Government credit will be maintained by refusal to exhaust it in the issue of securities." There is no reason to doubt Hoover's sincerity, but the plea was a shrewd one, designed both to tie Roosevelt's hands and vindicate Hoover's policies. That Hoover was well aware of the note's implication is verified by a letter to Senator David A. Reed several days later: "I realize that if these declarations be made by the President-elect, he will have ratified the whole program of the Republican Administration; that is, it means the abandonment of ninety percent of the so-called new deal. But unless this is done, they run a grave danger of precipitating a complete financial debacle. If it is precipitated, the responsibility lies squarely with them for they have had ample warning—unless, of course, such a debacle is part of the 'new deal.' " The letter is a curiously revealing one, written by a man who was not above playing politics with the nation's future, confident, apparently, that history would vindicate him. That he should have appealed to his soon-to-be successor to help allay the nation's fears was certainly understandable, but that he should have devised the proposed declaration with a view to compromising Roosevelt's incoming administration and justifying his own is far less creditable. We would not even be sure that those thoughts had been in his mind had he not undertaken to make them explicit in his letter to Reed.

Moley used all his influence with Roosevelt to prevent him from making any concessions on the debt issue, and when Roosevelt agreed, Moley wrote exultantly that it was his, Moley's, influence that "maintained the integrity of the debts as living obligations which . . . prevented the use of the United States as a war treasury by Europe" and had thereby "done more to stave off a general war than a dozen alliances. . . ." It was a curiously obtuse observation for a man of Moley's sophistication: the notion that the determinant in the outbreak of a European war was whether or not the United States could be counted on to finance it. In Moley's view, the position on the debts that he prevailed on Roosevelt to adopt distinguished his "foreign policy from that of the internationalists [of whom Hoover, of course, was one]" and also "served notice on the League advocates, the pro-sanctionists, and those who desired a revival of foreign lending that Roosevelt was likely to be no Herbert Hoover or Henry Stimson on foreign affairs."

Moley wrote: "Between February 18th and March 3rd, I detected nothing but the most complete confidence in his ability to deal with any situation that might arise—a confidence fed by the scandalous inability of the bankers to suggest any practical measures for blocking off the panic. . . . Roosevelt went serenely through those days on the assumption that Hoover was perfectly capable of acting without his concurrence; that there was no remedy of which we knew that was not available to the Hoover Administration. . . ." Roosevelt, in any event, had little sympathy with the bankers; they had contributed to the crisis by their reckless use of their depositors' funds. When the complaint was made that the Senate investigation into dubious or illegal banking practices was undermining public confidence in the banks, Roosevelt replied, "The bankers should have thought of that when they did the things that are being exposed now."

Just when Roosevelt became persuaded that his plans for relieving unemployment, helping the farmers, and feeding the hungry could not be reconciled with his frequently announced determination to balance the budget is unclear. When Tom Connally, the Texas Senator (whom Howe had listed in his file of influential Democrats as a man "without strong convictions, conservative. . . . Tremendously influential"), called on Roosevelt at Warm Springs, Roosevelt gave him a little lecture on fiscal soundness. Connally replied by arguing that in the crisis of the World War the nation had not hesitated to go heavily into debt in the cause of freedom. The Depression was another crisis. "If it was constitutional," Connally declared, "to spend forty billion dollars in a war isn't it just as constitutional to spend a little money to relieve the hunger and misery of our citizens?"

"When we arrived in Washington on the night of March 2nd, terror held the country in grip," Raymond Moley wrote of the arrival of the presidential party. Gold reserves were at an all-time low, and twenty-one states had total or partial bank holidays. The Federal Reserve had lost $226,000,000 in gold in four days. New York and Chicago were the last major cities where the banks stayed open, but the governors of New York and Illinois closed the banks in their states as well on the eve of Roosevelt's inauguration. Governor Ritchie of Maryland ordered the banks of that state closed also.

Hoover persisted in his efforts to pressure Roosevelt into identifying himself with his policies by some last-minute joint statement. He asked Roosevelt to come to the White House. Moley got a hasty telephone call from a Roosevelt aide. Ike Hoover, the chief usher at the White House, had whispered to Roosevelt as he entered that Hoover had his secretary of the treasury, Ogden Mills, and Eugene Meyer, governor of the Federal Reserve Board, with him. Roosevelt told the aide to summon Moley for his support. Moley rushed to the White House. "There," Moley wrote, "stood Hoover, grave, dignified, and somewhat uneasy. . . . Everyone smoked somewhat nervously, Hoover on a fat cigar." Moley was startled by Hoover's appearance; "he seems to me close to death," he told Tugwell. "He has the look of being done, but still of going on and on, driven by some damn duty."

Roosevelt stated that he would view most sympathetically anything that Hoover undertook to do to avert the impending debacle, but he would not associate himself with such action. Reports came in from around the country while they talked. Thomas Lamont, a Democratic financier, called from New York to report that the leading bankers in that city thought that the banks could hold out until noon the next day, until after Roosevelt had been sworn in as President.

Roosevelt and Moley had worked on the inaugural address at Hyde Park. Roosevelt went over Moley's text sentence by sentence and, conscious of Howe's sensitivity, made a mental note to copy the final version in his own handwriting so that Howe would not know of Moley's role. He did so on a yellow legal pad. The next day the pages were turned over to Howe, who added the clause "the only thing we have to fear is fear itself."

At the inauguration Roosevelt used his old family Bible in Dutch for the swearing-in ceremony. He then moved forward to deliver his address. "This is a day of national consecration," he began. "I am certain that my fellow Americans expect that on my induction into the Presidency I will address them with a candor and a decision which the present situation of our Nation impels. This is preeminently the time to speak the truth, the whole truth, frankly and boldly. Nor need we shrink from honestly facing conditions in our country today. This great Nation will endure as it has endured, will revive and will prosper. . . . So, first of all, let me assert my firm belief that the only thing we have to fear is fear itself. . . .

"Our distress comes from no failure of substance. . . . Plenty is at our doorstep, but a generous use of it languishes in the very sight of the supply. Primarily this is because rulers of the exchange of mankind's goods have failed through their own stubbornness and their own incompetence, have admitted their failure, and have abdicated. . . . True they have tried, but their efforts have been cast in the pattern of an outworn tradition. . . . They know only the rules of a generation of self-seekers. They have no vision, and when there is no vision the people perish.

"The money changers have fled from their high seats in the temple of our civilization. We may now restore that temple to the ancient truths. The measure of the restoration lies in the extent to which we apply social values more noble than mere monetary profit. . . . Restoration calls, however, not for changes in ethics alone. This Nation asks for action, and action now." His listeners could be sure he would "act and act quickly. . . . With this pledge taken, I assume unhesitatingly the leadership of this great army of our people dedicated to a disciplined attack upon our common problems." He hoped that "the normal balance of Executive and legislative authority" would be "wholly adequate," but if it proved not to be, he would not hesitate to ask "for temporary departure from that normal balance of public procedure. I am prepared under my constitutional duty to recommend the measures that a stricken Nation in the midst of a stricken world may require. . . ." He was prepared to ask for broad executive powers "to wage a war against the emergency, as great as the power that would be given to me if we were in fact invaded by a foreign foe." Finally, the nation could be strengthened by adversity: "These dark days will be worth all they cost us if they teach us that our true destiny is not to be ministered unto but to minister. . . .

"In this dedication of a Nation, we humbly ask the blessing of God. May He protect each and every one of us. May He guide me in the days to come."

Raymond Moley was sitting beside Eleanor Roosevelt. He said, "Well, he's taken the ship of state and he's turned it right around. We're going in the opposite direction."

Like Lincoln's first inaugural, to which it was compared, Roosevelt's resonated with biblical overtones. The "money changers" had "fled from their high seats in the temple of our civilization. . . . We may now restore that temple to the ancient truths. . . ." The eleventh chapter of the Gospel according to St. Mark tells of the arrival of Jesus at Jerusalem to endure his trial and persecution. There he went to the temple and drove out the money changers, excoriating the priests for having made the temple a "den of thieves." It was this act, which struck at the wealth and privileges of the priests, which caused them to seek "how they might destroy him: for they feared him, because all the people were astonished at his doctrine." The analogy between the corrupt priests of the temple in Jerusalem and the financiers and corporate tycoons who had betrayed their trust was inescapable.

The injunction to Americans to "minister" to each other came also from the Gospel according to Mark. Jesus told his disciples that "whosoever will be great among you, shall be your minister. And whosoever of you will be the chiefest, shall be servant of all. For even the Son of man came not to be ministered unto, but to minister and to give his life a ransom for many."

To Frances Perkins the inaugural had an unique significance that set it apart from Roosevelt's other speeches and addresses. Whenever she mentioned it to him, she noted, he would talk of it in a way "that made you realize you were on sacred ground so far as he was concerned. He would never claim credit for that. It was something not of his own making. I'm sure he thought of it," she wrote years later, "as direct divine guidance."

Aubrey Williams, a member of the new administration, recalled his emotions on hearing Roosevelt's inaugural address. The "government suddenly became real. He brought me into a circle which in many ways was totally new. It was a mutual community . . . with the government . . . becoming my government—a joined and connected amorphous mass, a continuum. In short he made me a member of the nation. I belonged."

Eleanor Roosevelt called the inauguration ceremony "a little terrifying . . . because when Franklin got to that part of his speech when he said it might be necessary for him to assume powers extraordinarily granted to a President in wartime, he received his biggest demonstration."

The fact was that all across the political spectrum there had been calls for the newly elected President to assume dictatorial powers. *Barron's,* the weekly business journal, espoused "a mild species of dictatorship," and Walter Lippmann in his columns exhorted the new President to pay as little attention to Congress as possible. "The situation is critical, Franklin," Lippmann told him. "You have no alternative but to assume dictatorial powers." Indeed, it was as though the country, in some collective manner, were beseeching him to become a benign dictator and save it from itself. Certainly the phenomenon, if new to the United States, was familiar enough in the long reaches of history. The Founding Fathers had been spurred to draft the framework of a Federal government by the fear that the hard times and general demoralization that followed the American Revolution would create sentiment for a dictator or king; there had been hundreds of thousands of Americans who hoped that Washington would assume such a role.

In the inaugural parade Gifford Pinchot, governor of Pennsylvania, was conspicuous in his grand governor's limousine. It must have given the old man a special thrill to see his *second* disciple in the White House, a man as devoutly committed to the Pinchot principles of conservation as his cousin Theodore had been.

For four hours the parade streamed by while Roosevelt sat on a shooting stick or stood with the aid of his crutches, smiling and waving to the marchers. With his feeling for ceremonial events, he knew what a parade could do for the drooping spirits of a people. Especially important to Roosevelt were the fourteen boys and girls who were victims of polio and had been invited to come from Warm Springs for the inauguration.

Edmund Wilson described the inauguration in a sardonic, contemptuous tone. The White House looked like "a replica of itself in white rubber. . . . The people seem dreary and are curiously apathetic. . . . They wait in the park in front of the Capitol. . . . They wait till they see Roosevelt's dim figure on the platform on the Capitol steps, hear dimly the accents of his voice—then the crowd rapidly thins." To Wilson "the phrases of the speech seem shadowy—the echoes of Woodrow Wilson's eloquence without Wilson's exaltation behind them. The old unctuousness, the old pulpit vagueness. . . . The old Wilsonian professions of plain-speaking followed by the old abstractions. . . . There is a warning, itself rather vague, of a possible dictatorship."

The inaugural parade appeared to Wilson simply bizarre, a parade of clowns. After the bands and the planes flying over the reviewing stand, "the procession crazily degenerates . . . [and] as the weather grows darker and more ominous, the parade becomes more fantastic. . . . Comic lodges and marching clubs go by. Men appear in curled-up shoes and fezzes, dressed in hideous greens, purples, and reds. Indians, terribly fat, with terribly made-up squaws. A very large old Negro in a purple fez and yellow-edged cloak. . . . An uncanny music now tickles the ear, the ambiguous figures loom out of Little Nemo's Adventures in Slumberland . . . a drunk with Leon Errol rubber legs, who ricochets back and forth and shakes hands with people on the sidelines. . . . You are glad when it is over. . . . The America it represented has burst, and as you watched the marchers, you realized that it had been getting sillier and sillier all the time."

Wilson's report on the inaugural told more about his state of mind and that of his fellow writers of the left than it told about the event itself. His point was that the zany, eccentric America represented by the parade was over and unregretted, at least by him. It had "burst." The new revolutionary order, its form as yet not clearly perceived, was waiting in the wings. The inauguration of the new President was not a new opportunity for America but a meaningless pageant, an interlude in the vast movement of history toward the future foretold by Marx and Engels.

The comments of the liberal press on the inaugural address were, in the main, unflattering. Bruce Bliven wrote in the *New Republic:* "In none of this is there anything surprising to those who understand Mr.

Roosevelt's character or followed closely his speeches in the campaign. . . . Much of his inaugural address has an odd sound, as though it were not a statement by the President to the people, but a statement to a President by, let us say, an editorial writer or an expert press agent, telling him what line would be most popular just now."

In the words of the historian Richard Hofstadter, "When Hoover bumbled that it was necessary only to restore confidence, the nation laughed bitterly. When Roosevelt said: 'The only thing we have to fear is fear itself,' essentially the same threadbare half-true idea, the nation was thrilled." Hofstadter and like-minded intellectuals wanted a bold program of socialism outlined; anything less was simply the propping up of an outworn and discredited economic system.

Roosevelt, with his fondness for ceremony, decided to have the entire Cabinet, accompanied by families, sworn in in the Oval Office by Supreme Court Justice Benjamin Cardozo. Again he used his old Dutch family Bible. "No cabinets have ever been sworn in before in this way," he announced. "I am happy to do it because it gives the families of the new cabinet an opportunity to see the ceremony. It is my intention to inaugurate precedents like this from time to time." Frances Perkins, he announced, would be addressed as "Madam Secretary."

After the swearing in, Roosevelt asked the new Cabinet members to join him at St. John's Episcopal Church across Lafayette Square from the White House for a service of prayer to start his administration. Endicott Peabody, his old headmaster from Groton days, had been invited to officiate. Two of Roosevelt's favorite hymns were included in the service: "Oh God Our Help in Ages Past" and "Faith of Our Fathers." Peabody prayed: "May Thy son Franklin, chosen to be our President, and all of his advisers, be enlightened and strengthened for Thy service." When the service was over, Roosevelt remained for a few moments in prayer.

The head of the White House Secret Service noted that the White House was instantly transformed "into a gay place, full of people who oozed confidence. . . . The President was the most happy and confident of them all." Seventy-five Roosevelt relatives, including Theodore Roosevelt's three children—Archie, Kermit, and Alice Longworth—assembled.

FDR worked far into the night with William Woodin and Homer Cummings on the bank holiday proclamation. The atmosphere grew, in Moley's words, "indescribably tense." Even Roosevelt's nerves were taut. After the meeting broke up, the lights in the Treasury building burned far into the night as Secretary Woodin, frail and in bad health, sat with a hastily improvised staff pouring over reports from around the country and discussing the detailed provisions for a national bank holiday. They had already agreed that it should include a prohibition against the withdrawal, transfer, or domestic use of gold and silver. A critically important question concerned the provision under which the President was to claim the authority to close the banks. Although there was "furious disagreement about purposes and methods," there emerged a consensus that the order closing the banks should stress that conventional banking methods—nothing "unusual or highly controversial"—would be followed. At the end of the "holiday" as many banks as possible should be allowed to open. It was also agreed that the "reputedly left-wing presidential advisers"—Berle, Tugwell, and Moley—should be "blacked out." The notion of issuing scrip in place of money seemed to have a curious appeal. Will Woodin inclined to it, and when the little Treasury band scattered late on Monday night, the opinion had tilted in its favor, but Tuesday morning, when Moley came to have breakfast with Woodin, the secretary of the treasury cried out triumphantly, "I've got it! I've got it!"

"Got what?" the startled Moley asked.

"Well, after you left, I played my guitar a little while and then read a little while and then slept a little while and then awakened and then thought about this scrip thing and then played some more and read some more and slept some more and thought some more. And, by gum, if I didn't hit on the answer that way! . . . We don't have to issue scrip. . . . We don't need it. These bankers have hypnotized themselves and us. We can issue currency against the sound assets of the banks. The Reserve Act lets us print all we need. And it won't frighten people. It won't look like stage money. It'll be money that looks like money." And so it was.

The next morning the executive mansion seemed to Roosevelt strangely deserted. Here he was at last in the office toward which his ambition had so long yearned, faced with the greatest crisis in the nation's history since the Civil War, to test whether, in Lincoln's words "a nation so conceived . . . can . . . endure." Everywhere around the world the political tide was flowing toward dictatorships of the right or left. Millions of Americans feared and many hoped that what had been called capitalism or Americanism was at an end, crumbling away in the face of economic problems with which it seemed unable to deal. Now the task was on his shoulders.

January 30, 1933, five weeks before the inauguration, was Roosevelt's birthday. It was also the day that Adolf Hitler became chancellor of Germany. Of Hitler's accession to power in Germany, the *New York Times* reported: "Herr Hitler was maneuvered into a coalition government of the National Socialists and Nationalists by Lieutenant-Colonel Franz von Papen, former Chancellor." Hitler at once called for new elections. In the campaign he made skillful use of the government's radio network under the control of Hermann Göring. When it still appeared that the Nazis would lose, the National Socialists (Nazis) set fire to the Reichstag, or Parliament, Building and laid the blame on the Communists. Hitler persuaded President von Hindenburg to issue a decree suspending civil liberties. Armed with that document, Hitler had some 4,000 Communist officials arrested. Many were tortured and beaten, and all were herded into concentration camps.

# 19

## Roosevelt's Special Session of Congress

Roosevelt had prepared two dramatic initial steps to begin his administration. The first was to declare a nationwide bank closing, or, as it was euphemistically called, a holiday, to give public fears a chance to subside and to allow the banks to put their own houses in order; the other was a call to Congress for a special session to pass a series of bills designed to alleviate the economic distress.

It had been Secretary Woodin's inspiration to "issue currency against the sound assets of the banks." The result was the Emergency Banking Act, which authorized the Treasury to print sufficient currency to assure that depositors could get money when it was needed.

Roosevelt, who as governor of New York had used radio fireside chats to rally public support for his legislation, followed the same procedure with the nation. It was estimated that some 60,000,000 people were tuned in at ten o'clock on that Sunday evening in March when Roosevelt began to speak in his informal, reassuring way. "I want to talk for a few minutes with the people of the United States about banking. . . . I want to tell you what has been done in the last few days, why it was done and what the next steps are going to be." People should put their money back in the banks. It would be safe there, Roosevelt assured them, far safer than under a mattress. "Let us unite

437

in banishing fear," he concluded. "We have provided the machinery to restore our financial system; it is up to you to support and make it work. It is your problem no less than it is mine. Together we cannot fail."

There was much inconvenience as a consequence of the closing of the banks. Many people, among them some of the nation's wealthiest individuals, were caught without cash. Subway tokens, stamps, and IOUs took the place of hard money. "This is the happiest day in three years," Will Rogers declared. "We have no jobs, we have no money, we have no banks; and if Roosevelt had burned down the Capitol, we would have said, 'Thank God, he started a fire under something.' "

When the New York Stock Exchange opened on Wednesday, there was a sharp rise in prices; the first words printed on the ticker tape were "Happy Days Are Here Again."

Although the Emergency Banking Act, drafted by Woodin, was a startling financial innovation, Congress, when it convened on March 9, was in no mood to dally, and after a half hour of desultory debate, the bill was approved by a large margin. In the Senate La Follette objected that there were not enough restraints on the banks, but the bill was approved, 73 to 7, before the day was over.

The results of the bank holiday were startling. It had been anticipated that even with Roosevelt's appeal the need for cash at the end of the four-day holiday (which, in fact, was six days when the weekend was counted) would result in substantial withdrawals, but $10,000,000 more were deposited than withdrawn. Moreover, 75 percent of the banks that had closed opened. The California banks were generally shaky, but Woodin ordered enough of them opened to prevent dislocation of the state's economy. "The week before inauguration," Tugwell wrote, "was one of despair. The sinking spell seemed to be more and more beyond human control and fright was almost palpably present in the air. The week after the inauguration, the reversal was like the incoming of an ocean tide in high latitudes." Moley put it more succinctly: "Capitalism was saved in eight days." Certainly the psychological effects were profound. If the question of whether or not capitalism was "saved" by the closing of the banks must remain moot, it is clearly the case that the New Deal program in general rode on the back of the success of the "holiday." One might indeed say that since the impetus given to the entire New Deal by the bank holiday "saved" capitalism, Moley was not too far off the mark.

The bank bill was followed by "A Bill to Maintain the Credit of the United States," which had been drafted by Lewis Douglas, director of the budget. The bill gave the President authority to cut more than $100,000,000 from government salaries and $400,000,000 from veterans' pensions and compensation with the hope of balancing the budget. Many Democrats deserted the President on the economy bill. When trouble loomed in the Senate, it occurred to Roosevelt that the chances for its passage might be improved if it were accompanied by a bill making beer and wine legal. The strategy worked. In the enthusiasm created by the prospect of once again being able to quaff those consoling beverages unimpeded by the law, the bill was approved. It helped lay to rest, at least for the moment, the fears of the business community that Roosevelt was a wild-eyed radical.

On March 14, at breakfast at the White House, Frances Perkins described her plan for grants-in-aid to the states for work relief, a plan to be incorporated in a bill being drafted by Wagner, La Follette, and Edward Costigan. According to Moley, when he reported the proposal to Roosevelt, the President replied with "the stunning idea of putting an army of young men, recruited from the unemployed, to work in forests and national parks." Moley reminded Roosevelt of William James's essay "The Moral Equivalent of War." Had Roosevelt perhaps picked up the notion from James when he was a student at Harvard? In Moley's words, "He admitted there might be some connection, though he wasn't consciously aware of it." The problem with Moley's story is that Roosevelt had instituted a similar program while he was governor of New York. Tugwell, Perkins, and others in the administration had been pressing the President since the inauguration for a direct relief bill. Roosevelt, uneasy about the cost, had resisted. The Civilian Conservation Corps proposal opened the way for the consideration of other relief measures. When the draft bill for the CCC was sent to the secretaries of agriculture, war, and the interior, they replied urging a "package" of relief measures—"the whole program of relief for industrial unemployment." The secretaries wrote: "We are of the opinion that there are three items to be considered in this program." The other two were direct relief payments and public works. Three days of discussion followed.

What emerged was a twofold plan for dealing with the massive unemployment. First was "relief" that is to say, payments by the Federal government through the states and municipalities to individuals and families that were actually in danger of starving to death. The other was "work relief" in the form of jobs created by undertaking necessary "public works." The relief was money paid out on an emergency basis without hope of return. It was intended not only to assist individuals in desperate need but to pump money into the moribund economy. Public works, on the other hand, would be undertaken in conjunction with particular states and municipalities, with the states and cities submitting proposals to be approved by the Federal government and providing, through bond issues, a substantial percentage of the cost, an amount usually ranging from 30 to 60 percent. Federal government subsidies would provide the balance. It was a requirement that the workers employed on public works projects must come from the rolls of the unemployed. The advantage of public works over relief was that as a project was completed and its cost began to be amortized through bond retirement, the government would be repaid at least a portion of its subsidy.

It was estimated that some $3,000,000,000 in various public works projects could be started in six months; among them were road repair, low-cost housing, public bathrooms, and projects aimed at getting electricity to farms. Lewis Douglas was the principal opponent in the Cabinet. The crucial debate, in Perkins's mind, was over whether public works, referred to as Title II, should be included in a general bill designed to stimulate industrial recovery. If public works were separated from what emerged as the National Industrial Recovery Act (NIRA), Perkins was convinced the proposal would be defeated in Congress. That was also Lewis Douglas's conviction and he tried to prevail on Roosevelt to present it in a separate bill for that reason. Charles Wyzanski, a young Baltimore lawyer whom Perkins had signed on as a Department of Labor attorney, was present when Perkins prevailed on Roosevelt to accept Title II as part of a "recovery" act being drafted by Hugh Johnson (and half a dozen others). "This really is a most revealing thing," Wyzanski told Perkins as they left the President. "I've studied law. I've studied political science. I never could have conceived that important matters were settled like this, but this is the way the government operates apparently."

On March 19 Roosevelt gave Moley a handwritten outline of his message to Congress to accompany the proposed Civilian Conservation Corps legislation. The CCC combined Roosevelt's passion for reforestation with his and Eleanor's concern for young people, especially for unemployed youth. The intention was to put some 250,000 young men in camps spread throughout the nation's forests to do flood control and soil conservation work under the direction of experienced foresters. The camps themselves were to be organized on semimilitary lines to ensure proper discipline and to be run by reserve officers recruited for the purpose. The legislation passed Congress on March 31, and in a few weeks the first camp was started in Luray, Virginia. Some 2,500 enrollees (who had to pass a "means test" asserting that they were unemployed and, in effect, destitute) turned out dressed in ill-fitting army surplus uniforms left over from the World War. It would be almost a year before each was issued his handsome CCC uniform of forest green with a green and yellow shoulder patch. In the eastern United States many of the initial enrollees were juvenile delinquents from the larger cities—Boston, New York, Philadelphia, and Baltimore—who had been in trouble with the law in varying degrees for petty crimes and were given the option by a judge of going to reform school or to the "Three Cs," as the camps were soon called. Enrollees received $1 a day for their healthy, outdoor labors, but aside from pocket money, the balance of their pay was sent to their parents to help them make ends meet or, if possible, to be put away for the end of the enrollees' terms of enlistment.

The CCC was loudly, if belatedly, opposed by labor. William Green declared that it smacked "of fascism, of Hitlerism, of a form of Sovietism." The Congress that passed such a bill would be execrated as one that had "established a dollar a day wage for the payment of labor on the public domain." The official Communist position was that the corps undertook "to establish and legalize a system of forced labor."

A flood of legislation meanwhile threatened to inundate Congress. Hardly a day passed without a new bill finding its way into the congressional hopper. On March 16 the Agricultural Adjustment Act, the work primarily of Wallace and Tugwell, was presented to Congress. Bitterly criticized, it nonetheless laid the groundwork for agricultural policy for the next half century or more. Tugwell had proposed such a plan to Roosevelt while he was still governor of New York. It provided for an allotment system and paid the farmer subsidies for restricting the number of acres that he planted. When Roosevelt presented the bill to Congress, his accompanying message declared, "I warn you that this is a new and untrod path." If it were the wrong one, he would be the first to acknowledge the fact, he assured that body. Underlying the Triple-A in Moley's words was the "revolutionary assumption of public responsibility for the economic well-being of the thirty-million farmers and farm dependents of the nation."

The Federal Emergency Relief Act (FERA) was submitted to Con-

gress on March 22 and passed six weeks later. It provided for
$500,000,000 in Federal funds to be disbursed to the states to initiate
work programs for the unemployed. In the debate over the bill, Congressman Robert Luce of Massachusetts declared, "It is socialism.
Whether it is communism or not I do not know," and Simeon D. Fess
of Ohio could hardly find "parliamentary language to describe the
statement that the States and cities cannot take care of conditions in
which they find themselves but must come to the Federal Government
for aid."

Harry Hopkins, who had headed Roosevelt's Temporary Emergency Relief Administration in New York State, waited impatiently to
be summoned to Washington and given, he hoped, a similar assignment. He had come to Washington with an aide a few days after the
inauguration to show Frances Perkins "a plan for the immediate appropriation by the Federal Government of grants-in-aid to the states
for unemployment relief." In Perkins's words, "I was impressed by the
exactness of their knowledge and the practicability of their plan." But
weeks passed without the expected call. Finally, in May, when the FERA
had passed a reluctant Congress, Hopkins was summoned to Washington to become head of the Federal counterpart of the state agency
he had headed; the word "Federal" had replaced "Temporary," and
there were, of course, vastly larger sums to be spent. It was a dizzy
ascent for someone of Hopkins's background. His mature life had been
spent as a social worker. He had little political experience and no
political constituency. His friends were co-workers in the world of
philanthropy and reform. Some were, to be sure, wealthy and powerful
men, but Hopkins stood in relation to them as employee to employer.
Although he was highly intelligent and had considerable charm, his
physical presence was far from impressive; he had acquired the ca-
daverous look that was the mark of his indifferent health. Someone
described him as having the "sardonic manner of a bored police court
judge who has heard it all before," and Joseph E. Davies spoke of him
as combining "the purity of St. Francis of Assisi with the sharp shrewdness of a race track tout."

Frances Perkins felt that Hopkins could be "arrogant, cynical,
ungrateful, self-centered—almost anything bad." But like Roosevelt,
he was intuitive, and his intuitions were often sounder than his reasoned analyses. He believed that the "present system" was "capable of
giving to all its workers those things which are now the expectations
of a comparative few: a warm, decent place to live in; a liberal diet;

suitable clothes; travel, vacations, automobiles, radios, and college educations for those who want them."

Of Hopkins's sympathy with the poor and oppressed there could be no question, but prudence was foreign to his nature. People were in want, hungry and ill housed. They must be provided for; it was as simple as that. He set up shop in a run-down commercial building on New York Avenue. It was ostentatiously seedy, in need of paint, with exposed heating pipes and a carpetless floor. Without waiting for furniture to be moved into his office, he began business in the hall outside, and by evening he had made grants to six states—Illinois, Iowa, Michigan, Mississippi, Texas, and Colorado. "I'm not going to last six months here, so I'll do as I please," he announced. Under the headline "Money Flies" the *Washington Post* editorialized: "The half-billion dollars for direct relief of States won't last a month if Harry L. Hopkins, the new relief administrator, maintains the pace he set yesterday in disbursing more than $5,000,000 during his first two hours in office."

The journalist Marquis Childs wrote that when he finally got to see Hopkins, "he had a sort of trapped look. . . . He barricaded himself behind his shabby desk, his feet up, inhaling deeply on a cigarette, snarling back at his persecutors [the press]." Oddly the press liked him despite his defensiveness. "He was rarely tactful or tactical," Childs noted, and reporters, accustomed to discreet evasions, appreciated his bluntness. "Only half trying, you could get out of him a fine, angry contempt for all that was contented and Republican. It was an act, but on the whole it was a good act. He was sensitive, impressionable, and he looked as though he belonged on the other side of the desk from his tormentors," Childs concluded. He was so obviously not the typical bureaucrat, and he skillfully cultivated the maverick style.

A bill to create the Farm Credit Administration was sent to Congress a week after the Federal Emergency Relief Act. It combined a number of agencies with responsibilities for farm relief into one, and an accompanying bill—the Farm Mortgage Act—authorized Federal loans to farmers in danger of losing their farms through foreclosure.

As the President explained what came to be called the Truth in Securities Act, which was sent to Congress two days after the proposed farm legislation, "This proposal adds to the ancient rule of *caveat emptor* [let the buyer beware!] the further doctrine 'Let the seller also beware.' It puts the burden of telling the whole truth upon the seller." The Federal Trade Commission was made the policeman of the securities market. Anyone who wished to sell securities was required to provide detailed information to the commission. False statements could result in severe penalties.

Roosevelt had long been an advocate of public power. He believed that government initiative should be used on energy projects too vast to attract private capital or covering several different states. The "father" of the idea of a "regional authority" to make and sell cheap power and, indeed, to enhance the lives of inhabitants in the entire area through government planning was Senator George Norris, the old-time Progressive from Nebraska. During the war the Federal government had built a hydroelectric plant at Muscle Shoals on the Tennessee River to provide power for a nearby munitions factory. When attempts to sell the Muscle Shoals facility to private power companies failed, Norris set out to establish a model of public power in the Tennessee Valley. He steered legislation through Congress in May, 1928, and three years later in March, 1931, but Coolidge vetoed the first bill, and Hoover the second.

Roosevelt, while still governor of New York, showed a strong interest in the development of public power and lent a sympathetic ear t Norris's plan for a large public power complex extending over parts f North Carolina, Kentucky, Virginia, Mississippi, Tennessee, and Alabama that would involve land reclamation, conservation, flood control, and the reforestation of marginal farming lands withdrawn from use. It was just the kind of scheme that appealed to Roosevelt's visionary idealism.

During the campaign of 1932 Eleanor Roosevelt had accompanied her husband through the Tennessee Valley, primarily at the instance of Norris. The crowds that waited at the train stations had seemed to the Roosevelts particularly poor and undernourished. "Their houses were unpainted, their cars dilapidated, and many grownups as well as children without shoes or adequate garments," Eleanor Roosevelt wrote. Franklin and Eleanor Roosevelt both were much affected by the poverty of the region. Roosevelt promised Norris to push for legislation to set up the Tennessee Valley project.

Submitted to Congress on April 19, a bill establishing the Tennessee Valley Authority was hurried through Congress in slightly more than five weeks. No single piece of New Deal legislation aroused more fear and anger in the breasts of those Americans who believed that Roosevelt was, in all but name, an agent of the Kremlin, a Bolshevik in the disguise of a gentleman farmer. No single act of Congress, with the possible exception of the Civilian Conservation Corps, more clearly symbolized the radically innovative character of the new administration or was acclaimed a greater success by the general public.

Three days after the passage of the Tennessee Valley bill, Congress received the Home Owners' Loan Act which, like the Farm Mortgage Act, was designed to save the homes of the unemployed from foreclosure. It has been calculated that millions of mortgaged homes were saved by the act.

Meantime, the President was faced with an acute fiscal crisis. When banks opened after the holiday, prices had continued to fall. Any notion of inflation was anathema to conservatives, but deflation caused severe hardship, especially among farmers, and proinflation forces combined in an organization called the Committee for the Nation. Once more the free coinage of silver faction raised its by now hoary head; its leader was Burton K. Wheeler, Senator from the silver state of Montana. Will Woodin listened patiently to Wheeler's arguments and later composed "Lullaby in Silver" on his piano and played it for Raymond Moley. The only questions were, in Walter Lippmann's words, "how inflation was to be produced and whether or not it could be managed and controlled."

In addition to the problem of deflation, and related to it, was a growing drain of U.S. gold reserves. The loss of gold through shipment abroad to foreign investors reached $250,000,000 in the week before the inaugural. Roosevelt reportedly asked William Bullitt what should be done to check deflation and stop the drain of gold, and Bullitt promptly replied, "Go off gold." Senator Key Pittman gave the same advice. Raymond Moley echoed it, and when the secretary of the treasury, Will Woodin, appeared, Roosevelt hailed him: "Hello, Will, we have just gone off gold." The startled secretary replied, "Have we?" When Roosevelt informed a group of government advisers of his intention, "hell broke loose in the room," in Moley's words. Lewis Douglas and James Warburg "began to scold Mr. Roosevelt as though he were a perverse and particularly backward schoolboy." Douglas expressed the opinion that such a step would cause panic in the money markets. When Roosevelt made it clear that he was determined to proceed, Douglas turned to Warburg and said, "This is the end of Western civilization." Bernard Baruch called it a victory for "mob rule," which, he predicted, would help only the "unemployed, debtor classes—incompetent, unwise people."

To reassure a glum Secretary of State Hull, Roosevelt took a $10 Bill out of his pocket, noted it was issued by a bank in Hull's home state of Tennessee, and said, "How do I know it's any good? Only the fact that I think it is makes it so."

After the meeting had broken up, Douglas and Warburg wandered along the Washington streets until five in the morning, when they returned to their hotel and awakened Bill Bullitt to discuss with him the terrible consequences that lay ahead as a result of the President's decision. On April 19, Roosevelt issued an executive order forbidding the export of gold and making it no longer the support of the dollar. The Thomas amendment passed the Senate nine days later by a vote of 64 to 21 and the House a week later by 307 to 86. It authorized the President to negotiate with the Reserve banks to sell government obligations on the open market and buy Treasury bills up to the value of $3,000,000,000, to issue greenbacks (unsupported by gold) to the sum of $3,000,000,000 to retire outstanding Federal obligations, to reduce the gold content of the dollar up to 50 percent, and to fix the ratio between gold and silver. While Roosevelt was praised and reviled for taking the United States off the gold standard, Raymond Moley remained convinced that he had done so "only to circumvent uncontrolled inflation by Congress."

Undersecretary of the Treasury Dean Acheson disagreed strongly with the President's policy on gold and resigned. Woodin, plagued by health problems, resigned also and was succeeded as secretary of the Treasury by Henry Morgenthau. Morgenthau had originally hoped to be secretary of agriculture, as noted.

To anyone familiar with the role of gold in the nation's history, Roosevelt's decision to go off the gold standard was one of the most significant of the century. Generation after generation gold had had the sanctity of divine law to millions of Americans, many of them creditors. To accept any other basis for the currency would be, they believed, to invite divine retribution in the form of runaway inflation and economic disaster. To other millions, gold was the cross on which rapacious capitalists had nailed farmers specifically and debtors generally. Gold and the devil and 10 percent interest were in league to pillage the nation. No issue had inflamed political (and even theological) passions more fiercely and persistently from the beginning of the Republic. Elections had been won and lost on the issue; new parties had been formed for no other ostensible reason than to fight for "silver" or "greenbacks" and against gold. One of the greatest politicians of the age—William Jennings Bryan—had risen to international fame on the issue and tied his party to it in one disastrous presidential election after another. Now, in the face of unprecedented economic disaster, gold was abandoned almost incidentally. J. P. Morgan the Younger was quoted as supporting the move. Opposition was confined largely to gloomy mutterings in board rooms and such centers of reaction as Union League Clubs.

One of the side effects of Roosevelt's taking the United States off the gold standard was that it prompted the return of the last of the American expatriates living in Europe, most commonly in Paris or Rome. John Peale Bishop, Edmund Wilson's Princeton classmate and close friend, was among the returnees. Louis Bromfield bought a farm in Ohio, his home state. One of the last returnees was Harold Stearns, who had achieved a kind of mythical status as an expatriate through such books as *America and the Young Intellectual*. Too poor to afford a steamship ticket, Stearns appealed to the American Aid Society, which got him passage home on a freighter.

While Roosevelt was authorized to fix the ration between gold and silver, there were no guidelines to how this was to be done. The consequence was considerable fluctuation in the value of the dollar. A gold purchase plan was devised by George Warren, a Cornell professor. It was Warren's theory that if the government bought up substantial amounts of "new" gold and then raised the price periodically and unpredictably, the value of the dollar would be lowered and the price of farm commodities raised proportionately. In October Roosevelt adopted the Warren plan. The method followed by the President and his closest financial advisers in setting the daily price of an ounce of gold was described by Henry Morgenthau. One typical morning, when Morgenthau proposed 19 cents an ounce, Roosevelt countered with 21 cents on the ground that 21 was three times seven and seven was a lucky number. "If anybody ever knew how we really set the gold price through a combination of lucky numbers, etc., I think they would really be frightened," Morgenthau wrote. On January 15, 1934, three months later, the President swore off the Warren plan and asked for a stabilization fund of $2,000,000,000.

Not all so-called New Deal legislation was proposed by the administration. Senator Hugo Black of Alabama introduced a bill on April 6 to cut the workweek from forty-eight hours to thirty. The idea was to create more jobs by reducing the hours of labor. Roosevelt was wary of the bill, believing that the result would simply be lower pay for those still employed. But the Black bill brought to the fore the issue of measures designed specifically to stimulate industry. Rather reluctantly

Roosevelt turned his attention to that problem. He found himself besieged by advisers of various, and often diametrically opposed, persuasions as well as by very different "interests." The spokesmen of labor wanted, above all, work, if not from industry, then from the government in the form of vast public works projects. They also demanded that the Federal government throw its weight behind the principle of industry-wide collective bargaining. The captains of industry, on the other hand, badly demoralized as they were, wanted government assistance in the form of loans and incentives and what they perceived as possible stimuli to business activity. Above all, they wanted labor kept in a dependent and supine state. "Labor" was their problem, not the government's.

Faced by the challenge of Hugo Black's thirty-hour-a-week bill, Roosevelt assigned Hugh Johnson the task of writing a substitute designed to avoid the pitfalls of Black's proposed legislation. Moley found a desk for Johnson in his office, and as he later recalled, "Hugh took off his coat and necktie, unbuttoned the collar of his shirt, and sat down. That was the beginning of the N.R.A." Soon Johnson found that Roosevelt had given the same assignment to half a dozen others— Secretary of Labor Perkins, Senator Wagner, Tugwell, and the labor lawyer, Donald Richberg. Presented with half a dozen different proposals, Roosevelt ordered their authors to "get together, shut themselves up in the room, iron out their differences, and come back to him with a bill." The outcome was the National Industrial Recovery Act, the NIRA as it was called.

Theodore Roosevelt had proposed a partnership between government and business in the Bull Moose campaign of 1912, hoping thereby to reassure the business interests. Woodrow Wilson, on the other hand, had favored what might be called an adversary relationship with business, arguing that government's proper role was to regulate business and particularly to prevent it from growing so big that it could not be regulated. As FDR's inner circle debated the various versions of the National Industrial Recovery Act, one member of the group said to Roosevelt, "You realize . . . that you're taking an enormous step away from the philosophy of equalitarianism and laissez-faire?" The President replied after a moment of reflection: "If that philosophy hadn't proved to be bankrupt, Herbert Hoover would be sitting here right now. I never felt surer of anything in my life than I do of the soundness of this."

When the President took to the airwaves to explain to the American people the philosophy behind the National Industrial Recovery Act, he assured his "friends and fellow-citizens" that the government would go into partnership with business and industry. Under its terms businessmen and industrialists could form trade organizations and devise their own rules. The President denounced unfair labor practices, long hours, and child labor. In certain areas—he used cotton as an example—the government had to intervene to assure decent conditions of labor. In the process of experimenting with new methods to meet the crisis, he did not expect to make a hit every time he came to bat. Some of the measures would doubtless fail of their purpose, but the important thing was to keep trying for hits until the game was won. "The old reliance on the free action of individual wills" was no longer adequate. The intervention of "that organized control which we call government seems necessary to produce the same results of justice and right conduct" that were "formerly achieved by the ethical conduct of individuals." While Roosevelt spoke reassuringly of a partnership, the NIRA provided that if the representatives of a particular industry could not agree on hours, wages, production and marketing quotas, etc., the government could impose its own code. The NIRA, by suspending the antitrust laws, challenged business to replace competition with cooperation.

Section 7(a), which guaranteed labor's right to collective bargaining and union organizing, was the most enduring and significant part of the NIRA. Largely the work of Senator Robert Wagner of New York, Section 7(a) came to be known as Labor's Bill of Rights.

Almost as important as Section 7(a) was the provision of Title II, which authorized a $3,300,000,000 public works program. The purpose of Title II was both to provide work for the unemployed and to create purchasing power as a stimulus to business. The comprehensiveness of the bill was both its strength and weakness. It dramatized the notion of the partnership between government and business of which we have already spoken, a partnership which seemed to many businessmen more window dressing than reality, more appearance than substance. On the other hand, it made the NIRA vulnerable to attack from the left. To those already convinced that Roosevelt was sweeping the country toward socialism/communism, the bill was confirmation of their worst fears; it envisioned a governmental involvement in the economy on an unprecedented scale. Will Woodin made no bones about his opposition to the NIRA. He told Harold Ickes that "the big financial men in New York were all down in the mouth . . . As they look at it, it [the NIRA] is going to put the country entirely in the hands of labor."

Perhaps more than any other piece of early New Deal legislation, the National Industrial Recovery Act bore the imprimatur of the disbanded Brain Trust. It had been Roosevelt's notion for some time that there might be worked out a plan for cooperation between government and industry that would provide for a degree of Federal supervision and regulation but would, essentially, involve cooperation by specific industries in establishing fair prices and wages and sensible levels of production. Such partnerships seemed to him a logical alternative to the ruinous competition of the marketplace. Since the days of populism there had been talk of a new era of cooperation rather than competition. Now, Roosevelt believed, with the economy in disarray caused at least in part by the competitive—some would have said predatory and exploitative—activities of business, the time had come to try cooperation. Under the spur and lash of the Depression, business and industrial leaders might at last be prevailed upon to modify their ethic of rugged individualism—in Darwinian terms, the survival of the fittest—for a more rational and harmonious approach. As Moley put it, the NIRA embodied "the idea of substituting, for the futile attempt to control the abuses of anarchic private economic power, . . . a policy of cooperative business-government planning to combat the instability of economic operations and the insecurity of livelihood . . . [and] it was the duty of government to devise, with business, the means of social and individual adjustment to the facts of the industrial age. . . . Its fundamental purpose was . . . to modify the characteristics of a chaotic competitive system that could and did produce sweatshops, child labor, rackets, ruinous price cutting, a devastated agriculture and a score of other blights," as evident in boomtime as in depression. It was no less than the blueprint of a new national economy, a radical (or, more accurately, a conservative) reordering of traditional capitalism—national socialism or state capitalism. Determined to increase the cost of farm products and thereby improve the economic status of the farmers, Roosevelt believed that his farm program must be accompanied by a "parallel stimulation of industrial activity," in Moley's words. It was this that the NIRA was designed to accomplish.

While the House of Representatives, now thoroughly under Roosevelt's spell, passed the NIRA with little debate, serious opposition developed in the Senate, not all of it from conservatives. Old Progressives attacked the bill on the ground that by suspending the antitrust laws, it would encourage the consolidation of capital and damage the interests of the workingman and workingwoman and the middle class as well. Hugo Black declared: "This bill, if it shall pass and become law, will transfer the lawmaking power of this nation, insofar as control of industry is concerned, from Congress to the trade associations. There is no escape from that conclusion. That is really what happened in Italy, and as a result, the legislation passed by the parliamentary body of Italy, as expressed by one economist, has reached the vanishing point."

It was not surprising that perceptive individuals like Louis Brandeis and Hugo Black, whose liberal credentials were unshakable and who were friendly to both Roosevelt and the general goals of the New Deal, were alarmed. To them it seemed that despite his antibusiness rhetoric, Roosevelt's solution to the Depression was to hand power to the men who had, in large measure, brought it about.

In a fireside chat, largely written by Moley and delivered on June 28, 1933, the President called for "harmony" and "orderly, peaceful progress. . . . In this modern world, the spreading out of opportunity ought not to consist of robbing Peter to pay Paul. We are concerned with multiplication . . . of wealth through cooperative action, wealth in which we all can share." The problem was, of course, that since the Populist movement, reformers had been trying unsuccessfully to prevail on those with wealth to share it, arguing that there was not a limited, finite amount of the world's goods so that if some gained, others must lose but that higher wages and better working conditions created greater wealth for all. The President assured his listeners that the NIRA was "the most important and far-reaching Legislation ever created by the American Congress."

In this he was perhaps somewhat less than candid. The broad general principles and even some of the specific pieces of legislation that Roosevelt had rushed to Congress in the preceding weeks were well grounded only in the sense that they were the fruit of Roosevelt's general political (and moral) principles, principles that had taken shape over twenty years or more of conversation, reflection, and political experience. By any other standard they were, of necessity, hastily improvised, if not precisely thrown together, as the critics of the administration claimed. As Raymond Moley put it, the President was "experimenting with government control over concentrated economic power in the interests of the wage earner, the salary earner, the consumer, and the employer."

With the passage of the NIRA in the Senate by a margin of five votes, the main outlines of the New Deal were clearly, if not precisely, defined. There would, to be sure, be further advances and some retreats (the latter largely as a consequence of Supreme Court decisions ruling various parts of the New Deal program unconstitutional), but the basic principle of the New Deal that underlay all specific measures was writ large for all who had the wit to read: The government not only had the power to intervene in the nation's economic life but had the responsibility to do so in order to help, as it would in wartime, to meet a crisis. That was a simple enough proposition, even though it had been spurned by Hoover and continued to be denounced by a major portion of the business community. But there was another more basic and far more radical implication: Not only had the government the responsibility to do all in its power to alleviate want and suffering in an economic crisis, but it had the responsibility (and the requisite constitutional powers) to do all that was necessary to achieve a more just and humane society, depression or no depression.

For Tugwell and the collectivists, the NIRA was a disastrous setback. In Tugwell's words, "Big business and 'the money power' were enlisted as partners, if not wholly trusted ones, in the national effort. . . . To the collectivists it was clear enough . . . that Roosevelt could be persuaded to depart from the old progressive line only in the direst circumstances and then only temporarily."

The National Recovery Administration (NRA) codes established maximum hours and minimum wages for every major industry. Equally important, the NRA abolished the sweatshop and child labor in industries such as textiles, gave workers the right to bargain through their own union representatives and specified that businesses must open their books to government inspection. Minimum wages were fixed at between $12 and $15 per week. More than half the codes adopted specified uniform prices, and a number limited production and assigned quotas to particular companies. Of the Blue Eagle, the highly publicized insignia of the NRA, Roosevelt said in a fireside chat, "In war in the gloom of night attack, soldiers wear a bright badge on their shoulders to be sure that comrades do not fire on comrades. On that principle, those who cooperate in this program must know each other at a glance."

Hugh Johnson, by virtue of his role as chairman of the group that put the NIRA together, expected to head the vast new program, but there were doubts among Roosevelt's advisers about his suitability.

When Frances Perkins asked Bernard Baruch his opinion about Johnson as head of the NRA, Baruch, who had been Johnson's employer, said, "You'd better interpose. Hugh isn't fit to be head of that. . . . He's been my number three man for years . . . [and] he's a good number three man, maybe a number two man, but he's not a number one man. He's dangerous and unstable. He gets nervous and sometimes goes away for days without notice. I'm fond of him, but do tell the President to be careful."

Perkins conveyed the message to Roosevelt, but FDR was no admirer of Baruch and gave it little credence. Besides, he felt he was already in too deep with Johnson to back out. As a compromise the PWA (part of the NIRA) was taken away from Johnson and given to Ickes, a move that irritated Johnson to the point where he considered refusing to accept the job as head of the NRA. Ickes, for his part, thought it was a great mistake to make Johnson head of the industries control section of the public works industrial control bill. Johnson immediately alarmed liberals by appointing Walter Teagle, president of the Standard Oil Company of New Jersey, Gerard Swope, president of General Electric, and Henry Ford as his advisers. Ickes considered Johnson "especially dictatorial and absolutely beyond control."

Finally reconciled to his diminished power, Johnson devoted his attention, initially, to steel, textiles, automobiles, coal mining, and construction, pressing for codes in those industries. Within a few months 260 different codes were applied for. In the words of Roosevelt's biographer Nathan Miller, the textile code, which was the first major code adopted, "stabilized production, set prices, established uniform wages and hours and ended child labor in the mills." Frances Perkins declared of the child labor prohibition: "That makes me personally happier than any other thing I have been connected with since I came to Washington."

When Perkins called the heads of the various major steel companies together to iron out points at issue in a code for the industry, she included along with such tycoons as Eugene Grace of U. S. Steel and William A. Irwin of Bethlehem Steel, William Green, president of the AFL and "labor adviser to the NRA." The steel executives were horrified to find themselves in the same room with Green. Most of them refused to be introduced to Green or to speak to him. "They backed away into a corner like frightened boys," Perkins wrote." . . . They did not see how they could meet with the president of the A.F. of L. . . . If it were known that they had sat down in the same room with

William Green and talked with him, it would ruin their long-time position against labor organization in their industry."

Perkins expostulated with them. Green had nothing to do with the steelworkers. He had come on behalf of labor to state its approval of the steel code. "This backing and filling went on for almost three-quarters of an hour," Perkins recalled. When Green realized what the frantic huddle at the other end of the room was about, he was "courtesy itself," but in the end he withdrew in an understandable "huff." Perkins wrote: "As the great barons of steel filed out, still looking solemn and sorrowful, I could not resist the temptation to tell them their behavior had surprised me and that I felt as though I had entertained eleven-year-old boys at their first party rather than men to whom the most important industry in the United States had been committed." It was the "most embarrassing social experience of my life," she added. "I had never known people who did not know how, by hypocrisy perhaps, but with an outward surface of correct politeness, to say how do you do even to people they detested."

The steel code called for the industry to work toward an eight-hour day. Wages were set at a minimum of forty cents an hour. The price for these concessions was that the industry could set prices and divvy up the market in an exemption from antitrust laws.

Whatever Hugh Johnson's shortcomings as an administrator may have been, he was certainly not lacking in dramatic flair. On Saturday, September 13, 1933, NRA parades were held in many cities across the country. The schoolchildren of Boston were assembled on the Common, and Mayor James Curley read the Blue Eagle oath: "I promise as a good American to do my best for the NRA." In New York City the parade lasted for ten hours and there were a quarter of a million marchers and a million and a half spectators. Included were 35,000 municipal employees, 20,000 garment workers, and 6,000 marchers from the film industry, led by Al Jolson. There was a Miss Liberty and a Miss Nira (National Industrial Recovery Act). There were Civilian Conservation Corps enrollees. Bands scattered throughout the march played "Happy Days Are Here Again." It was midnight before the artificial-flower makers and the Chinese waitresses passed the reviewing stand. It was just such a spectacle as Americans dote on. To the historically minded it recalled the Grand Procession in Philadelphia on July 4, 1788, celebrating the framing of the Federal Constitution and the Declaration of Independence. The National Industrial Recovery Act was designed to rescue the nation that the Constitution had launched. General Johnson was not bashful in his claims for the NRA. "Nothing like it has ever happened in the history of the world," he declared, with characteristic flamboyance. "It is as important as the Council of Nicaea or the Treaty of Verdun."

Eventually some 550 codes were approved, including the Burlesque Theater Code, limiting burlesque shows to four striptease acts.

Johnson managed to prevail upon 2,000,000 employers, from proprietors of corner grocery stores to the heads of giant industries, to sign the blanket code, but when it got down to the particulars of each industry, the going turned out to be much harder. Many industries were willing to accept price controls but balked at the labor provisions of Section 7(a) or simply ignored them. Their employees, however, encouraged by the strongly prolabor bent of the administration, were disposed to insist on strict observance of the labor clauses. The result was three times as many strikes in 1933 as in the preceding year. Most of the strikes were unsuccessful. The AFL was as alarmed by Section 7(a) as the employers. When the rubber workers in Akron, Ohio, tried to start a "vertical" or "industrial" union of all the workers in a plant, the AFL split them into nineteen separate unions, more readily controlled by its council.

The response of industry to the clause in the NIRA calling for collective bargaining was to form company unions, which led to war rather than, as the drafters of the bill had intended, to peace on the labor front. One suspects that it was Roosevelt's evident determination to support the workers' right to collective bargaining and union membership that did more than anything else to make business interests the enemies of the New Deal.

With the passage of the NIRA the organization of the steel and coal miners received an important stimulus. "We began to build the [Communist] Party among the coal miners and the ore miners," Hosea Hudson told Nell Painter. " . . . We had some big struggles." The companies had "shack rousters." If a worker reported sick and failed to turn up on the job, the shack rouster visited his house to confirm the illness.

When the second expedition of the Bonus Army trooped into Washington in early May, they met a very different reception from a year earlier. The President ordered them convoyed to Fort Hunt. There they were issued army blankets, fed army rations, and housed in a tent city with showers and electric lights. They even enjoyed a navy band concert. Egged on by Louis Howe, Eleanor Roosevelt visited their camp and joined them in singing "There's a Long, Long Trail." Veterans were authorized to enroll in the Civilian Conservation Corps although they were well past the maximum age. The treatment given the two contingents was an instructive measure of the two Presidents. To Roosevelt the ragged veterans were symbols of suffering humanity, fellow citizens grievously injured by forces beyond their control or understanding. His handling of the problem they presented was both humane and politically astute.

When Congress adjourned in June after passing the NIRA, it had accomplished more in a period of 104 days than any of its predecessors. It had enacted into law fifteen major pieces of legislation constituting the most fundamental change in relationship of the Federal government to its citizens in the history of the Republic or, it may be suspected, of *any* republic or, indeed, of any nation with a more or less representative government. Roosevelt had made ten speeches and sent fifteen messages to Congress explaining and justifying legislation submitted to it—a "record," in Moley's words, "of sheer effort, if not achievement, that has no parallel in the history of American Presidents." The Cabinet and inner circle of FDR's advisers were exhausted. "Only Roosevelt," Moley wrote, "preserved the air of a man who had found a happy way of life." From his inauguration to the end of the special session of Congress, Moley saw him lose "his poise, self-confidence, and good humor but once." That was when Bronson Cutting refused to compromise on the veterans' bonus issue. "In short," Moley wrote, "he was like the fairy-story prince who didn't know how to shudder. . . . Not even the realization that he was playing ninepins with the skulls and thighbones of economic orthodoxy seemed to worry him," Moley added. He took his rare defeats in Congress in good spirit. The economy seemed to have been infused by Roosevelt's optimism. The *New York Times* weekly business index rose from 52.3 at the inauguration to 87.1 by the time of the adjournment of Congress.

What remained to be seen was if the country was willing or able to absorb (or cope with) the practical consequences of the remarkable flood of legislation passed in the special session of Congress. Enemies of the New Deal and defenders of the Old Order (usually the same individuals) argued with considerable logic that Franklin Roosevelt had deliberately accentuated the atmosphere of crisis and, under the pretense of alleviating it, had carried the nation far down the path of state socialism. Congressmen and Senators returned home exhausted from their labors and uneasy about the response of their constituents. Most of them discovered that their constituents had been listening to the radio and were already, in varying degrees, under the spell of the President's intimate and confidential voice, which made complicated matters disarmingly simple. The President's utilization of the radio had about it a good deal of the air of the miraculous. It was as though Roosevelt, a modern Joshua, had marched seven times around the citadel of archaic ideas, blowing the New Deal trumpet, and the walls of Jericho had come tumbling down. There was more to it than that, of course. First, the hitherto invincible legions of capital had to be thoroughly discredited, their morale broken and their ranks thinned by death and desertion. Only then could the foundations of the new social and economic order be solidly laid.

William Allen White, who had castigated Hoover for doing nothing, was alarmed by his successor's headlong course. "The country seemed to want dramatic action," he wrote. "Roosevelt is supplying the want. It isn't in the books. The Constitution is straining and cracking. But, after all, the Constitution was made for the people and not the people for the Constitution. We are toying gayly with billions as we once played cautiously with millions. We are legerdemaining a huge national debt which is to be paid Heaven knows when or how. It is bewildering—this new deal—the new world. How much is false, how much is true, how much is an illusion of grandeur, a vast make-believe, only time will tell."

White asked Ickes, referring to Roosevelt: "How do you account for him? Was I just fooled in him before the election or has he developed?" It seemed to White that Roosevelt had shown "magnitude and poise, more than all, power! I have been a voracious feeder in the course of a long and happy life and have eaten many things, but I have never had to eat my words before. I shall wait six months and . . . if they are still on the plate, down they go with a gusto. And I shall smack my lips as my Adam's apple bobs."

While Walter Lippmann assured his readers that the New Deal measures were "practical expedients rather than revolutionary processes," he also warned against smuggling in social and economic reforms under the guise of curing the Depression. Such policies might alarm the business sector and inhibit the "free enterprise upon which an essential part of recovery depends." Roosevelt's intention, of course, was precisely that: to create a more just and equitable society while trying every expedient to lift the country out of the Depression. In the

President's view, there was no contradiction involved. In the long run the health of the society depended on the degree to which it became a more just society. Sweeping reforms were thus as essential as, or, indeed, more essential than, those measures adopted to deal with the current economic crisis. Severe as that crisis was, it would in time pass. If, in the meantime, under the extreme pressures created by the crisis, the nation had become educated to a larger and more generous view of the relationship of citizens to each other and of the obligations of the government to all citizens, the nation could face the future with the hope and confidence that had long been a dominant element in the American character.

Relatively few Americans saw things in that light. The great majority of practical politicians, Democrats and Republicans alike, clung doggedly to the old shibboleths. The business interests, in the main, were no more enlightened. From the left came strident cries for the reconstruction of American society along Marxist lines. Piecemeal reforms only delayed the coming of the revolution by deluding the masses with the hope of achieving that equality which could be attained only under communism. The Trotskyite journal *The Militant* declared that "the working class will only sink deeper into its misery unless it sees clearly the hypocritical nature of the Roosevelt program. . . . " To Earl Browder the New Deal was "a policy of brutal oppression at home and of imperialism abroad." The President was simply "carrying out more thoroughly, more brutally than Hoover, the capitalist attack against the living standards of the masses."

When Frazier Hunt returned from Russia in 1933 to the opening phase of the New Deal, the spirit in Washington reminded him "of the spirit of Moscow in the days when the Russian revolution existed only from day to day, and then largely in men's minds." There was an air of frantic improvisation. Much was done hastily, inefficiently, inadequately, or simply foolishly, but there was an electric quality in the atmosphere, the sense that a new and brighter future lay ahead, that Americans had finally seized on the Depression problem with a determination somehow to solve it even if they had to employ every notion of revolution or reform that came to hand or mind. "Brave men," Hunt wrote, "were at last to have a new chance. Things were no longer to be allowed to drift aimlessly with the current." It was twenty-five years since Herbert Croly's *Promise of American Life* had appeared with its exhortations to government to undertake responsibility for the social and economic well-being of its citizens. It was twenty years since Walter

Lippmann's gloss on Croly, *Drift and Mastery*, had appeared. Now it seemed as though at last the effort at "mastery" would replace the faith in "drift."

The New Deal, Frazier Hunt speculated, was able to seize the initiative only because "the true rulers of America—Wall Street, banks, railroads, insurance, steel, mines, industry, processors, public utilities"—were too frightened and demoralized to rally "their private senators and congressmen, their stool pigeons in government, their lobbyists and lawyers. . . . For once they went with the winds of public demands." Hunt was not sanguine about the long-term consequences. Soon the interests would get back their nerve and withdraw behind their barricades, "the courts and the Constitution." But for the moment Roosevelt was clearly in command. He continued "to preach his new faith in the common man. It was a new religion," Hunt wrote. "To me it was a thrilling one."

The President took advantage of the adjournment of Congress to plan an expedition to CCC camps in neighboring Virginia. A presidential motorcade was organized with Henry Wallace, Harold Ickes, and Louis Howe as members of the party. The first camp visited was in the Shenandoah Park in the Blue Ridge Mountains. The men were working on the Skyline Drive, and the company commander proudly told his visitors that the average gain in weight had been fifteen pounds. At a camp where they stopped for lunch they had steaks, mashed potatoes, green beans, a salad, iced tea, "and a so-called apple-pie," in Ickes's words. In all the party visited five camps during the day. Ickes described them as "well set up, sanitary, comfortable, and clean." The trip of inspection was Ickes's first prolonged contact with Roosevelt. "The President is a fine companion to be out with," he noted in his diary. "He is highly intelligent, quick-witted, and he can both receive and give a good thrust. He has a wide range of interests and is exceedingly human."

With Congress adjourned, the administration had two major tasks. The first, stated simply, was to keep people from starving to death. That was an immediate and pressing need, and Harry Hopkins was charged with accomplishing that goal by distributing money through the states. This "dole," as its opponents called it, was seen as a strictly temporary measure to be followed by the creation of jobs. Phase two of the administration's primary task was the creation of jobs through large-scale public works. That was Harold Ickes's responsibility under Title II of the National Industrial Recovery Act, or NIRA.

The second "major task" was to stimulate recovery through such measures as the Agricultural Adjustment Act and, above all, the NIRA. The NIRA was thus a crucial element in the whole New Deal program. Direct relief and relief through public works projects were perceived as expedients, measures intended to tide the country over until the cooperation between government and business had a chance to prove itself and put the country on the road to recovery. But it was soon evident to many observers, within and without the government, that the National Recovery Administration (NRA) was encountering serious problems. A recession in the fall was disheartening. Harold Ickes, charged with negotiating critically important agreements, or codes, for the oil industry, found it tough going. The whole system was enormously cumbersome, with endless hours consumed in wrangling over the specifics of various codes. Laboriously fashioned, codes were often ignored since the means of enforcement were virtually nonexistent.

In October, Roosevelt, alarmed over the continuing low prices of wheat, urged Morgenthau to buy 25,000,000 bushels for Harry Hopkins to distribute to the needy through the FERA. For several days Morgenthau bought wheat at a cost of more than $1,000,000 per day, while Hopkins and Wallace bought up some $10,000,000 worth of butter.

By the end of 1933 it was clear that little or no progress had been made in ending the Depression. More than 12,000,000 men and women were out of work, farm prices were still depressed despite the United States having gone off the gold standard, the stock market was in the doldrums, and the "leading economic indicators" offered little encouragement for the months ahead. In addition, there were natural disasters to supplement the economic ones. On Armistice Day Lorena Hickok, Harry Hopkins's "eyes," experienced one of the early dust storms that seemed destined to blow away much of the farmland of the Middle West. Hickok wrote a description to Eleanor Roosevelt: "All night the wind howled and screamed and sobbed around the windows. When I got up at 7:30 this morning, the sky seemed to be clear, but you couldn't see the sun! There was a queer brown haze— only right above the sky was clear. And the wind was blowing a gale. It kept on blowing harder and harder. And the haze kept mounting in the sky. By the time we had finished breakfast and were ready to start out, about 9, the sun was only a lighter spot in the dust that filled the sky like a brown fog." Hickok and her friends had to turn back. By the time they got home they couldn't see a foot in front of their car. "They had the street lights on when we finally groped our way back into town," she wrote. "They stayed on the rest of the day. By noon, the sun wasn't even a light spot in the sky anymore. You couldn't see it at all. It was so dark, and the dust was so thick that you couldn't see across the street. . . . I was terrified for a moment. It looked like the end of the world."

For many marginal farmers of the northern plains it was the end of their world. They watched in dismay as their farms blew away. When winter came, it was the coldest in fifty years. The thermometer dropped below zero in Washington, D.C. In the Rocky Mountain states it registered fifty below zero on occasion, and hundreds of thousands of cattle froze to death.

Yet despite these grim facts, the American people had begun to recover their morale. Hope and optimism revived. Times were still desperately hard, *but something was being done.* The administration and, above all, the President were clearly determined to do all in their power to relieve human misery and suffering; just that fact was enormously reassuring. Before his inauguration Roosevelt had told Anne O'Hare McCormick, a columnist for the *New York Times,* that in his view the presidency was "preeminently a place of moral leadership." He had demonstrated that it could indeed be so used and in doing so had lifted the spirits of the nation.

One of the more spectacular events of 1933 was the Century of Progress Exposition in Chicago. With that curious capacity for planning in advance national celebrations that subsequently took place in depressions, the Century of Progress was put on in the depths of a depression that made a mockery of the very notion of progress. The World's Columbian Exposition of 1893 had taken place in the depths of *that* depression, a depression far less disastrous and prolonged than the Great Depression. The Centennial Exposition of 1876, held in Philadelphia, had run concurrently with the serious depression of *that* year.

The introduction to the official program of the Chicago Exposition made no reference to the depression that gripped the country. Its accents were those of a cautious and muted optimism. It spoke primarily of the great advances of science, particularly electricity and chemistry. In the new century, the secretary of the architectural committee wrote, "humanity has only to voice its desires and the resourcefulness of its servants of science will gratify them." The Hall of Science and the Hall of Religions were the centerpieces of the exposition. "Look into the tomorrow!" the introduction concluded. "With our help the new day can be made so much more rich than the old! The views have the look of romance. Romance may become a reality if we humans will it to be so."

The style was Art Deco mixed with a liberal portion of Bauhaus. The sample homes were severe structures of steel, stucco, and glass. The amusement section, featuring the Children's Island, was perhaps the most successful. In the travel and transportation group, General Motors and Chrysler boasted large structures; General Motors had an assembly line, one of the most popular of the exposition's displays. There was a "restoration" of the Great Temple of the Mayas juxtaposed with "Old Belgium" and the famed belfry of Bruges. The Oriental Village vied with Medieval Paris, and the Hall of the World a Million Years Ago featured prehistoric mechanical monsters that "hiss, growl, roar and stamp the earth . . . in what we are told was the manner of their life in the long-ago." There was a section of the Great Wall of China, a Moroccan pavilion, and a Polish exhibit that told the story of that nation's "rare inheritance and its eager modernity."

It was all splendidly and triumphantly American—the notion that you could assemble in one place and one time all the styles of the world, past and present, and stare at them until you somehow possessed them. Presumption and innocence in equal parts. And extravagant fun in defiance of the nation's and the world's misery.

# 20

# The White House

One of the commonest accusations leveled against the New Deal was that it was hopelessly inefficient—a vast, inept, and inexperienced bureaucracy made up of amateur do-gooders. That there was considerable confusion and disorder, duplication of efforts, and overlapping of responsibilities and jurisdiction was not only true but, one suspects, inevitable in view of the magnitude of the task taken on. The surprising thing was not that the New Deal was wasteful and disorderly but that its accomplishments were extraordinary, if not heroic. It may thus be well to take a closer look at the inner workings of the New Deal, at what is often called the decision-making process. That process was often characterized by an air of frantic improvisation.

The President had a two-tiered system of advisers. The first—in many ways the less important—was the Cabinet. The second tier of presidential advisers was a loose and often shifting company made up of individuals whom Roosevelt found personally congenial and whose advice he valued. Louis Howe and Sam Rosenman were, of course, two such intimates. Harry Hopkins, as head of the Federal Emergency Relief Administration (FERA) and subsequently the Civil Works Administration (CWA) and the Works Progress Administration, later renamed the Work Projects Administration (WPA), was not a Cabinet

463

member, but he had more influence than any Cabinet members except Wallace, Ickes, and Perkins. Hopkins became one of Roosevelt's closest advisers and confidants. Raymond Moley, although he grew increasingly alienated from the New Deal measures, was another. Rexford Tugwell, located uneasily in the Department of Agriculture, was a third, although as a "holistic" thinker and a "collectivist" he found his influence waning. Adolf Berle was consulted, and Frankfurter, through his various protégés as well as directly, exerted considerable influence (although not as much as he believed he did). He was, in any event, not available on a day-to-day basis since he still held his chair at Harvard. As we have noted, two of his former students, Ben Cohen and Tom Corcoran, soon became New Deal "insiders." They kept their mentor informed of the course of events and, more important, the trends in policy within the administration. "The Tugwell crowd," they wrote Frankfurter, "has been pushed by its enemies—and its own loose talk—away over to the left. Ray [Moley] is vacillating considerably toward the right. Isaiah [Brandeis] is militant and impatient in the middle."

To Adolf Berle there were three competing groups in the Roosevelt inner circle: those "radicals" who wished for "wholesale change" (they were the non-Russian Socialists of the Norman Thomas, Eugene Debs stripe); then a group that advocated "making peace with business and letting matters run" in the hope that the economy would right itself if not excessively tinkered with; and finally, those who saw capital as the villain and believed that the Depression might be used as the means of breaking the hold of capital on the country. In this latter category, with which Berle, incidentally, had little sympathy, he placed Ickes, Cohen, and Corcoran.

Henry Wallace presided over the department closest to the President's heart. Under Wallace's leadership the Department of Agriculture became a refuge for the New Deal's most passionate idealists. Intellectuals who were sympathetic to the ideals of the Russian Revolution and a number who were members of the Communist Party found a home there or, perhaps more accurately, a base of operations. Under Wallace's benign, rather disorganized direction, eccentric ideas generally found a sympathetic hearing. George Creel wrote that as secretary of agriculture, Wallace "surrounded himself . . . with a weird collection of nuts that even included cultists," and there were stories that he "consulted astrologers and sought guidance from the stars." In the words of one old-line politician, "Henry's the sort that keeps you guessing as to whether he's going to deliver a sermon or wet the bed." Harold Ickes made much the same charge. "Henry Wallace is not a good administrator," Ickes wrote, "in addition to which he is a good deal of a religious mystic." Wallace was apparently a theosophist. Since Roosevelt was himself a visionary idealist, he got along well with Wallace. One of the President's pet projects was a plan for homesteading. Undeterred by the failure of the Val-Kill project at Hyde Park, designed to keep young farmers on the farm by enabling them to supplement their farm income by manufacturing furniture, Roosevelt pressed on with a plan to "resettle" both rural and urban families on subsistence farms, while reclaiming marginal farmlands for reforestation.

As secretary of the interior Harold Ickes presided over a vast empire. He had responsibility for protecting the nation's natural resources—grazing lands and forests, mineral wealth (primarily coal and oil), and water—from the grasp, in his view, of predatory capitalists.

Ickes was determined to clip the wings of the big cattle ranchers who grazed their stock on Federal land. "The public range," he noted, "is being overgrazed to an alarming extent. Part of it has already been destroyed and there will be more of this until there is some control. Some of the Western states are opposed to it because their stockmen in their greed want to turn their flocks and herds onto the range without the aye, yes or no of anyone." The Taylor Grazing Act authorized the Department of the Interior to set up a Division of Grazing, which in turn was given the assignment of working out a program of conservation for some 140,000,000 acres of public land on which sheep and cattle had been allowed to graze with little control or supervision. Such grazing rights constituted a kind of subsidy to cattlemen and sheepmen. The President authorized Ickes to take the necessary steps against Arizona and New Mexico cattlemen who had fenced in for their own private use "many, many acres of the public domain."

Harold Ickes took a special interest in the plight of Indians. He noted that the Congressman most active in Indian matters, who had maintained for years that eleven cents a day was enough to feed an Indian child, had been given a job in the Department of the Interior when he lost his bid for reelection. He had "crowded himself into this department, at a fine salary," Ickes wrote, "and . . . it gave me great joy, as one of my first official acts after I came to Washington, to fire him."

Ickes delighted in using his role as a member of the administration to lecture tycoons on their iniquities. In November, 1933, when he was invited to give the principal address at the hundredth anniversary of the Philadelphia Board of Trade, he told an audience that included the president of the Pennsylvania Railroad, the president of the Baldwin Locomotive Works, and dozens of other capitalists "how ruthlessly we had exploited the natural resources of the country and then the human resources, including women and children. I went on to say," Ickes noted in his diary, "that we were in the midst of a social revolution and that the days of rugged individualism and ruthless power were over forever."

The low esteem in which the Republican Party held the needs and concerns of labor was dramatically illustrated by the disorder and corruption that Frances Perkins found when she took over the administration of the Department of Labor. The department itself was characterized by a general air of dishevelment. The windows had not been recently washed, the chairs were old and dilapidated, and Perkins found an enormous cockroach in her desk. There was no sign that her predecessor, William N. Doak, was in any hurry to depart, but Frances Perkins hustled him out and sent his belongings after him. An old black man named Callus, who was Doak's factotum, offered to wash her gloves for her every morning. It turned out that his desk was the source of the cockroaches. Since there were no restaurants in the vicinity that would serve blacks, he was forced to bring his lunches, and the food stored in his desk attracted the roaches.

When Perkins attended a department party given in her honor, she made a point of meeting all those employees present. Then she initiated the dancing by inviting one of her assistants to be her partner. "We'll dance just a moment or two," she told the startled man, "and that will start the others." Her bold foray "created great astonishment," she noted with satisfaction. Soon the others joined in.

The supervision of the immigration laws was the principal responsibility of the Department of Labor. A series of laws, passed during the twenties, had imposed increasingly severe restrictions on immigration. The first so-called Quota Law had been passed in 1921. It limited immigration in any one year to 3 percent of the number of each nationality according to the census of 1910, with a maximum of 356,000. Its unabashed purpose was to limit the number of Southern and Eastern European immigrants. Three years later the quota was cut in half, and immigration further restricted to 2 percent of the "nationals" in the 1890 census. Although the new quota did not go into effect until July, 1929, it demonstrated the growing hostility both to immigration per se and to such nationals as Italians, Poles, Serbs, and other Slavs. Charles Edward Russell denounced the bill as "abominable." It sought, in his view, "to make this an exclusively Anglo-Saxon country and to hell with these dirty dagoes. On various pretexts immigrants arriving from the south of Europe were . . . denied admission and must be carried back."

Perkins soon discovered that the bureau's investigative arm, the notorious Section 24, was thoroughly corrupt. The job of Section 24, headed by an unsavory character named Murray Garsson, was to hunt down illegal immigrants and immigrants with dangerous or subversive ideas and deport them. Among Section 24's employees were Doak's son and nephew. The bureau accounted for 3,659 of the department's 5,113 employees, and took up $10,000,000 of its $13,500,000 budget. Doak seemed to have been obsessed with the "radical element" among the workers. In one of the section's raids to round up illegal immigrants, its agents, aided by the police, cleaned out an entire block, arresting 606 suspects, of whom only 2 were found to be deportable.

When Perkins told Roosevelt about Section 24 and her desire to get rid of the investigative unit headed by Garsson, he gave her the green light: "Go ahead and clean them out." Fortunately they had used up their funds and were expecting a supplemental appropriation from Congress, but Perkins declined to request the appropriation and dismissed the principal offenders on the ground that there were no more funds. Sixteen were put on furlough, and the jobs of seventy-one abolished.

Aside from abolishing Section 24, one of Frances Perkins's most notable achievements was the reform of the entire Immigration Service. In the words of her biographer, her purpose was "to simplify the immigration laws, which were a maze of technicalities often producing cruel and ludicrous results, and to treat aliens in a manner worthy of the dignity and professed humanity of the United States." It was a goal achieved in the face of general indifference and often overt hostility. The fact was that no actions of hers aroused more public resentment and criticism than her efforts to be fair in the treatment of aliens. In a hundred small and large ways she made clear to the timeservers in her department that there was to be a new regime.

It was Frances Perkins's fate to be, perhaps second only to Harry Hopkins, the most controversial and frequently criticized member of the New Deal. Congressmen delighted in interrogating and haranguing her. Part of the problem was that she usually knew considerably more than her interrogators and told what she knew in upper-class accents that grated on the nerves of run-of-the-mill politicians. She was inclined to lecture, and lectures from women were not taken kindly to by most Congressmen and Senators. The Washington *Evening Star* pointed up the dilemma in an editorial on her testimony before a congressional committee: "Call it a day, boys; call it a day. The lady is better than you are and we should be a bit surprised if higher compliments could be paid her. What's more, she is not afraid of you. And that makes an awful combination. A woman smarter than a man is something to get on guard about. But a woman smarter than a man and also not afraid of a man, well, good night!"

Another point of friction between Perkins and members of Congress was patronage. No novice to politics, she was well aware of the importance and function of patronage, but she had the stubborn and, to most politicians, wholly unreasonable determination that persons appointed to offices under the purview of her department should have some minimum degree of competence. Such an attitude enraged some Congressmen. Rather surprisingly, the press was in the main hostile toward her. The journalists who most frequently singled her out for attack were George Creel, Marquis Childs, both "liberal" newsmen, and Westbrook Pegler, a bulwark of reaction. *Time* magazine noted that "of all the game in the Roosevelt preserve, Secretary of Labor Perkins has been the most frequently chased and the most savagely harried."

Under the batterings of Congress and the press, the firm support of the President and her religious convictions were Frances Perkins's principal consolations. To her the most basic imperative of the Christian faith was "to see that the state does care about what happens to the individual and doesn't say—'Oh, well, it can't be helped.' " The task of the Christian, which included of necessity the impulse of reform, was "to know, love and serve God, and finally be joined with him in eternity." A Christian society was, by definition, one "of social cooperation and social justice."

There was yet another circle of intimates with whom the President relaxed. They were, in large part, his poker-playing companions, a lighthearted social company with whom wit, conversation, and that curious American custom of "teasing" prevailed. The President was the teaser in chief, passing out nicknames like Tommy the Cork for Tommy Corcoran and Henny Penny and Henry the Morg in reference

to Morgenthau's gloomy apprehensions that "the sky was about to fall."
When William O. Douglas came to Washington as an administrator in
the Securities and Exchange Commission, he soon became a poker-
playing White House regular. Corcoran was valued for his wit but
perhaps even more for his skill with the accordion and guitar. The
President loved to sing. Jokes, stories, banter, laughter, a constant flow
of good spirits—that was the President's style.

The poker games took place, in Bill Douglas's words, in an "atmosphere of relaxation and gaiety. Anyone who brought up business
was never invited back. A serious word was taboo because these were
the President's nights out—free of worries and concerns. . . . It was,
all in all, a happy crowd. . . ." Other poker players were Ickes, Garner,
and Morgenthau. Assessments of Roosevelt's skill as a poker player
varied, but most of those who played with him considered him a formidable opponent when he concentrated on the game and forwent the
jokes and stories that were usually a running accompaniment. Garner
was reputed to be the best poker player in Washington, but "the President took him into camp," Ickes noted. On one jackpot the President
outbluffed Garner, inducing him to lay down two pairs topped by kings
when Roosevelt held only sevens and fours. This setback "just about
broke the heart of the Vice President," Ickes reported.

One of the secrets of Roosevelt's remarkable energy was his ability
to escape completely from the burdens of office. After a trip to Hyde
Park the President told Ickes that he had stayed up one night until six
in the morning, drinking beer and playing poker.

Neither of the Roosevelts had the slightest aesthetic sense (several
friends noted that the President's idea of art was a ship in a bottle or
a nautical print). Of the formal social events at the White House,
Harold Ickes found the "musicales" that followed formal White House
dinners the toughest to take, in part because the spindly gold chairs
the guests sat upon were hideously uncomfortable.

The White House routine was a simple one. The President had
his breakfast in bed and remained in bed until late morning, reading
the newspapers, signing official documents, and receiving visitors. A
reporter who penetrated the Roosevelt bedroom noted the old-fashioned wardrobe and several worn chairs, including a rocker. On the
night table by his bed were the Book of Common Prayer, nose drops,
a glass of water, some aspirin tablets, cigarettes, and a telephone. The
mantel had a collection of china pigs and the array of family snapshots.

When the President first conferred with Harold Ickes, Ickes noted:

"When I got up to his study, his valet ushered me into his bedroom, telling me the President was showering . . . the President called out to me to come in. There he was, sitting before a mirror in front of the washstand, shaving. He invited me to sit on the toilet seat while we talked. When he was through shaving he was wheeled back to his room where he reclined on his bed while his valet proceeded to help him dress. . . ." He had to put on his cumbersome and uncomfortable braces to go downstairs to greet a group of men and boys who had come across the continent in the fashion of the pony express. When he had performed that ceremony, he returned to his room to have the braces removed. "I was struck all over again," Ickes wrote, "with the unaffected simplicity and personal charm of the man . . . His disability didn't seem to concern him in the slightest degree or disturb his urbanity." Everyone who saw Roosevelt "informally" was keenly aware of the enormous physical effort required for the simplest tasks: from bed to wheelchair and back to bed again; the strapping on of the cruel braces that pressed into his flesh and that had to be supplemented by crutches if the President was to take even a step.

Roosevelt would often talk with visitors in his bedroom before a lunch meeting with a Cabinet member or Senator to discuss the strategy involved in securing the passage of a piece of legislation. When the guest was a petitioner, he sometimes found it difficult to press his case because of the President's stream of conversation. Lincoln Steffens had hit on the strategy of talking to Theodore Roosevelt when he was being shaved on the ground that it was difficult for Roosevelt to talk back with a razor at his throat. Tugwell, experiencing the same difficulty with FDR, timed his visits to coincide with Roosevelt's lunch (Roosevelt often invited a guest to share his simple meal with him on his study desk). Tugwell would eat before he came and then do his talking while the President's mouth was full.

Afternoons were generally given over to appointments, Cabinet meetings, conferences with Roosevelt's speech writers or inner circle of advisers, and, on Fridays, press conferences.

Dinner was always preceded by a cocktail hour, at which the President himself mixed generous old-fashioneds. Grace Tully, Missy LeHand, and Louis Howe, who had a room in the White House and remained the President's closest friend and counselor, were usually present. Eleanor Roosevelt, when she was not off on some assignment for her husband, often had guests staying at the White House who joined in the evening ritual.

After dinner the President usually retired to his bedroom to read, work on his stamp collection, or do crossword puzzles. His favorite reading was biography and history, but he loved detective stories and exercised his ingenuity by trying, in his wife's words, "to figure out ways you could disappear with $50,000."

Undoubtedly much of the President's energy came from his easy and untroubled slumbers. "During my waking, working hours," he observed, "I give the best in me. . . . When the time comes for rest, I can reflect that I could not have done it better if I had to do it all over again. . . . There is nothing left for me but to close my eyes and I am asleep." Moley wrote: "An observer of Roosevelt gets the sense that he has the completely integrated nervous system of a great athlete. There is never any taking or asking of odds."

Roosevelt's routine at Warm Springs was much as it was at the White House. He read the morning papers in bed, spoke with his aides about pressing problems, and then had a therapy session, in effect a swim, at the pool at eleven. Roosevelt would next get into a little cart that had been built with hand controls so that he could drive it himself and go to the press cottage for an interview or conference. After lunch he took a nap and then drove out to his farm to inspect his cattle and the varieties of trees with which he was experimenting. Back at his cottage he would dictate for an hour or so to Missy LeHand and then enjoy the "ceremonial cocktail," made of gin and grapefruit juice, "and a vile drink it is!" Hopkins added. The President made a "first rate 'old fashioned'—and a fair martini." But he showed the same disposition in cocktails as in social programs; he was constantly experimenting with less agreeable portions, and in Hopkins's opinion, the President's "low and uncultivated taste in liquor leads him woefully astray."

When Harold Ickes accompanied the President to Warm Springs for the first time, he was struck by the obvious affection of the residents of the little Georgia town for their benefactor. "Everyone there loves him," he wrote, "and crowds hang outside the gate . . . just to see him and cheer him as he drives in and out occasionally."

The President loved impromptu outings and expeditions and invariably imbued them with a festive air. He was happiest on board the presidential yacht cruising the Chesapeake or on a navy cruiser. Ocean fishing was the only sport he was able to engage in, and his pleasure in that was vast. With his powerful arms and shoulders he could play large fish skillfully.

Eleanor Roosevelt found housekeeping a distraction and did as little of it as possible. There was general agreement that neither of the Roosevelts cared a bit about food; consequently the fare at the White House (as well as at Warm Springs and Hyde Park) ranged from indifferent to bad. Ickes was only one of a number of critics of the White House cuisine. He grumbled that while he was not "very fussy" about his food, he felt the White House staff could do better. It seemed incongruous to eat such fare with gold knives and forks. Wine was served in the White House for the first time since Wilson's administration, but the champagne that was produced after dinner was the worst that he had ever tasted. Ernest Hemingway was another critic of the White House food. He described a meal there as "the worst I've ever eaten. . . . We had rainwater soup followed by rubber squab, a nice wilted salad and a cake some admirer sent in."

Talking was both an important psychological release for the President and a way in which a crippled man could exercise a remarkable degree of control over the people and the world around him. No President with the possible exception of his cousin had been such a tireless talker. Moreover, not since Lincoln had there been such an indefatigable teller of stories in the White House. They were told, most typically, to politicians and reporters to make a point or to illustrate an idea. The storytelling was one of the things about Roosevelt most attractive to Southerners. They lived by and for the stories of politicians. Roosevelt also indulged himself in gossip, but such indiscretions were usually calculated. He would tell a visitor some mildly scandalous item as a test. If the visitor hurried to spread the story, Roosevelt would make a mental note that he could not be trusted with confidences.

Reading aloud was another favorite Roosevelt pastime. Harry Hopkins described a typical Roosevelt family Christmas when the President read, as he always did, Charles Dickens's *A Christmas Carol*, "and the cold, heartless Scrooge was unhappier than ever and his reformation the pleasanter." Hopkins, writing his daughter of the ceremony, added: "The President reads aloud better than anyone I know—he takes infinite pains with each word and phrase—placing the emphasis just right—and withal reading with such obvious pleasure to himself. And you laughed when he said 'humbug' in a loud voice and 'good afternoon' even louder. . . . The President had read this story to his children every Christmas for many years—and the little book is one of his priceless possessions."

Roosevelt's press conferences were held regularly at four o'clock every Friday afternoon. Like TR, he took a genuine interest in the reporters and in their wives and children. In his years as President he met the press 998 times, far more often than any President before or since. Most Presidents distrusted the press and developed adversarial relations with White House reporters, accusing them of distorting their remarks or seeking to embarrass them. Roosevelt, conscious of his ability to play upon their sympathies, not only liked newsmen, but saw them as having an essential role in the educational process he believed himself to be conducting. They were an extension, as it were, of his fireside chats. Each friendly reporter or journalist was a spokesman for his programs and, equally important, for his ideas. Since the editors of most of the newspapers were hostile to Roosevelt and the New Deal in varying degrees, it was especially important for the President to win over the reporters.

The columnists were another matter. Their political views and loyalties had been formed, in large part, during the Progressive era, the intoxicating days of Teddy Roosevelt and the early years of Woodrow Wilson's administration. They were, in a sense, inoculated against the Roosevelt magic (we usually have only one consuming political passion in a lifetime). Men like Walter Lippmann, William Allen White, Arthur Krock, and Mark Sullivan treasured their independence and objectivity (as well, it might be said, as their influence on Presidents). H. L. Mencken was perhaps the President's most relentless political foe. At the Gridiron Club's 1934 dinner, to which Roosevelt was invited, Mencken gave the principal address, which began "Fellow Subjects of the Reich." He then went on to attack the New Deal on the ground that it was depriving Americans of their freedoms. Roosevelt responded with a denunciation of the stupidity and venality of the press. His listeners grew increasingly restless and hostile; then Roosevelt made it clear that he was simply quoting from an article by Mencken himself. Mencken, who was sitting next to his fellow Marylander Governor Albert Ritchie, whispered, "I'll get the son of a bitch."

Much of the misunderstanding about Roosevelt's own views on a wide variety of issues stemmed from his affability, from his innate disposition to listen rather than to argue. Individuals with different political perspectives and ideological persuasions, having unburdened themselves of their opinions and been encouraged by the friendly and encouraging nods of the President's head, would leave his presence in the firm conviction that he thoroughly agreed with the opinions they had expressed. In addition, Roosevelt liked to act as a kind of mediator between members of his administration who had sharply differing views and, in some instances, strong personal hostilities to each other. It helped keep things fluid, open to change of mind or direction. In this rather limited sense the President was "pragmatic." Given a general policy or direction, there was often a variety of paths by which a particular goal could be arrived at. These options Roosevelt wished to keep open until the last moment and, in fact, often somewhat beyond the last moment, helping give him the reputation of fickleness and driving his advisers to the edge of despair.

A common complaint of Roosevelt's subordinates was that he was undependable, especially in the matter of appointments to offices. He would often agree to the appointment of a particular individual and then change his mind to the distress or rage of the person to whom he appeared to have made the promise. The reason was less deceitfulness than his disposition to please and his considerable difficulty in saying no to petitioners.

"You are a wonderful person," Harold Ickes told Roosevelt, "but you are one of the most difficult men to work with that I have ever seen."

"Because I get too hard at times?"

"No, you never get too hard but you won't talk frankly even with those people who are loyal to you and of whose loyalty you are fully convinced. You keep your cards close up against your belly."

Eleanor Roosevelt told Harold Ickes that, in Ickes's words, "the President shrank from saying anything to anybody of an unpleasant nature. He does not like to hurt people's feelings. In family matters she has to assume the unpleasant duties because of his tender-heartedness. . . ." Ickes had never seen him angry. "His patience and understanding are really remarkable," he added.

By the same token it was painful to Roosevelt to fire anyone. Raymond Moley recalled a session with the President prior to his giving someone the ax: "Roosevelt sat with his chin cupped in his hand, rehearsing speeches under his breath. He played with the pencils and ash trays on his desk. He smoked. He fidgeted. At last, he shook his head despairingly. He turned to me. I shook my head just as hopelessly. . . . Roosevelt sent for Louis [Howe]. It was Howe who did the job."

One of the President's qualities that most touched his subordinates was his genuine concern for their health and well-being. He noticed when they looked tired or seemed depressed. He insisted on their taking vacations to restore their strength and regain their good spirits. He told Ickes he must take a vacation; "it was beginning to worry him just to look at me and [he said] that if I didn't go away he would get mad." FDR was tirelessly solicitous, bearing various members of his staff off on the presidential yacht or to Hyde Park or Warm Springs, taking them on train rides with him and sometimes on extended cruises, buoying them up with his apparently unquenchable spirits. "I can never forget his kindness and understanding," Ickes wrote after a session with the President. "I have never been given to hero worship, but I have a feeling of loyalty and real affection for the President that I have never felt for any other man, although I have had very deep attachments for other men." One of the "loveliest facets of Roosevelt's character," Moley wrote, was that "he stood by his people when they got into a jam—sometimes even when they got him into a jam."

Tugwell was fascinated by Roosevelt's ability to accept defeat and failure in good spirit. He made decisions and "genuinely did not worry lest they be wrong. He had a source of support beyond the reach of ordinary judgments." That was clearly, in Tugwell's view, his Christian faith. In Frances Perkins's words, "If things went wrong, he took another tack."

When any of Roosevelt's extremely various top aides became acutely unhappy over his loose and haphazard way of doing business, the President called the distressed individual in for a session of what he called "holding hands," a process which consisted of reassuring words, entertaining anecdotes, and generous helpings of pure charm. The individual almost invariably left comforted, if slightly bewildered. If "holding hands" did not suffice, Roosevelt, in Tugwell's phrase, "resorted to promotion." He gave the person in question an ostensibly "higher" office to help soothe his ruffled feathers. The tough-minded old pros, most of whom had relatively low-level ideological concerns— men like Early, Farley, and Marvin McIntyre—saw, again in Tugwell's words, "an extraordinary procession of sensitive and dedicated natures coming up out of obscurity, being revealed momentarily in the presidential sun, and declining again into baffled obscurity." This was not, indeed, far from what happened to Tugwell himself. What was remarkable was Roosevelt's openness to the ideas put forth by these "sensitive and dedicated natures," most of whom were men and women of a type that would ordinarily have had no chance of gaining a presidential ear.

There was another presidential tactic that Tugwell called the "squeeze." It permitted administrators who had come to be out of step with Roosevelt's current line or who felt that they no longer had access to him to "go on until the tortured victim cried out in pain," meaning that he attacked some member of the administration who was, in effect, carrying out the President's policy. Eventually, feeling his position impossible, he would resign (Tugwell cited Arthur Morgan of the Tennessee Valley Authority as an example) to become "the momentary hero of the opposition press" or of some other anti-Roosevelt faction, like the Liberty League. While Tugwell gave Morgan as an example, it seems clear that his real target was his friend and former colleague Raymond Moley.

The relationship between Eleanor Roosevelt and her husband was a complex one. Franklin, typically, had a tender, jesting way with her. Like most husbands, he found the buying of birthday and anniversary presents for his wife somewhat beyond him, particularly since shopping was impossible. March 17, 1933, two weeks after the inauguration, was the Roosevelts' twenty-eighth wedding anniversary. He gave his wife a check with a note that read:

> "Dear Babs:
> After a fruitless week of thinking and lying awake to find whether you need or want undies, dresses, hats, shoes, sheets, towels, rouge, soup plates, candy, flowers, maps, laxation pills, whisky, beer, etching or caviar
> I GIVE UP
> And yet I know you lack some necessity of life—so go get it with my love and many happy returns of the day!"

That the Roosevelts were devoted to each other was indisputable, but like most husbands and wives, they sometimes got on each other's nerves. Walter Lippmann recalled a visit to Hyde Park to discuss the New Deal program. In the midst of their talk Eleanor Roosevelt came in and interjected some comments which, in Lippmann's view, were irrelevant. Franklin snapped, "Oh, Eleanor, shut up. You never understand these things anyway." (Lippmann, incidentally, went from considering Eleanor Roosevelt "something of a goose about public affairs" and "a rather silly woman" to thinking "she's one of the great people of our time.")

Most notably, both Roosevelts had their strong bonds of mutual interest. She shared, for example, her husband's infatuation with the idea of settling poor urban families in cooperative farm communities.

"I am very fond of Mrs. Roosevelt," Ickes wrote. "She has a fine social sense and is utterly unselfish, but as the President has said to me on one or two occasions, she wants to build these homesteads on a scale we can't afford. . . . " The President's notion was bare, "subsistence" housing without even indoor plumbing (to be installed later by the occupants), but Mrs. Roosevelt insisted on houses "with all modern improvements."

As she had done during her husband's governorship, Eleanor Roosevelt served as an extension of his powers of observation. When she traveled to Maine, her husband wanted to know everything she had seen on the farms she had visited, "the kinds of homes and the types of people, how the Indians seemed to be getting on and where they came from." She descended into coal mines and walked the corridors of prisons and asylums to inspect conditions. Champions of every conceivable cause besieged her with requests for support, confident that if they could enlist her interest, the chance for reform would be vastly improved. On one occasion when Roosevelt asked her secretary, Malvina Thompson, where his wife was, she said, "She's in prison, Mr. President." The President was said to have replied: "I'm not surprised, but what for?" It became a cartoonists' genre to depict the First Lady in improbable situations; Roosevelt spoke of his "Will o' the Wisp wife."

As a young woman Eleanor Roosevelt had driven past the White House and thought "how marvelous it must be to live there." Her gifts were not essentially those of a conventional housekeeper. Her modifications of the White House decor were modest. She put in "good substantial furniture" and hung her uncle's portrait in the Monroe Room. The President's bed had been made under Nancy Cook's supervision at Val-Kill, as had her own. Eleanor Roosevelt found the White House more demanding than running a hotel. In one year 4,729 people came to meals and 323 were houseguests. More than 9,000 people came to tea, and 14,056 were received at receptions and had light refreshments. More than 1,300,000 visited the public rooms of the White House, and 264,060 got special passes from their Congressmen to see the state dining room, the Red Room, the Blue Room, and the Green Room. The average attendance each Easter at the egg rolling was 53,108, in the course of which 180 children were lost and found and 6 persons fainted.

Mrs. Roosevelt's favorite recreation was horseback riding. She often rode in Rock Creek Park before breakfast, sometimes with Elinor Morgenthau and occasionally with Missy LeHand.

The President's wife had her own strong convictions, and she did not hesitate to voice them. William Douglas told of her returning from a trip to Alabama and Georgia to announce to her husband, "Franklin, we must do something about those sharecroppers. Wallace and Tugwell brag about their farm program, but I tell you, Franklin, the beneficiaries are *not* the men who do the work but only those who own the property." She was equally outspoken about the minimum wage. "They [wages] are awful, Franklin. Simply awful," she reported after a tour through New England and Pennsylvania. "Why, people can't live on them and raise a family as they should."

The Roosevelt children were often a problem for their parents. James, handsome and affable and disposed to try to trade on his father's office, was Roosevelt's severest cross. When William Douglas, as head of the SEC, was pressured by Jimmy Roosevelt to accept a shady stock deal, Douglas went to the White House and offered his resignation to the President. "FDR," Douglas wrote, "put his head on his arm and cried like a child for several minutes. Finally, wiping away his tears, he said 'Jimmy! What a problem he is. Thanks for telling me . . . of course you're not resigning.' "

Intense and loving relationships with other women remained important to Eleanor Roosevelt. Lorena Hickok was a woman reporter, stout and mannish, who wore shirtwaists and dark skirts, and smoked pipes and cigars. Someone said of her that she dressed like a police matron. She had had a bitterly unhappy childhood in South Dakota under the dominance of an overbearing father, who had apparently abused her and had succeeded in making her "dislike and distrust all men."

The friendship of Eleanor Roosevelt and Lorena Hickok began during the campaign of 1932 and soon became intense. In March, 1933, Mrs. Roosevelt wrote: "Hick darling, All day I've thought of you & another birthday I *will* be with you & yet to-night you sounded so far away and formal. Oh! I want to put my arms around you. I ache to hold you close. Your ring is a great comfort. I look at it & think she does love me, or I wouldn't be wearing it." One letter began: "Hick darling, I cannot go to bed tonight without a word to you. I felt a little as though a part of me was leaving tonight. You have grown so much to be a part of my life that it is empty without you. . . . Oh! darling. I hope on the whole you will be happier for my friendship. . . . All my love I shall be saying to you over thought waves in a few minutes

'Good night my dear one
Angels guard thee
God protect thee
My love enfold thee
All the night through.' "

The relationship between Eleanor Roosevelt and Lorena Hickok brings to mind that of John Hay and Henry Adams or John Jay Chapman and William James. There was, we are reminded, an era—before overt sexuality had become a problematical element in relationships—when upper-class intellectuals with an impulse to break free of social constraints, delighted in what James called "loving affections." Men wrote to other men and women to other women in terms of endearment that would hardly have been used between members of the opposite sex in the traditional language of courtship. Such relationships between women were so common in Boston that they were called "Boston marriages." Today we can hardly understand them.

In some ways Eleanor Roosevelt was far more radical than her husband. She could, of course, afford to be. While the often unpopular causes she espoused were sometimes embarrassing to her husband, he made no effort to deter her. Harold Ickes recalled an argument between Eleanor and her sons on board the presidential train during a trip to the Grand Coulee Dam. Mrs. Roosevelt, in Ickes's words, "expressed belief in a strict limitation of income, whether earned or not, and the boys insisted that every man ought to have the right to earn as much as he could."

The story of the New Deal can, of course, be told in terms of legislation passed, work projects undertaken, men and women given jobs or relief in one form or another. But that is clearly only part of the story. The temperament and personality of Franklin Roosevelt and of his wife were essential elements. The spirit that emanated from the White House set the tone of official Washington and gave the New Deal a quality unique in the history of presidential administrations. And because it was so difficult for the President to get about, the White House was, far more than in most administrations, the command post and nerve center of his administration.

"Under Coolidge and Hoover," George Creel wrote, "the White House had held the solemn hush of a mortuary establishment, but now it lacked nothing but a merry-go-around and a roller coaster to be a Coney Island. High-domed 'planners,' home-grown economists, overnight sociologists, magic-money nuts, social workers, and campus experts elbowed and shouted, and even the minstrel touch was provided by Tommy Corcoran's accordion. . . ." With all that, Creel was ready to admit that "despite the President's almost juvenile joy in the ferment, it was still the case that he drove with a firm hand, and out of seeming confusion had already come many sound laws."

# The United States
# and the World

I f the country was divided about most issues, it was of virtually one
mind on foreign affairs, and that mind was isolationist. Roosevelt
himself was one of a small group of what we have called closet internationalists. He had been a champion of the League of Nations and
had alarmed his advisers by supporting Henry Stimson's policy of
nonrecognition of Japan's Manchurian conquest. When Stimson pressured the League of Nations to condemn the Japanese invasion of
Manchuria, Roosevelt, as President-elect, had issued a public statement
of support. "It was a very good and timely statement and made me
feel better than I had in a long time," Stimson wrote in his diary on
January 7, 1933. Several days later, when he met with Roosevelt, the
latter remarked, "We're getting so that we do pretty good teamwork,
don't we?"

On March 4, 1933, the League concluded that Japan was ruthlessly
exploiting its puppet state in Manchuria (Manchukuo) and refused to
recognize it. The doctrine of nonrecognition promulgated by Stimson
thus became the official policy of the League.

Roosevelt's own predilections toward international cooperation
were indicated by the fact that he sent Norman Davis and Allen Dulles,
two well-known advocates of the League, to the Disarmament Con-

ference in Geneva in March, 1933. The American delegates agreed that the United States not only would "consult" with other nations on action against an aggressor but would not oppose a "collective effort" made by other nations to preserve peace. Mild as this gesture toward international cooperation was, it aroused so much alarm among the isolationists that Hiram Johnson added an amendment to the Arms Embargo Resolution of 1933, specifically ruling out U.S. participation in collective action for peace.

The strength of the Progressive movement lay in the Middle West. The Progressives had, in the main, supported Wilson's domestic reforms, but they split with him sharply, as we have had ample occasion to note, on the issue of the war, on the Treaty of Versailles, and on the League. The consequence was that the support of the old Progressives had to be negotiated for constantly. The Democratic taint of internationalism kept them at arm's length and made them a problematical element in the politics of reform.

The internationalist issue was closely tied to the tariff issue. As we have seen, the low-tariff/high-tariff conflict had plagued the nation since the beginning of the Republic. It was one of those "religious" issues which, generation after generation, had more to do with faith than with demonstrable political and economic realities. By and large, the old Progressives who feared foreign entanglements also supported high tariffs; they were indeed the reverse side of the same coin. If you disliked and distrusted foreign nations, if you believed they were greedy and aggressive powers eager to corrupt pure and high-minded Americans, you need have no qualms in erecting high tariffs to their products. They must shift for themselves. Even such sophisticated academics as Raymond Moley were virtually indistinguishable in their isolationist sentiments from a dirt farmer in Iowa or Indiana; certainly the practical effects were the same. Moley was strongly, one might say bitterly, opposed to any substantial reduction in European debts owed to the United States. The reason: Great Britain and France, primarily, must be taught that they could not count on the United States to finance their wars. In Moley's view, insistence on strict and complete payment of foreign debts was thus a "peace" measure, a way of discouraging future European conflicts.

To Colonel House, the American policy of "selfish isolationism" had resulted in chaos and disorder in Europe, while the United States itself had sunk to "a low level of materialism and official ineptitude." House argued that all the issues that the League addressed itself to—

disarmament, finances, economics, and the fate of the mandates—were of concern to the United States. The fact was that the League, as its opponents charged, was relatively impotent. It had no magic powers to suppress national greed and ambition, or, indeed, as facts proved, to prevent aggression against the defenseless, and it is doubtful if the official participation in the League by the United States would have substantially altered the situation. What was lacking was to be found not in the cumbersome structure of the League but in the lack of will on the part of its dominant members, Great Britain and France, and that is not to be wondered at. Both countries had suffered such a dreadful attrition of men and wealth that they remained, as one might say, in a state of shell shock for two decades. They simply could not consider the possibility of having to fight another war *under any circumstances*.

The abstention of the United States from the League was less a practical matter than a moral one. By refusing to join the League, the United States rejected the ideal of international cooperation and lapsed into its classic suspicion of the rest of the world, particularly of Europe. It was a failure of imagination and, indeed, of faith in a common future; it was a retreat into a form of xenophobia, always one of the least attractive vices and one to which Americans have been peculiarly susceptible.

When Hamilton Fish Armstrong had talked with Viscount Cecil in London in 1927, the British diplomat reflected on the irony of the fact that the League of Nations "had been the conception of an American President more than anything else, but the United States had then decided to disown responsibility and left others to try to make it work. It could not be done." Cecil pressed Armstrong to explain what had become of "traditional American idealism. Even more strange . . . was the disappearance of the liking Americans had always had for adventure and experiment. They used to be tireless . . . in searching out new ways to get things done. It had been what made the country great. What had made them so cautious?" Armstrong had no answer.

The Neutrality Laws of 1935 and 1936, which should have been called collectively the Isolationist Laws or even the Wishful Thinking Laws, declared in effect that the United States was not, should not, and would not become involved in any foreign war under any circumstances. To guarantee that policy the Neutrality Acts forbade government loans to belligerents, the sale of arms and munitions, and the use of American vessels to carry supplies of any kind to any warring nation. The acts were, in many ways, a direct outgrowth of the investigations of the Nye committee, which, under the chairmanship of Senator Gerald Nye, demonstrated that munitions manufacturers had made enormous profits out of the devastation of the World War. It was even argued that they had helped bring it about in order to make profits and had prolonged it for the same reason. The Johnson Act (sponsored by Hiram Johnson) of 1934 prohibited loans to any foreign government that was in default on its war debts. The Neutrality Act of 1935 was supplemented by the Neutrality Act of 1936, passed on February 29. The effect of the two acts was to place an embargo on all shipments of arms when the President declared "a state of war." American citizens were also forbidden to travel on the vessels of belligerent nations or to make loans to nations at war.

One of the sharpest controversies within the administration was over the issue of tariffs and war debts. A proposal backed by the British and French called for the canceling or scaling down of the debts. The administration advanced a proposal that the interest charges be canceled and the debts then reaffirmed by the debtor nations and a note for the remaining sum deposited with the Bank for International Settlements. The bank would then establish a sinking fund to be used to buy United States government obligations (the plan was known as the Bunny). The resistance of the French and British led to the abandoning of the Bunny, and most subsequent discussions revolved around the efforts of the French and British to link war debts with reparations and of the United States to oppose such linkage. Moley led the faction in the administration that argued against any substantial reduction in tariffs, any concessions on war debts, and any cooperative effort to stabilize the international money market or exchange rate. Moley wished for a "self-contained economy," independent of other nations, and he was supported by such men as James Warburg and Herbert Bayard Swope. On the side of lower tariffs—and that dreadful word "internationalism"—were Cordell Hull and those members of Congress and the administration who advocated international cooperation.

What brought the issue to a boil was the impending World Economic Conference, to be held in London in June, 1933. The "ultimate objective" of the conference was the "stabilization of [world] currencies on a gold basis." Since Roosevelt had taken the United States off the gold standard, he was understandably reluctant to make any such commitment. As Moley (and he believed the President) saw it, the way was open for some sort of agreement to calm the gold standard countries and "steady the dollar," provided that such an agreement did not check "the magnificent advance of American prices which had followed [the U.S.] departure from gold. . . . "

The issue of the World War debts owed to the United States hung over the conference like a dark cloud. Of the British debt to the United States of $4,277,000,000 about $1,447,270,000 had been paid by June 15, 1933. The French, who had owed almost as much, had paid less than a seventh of the British payments. The British sought some relief. They proposed paying $10,000,000 as "an acknowledgment of the debt pending a final settlement." The Italians, who owed $13,545,438, offered to pay $1,000,000, "the kind of a tip," Moley noted, "which one gave in a very unfashionable restaurant." While the internal struggle in the administration over the position of the U.S. was still going on vis-à-vis the questions on the conference's agenda, Roosevelt had to appoint the members of the American delegation. He appointed a mixed bag of protectionists and low-tariff men. James Cox of Ohio, Roosevelt's running mate in the 1920 presidential campaign and a low-tariff man, was a delegate, as was Key Pittman, chairman of the Senate Foreign Relations Committee and a high-tariff man. When Hiram Johnson refused to serve, Roosevelt appointed Senator James Couzens of Michigan, another high-tariff man. Pittman was often drunk at the conference, shooting out the streetlights in London with his six-gun. Another delegate was Roosevelt's cousin Warren Delano Robbins, who wore a monocle while his wife sported purple hair. Cordell Hull was the unhappy leader of the delegation. Small wonder that confusion distinguished the deliberations of the delegation and its relations with the delegates of the other nations attending the conference.

When it was clear that things were hopelessly confused in London, Roosevelt dispatched Moley and Swope to convey his sentiments and try to help get things back on course. The press took the line that Moley was being sent to supersede or, in effect, to replace Hull. When the American delegates finally agreed on an innocuous statement that it was believed would give some reassurance to the other conferees and sent it off to Roosevelt for his approval, he rejected it. Apparently under the influence of Howe and Morgenthau, he issued a statement rejecting "a rigid stabilization" of international currencies on the ground that the United States must remain free to stabilize domestic prices regardless of foreign exchange rates. "I would regard it as a catastrophe amounting to a world tragedy," Roosevelt wrote, "if the great conference of nations, called to bring about a more real and permanent financial stability and a greater prosperity to the masses of all nations . . . should allow itself to be diverted by a proposal of a purely artificial and temporary experiment affecting the monetary exchange of a few nations only." The President then went on to deliver a patronizing lecture on international economics.

As the journalist Ernest Lindley put it, "Europe exploded with resentment and wrath." The shock waves created by Roosevelt's quixotic response effectively broke up the conference. The press crowed that Moley, having gotten too big for his breeches, had been slapped down by the President. Moley wrote a book to vindicate his actions; he never forgave Roosevelt for his intervention. Hull, for his part, blamed Moley for the failure of the conference to achieve anything substantial. "That piss-ant Moley, here he curled up at mah feet and let me stroke his head like a huntin' dog and then he goes and bites me in the ass!" someone reported Hull as saying. A few weeks later Moley resigned from the State Department and became editor of the magazine *Today*. Historians and economists have debated Roosevelt's action in rejecting the work of the conference, but John Maynard Keynes called him "magnificently right" in not agreeing to stabilize prices at a low level.

Taking what comfort he could from the general debacle of the conference, Moley expressed himself as "gratified that the President's newly strengthened distrust of international 'cooperation' even in its mildest form had been, at last, unmistakably proclaimed." Moley also claimed that the American response "bought some rather fine insurance against further involvement in European wars."

It was hard to gainsay Walter Lippmann, who wrote that however excellent the President's purposes, he "completely failed to organize a diplomatic instrument to express them." Lippman asked: "How can a delegation, which lacks authority, which lacks technical competence, which lacks unity, which lacks contact with the President, hope to undertake the kind of difficult negotiation for far-reaching reforms which the President desires?"

When the Allies wrote into the Versailles Treaty the stricture against a German military force, they rationalized it as the first step in a program of general disarmament. But the fact was that nothing else had been done. The Washington Conference of 1922 had, to be sure, set limits on naval construction, but the League of Nations had failed to make any substantial progress in reducing or even controlling the size of armies. At the Geneva Conference in February, 1933, discussions were given a sense of urgency by German statements that unless significant reductions in armies and armaments were agreed to by the other signatories to the treaty, that nation would begin to rebuild its army and navy. That was the French nightmare, the one development that Georges Clemenceau had employed every stratagem to avoid. France, fearing a revived Germany above all else, showed not the slightest disposition to reduce its own land forces. By its obduracy it produced the very thing it most feared. Had France agreed to the reduction of its army, there was, of course, no guarantee that Germany would, in the long run, have abstained from building up an army of its own. If one assumes that Hitler's rise to power was inevitable, the whole question becomes moot. If, on the other hand, a more generous and enlightened policy had been followed by France, one less dictated by fear and the desire for revenge, the appeal to the German people of an Adolf Hitler might have been rendered nugatory and the course of German (and world) history might have taken a different turn. Hitler had, after all, made an attempt to seize power ten years before and was a thoroughly discredited figure in the years that followed his abortive *putsch*.

The delegates to the Disarmament Conference adjourned without having accomplished their declared objective. There was considerable support for outlawing certain weapons, like poison gas, which could not be controlled. There was also agreement on the principle that standing armies should be reduced, but no one could decide how this was to be done. A few months later Germany, true to its warning, announced that it would no longer participate in such discussions unless, in Armstrong's paraphrase, its "right to equality with other nations in all respects was recognized." The other nations accepted that condition, and when the conference reconvened on February 2, 1933, German representatives were present. But it was already too late; three days earlier Hitler had become chancellor.

Hindenburg had appointed Hitler chancellor on January 30, but the National Socialists were unable to form a government without the cooperation of the Center Party, and Hitler refused to make any compromises. The Reichstag was thereupon dissolved, and new elections were set for March 5. Hitler and his lieutenants used the intervening weeks to discredit and intimidate the opponents of the National Socialist German Workers Party, to give the Nazis their full title. The by now familiar theme that all of Germany's woes were due to intellectuals, pacifists, Communists, and Socialists, most of whom were Jews, was tirelessly reiterated. It was they who betrayed Germany by accepting the Versailles Treaty; it was they who kept Germany weak and impotent. Thousands of unemployed young men were enrolled in the storm troopers and dressed in uniforms. Hitler insisted he was the workingman's true friend; he assured the business interests that he was their only bulwark against communism.

On February 27 a fire partly destroyed the Reichstag building where the German Parliament met. Hitler at once announced that the Communists were responsible, and President von Hindenburg suspended all guarantees of free speech and assembly, allowing the storm troopers to bully and intimidate without restraint. The Communist Party was outlawed.

The Reuther brothers, Walter and Victor, on their way to Russia to help train workers in the Gorky automobile factory, arrived in Berlin at the time of the Reichstag fire. They saw the "smoldering remains of the old parliament, surrounded by armed guards, the whole center section gutted and the great glass dome collapsed. Brown shirted storm troopers were everywhere," Victor wrote, "hawking special editions of the Nazi-controlled newspapers. . . . The circus atmosphere around the ruined building—swastika flags flying in the smoke, barkers shouting to the crowd to buy the Nazi paper—would have been ludicrous if it had not been so tragic." The Reuthers found the Socialists, to whom they had letters of introduction from Norman Thomas, highly demoralized. The day before the election, March 4, at the time Franklin Roosevelt was being inaugurated on the other side of the Atlantic, they mixed with a crowd of some 25,000 Germans crowded into the Franz Joseph Platz to hear Hitler on the radio. There was martial music, church bells rang, and the crowd sang with fierce enthusiasm "Deutschland über Alles." Ecstatic Germans believed that their nation was rising from the humiliations of the Versailles Treaty, to hold its head high again among the nations of the world. Returning to the housing cooperative where their Socialist friends lived, the Reuthers found them barricading their doors and windows. A rope ladder was fashioned and hung out a back window for escape if necessary. There was no raid that night, but student activists began burning incriminating papers and packing to flee the city. The next night the raid came, and the best-known opponents of the Nazis were helped down the rope ladder. "That night we faced the reality: political and civil rights were dead in Germany," Victor Reuther wrote. At Dresden and Nuremberg the brothers saw more of the same, with swastikas flying everywhere and Nazi toughs patrolling the streets. Even in the little rural Swabian village of Ruit it was already dangerous to speak a word of criticism of Hitler. While the Reuthers waited for their Russian visas with relatives in Stuttgart, there were storm troopers everywhere and the "Horst Wessel Song" was sung constantly. Hermann Göring addressed a huge throng at the Sportpalast and the Reuthers heard the aged Hindenburg "repeating like a child the ideological clichés of the new regime." Trucks carrying movie projectors and large screens were placed in parks to show propaganda films. The Hitler slogan—"For peace, work, bread, honor, justice"—was reiterated endlessly. With the help of the Catholic center, Hitler forced through the Reichstag the so-called Enabling Act, which gave him dictatorial powers until April 1, 1937.

The Socialist trade unions, active in Germany for more than fifty years, were broken up. Their headquarters in Berlin were occupied by storm troopers, and their officers arrested as "Red criminals." The Freemasons and Jesuits fared no better. Judges who resisted Nazi edicts were forced to resign, and it was announced that in the future judges would be chosen for their "patriotism and martial ardor." They would also be sent to camps for training in "martial sports." The leaders of the Nationalist Party—landowners, former army officers, and industrialists—who had hoped to use Hitler, found themselves out of office and out of power. The plight of the Jews, less than 1 percent of the German population, was desperate. Dr. Alfred Rosenberg, the "philosopher" of nazism, had boasted that the head of a Jew would be stuck on every telephone pole from Munich to Berlin. It was rumored that more than 20,000 people had been imprisoned without formal charges or legal proceedings of any kind against them, and it was estimated that 50,000 had escaped.

When Hamilton Fish Armstrong visited Berlin later in 1933, it was Hitler's birthday. Outside the Adlon Hotel groups of shouting brownshirts passed on their way to rallies. A crowd assembled at the Pariser Platz, where a loudspeaker barked Nazi slogans. Armstrong discovered that "[a]lmost every German whose name the world knew as a leader in government, business, science or the arts . . . of the past fourteen years was gone . . . [and that] day by day, one by one, the last specimens of another age, another folk, were toppling into the Nazi sea." When he returned home, he wrote a prophetic book, *Hitler's Reich: The First Phase*. Its opening sentence read: "A people has disappeared." When he inquired about old friends or acquaintances, he was given vague answers: "Oh yes, but is he still alive? Maybe he is abroad. Or is he in a nursing home?" Armstrong added: "This was true not just of Jews or Communists, fled, imprisoned or being attacked in the streets, but of men like Otto Braun, leader of the Social Democratic party, perennial Premier of Prussia, the strong man of whom Germans used to say, 'When Hindenburg dies, we will have him.' " Heinrich Brüning, the last chancellor of the Centrist Party, was in a Catholic clinic. Some months later, when he escaped to Holland, a Dutch customs official who was a German agent tried to kill him with a poisoned cigar, but the scheme failed. Brüning got to England and then to the United States, where, in constant fear of his life, he lived in a seminary on Long Island under the name of Henry Anderson.

Armstrong's old friend, Ernst "Putzi" Hanfstaengl, was a graduate of Harvard whose mother had been a Boston Sedgwick. Hanfstaengl had befriended Hitler in his early days, lent him money, and played the piano for him when he was despondent. Now he was a rather disheveled Nazi functionary who came to the Adlon to escort Armstrong to an interview with Hitler. "Why, Putzi," Armstrong exclaimed, "I've never seen you in uniform before. How magnificent!"

"Yes, it is rather good, isn't it? Don't tell anyone, but it's English stuff. That does make a difference."

Hanfstaengl was the interpreter, but Armstrong noted that he was reluctant to translate awkward questions into German. Hitler, foregoing his usual histrionics, looked at Armstrong with "rather nice, wide-open eyes" about the color of which visitors disagreed. Dorothy Thompson, the American journalist, said they were gray. To Armstrong they appeared to be "a light brown with perhaps a greenish cast." Armstrong added: "His general appearance was insignificant." He kept his eyes "fixed on the upper distance," only looking down when Armstrong asked a question. While Hitler spoke calmly for the most part, his voice rose to the breaking point when he referred to some indignity inflicted on Germany, and he seemed in danger of losing control of himself. "We have waited months and years for justice. To get it, we must rearm. We cannot and will not wait longer. The *sine qua non* of any agreement which Germany will join must be, at the very minimum, equality in arms." To Armstrong's queries about his treatment of the Jews Hitler made no reply. When the brief and unsatisfactory audience was ended, Hanfstaengl was ecstatic. He repeated two or three times: "Wasn't he lovely to you?" Armstrong wrote: "He didn't ask questions or answer questions. He lived by and for himself alone. He was impervious to world opinion and cared for it so little that he didn't even inquire about it."

Hitler indeed made no bones about his objectives. He wanted the Polish Corridor and Danzig and Silesia back. He wished *anschluss* with Austria, North Schlesig from Denmark, Memel from Lithuania, and Malmédy and Eupen from Belgium. Also, he wanted back the colonies Germany had been divested of at the end of the war. He vowed "never to rest or relax until the Rhine flows to the sea once more as Germany's river, not Germany's frontier." The revolution would "only be complete when the entire German world is inwardly and outwardly formed anew." Russia was the great and ultimate enemy. The Jews and Communists must be exterminated.

Hitler was not the end of the bad news. Fascism seemed everywhere ascendant. In Rumania the Fascist Iron Guard seized power and began the systematic extermination of the Gypsies. They hunted them down in the marshes of the Dobruja. In France it was the Croix de Feu ("Cross of Fire"), growing daily in numbers and in acts of violence. Even Britain had the Mosleyites, followers of Sir Oswald Mosley.

Then, of course, there was the original Fascist, Mussolini, the longest-lived dictator in Europe, apparently impregnably ensconced. As the twenties wore on and the true nature of Mussolini's regime became more evident, many of his American admirers signed off. William Randolph Hearst, on the other hand, waxed positively rhapsodic. "Mussolini," he wrote, "I have always greatly admired, not only because of his astonishing ability, but because of his public service." The admiration was mutual, it turned out. When Hearst visited Italy in 1931, the dictator gave him the red carpet treatment. "He is a marvelous man," Hearst wrote a friend.

On a trip to Italy Harry Hopkins made an appointment with Mussolini. When Hopkins entered the long, ornate room that was the Italian dictator's office, Mussolini came "striding forward half way across the great room," wearing a "gray—rather flashy suit, light blue tie—soft shirt—and a broad smile. . . . Mussolini talks with his eyes and his hands—his gray eyes grow enormously big—like monkeys'—they flash—roll in the most amazing fashion. His hands and arms move constantly. . . . His questions were like sharp knives . . . ; he has the jaw of a strong man and a personality of great fervor," Hopkins wrote.

Hitler's persecution of the Jews made Mussolini nervous. He told

Hamilton Fish Armstrong that he had sent word to Hitler "personally" on the issue. "[I] told him it is a great error. I said he will have all the Jews in the world against him, and the Christians also." Hitler, Mussolini thought, was going too fast. "Remember, what I do now I do after ten years of experience." Mussolini agreed that France was finally frightened. The Maginot Line no longer seemed such an impregnable barrier. The French Socialists had voted for the war budget for the first time since the Versailles Treaty. "The economic crisis will continue," he told Armstrong, "and the political crisis will get worse. Anything can happen. But I do not believe in war."

Mussolini sensed that in tying his wagon to Hitler's insane ambition, he was getting into water that might well turn out to be over his head. He seemed uncertain and somewhat apprehensive to Armstrong. In contrast with Hitler he seemed quite human, able to "grin and carry on an ordinary conversation." If anything, he was too ingratiating. "Nothing was sincere, whether his friendly arm on your shoulder, or the grim visage and jut of chin with which he reviewed his troops . . . or his harangues from the balcony of the Palazzo Venezia, where his chest puffed out to incredible dimensions as the roar reverberated across the square: 'Duce! Duce! Duce! Duce!' "

In Brussels, Belgium, Armstrong met Count Carlo Sforza again. Sforza saw little change in Italy. The majority of Italians, he thought, were anti-Fascist but passive. Gaetano Salvemini, holed up with his books in a Paris garret, described the contest between Britain and France for Mussolini's favor. Britain, he declared, encouraged Italy and Germany to resist France. The British did not wish a crisis that would bring on "war or chaos," nor did they consider it "in the British interest for a thoroughgoing reconciliation to take place. The basis for the entente between MacDonald and Mussolini is that neither likes France, and both find material support for that dislike in German hostility to France." Lord Tyrrell, the British ambassador, rejected Salvemini's account of British double-dealing; not exactly pro-Italian, he recalled Lord Salisbury's description many years earlier: "The Italians, a nation of sturdy beggars."

In the United States, American Fascists appeared in the form of the followers of such exotics as George Sylvester Viereck, who made no bones of his admiration for Hitler. The Fascists seemed addicted to shirts. William Dudley Pelley's followers were termed Silver Shirts; another native Fascist was Arthur Smith, who led the Khaki Shirts. There were Blue Shirts, White Shirts, Minute Men, and dozens of other organizations. The Brown Shirts or Bund (largely German in membership) and the Black Shirts (largely Italian) corresponded to such groups in Europe. Lawrence Dennis's *The Coming American Fascism* was the Bible of the various Fascist groups. Dennis recommended purging the United States of both capitalism and communism in favor of a ruling elite.

Mussolini's influence in the United States, in part through Italian-American Fascists who did not balk at political assassination and other terrorist acts, was indicated by the fact that when the respected American journalist Gilbert Seldes wrote a highly critical biography of Mussolini entitled *Sawdust Caesar*, British and American publishers confessed they were afraid to publish it.

The spread of fascism in Europe and its appearance in the United States posed a serious dilemma for American radicals. They had no place in their philosophy of progress, a philosophy made up of faith in reason and science and the progressive enlightenment of the people through education, for the fact that in the "Century of Progress" evil should come back on the world compounded. In their view of the world, capitalists were "bad" and the people were "good." But fascism was clearly a popular movement. While it was led or at least encouraged by capitalists in the name, commonly, of opposing communism, it had the capacity to evoke the most wicked and rapacious impulses in ordinary folk. Moreover, it threatened to sweep everything before it. In nation after nation its barbaric doctrines found eager recruits. In Steve Nelson's words, "Those of us around the [Communist] movement followed the ascent of fascism in Italy and Germany with a mixture of horror and resolve; horror at the rapid and thorough destruction of the trade unions, civil rights, and the Italian and German radical movements; resolve that we would be more than idle spectators. As the picture appeared to me, there were two rivals on the world scene. There was an increasingly menacing fascist bloc and the countering force of the Soviet Union. The intensity and scope of the crisis suggested that the Western nations would be unable to sit this one out. They would have to go one way or the other . . . we raised these questions in the anthracite fields. At meetings, in our paper, and on our radio show, we urged a boycott of German goods, condemned Germany's racial theories, and tried to explain what was going on there."

The more or less official Communist line was that fascism was the final form of decadent capitalism. William Foster, chief theoretician of the American party, wrote that "in the days to come, Fascism may, in retrospect, be looked upon as a blessing in the guise of a setback. Who knows? Strange things, much stranger than fiction, are happening in this world of ours." In April, 1934, the Comintern declared that Hitler, "by destroying all the democratic illusions of the masses and liberating them from the influence of Social Democracy, accelerates the rate of Germany's development towards proletarian revolution."

In November, 1933, Roosevelt undertook a dramatic diplomatic initiative: the recognition of Soviet Russia. The negotiations with the Russians leading toward recognition were conducted in utmost secrecy by Henry Morgenthau and William Bullitt through Amtorg, the quasi-official Russian trading company.

If President Roosevelt sent Boris E. Skvirsky a letter, a draft of which Bullitt showed the head of Amtorg, to Chairman Mikhail Kalinin of the USSR, would it be favorably received? Having received that assurance, Bullitt, it was said, took the official letter from his pocket and handed it to Skvirsky, and the thing was done. On November 16, when Roosevelt announced recognition of the Soviet Union, his mother was so incensed that she threatened never to visit the White House again, and many conservative Americans felt equally strongly.

Rexford Tugwell was convinced that an important element in Roosevelt's decision to recognize Soviet Russia was his hope that such a step might help lessen the persecution of Russians who clung to their religious faith. Roosevelt talked at length with Tugwell about his concern regarding Stalin's merciless campaign against all religions. When Maxim Litvinov met with the President to conclude the final details of recognition, FDR said to him, as they finished their discussion, "There is one other thing; you must tell Stalin that the anti-religious policy is wrong. God will punish you Russians if you go on persecuting the church." An incredulous Litvinov told Tugwell and several American friends of the President's injunction. "Does he really believe in God?" Litvinov asked Tugwell. Tugwell assured him that he did.

A factor in Roosevelt's decision to recognize Soviet Russia may well have been his desire to deliver a rebuke to Hitler. The United States had diplomatic relations with Germany, hence with Hitler. This relationship could not be broken except by an act tantamount to war. But Roosevelt could at least recognize a nation marked by Hitler as his foremost enemy. For those who wished to read it so, recognition said, in effect, "Soviet Russia is the lesser of two evils."

The newly established U.S.-Soviet relations had a promising beginning. Litvinov, commissar for foreign affairs of the Soviet government, turned out to be an intelligent and urbane man. More important, he was an avid stamp collector and brought the President a veritable treasury of Russian stamps (he gave some to Harold Ickes, too).

Roosevelt gave considerable thought to the selection of the first American ambassador to the Soviet Union. He finally settled on William Bullitt. Bullitt was a wealthy upper-class intellectual who, like Roger Baldwin, was deeply committed to "social reconstruction." His marriage to Louise Bryant, John Reed's widow, had an almost symbolic significance. Rather like Felix Frankfurter's marriage, it marked the union of old Philadelphia aristocracy with transplanted West Coast bohemia (Louise Bryant had grown up in Portland, Oregon).

Bullitt had been one of that company of brilliant young men in the Peace Commission who went to Paris to negotiate the Versailles Treaty. If he was not an avowed Socialist, he shared the hopes and aspirations of his generation for a new political and economic order. He was a friend of Walter Lippmann, Lincoln Steffens, Bernard Berenson, and Jack Reed. To him, as to so many of his contemporaries, the Russian Revolution was full of promise, the harbinger of world revolution and a new day for the toiling and oppressed masses. He had wangled the famous and abortive mission to the Bolsheviks in 1919 with Lincoln Steffens to try to open negotiations with the Russians, and he and Steffens had come back to Paris convinced, in Steffens's words, that they had "seen the future and it works." After Bullitt's angry resignation from the peace delegation he continued to believe that if Wilson and other Allied leaders had responded positively to Lenin's initiatives, much of the hostility and misunderstanding that subsequently marked relations between Russia and the wartime Allies—France and Great Britain—could have been avoided.

Bullitt was in Vienna in late 1931 working with Sigmund Freud on a book that attempted to psychoanalyze Woodrow Wilson as an explanation of the rigidity he displayed in the matter of the League. Although the book was not published for some thirty-five years, it marked the beginning of what has come to be known as psychohistory, the effort to explain the behavior of leading historical figures (and thereby explain history) in terms of the childhood conflicts and traumas so dear to Freudians.

Raymond Moley described Bullitt as "pleasant, keen-minded, idealistic, and widely informed." On the negative side he "had a somewhat disturbing strain of romanticism in him. . . . Foreign affairs were . . . full of lights and shadows, plots and counterplots, villains and a few heroes." His was not, in Moley's view, the ideal diplomatic temper. But a place had to be found in the new administration for Bullitt, and Moley had persuaded a dubious Roosevelt to appoint Bullitt as a special assistant to Hull. Roosevelt believed that Bullitt had been disloyal to Wilson and complied with reluctance, but he soon fell under the spell of the Philadelphian's charm. It would be appropriate, FDR believed after his recognition of the Soviet Union, to appoint as ambassador someone known to be sympathetic to the ideals of the Russian Revolution.

Bullitt was happy in his aides, Charles "Chip" Bohlen and George Kennan. Bohlen was a classic representative of the Eastern establishment in the diplomatic service. A graduate of Harvard in 1927, he entered on the career of a diplomat in an era when isolationist sentiment was at a high tide in the United States. With no interest in the business world, which had attracted most of his college classmates, and no inclination to be a lawyer, he settled on the small and neglected Foreign Service by default rather than conviction. (His maternal grandfather had been named ambassador to France by Grover Cleveland.) Having passed the examinations and been admitted to the service, he found that the State Department had decided that each Foreign Service officer should specialize in a particular area of the world or a particular country. Bohlen chose Russia, as did five other young officers.

When Bohlen joined the Foreign Service, it was only three years old, having been established by the Rogers Act of 1924. It was, Bohlen noted, made up in the mid-twenties of a handful of dedicated diplomats interspersed with "eccentrics and misfits." The whole department consisted of only 614 people and had a budget of $14,000,000, most of which was recovered from fees for visas and passports. After his decision to specialize in Russia, Bohlen was sent to Estonia to master the language. It was not a taxing assignment. Quartered in a former Russian resort, he and the other students studied in the morning, had lunch at four in the afternoon, took a nap and then a walk, had a late and lavish supper, and then sat about a bubbling samovar, conversing "like characters in the stories of Chekhov, discussing philosophy and morals, reciting poetry, talking politics, and sipping tea." Bohlen's path was smoothed by his own cosmopolitan background (he had spent much of his youth in Paris with his mother) and his striking good looks. After two delightful summers in Estonia Bohlen, having acquired a considerable fluency in Russian, returned to the United States just in time for Roosevelt's recognition of the Soviet Union.

George Kennan, only slightly less handsome and aristocratic-looking than Bohlen, was described by his fellow diplomat as "tall, thin, and slightly balding, with a faintly ascetic expression." He was the son of a Midwesterner with strong ties to the East. A graduate of Princeton, he was the most brilliant of the younger members of the embassy. Kennan's first love was Russian literature. His namesake and distant relative, George Kennan, had been a Russophile and a friend of Leo Tolstoy's.

Kennan described Bullitt as "a striking man: young, handsome, urbane, full of charm and enthusiasm, a product of Philadelphia society and Yale but with considerable European residence, and with a flamboyance of personality right out of F. Scott Fitzgerald—a man of the world, . . . fluent in French and German, confident in himself . . . confident that he will have no difficulty cracking the nut of Communist suspicion and hostility which awaits him in Moscow. He is not a radical, but he is not afraid of radicals."

The Russia that Bullitt returned to was very different from the one that he had visited in 1919 and that he had continued to hold in memory. Lenin, however uncongenial his ideological persuasion may have been, was a towering figure, a man who emanated intellectual power. His successor, Joseph Stalin, was a brutal and ruthless man bent on eliminating all those he fancied were his enemies. But Bullitt's initial reaction to the Russians was that "as a nation they had become brotherly, open-hearted, free from conventions and unafraid of life." It was still possible to believe, in Charles Bohlen's words, "that the Soviets were emerging out of the difficult years of the civil war, the collectivization, and the beginnings of industrialization and were entering a plateau of relatively stable, pacific development."

Bullitt encouraged informal contacts with Russians and prodded his young staff to introduce baseball. Gloves and bats were ordered, and once a week Bohlen and his fellow diplomats would meet in a nearby park to give instruction to some bemused Russians, who had evidently been ordered to cooperate perhaps in the hope that learning the American game would provide some clue to the character of its citizens. The experiment was not a success. A Russian who was learning to catch missed a fast ball and was knocked out. The baseball school was abandoned.

Young Charles Thayer, another upper-class gentleman who had been on the polo team at West Point, undertook to introduce polo. The consent of Marshal Semyon Budenny, inspector general of the cavalry, was secured at the cost of large amounts of vodka. When Thayer finally trained two teams of Cossacks, a match was played before Marshal Kliment Voroshilov, commissar for defense. The results were no more encouraging than with baseball. After two or three rather ineptly played games, polo was also abandoned.

The most successful contact between the members of the American Embassy and the Russian people was with the members of the Moscow Ballet. When Bullitt invited the director of the ballet to the embassy to see a film on Balinese dancing, she was so impressed that she asked if he could arrange a showing for the corps de ballet. The result was a kind of alliance. While most of the members of the corps turned out to be disconcertingly plain, a "scrubby-looking group of young ladies . . . abominably dressed . . . without makeup; their hair indifferently combed," friendships were quickly formed, and soon "there were," in Bohlen's words, "usually two or three ballerinas running around the Embassy." When a Russian theater company undertook to put on the American play *The Front Page*, Kennan and Bohlen became advisers for the production.

The general atmosphere of Moscow was depressing to the Americans. In addition to the lowering skies, Bohlen noted that Moscow had a strange, penetrating odor, a "combination of sheepskin, sawdust, pink soap, disinfectant . . . —a ghastly Russian perfume. . . ." Foreigners called it "Stalin's breath." At the same time the members of the embassy staff liked the Russians they met. Bohlen wrote: "I know of no one who has been in Russia, whatever his attitude toward the regime, who felt anything but affection for the Russian people as a whole. They are simple and unaffected—primitive in the best sense of the word— and dislike many of the niceties of more sophisticated societies. They are natural, their characters and attitudes not having been frozen into molds by centuries of convention. I have always felt that a Russian is an individualist who gives his personal reaction to situations and people."

Bullitt cultivated the friendship of the old Bolshevik Nikolai Bukharin, who had been expelled from a leadership position in the party and then later restored. On one visit Bukharin, who was editor of *Izvestia*, was accompanied by Karl Radek, "a man of surpassing ugliness, with a brilliant and cynical mind." Radek had paid for his friendship with Trotsky by exile in Siberia. He had recanted and was now an editorial writer for various Soviet papers. Radek told Bohlen, "You Westerners will never understand Bolshevism. You consider Bolshevism as a hot bath whose temperature can be raised and lowered to suit the taste of the bather. This is not true. You are either a hundred percent in the bath and a hundred percent for it, or you are a hundred percent outside and a hundred percent against it."

Gradually it became apparent to Bullitt that Russia was no longer the nation pulsing with revolutionary zeal that had so appealed to him and Lincoln Steffens on their expedition in 1919. It was a rigid dictatorship more interested in consolidating power than in advancing the cause of humanity. Bullitt discovered that he could not trust the Russian officials with whom he dealt. Evasion and deceit characterized their words and actions. The change was profoundly disheartening to Bullitt, who had begun his mission with such high hopes. In Bohlen's words, the new Russia "violated his [Bullitt's] idealism and his old-fashioned American morality." The Soviets, victims of their faith in a Marxian dialectic that must, inevitably, like a law of nature, bring about the overthrow of capitalism, took the line that in their relations with any capitalist nation they were dealing with a transitory phenomenon. A corollary of this view was that the depraved nature of capitalism justified any tactic, however devious, that might weaken or discomfort the capitalist nations, already tottering to their graves.

The New Economic Policy (the famous NEP) was in danger of running aground in the face of the obduracy of the peasants, especially the kulaks, the larger landed farmers. They had reacted to the forced requisitioning of their crops by refusing to grow more than enough produce to feed themselves. Government officials were attacked by furious peasants, beaten, and, in some cases, killed. Cooperative property was burned, and even in coal mines there were numerous instances of sabotage. Many experienced observers predicted the collapse of the Bolsheviks. There was a terrible famine in 1933 as a result of the collectivization of the farms and the liquidation of the kulaks. American reporters in Moscow were aware of the rumors that 3,000,000 rebellious peasants had starved to death in the Ukraine, but no word of the tragedy was permitted to be cabled out of Russia.

The depth of Bullitt's disappointment with the Soviets can perhaps best be measured by the intensity of his hostility when he found all his advances rebuffed. He reacted, in Bohlen's words, "with violence, prejudice, and unreason." From having been a warm advocate of the new Russia, he became its bitter enemy. In both attitudes Bohlen, and Kennan as well, believed that the ambassador, whom they genuinely liked, had been at fault.

One of the problems in relations with the Soviets was that liberal opinion in the United States and within the Roosevelt administration (particularly Eleanor Roosevelt herself and Harry Hopkins) was friendly to the declared aims of the revolution and believed that the principal obstacle to friendly relations with the Russians was to be found in the profound and persistent hostility of those Americans of conservative persuasion, who saw the world in terms of a life and death struggle between capitalism and "godless communism." The unreasoning hatred and fear of communism in the United States thus produced in this country, as an antidote, a somewhat naïve view, even among non-Communist liberals, of the nature of the Soviet system. This complicated the task of American diplomats in Russia, who found that their efforts to describe realistically the aims of Russian policy and the often duplicitous means used to attain them were interpreted by liberal members of the administration as evidence of anti-Soviet prejudices. The generally sympathetic attitude of the members of the administration toward Soviet Russia is suggested by a letter of John Herrmann to his wife, Josephine Herbst, in the fall of 1934: "Was invited to the Sov. Embassy last night for buffet supper and to meet Ossinsky head of state planning board there in Russia . . . the entire new deal was there with the exception of the President. Tugwell, Frank, Howe and etc etc. . . . "

As we have had occasion to note, Americans had been making their way to Russia in considerable numbers since the revolution. Theodore Dreiser, after a visit in 1928, complained of the "inescapable atmosphere of espionage and mental as well as social regulation which now pervades every part of that great land." With diplomatic recognition, Americans came in larger numbers; their reactions varied, as did their temperaments and expectations. Many were impressed by the attention to the welfare of the workers and their families. There were health centers and kindergartens attached to every factory and collective farm, and women were encouraged to develop their capacities on the same basis as men.

Albert Coyle, head of the Brotherhood of Locomotive Engineers, organized one of the best-known expeditions to visit the Soviet Union, a so-called American labor delegation. Among its members were John Brody of the United Mine Workers, Lillian Herstein of the Chicago Teachers' Union, James W. Fitzpatrick, president of the Actors & Artistes Federation, and, on the intellectual and academic side, Stuart

Chase, Rexford Tugwell, and Paul Douglas from the faculty of the University of Chicago.

Josephine Herbst had mixed feelings about her Russian visit. "Some of their new cities terrified me," she wrote Katherine Anne Porter, "and convinced as I am that communism is coming whether we like it or not, and convinced also that it will save many while it damns a few, still I did shiver, being more of an anarchist and I am sure that as soon as it comes in the world little groups will revolt to get off by themselves and to be Alone."

Like Chip Bohlen and George Kennan, Hamilton Fish Armstrong was oppressed by the general feeling of grayness in Moscow. From his hotel window he watched the people below; "they were mere trickles of black ants in all that space, not hurrying like ants to a destination they wanted to reach but just going there doggedly. . . . " The impression was "not of lassitude or physical weakness, but of activity without spontaneity. . . . Nobody called out a greeting to a friend in the morning or waved a farewell at night." Paul Scheffer, a German newspaper correspondent, told Armstrong that all his old friends had disappeared or were inaccessible to him; in their place were "half a dozen Russians he didn't want to see but who were assigned to come and see him all the time." Most of the men, Armstrong noted, "wore black shirts and knee breeches, some leather jackets, almost all high boots. The only color was in the kerchiefs on the women's heads. . . . Beggars were sometimes as many as six or eight to a block (they were eliminated later by being shipped off to Siberia). . . . At night one saw homeless wanderers without enough spirit even to beg." Long queues were lined up at the state stores "to buy such elementary things as milk, eggs, ham. . . . "

The journalist Walter Duranty had a different impression. In Armstrong's words, "he thought that patriotic pride and faith in a socialist future compensated to a considerable degree for the crowding, deprivations and bleakness of daily life," while Louis Fischer was "inspired in the presence of this spectacle of creation and sacrifice."

In addition to those idealists who went to Russia to see the "future" (and often came away disillusioned), a number of Americans came to "make a buck." American capitalism, with a splendid indifference to ideological matters when there was money to be made, stood ready to assist its avowed enemy with American technology and "know-how." Henry Ford's Russian contacts went back before the revolution, when he had an agency in Russia for the sale of Model Ts. After the revolution the Bolsheviks immediately began negotiations for the purchase of Fordson tractors and cars (20,000 had been sold prior to 1933). The Russians were determined to enlist Ford's help in making their own Model As. The first step was to send fifty Russian technicians to the River Rouge plant to learn the ropes, or the machines. In 1928, at the beginning of the Five-Year Plan, a delegation of Russians had come to the United States to arrange for the construction of an automobile plant in the Soviet Union. Charles E. Sorenson, Ford's production manager, was sent to Russia to survey the situation there. In the words of Ford's architect friend Albert Kahn, who collaborated in the design of the Gorky plant, "Our attitude has been this—that we are not interested in their politics. We feel, as Mr. Ford has so well expressed it, that that which makes for the upbuilding of Russia is bound to prove a benefit to all nations, America included."

Sorenson and his aides were given the red-carpet treatment by the Russians, who provided a luxurious Pullman car for their travels. Stalin, who took a shine to down-to-earth Sorenson, greeted him, it was said, "Allo, Sharley." On May 31, 1929, Ford agreed to ship 72,000 disassembled vehicles to Russia over a three-year period, to train Russian technicians at the River Rouge plant, and to send experienced engineers to the Soviet Union to oversee the assembling of the trucks and cars and the installation of machinery to make cars at the Gorky plant. The Austin Company of Cleveland, an engineering and construction firm, accepted a contract to build a town to house 50,000 workers at the site of the Gorky plant. Included were a giant steam-generating plant, railway sidings, docks on the Oka River, apartment houses, a hospital, schools, theaters, stores, and social centers.

In 1931 one of Henry Ford's most experienced production men, Frank Bennett, sailed on the *Leviathan* with forty Ford technicians. "When the first car comes off, would you send me a cable? It means very much to this company," Ford told Bennett. When the first car had been assembled, the exuberant workers tossed Bennett in a blanket, a traditional Russian form of approval. Soon Bennett was complaining that so many Russian officials poured through the new plant that the men were unable to do their jobs.

When John Rushton, a Communist worker in a Ford plant, sold his home and took his family to Russia to help start up the Gorky factory, Walter Reuther was taken with the notion, and when he was fired by Ford, apparently for his work in the Norman Thomas campaign in 1932, Walter persuaded his brother Victor to follow in Rushton's footsteps. Armed with two sets of diemakers' tools, the brothers departed early in 1933 for the Soviet Union by way of Germany.

It was late November before the Reuthers finally arrived in Russia. They were given cramped quarters in the "American Village" and met John Rushton, comfortably settled in a house near the plant. The village had been built to accommodate the large number of American technicians—machinists and engineers—from Detroit, Chicago, Youngstown, and other U.S. cities. It was made up of some twelve two-story barrackslike buildings, a "number of small, jerrybuilt single houses, some communal rooms, and a special store where only foreigners were allowed to shop." A group of Finnish-Americans had built a sauna which the Reuther brothers were invited to use. In addition to some thirty or forty Americans, the village housed Italian refugees from Mussolini and British, Poles, and Germans.

The Reuther brothers encountered many hardships in their living arrangements and frustrations in their dealings with the Soviet bureaucracy, but they made firm friends with many of their Russian pupils and counterparts. "In the *Red Corner*," Walter Reuther wrote, "at lunch intervals, a wonderful spirit is to be found among the workers. A foreman produces a guitar, strums a few chords. A greasy mechanic and a red-kerchiefed *Komsomolka*, forgetting work, swing into gay dancing. Everybody keeps rhythm, shouts and laughs." The Reuthers were especially moved by the spectacle of Russian peasants from virtually medieval farming communities trying to adjust to factory labor. Modern heating and plumbing were unknown to them. One family nearly set a building ablaze by making a fire in the middle of the floor to cook dinner. Others had such difficulty learning to use indoor plumbing that they preferred to relieve themselves outdoors until the factory officials were forced to forbid the practice.

The Reuthers' principal contribution to civilization was organization of a volunteer group to make metal spoons out of scrap from the fender dies. These replaced unsanitary wooden spoons, and the workers celebrated their appearance with "a band, placards and banners, and speeches commemorating another milestone on the way to culture." When Victor Reuther's son went to Moscow thirty-four years later to study U.S.-Soviet relations at the university, he wrote his father that the famous spoons were still being used.

The training of workers went slowly at first, but by 1934 the Gorky plant was turning out 130 cars a day. The assistance given by Ford to the Soviets was not unique. Other industrialists, American and European, provided important machinery, as well as technicians and engineers, but Ford's contribution was the most extensive. It saved the Russians many months and even years in the industrialization of the country and, even more important, in the building of the tanks, trucks, and heavy equipment required for a modern army. Indeed, it may well have been that Henry Ford's greatest contribution to the world was not his car but the transmission to the Soviets of the technical knowledge and training which might be said to have provided that narrow margin by which Russia avoided defeat at the hands of Hitler's invading army.

# 22

## Communism and the Intellectuals

The segment of American society that proved most susceptible to communism was the new intellectual class. Communism appealed to it through the heart and the head. Although many members of the new class had renounced political activity to explore the darker realms of the psyche, they were predisposed, as the case of Sacco and Vanzetti demonstrated, to feel a special indignation at what appeared to be (and often were) miscarriages of justice. They were at heart reformists and, since that avenue seemed closed by the dominance of a reactionary capitalism, revolutionists. Communism, however brutal its actions, preached the universal brotherhood of man and did so in the guise of science. In addition, Marxist doctrine provided innumerable theoretical bones of the kind that intellectuals delight to gnaw on. Soon the stampede was on. Some rushed to join the party; many others were content to work in one of the numerous fronts the party was ingenious in devising, and they became fellow travelers. Often the distinction between a party member and a fellow traveler was a matter of degree. Being a party member involved, as we have seen, a dedication and, above all, a discipline that was basically uncongenial to the way writers, artists, actors, and intellectuals in general thought of themselves. It is thus the more remarkable that so many of them placed themselves under the formal discipline of the party.

Surprisingly, the advent of the New Deal, instead of checking the growth of communism by offering an alternative, initiated a period of unprecedented growth for the Communist Party. For those who believed in an inevitable revolution leading to the overthrow of capitalism, the New Deal was simply a straw in the wind or, conversely, a temporary impediment to the anticipated revolution, since it merely ameliorated, without curing, the basic defects—the inherent "inconsistencies," in Marxist terms—of capitalism. Moreover, on the two issues that radicals cared most about—checking the growth of fascism and insuring the civil rights of black Americans—Roosevelt was able to make only the most cautious and modest gestures.

After 1934, the new popular front line emanating from Moscow was also a great stimulus. People of intelligence and conscience who were sympathetic to communism but who wished to be able to work with other radical as well as liberal and reform groups welcomed the new line. By the same token it encouraged them to become Communists if they were not already party members because they were no longer required to denounce friends (or relatives) as "social fascists" and the "running dogs of capitalism."

Edmund Wilson was a kind of bellwether of the intellectuals' movement to the left. Despite his skepticism about the suitability of European socialism or communism for America, he found himself, as he wrote to Allen Tate in May, 1930, "going further and further to the left all the time and I have moments of trying to become converted to American Communism in the same way that Eliot makes an effort to become converted to Anglo-Catholicism. It is not that Communism in itself isn't all right, but that all that sort of thing in America seems more unrelated to real life than Catholicism does in England."

A year later Wilson wrote to Christian Gauss, his teacher at Princeton, that he had been (like many other intellectuals) reading Marx, "and so far as I can see," he added, "his prophecy is now being fulfilled and he ought to be turning in his grave with glee: combined overproduction and destitution, the complete divorce between the country and the city, with the people in the cities cut off from the earth and physically and spiritually enfeebled and the people in the country not able to make a living, and the concentration of money and means of production in a very few hands, with more and more of the rest of the people finding themselves dispossessed." A few months later Wilson was urging his Princeton classmate John Peale Bishop to read Marx and especially Trotsky's *Literature and Revolution*. Wilson expressed his conviction that intelligent people could not ignore those writers "any more than people of the eighteenth century could ignore . . . Voltaire and Montesquieu and Rousseau."

By the summer of 1931 things seemed much clearer to Wilson and, in consequence, much simpler. "The point is that it seems to me that the world is in for a big struggle between capitalism and Communism," he wrote to Allen Tate. "America is just beginning to be affected—having . . . definitely come to the end of her period of capitalist expansion. . . ." Soon other writers and intellectuals were taking the same path. Wilson wrote to John Dos Passos: "I found Sherwood Anderson all full of Communism. He doesn't know much about it, but the idea has given him a powerful afflatus. He has a new girl, a radical Y.M.C.A. secretary who took him around to the mills. He is writing a novel with a Communist hero and I have never seen him so much aroused." The artist Rockwell Kent was typical of those socialists (he had begun his radical career as a Christian Socialist) who moved readily in the direction of communism. "When the . . . revolution in Russia happened," he wrote, "I changed the name of what I believe in to Communism. Communism is coming. Capitalism is an outrageous, silly, cruel farce. . . . We can make the change—the revolution—peacefully: preserving democracy, not as Russia has done." At the same time Kent refused to join the Communist party, to the "discipline" of which he had no intention of submitting.

Malcolm Cowley was also an early recruit. In Cowley's words, "Communism offered at least the possibility of being reborn into a new life." Cowley recalled that Waldo Frank attributed *his* conversion to watching a parade in Moscow where he heard schoolgirls singing "We are changing the world." Granville Hicks and his friend Newton Arvin walked the streets of the college town where Hicks taught far into the night, debating the pros and cons, not so much of Marxism itself, about which they were generally in agreement, as of making a commitment to the Communist Party. In a letter written to Cowley in the summer of 1932 Arvin reflected that "it is a bad world in which we live, and so even the revolutionary movement is anything but what (poetically and philosophically speaking) it 'ought' to be. God knows, I realize this, as you do, and God knows it makes my heart sick at times; from one angle it seems nothing but grime and stink and sweat and obscene noises and the language of beasts. But surely this is what *history* is. . . . I believe we can spare ourselves a great deal of pain and disenchantment and even worse (treachery to ourselves) if we discipline ourselves to accept proletarian and revolutionary leaders and even theorists for what they are and must be: grim fighters in about the most dreadful and desperate struggle in all history—*not* reasonable and 'critically-minded' and forbearing and infinitely far-seeing men." Writers and intellectuals should salvage what they could of the things of the mind, the "rather abstract things we care for," but as long as people were starving and exploited, they should do "absolutely nothing, at any moment, to impede the work of the men who are fighting what is really our battle *for us.*"

It often seemed to Cowley that being a Communist resolved itself into walking picket lines, marching in parades, attending innumerable demonstrations, fund-raising events for unjustly incarcerated union organizers, blacks, farmworkers, and other victims of capitalist oppression (the list seemed unending), and, of course, meetings, constant and interminable meetings, most of them marked by bad-tempered exchanges between friends and ex-friends. Beyond all this there was what Cowley called the "religious element" present "in the dreams of those years." They made "everything else seem unimportant, including one's pride, one's comfort, one's personal success or failure, and one's private relations [which on the whole, as we have seen, usually ranged from bad to disastrous]. There wasn't much time for any of these things. . . . All one's energies turned outward, and they seemed to be vastly increased by being directed toward purposes shared with others. One borrowed strength from the others and gave it back twofold."

Meetings had a form as strict as any religious ceremony. Whenever a new committee was formed (and committees proliferated beyond counting), it was noted that "There should be a woman on it," and a black, and a real worker, preferably a union organizer. Someone suggested that the ideal solution would be a multipurpose black-woman-organizer.

The principal Communist front for writers was the John Reed Club. The clubs, scattered across the country, were designed to encourage the promising young authors of radical inclination and instruct them in the principles of "prolit," short for "proletarian literature."

The original John Reed Club was founded in New York City in October, 1929, the month of the crash, by writers associated with the *New Masses.* Its purpose was to "clarify the principles and purposes of revolutionary art and literature, to propagate them, to practice them."

The idea spread rapidly. Soon there were other clubs in other cities—in Chicago, San Francisco, Philadelphia, even in the little resort town of Carmel, California, where a club was started by Lincoln Steffens and Ella Winter. A year after the clubs had been founded and taken under the wing of the party, they sent half a dozen delegates to the Second International Conference of Revolutionary Writers in Kharkov. John Herrmann and Josephine Herbst slipped in as observers. Herbst found herself resisting the prolit cant that poured forth in such abundance. As she paraphrased the official line, "There was no time in this era of great depressions or threatened war to write long novels, poetry, or plays. . . . What was required were stories of their struggles and their aims: thus building the literature of the new class with the new man." Such pronouncements were painful to Herbst. She left the hall to smoke a cigarette, and Louis Aragon, the widely admired French poet and critic, followed her, took her arm, and said, "We all know what your position is. You mustn't mind that kind of talk. It's a kind of infantile disease and will wear out."

The proceedings of the conference were published in English in a special edition of *Literature of the World Revolution*, the masthead of which carried, among other names, those of John Dos Passos, Upton Sinclair, Michael Gold, Josephine Herbst, and John Herrmann.

Despite the absurd instructions issued from Moscow on the proper subject matter of revolutionary literature, the John Reed Club flourished. Young Richard Wright found a literary "home" in the one in Chicago, where his work, immature and tentative as it initially was, was praised and, most important of all, published. The individuals Wright met on his first visit ranged from "a Jewish boy who was to become one of the nation's leading painters to a chap who was to become one of the eminent composers of his day, to a writer who was to create some of the best novels of his generation. . . ."

Jerre Mangione, a member of the New York club, wrote: "Argumentation . . . was the John Reed Club's chief activity. The debates usually centered on differences of Marxist interpretation as precipitated by recently published books and articles." Most of the larger clubs put out their own literary magazines—the *Anvil*, *Hammer*, *Red Pen*, none very original, their titles generally more militant than their contents.

In addition to the other sources of conflict, there was, in most John Reed clubs, an age gap. Older, established writers, however sympathetic to the party's aims, had no intention of being told, often by doctrinaire young theorists who had written nothing very considerable themselves, what they should write about and how they should write. The younger writers often resented the success of their elders and believed that it had been achieved by compromises with capitalism and the literary bourgeoisie. Prolitcult dictated that all novels and stories should promote the coming revolution by focusing on the workers and the class struggle. As we have seen, America abounded in novels about workers and strikes in the decade of the nineties and in the first decade of the new century. Indeed, it could be said that the first proletarian novel was Harriet Beecher Stowe's *Uncle Tom's Cabin.* Herman Melville's novels had dealt with the lives of ordinary seamen who certainly qualified as proletarians, and aristocratic Richard Henry Dana's *Two Years Before the Mast* was as proletarian as one could wish except for the fact that it did not recommend revolution or, to be sure, stress the class struggle. Albion Tourgée's novel *Murvale Eastman, Christian Socialist,* published in the 1880s, was about a socialist minister who preaches to his congregation on the iniquities of capitalism, asking why there are two distinct classes in America, the rich and the poor. "Are the Rich to grow richer forever, and the poor to grow feebler and more dependent? . . . Is the dollar mark the real measure of human values?" Edward King in *Joseph Zalmonah,* published in 1893, had told the story of a radical union organizer in the New York garment trades and his fight for a socialist America. So there was, in fact, no dearth of novels dealing with the lives of working people. Jack London had tried his hand at them, and of course, Upton Sinclair's *The Jungle* was the prototype of the proletarian novel. But that particular crop of proletarian novels, written before the word was in common usage, had been largely forgotten and doubtless would not, in any event, have satisfied the strict new rules. The fact was that the most conscientious efforts to comply with the rules were often unsuccessful. Party theoreticians were constantly on the lookout for heresies and deviations.

In 1933 Granville Hicks's survey of American writers entitled *The Great Tradition* was published. It took the line that American writers had failed to understand the nature of the class war and had thus distorted reality in their books. Malcolm Cowley reviewed it in the form of a letter to Hicks: "Both of us believe that the central feature of modern life is a struggle between classes which is also a struggle of the working class against all forms of exploitation. . . . Both of us are convinced that literature and politics, art, science and education are all departments of life, and that no artist or writer can divest himself of his role in life. He takes, or eventually will be forced to take, one side or the other, and both of us have made the same choice." But Cowley went on to take his friend Hicks to task for applying too rigid a Marxist standard to the writers he criticized.

The most famous assault by a Communist critic on an established non-Communist writer was undoubtedly that of Mike Gold on Thornton Wilder, which appeared in the *New Republic* in October, 1930. Wilder was chosen as the symbol of a decadent upper-class culture that prescribed "love" rather than class war as the solution to the problems of mankind. The attack, ferocious even for the literary world, was entitled "Wilder: Prophet of the Genteel Christ." Wilder was a "diluted . . . Anatole France" presiding over a "historic junkshop," while neglecting the "facts of . . . working-class martyrdom." He combined "chambermaid literature, Sunday-school tracts and boulevard piety" with "a dash of the prep-school teacher's erudition." He served the bourgeoisie with an "air of good breeding . . . decorum, priestliness, glossy high finish . . . love of the archaic, etc. . . ."

At the end of his best-selling novel *The Bridge of San Luis Rey*, Wilder had written: "For there is only the land of the living, and the land of the dead, and the bridge is love, the only survival, the only meaning." Gold quoted the sentence to ridicule it: "And nobody works in a Ford plant, and nobody starves looking for work, and there is nothing but Love in God's ancient Peru, Italy, Greece, but not in God's capitalist America in 1930!"

In addition to the John Reed clubs a number of Communist-inspired organizations appeared on the literary and artistic scene. Malcolm Cowley in his memoir recalls the Workers Film and Photo League ("workers" and "league" were favorite party words), the Workers Dance League, Red Dancers, Rebel Dancers, American Revolutionary Dancers, the Theater Union, the Theater Collective, the Theater of Action, the Workers Laboratory Theater, the Harlem Prolets, the Music Vanguard, the Workers Music League, and the League of Workers Theaters. The last were in fact looked on as major agents of the revolution. In them the class struggle would be enacted with dramatic effect. There the workers would see radical ideas illustrated in unmistakable power and simplicity. It was the ambition of every aspiring radical playwright and director to produce such plays. It was hoped that in time the workers would write and act in their own proletarian dramas. Workers might not read books, but they could watch plays. Hallie Flanagan, the leading American "Marxist theoretician" of revolutionary drama, declared that the producer of plays for the worker must be "Strong, . . . for the theater, if it is to be of use to the worker, must be divorced from the nonessentials which have become synonymous with it—divorced from expensive buildings, stage equipment, painted elaborate costumes and properties . . . above all, divorced from actors who want to show off or make money." The proponents of the new revolutionary theater were advised: "Start dramatic groups in unions, in fraternal organizations, in social clubs, in company unions, in YMCAs. . . . Don't expect profit in money. These theaters exist to awaken the workers."

Flanagan anticipated workers' companies everywhere, performing in "street plays and pageants . . . on trucks and on street corners. . . ." The plays would doubtless be "crude, violent, childish and repetitious," but Americans need not "deplore the lack of art in the workers' theater"; bourgeois audiences would not even see such plays. "It is only in the event of the success of its herculean aim—the reorganization of our social order—that we shall become an involuntary audience," Flanagan added.

"How are they to be trained, these workers, unused to the simplest technique of the stage," Flanagan asked, "men and women who work by the day in shops, factories or mines, and come together at night to make a theater?" They should not be trained in the "act of illusion," for their purpose was to grasp reality more firmly by enacting the drama of their own lives, "expressing workers' problems," attacking "those evils from which they themselves are suffering, wage cuts, unemployment, deportation, lynching, racial prejudice, legal discrimination, war, and all oppression and injustice."

In June, 1931, a conference of so-called workers' cultural societies, sponsored by the John Reed Club of New York, brought together 224 delegates from groups in New York City and the vicinity. Hallie Flanagan, who was present, reported that there were "some two thousand cultural organizations of workers," but just what that phrase meant was left vague.

Since the primary task of Communist writers was to produce proletarian literature, a vast amount flowed from the presses. Joseph Freeman's *Proletarian Literature in the United States*, published in 1935, contained the pro forma attack on liberals. The typical liberal (if one could find him), "wrapping himself in linen, donning rubber gloves, and lifting his surgical instruments—all stage props—the Man in White, the 'impartial' liberal critic, proceeds to lecture the assembled boys and girls on the anatomy of art in the quiet, disinterested voice of the old trouper playing the role of 'science.' " Behind the mask of science was the "bitter gall of partisan hatred." Freeman concluded: "In the past five years, American proletarian literature has made striking progress. The arguments against it are dying down in the face of actual creative achievement. Life itself has settled the dispute for the most progressive minds of America."

Jack Conroy was a leading proletarian novelist. The son of a coal miner, Conroy grew up in the classic Midwestern town of Moberly, Missouri. His proletarian origins and his rough style made him something of a hero in New York literary circles. His shoes were "chronically untied," and he had a "thoroughly disheveled manner," a friend noted. Mencken, taken with an article Conroy submitted to the *American Mercury*, became his patron, and Conroy solidified his position as a Communist writer and critic by editing radical literary journals (first the *Anvil* and then the *New Anvil*) of the Chicago John Reed Club. John Dryden was Conroy's favorite poet, and Charles Embree, also a Moberly native, remembers Conroy reciting "long batches" of the English poet in his "fog-horn" voice in a working-class bar in Moberly to the obvious irritation of the other patrons.

In 1933 Conroy published his obligatory proletarian novel, *The Disinherited*, which described the struggle of young Larry Donovan to survive in a mining camp called Monkey Nest. After a bitter winter in New York Donovan returns to his Missouri hometown to find farmers facing starvation and the loss of their homes. He decides to devote his life to the revolutionary struggle. "To me," Conroy declared, "a strike bulletin or an impassioned leaflet are of more moment than three hundred prettily and faultlessly written pages about the private woes of a gigolo or the biological ferment of a society dame as useful to society as the buck brush that infest Missouri cow pastures."

One of Conroy's closest Moberly friends was the black poet Melvin Tolson. Tolson became a professor at a black university and was appointed the poet laureate of Liberia at that African nation's centennial celebration. Years later Tolson wrote Conroy a "birthday poem":

> Perhaps when we are dust and stone
> Our epitaphs decayed, unknown,
> In tomorrow's century,
> Some Ph.D. with pick and spade
> And literary masquerade
> Will excavate knoll or glade
> In ancient Moberly.

> Our ghosts now guzzle Olympian brew
> With Heine, Whitman, Homer, Shakespeare too
>     And listen to Voltaire's jest.
> In heaven you and I look down
> Upon the site of our home town
> Whence kith and kin and sage and clown
>     Departed are, we hope, to rest!

The poem ended on a cheerful note:

> Ghost talk! I say: Remember when
> Jack Conroy wrote *A World to Win*
>     And *The Disinherited?*
> Now, look at Moberly! Ah, Jack,
> I see no hovels by the track,
> No crummy miners, white or black,
>     No children underfed.

When William Rollins's proletarian novel *The Shadow Before* was published to laudatory reviews, it sold fewer than 2,000 copies, but it was translated into Russian, and Rollins was invited to visit the Soviet Union as its guest and stay as long as he liked (he stayed a year). Before he departed, he was lionized in the leftist literary circles of New York, which were, for all practical purposes, the only literary circles in the United States, and he complained to Jerre Mangione that cocktail party guests "talk about my book as if I weren't present, as if the novel had been written by some extraordinary writer that I hadn't yet met." He even found himself, after a few drinks, talking about himself in the third person.

Robert Cantwell had left college at the age of seventeen to work in a plywood mill. He told Malcolm Cowley that he had taught himself to write by reading Henry James's prefaces. He had published his first novel, *Laugh and Lie Down*, at the age of twenty-three, making him the prodigy of the New York literary world. It was followed by his widely acclaimed *The Land of Plenty*. In Cowley's words, "he was a slight, sallow, hungry-looking young man who dressed neatly in suits that were always too large, as if he had shrunk since buying them. . . ."

James T. Farrell was a proletarian novelist in good standing. At the end of his *Studs Lonigan* trilogy, Farrell used Studs's death as a symbol of the collapse of capitalism. As Studs is dying, his father is watching a Communist demonstration.

Waldo Frank's two novels, five years apart, traced an aeon of intellectual travel. *The Dark Mother*, published in 1928, told the story of the young manhood of David Markand (plainly Waldo Frank)—his search for himself and his first timid experiences of sex, ending with the mature love of Helen, the woman he would marry, and the suicide of the woman whose love for him was unrequited. *The Death and Birth of David Markand*, published in 1934, told of Markand's abandoning his wife and his successful middle-class professional career to "find himself," as we say today. A major revelation comes to Markand at the graves of two men who have been murdered for leading a strike of coal miners in Kentucky, an episode based, obviously, on Frank's own experience with the Harlan County strike. He thinks, as he stands beside their graves, "I envied you, knowing how different I am. I will no more envy you. I will be like you. I will do like you. . . . I will embrace your class. All men who want to live today must embrace it to live. I have only the dead body of a class that dies. I need, that I may live, the living body of the class which is now life." Markand's rebirth included sexual intercourse with a black woman who represents joyful and uninhibited sexuality, in contrast with Markand's earlier guilty and uncertain gropings. In one of the more touchingly romantic notes of the time, Frank dedicated his novel "To the American worker who will understand."

In addition to proletarian novelists by the dozen, there were hundreds of Communist critics and journalists (often, to be sure, the critics and journalists wrote proletarian novels). Heywood Broun, while he may not have been a party member, was a conspicuous Communist journalist. Scion of an old New York family, Broun had been a leader in the fight to save Sacco and Vanzetti and was the founder of the left-leaning Newspaper Guild. "There seemed to be a tremendous lot of him," Malcolm Cowley wrote, "in height, girth, features, appetite, rumpled clothes, untied shoelaces, and social conscience." Westbrook Pegler, a rival conservative journalist, called him the "one-man slum." The Broun apartment, which featured an enormous couch called the Maine Bunk and numerous pillows scattered about the floor "for those who live close to nature," Taylor Gordon noted, was a gathering place for radical artists and intellectuals, invariably including blacks and black entertainers.

Broun's circle included Kyle Crichton, another large, untidy man, who was a humorous writer—a hard trade—for thoroughly bourgeois *Collier's* and wrote under the pen name of Robert Forsythe for the *New*

*Masses.* Orrick Johns was a fierce cripple with a reputation as something of a Communist theoretician. His wife, Peggy Baird Johns, divorced him and married Malcolm Cowley, but she did not in consequence limit her affairs, of which she constantly boasted. After twelve stormy years her marriage to Cowley broke up, and she went off to Mexico as a kind of companion-nurse to Hart Crane.

Among the prominent literary converts to communism was that exotic figure of the twenties Max Bodenheim. Like many other hedonists, Bodenheim accepted communism's Puritanism in sexual matters and became notably straight.

Theodore Dreiser believed that it was not enough for writers committed to communism to turn out proletarian novels and plays; they should become directly involved in the workers' struggle for justice. He thus early in 1931 assembled a number of literary figures at his apartment on West Fifty-seventh Street. There Malcolm Cowley encountered "novelists, critics, liberal editors, crusading journalists, almost everybody in the literary world—except Red Lewis and Dorothy Thompson. . . ." Passing a large white handkerchief through his plump pink hands, Dreiser told the assembled literati that in his view, "the time was ripe for American intellectuals to render some service to the American worker." Others spoke: Louis Adamic and, notably, Lincoln Steffens, dean of reform journalists, "small, trim, with a little white chin-beard and a Windsor tie tucked loosely into his collar," looking like "a cartoonist's notion of a dapper French artist."

Out of the meeting came an organization called, somewhat misleadingly, the National Committee for the Defense of Political Prisoners. The secretary of the committee was Alfred Hirsch, a graduate of Harvard, class of 1926. It recognized the "right of workers to organize, strike and picket, their right to freedom of speech, press and assembly, and it will aid in combating any violation of those rights, through legal means, and above all, by stimulating a wide public interest and protest." It invited "writers, artists, scientists, teachers and professional people . . . to join its ranks and aid its work." It was, for all practical purposes, the literary arm of the International Labor Defense, and like that body, it was allied with the Communist Party. Its purpose was to send teams of writers wherever the rights of workers, union organizers, or strikers were denied, to draw public attention and muster support. The national committee was soon dispatching teams of well-known writers to the scenes of labor conflicts.

In July, 1931, Dreiser traveled to the coalfields of western Pennsylvania to offer aid and comfort (and publicity) to the National Miners Union, the Communist Party alternative to Lewis's United Mine Workers. Dreiser denounced the AFL for its reactionary policies and for its refusal to support the strike, which failed miserably.

In Harlan County, Kentucky, the Communists had come in to support striking coal miners and, they hoped, to win recruits. The conditions in the coalfields were execrable. The miners, for their dirty and dangerous work, earned less than $35 a month, which was usually paid in company scrip that had to be spent at a company store where everything was overpriced. The circumstances of the miners were essentially what they had been sixty years earlier, when the Molly Maguires began their deadly strike. The Harlan County strike, like that in the western Pennsylvania coalfields, was a reminder, if any was needed, of how precarious the situation of workers was in industrial America. Since the coal strike of 1902, when Theodore Roosevelt's intervention had won the miners in the anthracite fields some grudging concessions, their wages and conditions of labor had regressed.

Dreiser gathered a little band of writers that included John Dos Passos, Edmund Wilson, and Charles Rumford Walker and Walker's wife to go to the aid of the embattled miners. When the group arrived in Pineville, Kentucky, they found machine guns emplaced around the courthouse. The appearance of *Northern Communist Writers*, who combined in their respective persons three of the most feared and hated categories in the South, enraged the mineowners and their dutiful accomplices, the law enforcement officers of the county.

Followed everywhere by armed deputies, the writers "held hearings" like some congressional committee, presided over by Dreiser, "like a goofy old senator," in Dos Passos's words. The stories that they heard from miners and their families were grim: starvation wages, long hours, warrantless searches for weapons, jailings on even a rumor of union activity, and brutal beatings. A miner's wife, asked by Dreiser what she thought of the law, replied that it was "a gun thug in a big automobile." A nurse testified that three to seven babies a week were dying of inadequate diet in the little community of Straight Creek. She sang for the writers a song, "The Kentucky Miner's Wife Ragged Hungry Blues":

> All the women in this coalcamp
> are a-sittin' with bowed-down heads,

> Ragged and barefooted
>> and their children a-cryin' for bread.
> No food, no clothes for our children,
>> I'm sure this ain't no lie.
> If we can't get no more for our labor
>> We will starve to death and die.

When the writers escaped from Harlan County to tell their tales of terrorism by law, the officials of the county belatedly indicted them for criminal syndicalism. Dreiser was also charged with having sexual commerce with a woman named Marie Pergain. A detective testified that he had seen the woman go into Dreiser's room and had placed toothpicks against the door. They were undisturbed in the morning, indicating that Pergain had spent the night in Dreiser's bed. In view of Dreiser's insatiable sexuality, which had only slightly diminished with age, the story was not unlikely, but it seemed irrelevant to the issue at hand. Dreiser added unintended levity to the whole situation by denying the charge of immorality, Kentucky-style, on the ground that he was "completely and finally impotent."

Meanwhile, the strike dragged on. The mineowners were determined to starve the miners into returning to work. Kitchens organized to feed the miners and their families were dynamited or burned, and trucks carrying food were turned back. Charles Rumford Walker undertook to round up another band of writers, arguing that the visit of the Dreiser group had had very positive results in creating national publicity. This time the group was made up of Malcolm Cowley, Edmund Wilson, Waldo Frank, Quincy Howe, and that veteran of innumerable strikes and labor wars Mary Heaton Vorse. Since, in Cowley's words, Frank had written more books than the others, he was made chairman. Assembling at Knoxville, Tennessee, on February 10, 1932, the group received the disheartening news that Harry Sims, a young Communist union organizer, had been shot by a sheriff's deputy and was dying in a nearby hospital. On the road the writers encountered thirty armed men, and their driver warned them: "They're fixing to keep you out of Harlan County. It's a tough county and Harlan is a tough town. I went there once, but I didn't stay long. A man came up to me in the street and said, 'I'll give you ten dollars for your gun.' I said, 'But you've got a gun already.' He said, 'A man ain't safe here withouten he has two guns.' So I took his ten dollars and got out of town."

At Pineville things seemed hardly less threatening. There were more heavily armed men, and visiting the office of the only lawyer in town who would speak for the strikers, Cowley saw machine guns protruding from the windows of buildings across the street. The union, more concerned with using the visitors to generate sympathy for the cause than with the safety of the writers, had called a public meeting in defiance of the Pineville officials. The townspeople, alarmed by rumors that the miners, led by Communists, intended to set fire to Pineville, all were armed to the teeth. At a meeting with merchants, mineowners, and the mayor, Frank explained that the writers simply wished to deliver three truckloads of food to the striking miners for distribution to their families and to hear the miners' grievances. The mayor refused. If they attempted to distribute any food, they all would be arrested. They must not have a meeting or talk with the miners or distribute any printed material. If miners were invited to their rooms in the local hotel, they would be arrested for holding a meeting. A coal operator with, in Cowley's words, "a steel-trap mouth," told the writers, "This is another war. I admire your nerve in coming here where you don't know anything about the conditions or the feeling of the people. If you don't watch out, you'll find out how ugly we can be. . . ." Cowley learned that at a meeting of mine operators that afternoon some had urged that the writers all should be shot as a warning to outsiders and radicals in general that nobody should mess with Harlan County's business, but cooler heads prevailed.

Meanwhile, the county attorney had given permission to distribute the food on a county road. When the food had been passed out, a miner tried to speak. The sheriff, with revolvers in both hands, chased the miner, who escaped into the crowd. That evening the baggage of the party was searched for subversive material at the hotel, and at ten-thirty at night the writers were roused from their hotel rooms and told that they all were under arrest. Released after several hours, they returned to their hotel to find armed citizens awaiting them. They were hustled into waiting cars to be driven to the state line. During the trip their abductors carried on conversations designed to unnerve them further. In Cowley's car the driver declared: "They shot one of those Bolsheviks up in Knox County this morning. . . . That deputy knew his business. He didn't give the redneck a chance to talk, he just plugged him in the stomach. We need some shooting like that down here. . . . Let me tell you, I've got eight men with rifles waiting on the hill, and if any redneck tries to picket my mine, he's going to be dead before he knows it. . . . Listen," the driver said to his silent passengers,

"I want to ask you a question. Do you two fellows believe in a Supreme Being?"

Deposited at the state line, Cowley and his companions heard screams coming from the car carrying Frank and a lawyer for the International Labor Defense, Allan Taub. The two men were being beaten and pistol-whipped. When Frank was half pushed, half carried from the car, blood was streaming from wounds on his head.

The trip, quixotic and dangerous as it had been, did bear fruit. Cowley, as editor of the *New Republic*, carried some weight. He got a hearing from Bronson Cutting, the liberal Senator from New Mexico, whose aide was the radical young poet Phelps Putnam, a Yale man who persisted in wearing a black Stetson around the Senate Office Building. Cutting agreed to call for hearings on the strike. The writers wrote voluminously about their experience in Pineville and talked extensively.

The Pineville episode accelerated the movement of Edmund Wilson and Waldo Frank to the left. A few months after their ordeal Wilson and Frank, with Lewis Mumford, Sherwood Anderson, and Dos Passos, drew up a manifesto "without the collaboration or knowledge of the Communists," in Wilson's words, and circulated it to other writers—Dreiser, Edna St. Vincent Millay, and Paul Green among them. The manifesto began: "The present crisis of the world—and specifically of the United States—is something more than a mere crisis of politics or economics; and it will not pass with the depression. It is a crisis of human culture. What faces us today is the imperative need for new social forms, new values, a new human order." The economic system was "based on the subordination of human values to motives of anarchic self-assertion . . . the exploitation of the many for the profit of the few. . . . The need of human growth is . . . inextricable from the need for a new social-economic order. . . . The ruling castes . . . must be expelled from their present position. A temporary dictatorship of the class-conscious workers must be set up, as the necessary instrument for abolishing all classes based on material wealth." The revolution, the manifesto argued, was not simply "a revolt against the economic chaos of today." It was "an immediate organ of creation." As writers the drafters and signers of the manifesto supported the "social-economic revolution" as the first step toward the creation of "a new human culture . . . which shall release the energies of man to spiritual and intellectual endeavor." The authors recognized the "fundamental identity of [their] interests with those of the workers and farmers of the nation" and called on "our fellow writers, artists, teachers, scholars, engineers, and intellectuals of every kind, to identify their cause with that of the workers, in whose ultimate capacity to rise and to rule rests the destiny of America and mankind."

The manifesto, which was warmly debated and substantially modified before several hundreds of America's best known writers and artists signed it, was perhaps the high point of the delusional politics of the left. Certainly there were things profoundly wrong in America. In the ruthless suppression by violence and intimidation of all efforts by workers in mines and factories to raise their wages and improve their conditions of labor there was ample indication of the determination of the rich and powerful to exploit the poor and weak. The war between capital and labor, in its more extreme and dramatic form, was at least as old as the Great Strikes of 1877. It had been a constant preoccupation of reformers and socialists of various persuasions for more than half a century. But there was much else wrong as well, and the notion that the infallible cure for the manifold ills of American society was a "temporary dictatorship of the class-conscious workers" revealed a startling lack of understanding of American society and American history.

John Dos Passos was a strong critic of the manifesto. He pointed out what hardly needed emphasis: It read like a pronouncement by the Comintern. Wilson wrote to Waldo Frank that Dos Passos felt that "in spite of our efforts to keep clear of the Communist formulas we have followed them too closely." The formulas did not, for example, allow for the large number of white-collar workers in the United States. Dos Passos believed that an identity of interests between the "petty bourgeois" and the "proletariat" should be emphasized, "rather than the possible class dictatorship of the proletariat over the bourgeoisie," certainly not an unreasonable suggestion. A number of well-known writers, among them Sinclair Lewis and Van Wyck Brooks, balked at signing.

The interventions of nervous bands of writers spouting revolutionary rhetoric often bordered on the absurd. In 1922 the Italian marble workers in Barre, Vermont, had gone out on strike to protest unhealthy working conditions, specifically the dust from the marble-cutting operations which collected in the lungs of the men and often resulted in early death from lung diseases. The companies brought in French-Canadians and broke the strike. When the marble workers went out on strike again in 1935, the defense committee dispatched a contingent of writers to Barre. Josephine Herbst was among them. In Barre she encountered a group of New York party members that included the Max Lerners and Rockwell Kent. Kent's speech to the strikers was so patronizing, Herbst wrote to William Phillips, that "I wanted to sink through the floor. . . . All the other smuggies got up and told them 'to fight' etc etc ad nauseam." Budd Schulberg, a student at Dartmouth College, tried to enlist Sinclair Lewis, who lived in nearby Woodstock, Vermont, but Lewis was wary.

Observing a textile strike at New Bedford with Mary Heaton Vorse, Waldo Frank thought "of the heroic tiny groups of revolutionary organizers throughout the nation: individuals, isolate, threatened, resourceless save for their own luminous spirit. Pleading with the workers, against the workers, to know themselves, to be themselves, to fight the good fight," Frank wrote, "while the official leaders and the pack of papers and the towns and the churches vomit their fear of the new world in the form of insults and lies. . . . When the collectivist era has done its work—the abolition of economic classes and of animal want—men will turn, as only the privileged of the past could ever turn, toward the discovery of Man."

Other writers journeyed to other strikes in North Carolina, Alabama, Mississippi, and the Imperial Valley of California. They invariably encountered hostility and were often in danger; they seldom, if ever, affected the outcome of a strike, and many of them came to realize that they were being used by the Communist Party for its own ends, which were not necessarily those of the strikers. But in the aggregate they performed somewhat the same function that the muckrakers, men and women like Lincoln Steffens, Charles Edward Russell, and Ida Tarbell, had at the turn of the century; they increased the public awareness of terrors and brutalities experienced by workingmen and workingwomen.

One of the first fruits of the new Comintern policy of the popular front was the American Writers' Congress, called in 1935 by a group of writers, most of whom had supported the Communist presidential ticket in 1932. A full page of the *New Masses* of January 22, 1935, was taken up with the "call." The congress was to be devoted to an "exposition of all phases of a writer's participation against war, the preservation of the civil liberties and the destruction of fascist tendencies everywhere. . . . The capitalist system crumbles so rapidly before our eyes that, whereas ten years ago scarcely more than a handful of writers were sufficiently far-sighted and courageous to take a stand for proletarian revolution, today hundreds of poets, novelists, dramatists, critics, short story writers and journalists recognize the necessity of personally helping to accelerate the destruction of capitalism and the establishment of a workers' government." The call assured its readers: "A new renaissance is upon the world; for each writer there is the opportunity to proclaim both the new way of life and the revolutionary way to attain it." All writers "who have achieved some standing in their respective fields, who have clearly indicated their sympathy to the revolutionary cause, who do not need to be convinced of the . . . inevitability of revolution" were invited to the congress. The intention was to form a League of American Writers that would be affiliated with the International Union of Revolutionary Writers. Sixty-two writers signed the call; they included Theodore Dreiser, Sherwood Anderson, John Dos Passos, James T. Farrell, Waldo Frank, Langston Hughes, Malcolm Cowley, Granville Hicks, Ella Winter, Nelson Algren, Erskine Caldwell, Josephine Herbst, Nathanael West, and Richard Wright.

When the congress met on April 26, the Mecca Temple in New York City, which held 4,000 people, was filled. On the stage were seated 216 writers. Malcolm Cowley suspected later that many of the 4,000 in the audience were there not because of their devotion to literature but because it was a required exercise for the party faithful. The German playwright Friedrich Wolf reported on the writers who had been beaten and tortured in Hitler's concentration camps. Waldo Frank gave a scholarly address on "The Values of the Revolutionary Writer," and Earl Browder, "a gray-faced man in a rumpled gray suit," with the "honest face of a clerk in a Kansas feed-and-grain store," in Malcolm Cowley's words, reassured writers that the party had no intention of telling them what or how to write (a less than candid statement, as events were to prove). "We must dig deep into the treasures of our national tradition and cultural heritage without succumbing to narrow chauvinism," Browder declared.

The opening session was followed by smaller sessions on particular areas—drama, poetry, the short story, etc. Edwin Seaver, Harvard graduate and descendant of an old New England line, declared that "the most valuable contributions to the American novel during the last several years are to be found in the work of our writers in the left sector. . . . It is not style, not form, not plot, not even the class portrayed that are fundamental in differentiating the proletarian from the bourgeois novel. . . . It is the present class loyalty of the author that is the determining factor." Martin Russak, who had gone to work in a silk mill when he was thirteen years old and become a party member and labor organizer, took the line that a proletarian novel was, quite simply, "a novel that deals with the working class. . . . In the working class we have a distinct kind of human being, a new type of human being, with an emotional life and a psychology that is different, and distinct."

Jack Conroy talked on "The Worker as Writer." There were other talks on "Proletarian Poetry" and the proper topics for novels. Granville Hicks spoke on "The Dialectics of the Development of Marxist Criticism." Josephine Herbst and James Farrell quietly mocked the self-important solemnity of the proceedings, but Herbst gave an eloquent account of her trip to a New World "soviet" in the mountains of Cuba.

Richard Wright reminded his white colleagues that they could have very little notion of the isolation in which the black writer worked. "You may not understand it. I don't think you can unless you feel it. You can understand the causes, and oppose them, but the human results are tragic in peculiar ways. Some of the more obvious results are lack of contact with other writers, a lack of personal culture, a tendency toward escape mechanisms of ingenious, insidious kinds."

Kenneth Burke urged that the revolutionary writers cast their net somewhat wider than simply the "workers." Would they not better speak of the "people" as a more comprehensive category, at least in the United States, where there were so many reform-minded members of the middle and upper classes who were, if anything, more alienated from "capitalism" than the workers themselves. For this heresy Burke was denounced by John Howard Lawson: "To attempt to substitute 'people' for 'worker' is very dangerous. . . . Historically, it has been the ruse of the exploiting class to confuse the issue. Moreover, the word 'people' is historically associated with demagoguery of the most vicious sort. . . . The worker has nothing to lose but his chains. He alone is forced by his position to be revolutionary, and he alone can liberate the people. If we do not get lost in 'myths,' if we stick to the reality, it is only in the working class that the other exploited classes of society— including the intellectuals—can find leadership."

Burke was plainly distressed. He had shown the text of his talk to a friend respected for his knowledge of party doctrine before he delivered it and had been assured it would not offend. "I had a terrific desire to belong . . . you know, 'togetherness,' " he recalled later. But he was nonetheless raked over the coals and denounced as "a snob."

Manuel Gomez reported that the Theater Union in New York had produced four plays that had been seen by 500,000 people, 75 percent of whom had been workers. Peter Martin listed the accomplishments of the Theater of Action, formerly the Workers' Laboratory Theater, which had begun and still functioned as a "mobile theater" where the actors carried the scenery around in their arms and erected their simple sets in union halls and in front of picket lines and factory gates and for stevedores on the waterfront; they gave 500 performances before an estimated 250,000 workers. Starting out with "cartoon" forms, the Theater of Action was planning "short and long realistic plays."

In summary, it was stated that there were in the United States "three hundred functioning workers' theaters." They were "springing up everywhere with a vitality so tremendous that in a great many places they are taking over the old little theaters which have been functioning for many years." One speaker declared: "This new theatre in America is booming as no other revolutionary art today. Write for it and help it grow." Friedrich Wolf told the delegates that "in two or three years the revolutionary theaters of the United States had accomplished what had taken sixteen years in Germany."

John Howard Lawson reported on "workers' movies." Pudovkin's *Mother* had been shown "in almost every industrial center, small town and farming community in the country," according to Lawson, and thereby demonstrated "in one stroke . . . an example of how a worker's art can reach not thousands but millions of people." Two radical film companies were operating in New York: the Film and Photo League and the New York Kino. "The future of cheap workers' films of high artistic quality," Lawson concluded, "is within our hands if we take it. The result can only be something that will surpass all previous attempts at developing a working-class art which can reach wide masses of people."

Taken together, the "revolutionary" efforts of the filmmakers and dancers, actors and playwrights, modest and infatuated as they were, had an important, if unmeasurable, role in strengthening the resolution and solidarity of tens of thousands of working-class men and women, many of whom emerged as leaders in that struggle. Seeing their situation dramatized and represented as art gave them a precious dignity. The unionization of American workers, partial and nonrevolutionary as it was, was both heroic, in the fullest sense of that word, and of profound importance. The contribution to the future of America of those who conceived of themselves as "revolutionary artists" in fanning into flame the embers of union zeal that had blazed so brightly in the last decades of the nineteenth century was much more considerable than we have acknowledged.

Waldo Frank was elected chairman of the League of American Writers at the conclusion of the congress. He was the chief delegate of the league when the Writers' International Congress for the Defense of Culture met in Paris in the fall. Some 200 writers from many countries attended, and the common theme was antifascism rather than adherence to communism and Stalin. The French delegates included André Gide, André Malraux, and Louis Aragon. The Soviet delegation was led by Boris Pasternak, Isaac Babel, and Aleksey Tolstoy, while the English delegates included E. M. Forster, Aldous Huxley, and John Strachey. Malraux declared: "Art, ideas, poems, all the old dreams of man: if we have need of them to live, they have need of us to live again. . . . Whether or not we wish to do so, we create them at the same time that we create ourselves. . . . The cultural heritage does not transmit itself, but must be conquered."

The harmony that generally prevailed at the American Writers' Congress was not maintained for long. It soon degenerated into the most unseemly wrangle about the proper literary line for radical writers to take. The Trotskyite split was the bitterest. Jerre Mangione committed the unpardonable sin of reviewing favorably the first novel of the Italian writer Ignazio Silone, who had been charged with Trotskyite inclinations. "One of the editors [of the *New Masses*] turned away from me as though I were a dirty heretic," Mangione wrote. "Another smiled at me benevolently, pity in his eyes."

John Dos Passos's conviction that writers and intellectuals must identify themselves with the struggle of the workers for social justice was shaken by his experience with the communistic New Playwrights group, which, in Edmund Wilson's words, had "kept trying to high-hat him by giving him to understand that *Airways* [a play he had written for it] was insufficiently social-revolutionary. . . ."

Sinclair Lewis, who had recently been awarded the Nobel Prize for literature, the first American so honored, remained aloof from the League of American Writers, but with the appearance of his *It Can't Happen Here*, a lively anti-Fascist tract, if an inferior novel, the League laid on a dinner for Lewis and his wife, Dorothy Thompson, apparently hoping to enlist him publicly as a member. It was not a success. At one point, according to Horace Gregory, Lewis broke out, "Boys, I love you all, and a writer likes to have his latest book praised. But let me tell you it isn't a very good book—I've done better books—and furthermore I don't believe any of you have *read* the book; if you had, you would have seen I was telling you all to go to hell. Now, boys, join arms; let us all stand up and sing, 'Stand Up, Stand Up, for Jesus.'" Thereupon most of the company stood up and slipped away as quickly as possible.

The involvement of upper-class and intellectual women in the party and its affiliates was striking. Women were encouraged to join the party and often elected or appointed to important offices since Marxism called for the equality of women. On the other hand, the secret-club-like conspiratorial character of party meetings seemed to the more sophisticated women faintly ridiculous. John Herrmann joined the Communist Party in 1931 while his wife, Josephine Herbst, although as dedicated to the cause as he, did not. She believed the party to be a kind of boys' club. Herrmann was obsessed with the party's secret life, with the transmission of government documents and information on such vital matters as estimated wheat and cotton production, and with what seemed to Herbst the party's mumbo jumbo. Herrmann worked closely with Harold Ware and a man Herbst knew simply as "Karl," who later turned out to be Whittaker Chambers; his close friend Alger Hiss was also involved in some way that was not entirely clear to her. She wrote to Katherine Anne Porter that Edmund Wilson, Malcolm Cowley, and Mike Gold patronized her. "Miss Porter you and me received much the same gentle stay-in-your place which may or may not be the home, as I receive now. . . . Mr. Herrmann departed for hence [a party meeting] full of a masculine importance you and I will never know, alas, and came back somewhat boozy but so far as I could see with not one idea the smarter."

Most women were committed to the party without Herbst's reservations. We have already encountered Vincent Sheean's Rayna Prohne, who died so dramatically in Moscow. A despairing Sheean had written: "No decision in life could be more final. The vows of a nun, the oaths of matrimony, the resolutions of a soldier giving battle, had not the irrevocable character of this decision."

At a dinner given by the National Committee for the Defense of Political Prisoners, Agnes Smedley was the guest of honor. Malcolm Cowley, who attended the dinner, described her as "fanatical." She had grown up in a coal-mining town in Colorado. When she arrived in New York, determined to become a journalist, she took up with a

"Hindu revolutionist." From Germany during the days of the Spartacist uprisings, she was sent to China by the *Frankfurter Zeitung* to report on the progress of the revolution there. She wrote speeches for Madame Sun Yat-sen, barely escaped with her life, made her way across Siberia, and arrived in New York a much acclaimed heroine of the left. "Her hair grows thinly above an immense forehead," Cowley noted. "When she talks about people who betrayed the Chinese rebels, her mouth becomes a thin scar and her eyes bulge and glint with hatred. If this coal miner's daughter ever had urbanity, she would have lost it forever in Shanghai when her comrades were dragged off one by one for execution."

Mary Price, born in Greensboro, North Carolina, and a member of a proud old Southern family, had been a Communist for some years under the name of Mary Watkins. She was also a charter member of the United Office and Professional Workers of America and the Washington secretary of Walter Lippmann. Price was instructed to search Lippmann's files for information of interest to the party, and Elizabeth Bentley, by her account, assisted her in the task while Lippmann was away on a trip.

Grace Hutchins of Boston's Back Bay was a classmate of Alger Hiss's wife and the wife of Carl Binger, the psychoanalyst. Another Grace, active in the party, was Grace Lumpkin, a novelist whose book *To Make My Bread* was judged sufficiently proletarian to win the Maxim Gorky prize for literature. Lumpkin was the sister of Senator Lumpkin of South Carolina and a close friend of James F. Byrnes, then a Senator and later a Supreme Court justice, secretary of state, and governor of South Carolina.

Vassar rivaled, if indeed it did not surpass Bryn Mawr, in producing radical graduates. Mary McCarthy, who became Edmund Wilson's second wife, was a Vassar graduate, as were Muriel Rukeyser and the sisters Eleanor and Eunice Clark, transplanted Southerners and both "strikingly handsome," in Malcolm Cowley's words, and both wholeheartedly committed to the cause.

Mary Heaton Vorse was another "refined" upper-class woman who had devoted her life to Socialist and, later, Communist causes as a journalist.

Juliet Stuart Poyntz was a graduate of Barnard College, a veteran Communist, and a member of the Central Committee of the Communist Party. Whittaker Chambers had first met her when he joined the party in 1925. He described her as a "heavy-set, dark, softly feminine woman," who later went underground and became, in her new role, "a little absurdly imperious and mysterious . . . sagging self-consciously under the weight of so much secret authority and knowledge," a description not unlike the one that Josephine Herbst gave of Chambers when she met him in Washington in 1936. When Poyntz "deserted" the party and disappeared, Chambers was sure she had been killed by Russian agents.

Elizabeth Bentley was another Vassar graduate who joined the party. She dated her interest in social reform from a visit to Vassar College by a group of strikers from Gastonia, North Carolina, who had come to solicit money to keep their strike going. Bentley never forgot their descriptions of the "horrible . . . conditions then prevalent in the textile industry." Although she was only twenty-five, she had seen two depressions. "Each," she wrote, "had left in its wake suffering, starvation and broken lives." What lay ahead seemed to her nothing less than chaos, "undoubtedly . . . succeeded by a Fascist state." Taking a business program at Columbia University, Bentley found herself rooming with Lee Fuhr, a young woman from the Midwest who was working for a nursing degree. Impressed with the unselfish idealism of her friend, Bentley began going with her to meetings of the American League Against War and Fascism, where social and political issues were discussed. The Columbia branch of the league seemed to be made up largely of graduate students and professors. She found the atmosphere intellectually stimulating and enjoyed the companionship of the group, whose basic commitment, she was told, was to fight fascism. "From then on," Bentley wrote, "my life took on a new zest. I seemed to have cast off the old feeling of listlessness and despair. As I threw myself ardently into the work of fighting Fascism, I found that my own personal problems faded further and further into the background." She was impressed by the character of the people in her group. "They seemed to have an heartfelt concern for the welfare of other human beings." Bentley attributed this "to the fact that many of them came from small towns where neighborliness is taken for granted. . . ." Then she discovered that "it was more from their profound belief in the essential brotherhood of man. This explained, too, their curious lack of the usual prejudices against people of another religion, race, or color. They seemed to have no interest in whether a man was Protestant or Catholic, Jew or Gentile, Negro or White." When Bentley discovered that most of the members of the group were Communists or closely identified with the party, it somehow seemed both natural and inevitable. She remembered Hallie Flanagan's enthusiasm. Flanagan had told her students of the remarkable changes in Russia. "Indeed, her enthusiasm had been so contagious," Bentley wrote, "that I had wanted to go over there and see for myself." Most of the "liberals" on the Columbia campus, Bentley wrote, "hung around the outskirts of the Communist Party. Many of them became members, as I . . . did. Those who escaped did so not because of their intelligence or good intentions but, ironically enough, because they felt unable to make the sacrifices involved."

When Elizabeth Bentley joined the Communist Party, she took the "party" name of Sherman after her ancestor Roger Sherman, one of the signers of the Declaration of Independence. The head of the Columbia University "shop unit," made up largely of professors and graduate students, was a worker in the university cafeteria, a fact frequently cited to Elizabeth Bentley as evidence of the democratic, worker-oriented character of the party.

After a trial period as a covert party member in the Italian Library of Information, an agency of the Fascist government, Bentley found herself on the way to becoming a "steeled Bolshevik"—that is, one who by his or her dedication and discipline was considered worthy of more and more demanding assignments for the party. Somewhere the decision was made to send her underground. She would have to adopt a ceaseless watchfulness and make herself as inconspicuous as possible outside her assigned "open" job.

She was introduced to a mysterious individual, apparently a Russian who spoke English with only a trace of an accent. He quizzed her about her dedication to the party. "The life of a Communist . . . is not easy—only the strongest, mentally and physically, can survive. That is why . . . we lose so many people. They cannot take the hardships involved. . . . You are now no longer an ordinary Communist but a member of the underground. You must cut yourself off completely from all your old Communist friends. If you happen to meet them and they get curious, you will have to tell them that you have dropped out of the Party. You cannot even be known as a 'liberal' and move in progressive circles."

As in all good romances, Elizabeth Bentley and her N.K.V.K. contact fell in love, which was a no-no in the underground. They were forced to be as furtive in their lovemaking as in their work as couriers in the Washington spy apparatus.

Hede Massing was another important member of the Washington

apparatus; like Bentley, she became an FBI informer after World War II.

In sexual matters there was a good deal of ambiguity. The official party view was puritanical. Sex, like everything else, should be rigorously subordinated to the revolution. Hosea Hudson was especially attracted to the party teaching that members should live moral, upright lives and not covet the wives of other party members or indeed any other wives. On the other hand, conventional marriage was considered a repressive, bourgeois institution, and the "free love" spirit of anarchism largely prevailed in intellectual circles. Communist marriages often suffered from the classic deficiency of American marriages—the husband too much away from home, not in this instance making money but preparing for the revolution.

Drinking and having sexual adventures to excess were, it sometimes seemed, almost obligatory. They were ways of asserting one's defiance of middle-class values. There was also a good deal of homosexuality and a number of ventures into lesbianism. Josephine Herbst had a passionate love affair with a young woman musician named Marion Greenwood, whom she met at the artists' colony at Yaddo. Herbst told her husband, John Herrmann, "I never would have gone to a woman for caressing love if I had got it much from you." The affair continued after Herbst had rejoined her husband; he seems to have been a remarkably good sport about it, although it did not conform in any degree to teachings of Karl Marx, a devoted family man and a bitter opponent of free love.

In 1931 there was, in Malcolm Cowley's words "an epidemic of divorces in the literary world." Often it seemed to be related directly or indirectly to radical politics. Husbands or, less frequently, wives who, like John Herrmann, had given their hearts to the "party" seemed to have had insufficient time for their spouses. Not simply devotion to the party or to the "cause" but the particular form that devotion took imposed a severe strain on marriages that were often already clouded by emotional conflicts. Husbands and wives quarreled and parted over the role of women in the party (or one of its factions or schisms), as well as over fine points of doctrine. In some cases couples, married or unmarried, split over the issue of joining or not joining the party.

The rigors of life among the proletariat were softened by the largess of rich radicals, who allayed their uneasiness over their luxurious style of living by giving money to radical causes and giving parties for hungry intellectuals, writers, and artists. "On Friday evenings we would drive to Baltimore [from Washington]," Sidney Lens recalled, "for a big splash at the lavish home of V. F. Calverton. . . . The discussion and the arguments and the drinking would go on to early morning, unless the party was broken up by a fist fight which sometimes happened."

In Philadelphia it was John Frederick Lewis, Jr., a wealthy radical full of guilt over the ill-gotten capitalist millions he had inherited and anxious to make amends, who contributed to various radical causes and entertained Communist intellectuals at his handsome mansion.

In New York City there were a number of guilt-ridden or simply radically disposed rich men and women who contributed generously to a wide range of Communist-front organizations and made their houses and apartments available for fund-raising events or simply luxurious parties for the cohorts of the left. Cornelius Vanderbilt, Jr., was one of the best known, but he had numerous counterparts. In the words of a disenchanted Ben Gitlow, "cocktail parties for good causes were held to which the golden butterflies [of New York society] were invited. One night of each week was set aside for open house. Here penthouse society mingled and rubbed shoulders with Red Bohemia. . . . The money rolled into the Communist party coffers. United front movements could be organized and financed for every kind of cause. . . . The Communist party in society was an organization with the kind of influence that counted in dollars and cents."

At such parties toasts were drunk "To the Red Dawn," and a parting remark at the end of an evening of dancing was often "See you on the barricades." Another popular toast was "To the last hour of capitalism. Let's make the most of it."

In addition to wealthy individuals who bankrolled the party and its various fronts, there were a number of philanthropic foundations which were favorably disposed to Communist causes. Many party fronts were bankrolled by the American Fund for Public Service, established by Charles Garland, a wealthy Massachusetts radical. In a period of twelve years the fund gave grants of more than $2,000,000 to various left-wing causes, from the Socialist Party to the Communists and the IWW. Among its directors were Roger Baldwin, Elizabeth Gurley Flynn (a member of the Communist Party), William Foster, Norman Thomas, and Scott Nearing. Sidney Hillman was a director for a time, and the fund gave money to assist his union. Another beneficiary was the Federated Press, under the direction of Carl Haessler. An important "left" foundation was the Robert Marshall Foundation, a majority of the directors of which were sympathetic to the Communist cause.

It is interesting to speculate on why so many members of the new intellectual class, perhaps most conspicuously writers, were drawn to the Communist party. Eugen Rosenstock-Huessy has written: "The heart of man either falls in love with somebody or something, or it falls ill. It can never go unoccupied. And the great question for mankind is what is to be loved or hated next, whenever an old love or fear has lost its hold." The "old love," liberalism, had been dissolved by the acid of skepticism. That at least was the argument of one of the most brilliant young Communist critics, V. F. Calverton. Calverton read the burial ceremony for liberalism a few weeks before Roosevelt's inaugural: "The Retrogressive Role of American Liberalism." His principal charge was that liberalism had encouraged the movement to "debunk" American history. "The achievements of the Revolutionary War were debunked; the importance of the Civil War was debunked; the pertinence and place of various individuals in the historical process was debunked—in fact, everything was debunked with an indiscriminate enthusiasm which betrayed the lack of historical insight involved in the whole approach." The liberal historians were especially at fault for "stressing with a narrow-mindedness culpably characteristic of defeatist historians the corruption involved in the *means* but neglecting entirely the significance involved in the *ends*." While it may seem ironic for a Communist theoretician to attack liberals for debunking American history, Calverton's essay reinforces the point that one of the appeals of communism was that it restored, or at least attempted to restore, the element of the heroic to the lives of the "workers" and their middle-class champions. Lives that had been without hope or purpose suddenly took on a vital new meaning. Since the events of 1914 to 1919 had brought shattering disillusionment to American intellectuals—progressives, liberals, socialists, radicals, anarchists, whatever—they were bound to find a new faith. For most that faith was communism. Communism made whole, if only briefly, the hearts that had been broken by the terrible disillusionment of the years from 1914 to 1919.

"Values exist again," Malcolm Cowley wrote in the spring of 1934, "after an age in which they seemed to be lost; good and evil are embodied in men who struggle." Joseph Wood Krutch had written in the twenties that "we have come, willy-nilly, to see the soul of man as commonplace and its emotions as mean." To Krutch, modern man had lost the "tragic sense of life." But communism, Cowley argued, had restored that sense. "Tragedy lives in the stories of men now dying in Chinese streets or in German prisons for a cause by which their lives are given dignity and meaning."

Thinking back over the times, Cowley was most impressed by the "religious" or "conversion" aspect of communism. Meridel Le Sueur, who came from a middle-class family in Minnesota, wrote that the experience of joining the Communist Party was "difficult because you are stepping into a dark chaotic passional world of another class, the proletariat, which is . . . like a great body of sleeping, stirring, strange and outside the calculated, expedient world of the bourgeoisie. It is a hard road to leave your own class and you cannot leave it by pieces or parts; it is a birth and you have to be born whole out of it. It is a complete new body. None of the old ideology is any good in it." Cowley added that the party "performed for its members the social and institutional function of a church, and communism was, in effect and at the moment, the only crusading religion." It had its sacred texts in Marx and Engels; *Das Kapital* was its Bible (and later commentaries such as Lenin and Trotsky); its Pope was Stalin, and its holy city, Moscow. It was a worldwide universal order that promised earthly instead of heavenly bliss. It was made up of the elect (party members and fellow travelers) and the damned or unregenerate, those outside the faith. Its dogmas covered every aspect of life: what writers should write and painters should paint; even the relationships of husband to wife and the individual to the state. It was as merciless to schismatics and heretics as the medieval church. It practiced group examination to root out deviant thinking and behavior, and it required confession and penance. The punishments for doctrinal deviation or other less serious failures were reprimand and expulsion. "There was also, in many cases," Cowley wrote in retrospect, "the personal specter of isolation and nervous breakdown." Moreover, once a critical mass of writers and artists had opted for communism, to remain aloof was to increase that sense of isolation, the overcoming of which was one of the party's main attractions. In other words, it took great self-confidence and even courage not to be part of, as it seemed, the vanguard of the future. "The progress of the Communist faith among our writers since the beginning of the depression has followed a peculiar course," Edmund Wilson wrote. "That the aims and beliefs of Marx and Lenin should have come through to the minds of the intellectuals who had been educated in the bourgeois tradition as great awakeners of conscience, a great light was quite natural and wholly desirable. But the conception of the dynamic Marxist will, the exaltation of the Marxist religion seized the members of the professional class like a capricious contagion or hurricane. . . ." Later they began to shake off the grosser delusion. "But for many there was at least a moment when the key to all the mysteries of human nature seemed suddenly to have been placed in their hands, when an infallible guide to thought and behavior seemed to have been given them in a few easy formulas."

On the most basic level the Communist Party functioned for intellectuals as Rotary or the Lions Club did for middle-class businessmen. There was a sense of social as well as intellectual camaraderie. American intellectuals and artists may well have suffered more from the disintegrative effects of American life than other middle-class Americans. Many of them, as we have had occasion to note from time to time, were obsessed with the question of what it meant to be an American. The standard answer—competition and material success— was clearly not sufficient, especially since many were conspicuously not successful. Living, for the most part, in cities far from their predominantly small-town origins, they felt excruciatingly alienated. Willa Cather comes to mind; a lifelong refugee from Red Cloud, Nebraska, she could not live there or ever free herself of the hold it had upon her. Much the same could be said for any number of writers. Sinclair Lewis, Theodore Dreiser (Terre Haute was a *large* small town), Sherwood Anderson, Floyd Dell—the list is almost endless. For many such dispossessed spirits the Communist Party provided a desperately needed "home away from home," a sharing of perils and joys with "comrades." Even the bitter wrangles over party doctrines were better than loneliness and isolation.

Karl Marx had predicted that when "the process of dissolution going on within . . . the whole range of the old society" reaches a certain point, "a small section of the ruling class . . . joins the revolutionary class." The only trouble with that formulation was that there was no "revolutionary class" for the middle- and upper-class intellectuals to join; they were the "revolutionary class" so far as there was one.

A part of the attraction of communism for writers and artists was undoubtedly a consequence of the modern romanticism of the arts (also called bohemianism), which held that the writer or artist was at war with the philistine spirit of the bourgeoisie. This, of course, had been the main theme of Henry Mencken and the *American Mercury*. As allies of the worker, artists and writers would have the status that they deserved; they would be honored as vital elements in the new society. Meanwhile, they must join the final, apocalyptic struggle against the capitalists and their bourgeois supporters. It might thus be argued that communism was, above all, a literary and poetic movement. Not only did Communist writers compose poems about the struggle of the working class and other approved subjects, but even their essays and dialectical excursions were a kind of poetry—that is to say, the content was more emotional than rational, and the appeal was to the sentiments rather than to the brain or the critical faculties. That, at least, was the opinion of union organizer Len De Caux. To De Caux, with his background in international communism, the American variety was "extremist, romantic, impossibilist," in contrast with, for one, the British Communists, who were "practical working folks, not so wild and up in the air." A major problem for most writers and artists is what they should write about or paint or sculpt. The Communist Party solved that perpetual and perplexing question with one conclusive word: workers. Finally, there was the not inconsiderable fact that Soviet communism was a fad. It was, above all, fashionable. Many of the rich, the famous, and the wellborn embraced it with as much enthusiasm as a Jack Conroy or a Robert Cantwell. Enthusiasm for, or at least intense interest in, Soviet Russia reached into unlikely places. The Book-of-the-Month Club distributed *New Russia's Primer* in 1931. The great Russian director Sergei Eisenstein was lured to Hollywood to make a film. Boris Pilnyak was invited to the United States by the editor of *Cosmopolitan* and given a glittering dinner at the Metropolitan Club, to which most of America's literary luminaries were invited. During the dinner Sinclair Lewis accused Theodore Dreiser of having lifted some 3,000 words out of Dorothy Thompson's book on Russia, and Dreiser slapped Lewis's face.

There were, of course, significant literary figures, reformers, and intellectuals who remained aloof from the Communist Party and from communism in its various forms. They were, for the most part, members of an older generation of reformers and radicals, men like Charles Edward Russell, Frederic Howe, and Hutchins Hapgood. Communism was, in the main, a young man's and woman's game. Where Hapgood differed from "the young enthusiasts" about him was that they were convinced that they could "work out a general propaganda or political faith by which good is assured and will continue. I not only have no faith in that," Hapgood wrote, "but just there I detect an ever-existing danger. Just there I see the vital process threatened by the death-dealing fanatical generalization." The "death-dealing fanatical generalization" was for Hapgood communism, which aligned itself with the Soviet Union without cavil or question. To him "the Russian government's impulse" was "not primarily a communistic impulse but a dictatorship of the few, without any particular reference to democratic principles." What depressed Hapgood about the Communists he knew was their grimness. There was about communism none of the joyful exuberance that had distinguished the great days in the Village and at Provincetown. "At the age of sixty-nine," he wrote in 1938, "I find myself surrounded by young men and women who seem to me fanatical, in the sense that they are willing to destroy life for the sake of ideas." Hapgood had only one faith left: "what may be called . . . the faith in the labor movement. As far as I have been able to think and observe, the unassailable and inevitable good rests in the attempt by the masses of men to improve their physical, moral, and spiritual condition."

Emma Goldman had much the same reaction. She wrote to Carlo Tresca, who was outspoken in his denunciations of Stalin, that he had a difficult task trying to defend Trotsky "because Russia has poisoned all the wells of decent public opinion and one cannot hope to get a hearing even in the so-called liberal press . . . you will become a target for the rotten Communist gang not only to besmirch your character but also to endanger your life. For they are capable of murder open and underhand as they have proven for a very considerable number of years."

Perhaps the shrewdest analysis of communism in America was that of Karl Radek, the old Bolshevik and one of the party's leading theoreticians. Hamilton Fish Armstrong, attending the Geneva Disarmament Conference, took the occasion to talk with Radek about the future of communism in the United States. "We did not succeed in Germany, a country where Marxism had been nourished and propagated for years, even after a fearful war and defeat, and following a civil war in which we lost thirty thousand men," Radek reminded Armstrong. "And in England, where the roots of economic distress go deep, we see as the socialist leader a mild and tired man like Arthur Henderson. What, then, can we think our prospects are in a country with twenty-four million automobiles? Labor troubles will come there, of course, and there will be unemployment insurance and various kinds of state socialism, but the structure will remain as it is for some time to come. The pioneering spirit is not dead, there will be energetic adaptations to new conditions and these will meet with comparative success due to the large home market and the wealth of the population."

Such heretical notions cost Radek his life. He was tried for treason, convicted, and executed as an enemy of the state.

# 23

## The Scottsboro Boys and Angelo Herndon

While intellectuals flocked to the standard of the Communist Party, the party gave special attention, as we have seen, to recruiting blacks. The Communists had some success north of the Mason-Dixon Line in attracting black members, but south of that famous line the going was much tougher and far more hazardous. There Communist organizers operated in actual danger of losing their lives. In 1930 a young Communist named Donald Burke opened a party office in Birmingham, the leading industrial city of the South. When he tried to recruit in the black areas of the city, the police raided his office and dogged his footsteps. He was arrested a number of times but, since being a Communist, perilous as it was, was not defined as a crime, he was released each time at the insistence of an International Labor Defense lawyer who always appeared promptly.

In 1929, at the beginning of the Depression, there were fewer than 200 black Communists in the South, most of them in Birmingham and Atlanta. By 1930 more than 20 percent of the new members of the party in the South were black—1,300 out of 6,000. One of the first recruits was a young Birmingham black, still in his teens, named Angelo Herndon. As Herndon described his involvement, he was on his way home from work one evening in June, 1930, when he saw some tattered handbills lying in the street. He picked one up. It "discussed unemployment, hunger and suffering of both Negro and white workers in Birmingham and throughout the whole country." It announced a meeting of the Unemployed Council for that afternoon. Herndon went and met Frank Williams, the white organizer of the council. Williams was a large, powerful man who spoke eloquently of the hardships endured by workers in the mines and factories of Birmingham. Those who suffered most were the black workers. "They are denied the rights of citizenship," Williams declared; "they are lynched and terrorized in open violation of the United States Constitution." To the uneasy little group of white and black workingmen in the room, Williams described the aims of the Communist Party. "If you want to maintain your human dignity instead of being looked upon as vagabonds and paupers, there is only one way to do it, and that is to establish unity among all workers, Negro and white. You have been told that the Reds are dirty foreigners and 'Nigger Lovers,' but why have you come to this meeting today?" It could be only because they wished to improve the conditions under which they lived and worked.

Herndon was thrilled by Williams's message. He turned to a black friend who had come with him and exclaimed: "He's right! He does nothing but tell the truth. He's the first honest white man I've seen. Have you heard of another white man who has the courage to publicly tell the truth about the conditions of Negroes?"

In the months that followed Herndon became an enthusiastic organizer for the Unemployed Council, which had been set up by the Communist Party. He heard William Foster and Bill Dunne, head of the International Labor Defense. When a white worker at a meeting addressed by Dunne called out, "Would you want a nigger to marry your daughter?" Dunne replied, "Listen, mister, my daughter will marry any man she likes whether white, Negro or Chinese. That will be her affair, not mine. But one thing you can rest assured of: I would rather that she jump into a lake than to marry such a yellow-bellied Negro-hater like you." The story spread and proved an added incentive for blacks to work with the Communists.

Herndon wrote: "All of a sudden I found myself in an organization which fought selflessly and tirelessly to undo all the wrongs perpetrated upon my race. . . . Now, as if by a miracle, a new world had unfolded itself before my eyes. It, too, was a part of the white man's world, but it did not leave us Negroes standing like beggars outside in the cold. Welcoming brotherly hands were outstretched to us. We were called 'comrades' without condescension or patronage. Better yet we were treated like equals and brothers. . . . At last I had found my true friends in the world and I was happy."

When the word spread in the white community of Birmingham that efforts were being made to organize black workers and, most alarming of all, that the organizing was being done by Communists, the white agencies of intimidation were mustered. In Herndon's words, "The Ku Klux Klan and the American Legion now got busy. . . . They paraded up and down the streets, especially in the Negro neighborhood, night after night. They dressed in their full regalia, like spooks in funny pictures, with nightgowns and pillow cases and flaming torches. Everywhere they went they howled in unearthly voices the warning that Negroes better keep away from the Communists. . . ."

Herndon, as a Communist organizer, was the special object of white attentions. He found a leaflet lying on his doorstep that read: "Communists must be wiped out. Drive the foreigners back to the North and Russia where they came from. Alabama is a good place for good Negroes, but a bad place for bad Negroes who want social equality."

When Herndon attended the National Convention of the Unemployed Councils in Chicago, the police attacked a demonstration by the delegates and their sympathizers at Union Park. Men, women, and even children were clubbed to the ground. The police fired into the crowd, and dozens were injured and some killed. The next day the newspaper headlines proclaimed "Twelve Thousand Cops Quell Riot of Twenty Thousand Reds." The speakers at the convention included Bill Dunne, who, with William Foster, had been one of the leaders of the steel strike in 1919, and Nels Kjar, a Swedish immigrant and head of the Unemployed Council in Chicago, who was soon to be deported for his party activities.

When Herndon returned to Birmingham, full of zeal for the cause and determined to sign up workers for the National Miners Union, he found himself the object of attention by mine guards as well as the police. He and a companion were locked up in the Big Rock prison on a charge of vagrancy, and Herndon was put in solitary confinement. When their case came to trial weeks later, the judge declared: "I find that both of you are guilty. I am only sorry that we haven't got an insurrection law here in Alabama as they have in Georgia, so we could have your necks broken . . . without delay. I, therefore, now sentence both of you defendants to twelve months on the chain gang at hard labor. You are also to pay a fine of $500 each." Herndon and his friend had been represented by a lawyer named Rosenthal, hired by the Unemployed Council. Herndon's lawyer appealed, and the circuit court threw the cases out. The next day Herndon returned to his task of organizing the black miners. There were in greater Birmingham more than 10,000 miners, some 75 percent of whom were black. "The difficulties I faced in organizing them," he wrote, "were insuperable, so it seemed to me. . . ." But gradually his efforts began to bear modest fruit. He organized union locals in four of the mines, with approximately 35 black and white workers in each. Meanwhile, police harassment continued. Every time he was arrested he was knocked about and threatened, but he consoled himself with the recollection of his grandmother's tales of the Christian martyrs: "the greater and more cruel the trials of the saints of old, the more obstinate they became in their resistance to the authority of the Roman Empire. Although I was only seventeen years old," Herndon wrote, "I had the conviction that only death could stop me from working for the social revolution in America."

Even so, Herndon was a marked man, and the repeated arrests severely limited his effectiveness. The Trade Union Unity League dispatched him to New Orleans, where a strike involving 7,000 white and black longshoremen had broken out. The longshoremen, who were paid a comparatively high wage of sixty-five cents an hour, were fighting a twenty-five-cent-per-hour cut in pay. The steamship and dock owners had brought in armed guards to protect the desperate scabs they had hired to replace the strikers. When the strikers tried to picket the docks, the company guards without warning opened fire with machine guns and sawed-off shotguns, and 118 strikers were wounded, some fatally. Herndon was arrested for distributing the *Marine Workers' Voice*, but after he spent four days in jail, a judge dismissed the charges against him.

Herndon's next assignment was in Atlanta. In that city some 20,000 unemployed whites had joined the American Fascisti Order of the Black Shirts, modeled on Mussolini's black-shirted legionnaires. One of their projects was to "Run the niggers back to the country where they came from—Africa!" It was blacks who, by working for lower wages, stole the jobs of white men—"no real white man will work for nigger wages!" Those whites often referred to as "po' white trash" made up the principal recruits of the American Fascisti. Mob violence against blacks who had jobs mounted month by month until, in Herndon's words, the "whole Negro population of the city lived in constant fear of their lives."

The authorities in Fulton County, Georgia, where the city of Atlanta is located, grew increasingly alarmed over the growth of Communist influence among that city's blacks. Matters came to a head with the announcement by the county commissioners of plans to cut 23,000 families, the majority of them black, from the relief rolls on the ground that the county was bankrupt. The Atlanta Unemployed Council issued a call to all organizations of the unemployed and all those who would be affected by the commissioners' decision for mass protest meetings. By ten o'clock on the appointed day more than 1,000 men and women, more than half of them white, marched into the county courthouse to present their demands. Angelo Herndon believed it was the largest gathering of black and white workers in the history of the South. Still more astonishing, it achieved its purpose. Additional money was appropriated for the needy, and the order dropping families from the relief rolls was rescinded.

Despite the risks, beatings, and harassment, the party had little to show for its efforts by the spring of 1931, when fortune smiled on it. On March 25, 1931, on a freight train going from Chattanooga to Memphis, Tennessee, a group of five or six white youths were ousted, after a short scuffle, by a band of nine young blacks. On the train were two white women dressed in overalls and men's coats. The ousted whites contacted a local sheriff, who in turn notified the sheriff at Scottsboro, Alabama, that young blacks had attacked white boys and should be taken into custody and charged with assault and battery. The two young women on the train, Ruby Bates and Victoria Price, were millworkers and part-time prostitutes. When their presence on the train was discovered, they claimed they had been raped by the blacks.

The only one of the nine who was not a teenager was Charles Weems. Olen Montgomery was blind in his left eye and had only partial sight in his right eye. Will Robertson had syphilis and gonorrhea, for which he had been unsuccessfully seeking treatment for some six months; a doctor later testified that he could not have had intercourse without extreme pain. Weems, Robertson, Montgomery, Ozzie Powell, and Clarence Norris all were from Georgia but insisted that they had not known each other before they boarded the freight train in the Chattanooga freightyards. Heywood Patterson and Andrew Wright were nineteen. Eugene Williams was thirteen, and Leroy Wright was four-teen.

The women were from Huntsville, Alabama. They explained their presence on the train by saying that they were headed for Memphis to try to find work in the cotton mills there. They were sent to two local doctors to be examined and, if necessary, treated. Neither of the doctors found evidence that they had been raped. There were no signs of violence, no serious bruises or abrasions such as rape might have been expected to produce, and one of the examining physicians had trouble obtaining motile semen from Victoria Price, a fact which suggested that she had had intercourse sometime before the alleged rape occurred. But for the community of Scottsboro the fact that the two white women claimed to have been raped was prima facie evidence. Nothing more in the way of proof was needed. The *Huntsville Daily Times* called the alleged rape (the papers did not bother to preface "rape" with "alleged"; it was simply taken as a fact) "the most atrocious ever recorded in this part of the country, a wholesale debauching of society . . . so horrible in its details that all of the facts can never be printed." It "savored of the jungle" and the "meanest African corruption." The white men of the South, the editor of the paper declared, "will not stand for such acts."

The *Jackson County Sentinel* also did its best to fan the fires of public anger. A headline proclaimed: "All Negroes Positively Identified by Girls and One White Boy Who Was Held Prisoner with Pistol and Knives While Nine Black Fiends Committed Revolting Crime." The story accompanying the headline declared that the two women were "found . . . in a terrible condition mentally and physically after their unspeakable experience at the hands of the black brutes." Far from being in a "terrible condition," Victoria Price had laughed when one of the doctors who had examined her told her that he believed she was lying. She had not denied his charge.

An angry mob of several thousand people gathered at the jail and demanded that the boys be turned over to them for a proper lynching. The sheriff deputized a number of men, armed them with guns, and announced his determination to defend the prisoners at all costs, meanwhile sending word to the governor of the state, requesting reinforcements.

In order to quiet those citizens intent on lynching, a trial was hastily scheduled, so hastily in fact that the defense attorney, an elderly Chattanooga lawyer with a drinking problem, did not have time to consult with the defendants before the trial began. It opened in an atmosphere of extreme hostility, the courtroom crowded and several thousand townspeople gathered outside. The attitude of the authorities was that the nine blacks were undoubtedly guilty of a gang rape, and the sooner they were convicted and executed, the better the chance of avoiding a mass lynching that would besmirch the state's good name.

The terrified defendants gave conflicting testimony. Some, while denying that they had been involved in the rape of the two women, said that they had seen others so engaged. The cases of the nine were divided into three groups according to their ages and the strength of the evidence against them. Heywood Patterson was the first to be tried.

Victoria Price, obviously delighted with her prominence, gave a lurid, if often contradictory, account of her ordeal. It took two of the defendants to take her clothes off, "and three of them to ravish me" while holding a knife against her throat. One held her legs while another ripped off her step-ins. "They would not let me up between times, not even let me up to spit [snuff]," she declared as a further measure of their depravity. She was "beaten up," battered and bruised, she declared, bleeding from her "privates" and her head. Dr. R. R. Bridges testified that while both women had semen in their vaginas, there was only a trace of semen in Victoria Price's vagina and no evidence that either woman had been raped. They were not "bloody" or lacerated, and there was no sign of the emotional distress or hysteria which might have been expected after such an ordeal. Dr. Bridges, a graduate of Vanderbilt and a member of Scottsboro's small upper class, was supported by the testimony of a young doctor named Marvin Lynch, who had graduated from the Medical College of South Carolina a few years earlier.

When the defense lawyer asked Mrs. Price if she had ever practiced prostitution, she replied indignantly, "I don't know what you are talking about. I do not know what prostitution means. I have not made it a practice to have intercourse with other men. I have not had intercourse with any white man but my husband." The fact was that she had recently served a jail term in Memphis on a charge of adultery with a man named Jack Quilley.

Victoria Price had earned twenty cents an hour on a twelve-hour night shift. In 1931 the mill reduced wages to $1.20 a day, for three days every other week. "You know nobody can live on wages like that," she said. Although she did not admit it, it was evident at that point that she had become engaged in part-time prostitution.

When the brief testimony was completed, the jury took twenty-five minutes to agree on a verdict of guilty for Patterson, the punishment to be death by electrocution. It was later disclosed that the verdict had been virtually instantaneous and unanimous, the additional twenty minutes being taken up to give an impression of deliberation. The word of the verdict in Patterson's trial was announced during the trial of the next defendant and greeted with loud and prolonged cheering by those outside the courthouse. Weems and Norris were next convicted, followed by the three remaining defendants. In the case of Leroy Wright, who was only thirteen, the state asked only for life imprisonment, but seven of the jurors held out for the death penalty for him, and a mistrial was declared by the judge. The others were sentenced to death by Judge Hawkins.

Alabama newspapers, with certain notable exceptions, engaged in an orgy of self-congratulation. The men had, after all, not been lynched. They had instead received a trial which was a tribute to the "patience and chivalry" of the citizens of the state. "If ever there was an excuse for taking the law into their own hands," the *Scottsboro Progressive Age* declared, "surely this was one." But the people had remained "calm" and allowed "the law to take its course." The *Jackson County Sentinel* averred that "in the face of one of the most atrocious crimes ever committed in this section," white Alabamans had "shown the world that they believed in justice, regardless of color." Praise for Scottsboro's handling of the episode was not limited to Alabama. The dean of Mississippi's Blue Mountain College pointed out, somewhat gratuitously it seemed, that blacks were inferior to whites and that this truth was "incontestable." Even when a black man learned to read and write, he remained "a creature of the jungle."

On the day that the trials ended, the Central Committee of the Communist Party issued a statement denouncing them as "cold blooded 'illegal' lynching by the parasite landlords and capitalist classes of the South." There was much more, of course, including calls for solidarity among poor black and white Southerners against their exploiters. Through its legal arm, the International Labor Defense (ILD), the Communists announced that they would provide proper counsel for the nine men who had been convicted. An appeal was made at once to the Alabama Supreme Court.

Other Communist-front groups rallied to the defense of the "Scottsboro boys," as they were soon called. The Trade Union Unity League and the League of Struggle for Negro Rights, the Young Communist League, and the Anti-Imperialist League (all more or less interchangeable Communist-front organizations) flooded the office of the governor of Alabama with telegrams and letters. An Atlanta lawyer wrote the governor that while he was "not a 'nigger-lover,' or a Communist or anything other than a Georgia cracker who enjoys being a neighbor of Alabama," he considered the sentence "a barbarous penalty . . . to be applied to these children, for children in years and mental development is exactly what they were." He could understand how "such savagery could exist in a state like Mississippi," but he could not believe that "a civilized community like that of your state" would "be guilty of such an atrocity."

The call to arms issued by the Communist Party, primarily through the *Daily Worker*, brought a surprisingly strong reaction. Public figures along the whole political spectrum joined in protests and pleas for executive clemency. Only the NAACP hung back, afraid of committing itself to the defense of the condemned until it knew more of the circumstances. But it soon found itself besieged by branches of its own organization, urging it to take a strong public stand and, more important, to provide legal assistance for the "boys."

An unseemly tussle between the aroused NAACP and the International Labor Defense took place, with each organization vying for the right to defend the condemned men. Clarence Darrow, seventy-four years old and ailing, was prevailed upon to represent the NAACP on behalf of the boys in cooperation with the ILD, but in several days of tense negotiations it became clear that the ILD would not compromise its demand that its lawyers direct all further legal proceedings. Darrow withdrew, and the case or cases were left in the hands of the ILD, which, working through the mothers of the defendants, had obtained statements from them designating it their legal representative.

The *Daily Worker* called the NAACP "the Nicest Association for the Advantage of Certain Persons" and declared that Walter White has "as much to do with the black masses of workers and sharecroppers as any similar group of scented, spatted, caned and belly-filled white parasites have to do with the white masses," an unkind reference to the fact that both White and W. E. B. Du Bois, editor of the NAACP paper the *Crisis*, were notoriously natty dressers.

Southerners were, of course, delighted by the unseemly contest between the ILD and the NAACP. The *Birmingham Age-Herald* observed that it was a "nauseating struggle between the Communist group and the negro society, not so much that justice may be done as that selfish interests may be advanced through the capitalization of the episode."

The principal concern of those opposing the ILD was that the Communist Party would sacrifice the boys for propaganda purposes. The party took the line, after all, that the American judicial system was a hopelessly corrupt tool of the exploiting class that, in Scottsboro, was being used for a "judicial lynching" more odious because it was more hypocritical than an outright lynching. This was not an attitude well received in Alabama or in the South generally. In some Southern cities the possession of "radical" literature such as the *Nation* and the *New Republic*, not to mention the *New Masses*, was enough to warrant arrest on suspicion of Communist affiliation.

Those Southerners who took an interest in the case stressed to Northern liberals and especially to Walter White and the NAACP that it was essential to have Alabama lawyers or at least Southern lawyers as prominent members of the defense team in appealing the case to higher courts. Will Alexander, a member of the Commission on Interracial Cooperation, was active in securing the services of a prominent Chattanooga lawyer, George W. Chamlee, whose grandfather had been a Confederate general and who had himself been an officer in the U.S. Army in the World War. Chamlee and the ILD received the support of a number of black ministers in Chattanooga, who were unaware that the ILD was the legal arm of the Communist Party but who were relatively unconcerned when they found out. Their primary interest was in trying to save the lives of the nine defendants. For the record, the Chattanooga Ministers' Alliance, while characterizing the ILD as "communistic on the doctrines and principles which it advocates . . . ," endorsed that organization's commitment to "justice and fair play to all mankind, regardless of race or previous condition." It believed this could best be attained by "a due regard for the principles which are fundamental to the good of all mankind as embodied in the Constitution of the United States." With this proviso, the Ministers' Alliance and other black ministerial groups cooperated with the ILD.

As the involvement of the ILD became known, Judge Hawkins told one of the defense attorneys that he did not "really think the boys should be put to death, but . . . the Communists are more of an issue than are the FACTS of the case," the implication being that the defendants should be put to death in order to put the Communists in their place. Increasingly the line taken by the more intractable whites

was that, regardless of their guilt or innocence, the freeing of the
Scottsboro boys was impossible because it would encourage other blacks
to rape white women.

In an effort to find a public figure in Alabama willing to identify
himself with the defense of the nine young blacks in their second trial,
representatives of the NAACP approached a Congressman, George
Huddleston, reputed to be a "fiery left-winger." When Huddleston was
asked to join the defense, he shouted that he did not care whether the
defendants were guilty or innocent. It was enough that they had been
apprehended in the same freight car with two white women. "You can't
understand," he declared, "how we Southern gentlemen feel about this
question of relationship between negro men and white women."

It was significant that the mothers (and in some instances fathers
as well) of the condemned young blacks felt that they had been patronized and condescended to by representatives of the NAACP as
simple and uneducated blacks, while the ILD members treated them
with far more consideration. In addition, the ILD gave the mothers
small sums of money and arranged for them to travel around the
country to speak at rallies to raise money for the defense of their sons.
Janie Patterson, the mother of Heywood, was brought to New York
to address a rally in Harlem at the corner of Lenox Avenue and 104th
Street. In a parade down Lenox Avenue marchers carried placards
that read: "Death to Lynch Law," "Smash the Scottsboro Frame-up,"
and similar sentiments. When police tried to block the line of march,
a fierce fight broke out, with the lawmen cracking heads indiscriminately with their nightsticks. The headlines in the *Times* read: "Police
Clubs Rout 200 Defiant Reds Who Attacked 'Lynch Law' in Alabama."
Soon much the same scene was being repeated in other cities with large
black populations, Philadelphia, Chicago, and Detroit, among others.

Along with its attack on the "Southern capitalist classes," the Communists kept up a drumfire against the NAACP as "traitors to the
Negro masses and betrayers of the Negro liberation struggle." The
traditional May Day parades in cities all around the nation provided
a golden opportunity to utilize the Scottsboro boys in the class war. In
speech after speech the Scottsboro case was the major item in the
condemnation of capitalism. The members of the NAACP were denounced as "Murderers of Negro and White Workers," which was a
bit strong. The NAACP was more interested in its "respectability . . . in
the eyes of the liberal white millionaire and upper class people" than
in "saving the lives of nine children being murdered in Alabama."

While taking all available legal means to save the Scottsboro boys from the electric chair, the ILD called, rather inconsistently, on the "workers" to "throw off their blind faith in the ruling class courts of law. . . . So deeply ingrained is the superstitious respect for the paraphernalia of capitalist class government that [American workers] . . . will kiss the rope that hangs their brothers, if only the rope is blessed by a ruling class judge."

After the Scottsboro case broke into the headlines, the party assigned three assistants to help Donald Burke in his efforts to recruit blacks in the Birmingham area. The League of Struggle for Negro Rights called an "all-Southern Scottsboro Defense Conference" for May 24, 1931, in Chattanooga, but efforts to turn out a large crowd of blacks failed. The Chattanooga police arrested the president of the league and two other black Communists for loitering when they left the meeting hall during a recess. Burke and a group leaving Birmingham early in the morning of May 24 to drive to Chattanooga were arrested for violating the curfew.

The case provided an opportunity for Southerners to restate the racial inferiority of blacks. M. J. McCary of Anniston, Alabama, writing to the *Birmingham Age-Herald*, declared that although exposed to white civilization in America for several hundred years, blacks "have not lost a single one of their ape-like characteristics nor developed the slightest shade of mentality."

What was, of course, most resented throughout the white South as well as Alabama was the intrusion of "outsiders." It was a familiar refrain from so-called Southern moderates that such interference must "result in . . . organizations like the Ku Klux Klan and in violent retaliation against the Negroes—themselves often innocent." No one could understand the problem of race in the South except Southerners. Yankees who had lived long enough in the region might begin to get a glimmering of the truth. "Nothing has done more to aggravate the race question in this section," the *Chattanooga Daily Times* stated, "than just such meddling by outside agencies."

Zebulon Judd, dean of the Auburn University School of Education, wrote: "The whole state seems satisfied not only that justice was meted out, but that it was done in an orderly legal fashion" despite the "pestiferous interference from the outside world that knows little or nothing about the case."

New York City was not simply the name of a metropolitan area; it was, in much of the South, a term of invective. It was a place generally considered swarming with Jewish Communists and insolent blacks. There were certainly more enlightened views expressed in some Southern newspapers and journals, and as more and more evidence was made public of the shoddy nature of the first trial, a note of uneasiness crept into reflections on the case, especially in Birmingham papers.

In New Orleans the secretary of the Marine Workers' Industrial Union called a protest meeting over the Scottsboro boys, and 500 longshoremen and seamen turned up, many of them white, including the crew of a German freighter tied up at New Orleans. The black Methodist and Baptist churches of New Orleans called special church meetings, at some of which Angelo Herndon spoke, and the Provisional Committee for the Defense of the Scottsboro Boys was formed with several thousand members. A correspondence committee was organized to write encouraging letters to the imprisoned youths.

The first All-Southern Conference for the Scottsboro Defense met on May 31, 1931, in Chattanooga, Tennessee. There were delegates from Alabama, North and South Carolina, Georgia, Tennessee, and Kentucky. "It was a strange gathering of shabby and undernourished sharecroppers, and of miners and mill workers who fraternized without any self-consciousness with well-dressed white and Negro middle-class liberals and intellectuals." Black and white speakers shared the platform. The principal address was given by Robert Minor, the upperclass maverick who had been rescued from a World War firing squad by Lincoln Steffens and Bainbridge Colby and was an editor and cartoonist for the *New Masses*. Another speaker was B. D. Amis, secretary of the League of the Struggle for Negro Rights and an editor of the *Liberator*. Amis called on Southern blacks "to fight with the same might and determination as did Nat Turner, Frederick Douglass and other Negro heroes in the days of slavery."

Langston Hughes wrote a poem entitled "Scottsboro" for the December, 1931, issue of *Opportunity* while the case of the thirteen-year-old Roy Wright was still pending:

> 8 Black Boys in a Southern jail.
> World, turn pale!
> 8 Black Boys and one white lie.
> Is it much to die? . . .

At the University of North Carolina, where Hughes had gone to give a poetry reading at the height of the excitement over the case, his life was threatened. Paul Green, Chapel Hill's writer-in-residence, author of the play *In Abraham's Bosom*, helped procure police protection, and when Hughes read his poetry at the campus theater, it was packed to overflowing.

When Hughes visited the Scottsboro boys in their jail cells to read his revolutionary-racial poems to them, they looked at him dully. Only Clarence Norris came over to shake his hand and thank him. He wrote "A Poem for Clarence Norris," included in a pamphlet, *Scottsboro Limited*, that was largely a reiteration of the date, August 19, when Norris had been condemned to death in the electric chair.

A benefit for the Scottsboro boys was held at the Rockland Palace in New York under the auspices of Theodore Dreiser's National Committee for the Defense of Political Prisoners. Among the speakers were Waldo Frank, James Ford, the black Communist candidate for Vice-President of the United States, and the black journalist Eugene Gordon. Louise Thompson spoke also, and the cast of *Porgy* performed, as did Martha Graham and her dancers. The Hall Johnson Choir sang, and Cab Calloway played for a largely white audience of some 2,000 who contributed $2,500 to the Scottsboro Defense Fund. Thompson's speech displeased Alain Locke, who wrote to Charlotte Mason that it was a "masked harangue mixed with social service and lynching statistics and weak Communist platitudes about the solidarity of black and white labor."

The Scottsboro Unity Defense Committee decided to put on another dance and benefit primarily for blacks. This time there was assembled an array of almost exclusively black talent, including Duke Ellington, Fletcher Henderson, Fats Waller, the Mills Brothers, and Ethel Waters, along with the white bandleader Paul Whiteman. Again several thousand dollars were raised. It was ironic that the benefit was put on primarily by the Harlem Communists, since the Comintern had condemned jazz as decadent and prohibited party members from playing it or dancing to it.

Among the backers of the Scottsboro defense was the New York Interdenominational Association of Preachers, made up of the twenty largest black churches in the city, and the American Scottsboro Committee, composed of prominent blacks and a number of white leaders.

Black colleges were largely passive in regard to the Scottsboro case. Many of them had white presidents and faculty that discouraged protests. When students at the Hampton Institute proposed a march of silent protest, they were denied permission by the president, who declared, "We educate, not protest."

Petitions calling for the freeing of the Scottsboro boys were circulated everywhere, and those who signed read like a who's who of the famous. In addition to such names as Dreiser, Steffens, Sinclair, Anderson, and Dos Passos, Albert Einstein, Thomas Mann, and 300-odd German intellectuals called on President Hoover and Governor B. M. Miller of Alabama for clemency. In Britain, H. G. Wells and thirty-three Members of Parliament added their voices. In Dresden, Germany, young Communists attacked the U.S. consulate and hurled bottles through the windows containing the message "Down with American murder and imperialism. For the brotherhood of black and white young proletarians. An end to the bloody lynching of our Negro co-workers." There were similar demonstrations in Leipzig, in Berlin, and in Geneva, Switzerland.

In March, 1932, the Alabama Supreme Court upheld the verdict of the Scottsboro court by a margin of six to one. The case was thereupon appealed to the U.S. Supreme Court, which agreed to hear it. Five months later arguments in the case were heard, and on November 7, the Court reversed the decision on the ground that the defendants had been denied adequate counsel and remanded the case to the lower court. Another trial was ordered.

For the second trial the ILD engaged one of the nation's best-known criminal lawyers, Samuel Leibowitz, a Rumanian-born Jew whom many people considered the successor to Clarence Darrow because of his commitment to civil rights issues. The second trial began with a request for a change of venue on the ground that public opinion in Scottsboro was too inflamed for a fair trial there. The defense requested that the trial be moved to Birmingham, but Judge Hawkins designated the town of Decatur, another rural town, some fifty miles from Scottsboro. The judge there was James Edwin Horton, Jr., one of the most respected and independent jurists in the state. Once again Patterson would be tried initially.

As the second trial opened, Leibowitz made clear that he would undertake to prove that blacks were routinely excluded from juries in Decatur, despite the fact that this tactic would increase hostility toward him and the defendants. He did this skillfully, first producing respected white witnesses to establish the fact that no one could recall ever having seen a black man serve on a jury, then dramatically calling to the witness stand a number of black doctors, lawyers, and businessmen, some of them college graduates. One white witness excused the omission of black jurors on the ground that "they will nearly all steal." Leibowitz asked him if he meant that every black in Jackson County would steal—ministers, doctors, community leaders? The witness twisted and perspired and then acknowledged that he would not admit blacks to a jury simply because they were blacks. Mary Heaton Vorse, covering the trial for the *New York World-Telegram*, noted "Almost all [the blacks called by Leibowitz] have college degrees, some more than one." Leibowitz then called on the jury commissioner to produce the county's jury rolls and demonstrated that here and there the name of a black man had been added by forgery.

As the trial itself proceeded, Leibowitz led Victoria Price, the state's star witness, whom Vorse described as "terrifying in her depravity," into a maze of contradictions and confusions, but instead of discrediting her testimony to the jurors and the courtroom spectators, his grilling evoked hostility toward the lawyer on the part of jurors and spectators alike. One newspaper later editorialized: "One possessed of that old Southern chivalry cannot read the trial now in progress in Decatur . . . and publish an opinion and keep within the law." The "brutal manner" in which Leibowitz questioned Mrs. Price "makes one feel like reaching for his gun. . . ."

At a recess in the trial one of the doctors, Marvin Lynch, told Judge Horton that in his opinion, the women could not possibly have been raped. "Judge," he declared, "I looked at both the women and told them they were lying, that they knew they had not been raped and they just laughed at me." The judge was horrified. He urged the doctor to testify for the defense, but Lynch replied that to do so would ruin him professionally. Suppressing his misgivings, Horton allowed the trial to proceed in the hope that the testimony of the other doctor, Bailey, and Victoria Price's poor performance as a witness, would induce the jury to bring in a verdict of not guilty, which he was now convinced was proper. One by one, Leibowitz, with the skill acquired in years of courtroom experience, demolished the testimony of the state's witnesses. One farmer, who claimed to have seen the women struggling with a group of blacks as the train passed, referred to their "dresses" when it had been established that they were wearing overalls and men's jackets. Leibowitz produced witnesses who asserted that both women had had intercourse with casual acquaintances within the twenty-four hours preceding the alleged rape. As Leibowitz proceeded to build what he was convinced was an unshakable case for the innocence of the defendants, the tension in the courtroom mounted. Mary Heaton Vorse heard one spectator whisper, "It'll be a wonder if ever he leaves town alive." Word reached the judge that some 200 local whites had met to plan the abduction of Leibowitz. He was to be ridden out of town on a rail, and the defendants were to be lynched. Judge Horton thereupon delivered a blistering denunciation of all those contemplating taking the law into their own hands and ordered the security around the courtroom and jail increased.

The most sensational moment of the second trial came when Leibowitz produced Ruby Bates, who had disappeared after the first trial. She declared that she had gone to New York with a "Jewish lady" and there had been prevailed upon by Harry Emerson Fosdick, the famous minister of the Riverside Church, to return to Alabama and tell the truth. The truth was that neither she nor Victoria Price had been raped or otherwise molested by the defendants. The prosecution managed to imply that she had been taken over by New York Jewish Communists and convinced to commit perjury. Bates indeed announced after the trial was over that she had become a convert to communism, and as such she became a star speaker at ILD meetings. But her testimony did nothing to sway the jurors or change public opinion in the South.

In his summation to the jury, one of the prosecuting attorneys, Wade Wright, taking little notice of testimony, pointed to Leibowitz and the ILD attorney Joseph Brodsky and orated, "Show them that Alabama justice cannot be bought and sold with Jew money from New York." If the jury acquitted Patterson, Wright declared, "put a garland of roses around his neck, give him a supper and send him to New York City," where "Dr. Harry Fosdick [will] dress him up in a high hat and morning-coat, gray-striped trousers and spats." Once more the state called for death in the electric chair. Once more the jury, determined to defend the honor of Southern womanhood, returned a verdict of "guilty as charged and fix[ed] the punishment at death in the electric chair." Leibowitz, shocked at the verdict, congratulated the judge on his fairness.

As the verdict was announced, Mary Heaton Vorse heard one old man say matter-of-factly, "Anyone would have to [convict] after hearin' her say that nigger raped her." Testimony to the contrary didn't "count a mite." As another spectator put it, Victoria Price "might be a fallen woman, but by God she is a white woman."

When word flashed over the wires that Patterson had been sentenced once more to the electric chair, the editor of the *Amsterdam News* in Harlem issued a call for blacks to march to Washington to protest the trials. The next day 3,000 blacks met Leibowitz when his train arrived in New York, and within twenty-four hours more than 20,000 signatures had been obtained protesting the proceedings in Decatur. When someone asked him how the jury could have convicted Patterson in the face of the evidence, the angry Leibowitz declared, "If you ever saw those creatures, those bigots whose mouths are slits in their faces, whose eyes pop out like a frog's, whose chins drip tobacco juice, bewhiskered and filthy, you would not ask how they could do it." It was not a tactful response. It was soon spread about the South, and the *Alabama Courier* replied, "The New York Jew says there is no such thing as a fair trial in Alabama. It seems to this paper this recent recruit from Russia is a poor sort of a chap to try to blight the good name of Alabama."

Kid Davis soon found that the Communist Party and the ILD had wrested the protest march on Washington from him. The "march" was actually a bus and motorcar cavalcade, preceded by a rally at the St. Nicholas Arena in New York, which was attended by about 5,000 white and black protesters. The rally featured Ruby Bates, who repeated her denial that she and Victoria Price had been raped. On Sunday protesters from a number of Eastern cities, including Baltimore and Philadelphia, gathered outside the White House. A delegation of black leaders that included James Ford and William Patterson asked to confer with the President. They got Louis Howe instead and then marched on to the Capitol, where they delivered the draft of a civil rights bill to the Vice-President and the speaker of the House. Cyril Briggs wrote exultantly: "The march marks a new stage in the struggle of the Negro people, with the workers emerging as the leaders of these struggles and . . . supplanting the businessmen, preachers, and professional self-elected leaders who have consistently betrayed our struggle in the past . . . the Negro people [have] come forward clearly as an active force . . . in the mass fight to free the Scottsboro boys and put a stop to the flagrant violations of Negro rights. . . . Harlem during the past few weeks has given the Negro people of the whole world a wonderful demonstration in the effectiveness of militant and united struggle."

The second trial had shifted the emphasis from protecting white womanhood from "niggers" to rebuffing communism and Northern influence. A Harvard classmate of Carl Carmer told him, "I might have been for acquittin' them at the first trial but now after all this stink's been raised, we've got to hang 'em." A correspondent of the *Chattanooga Daily Times* wrote that "as yet, communism is not running the courts of Alabama, the mutterings and ravings of foreign 'reds,' Bolsheviks, revolutionaries, busy-bodies, meddlers . . . and other undesirables to the contrary. . . ." The *Wiregrass Journal* editorialized: "Leibowitz in the Scottsboro Case has thrown down the challenge to the Democratic party to maintain white supremacy in the South."

At the same time a number of the more responsible Southern newspapers began to accept the fact that the Scottsboro nine were innocent. One of the most vocal journalists was Douglas Southall Freeman, historian and editor of the *Richmond News-Leader*. For him the second trial confirmed all the suspicions aroused by the first hearing. Patterson had been the victim of the " 'unwritten law' that when a white woman accuses a white man she must prove his guilt, but . . . when she accuses a Negro he must prove his innocence." Josephus Daniels, former secretary of the navy and editor of the *Raleigh News and Observer*, wrote: "Southerners have a deeper interest in the case than people elsewhere since all Southern justice will be discredited by the shocking verdict." Even the *Chattanooga News* declared, "We cannot conceive of a civilized community taking human lives on the strength of this miserable affair," while the *Birmingham Post* noted: "We love justice enough to want it done regardless of the fact it may seem to play into the hands of unfair radicals."

But when four prominent white men spoke at a rally to protest the conviction of Patterson, they all suffered for their outspokenness. Kenneth Barnhart, professor of sociology at Birmingham-Southern College, was fired from his academic post. Rabbi Benjamin Goldstein of Temple Beth Or in Montgomery was told by his congregation, dismayed at the rise of anti-Semitism in a region that had been notable for its absence, to cease all involvement with the Scottsboro case or resign. He resigned. He had planned to remain in Montgomery for a time at least, but the mayor informed him that he would be liable to prosecution under a "criminal anarchy" law.

Mrs. Craik Speed and her daughter, Jane, were members of one of Montgomery's oldest and proudest families, but when the two women announced their support for the ILD, and Jane Speed addressed a May Day rally of blacks and whites in Birmingham calling for racial justice, she was arrested and fined $50 for speaking without a permit and "addressing a meeting at which there were no physical barriers erected between white and Negro auditors." She served fifty-three days in jail. Police placed Mrs. Speed's house under surveillance, and when her daughter was released from prison, the two women left the state.

The tenderest shoots of liberal sentiment appeared here and there in Birmingham. Jere King, a retired UCLA history professor who grew up in Birmingham, recalls meetings at the home of Joseph Gelbers and his wife, Estelle, to discuss John Strachey's socialist book *The Coming Struggle for Power*. He traced his own conversion to a more liberal view of racial relations to reading Robert Russa Moton's book *What the Negro Thinks*, placed in his hands by William Kyle Smith, secretary of the University of Virginia chapter of the YMCA. "Until I read Moton's book," King later wrote, "my world view was as racist as that of George Wallace. I never met a white Southerner who believed in racial equality during that period [1931–1933]. I continued to fear and hate blacks. . . . I . . . considered them subnormal by natural and divine decree." The process of conversion, begun by Moton's book, was completed when King heard Howard Thurman speak at an interracial YMCA conference in Atlanta, Georgia. "I became a lay racial and socialist missionary," King added, "winning only one convert, my mother." With the Scottsboro case, King and his mother formed a defense committee of a half dozen like-minded whites, who resolved that their best contribution to the cause would be to have the transcript of the trial reproduced and sent to the editors of all Alabama newspapers so that their editorials would at least "not be written in ignorance of the 'best evidence.' "

In addition to pressing the petition for a new trial, the ILD went to Tuscaloosa, Alabama, to defend three blacks charged with raping and killing a young woman. Word spread that the "Communists had come to town," and a crowd promptly assembled at the courthouse. A heavily armed national guard unit got the ILD lawyers out of town, and the three accused men were turned over to a party of white men, who shot them. One survived and crawled to a nearby farmhouse. He was jailed without a trial and then released months later with the understanding he would leave the county once and for all.

Another murder took place two months later in Tuscaloosa when a mentally retarded white woman accused "an elderly syphilitic cripple" of rape. When the police refused to act on her charges, seven white men kidnapped the accused and filled his body with bullets. When the National Committee for the Defense of Political Prisoners undertook to launch an investigation of the murder, the Citizens' Protective League was organized to "keep communists out of the county." The League's members made thirty-two raids on black homes, searching for subversive materials. The *Tuscaloosa News* blamed the deaths of the blacks in the two episodes on the ILD. They had been killed by "hotheads who . . . fear[ed] that outside interference would block the course of justice. . . . But the maggoty beaks of the bellied buzzards of the International Labor Defense are stained with the blood of the three Negroes. . . ." The Communists had clearly met their match in invective.

In June, 1933, Judge Horton received a defense motion for a new trial for Patterson. The defense attorneys considered it no more than a step toward appeal to the State Supreme Court and subsequently to the Supreme Court, this time primarily on the ground that blacks were excluded from the juries that had heard the case. To their surprise the judge addressed himself directly to the question "Is there sufficient credible evidence upon which to base a verdict?" His conclusion, carefully spelled out, was that no such evidence existed. Horton therefore accepted the motion of the defense, set aside the jury verdict, and ordered a new trial. Prominent among the reactions to Horton's decision was that of the former Alabama Senator Thomas Heflin, who wrote to the attorney general that "this dallying about with the Scottsboro rapists is a humiliating insult to the white race in Alabama and the very worst thing that could happen to the law-abiding negroes of this state."

Horton, for his forthrightness and courage, was removed from the case, which was transferred into the jurisdiction of a "hanging judge" noted for his intolerance and severity. Running for reelection later, Judge Horton was defeated.

The judge at the third trial, which was held in November, made it clear that he would tolerate no nonsense. "There ain't going to be no more picture snappin' around here," Judge William Washington Callahan warned newspaper photographers. Leibowitz was back as the principal attorney for the defense. The judge's bias was evident. From the first he upheld almost all of the prosecution's motions and denied those of the defense. His manner toward Leibowitz was blatantly hostile, and he refused to admit evidence designed to show that the two women had had intercourse prior to boarding the train.

Leibowitz gave special attention to evidence that blacks were excluded from the jury lists. The same evidence was reviewed. Victoria Price testified again, and once more Leibowitz made a shambles of her testimony. The expressions on the faces of the jurors revealed their hostility to his cross-examinations. The judge did his best to inhibit Leibowitz's questioning. His charge to the jury was equally prejudicial, and the conclusion was foregone. The earlier convictions were upheld.

Once more the case was appealed to the Alabama Supreme Court, which unanimously denied the defense motion for a new trial or trials. It was then taken once again to the U.S. Supreme Court. On April 1, 1935, Chief Justice Charles Evans Hughes read the Court's opinion in *Norris* v. *Alabama*. Clearly, by the exclusion of blacks from juries, "a federal right has been denied," Hughes declared. The facts were beyond dispute. The case of Norris was returned to the Alabama courts. Public clamor for throwing the case out on the ground of inadequate evidence rose. The *New York Times* declared, "Wisdom—even the most shallow and opportunistic kind of wisdom—would certainly indicate that the case be dropped now and forever." Letters and telegrams urging pardons or at least clemency flooded the office of Alabama Governor Bibb Graves. His only response was to notify the courts of the state "that we must put the names of Negroes in the jury boxes in every county." The decision of the Supreme Court was one of the most significant in its long history. But while the names of black residents were placed on jury rolls, excuses were found not to call them to duty or, if they were called, to challenge their service on juries. Southern newspapers and politicians continued to insist that juries with black jurors were "out of the question" and to call for the evasion of the law as "not binding on honor or morals." Despite the decision of the Supreme Court, it would be decades before blacks were impaneled on Southern juries.

The new Soviet line of popular front cooperation now made possible an alliance in defense of the Scottsboro boys which included the ACLU, the ILD, the NAACP, and the Methodist Federation for Social Service. It was headed by Allan Knight Chalmers, pastor of the Broadway Tabernacle Congregational Church, a graduate of Johns Hopkins University and the Yale Divinity School, and a man of singular tact, courage, and tenacity, who now became the principal figure in the long, drawn-out fight to secure a measure of justice for the Scottsboro boys, most of whom were now men.

Fresh indictments were brought, and new trials were scheduled for January 20, 1936. They opened, still under Judge Callahan, and Victoria Price once more gave her muddled and unconvincing testimony. At the end of Patterson's trial the prosecuting attorney exhorted the jury "to protect the sacred secret parts of the female" lest all Alabama women would have "to buckle sixshooters about their middles. . . . Don't go out and quibble over the evidence," he shouted.

". . . Get it done quick and protect the womanhood of this great State."

The jury was as determined to protect the "womanhood of this great State" as its predecessors had been. It found Patterson "guilty as charged." But this time there was a surprise. The punishment recommended was not death but merely seventy-five years in prison. The *Birmingham Age-Herald* hailed it as a notable breakthrough for Southern justice, undoubtedly the first time in the history of the state that a black man "convicted of a charge of rape upon a white woman has been given less than a death sentence." The recommendation for a long prison term—in effect, life—was the accomplishment of the foreman, John Burleson, a famous athlete and a prosperous farmer with intellectual interests and liberal inclinations. Convinced that Patterson was innocent, he had held out stubbornly for less than the death penalty. It marked a turning point in the case or, more accurately, cases. Callahan granted a postponement in the trials of the other defendants, and for months negotiations went on behind the scene between Chalmers and Southern liberals anxious to see justice done. The governor at one point agreed to issue a pardon, but then, afraid of the political consequences, he reneged. One suggestion was that if Patterson, Norris, and several others would plead guilty to rape, the remaining defendants would be released. That proposal was indignantly rejected. The governor seemed time and again on the verge of some kind of compromise.

In the end all such efforts fell through, and the trials of the remaining defendants were resumed on July 12, 1937, six years after the alleged rape. This time the first defendant was Clarence Norris. A number of individuals originally connected with the case had died or moved away. Some witnesses could not be found, but once more the wheels of justice ground on, and once more the jury, after two hours and a half of deliberation, returned a verdict of guilty and the "punishment of death." When Allan Chalmers heard the verdict he was attending an ecumenical service in Oxford, England. He had not, he wrote later, felt such an "indescribable loneliness" since a friend had been killed beside him at Verdun in the World War. He leaned against the door of the church and wept.

The rest of the defendants remained to be tried. The first was Andy Wright. The state agreed not to ask for the death penalty. The jury returned a verdict of guilty, after deliberating an hour and fifteen minutes, and recommended a sentence of ninety-nine years. The trial of Charley Weems followed. The same grim farce was repeated. The state did not ask for death; the verdict was guilty, the term of imprisonment seventy-five years.

A weary and bitter Leibowitz castigated Southern justice mercilessly, knowing he could do the defendants no harm since their respective fates were already sealed. But the prosecution, by now as weary as the defense, dropped the rape charge against Ozzie Powell (he was sentenced to twenty years for assault) and then, in a surprise move, dropped all charges against the rest of the defendants: Willie Robertson, who had a severe venereal disease, Olen Montgomery, who was virtually blind, and Eugene Williams and Roy Wright, who had been thirteen years old at the time of the "crime." Three men had been convicted of rape and given in effect life terms, and Norris had been sentenced to death; now four were discharged on the same evidence that had convicted the others. The *Richmond Times-Dispatch* was among those papers that commented on the incongruity. Dropping charges against the four, Douglas Southall Freeman wrote, "serves as a virtual clincher to the argument that all nine of the Negroes are innocent."

Efforts on behalf of the five convicted men were now concentrated on an executive pardon. Chalmers's hopes soared when Bibb Graves was quoted as saying, "I have already stated my feeling that the position of the State is untenable with half out and half in on the same charges and evidence. My mind is clear on the action required to remedy this impossible position." But Graves dragged his feet and finally, after meeting with several of the defendants, announced that he was unwilling to pardon them. At this stage President Roosevelt intervened with Graves, a politician who had made a notable record as a reform governor and as an ardent New Dealer. Enlisted by Walter White, Eleanor Roosevelt had urged the President to do what he could to prevail on Graves to pardon the men. FDR responded by inviting Graves to visit him at Warm Springs to discuss things informally. Aware of Roosevelt's powers of persuasion, Graves declined on the ground of pressing business. Roosevelt then wrote him a letter: "Dear Bibb, I am sorry indeed not to have seen you while I was at Warm Springs because I wanted to give you a purely personal, and not in any way official, suggestion. You have been such a grand governor and done so much for the cause of liberalism in the State of Alabama that I want you to go out of office without the loss of the many friends you have made throughout the nation." He had given a number of people the "real feeling . . . that you said definitely and positively that you were going to commute the sentences of the remainder of the Scottsboro boys. . . . As I said before, I am writing this only as a very old and warm friend of yours, and I hope you will take it in the spirit it is said."

Apparently a group of Alabama politicians, who included the adamant Heflin, a major power in the state, told Graves he was through politically if he pardoned the men still in prison. The word of Graves's change of heart brought a storm of criticism, much of it from Southerners. The *Richmond Times-Dispatch* upbraided him for "capitulating to the forces of obscurantism and bigotry which already have dragged his Scottsboro case through the courts for over seven years and disgraced Alabama and the South in the eyes of the civilized world."

The case of the Scottsboro boys was to drag on for eleven more years while the faithful Chalmers tried one recourse after another to prevail upon Alabama officials, who, in the words of a historian of the case, "were timid, fearful, and sometimes malicious." The four men who were freed had checkered careers, drifting into obscurity after they had served the purposes of the ILD and the Communist Party, which exhibited them widely as living evidence of the party's commitment to justice for American blacks.

In November, 1943, the Alabama Board of Pardons and Paroles, after six years of tergiversation, released Charley Weems, and several months later released Andy Wright and Clarence Norris, although they were forbidden to leave the state. When they did flee, Chalmers persuaded them to return, but the board put them back in prison for violating the terms of their parole. Norris wrote, "I don't Believe I have a white friend in the world I believe all Races of white hate negroes Especially in the United States."

At the end of 1946 Ozzie Powell was released, and Norris was given another parole. Patterson, who was described as "sullen, vicious and incorrigible," escaped from a work gang in the summer of 1948 and, eluding airplanes and bloodhounds, made his way to Detroit. Andy Wright was paroled in June, 1950, after nineteen years in the state penitentiary.

The trials of the Scottsboro boys held the attention of Americans for almost a decade. Although public interest waned rapidly after the fourth trial, the case itself became a kind of shorthand reference for racial injustice in the United States. As we have seen, poets wrote poems about it, artists painted pictures, cartoonists drew innumerable cartoons. Thousands of news stories flooded the press of the world and innumerable essays and articles were written about every aspect of the case. It dramatized, year after year on the stage of world history, as nothing else could have, the condition of blacks in the South. It gradually awakened Southerners of liberal or moderate inclination to the racial horrors of their segregated homeland. The activities of the Communist Party (and its legal arm, the International Labor Defense) contributed greatly to the party's standing among liberals, radicals, and civil libertarians, and, of course, above all, blacks. It seems reasonably fair to say that without its intervention the Scottsboro boys all would have been electrocuted for a crime they did not commit. In the case of *Norris* v. *Alabama*, it elicited the important decision that blacks must be included on jury rolls.

Heywood Patterson's mother told an enthusiastic crowd in New Haven, Connecticut, "I haven't got no schooling, but I have five senses and I know that the Negroes can't win by themselves." As for the charge that the ILD was a Communist organization, she said, "I don't care whether they are Reds, Greens or Blues. They are the only ones who put up a fight to save these boys and I am with them to the end."

Eugene Gordon, a black journalist for the *Boston Post*, wrote in the *New Masses*: "Negro workers think of the countless times Communists have been beaten insensible for defending . . . Negro workers. . . . They see the ILD . . . supported by the Communist Party, rushing to the defense of the nine Negro youths at Scottsboro before other Negro organizations in the country condescend to glance superciliously in their direction. . . . Seeing and hearing all these things, the Negro worker in the United States would be a fool not to recognize the leadership he has been waiting for since his freedom."

Most important of all, the Scottsboro case gave black Americans a new confidence that the bonds of racial oppression might in time be broken. It brought hope where before there had been only hopelessness, and where there had been hope of better days that hope was strengthened. Finally, the nation's conscience was touched by the plight of black Americans as it had not been since the Civil War. In summary it seems as safe as any historical generalization to say that the sufferings of the nine young blacks and the tireless labors of their advocates, extending far beyond the ILD and the Communist Party itself to include innumerable black congregations and many white organizations dedicated to the eradication of injustice, changed the racial situation in the United States or at least laid the essential psychological foundation for change. "All revolutions," John Adams wrote almost two centuries earlier, "begin in the hearts and minds of the people." Many of the same people who had enlisted in the cause of Sacco and Vanzetti made the cause of the Scottsboro boys their own as well. The vast ice jam of white prejudice and, equally important, indifference began to break up. Although horrendous racial episodes continued in the South and elsewhere, although bright and able young blacks continued to find the doors of that famous American opportunity closed to them, although things seemed "objectively" much as before, they would in fact never be the same again.

The Scottsboro case was highlighted by an only slightly less sensational case involving Angelo Herndon, the young Communist organizer. Herndon was arrested in Atlanta, Georgia, and subjected to a brutal interrogation about his Communist connections. For eleven days he was held without charges and without the opportunity to communicate with anyone outside the jail. As soon as he could smuggle out word of his plight through a released prisoner, the International Labor Defense sent a lawyer with a writ of habeas corpus. The judge rejected it but ordered that an indictment be drawn up at once or he would order Herndon released. On July 22, 1932, Herndon was indicted for attempting to incite insurrection on July 16, at which time he had been in the Fulton County jail for two weeks. The indictment charged that the accused did "organize . . . establish and . . . set up a group and combination of persons white and colored, under the name and style of the Communist Party of America, for the purpose of uniting, combining and conspiring to incite riots, to embarrass and impede the orderly processes of the courts and for the purpose of offering and making combined opposition and resistance to the lawful authority of the State of Georgia and for the purpose of overthrowing and defeating by force and violence the lawfully constituted authority of the State of Georgia. . . ."

The statute under which Herndon was charged had been originally drawn up in 1861 to discourage slave insurrections and modified after the war to omit specific mention of blacks.

After his indictment months passed without a date being set for the trial. Meanwhile, Herndon was encouraged to write a letter to the *Liberator* giving the facts of his arrest and imprisonment. Given wide publicity by the various journals and papers of the Communist Party, his arrest and indictment became first a national and then an international issue. On December 24, 1932, two black druggists in Atlanta posted bail for Herndon, and for the first time in six months he was free from his jail cell.

When his trial opened on January 16, 1933, the courtroom was crowded with curious spectators, eager to see a "black Red." The prosecutor was a classic Southern lawyer, Colonel *and* Reverend John H. Hudson, officer of the state's national guard and minister of the Gospel, a lawyer with the orotund tones of a full-voiced Methodist preacher. Hudson was confident he could prove "that the defendant, Angelo Herndon, is guilty of trying to overthrow the lawfully constituted authority of the State of Georgia." Already alerted by the Scottsboro case to the issue of no blacks on the jury, Hudson was at pains to argue that despite an industrious search, "there isn't a single one . . . that comes up to the requirements. . . ."

Among the documents taken from Herndon's room and submitted to the jury to prove that the accused was a Communist were *The Communist Position on the Negro Question, Communism and Christianism* by an Episcopal minister, the *New York Times,* the *Wall Street Journal,* and *Red Book* magazine. The trial, Hudson made clear, was the trial not simply of a young black man named Angelo Herndon "but of Lenin, Stalin, Trotsky and Kerensky, and every white person who believes that black and white should unite for the purpose of setting up a nigger Soviet Republic in the Black Belt." An example must be made of Herndon by specifying the death penalty for spreading Communist propaganda so that the message would be unmistakable: "As fast as the Communists come here, we shall indict them and I shall demand the death penalty in every case."

Herndon's black lawyer was Benjamin Davis, a graduate of Amherst College, where he had been an all-American football player, and of Harvard Law School. When Horace Cayton visited Atlanta, he met Davis, who, to Cayton's "great envy," was smoking a Dunhill pipe, a mark of his family's wealth. Davis, who had all the easy, outgoing charm of a Southern politician, was described by his friend Henry Lee Moon as a "good old boy."

Davis's self-appointed bodyguard was the Reverend Martin. Hosea Hudson described him as "a great big man, large, robust." Martin and two or three of his deacons would put on their overalls, with pistols concealed in their pockets, and sit in the courtroom, ready to act if there was any attempt on Davis's life. "Ben didn't know it. Nobody know it, but him and his deacons was armed, sitting in the courthouse like workers, while the case was going on. When Ben would leave the courthouse, they'd leave, follow him, stay some distance, see that nothing happen to him."

In his address to the jury Davis declared: "Angelo Herndon is charged with attempting to incite insurrection. According to the Reverend Hudson, it's insurrection to fight for bread—and when you fight, the Reverend Mr. Hudson, lord and master of the Methodist pulpit, wants to send you to the electric chair.

"Gentlemen of the Jury, this is not a case of prosecution; it is one of persecution. Which one of you can say that he also will not be sitting in the scornful seat, listening at the righteous bellowing of Reverend Hudson, merely because you demanded food for your loved ones. . . . Gentlemen, this very case is a blot upon American civilization which boasts of liberty, democracy, freedom of speech and press. And it is in the name of this very liberty and democracy that the Reverend Hudson is asking you to send this Negro youth to a horrible and unjustifiable death—merely because he fought for the rights of the poor and needy without regard to their race or color."

The jury's deliberations were brief. Its verdict: "guilty as charged." But the judge sentenced Herndon to twenty years on the Georgia chain gang instead of death.

Many Southern newspapers applauded the conviction of Herndon, agreeing with the *Mississippi Meridian Star*, which declared: "We white people of the South, having lived in close touch with the Negro race for years and years, are well aware of the fact that Communism is a deadly 'intoxication' that leads to trouble, not only for Negroes who listen to its tempting lies, but for law and order as well. Under the old Georgia law by which Herndon was tried and convicted, the death penalty is possible, but the jury, as well as the judge, feels that a command to 'halt'—brought by an eighteen to twenty year prison sentence—will effectively curb the culprit's teachings."

Some newspapers in the South expressed serious doubts about the constitutionality of the law under which Herndon was tried, but the black *Pittsburgh Courier* noted that the responsibility for Herndon's conviction lay not only with "the planter-manufacturer dictatorship of Georgia, but upon the Communist Party which persists in callously sending these youngsters down to certain imprisonment and death." His jailing and that of others in adjoining states were "not only a disgrace to American civilization, but a severe indictment of the Communist Party policy, which persistently ignores realities while chasing Marxist will-o'-the-wisps."

The *Macon Telegraph* attacked the trial and the verdict and reminded its readers that the strength of the Communist Party in the South was derived from its efforts "to provide food and clothing and shelter for oppressed people. . . . The *Telegraph* hopes that the Supreme Court of this state will substitute common sense for the Bourbonism of the jury that tried Herndon."

The International Labor Defense filed a motion for a new trial before the judge who had presided over the initial trial. He denied it, and the case was appealed to the State Supreme Court. As his case awaited appeal, Herndon became convinced that there was a conspiracy on the part of the prison officials to subject him to such hardships as to kill him or drive him insane. He was kept on death row although his sentence had not been death, and he found it a shattering experience to see one after another of his fellow prisoners, most of them black, being led away to the death chamber. After numerous delays and procrastinations and persistent pressure by a committee, headed by the playwright John Howard Lawson, that visited Governor Eugene Talmadge to protest Herndon's treatment, a doctor was allowed to examine him. His physical condition was so poor that he was admitted to the prison hospital, but his treatment was little better there. "Every minute became an eternity of suffering," Herndon wrote of that period of his incarceration.

As word of Herndon's treatment was spread by the liberal and radical press, at mass meetings and rallies, contributions of money, letters, essays, and poems flooded Herndon's cell. One poem was by a sixteen-year-old white girl in Atlanta, Belle West:

> Listen, white bosses-lynchers!
> I'm white, too!
> I'm sixteen.
> You love to call me
> "The Flower of Southern womanhood!"
> And breed hate in my heart
> With sneaking lies of
> "Nigger rape."
> But I laugh in your face,
> And stretch my hand
> To a black boy in Georgia's jail
> Whose courage

You cowards can't break!
Angelo Herndon, do you hear us?
Do you hear our tread?
It shakes the lynchers
Like a reed in the wind.
Listen to our step-Negro
White!
All in time—the same rhythm.
We are coming, Angelo.
Listen!

In May, 1934, the Georgia Supreme Court upheld Herndon's conviction. The sentence to the chain gang was suspended, awaiting the result of the appeal to the Supreme Court of the United States. The judges' motivation was apparently the rumor that Herndon would be killed as soon as he was beyond the jurisdiction of the prison officials. Bail was set at $15,000, and the International Labor Defense, the Communist Party, and various liberal and radical groups set about to raise the money.

Herndon packed his modest belongings to indicate to his outraged jailers that he was confident the $15,000 required for his bail would be raised. A friendly prison guard informed Herndon that he had heard talk in the "front office" of plans to lynch him before he could get out of the state if the bail was raised. When word reached the ILD, it enlisted Theodore Dreiser, who called Governor Talmadge on the telephone. "We are sending a man down to take Angelo Herndon out of jail in a few days," Dreiser told the Georgia governor. "We are informed that he has been threatened with lynching in case he is released." The governor expressed skepticism, and Dreiser replied, "We demand protection for him."

Talmadge replied: "People down here don't get excited about things like that. We never molest a nigger unless he rapes a white woman. My nigger servants who are standing right here now can testify to that. . . ." Talmadge assured Dreiser that Herndon would be perfectly safe in Georgia as long as he "behaves himself."

Herndon's trip from Atlanta to New York was a triumphal procession that recalled to some Big Bill Haywood's trip from Caldwell, Idaho, to Chicago in 1907 after his acquittal for the murder of the ex-governor of that state. At every stop Herndon was greeted by enthusiastic crowds of blacks. When he reached New York, a delegation made up of the various groups that had worked to raise bail met him, and Pennsylvania Station was jammed with thousands of cheering blacks and whites.

Robert Minor and Benjamin Davis lifted him onto their shoulders, and he was pelted with flowers.

Herndon proved an effective speaker, and he was soon in demand at political rallies and before black congregations in major Northern cities. At the Pilgrim Baptist Church, one of the largest black congregations in Chicago, its pastor, the Reverend J. C. Austin, told a meeting of 3,000, "Any man who does not want freedom is either a fool or an idiot, and if to want freedom is to be a Communist, then I am a Communist and will be until I die. From all I have learned of Communism, it means simply the brotherhood of man, and as far as I can see Jesus Christ was the greatest Communist of them all. A few weeks ago I stood in Red Square, Moscow, and raised my voice to the tune of the National Anthem of Russia. Just a week ago I stood in this church and talked to my congregation on the subject 'Russia, the hope of the Negro.' " He had been warned not to let his church be used as a forum for Herndon, but Herndon was welcome any time he wished to come—"you will find me always willing to stand shoulder to shoulder with you, preach with you, pray with you, march with you and, if necessary, die with you for the common good of us all."

At an American Federation of Labor convention A. Philip Randolph, the president of the Brotherhood of Sleeping Car Porters, presented a resolution which called for the freeing of Herndon and stated that "the conviction of Herndon is equivalent to the conviction of the labor movement, since any labor organizer, white or black, may be picked up and sentenced to the chain gang under this archaic and barbaric law."

On April 12, 1935, the Supreme Court heard the case of Angelo Herndon argued on appeal by Whitney North Seymour. J. Walter McCraw, attorney for the state of Georgia, harangued the justices, waving a copy of the *Daily Worker* and expatiating on the worldwide menace of communism. The justices' impatience with such tactics was obvious. What was the specific charge? Justice Van Devanter asked. "He [Herndon] tried to set up a Nigger Republic in the Black Belt." McCraw hinted that in the event of an adverse decision, Georgia might once again secede from the Union. The Court, after due consideration, rejected the appeal on the ground that the "Federal question" had not been raised by the defense or considered by the state court. In other words, the points of law at issue did not enter the Court's jurisdiction. Cardozo, Brandeis, and Stone challenged the majority of the Court, arguing that there was a perfectly legitimate reason to consider the serious constitutional questions involved.

The attorneys for Herndon appealed to Justice Owen Roberts for a stay of execution pending a motion for a rehearing by the Court, and Roberts granted it, once more delaying Herndon's being remanded to a Georgia chain gang. By now the attention of radical groups in every industrial nation was directed at the Herndon case. Many newspapers, hitherto neutral or noncommittal, threw their weight into the scale on Herndon's side. The *New York Post* pointed out that Georgia made no bones of the fact that it would use Herndon's conviction "against all who can be regarded as advocates of Negro equality or the right of Negroes and whites to organize in the same union." Eighteen other persons, six of them women, were under indictment under the same law. Their only offense was that they were union organizers.

Petitions arrived on the desk of the governor of Georgia from as far away as Johannesburg, South Africa, from Mexico and from France. The City Council of Cleveland passed a resolution calling for justice to Herndon, and many other towns and cities followed suit. When the Joint Committee of Aid for the Herndon Defense was formed in September, 1935, its executive committee read like a roster of civil libertarians: Thurgood Marshall for the NAACP; Arthur Garfield Hays and Morris Ernst for the American Civil Liberties Union; Bethuel Webster, Jr., of the Council of the Church League for Industrial Democracy; Winifred Chappell of the Methodist Federation of Social Service; the Justice Commission of the Central Conference of American Rabbis; representatives of the Federal Council of Churches, including the Reverend Allan Knight Chalmers, who was leading the fight for the Scottsboro boys; and Harry Emerson Fosdick. The Socialist and Communist parties had representatives on the joint committee, as did numerous religious and civic groups.

On October 13, 1935, the Supreme Court rejected the petition of Herndon's lawyers for a rehearing. Herndon was ordered to report to the Georgia authorities to start serving on a Georgia chain gang. The New York leftist Congressman Vito Marcantonio became an active champion of Herndon, circulating a petition among his fellow Congressmen and calling "an emergency defense conference" in Harlem. "Freedom for Angelo Herndon represents the cause of the right of the American working class, irrespective of race or creed to protest,

to demand, and to agitate for a better deal in these United States,"
Marcantonio told those who attended the conference. Herndon was
present, and after the Reverend William Lloyd Imes had addressed
him as "fellow-worker and brother" upon whom had fallen "the agony
and the glory of symbolizing those heroic workers of America
who . . . must bear the onslaught of all the dark and evil forces in this
country. . ." Herndon replied: "The period in which we are living today
is so crucial that the fate of the whole human race is at stake. And it
seems that my fate has already been decided by the cruel lynchers and
despots of the State of Georgia. Within a few days I must give myself
up to be tortured for twenty years on a chain gang because I was born
with a black skin, and above all because I had the courage to challenge
their rule." But the fight for the rights of black people would go on.
"We love this country," Herndon declared. "Why not? We have built
it, we have made it what it is. The blood and bones of our forefathers
are mingled in its soil. . . . The fact that I am a Communist infuriated
the rulers of Georgia. They would rather see their Negro servants
come crawling on their knees asking for their hypocritical mercy. But
let me say this: Before I would get down on my knees and beg them
for mercy, I would rather see myself put to death. . . . You and the
other justice-loving people of America must be the ones to smash the
insurrection law, to free the Scottsboro boys, to free me, to put an end,
at last, to the barbarous regime of the South. Continue that fight; it is
a fight for your own freedom as well as for mine."

Returning to Georgia after almost a year of freedom, Herndon
saw signs of poverty everywhere the train passed: bales of rotting
cotton; the tumbled-down, often windowless shacks of black sharecroppers; lean mules and dispirited men and women. Back in Fulton
County prison, Herndon found miraculous changes. The clamor raised
by his imprisonment and the public attention it focused on prison
conditions had led to extensive reforms. The inmates slept on cotton
mattresses instead of the cement floor. They got clean linen and were
allowed to bathe twice a week. The food had improved. On Sunday
the prisoners had fresh vegetables and ice cream and cake. Even though
he was once more on death row, reading material was available. During
his stay in the Fulton County prison, he organized classes in black
history, unionization, fascism, and war.

A little more than a month after Herndon returned, Whitney
Seymour brought a writ of habeas corpus before a judge of the Georgia
Court of Appeals. A month later Judge Hugh Dorsey ruled that the

charge against Herndon was "too vague and indefinite to provide a sufficiently ascertainable standard of guilt" and that it was also in conflict with "Article 1, Section 1, Paragraph 3 of the Constitution of the State of Georgia . . . and that his conviction and sentence are unconstitutional, illegal, void and of no effect. . . ." Herndon's bail was set at $8,000 while the verdict was appealed to the State Supreme Court, and the ILD promptly posted the bail. Herndon was free again. When the State Supreme Court in June, 1936, reversed Judge Dorsey, Seymour at once filed an appeal to the U.S. Supreme Court and obtained a stay of execution.

In February, 1937, five years after Herndon had been arrested in Atlanta on the charge of plotting to overthrow the government of the state of Georgia, the Supreme Court, by a vote of 5 to 4, overturned the decision of the Georgia court.

Justice Roberts, who wrote the opinion for the one-justice majority, declared: "[Herndon's] membership in the Party wholly fails to establish an attempt to incite others to insurrection. . . . In these circumstances to make membership in the Party and solicitation of members for that Party a criminal offense . . . is an unwarranted invasion of free speech." Herndon was free.

By its verdict in the case of Herndon, the Supreme Court began the process by which the protections of the Fourteenth Amendment, so long ignored by state courts, were brought within its jurisdiction and were eventually invoked to override state laws in conflict with the Fourteenth Amendment. The particular application was to the First Amendment, and it established that "Speech may not be punished because of its dangerous tendency to induce violations of law." The lawyer who argued the case before the Court on this principle was the former assistant solicitor general under Herbert Hoover, Whitney North Seymour, Sr. Herbert Wechsler of the Columbia Law School faculty, who had been a clerk to Supreme Court Judge Harlan Stone, was associated in the case with Seymour. The moving spirit behind the campaign to carry Herndon's case to the Supreme Court was a lawyer named Carol Weiss King.

After Herndon's release he moved to New York, where he was much featured by the Communist Party. The four American delegates to the Second International Writers Congress in Paris, in July, 1937, were Langston Hughes, Malcolm Cowley, Anna Louise Strong, and Louis Fischer. Anglo Herndon, invited to attend, was unable to get a passport. Hughes gave the concluding address at the congress. Referring to Herndon's difficulties in securing a passport, Hughes denounced the reactionary forces of the world and spoke of the "great longing . . . in the hearts of the darker peoples of the world to reach out their hands in friendship and brotherhood to all the white races of the earth. . . . We represent the end of race," he declared. "And the Fascists know that when there is no more race there will be no more capitalism, and no more war, and no more money for munition makers, because the workers of the world will have triumphed."

Herndon decided to devote a major part of his energies to trying to tell the story of the role of blacks in the nation's history. He deplored "the unfortunate contrast of American history over against Negro history. . . . The time is long overdue when the story of America's unsung heroes must be told." His first project was to reprint the autobiography of the greatest hero of them all, Frederick Douglass. The project failed. White America was not interested, and black America not self-conscious enough.

Daughters of Revolution. Painting by Grant Wood. (*Cincinnati Art Museum*)

"Gods of the Modern World," panel from The Epic of American Civilization. Fresco by Jose Clemente Orozco, 1932–1934. (*Courtesy of the Trustees of Dartmouth College, Hanover, N.H.*)

City Activities with Subway. Mural by Thomas Hart Benton. (*Courtesy of Equitable Assurance*)

Lenin and the Workers of the World, detail from mural by Diego Rivera. (*Courtesy of the Rockefeller Center*)

The Night Wind. Painting by Charles Burchfield, 1918. (*Collection of the Museum of Modern Art, New York: Gift of A. Conger Goodyear*)

"The Bridge," panel from New York Interpreted. Painting by Joseph Stella, 1922. (*Collection of the Newark Museum*)

Nighthawks. Painting by Edward Hopper, 1942. (*Courtesy of the Art Institute of Chicago: Friends of American Art Collection*)

Aucassin and Nicolette. Painting by Charles Demuth, 1921.
(*Columbus Museum of Art: Gift of Ferdinand Howald, 1931*)

American Landscape. Painting by Charles Sheeler, 1930. (*Collection of the Museum of Modern Art, New York: Gift of Abby Aldrich Rockefeller*)

Baptism in Kansas. Painting by John Steuart Curry, 1928. (*Collection of Whitney Museum of American Art, New York*)

# 24 ※

# Black America and the Communist Party

While Angelo Herndon fought to avoid a life sentence on a Georgia chain gang, another black Communist union organizer, Hosea Hudson, enjoyed some success among black steelworkers in Birmingham, Alabama. When Hudson was an old man, he told the story of his party activities to a patient and skillful interviewer, Nell Irvin Painter. The son of pious sharecroppers, Hudson grew up an illiterate farm boy, in Wilkes County, Georgia. In 1923 he went to Atlanta to try to find work. "When I got in the city," he told Painter, "I wouldn't associate with nobody, gamble, or drink. That's why I stayed out of trouble." From Atlanta he moved to Birmingham in search of better wages, and there, after the Scottsboro case had become front-page news, he was approached by Al Murphy, a black organizer for the Communist Party. Murphy, who was in his early twenties, had attended night school and had the rudiments of an education, while Hudson could still neither read nor write. Murphy, in turn, had been recruited by Frank Williams, Angelo Herndon's recruiter, who, though illiterate himself, gave Murphy Communist leaflets. Impressed, Murphy wrote to the address on the leaflet and received some pamphlets and copies of the *Daily Worker*. Williams took him to a party meeting, "held in a standing room only smoke-filled room somewhere not far from the [foundry]." A white party organizer talked about black rights and the party's notion of an autonomous Black Belt. He pointed out that the Depression was a sure sign of the demise of capitalism. After signing up, Murphy looked for other recruits and hit on Hudson. "He knew the workers and about their conditions. Hosea was a large hunk of somebody," Murphy wrote, "about six feet tall or more, his complexion was medium brown. He was popular in the black community because he was well-known as a fine singer and music group leader."

During a lunch break, Al Murphy "got to outlining about the role of the Party and the program of the Party—the Scottsboro case and the unemployed and the Depression and the imperialist war. . . . He was explaining about how the Scottsboro case is a part of the whole frame-up of the Negro people in the South—jim crow, frame-up, lynching all that was part of the system. So I could understand that all right, and how speed-up the unemployment, and how the unemployed people wouldn't be able to buy back what they made, that they was consumers and that it would put more people in the street." For the first time in his life Hudson began to see the plight of black Americans in a larger context. Whether the context was accurate was far less important than the fact that Hudson was able to see his own woes and those of black Americans generally in a larger perspective—a perspective, moreover, that brought hope. It was especially encouraging to be able to understand Southern racial prejudice as part of a social and economic problem that affected dark-skinned peoples all over the world.

Hudson was a willing recruit. "It look like the thing I been looking for," he told Painter. Soon he was busy recruiting other blacks who seemed bold and rebellious. Hudson was especially attracted by the idea of the nation of the Black Belt. "Out in the rural area . . . where the Negro farmers was in the majority, we felt that there, many places that the Negro would be able to get, enjoy the land, the land would be, you know, the rights of the land, before socialism." In those areas where there was a substantial majority of blacks, it seemed simple enough. "We say," Hudson told Nell Painter, "the whites will be recognized on the basis of their percentage represented on all bodies and committees. But the Negroes at all times would be in the majority." The problem of the cities was more perplexing. In most of the cities of the Black Belt whites not only were a majority but controlled all the economic life of the cities. The blacks would have to take measures, in any event, to be sure they did not replace white capitalists with black capitalists, who would exploit the "Negro masses just like the white under such system."

When Hudson and some of his fellow black Communists met with a white organizer from New York, the organizer told them, "You all get something started here. . . . If you get in jail, we'll come and get you out. Don't worry about getting in jail. Get something started." Getting in jail was, of course, the easy part; the hard part was that jail almost invariably meant a severe beating. The danger was that "starting something" might well mean getting shot or lynched, in which case the ILD was not of much help.

"The Negroes," Hudson recalled, "was easier to recruit. They was ready to come. The whites had a whole lot of hang-ups. The ordinary whites in Birmingham, they were sympathetic, but they could not turn that racist sugar-tit loose. . . . Up in the top years, '33, '34, '35, the Party in Birmingham and Alabama was dominated by Negroes." He estimated that 600 or 700 Birmingham blacks were party members or closely associated with the party at its height, with perhaps 1,000 members in the state. "We only had a few whites and I mean a few whites," he added.

A party meeting in Birmingham in the spring of 1932 was attended by Angelo Herndon and Otto Hall, an organizer from Atlanta. The party's district organizer (DO) was a white man named Don Rose. The district was District 17. The "bureau" for the district was made up of the DO and members of the party representing various organizations: Joe Howard Black for the steelworkers; Hudson for the unemployed; Cornella Hibbard for the women. Hudson recalled: "Coal was a black person. Steel was a black person. . . . Youth was two people, black and white. And the ILD was a white person, Southern white." The bureau met every week, always secretly and usually in private homes. Members entered the house where the meeting was held one at a time, at intervals, to avoid suspicion. They left the same way, whites always leaving last so that if they were seen, they could explain that they had been there on business. Several members suspected by the police of being Communists were frequently under police surveillance, but they became adept at eluding them and police detectives were reluctant to go into black neighborhoods alone.

In the words of Hudson, "I lived under terror. . . . Police would ride by. I'd come home this evening, and I'd look for the police to raid my house before day in the morning, just like going to bed. . . . They was regular raiding different Party members' houses all over the city. . . . They'd ride by, and I'd be setting on the porch." But Hudson's house was never raided.

Hudson had been a reasonably pious Baptist and active church singer before his conversion to communism. One of the things that appealed to him and his friends was that the party had a code of ethics as strict as the Baptist Church. "We all thought, 'Well, now, this is the real religion, 'cause they said that Party members shouldn't mess around with another party member's wife or his daughter, and all like that, and live a clean life, get out and meet the public, people look upon you as a leader. So that was what we came up in the Party in, and not drinking no whiskey, not being half-drunk. . . . My first time seeing Party people drink was at a Christmas party."

Since the churches were the crucial institutions for black organizers, most of them were members of black congregations, and some, like Hudson, were singers or members of church choral groups. More sophisticated party members tried to discourage Hudson from going to church. When he declared that he was "going there to serve the Lord, to sing and pray," his atheistic friends confused him by asking such questions as "If God's all good, how come he don't stop police from killing Negroes, lynching Negroes, if God is all that just?" Hudson had no answer. His faith weakened.

Hudson stressed the enormous difficulties of inducing Southern blacks to take up the battle for their rights. "The Negroes wouldn't back me up," he told Nell Painter, "cause at that time, the Negro in the South, you had to pick out certain Negroes to stand up and speak out. When Negroes set down, they mind set down, they thoughts set down. They went to sleep, like, and they just couldn't think, cause they wouldn't think. These things they ought to talk about, they wouldn't talk about it." It was too painful; they were benumbed. "The regular saying was that what the Negroes was lacking was some good leaders," Hudson reflected. "So when I got to developing and found I could be somebody, from not being able to read and write and still coming forward, I set out to be a leader among the Negro people in Birmingham. I thought, I really thought, that the Negro, all he needs is somebody to stand up and speak, and he would fall in line." It was a false hope, Hudson discovered; "that's where I was let down." There were layers of fear and suspicion that had to be penetrated. One of the most formidable and disheartening was the conviction of racial inferiority that made most blacks prefer white lawyers and doctors and teachers and leaders to those of their own race. That was, in some ways, the longest and slowest and bitterest struggle of all: to prevail on the black brothers to believe in their race and themselves.

"I found this Party, a party of the working class, gave me rights equal with all others regardless of color, sex, or age or educational standards. I with my uneducation could express myself, without being made fun of by others who could read well and fast, using big words. I was treated with respect. I had a right to help make policy," Hudson recalled. "We would read this paper [the *Liberator*] and this would give us great courage. We had classes reading these articles and editorials. . . ." It mattered little in the South "whether an individual was actually a party member or not," as Hudson put it. "Anytime you begin to talk too militant, too progressive about certain things that favors the poor people, you automatically you's a communist . . . whether you want to believe it or not, it ain't no way for an honest person who wants to see real progress made to avoid being called a communist. Automatically you fall in that category. Cause communists is the onliest ones fighting for such things as that. I mean fight. Some of them make a lot of noise, then they back up. But the Party fight all the way through. It's like a bulldog. We don't give up. . . ."

In Hudson's view, Stalin had done more than anyone else for the rights of blacks in the South, "cause Stalin, way back there in the early stages of the Party, along about the late '20s, first of the '30s, he called a conference of some of the Negro American comrades. . . . Stalin did something that nobody else hadn't done, to make it possible for us to struggle."

Hudson rejected the argument that the Communist Party was using blacks. The party was "a working class, political party, and it takes in all workers, and Negroes happen to be part of that working class. How they going to use them? . . . [H]ow they going to use us when we're part of this working class? . . . What the Party was doing was taking this lower class like myself and making people out of them, took the time and they didn't laugh at you if you made a mistake. . . . There was always something to bring you forward, to give you courage."

While most of the black Communists in the South were industrial workers and farmers, there was a sprinkling of middle-class black intellectuals, men like Benjamin Davis, the defense lawyer for Angelo Herndon. In the opinion of Hudson, the mixing of middle-class and working-class blacks in the party helped change the middle-class prejudices against rural blacks and black workers. He told Painter that he and his friend Henry Mayfield were "the ones that woked them so-called better class of Negroes up that the lower-class Negroes had some sense. They was shocked, they was surprised to hear what we had to say. They wonder, 'where did that fellow Hudson come from? I didn't know we had people like that.' That was the kind of admiration they made. We'd get up and talk, and they'd just sit there with they mouth open. They didn't know what to say. . . ."

Hudson told Painter: "The Scottsboro case had got me interested in trying to read." After he had joined the Communist Party, Hudson continued his efforts to learn to read, "but I had a very hard time," he recalled. The party decided to send him to New York to the National Training School for ten weeks of intense schooling in Marxist theory and, for Hudson, reading and writing. The school, called Nitgedaiget, a Yiddish word for "not to worry," was run by the International Ladies' Garment Workers' Union. Hudson and two others were told they would have to reach New York by hoboing; moreover, they could not ride a freight through Virginia because that state had very strict laws about black hoboes. They had to go west in the dead of winter through Ohio and then via Pittsburgh and Philadelphia. The three men arrived in New York, more dead than alive after having barely survived the bitter cold and the attentions of freightyard dicks.

At the National Training School the students "studied the history of the trade union movement, the history of the Party, the whole question of China, and . . . Roosevelt in that period," in Hudson's words. The Communists considered that Roosevelt's "position was reactionary, at that time, that he was taking a semi-fascist position [a reference, doubtless, to the NIRA]." The teaching at the school was "that Britain and France and the United States was building Hitler up to attack the Soviet Union."

When Earl Browder called an extraordinary plenary session of the Communist Party to meet in New York on July 4, 1933, Hosea Hudson drove North with Benjamin Davis in the latter's Ford. Besides Davis and Hudson, five party delegates from Atlanta and Birmingham were packed into the car. Of the seven passengers, four were white: Don Rose, the District 17 organizer; his wife; a man named Ted Mebber; and a Texas delegate simply known as Lee. The trip to New York and back by the crowded carload of whites and blacks was full of peril. Traveling mostly at night, they tried to be as inconspicuous as possible, but every stop for gas or food was hazardous. Several times they were stopped by police and questioned closely.

Dangerous as organizing was for black party members living in cities like Birmingham and Atlanta, it was far more perilous in rural areas. In the cities black party members might blend in with the black population, but in the country they were far more conspicuous. The Communist Party's major effort at organizing black sharecroppers took place in Tallapoosa County, Alabama, in the summer of 1931. It was a cotton-growing county and one of the poorest in the South. One-third of the residents of the county were black, most of them share-croppers. A black organizer arrived at Camp Hill to undertake the task of forming a union of black and, it was hoped, white sharecroppers. Union fees were five cents, and the organizer assured the members that they could force the landowners to double the wages for picking cotton if they would join the union. Someone informed the sheriff, J. Kyle Young, of the activities of the organizer and of a meeting of 200 blacks at Mary Church, near Camp Hill, to draw up a protest against the conviction of the Scottsboro boys to send to the governor. The sheriff, accompanied by the Camp Hill chief of police and two deputies, went to Mary Church. On the road to the church they intercepted a young black sharecropper named Ralph Grey, who was carrying a shotgun and a bundle. When the sheriff asked what was in the bundle, Grey replied that it was none of his business. When the sheriff reached into the back of his car for his gun, Grey fired at him, and several pellets struck Young in his side and arm. The deputies fired back at Grey, seriously wounding him. The noise of the gunfire scattered the blacks meeting at the church. The police chief thereupon gathered a posse of some 500 men armed with pistols, rifles, and shotguns on the ground that a black uprising was in progress. County roads were pa-trolled, and the shacks of black sharecroppers were searched amid mounting hysteria among the county's whites. When the sheriff re-ceived word that eight cars filled with black Communists were on their way from Birmingham to Camp Hill to reinforce the blacks there, roadblocks bristling with guns were set up. "Negro Reds Reported Advancing," the *Birmingham Age-Herald* announced. When a convoy of cars filled with blacks was intercepted, it turned out it was a funeral procession headed for a county graveyard. The Camp Hill chief of police meanwhile reported he had found a list of the names of 170 blacks who had joined the union for the avowed purpose of "de-manding social equality with the white race" and $2 a day as wages. They had also demanded that the governor release the Scottsboro boys, thereby in effect approving the rape of white women. The church in which the men met was burned down, along with the house of one of those who had been present at the meeting.

The Alabama chapter of the American Legion expressed alarm over the "horde of communists" who had poured into the state, "spreading a flood of propaganda opposing our form of government and social conditions, our race relationships and all the bases upon which our society rests, advocating racial equality and destruction of law and authority by force and violence." The Legionnaires volunteered their services to help drive out the alien "hordes," most reputed to be from New York City. Gun stores reported a large jump in sales to an already heavily armed population, and levelheaded Will Alexander declared, "If we can escape violence on a large scale, or a break between white and colored people in the next two or three years, we shall be very fortunate."

A year after the shooting of Ralph Grey at Mary Church in Tallapoosa County, two black Communists from Chattanooga returned to try once more to organize a black chapter of the sharecroppers' union. This time a farm owner named Clifford James undertook to organize the union. When word reached Sheriff Young, he searched James's house and found "radical literature" and membership blanks for the union. Young then contacted a merchant, W. S. Parker, who held the mortgage on James's farm. Parker issued a writ of attachment against James's two mules and two cows.

When Ned Cobb, a prosperous black farmer, heard talk of a sharecroppers' organization "workin' to bring us out of bad places where we stood at that time . . . I felt it, I could feel it was somethin' good," he told an interviewer. "It was goin' to rise us out of these old slum conditions that we had been undergoin' since slavery times, bring a clear life to live, push the white man back." These were the promises of the organizer of a union for black sharecroppers. He told Cobb and his fellow farmers "if we didn't do somethin' for ourselves today, tomorrow wouldn't be no different." Cobb found his fellow farmers "shy like rats. . . . They was keepin' their eyes open for stool pigeons and giveaways." Cobb was eager to sign up. He paid a small dues, "nothin' to hurt me, not more than a few cents." And he put up and fed the "teacher," the union organizer who "had more knowledge and authority than we had and from his words I went out and talked it over with folks. . . . Some of 'em went in, too, by my descriptions. I told them it was a good thing in favor of the colored race. . . . I recommended it thoroughly to particular ones I knowed—some of 'em was too scared to join and some of 'em was too scared not to join; they didn't want to be left alone when push come to shove."

The first test of the infant organization came when the sheriff sent a deputy to seize the stock of Clifford James. Cobb was convinced that if he and the "union" failed to come to James's aid, it would be a severe setback for union organizing. Confident that he would be next, Cobb rounded up a half dozen armed members of the union and stationed them in James's house. He armed himself with a .32 revolver and went out to meet the deputy and the three armed men who had accompanied him. "Please, sir, don't take what he got. . . . Go to the ones that authorized you to take his stuff, if you please, sir, and tell 'em to give him a chance. He'll work to pay what he owes 'em," Cobb said. The deputy cursed Cobb and told him to stand aside.

"Well, if you take it, I'll be damned if you don't take it over my dead body," Cobb told him. "Go ahead and take it."

"Somebody got to stand up," Cobb later told Theodore Rosengarten, explaining his actions. "If we don't we niggers in this country are easy prey. Nigger had anything a white man wanted, that white man took it; it made no difference how the cut might have come, he took it."

The deputy told Cobb he had already done enough, by defying the law, to be killed.

"Well, if you want to kill me, I'm right before you. Kill me, kill me. Ain't nothing between us but the air. Kill me."

The deputy raised his voice. "I'll just go and get Kurt Beall [a deputy sheriff]; he'll come down here and kill the last damn one of you. . . . When he comes in he comes in shootin'."

"Go ahead and get Mr. Beall, I'll be here when he comes."

While the men in the house waited apprehensively, Cobb bucked himself up with the thought that "an organization is an organization and if I don't mean nothin' by joinin' I ought to keep my ass out of it. But if I'm sworn to stand up for all the poor colored farmers . . . I've got to do it."

Four men came back in a few hours. Virgil Logan, the deputy, pointed to Cobb, who stood in front of the house. He pointed him out to the others. "That's him right there." The four men with guns drawn surrounded the house. Cobb stood with his hands in his overalls pockets, his right hand holding the .32 Smith & Wesson revolver. For what seemed an interminable time the four men confronted Cobb. Finally Cobb turned to go back to James's besieged house. As he did so, one of the deputies, Byron Ward, put his hand on his arm as though to stop him. Cobb flung his arm aside and continued toward the house. A deputy named Platt fired at his back with his shotgun. Cobb continued walking. The deputy fired twice more. "He filled my hind end up from the bend of my legs to my hips with shot," Cobb recalled. "Blood commenced a flyin'."

At the door to the house Cobb turned and began firing at the deputy, who ducked behind a tree. The others turned and fled for their lives, convinced that the house was filled with armed blacks. Cobb's boots were full of blood: "Wonder they hadn't shot my secrets out."

Cobb returned to his own home, and from there his wife and sons managed to get him to a black hospital at Tuskegee, where his wounds were dressed by frightened doctors who refused to keep him in the hospital. Cobb's wife drove him to her cousin's house in a nearby town. When they returned home, they found it surrounded by a mob of whites shooting into it with rifles and shotguns. Four or five terrified Cobb children were in the house, but miraculously only his small daughter Leah was injured, and she only slightly. Cobb's brother-in-law, Milo Bentley, appeared with an old breech-loading musket to defend himself against the whites hunting him. As Bentley ran from the house with his gun, four shots hit him. "I was listenin' at the rifles cryin' behind that boy," Cobb recalled years later.

The sheriff knew Cobb well. He entered the house and found him sitting in a chair. Cobb walked out, picked up Bentley, who was still breathing but unconscious, and put the bleeding boy in the back of a deputy's car. The sheriff said, "Ned, I wouldn't a thought that of you. We didn't know that there was such tricks in you. We always taken you to be the leadin' darky for [Tallapoosa] County." Cobb was placed under arrest.

As long as he had been docile and obedient, he had been left alone. "But when I wouldn't stand under their whip," Cobb told Rosengarten, "they arrested me for *bad* crimes—that's the way they termed it, *bad*—fighting a crowd of sheriffs over what was mine and what was my friend's. O, that was terrible." After Cobb had been put in prison, Bentley, his wounds untreated, was left to die in jail, and Clifford James, over the seizure of whose mules and cows the whole affair had started, was shot and killed. LeRoy Roberts, who had been in James's house and escaped when the sheriffs arrived, was caught and shot. Cobb's two oldest sons were jailed. After questioning Cobb about whether they belonged to the "organization," the sheriff freed them with the order "Go on back home and work." A lawyer named Stein working for the ILD appeared as Cobb's defense attorney. "Cobb, you the best man we got, we goin' to stick with you," Cobb recalled Stein saying. ". . . We can't pull you out of it but we goin' to stick with you."

At the funeral of Clifford James and Milo Bentley, two white women, Jane Spears and Mary Stevens, went to the mourning room filled with blacks. The police, learning that the white women were in the same room with black women, entered the house and told Spears and Stevens, "All right, come out from here, little ladies. You all come out, you can't sit up there among them niggers." When the two women refused to budge and the police started to remove them, "a lot of the people commenced to screaming and going on over the dead, and the police got scared and came out, left out of there," Hudson told Nell Painter.

The trial of Ned Cobb and four others accused of having come to the support of Clifford James lasted only a day. Cobb's lawyer was not allowed to cross-examine witnesses or present a proper defense. It was evident to Cobb that the trial was "just a sham," in his words. "The nigger was disrecognized; the white man in this country had everything fixed and mapped out. Didn't allow no niggers to stand arm and arm together. . . . The nigger's voice just wasn't just substantious to stand up for hisself."

In jail Ned Cobb had an experience of conversion. "Any person that have never received the love of Jesus in his soul, he can't imagine it until it hits him. When it hits you, you'll know it. There's a great undiscussible change takes place within you, somethin' that I never had before . . . couldn't help myself, couldn't do nothin' but laugh and cry and talk and study over my troubles. O, I tell you it was bluesy times. Right there I was converted; right there I received the love of Jesus." Cobb was convinced that it was his experience of conversion that enabled him to survive the twelve-year sentence imposed on him. He was forty-seven years old when his sentence began.

Through the ILD Cobb's case got worldwide attention. Less spectacular than the case of the Scottsboro boys or Angelo Herndon, it nevertheless became an important part of the record of abuse of Southern blacks who made any effort to improve their desperate situation. Cobb got a letter from "a white gentleman in prison in some part of California," Tom Mooney. "I taken that to mean that my name was known for what I was and what this work was about—newspapers carried my name to distant states. And the beauty part about it, for—stuck there and stickin' there today. I stuck there so good and tight, and this white gentleman that wrote to me, he had confidence in me that I would."

During Cobb's imprisonment the ILD sent him $5 a month and helped his family: "That's what the organization believed in—takin' care of a man's family when he's pulled away from 'em."

The Camp Hill affair, coming in the wake of the Scottsboro case, had an enormous impact on the black community. "It was the first time I ever known where Negroes tried to stand up together in the South," Hosea Hudson told Nell Painter. The authorities blamed the Camp Hill episode on Reds and Bolsheviks, and the newspapers took up the cry. Blacks in Tallapoosa County had been perverted by advocates of social equality, and a bill was introduced into the state legislature to make it illegal for "two or more persons to bind themselves together in order to resist the enforcement of any civil or criminal law. . . . " Yet in spite of all such efforts, the black sharecroppers' union continued to grow until more than 5,000 black sharecroppers in Tallapoosa and adjacent counties were enrolled.

Some of the bolder party members undertook to get blacks to register to vote. Joseph Gelbers, the Communist physics professor at the University of Atlanta, proposed to Hosea Hudson that they mount a campaign in Birmingham to register black voters. They printed a pamphlet containing the Constitution and the Bill of Rights with explanations of the various articles and amendments. These were distributed among blacks and discussed at public meetings. It was slow, uphill work. Becoming a registered voter was in itself a major undertaking; it took Hudson weeks and the intervention of a lawyer before he was finally registered. Once poor blacks (or poor whites, for that matter) succeeded in overcoming all the hurdles placed in their way, they had to pay poll tax of $1.50 *for every year since their twenty-first birthday* and, of course, a dollar and a half at every election thereafter.

The Right to Vote Club distributed sample registration forms to those who came to the club meetings, explaining the forms, and provided answers to the questions that could be asked. When the Board of Registrars discovered that applicants were prepared for the standard questions, "the board [would] ask them who was the president in such-and-such a year of the United States, which wont no part of the blank," Hudson recalled. Despite these obstacles, the club managed to qualify almost 100 voters for the spring elections of 1938. "Twas a hard nut. . . . Some was afraid, some was bashful. . . . You'd be surprised how people felt. I know how I felt, and that's the way I know them people felt. You just get nervous, you just nervous. It's a very uncomfortable feeling. Going down to a new place, you don't know whether you going to make mistakes, going down among these white folks, to face these white folks, you ain't been used to facing white people. You was just nervous, that's all. . . . Going down to the white people, to walk in there, just walking in now, and say, 'I came down to register to vote.' It took courage. You all don't have no idea! I can't explain how deep the oppression of the Negro people was, and how backward the poor whites was. . . . You had to preach to the whites just like you had to preach to the Negroes. They didn't feel comfortable at all. You'd be surprised the problem we had among the poor white." Better-educated blacks, teachers, and those dependent on employment by whites hesitated to register for fear of losing their jobs. The black Democratic club was almost equally unsympathetic. The club president had been told by the registrar of voters, "Your friends, we'll qualify them. But don't sent everybody down. Don't bring no common nigras, and don't bring over fifty a year. We ain't going qualify everybody." Industrial workers, preachers, and teachers would register or attempt to register, but it was hard to prevail upon what Hudson called "them piebacks, domestic workers, bootblacks, common laborers."

As Langston Hughes put it, "If the Communists don't awaken the Negroes of the South, who will? Certainly not the race leaders whose schools and jobs depend on white philanthropy and who preach 'be nice' and keep quiet."

While the New Deal exerted a strong attraction for many American blacks, black intellectuals and writers like Langston Hughes and Claude McKay were skeptical or hostile toward it and impatient with Roosevelt's unwillingness to take public stands that would alienate Southern Congressmen, whose support he considered essential if he was to steer his program through Congress. Langston Hughes expressed his disenchantment in a poem, "Ballad of Roosevelt":

> The pot was empty,
> The cupboard was bare.
> I said, Papa,
> What's the matter here?
> I'm waitin' on Roosevelt, son,
> Roosevelt, Roosevelt,
> Waitin' on Roosevelt, son.

> The rent was due
> And the lights was out.
> I said, Tell me, Mama,
> What's it all about?
> > We're waitin' on Roosevelt, son,
> > Roosevelt, Roosevelt,
> > Just waitin' on Roosevelt.

To Southern blacks the most appealing aspect of the Communist Party, aside from its insistence that blacks receive equal treatment with whites in all aspects of American life, was the simple physical courage of white Communist organizers, who actually took their lives into their hands when they ventured much south of the Mason-Dixon Line. However armored by loyalty to the party and its creeds and doctrines, the organizers were entirely human and knew the fear of bloody beatings and violent death. With the odds overwhelmingly against them, bearing the stigma of being Yankees and, frequently, Jews as well, they went, time and again, into the no-man's-land of Southern hostility to bear witness to their solidarity with black Americans. Not since Northern abolitionists had risked their lives to help slaves escape had whites endured such hardships for black men and women.

Poor as black sharecroppers and tenant farmers were in the South, theirs was a common misery experienced by their white counterparts. In the great Northern cities—Philadelphia, New York, and Chicago—the suffering was, if possible, greater and the Communist Party more ubiquitous. In New York City a special effort was made to attract Harlem blacks to the party. The *Liberator* demanded "WORK or WAGES"; "Fellow Negro workers! Are we going to allow ourselves to be kicked out into the streets by greedy landlords? . . . We have only one choice! Fight or starve." Among the thousands of demonstrators who turned out were a number of blacks. Cyril Briggs wrote in the *Crusader* that blacks and whites "stood shoulder to shoulder against the brutal attacks of the police," giving thereby "smashing refutation of the lying slanders . . . that Negro workers are too stupid to organize and too cowardly to resist oppression."

In March, 1935, a riot started in Harlem over the rumor that a boy caught stealing had been beaten by police. The riot was led by a group of young black radicals who called themselves the Young Liberators; a number were Communists. In the view of Claude McKay, it was the culmination of two years of agitation for blacks "to organize and demand of the white merchants [of Harlem] a new deal: that they should employ Negroes as clerks in the colored community." The most expressive voice was that of Sufi Abdul Hamid, who headed the Negro Industrial and Clerical Alliance. Hamid and his followers began picketing Harlem stores and demanding that they employ black clerks. Although black newspapers ridiculed Hamid for his eccentric dress (he wore a bejeweled turban and flowing robes), he continued to attract adherents, the best known of whom was the Reverend Adam Clayton Powell, Jr., assistant pastor of the largest church in Harlem, the Abyssinian Baptist. When Powell joined the picket lines, upper-class Harlem took notice; churches joined the movement, and A Citizens' League for Fair Play was formed. When some of the larger department stores employed a few black clerks, the movement received greater impetus. Meanwhile, since most of the stores were owned by Jewish merchants, an element of anti-Semitism crept into the controversy. Hamid denounced Jewish merchants and was denounced in return as a "black Hitler." A group calling itself the Jewish Minute Men complained to the mayor that Hamid was stirring up anti-Semitic feelings. A predominantly Jewish Harlem Merchants' Association was formed to resist Hamid's demands. Meanwhile, members of the Citizens' League fell to quarreling about whether the clerks employed should be light-skinned or dark-skinned, and Judge Samuel Rosenman enjoined the league's pickets. The March, 1935 riot, McKay argued, was the aftermath of the movement, the act "of a defeated, abandoned, and hungry army . . . the gesture of despair of a bewildered, baffled, and disillusioned people." An interracial dance at the Rockland Palace Ballroom in Harlem followed the riot. There were speeches by black and white party leaders. Duke Ellington's band played, and everyone sang the "Internationale."

One result of the riot was the formation of the Negro Labor Committee, made up of representatives from white and black unions. Its purpose was, in McKay's words, "to remedy the acute problem of the Negro worker's relationship to organized labor. . . . " Another black labor enterprise was that of Ira Kemp, a tall, thin, dark-skinned black man whose Harlem Labor Union was less exotic than Hamid's organization. John L. Lewis's CIO also entered the picture, announcing its intention to organize black workers in integrated industrial unions.

Another important figure who emerged through the Negro Labor Committee was Frank Crosswaith. Crosswaith, "a nervous, intellectual type," in McKay's words, given to wearing a rose in his buttonhole, had been a member of the Socialist Party for more than two decades and had had wide experience with the Pullman porters' union and the International Ladies' Garment Workers.

When Sufi Abdul Hamid's Afro-American Federation of Labor collapsed, Hamid shaved off his beard, shed his uniform, and took up the study of Buddhism.

One of the leading black Communists in Harlem was aristocratic-looking Max Yergan, who held a doctorate in education and who had been a director of YMCA work in South Africa for fifteen years. He returned to the United States in 1936, deeply offended by South Africa's racial policies, and offered his services to the Communist Party. He at once became a spokesman for black culture and gained fame as the teacher of the City College of New York's first course in Afro-American history. He was also active in the International Committee on African Affairs and was one of the sponsors of the Suitcase Theater, for which Langston Hughes and other black authors wrote plays dealing with black life.

The story was much the same in Chicago. Horace Cayton wrote of it: "All the city suffered from the depression, but the black belt suffered more and differently. The first reaction was panic and a deep sense of frustration, followed by spontaneous, unorganized demonstrations. . . . " To Langston Hughes it was "a savage and dangerous city. It's a kind of American Shanghai. And almost everybody seems to have been held up and robbed at least once. . . . 85% of the Negroes are on relief. And there were whole apartment houses packed with people who haven't paid rent for months, and the landlords letting the houses go to rack and ruin, so that they look like nothing you ever saw inside and out. Kids rove the streets at dusk snatching women's pocketbooks, so people are even afraid of children. And when you go to call on somebody, they never open the door until they have hollered out to ask who it is, and are sure they recognize you. I really never saw anything like Chicago!!!"

In that city protests were organized, in Horace Cayton's words, "against white people who did business in the black belt and hired only white help, and one could see groups of ragged pickets walking in front of the chain stores, the beginning of a movement which stirred the community as nothing had since the race riot." Black newspapers carried headlines such as "Spend Your Money Where You Can Work."

A boycott against the most conspicuous offenders was organized, and a few victories were won. The Woolworth five-and-ten-cent stores increased the number of black clerks to 25 percent in stores in black neighborhoods.

As the Communists came to dominate the Unemployed Councils in Chicago, the protests and demonstrations grew more violent. When about 5,000 blacks gathered to block an eviction and refused police orders to disperse, the police fired on the crowd, killing 3 and wounding several dozen. Fifty thousand leaflets were distributed around black Chicago in a few hours. "DEMAND THE DEATH PENALTY FOR THE MURDERERS OF THE WORKERS!" they proclaimed. Whites and blacks turned out in large numbers for the funerals of the slain, and the threat of a race riot or, some said, a Communist-inspired uprising hung over the city. The renters' court suspended evictions, and plans were made for a large-scale relief program.

The Communist Party helped organize the National Negro Congress that was called in Chicago in February, 1936. A gathering of "political, civic, fraternal, and religious organizations," it had as its purpose the formation of a united front against all forms of discrimination. The delegates drew up an inclusive list of reforms that extended from desegregated schools and civil rights for all Americans to opposition to fascism. The first president of the National Negro Congress was A. Philip Randolph.

In addition to the activities of black and white Communists in black areas of major cities, every party gathering featured blacks. When Horace Cayton was in Paris, a Swedish friend took him to a conference "In Defense of Culture," a gathering of left-wing intellectuals from around the world, dominated by the Communist Party. Mike Gold, editor of the *New Masses,* was one of a number of well-known writers seated on the speakers' platform. When Gold saw Cayton, he sent him a note asking him to join the platform group. "Come up to the stage," it read. "We need a Negro badly." There he was introduced as "the celebrated American Negro author." Among the authors present Cayton recognized John Dos Passos, Aldous Huxley, and André Gide.

Langston Hughes continued to praise the Communist Party. Visiting Carmel, he joined Ella Winter and Lincoln Steffens in declaring that the "*Daily Worker,* so far as I know, is the only daily voice in America that consistently and without deviation constantly calls for the complete liberation of the Negro masses, and works for their full and equal place in American life. Every Negro receiving a regular salary in this country should subscribe to the *Daily Worker,* and share it with his brothers who are unemployed."

Paul Robeson, because of his fame as a singer and actor, was the best-known black Communist. He was also the leading apostle of the potency of the African cultural heritage. He is said to have learned ten African languages during his years in France, and he constantly called attention to African art and music.

The power and confidence of Harlem blacks by the end of the decade of the 1930s was demonstrated by the success of Benjamin Davis's campaign against the movie *Gone with the Wind.* Davis, an editor of the *Daily Worker* and an avowed Communist, forced the resignation of the newspaper's film critic for reviewing it favorably and started a seven-part series on the "Negro in Hollywood Films," analyzing the stereotyped representation of blacks. When the film was shown in Harlem, Davis led a picket line at the theater and denounced it as counter to the best traditions of "Lincoln and America."

The Harlem chapter of the Communist Party launched a campaign to force the admission of black patients to all the hospitals in the city and to win the right for black doctors and nurses to be promoted on the basis of their competence.

One of the causes taken up with special vigor by black Communists, especially those enrolled in the Young Communist League, was that of integrating sports. *As we have already noted,* collegiate sports, except in the South, were, to a degree at least, integrated, and a number of black leaders like Benjamin Davis and Paul Robeson had been outstanding athletes in white colleges. But after a brilliant beginning blacks had been excluded from professional sports, boxing excepted. It was clear enough from the performance of black athletes that blacks were, for whatever reasons, considerably more gifted athletically than whites. The Young Communist League concentrated its attention on segregation in professional baseball, joining forces with a party front, the Trade Union Athletic Association, to sponsor an "End Jim Crow in Sports" day at the New York World's Fair and to collect more than 10,000 signatures calling for an end to racial discrimination in big-league baseball. "If we are to preserve democracy," Richard Moore, a black Communist leader, told a union meeting, "we must stand firm . . . against those forces who trample on the principles of sportsmanship."

It is small wonder that Marcus Garvey's *Negro World* complained that the Communists were "capturing hundreds of Negro workers by promising them Garveyism with a wrapping of red tissue."

As we have noted, the Soviet Union played host to a stream of black Americans, many of whom were featured and lionized. Hudson's party unit in Birmingham was told by headquarters in New York to select three members to go to Russia for eighteen months to study at the Lenin School. Cornella Hibbard, an ardent party member and wife of West Hibbard, also active in the party, was chosen, along with Hudson's pal Henry Mayfield and Archie Mosley, active in the International Labor Defense. One of the leaders at Camp Hill had been Mack Coad. After Camp Hill the party sent Coad to Russia for almost three years. When he returned to Birmingham, Coad moved in with Hosea Hudson, much to Hudson's wife's displeasure. Coad and Hudson were constantly away on party business. Once Hudson's wife challenged Coad. "What are you trying to do to me? Why don't you . . . let Hosie stay here with me?"

"Why do you want him to stay with you?"

"I'm in love," Hudson's wife replied.

Coad's answer was that there was no such thing as love. The plain implication was that there was only sexual attraction and party loyalty.

In an effort to make propaganda out of the plight of American blacks, Joseph Stalin approved a film project which called for a company of black actors and writers to travel to Russia to make a film of black life in America directed by a Russian director. In addition to Loren Miller, Louise Thompson, and Langston Hughes, the group included a divorcée who traveled on alimony, a female swimming instructor, and various clerks and stenographers—all distinctly from the white-collar and student classes. Wayland Rudd was one of the few with acting experience; he had appeared in DuBose Heyward's *Porgy*. On board the ship carrying the company to Europe was Ralph Bunche, a Howard University graduate, bound for study abroad.

In Moscow Langston Hughes felt a special affinity for Boris Pasternak, who was in trouble with the official arbiters of Soviet culture. Hughes found Pasternak "a gentle likable man, cultured in appearance and shy with strangers." He translated the Russian's poem "Beloved."

The film project, however, was doomed from the first. The script, such as it was, was "so interwoven with major and minor impossibilities and improbabilities that it would have seemed like a burlesque on the screen," Hughes wrote. The venture soon collapsed in bitter recriminations (rumor had it that Stalin canceled the project because he did not wish to do anything that might interfere with the diplomatic recognition of Russia by the new Democratic administration of Franklin Roosevelt), and most of the group returned home, but Hughes and several others, provided with contracts, took the opportunity to tour Russia and proclaim its achievements. Hughes wrote in a dispatch to the *Afro-American*: "A better world's in birth! Look at Russia—nobody hungry, no racial differences, no color line, nobody poor. Listen to Foster and Ford. . . ."

While Hughes was visiting the Uzbek Soviet Republic of the Soviet Union, he was taken to a cotton farm, where he found "about a dozen American Negroes attached to this . . . experimental farm, most of them from the South. Some were agricultural chemists, graduates of Tuskegee or Hampton, others were from Northern colleges, and some were just plain cotton farmers from Dixie, whose job it was in Soviet Asia to help introduce American methods of cultivating cotton. . . . It was an oddly assorted group of educated and uneducated Negroes a long way fom Dixie—and most of them not liking it very well. Conditions of the Soviet collective, while a great change for the better for the Uzbeks, were for Negroes from America more primitive than most of them had known at home, especially for the younger college people. . . ."

Among those who lingered on in Russia was Wayland Rudd, who took the opportunity to study music, singing, fencing, and dance. Another member of the party, Homer Smith, stayed to supervise the establishment of a special delivery system for Moscow mail and remained for fifteen years. Louise Thompson told the correspondent for the *Amsterdam News*, "Russia today is the only country in the world that's really fit to live in. I'd live here any time in preference to America." She had returned to care for her sick mother, she explained.

The black writers and intellectuals and the black union organizers and labor leaders (most of whom were Communists) gave up the hope of "normal" lives, of families and children, of enduring relationships with women, of conventional jobs and common pleasures, for the intoxicating venture into unexplored social spaces. Like the first generation of women's rights leaders, the first generation of black men and women to become "visible" as leaders of their race had to live the lives of mobilized soldiers in their war against racial prejudice. The strains of working with whites were intense and continual. Every hour or day spent with white friends or colleagues was edged with anxiety, yet such friendships were essential both for the "cause" of black equality and for the party. If the Communist Party did nothing else, it provided an essential organizational framework where whites and blacks could come together less self-consciously than would have otherwise been the case for joint tasks, whether it was Claude McKay and Max Eastman editing the *Liberator* or Bill Dunne and Hosea Hudson organizing miners and steelworkers or working with Joseph Gelbers to register black voters.

Carl Murphy, editor of the *Baltimore Afro-American,* wrote that the Communists were "the only party going our way." Since the abolitionists "no white group of national prominence has openly advocated the economic, political and social equality of black folks." William H. Davis, editor of the influential *Amsterdam News,* Harlem's principal black paper, wrote: "Oppressed on every hand, denied equal educational facilities, discriminated against in public places and in employment, Jim-Crowed on street cars and railroad trains . . . even lynched, it would seem that any program—Communistic or Socialistic— . . . should readily find converts among American Negroes."

It may be that the greatest accomplishment of the Communist Party of the United States, an accomplishment that perhaps compensated for its insane rhetoric, its ideological tergiversations, and its slavish adherence to the edicts of Stalin, was, indeed, to "raise the consciousness of American blacks." This was done in an inept way (the party line that blacks must have their own "nation" within the United States had little appeal to the great majority of black Americans) and less in the interest of the blacks themselves than in the interests of the worldwide proletarian revolution of the "masses." But the fact remains that whatever their motives, the Communists did in fact treat black Americans as "comrades," something that white Americans had not done in any discernible and consistent way since abolitionist days. When they came into contact with blacks, the Communists not only treated them as nearly as equals as whites with the best of liberal intentions have been able to treat blacks but also made them a part of the lively social life of the party. The experience of the mothers of the Scottsboro boys is highly instructive in this regard. The International Legal Defense front certainly exploited the boys' mothers at hundreds of party rallies. On the other hand, it treated them more humanely than the patronizing agents of the NAACP, who considered them ignorant and gullible; most of the mothers had nothing but praise and gratitude for the efforts of the ILD. The Communist Party, considering the effort it expended to sign up blacks, was not notably successful. Southern (and Northern) blacks welcomed the assistance of the party and its various fronts in their struggle for even a modicum of justice; they refrained from joining in the anti-Communist refrain; and above all, they refrained from joining the party. At the same time they picked up those elements of the Marxist theory which helped them understand and define their relationship to American society. In this sense membership in the party was irrelevant. In the manifold ironies of history few are greater than the fact that the invasion of black nightclubs in such cities as New York and Chicago by white socialites looking for expensive thrills, along with the largely unsuccessful efforts of the Communist Party to recruit black members for the anticipated revolution, combined to make blacks both more visible and more conscious of their own latent power.

# 1934

A critical year for the New Deal and for the nation was 1934. The country was still gripped by the Depression. The midterm congressional elections in the fall would constitute the first public referendum on the New Deal. The NRA, from which so much had been expected, had encountered rough sailing. The recession at the end of 1933 indicated that it was no panacea (although Hugh Johnson, of course, insisted that the slump was due to the failure of American businessmen to cooperate wholeheartedly with the program). The NRA was under attack from the left as well as the right on the grounds that it resembled Mussolini's fascism and that it strengthened the hands of the capitalists at the expense of the workingman. Johnson himself became increasingly belligerent and erratic under the pressures of his office, which was, in a considerable degree, that of running the nation's economy or at least a large and crucial part of the nation's economy.

When the economy slumped, the problem of relief became acute. Aubrey Williams was Hopkins's chief assistant. He was out of the Hopkins mold, a dedicated and unselfish laborer in the cause of reform. His experience was primarily in the area of trying to alleviate the harsh conditions of rural life. Williams, detailed by Hopkins to prepare a "work relief" plan, discovered that Samuel Gompers had proposed such a plan during the Depression of 1907, calling it the "day labor plan." When Hopkins laid it before Roosevelt, he asked how many jobs it would provide. Hopkins estimated some 4,000,000. That would mean a Federal expenditure of roughly $500,000,000. Roosevelt, suppressing his anxiety about balancing the budget, gave his assent. The program would be called, it was decided, the Civil Works Administration (CWA), and it would, so far as possible, take over, if not replace, much of the Federal Emergency Relief Administration work. The CWA would undertake no contract work, such as sewers and bridges. It could only put men to work on clearing and cleaning wasteland, refurbishing run-down neighborhoods, ditching, soil erosion prevention work and similar tasks requiring little or no capital outlay. Hopkins announced that his goal would be to put 2,000,000 men and women to work in less than two weeks and another 2,000,000 by the first week of December, a month away. That proved impossible, but the reality was hardly less spectacular than the aspiration. Within a month 1,976,625 people were at work, and by January 18, 1934, nine weeks after the official birth of the CWA, 4,263,644 men and women were at work on a wide range of jobs and projects.

At the same time almost 20,000,000 men and women depended on some form of government assistance. In South Dakota it was estimated that one-third of the population was receiving direct Federal aid. The problem in the agricultural states was that it was far more difficult to create jobs or "public works" there than it was in urban industrial areas. More farmers were, in consequence, on direct relief. It was plainly impossible to develop well-thought-out plans for public work projects, assemble the necessary materials, and train a work force in a few weeks. In the press to get men off relief and to work, much of the work was of the "made" or improvised type, such as, most notoriously, raking leaves or mowing grass. An enterprising reporter found some men paid to frighten pigeons from the eaves of public buildings. The criticism of the Civil Works Administration centered on rakes and shovels; these two instruments became weapons in the hands of all those opposed to the program, which were the vast majority of the newspapers of the country. Roosevelt, stung by the criticism, insisted that there be a program of "real public works, which, at the same time, would give work to practically all idle employables in socially useful structures." The unemployables would be taken care of by the states and local communities with help, where necessary, from the Federal government.

Hopkins described the difference between what he called "work relief" and a job on a "work program." He said: "To the man on relief the difference is very real. On work relief, although he gets the disciplinary rewards of keeping fit, and of making a return for what he gets, his need is still determined by a social worker, and he feels himself to be something of a public ward, with small freedom of choice. When he gets a job on a work program, it is very different. He is paid wages and the social worker drops out of the picture. His wages may not cover much more ground than his former relief budget but they are his to spend as he likes. . . . The wife of the WPA worker tossed her head and said, 'We aren't on relief any more, my husband is working for the Government.'"

As public criticism of the CWA mounted, an uneasy Roosevelt dispatched an old friend, Frank Walker, one of the most effective, if least-known, members of the New Deal, to report specifically on the CWA. From Montana Walker wrote poignantly: "I saw old friends of mine I had been to school with—digging ditches and laying sewer pipe. They were wearing their regular business suits as they worked because they couldn't afford overalls and rubber boots. If I ever thought, 'There but for the Grace of God—' it was right then." One of his friends took a few coins out of his pocket and told Walker, "Do you know, Frank, this is the first money I've had in my pockets in a year and a half? Up to now, I've had nothing but tickets that you could exchange for groceries."

Walker advised the President to pay no attention to the critics of the program. "Hopkins and his associates are doing their work well. They have done a magnificent job. It is amazing when you consider that within the short time since the CWA was established four million idle have been put to work. During Christmas week many of them were standing in a payroll line for the first time in eighteen months. You have every reason to be proud of CWA and its administration. It is my considered opinion that this has averted one of the most serious crises in our history. Revolution is an ugly word to use, but I think we were dangerously close at least to the threat of it." But Roosevelt, concerned by the expense of the program and smarting from the widespread criticism, especially in the Northeast, where it came under attack from labor leaders and capitalists alike, ordered Hopkins to phase out the agency. "We cannot carry CWA through the summer. We all agree that there has to be a limit . . . and the people must assume more or less that things are going to straighten themselves out." Hopkins went back to administering the Federal Emergency Relief Administration, but convinced that a high level of unemployment was "structural"—that is to say, a consequence of continued improvement in laborsaving machinery—he continued to plan for a large-scale program of public works, confident that it would be needed sooner or later.

Amid widespread criticism of the NRA and the CWA, Roosevelt was pleased by William Allen White's cautious endorsement. "We have clamored," White wrote, "for higher income taxes, for devastating inheritance taxes, for workmen's compensation, unemployment insurance, old-age pensions, for all the measures which Colonel Theodore Roosevelt used to call 'social and industrial justice.' . . . It is plain as a barn door that we are getting our revolution through the administrative arm of the government, without legislation. . . . These are great days— if not happy ones." White delighted in the unhappiness of the conservative Democrats, especially the states' righters who were horrified witnesses of the greatest centralization of power in the Federal government since Lincoln. It seemed evident to White that Roosevelt was "aiming at something of the same target at which both the fascists and the communists are shooting; that is to say, the socialization of capital, the regimentation of industry and agriculture, and finally, a more equitable distribution of wealth, a guarantee of a minimum standard of living for all who have worked honestly. . . . No one can deny that he is seeking the larger good of the American people. It is evident that he is no dictator. He has none of the faults and few of the virtues of a tyrant. Instead . . . [he has] a yearning for peace, for justice and for self-respect, for the people of this country and for the world. . . . Probably America can do this strange thing—establish a new revolution of free men with their dollars in shackles."

As the new year turned, Roosevelt seemed as confident and ebullient as ever. "The President was in fine form at Cabinet today," Harold Ickes noted on February 2, 1934. "His spirits soared high and he was full of good humor which expressed itself frequently in that infectious laughter of his." When Congress convened, the President had a number of new measures to present to that body. The Farm Mortgage Refinancing Act was, as its name suggests, designed to refinance heavily mortgaged farms to save them from foreclosure.

The President also proposed a number of subcommittees to study various aspects of flood control and conservation. One committee was to concentrate on the Atlantic watershed; another, on the watershed that drained into the Gulf of Mexico. They were to consider "not only flood control but navigation, soil erosion, irrigation, reclamation, sewage, power, and reforestation." Each subcommittee was to list in order of importance ten long-range projects for each major watershed area.

Roosevelt invoked powers given him under the Reconstruction Finance Corporation and the NRA to encourage foreign trade by short-term agricultural loans and by extending credit to American firms to facilitate exports. One bank was established to expedite trading with the Soviet Union and another for Cuban-U.S. trade.

In March Congress overrode the President's veto of a bill restoring the cuts made in the salaries of Federal employees by the Economy Act a year earlier.

The Home Owners' Loan Act provided funds for the repair and refinancing of home mortgages, and a series of bills extended the list of enumerated crops under the Agricultural Adjustment Act.

The most important piece of legislation presented to Congress was the Securities Exchange Act, which provided for Federal regulation of exchanges dealing in securities. The intention of the act was to prevent the wild stock market speculation that had brought on the crash. The initial act of 1933 had been concerned with the sale of securities; the 1934 act regulated stock exchanges and brokers.

The first chairman of the Securities and Exchange Commission was Joseph Kennedy, himself a notorious speculator. Kennedy protested his appointment as chairman of the SEC: "Mr. President, I don't think you ought to do this. I think it will bring down injurious criticism." To those who objected to the appointment, Roosevelt is said to have replied, "Set a thief to catch a thief," not very flattering to Kennedy.

William O. Douglas was recruited to head a study of reorganization committees which had been charged with manipulating bankruptcies and receiverships under their jurisdiction. Douglas hired Abe Fortas, his prize student at Yale, and tried to employ a bright young lawyer named Alger Hiss.

Frances Perkins had never let the President forget his promise to support unemployment and old-age insurance. "It is probably our only chance in twenty-five years to get a bill like this," she reminded him. At a Cabinet meeting in April FDR devoted most of the time to a discussion of the two measures. "It is evident," Ickes wrote, "that he has thought deeply on the subject. He is looking forward to a time in the near future when the government will put into operation a system of old-age, unemployment, maternity, and other forms of social insurance." Ickes wrote a few days later: "What I like particularly about the President is that he has imagination and is always looking into the future."

Roosevelt included a reference to "social insurance" in a message to Congress in June. "Next winter," he warned the legislators, "we may well undertake the great task of furthering the security of the citizen and his family through social insurance." Many modern nations had such plans, and it was time for the United States to provide "security against several of the great disturbing factors in life—especially those which relate to unemployment and old age." Such a program would call for a maximum of cooperation between states and the Federal government.

Having put Congress on notice, Roosevelt appointed a Committee on Economic Security to prepare a comprehensive social security bill. On it were Morgenthau, Cummings, Wallace, and Hopkins. There were, not surprisingly, divisions in the committee. Hopkins, at one end of the ideological spectrum, wanted relief and all forms of social insurance to be combined under a Federal agency. Anyone unemployed, old, or ill would receive payments from the government. The money would come out of general tax revenues. One purpose of Hopkins's plan was to redistribute income. Frances Perkins thought that the notion was much too extreme to win acceptance from Congress and gave her backing to a plan which required payments by employers and employees into a general fund.

The Communist May Day parade in New York City in 1934 was the largest and most exuberant ever. Starting at the Battery, the marchers filed into Union Square for the usual speeches. The vanguard arrived at 2:00 P.M., and the last contingents at 6:30. There were banners scattered among the march depicting the Blue Buzzard of the NRA and denouncing Mussolini, Hitler, and Roosevelt. Capitalism was represented by a yellow dragon fifty feet long. More than 1,000 policemen, reinforced by 300 plainclothesmen, lined the route of march to be sure revolution did not break out then and there. Malcolm Cowley took the occasion to write an editorial for the *New Republic* lauding communism. "First of all," he wrote, "it can offer an end to the desperate feeling of solitude and uniqueness that has been oppressing artists for the last two centuries, the feeling that has reduced some of the best of them to silence or futility and the weaker ones to insanity or suicide. It can offer instead a sense of comradeship and participation in an historical process vastly larger than the individual." The Communist Party was not only growing rapidly but becoming increasingly respectable—indeed, it might be said, even fashionable.

With Congress adjourned after having passed another mass of legislation, the President departed the White House like a small boy let out of school. Having stated his determination to remain above the midterm congressional elections, he boarded a navy cruiser and proceeded down the Atlantic coast, through the Panama Canal, and up the West Coast to Oregon and Washington.

In the Pacific Northwest there were, of course, Indians. All American Presidents have paid particular attention to Indians; they have been, after all, the great chiefs of the Indian tribes. Franklin Roosevelt was no exception. The President made ritual visits to the Yakima and Klamath Indians.

The Yakimas had more than 6,000 members, of whom only 706 were full-blooded. To qualify as a Yakima, only one sixty-fourth Indian blood was necessary.

The Klamath Indians, with some 1,500 or 1,600 members, had the greatest per capita wealth of any Indian tribe. The tribe owned more than 1,000,000 acres of land, much of it covered with yellow pine. This lumber was exploited by large lumber companies, and Harold Ickes was anxious to have logging and milling operations conducted by the Indians themselves, "solely for the benefit of the Indians."

The Blackfoot Indians were waiting for the presidential party at the edge of Two Medicine Lake. They chanted and danced in the prescribed manner of Indians meeting politicians, and they proceeded to make the President and Mrs. Roosevelt and Harold Ickes members of the tribe. Roosevelt's tribal name was Lone Chief, and Ickes, Omuc Ki Yo or Big Bear. Enrollees from nearby CCC camps were present and sang camp songs. One group was made up of young blacks—a reminder, if any was needed, that the CCC camps were segregated. There were about 4,000 Blackfoot Indians on a reservation of more than 1,200,000 acres. Many members of the tribe raised cattle on their own farms, and the tribe had recently built a "community house" as a tribal center. When the prescribed war bonnet was placed on Roosevelt's head, the President, in dramatic contrast with his immediate predecessors, looked the part—a "Great Chief" or, to borrow Al Smith's nickname, a "Happy Warrior."

The presidential train was made up of a private car for the Roosevelt family and Louis Howe and six sleepers, filled with "governors, Senators, members of Congress, newspaper correspondents, etc., etc.," in Ickes's words. It was not a campaign trip, the President told reporters with his roguish, knowing smile; he was simply educating the electorate by explaining his program.

In addition to those more honored supporters invited to join the presidential party for travel between stations or sometimes for days, thereby sharing in the glow that enveloped the hero, hundreds of aspiring politicos had their hands warmly shaken and their photos taken basking in that famous smile. Everywhere "the reception was grand," Roosevelt wrote Garner, "and I am more than ever convinced that, so far as having the people with us goes, we are just as strong—perhaps stronger—than before."

Back home in Washington, the more conservative members of the administration urged the President to placate the business community. The fear and rage of businessmen, the capitalists large and small, were more pathological than rational; they were ideologues as fierce and passionate as the Communists. It was not with them simply a matter of profit and loss. Most would have preferred to lose money, to lose everything and drag the country down with them rather than surrender one article of their faith in the sanctity of property and the inviolability of the various tenets of capitalism, as defined by them.

Roosevelt had, to be sure, denounced the speculators and money manipulators in unsparing terms, but he had been at pains to insist that he not only believed in American business but was determined to do all in his power to save it from its own folly. His poker partner William O. Douglas, who, incidentally, blamed Roosevelt for not going further in his programs of reform, recalled that the President frequently expressed bewilderment that the class he was doing his best to bolster up was arrayed so solidly and so bitterly against him. Even the Federal Deposit Insurance Act, designed to protect depositors from losing their savings from a bank failure, was vehemently denounced on the ground that it would weaken the character of bankers by bailing them out of their mistakes. In the words of Douglas, it was criticized for making "people more and more dependent on government, when what is needed is strong and independent men; it is a form of socialism that is dangerous; free enterprise cannot remain free if its mistakes are underwritten by . . . government. . . . This was the essence of the hardcore reaction against FDR."

Ed Flynn told Claude Bowers of an evening spent at a fashionable resort where the guests knew of Flynn's close relationship to the President and took the opportunity to pour out the "most venomous personal abuse" of Roosevelt. Some of the less fanatical Roosevelt haters complained that he had ruined upper-class social life. Virtually the only topic of conversation in those circles was the iniquities of the squire of Hyde Park. Their hostility toward Eleanor Roosevelt was only slightly less virulent. It seems safe to say that not since Andrew Jackson had a President been the object of so much personal abuse. The Chamber of Commerce entertained itself at its annual conventions by bitter attacks on the New Deal and all its works. The usually equable Roosevelt, who prided himself on his thick skin, was upset by the vitriolic words showered upon him by the chamber's speakers. He was relatively inured to the denunciations of the big industrialists and financiers as well as the conservative politicians. But the Chamber of Commerce was, after all, the stronghold of small business, and Roosevelt felt he deserved better at its hands. "The interesting thing to me," he declared, "is that in all of these speeches made, I don't believe that there was a single speech that took the human side, the old age side, the unemployed side."

In Rexford Tugwell's words, "Roosevelt was considered a crazy reformer for continuing to insist, when the better times of partial recovery came, that what they [the businessmen and financiers] had weepingly promised in the fake repentance of a stormy day should now be carried out. . . . Most of all [the businessmen] hated and feared the reformer who wanted to improve their morals."

Raymond Moley, on the other hand, blamed Roosevelt's truculent rhetoric directed at his corporate enemies on the fact that he was "surrounded by men with a genius for arousing his antagonisms toward business." At the same time Moley had to admit that the virulent attacks on the President did little to promote the government-business harmony that Moley was constantly proclaiming as the only viable basis for economic recovery.

"It was no accident indeed," Tugwell wrote, "that [Roosevelt] would inherit this same hatred [that of the moneyed class for "deep" reformers] multiplied a thousand-fold. No attempt to recapture for government its lost powers could escape this division. No reformer who sought to reform 'conditions' rather than people could remain respectable."

Roy Howard, president of the Scripps-Howard newspaper chain, wrote to Roosevelt on the day that Congress adjourned, August 26, 1934, telling him that "throughout the country many businessmen who once gave you sincere support are not merely hostile, they are frightened." Such men believed "that there can be no real recovery until the fears of business have been allayed through the granting of a breathing spell to industry, and a recess from further experimentation until the country can recover its losses." The message was clear enough: no more legislation objectionable to business, which meant, in effect, no more legislation designed to curtail dubious business activities such as constraints on stock market and securities manipulation and holding company operations.

The opposition to Roosevelt was not limited to businessmen. It was no secret that he had almost as many enemies in his own party as in the Republican opposition. In the words of Frank Kent, a columnist for the *Baltimore Sun*, "It is difficult today to name any outstanding Democratic leader of the pre-New Deal period who is in sympathy with the Roosevelt policy. . . . Except in the most perfunctory manner, none of them have been consulted by the President. Most of them have been completely ignored."

A potentially serious threat came from the American Liberty League. A group of disenchanted Democrats (the breed Frank Kent described) led by Al Smith and John W. Davis, Jouett Shouse and John J. Raskob, joined Irenée du Pont and other Republican bigwigs to oppose Roosevelt's reelection in 1936. Smith and Davis were, of course, ex-presidential candidates, and Shouse had been chairman of the Democratic National Committee. Two thousand members of what a sociologist later termed the "power elite" gathered at the Mayflower Hotel in Washington to hear Smith attack Roosevelt as a radical and subversive. "There can be only one capital," Smith said in an odd phrase, "Washington or Moscow."

Many of the attacks on Roosevelt had a strongly anti-Semitic character. He was called "Rosenvelt" and charged with filling his administration with Jews of a radical persuasion. It was rumored that Frances Perkins was a Russian Jew named Matilda Watski who had changed her name. She was denounced for having "decreased alien deportation 60 percent" and having allowed Emma Goldman to visit the United States.

It would be a mistake, of course, to suggest that American businessmen were solidly opposed to Franklin Roosevelt. Hostility to Roosevelt was centered in Eastern capitalists, men of great wealth and power. Businessmen in various parts of the country, especially those in regions that had plainly benefited from New Deal measures, gave substantial support to the President. Outside the South almost 40 percent of the businessmen polled by Gallup supported Roosevelt, and in the South the figure was 72, more or less that of the South generally.

More troubling than the barrage of criticism from the right—from businessmen and politicians—were the difficulties within the NRA. Roosevelt returned from his noncampaign to face mounting criticism of his administration. The NRA was the particular target. Whatever one called the NRA, "holistic," "collectivistic," "corporate," "cooperative," or, more simply, "state capitalism," it was plainly not working. General Johnson, after his extraordinary and flamboyant launching of the agency, became one of its principal problems. He suffered fits of depression, drank to excess, disappeared for days. Among other things, Ickes noted, Johnson had developed a "relationship with an administrative assistant" that had been "distinctly detrimental." She was "as obtrusive as a certain type of wife is in the private affairs of her husband." Ickes's own mistress apparently knew her place.

The progressives and the more pragmatic members of his administration were after Roosevelt to jettison the NRA, pointing, among other things, to Johnson's egregious maladministration. But Tugwell wanted it kept at all costs as the centerpiece of the new order: "It could still be the industrial counterpart . . . of the Agricultural Adjustment Administration." It was a striking analogy. Tugwell lived long enough to observe that the agricultural policies initiated by the AAA, while they maintained a certain level of prosperity for the farmer, did so at a heavy cost, both to the taxpayer and to the farmer himself in terms of enmeshing him in a rigid and often arbitrary system, the deficiencies of which he was, in a sense, paid to ignore. To assume that the vastly more complex industrial segment of the economy could be subjected to a similar process of rationalization and control was dangerously naïve.

By the fall of 1934 Hugh Johnson had become, in the opinion of most of the Cabinet members, a distinct liability to the administration. Yet, typically, Roosevelt was too tenderhearted to fire him, so matters went from bad to worse. There were days at a time when Johnson did not even put in an appearance at the offices of the agency he was in charge of. Finally he was prevailed on to resign. Robert Hutchins, the precocious and brilliant young president of the University of Chicago, was proposed as a replacement, but there was strong opposition to him by some members of the administration on the ground that he was "arrogant and dictatorial." Donald Richberg, a well-known labor lawyer who had served a brief novitiate as a member of the Brain Trust, was chosen to replace Johnson. He was as colorless as Johnson had been flamboyant.

As the congressional elections approached, there were important defections from the New Deal ranks. James Warburg, who had turned against Roosevelt after the abortive London Economic Conference and written two "bitter books" denouncing the New Deal, returned to the Republican fold. Dean Acheson followed suit.

Not only did Lewis Douglas, the director of the budget, resist virtually every New Deal measure, but Roosevelt was disturbed to learn that he was making a written record of disputes with the President on fiscal matters. Roosevelt got the distinct impression that his budget director was preparing a case against him in anticipation of the day that he would resign and level various charges against the administration. In September Douglas finally resigned. "While an attractive young fellow," in Harold Ickes's words, ". . . he was not in step with the administration." Wallace and Tugwell fell out, and Tugwell departed for Europe. Hopkins told Ickes that in his opinion, Wallace had the presidential bee in his bonnet and was becoming more conservative all the time. (Hopkins had the presidential bee in *his* bonnet, and it was clear that Ickes did, too.)

Raymond Moley was a major defector. In the words of his friend and colleague Rexford Tugwell, "Moley came to the point of regarding demands for plain ethical behavior as somehow threatening and unusual." It might imperil that business "confidence" that Moley had come to believe was essential to recovery but that was, in fact, a kind of moral blackmail which Roosevelt refused to bow to. Moley made clear, in his truncated autobiography (which was really an account of his personal break with Roosevelt), that he had never been a reformer. "I had a horror," he wrote, "of the humorlessness, the intentness, and the intolerance of most reformers." Moley's conservative predilections are perhaps best indicated by his resentment over Senator Hugo Black's investigation of the utilities' lobbying against the holding company bill. Black, Moley wrote, was pursuing the lobbyists "with a fanaticism not surprising in a one-time Klan member."

Moley, of course, missed the historical point (or did not know it) when he argued that social and economic reform had to come through cooperation with business rather than confrontation. The reader of these volumes can be in no uncertainty on the fact that the rise of industrial America brought with it the exploitation of men, women, and children on a scale and to a degree that can hardly be imagined today; furthermore, every substantial reform was bitterly resisted by the great majority of the owners of mills, mines, and factories. This is not, of course, to say that the exploitative industrialists were consciously and deliberately "bad" men; some doubtless were, but the great majority thought they were doing the Lord's work by providing jobs for the needy and protecting the institution of private property by every stratagem at their disposal, including hired thugs and Pinkerton agents.

When Moley withdrew from the administration, it was undoubtedly the result of mutual disenchantment. Moley was as stubbornly opinionated as he accused the President of being; indeed, it could be argued, considerably more so. He was convinced he was dealing in eternal verities and accused FDR of persisting in thinking that there were at least two (and often many more) sides of every question. But Moley comforted himself with the thought that if the marriage was over, he had been able, during the months he had worked as one of Roosevelt's closest and most trusted advisers, to "insist upon his thinking a bit longer before the inevitable moment when his pragmatic oversoul summoned him to action." That, he told himself, "was good for the country." Nevertheless, for the next two years, until Roosevelt ran for reelection in 1936, there were few speeches or messages that Moley did not have a hand in.

By the fall of 1934 Roosevelt had decided to do away with direct relief altogether and undertake a public works program that would give employment to "all who are willing and able to work." That was in itself an enormous undertaking since the number of unemployed was estimated at something in excess of 12,000,000. Harry Hopkins persuaded the President that thorough, honest, and conscientious as Ickes was, he did not move fast enough, nor could he, given the nature of the public works program, to get large numbers of unemployed to work. Moreover, there were whole categories of people unaffected by the public works program: teachers, writers, artists, actors, students, men and women who had as much claim on the assistance of the government as machinists and coal miners.

By the late fall in 1934 it was evident that the hope of "self-liquidating" public works projects was a vain one. The vast majority of major projects would have to be heavily subsidized by the Federal government. About the same time Roosevelt became convinced that "big business is out on a deliberate policy of sabotaging the Administration," in Harold Ickes's words. Big business, FDR believed, had gotten its "own people" into various government agencies not only to keep their principals informed of what was going on but in order to block New Deal programs whenever they could.

The midterm elections solidified the authority of the New Deal. As Jim Farley had predicted, the Democrats won 26 out of 35 Senate seats, giving them a 69 to 25 majority in that chamber, while in the House 322 Democrats were elected to 103 Republicans. Even the gubernatorial races went heavily Democratic, leaving the Republicans with seven governors out of the forty-eight states. A number of conservative Republicans fell by the wayside. Simeon Fess of Ohio, who had been an outspoken critic of the New Deal, was defeated, and Roscoe Patterson of Missouri was replaced by a loyal member of the Democratic machine, Judge Harry Truman. "The President," William Allen White wrote, "has all but been crowned by the people."

When Dan Roper, the secretary of commerce, assured the President, in the aftermath of the congressional elections, that the business community in general was ready to go along with him and "work for the economic recovery of the country," the President's sharp response was that "business will have until January 3 [when the Seventy-fourth Congress convened] to make up its mind whether it is going to cooperate or not." Several years ago, Roosevelt told Roper, a study had listed eighty men who controlled the business and finances of the United States. He was "tired of eighty men controlling the destinies of one hundred and twenty million people. . . . " In his opinion, "the only way to curb this control was to do away with holding companies."

Rexford Tugwell reported a conversation with Roosevelt following the elections in the course of which the President said: "You know we ought to have eight years in Washington. At the end of that time we may or may not have a Democratic party, but we will have a Progressive one; and some day we will have the planning you want." To Tugwell's fears that conservative Southern Congressmen would defeat his best-laid plans, Roosevelt replied that as much as they might be opposed to his measures, they had no place to go. "They will have to go along. You'll see, we will get our job done in the time we have."

Harry Hopkins, elated by the election results, was reported to have said to Aubrey Williams and several of his aides in the FERA: "Boys—this is our hour. We've got to get everything we want—a works program, social security, wages and hours, everything—now or never. Get your minds to work on developing a complete ticket to provide security for all the folks of this country up and down and across the board." His staff provided a plan shortly with the imposing title a Plan to End Poverty in America, known as EPIA for short. Hopkins, after conferring with Ickes, set off for Warm Springs to lay it before the President. He found Rexford Tugwell and Donald Richberg there. They swam, played poker, and talked about the age-old dream of ending inequality and hardship in America. The newspaper reporters who swarmed around Warm Springs got word of what was up, and the *New York Times* observed: "The fire-eating Administrator of the Federal Emergency Relief, Harry L. Hopkins, may safely be credited with spoiling the Thanksgiving dinners of many conservatives who had been led to believe that President Roosevelt's recent zig to the right would not be followed by a zag to the left."

The EPIA report argued that with the disappearance of the old frontier, which had absorbed millions of Americans seeking work and land and their fortunes, a new frontier "of idle men, money and machines" had appeared. Conquering this new frontier would require "all the resourcefulness, ingenuity and courage . . . in twelve or thirteen million unemployed men." But even with courage and enterprise they were helpless without the "tremendous organization of productive forces such as only Government can supply when business is in the doldrums. . . . " Moreover, such a program must be one that carried no stigma of "social inferiority" with it but that was accepted "as a matter of right."

The plan listed six elements in the program of the new frontier. Unemployed young people must, above all, be spared the demoralizing consequences of idleness by such agencies as the Civilian Conservation Corps. There must be a system of unemployment insurance for those who, through no fault of their own, were laid off by industry. When unemployment insurance ran out, the unemployed must be able to find work on Federal projects such as those administered by the WPA. The aged should have security through pensions, and those persons who could not work, especially mothers with young children and the physically and mentally handicapped, must be provided for.

The EPIA included the expansion of "subsistence homesteads" and "rural rehabilitation" to include all the families willing to enter the program. In addition, families farming marginal land would be assisted in establishing themselves on "home sites," where they could live on a more civilized scale with government loans or subsidies to buy tools and livestock. Another provision of the EPIA was for the establishment of "centers" where the unemployed could carry out their own small-business enterprises—canning for farmers; needlework and craft activities for their wives. Finally, the plan called for an extension of low-cost, publicly subsidized housing for the poor in large cities. Since most of the ideas were Roosevelt's, it is not surprising that he responded enthusiastically.

On the train back from Warm Springs to Washington a month after the elections a party atmosphere prevailed. "It is delightful," Ickes wrote, "to see how the President can enter in at a party. He had as good a time as anyone there, laughing and talking and joking. . . . Yet in spite of all his fun-making, no one ever presumes to treat him with familiarity, although everyone knowing how friendly and approachable he is looks on him as a real friend and a desirable companion."

Roosevelt, armed with the Williams-Hopkins blueprint, was ready to issue the order "Full speed ahead." Many of the EPIA proposals were included in the President's State of the Union message to Congress on January 4, 1935. He recommended direct relief for the ill, the aged, and the handicapped be returned to the states, while the program of Federally funded work relief be greatly expanded. "The Federal Government," he declared, "must and shall quit this business of relief. . . . Work must be found for able-bodied but destitute workers." He was not willing, the President insisted, "that the vitality of our people be further sapped by the giving of cash, of market baskets, of a few hours of weekly work cutting grass, raking leaves or picking up papers in the public parks. We must preserve not only the bodies of the unemployed from destruction but also their self-respect, their self-reliance and courage and determination." There were some 5,000,000 Americans on the relief rolls as he spoke; they were under the aegis of the Federal Emergency Relief Administration. That agency should be replaced by "a coordinated authority which will be charged with the orderly liquidation of our present relief activities and the substitution of a national chart for the giving of work." Hopkins, listening to the address on the radio, observed in his diary, "Fortunately he means all that he says and more."

One outcome was the Works Progress Administration, charged by the President with carrying out projects "in which a considerable proportion of the money spent will go into wages for labor." That agency would also seek projects in which there was promise of "ultimate return to the Federal treasury of a considerable proportion of the costs." The funds allocated should be spent promptly so as to have the maximum effect on the economy. All projects should be designed to get people off the relief rolls, and they should be undertaken in areas where unemployement was highest. Roosevelt asked for $4,000,000,000 to run the program, with an additional $880,000,000 to carry on the existing relief program until the new plan was in full operation.

The Civil Works Administration, which had been phased out, had compiled an impressive record. Many rural roads that had been virtually impassable were graded and covered with gravel. Fifty thousand teachers had been given employment in 40,000 newly built schools. Five hundred airports, many of them in small and otherwise inaccessible towns, had been constructed. In the midst of the nation's worst economic crisis much of the country had been refurbished. Decaying and dilapidated public facilities, from sewers to parks, had been renovated.

The opening gun of the last great campaign in the war between capital and labor occurred in 1934. It took place not in the familiar precincts of Eastern industrial cities but on the distant West Coast, in the gracious city of San Francisco, long a labor stronghold. Its leader was a tough, wiry longshoreman, who was an Australian immigrant, an avowed Marxist, and a close collaborator with the Communists but not a member of the party: Alfred Renton "Harry" Bridges.

The longshoremen on the West Coast, under Bridges's leadership, called a strike in May. It involved some 3,500 men in San Francisco and approximately 15,000 on the entire West Coast, from Los Angeles to Seattle. Taking advantage of the provisions of Section 7(a) of the NIRA, the usually anarchic longshoremen had formed a union—the International Longshoremen's Association—and when the shipping companies refused to recognize or bargain with it, the union called for a strike. The Teamsters' locals voted not to carry cargoes into the port loading areas. They were followed by sailors, firemen, cooks, pilots, and other ship personnel; in a few weeks all major West Coast ports were shut down. The owners, determined to break the strike, offered inducements to scabs far in excess of those given the longshoremen themselves: bonuses, free meals, and lodging. (The coach of the University of California football team urged his players to offer their services.) Many of the scabs lived in luxury on board ships. But if they were caught by the strikers, punishment was merciless; the scab had his teeth kicked out or his leg broken. Alarmed by the strike, the San Francisco Merchants' Committee declared that the government should "register, fingerprint and photograph all persons over eighteen."

Bridges's Communist sympathies and the fact that he was an alien, and, many of his critics insisted, a deportable alien, were played up by the press in a largely successful effort to give the strike a Communist tinge. The president of the American-Hawaiian Line insisted that the strike "was to get power. To get control on the part of the Communist Party." Most of the newspapers in San Francisco echoed him.

Sidney Lens credited Bridges with introducing three "creative tactics" in the longshoremen's strike. Mass picketing was the first. A thousand men filled San Francisco's waterfront Embarcadero in twelve-hour shifts to guard against the use of strikebreakers by the shipping companies. In Portland in one day twenty-five strikebreakers were thrown into the Willamette River; in San Pedro, near Los Angeles, a strikebreaker was killed.

Another of Bridges's tactics was to involve unions in related fields, such as the Marine Workers and Industrial Union and the Teamsters. He also organized a Joint Strike Committee of fifty members, with five representatives from each union on strike. Under the firm control of Bridges they formed a solid front against all those opposed to the strike. When a secret agreement to end the strike was made between "King" Joe Ryan, a rival of Harry Bridges in the longshoremen's union, and the assistant secretary of labor, Edward McGrady, the strikers repudiated the agreement.

A crisis came on July 3, when an effort was made to force five trucks through the picket line on the Embarcadero. A four-hour battle followed. In a scene reminiscent of the Battle of Bunker Hill in the American Revolution, thousands of San Franciscans gathered on the hills above the bay to watch the conflict. One picket was killed, and several dozen were badly wounded.

The police returned to the fray with reinforcements and vomit gas. Firing their revolvers in the air, they dispersed the pickets, but the longshoremen were soon reinforced by workers from other unions. This time 2 strikers were killed, and 2 more mortally wounded. More than 100 police, pickets, and bystanders were carted off to hospitals, while hundreds more nursed lesser injuries. The following day the governor called out the national guard. An estimated 15,000 sympathizers with the strike, most of them workingmen and workingwomen, marched in protest. A few days later the San Francisco Labor Council voted for a general strike to take place. The business community responded to a call by Hearst's man in San Francisco, John Francis Neylan, for a pact among newspaper publishers "to protect our community from communism" by forming a committee to censor all stories about the strike. The *Chronicle* was forbidden to publish an interview with Bridges. Such heroes of the old Progressive era as Hiram Johnson joined in the chorus of alarm. Johnson wired Harold Ickes: "Here is revolution not only in the making but with the initial actuality. . . . Already a food shortage exists. Unless a miracle happens, Monday will bring discomfort, possible disaster and actual want. . . . Obviously Washington doesn't understand a general strike." If the President failed to act, presumably by calling out Federal troops, Johnson predicted the "possible ruin of the West Coast." Roosevelt was on board a navy ship headed for Hawaii. Frances Perkins, who found herself in the middle of things, was anxious to prevent the President from any step that might compromise the administration. In Roosevelt's absence, Cordell Hull, as secretary of state, was in charge. He and Homer Cummings seemed to Perkins near panic. "We think that we should do something," Hull told Perkins. " . . . I think we should take some severe and drastic steps immediately." When she went to Hull's office to confer with the two men, their faces seemed to register "total disaster, total defeat of themselves and the end of the world," she wrote.

As attorney general, Cummings had come up with a definition of a general strike as one intended to "overthrow the ordinary procedures of government." The San Francisco general strike seemed to him to fit this definition. Perkins argued that it was, on the contrary, intended as a peaceful act of protest. To call in Federal troops would be to turn it into a confrontation between the working people of San Francisco and their sympathizers and the Federal government. What, asked Perkins, did Hull and Cummings expect the soldiers to do? Drive trucks and bake bread? "I cannot tell you how serious it would be politically, morally and for the basic labor-industry and labor-government relationships of the country, if we were to do this," she declared. "What's more, if the cabinet does this while the President is out of the country, imagine the bedlam and trouble he'll be in!" She wished it to be part of the record that she demanded they wire the President and get his authorization before acting.

Mercurial Hugh Johnson, who had appeared in Berkeley to speak at his alma mater, the University of California, poured oil on the fire. After affirming the right of labor to organize, he went on to denounce the general strike as "a threat to the community" and "a menace to government. It is civil war," he proclaimed. Children would be without milk. It was "bloody insurrection . . . a blow at the flag . . . and it has got to stop." If the Federal government failed to act, "the people would act, and it would act to wipe out this subversive element as you clean off a chalk mark on a blackboard with a wet sponge." Coming from one of the most important figures in the administration, this was hardly the kind of talk calculated to dampen passions on both sides. It was especially dangerous talk in California, which had a long tradition of vigilante action stretching back to the gold rush days and including attacks on Chinese immigrants.

Inspired by Johnson's heated rhetoric, vigilante groups in numerous towns and cities descended on Communist headquarters and meeting halls, destroyed property, and attacked Communists and radicals indiscriminately while the newspapers applauded their actions. Johnson had agreed to meet with John P. McLaughlin, the conservative head of the San Francisco Teamsters' Union, to try to work out some kind of a compromise. But he arrived at the meeting drunk and denounced the strikers and labor generally. Several days later Bridges drew Johnson's particular animus. Johnson called for Bridges's deportation and the deportation of immigrants generally, declaring that if sufficient numbers were deported, "the unemployment and destitution problems of the United States would be reduced by at least one-third. . . . [A]ny alien who pretends to lead an economic group of our people in the direction of strike and bloodshed has no place here and should be no more tolerated than an armed enemy under a foreign flag," Johnson announced.

The Great Strike was, it turned out, a demonstration, not the beginning of a revolution. Largely through the efforts of Frances Perkins, Federal troops were not called out, and a possibly bloody confrontation was avoided. Most of the strikers' demands were met. The strike itself had far-reaching consequences. Workers all over the country were encouraged to take up the battle for unionization. Bridges, a complete outsider in the labor movement, became a national figure, much admired and much feared. The final campaign had begun in spectacular fashion. Soon other hands would take it up, and other soldiers join the battle.

The deportation of Harry Bridges became a major political issue. The only ground for deportation was that he was a Communist. That the United States immigration officers in San Francisco could find no evidence that Bridges was "a card-carrying member of the Communist Party" cut no ice with those patriots who were indignant over his role in the Longshoremen's Association and considered him a dangerous radical in any event. They raised a hue and cry that Frances Perkins was protecting Communists (whereas she was simply upholding the law) and demanded her impeachment. One of the stories spread by her enemies was that the reason she failed to act was that she and Bridges were secretly married and that both were Communists.

One of the most significant events of 1934 was little noticed in the United States. At an international conference of radical writers in Paris the Bulgarian spokesman for the Comintern, Georgi Dimitrov, hinted at a change in the third period dogma. Wild riots in that city had brought about the downfall of the mildly reformist government of Edouard Daladier. The Communists, acting on the doctrine that all liberal and radical non-Communist groups were "social Fascists," to be as strongly opposed as any right-wing faction, had more or less conspired in the downfall of the Daladier government. The government that succeeded it was enthusiastically anti-Communist. For a time it seemed as though Stalin and the Comintern had not learned the lesson of Germany. There the Communists, confident that they could oust Hitler once he had taken power, had acquiesced in the Nazi takeover. The results of that miscalculation were all too apparent. If Russia were to have any allies against the dangerous aggressions of Hitler, it must abandon the third period policy and seek friends where it could find them. What was required was a popular front of all anti-Fascist groups against the rising menace of fascism-nazism.

# 26

## On the Fringe

As Roosevelt and his close advisers looked ahead to the presidential election of 1936, one of the most disturbing developments was the remarkable growth of Huey Long's Share Our Wealth movement. It was said that twenty-five aides were needed simply to open and answer Long's mail.

If politics was mother's milk to Southerners, Huey Long was the most successful practitioner of the art. Long was born in Winnfield, Louisiana, in 1893 "in a comfortable, well-built, four-room log house" on a small farm. His moderately prosperous father and mother had nine children. From an early age, he wrote, "my sympathies were attracted to persons . . . whose fight for existence was one of living from hand to mouth. . . ." One of his earliest memories was of the auctioning off of a neighbor's farm for a debt owed to a local store. At the farmer's plea no one bid on the farm. Finally the creditor plucked up courage to bid. The farmer lost his farm. "I was horrified," Long wrote, "I could not understand. It seemed criminal. This marked the first sign, in my recollection, of a neighborhood where the blessings of the Creator were shared one with the other, being transformed into a community yielding to commercial enticements."

Long hated farmwork. "In the field the rows were long; the sun was hot; there was little companionship. Rising before the sun, we toiled until dark, after which we did nothing except eat supper, listen to the whippoorwills, and go to bed." At the age of ten Long tried to run away. He was caught and given a beating.

On Sundays Long and his brothers and sisters went to Sunday school at nine o'clock. Church services followed and in the afternoon there was a meeting of the "young people's religious society." Sunday night there was another service and on Wednesday night there was a prayer meeting. "We went to every funeral within ten miles," Long wrote. "Most of us read Scripture from cover to cover." At thirteen Long went to work part-time as an apprentice printer, thus beginning what proved to be a lifelong association with books. His next job, while he was still attending high school, was with a book auctioneer. In school he became a luminary of the debating society, a runner, and a declaimer. His debating skill won him a scholarship at Louisiana State University, but Long was too poor to be able to accept it. At eighteen he became a traveling salesman, and he saved enough to attend the University of Oklahoma for five months, "the happiest days of my life." Still working as a traveling salesman, or drummer, with his headquarters in Shreveport, Long invited Rose McConnell to see the opera *Lohengrin* at the Grand Opera House. They were married a year later. Long was nineteen. He borrowed $400 from a brother and entered the law program at Tulane University. In a desperate race with his dwindling funds, he studied as many as sixteen to twenty hours a day. His weight fell to 112 pounds, but he completed three years' work in one year, and with the cooperation of a kindly bar committee, which waived a rule requiring at least two years' attendance at the law school, he passed his bar examination and was sworn in as "a full-fledged lawyer in the State of Louisiana at the age of twenty-one." Long hung out his shingle in Winnfield, promising never to turn away a client because of inability to pay.

When Winnfield proved too small a field for Long's talents, he moved to Shreveport. At the same time he began to dabble in local politics, finding, at every turn, the presence of Standard Oil, which, it soon became evident to Long, for all practical purposes owned the state of Louisiana. Long's first crusade was against a law, backed by the state's industrial interests and particularly by Standard Oil, which "severely restricted the right of recovery for industrial accidents." When Long testified before the legislature's Committee on Capital and Labor in defiance of the chairman's effort to rule him out of order, he declared: "For twenty years has the Louisiana Legislature been dominated by the henchmen and attorneys of the interests. Those seeking reforms have bowed their heads in regret and shame when witnessing these corrupting influences in this capital." The law under consideration would prevent a family from receiving more than $300 for the death of a laborer, "upon whom they depend for education and support. . . . There are hours when the infidel invokes God and the anarchist calls on the government. There are times when the people cling to what they have repudiated. Can it be that these gentlemen, after exposure seems imminent, will now attempt to invoke the term 'justice' after their continued practices of fraud and deceit?" With the reputation of a radical and a troublemaker, Long found his path blocked by "all the corporations of my territory" when he tried to become assistant United States attorney in Shreveport.

Long was determined to find his own way past such obstacles. In March, 1918, the *New Orleans Item* and other papers in the state printed a letter from him under the headline "THINKS WEALTH SHOULD BE MORE EVENLY DISTRIBUTED." Long wrote: "A conservative estimate is that about sixty-five or seventy per cent of the entire United States is owned by two per cent of the people. Sixty-eight per cent of the whole people . . . own but two per cent of its wealth. From the year 1890 to 1910, the wealth of this nation trebled, yet the masses owned less in 1910 than they did in 1890." Only 14 out of every 1,000 young men and women received college educations. "Does such a condition give the ordinary man his proper return of the nation's prosperity?" Long asked. "What do you think of such a game of life, so brutally and cruelly unfair, with the dice so loaded that the child of today must enter it with only fourteen chances out of a thousand in his favor of getting a college education? . . . How can this Nation prosper with the ordinary child having only twenty chances in the thousand of securing the first part of the game [completing high school]?" Under such circumstances there was not "the opportunity for Christian uplift and education and cannot be until there is more economic reform." Long was twenty-four, and the letter was his political manifesto; he was determined to make his weight felt politically in the state of Louisiana. That meant, in effect, taking on the state's most powerful vested interest, Standard Oil.

Long found that the state constitution put no minimum age on members of the Railroad Commission. He ran for that influential body in 1918, his headquarters the house of his father-in-law in Shreveport.

From the first moment he appeared a formidable campaigner. When he found his campaign posters were being torn down by his enemies, he borrowed a flatbed truck and tacked the posters high up on trees and telephone poles. He called farmers on the phone late at night to make his pitch and solicit their support on the ground that they would not likely forget him. Surprisingly, it worked. Long could charm even a sleepy farmer. He won election and found an immediate cause in the support of small oil companies and independent producers, squeezed by the big oil companies, which refused to let the small guys use the oil companies' pipelines to carry their oil to refineries. Soon the issue was attracting widespread attention around the state. When Long attacked the oil companies, a friendly newspaper termed his speech " 'as hot as this boiling water that bubbles up from Hot Wells at 116 degrees.' . . . Mr. Long said that if there ever was an institution that stood convicted before the people, that is Standard Oil. 'This octopus is among the world's greatest criminals. It was thrown out of Texas following its raid in Spindle Top; it was ousted from Kansas; it was forced to terms in Oklahoma. . . .' " It also was to make Huey Long governor and Senator. Meanwhile, he was active in a number of lawsuits against larger corporations: to limit street railway fares, to impose a 3 percent severance tax on oil, and to shift the tax burden from poor citizens to rich corporations.

Long became chairman of the Railroad Commission and used the office to increase his political leverage in the state. The State Supreme Court upheld a commission decision to lower phone rates and the cut was hailed by the *New Orleans Item* as "manna from Heaven." Long made sure the voters of the state knew who their champion had been. His fight with Standard Oil continued until the courts decided the issue in his favor by declaring the pipelines "common carriers," available to all oil producers.

Long sounded more like the Populists' James Weaver or Tom Watson than a Democratic politician when he wrote: "The bowels of the earth are filled with oil and gas and minerals. The face is covered with forests and natural resources. When these are extracted from the ground they should leave on top of the ground blessings to speak for the things that have been taken. The blessings should include schools, hospitals, etc."

In 1923, on his thirtieth birthday, Long announced his candidacy for governor. He found himself opposed by the closed ranks of the more conservative, business-oriented politicians of the state as well as by the newspapers. The Klan issue was promptly injected into the campaign. One of Long's rivals was supported by the Klan; the other received the anti-Klan vote. Long was the man in the middle. Long carried the "country" over both his opponents, well-known political figures with large campaign chests, but he lost the election in New Orleans, the voters of which feared his Populist principles and fiery denunciations of the corporations responsible for the city's prosperity.

In one of Huey Long's encounters with his bitter rival L. E. Thomas—the creature, in Long's view, of the sugar interests—Long told a long story of a fretful infant at a camp meeting whose mother finally quieted it with a "sugar tit," a piece of cloth wrapped around a biscuit with butter and sugar added. Every time Thomas became fretful, Long concluded, the sugar interests provided him with a "sugar tit," a bribe to keep him quiet.

Thomas replied in kind with the story of a man passing through hell who saw a large iron box locked and shackled. What was in it? he asked the devil. Huey Long. Why not let him out? "Oh, no! . . . We can't let him out. He'd take charge of hell if we did."

In 1928 Long was on the hustings again, determined to win the governorship this time around. His principal issues were corruption and cronyism. Governor Henry L. Fuqua had awarded the so-called Watson-Williams syndicate the right to build a toll bridge over Lake Pontchartrain to New Orleans. Long insisted that the state should build the bridge in question and make passage over it free. If he were elected governor, Long said, he would build a free bridge parallel to it, thereby rendering the Watson-Williams toll bridge an expensive disaster. In the gubernatorial campaign Long developed those campaign tactics that were to distinguish his brief political career. With the press almost solidly against him, Long produced his own newspaper, the *Louisiana Progress,* and developed a distribution network for circulars and pamphlets that extended into every village and hamlet in the state. He also came up with the slogans "Share Our Wealth" and "Every Man a King." His famous phrase "Every man a king" was taken from his hero William Jennings Bryan, who had said, "Behold a Republic! where every man is a King, but no one wears a crown." Long also made reference to a law in Leviticus which provided for "freeing and refreeing," in Long's words, "all persons of debts every seven years and distribution and redistribution of wealth every fifty years."

Long's flare for the dramatic was demonstrated by his choosing the Evangeline Oak at St. Martinville to launch his campaign. Legend had it that Evangeline, immortalized by Longfellow's poem, had waited faithfully there for her lover, Gabriel, who never came. "Evangeline is not the only one who waited here in disappointment," Long told his audience. "Where are the schools, the roads and highways, the institutions for the disabled you sent your money to build? Evangeline's tears lasted through one lifetime—yours through generations. Give me the chance to dry the eyes of those who still weep here!"

His opponents, increasingly bitter and vituperative, promised that if he were elected, he would be impeached within a year. But Long polled 126,842 votes to 81,747 and 80,326 for his two rivals respectively. The vast majority of Long's votes came again from rural areas of the state. In the runoff election Long won by a large majority, and he soon made clear that he intended to carry out his campaign pledges to provide extensive services for Louisiana's poor, black and white alike. In present-day America, with uncounted miles of paved roads and highways, it is difficult to convey what roads meant to farm communities in the South. They were essential links with towns and cities, connecting tissue between communities, and, most important of all, the means of transportation of farm produce to market and of needed supplies to farms. Rutted and often impassable roads meant serious hardship to farmers and their families. The automobile was, in the South, a potent symbol, if not precisely of success, of at least a fragile connection with the outside world, with progress and a modicum of dignity. Poor black and white farmers undertook desperate expedients to buy rickety old Model Ts or Oldsmobiles even in areas where the roads were virtually impassable and even though they seldom had the hard cash to pay for gasoline. Their cars sat, like cherished statuary before an Italian villa, in front of weather-beaten four-room shacks where meat was a luxury. Muddy, unpaved roads not only slowed transportation to a crawl when they did not stop it entirely, but they took years off the useful lives of the cars and trucks that bounced and shook over them. So paved roads were the most essential desire of the Louisiana farmers, and Long set out to build them, driving often reluctant or inept state officials mercilessly. "We are building roads ten times as strong and for less than half the cost of the roads built by other administrations before us," he boasted. The state had also had the smallest number of bank failures during the early years of the Depression, and the death rate in state hospitals had been dramatically lowered. One enthusiastic supporter declared near the end of Long's term as governor: "The highway system that Long will leave will be a greater monument to his foresight than the Appian Way of Rome."

It was much the same with passage over the rivers and creeks that crisscrossed the state, most of them served by ferries, as they had been since the state was first settled. Long built bridges to bear the farmers' cars and trucks. In so doing, if he did not make every man a king, he vastly accelerated his movement. The most poignant feature of Long's quasi-autobiography, *Every Man a King*, are the photographs of Louisiana roads "before and after." There are five such "before and after" roads and three photographs showing river crossings "before" (dilapidated ferries) and "after" (gleaming new bridges). In addition, there are photographs of rural health clinics (some with no "before," others filled with the most modern equipment) and mental institutions. Long also built a skyscraping state capitol, but the principal object of his largess was Louisiana State University. There he built a medical school which he hoped would rival Johns Hopkins or Harvard, an imposing structure incorporating the most advanced medical technology and committed to appointing a distinguished faculty.

Long was a conspicuous figure at most LSU football games, conducting the band, addressing the crowds, surrounded by cheerleaders and beauty queens. On one occasion, as the LSU band was marching through town on the way to the stadium, Long intercepted it and assumed the role of drum major.

Such antics horrified the old blood, who felt their aristocratic state, which had prided itself on its good manners and good breeding, was being made the laughingstock of the country. Long's vulgarities made proper New Orleanians cringe. He dressed in flamboyant white suits and smoked wicked-looking black cigars. He looked rather like a clown, with a little plume of wiry hair and a bulbous nose—an impression which he deliberately created by his clownish behavior.

Long's enemies were determined to make good on their threat to impeach him. Impeachment proceedings were instituted in the state legislature, on the ground of malfeasance in office, and public meetings condemning him and his policies were held around the state. His proposal to tax each gallon of lubricating oil, gasoline, or kerosene produced in the state one-seventh of a cent set off a furor. His enemies made no bones about their stand. They condemned, as "vicious, dangerous and utterly without merit, any and all systems of taxation . . . which directly or indirectly seek to impose tax burdens upon industries within the State of Louisiana." Long noted that at his opponents' political rallies the sixty-piece Standard Oil band, dressed in mufti instead of the usual brilliant uniforms, provided the music.

Long's reply, circulated through his network, declared to the "People of Louisiana: I had rather go down to a thousand impeachments than to admit that I am the Governor of the State that does not dare to call the Standard Oil Company to account so that we can educate our children and care for destitute, sick and afflicted. If this State is still to be ruled by the power of the money of this corporation, I am too weak for its governor."

Another no-win cause taken up by Long's opponents was stubborn opposition to his program of free schoolbooks for the state's children. It was, they declared, a socialist measure that would bankrupt the state. Once more Long outmaneuvered the opposition. The schoolchildren got their books, and Long enhanced his reputation as a friend of the poor. To the rage of his enemies, most of the legislation that Long initiated was upheld by the state courts. Fighting off the promised effort to impeach him, an effort in which malice was more evident than were impeachable offenses, Long turned Louisiana upside down and, in the process, made himself a national figure. Reporters descended on the state capitol at Baton Rouge to interview the new political phenomenon. Frazier Hunt came back from a session with Huey Long with confused feelings about the Louisiana "dictator." Hunt had no illusions about Long's dictatorial reign. He referred to his "Fascist" tendencies and had no apology to make for its "brutality and its mistakes." He was "only sure that here was a man of immense talent and possibilities. In many things he was right; it was criminal to let men go hungry in a land overflowing with milk and honey . . . great concentrations of wealth and privilege must be broken up; the good things of life must go to all. . . . His greatest crime was that he dared join with the poor white trash against the rule of Southern aristocracy. He wore bright clothes and diamond rings, and spent money as if it were so much Mississippi River water, but he meant what he said about poverty and hunger."

Whatever upper-class Louisianans or others thought about Long, the common citizens, black and white, gave him their hearts. Paul Anderson noted, "They do not merely vote for him, they worship the ground he walks on. He is part of their religion." A Long supporter used a biblical image—"They felt the hand of Huey"—and many thought they recognized in his angry cadences the voice of an Old Testament prophet. Of blacks Long said, "Treat them the same as anybody else, give them an opportunity to make a living." His black chauffeur said of him, "There was not a finer man. Nothing wrong with him. He always treated me fine." A black farmer said, "He was fair to colored people, good to poor people. He walked the land like Jesus Christ and left nothing undone." A black schoolteacher declared, "We felt he had no prejudices. He gave Negroes and all poor people hope."

Elected to the U.S. Senate in 1930, Long left the state in the hands of a loyal lieutenant. He came to the Senate, he wrote, "with only one project in mind, which was that by every means of action and persuasion I might do something to spread the wealth of the land among all of the people. . . . There is no rule so sure as that one that the same mill that grinds out fortunes above a certain size at the top, grinds out paupers at the bottom. The same machine makes them both." It seemed clear to him that "God Almighty had warned against this condition. Thomas Jefferson, Andrew Jackson, Daniel Webster, Theodore Roosevelt, William Jennings Bryan and every religious teacher known to this earth had declaimed against it." Long did not delay in describing to his bemused Senate colleagues his program for sharing the wealth. In a speech in April, 1932, he described how machines had vastly improved human productivity: "[M]ore is produced by the labor of one man than was formerly produced by the labor of a thousand men, but instead of producing prosperity, ease and comfort, they have meant unemployment; they have meant idleness; they have meant starvation; they have meant pestilence; whereas they should have meant that hours of labor were shortened, that toil was decreased, that more people would be able to consume, that they would have more time for pleasure, time for recreation—in fact, everything that could have been done by science and invention and wealth and progress in this country should have been shared among the people. . . . " If the fabulous wealth of the country concentrated in the hands of a few could be distributed, "while leaving these rich people all the luxuries they can possibly use, what a different world this would be." Long's rather modest proposal was for laws that would allow no one an income of more than $1,000,000 a year; inheritances would be limited to $5,000,000 per person. It was hardly a revolutionary program, but it raised a fever of anxiety among the wealthy.

Long's most important recruit was an ex-preacher named Gerald L. K. Smith. None other than Henry Mencken hailed Smith as "the gutsiest and goriest, the deadliest and damnedest orator ever heard upon this or any other earth—the champion boob-bumper of all epochs." Smith was born in 1898 in Pardeeville, Wisconsin, the offspring of three generations of evangelical preachers. After his graduation from Valparaiso University he, too, was ordained and served in several churches in Indiana before he accepted, in 1928, a call to a fashionable church in New Orleans. There he promptly fell under the spell of Huey Long.

Long's program for redistributing the wealth—"making every man a king"—called for confiscatory taxes on great wealth to provide pensions for the elderly, a veterans' bonus, and an automobile, radio, and home for every American. Long directed his fire increasingly at the New Deal, charging that Roosevelt, despite his tough talk, was actually capitulating to Wall Street. He compared the NRA's Blue Eagle with the Nazi swastika, derided the secretary of agriculture as Lord Corn Wallace, and described Ickes as the "Chicago Chinch Bug." When Long threatened to head a third party in 1936, thereby sabotaging the Democratic Party, Roosevelt directed the Internal Revenue to examine Long's tax returns and put out the word that no one "working for Huey Long and his crowd" was to receive a government job or government patronage. "Anybody working for Huey Long is not working for us," he declared. Suddenly Long began to have bad press. The *Memphis Commercial Appeal* reported in January, 1933: "Secret service agents are investigating Senator Long's personal income tax over a period of years; they are trying to find irregularities in a loan which he obtained from the Reconstruction Finance Corporation. . . . No stone is being left unturned. . . . Long's bank accounts everywhere are being scrutinized. When he made a trip to New Orleans during the Christmas holidays he was shadowed by government agents, his telephone tapped and every movement watched."

Long knew very well the hatchet job was on. At the end of *Every Man a King*, he inserted two parallel columns on him by the same writer from the same magazine. One, written in 1930, when he was governor of Louisiana, was highly laudatory; the other, three years later, was an all-out assault; he had become "Hotcha Huey (Tell 'em nothing and make 'em like it), Get-'em-while-they're hot Huey . . . the hardest-working demagogue in America," a man so lacking in physical courage that he slept behind a machine gun.

When Hugh Johnson attacked Long in a radio address in March, 1935, the Kingfish replied. Johnson responded, and Father Charles Coughlin, the "radio priest," got into the act. It was not an edifying exchange. The income tax people were after Huey, and political patronage in Louisiana was channeled to his opponents. Long's response was to carry his warfare into neighboring states. He mounted a campaign to defeat the New Deal war-horse Senator Joseph Robinson in Arkansas and threatened Pat Harrison in Mississippi. Secret polls taken by the Democrats showed considerable Long strength in the whole lower Mississippi Valley. To Moley Roosevelt talked of measures to "steal Long's thunder"; Moley was convinced that fear of Long stimulated the second wave of New Deal social legislation. In his words, "the Democratic leaders began to get an acute attack of jitters about the apparently growing political strength of the Kingfish."

Not only were the congressional elections of 1934 the first serious testing of the popularity of the New Deal, but they marked the high-water mark of political movements spawned by the Depression. In addition to Huey Long's Share Our Wealth campaign, Father Coughlin posed a serious challenge to the Democrats. Coughlin was an oddity on the American political stage, a kind of Catholic Populist who denounced capitalists and Communists with equal fervor and mixed in a substantial helping of chauvinism and anti-Semitism. Coughlin was parish priest at the Shrine of the Little Flower just north of Detroit, and his skillful use of the radio made him a national fixture. A Gallup poll showed that some 8,500,000 families listened to Coughlin's radio sermons "regularly" or "from time to time," and 83 percent approved of his message. His "sermons" were carried initially on the CBS radio network, but after CBS had dropped him as he grew increasingly controversial, Coughlin started his own network, which reached an audience of an estimated 40,000,000 people. In addition, he had a kind of private army of enthusiastic racists who armed themselves and drilled in preparation for the day when the Jews and capitalists would try to take over the country. The story was told that newsboys selling his newspaper "Social Justice were instructed to sob, and when questioned about the reason, to say, 'A big Jew hit me.' "

Coughlin never tired of berating the godless Communists of Russia and depicting the United States as locked in final and mortal combat with the Soviet Union, but at the same time he attacked capitalism, especially the international bankers, an approach which, as we have noted, was a classic, anti-Semitic ploy. Joe Kennedy, a loyal Democrat, spent an inordinate amount of time, in Ickes's view, "trying to reconcile the President to Hearst and Father Coughlin." Coughlin visited the White House, and Roosevelt exercised his charm upon him. Coughlin, in turn, gave his support to some of the early New Deal measures, but he was hopelessly mercurial, and as his anti-Semitism became increasingly virulent, William Douglas was puzzled by the President's acceptance of Coughlin's intermittent and unpredictable support.

But it was in faraway California that what were in some ways the most far-out political movements arose. "Until 1933, the climate of California completely satisfied every physical, mental, and emotional need of the state's inmates," George Creel wrote, "but the effects of the Depression were particularly devastating in that golden land. Not only were the economic consequences especially severe, the state was full of refugees from harsher psychological and geographical climes. Californians were inclined to the view that whatever evil and ambiguity there might be in the world was suspended when one crossed the borders of the state. Every economic nostrum found a ready ear there at the continent's western rim."

The state was a mecca for the retired. Farmers and their wives, worn out by the bitter winters and summers of Nebraska, the Dakotas, and the farm states of the Middle West, flocked to Long Beach, Los Angeles, Pasadena, Whittier, and Azusa by the tens and then hundreds of thousands. There they clustered—the Quakers in Whittier, the Baptists in Long Beach, the Presbyterians and Methodists in Pacific Palisades, the Episcopalians in Pasadena. Their prophet was Dr. Francis Everett Townsend of Long Beach. His remedy for the Depression was to give every person over the age of sixty a pension of $200 a month, with the proviso that it must all be spent within the month. This, he argued, would provide such a stimulus to the economy (not to mention the stimulus it would provide to those over sixty) that the Depression would be immediately ended.

Townsend soon had a new program and two new slogans: "Thirty Dollars Every Thursday" for everyone over fifty (Thomas Paine had made substantially the same proposal almost 150 years earlier) and "Ham and Eggs for California." The $2,000,000,000 required to launch the program could, Townsend declared, be raised by a 2 percent tax on all incomes. The appeal of the Townsend Plan was such that it captured the legislatures of seven Western states in 1934.

The technocrats were also heard from. Howard Scott was an engineer whose contribution to the thinking of the day was technocracy, a society in which engineers ruled and no one had to work more than two or three hours a day. Money would be replaced by "units of energy" called ergs and joules. William Douglas and his friend Jerome Frank had often discussed the consequences of the newer technologies, which, they believed, would change the whole concept of work and unemployment. "Unemployment would be normal and not occasional; the regular pattern, not a mere emergency." The technocrats also anticipated such a day in the not far distant future. They advocated replacing the price system and "supplying everyone with the basic necessities and lifetime personal security." Radical journalist Stuart Chase took up the cause, but Frank and Douglas became disenchanted with Scott when he began to hold up the military services as "the only efficient and disciplined bodies, and the least affected with business values. . . . " If any minority, "racial, religious, or economic," opposed the reorganization of society along the lines of technocracy, Scott declared, young Americans committed to it, "will concede nothing short of that minority's annihilation."

In California another group called simply Utopians, flourished. The Utopians were founded by a gasoline salesman, an investment banker gone broke, and a promoter. Initially conceived as a kind of fraternal order, the group soon produced an ambitious platform that called, in effect, for a new social order based on Edward Bellamy's *Looking Backward,* Henry George's various works, Plato's *Republic,* and Sir Thomas More's *Utopia.* The Utopians' most effective recruiting technique was what we call today "guerrilla theater," simple morality plays which depicted a capitalist as "a fat, oily creature, exuding avarice from every pore," in George Creel's words. In one such skit the Capitalist refused bread to starving men, women, and children who appealed to him for help. The Food Merchant is likewise indifferent to the pleas of those clothed in rags, and the Moneylender, when appealed to, "bursts into fiendish cackles and tells them that to borrow money they must first become his slaves. . . . Desperate, hopeless, sobbing, they accept his terms and are loaded down with chains." Finally, the Hermit Reason appears and tells the enslaved multitudes that if they will cooperate collectively toward abundance, he can bring them to the Land of Plenty for All where a man "produces what he uses and uses what he produces." It was said that the Utopians had enlisted 600,000 members in California, and they claimed 30,000,000 members nationwide. Allowing for considerable inflation, the figures are a measure of the country's desperate search for an answer to the Depression.

Among California's immigrants was Upton Sinclair, one of the earliest and most famous muckrakers, a formidably prolific writer. Sinclair decided in 1934 to run for governor of California on the

Democratic ticket. The shift in the political spectrum from right to left was indicated by the fact that his "conservative" rival for the Democratic nomination was George Creel, a Theodore Roosevelt Progressive and Wilsonian liberal. Sinclair devised a program to End Poverty in California, or EPIC, as it came to be called. "I say positively and without qualification we can end poverty in California," Sinclair announced. "I know exactly how to do it, and if you elect me governor, with a legislature to support me, I will put the job through, and it won't take more than one or two years of my four years." He added: "I am one of those old-fashioned persons who still have hope that in countries such as Britain and the United States where people have been accustomed to self-government, the change from capitalism to socialism can be accomplished without the overthrow of the government."

Bizarre as much of the EPIC program sounded, it had elements of serious and practical reform that attracted people who had little faith in Sinclair's more extravagant promises. The California Authority for Land was assigned the prospective role of taking over all unused land and all land sold for taxes; it would all be used for agricultural colonies. Each colony would feature a community dining hall and a kitchen with the most modern equipment. There would be a community laundry, a hospital, and a hall for concerts, lectures, and films; a nursery, or, as we would say today, a day care center, would be provided so babies would be cared for while their mothers worked or engaged in "learning in library, concert hall or theater." Such notions were not new, of course; they were as old at least as Robert Dale Owen's New Harmony, Brook Farm, or John Humphrey Noyes's Oneida Community. Charlotte Perkins Gilman had envisioned similar communities at the turn of the century.

The California Authority for Production was designed to run idle factories in which the unemployed would turn out products for themselves as well as for the "land colonies." The California Authority for Money was the weakest link in the EPIC chain. It would, when put into effect, issue $300,000,000 in bonds, but it was unclear who would buy the bonds. A tax of 10 percent would be placed on all unimproved land, and a state income tax would be enacted on all incomes over $5,000. Much of the cost of the EPIC program was to be covered by a 4 percent tax on stock sales. The centerpiece of Sinclair's program was the Central Valley Water Project. There 50,000 unemployed would be put to work. They would be fed by nearby farmers, who would accept scrip redeemable on completion of the project, in return for supplying food. For a time EPIC seemed irresistible. It was estimated that 8,000,000 Californians joined its ranks.

Although Creel's writer friends, Irvin Cobb, Rupert Hughes, and Kathleen Norris among them, turned out to assist him in his campaign for governor (Norris wrote a pamphlet entitled *My Friend—George Creel*), he encountered hostile audiences whenever he tried to subject the extravagant notions of his rival to critical analysis. Clarence Darrow and Theodore Dreiser were only two of a notable array of public figures who endorsed Sinclair and EPIC. In the Democratic primaries Sinclair polled more votes than the total of eight other candidates. The stage was thus set for a contest between Sinclair and Frank Merriam, "reactionary to the point of medievalism," in Creel's words. Creel promised Sinclair his support if he would trim his sails a bit and present a less radical stance to the voters. Sinclair agreed to abandon his more extreme proposals, but he was soon singing the familiar tunes, and Creel wrote to him charging him with "optimism carried to the point of delirium." Sinclair's call for "immediate EPIC," Creel added, ". . . puts me back, exactly where I was in the primary campaign. In its essence it is the original EPIC that I attacked as unsound, unworkable, and un-American, designed to appeal to credulities, ignorance, and despair, and immeasureably hurtful in its effects on true progressivism." "Unsound" and "unworkable" EPIC may indeed have been, but "un-American" it certainly was not.

Among Sinclair's ardent supporters were two young graduate students in political science at the University of California, Dean E. McHenry and Clark Kerr. McHenry and Kerr and their girlfriends worked part-time in the Division of Self-Help Cooperatives of the State Emergency Relief Administration. McHenry, who had been a Progressive Republican, switched to the Democratic Party, and he and Kerr became workers for Sinclair. McHenry's role was to organize a "brain trust" for Sinclair in Northern California. He described the venture as an "informal group of educators, businessmen and professional people with both EPIC sympathies and technical training and ability to contribute to planning."

Robert Gordon Sproul, president of the University of California, invited McHenry to speak on Sinclair's behalf at a university convocation. McHenry's talk "stressed the relative success of the self-help cooperatives and the common sense of providing the unemployed with productive work." McHenry had helped start "small-scale bakeries, dairies, garment factories, and other enterprises," and he believed that the principle was a sound one.

For a time it seemed that Sinclair and EPIC were irresistible. Sinclair visited Roosevelt at Hyde Park and reported a cordial and friendly session with the President. Harry Hopkins put in a good word for him: "He's on our side, isn't he?" Jim Farley wrote a letter urging California Democrats to support Sinclair. There was a terrific flap among more orthodox party members, and Farley explained that the letter had been sent by a secretary who had used a stamp for his signature. The conservative elements in the state experienced something akin to panic. A vast campaign of abuse and innuendo was mounted against Sinclair. It was evident everywhere, often in the form of outright coercion. Louis B. Mayer deducted a day's pay from everyone working for MGM to check the "Bolshevik sacking of California" by the EPIC forces. When the Communist playwright John Howard Lawson went to Columbia Pictures to work as a screenwriter, Harry Cohn, head of the studio, rebuked him for his radical leanings and, suspecting that Lawson supported Upton Sinclair, ordered him to contribute at least a dollar to Sinclair's rival for the California governorship. When Lawson refused to obey Cohn's order, he was fired. "I am king here," Cohn declared. "Whoever eats my bread sings my song."

Sinclair was denounced by the Democratic Party, with which he had sought an alliance. The leading papers of the state refused to print any news of the EPIC campaign (Sinclair put out his own paper), and documents that purported to prove that he was in the pay of Moscow were forged and distributed widely. MGM produced a newsreel depicting an invasion of California by Okies and Arkies if Sinclair were elected. Townsend declared for Merriam, and Sinclair's support began to crumble. He was resoundingly defeated by Merriam, and six months later EPIC was dead beyond recall, one of the most ephemeral political movements in our history. Utopia died as quickly. Only the Townsendites, based on the nation's elderly, lingered on.

# 1935

Harry Hopkins's euphoria over the smashing Democratic victory in the congressional elections proved premature. Despite the huge Democratic majorities in Congress, there were danger signals for the administration in the early days of the new year. On January 7, 1935, Section 9(c) of the National Industrial Recovery Act was declared unconstitutional by the Supreme Court. It was a taste of what was to come. Roosevelt, nonetheless, had little choice but to push on with the rest of the act, though there was little recovery to show for it and a vast amount of bureaucratic confusion. When Congress convened, he requested its extension for two more years. He recommended fewer codes more strictly enforced.

In addition to the extension of the NIRA, the seventy-fourth Congress found itself faced by a flood of new legislation. The President had promised a pension system for the elderly—social security. He proposed a long-needed bill to supplement the Security and Exchange Commission acts by regulating the public utility holding companies that systematically bilked the public, and he also presented a bill—the Emergency Relief Appropriation Act—that was intended to take the place of the Civil Works Administration, which had expired. The bill established a greatly extended program of "work" rather than "relief."

Direct relief was described as a "narcotic," a subtle destroyer of the human spirit. Public works programs must be expanded to take the place of the "dole." Those who could work must be given work under the aegis of the Federal government, while those incapable of working would have relief administered by the states which were better able to judge what their disabilities were.

The submission of the bill was a clear indication that the Depression still held the country in its grip and that the administration had accepted that fact. Congress proved surprisingly recalcitrant. Ironically, the large Democratic majorities encouraged some Congressmen to kick over the traces. The fight for the passage of the bill establishing the Works Progress Administration turned out to be bitter. Vice-President Garner, who managed the bill in the Senate, confessed that he was "having lots of trouble, that he no sooner had put out a fire in one spot than another one broke out somewhere else. . . . [He] had never had so much trouble since he had been in Congress." Ickes was convinced that the administration itself was in serious trouble. The Senate gave "distinct indications of getting out of hand."

One consequence of the increasingly bitter struggle was a mood of stress and anxiety in the administration. A weary and discouraged Garner confided to Ickes that he had lain awake most of the previous night, worrying about the state of the country and the rapid decline of the New Deal's popularity. Like Ickes, he was convinced that Jim Farley "hasn't the slightest idea of what the state of mind of the country is." Garner wanted the United States "to be a country of a happy, contented, and prosperous people." If Roosevelt was not reelected in 1936, he told Ickes, "a reactionary Republican will succeed him and that then will follow either a fascist government or a communist one. He could actually foresee a revolution in certain circumstances. He spoke with deep feeling and sadness," Ickes added. Ickes felt that Roosevelt had "done little to satisfy the expectations of the people for a liberalized Government . . . [and] practically nothing [had been done] along liberal lines." His diary was full of gloomy forebodings, caused, in large part, by the increasing prominence of Harry Hopkins and the correspondingly shrinking funds for the PWA. But his anxieties were shared by other Cabinet members and Democrats in and out of government. Only the President seemed unaffected. A deputation of Cabinet members, which included Cordell Hull and Homer Cummings, failed to impress on him what they at least viewed as the seriousness of the situation. Colonel House, consulted by Ernest Gruening, formerly editor of the *Nation* and now director of the Division of Islands and Territories, "thought the situation not a healthy one." Finally, even Roosevelt began to show the effects of the general demoralization around him. Ickes thought he had never seen him look so tired. "[He] seemed to lack fighting vigor or the buoyancy that has always characterized him." For the first time Ickes had doubts that the President could "fight his program through" Congress. Ickes himself was exhausted. He wrote in his diary on March 17, 1935, that he was "so tired and nervous that I literally couldn't sign my name any more. My arm had a numb ache. . . . " Roosevelt told Ray Stannard Baker that "people tire of seeing the same name day after day in the important headlines of the papers and the same voice night after night over the radio. . . . I am inclined to think . . . that the time is soon at hand for a new stimulation of united American action."

When the bill to establish the Works Progress Administration finally passed Congress in April, it carried a number of amendments, one by that indefatigable isolationist, William Borah, which stipulated that "no part of the appropriations . . . shall be used for munitions, warships, or military or naval material." Borah's anxieties, whether right or wrong, were justified. The aircraft carriers *Enterprise* and *Yorktown* were, in fact, built by PWA funds; they helped sink four Japanese carriers in the Battle of Midway.

The President asked for and received from Congress $4,880,000,000 to be dispensed largely at his own discretion. The FERA was phased out and replaced by the Work Progress Administration (WPA) under Harry Hopkins. The PWA continued, but now its funds came from the President's allocations, rather than from a direct congressional appropriation. Under the rubric of "emergency relief," almost $5,000,000,000 were allocated as follows: $800,000,000 to construction of highways and grade crossings; $500,000,000 to rural relief, including irrigation and reclamation projects; $450,000,000 to housing; more than $1,000,000,000 to rural electrification; and $300,000,000 to aid to education. The Civilian Conservation Corps was allocated $600,000,000, while $900,000,000 were lent to local agencies for "self-liquidating projects." Reforestation, erosion and flood control received $1,350,000,000. What was particularly galling to Ickes was that Hopkins was given the authority by the President to decide whether or not particular PWA projects were designed to employ a high enough number of workers. Since many PWA projects, which through funding by municipal bond issues could be counted on to satisfy the requirement of promising an "ultimate return to the Federal Treasury of a considerable proportion of the costs," also required a relatively small and highly skilled work force, Hopkins was in a position, in effect, to veto certain of Ickes's projects. WPA projects were to be limited to those costing no more than $25,000. But Hopkins got around this provision by dividing projects in which he was interested into numerous segments, each one estimated to cost $25,000 or less.

While Ickes was carefully developing plans for various projects, Hopkins rushed in to enlist artists, scholars, writers, students—a vast corps of mostly young men and women who had been largely overlooked in concern for the farmer and the blue-collar worker. It has been calculated that from mid-1935 to the beginning of World War II (and the end, correspondingly, of the Great Depression), 8,000,000 individuals were employed by the WPA.

A piece of legislation dear to the President's heart produced the Subsistence Homestead Corporation under the director of the Resettlement Administration. It was one of the most utopian of the New Deal programs, taking impoverished families and resettling them in new communities, building modest houses for them, and providing them with farm tools and equipment as well as with instructors to teach them how to farm. It was estimated that each homestead, consisting of a house and several acres of land, would cost the government between $2,500 and $2,800. The cost was to be amortized over a period of thirty years on government-held mortgages at 3 percent interest.

Rexford Tugwell was placed in charge of the program, thereby strengthening the conviction of critics of the New Deal that the Socialists/Communists were taking over. The Resettlement Administration planned to resettle a half million families, not limited, of course, to farm families. Some 4,000 were moved, a major undertaking in itself, but not enough certainly to effect any major change in the social structure or even the consciousness of the nation. Part of the difference between the intention and the achievement may be charged to Tugwell's deficiencies as an administrator. Under Tugwell, the rural resettlement program became, at least in Harold Ickes's view, "a shambles." It turned out for one thing to be far more expensive than had been anticipated. There were, indeed, problems from the beginning—poor leadership, high costs, demoralized settlers, and, at least at Reedsville, West Virginia, one of the first and most widely publicized projects, a flood of bad publicity. The cost of resettlement turned out to run in excess of $10,000 per family, far above the estimated figure.

Oscar Ameringer complained that it took him months and eventually years to secure approval and then funding for his own resettlement project in Louisiana. He described, with considerable feeling, the labyrinthine bureaucratic maze that he had to find his way through to get a few thousand dollars to sustain his community. At every step he bumped into professors on leave and assorted experts who demanded reports and studies and specifications before anything could be done. When, after long, weary months of compliance with "guidelines" established by theoreticians short on practical knowledge, Congress at last voted funds for the Subsistence Homestead Corporation, the agency was abolished, and its responsibilities were turned over to the Resettlement Administration. The whole laborious process had to be initiated again. There were new guidelines and new reports to be submitted, new bureaucrats to contend with. "When I next entered the new setup territory," Ameringer wrote, "a conclave of Ph.D.'s was reading my book [on the resettlement project]." The judgment was favorable. At last it seemed that action might follow, but delay followed delay, and finally a "political agronomist in the employ of Boss Crump" vetoed the project in favor of one supported by Edward Crump. Ameringer persevered on the land, raising cotton, corn, cows, pigs, chickens, and vegetables.

Rexford Tugwell's principal monument was the greenbelt towns. The idea was borrowed from the British garden city movement founded by Ebenezer Howard at the turn of the century, which resulted in the cities of Letchworth and Welwyn. "Town and country *must be married, and out of this joyous union,*" Howard wrote, "will spring a new hope, a new life, and new civilization." The idea behind the garden city movement was a highly idealistic one: that people of different social and economic classes should be encouraged or persuaded to live together in carefully planned communities that combined the best of urban and rural environments. The dream was of a new, more or less classless, society in which the principle of cooperation would replace competition and class war. "My idea," Tugwell wrote, "is to go just outside centers of population, pick up cheap land, build a whole community and entice people into it. Then go back to the cities and tear down whole slums and make parks of them." Such greenbelt communities were built outside Washington, Cincinnati, and Cleveland. The notion was that they would provide clean air and open spaces for working-class and lower-middle-class families. The expectations were only partially fulfilled. The towns did indeed incorporate a bold new vision. To the residents lucky enough to win a place in one of them, the rows of neat brick apartments, sparkling and modern, seemed a foretaste of paradise. Today they remain as substantial reminders of a utopian dream that was briefly realized, but they are occupied, for the most part, by middle-rank bureaucrats and young professionals.

Meanwhile, there were rumors that the Supreme Court was preparing to declare important New Deal legislation unconstitutional. On Monday, May 6, the Court invalidated the Railroad Retirement Board Act of 1934 on the grounds that it violated due process. But worse was yet to come. Three weeks later the Court struck down the Frazier-Lemke Act, designed to assist debt-ridden farmers by preventing foreclosures and, in the "sick-chicken case," known officially as the *Schechter Case,* ruled large portions of the NIRA in effect unconstitutional. The Schechter brothers had been charged with selling diseased chickens and failing to observe the wage and hour regulations of their NRA code. The Court ruled that since the Schechters were not engaged in interstate commerce, the government lacked the power to set working conditions. To the administration the day of the Court's decision was known as Black Monday. Not only did it invalidate a major part of the principal New Deal legislation, it called into question the entire program for dealing with the Depression and extending the powers of the Federal government through measures intended to ameliorate the hardships endured by working men and women. Dismay ran through the administration. Some New Deal lawyers, Charles Wyzanski among them, believed that much of the NIRA could be preserved since many of the regulated industries were engaged in interstate commerce. The attorney general took the more extreme view that the decisions in effect nullified the NIRA. To him it was "in line with [the justices'] old-fashioned, their archaic, their reactionary decisions . . . in all the other cases we have taken up." The votes of the Four Horsemen, the most conservative justices (McReynolds, Van Devanter, Butler, and Sutherland) were anticipated. The shock came with the concurring votes of those justices of unimpeachable liberal credentials—Brandeis, Cardozo, and Stone. Brandeis had become increasingly hostile to the New Deal. Word reached Tugwell that Brandeis was "declaring war" on the New Deal on the ground that it favored big business at the expense of ordinary Americans. As Brandeis wrote Adolf Berle, "unless he could see some reversal of the big business trend, he was disposed to hold the governmental control legislation unconstitutional from now on."

Claude Bowers met with Roosevelt just after the Supreme Court *Schechter* decision. The President was furious and puzzled at the "almost incredible bitterness" against him on the part of the business community. "The people have not been in control of this country since the Civil War," he said to Bowers. "First the railroads were in the saddle, and then the industrialists, and then the big bankers took control of industry and the railroads. For a long time now the bankers have had the people by the throat." Two years before the bankers had come to him on their knees begging for help; now they were opposing everything he was trying do, and the Court was their instrument. He paused in the midst of his angry tirade and laughed. "It's amusing how little some really intelligent big-moneyed men know of the country and the spirit of the times."

Bowers had heard that Brandeis was anxious to send a message of encouragement to the President. He assured Roosevelt that Brandeis was still "a liberal and his friend."

"Ah, yes, he is. But once he wrote a book against monopoly and the concentration of great economic power, contending that the resulting problems were too big for one man to handle. That's in his mind. He feels the same about the NRA." Bowers noticed that the President's hand shook as he lighted his cigarette. Later he asked Daniel Roper, the secretary of commerce, if he had noticed Roosevelt's "nervousness." Roper replied that it had become evident since the Supreme Court decision.

Frances Perkins's reaction to the *Schechter* case was that "the people of the United States may not be expected to give up the philosophy of fair play and cooperation simply because that philosophy has not yet found adequate legal expression." Anticipating the Court's decision, Perkins had ready the Walsh-Healy, or Public Contract, Act. This authorized the government to set standards for wages, hours, and conditions of labor in all its contracts with industry. It covered contracts for goods and services worth more than $10,000. It provided specifically for an eight-hour day and a forty-hour week, no child or convict labor, safety standards, and a minimum wage to be set by the secretary of labor in accordance with prevailing wages in a particular region and industry.

Perkins, watching the President's face in a Cabinet meeting during discussion of the Court's decision on *Schechter*, thought that he was secretly relieved at being rid of an administrative Frankenstein that had grown so large and complex that it threatened to collapse of its own weight. That certainly was Walter Lippmann's view. He wrote to Hamilton Fish Armstrong: "Politically the destruction of the NRA was Roosevelt's greatest stroke of luck since 1933"; it saved him the "embarrassment of trying to enforce codes that were breaking down of their own inherent foolishness." William Douglas wrote: "Any Supreme Court that ever sat would have so ruled, because lawmaking under the Constitution is a matter for Congress, not for private parties."

When the NRA went down, it was a devastating blow to Rexford Tugwell, who had been one of its major architects and strongest advocates in the inner circle. Yet, in his tireless "search" for Roosevelt, Tugwell followed the statement of his acute disappointment over the fate of the NRA with the comment that Roosevelt "saw the nation, as none of the others did; he saw part working with part, all functioning together [what he had called in one of his speeches a "concert of interests"]: the men in the cities, the men on the farms, the men at sea, all working for each other as they worked for their families; and he the conjunctural center. He could not make the nation over. He could not make it other than it was. He could only make it more consciously what it had been trying to become." But there are paradoxes even within Tugwell's moving sentences. The President could and did "make the nation over," but he was always acutely conscious of how slow and laborious a task that was, that it was essentially an educational undertaking, the rooting up of old and obsolete ideas, the planting of new ones.

In the context of American politics, the NRA was as radical as one could have wished, though to many liberals and radicals it was radical toward, or in the direction of, capitalism. It envisioned a kind of corporate or state capitalism without, to be sure, the repressive features of Mussolini's Fascist state. It was clearly the work of the "holistic" theorists. What was perhaps most notable about it was that it appealed to Roosevelt's "visionary idealism" and may thus be fairly taken as an indication of how venturesome he was in the realm of novel social and political ideas. The surprising thing is not that the NRA failed but that, Alice in Wonderland prospect that it was, it was even tried.

What historians have chosen to call the Second New Deal dealt directly with social issues that had been the concern of Progressives since the beginning of the century (and of the Populists before them): unemployment insurance, old-age pensions, the prohibition of child labor, and the rights of labor. "As time passed and the crisis lightened,"

Tugwell wrote, "progressives of the older, more orthodox persuasion became the trusted helpers. These were the Second New Dealers. By the end of 1934 the First New Dealers had mostly departed and with them the conception of an organic economy." The reversion, in Tugwell's view, to the "old individualism" was a step backward into the ethics of the nineteenth century.

In fact, the First New Dealers, with their notion of a planned economy, were only briefly in the ascendancy. Aside from the NRA, which was an odd bag of somewhat contradictory elements, President Roosevelt from the first moment of his administration had in mind a series of measures, most of which he had already tried out in New York State and which were essentially his own.

Raymond Moley, on the other hand, perceived Roosevelt as falling increasingly under the spell of his radical (or old Progressive) advisers. In his magazine *Today* Moley continued to insist that the "public is developing a terrific thirst for a long, cool swig of political quiescence. The danger to liberalism at such a moment is that a reactionary party will offer it a long, cool, but narcotic swig of 'normalcy.' " The Democrats "must recognize that every social crusade, from Cromwell to Wilson, has sooner or later come face to face with the stubborn refusal of human nature to rise too high or stay high too long." It was the same argument Moley had used in talking with Roosevelt the past winter, and it became the principal theme of the "conservative liberals."

Walter Lippmann took the Moley line. He was for only a little reform, and he was alarmed by what was already being called the Second New Deal, the flood of reform legislation passed in the summer of 1935. "[A]n overpowering desire for the improvement of society leads to policies that put too great a strain on institutions," he wrote. "The people gave Mr. Roosevelt a sword to lead them in a particular battle," he wrote in another editorial. "That battle is over, and that sword should now be returned to its scabbard." From Lippmann's point of view, the crisis was past, the country was on the road to recovery, and it was no time to start tinkering with the machinery of capitalism.

While the Moleys and the Lippmanns exhorted the President to "go slow," dozens of radical panaceas flourished around the country, from Huey Long's "Every Man a King" to Father Coughlin's Fascist fantasies, Dr. Townsend's plan, and Upton Sinclair's EPIC. Harold Ickes warned the President, with some reason, that the people in general were far more radical than the government.

The most important bill passed by the Seventy-fourth Congress was the Wagner, or National Labor Relations, Act. It was of primary importance since the Supreme Court's striking down of the NIRA had thrown a cloud of uncertainty over Section 7(a), which had already served to encourage labor organization. Robert Wagner was the father and untiring promoter of his bill, one of the most important in the nation's history. It may be taken as the official peace treaty in the long war between capital and labor. Capital did not, to be sure, sit down with labor and "sign" in a spirit of reconciliation. The treaty was imposed on a demoralized enemy or at least an enemy rendered too weak by its own failures and defeats to resist it. But imposed or not, it marked the beginning of the end of the second longest and most desperate conflict in the nation's history, the first being the abolition of slavery. Many skirmishes and some battles remained to be fought, and a basic conflict of interest was perhaps built into the relationship as long as business enterprise should be more or less free, but the war was for all practical purposes over.

Wagner's bill, besides providing those protections for labor already spelled out in Section 7(a) of the NIRA, stipulated that a three-member National Labor Relations Board be appointed to hear complaints of workers against their employers, especially in regard to antiunion measures and refusal to bargain with a union.

Roosevelt and Perkins did not initially support the bill. They would have preferred to have it administered by the Department of Labor rather than by an independent board, but Wagner pushed their objections aside. The bill passed the Senate, and when it seemed likely to pass the House, FDR announced his support. It might thus be said that what was in many ways the most important piece of legislation passed in the New Deal era was not the work of the administration and had only belated support from the President and his secretary of labor. To put the matter thus would be to misstate it seriously. Section 7(a) of the NIRA had already staked out the administration's policy of support for the principle of unionization. Its chief weakness was that, depending on the goodwill of the business community, it had provided no effective machinery for enforcement (except withdrawing the Blue Eagle). But the essential fact was that the New Deal created the climate of political opinion in which a measure like the Wagner Act could be passed, and Roosevelt's rhetoric contributed substantially to its passage. Raymond Moley spoke of the Wagner bill's "palpable one-sidedness," but the fact was it was a bill intended to redress the "palpable one-sidedness" of laws and judicial interpretations so prejudicial to labor.

Crucial to the success of the act was Section 8, which specifically defined unfair labor practices. Armed with Section 8, Senator La Follette's subcommittee on civil rights was able to act as a watchdog over efforts by industry to stifle union activity.

In June, 1935, a somewhat awed Lippmann wrote to Hamilton Fish Armstrong that Roosevelt was "now in the incredibly strong position where in about a month he will have completed the most comprehensive program of reform ever achieved in this country in any administration, and at the same time he is well set for a very substantial business recovery. If he wants to play the cards that are now in his hand, I believe that he can come to the election next autumn with reform and recovery both achieved, with the currency stabilization well in hand."

Roosevelt undertook during the first session of the Seventy-fourth Congress to make good his promise to provide social security legislation. "You want to make it simple—very simple, so simple that everyone will understand it," he told Perkins. "And what's more, there is no reason why everybody in the United States should not be covered. I see no reason why every child, from the day he is born, shouldn't be a member of the social security system. . . . This system ought to be operated through the post offices. Just simple and natural—nothing elaborate or alarming about it. . . . And there is no reason why just industrial workers should get the benefit of this. Everybody ought to be in on it—the farmer and his wife and family. . . . I don't see why not. Cradle to the grave—from the cradle to the grave they ought to be in a social insurance system."

Perkins replied that "the political climate was not right for such a universal approach." Social security was seen as simply a supplement to personal savings and private pension plans. Hopes for a comprehensive plan of health insurance, such as that which had been adopted by Britain, Germany, and Sweden, was considered much too radical and was strongly resisted by the American Medical Association and other powerful opponents. Roosevelt would have to settle for much less. Still, the bill was a milestone of the New Deal. The Social Security Act contained ten provisions. Eight were direct relief—for the blind and for dependent children, for grants-in-aid to the states and to the U.S. Public Health Service. The old-age insurance was the only entirely Federal program; the other nine required cooperation between the states and the Federal Government. The argument used was that Americans were so mobile that to attempt to administer the old-age

insurance on the basis of the state-Federal partnership would be hopelessly complicated; an eligible recipient could have lived in a dozen
states by the time he or she reached retirement age.

Agricultural and domestic workers were dropped from the plan,
as were workers in educational, religious, and charitable organizations.
The legislation applied to employers who hired ten or more workers
for at least twenty weeks of the year (this as a consequence of pressure
from canneries, which were in effect exempted). Congressmen were
jealous of the degree of Federal control; Fred Vinson of Kentucky
declared, "No damn social workers are going to come into my State
and tell our people whom they shall hire." Passed on August 14, 1935,
the bill covered only about half the work force. Inadequate as the
legislation was in terms of Roosevelt's visions, he was pleased with it;
it was at least a beginning.

Replying in part to the criticism of Brandeis and other liberals
that he had been too easy on the rich, Roosevelt proposed a tax bill
designed to redress the income balance. It included an inheritance and
gift tax and increased individual and corporate income taxes. "Our
revenue laws have operated in many ways to the unfair advantage of
the few," the President wrote in the message acompanying the bill,
"and they have done little to prevent an unjust accumulation of wealth
and economic power."

The rationale for the tax reform measure, soon known publicly
as soak-the-rich taxes, was that social unrest and a deepening sense of
unfairness called for a "wider distribution of wealth." The bill provided
for an increase in personal income taxes for those making over $50,000
a year (the equivalent of at least four times that sum in 1986 dollars),
a graduated corporate income tax, and the taxation of "unwieldy and
unnecessary corporate surpluses." A constitutional amendment taxing
interest on national, state, and municipal bonds was also proposed.
Outlining his tax plan to Harold Ickes, the President looked up, smiled,
and said, "That is for Hearst." Hearst was not slow to respond. He
ordered his papers to attack the bill as the "Soak the Successful Act."
Far from redistributing the wealth, as Roosevelt's corporate enemies
charged, the bill as written would have brought in little more than
$250,000,000. In its final, watered-down version, it brought in consid-
erably less than that.

When Charles M. Schwab, the chairman of the board of Bethlehem Steel, complained to Roosevelt that his responsibilities were to the
company's stockholders, Roosevelt asked him if that was why he paid

Eugene Grace, the president of Bethlehem Steel, $1,000,000 a year in salary. As Schwab departed, Roosevelt sent his warm regards to Grace and instructed Schwab to inform him he would never again be allowed to make $1,000,000 a year. The President wrote to Colonel House in reference to the tax bill: "The real truth of the matter is, as you and I know, that a financial element in the larger centers has owned the government ever since the days of Andrew Jackson—and I am not wholly excepting the Administration of W.W. [Woodrow Wilson]. The country is going through a repetition of Jackson's fight with the Bank of the United States—only on a far bigger and broader basis."

The fight over the holding company bill was one of the bitterest of Roosevelt's presidential years. Lobbyists were everywhere, and no practice was considered too devious to use in the efforts of the holding utility companies to protect their interests. "You talk about a labor lobby," an angry Roosevelt exclaimed. "It is a child compared to this utility lobby. You talk about a Legion lobby. Well it is an infant in arms compared to this utility lobby."

There were more than 140 holding companies owning or controlling some 1500 subsidiaries. Bond & Share held properties, for example, in thirty-two states; Associated Gas, in twenty-five. The holding companies exacted all kinds of special charges and fees from the companies that sold power to individuals and corporations. In the words of William Douglas, "Through exaggerated fees, the [holding] company saddled the operating companies with enormous charges, which . . . in turn were paid by the consumers of gas and electricity." In Douglas's opinion, it was only through the combined efforts of Burton Wheeler, the Senator from Montana, Hugo Black, then in the Senate, and Sam Rayburn in the House that the Public Utility Holding Company Act of 1935 was pushed through Congress "by a squeak," in the face of one of the most massive lobbying campaigns ever mounted by an industrial interest. "Amiable, though rigorous, treatment was given the opposition," in Douglas's words. The aim was not destruction but control. John Foster Dulles became the lawyer for the holding companies. In the aftermath of the passage of the act Dulles called together the heads of the major holding companies and argued that the act was unconstitutional and that the Supreme Court would rule it to be so. Meanwhile, he advised the companies to comply.

The passage of the act helped appease Brandeis. "F.D. gives evidence of appreciation of the 'irrepressible conflict with bigness'—and of growing firmness," he wrote a friend.

The Banking Act was almost as important in its effects. Its author was a maverick Utah financier and Mormon elder, Marriner S. Eccles. Eccles shared the general suspicion of Wall Street and Eastern financiers that was characteristic of the West. Although he had apparently not read John Maynard Keynes, he had concluded that it was simply common sense to accept large Federal deficits in periods of acute depression under the assumption that they would be reduced in good times. It was Eccles's intention to insulate the country's financial system from the bankers by giving the power to set discount rates and reserve requirements to the Federal Reserve.

Roosevelt, ever solicitous for the farmer, pressed for the establishment of the Rural Electrification Administration to provide electricity for farmers and their wives. Other pieces of legislation were designed to repair the damage done by the Supreme Court's striking down of the NIRA.

The President's only real setback came on the issue of the World Court, a bone of contention since 1926. One of the last hopes of the internationalists, those Americans who had been the enthusiastic supporters of the League of Nations and for whom its defeat had been one of the darkest moments of their lives, focused on U.S. membership in the World Court. Despite the country's generally isolationist mood, Roosevelt decided to stake his own prestige on the issue. It was doubtless for him an act of respect and propitiation to the Wilsonian dream of an international order. Both the President and his wife pressed for United States participation in the court. Eleanor Roosevelt made the cause of the court her own. She spoke and wrote in its behalf and did not hesitate to exercise her considerable powers of persuasion to muster support for American involvement. Her activities irritated the isolationist Ickes, who noted in his diary that Senators opposed to American participation had been flooded with telegrams, a great many of which "were bitter in their criticism of Mrs. Roosevelt for mixing up in the fight. . . . It does seem to me," Ickes added, "that she is not doing the President any good. She is becoming all too active in public affairs. . . . After all, the people did not elect her President, and I don't think the country likes the thought of the wife of the President engaging prominently in public affairs to the extent that she does."

The opposition to the Court was led by Huey Long, but he had willing allies in Senators Johnson and Borah. The treaty fell seven votes short of the necessary two-thirds required for ratification. Ickes was confident that the "sentiment of the country is overwhelmingly opposed to going into the League Court." In Jim Farley's mind, it was one of the administration's most serious mistakes. In Garner's opinion, a popular vote would show the American people opposed to the court by a margin of two to one. Ickes credited Hiram Johnson with defeating the treaty. When he called him up to congratulate him, Johnson was, in Ickes's words, "happy as a boy." It seemed evident to Ickes that the failure of the Senate to ratify the World Court treaty had "cut pretty deeply." The President's laughter seemed forced, and untypically, he revealed "a little . . . willingness to hurt those who brought about his defeat."

Despite a considerable degree of balkiness, Congress gave the President most of what he asked for: a nine and a half months' extension of what was left in the NIRA; the beginnings of a social security program; a somewhat less than $500,000,000 work relief, or WPA, program; important modifications of the Federal Reserve Act; the Wagner National Labor Relations Act; legislation regulating bus, railroad, and air transportation; and a revised Railroad Pensions Act.

"This administration," the President wrote Roy Howard, "came into power pledged to a very considerable legislative program. This basic program, however, has now reached substantial completion and 'the breathing spell' of which you speak is here—very decidedly so." If there was what could be described as a "breathing spell," it did not allay the rancor of the President's more vociferous opponents. Raymond Moley was appalled by the "continuation of intemperate attacks" upon the President, especially the "practice of passing around stories about the President or his family"; Moley could not recall "a more vicious crop of them than that spring produced."

In November, 1935, at a meeting of the American Bankers Association in New Orleans, Roosevelt was unmercifully attacked by a series of speakers. One of the vice-presidents of the association urged his fellows to refuse to accept or handle government bonds. "He talked," Harold Ickes noted, "like the ruler of an independent kingdom." When William O. Douglas addressed the Chicago Bond Club, a furious investment banker followed him from the room, shouting, "Why are you trying to destroy America?," and when Jane Addams and Frances Perkins received honorary degrees from the University of California at Berkeley (Herbert Hoover received one at the same time), a man in the receiving line glared at Perkins and declared, "I will *not* shake hands with a communist," referring to Perkins's support for unions and collective bargaining.

Henry Luce, the son of missionaries to China and a graduate of Yale, had recently started a newsmagazine called *Time*, that was, in Harold Ickes's words, "especially strong in . . . opposition to the President. [Luce] thinks that Roosevelt has offended and hampered business. . . . Roosevelt, according to these very rich people, is penalizing business and tearing it down because he has increased the income taxes in the higher brackets and because he is taxing surpluses in corporation treasuries."

At a dinner where the younger Hearst was present along with a number of other prominent business figures, Ickes challenged the company to explain how Roosevelt had hurt business. "I took two or three occasions . . . " Ickes wrote, "to show how I felt about men being called communists who were simply trying to improve the social order and give the underdog a chance." He insisted that the President "really had saved capitalism. However," he added, "there is no use trying to talk to men of that type. They do not know what has happened in the world, they haven't sense enough to appraise the social forces of this generation, and they cannot see ahead into the future any further than the end of their noses."

George Gallup began his famous poll in October, 1935, and the first question he asked was if the people of the country thought "expenditures by the Government for relief and recovery" were "too little, too great, or just about right?" Of the respondents, 9 percent said "too little," 60 percent said "too great," and 31 percent said "about right." The second question was "Did you vote for Franklin Roosevelt in 1932? Would you vote for him today?" The results were encouraging to the Republicans. Of those who had voted for Roosevelt in 1932, substantially fewer indicated that they would vote for him again or, more precisely "today." The loss varied from 13 percent in New England (a drop from 51 to 38 percent) to a drop from 55 to 51 percent in the East-Central region. Roosevelt lost 6 percent in the South (from 76 to 70 percent), still by far the highest percentage of any major region of the country. Only in the Rocky Mountain states was there an increase— from 60 percent in 1932 to 65 percent three years later. In a poll taken a month later which asked simply, "Would you vote for President Roosevelt today?" 53 percent said yes, 47 percent no, a far more comfortable margin. At the same time there were only six firm Republican states and eight "borderline," as opposed to twenty-seven "definitely Democratic" states and six "borderline" Democratic. Mississippi, 88 percent Democratic, was followed by South Carolina with 85 percent. The South, the Rocky Mountain states, and the North-Central States—the Dakotas, Nebraska, Wisconsin—were solidly Democratic.

Despite substantial backing for the New Deal, when voters were asked by George Gallup if they considered themselves conservatives or liberals, 53 percent chose the conservative label. Only in the South, Mountain states and Pacific states was there a small margin in favor of "liberal," but young people (twenty-one to twenty-four) considered themselves liberal by a margin of 66 to 34 percent.

The fact that Roosevelt's popularity sank to a new low in September, 1935, suggests that he had expended his political capital to get his social programs through Congress. It was clear that in the process he had stepped on a number of toes and outraged quite different factions around the country. The effects of Section 7(a) and, following its invalidation, the Wagner Act, were beginning to be felt in a wave of strikes that swept the country.


One of the most notable events of the year was a dinner at the Willard Hotel in Washington in honor of Jane Addams on her seventy-fifth birthday. It was also the twentieth anniversary of the founding of the Women's International League for Peace and Freedom. It was, the manager of the Willard told Harold Ickes, the biggest dinner ever given at the hotel; 500 people had been turned away. Eleanor Roosevelt was the principal speaker, followed by Harold Ickes. Then came Gerard Swope, president of General Electric; Oswald Garrison Villard; Sidney Hillman, head of the Amalgamated Clothing Workers of America; and Alice Hamilton, one of Addams's earliest recruits and more recently the first (and rather badly treated) female member of the Harvard Medical School faculty. Three weeks later, on May 27, Jane Addams died. Her funeral was held at Hull House, and the streets around that famous institution were filled to overflowing with crowds that came to pay their respects to one of the most remarkable individuals in the nation's history. Halsted Street was then predominantly Greek, and shops of Greek merchants and the Greek restaurants displayed strips of purple cloth in her honor. The service was a simple one, with several of Addams's favorite musical pieces and a talk by the dean of the University of Chicago. "All of us felt the occasion very deeply," Harold Ickes noted in his diary. "She was a great spirit, gentle and simple, and yet able and with rare vision. I have never known anyone like her, nor shall I ever. Hers is really an irreparable loss, not only to Chicago and the United States but to civilization."

When Congress adjourned after a session that was second only to the special session in the spring of 1933 in terms of significant legislation passed, the President reversed his vacation procession. He traveled by train to Los Angeles and there boarded the *USS Houston* of the Pacific Fleet. With him were Hopkins and Ickes and his personal staff—his military and naval aides, his physician, Ross McIntire, and his personal secretary, Colonel Edwin [Pa] Watson. The presidential party visited Lower California (Baja California), the Cerros and Cocos Islands, and Magdalena Bay. Roosevelt's obvious delight in everything about him was infectious. He was a tireless cruise director, involving everyone in his games. Even Hopkins tried his hand at fishing. The President hooked a 134-pound sailfish and played it for more than two hours, in the course of which Hopkins threw up from the motion of the launch. Hopkins edited an issue of the ship's paper *The Blue Bonnet* and wrote: "The feud between Hopkins and Ickes was given a decent burial today. With flags at half mast—the bands muted—Pa freshly shaved—the Officers half dressed—the President officiated at the solemn ceremony which we trust will take these two babes off the front page for all time. . . . Ickes wore his faded grays, Mona Lisa smile, and carried his stamp collection." The "burial" was short-lived. Back on dry land Hopkins and Ickes were soon fighting over who had the right to distribute the spoils, but the "burial" or truce took much of the bitterness out of their quarrels, and from then on they professed to "like" each other whatever the issues between them.

Reviewing the past session of Congress in a reflective mood, the President said to Ickes "that we were doing in this country some of the things that were being done in Russia and even some of the things that were being done under Hitler in Germany. But we are doing them in an orderly way." After Ickes's assurance that no one could lead the country as he was doing, the President responded "that . . . he had been thinking along these lines for a good many years, but . . . he himself had not anticipated the problems that have arisen. . . ."

When Huey Long was assassinated on September 8 by a young doctor, the Democrats breathed a sigh of relief. Gerald L. K. Smith delivered the oration over Long's grave, at what he called "the largest public funeral in American history." An estimated 250,000 people crowded into the cemetery, and cars were backed up for eight miles waiting to cross on the Mississippi River ferries. The floral contributions covered three acres.

Long was by no means the semiliterate redneck, or peckerwood, that he often presented himself as to his rural constituents. As though to dispel the rumor, he opened his autobiography *Every Man a King* with references to Benvenuto Cellini, the famous Florentine sculptor and autobiographer, and Jules Mazarin, the great seventeenth-century French cardinal. According to the story told by Alexandre Dumas and repeated by Long, Mazarin, dying at the age of fifty-two, was comforted by his physician, who assured him that every year of Mazarin's contention with the Fronde, a party of rebellious nobles during the regency of Louis XIV, was the equivalent of four normal years. Since the struggles with the Fronde had lasted some ten years, Mazarin should add forty years to his fifty-two, making a very respectable old age. That Long should open his own biography with the Mazarin story was striking. Two years after the book's publication in 1933 Long was dead by an assassin's bullet. It could well be said of him that in his ten years as a rising politician in Louisiana, as governor of that state, and as U.S. Senator, he might well, like Mazarin, have been credited with four years for every one.

History has not dealt kindly with Huey Long. The general image of him is that of a ruthless and dangerous demagogue who trampled all those who opposed him. If toward the end he did give evidence of a kind of growing megalomania, it is clear enough that he accomplished a great deal in the way of good in his home state, that he humbled, if he did not break, the power of Standard Oil and the "interests" in Louisiana, and that he touched, in his modern populism, one of the deepest chords in our history: the fight of the poor and exploited against their exploiters. He was, obviously, very far from being a Socialist or a Communist or even particularly radical, though it is a measure of the basic conservatism of the nation that he appeared so. Southern blacks loved him in part because he scrupulously refused "nigger baiting" and insisted that poor blacks and whites alike must have the advantages of a decent education and access to adequate health facilities. He refused to engage in racist politics of any kind, and when a reporter asked him if he was not an advocate of a form of American fascism, a native Hitler, he replied hotly, "Don't liken me to that sonofabitch. Anybody that lets his public politics be mixed up with religious prejudice is a plain Goddamned fool." On another occasion when the issue came up again, he said, "I don't know much about Hitler. Except this last thing, about the Jews. There never has been a country that put it[s] heel down on the Jews that ever lived afterwards."

H. G. Wells, who visited the United States in 1935 and heard Long speak in the Senate, called him "a Winston Churchill who had never been to Harrow," but Wells's common-law wife, Rebecca West, was not so favorably impressed. She thought him "the most formidable kind of brer fox," a man with a dangerous sense of destiny and an animal vitality. The newspaper correspondent Paul Anderson concurred. There was "a charged atmosphere which envelops, the sense of danger that pervades the air around him. . . . If events fail to occur naturally, he produces them."

No less a figure than the chief justice of the Supreme Court, William Howard Taft, declared, "Huey P. Long is the most brilliant, competent and intelligent attorney to have appeared before me during my term as the Chief Justice of the Supreme Court."

In the words of W. J. Cash, Long "was full of the swaggering, hell-for-leather blather that the South demanded of its heroes and champions; and in addition he had a kind of quizzical, broad, clowning humor, and a capacity for taking on the common touch, that had characteristically been the stock-in-trade . . . of the more successful demagogues . . . he was the first Southern demagogue to leave aside nigger-baiting and address himself mainly to the irritations bred in the common white by his economic and social status."

It seems safe to say that Long so polarized emotions that he left the air charged behind him. Love and hate created a dangerous static electricity, as dangerous for him perhaps as for the country. The classic tactics of Southern politics, ratified by generations of in-house use, were not readily transferable to the larger stage of national politics. There they were so unfamiliar as to appear both exotic and alarming.

From his youth Long committed himself to the cause of the poor and underprivileged. His heroes were exemplary; his practical achievements, great; his pronouncements, in a great tradition of popular oratory. He was beloved by his "people." So why do we hesitate to claim him unambiguously as an authentic American hero? Perhaps in part because of the way he looked and dressed, because of his clownish face and constant buffoonery. Perhaps because he was Southern and the agencies of judgment were, in the main, Northern. Finally, because we sense in him, as Rebecca West did, a growing megalomania, more than a hint of the fearful lust of idealism that has so often shown itself capable of producing dictators.

On the international scene the year 1935 started off badly when Hitler denounced the clauses in the Versailles Treaty which forbade Germany to rearm and announced that the Germany Army would be increased to thirty-six divisions. The French response was a five-year treaty of alliance with Soviet Russia, each party agreeing to come to the aid of the other in the event of an attack; it was clearly aimed against Germany.

When Josephine Herbst visited Germany for the second time in the summer of 1935, she sensed a strange disquiet that seemed to lie just below the surface: "The newspapers, the radio and the newsreel repeat that all is quiet in Germany, everything is in order. To the eye the streets are clean, window boxes are choked with flowers, children hike in the country in droves, singing songs." Yet in the undercurrents "tiny leaflets inform the uninformed. . . . Boys bicycle in the country roads. Who sees a concentration camp? Yet silence is over the very country-side, in little inns where one is sharply scrutinized, in trains, along streets." Everyone was wary; everyone was looking over his or her shoulder. The magazines were full of pictures and stories of "our animal friends, the birds and the bees, the pictures of Hitler smilingly accepting a nosegay from a little girl." The papers were full of accounts of rainstorms and other natural phenomena, but nothing of politics. Jokes circulated cautiously about Hitler. A customer says to a barber, "My hair lies too flat. How can I make it stick up more?" The barber replies, "Look out the window at what is going on in Germany and your hair will stand on end for the rest of your life."

At the end of the year Roosevelt received a long, gloomy letter from Ambassador William Dodd in Berlin. To Dodd Europe was on the edge of a precipice. He could see no possibility of restraining Hitler. Intelligence sources informed the President that there was evidence of "an understanding between Germany and Japan" which might result in "a squeeze play against Russia." Great Britain, alarmed at the danger such an alliance might pose to its Far Eastern colonies, was thought to be seeking an "understanding" with Hitler as well as with Japan.

The event that paved the way for the abandonment by Stalin of the third period dogma was the French-Russian pact of "mutual assistance," which made them allies if either nation was attacked by a

"European state," specifically, of course, Germany. A few months after announcement of the pact the Seventh Congress of the Comintern, meeting in Kharkov, produced the official popular front doctrine calling on the party members to cooperate with all liberal and left-wing factions to oppose fascism. Entitled "The Offensive of Fascism and the Tasks of the Communist International in the Fight for the Unity of the Working Class Against Fascism," the new line was laid down by Georgi Dimitrov, the Bulgarian Communist who had been accused by Hitler of setting fire to the Reichstag and had narrowly escaped with his life. Dimitrov called for a "people's anti-fascist front." Even if farmers and lower-middle-class elements were politically unsophisticated and lacking in class consciousness, they "must be taken as they are and not as we should like to have them." Dimitrov added: "We are even prepared to forgo the creation of communist groups in the trade unions if that is necessary in the interests of trade union unity." The party should work with "all democratic elements" in the struggle for "partial economic and political demands."

The new line was greeted ecstatically. A report of the congress read, "The entire hall rises and gives Comrade Dimitrov a rousing ovation. Cheers coming from the delegates are heard on all sides and in various languages. . . . The strains of 'The International' sung in every language fill the air. A new storm of applause sweeps the hall." Needless to say, such exercises were more than therapeutic. They touched chords of the longing for human unity that lie at the deepest level of our consciousness. On his return from the Kharkov conference, Mike Gold, the commissar for letters in the United States, announced: "Every door must be opened wide to fellow travelers. We need them. We must not fear they will corrupt us with their bourgeois ideas." Hal Draper, an active leftist of the time, wrote, "I can myself testify to the staggering impact of the Franco-Soviet pact and communiqué on the CP's ranks." Parallel organizations were "out"; "boring from within" was "in"—that is to say, working with and through established liberal/radical organizations and parties was approved. The American party, always opposed to third period doctrines (the Trotskyites had broken off in part on the issue), welcomed the new line with enthusiasm. It was much more congenial to the American temper, which was only mildly conspiratorial. American Communists had found the requirements of the third period desperately hard and profoundly alienating. With the changed political atmosphere in the United States as a consequence of the New Deal, it did not seem beyond imagining that the Communists might in time take over the New Deal. What it meant for the New Deal, on the other hand, for the labor movement, and for liberal and radical causes in general was that thousands of seasoned, dedicated, and, for the most part, intelligent men and women were available to be deployed in every good cause, ready to endure any hardship, even to the hazard of their lives.

One immediate consequence of the new popular front doctrine was the American League Against War and Fascism, dedicated to educating the public to the dangers to world peace posed by the fascism of Germany and Italy. Its chairman was usually a Protestant minister of radical inclinations. Roger Baldwin was an important member of its board, along with James Waterman Wise, the son of the respected Rabbi Stephen Wise. Dorothy McConnell, daughter of the Methodist bishop, was another prominent member, as was Margaret Forsythe of the International YWCA. Earl Browder was the only Communist member of the board until he was joined by Clarence Hathaway. Harry Ward, a member of the faculty of the Union Theological Seminary, was chairman in 1935, and Meta Berger, the widow of Victor Berger, the Milwaukee Socialist, became vice-chairman. Several of Roosevelt's Cabinet members were also active in the league, which at the height of its influence claimed "an affiliated membership of seven million."

At the same time that the Comintern announced the new popular front policy it called for continuing efforts on the part of the faithful to destroy capitalism. Ambassador Bullitt made an angry protest to Litvinov, who replied blandly that neither he nor Stalin had any control over the actions of the Comintern—whereas it was transparently the case that the Soviets dictated every action of that body. Bullitt, in his anger and disillusionment with Soviet actions, leaned for a time toward détente with Germany. In April, 1936, he wrote to Secretary of State Cordell Hull: "We should neither expect too much or despair of getting anything at all. We should take what we can get when the atmosphere is favorable and do our best to hold on to it when the wind blows the other way. We should remain unimpressed in the face of expansive professions of friendliness and unperturbed in the face of slights and underhand opposition. We should make the weight of our influence felt steadily over a long period of time in the directions which suit our interests. We should never threaten. We should act and allow the Bolsheviks to draw their own conclusions as to the causes of our acts.

"Above all, we should guard the reputation of Americans for business-like efficiency, sincerity and straightforwardness. We should never send a spy to the Soviet Union. There is no weapon at once so disarming and effective in relations with the Communists as sheer honesty. They know very little about it."

Besides being excellent on relations with the Russians (or any other foreign power), Bullitt's advice marked the high tide of his own disillusionment and the abandonment of his hopes for a genuine rapprochement with the Russians marked by friendliness and trust.

In Russia the purges, the public trials which were to amaze and horrify world opinion, began in the aftermath of the murder of Sergei Mironovich Kirov, a member of the Politburo in charge of the Leningrad area. It was the first time since the revolution that a leading Bolshevik had been assassinated. In the words of Victor Reuther, "Kirov was the only leader with the qualities and stature to present a serious challenge to Stalin. He was a remarkable and unpretentious man who had established rapport with both intellectuals and workers." In the wake of his assassination a reign of terror began in Russia. Anything less than complete loyalty to Stalin could mean exile to Siberia or even death. "The lynching urge was encouraged in every factory in Russia," Victor Reuther wrote. "Anyone in the least suspect was placed on trial for conspiracy and some workers were removed without any trial at all. Under the circumstances, political talk was taboo in the tool room. . . ."

In September, 1935 Mussolini's forces invaded Ethiopia, one of the few African nations not already under the control of some European nation. It was an unabashed act of aggression against a small, weak country, and fifty-one nations in the League of Nations voted to impose on Italy sanctions covering arms, credit, and raw materials of various kinds, oil excepted. Imports from Italy were also prohibited to the member nations. For a moment it seemed that the League might at last take resolute action against an aggressor nation, but there were soon numerous evasions. Anxious to use Mussolini as a counter to Hitler, Britain shipped oil to Il Duce for his trucks and tanks and allowed him to use the Suez Canal for his troopships. The French were equally irresolute. The fear of a general war undermined the resolution of the League. Italy continued its "war" against the courageous but ill-equipped Ethiopian Army.

In the United States the invasion of Ethiopia brought a rash of outbreaks between blacks and Italians. In spite of the fact that Mayor Fiorello La Guardia of New York City assigned some 1,200 police to patrol Italian neighborhoods, angry blacks smashed the windows of Italian stores. Adam Clayton Powell's Abyssinian Baptist Church joined with other black congregations to protest the invasion. Efforts were made to organize a regiment of black Americans to fight for Ethiopia. The State Department discouraged the move by threatening to revoke the citizenship of those who volunteered, but Colonel Hubert Julian, a follower of Marcus Garvey known as the Black Eagle of Harlem, went to Ethiopia anyway. He offered his services as a flier to Emperor Haile Selassie, but the Ethiopian Air Force never got off the ground. As it turned out, Ethiopians, and Haile Selassie in particular, were hostile to American blacks.

Wallace Stevens, one of America's foremost poets, delcared, "I am pro-Mussolini personally." In his opinion, the Italians had "as much right to take Ethiopia from the coons as the coons had to take it from the boa-constrictors."

On Armistice Day in 1935 Roosevelt noted that Americans who had lived through the World War knew that "the elation and prosperity which may come from a new war must lead—for those who survive it—to economic and social collapse more sweeping than anything we have experienced in the past." In a letter to Ambassador Dodd, Roosevelt wrote, "I do not know that the United States can save civilization but at least by our example we can make people think and give them the opportunity of saving themselves. The trouble is that the people of Germany, Italy and Japan are not given the privilege of thinking."

# 28

# The Election of 1936

On January 3, 1936, Roosevelt opened his drive for reelection with an address to a joint session of Congress, the first since Wilson's call for war against Germany in April, 1917. In his first term Roosevelt had devoted much time and thought to winning the support of the country's business interests. Indeed, he had risked the displeasure and disenchantment of such liberal supporters as Louis Brandeis and Rexford Tugwell by, in their view, currying favor with business rather than taking for granted their opposition and getting on with the formidable task of lifting the country out of the Depression. Now Roosevelt challenged his critics. He was careful to distinguish between the "good" capitalists and the "bad" capitalists, but his message was unmistakable. He had given business its chance with the NRA and the Reconstruction Finance Corporation. It had resisted his blandishments and his pleas. Instead of accepting his invitation to join in the work of reconstruction, it had stubbornly opposed its will to his and denounced every measure designed to help the desperate and the hungry as socialistic or as an effort to "Sovietize" the United States. Now it must be clearly identified as the enemy, as "discredited special interests." Roosevelt declared: "We have invited battle, we have earned the hatred of entrenched greed."

Roosevelt also took note of the international situation—the aggressions of Japan and Germany: "A point had been reached where the people of the Americas must take cognizance of growing ill-will, of marked trends toward aggression, of increasing armaments, of shortening tempers—a situation which has in it many of the elements that lead to the tragedy of a general war." His solution was a "two-fold neutrality" that would bar the sale of military supplies to aggressor nations. Help to other nations threatened by aggression on the part of their neighbors must be "confined to moral help." They could not expect the United States "to get tangled up with their troubles in days to come." The *New Republic* of January 15, 1936, criticizing Roosevelt's speech for its lack of specifics, noted that "in the long run, [the President] cannot hope to hold the masses of the people by expressions of sympathy which, no matter how brilliantly or movingly expressed, give hardly an inkling of what, after nearly three years in office, he proposes to do for them."

A few days after his joint address to Congress the Supreme Court struck down the Agricultural Adjustment Act by a 6 to 3 vote, Brandeis, Cardozo, and Stone dissenting. The Court's decision had the practical effect of ruling that neither the Federal government nor the states could regulate interstate commerce. When Roosevelt got word of the decisions, Harold Ickes noted that he smiled. "It is plain to see . . . " Ickes wrote in his diary, "that he is not at all averse to the Supreme Court declaring one New Deal statute after another unconstitutional. I think he believes that the Court will find itself pretty far out on a limb before it is through with it and that a real issue will be joined on which he can go to the country." It was the first intimation that the President had decided to chasten the Court. The Triple-A decision was useful ammunition. Yet Ickes was seriously concerned about the President's health and the prospects for reelection. At the Cabinet meeting on January 17, 1936, Ickes noted that the President did not look well. "He looks many years older," Ickes wrote, "and his face looked drawn and tired." He seemed nervous, and his laughter forced. Ickes predicted doom and disaster in the fall elections. He was convinced that the political tides were running against the President. Hopkins also felt the strain. Ickes thought Hopkins looked fifteen years older than he had at the beginning of the administration, fewer than four years ago; Ickes himself was near exhaustion.

While Ickes and others in the administration continued to be pessimistic about the President's chances of reelection, Roosevelt exuded confidence. He assured Ickes in February that he would be re-elected, "but that the next four years would be very tough ones, with a crisis in 1941." Reviewing the achievements of his administration, he told the secretary of the interior that the prior four years marked "the longest period since [Chester] Arthur was President in 1882 that Federal troops had not been called out in some part of the country on account of labor troubles." The fact that the President was proud of this statistic tells a good deal about his own attitude toward the aspirations of labor. He also reminded Ickes that it was the longest period since 1892 "that Marines or soldiers had not been landed by the United States on foreign soil." But Ickes refused to be reassured. "It passes all my comprehension," he wrote in his diary; "I have thought all along that the President was really an able politician. . . . I think he is defeating himself, . . . We are losing ground every day, and the longer this goes on, the less chance there will be of winning. . . . Father Coughlin . . . last week denounced the President as a liar and not a word in reply from anyone! The President is having too much fun sailing and fishing to resent a gross insult. . . . " According to Ickes, Eleanor Roosevelt was worried, and so was Jim Farley, "but the President . . . seems to be up in the clouds with his mind on more spiritual things than his own re-election."

The fact was that Coughlin had finally overreached himself. Wyndham Mortimer recalled hearing Coughlin on his car radio one Sunday afternoon. After criticizing various New Deal measures, Coughlin declared, "I tell you, ladies and gentlemen, that Franklin Delano Roosevelt is a liar!" That did it, as they say. Coughlin's influence declined rapidly thereafter. The revelation that he and his secretary had gambled in the silver market with money contributed by his followers helped substantially in his eclipse.

As late as the end of July Ickes considered the situation very serious and the chances of the President's reelection slim. There seemed little chance of his carrying New York, and only an outside chance for Ohio, Indiana, and Minnesota. By Ickes's calculations, the President would fall short by some thirty-six electoral votes of the needed majority.

Lorena Hickok, Eleanor Roosevelt's friend and Harry Hopkins's "private eye," warned Hopkins that Roosevelt was in trouble in Ohio because of the continuing high rate of unemployment. "I don't see how he can carry Ohio if things go on as they are," she wrote.

Al Smith let it be known that he was prepared to leave the Democratic Party if Roosevelt was nominated. "It's all right with me if they want to disguise themselves as Karl Marx or Lenin or any of that bunch but I can't stand for allowing him to march under the banner of Jackson or Cleveland," Smith declared. Encouraged by indications of Roosevelt's declining popularity, Smith and the Liberty Leaguers redoubled their efforts.

As the dates of the nominating conventions drew closer, George Gallup had the notion of polling Americans on their support for the President by "class" or economic status. Of the persons listed in *Who's Who*, 69 percent expressed themselves as opposed to Roosevelt, while of those on relief, 77 percent favored the President. One interesting poll asked the question "Which theory of government do you favor— concentration of power in the Federal Government or concentration of power in the state governments?" Of those who responded, 56 percent favored the Federal government. Interestingly enough, in the South, long considered the stronghold of states' rights sentiment, 58 percent favored the Federal government. In a category called "Leading citizens," 75 percent favored the states. If business interests constituted a major element in the "Leading citizens" category, it seems clear that they thought they could best preserve their special privileges and prerogatives at the state level. Although a significant majority of voters described themselves as "conservative," Gallup polls continued to show Americans supporting by large margins such "socialistic" measures as the distribution of birth control information by the Federal government, Federal old-age pensions, unemployment insurance, and Federal assistance to provide "medical care for mothers at childbirth" (81 percent in favor).

The spring of 1936 was shadowed for the Roosevelts by the illness of Louis Howe, who was plainly dying. Tiny and simian, he spent much of his time in bed on his hands and knees, the most comfortable position that he could take. Finally, when he could no longer be cared for in the White House, he was moved to the Bethesda Naval Hospital. There Eleanor Roosevelt visited him almost daily, and the President came frequently to see his friend.

Howe died on April 18, 1936. Eleanor Roosevelt wrote of him: "This little man was really the biggest man from the point of view of imagination and determination I have ever known; his body was weak but his mind never stopped working for a second. . . . I used to laugh at Louis," she noted, "and say that one could not plan every move in this world; one had to accept circumstances as they developed. That was one thing that Louis hated to do. He liked to feel that he dominated circumstances and, so far as it was humanly possible, he often did. . . . Louise Howe's death left a great gap in my husband's life." Howe had been careful to see that Roosevelt talked to "a cross-section of people and heard a variety of points of view," in Mrs. Roosevelt's words. "I do not think he purposely brought in people who particularly agreed or disagreed with Franklin, but he did try to see that all points of view reached him, so that he would make no decision without full consideration," she added. Mrs. Roosevelt noted that Howe gave her often imperious husband "the benefit of his sane, reasoned, careful political analysis and even if Franklin disagreed and was annoyed, he listened and respected Louis's political acumen. Whether he ignored Louis's advice or not, at least all the reasons against the disputed action had been clearly stated and argued. . . . Consequently, after Louis's death, Franklin frequently made his decisions without canvassing all sides of a question."

In Tugwell's view, Howe's influence on Roosevelt was far less in the direction of urging the President to undertake particular programs or courses of action than in checking his propensity for "projects of a weird or grandiose sort much better not undertaken." The phrase is worth lingering over. There was in Roosevelt, the country squire and ambitious politician, an extravagance of imagination more common to romantic poets than to politicians. Again it was a quality that he shared more with Jefferson than with any other American President with the exception of Woodrow Wilson, who, after all, wished to make the world over all at once.

Howe's greatest contribution, in Tugwell's opinion, was "to sustain Roosevelt through the most difficult years of his career with such un-wavering devotion as has to be studied to be believed." After 1925 (by which time Howe had been Roosevelt's political alter ego for more than ten years), Howe's place was, again in Tugwell's view, that of "First Political Representative . . . [but] the direction would be Roosevelt's own. . . . His old association with Roosevelt had been based on the conception he had in Albany of a surrogate for his own ambitions. His new one had its source in the love and loyalty he felt at seeing his handsome hero lying helpless and alone with his dreams crumbling about him. This had the curious and paradoxical effect of bringing Howe to accept a secondary role. Roosevelt was no longer a puppet to be manipulated; he was a loved object to be treated with tender-ness. . . . From pusher he [Howe] became a follower." It was Tugwell's conviction that the "conspiracy to exploit the common folk for the benefit of the few who knew how to get and manage the power of the state had generated in [Howe] a kind of unresting rage. He was the child of the muckraker's era." Tugwell believed Howe had picked Roosevelt as the agent of his will to bring the exploiters to account.

Ickes also testified to Howe's influence. "Howe," he wrote, "was the only one who dared talk to [the President] frankly and fearlessly. He not only could tell him what he believed to be the truth, but he could hang on like a pup to the root until he got results."

After Howe's death the influence of Harry Hopkins increased substantially. The President, Eleanor Roosevelt wrote, "found in Hopkins some of the companionship and loyalty Louis had given him, but not the political wisdom and careful analysis of each situation." Hopkins, in her view, bent too readily to the President's will. "This was not as valuable a service as forcing Franklin . . . to hear unpleasant arguments."

All the old familiar parties nominated candidates for the presidential election. The Socialist Labor Party, a mere handful; the indefatigable Prohibitionists (they met at watery Niagara Falls early in May); the Socialist Party which nominated Norman Thomas once again.

The most difficult problem Thomas had to deal with was the charge that the New Deal was "socialistic." If that was indeed the case (and many Americans, both liberals and conservatives, thought it was), there was little use for the Socialist Party. When Al Smith attacked the New Deal as "socialistic," Thomas was stung to respond with a pamphlet refuting the notion. Thomas was "concerned to point out how false the charge [was] that Roosevelt and the New Deal represent socialism. . . . What is at stake is a clear understanding of the issues on which the peace and prosperity of generations—perhaps of centuries—depend. A nation which misunderstands socialism as completely as Al Smith misunderstands it is a nation which weakens its defense against the coming of war and fascism." While Thomas did not charge Roosevelt with Fascist inclinations, he argued that the New Deal was simply a way station on the road to the corporate state on the model of Italy. Roosevelt's cry had not been "Workers of the world . . . unite!" It had been "Workers and small stockholders, unite, clean up Wall Street." Roosevelt had failed to attack the profit system, which was the heart of capitalism. Instead of a cure, he proposed palliatives. When a reporter asked Thomas if the New Deal had not carried out the Socialist program, he replied sharply that the New Dealers had carried it out on a stretcher.

With Huey Long dead, Gerald L. K. Smith and Father Coughlin joined Dr. Townsend to form the Union Party and nominated ancient William Lemke, a reformed North Dakota radical from the days of the Nonpartisan League. Coughlin assured Lemke that he could win 9,000,000 votes for the Union ticket. He hoped to form an alliance of all the extremist political movements: the Townsendites, the remnants of Upton Sinclair's EPIC followers, the adherents of Huey Long, Catholic labor unions, and the more conservative farmers.

The Farmer-Labor Party also endorsed Lemke, and some of his more radical supporters announced that he had Communist backing through the Farmer-Labor Party. Lemke deplored the open assertion of Communist affiliation. "Some ass in this state is sending out literature . . ." he wrote, "openly boasting that the Farm-Labor party is communistic. Of course this fool thinks he is doing some good for the cause, but he is just giving the ammunition to the opposition that they want."

The Republican National Convention met at Cleveland early in June. The leading candidates for the party's nomination were Hoover himself, who longed for a chance to vindicate his administration, Senator Borah of Idaho, Arthur Vandenberg of Michigan, Alfred Landon of Kansas, and Frank Knox, Republican war-horse since the Bull Moose days. It was not, on the whole, a formidable field and after three lackluster days the Republicans nominated Alf Landon for President and Frank Knox for Vice-President. It was a little like running a stakes' claimer against the winner of the Kentucky Derby. Landon was "an oilman," and Harold Ickes took a dim view of oilmen in general. "An honest and scrupulous man in the oil business is so rare as to rank as a museum piece," he wrote in reference to Landon. William Allen White, who had known Landon for years, told Ickes that his family considered Landon a terrible bore. The word that he was coming for dinner or to spend the night brought a collective groan from the Whites. According to White and his wife, Landon had little claim to be called a Progressive. It was their opinion that he was "mediocre in ability and on every account a poor man to put in charge of the nation at this time." Yet White, an unreconstructed Midwesterner, wrote a long article for the *Saturday Evening Post* praising Landon as a Republican candidate in the Progressive tradition.

On the eve of the Democratic Convention the Supreme Court struck down legislation guaranteeing the right of unions to bargain collectively. "This is positively medieval," an angry Ickes wrote in his diary, "and I am frank to say that if this decision is constitutional, then we need either an entirely new or a radically amended Constitution. If it isn't constitutional, then we need a different Supreme Court."

The Democrats met in Philadelphia on June 23, abolished the two-thirds rule which had plagued the party for a generation or more, adopted a platform, and renominated Roosevelt and Garner by acclamation. According to Raymond Moley, one of the most controversial planks in the Democratic platform was drafted by the President himself. In its original form it contained a sentence which read: "We have begun and shall continue the successful drive to rid our land of kidnapers, bandits, and malefactors of great wealth who defraud and exploit the people."

It was estimated that more than 100,000 people crowded into Franklin Field in inclement weather to hear Roosevelt's acceptance speech. As he made his way laboriously through the crowd to the speakers' platform, he saw the old poet Edwin Markham, author of "The Man with the Hoe." Roosevelt reached out to shake his hand. His brace buckled and he fell, scattering the manuscript of his speech. Hauled to his feet by Secret Service men, furious at his body's betrayal of him, he saw Markham's anxious face and stopped once more to shake his hand.

A militant Roosevelt attacked the "economic royalists." They had "conceded that political freedom was the business of Government, but they have maintained that economic slavery was nobody's business. They granted that the Government could do anything to protect the citizen in his right to vote but they denied the Government could do anything to protect the citizen in his right to work and his right to live. . . . These economic royalists complain that we seek to overthrow the institutions of America. What they really complain about is that we seek to take away their power.

"Governments can err. Presidents do make mistakes, but the immortal Dante tells us that divine justice weighs the sins of the cold-blooded and the sins of the warm-hearted in different scales. Better the occasional faults of a Government that lives in a spirit of charity than the consistent omissions of a Government frozen in the ice of its own indifference. . . . There is a mysterious cycle in human events. To some generations much is given. Of other generations much is expected. This generation has a rendezvous with destiny."

It was, for a certainty, a splendid speech. If Roosevelt was too severe on his unhappy predecessors, his assertion that "This generation has a rendezvous with destiny" rang out as memorably as the great sentences of the Gettysburg Address or Lincoln's Second Inaugural.

Harold Ickes thought it "the greatest political speech I have ever heard. It was really a strong and moving statement of the fundamental principles underlying our politics today. . . ." Roosevelt had enunciated what Ickes had "believed in and stood for all of my life." But some of Roosevelt's warmest supporters, Frances Perkins among them, were disturbed over the militancy of the speech and the use of such phrases as "privileged princes of . . . economic dynasties." They smacked of Marxist rhetoric. Raymond Moley, already alienated, was especially offended. But Roosevelt, as we have noted often, saw himself as the nation's schoolmaster. In his view, he was doing no more than describing the course of American history and doing it with words reminiscent of his heroes, Thomas Jefferson, Theodore Roosevelt, and Woodrow Wilson, not, of course, to mention the great orators of the Populist movement and William Jennings Bryan, who had built his political career on attacking Wall Street. Roosevelt was trying to put his enemies in the context of American history and shatter whatever remained in the popular consciousness of deference to big business. From the beginning of U.S. involvement in the World War in 1917 to the onset of the Depression, big business, through such agencies as the National Association of Manufacturers (and with a notable assist from Soviet communism)and innumerable Chambers of Commerce, had been remarkably successful in identifying its interests with those of the nation as a whole. What was good for business, or what business thought was good for it, was good for America. If shorter hours and higher wages, unions and decent working conditions were "bad"—i.e., more costly and inconvenient—for manufacturers, they were, of necessity, "bad" for America, and those who proposed them were dangerous, un-American, and probably Communists. That was, in essence, the view that had been dinned into the minds of many Americans, and now, if the New Deal social programs were to become permanent parts of the American system, it had to be "dinned" out. Roosevelt believed that it was his responsibility to take the lead in shattering the illusion that the will of the business community was synonymous with the will of the people. There were deep and profound conflicts and differences between the interests of business and the interests of workers. To minimize or gloss over them was to deceive and mislead the American people. Education was a function of leadership. Roosevelt was committed to reconciling those differences and healing those schisms—in short, to saving so-called capitalism from destruction. That had been the basic assumption behind the NRA—a partnership of business, government, and labor to lift the country out of the Depression. But business had been recalcitrant, increasingly hostile, and, finally, bitterly opposed. Big business had challenged the New Deal and all its works, had put impediments in its way, and week in and week out had denounced it through the media it controlled.

At least one of Roosevelt's advisers was deeply disappointed by the acceptance speech. In Tugwell's words, "Holistic ideas were ditched for the campaign." He remained convinced for the rest of his life that Roosevelt had "missed the best opportunity we would ever have in our lifetimes to recast the economy and redefine the objectives of our people."

The Communist Party met in New York at the end of June and nominated Earl Browder (William Foster was in disgrace) and James Ford, for President and Vice-President respectively. The convention's mood was optimistic, not to say euphoric. No one anticipated victory in November, but the party was growing rapidly, and more important, it was proud to count in its ranks, or closely allied with it, most of the new intellectual class, young collegians by the thousands, and many of the rich and well-to-do, who contributed generously to its coffers. The future, it was confident, belonged not to the liberal legions of the New Deal but to it. It was, in practical fact, ready to do business with the New Deal while continuing ritually to denounce it. According to Benjamin Gitlow, longtime Communist and historian of the party, "negotiations were proceeding behind the scenes, between certain elements in the New Deal and representatives of the Communist party." The Hearst papers published a front-page box announcing that orders had been issued by Moscow to the members of the Communist Party of the United States that it was to support Roosevelt. The *Daily Worker* denied the story. "Is it true that the Communist party will support Roosevelt as a lesser evil to the more reactionary groups like Hearst and the Liberty League?" the newspaper asked rhetorically. "No! The Communist party from the very outset of the New Deal has consistently exposed Roosevelt's anti-working-class aims. The development of the New Deal is towards fascism and the war and not towards 'socialism' as is claimed by Hearst and his crew of red-baiters." Gitlow insisted that the party nonetheless gave substantial support to Roosevelt by encouraging workers and the unemployed to vote for him.

The Republicans compaigned largely on the theme that the New Deal was hardly to be distinguished from Soviet communism. A thousand changes were rung on that single key. Frank Knox declared: "We are not in a political campaign. We are in a campaign to save America" from "fanatics, theorists and impractical experimenters." In another talk he warned Americans to "be on your guard. Silently in the night they are creeping up, seeking to impose upon us, before we realize it, a new and alien kind of government."

The Liberty League played subtly on the theme of racial prejudice. Doubtless hoping to stir up the same kind of storm that had greeted the news that Theodore Roosevelt had invited Booker T. Washington to a meeting at the White House, the League circulated a photograph of Mrs. Roosevelt standing beside two blacks. A caption pointed out that blacks had been invited to eat and even sleep at the White House. The league also distributed literature implying that social security (which required a matching deduction from employees' wages) was, in fact, a government-mandated pay reduction. Much was also made by the league of the fact that John L. Lewis and the United Mine Workers had thrown their moral and financial support to Roosevelt. At their convention in Washington in 1936 the UMW delegates had declared, "We are for Roosevelt, the greatest humanitarian of our time. . . . " Before the campaign was over, the UMW had contributed $400,000 to the President's campaign.

Outside of the South the major newspapers and the great newspaper chains like the Hearst and Scripps-Howard papers were virtually unanimous in their opposition to Roosevelt and their support of Landon. Harold Ickes wrote in his diary that if Roosevelt were reelected, it would be "over the hateful and violent opposition of practically every conservative interest in the country." To Ickes "the fundamental issue was whether we are to have real freedom for the mass of people, not only political but economic, or whether we are to be governed by a small group of economic overlords."

A few weeks after the nominating convention Roosevelt sought refuge at Harold Ickes's home in Maryland. The President and his party, which included Grace Tully and Missy LeHand, had dinner on a steaming summer night on the lawn in front of the house. Tom Corcoran had brought his accordion, and he played and sang much of the evening, with the others joining in on familiar songs. "The President certainly carries his liquor well," Ickes observed, noting that Roosevelt had five gin and ginger ale highballs after dinner without showing the "slightest effect." The table was lit by candles, and a late moon lent its light to the party. There was honeydew melon, cold salmon with mayonnaise dressing, squab with peas, and Ickes's own black raspberry ice cream with cookies and coffee, Château d'Yquem, a good claret and a vintage champagne. Ickes was delighted with the evening, Corcoran's music, and the good talk and laughter. "It was difficult to realize," he wrote, "that this man who was so friendly and delightful and who entered into the affair so wholeheartedly was President of the United States."

Either the mood of the public was highly volatile or the polling techniques of Gallup were very imprecise (possibly both were true), but a "Presidential Trial Heat" in July, 1936, three months before the November elections, indicated that only 50.8 percent of the electorate would vote for Roosevelt if the election were held "today," while 48.2 percent intended to vote for Landon. Only in the South and the Pacific states did the President have comfortable margins—almost 70 percent in the South and 59 percent on the Coast.

The polls alarmed Roosevelt's advisers, but he remained as confident as ever. One of his favorite gambits during the campaign was to tell his audience of the tycoons who had come to him in 1933 at the beginning of his administration begging to be saved. "In the summer of 1933, a nice old gentleman wearing a silk hat fell off the end of a pier. He was unable to swim. A friend ran down the pier, dived overboard and pulled him out; but the silk hat floated off with the tide. After the old gentleman had been revived, he was effusive in his thanks. He praised his friend for saving his life. Today, three years later, the old gentleman is berating his friend because the silk hat was lost."

Roosevelt declared: "The New Deal . . . seeks to cement our society, rich and poor, manual workers and brain workers, into a voluntary brotherhood of free men, standing together striving together for the common good of all. It was this administration which saved the system of private profit and free enterprise after it had been dragged to the brink of ruin." In a broadcast address Roosevelt insisted that the government should "spend money when no one else had money to spend." The normally reserved Hoover, who was listening to the broadcast with Republican candidate Alf Landon, called out, "Boo! Boo!" at such outrageous sentiments.

At Chautauqua Roosevelt promised to protect the United States from the threat of war in the Far East. "I have seen war," he declared in one of his most famous passages. "I have seen war on land and sea.

I have seen blood running from the wounded. I have seen men coughing out their gassed lungs. I have seen the dead in the mud. I have seen cities destroyed. I have seen two hundred limping, exhausted men come out of the lines—survivors of a regiment of one thousand that went forward twenty-four hours before. I have seen children starving. I have seen the agony of mothers and wives. I hate war." He assured his listeners, "I have passed unnumbered hours, I shall pass unnumbered hours thinking and planning how war may be kept from this nation." We must have "the courage to say 'no' to those who selfishly or unwisely would let us go to war."

As Roosevelt's campaign crossed the country, it became a kind of triumphal procession. The Depression was far from over, but conditions were vastly better than they had been four years earlier. It was estimated that 6,000,000 more men and women had jobs. Corporate profits were up, and even Detroit was reviving as car sales increased. At a Chicago rally, Harold Ickes recorded in his diary, "there was the greatest political demonstration that the city had ever seen." And so it went throughout the trip as confidence grew that Roosevelt would score a substantial victory. Everywhere the crowds were large and delirious. Their enthusiasm both pleased and chastened the President. He told Ickes that "there was something terrible about the crowds that lined the streets. . . . " Many individuals called out such things as "He saved my home," "He gave me a job." It troubled the President to think that people had been reduced to such desperate straits.

On October 2 in San Diego, a city often racked by the activities of antilabor vigilantes, Roosevelt declared: "Never was there more genuine reason for Americans to face down these principal causes of fear [domestic violence and foreign war]. 'Malice domestic' from time to time will come to you in the shape of those who would raise false issues, pervert facts, preach the gospel of hate, and minimize the importance of public action to secure human rights or spiritual ideals." While Mussolini's invasion of Ethiopia had raised the specter of "a foreign war," the United States, following the admonitions of the "Father of our Country," was "determined to avoid those perils that will endanger our peace with the world." Raymond Moley interpreted Roosevelt's words, some of which he had written, as conciliatory toward business.

Back on the East Coast for the last phase of the campaign Roosevelt toured Pennsylvania. At Forbes Field, Pittsburgh, George Earle, the governor of the state, prepared the crowd for the President's arrival by reciting the names of the "economic royalists" who were outspoken opponents of the New Deal. After each name the journalist Thomas Stokes recalled, the governor "was forced to pause as the crowd vented its scorn on its enemies, like the whine of a hurricane before it strikes. He stood, smiling and confident, enjoying the tempest he had produced." When Roosevelt finally appeared, the crowd "drowned him with paeans of joy." It was all a bit scary, at least to Stokes, somewhat of a tycoon himself.

It was at Pittsburgh that Roosevelt, four years earlier, had attacked Hoover for reckless spending and promised to balance the budget if it could be done without undue hardship for the hungry and unemployed. When he asked Sam Rosenman to look up what he had said there in the 1932 campaign and Rosenman told him, Roosevelt asked Rosenman what he thought he should say in the light of the accumulating New Deal deficits. Rosenman advised him to deny that he had ever been in Pittsburgh. It was just the kind of response that delighted the President. He threw back his head and roared with laughter.

The Democratic strategists did all they could to appeal to black voters. Roosevelt, often in response to pressure from his wife, had appointed more blacks to Federal offices than any President since Grant. More important, Eleanor Roosevelt, out of the generous impulses of her heart, had made the cause of black Americans her own. In numerous small but, to blacks profoundly important ways, she made evident her sympathy and concern. Each episode of simple friendliness, while it often passed virtually unnoticed by the Northern press and invariably inflamed Southern opinion, made a deep impression on blacks. It is probably not too much to say that when Eleanor Roosevelt invited the black woman activist Mary McLeod Bethune, head of the Negro Affairs Division of the National Youth Administration, to be her guest at the White House, more black Americans were drawn to the Democratic Party than by any single piece of congressional legislation or any official presidential edict favorable to blacks. At a rally in Madison Square Garden attended by an estimated 20,000 blacks, a twenty-foot-tall painting of Roosevelt, his hands outstretched over kneeling blacks with Abraham Lincoln's figure in the background, was unveiled.

When Roosevelt went to a World Series game between the Giants and the Yankees with Senator Wagner, the presidential party drove through the Bronx. "It was especially interesting," Harold Ickes noted, "to see the turnout of Negroes." Senator Wagner told Ickes that "in former times Negroes would not turn out to see any Democratic candidate. There were thousands of them and they displayed great enthusiasm."

The black newspaper the *Pittsburgh Courier* summed up the black attitude toward the New Deal: "Armies of unemployed Negro workers have been kept from the near-starvation level on which they lived under President Hoover.... Armies of unemployed Negro workers have found work on the various PWA, CWA, WPA, CCC, FERA, and other projects.... Critics will point to discrimination against colored sharecroppers, against Negro skilled and unskilled labor.... This is all true. It would be useless to deny it even if there were any inclination to do so, which there is not.... But what administration within the memory of man has done a better job in that direction considering the very imperfect human material with which it had to work? The answer, of course, is none."

Many liberals continued to remain aloof from the President. Walter Lippmann decided that he was rushing the country along too fast on the path of social reform. It needed that famous "breathing spell." He grew increasingly persuaded that it might be "absolutely necessary not to re-elect Mr. Roosevelt." He professed to discern a powerful but "entirely inchoate" movement to block his nomination. Lippmann found himself in a kind of unholy alliance with Lewis Douglas, former director of the budget, whose covert campaign from within the administration against the New Deal had led to pressure on him to resign. Dean Acheson was another recruit to the cause. By midsummer Lippmann had decided that the Kansas governor, Alf Landon, "a dull and uninspired fellow, an ignorant man," was the country's best hope and indeed only hope of ridding itself of Roosevelt and the New Deal. To Roosevelt's opponents the odds seemed encouraging.

There was alarm in Democratic circles (and joy among Republicans) a few weeks before the election at the result of a poll circulated by the *Literary Digest*. Contemptuous of Gallup's "scientific" polling, where a few thousand voters were queried, the *Literary Digest* sent out 10,000,000 ballots and, after counting the returns, announced confidently that Landon would win in a "landslide" with 57 percent of the vote (and thirty-two states) to 43 percent for Roosevelt and sixteen states. Jim Farley, counting the votes far more accurately than any pollster, predicted that Roosevelt would carry every state but Maine and Vermont.

The *New York Times* of October 1, 1936, reluctantly conceding a Roosevelt victory, editorialized: "[We] believe that Mr. Roosevelt is a keen enough judge of public opinion to make his second administration more conservative than his first, in the sense that conservatism means consolidating ground already gained and perfecting measures hastily enacted. We believe this both because the tide of public opinion is running with steadily increasing strength against hasty experimentation and because the President himself has moved definitely in this direction. . . . We believe that in this case conservatives and radicals can compose their differences within that [the Democratic] party. . . ."

At the end of his campaign tour Roosevelt was greeted in New York by huge crowds in a procession up Fifth Avenue. It was said that the only boo heard was when Roosevelt passed the Yale Club. He wound up his campaign with a speech at Madison Square Garden. It was a final vindication of the New Deal before the election, and Roosevelt was at his oratorical best. "For twelve years" he told the enraptured Democrats, "this Nation was afflicted with hear-nothing, see-nothing, do-nothing Government. The Nation looked to the Government but the Government looked away. Nine mocking years with the golden calf and three long years of the scourge! Nine crazy years at the ticker and three long years in the breadlines! Nine mad years of mirage and three long years of despair! Powerful influences strive today to restore that kind of government with its doctrine that Government is best which is most indifferent.

"For nearly four years you have had an Administration which instead of twirling its thumbs has rolled up its sleeves. We will keep our sleeves rolled up." There was no equivocation about who the enemies of progress were. They were named: "business and financial monopoly, speculation, reckless banking, class antagonism, sectionalism and war profiteering"—the rulers of America. "Never before in all our history have these forces been so united against any one candidate as they stand today. They are unanimous in their hatred for me—and I welcome their hatred.

"I would like to have it said of my first Administration that in it the forces of selfishness and lust for power met their match." The audience, rising to their feet, broke forth in a storm of applause, thrilled by the vision of a nation free at last of the dominance of the "capitalists." "I should like to have it said—" Roosevelt cried above the turmoil. "Wait a moment! I should like to have it said of my second Administration that in it these forces met their master!" The Garden erupted in fresh ecstasies of emotion. There was, in the response, something of the joy roused by the shattering of idols. Americans had been arrested and accused of Bolshevik sympathies or, in effect, treason for less. Now the President of the United States had thrown down the gauntlet. It is human nature to search for a scapegoat in bad times. The bankers, financiers, and industrialists were ideal scapegoats. Locked in the mental world of Darwinism and classical economics, they were stubbornly resistant to any larger view of reality, and their rage and bitterness at Roosevelt's efforts to lift the country out of the Depression while at the same time creating a government more responsive to the needs of its citizens made them the perfect scapegoats—the kinds of enemies a politician dreams of having. They were, in the main, not wicked or evil and probably no more greedy and selfish than the ordinary run of humanity. Brooks Adams had argued in his *Theory of Social Revolution,* written in the aftermath of the Republican Party's rejection of Theodore Roosevelt, that throughout history no class that held power had ever surrendered it or even shared it. It had invariably been torn from it in bloody revolution by the excluded and exploited majority. Now it appeared that under the pressures of an economic catastrophe of unprecedented proportions—a catastrophe for which, rightly or wrongly, the capitalist class had been blamed (and correspondingly discredited)—there might, after all, be a "social revolution," in which the holders of power had it wrested from them by a majority of the people led by a master of political persuasion.

Walter Lippmann, feeling like the Dutch boy who put his finger in the dike, voted "with a sick heart" for Landon, convinced that nothing could be worse for the country "than another Democratic landslide." William Allen White's Democratic sympathies, it turned out, were only skin-deep. He had been a Republican delegate to the party's national convention, and he threw the full weight of the *Emporia Gazette* behind Landon. He denounced the President as a "slick old thimblerigger" and scorned his suggestion that the Democrats cared more about helping the needy than the Republicans. The difference was the Republicans would work through state, municipal, and county agencies in the true spirit of democracy, whereas the Democrats were dedicated to building the power of the Federal government and thereby creating "a great political machine centered in Washington" and paid for "with waste and extravagance. . . ."

The President received the election returns at Hyde Park while Tommy Corcoran played his accordion and the return watchers sang songs; it soon became clear that a landslide was in the making.

Confident of the accuracy of the *Literary Digest* poll, Republican leaders in New York met to celebrate the election returns at the Iridium Room of the St. Regis Hotel. Dorothy Thompson, the journalist and wife of Sinclair Lewis, was present with the Harry Hopkinses. She wrote an account of the evening to Robert Sherwood. The glittering assembly danced to a Russian balalaika orchestra as the returns were flashed on a large screen. From the first hour they were extremely disheartening to the Republican faithful. When word came that Landon had conceded, Dorothy Thompson urged Hopkins to propose a toast to the President. "Here?" he replied. "Are you crazy? We'd probably be lynched." Thompson, avowing her neutrality as a journalist, thereupon rose and proposed a toast, but no one except the Hopkinses responded. "We drank our toast," she wrote, "and Harry choked on his, he was so amused, and spurt champagne just past my nose. . . . Still, I thought Harry's feelings a little hilariously vindictive. Whereas I was perturbed by the attitude of the crowd, he was delighted with imagining the further chagrins they would feel before the next administration was over."

Roosevelt's victory was indeed sweeping. He took every state except Maine and Vermont. Maine had always prided itself on the slogan "As Maine Goes, So Goes the Nation." Now wags rewrote it: "As Maine Goes, So Goes Vermont." Roosevelt's majority was more than 10,000,000. "There has been nothing like it in the history of American politics," Harold Ickes wrote in his diary. "Never have the newspapers, in my recollection, conducted a more mendacious and venomous campaign against a candidate for President, and never have they been of so little influence." It *was* a strange moment; it demonstrated in the most dramatic fashion the gulf between the people of the country and their erstwhile masters, the businessmen and power brokers of the old elite. Clearly there *were* two Americas. One included most of those individuals, but by no means all, who were well-to-do or rich. This America was profoundly conservative in temperament and in political philosophy. It believed that the business interests should run the country much as they pleased. It subscribed to a mixed bag of timeworn political shibboleths: free enterprise; rugged individualism; competition; survival of the fittest. It was of a mind with George Baer, who told the church group that undertook to investigate the facts of the steel strike of 1902 that God in His wisdom had placed the running of the country in the hands of him and his fellow corporate leaders, and they should mind their own business.

There was, as we well know by now, another America, an America of tenant farmers, industrial workers, farm laborers, immigrants from fifty nations, blacks, women. That America, the second America, had waged a long and bitter war for justice and equality. Even in the so-called Progressive era and the days of Wilsonian reform they had had to be satisfied with crumbs from the table of capital. If they were not precisely on top, they now had a voice and a spokesman and, above all, hope. Until the presidential election of 1936 it had been by no means clear whether the country as a whole would accept the New Deal. Only one thing was clear: the business community approached unanimity in its rejection of the New Deal and so, not surpisingly, did its organs and agencies, its associations, chambers, leagues, clubs, newspapers, and magazines. They had constituted a chorus, a drumbeat of angry denunciation. Would that endlessly repeated refrain penetrate the consciousness of the mass of Americans? Would they succumb to the arguments of the editorial writers, the conservative press, the political soothsayers, or would they perceive where their true interests lay? Polls had shown the New Deal declining rapidly in voter approval. Roosevelt's popularity, the pollsters announced, had sunk to new lows as the people of the country began to recognize the President for what he was. There were, of course, debates over just what he was. A mercurial political playboy? A power-mad potential dictator? An agent of Soviet Russia? A crazed syphilitic? A well-intentioned but shallow experimenter with the nation's future? A cynical fomenter of class bitterness? A traitor to his class? The latter was the most revealing denunciation of all. "Traitor" implied war: between capital and labor, or between the haves and have-nots, or, in Jefferson's (and William Manning's) term, between "the few and the many." The outcome had been by no means certain. As late as April and May, 1936, Harold Ickes was close to despair, ready to concede Roosevelt's defeat. Whether there was some ground swell of popular sentiment between May and November that swept the President to one of the most one-sided victories in our history, or whether there had been all along beneath the surface of the media, quite invisible to the political prognosticators, a deep affection for the President and confidence in his leadership, it is impossible to say.

Undoubtedly the election of 1936 marked one of the major turning points in American history. As we have noted from time to time throughout this work, the Civil War had left the nation virtually immobilized as far as any possibility of comprehensive social and economic reform was concerned. One European nation after another—Britain, France, Italy, even Germany with its notable lack of democratic institutions—instituted such reforms as unemployment insurance, old-age pensions, and state assistance for the indigent, not to mention Australia and New Zealand, which were models for the rest of the world. Only the United States lagged. The major cause of such backwardness was, as we have said, the legacy of the Civil War, which had vastly diminished the power of the odd Democratic alliance between the big-city bosses of the North, with their largely immigrant constituencies, and the slave-holding South. The "agreement of 1876" left the South to go its own way, which, in practical fact, meant to destroy whatever political power the war had given the freed slaves. To this task the South devoted the greater part of its political attention, and while there were certainly radical farmers and politicians in the South, viz., the Farmers' Alliance and Tom Watson, they were isolated from the radical movements of the North and Midwest. The Republicans, meanwhile, abandoning their early tradition of reform, became increasingly the voice of the most conservative interests in the country. At the same time they retained (and neutralized) the reform-minded, who would have sooner formed a league with the devil than have voted Democratic. The consequence was that from the Civil War to the Great Depression the nation was, for all practical purposes, a one-party nation. The dissident elements coalesced briefly and spectacularly as the Populist Party, but the party could not sustain itself in the face of the patronage that the Democrats and Republicans controlled. With the exception of Cleveland and the "accident" of Wilson's election, made possible by the split in Republican ranks in 1912, the Democrats existed largely by virtue of the power of the big-city bosses and the intractability of the Solid South, a region whose concerns were only fitfully congruent with those of the rest of the nation. The election of 1936 created, for the first time since the Civil War, a true second party. Not only that, but it made that second party the dominant party for a generation. The political situation which had obtained from the Civil War to the Great Depression was now almost exactly reversed. From 1932 to 1972— forty years—the Republicans would hold office for only twelve years, eight of those being the administration of Dwight Eisenhower, a Republican more by chance than conviction, elected not for his Republicanism but for his popularity as a war hero.

The lesson was familiar and instructive: any group or party that holds power, virtually unchallenged, over an extended period of time becomes fixed and rigid in its policies and what we might call its disposition. It thus prepares the way for its own demise, and it not infrequently brings down the larger political entity of which it is a part. The price of getting rid of obsolete ideas (while holding fast to ancient values) is usually bloodshed and destruction. It was just such reflections that led Jefferson to recommend "a little rebellion, now and then," to avoid those devastating upheavals that come when pressure builds up along the fault line of a society by virtue of the increasing discrepancy between outmoded ideas and the demands of the deprived groups for social and economic justice. The earthquake analogy is a useful one. Geologists tell us that a series of small quakes along a fault can relieve pressure and thereby lessen the danger of a catastrophic earthquake. At one instant—in 1936—Americans, abetted by the Depression and educated by a master pedagogue, discarded a vast baggage of ideological propositions no longer, if ever, relevant to the conditions of the modern world. Human beings cling to "value systems," ideologies, and odd congeries of notions hardly to be dignified by the word "philosophy" for centuries and, in some instances, millennia, through thick and thin and then, on occasion, abandon them, or appear to, as casually as one would cast off a wornout garment. The latter phenomenon we rightly speak of as revolutionary. We are certainly justified in using that word to describe what took place in 1936.

Ed Flynn, a shrewd observer of the political scene, had given his analysis to Raymond Moley before the election: "There are two or three million more dedicated Republicans in the United States than there are Democrats. The population, however, is drifting into the urban areas. The election of 1932 was not normal. To remain in power we must attract some millions, perhaps seven, who are hostile or indifferent to both parties. They believe the Republican Party to be controlled by business and the Democratic Party by the conservative South. These millions are mostly in the cities. They include racial and religious minorities and labor people. We must attract them by radical programs of social and economic reform." Flynn's analysis could hardly be improved upon. The fact was that millions of Americans, seeing little difference between the two major parties, had ceased voting. The

New Deal did not so much convert Republicans into Democrats as draw millions of Americans into the political process by convincing them that it had their interests at heart.

The weather at Roosevelt's second inaugural was as daunting as it had been at his first. A drizzle of cold rain fell on the crowd that gathered in front of the Capitol without noticeably dampening its enthusiasm. Cellophane covered the Roosevelt family Bible, on which the President took the oath of office from his adversary Chief Justice Charles Evans Hughes. Some spectators noticed that Hughes put special emphasis on the President's responsibility "to preserve, protect and defend" the Constitution. Roosevelt told Sam Rosenman later that he was tempted to reply, "Yes, but it's the Constitution as *I* understand it, flexible enough to meet any new problem of democracy—not the kind of Constitution that your Court has raised as a barrier to progress and democracy."

"In this nation," Roosevelt declared in his inaugural address, "I see tens of millions of its citizens—a substantial part of its whole population—who at this very moment are denied the greater part of what the very lowest standards of living today call the necessities of life.

"I see millions of families trying to live on incomes so meager that the pall of family disaster hangs over them every day. . . .

"I see millions denied education, recreation, and the opportunity to better their lot and the lot of their children.

"I see millions lacking the means to buy the products of farm and factory and by their poverty denying work and productiveness to many other millions.

"I see one-third of a nation ill-housed, ill-clad, ill-nourished.

"It is not in despair that I paint you that picture. I paint it for you in hope—because the Nation, seeing and understanding the injustice in it, proposes to paint it out. . . ."

For all his awesome majority, there was trouble ahead for the President. In addition to the fact that economic recovery was still painfully slow, the Supreme Court was busy nullifying many of the most important New Deal measures. To Roosevelt the question became increasingly, Could nine old men, a majority of them rooted in the discredited ideas of the past century, frustrate his program, delay recovery, and defeat the wishes of the electorate?

Soon after the election Gallup asked the voters, "Shouid President Roosevelt's second Administration be more liberal, more conservative, about the same?" Only 15 percent said "more liberal," while 50 percent said "more conservative," and 35 percent said, "about the same." Of the Republicans polled, 88 percent said "more conservative," as did 40 percent of the Socialists. Such statistics were not encouraging for the future of the New Deal.

On May 5, 1936, Italian forces had seized Addis Ababa, the capital of Ethiopia, and deposed the emperor, Haile Selassie. Mussolini claimed his title. The campaign had taken seven months and reflected little glory on Italian arms. The ineptness of the League of Nations in the face of the Italian dictator's unabashed aggression marked its virtual demise. Five months later Hitler and Mussolini formed an alliance, to the dismay of those powers who had hoped to use Mussolini to block Hitler. British and French leaders of that persuasion then pinned their hopes on Russia. Perhaps Russia could be maneuvered into a situation where the two dictatorships, one of the right and one of the left, would destroy each other.

# 29

# The Court-Packing Fight

The first item on the agenda of the reelected President was the Supreme Court. By the end of 1936 the Court had declared nine major New Deal measures unconstitutional (out of sixteen cases). If Brooks Adams had been alive, he would have felt assured that his *Theory of Social Revolutions* had been proved correct. As we have noted, Adams argued that no ruling class in history had ever surrendered or even shared its powers and that in all such historic cases the courts and legal systems had been the last stronghold of entrenched wealth.

Six of the nine justices were over seventy. The most conservative—Pierce Butler (descendant of the slaveholding South Carolinian of the same name who signed the Declaration of Independence and whose son married Fanny Kemble), James Clark McReynolds, Willis Van Devanter, and George Sutherland—were called the Four Horsemen because they usually voted as a bloc and, invariably, on the conservative side of every issue. They represented the hold that corporate interests had on the Court and on the nation by virtue of the process that recruited members of the state and Federal courts from the ranks of corporation lawyers. The other justices were Harlan Stone, Chief Justice Charles Evans Hughes, Owen Roberts, Benjamin Cardozo, and Louis Brandeis.

Roosevelt was convinced that efforts to prevail on the antediluvian justices to retire would prove fruitless. They had a mission in life, which, in their view, was to prevent the country from sliding into socialism on a tide of New Deal legislation. "Although it had become, on the average, the most aged Court in our history," Roosevelt wrote in a review of his conflict with the justices, "though six justices had passed the age of seventy, not a single vacancy had occurred during my first term of office." What Roosevelt did not know was that when Justice Van Devanter, one of the most reactionary members of the Court, tried to retire in 1934, Brandeis had urged him to remain.

Roosevelt had hinted to Ickes shortly after the fall elections that he was determined to clip the wings of the Court. Ickes was entirely in agreement. He had written in his diary in November, 1935: "I am firmly of the opinion that we cannot work out an adequate and modern social system in this country so long as we are held in the present strait jacket of the Supreme Court." And six months later he noted: "Now that business is in the saddle and only the Federal Government can hope to cope with it, the Supreme Court has swung away from the theory of nationalism and is trying to divide up the United States into forty-eight states of different ideals and background and different laws. We are no longer one nation. The big corporations operate as entities in the whole country, but the United States, according to Chief Justice Hughes and his four reactionary associates, is not to be allowed to exercise powers commensurate with the social and economic needs of the people."

Roosevelt had reached the conclusion that "substantially all of the New Deal bills will be declared unconstitutional by the Supreme Court." "This," Ickes noted after a somber Cabinet meeting in December, 1935, "will mean that everything that his Administration has done of any moment will be nullified." The President suggested three possible solutions: "packing" the Court by adding ostensibly liberal justices; amending the Constitution, a prolonged and uncertain process; or passing a law specifically giving the Court the power to declare acts of Congress unconstitutional (a power not granted by the Constitution but assumed by the Court in its early years), with the additional proviso that a congressional election having intervened, Congress could then repass the law, in effect overriding the Court's veto.

Roosevelt was delighted when Homer Cummings discovered the "Wilson-McReynolds" plan to add liberal justices to the Court in order to produce a majority favorable to Wilson's legislative program. In

1913 James Clark McReynolds, Wilson's attorney general, had described the problem of ancient and reactionary justices: "Judges of the United States' courts, at the age of seventy, after having served ten years, may retire upon full pay. In the past, many judges have availed themselves of this privilege. Some, however, have remained on the bench long beyond the time when they were capable of adequately discharging their duties. . . . " As a consequence the administration of justice had suffered. The McReynolds solution was to allow the President to appoint another justice when one who had reached the age of seventy refused to retire. Now McReynolds was one of the ancient and reactionary justices who were declaring New Deal legislation unconstitutional by the yard.

The number of justices was not, in any event, a sacred number sent down from on high. The original six justices had been reduced to five by Congress during John Adams's administration and increased to seven by Jefferson (in order to get some Jeffersonian Republicans— i.e., Democrats—on the Court; they had then proceeded to vote with the Federalists on most issues). Two more had been added in 1837, and Lincoln had prevailed on Congress to add one (for ten) in 1863 to stop the Court from declaring essential war measures unconstitutional. The black Republicans in Congress had reduced the number to eight in order to prevent Andrew Johnson from making two appointments, and one had been added in 1869 in order to get support for the Legal Tender Act. Thus, in the context of our history adding or subtracting justices for essentially political reasons was a well-established practice, and although each change in the number of justices had aroused the fears of defenders of the Constitution, the outcry had been short-lived, and the effects on the Court over the long run negligible. But collective memories are usually short. The last change had been, after all, in 1869 by the generally discredited Reconstruction Congress, and for sixty years a series of Presidents had endured the vagaries and, on the whole, profoundly conservative character of the Court with more or less equanimity. The first Roosevelt, the reader may recall, had launched an attack on the judiciary and even gone so far as to suggest that some mechanism be established to overrule their decisions or recall obnoxious judges. The idea had horrified his friend Henry Cabot Lodge, who took him severely to task for such a radical suggestion. TR had had to satisfy himself with using the tactics of intimidation. He might, he told a friend, not know much about law, but he knew how to scare the hell out of recalcitrant justices.

In a conference held on January 30, 1937, attended by Cummings, Donald Richberg, head of the NRA, and Judge Rosenman, Roosevelt decided to push the "court-packing" bill. The President wrote to Felix Frankfurter: "Very confidentially, I may give you an awful shock in about two weeks." On February 3, 1937, Roosevelt held the customary annual reception for the justices. It was a lively affair. The President was in excellent spirits. Two days later he summoned members of the Cabinet and key Congressmen and Senators, among them the chairmen of the respective Judiciary committees. Roosevelt informed his startled audience of his plans to reform the judicial branch of the government. "The personnel of the federal judiciary is insufficient to meet the business before them," he declared. The principal reason was that the justices had clung to their offices "far beyond their years or physical capacity. . . . A constant and systematic addition of younger blood will vitalize the courts and better equip them to recognize and apply the essential concepts of justice in the light of the needs and facts of an ever-changing world." His plan was essentially that of McReynolds, applied this time to the Supreme Court as well as to the Federal judiciary as a whole. If a judge or justice reached the age of seventy and did not retire in six months, the President would have the right to appoint an additional judge. Roosevelt's proposal was embodied in the Judiciary Reorganization Bill of 1937.

The President sent Tom Corcoran to assure Brandeis, at eighty the oldest justice on the Court, that the scheme was not directed at him, but Brandeis received the word coldly and told Corcoran that he believed that Roosevelt had acted unwisely.

"Now you have blown me off the top of Vesuvius," Frankfurter wrote to Roosevelt when he heard of the court-packing plan. "Dramatically and artistically you did 'shock' me. But beyond that—well, the momentum of a long series of decisions not defensible in the realm of reason nor justified by the settled principles of Constitutional interpretation have convinced me . . . that means had to be found to save the Constitution from the Court, and the Court from itself. . . . There was no perfect way out." Frankfurter, somewhat to the surprise of his friends and to the relief of his many former students scattered throughout the New Deal, kept whatever reservations he might have had to himself.

The President summoned George Creel for a "background story" on his reasons for attempting to alter the composition of the Court. As Creel reported the interview, "It is the deep conviction of Franklin D. Roosevelt that the Constitution of the United States was never meant to be a 'deadhand,' chilling human aspiration and blocking humanity's advance, but that the founding fathers conceived of it as a living force for the expression of the national will with respect to national needs. Sincerely, steadfastly, the President refuses to believe that the framers meant to tie the hands of posterity until the end of time. . . . The thing that has been called the New Deal is Franklin Roosevelt's conscientious, deliberated effort to continue the Constitution as a truth and as a hope, not as a mere collection of obsolete phrases." If the enemies of change and of progress insisted on invoking the Constitution as an impediment to remedies for social and economic problems, the President declared, he would "have no other alternative than to go to the country with a Constitutional amendment that will lift the Dead Hand, giving the people of today the right to deal with today's vital issues." Since the amending process was so protracted, the President pointed out, his only recourse was to add enough liberal justices to the Court to forestall the efforts of the conservatives to block his programs. "Fire that," he told Creel, "as an opening gun." When the article appeared in *Collier's* magazine, the President and Creel both were surprised at the mildness of the public reaction.

The first defection from the administration ranks was Vice-President Garner, long restive over the course of the New Deal. Now he denounced Roosevelt as "the most destructive man in all American history." Hatton Summers, chairman of the House Judiciary Committee, bailed out with the declaration "Boys, here's where I cash in my chips." A serious defection was that of Burton K. Wheeler, the Montana maverick, who had been one of Roosevelt's earliest and most enthusiastic supporters. "I am not in sympathy with the plan to enlarge the Supreme Court," Wheeler declared. When Roosevelt twisted Wheeler's arm, he responded, "A liberal cause was never won by stacking a deck of cards, by stuffing a ballot box, or packing a court," a splendid sentiment but a dubious claim.

Day by day the chorus of indignation mounted. Carter Glass broke with the President, denouncing the scheme as "destitute of moral sensibility and without parallel since the foundation of the Republic," a statement which, as we have seen, was simply factually wrong. The *New York Herald Tribune* predicted the "end of the American state as it has existed throughout the long years of its life."

The judiciary reorganization bill was an undisguised blessing to Roosevelt's enemies. But it also pained his friends and put many of them in an awkward position. They did not wish to become open opponents of the plan, thereby weakening the President and his program and lending support to the opponents of the New Deal. On the other hand, they considered the proposal divisive and unwise. Some, while strongly opposed, kept silent—in the case of Frankfurter, his friends surmised, because he aspired to succeed Brandeis as the "Jewish" member of the Court. In addition to Wheeler, George Norris, architect of the TVA and one of the "Sons of the Wild Jackass" who had held the banner of the Wilson Progressives aloft through the long, dry years of Republican ascendancy, announced his opposition. Meanwhile, Walter Lippmann checked in with the charge that Roosevelt was "drunk with power" and bent on a "bloodless coup d'etat which strikes a deadly blow at the vital center of constitutional democracy." In thirty-seven different columns he denounced the plan to "pack" the Court.

Meanwhile the opponents of the court-packing plan in Congress passed the Retirement Act on March 1, 1937; it provided a generous retirement program for the justices and was plainly intended to weaken the argument for adding extra justices by encouraging the older members to retire.

Roosevelt's reaction was, like Admiral David Farragut's in the Civil War battle of Mobile Bay, "Damn the torpedoes—full speed ahead!" At a Democratic Party victory dinner he declared that the future of the New Deal programs and, indeed, of the nation itself was at stake. Should the justices of the Supreme Court be the final arbiters of the country's destiny? It would be a hollow triumph to preserve at least the justices' notion of the Constitution and lose the nation to chaos and revolution. The President took to the air to explain to the American people the rationale behind his action. He was not attacking the Court as an institution, as the third branch of the government; he was merely trying to prevent it from obstructing the administration's efforts to respond to the wishes of the electorate as expressed in his overwhelming victory in the recent elections. "We cannot yield our Constitutional destiny to the personal judgment of a few men who, being fearful of the future, would deny us the necessary means of dealing with the present." Having made his appeal to the public, Roosevelt proceeded to demonstrate the proposition that "the children of light must be as cunning as the children of darkness." He employed all the ancient means of persuasion to prevail on reluctant legislators to support legislation they disliked or abhorred. Political threats were supplemented with political promises. Senator Wheeler found that his income tax returns were being audited. A Democrat rumored to be a homosexual was investigated.

Despite the President's best efforts, a majority of the Judiciary Committee of the Senate issued a report on June 14 attacking the Court plan in detail. The scheme, according to the Senators, "stands now before the country, acknowledged by its proponents as a plan to force judicial interpretation of the Constitution, a proposal that violates every sacred tradition of American democracy.... Its ultimate operation would be to make this government one of men rather than of law.... It is a measure which should be so emphatically rejected that its parallel will never again be presented to the free representatives of the people of America."

Roosevelt was not without his defenders. The dean of the Notre Dame Law School, Thomas F. Konop, came to his support. The President had been accused of being an usurper, "a dictator and an autocrat," but, Konop argued, it was actually the Supreme Court that was "usurping the power of Congress and the President. It is the Supreme Court that has been destroying laws providing for a better life, more liberty and equality, social justice, and the pursuit of happiness of 130,000,000 people." Senator Borah was another supporter of the judiciary bill. "The driving power in politics in this country for years to come," he declared in the Senate, "will come from labor, from the producer, from small business, and from millions who have, through no fault of their own, been stripped of their life's savings and life's opportunities.... They are offered the Constitution. But people can't eat the Constitution."

Some critics of the Court, like the well-known lawyer, Morris Cohen, were far more radical in their approach. Seeing the Court as an obstacle not simply to reform but to all efforts to save the nation from revolutionary change to the right or left, they wished in effect to destroy it or to change it in so fundamental a fashion as to make it subservient to the executive and legislative branches. Cohen reproached Frankfurter for not supporting a more basic reform of the judicial system. "I should be lacking in candor," he wrote, "if I did not say frankly that the fundamental weakness of your position in this matter is due to your thinking in terms of personalities and neglecting ultimate issues. You think in terms of Holmes, Brandeis and Cardozo, and you think more men of that type would make the Supreme Court a good institution." Frankfurter ignored the fact that such men were, properly speaking, exceptions who got on the Court "only by accident" and were usually on the minority side. The real problem, in Cohen's view, was that the system was fundamentally dishonest. The Court " 'pretended' to say what the Constitution lays down," while in actual fact, as any rational person knew well enough, the justices simply imposed their own prejudices upon the rest of the country. "I am persuaded," Cohen wrote, "that if we are to emerge from the present economic and social chaos without resort to a communist revolution or a fascist dictatorship, it can only be by easing up the restraints which the present idolatry of the Constitution and the Courts put in the way of national planning of production for use instead of profit."

Frankfurter replied that he was well aware of Cohen's arguments and in large part agreed with them. But it would be a pyrrhic victory to emasculate the Court or sweep it aside in the name of saving the nation from a dictatorship of the right or left only to discover that the result was "a unitary state." Certainly the Court must respond to the "felt necessities of the time," and it was apt to be subject to severe strains when a President representing a new spirit and with a strong electoral mandate from the people found his way blocked by its aged and reactionary members, appointed when the mood and problems of the nation were very different. The first Roosevelt had had his troubles with the Court. La Follette in 1924 had proposed that Congress be authorized by amendment to override judicial decisions by a two-thirds majority.

Meanwhile, Chief Justice Hughes, with support from other justices, undertook to refute the President's charge that the age and precarious health of the older justices had caused a serious backlog of cases to accumulate. If there had been delays, Hughes wrote in a letter to the Senate Judiciary Committee, they were due not to the age of the justices but to the inefficiency of the attorney general, Homer Cummings.

More important, the Court in its first case after Roosevelt's assault on it rendered a decision in favor of a Washington State minimum wage law that was similar to a New York law that it had declared unconstitutional a year before. Justice Roberts lined up with Brandeis, Cardozo, Stone, and Hughes to produce a 5 to 4 verdict. "A switch in time saves nine," some wit proclaimed. Roberts later confessed that he had been well aware of the "tremendous strain and threat to the existing Court."

The Railway Labor Act and the farm mortgage moratorium—the Frazier-Lemke Act—were also upheld. A month later the critically important Wagner Act, concern for which had been a major factor in Roosevelt's decision to try to change the composition of the Court, was also validated, as was the Social Security Act. Six weeks later, on May 18, Justice Van Devanter, seventy-eight years old, announced his retirement; he had served on the Court for twenty-five years. Joe Robinson, Senator from Arkansas and a loyal supporter of the New Deal, advised Roosevelt to call off his campaign against the Court. "The thing to do is to settle this thing right now," he told a presidential aide: "this bill is raising hell in the Senate. Now it's going to be worse than ever, but if the President wants to compromise I can get him a couple of extra justices tomorrow. What he ought to do is say he's won, which he has, agree to compromise to make the thing sure, and wind the whole business up." But Roosevelt refused to be deflected. The fight had become one between the hard-core supporters of the New Deal and the old-line conservatives in the party, who had grown increasingly restive as the New Deal program unfolded. Roosevelt saw the Court fight as an opportunity to purge the party of halfhearted supporters and prospective opponents.

It seems evident that the feeling among lawmakers in Congress was far stronger than in the country at large. In Texas an ambitious young politician named Lyndon Johnson ran for Congress in a special election on his support for Roosevelt's Court reform plan and won. "Spring has come to Washington . . . " Roosevelt wrote William Bullitt, who had recently been shifted from ambassador to the Soviet Union to ambassador to France, "and even the Senators who were biting each other over the Supreme Court, are saying 'Alphonse' and 'Gaston' to each other. I, too, am influenced by this beautiful spring day. I haven't a care in the world which is going some for a President who is said by the newspapers to be a remorseless dictator driving his government into hopeless bankruptcy."

When Vice-President Garner got back from a five-week vacation in Texas, which was generally understood to be a flight from the Court fight, Roosevelt asked him what he thought the chances were of getting the judiciary reorganization bill through the Senate. "Do you want it with the bark on or off, Cap'n?"

"The rough way."

"All right. You are beat. You haven't got the votes."

And so it turned out. It was the sharpest defeat the President would experience during his long tenure of office. But luck, as they say, is more important than talent. There could have been no clearer evidence that Franklin Roosevelt was the child of fortune than the events that followed the defeat of his efforts to alter the composition of the Court by statute. In Roosevelt's words, "The Court yielded. The Court changed. The Court began to interpret the Constitution instead of torturing it. It was still the same Court, with the same justices. No new appointments had been made. And yet, beginning shortly after the message of February 5, 1937, what a change!" To Roosevelt it was evident "that the change would never have come, unless this frontal attack had been made upon the philosophy of a majority of the Court."

Fortune followed on fortune. Van Devanter's retirement permitted Roosevelt to nominate Hugo Black to his seat. Cardozo's unexpected death created another opening, and Roosevelt, confident of Frankfurter's liberalism and grateful for his loyalty, offered the justiceship to the Harvard Law professor, after it might be said, skillful and energetic lobbying on the part of Frankfurter's "hot dogs" in the administration.

Not surprisingly, there was considerable opposition to Frankfurter's appointment. Those who opposed it were afraid that his reputation as a spokesman for the left and an advocate of unpopular causes, notably his defense of Sacco and Vanzetti, would give rise to charges that Roosevelt was soft on "Reds." A group of prominent Jews urged Roosevelt not to make the appointment on the ground that it might fan the anti-Semitic sentiment which seemed to be growing almost monthly in the country and to which the rise of Hitler in Germany had given dramatic emphasis. There was, after all, a liberal Jew, Brandeis, on the bench. To add another would be to reinforce the notion that Jews were radicals or at least liberals. Pat McCarran of Nevada, at the Senate hearings on Frankfurter's confirmation, tried to use the latter's friendship with Harold Laski to pin the label "Socialist" on the candidate, but Roosevelt stood fast. Frankfurter was effusive in his thanks. "And now, on your blessed birthday," he wrote the President, "I am given the opportunity for service to the Nation, which, in any circumstances would be owing, but which I would rather at your hands than at those of any President barring Lincoln."

The retirement of other "standpat" justices, old and broken in spirit, followed. Before his second term was over, there was an unmistakably "Roosevelt Court." The appointments of Black and Frankfurter were followed by those of Stanley Reed, William O. Douglas, and Frank Murphy. The President, who had complained that in his first four years of office he had had no opportunity to appoint a justice sympathetic to his own views, was able to appoint five in the next four years. Black, whose appointment had been opposed by liberals on the ground that he had been, briefly, a member of the Ku Klux Klan, turned out to be the most liberal justice (his only rival in that regard was Douglas), and Frankfurter the most conservative, of the five.

But there were important items on the debit side of the political ledger as a consequence of the Court fight. For only the second time in almost five years Congress had summoned up the resolution to oppose the President on a major issue (the World Court was the other major setback). Moreover, it had won the political equivalent of the shoot-out at the OK Corral. Instead of driving the conservative Democrats out of the party, the President had encouraged them to form an alliance with conservative Republicans. From this point on New Deal legislation met with increasing opposition in Congress. As for Roosevelt, despite his outward air of bravado, Ickes noted, "He is punch drunk from the punishment that he has suffered recently."

Historians are still debating (and will doubtless continue to debate) Roosevelt's judgment in attacking the Court head-on. A common argument is that if he had simply been a little more patient, he would, in the normal course of things, have had the opportunity to appoint liberal justices, who would have shifted the balance of the Court decisively in favor of the New Deal. But that is wisdom after the fact. The threat to New Deal legislation was certainly not an imaginary one. In Roosevelt's view, the peril to the nation was acute. The disposition of the Court to strike down major New Deal programs threatened the success of the fight against the Depression and, equally important, Roosevelt's social legislation.

The mood of Congress might be gauged by the renewed assault on Frances Perkins. Her principal tormentor was the Texas Congressman Martin Dies. Tall, blond, and aggressive, he was completely indifferent to the claims of justice or fair play in the indiscriminate pursuit of his victims. Relying on the testimony of self-appointed "Red" hunters before his Committee on Un-American Activities, he threw his net wide enough to take in virtually every individual of liberal sentiments in the country. On August 30, 1937, Dies declared that deportation proceedings against Harry Bridges "should be commenced without further delay." Perkins replied that the issue was in the hands of the courts. Dies's response was to threaten impeachment proceedings against her. "The responsibility for this breakdown in the enforcement of our deportation laws must be laid at the door of Secretary Perkins. The conclusion is inescapable that Secretary Perkins and those around her are not in sympathy with the deportation of radical aliens."

Dies also directed his fire at Governor Frank Murphy of Michigan for failing to call out the national guard to drive strikers out of the General Motors plant in Flint. Murphy, Dies declared, had been hand in glove with Communists in the CIO. Roosevelt, anxious to try to save Murphy's hide in the upcoming gubernatorial election, expressed his regret that the committee had allowed itself to be used "in a flagrantly unfair and un-American attempt to influence an election."

In addition to Pekins, Dies decided Harold Ickes and Harry Hopkins had filled their agencies with "many radical associates." He declared, "These satellites range in political insanity from Socialist to Communist. . . . " They were devoted to the "promotion of class hatred" and had "succeeded in spreading their venom far beyond the confines of their departments and in securing the passage of certain legislation bearing their unmistakable imprint."

Inspired by Dies's attacks, hate mail poured into Perkins's office. It was the most difficult period of her years in political life. Personal attacks were not new to her, as we have seen. She had, almost from the beginning of the administration, been criticized and ridiculed for being a radical and, perhaps worse, a woman. She had gotten little support from labor, at least from Bill Green and the conservative AFL, and even liberal journalists seemed to take a mean-spirited delight in sniping at her. She was asked such questions as "Are you a Communist?" and "Is your daughter married to Harry Bridges?" She found strength in her visits to the Episcopal convent in Maryland and in prayer. She drafted a statement on the Bridges case, and included in it a statement of her own philosophy. "Communism," she wrote, "has no place in American life. I am not an expert on Communist teaching but the concept of a dictatorship of the proletariat and the contempt for Christian ethics, concepts reiterated in communist literature, are contrary to all my beliefs, devoted as I have always been to the democratic principles of our own Constitution with the protection of individual liberties, freedom of religious worship and freedom of speech. . . . " J. Parnell Thomas, a New Jersey Congressman, as primitive a thinker as Martin Dies, introduced a resolution in the House at the end of January, 1938, calling for the impeachment of Perkins and two officials of the Immigration Service.

A special hearing on Bridges's deportation was set up by Perkins, who chose James Landis, dean of the Harvard Law School and ex-chairman of the Securities and Exchange Commission, to conduct it. After weeks of testimony from some sixty witnesses Landis concluded that "the evidence . . . establishes neither that Harry R. Bridges is a member of nor affiliated with the Communist party of the United States of America." Now Landis began to receive hate mail denouncing him as a "Goddamn Communist" and a "Goddamn Jew." Perkins was also denounced again as a Jew. Congressman Philip Bennett of Missouri spoke of "Frances (Wadski) Perkins" and her "native Russia" and referred to her as being "surrounded . . . by Communists."

Whatever the cost of the effort to alter the composition of the Supreme Court, it seems clear in retrospect that the one thing that the President could not have done was to have done "nothing." He could not stand by while the Court dismantled the program on which his administration had staked its reputation—a program which, it could be argued, had received the overwhelming approval of the American people. There was, it must be said, a good deal of misplaced piety and not a little hypocrisy in the outrage expressed by conservative politicians and indignant Liberty Leaguers. The simple fact was that the Supreme Court from its inception had, in the main, supported the status quo or the status quo ante and supported the rights of property far more consistently than the rights of individuals. If the Court was a coordinate branch of the government, it had never been intended by the Founders that it should dominate the other two—the executive and the legislative.

Granted that Franklin Roosevelt had to take some action to ensure that the Court did not continue to frustrate the will of the people as expressed through him, the plan he settled on—changing the number of justices—had, as we have seen, a respectable history behind it.

The impression is sometimes conveyed by hasty historians that the court-packing plan was defeated because the country, morally outraged, rose against it. The facts are somewhat different. The opinions of the electorate underwent a considerable change as it became clear that the Court was obstructing the New Deal. A Gallup Poll taken in November, 1935 (one of Gallup's earliest polls), purported to show that 53 percent of the American people were opposed to "limiting the power of the Supreme Court to declare acts of Congress unconstitutional," while only 31 percent expressed themselves in favor. But in February, 1937, another poll showed the voters closely divided on the Roosevelt plan to "reorganize" the Supreme Court—47 percent yes to 53 percent no. While the overall vote on the Supreme Court plan was close, among Democrats 75 percent favored it. At the same time the President's voter approval percentage rose to its highest level.

Packing the Supreme Court was primarily a political issue, not a moral issue, as its opponents charged. The Constitution, as we have noted, is vague on the function of the Court. It seems clear, for instance, that many of the Federalists in the Constitutional Convention intended the Court to declare unconstitutional state and Federal statutes which were contrary to the Bill of Rights as well as to specific provisions of the Constitution. The Court, throughout much of its history, had avoided civil rights issues by taking the line that these were the responsibility of the states. This was indeed the assumption that ended the Reconstruction era. Many Southern legislators deserted Roosevelt on the Court issue for three primary reasons. First, the South had a genuine reverence for custom and tradition (although it might be noted that Thomas Jefferson was the first President to try to emasculate the Court on the ground that it thwarted the popular will). Beyond that, the South was mortally afraid that a "liberal" Court would undertake to enforce the civil rights of black Southerners; that was the fear that kept Southerners awake at night. Finally, many Southern legislators, caught between their own conservative convictions and the enormous popularity of the President in their home states and districts, felt freer to vote for New Deal legislation because of their convictions (or hope) that the Supreme Court would throw it out. In other words, they counted on the Court to pull their consciences out of the fire.

One of the few positive accomplishments of Congress in 1937 was the Bankhead-Jones Farm Tenant Act, passed in July, replacing the Resettlement Administration with the Farm Security Administration, an agency with the more modest assignment of providing long-term mortgages for farm families as well as labor camps for migratory workers. The most important aspect of the Farm Security Administration was its commitment to giving black farmers equality with whites.

An effective measure of the FSA was the withdrawal of more than 20,000,000 acres of marginal farmland from production. As a consequence, in part at least, of the various New Deal farm programs, the price of cotton rose from five cents a pound to twelve, while corn rose from ten cents a bushel to seventy cents. As farm income increased, ancillary services for the farm—seed and fertilizers and farm machinery—also registered gains. But the gains were threatened by a recession.

One of the most devastating scandals to hit the financial community in its long history came early in 1937 with the revelation that Richard Whitney, president of the New York Stock Exchange, had appropriated a client's securities. William Douglas, head of the SEC, which had carried on a running fight with the New York exchange, was exultant. "The Stock Exchange," he wrote years later, still savoring the moment, "was delivered into my hands." Douglas hurried around to the White House with the news. Roosevelt, who had gone to Groton with Whitney, exclaimed, "Not Dick Whitney!"

"Yes, Dick Whitney."

"Dick Whitney—Dick Whitney, I can't believe it," Roosevelt kept repeating. Although Whitney had been one of his most vocal critics, Roosevelt took no pleasure in the news. Douglas realized he was close to tears. Whitney's brother *was* the House of Morgan; the Whitney family epitomized the Eastern upper-class establishment. One of the foundation stones of its claim to power and privilege was its subscription to the code of the gentleman, the code that Endicott Peabody had tried to instill in every young Groton student. Thomas Dewey, Douglas's Columbia Law School classmate, had recently been elected New York County district attorney. Dewey wanted to close the case as quickly and quietly as possible. Whitney could be arraigned before a judge, plead guilty, and be sentenced. Douglas was determined to use the occasion to "disclose the whole anatomy of Wall Street chicanery and corruption." He ordered a thorough investigation. The exchange's counsel was a suave representative of Whitney's class, Dean Acheson—"elegant, able, fastidious, and conservative." The scandal greatly strengthened the hands of those members of the administration who, like Douglas, wished to impose strict regulations on stock market manipulations.

In May, 1937, Roosevelt sent a fair labor standards bill to Congress. A child labor amendment that had been sent to the states years earlier was still short, by some eight states, of the number needed for ratification. The fair labor standards bill included a child labor clause, and the President in his accompanying message declared: "A self-supporting and self-respecting democracy can plead no justification for the existence of child labor, no economic reason for chiseling workers' wages or stretching workers' hours." The bill would authorize Congress to set minimum wages and maximum hours upon the advice of a Fair Labor Standards Board. When Congress was cool to the bill, Roosevelt persisted, urging that body eight months later, in January, 1938, to take action, noting, "We are seeking only, of course, to end starvation wages and intolerable hours. More desirable wages are, and should continue to be, the product of collective bargaining." One of the problems was strong labor opposition. Once again, this was based on the apprehension of labor leaders that if the government mandated minimum wages and maximum hours, there would be less incentive on the part of workers to join unions. As one labor leader put it, "If you give them something for nothing, they won't join the union."

While Congress vacillated, Claude Pepper in Florida and Lister Hill in Alabama won substantial victories based on their announced support for the administration bill. Congress capitulated and agreed on a compromise bill, which Roosevelt signed on June 25, 1938. "Everybody claimed credit for it," Frances Perkins wrote later. "The AFL said it was their bill and their contribution. The CIO claimed full credit for its passage. I cannot remember whether the President and I claimed credit, but we always thought we had done it." The standards it set were modest enough. Wages should begin at a minimum of twenty-five cents an hour, rising to forty cents in seven years. There should be a forty-four-hour week, falling to forty hours after three years. The Bureau of Labor Statistics calculated that in September, 1938, some 250,000 businesses, employing more than 11,000,000 workers, were affected.

In June Roosevelt, always concerned about deficits, cut spending sharply, curtailing public works and cutting thousands of workers from the public payroll. The budget was balanced for the first time since the crash. The result was a severe recession, announced by a sharp drop in the New York Stock Exchange on so-called Black Tuesday, September 7, 1937.

William O. Douglas, recently appointed head of the SEC, resisted pressure from Charles Gay, the president of the New York exchange, to close it, as Douglas had the power to do. If he did so, he replied, the New Deal would be charged with responsibility for the market's not operating. The market, he told Gay, would have to seek its own equilibrium. Gay then appealed to the President, who called Douglas to add his pressure to Gay's. Roosevelt believed that the market was dropping as the result of a conspiracy between "Business and Wall Street against yours truly." Douglas replied, "You're dead wrong. The market is going down because you cut spending." Marriner Eccles, head of the Federal Reserve, also urged Roosevelt to abandon his balanced budget mania and accept deficit spending as a practical necessity at least for the time being. Morgenthau was bitterly opposed, blaming the recession on that famous scapegoat the loss of "business confidence."

Alarmed over the deteriorating state of the economy and perhaps anxious to recoup some of the prestige he had lost in the Court battle, Roosevelt called Congress into a special session in November. When he was preparing his message for the session, Morgenthau said to him, "What business wants to know is: are we headed toward state socialism or are we going to continue on a capitalistic basis?" Roosevelt's answer was: "I have told them again and again." But it was never apparently enough. When Morgenthau spoke at the Academy of Political Science several days later, his audience included the "wealthiest and most conservative business men in New York City," and the atmosphere crackled with hostility. Morgenthau insisted that the administration wanted "to see capital go into productive channels of private industry. We want to see private business expand. We believe that much of the remaining unemployment will disappear as private capital funds are increasingly employed in productive enterprise. We believe that one of the most important ways of achieving these ends at the time is to continue progress toward a balance of the federal budget." When Morgenthau's remarks were greeted with hoots and derisive laughter, he was almost persuaded that Roovevelt's description of the business community as irreconcilable was accurate.

It was soon evident that the special session was a mistake. Roosevelt presented a bill for governmental reorganization as well as a national farm act to take the place of the emergency AAA. Congress fell savagely on the governmental reorganization bill, declaring it was evidence that Roosevelt wished to make himself a dictator. The response was clearly out of all proportion to the provocation, if the bill could be called provocative at all. It called for two new Cabinet posts—Social Welfare and Public Works—and recommended extending the merit system in Federal appointments "upward, outward, and downward to cover practically all non-policy-determining posts" (therefore, of course, depriving Congress of many potential patronage appointments). Walsh of Massachusetts called it a dagger plunged "into the very heart of democracy." Roosevelt was compared to Hitler in his lust for power.

The dictatorship charge was too much for Roosevelt. At Warm Springs Roosevelt called in reporters and issued a statement: "I have no inclination to be a dictator.... I have none of the qualifications which would make me a successful dictator.... I have too much historical background and too much knowledge of existing dictatorships to make me desire any form of dictatorship for a democracy like the United States of America."

Ickes attributed part of the resistance to the proposal for a Department of Social Welfare to the fear on the part of Congress that Harry Hopkins would be made secretary of the new department and use it to promote his radical ideas. The Roman Catholic hierarchy, Ickes believed, was afraid that Hopkins would disseminate birth control literature.

The President's farm bill fared no better. Congress adjourned without passing any of the legislation he had requested. His response was a cruise in the Caribbean on the *Potomac* with Hopkins, Ickes (who shared a stateroom with Hopkins), the assistant attorney general, Robert Jackson, and Pa Watson. The trip was not a great success. The weather was bad, Ickes and Hopkins were seasick, and the fishing was poor. To Ickes the President seemed tired—"He looked bad and he seemed listless." Ickes could not tell whether the trouble was "spiritual or physical."

For months the economy worsened while a debate raged in the administration over its cause and its remedy. In April, 1938, Harry Hopkins, out of the hospital after a serious stomach operation, tipped the balance in favor of renewed spending. When Henry Morgenthau, champion of the balanced budget approach, returned to Washington from a brief vacation, he reported to his staff that the spenders "have just stampeded him [the President] during the week I was away. He was completely stampeded. They stampeded him like cattle." The WPA, the CCC, and the National Youth Authority, which had been in the process of being phased out, were cranked up again. Programs of slum clearance and Federally subsidized housing were initiated, farm subsidies were increased, and a new program of naval construction launched. But 9,000,000 Americans were unemployed. As Hosea Hudson put it, "We had a Depression.... We got out of the Depression. Then we had a recession, last of '37. When that recession came in '37, everybody what had done got a job, practically, was throwed back out in the street." Just after the first of the year word came that unemployment compensation would be paid. It was, inevitably, a cumbersome bureaucratic process. An unemployed person had to apply, had to be approved, and often had to wait a month or more for the first payment. Meantime, there was a problem of eating and paying rent.

In the realm of foreign affairs Japan had turned on China in July as the first step in the creation of a "new order" in East Asia, an order clearly to be dominated by Japan. A special session of the League Assembly was called at the request of China to give attention to the occupation of Shanghai by the Japanese, during which, it was charged, many atrocities were committed by the Japanese Army. The Japanese delegation was headed by a woman, Tsuneo Matsudaira. As we have noted earlier, a faction of the British Conservative Party, led, at least according to William Bullitt, by Lord Beaverbrook and Winston Churchill, was indifferent to the fate of China and anticipated an "understanding" with Japan. France was also determined not to antagonize the Japanese, hoping that country would provide a counterweight against Russian ambitions in the Far East. The French representative was described by Hamilton Fish Armstrong as "verbose, rhetorical, sentimental," and Sir John Simon, the head of the British mission, was, again in Armstrong's view, "pompous and vacillating." The position of the small nations was anomalous. They were acutely conscious of the importance of preserving the ideals of the League as put forth in the Covenant, but if they pressed the moral argument, they risked alienating those nations that would, they hoped, provide a shield against aggression directed at any one of them. As Armstrong put it, "they had to vindicate the prestige of the League, but not at the risk of destroying the League." Not surprisingly, it proved a task beyond their modest capacities.

The United States had had a long and close relationship with China. American missionaries had made it their special field of Christian endeavor, just as New England merchants had made it a mainstay of their foreign trade. With the Japanese invasion in mind an indignant Roosevelt delivered in Chicago in October what came to be known as the Quarantine Speech. The President warned that "Innocent peoples . . . [and] innocent nations are being cruelly sacrificed to greed for power. If those things come to pass in other parts of the world let no one imagine that America will escape, that Americans may expect mercy, that the Western Hemisphere will not be attacked and that it will continue tranquilly and peacefully. . . . When an epidemic of physical disease starts to spread, the community approves and joins in a quarantine of the patients in order to protect the health of the community against the spread of the disease. . . . War is a contagion be it declared or undeclared. It can engulf states and peoples remote from the original scene of hostilities. . . . It is true," he declared, "that the moral consciousness of the world must recognize the importance of removing injustices and well-founded grievances, but at the same time it must be aroused to the cardinal necessity of honoring sanctity of treaties, of respecting the rights and liberties of others, and of putting an end to acts of international aggression. It seems to be unfortunately true that the epidemic of world lawlessness is spreading. . . ."

Roosevelt wrote Colonel House, "I hope you liked the Chicago speech, and the repercussions across the water. I . . . verily believe that as time goes on we can slowly but surely make people realize that war will be a greater danger to us if we close all the doors and windows than if we go out in the street and use our influence to curb the riot." Once again the nation's principal pedagogue was planning to educate the American people to the realities of international politics. He was criticized by some internationalists for not following his Quarantine Speech with specific measures, but Roosevelt believed the country needed time to come to the conclusion that aggression must be punished by the international community.

The reaction to the Quarantine Speech indicated how strongly the passions of the isolationists ran and how many Americans shared the isolationist sentiment. It was proclaimed in numerous newspaper editorials that all Europe was not worth the death of one American boy. "The President was attacked by a vast majority of the press," Sam Rosenman wrote. "Telegrams of denunciation came in at once. . . . " Rosenman recalled that the President said to him, "It's a terrible thing to look over your shoulder when you are trying to lead—and to find no one there." Hugh Johnson, ex-head of the NRA, criticized the President for nudging the country toward war "without taking this people into much more confidence than is displayed in this collection of warlike hints." Walter Lippmann was also alarmed. "We can well afford to say plainly," he wrote, "that the Chinese must defend their own country, and that we have no political interests whatever in Asia." The true center of American interest was in Europe, not in the Far East, and the guarantor of American security was the British fleet. "In the final test," Lippmann wrote in *Foreign Affairs*, "no matter what we may wish now or now believe, though collaboration with Britain and her allies is difficult and often irritating, we shall protect that connection because in no other way can we fulfill our destiny." While highly critical of the reluctance of the European powers to check Hitler's invasion of the Rhineland, Lippmann shrank from strong measures against Japan. He felt it would be a grave mistake for the United States "to take the sole responsibility and bear the whole onus of dealing with Japanese expansion."

The Japanese response was characteristic. On December 12, 1937, the well-marked gunboat USS *Panay*, while anchored in the Yangtze River above Nanking, was attacked by Japanese warplanes and sunk. As those aboard—crew, newsmen, and some executives of Standard Oil—tried to reach shore on rafts, they were strafed by the Japanese pilots, and forty were wounded. The act seemed a deliberate provocation, but the Japanese expressed their regrets and agreed to a substantial indemnity.

# 30

# The CIO

Following the World War, American workers lost ground, as we have noted. Most unions lost members, sometimes in considerable numbers. The AFL was highly conservative, and in many industries unions were virtually nonexistent. Prior to 1929, 55 percent of all strikes were over wages and hours; only some 24 percent were fought over the issue of collective bargaining. These figures point up the weakness of unions. Beginning in 1934, with the stimulus of the NRA labor codes, the number of strikes increased dramatically. But such modest successes as labor unions achieved came at a high price in battle casualties—in killed and wounded in action. From August through October, 1933, fifteen strikers were killed on picket lines, and hundreds injured, many seriously. Forty were killed in 1934, and forty-eight in the next two years.

Many communities had groups such as the Black Legion, formed specifically to wage war against "foreigners" and "Communists," with whom they equated union members, and radicals in general. The Ku Klux Klan was always ready for an antiunion foray, and citizens' committees made up of small-business men and professionals also stood ready to engage in tactics of intimidation and harassment.

Under the stimulus of Section 7(a) of the NIRA, the nation was swept by a wave of organizing activities and strikes, led, in many instances, by the Communists. Two of the most dramatic were the Toledo Auto-Lite strike and a national strike in the textile industry.

Early in 1933 there were a series of strikes in Detroit and Toledo auto plants, led by an organization that called itself the Auto Workers Union and functioned under the wing of the Communist-dominated Trade Union Unity League (TUUL). Wyndham Mortimer, struggling to unionize the White Motor Company and getting only indifference or open opposition from the AFL, had turned to the TUUL. The principal AFL contribution was a leaflet distributed at a meeting of the workers in the White plant that read: "All White Motor production workers under one charter now. CHOOSE BETWEEN FRANKLIN DELANO ROOSEVELT AND JOE STALIN," the implication being that a craft or "trade" union was American and an industrial union—"one charter"—Communist.

Frustrated by the AFL Metal Trades Council, Mortimer appealed to the newly appointed Automobile Labor Board, which had the responsibility for formulating a code for the automobile industry under the terms of the NIRA. There he found an unabashed open-shop philosophy, but encouraged by Section 7(a), union activists were busy in a number of auto plants, recruiting union members and applying for elections under the Automobile Labor Board. At every step of the way they encountered resistance from the AFL Executive Council. On one occasion, when leaders of the various locals seemed determined to strike, an AFL official produced a bogus telegram which he read: "Strongly urge against strike situation demands peaceful negotiations Franklin Delano Roosevelt."

At the Toledo Auto-Lite strike some 4,000 employees walked out. While a judge limited picketing to 25 strikers, the company rounded up 1,800 strikebreakers, many of them blacks. The Lucas County Unemployed League, led by two disciples of A. J. Muste, Sam Pollock, and Ted Selander, took over the picketing. By the third day they had mobilized 5,000 unemployed. Pollock and Selander were arrested, but as soon as they were released, they returned to the picket lines, which held firm despite further injunctions and police harassment. After two weeks a strikebreaker threw a bolt from a factory window that hit a woman picket and seriously injured her. Police arrived to escort more strikebreakers into the factory, and tear gas grenades were tossed into the picket lines. The angry unemployed, now entirely mixed in with the striking workers, formed such a dense mass around the factory gates that strikebreakers and police could get neither in nor out. The factory was in a state of siege. After fifteen hours 900 national guardsmen arrived at the plant to rescue the strikebreakers. For the next six days the soldiers, young and inexperienced, found themselves the object of the crowd's attention. Young women taunted them, and an occasional rock or bottle was hurled at them. Finally, frightened and demoralized, they fired into the crowd, killing 2 people and wounding 24 more. In a six-block area a battle raged between the strikers and their sympathizers and the beleaguered guardsmen. With talk of revolution commonplace, 40,000 people turned out in protest against the guards. The alarmed governor ordered the troops removed, and the plant gave up its effort to continue operation and negotiated a settlement with the union.

In Minneapolis three major strikes were conducted, in Sidney Lens's words, with "military precision." The leader of the truck drivers of that city was Karl Skoglund, a Swedish immigrant and a Trotskyite. Skoglund organized the drivers of coal trucks of sixty-seven coal companies and led them on a carefully planned strike that soon forced the companies to capitulate. Four other Trotskyite leaders, three of them brothers, Vincent, Grant, and Miles Dunne, signed up 3,000 "inside warehousemen" with Local 574 of the Teamsters. The Dunne brothers, a hard-bitten trio, organized flying squads, such as those used in the cotton mill strike in Gastonia, to cruise the city and be sure no coal companies were operating. When some gas stations persisted in remaining open, the flying squads, which were often composed of a dozen or more cars loaded with strikers, demolished their gas pumps.

The headquarters of the strike was in a large garage, where strikers were fed and where as many as 1,000 men and women could sleep. There were a hospital, a press headquarters, facilities for union meetings, and a dispatch center for the flying squads. Cabdrivers, unable to get gas, joined the strike, and they were followed by 35,000 building trades workers and, several days later, 10,000 streetcar employees.

As in other cities, businessmen and the more conservative elements formed a Citizens' Alliance to help break the strike; "to protect our homes and our wives and daughters" was the way it was commonly put. On May 21 and 22, 1934, the police, in anticipation of a clash between the Citizens' Alliance and the strikers, began to move perishable food from the central market. Local 574 had laid careful plans. Some 600 men were posted in the Central Labor Union headquarters; 900 more were held in reserve at the garage. At an agreed-upon signal the strikers, armed with clubs and bricks, surrounded the market and the police and attacked them. At one point in the fight a striker with 25 men on his truck drove into a squad of police who were about to open fire. As a result, 30 police were hospitalized. The next day it was estimated that 20,000 people took to the streets to do battle with 2,000 police and deputies. By evening the police and deputies had been routed, with 2 killed, one a lawyer for the Citizens' Alliance. Hundreds of law enforcement officers had been injured, along with a number of members of the Citizens' Alliance and many of the strikers and their supporters. The leftist governor of Minnesota, Floyd Olson, negotiated a truce and called off the national guard. The companies involved agreed to recognize the union, and the strike leaders claimed victory. But a few weeks later there was another violent outbreak, this time over the meaning of the word "recognition." It resulted in 55 pickets being shot and 2 killed. After five more weeks of sporadic violence, the employers accepted most of the union demands.

Under Section 7(a) of the NIRA, the textile industry, rather to everyone's surprise, had adopted a liberal labor code which increased wages by sixty-five percent, outlawed child labor, and established a board to hear labor disputes. But it was soon evident that the mill-owners had no intention of abiding by the labor provisions of the code. Out of 2,000 cases brought to the labor board for arbitration, only a handful had been acted upon in favor of the workers. Francis Gorman, a leader of the textile workers, called a strike in September, 1934. The strike was called on the ground that the industry was not only not paying the NRA minimum wage of $12 to $15 a week but was increasing work loads by as much as 100 percent. More than 350,000 workers in textile mills from New England to Georgia and Alabama were involved. Again with the union using the tactics of flying squads, mills were shut down, and open war was waged between armed strikers and police and national guardsmen, aided and abetted by the Ku Klux Klan and "cit-izens'" committees. At Greenville, South Carolina, a community with a long history of violence, in a battle between deputies and members of a flying squad a striker was killed. At Trion, Georgia, in a two-hour gun battle, a deputy sheriff and a striker were killed and 15 strikers were wounded; 3 were wounded at Augusta, Georgia, and 1 killed at Honea Path, South Carolina. Violence flared in Rhode Island and in Lancaster, Pennsylvania, and it was estimated that by the second week of the strike 15,000 national guardsmen had been called out in seven states. In Georgia Governor Eugene Talmadge set up a concentration camp for arrested strikers. In Fitchburg, Massachusetts, Powers Hapgood was checked by police when he tried to form a picket line with 50 pickets at a local mill. He mustered 500 workers drawn from other plants in a flying squadron, broke through the police barricades, and got his pickets in place around the plant. Finally, the leaders of the strike responded to President Roosevelt's request that they accept the arbitration of the Textile Labor Relations Board. The result was profoundly disappointing to the textile workers: They gained little or nothing, and 15,000 union members were denied reemployment. Some of those returning to work were required to sign the outlawed yellow dog contracts, promising not to join a union. Disillusioned members dropped out of the union by the tens of thousands.

As we have said before, the American labor movement, which, for all practical purposes, was the American Federation of Labor, was in the hands of a thoroughly conservative, not to say reactionary, group of leaders, most of them old-line union bosses more interested in their own powers and prerogatives than in the fate of workers. Nonetheless, the AFL profited from the growing militancy of workingmen and workingwomen. In the period of a year—July, 1933, to July, 1934—the AFL issued 1,300 charters for national unions, five times as many as in the previous five years. There were almost as many independent unions outside the AFL as there were affiliated with it. At the 1935 AFL convention, Charles P. Howard, one of John L. Lewis's lieutenants, declared, "I don't know, there is no one at this convention who knows . . . how many workers have been organized into independent unions, company unions and associations that may have affiliation with subversive influences during the past few years," but he believed the number was "far greater than any one of us would grant."

The refusal of the old-line AFL leadership to accept or cooperate with industrial unions created an acute crisis in the labor movement. "A few of the Old Guard," Len De Caux wrote, "were once union pioneers, even radicals, but in office lived down such juvenile delinquency. The once-radical were expert at sniffing and driving out the now-radical . . . [and] the union bosses continued indefinitely . . . to curb all inner-union critics as communists or in league with communists. . . . Union bosses saw in anti-communism a common ground for winning favor from employers who otherwise hated the unions' guts."

Prominent among these labor troglodytes was John L. Lewis, head of the United Mine Workers. Large, menacing, with black beetle brows and bulldog jowls, he appeared an exemplar of the old-fashioned labor boss. One of five intensely loyal brothers, of whom it was said that if you fought one Lewis, you had to fight them all, Lewis had the reputation in radical labor circles of being a ruthless suppressor of anyone who challenged his leadership. He had fought the Communists in his United Mine Workers and later, in the third period, in the "parallel" union, the National Miners Union, and he had loudly denounced William Foster as a union wrecker.

He spoke, orated, in a rich basso profundo, rolling the consonants and vowels on his tongue. One of his lieutenants, Len De Caux, recalled in later years a "broad, black-coated back. A black fedora atop a large head, made larger by back-bulging hair. A big and solid figure of a man walking slowly, black cane in hand." Saul Alinsky, another Lewis aide, told of Lewis's role in negotiations at the time of the Chrysler strike. The Chrysler legal counsel, Nicholas Kelley, "was so hostile and insulting" that Lewis took him down a peg or two with his most intimidating manner, at which Kelley jumped up and cried, "Stop it, stop it, Mr. Lewis! . . . Mr. Lewis, I want you to know, Mr. Lewis, that I-I-I am not afraid of your eyebrows."

Lewis was also, as it turned out, a man with an acute sense of the tides of history; he was the first and virtually the only old-line labor leader to perceive the possibilities inherent in Section 7(a) of the National Industrial Recovery Act. He was also well aware of a ferment among young union members, in incipient revolt against their standpat elders, and he decided to place himself at the head of it.

Lewis, De Caux insisted, was highly pragmatic. "He didn't adopt any of the social-reformist, radical, religious, capitalist philosophies current in the labor movement. . . . He was too complex and unrestricted to be a pure-and-simple unionist. . . . He carried a minimum of ideological baggage. . . . His mind ran to practical politics, personal psychology, conclusions from his own experience and observations, rather than to theories absorbed from books." Certainly he had a remarkable capacity for self-dramatization. One of his favorite sayings was "He who tooteth not his own horn, the same shall not be tooted." Alinsky wrote of him: "He is a great leader. The other so-called labor leaders I have worked under are like children compared to John. He can set you afire, he is the greatest of them all."

The initial engagement between the old-line unionists and the insurgents led by Lewis took place in 1934 at the AFL convention. There Lewis began to form the nucleus of rebellion, a rebellion that eventually led to the formation of a rival union, the CIO. Among his coadjutors were such liberal union leaders as Sidney Hillman, David Dubinsky, and Philip Murray. Hillman had been "a teen-age revolutionist" in Russia and had been jailed for his radical activities. Arriving in the United States in 1907, he plunged into the fight of his fellow immigrants in the garment trades for unions and for decent pay and working conditions. A friend of Hillman's told De Caux that the union leader thought that "the police of Chicago were more brutal than those of Russia; that its prisons were more loathsome; that the treatment of prisoners was more barbarous." The New Deal, De Caux wrote, "gave Hillman his big chance. It was made for him, and he for it." Hillman had already "pioneered in planning, industry-regulation, capital-labor adjustment, social welfare of every kind the New Deal had in mind. A brain trust? Hillman had his professors, economists, social workers, long before the New Deal. . . . He furnished a ready made model for the whole New Deal."

If that was something of an overstatement, it was certainly true that Hillman and Roosevelt seemed "made for each other." Hillman was a strong advocate of cooperating with employers. "That is what a union is for," he told an interviewer. "I even believe in helping an employer to function more productively, for then we have a claim to higher wages, shorter hours, and greater participation in the benefits of a smooth industrial machine."

The fact was that the Amalgamated Clothing Workers under Hillman's leadership had brought a degree of order out of the chaos of the industry, thereby benefiting both capitalists and workers. "He had won over many clothing employers," De Caux (whose wife, Caroline, worked for Hillman), wrote, "with his integrity, his realism, his practical business sense."

De Caux described Hillman as looking like an up-to-date professor or a rabbi: "He was emotional—high strung and nervous at times, a hand-wringer under reverses, but mostly eager and enthusiastic." Hillman's faction was predominantly Jewish, intellectual, Socialist or Communist and was referred to by conservative union leaders as pinko. His union had only recently been affiliated with the AFL. John L. Lewis told De Caux in a confidential moment, "I believe Sidney is really scared of them [the Communists]." The remark was a revealing one. Lewis was far from being a Communist himself, but he felt entirely capable of controlling the Communists and had, in consequence, no fear of them; he judged them by their works.

David Dubinsky, who had been an ardent Socialist and a bitter enemy of the Communists, was head of the Ladies' Garment Workers and a member of the AFL Executive Council. The "needle unions"— the garment workers of Dubinsky and Hillman essentially—"had used revolutionaries, socialists, anarchists, poets even, to get things started— for the bureaucrats to take over," De Caux noted.

Philip Murray was an important Lewis lieutenant. Murray had been born in Scotland in 1886. He had served as vice-president of the United Mine Workers since 1916 and was a member of an advisory board of the NRA. Murray told De Caux that he had no "ideology," but to De Caux that was only half true. As a devout Roman Catholic Murray had, if not an ideology, a loyalty and a political philosophy which "called for reforms within the capitalist structure, without challenging capitalism itself. . . . Murray based his philosophy on church doctrine" which envisioned "tripartite government-employers-labor councils in each industry," a plan consistent with "Papal perspectives of reconciling labor and capital under more orderly and humane capitalist conditions." Although De Caux called Murray "a compromiser, an adjuster," who "typically counseled moderation," he considered him "a high type of conventional labor leader—intelligent, experienced, with some vision."

The historian Philip Foner has estimated that in the early decade of the century half the AFL members were Roman Catholics. De Caux believed that the proportion of Catholics in the CIO was substantially higher, "and of Catholic leaders still higher again." The importance of the Catholic establishment in the unions that made up the CIO is hard to overestimate. Certainly it presented the principal stumbling block to the Communists. At the same time it must be said that many of the Catholics in the Association of Catholic Trade Unions were Socialists. It was communism, with its doctrinal hostility to all religions, that was objectionable to Catholics; many had no difficulty with any of a number of non-Marxist socialisms. To Catholic workers Philip Murray was just this side of a saint.

The "new men" were individuals like excitable, energetic Jim Carey of the United Electrical Workers (Carey said "yes, sir," to male elders, the mark of the parochial school, John Brophy noted), "brainy" Julius Emspak; and "darkly shy George Addes." "Red Mike" Quill of the transport union was a striking contrast with Ben Gold of the fur workers, a man who made no bones about his membership in the Communist Party. Joe Curran of the maritime union was a large, bold, blustering radical. "Not all the new-typers were communists, or sympathetic, though many were," De Caux wrote. "Not all were leftist enough to work with the communists though most did. Some were in-again-out-again, on-again-off-again, some factionally hostile."

Lewis's strategy at the AFL convention in San Francisco in 1934 was to discredit the old leaders with two minor resolutions calculated to serve notice of the prospective challenge. One, directed at Matthew Woll, stated that no union leaders could be members of the National Civic Federation (Woll was acting president). The other forbade the AFL magazine to run ads from antiunion corporations. De Caux, well aware of Lewis's longer-range intention, was deeply impressed by the patience and subtlety of his tactics. Without directly confronting the old guard, Lewis had managed to send to those disenchanted union leaders who yearned for a new and militant union movement a clear message that he was prepared to be their leader—determined to be in fact—and that in that new movement there would be no harassment for political views, however radical, as long as they were subordinated to the goal of building strong industrial unions.

At the 1935 AFL convention in Atlantic City the battle lines were clearly drawn. The faction of which Lewis was now plainly the head was determined to have "*unrestricted* industrial-union charters in mass-production industries," in De Caux's words. The challenge to the craft unions was to accept the principle and the fact that unionization by industry rather than craft was the rational way to organize the millions of nonunion workers in the nation. In De Caux's rather romantic formulation, "the conflict involved impatient youth against bossy old age, radicals against stand-pat conservatives, class struggle breaking through collaboration, poor kicking against rich, the downtrodden determined not to be doormats. The young, the rebels, the reds were on one side; the old, conformist, conservative, on the other."

Labor's old guard—the Matthew Wolls, Big Bill Hutchesons, and Daniel Tobins were much in evidence in Atlantic City, corpulent, tuxedoed, self-important. Hutcheson, De Caux wrote, was "a Harding-Coolidge-Hoover Republican." The second line of union bosses included the heads of the electrical workers, bricklayers, plumbers, railway clerks, musicians, streetcarmen, painters, hodcarriers, longshoremen, garment workers, and ranks of smaller craft unions. What the Young Turks of the union movement discovered to their pleased surprise at the 1935 convention was that Lewis, in De Caux's words, did not care "if they were right or left, red or pink, or whatsoever color." Already determined to cast his lot with the industrial unions,

Lewis was ready to waive, or at least suspend, ideological considerations. It was evident to him that the drive, energy, and intelligence of the young radicals were essential to the success of his campaign to circumvent the old-style labor bosses.

William Green was chairman of the convention, and he was bent on suppressing any sign of rebellion but it bubbled up irrepressibly. The Communist-dominated Mine, Mill and Smelter Workers Union complained about craft unions scabbing on the metal miners' strike. Wyndham Mortimer tried to get the floor to propose a program of industrial organization, but Green refused to recognize him. Lewis then told Mortimer to go to the stage and stand beside the microphone until Green let him speak.

When the leader of the rubber workers argued for an unrestricted—i.e., noncraft—charter for his union, Big Bill Hutcheson, the leader of the carpenters, rose to a point of order: The question had already been settled—no unrestricted charters. Lewis at once objected to Hutcheson's objections. It was "pretty small potatoes," he declared. Hutcheson, six feet three inches and some 300 pounds, replied that he had been raised on small potatoes. Lewis approached Hutcheson, they exchanged some words, and Lewis punched Big Bill, knocking him down and bloodying his nose. It may well have been the most famous punch in American history. Its symbolic significance was enormous; its practical consequences were vast. It was the kind of act that workers could understand and appreciate. In the simplest terms industrial unions had knocked down craft unions. The workers, Len De Caux wrote, "did follow sporting events." But Lewis was too shrewd a politician to suggest that himself or to do other than to appear to minimize the clash. When an alarmed Bill Green, who owed his elevation to the presidency of the AFL primarily to Lewis, rebuked his master, Lewis said, "He called me a foul name."

"Oh, I didn't know that," Green replied, relieved to hear what appeared to be an acceptable excuse.

Students of Lewis debated then and later whether the blow was premeditated. There was a consensus that it was. Formidable and seemingly choleric as Lewis was, his most casual gestures were commonly intended for effect. "His was a calculated strategy," De Caux wrote, "long thought out and much subtler than some of his bold crudities made it appear."

Lewis, in effect, told the old guard, "At the San Francisco convention I was seduced by fair words. Now, having learned I was seduced, I am enraged, and I am ready to rend my seducers limb from limb." As Lewis had predicted, Green, unnerved by Mortimer's stance beside the microphone, gave him the floor, and Mortimer presented his motion for industrial unions. The motion lost by a vote of 18,024 to 10,993. Lewis's response was to join with Sidney Hillman, Charles P. Howard of the International Typographical Union, and five other union leaders to form a Committee for Industrial Organization. The CIO was formed "to encourage and promote the organization of the unorganized workers in mass production and other industries upon an industrial basis. Its aims are to foster recognition and acceptance of collective bargaining in such basic industries; to counsel and advise unorganized and newly organized groups of workers; to bring them under the banner of and in affiliation with the American Federation of Labor as industrial organizations."

Lewis's strategy was not to split the AFL (so-called dual unionism—rival unions—was the bugbear of all good union members) but to force the AFL old guard to accept the principle of industrial unions *within* the AFL.

The Committee for Industrial Organization was an instant success. "The workers," De Caux wrote, "were waiting for the CIO, pounding on its doors long before the CIO was ready for them." Its offices had hardly opened before it was flooded with inquiries and requests for support. "We heard from auto and rubber workers, seamen; from radio, electrical, shipyard, furniture, textiles, steel, lumber workers; from gas, coke, glass, and quarry workers, from sharecroppers, newspapermen. . . . All said, 'CIO, let's go!' "

There was soon a union song that went:

> CIO it to my country,
> CIO it to my home
> CIO it to my fellow-workers
> To be a union man
>
> A union for the masses
> To include every craft,
> Better wages for each worker,
> In CIO there is no class
>
> If I want to help all workers
> To enjoy a better life,

> I CIO it to my union
> To be a CIO man.

The most popular song was an old Socialist ballad, "Just Like a Tree That's Standing by the Water, We Shall Not be Moved." There was not much more to it than that, but it bore endless repetition.

The itinerant radical poet Woody Guthrie wrote:

> Quit beating that woman, Officer! We're peaceable folks
> Out on the hunt of a job of work.
> Thirty days we got to spend in jail
> 'Cause we spoke at a union and we ain't got bail.
> Come on, black man! Come on, white!
> Show these rich how the poor can fight!
> Stand up, woman, and meet a man!
> Gonna make this country the promised land!
> Gonna have a house with strawberry pie!
> I aim to live some before I die!
> Gonna have a meeting and all talk free!
> Come on, you cops, and be like me!

"It was a mass movement with a message, revivalistic in fervor, militant in mood . . ." De Caux wrote. In the words of the Trotskyite organizer Sidney Lens, writing many years after the event, "It is difficult to impart on ordinary paper the magic that surrounded the letters *C-I-O* in 1937." John L. Lewis was soon synonymous with the CIO. Union leaders who arrived in Washington would say to the cabdriver at the station, "Take me to John L. Lewis."

Among those who rallied to the banner of the CIO were a disproportionate number of Communists. They were the seasoned and dedicated organizers, the battle-tested and battle-scarred veterans of dozens of bitter clashes, defeated strikes, lost causes. Len De Caux was one; John Brophy, Carl Haessler, and Wyndham Mortimer were others, but there were dozens, indeed hundreds, more.

De Caux, who had worked with Carl Haessler on the Communist-dominated Federated Press, a radical counterpart to the Associated Press, at once applied for a job editing the *CIO News*. David Dubinsky was unwilling even to talk to members of the Federated Press on the ground that it was a Communist-dominated organization, but Lewis plainly did not care. He hesitated only briefly before giving the OK to John Brophy's proposal to hire De Caux as editor of the *CIO News*. Lewis knew that De Caux, as Oscar Ameringer's assistant on the *Illinois*

*Miner,* had been a harsh critic, and he suspected, if he did not know, that De Caux was a Communist Party member, but that was less important to Lewis than the fact that De Caux was an enthusiastic supporter of the CIO and of the principle of industrial unions. Under Lewis's questioning, De Caux told him that he had "close sympathies with the communists, had many friends among them, and associated myself with them in a number of ways, though not organizationally." Lewis, for his part, undoubtedly considered that giving De Caux the job of editor of the *CIO News* was a way of sending a message to the Reds: Play ball with us, and we will be square with you. As De Caux put it, "Lewis threw out his arms to welcome all who could or would help the CIO. He gave credit, where due, on the basis of performance. He wasn't finicky about a man's shade of pink or red, if he was a fighter in the ranks." Much the same could be said, of course, about the New Deal itself. There the question was not the shade of a man's and a woman's ideas, but their competence and their commitment to the goals of the administration. As with the CIO, the New Deal took its moral and intellectual bent from the character of its leader. If Roosevelt and Lewis were strikingly different in almost every other way, they were alike in their receptivity, their responsiveness to new ideas, and, perhaps, above all, their ability to win and hold the devoted loyalty of those who worked for and with them.

De Caux himself was a representative of a new breed of itinerant international revolutionary. An upper-class Englishman, a graduate of Harrow and Oxford, he had been editor of various Communist newspapers and journals in Britain, France, Canada (where he belonged to the Canadian branch of the IWW), and Germany. In 1926 an American friend, Carl Haessler, wrote offering him a job as assistant editor to Oscar Ameringer on the *Illinois Miner,* a strong anti-John L. Lewis paper. De Caux called Ameringer a "reformist socialist," in reference to his adherence to a kind of Americanized, Midwestern version of Marxism. De Caux had witnessed Lewis's invasion of the Illinois branch of the United Mine Workers, which he wrested from the leadership of Frank Farrington. To the battered Illinois union officials Lewis appeared "Reactionary. Red-baiting. Autocratic. Brutal. Lacking in vision and labor statesmanship. Certainly," De Caux wrote, "he went out for personal, dictatorial, centralized control over his union—and did so ruthlessly."

Another recruit to the "new" Lewis was Powers Hapgood. Powers was the nephew of Hutchins Hapgood, son of his brother, William

Powers Hapgood, who headed a small family venture called the Columbia Conserve Company. When Powers Hapgood and several fellow Communists were beaten up and expelled from the United Mine Workers on the orders of John L. Lewis, William Powers Hapgood took them into the family business, which was largely worker-owned. There Powers Hapgood and friends worked early and late to persuade the 100 or so workers in the conserve factory that they were the exploited victims of capitalist oppression and must form a union. With some prodding from another of his brothers, who was one of the few non-worker stockholders in the company, William and the company "council" fired his son and his "red" companions. When Lewis formed the CIO, he took in Powers Hapgood, who was soon a trusted lieutenant of Philip Murray.

Lee Pressman, chief counsel of the CIO, was a Harvard Law School graduate and an ardent Communist. Well tailored, with an abrupt, arrogant manner, he was so abrasive that Frances Perkins asked Lewis not to bring Pressman with him to meetings that she attended.

John Brophy, a veteran coalfield organizer, had spearheaded the drive to oust John L. Lewis as head of the United Mine Workers, but Lewis, recognizing Brophy's organizing ability and anxious to recruit his Communist supporters, made him head of the Committee for Industrial Organization. "Lewis," De Caux wrote, "tended to shrink his associates—inevitably more than deliberately. . . . Brophy [a small man in contrast with Lewis's bulk] came to his CIO job pre-shrunk."

Albert Coyle, head of the Brotherhood of Locomotive Engineers, had supported John Brophy for president of the UMW in 1926. Lewis in turn had denounced Coyle as a master of "red intrigue" and as leader "of a scabbing, strike-breaking organization, to-wit, the Brotherhood of Locomotive Engineers, which was boring from within to break up the United Mine Workers." Now Coyle, too, found a job with the CIO.

Wyndham Mortimer, like De Caux an Englishman, was born in 1884 in a rural village, the son of a brewer who brought his large family to Bitumen, Pennsylvania, where he found work as a miner. Young Mortimer entered the mines at Bitumen when he was twelve. It, he recalled, "was the nearest thing to peonage to be found anywhere in America." From mining, Mortimer progressed to working in a steel mill, to driving a streetcar and, finally, to a job as a machinist with the White Motor Company.

Carl Haessler was the beau ideal of the left. The son of German parents who were Socialists, Haessler was graduated from the University of Wisconsin, won a Rhodes Scholarship, studied the classics, and prepared for a career as a college professor. At the same time he became a protégé of Oscar Ameringer and active in Socialist circles in Milwaukee. He was teaching philosophy when the United States entered the European war in 1917. Haessler refused to be drafted and was convicted and sentenced to fifteen years in prison. Sent to the Federal prison at Leavenworth, he organized a strike against prison conditions and started a radical prison newspaper. From Leavenworth he was shipped to Alcatraz as a hard case, and there he again became a leader, organizing the Wire City School, an inmate-run enterprise, and publishing a clandestine paper. Freed from prison at the end of the war, Haessler found it impossible to get a teaching position and decided to embark on a career as a journalist. With several other Communist friends, he started a radical news service, an alternative to the Associated Press, to provide left-wing and labor newspapers with stories and information that they could not get from the "capitalist press." In 1926 Haessler took the almost obligatory trip of a young radical to Russia. He returned a dedicated champion of the Soviet Union, but when he was urged to join the Communist Party, he replied, "If I become a member, it will soon be whispered around and then people will think I am under Communist party discipline, something which I would not allow even if I were a member and were still manager of the Federated Press. The only value to the revolutionary movement of the Federated Press is the fact that it is managed not under the discipline of the Communist party and that it has sufficient entrée in other circles to carry news of what's going on in the Communist wing of the labor movement and elsewhere. And there is no sense in sacrificing that." Party officials evidently agreed because the party remained a major source of funds throughout the existence of the Federated Press. Of Haessler's own convictions there was no doubt. To a friend who left to take a job with the Russian news agency Tass, Haessler wrote congratulating him on having an "assured job" while "FP will always remain precarious until the great day when it becomes the Soviet-American Tass."

The board of directors of the Federated Press always had several Communist officials on it. William Z. Foster, who edited the *Workers Monthly,* and Earl Browder, editor of *Labor Unity,* were members at various times, as was Charles Hathaway, for years editor of the *Daily Worker.* Florence Curtis Hanseon, editor of the *American Teacher* for eight years, was also a member of the board of the Federated Press. If the board had members covering a wide range of the left, the Communist influence was dominant. With the rise of the CIO, Carl Haessler and the Federated Press tied their wagon to John L. Lewis's rising star, and the press enjoyed its most productive period.

Discussing the prominence of Communists in the early years of the CIO, De Caux wrote: "In those days, only company stooges or spies asked precise questions about political affiliation." In his autobiography De Caux always spelled "communist" or "communism" with a small *c*, the point clearly being that party membership was primarily a technical issue. Those communists who joined the party were, for the most part, less vulnerable individuals who were self-employed or who held jobs where the matter of their political affiliation was unlikely to arise. Other equally dedicated communists, who needed to be able to reply to the question, "Are you a member of the Communist Party?" with a confident and emphatic no in order to be able to continue to function as a union official or the head of a front organization, stayed out. Of course, the line was never so clearly drawn. Simple ardor often induced men and women to join the party at considerable risk to their effectiveness if pursued by "Red hunters." A simpler division was between the "good guys" and "bad guys," in De Caux's words. "The good guys were on the working-class side; the bad guys were on the capitalist side. The good guys ranged from class-conscious radicals, through all shades of sincere pink and humanitarian fervor, to stodgy conservatives who really wanted the workers to win."

If one asked a Communist "the good-guy question, 'He's 100 percent' might mean a real communist; 'He's okay,' some other kind of left-winger; 'Okay, I guess,' a not-too-guaranteed united-front attitude. . . . Among the younger brighter union pioneers, some kind of radical affiliation was the vogue. The Communist party had the widest influence and prestige." De Caux vigorously defended the Communists from the charge that they were a constant source of disruption in the various unions in which they often played a central role. They had little to gain by factionalism, he argued, since they usually represented the "in" group. The other radical organizations like the Socialists, the Lovestoneites, the Trotskyites, and the so-called Proletarian Party were more often the troublemakers, as well as the most active Red baiters.

William Foster stated that of the staff of 200 employed by the CIO's Steel Workers Organizing Committee, 60 were party members, among them Gus Hall. This did not count those organizers who, while not party members, were sympathizers. Sidney Lens notes that of the 33 Steel Workers Organizing Committee staff in Chicago, 31 attended Communist caucuses. In Lens's opinion, while James Carey was the attractive young head of the electrical workers, Julius Emspak, a long-time Communist, really ran the union. There is thus considerable evidence to support the statement that "there were few areas of new organizations where lefts didn't exert some influence by being among the first, most active, and most militant in union organizing."

When someone asked John L. Lewis why he had hired so many Communists, he replied, "Who gets the bird, the hunter or the dog?" Lewis was the hunter; the Communists were the "dog."

Hardly to be distinguished in the popular mind from the Communists were the Socialists. Among the latter the ablest were the Reuther brothers—Victor, Roy, and Walter. The Reuthers were sons of a German Socialist and brewery union organizer in West Virginia. The boys were reared in an atmosphere of political activism. Walter and a friend, Merlin Bishop, organized the Social Problems Club, the "reading list" of which included most of the works of Scott Nearing and a number of Upton Sinclair's books, along with several works of Will Durant and Norman Thomas. Walter, Victor, and Roy threw themselves enthusiastically into campaigning for Norman Thomas in the election of 1932, and their father gave them his blessing, congratulating them for recognizing the "existence of a class struggle" and taking their place "on the side of labor politically. . . . To me," the elder Reuther added, "Socialism is the star of hope that lights the way, leading the workers from wage slavery to social justice, and to know that you boys have joined the movement, and are doing all in your power to spread a doctrine of equal opportunities for all mankind, only tends to increase my love. . . . " When Walter Reuther got a job as a machinist with the Ford Motor Company, he did his best to stir up some sentiment for a union. His only reward was to be fired. He assumed it was because of his prominence in the Norman Thomas campaign, but no reason was given him.

Walter and Victor, the reader may recall, had spent two years working in the Gorky automobile plant in Russia. When they returned to the United States, the brothers had no jobs and no base of operations in the automobile industry. Victor visited his brother Roy, who was enrolled at A. J. Muste's Brookwood Labor College at Katonah, New York. The emphasis of the college at that time was very strongly on the Quaker-inspired Emergency Peace Campaign. Victor became a lecturer on pacifism for Brookwood. Walter, unable to get a job in an automobile plant because of his reputation as a union organizer, lectured on his experiences in Russia and considered an offer to join the faculty of Brookwood College. Meantime, Victor met, fell in love with, and married a young Polish Catholic named Sophia, or Sophie Goodlavich. Walter fell in love with a Jewish schoolteacher named May Wolf, whose immigrant Russian parents were Socialists and who had been active in the Detroit teachers' union.

Victor's wife, Sophia, had been wooed from the Roman Catholic Church by the political activism of the Methodists' Epworth League. As a leaguer she had collected food and money for the striking Camden Shipyard Workers. Soon after she had been admitted to Brookwood College on the recommendation of Norman Thomas.

Walter Reuther's Socialist friends in Detroit, who had a United Auto Workers' charter for the Ternstedt plant there, sent Reuther as that plant's delegate to the United Auto Workers' convention at South Bend, Indiana, in 1936. Reuther and five fellow delegates hitchhiked to South Bend and checked into the town's cheapest hotel. They rented a room with a double bed, put the mattress on the floor, and slept three on the springs and three on the mattress. The convention was the beginning of Reuther's spectacular rise as a union leader, "all on the foundation of a questionable credential plus the uncanny knack of a radical to deal with rank-and-file problems," in De Caux's words.

The secret of Walter Reuther's success, according to De Caux, was "his concentration. Others might sometimes relax. . . . Not Walter. He didn't drink, smoke or dillydally in any way to distract him from giving his all to his purpose." De Caux called him "a radical united-fronter, in the spirit of the CIO uprising."

One of David Dubinsky's most determined and successful organizers in the International Ladies' Garment Workers' Union was Rose Posetta, a dedicated Socialist. Born in Derazhnja in czarist Russia, Posetta came to the United States in 1913 as a seventeen-year-old immigrant. Her sister, Esther, was already in the United States. She got Rose a job in a shirtwaist factory, and the young woman soon found herself involved in union activities and workers' education. Carey Thomas, the president of Bryn Mawr College, had established the Summer Institute for Women Workers in Industry, "to stimulate an active and continued interest in the problems of our economic life which so vitally concerns industrial women as wage earners. . . . " Rose

Posetta was one of 104 young women from all over the country who met at Bryn Mawr in the summer of 1922. "We are aided in our studies by tutors," she wrote, "daughters of wealthy families, young women amazingly tall, who never had to bend over a sewing machine in their growing years. . . . " Broadus Mitchell, the economist, was one of her teachers. A year later Posetta won a scholarship to continue her studies at the Brookwood Labor College. A. J. Muste then was dean of Brookwood and taught the history of civilization and public speaking. "Organizing the unorganized" was the main goal of the college; students came from steel, textile, and automobile factories.

When Rose Posetta was sent to Buffalo to help organize the Polish garment workers there, she found the women afraid to discuss unionization. They were sympathetic but had such replies as "I couldn't afford to get mixed up in it," "I'd hate to go back on relief," "My family depends upon my earnings," "This might cost me my job." Posetta wrote: "This fear was based on what had happened to some of their more outspoken friends, who early in 1934 had tried to establish a union in the cotton dress factories in Buffalo. These were gradually eased out of their jobs and never again could get work in their trade. This threat hung over the heads of young girls who had recently begun to earn a living, and over mothers of large families, whose earnings kept the home pots boiling." Rose Posetta put out a weekly newspaper entitled *What Now?* for the garment workers, but months of painstaking work in a grim winter brought no tangible result. Buffalo seemed unionproof.

Planning and running a strike in a large factory of a major industry was as complex and arduous an undertaking as a major military campaign. Often involving thousands of workers, it required battle-seasoned leadership, a high level of organization, the assembling of a substantial general staff assisted by numerous "field soldiers" and volunteers, and, above all, the development of a strike strategy: what were the aims of the strike and how could they best be achieved? Logistics— supply and communication—were of critical importance. Special attention also had to be given to public relations. How the public, both local and national, perceived the goals of the strike and the justice of the strikers' cause had a major bearing on the strike's success or failure. A strike also required, like battle, a high degree of physical courage.

The enemy, the employer, usually had at his command vast resources. The local law enforcement agencies were commonly at the call of the employer to protect his property and suppress riot. The news media were almost invariably allied with the employers, on whom they depended, among other things, for advertising. In large industrial plants there were often company spies and strong-arm men, sometimes workers in the plants who received special pay or privileges, sometimes—especially when strikes broke out—hired thugs and, not infrequently, gangsters.

William S. Knudsen, president of General Motors, testified that his company had spent $839,764 on spies over a two-and-a-half-year period. Wyndham Mortimer suspected that Ford and Chrysler had spent comparable sums. Certainly the Ford spy and intimidation system of Harry Bennett was a model for the industry. Workers with union sympathies often had as many names as they had jobs, assuming different names whenever they sought employment in order to evade industry blacklists.

Black workers had special problems. Wyndham Mortimer, trying to organize an auto workers' local in Flint, Michigan, listened to the complaint of a black worker known as Old Jim. Jim told Mortimer the various ways in which the union discriminated against blacks: They were "refused admittance to dances, picnics, or any other social activities sponsored by the federal unions. . . . They were limited to janitorial and foundry work, where the labor was hot, hard, and heavy." Mortimer was sent an unsigned message asking him to meet at a black church. When he arrived, he found eighteen blacks gathered secretly; all were employed by the Buick division of General Motors. They told Mortimer a grim story of hardship and prejudice, concluding, "You see, we have all the problems and worries of the white folks, and then we have one more; we are Negroes."

Akron, Ohio, the rubber capital of the world, was an important target for unionization. In a Firestone rubber plant in January, 1936, the firing of a union member for fighting was met by an immediate sit-down. Without planning or discussion men simply shut off their machines. There was silence; one man called out, "Jesus Christ, it's like the end of the world." A roar of laughter followed his exclamation. Three days later the company capitulated, and 400 workers who had dropped out of the union signed up again.

A Goodyear plant was marked for unionization. It proved a tough nut to crack. When the workers went out on strike, the company obtained an injunction against picketing. The sheriff had deputized 30 men, and the city police contributed another 150 to break up the picket lines. By Rose Posetta's estimate, some 10,000 pickets, many of them unemployed men and women, gathered at the factory, each armed with "a billy—a baseball bat, a bowling pin or a piece of broomstick." At the last minute the police chief, realizing that a clash would mean lives lost, withdrew the police. In front of the forty-five gates of the Goodyear plant the strikers had erected more than 300 tents or hastily constructed shanties; a picket line stretched for eleven miles. Each structure had a name: "Strike Post No. 1"; "Camp Roosevelt"; "John L. Lewis Post"; "Senator Wagner Post"; "Mae West Post"; "House of David Post." The strike was led by John House, a tall, soft-spoken Georgian in his twenties. When Rose Posetta introduced herself and offered her services, he proudly conducted her on a tour of strike headquarters: the first-aid station; the commissary; the cash relief department; the public information office. The commissary, with a 13-burner stove, a battery of coffee urns, and a hotel-sized refrigerator, was doing a twenty-four-hour business. Powers Hapgood had been sent to Akron by the CIO to assist in the strike. Skip O'Harra, who was in charge of "field operations"—that was to say, the pickets—had been given the title of field marshal. He told Rose Posetta that six months before, he had been a leader of the Akron Ku Klux Klan. When Posetta went through the food line in the commissary, her "plate" consisted of baked beans, kidney beans, spaghetti with meat sauce, potato salad, fresh baked corn bread, homemade jam, coffee, and cottage pudding covered with custard sauce.

Rose Posetta and Powers Hapgood visited the strike posts and talked with the men manning them about the strike and the long-range goals of the workers; they shared their coffee and listened to the men's stories of their lives. Many were from the South, and they argued good-naturedly about the merits of their respective states. Posetta and Hapgood distributed "little red booklets" of union songs and taught the strikers to sing them. Old tunes were given new words appropriate to the strike. "She'll Be Comin' 'Round the Mountain" was directed at the sheriff, whose name was Flower:

Flower'll be comin' 'round the shanties, yes he will;
Flower'll be comin' 'round the shanties, yes he will;
He'll be shiv'ring in his panties when he's comin' 'round the shanties,
He'll be shiv'ring in his panties, yes he will.

When Posetta was put in charge of entertainment, she rounded up "elderly fiddlers and accordionists . . . men and women close to their seventies," who demonstrated "the old fashioned dancing . . . and young boys and girls gave us tap dancing, yodeling and guitar music." Ballads from the Appalachians were sung by older men and women:

> When I can read my title clear
> To mansions in the skies,
> I bid farewell to ev'ry care
> And dry my weeping eyes.

Other familiar songs were "Solidarity Forever" and "Hold the Fort," sung to the accompaniment of a banjo:

> Hold the fort, for we are coming
> Union men, be strong;
> Side by side we battle onward—
> Victory will come!

Ironically, many of the younger leaders of the strike had been trained by Goodyear as potential strikebreakers.

After two weeks the president of Goodyear, Paul Litchfield, emerged from the besieged plant, looking gaunt and tired, took a room in the Mayflower Hotel, and announced, "The Goodyear Tire and Rubber Company will not sign an agreement with the United Rubber Workers of America under any circumstances." It turned out that two strikers had stationed themselves under the window of his office in the plant and had played a guitar and sung there for hours on end "Old man Litchfield had a shop, E-i, E-i, O!" The company's principal reliance was on the charge that the strike leaders were "outside agitators" in the pay of Moscow, to which the strikers replied, "The two agitators in this strike are Goodyear hours and wages. They are native products. They are not imported from Moscow."

Leaflets exhorted the strikers, "Be orderly! Be peaceful! Be polite! Be sober! Our record is clear . . . let's keep this America's most peaceful and orderly strike." The company's response was to import a trainload of what Posetta called "hired thugs," professional strikebreakers. Their task was to foment trouble in order to provide an excuse for calling in the police and national guard. To counteract the flood of antiunion propaganda from the company, the CIO dispatched a seasoned public relations man, McAllister Coleman, who had worked for the *New York Sun* and for the *New York World*. "Systematic personal contact with the strikers and their families was carried on, as the best method of keeping the strike lines intact, and allaying any misgivings that might arise among the rank-and-file . . . " Rose Posetta wrote. Her movie camera was also put to use, taking pictures of the strikers and then editing them into a film which emphasized that the Akron strike was part of a much larger movement by workers all over the United States and which got an enthusiastic reception when it was shown to the strikers and their families.

On the morning of March 7, the mayor of Akron sent seventy-five policemen and street cleaners to tear down the pickets' shanties and tents on the ground that they were obstructing traffic, but they were soon beaten back by the pickets, augmented by hundreds of strikers and by workers from the nearby Goodrich and Firestone plants.

The final crisis in Akron came with the organization of a citizens' vigilante committee called the Akron Law and Order League, headed by ex-mayor C. Nelson Sparks. Sparks claimed 30,000 members. He began drilling his forces in the parking lot behind the Mayflower Hotel. Many of the strikers and their supporters from other rubber plants were already armed, and it was generally assumed that the vigilantes were armed. Veterans' organizations, appealed to by the strikers, began drilling in union halls. Wilmer Tate, head of the American Civil Liberties Union, who had come to Akron, declared on the radio, "Never have I heard a more direct incitement to lawlessness than that uttered today by ex-Mayor Sparks. . . . There is talk of lynching parties and ganging-up buzzing around the lobby of the Mayflower Hotel."

Sparks's response was to announce that his vigilantes would break the picket lines and force the reopening of the plant; he would reveal the time over the local radio station. Rumors spread that the attack would come on March 17. The union bought radio time for the night of March 16–17 and improvised an all-night program, alternating union songs and music provided by barber shop quartets, "players of ukuleles, harmonicas, bazookas, and accordions," with talks on the need for organization, American labor history, and the strikebreaking techniques being used by Goodyear. A drama of Papa Fink and Baby Fink was hastily produced. At dawn all was quiet. The threatened attack failed to materialize, and the union added the all-night radio show to its inventory of strike tactics.

Finally, on March 20, the negotiators produced an agreement which Rose Posetta considered a triumph for the union. When Louis Budenz, labor editor of the *Daily Worker,* appeared in Akron and asked

Posetta for a copy of the agreement between Goodyear and its workers, she firmly rebuffed him. "Why are you so belligerent?" a party organizer with Budenz asked.

"Because you have no business here. . . . My advice to you both is to lay off this strike and let us settle it our own way."

Posetta wrote at the conclusion of the strike: "Not since Armistice Day in 1918 had there been such jubilation in Akron." Homer Martin, Walter Reuther, and George Addes of the autoworkers arrived from Detroit to observe the triumph. "We'll be next," Martin told Posetta. "Will you come and help us?" he asked her and Powers Hapgood. They assured him they would be there when they were needed.

"During the rise of the CIO," Len De Caux wrote, "American communists followed the general policy of the Seventh World Congress (July–August, 1935) of the Communist International. The sixty-five parties represented, including that of the United States, agreed that fascism and the war it threatened were the main danger. . . . As applied to the labor movement, the policy was to build and strengthen trade unions, as a major bulwark against fascism." Instead of persistent and vituperative attacks on the "social-fascist" leaders of labor—of, indeed, every non-Communist liberal or reform movement—"the communists were now eager to work with nonred leaders for working-class solidarity." The problem was that many Socialist labor leaders could not readily forget that only yesterday they had been the targets of remorseless vilification. There was no guarantee that they would not be vilified tomorrow if that were proclaimed as the new Moscow line.

Rose Posetta could never forgive the Communists for their disruptive tactics, which, in her view, had virtually destroyed the International Garment Workers' Union by means of the Communist-dominated Needle Trades Industrial Union. After the popular front was proclaimed, the Needle Trades Industrial Union was liquidated, and its members were instructed to join the ILGWU in an attempt to take it over. "By placing party members in the best shops, giving them top positions and putting some of their leaders on important union committees," Posetta wrote, union officials were spared the "terrorizing tactics" of the Communists within the union. In Communist-dominated locals, Communist party organizers with no union duties were often paid by the union to carry on party activities.

# 31

# The Autoworkers

The attention and resources of the CIO now focused on General Motors, the largest and most powerful manufacturer in the nation, a symbol of successful and dynamic (and ununionized) capitalism.

The task of unionizing General Motors was complicated by bitter internal wrangling within the United Auto Workers, principally between the inept president of the union, Homer Martin, and the more able and experienced Communist officers of the union. UAW officials, such as the paunchy, cigar-chewing timeserver Francis Dillion, worked behind the scenes to undermine the union, urging the Detroit school board to refuse the use of the high school auditorium for union meetings and assuring the younger UAW officers that there was no chance of organizing the unskilled and often illiterate autoworkers. An earlier union, the United Automobile, Aircraft and Vehicle Workers, had claimed 45,000 members by 1920, but the loss of a strike and the demobilization of war industry—in addition to raids by the AFL—had destroyed it. The NRA code for the automobile industry contained a clause that made it possible for the companies to evade Section 7(a) of the National Industrial Recovery Act. The clause read that they could hire workers "according to merit—that is, competence on the job as judged by the employer." This was used as a cover for firing workers who indicated sympathy for a union. Nonetheless, strikes took place in seven automobile plants in January, 1936, and during the course of the year thirty-three plants in eight cities were affected by strikes or slowdowns. With the AFL uninterested or hostile, three independent unions struggled for the loyalty of the autoworkers. The AFL, alarmed by the challenge of the new unions, took them reluctantly under its wing, claiming the affiliation of some 210,000 autoworkers by 1934, but the failure of the federation to exert aggressive leadership brought about a sharp decline in union membership.

The first major step in the UAW campaign came with the UAW convention in 1936, in South Bend, Indiana, called largely at the instance of John L. Lewis. Rose Posetta was there with greetings and encouragement from the International Ladies' Garment Workers' Union. Powers Hapgood represented the CIO. Leo Krzycki, a veteran of union wars and vice-president of Sidney Hillman's Amalgamated Clothing Workers of America, was also present. One of the most impressive figures was young Richard Frankensteen, an ex-University of Michigan football star who sported a gold football on his watch chain. Frankensteen worked in the Dodge plant in Detroit and was president of the recently formed independent Automotive Industrial Workers Association. He was generally assumed to be a Communist. The officers who were elected on the third day of the convention represented a compromise between the far left and the center. Homer Martin's principal qualification was that he was not a Communist. Wyndham Mortimer, who had played such an effective role in organizing the White Motor Company, was clearly an able candidate to lead the new union, but he was too well known as a Communist to serve as president. George Addes, a veteran of the Electro Auto-Lite strike in Toledo, and Ed Hall from Milwaukee were elected to the AFL Executive Council and gave the Communists a preponderance of power in the new union. When the newly elected UAW officers attended a meeting of the AFL Executive Council, they found the members discussing their investments. Hutcheson of the carpenters was telling Ed Wharton of the machinists that he had just bought $50,000 worth of Consolidated Edison. "I think it's a good buy," he added. David Dubinsky's principal contribution was to ask Mortimer, "How many of your committee are Communists?" Mortimer's reply was: "I don't know and I don't give a damn.... Such a question is irrelevant and out of order." The opposition to Martin took the name of the Unity Caucus, arguing that a common front against the capitalist employers was far more important than political affiliations. In the words of Carl Haessler, the Unity Caucus "comprised left wingers, both socialist and communist, nonpolitical progressives. . . . " Its purpose was not so much to unseat Martin as to secure a majority of union officers on the board.

When a move was made to expel all Communists (that is to say, those who acknowledged membership in the party), Rose Posetta, who had often suffered from the disruptive tactics of the Communists in the ILGWU, strongly opposed it. "Regardless of the faults of Communism . . . our nation was confronted by an even greater danger—Fascism, whatever it might be called, on American soil." She pleaded with the delegates to avoid political conflicts among themselves. "A trade union was primarily an economic organization; members must work together for the good of all despite their political differences."

In response to the call for unionization, the car companies—with the exception of Ford, which always went its own way—began a heavily financed antiunion "educational" campaign. The sum of $100,000, Posetta wrote, "was to be spent within six months on radio broadcasts, press, school, recreation and social clubs in the plants . . . as well as financing company unions, which were being organized feverishly" in an effort to block an industrial union.

With a total membership of 25,000 out of some 1,000,000 autoworkers and a treasury of slightly more than $25,000 the UAW began its drive to unionize the automobile industry.

The initial UAW strike was directed at the Kelsey-Hayes Wheel Company, a Detroit plant that made brake drums primarily for Ford. The union Local 174 was a militant and well-organized one, but when Walter Reuther tried to meet with small groups of workers at Kelsey-Hayes to persuade them to join the union, "he discovered," in the words of his brother Victor, "that of the four or five present, one was sure to be a hired spy and as soon as a worker signed up for the union in this private session, he would be fired." After weeks of disheartening efforts Reuther finally found a group of men who had "developed a union loyalty and a courage that was unique in his experience. . . . " Arrangements were made to transfer these men to one unit of the plant. May Reuther, Walter's wife, met with the wives of union members to encourage them to support their husbands. Victor's wife, Sophie, who spoke Polish fluently, spent her honeymoon turning out bilingual leaflets and bulletins for Polish workers, many of whom could not read English.

The Reuthers and other organizers met regularly to hear reports on the situation within the various departments, hoping to find one in which there was both a strong union nucleus and serious grievances which might provide the basis for a successful strike. It was also important that the strike be called in a department that made some essential part, the unavailability of which would shut down production generally. The right combination was finally found in the hub and brake drum section, where a newly instituted speedup had been so severe that one woman had fainted. A strong union supporter, she agreed to faint again. Her feigned faint would be the signal for a strike in Department 49. The men would simply shut off their machines and sit down beside them. Elaborate plans were made to feed the men inside the plant and their families outside. Picket squads were organized, and a host of essential jobs delegated. May Reuther took a leave from her job as a schoolteacher. A former Brookwood student, Frank Winn, agreed to take on the job of publicity.

At the appointed hour everything went as planned. Rather to the surprise of the strike leaders, the company agreed to negotiate. "Our organizers were on hand with sound trucks, leaflets and membership applications," Victor Reuther wrote, "and many hundreds of workers signed up impressed by the fact that we had caught the company off-guard. . . ."

Despite this encouraging beginning, weeks of fruitless discussion with the company followed. It soon became obvious that management was determined to wait out the strike. When an informant passed the word that Kelsey-Hayes planned to remove certain essential machines to another location to resume production of brake parts, thousands of autoworkers from all over Detroit turned out to block access to the plant. The lack of brake assemblies began seriously to affect production at Ford's River Rouge plant, and just before Christmas a strike settlement was reached. It provided, among other things, for a seventy-five-cents-an-hour minimum wage; Victor Reuther's wages doubled. Kelsey-Hayes also agreed to a shop steward system and a seniority system. Within ten days Local 174 had increased its membership from 78 to 3,000. Within a year the union rolls had risen to 35,000.

At the moment when Walter Reuther was concluding an agreement with Kelsey-Hayes in the offices of the Ford Motor Company, his brother Roy was actively involved in the beginning of a far more dramatic strike at the Flint plant of General Motors. When the head of Kelsey-Hayes saw an article in the newspapers that mentioned the role of Roy Reuther as one of the organizers of the Flint strike, he burst out, "My God, how many of those Reuther bastards are there?"

In June Wyndham Mortimer set up his headquarters in Flint and began his efforts to organize Fisher Body Plant No. 1. He found a room in a cheap hotel and had hardly unpacked before the phone rang and a voice said, "You had better get the hell back where you came from if you don't want to be carried out in a wooden box!" The obstacles that Mortimer and his aides faced were considerable. All the GM workers belonged to a company union, the International Motors Association, and a city ordinance forbade the distribution of any kind of literature. The five auto union locals in run-down offices on Beach Street had a combined membership of 122. Compiling a mailing list of some 5,000 names of workers thought to be favorably disposed to a union, Mortimer wrote each one a letter pointing out the burdens the workers labored under without an effective union and urging each to sign up with the UAW-CIO.

One of Mortimer's first tasks was to identify, as Walter Reuther had done at the Kelsey-Hayes plant, those individuals who could be depended upon to assume leadership positions. They were instructed in the rudiments of labor history, in labor economics, and in such practical matters as conducting a meeting. But it soon became apparent that every meeting contained Pinkerton spies hired by General Motors. As soon as the good union prospects were identified to the company, they were given their pink dismissal slips.

The initial task of organizing the Flint workers had been assigned to Mortimer, but he was hampered by his reputation as a Communist, and he was soon replaced by Bob Travis, with Roy Reuther as one of Travis's principal aides. At the beginning of the organizing campaign there were fewer than 200 United Auto Workers in the whole city of Flint. Travis described the pending clash between GM and the UAW in military terms: "The situation as it stands now is comparable to a vast army on one side with all the hideous advantages of modern warfare—airplanes—poison gas—machine guns—long range guns, and hand grenades, and last, but not least, their secret service. . . . On the other side, we see scattered battalions, unskilled . . . in this modern warfare, armed with bows and arrows, spears and swords. They have no secret service working . . . in the enemy lines. . . . Regardless of how well founded their cause, these men are doomed to defeat, unless they concentrate their armies to enter upon the field equipped to fight fire with fire. . . . " After months of labor only 1,000 out of 47,000 GM workers had been prevailed upon to join the union.

In October two brothers named Perkins were fired from Fisher No. 1 for union activity. The workers, led by Bud Simons, a veteran union man and a dedicated Communist, walked off the job and refused to return until the brothers had been reinstated. The company at once called the Flint Police Department to enlist its help in locating the two men, but it was several hours before they could be found. Meanwhile, the plant was at a standstill. In Mortimer's opinion, the incident had an enormous impact on the rest of the GM workers in Flint. A mass meeting called at the plant the next day was heavily attended, and plans went ahead to call a strike in Fisher No. 1 after January, in order not to deprive the workers of their Christmas bonuses. But the impatient men refused to wait. On December 26, while Travis and Mortimer were sitting in the Dresden Hotel in Flint, making plans for the strike, word came from the Fisher Body local in Cleveland that the workers had gone on strike there. Trouble had begun in a division where seat-covering material was made when three inspectors were transferred to undesirable jobs because they refused to leave the union. At once a shift of 125 men staged a sit-down. When Mortimer arrived in Cleveland by train, he went at once to the Fisher Body plant and found it surrounded by mounted police. They refused to let Mortimer enter the plant, but by means of a loudspeaker he told the strikers that the international union would support them "all the way" and added, "Keep up the fight, fellows, we are going to win this one!" Mortimer then called Travis in Flint, told him to shut down Fisher Body No. 1, and issued a statement to the press. Before the day was over, a wire came from John L. Lewis pledging the support of the CIO.

Discovering on December 29 that GM, in anticipation of a strike, was starting to remove important dies from the plant, the men in Fisher Body No. 1 sat down the next day. The most important strike in American labor history, it might well be argued, had begun. The sit-downers, led by Bud Simons, began to organize the plant in anticipation of a long siege. A Communist, Walter Moore, was elected mayor of the plant with a council of ten advisers. Moore in turn appointed a police chief to keep order. He requested the company police to leave the plant, and they did. A sanitary engineer was appointed to take care of cleanliness. Food and medicine were smuggled into the plant, and the strikers were assured that the union would make sure that their families had sufficient food and fuel.

With the strike a week old, Judge Edward D. Black of the Detroit Circuit Court issued an injunction directing the strikers to vacate the plant. Lee Pressman and Maurice Sugar, another CIO lawyer, thereupon turned up the fact that Judge Black owned more than $200,000 of General Motors stock. A Michigan law prohibited any judge from ruling on a case in which he had a financial interest; the injunction was void.

The *Detroit News,* in common with most of the other newspapers in the city, took the line that the company's property rights were the paramount issue. The public's interest was in "getting the trouble settled before it affects irreparably the prosperity of the community." Union recognition was out of the question. "The UAW must realize that the corporation, however embarrassed by the union's temporary ability to shut down operations in key plants and departments, is not likely to yield on an issue that seems to it so fundamental." In the words of Victor Reuther, "Flint's Mayor, Chief of Police, clergy, newspapers, and even its judges were under the thumb of General Motors, which had become the world's richest and most powerful corporation." Reuther estimated that 80 percent of the families of Flint were dependent on Buick, Fisher Body, Chevrolet, or AC Spark Plug. Most of the rest were on relief.

Carl Haessler, put in charge of public relations for the union, not only turned out press releases daily but took special pains to cultivate the goodwill of the horde of reporters who poured into Flint to keep the public informed, or misinformed in some cases, about the progress of this sensational new technique, the sit-down strike.

In a spirit reminiscent of the Paterson strike in 1912, Flint teemed with radical luminaries, writers and artists and journalists. Josephine Herbst and her friend and fellow radical journalist Mary Heaton Vorse appeared. Vorse spoke, in Jerre Mangione's words, "with the cultivated inflection of a grande dame." She appeared "far too old, fragile and fastidious to have ever been near a strike," but when Mangione met her, she had just received a slight bullet wound over one eye during a skirmish between strikers and police.

Among the distinguished visitors who climbed the ladder to the second floor of Fisher No. 1 was Jennie Lee, a British Laborite, and Mrs. Gifford Pinchot, who was as enterprising as Eleanor Roosevelt in venturing into odd and unexpected places. Rose Posetta climbed into Fisher No. 1 through a window, and thin, earnest Bud Simons proudly escorted her around. He pointed out radical journals and newspapers and adventure magazines available for reading. The men had organized an orchestra and a chorus, and they held concerts each night, broadcast through a loudspeaker to the crowds that gathered outside. The most popular song was one composed for the occasion:

> When they tie a can to a union man
> Sit down! Sit down!
> When they give him the sack, they'll take him back,
> Sit down! Sit down!
> Sit down, just take a seat
> Sit down, and rest your feet
> Sit down, you've got 'em beat
> Sit down! Sit down!

Vigilante activity increased. A number of union organizers were attacked and badly beaten. There were rumors that the city manager of Flint was plotting the assassination of Roy Reuther and Travis; the Reuthers and other union officials slept with bodyguards outside their doors. The National Association of Manufacturers and the U. S. Chamber of Commerce organized campaigns of telegrams and letters to Governor Frank Murphy, demanding that he take action to oust the strikers and "restore law and order."

Murphy, a liberal and a staunch New Dealer, was the man in the middle. Like Philip Murray, Murphy was a devout Catholic, much concerned, in Len De Caux's words, "with matters of soul and conscience . . . thoughtful, philosophical to the point of introversion . . . a humanitarian, an idealist." De Caux admired Murphy's "big Irish head" and "his rich, soft voice." He had the Lewis eyebrows, reddish instead of black. Throughout the strike he showed commendable restraint.

Frances Perkins concentrated on trying to get the head of General Motors, Alfred P. Sloan, to meet with union leaders to undertake negotiations. Sloan's refusal to recognize the union had been a major cause of the strike, and he vacillated, agreeing to meet and then changing his mind on the ground that the strikers must evacuate his building first. "It is a procedure which brings no one any good," Perkins complained. "The American people do not expect [those at General Motors] to sulk in their tents because they feel that the sit-down strike is illegal. There was a time when picketing was considered illegal and before that strikes of any kind were illegal. The legality of the sit-down strike has yet to be determined," she told a reporter.

At a Cabinet meeting when Perkins urged that the government refrain from any action that might have a negative effect on the strike, John Garner exclaimed: "You don't think the employers should meet them while they're in the factories, do you?"

"Yes," Perkins replied. "I see no reason why they shouldn't. What good is it going to do to stick it out? If people are mad, they'll get madder. If they've made a mistake, they'll make it harder. I think the employers could solve this problem right now by meeting a committee. If it goes on much longer, they may not be able to solve it just by meeting a committee." But to Garner and several other Cabinet members it was a question of upholding the law. "Why," Garner asked, "didn't Murphy get out the troops and enforce the law?"

The strikers, Perkins countered, hadn't tried to seize or make use of the property of General Motors. "It's still there. It's unharmed, and it's there."

"These labor people have been too much coddled" was Garner's response.

Roosevelt himself was alarmed at the sit-down. "Well, it is illegal," he told Perkins, "but what law are they breaking? The law of trespass, and that is about the only law that can be invoked. And what do you do when a man trespasses on your property? Sure, you order him off. You get the sheriff to order him off. . . . But shooting it out and killing a lot of people because they have violated the law of trespass somehow offends me. I just don't see that as the answer. The punishment doesn't fit the crime. There must be another way. Why can't those fellows in General Motors meet with the committee of workers? Talk it out. They would get a settlement. It wouldn't be too terrible. . . . What do you think I'd better do?" he asked Perkins.

"Well, do you think it's reprehensible?"

"Yes, I do. Don't you?"

"Yes. . . . But after you've said it's reprehensible, then what? What do we do next? I'll say to you that it's reprehensible, and you say to me that it's reprehensible. So long as we say it only to each other, we don't have to do anything. But once you say it to the country, then what? . . . My advice is not to call it intolerable or reprehensible or illegal unless we have a course of action to put immediately into effect."

So, quite wisely, nothing was done. Perkins sent a negotiator to Flint to talk with the union leaders and with Murphy, and she called the governor almost every night to check with him on the state of affairs while doing her best to persuade Sloan to undertake negotiations. At this point John L. Lewis muddied the waters by calling on Roosevelt to side with the union on the ground that the CIO had made an enormous contribution to his recent presidential campaign.

When Sloan, having promised to come to a meeting, backed out,

Perkins lost her temper and gave him a piece of her mind. Sloan protested: "You can't talk like that to me! I'm worth seventy million dollars, and I made it all myself." Perkins's reply was that he was "a rotter" and that all his money would not save his soul.

Meanwhile, the strikers in the plant were divided into "families" of fifteen, each with a "captain." Each family set up housekeeping in its own "apartment," with car cushion wadding or unfinished automobile bodies serving as beds. Different "families" named their quarters the Hotel Astor, the Biltmore, etc. Each striker was expected to take a shower every day and put in six hours of work in the "kitchen," patrolling a designated area, and "housekeeping." Classes were taught on labor history and on such practical matters as how to conduct a meeting. There were sports events—boxing and wrestling—and games such as chess and checkers. One team manufactured clubs to be used in the event that the police tried to evict the strikers. On New Year's Day company police smuggled in two prostitutes and some liquor, but the strike committee took a hard line on such transgressions. A lounge area was designated, and soon it was equipped with playing cards, checkers, Ping-Pong tables, and a roulette wheel. Blankets and heavy clothes were smuggled in to the strikers. The commissary was Cook's Restaurant, across the street from Fisher No. 1, under the management of Mrs. Bud Simons, wife of the union chairman on Fisher No. 1. When the strike came, Cook had offered his restaurant to the union to be used for the duration. The hastily organized Women's Emergency Brigade, made up of wives, mothers, daughters, and sisters of the strikers, wore red berets. They helped prepare food, run the commissary, and man the picket lines.

Victor Reuther's assignment was the sound car, an old Chevrolet with speakers on the roof. He went from plant to plant and picket line to picket line, bringing the strikers up-to-date on the latest developments, playing music, and giving instructions on strike tactics. When police congregated at Chevrolet No. 9, where ball bearings were made, to oust the sit-down strikers inside, Roy Reuther and Powers Hapgood borrowed the sound truck to rally pickets and encourage the besieged strikers; at the same time reinforcements were rushed to Chevrolet No. 4, where it was rumored the police also planned a raid. When the police were beaten back at Chevrolet No. 9 with injuries to eighteen strikers, the Women's Brigade played an important role.

General Motors decided on an all-out assault on Fisher No. 1. First, the heat would be turned off in the bitterly cold weather, and then the delivery of food blocked. These steps would be followed by a police assault with tear gas. Victor Reuther saw the police cars advancing through a haze of gas, their "occupants holding short, stubby muzzled guns, look[ing] very strange in their gas masks." He saw more police on foot shielded behind the squad cars. As they got closer, they directed their tear gas at the second-floor windows of Fisher No. 1. The second-floor doors were barred with steel dollies; the strikers had made giant slingshots out of inner tubes. Their projectiles were pound and a half hinges; water hoses had been coiled by the windows to help repel invaders. Hoses and slingshots were soon in action. In the freezing temperatures the water which showered down on the police was an especially effective deterrent. Reuther meanwhile directed the defenders from his sound truck and urged the onlookers to join the picket lines. The police, driven back by the rain of objects that fell on them from the upper floor and roof of Fisher No. 1, re-formed and headed for Reuther. Reuther, his mouth and nose partially covered with a wet handkerchief, continued to exhort the pickets and the strikers. One observer wrote, "From the sound car emanated one steady unswerving note. . . . Reuther's voice was like an inexhaustible furious flood pouring courage into the men." Finally, the police, rebuffed in their second attack began to fire directly into the ranks of the pickets, seriously wounding thirteen men.

When they launched a third attack, the police were armed with long-range tear gas guns. At one critical moment, after a barrage that scattered the pickets, making them weep and vomit, the wind shifted and blew the gas back into the ranks of the police. By midnight the police had expended all their tear gas ammunition, and the fight, the Battle of the Running Bulls, as it came to be called, was over.

The next morning Chevrolet Avenue, in Victor Reuther's words, "looked like a battlefield of the industrial age—smashed and overturned vehicles, broken windowpanes, shattered bottles, stones, hinges, splintered picket signs, used tear-gas canisters, and everywhere the ice formed by the water that had served so effectively as a defense weapon." Chevrolet Avenue was indeed just that—"a battlefield of the industrial age"—and in many ways more significant, perhaps, than the Civil War engagement from which it took its mock-heroic name, Bull Run. There had been bloodier battlefields in the long, long war between capital and labor, and there would be others more bloody in the years ahead, but none more dramatic or momentous. For the embattled sitters-in it was the highpoint of the strike, just as the strike was the highpoint of the last great campaign of the war. It was also the beginning of the end of the strike. Now public opinion began to be more strongly felt. There *must* be serious, good-faith negotiations. General Motors appeared each day more brutal and more arrogant in the public eye; equally important, its output of cars had dwindled to a mere trickle. It was producing only 1,500 cars a week in all its plants, as contrasted with a prestrike figure of 53,000. Eighteen plants were closed in ten cities.

On January 28 Judge Paul V. Gadola of Flint issued an injunction prohibiting any form of picketing and ordering the strikers out of the plants under the threat of a $15,000,000 fine. The union responded by calling on union members from other cities to join the UAW in defying the injunction. Union members came from dozens of cities and towns—Toledo, Pontiac, Saginaw, Bay City, Lansing. The next day a huge crowd had gathered at the gates of Fisher Nos. 1 and 2, and a message was sent to Murphy: "Governor, we have decided to stay in the plant. We have no illusions about the sacrifices which this decision will entail. We fully expect that if a violent effort is made to oust us, many of us will be killed, and we take this means of making it known to our wives, our children, to the people of the State of Michigan and the country that if this follows from the attempt to eject us, you are the one who must be held responsible for our deaths."

Still the strike dragged on, with pressure mounting on Murphy to enforce the judge's injunction. All the familiar law-and-order arguments were trotted out. If the strikers were able to defy the law, the Republic would tremble on its foundations. Chaos would ensue if Communist-led workers were allowed to take the law into their own hands. On February 8 Lewis, who had come to Flint for what had been presumed to be the last stage of negotiations, sensed that Murphy was weakening under the relentless pressure; he drafted a telegram at the conference table and read it to Murphy: "I shall personally enter General Motors plant Chevrolet No. 4. I shall order the men to disregard your order. I shall then walk up to the largest window in the plant, open it, divest myself of my outer raiment, remove my shirt and bare my breast. Then when you [Murphy] order your troops to fire, mine will be the first breast those bullets will strike."

People present in the room reported that Murphy turned white, took Lewis's draft, and rushed from the room. The troops were not called out. Finally the logjam began to loosen. William Knudsen, head of the automotive division of GM, sent word to Frances Perkins that he would meet with a committee of workers if he were able to say that he had been urged to do so by the President. Roosevelt, in bed with a cold, called Knudsen. "Is that you, Bill? I know you've been through a lot, Bill, and I want to tell you that I feel sorry for you, but Miss Perkins has told me about the situation and what you are discussing and I have just called up to say I hope very much that you go through with this and that your people will meet a committee."

The next day Knudsen arrived in Detroit accompanied by John T. Smith, a representative of the Du Ponts, major GM stockholders, for discussion with Lewis and the officers of the UAW. Lewis at once took to his bed in his hotel room, announcing that he had the flu. Smith, known as a hard bargainer, was forced to confer with the ostensibly sick union leader at his bedside. Lewis, sprawled in bed, large and untidy, professed to have trouble hearing Smith. "What's the matter?" Smith asked.

"Move your chair closer," Lewis replied, "so I can tell my grandchildren how close I once was to one and a half billion dollars."

Smith and Knudsen, after conferring with the Du Ponts, agreed in principle to recognize the union, but the company wanted elections in a month. The union insisted on six months. For a time it looked as though the tentative agreement might break down. Roosevelt urged Lewis by phone from the White House to accept a one-month agreement. Lewis consulted with Mortimer and Travis, who in turn consulted with the workers. They would not budge for less than six months. "Come, John, this is no time to quibble," Roosevelt reportedly said.

"Mr. President, it must be a six-month contract," Lewis replied.

William Green, head of the AFL, hearing that GM was on the verge of an agreement with the UAW, sent Knudsen a telegram signed by the AFL Executive Council, demanding that the company not negotiate a contract with UAW-CIO on the grounds that it would "destroy the rights of AFL members in the General Motors plants."

At last the company yielded. When the news was flashed that GM had capitulated, Len De Caux and John Brophy joined the workers in the Fisher plant for the march out. There were evidences everywhere of the order and discipline that the strikers had maintained, for everything was "strangely neat," De Caux wrote. Rose Posetta was among the union leaders who climbed through a window at Fisher No. 1 to join the strikers in their triumphant exit. "The sit-downers were waiting just inside with their belongings," she wrote. "Everybody began shaking hands and talking all at once. Strikers embraced their officers like long lost brothers. Unshaven, many of them had the look of castaways rescued from a desert island. . . . When the main gate . . . was thrown open, they came out singing, led by their band, and with many carrying American flags." They were greeted with volleys of cheers from the waiting crowd outside: cheers for the union, for John L. Lewis, and for Frank Murphy.

At Chevy No. 4 another exuberant celebration took place. The strikers clustered on an outside stairway to sing "Solidarity Forever," amid confetti and free-floating balloons with colored streamers attached. The flashlights of newspaper photographers flared in the crowd. "The people sang and joked and laughed and cried, deliriously joyful," Posetta wrote. "Never had anything like this been seen in Flint. To great numbers of workers the UAW victory was more important than the ending of World War I, for it meant a freedom that they had never known before. No longer would they be afraid to join unions. . . . I suddenly realized that my face was wet. Tears of gladness were streaming down my cheeks."

Len De Caux told a revealing story of the victory celebration at the Flint stadium. When John L. Lewis entered the stadium where he was to speak, a crowd surged around him. Instead of walking toward the platform, Lewis headed in another direction. "At the head of this moving mass retinue, Lewis forged slowly ahead." When De Caux elbowed his way up to Lewis, he found the crowd "now standing back from him at a respectful distance. They were watching solemnly—as the historic occasion demanded—while the great man relieved himself at the urinal. No one cracked a smile or a jest. Least of all Lewis. He zipped up his pants and washed his hands. Then he headed into the ranks of his admirers, which parted to let him lead the way in all majesty out of the men's room."

The UAW was recognized by General Motors as the legitimate representative of the GM workers in the company's sixty factories. In Victor Reuther's opinion, the individual most responsible for the success of the strike was Bob Travis, who, in Reuther's words, "inspired confidence and loyalty everywhere he went." De Caux noted: "The sitdown was the stratagem of the man on the job." When union bigwigs were debating strike strategy, Lewis chuckled and said, "Leave that to the men on the job. They'll find a way—they're ingenious about things like that." So the sit-down was the autoworkers' invention, the most dramatic and successful strike technique since the picket line. There had been sit-downs by Communist workers in 1920 in Italy, but there the workers had run the plants in the name of the revolution. At Flint the more individualistic American workers took the line that the jobs were theirs, not the state's. They shut down production.

A number of factors contributed to the spectacular success of the Flint strike. The sympathetic attitude of Governor Murphy was certainly a crucial factor, as was the silent but tacit support of the President of the United States and his secretary of labor. The skillful tactics of the United Auto Workers, the all-out support of Lewis and the CIO, the essential contributions of the strike-toughened Communist leaders in the UAW, men like Mortimer, Travis, Addes, Frankensteen, and dozens of others—all played a part.

Finally, and perhaps in the last analysis most important of all, public opinion had been subtly but profoundly altered, not simply by the fact of the Depression and the concomitant discrediting of business enterprise in general and large-scale capitalism in particular but also and equally by what we might call the romanticization of the worker (note that he is no longer called the "laborer"; he is now the "worker"), vessel of light and bearer of hope in a darkening world. Frederic Howe, when every other cause and hope had failed, had turned to the "worker" as the true repository of unsophisticated wisdom, courage, and endurance. So, too, had Hutchins Hapgood. The Russian Revolution was in large part responsible for the romanticization of the worker. There had always been Americans like Wendell Phillips who had stoutly advocated the cause of laboring men and women and called for unions. As we have seen, thousands of reformers had devoted their lives to improving the lot of labor through legislation framed to protect lives and improve the generally wretched conditions under which Americans in major industries worked for their livelihood. Those efforts had been directed at egregious hardships and manifest injustices. Except for a handful of Socialists, Communists, and anarchists of doctrinaire Marxist brand, there had been no disposition to see the laboring man or woman as the "ideal human type." The issue had simply been one of creating a more just and equitable society in which everyone, laborers of all kinds and categories, would share in the abundance of the economy. For as ardent an anarchist as Emma Goldman, the revolution that was anticipated was one that would humanize society as a whole rather than simply put the worker on top and the bourgeoisie on the bottom. While the propaganda of the left, of the writers and intellectuals, of the Communists and Socialists, of the old Progressives and the new Progressives, had been heavily discounted by the mass of

Americans for almost a decade, plays, poems, short stories, novels, articles in center as well as left-wing publications had sounded variations on the theme of the worker as savior and uplifter, as the uncorrupted segment of a corrupt society. The old-line Protestant churches at their annual conventions had issued statements that sounded alarmingly like the pronouncements of the Comintern. The consequence was that there had formed a solid stratum of liberal-to-radical middle-class opinion which ranged from the idealization and romanticization of labor that we have noted to, more simply, a sympathy for and identification with the cause of workingmen and workingwomen. When all was said and done, that was perhaps the most valuable asset that the sit-down strikers at the General Motors Flint plant had.

The effect of the GM strike was electrifying throughout the ranks of labor. "Workers everywhere—AFL, CIO, and unorganized—began sitting down," De Caux wrote.

Sixty thousand workers sat down in the Dodge and Plymouth plants of the Chrysler Corporation. At one point there were eighteen sit-down strikes going on in Detroit alone. Meanwhile, violent clashes with the police occurred with increasing frequency. A wildcat strike that broke out in the Consumers Power Plant cut off electricity to most of northern Michigan. Wyndham Mortimer got a frantic call from CIO headquarters instructing him to try to get the strikers to restore power before Governor Murphy was forced to act. The threat of force was countered by a plan to open the sluice gates of the company's dams and release the water. Lewis called Mortimer with instructions to meet "Mr. Wendell Willkie. Mr. Willkie is the man who can settle your difficulty." Mortimer found Willkie at the Blackstone Hotel in his BVDs, drinking lemonade and trying to keep cool. Willkie agreed to most of the union demands, and following a meeting with Lewis himself in Washington, the two sides signed a contract that became a model for a number of other privately owned public power plants.

Anderson, Indiana, was another General Motors town. Guide Lamp and Delco-Remy were the two plants that dominated Anderson the way Fisher Body dominated Flint. When the United Auto Workers set out to unionize the plants, they encountered the same kind of opposition that they had encountered in Flint, except more so. At the first sign of union activity the enemies of unionization formed a vigilante group called the Citizens' League for Employment Security. Well supplied with liquor, the league set out to drive the union organizers out of town. Charles Kramer, an organizer, was given a brutal beating while the police watched. The vigilantes then wrecked the union head-quarters while the union officials fled for their lives. Among them was Sophie Reuther, Victor's wife, who had been sent to Anderson to work with the women employees of Guide Lamp. When Victor Reuther arrived the next day, he had trouble finding her; she was in hiding with a union family.

Reuther immediately called Detroit for reinforcements, and two experienced organizers were sent to Anderson to help him reestablish the union headquarters. When Reuther tried to repeat the Flint tactics of using a sound truck to exhort the workers in the GM plants, the city promptly passed an ordinance banning the use of sound equipment on the streets. With the headquarters functioning once more, the UAW organizers had to cope with familiar tactics of spying and intimidation. Meeting places were denied them, hotels refused to allow them to register for fear of retribution from the Citizens' League, and when Reuther finally obtained the use of an abandoned theater for a union rally, several hundred armed members of the league surrounded the building crowded with people, among them women and children, and began firing into it. Reuther's appeal to the police chief for protection was ignored, and Reuther had difficulty restraining some of the more militant, who, it turned out, had come to the meeting armed, from firing back. After a siege over much of the night, it was almost dawn before those who had attended the rally were able to make their way to their homes in relative safety. When word of the abortive rally reached Detroit, Walter Reuther and Bob Travis rounded up a caravan of some twenty automobiles loaded with strike-seasoned union men and set out for Anderson. "For some hours," Victor Reuther reported, "they made the rounds of the various bars and gathering places of the leaders of the Citizens' League, the Black Legion, and the Ku Klux Klan. Scuffles and shootings occurred. At that point the terrorizing of the UAW was broken."

Martial law was declared, and all meetings without special permits were banned. Reuther called on Roger Baldwin and the American Civil Liberties Union to intervene and asked Norman Thomas to visit Anderson in support of the right of free speech. The Midwest League for the Protection of Constitutional Rights brought pressure on the governor of Indiana: permission was finally granted for the union to hold "small meetings." With national attention focused on Anderson, the town authorities felt obliged to enforce the law. Once the terrorist tactics of the Citizens' League had been checked, however, employees in the two General Motors plants proved eager to join the union. Years later, when Victor and Sophie Reuther returned to Anderson, they were greeted by the mayor as visiting dignitaries.

Sit-down strikes occurred among hotel and restaurant workers; workers in hosiery, shoes, transportation, and shipbuilding; printers, pressmen, Woolworth store girls, farm hands, movie operators, food packers, janitors, and gravediggers. In addition to the new industrial unions that came in under the banner of the CIO, a number of independent unions and AFL unions joined the ranks of the CIO. The United Rubber Workers won a fifty-nine-day Firestone strike and held elections in the Goodrich and Goodyear plants in Akron, adding seven rubber plants to the CIO roster. The CIO also took in as natural allies the West Coast longshoremen and made rapid progress in the communications, shoe, cannery, and the older fur and mine-mill unions, where there was strong Communist involvement.

The CIO's 1937 conference, which met in Atlantic City in the fall, was, as Len De Caux put it, "a celebration." The CIO's spectacular success had exceeded all expectations, except perhaps Lewis's. "There was credit aplenty to go around. Congratulations were bandied to and fro. Never before, nor after, was there such togetherness organizationally, socially. Even politically, the factions were lulled into momentary truce." It had only been two years since, in that same city, John L. Lewis had floored the AFL heavyweight Big Bill Hutcheson and thereby ushered in a new era in union history.

In the fifteen months since the UAW convention at South Bend that union had grown from some 20,000 to more than 400,000 dues-paying members. "We had stormed and taken the most formidable fortress of capitalism, the General Motors-Du Pont combine whose influence dominated the entire automobile industry," Wyndham Mortimer wrote. Only Ford, among the major automakers, remained unununionized.

John Brophy reported that the CIO had grown from 1,000,000 members two years earlier to 4,000,000. In addition to the 400,000 UAW members, there were 75,000 members in rubber, 400,000 in textiles, and 100,000 in oil, with thirty-two affiliated national industrial unions. Len De Caux wrote that 1936 and 1937 were "years of liberation for American industrial workers. They felt as zestful as any newly liberated people. . . . Once a man had to slink into the men's room to voice a beef—and flush the toilet lest his voice be heard. Now he and his buddies might wear union buttons right on the assembly line and stewards vie to fight for their beefs. . . . If things got too bad, there might be a sitdown on the job, or a walkout from the job, with good prospects of walking in again. . . . All this, and more money, too— higher wages, shorter hours, paid vacations and holidays, fringe benefits." The word "union" which "to many workers," De Caux wrote, ". . . had meant only potbellied grafters with diamond stickpins—little cliques of gravy-train snobs with a corner on cushy jobs—high initiation fees, long apprenticeships, rituals, all sorts of tricks to avoid sharing the goodies," took on a new and potent meaning. "There was light after darkness in the youth of the movement—youth that was direct and bold in action, not sluggish and sly from long compromise with the old and the rotten. There was light in the hopeful future seen by the red and rebellious, now playing their full part in what they held to be a great working-class advance against the capitalist class. There was light, and a heady happy feeling in the solidarity of common struggle in a splendid common cause."

It was all too much for the AFL old guard. In the fall of 1936 the AFL Executive Council suspended the CIO, much to the relief of its devoted adherents. It was the AFL that now had to bear the stigma of separatism, of "dual unionism." It was true that Lewis had sorely provoked the members of the old guard, doubtless with the intention of forcing it to expel the CIO, but the break gave him much more freedom; in the eyes of liberals and radicals, "purifying" the CIO made it more than ever the idol of the idealists.

With the break with the AFL final, the CIO changed its name (but not its initials) from the Committee for Industrial Organization to the Congress of Industrial Organizations. David Dubinsky withdrew his Ladies' Garment Workers before the convention, which proved notably harmonious. The principal issue was a resolution barring Communists from holding offices in CIO unions. Lewis managed to sidetrack the controversy over the proposed resolution. He was determined, however, to advance the career of his daughter, Kathryn. To De Caux (and to many others) she seemed like a younger feminine edition of her father, even to physical size: the "political boss in embryo, with an egotism that reflected and magnified [her father's]."

The triumphs of the UAW were followed by bitter internecine warfare in the upper ranks of the union itself. Homer Martin, with Jay Lovestone at his elbow, expelled Addes, Mortimer, and Frankensteen for "conspiring to turn the international union over to the Communists," as Mortimer put it.

Henry Ford held out against the unionization of the Ford Motor Company long after General Motors and Chrysler had capitulated. His right-hand man in the war Ford waged against the UAW was Harry Bennett, who had started out in the Ford entourage as a bodyguard for the Ford children. He so ingratiated himself with the autocratic head of the company that Ford gave him free rein in his assignment to stymie the union by whatever means were necessary. Terror and intimidation were the weapons that Bennett chose to employ. These were familiar enough; Bennett's contribution was to raise them to a new level of violence. He arranged to have released convicts from the Michigan State Prison in Jackson paroled to him and signed them up as members of the Ford security force. He worked closely with known gangsters and Mafia figures in Chicago and Detroit. One of his known allies was Chester LaMare, the so-called Al Capone of Detroit. LaMare told Bennett, "I am the king. You deal with me and nobody gets killed." LaMare was a big-time drug dealer, a hijacker, and the owner of a number of brothels and nightclubs. The Ford service department was in actual fact a private army of several thousand men, some recruited, as we have noted, from ex-convicts, others chosen from workers in the plant. The tactics of terrorism were standard in all Ford plants. At Dallas, Texas, when the UAW hired an attorney, A. B. Lewis, he was waylaid by a dozen Ford "servicemen" and beaten and stabbed so severely that his life was in question for several days. Two Socialist Party men showing the labor film *Millions of Us* in a Dallas park were assaulted by Ford thugs, who wrecked the projector, beat one man, and left his companion covered with tar and feathers.

Henry Ford, it must be said, did nothing to help his cause in the court of public opinion. Notoriously anti-Semitic, he admired Adolf Hitler's enthusiasm for modern technology. Hitler was determined to produce the German equivalent of the Model T, a low-priced car for the "people," a Volkswagen. The admiration was mutual. Hitler presented Ford with a handsome medal.

For almost two years the UAW was virtually immobilized by the factional infighting. Then, with Martin ousted, the Communists neutralized, and the Reuthers in control, the final battle in the campaign to unionize the automobile industry began. Walter Reuther went to Detroit with his brothers to take personal charge of the drive to unionize the River Rouge, or home, plant of the Ford Motor Company. Once more the groundwork was carefully laid. Bulletins were issued in Polish, Serbo-Croatian, Hungarian, and Italian. Space was bought on billboards in working-class neighborhoods, and union commercials were inserted into foreign-language radio programs. A hundred or more "prominent citizens"—liberal clergymen, professors, lawyers, leaders in the Polish and Italian communities—were enlisted to distribute union literature. An airplane flew over the River Rouge plant with an amplifier exhorting the workers to organize. Union sympathizers would join in public tours of the plant and then pull out signs that read, "GET WISE, ORGANIZE."

A popular UAW ballad, written by Joe Glazer, went:

> They put me to work on the assembly line;
> My clock-card number was 90-90-9.
> The Fords rolled by on that factory floor,
> And every fourteen seconds I slapped on a door.
> CHORUS: You gotta fight that line
>                   You gotta fight that line
> You gotta fight that line . . . all the time.
>
> Those Fords rolled by all day and all night,
> My job was the front door on the right
> Foreman told me the day I was hired,
> "You miss one door, Mr. Jones . . . you're fired."
> I slapped those doors always on the run
> Every fourteen seconds, never missed a one.
> And I staggered home from work each night,
> Still slappin' 'em on front door right.

Reuther decided that the next step should be the distribution of union leaflets at the many gates to the plant. Volunteers were enlisted to assist in the operation. The central gate through which a majority of the workers entered was Gate 4. Reuther and his top aides chose that gate for their own post, taking care to notify newspaper reporters and photographers. It was approached by an overpass that crossed Miller Road. The time chosen for the leaflet distribution was May 26, 1937, at the afternoon shift change. Waiting on the overpass were some thirty or forty of Harry Bennett's strong-arm men. As Reuther and Dick Frankensteen reached the center, they were attacked. "I didn't fight back," Reuther wrote. "I merely tried to guard my face. The men . . . picked me up about eight different times and threw me down on my back on the concrete and while I was on the ground, they kicked me in the face, head and other parts of my body. . . . Then they would raise me up, hold my arms behind me and begin to hit me some more. . . . Finally they got me next to Dick who was lying on the bridge and with both of us together they kicked me again and then picked me up and threw me down the first flight of stairs." For almost a block the men drove Reuther and Frankensteen ahead of them, never letting them go, knocking them down, kicking them, and then slugging them when they struggled to their feet. Finally the two men were rescued by newspaper photographers in a car and spirited away. "I might add," Reuther wrote, "the police standing around did nothing to prevent the slugging."

Similar scenes were enacted at other gates; a number of women were among the leaflet distributors and were kicked and beaten. The newspaper photographers meanwhile recorded the epiphany of violence, and the next day the sensational photographs were spread over the front pages of most of the nation's newspapers. The Battle of the Overpass took its place beside the Battle of the Running Bulls in the legendary warfare of labor against capital. Among the hundreds of observers was the Reverend Raymond Sanford, chairman of the Committee for Church and Industry of the Chicago Church Federation; he recounted the brutal beating of Reuther and Frankensteen, "kicked in the groin and kidney. . . . A well-dressed man kicked one of the girls [distributing] leaflets in the abdomen and she fell at my feet." A woman named Mrs. Gelles testified before the National Labor Relations Board that when she appealed to a policeman to call an ambulance for a badly beaten woman named Stella, he replied, "Oh, let her go back the way she got here. We didn't invite her."

One of the Ford toughs told a reporter for the *Detroit Times*, "We were hired, as far as I know, temporary, to take care of these men that are to distribute these pamphlets." Four men had been assigned to each leaflet distributor, with instructions to beat them as badly as they could without killing anyone.

It is hard to understand how Bennett (and Ford) could have been so insensitive to the effect on public opinion of such tactics. They could hardly have devised a response better designed to create sympathy for the union and to blacken the reputation of the Ford Motor Company. Was it simply arrogance or a kind of extraordinary rectitude, a feeling that whatever Ford did must be right and be so perceived by the world? What Reuther had done, at the cost to be sure of great pain, was to stage, with the cooperation of Harry Bennett and Henry Ford, a transfixing public drama for the world. The theme of the drama was "capitalist thugs beating workers." *Time* magazine, giving an account of the battle, concluded that "it looked very much as if that brutal beating might hurt Henry Ford as much as it hurt Richard Frankensteen." (Frankensteen was, in fact, the more seriously hurt of the two men.) The reaction of the Ford Motor Company was again obtuse: It withdrew all advertising from *Time, Life,* and *Fortune* for a year and a half.

A few weeks later another distribution of leaflets was carried out at the gates of the River Rouge plant, this time without incident. It was described in a letter to a convalescing Reuther as a "magnificent success, in perfect order, and high union spirits. Ford employees taking papers in great numbers. West Side Local had 600 at hall." Upton Sinclair did his considerable bit by writing an exposé of Ford entitled *The Flivver King,* and the printers' union printed up 200,000 copies.

But the pursuit of Walter Reuther was relentless. In April, 1938, at a birthday party for Victor Reuther's wife, Sophie, at Walter and May Reuther's apartment, two men appeared with drawn revolvers, ordered the guests into one part of the room on threat of being shot, and tried to kidnap Reuther. One of the guests told the intruders, "You're not going to get him out of here. You may shoot some of us, but you won't get out yourselves." Reuther refused to leave, and when one of the guests escaped and raised a cry for help, the gunmen fled, but it was a somber reminder of how far Harry Bennett's arm reached. The Reuthers got permits to carry revolvers for self-defense; the gunmen were apprehended, tried by a jury, and set free.

Despite the Battle of the Overpass and the bad press that resulted for Ford himself, the old man remained obdurate. It was not until March, 1941, by order of the National Labor Relations Board *and* the Supreme Court, that the Ford Motor Company posted notices at the Rouge River plant declaring that the company no longer opposed the United Auto Workers. The order required the rehiring of several hundred union workers who had been fired from various Ford plants across the country in 1937. The CIO threw its weight behind the drive to organize Ford, establishing the Ford Organizing Committee, well funded and staffed by experienced organizers. On April 2, 1941, a majority of Ford workers at River Rouge went out on strike. After ten days the company capitulated, agreeing to recognize the UAW-CIO as the bargaining agent for its employees pending an election supervised by the National Labor Relations Board. Years later in an interview Harry Bennett recalled that Ford was furious over the strike. "I've never done anything against labor," he declared.

Walter Reuther's principal achievement with the United Automobile Workers was that he made his union into the liberal image of what a union should be (and all too seldom was): a force for social justice. His greatest accomplishment may well have been to eliminate discrimination against blacks. His union crusaded for housing for the poor, for integrated schools, and for expanded national parks. It is not too much to say that under Reuther's leadership a segment of America labor became, for the first time in our history, an advocate of large-scale social reform through political action. Labor's earlier battles had been, the socialist element in the labor movement aside, for higher wages and better working conditions. Under Reuther's leadership the United Auto Workers became a bellwether of liberal politics, and Reuther the heir apparent of Eugene V. Debs and John L. Lewis.

# 32

## The Last Campaigns

The steel industry had been intermittently unionized, but since the failure of the steel strike of 1919, it had been, in the main, immune to unionization. Now Lewis decided it was time to tackle the steel companies, starting with so-called Big Steel—Bethlehem Steel and the U.S. Steel Corporation, which had taken the lead in breaking the 1919 strike. The Steel Workers' Organizing Committee consequently received a lion's share of the available CIO funds and organizers, and Philip Murray was put in charge of the organizing campaign.

Once again Communists were actively involved. "In this New Deal period," Hosea Hudson told Nell Painter, "the party was different from before. Now we got this open Party office, and you go up there, walk in, have classes on a Sunday." The party units were called clubs, and word came down from Earl Browder that they were to encourage membership like "a community club or an industrial club, where all the coal miners and the steelworkers meet. . . ." Starting in 1937, the party in effect lent its most experienced and capable organizers to the CIO. In Birmingham, Alabama, Hudson put his energies into union organizing; the party was secondary. On the other hand, there was less fear of Reds. Before, "they had been cramped up," Hudson stated, "dodging and hiding to get to a meeting, [but now] they could come

751

to the union meeting and they wouldn't be bothered, wont afraid at the steel union. It was a devil of a turnaround," Hudson added. Noel Beddow, the organizer of the drive to bring the steelworkers into the CIO, was violently anti-Communist, according to Hudson, but his orders from Philip Murray and John L. Lewis, as Hudson interpreted them, were: "You got to work with these guys, 'cause they's good organizers. They's the ones that know how to organize, know how to contact people."

In Hosea Hudson's words, "The CIO came in and began to show these white and black workers the differential in the wages of the steelworkers in Birmingham and the steelworkers in Pittsburgh." The steelworkers in Birmingham got $12, compared with $16 in Pittsburgh, for eight hours of work. The difference was that the Pittsburgh steelworkers were members of the union.

Another important aspect of the CIO organizing drives in the South was that the union insisted that black and white workers belong to the same "big union" and that there be no racial discrimination in meetings. One tactic that proved successful in Birmingham was a mass march of black and white steelworkers through town. "We started down in the business section," Hosea Hudson recalled. ". . . We marched up the hill, went round, circled up across the streets . . . where the big shots lived. . . . We was four deep. I never did know how many people was in that march. . . . It was so long, it come twisting around. You look up, far as you could see, you see men, all the town. . . . That was something unusual, to see white and black together. We used everything to show them our strength."

When Lewis and Murray approached the president of U.S. Steel with a proposal that the company set the standard for the rest of the industry by accepting the CIO as the bargaining agent for the steelworkers, establishing a forty-hour week, and paying time and a half for overtime, the president, to their surprise, accepted. In March, 1937, the company announced that it had granted bargaining rights to the Steel Workers' Organizing Committee, increased wages 10 percent, cut the workweek to forty hours, and agreed to time and a half for overtime. It was said that two financiers closely tied to the Morgan interests had negotiated the agreement. Within three months 140 companies with some 300,000 employees had signed contracts with the steel union.

In Little Steel (the name given to the smaller companies), Tom Girdler, president of Republic Steel, set himself to check the union tide. Citizens' committees were formed, and various strategies devised to induce strikers to return to work; the number of company spies and provocateurs who urged the strikers to undertake violent and illegal actions that could be counted on to result in police attacks was greatly increased, and special efforts were directed at gaining the support of newspapers for the company. In Len De Caux's words, "Governors, mayors, sheriffs, police were suborned against the CIO, sometimes with hard cash, as the La Follette committee later revealed. . . . Millions were spent on every device to guide local opinion formation. . . . Anti-CIO propaganda flooded the land." Much of it emphasized the theme that the CIO was staffed with dangerous Reds—Bolsheviks who were the pliant tools of Moscow. Experts on subversion came forward to list the names and offices of communists with small or large C's among CIO officials. Lewis, as the symbol of the CIO, faced the storm defiantly, refusing to trim his sails or change course. Under constant pressure to denounce the Reds and weed them out of the CIO leadership, he compromised only to the extent of denouncing "commonists and fascists."

On Memorial Day, 1937, police fired on marchers near the Republic Steel mills in South Chicago; ten people were killed, and dozens wounded. Cleveland and Youngstown were the principal locations of Republic plants. In Youngstown company police fired from trucks on men and women pickets, killing two people and injuring dozens of others. The homes of the strikers were searched for guns and explosives, and strike leaders were routinely arrested, sometimes daily, taken to the police courts, detained for most of the day, and then released. Emil De Leo, a union official, would throw up in the police station every time he was arrested. The tactic worked; the police stopped arresting him. Every form of harassment was tried. A police order forbade the pickets from singing on the ground that it would disturb those workers in the plant who had not joined the strike; the union response was to send teams, consisting of six or seven women and several men, to sing. When these were arrested, they would be immediately replaced by a new team. After sixty-four women and ten men had been arrested, the police gave up. Rose Posetta, who had come to Youngstown to assist the strikers, was arrested each morning and taken to the police station in an effort to halt her work among the wives of the strikers. One morning she raised such a scene, shouting and yelling when the police arrested her outside the plant, that cars stopped and a crowd collected. At the police station she continued her outcry, denouncing the police captain as "a miserable coward, afraid for your own skin. I would not even say you were bribed. You couldn't sink so low for mere money. You are afraid of those thugs who are now breaking the strike, kowtowing to them, so you'll be safe." The alarmed police hustled her out of the station. Like Emil De Leo, Posetta was not arrested again.

Lewis, meanwhile, exhorted Roosevelt to intervene on behalf of the steelworkers, but Roosevelt, alarmed by the growing number of strikes, which many critics attributed to his coddling of labor, pronounced a "plague on both your houses." Lewis's response was prompt and angry: "It ill behooves one who has supped at Labor's table . . . to curse with equal fervor and fine impartiality both labor and its adversaries when they become locked in deadly embrace." The National Labor Relations Board took some of the sting out of Roosevelt's above-the-battle stance by supporting the union and ordering Little Steel to undertake collective bargaining. After many months and hundreds of casualties, including a number of deaths, Little Steel capitulated.

So the struggle went from plant to plant and industry to industry. Some employers capitulated without a struggle; others fought to the bitter end. Since the appearance of Upton Sinclair's *The Jungle*, describing the unspeakable conditions under which men and women worked in packing plants, there had been three major and unsuccessful strikes in Chicago packing plants. When the Packing House Workers' Organizing Committee tackled such houses as Armour and Swift, they had a reservoir of accumulated bitterness to draw on. Betty Burke, under the aegis of the Federal Writers' Project, interviewed men and women who worked "back of the yards" in the great Chicago packinghouses. As in the automobile, steel, coal, and textile industries, the union organizing effort was led by Communists, among them Victoria Kramer, a leader in the Young Communist League. "I was blacklisted under my real name for union activity at Armour's," she told Ann Banks. "I went right back to work in the same department under a different name. In the end I must have had about five different names." Although the packinghouses were cleaner as the result, in large part, of the revelations of *The Jungle*, the working conditions were little better. Estelle Zabritz worked in Wet Casings, also called the Gut Shanty, where the intestines of hogs were washed prior to being packed with meat. When tourists were escorted through the plant, Zabritz reported, "Lots of those ritzy ladies can't take it. . . . The pickle water on the floors gets them all slopped up, just ruins their shoes and their silk hose. And are they glad to get out! They bump into each other and fall all over themselves, just like cockroaches, they're so anxious to get out!" Rheumatism from the damp floors was the principal occupational ailment. Diseases of the skin were common from the chemicals used in curing. "That pickle water causes salt ulcers," Zabritz told Betty Burke, "and they're very hard to cure, nearly impossible if you have to keep working in the wet. The acid and salt just rot away a person's skin and bone if he gets the smallest scratch or cut at work." Another packinghouse worker, Anna Novak, told of having to buy presents for the foreman on "all the holidays, Christmas, Easter, Holy Week, Good Friday. . . . Your job wasn't worth much if you didn't observe the holiday custom. . . . You could get along swell if you let the boss slap you on the behind and feel you up."

In the canning rooms the "steam was so dense," Novak told Burke, "it's like a heavy fog and you can't breathe. In the winter the steam penetrates your clothing and turns cold and clammy on your skin; your hands and feet simply freeze. You should see the rash the girls who have to handle poisoned pork get. And the acids from cans get you so you can't stand up." Black women had black stars pasted on their time cards to identify them and ensure that they did not get any of the better jobs in the plant. "They hardly get a chance at anything but the dirtiest, wettest jobs, that even the white men can't stand or just wouldn't take."

Novak told Betty Burke that the Catholic priests told the Polish women who worked there that " 'the CIO is against religion and the Church! You have no business going to union meetings, you should stay home and be concerned with raising a family of good Catholics.' Around here they always yell about the married couples who have no children. They don't want to give them absolution. Raise children, raise children, raise children, that's all they know. But how to feed them— that they don't know." Sometimes, when Novak had gotten up early, she would "sit down at the window and watch old ladies, seventy years old and more, going to work in the yards, so bent over and shriveled up and sick it makes you want to cry just watching them. The bosses make it so miserable for them, too. . . . They have to sit down there on the floor and rest for half an hour after work before they have the strength to get up and go home at night." The salt water on the floors ate up the leather in the shoes of the women workers. "We kick about things like that and talk about the union, we make the boss mad,"

Novak said. Bosses were so anxious to push production that they ignored the health and the safety of the workers. "It's things like that the union is here to prevent," Novak told Betty Burke.

The Mexican workers in the Chicago packing plants were strong union supporters. Jesse Perez's efforts to organize a CIO chapter resulted in his being fired. "We talk all the time," he told Burke, "what the union going to do for us, going to raise wages, stop speedup." When the men in Perez's unit at the Armour packing plant stopped work in protest at a speedup, they all were summarily fired. "We took the case in the labor board," Perez told Betty Burke, "and they call the boys for witness. Labor board say we got to get jobs back, boss got to promise to put us back. . . ."

Jim Cole, a black man, worked in the "Beef Kill section." The company would not promote him or pay him the standard wage for the dangerous and difficult work that he did, and the AFL union, the Amalgamated Butchers and Meat Cutters, would not allow him to join because he was black. "Long about 1937," Cole told Betty Burke, "the CIO come. Well, I tell you, we Negroes was glad to see it come. Sometimes the bosses or the company stooges try to keep the white boys from joining the union. They say, 'You don't want to belong to a black man's organization. That's all the CIO is.' Don't fool nobody, but they got to spread lying words around. . . . I don't care if the union don't do another lick of work raising our pay, or settling grievances about anything," Cole concluded. "I'll always believe they done the greatest thing in the world getting everybody who works in the yards together, breaking up the hate and bad feelings that used to be held against the Negro. We all doing our work now, nothing but good to say about the CIO . . . . We try to get every person represented. President of the local, he's Negro. First vice president, he's Polish. Second vice president, he's Irish. Other officers: Scotchman, Lithuanian, Negro, German. Many different people can't understand English very well and we have to have union interpreters for lots of our members. But that don't make no mind; they all friends in the union, even if they can't say nothin' except 'Brother' and shake hands."

Elmer Thomas gave the same testimony. White butchers used to hate black butchers, who had the reputation of scabbing. "Well, that was a long time back," Thomas told Betty Burke, "—with the CIO in, all that's like a bad dream gone. Oh, we still have a hard row, but this time the white men are with us and we're with them."

The hostility of the South toward any union activity persisted. As late as 1937 the Memphis police chief warned that no CIO organizers would be permitted in that city. When organizers appeared in spite of his warning, they were driven out of town, and one was badly beaten. Klansmen marched through towns where CIO organizers were trying to form unions and burned their crosses in view of union meetings. Blacklisting and beatings of union members persisted in the South after they had become rarities in other parts of the country. In the words of Congressman Edward Eugene Cox of Georgia, "I warn John L. Lewis and his Communist cohorts that no second-hand 'carpetbag expedition' in the Southland under the banner of Soviet Russia . . . will be tolerated."

Yet despite all such bans and prohibitions, union activity persisted in the South, as we have seen, much of it under the aegis of the Communist Party. In July, 1934, seven blacks and eleven whites founded the first local of what became the Southern Tenant Farmers' Union at Tyronza, Arkansas. The union turned out to be one of those ideas whose time had come. Within a year it counted more than 10,000 members, and in September, 1935, it led a strike in Arkansas for sixty-five-cents-a-hundredweight pay for picking cotton. From Arkansas the union spread to Oklahoma, Texas, Tennessee, Mississippi, and Missouri, with some 30,000 members.

Much of its success was due to the leadership of H. K. Mitchell, a sharecropper who had turned dry cleaner. He had been a Socialist since the beginning of the Depression, and his Socialist connections won his union the support of Norman Thomas and the Socialist Party, which doubtless saw an opportunity for the Socialists to counter the gains of the Communists in the various farm organizations. The union was as poor as its members, many of whom were unable to pay their dues of ten cents a month. Mitchell himself did not receive a salary, and one of his organizers wrote, "If you know any Commie sources to appeal to for my support, for Gawd's sake do it."

The battle of the Southern Tenant Farmers' Union for survival was a desperate one. In addition to lack of funds, the members were constantly harassed by landlords and their agents, the local law enforcement officials. In January, 1935, a union meeting at Marked Tree, Arkansas, was broken up by sheriff's deputies; the organizer of the meeting, Ward Rogers, a Vanderbilt Theological Seminary graduate, was arrested, convicted of criminal anarchy, and sentenced to six months in jail. Once more the International Labor Defense came to the assistance of a union organizer. Students and faculty at Commonwealth College took up Rogers's cause, as did some of the Vanderbilt Seminary students, while the *Daily Worker* and the *New Masses* gave the case wide publicity.

Frazier Hunt, visiting Marked Tree, heard "incredible tales of how [the organizers and union members] were being beaten, thrown in jail, hounded and hunted down like runaway slaves." Union officials and organizers were careful not to venture into remote rural areas or, indeed, anywhere without bodyguards.

The Communist Party, in the person of Donald Henderson, made an effort to take over the Southern Tenant Farmers' Union. Henderson, a thin young man, had traveled to Soviet Russia in the twenties with Rexford Guy Tugwell under the auspices of the Workers' Party. He had done graduate work in economics at Columbia and taught there while he was working on his dissertation. Columbia had fired him, ostensibly for failing to make satisfactory progress on his doctoral dissertation; in the opinion of his friends and fellow students, he was actually fired for teaching radical doctrines. He soon joined the Communist Party and became an agricultural organizer.

Henderson had organized a union designed to absorb all existing farm organizations. It was given the awkward name of the United Cannery, Agricultural, Packing and Allied Workers of America, which, heaven knows, was comprehensive enough. Prominent in the founding convention were Harry Bridges of the longshoremen and Reid Robinson of the Mill, Mine, and Smelter Workers, a party-line union, Mary Heaton Vorse, and John Bosch, president of the Farmers Holiday Association. Pat Jackson, a Henderson lieutenant, was heir to a railroad fortune. A radical journalist, he had been one of the most ardent supporters of Sacco and Vanzetti. Through the Washington Committee to Aid Agricultural Workers, Jackson raised money to help Henderson put together the agricultural workers' union. Henderson offered to make Mitchell secretary of the new organization if he would clandestinely join the Communist Party. Mitchell refused and reluctantly accepted an affiliate status. Mitchell disliked Henderson from the first and wrote to Norman Thomas, "Two or three centuries ago such people as Henderson were out burning witches." A Southern Tenant Farmers' Union organizer complained to Mitchell that the Communists "always talk bourgesis and Proletariot when people don't even know what that means."

Howard "Buck" Kester was another Vanderbilt Seminary student, active in the tenant farmers' union, whose Socialist affiliations made him wary of Henderson's efforts to take over. Frustrated by Mitchell's resistance, Henderson tried to prevail on Odis Sweeden, part Cherokee Indian and head of the Oklahoma chapter of the Southern Tenant Farmers' Union, to switch his allegiance and his union to the Communist-led Farmers' National Committee for Action, headed by the Communist organizer Lem Harris. When Mitchell visited Commonwealth College, a Southern Tenant Farmers' Union organizer tried to shoot him. No connection was ever established between the Communists at Commonwealth College and the assassination attempt, but Mitchell believed that criticism of him for refusing to join forces with the Communists had incited the act.

After several years of an uneasy alliance with Henderson's catchall union, the Southern Tenant Farmers' Union voted to secede. A mock funeral service was held for the United Cannery, Agricultural, Packing and Allied Workers of America, and to the beat of a jazz pianist the STFU members sang:

> She's ashes to ashes, and dust to dust,
> Here lies a union we never could trust;
> Ashes to ashes and dust to dust,
> This man Henderson has hushed his fuss.

Years after the demise of the STFU a historian of the movement wrote that it "represented the most dedicated and sincere effort . . . to ameliorate the condition of southern farm workers, sharecroppers and tenant farmers, both black and white. Its amazing strength came from the faith of its humble members, manifested in the face of brutal beatings and persecution."

The situation of farmworkers in California was almost as grim as that in the South, since huge corporations, like the Southern Pacific Railroad and the Crocker Bank, and wealthy individual growers owned most of the state's rich farmland. In 1930 more than 30 percent of the large-scale cotton farms in the nation were in California, although it produced only 2 percent of the cotton crop. It also had 40 percent of the large-scale dairy farms, 53 percent of the poultry farms, and 60 percent of the large-scale fruit farms. In 1935, 62.5 percent of the farm acreage in the state was controlled by 3.5 percent of those engaged in agriculture. In the rich Imperial Valley 43 percent of the land was owned by 6 percent of the population (individuals and corporations). It was said, not wholly inaccurately, that the railroads and the large growers ran the state.

The task of union organization was greatly complicated by the fact that approximately 75 percent of the migratory pickers in the cotton fields were Mexican, and the rest were white migrants from Oklahoma and Arkansas with an inbred hostility toward Mexicans as well as an inability to speak Spanish.

Following the defeat of the Mexican Mutual Aid strike in the Imperial Valley, the Communists organized the Agricultural Workers' Industrial League. Plans to strike the cantaloupe harvest in the spring were revealed to the authorities by informers. The party headquarters were raided, and 103 workers, organizers, and officers were arrested; 8 were sentenced to prison terms for criminal conspiracy. By 1933 wages for migratory workers had dropped to fifteen or sixteen cents an hour. At a hearing of the state legislature a seven-year-old child said that working at cotton picking from seven o'clock in the morning until dark, he had made three cents an hour. The Agricultural Workers' Industrial League meanwhile metamorphosed into the Cannery and Agricultural Workers' Industrial Union. In the years from 1930 to 1932 in California there were ten agricultural strikes, in five of which the Communists were directly involved. Virtually all failed. But the NIRA stimulated new efforts. In 1933, the first year of the New Deal, a wave of strikes swept California farms. More than 48,000 agricultural workers went on strike, and the cannery and agricultural union provided the leadership in the great majority of the strikes. The growers' strategy was to drive the strikers off their ranches, to prevent picketing by the use of armed deputized growers, and, finally, to force the strikers out of the valley and replace them with a more docile labor force. The result was not what the growers had anticipated. Forced off the ranches, the strikers found refuge together in encampments where they were better able to protect themselves. In addition, they received food and medicine through Federal relief agencies. The growers decided to step up the violence against the strikers. At Pixley a skirmish line of growers fired on a union meeting, killing two persons and wounding nine others. In Kern County a striker was murdered by vigilantes.

A state-appointed fact-finding committee recommended pay of seventy-five cents a hundredweight of cotton and criticized the growers for infringing on the civil liberties of the strikers. Pressures were applied to both sides to settle the strike. The union, under Caroline Decker's leadership, held out for eighty cents, but on October 26 an agreement was reached, and the strikers went back to work. It was a costly victory. Raising the cry of communism, the Associated Farmers of California organized to fight the unionization of agricultural workers, and a large war chest was collected from the big corporate growers. By 1936 some $163,000 had been spent, most of it directed against the cannery and agricultural union. The situation was similar to that in the South. In both instances racial prejudice played an important part in the determination of the landowners to suppress unions. Mexicans in California (and the other Far Western states) were not as severely discriminated against as Southern blacks (they were, after all, technically white), but it was a matter of degree. In contrast with the Southern landlords, many of whom were not much better off than their tenants, most of the California agricultural land was, as we noted, owned by huge corporations, whose opposition to unions fell into the classic pattern of the war between capital and labor. When a fruit pickers' strike began in the Imperial Valley in January, 1934, the growers lost no time in wheeling in the heavy artillery. At Brawley, on January 9, 87 strikers were arrested, and three days later 100 Mexican strikers were tear-gassed by the police. A Civil Liberties Union lawyer who tried to speak was kidnapped and beaten along with attorneys for the International Labor Defense.

A strike by cherry pickers in Santa Clara succeeded in winning a wage increase and better working conditions, despite an attack by strikebreakers that wounded fifty strikers and resulted in the arrest of twenty-seven. A strike of El Monte berry pickers was broken, in part because of cultural conflicts between Mexican strike leaders and Anglo Communists. When the growers offered twenty cents an hour and union recognition, the strikers wanted to go back to work, but the Communists rejected the offer. When the strikers did resume work later, it was for less than the growers' best offer, and the Communists were blamed. Victories in pear and peach strikes were followed by growing vigilante activity and losses in a series of subsequent strikes. When the cannery and agricultural union struck the San Joaquin cotton fields, the growers went all out to break the strike and the union.

The police raided the Sacramento headquarters of the union and arrested Caroline Decker, Pat Chambers, and twenty others. They were held in jail six months before being tried on charges of criminal syndicalism, in a trial that began in January, 1935. Five men and three women were given lengthy jail terms; it was not until 1937 that the sentences were thrown out by a higher court on appeal. Meanwhile, the leadership of the Communist Party and, with it, much of the drive for unionization was effectively suppressed in the state.

The cannery and agricultural union was also active among the sugar beet workers in Colorado and Montana. It also organized the cotton workers, again most of them Mexican, in Arizona.

In 1938 and 1939 the Communist Party decided to concentrate its union activities in California, making another attempt to organize the farmworkers in that state. Steve Nelson and his wife were among the experienced organizers sent to help in the campaign. They found the party much livelier in California than in the East. Nelson wrote: "People talked back to you—they argued their points and did it in plain language, freer of leftist jargon than in most places." A young party worker named Dorothy Healey impressed Nelson. She was "a lively and quick-witted organizer blessed with a beautiful smile and lots of guts." Bill Bailey was active in the longshoremen's union and helped run the Seamen's Bookstore on the San Francisco Embarcadero.

Nelson was assigned to Los Angeles, a tough town on unions since the days of the McNamaras. Like Chicago, the city had a Red Squad in the police department, led by William "Red" Hynes, an enemy of Communists and unions, between which he seldom bothered to distinguish. Nelson's principal job in Los Angeles was to act as a liaison between the party headquarters and the Japanese Bureau of the party, which, with some 125 members, was the smallest nationality group. The Nelsons were attracted by the music on a country radio station of a young Oklahoman named Woody Guthrie, "handsome and gangly with a disheveled head of bushy hair." Guthrie's songs were about the Dust Bowl, poor farmers and rich bankers and the better day coming. When he was invited to the Nelsons' apartment, they discovered that he had never eaten spaghetti before. His questions about Russia and communism were endless. "It made me feel rejuvenated just to talk to him," Nelson wrote.

Spanish-speaking party members were sent into the fields and orchards of the Imperial and San Joaquin valleys as laborers to try to organize the Mexican workers. What followed was a classic campaign in the war between capital and labor. All the familiar tactics of harassment, intimidation, company spies, and "goons" were employed by the growers organized to protect their interests under the somewhat misleading name of the Associated Farmers. The party organizers were tracked down by the growers and fired after having first been beaten. It might be said that California was more ruthlessly efficient than Alabama, Georgia, or Mississippi in the tactics used to suppress farm-workers and any lawyers, Communist or otherwise, rash enough to try to come to their aid. Certainly the interventions of the Communists were a mixed blessing. As we have noted, there were often bitter disputes over goals and tactics between Anglo Communists and Mexican strike leaders. Moreover, the Communists were inclined to encourage violence on the part of the strikers, hoping that a crescendo of violence would draw public attention to a particular strike and help rally public opinion in favor of the strikers' cause. There was, of course, also the doctrine that an episode of violence, by dramatizing the inherent and ineradicable opposition between capital and labor, would deepen class consciousness and hasten the revolution. A strike therefore had, at least potentially for the Communists, this extra "educational" dimension that often had nothing to do with the immediate needs of the strikers; the question often was not how can this strike be settled most expeditiously and fairly but how can this strike be used to hasten the triumph of Marxism. This meant that the Communists were always difficult to work with, and sometimes impossible. By the same token the Communist strike leader served two masters. As a man or woman with deep and honest social convictions the strike leader had an instinctive concern for and sympathy with the real and almost invariably desperate needs of the workers who had risked their livelihood by going out on strike. On the other hand, if he helped them settle a strike on terms satisfactory to them, he might well have to answer to his superiors for some kind of doctrinal weakness or deviation from party policy.

In 1930 there had been 637 strikes involving 183,000 workers, one of the lowest totals of the century. In 1935, under the stimulus of the New Deal, there were 2,014 strikes involving roughly 1,120,000 workers. Two years later the number rose to 4,740 strikes and 1,860,000 workers. Union recognition was the most important issue in the great majority of strikes, and the number of union members rose from 3,632,000 in 1930 to almost 9,000,000 in 1937. But statistics tell only part of the story. The union members in 1930 were largely in AFL craft unions, highly traditional, as we have seen, and strongly opposed to industrial unions or indeed to any challenge to their hegemony. The new union members, recruited in the decade of the 1930s, were not only overwhelmingly in industrial unions under the banner of the CIO but also in industries that had been stubbornly resistant to unionization. It might well be argued that workers in nonunion plants benefited almost as much as unionized workers from the great wave of unionization that reached its peak in the years between 1935 and 1938. Employers who wished to avoid the unionization of their plants found that the most effective way was to meet or exceed the standards in union plants. Most important of all, as one union loyalist after another testified, was that, under the protection of the Federal government, workers were relatively free to organize unions without fear of retribution in the form of losing their jobs or being beaten by company thugs. Although union members and closed shops covered only a relatively small portion of the entire labor force, their influence was felt disproportionately by workingmen and workingwomen everywhere.

Perhaps the most notable fact about the strikes which increased so dramatically in number from 1933 on was the outpouring of bitterness and hostility on the part of the workers involved. The level of violence recalled the Great Strikes of 1877. Whenever practical, the Communists turned out members of the Unemployed Councils to act as reinforcements for the strikers. Efforts by local authorities to break the strikes or sometimes to do no more than preserve order almost invariably provoked violent encounters.

For two generations, from roughly the 1870s to the 1930s—a period of some sixty years, almost a third of the lifetime of the nation—workingmen and workingwomen had suffered a series of devastating setbacks. The Knights of Labor had promised much and ultimately delivered little. Debs's "horizontal" railroad union, the first major industrial union, had suggested the potentialities of that form of organization. But when the prize of general union organization seemed within the grasp of workingmen and workingwomen, it had time and again been snatched away, sometimes by a depression, sometimes by a massive counteroffensive by employers, sometimes by a combination of both.

In 1918 at the end of the World War there had been reason to believe that a new era had dawned for American labor, but capital, it turned out, had profited far more from that conflagration. The greed and selfishness that predominated in the 1920s did not provide a congenial environment for the growth of social justice. Triumphant capitalism was in the driver's seat, and it had no notion of sharing its sensational prosperity with its employees—in the rhetoric of the left, with the "workers." Underpaid, overworked, spied on, intimidated and harassed, large numbers of laboring men and women made the bitter best of a situation they seemed powerless to change. But the bitterness was there, deep and unsleeping, and when the opportunity came, for the most part quite unexpectedly, the bitterness gushed forth in torrents that frightened and disconcerted even labor's avowed friends. There was also a kind of angry *joy*, an exultation in speaking and, even more, in acting out the anger they had so long suppressed. The strikes that flared across the country were often spontaneous and out of control. That was not what top labor leaders—most of whom, like Lewis, Dubinsky, and Philip Murray, were basically conservative—had in mind. Union leaders found themselves spending much of their time rushing around to stamp out wildcat strikes. Once acclaimed as the spontaneous reactions of an oppressed class, they were now severely criticized as irresponsible.

Franklin Roosevelt viewed all these matters, as we have seen, with mixed emotions. So did the general public. While Gallup, the indefatigable pollster, reported that a majority of Americans favored unions, there was strong opposition to sit-down strikes, with 65 percent of those polled agreeing that "state and local authorities" should "use force in removing sit-down strikers." In addition, 55 percent thought that the New Deal had been "too friendly toward labor," while 42 percent said its approach had been "about right." (Among Republicans, 80 percent said that the New Deal had been "too friendly toward labor.") Unions were approved of by 76 percent, but 63 percent favored "craft unions"—the AFL type—while slightly more than 30 percent approved of industrial unions—i.e., the CIO. Of those polled, 67 percent preferred the conservative union leader William Green to John L. Lewis, and in July, 1937, 71 percent declared they were "less in favor of unions" than they had been six months earlier. The point hardly needed to be belabored: The popular support for labor unions, especially those of the militant, CIO type, was very thin.

Roosevelt was certainly committed in theory to the cause of improving the conditions of labor, primarily by guaranteeing the right to unionize and bargain collectively, but when the whole country seemed racked by prolonged and dangerous strikes in which the public interest received little attention, the President was well aware that labor unrest was being blamed on him. Not surprisingly, he wished "not so much and not so fast." Things seemed in danger of getting quite out of hand. In the words of Len De Caux, "No matter how much Roosevelt did for the workers, Lewis demanded more. He showed no gratitude, nor did he bid his followers be grateful—just put the squeeze on all the harder."

But even Lewis, conscious of the power of public opinion, knew that there were limits to the nation's tolerance. The economic slump of the fall of 1937 threatened to push the country back into a deep depression, and Lewis, sensing that the public was losing sympathy with the apparently endless strikes, pledged an end to sit-downs. The greatest era in the history of American labor was, for all practical purposes, over, but it had, in about three years, permanently changed the structure of American society.

It would be difficult in a discussion of the culminating campaign in the long war between capital and labor to overstate the importance of the Wagner Act and the role of the congressional committees that oversaw its enforcement. The National Labor Relations Board was strongly prolabor and prounion. Equally important, its staff, made up largely of young lawyers, was predominantly radical. By the mid-forties all the major industries in America had succumbed to unionization. In bringing this about, the NLRB supervised some 24,000 union elections, involving 6,000,000 workers. The AFL won 33.4 percent; the CIO, 40 percent. Independent unions won 10.5 percent, and in 16 percent of the elections no union was chosen. Moreover, 300,000 union members were ordered reinstated in jobs from which they had been fired, most commonly for union activity, and awarded $9,000,000 in back pay.

Almost equally important was Senator Bob La Follette's subcommittee on civil liberties violations, which protected workers' right to organize. "All through the early CIO years, all over the field," De Caux wrote, "I ran into men from the La Follette committee doing their brave, shrewd, and conscientious work."

# 33

## The Spanish Civil War

When Hamilton Fish Armstrong visited Madrid in August, 1931, there had been fighting between the supporters of King Alfonso and the champions of republican government, and the king had fled by the back door of the palace, rather ungallantly leaving the queen and other members of the family behind. A former professor of political science, Fernando de los Ríos, minister of justice in a Republican-Socialist coalition which had been formed after the king's flight, was busy making plans to break up the great estates in southern Spain. In Barcelona the radical syndicalists, determined to break away and form a separate Catalan republic, were engaged in a bitter struggle with the trade unionists, who wished to preserve strong ties with the republican government in Madrid. Jay Allen, an American journalist who had made Spain his special beat, was in Madrid, as was Ernest Hemingway. Hemingway was writing a book about bullfighting, which fascinated him, with the prospective title *Death in the Afternoon*. Sidney Franklin, the tall young Jewish bullfighter from Brooklyn, was a drinking pal of Hemingway and Allen, as was the Spanish artist and Socialist Luis Quintanilla. Drinking beer and eating shrimp, the four men talked of the promise of the new republican government. By the late twenties, Spain, specifically Madrid, had replaced Paris, Rome, and Berlin as the mecca for American intellectuals. The fame of Sidney Franklin and Hemingway's enthusiasm for bullfighting, combined with the emergence of Spanish republican politics, made the fall of that ancient, decadent monarchy seem the promise of a better day.

The departure of King Alfonso had been followed by almost five years of fighting among the parties of the left. The syndicalist-anarchists attempted a coup in Barcelona in December, 1933. It was suppressed after ten days of bloody street fighting. Six months later the Socialists took their turn at trying to seize power in Barcelona. Catalonia proclaimed its independence in the fall of 1934, and an insurrection by the miners of Asturias further complicated matters. Finally, in February, 1936, the republicans, Socialists, and Communists formed a popular front government that defeated a coalition of conservatives, clericals, and monarchists. Six months later a revolt against the government led by Francisco Franco began in Spanish Morocco. Within a few months Mussolini had thrown his support to Franco on the ground that it was essential to stop communism.

Liberals, Socialists, and Communists everywhere rallied to the cause of the Spanish republican government, the Loyalists. "The Spanish Civil War," Hamilton Fish Armstrong wrote, "tested liberal convictions everywhere. For me, and especially for those a few years younger, it became the embodiment of the struggle against Fascism and Nazism. . . . The Spanish War should have been the warning to civilized governments, but instead they adopted the strangling policy of nonintervention. . . ." As the British socialist Clement Attlee expressed it, the policy was "really devised to prevent the Spanish government from exercising its rights under international law," specifically the right to buy arms and munitions for its own defense.

In the United States, Congress, on January 8, 1937, put an embargo on all arms to Spain. Hitler and Mussolini, of course, had no such compunctions. A desperate Loyalist government turned to Russia for assistance, and Stalin was glad to respond. He announced that the defense of the Spanish republican government against Franco was not simply a Spanish issue but one that must enlist the sympathies of "progressive" people everywhere. Stalin's support of the Spanish Loyalists drew more American intellectuals into the ranks of the Communist Party than reams of Soviet propaganda. One nation in the world— and that nation the Soviet Union—was willing to come to the aid of the democratically elected government of Spain. To understand the psychological effect of this decision in liberal and radical circles, especially in the United States and Great Britain, it is necessary to bear in mind the shattering disillusionment that came in the wake of the Versailles Treaty. The darkest forces of reaction seemed everywhere in the ascendancy. In Europe repression, political terrorism, and assassination on both the right and the left (and within the right and the left) seemed to be the order of the day. The so-called civilized nations were engaged in the most shameless and cynical maneuverings for advantage or simply for security. In all that darkness of defeated hopes, Spain shone with a startling luster. The expectations that it aroused were doubtless naïve. The Loyalist government was not without its flaws and weaknesses, but the mere fact that it existed at all seemed, under the circumstances, a kind of miracle.

The Spanish church was undoubtedly the most reactionary ecclesiastical establishment in Europe. Opposed to every effort at reform, it symbolized for the parties of the left all that was most cruelly repressive in the ruling class. At the same time the fury with which the parties of the left turned on the church dismayed those of its friends still immune to the notion that the ends justify the means. During the early months of the war 13 bishops, 4,184 priests, 2,365 monks, and 283 nuns were murdered in the republican zone. One inevitable consequence was that the worldwide Catholic Church moved farther to the right than ever. In the United States it constituted a powerful lobby against any aid to the Loyalist (republican) government. Since Irish and Polish Catholics were a substantial element in the Democratic Party, their feelings were attended to. If the massacre of Spanish Catholic orders had not occurred, it would by no means have followed that the democratic nations would have given aid to the Loyalists. In the United States at least, isolationist sentiment would doubtless have made such aid impossible. But certainly the republican cause was seriously compromised in the eyes of moderate world opinion by the murders; they added one more dimension of horror to what rapidly became one of the most devastating chapters of twentieth-century history.

The majority of Americans showed little initial interest in the Spanish Civil War. A Gallup Poll in February, 1937, indicated that 22 percent favored the Loyalists, 12 percent favored the rebels (Franco's forces), and 66 percent were "neutral, no opinion." Although by February, 1939, more than 75 percent of the American voters favored the Loyalists' cause, 79 percent were opposed to providing any aid to them. Rather surprisingly, there was comparatively strong support for the Loyalists in the South (perhaps because they were the constitutionally elected government); the Pacific coast showed the highest level of Loyalist support.

The Insurgents, or Nationalists, led by General Francisco Franco and depending heavily on feared Moorish soldiers, set up the Junta of National Defense at Burgos and began a drive aimed at Madrid. By August they were at Toledo, which they captured after a ten-week siege of the ancient Alcázar fortress. On November 6 Franco's army was at the outskirts of Madrid.

Since most of the regular army had defected to Franco, the Loyalist government was forced to rely primarily on a hastily recruited and poorly trained militia of peasants and workers. They had proved ineffective against trained soldiers and the ferocious Moors, but they were soon reinforced by cadres of volunteers (no better trained) from other nations, the so-called International Column, later the International Brigade.

The defenders of Madrid, many of whom had only recently broken and fled ignominiously before Franco, turned now on their own ground and fought fiercely. The commander of the Madrid defenders, "a middle-aged, fat, bald-headed, owl-like general called [José] Miaja," in Bernard Knox's words, had apparently been authorized to surrender the city on the best possible terms. However, he was determined to defend it and to do so he called on the well-trained and highly disciplined Communist Fifth Regiment. Everyone not prepared to die should leave the city at once, he announced.

To the defenders of Madrid Dolores Ibarruri, "La Pasionaria," the Passion Flower, declared, "It is better to die on your feet than to live on your knees." She was the author of the Loyalists' most famous battle cry, *No pasarán* ("They shall not pass."). "Due to the miracle of 'No pasarán!' . . . the city did not fall—not that week, nor that month, nor that year. Madrid held out," Langston Hughes wrote. The battle turned on the defeat of the Moors. Their stronghold was a building in University City. Three hundred men of the International Brigade attacked and drove the Moors out, suffering the loss of two-thirds of their forces, killed or wounded, but dispelling the illusion that the Moors were invincible.

The International Brigade was the most dramatic manifestation of a collective will among the peoples (not, certainly, the governments) of the Western democratic nations to check the spread of fascism. In consequence, it became the focus of attention for legions of visiting journalists and liberal politicians, the subject of unnumbered plays, novels, and poems. Intellectuals, artists, and radicals of every description headed for Madrid. While the anarchists and Socialists were much in evidence, the Communists clearly dominated. In the words of W. H. Auden, the international volunteers "clung like burrs on the long expresses that lurch/Through the unjust lands, through the night, through the alpine tunnel/ They floated over the oceans./ They walked the passes; they came to present their lives."

In the United States the Communist Party set up a Committee for Technical Aid for Democratic Spain, the principal purpose of which was to recruit men who were willing to go to Spain. Steve Nelson, organizing for the party in the anthracite coalfields of Pennsylvania, took sveral busloads of miners from Wilkes-Barre to hear André Malraux, the French writer, and John Strachey, the British socialist, urge support for the Spanish Loyalists. Nelson was one of eight from the Wilkes-Barre area to volunteer. At thirty-four he was the oldest. All were active in the Unemployed Councils, the Young Communist League, or the party. Under the rubric of "tourists" Nelson and his companions joined hundreds of other volunteers making their way first by steamship to France and then through an intricate underground to the Spanish border, where they were joined by British and Canadian volunteers, all initially arrested by the French. Finally freed after several weeks, they managed to slip across the border into Spain. "By foot, truck, and finally train," Nelson recalled, "we made our way to Albacete, one hundred miles from the front and base camp for the International Brigade." The streets of the town swarmed with soldiers of various nationalities, back from the front. "They lounged on the streets, basking in the sun, flirting with the girls. . . ." It was from Albacete that the International Brigade had moved to the defense of Madrid. There were, in fact, five brigades: the Thaelmann Brigade, named after a German Communist leader killed by the Nazis, and made up of Germans; the Twelfth, composed of Italians, Germans, and French volunteers and called the Garibaldi; the Slavic Thirteenth, the Dombrowski; the Fourteenth, made up for the most part of Belgians and French; and the English-speaking Fifteenth, comprised of two American battalions, the Lincoln and the Washington, and a Canadian battalion.

From Albacete, the Americans in Nelson's party made their way by truck to the position on the front line held by the Lincoln Battalion. Nelson, as one of the older volunteers and an experienced party member, was at once made political commissar. His task was "to explain every situation, to see that military decisions and objectives are understood, and that the men's needs, physical and personal, are taken care of." When Nelson joined the battalion, it had just been pulled back from the defense of the Jarama, where it had suffered heavy casualties.

Oliver Law, a black man with six years' experience in the U.S. Army, was commander of the Tom Mooney Machine Gun Company. In Chicago he had worked in the building trades and been a leader in the fight for black rights. Law took Nelson on a tour of the battalion's position. In an olive grove six-foot-deep holes, large enough to hold one or two men, had been dug at intervals and covered over with branches and grass. The enemy lines were some 500 yards away, and the American positions were bombarded three times a day by the clock.

Nelson's headquarters were the "library," supplied with a store of books and magazines as well as checker games and Ping-Pong balls and paddles. He used a bundle of *Daily Workers* as a pillow.

After weeks at the front, the Lincoln Battalion was ordered to a rest area near the village of Ibáñez. The spokesman of the village was a cripple. He told the Americans, "Ours is a small and old village. We have done all we could. We have sent thirty-one men to the army, our teacher among them. . . . You have come to us from far away, and we accept you as our sons, our brothers, and our comrades. We know how badly you need rest, and we are honored that you come here." A flour mill had been cleared out as a barracks. When the welcoming talk was over, the villagers shouted, *"Viva los americanos!"* and the soldiers shouted back, *"Viva la República Española!"* The soldiers and townspeople were soon cheerfully involved with each other. Most of the battalion turned out to help harvest the barley crop. A picnic with games and prizes was organized for the children of the town. A Spanish-speaking soldier who had taught school in the United States reopened the village school and soon had thirty pupils, while a Canadian doctor provided much needed medical care.

When the battalion left the village in July, the church bells of the town rang and the people of Ibáñez turned out to see their American friends off. They were headed for the first major offensive of the republican army against Franco's forces. The Washington Battalion was one of the attacking units, while the "Lincolns" were held in reserve. For three days the attackers inched forward, taking the Fascist-held town of La Cañada and holding it against a counterattack. Oliver Law, who had succeeded to the command of the Lincoln Battalion, was fatally wounded in the July offensive. "It was perhaps the first time," Steve Nelson wrote, "that a black man had commanded white American troops." Steve Nelson replaced him as commander of the battalion. Another black volunteer was Angelo Herndon's brother, Milton, who died in the fighting at Fuentes de Ebro on October 13, 1937. For Langston Hughes, covering the war for the Afro-American Newspapers organization, Herndon's presence and his death had a profound symbolic significance. Angelo Herndon had become a figure of international renown during his long-drawn-out trial, in the course of which new constitutional principles had been enunciated. Now his brother, an equally dedicated Communist, had given his life in the fight against fascism and thereby dramatized the ideal of the solidarity of the "darker races" in their common fight against internal and external imperialism. One of Herndon's fellow soldiers told Hughes that before he died, Herndon had said, "Yesterday Ethiopia. Today Spain. Tomorrow, maybe America. Fascism won't stop anywhere—until we stop it." Langston Hughes wrote: "They were there in Spain in 1937–38, American Negroes. History has recorded it; before that time, the leading ambassadors of the Negro people in Europe were jazz-band musicians, concert artists, dancers or other performers. But these Negroes in Spain were fighters—*voluntary fighters*—which is where history turned another page."

Another casualty of the offensive was John Parks, "a tall, wiry sort of guy," as Nelson described him, "he was the personification of the small farmer from the hills of Tennessee or Kentucky. Working as a party organizer in Pennsylvania, Parks had been responsible for organizing a hunger march to the state capitol in Harrisburg to press the legislature for measures to alleviate suffering among the unemployed. Nelson also saw along the road the dead body of his friend George Brown, "a tall, handsome Irishman" who had been one of his classmates at the Lenin School in 1931.

The government drive on the Aragón front was directed up the valley of the Ebro River. The drive began promisingly with the capture of the town of Quinto. The next objective, Belchite, was far more formidable. German engineers had fortified it heavily. But the Lincoln-Washington Battalion, now consolidated because of casualties, got a foothold in the town before Nelson was badly wounded.

Convalescing from his wounds, Nelson became an escort for the stream of visiting American dignitaries. Ordered back to the United States by Earl Browder, he traveled around the country as a speaker for the National Committee to Aid Democratic Spain.

Different motives drew Americans (and others) to Spain. "There were two major reasons for my being there," the playwright Alvah Bessie noted, "to achieve self-integration, and to lend my individual strength (such as it was) to the fight against our eternal enemy—oppression; and the validity of the second reason was not impaired by the fact that it was a shade weaker than the first, for they were both part of the same thing."

Josephine Herbst wrote a friend that she was going to Spain to write "about the Spain that is living, in spite of the dying . . . how people hold together, live & eat & sleep under the barrage of fear." Spain, she wrote later, "put iron into me at a moment when I needed iron." When Herbst visited the International Brigade in its rest area, she was entranced. A number of the soldiers had gathered with the villagers in the schoolroom, which, crowded with soldiers of a half dozen different nationalities, had, for her, "the benign air of those paintings called 'The Peaceable Kingdom' made by the Quaker Hicks in Pennsylvania when he was trying to reconcile the animal world to the human, the invading whites to the Indians. . . . If the soldiers' chorus of Yugoslavians . . . reminded me of the frescoes in Italy where Fra Angelico's band of musicians resembled the choirboys who sang in the big cathedral, it was because everything during this evening reminded me of something else, and that something was always vibrant and living. . . . The Czech soldiers sang Goethe's 'Röslein, Röslein, Röslein roth' with the tenderness of men who were actually serenading a real sweetheart. . . ." A handsome Hungarian, who had been first violin in a Budapest orchestra, played a violin solo. He was followed by "two comic Rumanians, stamping and singing—of all things—'Who's afraid of the Big Bad Wolf'!"

Herbst never forgot the sight of soldiers in the front lines learning to read and write, using "little blue books of the kind we used to use in college for exams." One of the lines they wrote was: "The cause of the proletariat shall triumph."

But amid the romantic ardor, the determination to check fascism before it devoured the world, there were fermenting doubts about the true nature of the Soviet communism so dominant in the inner councils of the government and its fighting forces.

In the words of Bernard Knox, an Englishman who served in the Eleventh International Brigade, "The Communists owed their prodigious growth in membership and influence to the simple fact that they had (for the moment) only one objective: the creation of an army that could win the war. And in their formation and training of the Fifth Regiment . . . they showed how it could be done." The anarchists, on the other hand, followed what they called "libertarian discipline," which turned out to be no discipline at all. Thus, however brave, they were hopelessly outclassed by trained soldiers. Moreover, the anarchists, who initially formed the backbone of the Loyalist forces, were suspicious of the volunteers of the International Brigade and did their best to block their deployment. "It seemed to me a major weakness of Loyalist Spain," Langston Hughes wrote later, "that, even in regard to the conduct of the war, action and opinion varied so greatly between the Socialist, Communist, Anarchist, and Republican parties as to cause not infrequent confusion in military plans." In Barcelona one of the most disturbing events of the war took place. When the anarchists took over the docks and the telephone exchange, they were attacked by the feared Communist Fifth Regiment with heavy casualties. The episode was demoralizing in the extreme because it raised the question of whether factional quarrels within the republican army and its adjuncts would not fatally cripple the Loyalists' cause. When the bitter debates between Trotskyites and Stalinists were transferred to the battlefields of Spain, the result was the assassination of the Trotskyite leader Andrés Nin, apparently at the orders of the ominous Russian Marty.

"I would like to be able to question without having someone accuse me of disloyalty," Josephine Herbst wrote to Granville Hicks. "There are many things in Spain that are far from simple. I could see . . . quite clearly the role POUM [the Trotsky faction] was playing but I ask what is responsible for [Nin's] assassination? Why are the documents claimed to have been found not published clearly so we can see them? If there was an actual connection between POUM and Franco it would clear everything. While I think there were crooks in the leadership of POUM I know honest men followed too. Why are these things not cleared up? In the case of Russia, many developments leave me confused but I am willing to be patient. But this patience extends too far." Even to a magazine as committed to an evenhanded treatment as the *Nation*, Herbst's misgivings were unacceptable.

Another famous or infamous episode involved an American professor of language and literature from Johns Hopkins. Professor José Robles Pazos had gone to Spain to become a member of the republican Ministry of War. He had been abducted and murdered. When John

Dos Passos arrived in Madrid, he could find out nothing about his friend from government officials. After weeks of inquiry he learned that Robles was dead, apparently assassinated on the orders of the Communists. When Dos Passos expressed his horror to Hemingway, the latter took the news with what seemed to Dos Passos a chilling coldness, suggesting that Robles was doubtless collaborating with the Fascists. It would be a mistake, he declared, to push the matter further. Hemingway's response was the beginning of the end of their friendship.

Langston Hughes was one of the writers who made their way to Madrid. He had been commissioned to write about the war by the *Amsterdam News.* The Alianza, Hughes wrote, was "Madrid's House of Culture, the place where artists and writers gathered to make posters and write pamphlets, songs, poems for the cause." Its president, José Bergamin, was himself a well-known poet, and the Alianza seemed to Hughes a place where "creative miracles continually happen." It was, he wrote Arthur Spingarn, "a thrilling, poetic place to be. . . . There's surely nothing else like it in the world." In the few months that he was in Spain, Hughes "became acquainted with more white American writers than at any other period in my life," he recalled. Dorothy Parker "came quietly and went away quietly. Lillian Hellman came and made a broadcast to Americans from Madrid, exhorting them to give assistance to the Spanish people." Hemingway was the most conspicuous literary figure. "I found him a big likeable fellow whom the men in the Brigades adored," Hughes wrote. "He spent a great deal of time with them in their encampments." Hemingway was a journalistic superstar. In the words of Elinor Langer, Josephine Herbst's biographer, if other correspondents "had a room: he had a suite. If they had no cars: he had two. He had sex: his affair with Martha Gellhorn. He had food: delicacies scavenged for him by his aide Sidney Franklin. He had friends: even the Russians liked him. . . . Fame, fortune, a marriage, a mistress, even for the time being a purpose: Hemingway had them all."

Langston Hughes's friend Louise Thompson was in Spain working for a relief committee. The British poet W. H. Auden was for a time a stretcher-bearer. The novelist George Orwell fought with a Trotskyite unit. Orwell wrote: "When you have had a glimpse of such a disaster as this—and however it ends the Spanish war will turn out to have been an appalling disaster, quite apart from the slaughter and physical suffering—the result is not necessarily disillusion and cynicism. Curiously enough the whole experience has left me with not less but more belief in the decency of human beings. . . ."

Auden wrote a poem entitled "Spain":

> What's your proposal? To build the just city? I will.
> I agree. Or is it the suicide pact, the romantic
>     Death? Very well, I accept, for
> I am your choice, your decision. Yes, I am Spain.

And at the end:

> The stars are death. The animal will not look.
> We are left alone with our day, and the time is short, and
>     History to the defeated
> May say Alas but cannot help nor pardon.

In August, 1937, France closed its border with Spain for primarily political reasons. Loyalist troops were ordered to defend the town of Teruel. Without the assistance of the International Brigade, the town fell, and Franco on December 29, 1937, began a crushing offensive. The Haitian poet Jacques Roumain, living in Paris, expressed the feeling of those intellectuals who had made the cause of republican Spain their own when he said, despairingly, "I expect the world will end."

By December it was evident that the days of the Loyalists were numbered. Franco's forces had occupied the major cities and were threatening to cut the Madrid–Valencia road, the only open line of supply or escape from the city. Americans began to leave. Hemingway, Herbert Matthews, a correspondent for the *New York Times,* and Langston Hughes had a farewell party. From Valencia the trains north to Barcelona were booked for weeks ahead as thousands of men and women, Spanish and foreigners alike, tried to leave the country. The weight of Fascist arms from Italy and Germany, the skill of Franco, and the divisions within the republican army foreordained the outcome many months before the Loyalist forces were encircled by Franco and starved into submission.

In the years that the war lasted, some 4,000 Americans fought for the Loyalists, the great majority of them in the Lincoln and Washington battalions, later known as the Lincoln Brigade. Of that number, almost 2,000 died of wounds or disease, an enormous casualty rate, and many more returned home with wounds that they carried to their graves.

Steve Nelson, his wife, and two friends were in a Manhattan apartment when they heard on the radio that Franco's forces had entered Madrid. Nelson was too numb for tears; the others "cried like children." What now? they asked themselves. How could it have happened?

The consequences were beyond calculation. Thousands of republicans of all political persuasions were executed by Franco's firing squads; almost 1,000,000 were imprisoned; and many thousands were driven into exile. In Nelson's words, "And as night follows day, World War Two followed the defeat of the Spanish Republic." Saddest of all was the fact that many of the men who fought in Spain and could not return to their own countries—Germans and Italians specifically—found refuge in Russia only to fall victims, in many instances, to Stalin's purges. One of Hemingway's friends was Mikhail Koltsov, a correspondent for *Pravda*. Hemingway put him into his Spanish Civil War novel *For Whom the Bell Tolls* as Karkov. A year later Koltsov was executed in one of the purges.

A poet wrote of the martyrs of the war:

> for comrades dead, for having loved tomorrow,
> betrayed and bastinadoed, burned at the stake,
> slow-starved in prison or in exile, buried alive,
> beaten insensible, roused at the day's break,
> then hurried through the snow to execution. . . .

Dos Passos had come to Spain to work with his friend Hemingway on a documentary, *This Spanish Earth,* but the murder of Robles shattered his illusions. His months in Spain and his observation of what he considered the ruthless and cynical exploitation by the Communists of the idealistic volunteers from other countries completely disillusioned him. He came home and denounced what seemed to him the immoral and self-serving actions of the Russians in Spain and thereby made himself the special object of Communist vituperation.

"The Spanish business is so shocking and so horrible," Josephine Herbst wrote to Katherine Anne Porter, "and having been there I feel as if I had watched a boy grow up through sickness and with much promise only to be run over by a streetcar—the horrible treachery involved, in sheer lack of ammunition, all of it, is something one might as well harden oneself to, as the worst has only doubtless begun to happen in the world. . . . Is it totally mad to want to understand so passionately at this hour?"

Thirty years later, when Herbst went to see a documentary on the Spanish Civil War, she could not stop crying. After the film was over, she sat in the lobby of the theater trying to pull herself together. Sitting there, she wrote to her daughter, "[I]t came to me that in the most real sense my most vital life did indeed end with Spain. Nothing so vital, either in my personal life or in the life of the world, has ever come again. And in a deep sense it has all been a shadow picture for years and years." She had known before she left Spain that the war would end in defeat. "And that nothing was going to stop World War II. Nothing. And most of the time since then had been lived on the buried treasure of earlier years. . . . It is all too repetitive and too terrible, with no lessons ever learned. Yet, grim as my view has come to be, I think it absolutely necessary, to continue on any line available, the harassment and the protest. . . ."

As Elinor Langer has pointed out in her biography of Herbst, there is no understanding the thirties without achieving some mastery of the meaning of the Spanish Civil War, some sense of its emotional impact on those directly or even indirectly involved. It suddenly brought Communist dogma out of the pages of the *New Masses* and the learned formularies of Marxist apologetics into the real world—the world, in this instance, of suffering Spanish peasants and workers, of real bullets and cannon shells, of cynical and self-serving maneuvers behind the scenes and extraordinary courage and idealism in the villages and on the battlefields. The fact that so much hope had been invested in the cause of the republican government made its defeat all the more shattering. Even for those whose faith in the party and the Soviet Union remained unshaken, some savor had gone out of life; a fire that could never be rekindled had died.

Steve Nelson felt that the third period dogmas were in large part to blame for the divided councils of the Loyalists. They had been fatal to the party internationally. "We had been wrong," he wrote, "to use the label social-fascist, and the consequences were tragic. Even after we attempted to revise our appraisal, there was a lack of trust and respect. This interfered with the broadest possible support for the Republic." Nelson believed that "some of the anarchist attempts to create agricultural communes and establish worker ownership in all factories—large and small—were premature and hindered the fullest possible mobilization against the fascists." But one can hardly doubt that the real culprit was our old enemy, the Versailles Treaty, which had let loose so many demons in the world. In the failure of Woodrow Wilson's noble and extravagant dream lay the seeds of American isolationism. "Never again," Americans said collectively, and in saying that, they made "again" inevitable.

Idealists and dreamers from many nations—Communists, anarchists, Socialists, syndicalists, men, and occasionally women, speaking a dozen different languages—came together united in only one thing: their hope of a juster, kinder world. They lived among the simple people of their host country, who welcomed them as friends and saviors. The result was a kind of collective euphoria which cynical betrayals and bitter factional quarrels could not eradicate, nor time dim. It *was*, at its best and noblest, the promise of a new human order, and that promise was better than the cause, better than many of the leaders, better, as it turned out, than the stern imperatives of history would allow. Above all, it was *right*. For whatever mixture of motives the brigades and the individuals who made them up spilled their blood on the soil of Spain, they were on the side of justice and decency; they were the steadfast enemies of one of the most retrograde movements in all history. In serving as they did, they made evident in the most dramatic possible way, by offering their lives in trust, that the anti-Fascist cause was not a matter of conflicting nationalisms, of order versus disorder, of conservatism or capitalism against communism but of humanity against inhumanity, inhumanity of a degree as yet hardly imagined. They began to wake up the lazy and indifferent conscience of the world. That they were used or exploited by Stalin for his own purposes is beside the point. The purity of their actions and the sacrifices of their lives remain inviolate.

In dark and terrible counterpoint to the idealism of those who fought for the Loyalists in Spain, in Soviet Russia a new series of treason trials began. The public trials, which, of course, accounted for only a minute portion of those arrested, exiled, or executed, started in the summer of 1936 with the arrests of two famous Bolsheviks, Grigory Zinoviev and Lev Kamenev. They were charged with conspiring to topple the government, assassinate Stalin, and destroy the Soviet economy. They confessed, were convicted, and were executed along with fourteen other important but less well-known Bolsheviks.

When Charles "Chip" Bohlen and his wife (he had married the sister of his polo-playing fellow diplomat Charles Thayer) returned to Moscow in 1937 with the new U.S. ambassador, Joseph E. Davies, the trials were at their height. The Bohlens had in their Moscow apartment two servants, one of whom kept them informed of many of the arrests and exiles and both of whom, they suspected, reported regularly to the secret police. The purge was brought close to home when they discovered that the "genial old Bolshevik journalist" Pavel L. Mikhailsky, who lived on the floor above them and who wrote about America for *Izvestia,* had been carried off in the middle of the night by the NKVD. When the pipes in his abandoned apartment burst and water dripped into the Bohlen quarters, they went upstairs to investigate and found their neighbor gone and his books and papers scattered about his rooms.

Davies, who succeeded William Bullitt as ambassador to Moscow, had gone to his post, in Bohlen's words, "sublimely ignorant of even the most elementary realities of the Soviet system and of its ideology." Davies, a highly successful capitalist and longtime Democratic Party fat cat, was guilelessly pro-Soviet. Ironically, Bullitt, an intellectual, a liberal with socialist inclinations and an initially friendly attitude toward Russia and Russians, had been replaced because of his undisguised rancor toward the Soviets. He was succeeded by a man devoid of any real knowledge of Russia, past or present, who was determined to stay out of trouble with the Roosevelt administration by adopting what Bohlen called "a Pollyanna attitude." He took what the Russians said at face value and ignored the advice of his staff members, whom he had been warned against as being, like Bullitt himself, unduly hostile toward Stalin and his commissars. It was an eerie atmosphere. Bohlen did not dare look up Russian friends from his earlier tour of duty. He heard indirectly that a number had been executed or exiled, and he knew that any effort on his part to contact others would be like signing their death warrants. Before, Russians had been open and friendly toward Americans. Now they went out of their way to avoid them. When Bohlen's wife, dressed in her American-style clothes, joined a line at a department store, the Russian women who were in the line left it hastily.

The second public trial in January, 1937, featured as defendant Y. L. Piatokov, a close associate of Lenin's who had been in charge of the first Five-Year Plan in heavy industry and had been one of Zinoviev's principal accusers. Karl Radek, who three years earlier had assured Bohlen and Kennan that Americans did not understand bolshevism—that Russians were either 100 percent Bolsheviks or completely outside—was another prominent victim of the second trial. Edmund Wilson wrote to James Farrell, asking his opinion about the Radek trial. "My theory is that it has been brought home to them that the trials just before were an international flop, and they have decided to do the whole thing again and take more pains to make it seem plausible. The idea that the accused were plotting with Japan against the United States is a diplomatic gesture intended to cement the entente cordiale with us. . . ." Wilson had much the same words for Malcolm Cowley. "The victims had, I suppose, been guilty of some kind of opposition to the regime; and the technique evidently is to tell them that they can only vindicate themselves by putting on acts which will be helpful to the U.S.S.R."

The principal defendant at the third trial, which began in March, 1938, and was designed to mark the conclusion of the purges, was Nikolai I. Bukharin, one of the most prominent of the "old" Bolsheviks. Bukharin had been Lenin's favorite theoretician. With Stalin and Trotsky, he had been a pallbearer at Lenin's funeral and had become a member of the Politburo. But Bukharin had argued for Lenin's policy of good relations with the peasants and opposed Stalin's effort to coerce them. In a showdown between Stalin and the faction represented by Bukharin, Stalin won, and Bukharin was sent into exile in Siberia. Allowed to return to Moscow, he managed to ingratiate himself sufficiently to be made editor of *Izvestia* and given some status as "an oracle for the rank and file of the party." When Hamilton Fish Armstrong met him on a visit to Paris in 1936, he tried to persuade him to write an article for *Foreign Affairs*. Instead, Bukharin, "with the amiability of a tired professor," gave him a lecture. The essential harmony of Communist society was not, Bukharin insisted, a theory but "a spontaneous fact" (whatever kind of "fact" that is!). Rivalry between Communist states was thus impossible—"by definition an impossibility." Wars were created by the "competition of monopoly capitalism for raw materials and markets." Capitalist society was "made up of selfish and competing units and therefore is by definition a world at war. Communist society will be made up of unselfish and harmonious units and therefore will be by definition a world at peace. Just as capitalism cannot live without war, so war cannot live with Communism." Among the charges against the famous old theoretician was that he had sabotaged shipments of eggs and vegetables by blowing up the railroad cars.

Alelssey I. Rykov, another defendant, had been premier of the Soviet Union. G. G. Yagoda was formerly head of the NKVD. Charles Bohlen attended the trial held in the Hall of Columns of the Nobles Club in Moscow, as interpreter for Davies. The prosecutor was Andrey

Y. Vishinsky. The defendants, twenty-one in all, sat in an enclosed area like a jury box, guarded by soldiers with rifles and bayonets. Three judges presided. Vishinsky, a slight man with thinning reddish hair, reminded Bohlen of a ferocious ferret in his virulent pursuit of the defendants, whose lawyers made no serious effort to defend them but rather admitted their guilt and asked for "proletarian mercy." To Bohlen and many other observers the trials were "fantastic." Much of the evidence produced was too bizarre to believe, such as the charge that Yagoda had sprayed the walls of his office with poison so that his successor would be fatally injured. All the defendants had confessed, some to absurd or manifestly impossible crimes. How such men, long-time leaders in the councils of the party, had been prevailed on to confess could only be conjectured. One man, Nikolai N. Krestinsky, once vice-commissar for foreign affairs, withdrew his confession, declaring that it had been secured by threats and blackmail. The next day he repudiated his charge that his confession had been coerced.

When the trials ended at four o'clock in the morning of March 13, 1938, the death sentences were read by the chief judge of the court, who looked to Bohlen like "a sadistic pig." After each he repeated the words "To be shot, to be shot, to be shot." Eighteen of the defendants were so condemned; the three others received long prison sentences. Ambassador Davies was only one, if one of the most improbable, of those non-Russians who accepted the trial at face value. He commended the officials involved for the "dignity" of the proceedings and wrote that "a terrible, sordid picture of human nature at its worst is being unfolded," but for Davies the sordid picture was that of the defendants, not their prosecutors.

From those "old" Bolsheviks whose loyalty to Stalin was suspect, the purge extended to many of the highest-ranking officers of the Red Army. It has been estimated that more than 10,000 officers of the rank of colonel or above were executed or exiled. The purge of the army was carried out at the very time when Hitler's rapidly growing military forces posed an increasing threat to Russia. Indeed, it was the opinion of Kennan, Bohlen, and other Russian experts that the German-Russian nonaggression pact was in large part a by-product of Stalin's necessity to buy time to rebuild the army that he had destroyed.

The purges themselves continued; they continued until, by some estimates, between 9,000,000 and 10,000,000 Soviet citizens had been executed or had died in labor camps. The country was turned into a vast charnel house. Through it all the ordinary Russian closed his eyes and ears, so far as he could, to the interminable slaughter. The "purges" or "liquidations" were accompanied by a drumfire of charges against "counterrevolutionary terrorist" activity that must have given Soviet citizens an odd notion of the state of a revolution so besieged by internal enemies.

For Communists, radicals, and fellow-traveling liberals the world over, acceptance of the validity of the trials, despite the overwhelming air of spuriousness that attended them, became another test of faith in the Soviet Union and in Stalin himself. Those aspects of the trials that defied credulity were charged to deliberate distortions of the capitalist press. Individuals who expressed open doubts were written off as hopeless prisoners of bourgeois morality. In 1938 in the United States 100 writers signed a "Statement of American Progressives on the Moscow Trials," which read: "The measures taken by the Soviet Union to preserve and extend its gains and its strength . . . find their echoes here, where we are staking the future of the American people on the preservation of progressive democracy and the unification of our efforts to prevent the fascists from strangling the rights of the people. American liberals must not permit their outlook on these questions to be confused, nor allow their recognition of the place of the Soviet Union in the international fight of democracy against fascism to be destroyed. We call upon them to support the efforts of the Soviet Union to free itself from insidious internal dangers. . . ."

While only a handful of the writers who signed the statement were party members, most were dedicated Communists, like Langston Hughes and Donald Ogden Stewart. That they could have been persuaded to support such a statement with no more evidence than the official proclamations of the party may be taken both as a gauge of the general human capacity for self-delusion and as a measure of the degree to which American intellectuals had accepted the basic theses of the popular front: that fascism could be checked only by the concerted efforts of all those who loved freedom and justice and that the necessary leader in that fight was the Soviet Union. Their signatures on the "Statement" were less an index of their devotion to Stalin or their belief in communism per se than of their disillusionment with the failure of the non-Communist nations, the United States prominent among them, to give any firm indication of the will to resist fascism. In their view, however "fishy" the Moscow trials might be, the fate of a few old-line revolutionaries weighed relatively little against the world-wide menace of fascism. Both the *Nation* and the *New Republic* suppressed misgivings and accepted the trials as legitimate actions of the Soviet Union in its defense.

But there were doubts and significant defections. Edmund Wilson came back to the United States from a visit to Russia during the trials convinced that there was "a complete double standard of truth in the Soviet Union, one for the official groups among themselves and another for manipulating the people. Nobody who hasn't seen the Russians at home will ever believe this, but the gap between the informed and intelligent and the ignorant and dumb is still so great that the latter are always treated as children by the former." *Izvestia* and *Pravda* were "as bad as the Nazi papers. . . . The higher-ups simply agree among themselves on what it is expedient to tell the boobs. The procedure is totally undemocratic." Wilson perceived "a kind of snobbery which enables intelligent people to condone all this hornswoggling of the masses in the name of whom everything is being done."

Wilson wrote to A. J. Muste that he suspected that while the "inefficiency and unreliability of the Russians" were responsible for much of what was happening in Russia, Marxism itself was also "partly to blame." The degradation of Zinoviev, Radek, etc. was part of a tradition that went back to Marx himself, who had attempted to destroy the credibility and good names of those who opposed him on ideological grounds. Wilson added, "[T]he Marxists have been—and are still being—sadly misled through believing in the dialectic as a supernatural power which will bring them to salvation if they trust in it, without the necessity of thought or virtue on their part." It had taken some six years for Wilson to make the journey from enchantment to disillusion.

Katherine Anne Porter wrote to Josephine Herbst that the trials were, in her opinion, merely symptoms of deeper ills. "Josie," she wrote, "you know well that the original aim of the Russian Revolution was the best thing that had happened to the mind of men . . . in all the history of social theory. . . . But . . . all revolutions have had noble aims, and without exception they have all collapsed and gone corrupt and for exactly the same reason, over and over. . . . The real revolutionists are betrayed and kicked out or killed by demagogues, the dictator, the man, or the party, who will stick at nothing to get power. . . ." A troubled Herbst replied: "It is all I ever did want, any place, any time, and throwing myself into the movements that seem in the vital direction of history were only to understand. Now I truly feel that the real thing wrong in Russia is not its original aim, that is still the one aim worth striving for, but that it has somehow been unable to work it out, that we expect too much and understand too little, and what I know is that Russia should not have let Spain down, not for anything."

When Waldo Frank joined in the call for an impartial investigation of the trials, he was fired as chairman of the League of American Writers by Earl Browder at the second Congress of American Writers in 1937. Claude McKay was on the platform when Browder began his attack on Frank. McKay rose and left the platform to make his disgust evident. He was surprised that the attack on Frank did not start "a revolt against League members—at least all those who entertain serious ideas about the business and purpose of writing." Yet there were few defections. McKay described those who suppressed their misgivings as persons who took the line that since "Russia is a proletarian state they should suspend criticism of its mistakes and criticize only the fascist dictatorship maneuvers which menace the social progress of the world." To McKay it seemed "that more than any [other state] the Soviet state stands in need of radical criticism and analysis always and precisely because it is generally admitted by radical workers that it is perhaps the greatest social experiment in the history of the human race." McKay was against all dictatorships, whether of the right or of the left, but he added: *"I believe in the social revolution and the triumph of the workers' democracy, not the workers' dictatorship."* He soon announced his own break with the party.

A "countertrial" was conducted in Mexico by a group of American liberals and radicals that included John Dewey and Carlo Tresca. The "jury" cleared Trotsky of the charges against him and went on to denounce the Russian purge trials. A grateful Trotsky wrote to Tresca, "I hope you will permit me to express the deepest esteem for you, as a man who is every inch a fighter." Not long afterward Tresca himself was assassinated, whether by agents of Stalin or Mussolini was never determined. The most tangible consequence of the trials in the United States was a deep rift among the intellectuals in the Communist Party or allied with it. Edmund Wilson, James T. Farrell, Dos Passos, William Phillips, James Burnham, John Chamberlain, and Lionel Trilling were among those who supported an impartial investigation of the trials. A number thereafter aligned themselves with the Trotskyites, and others, like Wilson and Dos Passos, moved away from the party.

Today, nearly fifty years later, the trials remain almost as mysterious and impenetrable as they were when they took place. The only general agreement is that they were trumped up. That there was opposition to Stalin's bloody regime among old Bolsheviks is not surprising. Indeed, it would have been surprising (and disheartening) if that had not been the case; if ever a ruler merited opposition, Stalin did. But it is highly unlikely that the opposition took the form that the prosecution charged—of a widespread, well-coordinated counter-revolutionary terrorist plot. Certainly no evidence of the kind that would stand up in a Western court of law was then adduced, or discovered later, to prove such a charge. The question remains why the farce of the trials. What purpose did Stalin intend to serve by the trials and confessions? For one thing they provided a highly publicized rationale for the sub rosa execution and exile of millions of Russians, the great majority of whom we must, I think, assume were innocent of anything that could properly be called treason. Charles Bohlen speculated that Stalin was anxious to find a pretext to rid the party of "those who, in the tradition of Lenin, possessed a Western-based intellect." The result, in Bohlen's view, was a sharp drop in the quality of Russian leadership and a genuine moral and intellectual break with what we call, rather loosely, Western civilization.

Like all thoughtful students of Soviet Russia, Bohlen was at pains to distinguish between the Russian people, whom he admired and who seemed to him much like Americans in many ways, and their leaders, whom he deplored. "Such a mindless and all-pervading bloodbath could take place only in a country where the actions of the authorities are outside the influence of the ordinary citizen," Bohlen wrote. He was struck by the degree to which ordinary citizens were able "to go on without being affected by the policies, if not the actions, of the regime."

The weather had, in Bohlen's view, a critical influence on Russian character. The winter in Moscow lasted seven generally dismal months, with slate gray skies and discolored snow. The result was "lethargy, broken by outbursts of energy, and occasionally by violence." Americans were "quicker, more nervous, more active," while Russians were "generally . . . slower, more thoughtful, more patient. The American lacked the endurance of the Russian, especially his extraordinary stoicism in bearing hardship"; Russians and Americans shared a "frankness and generosity" and a freedom from "convention and tradition."

As the most experienced member of the American Embassy Bohlen sensed a subtle change in the atmosphere of the Kremlin. There were bits of evidence that Stalin and his inner circle were considering some kind of understanding with Hitler. Matters were further complicated by a growing tension in the official relations between the United

States and the Soviet Union. The Roosevelt-Litvinov agreement in 1933 leading to diplomatic recognition stipulated that the Soviets acknowledge American debts from the era of the czar, ban organizations dedicated to the overthrow of the U.S. government, and allow freedom of worship to Americans living in Russia. The latter was not a problem, but the other agreements the Soviets refused to honor. The result was a certain chill. In defense of the Russians it might be said that if they had reached an agreement with the United States on the relatively small sums claimed by the Americans, they would have made themselves susceptible to far larger claims on the part of France and Great Britain. Moreover, they could hardly ban organizations dedicated to the overthrow of the U.S. government without abandoning the whole theory of world revolution.

When Joseph Davies departed in 1938, he was succeeded by Alexander Kirk, chargé d'affaires, who took over the embassy on an interim basis. With this change Bohlen became primarily responsible for drafting the dispatches on the intentions of the Soviet Union for Secretary of State Hull and the President. Bohlen soon began to pick up further hints that the Soviet Union was moving toward some sort of accord with Hitler, but he was hesitant to pass along such rumors, well aware that they would be greeted with incredulity by many members of the administration. Moreover, if they proved wrong, Bohlen would lay himself open to the charge of being anti-Soviet.

There were other disheartening events abroad. In France, Léon Blum's popular front government fell. Walter Lippmann, who had been traveling in Europe, returned to the United States with the impression that "the Western democracies were amazingly complacent, distracted, easy-going and wishful." It was much like the impression of Charles Edward Russell after his trip to Europe on the eve of the European war of 1914. "If the democracies *are* decadent, then the future of the Old World is once more in the hands of the warrior castes, and the civilian era which began with the Renaissance is concluded," Lippmann wrote.

# 34

## Federal Project No. 1

Perhaps in the last analysis the most novel aspect of the New Deal was its patronage of the arts. From the beginning of the Civil Works Administration (CWA) and the Works Progress Administration (WPA), Harry Hopkins had encouraged projects that employed writers and artists. Some 3,000 had found work under the aegis of those agencies, but writers wanted a more formal and comprehensive program.

In the last year before the crash publishers had taken in an estimated $42,000,000 from the sale of fiction and general interest books. Four years later their revenues had shrunk by one-half, while library borrowings had increased by almost 40 percent. By the same token, the number of books published had fallen sharply year after year. Only fifteen writers sold 50,000 or more copies of their books in the United States in 1934. Newspapers also failed in record numbers, throwing newspapermen and newspaperwomen out of work.

In February, 1935, some twenty men and several women picketed the New York Port Authority Building, which contained Federal offices; they carried placards calling for Federal assistance to writers. One sign read: "CHILDREN NEED BOOKS. WRITERS NEED BREAD. WE DEMAND PROJECTS."

As we have had frequent occasion to note, virtually all red-blooded middle-class (and up) American males since the beginning of the Republic had wished, above all things, to become "writers." Relatively few had been able to make a living in that trade, and recently their numbers had been swollen by growing numbers of young women who were equally determined. In ordinary times, good and bad, writers and would-be writers took their economic lumps, a few becoming rich and famous, thousands scraping by, and thousands more falling by the wayside, reduced to such mundane callings as the law, teaching, and even business.

Since large numbers of the population either considered themselves writers or aspired to be, the problem that faced those public officials who were assigned to do something for writers was to determine who was really a writer and who simply desired to acquire that magic status. Muriel Rukeyser, a Vassar student numbered among the aspirers, wrote bitterly that the public saw writers "as trash. . . . Living meant going to the office. Writing for magazines was jeered at, unless it was for the *Saturday Evening Post.* That meant acceptance, money and the proper capitalist virtues." Rukeyser, it should be said, was indulging in that self-pity to which American writers are especially prone; Henry Adams was one of the most prominent lamenters of the public indifference to the work and the fate of writers. It was certainly not surprising that a working stiff who rushed off to some demanding and debilitating job did not look kindly upon someone who stayed at home, pecking away intermittently at a typewriter in the hope that someone would read what he or she had written. Henry Seidel Canby, editor of the *Saturday Review of Literature,* described the public's attitude toward writers: "No writer is worth shucks until he can and has taken punishment. He's supposed to go hungry and ragged and cold, to drudge at chores he loathes, to suffer endless humiliation and rejection doing the thing he loves in infrequent, stolen moments or baking beans. It MAKES a writer, and weeds out the POSEURS, the people with a smattering of talent but no salt or spunk, lacking which no writer is worth a hoot." In Canby's opinion, "no good (and celebrated) story-teller or playwright, even in 1932, can fail of a decent reward." The *New York Times* was equally unsympathetic, editorializing that the problem of writers might well be that they spent too much time at literary teas.

Unemployed writers had, of course, as much right to go on relief as unemployed plumbers, and by March, 1935, 1,400 journalists had done so. But thousands of writers clung to their status as writers and took any jobs they could get. Harry Roskilenko, a respected journalist, worked as a ditchdigger on the Eighth Avenue subway in New York City. Studs Terkel wangled a clerkship in the Treasury Department.

Projects begun by the CWA were greatly extended. The Connecticut Planning Board undertook a survey of historic sites. In New Mexico a team of writers began the translation of the Spanish archives of the state. In New York City seventy-five unemployed newspapermen and newspaperwomen informed the public of the work of some thousand social service agencies.

A majority of unemployed writers lived in New York City. Not only was that city the center of publishing, but many writers had the notion that the creative juices flowed more abundantly in the metropolis. Consequently, it was in New York that the first writers' organization was formed, under the wing of the Communist Party, to seek Federal assistance specifically for writers. In January, 1934, some 25 established writers formed the Unemployed Writers' Association (UWA), modeled on the Unemployed Councils. In a short time it had 500 members and a mailing list of 1,200. The association demanded a "national plan for writers" and the development of programs which would employ writers, each at a minimum of $30 a week. Theodore Dreiser, Ida Tarbell, Waldo Frank, and Sherwood Anderson were among the writers endorsing the proposal. The Author's League joined forces with the UWA to lobby in Washington, and over a period of two years the groups raised $100,000. The Author's League had, moreover, a specific plan to put forward: "a survey of the varying aspects of everyday life as it is lived in all parts of the United States." The league estimated that the project could utilize the talents of 500 writers for ten weeks. There was soon no dearth of projects, from regional magazines to guidebooks and state histories, the latter the suggestion of the poet Marianne Moore. The doctor-poet William Carlos Williams added: "Wonders might come from such a move . . . , for letters are the wave's edge in all cultural advance, which, God knows, we in America ain't got much of."

By 1935 considerable political pressure had developed for "assistance for educational, professional, and clerical persons," and $300,000,000 in WPA funds were allocated for projects designed to involve the unemployed in those categories. That was called Federal Project No. 1 and covered the four fields of the arts: the theater, music, the visual arts, and writing. The Federal Writers' Project called initially for three specific undertakings designed to employ 6,742 "relief workers," not all of them writers, for a year, at an average salary of $912.54

per year. The total budget was $6,285,222.72. Hallie Flanagan, Harry Hopkins's college mate, was placed in charge of the Federal Theatre; Holger Cahill was put in charge of art; Nikolai Sokoloff was responsible for music. The man chosen to head the Federal Writers' Project was Henry Garfield Alsberg. Born in New York City of German-Jewish immigrant parents, Alsberg had entered Columbia at the age of fifteen, gone on to the Columbia Law School, and, after practicing law for three years, decided it was "a dirty business" and begun graduate work in English at Harvard. His real ambition was to be a writer. During the war he served as a correspondent for the *Nation* and the *New York World,* met Prince Kropotkin, decided he was an anarchist, and became a close friend of Emma Goldman and Alexander Berkman. After spending most of the twenties as a kind of roving intellectual, Alsberg was given a job with the Federal Emergency Relief Administration. From this vantage point he pushed the notion of the state guidebook series with Harry Hopkins, who lent a sympathetic ear (some writers have even credited Hopkins with the original notion; in any event it was "in the air"). Another promoter of the guidebook idea was Katherine Kellock, a graduate of Columbia in history, who had done relief work with the Quakers in Central Europe after the war, worked as a nurse in the Henry Street Settlement House, and been given a job by Hopkins in the Resettlement Administration.

Something over $27,000,000 was allocated to Federal No. 1. Guidebooks became at once the primary task of the Federal Writers' Project (FWP).

What had been anticipated from the first—namely, that a vast company would seek employment with the writers' project—proved true. An unemployed mail carrier, who had been described as "a man of letters" by a social worker, insisted that he was qualified for a job on the project. Thousands of writers appeared with voluminous manuscripts that they wished the government to publish. One applicant wrote to Alsberg: "Kind of work: will accept any position. Salary: Enough to make a living on. At present: Broke." Another applicant wrote, "I'm not a Ph.D. or a G-man, but I don't see why I haven't as much right to the work as they have," referring apparently to two acquaintances who had gotten jobs with the writers' project.

By November, 1935, 4,016 men and women had been employed by the Federal Writers' Project, and the number rose to 6,000 by the first of the new year. The historian of the project, Monty Noam Penkower, estimates that at any one time between 4,500 and 5,000 people were on the FWP payroll during the four years it existed. Out of that number, a survey indicated that there were 106 blacks. Most black writers were assigned to projects in New York, Illinois, or Louisiana, where they worked on the history of blacks in those states. "For the first time since the Harlem period of the '20's," Arna Bontemps wrote, "Negro writers had a chance." Virtually all the established black writers found jobs with the writers' project; among them were Claude McKay, Ted Poston, Ralph Ellison, Willard Motley, Bontemps himself, and the black author of romance novels Frank Yerby. Richard Wright began *Native Son* as an FWP author.

Black historians from the Hampton Institute organized a project which was centered in New Orleans and collected ex-slave narratives. The black dancer and ethnographer Katherine Dunham worked with Horace Cayton on black religious cults in Chicago. The project, in the words of its historian, "pioneered in giving a fairer appraisal of the Negro's role in American history through the guides, specialized volumes, and valuable ex-slave narratives." Three or four significant books on black life came directly or indirectly out of the project, among them Horace Cayton and St. Clair Drake's *Black Metropolis*, a study of Chicago blacks, and *Any Place but Here* by Arna Bontemps and Jack Conroy.

Another project, suggested by New York's Mayor Fiorello La Guardia, collected some 2,000 documents on city finances, public safety, and related municipal concerns. The Museum of Modern Art sponsored an index to the history of the motion picture, which included 9,000 references. Other projects included the writing and installation of historical markers and the publication of *Who's Who in the Zoo*, a guide to the city's zoos. A Survey of State and Local Archives, known as the Historical Records Survey, was also undertaken.

The project allocated some of its resources to a study of American folklore, with special emphasis on American songs. John Lomax was an adviser. Ben Botkin, an expert on folklore, helped guide the project and enlisted Nelson Algren, the Chicago author. Many of the tales collected were used by Botkin in his *A Treasury of American Folk-Lore*. A number of books resulted from detailed studies of various immigrant groups: Armenians in Massachusetts, Swedes in New Jersey, Greek sponge fishers in Florida, Russians in Alabama, and Albanians scattered about the country. Pioneering work was also done in oral history. Interviews with Southern millworkers were published under the title *These Are Our Lives* to enthusiastic reviews.

Many of the Federal Writers' Project interviewers had had lives as hard as those they interviewed. Ned DeWitt, in the Oklahoma writers' project, had worked as a newsboy, truck driver, and rig builder in the oil fields. Jack Hartley told him that where he grew up "we didn't know anything but oil—oil and gas. We smelled it all the time, had rigs all around our house, used crude for syrup on our pancakes, and had so darned much in us we have a good grade of wax-free oil for blood. There wasn't anything but oil to think about or work in." Daniel Garrison had been a tobacco farmer in Maryland, a deck boy on a freighter, and an oil field roustabout before he joined the Oklahoma writers' project.

Some of the project interviewers gathered material that they used in short stories and novels of their own. Nelson Algren developed a character named Highpockets out of his interviews with country boys who came to the city seeking work. It was Leo Gurley, a black Harlem storyteller, who sowed the seed in Ralph Ellison for *The Invisible Man*. Gurley told Ellison about Sweet-the-monkey. "He wasn't no big guy. He was just bad. My mother and my grandmother used to say he was wicked. He was bad alright. . . . It was this way: Sweet could make hisself invisible. You don't believe it? Well here's how he done it. Sweet-the-monkey cut open a black cat and took out its heart. Climbed up a tree backwards and cursed God. After that he could do anything."

Another inadvertent contributor to *The Invisible Man* was a Pullman porter to whom Ellison gave the pseudonym Lloyd Green. Green told Ellison in a kind of refrain, "I'm in New York, but New York ain't in me. You understand? I'm in New York, but New York ain't in me." Green was from Jacksonville, Florida, and although he had lived in New York for twenty-five years, he had kept its wicked ways at bay: "Pimps, Numbers, Cheating these poor people outa what they got. Shooting, cutting, backbiting, all them things. Yuh see? . . . *I'm* in New York, but *New York ain't in me!*"

John Cheever was an employee of the writers' project. Kenneth Patchen and Kenneth Fearing in New York and Kenneth Rexroth in San Francisco were beneficiaries of the project, along with Max Bodenheim, Conrad Aiken, and George Willison. Cheever wrote: "The Washington rooming-houses where one lived, the social and athletic life of the project, the diversity of the cast—drunken stringers and first-rate men—the bucking for power, the machinations of the Dies Committee and the sexual and political scandals all make an extremely interesting story but it doesn't seem to be my kind of thing."

The black writer Henry Lee Moon expressed the attitude of many of the more established professional writers in New York: "Stay on as long as you had to and get off as quickly as you could." Most of the "creative writers" were assigned jobs editing poorly written manuscripts from various projects and found the job little to their liking. Rexroth read "some of the most atrocious prose" he had ever encountered. Cheever was assigned to tasks that "seemed neither interesting nor useful." Under the category of "creative projects" some writers, Claude McKay and Richard Wright among them, were allowed to pursue their own writing. Algren, a supervisor of the Chicago industrial folklore project, wrote most of the Galena guide, but spent more and more time at a nearby bar and described his practice of reporting to the relief office, to "establish myself as a pauper, and get a free bag of potatoes. This qualified me to get back on the payroll [of the writers' project]. It usually only took about three days to get back on, so I'd manage to get fired toward the end of the week and get my bag of potatoes on Saturday morning, so I could get back to King's Palace [the name of the bar], via the project, by Monday afternoon. This worked out pretty good until the army got me when I wasn't looking."

A project magazine called *American Stuff* was intended to demonstrate the range and variety of American life and, not coincidentally, of the writers' project itself. It ran aground on ideological shoals. The Communists, who were so numerous in the New York section of Federal Project No. 1, tried to take over *American Stuff* so that, in the words of one critic, they could "boast in Moscow that they had a magazine with funds from the U.S. government." When they could not control its editorial policy, the Communists sabotaged the venture on the ground that the magazine's content was not determined "democratically."

The state guides were the best known and most notable fruit of the Federal Writers' Project. Critics almost unanimously praised the guides as they appeared. One reviewer called them "the biggest, fastest, most original research job in the history of the world," which may well have been true. But the guidebook project encountered serious difficulties, as suggested by a poem by one state editor:

> I think that I have never tried
> A job as painful as the Guide,
> A guide which changes every day
> Because our betters feel that way,
> A guide whose deadlines come so fast
> Yet no one lives to see the last,
> A guide to which we give our best

> To hear: "This stinks like all the rest!"
> There's no way out but suicide
> For only God can end the Guide.

Robert Littell, a project writer, observed: "It is Baedeker's business to steer his readers to flawless churches and flealess hotels. I'm afraid the U.S. Guidebook, compiled with funds derived from taxes paid by its eventual readers, will not say much about flaws and fleas. If the Squeedunks and the Linoleumvilles of the United States are omitted from the Guidebook, or truthfully described as being of small interest, they will raise enough hell to ripple all the way to Washington. . . . I shall want a guidebook that can stifle its passion for statistics and arrowheads long enough to leave some room to write about American people. But I'm afraid I'll be disappointed, and that the guidebooks will continue to treat people as they always have—as ethnological wax groups frozen behind the glass exhibit-cases of a natural-history museum."

Writers did often feel pressure to omit unpleasant facts and emphasize the positive. This was especially true in those volumes dealing with Southern states, where saccharine prose about the delights of the Old South constantly threatened to creep in. Copy for the Georgia guide (subsequently deleted) described the slaves as "cherishing only affectionate regard" for their masters. In Alabama blacks were "engaged in friendly and stimulating rivalry" with whites. The state director of the Mississippi guide protested that the book would be ignored in the South if it contained a "sociological treatise" on "any of the many debatable phases of the race question." The Connecticut director was told he would have to remove references to the Ku Klux Klan, beer halls, and Colchester's Jewish population. One directive involved an account of a battle in the Revolutionary War which ascribed a patriot rout to the fact that the soldiers were "reputedly drunk"; instead, "troop movements were confused by a dense fog" was proposed.

But Alsberg and Katherine Kellock, who became his principal assistant, were persons of talent and discrimination, and they surrounded themselves with equally talented friends. Floyd Dell was on the advisory staff of Federal Project No. 1, and a number of able historians contributed their skills to the project. Frank Manuel of the Harvard history faculty was regional director of the New England guide, and Ray Allen Billington supervised the Massachusetts guide. In some states finding qualified writers proved difficult. Vardis Fisher, the novelist, could find no other writer in Idaho. Another state project director wrote that it required "a great deal of scratching among the cornfields of Iowa to turn up three people with writing experience." Since Iowa was not a state short of literary talent, all the rest had gone to New York presumably. Only 7 of 104 professed writers in Texas could turn out copy ready for the printer, and in South Carolina there were said to be only 3.

Robert Cantwell wrote of the guide series: "How has it happened that nobody ever thought to trace the careers of the vast majority who guessed wrong—the leading bankers who put their money in canals in 1840 and in Maine shipyards in 1856, who plunged on slaves in 1859, and bet that Florence, in Baboon Gulch, Idaho, would be the leading city of the state: What a fine group of far-sighted financiers have really turned up in the Guides! . . . [The series] is a grand, melancholy, formless democratic anthology of frustration and idiosyncrasy, a majestic roll call of national failure, a terrible and yet engaging corrective to the success stories that dominate our literature."

Jerre Mangione, who had transferred from the Farm Security Administration to the Federal Writers' Project, wrote that despite the hostility of the press and most politicians, "we were like a gang of inspired revolutionists who, determined to give substance to a dream, recognized no obstacles. Each of us suspected that never again might we know a means of earning a livelihood that involved us as fully and selflessly."

When pressure, primarily, it might be said, from the press, caused the curtailment of the program, angry writers showed that they were prepared to employ the tactics of the labor unions they admired by "sitting in" in protest and staging demonstrations that on several occasions ended in bloody confrontations with the police. At the demonstrations they sang a song:

> Roosevelt! you're my man.
> When the time comes
> I ain't got a cent
> You buy my groceries
> And pay my rent
> Mr. Roosevelt, you're my man.

As William Douglas put it, "While the communist-oriented writers were talking about this ugly earthly existence and the good times coming, these starving writers wrote about the greatness of America and

its future, and at the same time they unfrocked phony figures, promoted racial understanding, and made articulate the lower third of
this society." If that somewhat overstates the case, it was nevertheless
true that the writers' project marked a unique event in the nation's
history and underlined the New Deal's commitment to the artistic and
literary aspects of American life.

When the writers' unit of the WPA shut up shop in early 1943,
it was described as the "biggest literary project in history"; its output
filled seven twelve-foot shelves in the Department of the Interior. It
had been in existence for seven years and spent something in excess
of $27,000,000 (or one-fifth of 1 percent of the WPA expenditures).
Its indirect consequences were substantially larger. It established the
principle of government interest in and sponsorship of the arts, an
entirely novel idea which led, after the war, to the establishment of
the National Endowment for the Arts and the National Endowment
for the Humanities, with budgets of millions of dollars a year for
encouragement of the arts and of scholarship and intellectual activity
over a wide range of fields in the humanities. Involved both as writers
and artists and as administrators were a number of able women, among
them Katherine Kellock, Ellen Woodward, and Florence Kerr. Federal
Project No. 1 stimulated interest in America's past and its rich traditions
of folklore. Above all, it made a modest beginning in acknowledging
the role of black Americans and their contributions to a uniquely American culture. Muriel Rukeyser told an interviewer, "The key to the '30's
was the joy to awake and see life entire and tell the stories of real
people."

More visible and even more political than the Federal Writers'
Project was the Federal Theatre Project (FTP). It was headed, as we
have noted, by fiery, diminutive Hallie Flanagan. Flanagan had been
born in Redfield, South Dakota, in 1890. After her parents had settled
in Grinnell, Iowa, she attended high school there and then Grinnell
College, a year behind Harry Hopkins. Only four feet eight inches in
height, red-haired and freckled, she was actively involved in dramatics
at Grinnell and after graduation married an Irish classmate, Murray
Flanagan. In 1918 her father suffered heavy financial losses. A year
later her husband died of tuberculosis, leaving her with two children
to support. She got a job teaching drama at Grinnell. There she wrote
a prizewinning play which won her a job as an assistant to George
Pierce Baker, the head of Workshop 47 at Harvard. Another well-

received play and a growing reputation as a drama teacher won her, in 1926, the first Guggenheim Fellowship awarded to a woman, permitting her to do a comparative study of the modern theater in various countries. She was thrilled by the productions of the Moscow Art Theatre, which had toured in the United States. From the Russian director Vsevolod Meyerhold she took the idea of using clowning and acrobatics to break down the barriers between audiences and actors.

After her year of study, which included three weeks in the Soviet Union, she devoted her principal efforts to writing and producing plays that dealt with social problems. In collaboration with a Vassar graduate named Mary Ellen Clifford, who shared her radical proclivities, she wrote a play based on a story by Whittaker Chambers. *Can You Hear Their Voices?* was a kind of documentary recounting the desperate circumstances of poor farmers during the 1930s drought. In the play Flanagan and Clifford used mixed media—short scenes of the farmers interspersed with reports of congressional ineptness flashed on a large white screen. A farmer who has led an uprising is sent to jail at the end of the play and advises his son to throw in his lot with the Communists as the only hope for radical change. The Voice of the Loudspeaker, which provides a kind of running commentary during the play, announces: "These boys are the symbols for thousands of people who are turning somewhere for leaders. Will it be the educated minority? Can you hear their voices?" Despite the radical theme of the play, it was produced at Vassar with the backing of the president, Henry Noble MacCracken, a radical educator who shared Flanagan's enthusiasm for "social theater" and sometimes acted in student plays. A number of Vassar graduates, like Elizabeth Bentley, responded to the Flanagan-Clifford exhortation and either joined the Communist Party or threw themselves into other left-wing causes. Flanagan wrote in the *Theatre Arts Monthly* of November, 1931: "The theater being born in America today is a theater of workers. Its object is to create a national culture by and for the working class of America. Admittedly a weapon in the class struggle, this theater is being forged in the factories and the mines."

Flanagan was forty-five, a darling of the revolutionary theater, when Harry Hopkins swore her in as head of the Federal Theatre Project. She at once threw into the project her remarkable energy, her skill as a dramatist, her dedication to the theater as a medium of social change, and, perhaps above all, her unique organizational skills. The productions of the Federal Theatre were not aimed at the regular theatergoing public, catered to by the commercial theater, but at the "people": the poor; the blue-collar worker (referred to, of course, simply as the "worker"); children, especially children; and the unemployed. Tickets ranged in price from $1 to as little as ten cents. In the New York City project, set up by Flanagan and her old friend Elmer Rice, there were five major units: the Living Newspaper; the Popular Price Theatre to produce plays by "new" writers; the Experimental Theatre with the mission of putting on far-out dramas; the Negro Theatre, headed by John Houseman and Rose McClendon, assigned to put on black plays for Harlem audiences; and the Try-Out Theatre, devoted to trying out potential commercial plays for Broadway production.

In addition to dealing with irate politicians who denounced the Federal Theatre productions as Communist or New Deal propaganda, Flanagan had to cope with twelve old-line unions that demanded a piece of the project pie. She was as firm with them as with the politicians. The Federal Theatre was for all the people; it could not place itself under any yoke or constraint on what it produced and how.

The most successful and controversial production unit was that of the Living Newspaper. It was the undertaking closest to Flanagan's heart, modeled as it was on *Can You Hear Their Voices?* It had its own extensive research wing, where material was gathered from scholarly studies, government reports, and newspaper accounts and turned into lively documentaries. The Bureau of Research and Publications employed some fifty men and women, "reading, editing, writing, and translating plays." One of its first ventures was *Ethiopia,* directed by Elmer Rice, a damning account of the Italian invasion of that weak African country, which employed the talents of African drummers and musicians who were caught in America by the outbreak of the war. When objections were raised that the play might be offensive to Mussolini, Flanagan appealed to Eleanor Roosevelt, who used her influence to block censorship. The play could be done, Hopkins decided, if it did not present actual Italian officials. Rice refused that concession and left the project.

The second, and in many ways, the most exciting year of the brief lifetime of the Federal Theatre, was 1936. The month of March witnessed the opening of three vivid and controversial dramas. One of its first productions was *Chalk Dust,* an indictment of the grim and joyless atmosphere of the contemporary high school, which was enthusiastically supported by John Dewey. It was followed by *Triple-A*

*Plowed Under,* a production reminiscent of Flanagan's play *Can You Hear Their Voices?,* which used the same skit-blackout-loudspeaker (and music) format to recount the story of the woes of the American farmer, ending with the Supreme Court's invalidation of the AAA.

The Living Newspaper was heavy on footnotes, which made it popular with professors. *Triple-A Plowed Under* noted that it was a "Digest of an article on 'A.A.A. Philosophy' by Rexford G. Tugwell, *Fortune Magazine,* January, 1934." The curtain rose with four spotlights illuminating "a FARMER, a DEALER, a MANUFACTURER, a WORKER." It included a speech by Henry Wallace calling for a fuller share in American life for the farmer and one by Earl Browder which attacked the Supreme Court. When the play opened at the Biltmore, the *New York Times* reported, "the actors were full of misgivings, the audience full of tension and the lobby full of police." The audience that poured into the Biltmore night after night was a new kind of audience—an audience, in Harold Clurman's words, "with a smouldering conviction uncharacteristic of the usual Broadway audiences. . . . It was essentially an audience for a national theatre." The *New York Sun* critic took note that it was "an enjoyable audience. It is young, lively, and I suspect hard up."

*Power,* plainly intended to create favorable sentiment for public ownership of power, was another Living Newspaper:

"Loudspeaker: What do you pay for electricity, Mister?
"Consumer: Too much. Seventeen cents a kilowatt hour.
"Loudspeaker: What's a kilowatt hour?"

The consumer confesses ignorance, and the Loudspeaker goes on to educate him (and the audience) on the mysteries of the generation of electricity and the iniquities of public utility holding companies.

*Medicine* exposed the shortcomings of the medical profession and contained a pitch for public health insurance. It infuriated the American Medical Association.

One of the most controversial of the Living Newspapers was *Injunction Granted,* a documentary history of the struggles of workers to unionize, struggles often ended by court injunctions against the strikers. Critics of the play fulminated that it destroyed confidence in the American system of justice and was another example of Communist propaganda. Defending it and plays like it, Flanagan wrote: "Art in America had hitherto been apart from politics, but these projects were at the core of life. If they were mixed with politics, it was because life in our country was mixed with politics. . . . These Arts projects were coming up, through, and out of the people. They were affected by everything affecting American life."

Perhaps the most traumatic effort of the New York City project was the attempt to produce a play based on Sinclair Lewis's novel *It Can't Happen Here*, about how America might go Fascist. First attacked as radical propaganda, then examined, debated, and cleared of bearing a Communist message, it encountered every possible difficulty. When it finally opened, it proved a critical failure but a popular success. Soon it was playing all over the country.

By no means were all the Federal Theatre productions political. Hopkins had set up theatrical production companies of unemployed actors and directors under the aegis of the FERA and CWA. The latter had been especially successful with a series of Gilbert and Sullivan light operas. These now became a valuable part of the Federal Theatre Project. There were also vaudeville shows and circuses. A Negro Youth Theatre was started. There was a company that produced exclusively poetic dramas, a Yiddish vaudeville group, a German company that produced plays in German, and an Anglo-Jewish theater. The poet and critic Alfred Kreymborg, head of the Poetic Theatre, produced *The Dance of Death* by the British poet W. H. Auden. Flanagan had directed T. S. Eliot's *Sweeney Agonistes* while she was at Vassar, and Eliot had recommended Auden's work to her.

On March 20, 1936, T. S. Eliot's verse play *Murder in the Cathedral*, about the martyrdom of Thomas à Becket, opened at the Manhattan Theater under the auspices of the Federal Theatre. *Battle Hymn*, written by Mike Gold and Michael Blankfort, both professed Communists, was ostensibly about John Brown's raid on Harpers Ferry. Another successful play was Maxwell Anderson's *Valley Forge*, which opened at the Plymouth and was promptly denounced as propaganda, although it had been endorsed by the American Legion and the Massachusetts Historical Society.

In Harlem Orson Welles, the boy wonder of the theater, joined forces with John Houseman to produce a black *Macbeth*, set in Haiti, with voodoo doctors for witches and drummers from the stranded African troupe. A company of brilliant black actors was assembled, and the play became an instant hit. *Conjur' Man Dies* was directed by Joseph Losey and starred the black actor Dooley Wilson, playing a detective song-and-dance man. (Wilson later starred with Ethel Waters in *Cabin in the Sky* and was Sam, the piano player, in the film *Casablanca*.)

Meanwhile, the Children's Theatre put on *Cinderella* and *Mark Twain* and a marionette performance of *Treasure Island*, which, like the Gilbert and Sullivan operettas, had begun as a CWA project.

The Federal Theatre Circus played for an audience of 14,000, predominantly children, at the Field Artillery Armory in Brooklyn. The circus was also an inheritance from the CWA. One of the performers on the horizontal bar was young Burt Lancaster.

The newspaper attacks on the productions of the Federal Theatre were unceasing. When plans were made for a project in Minneapolis featuring plays and actors with Scandinavian backgrounds, a Minneapolis newspaper turned up the fact that one of the prospective actresses who had been interviewed (but not employed) had been a fan dancer. A photograph of her captioned "Federal Fan Dancer No. 1" was printed in papers all over the country. An alarmed state administration thereupon dropped the Minneapolis project. In the words of Elmer Rice, the Federal Theatre "was constantly attacked in Congress as wasteful, immoral and Communistic. . . ."

The critical (as opposed to the political) response to the Federal Theatre was, in the main, highly favorable. Burns Mantle wrote: "The WPA has turned the theatre back to the people to whom it rightly belongs and taken it from the moneyed aristocracy that has for years dictated its course and definitely influenced its productions. For years playwrights have been told by commercial producers what the public did and didn't want—with no appeal from the decisions." Free of the inhibitions of commercialism, "Uncle Sam had established a whole set of new ideas of what constitutes popular theatre." The Hearst papers on the other hand denounced the plays as "the most outrageous misuse of taxpayers' money that the Roosevelt administration had been guilty of," while the *Herald Tribune* declared the productions were "run by reds," a charge which, while irrelevant to the quality of the productions, had at least a grain of truth in it.

New York City, the nation's theater capital, employed some 4,000 actors in forty-nine companies or units. California had 6,680 people employed in thirty-two companies. Boston had thirty-three companies; St. Louis and Dallas, two each. More than 9,000 men and women were involved in the Federal Theatre nationwide. It was estimated that during the heyday of the FTP in 1936 and 1937 its productions had a weekly audience of more than a half million. Not included were the tens of thousands of Civilian Conservation Corps enrollees who witnessed Federal Theatre productions in their camps and, in the case of a play entitled *CCC Murder Mystery,* participated themselves in dramatic performances.

In Little Rock, Arkansas, in a huge outdoor amphitheater, 40,000 people witnessed the pageant *America Sings.* John Houseman produced an antic comedy, entitled *Horse Eats Hat.* As he described it in his memoirs, "Madness followed madness through the crowded acts—with actors by the score hurtling across the stage . . . in endless circular pursuit, in carriages and cars, tricycles and roller skates, walking, trotting, galloping, like a herd of hysterical elephants, leaving ruin in their wake. . . . I can still see Joe Cotten . . . leaping from sofa to table to piano top to chandelier in a wild, forty-foot flight till he vanished in the skyloft . . . Cotten himself . . . squirting streams of soda water over the madly whirling crowd below."

There was, in fact, hardly an area of American life that was not affected by the FTP. Hallie Flanagan listed the groups involved with Federal Theatre productions. Among them were 263 social clubs, 264 welfare and civic organizations, 271 educational organizations or institutions, 95 religious organizations, 66 trade unions, 62 professional unions, 17 consumers' unions, and 15 political organizations. Between 1935 and 1938 the Federal Theatre produced 924 plays, which were seen by "something like forty-five million Americans," by Flanagan's estimate.

When Hallie Flanagan was called before the Dies committee in December, 1938, as one of its first witnesses, she was grilled unmercifully on her radical political sympathies. She did the best she could under the questioning of hostile congressional interrogators to explain away or gloss over both her radical orientation and that of the Federal Theatre under her direction. The Dies committee charged "that numerous people working on the [Federal Theatre] Project were Communists. We got that from one or two who are members of the Communist Party themselves . . . and received testimony that Communist literature was disseminated through the premises during Project time, that they were printed on the bulletin board . . . [and] that meetings of the Communist units were held on Project time in the premises." All this was doubtless true, but the fact was that the record of the Federal Theatre needed no defense, certainly not from the primitive opinions of the Committee on Un-American Activities. Its record spoke for itself.

Music and the dance were, as we have noted, profoundly affected by the doctrines of the popular front era. Suddenly it was not only acceptable to praise America, American history, and the American radical movements, but it was mandatory. Aaron Copland abandoned avant-garde music to write "a good marching song for May Day, 1934," which included such lines as "Up with the sickle and hammer" and "Down with the bourgeoisie!" He also turned out a number of ballets and other compositions celebrating America—*Billy the Kid, A Lincoln Portrait, Fanfare for the Common Man*—and the scores for documentaries. He believed his proper mission was to write "music for the people, for as large an audience as possible." *Fortune* magazine, the journal of capitalism, agreed. Federal Project No. 1 had achieved "a more immediate contact with the people" and had evoked "a greater human response than anything the government has done in generations."

The music division hunted down folk songs by the thousands: Creole songs; Maine sea chanteys; spirituals; cowboy songs; Elizabethan songs from Appalachia, preserved for generations in the hills of West Virginia, Kentucky, and Tennessee.

In the late twenties and early thirties Martha Graham announced her task as that of dealing with the timeless and archetypal. But she, too, was caught up in the passion to capture the essence of radical America by words and music and movement. From such pieces as *Désir* and *Four Insincerities: 1. Petulance 2. Remorse 3. Politeness 4. Vivacity* (created between 1926 and 1929), she turned, with Copland as her collaborator, to *Frontier: An American Perspective on the Plains,* subtitled "A Tribute to the Pioneer Woman . . ."; *American Lyric;* and, best known perhaps, *American Document,* in which passages from great American documents—the Declaration of Independence and the Emancipation Proclamation among them—alternated with dances on Indian themes and themes of the land. As three women danced, a voice declared: "We are three women; we are three million women. We are the mothers of the hungry dead; we are the mothers of the hungry living." *Appalachian Spring* used themes from the Shaker hymn "Simple Gifts," figures from folk dances, the Virginia reel, and ragtime to weave dance and music together.

In the visual arts the work done under the auspices of the New Deal was less obviously polemical than in the theater. Nonetheless, the subject matter often had a strong ideological content. Like that of the Federal Writers' Project and the Federal Theatre Project, the work of the painters and sculptors was heavily documentary—that is to say, it dealt most typically with the themes of workers and farmers, strikes and hunger marches. Much of it was public or mural art. Inspired by the radical Mexican revolutionary muralists Diego Rivera and José Clemente Orozco, North American artists turned from easel painting to broad political and social themes. Even the conventional canvases often treated social themes and scenes of everyday life. One of the best known paintings of the day was "Trouble in Frisco," depicting strikers battling with police and referring specifically to the San Francisco longshoremen's strike. The more radical painters sometimes scattered Communist symbols about—red stars or hammers and sickles.

The Mexicans had revived the classic Italian mural technique of painting on wet plaster. The use of "earth colors," ground by the artists themselves, was preferred to commercial colors.

The project of employing artists to produce works of art to enhance public buildings was born in the early months of the New Deal. George Biddle was a better than average artist who, as a member of the famous Biddle family of Philadelphia and a Harvard classmate of Roosevelt, had access to the President. Hearing that a new Department of Justice building was in the process of construction, Biddle wrote to Roosevelt proposing that artists be employed to paint murals on the principal interior walls of the building. Alfred Barr, the director of the Museum of Modern Art in New York, pressed a similar idea upon Frances Perkins's daughter, Susanna, and she, in turn, besieged her mother to take up the idea with Roosevelt and Hopkins. She told her mother "that the public buildings of America were dreary and gloomy and that artists should decorate their walls. Then the buildings would be interesting and cheerful and make people happy as they entered."

Roosevelt responded with characteristic enthusiasm. "A lot of artists are out of work," he told Henry Morgenthau. "Let us hire these people and put them to work painting pictures on public buildings." The result was the Public Works Art Project, a division of Harry Hopkins's commodious Civil Works Administration. The man chosen as technical director of the PWAP was Forbes Watson, a brilliant art critic who believed that art was an essential part of any true civilization. Launched in December, 1933, the project had, within a few weeks, sixteen regional directors, artists on the payroll, and projects under way. In Watson's words, "a system, new to the world, had been evolved for employing artists." During the first five months of its existence

3,749 artists received payment for 15,663 works of art and craft, among them almost 4,000 oil paintings, 3,000 watercolors, and 1,500 prints. More than 700 murals or sketches for murals were produced, and 400 murals were completed. Any building supported at least in part by Federal, state, or local taxes was eligible for a mural. The expiration of the Civil Works Administration, under the aegis of which the Public Works of Art Project had bloomed so extravagantly, meant the end of the PWAP. A show of work done by artists during its brief lifetime was assembled at the Corcoran Gallery in Washington. Forbes Watson announced: "This will be the greatest art event in this country since the Armory Show. . . ." With the expiration of the CWA the sponsorship of the arts passed to the jurisdiction of the Treasury Department under a sympathetic Henry Morgenthau (and especially his wife). There, with the support of the Roosevelts, it was known as the Section of Painting and Sculpture. Its mission was to adorn Federal buildings with art, most commonly murals of the "best quality available."

Meanwhile, Harry Hopkins kept artists on the WPA payroll under the newly established Federal Art Project (FAP). Between 1934 and 1943 the Section of Fine Arts (originally the Section of Painting and Sculpture) received 40,426 sketches from 15,426 artists in some 190 competitions and awarded 1,371 commissions.

Rockwell Kent was commissioned to paint a mural for the Washington post office. It depicted various forms of carrying the mail, including Eskimo dog sled. Puerto Rican Communists had recently attempted to overthrow that island's government. Kent had Eskimo words in the mural, which, translated, read: "To the people of Puerto Rico, our friends. Go ahead, let's change our chiefs; that only will make us free and equal." When the meaning became known, there was an uproar, and the message was changed to something less provocative.

Soon public buildings—post offices, meeting halls, auditoriums, the dining halls of Federal buildings—blossomed with murals. Daniel Rhodes, a young painter who had grown up in Fort Dodge, Iowa, studied at the University of Chicago, and worked under the direction of Grant Wood at the Stone City art colony near Cedar Rapids, was lured to Washington to paint a mural in a Navy Department cafeteria. From Washington Rhodes went off to a black CCC camp near Gettysburg, Pennsylvania, to paint more murals. That stint over, he visited Mexico with a benefactor and saw at first hand the murals of Rivera, Orozco, and David Siqueiros. "They had a powerful effect on me," he wrote, "not only as paintings but as examples of how art can function in a society. I was staggered by Orozco's paintings at the Preparatoria in Mexico City, by their monumentality and deep expression of both tragedy and hope. . . . I began to think of mural painting as a solution to the problem of the artist's role." Rhodes returned to Fort Dodge, "determined to work out my career there . . . [as] an Iowa artist and mural painter." Rhodes, who had earlier abandoned regionalism and then abstractionism, now developed a "kind of dark, earthy realism," and won a number of commissions for murals, many of them in Federal buildings in the state. It was a path followed by hundreds of other young painters (and older painters as well), many of them enrolled in the Federal Art Project.

Ben Shahn was hired by the Farm Security Administration (which stressed photographic documentaries of farmers and farm workers) to design posters "showing the sad plight of the rural population."

Perhaps the mural project that best demonstrated the prevailing attitudes toward the role of the artists was one started under the Civil Works Administration several years before Federal Project No. 1 was launched. In San Francisco a rather ungainly tower had been erected in 1933 on Telegraph Hill with money bequeathed to the city by Lillie Hitchcock Coit. (The novelist Gertrude Atherton, who was a member of the San Francisco Art Commission when the plan of the tower was submitted to it, had protested vigorously against the ugliness of the design, but the men on the commission, she wrote, brushed her objections aside.) In an effort presumably to counteract the rather bleak character of the concrete structure, the Public Works Art Project commissioned twenty-six artists and nineteen assistants to paint murals on the interior walls of the tower's ground floor. The facts that both men and women artists worked on the murals, that it was a cooperative project (since the murals had to relate to one another thematically and, to a degree, in style), that the artists themselves were of at least five different nationalities, that they all were strongly influenced by the Mexican muralists (three had actually worked with Rivera) and were uniformly of a radical political persuasion—which meant, in most instances, that they were either Communist Party members or sympathizers—made the project a classic example both of New Deal art and of Marxist art.

In scenes that ranged from industrial activity to the picking of fruit in the Imperial Valley, the artists preserved a remarkably harmonious tone, scattering about little signs and symbols of their Communist bent—a news rack with issues of *Masses* and the *Daily Worker* prominently displayed; a reader in a library reaching for a copy of Karl Marx's *Das Kapital*; a hammer and sickle incorporated into another panel. Even before the murals were opened to the public, controversy broke out over their "revolutionary" content. Clifford Wright, one of the muralists who had worked with Rivera, had painted three figures, one labeled "Rugged Individualism," one the "New Deal," and the third "Communism," the implication being that these were the choices facing the nation and, apparently, that communism was the final step in the nation's progress (Wright's panels were the ones that bore the hammer and sickle). Despite widespread agitation to have the murals removed, they remained and can be seen today as a classic visual representation of "art and the Great Depression."

In addition to hundreds of murals in parks and post offices (a number of exterior murals were done in ceramic tile), the Federal Art Project had on its rolls more than 900 easel painters. In New York City 300 FAP artists won important awards. Ivan Le Lorraine Albright, a project artist, won first prize in the Metropolitan Museum of Art national show in 1941. Second prize went to the painter Jack Levine, while Marsden Hartley took fourth prize and Mark Tobey won a $500 award. At the Whitney Museum of American Art, out of 200 works selected for a national show in 1937, 72 were by project artists. In the words of the historian of the New Deal's various art projects Richard McKenzie, 240,000 of the prints produced by graphic artists "found their way to schools, colleges, libraries, and government offices."

The Index of American Design was undoubtedly the most ambitious single undertaking of the Federal Art Project. It employed some 300 men and women for a period of six years, tracing and cataloging the decorative arts from colonial times to the thirties. Included were quilts, Shaker furniture, weather vanes, ship figureheads, cigar store Indians, cowboys, and carousel horses. Three women—Romona Javitz, head of the picture collection of the New York Public Library; Frances Pollack, a Federal Art Project administrator; and Ruth Reeves, an artist—took the lead in pressing the idea of a comprehensive index of American folk art.

Besides projects designed to keep artists from starving, the CWA and WPA sponsored a vast program of teaching and instruction in the arts. Community arts centers were established in many cities and towns. In the words of Richard McKenzie, "The art centers provided frequent exhibitions of local and national art, free lectures and films, free classes, free workshops, free meeting rooms for clubs, political rallies, and cultural events." By 1940 there were 100 such centers. Local communities had contributed more than $850,000 to maintain them, and an estimated 8,000,000 people of all ages utilized them. Some 2,000,000 students had attended art classes in the centers. In New York City alone 465 art teachers were assigned to 180 settlement houses and social centers to teach art to children and adults. There were also traveling workshops, trucks equipped with art supplies and driven by teachers, which visited isolated rural areas and city ghettos. Holger Cahill, director of the Federal Art Project, declared: "We are interested in raising a generation . . . sensitive to their visual environment and capable of helping to improve it."

As more and more work in various media accumulated, it became evident that the government was faced with a vast surplus of art that, unlike wheat and corn, was difficult to store and could not be held for higher prices. The increasingly urgent question was: How was the art produced by artists on one form or another of work relief to be gotten into the hands of the public? Americans spent less than $500,000 a year on contemporary art (as against $20,000,000 for chewing gum), and it was estimated that only 150 American artists made as much as $2,000 a year from their work.

In 1940 President Roosevelt hit on the notion of a national Art Week. He was convinced that with sufficient publicity and modest prices, millions of Americans might be persuaded to buy original contemporary art. The week of November 27–December 3 (before Christmas) was set. With the enthusiastic support of Mrs. Roosevelt, committees were formed all over the country to arrange for exhibitions. More than 1,600 exhibitions were organized; 134,255 "objects" created by 31,403 artists and craftsmen and craftswomen were assembled for sale. Francis Henry Taylor, director of the Metropolitan Museum of Art, hailed the week "as one of the most significant events in the history of modern art and in the history of our American civilization." The public response, at least as far as attendance was concerned, was encouraging. It was estimated that over the entire country some 5,000,000 people turned out. However, they only spent, on the average, two cents each, for a total return of $100,018.45. Still, they had come and looked, and doubtless by some modest increment, the nation's artistic consciousness was raised. The next year there was another Art Week, scarcely more successful, before the exigencies of war brought an end to the effort. Many well-known artists refused to participate on the grounds that genuine art should not pander to mass tastes and that the very notion was a degradation of the muse.

Art Week aside, the list of artists who painted under the aegis of the Federal Art Project was impressive. It included, besides those men and women already mentioned, Morris Graves, Jackson Pollock, Yasuo Kuniyoshi, Stanton McDonald Wright, and Stuart Davis.

At the initiation of the Works Progress Administration, Roosevelt and Hopkins had agreed that the agency would not take into account the political beliefs of those who applied for jobs. When Federal Project No. 1 was launched, Hopkins reaffirmed the policy. The fact was that a substantial portion of the writers and artists in the project were members of the Communist Party or sympathizers. Some, like Max Eastman, inclined to the Trotskyite side of the radical political spectrum. In New York and Los Angeles militant radicals pretty much ran the show, and Communist orthodoxy was virtually a requirement for a job. Writers who were Communists sometimes carried on party activity while on government payroll, and party publications and pronouncements were much in evidence in offices and on bulletin boards. The party, through the League of American Writers, tried actively to recruit other Communists into the project, as well as to enlist volunteers for the Spanish Loyalists. They also lobbied energetically in Washington to enlarge the project, hoping to use it as the nucleus of a kind of American agitprop, or party propaganda, agency for Russia and the revolution. In familiar tactics they denounced their opponents in Federal Project No. 1 as Fascists and picketed the New York office. The director of the New York branch was replaced by Orrick Johns, a former editor of the *New Masses.* Finally, the internal struggle for control of the New York project went public. Members of the league sat down in the project's office in imitation of the Flint autoworkers; there they burned red candles, sang party songs, and sported red armbands. The Trotskyites, on the other hand, were not allowed to distribute their magazine, the *Militant,* outside the project office. The union's paper, the *Red Pen,* meanwhile circulated freely, attacking all those suspected of "deviation." When Liston Oak, a writer on the project, returned from Spain and publicly criticized the suppression by assassination of anarchist leaders by the Soviet faction, he was unable to get his project job back. John Dos Passos was rejected as head of an advisory committee on the same ground: He had expressed his dismay at the ruthless methods of the Soviet "advisers" in Spain. The writer Edward Dahlberg quit when his opposition to the party line on literary issues made him the object of bitter denunciations. The struggle completed Claude McKay's disenchantment with the party. McKay blamed the League of American Writers for its "rule or ruin" policy. "It sabotaged the New York Writers' Project in an attempt to gain control of it through its stooges," he wrote.

The activities of the Communists in the Federal Theatre Project and the Federal Writers' Project inevitably drew the attention of the media. The new profession of Red-hunting flourished as right-wing journalists, ex-FBI agents, and even a former funeral director emerged as experts on subversion. The Dies or House Un-American Activities Committee, established in 1938, was soon hot on the trail of Reds. A number of reformed Communists joined their ranks. Ralph De Sola, secretary of the party unit in the New York project, testified on the party's control through the local Workers' Alliance, estimating that no fewer than 106 out of the 300 members of the project were card-carrying members of the Communist Party. J. Parnell Thomas, one of the members of the Dies committee, announced that the "New Deal masterminds," a category that included Hopkins and Ickes, had "pawned themselves out to the Communist strategists," and he demanded that they and Frances Perkins resign.

The guidebooks of the writers' project were examined minutely for subversive phrases. Mention in the Washington, D.C., guide of the fact that George Washington's stepson, Parke Custis, had left a tract of land in Arlington to a black daughter was fastened on by Representative Frank Keefe, a Wisconsin Republican, as an effort to stimulate "racial intolerance." The reference to Custis, as well as quotations from black Reconstruction Congressmen, was removed from future editions of the District guide.

The inquisitorial tactics of the Dies committee marked the beginning of the end for Federal Project No. 1, but it had remarkable accomplishments to its credit. In the words of the critic Grace Overmeyer, the Federal No. 1 projects were "a sort of road map for the cultural rediscovery of America from within." That rediscovery did not, to be sure, start with the Federal arts projects. Waldo Frank had been calling for it since the early 1920s, and many writers and poets had taken it up with enthusiasm even before the end of the Moscow-proclaimed third period. But Federal Project No. 1 gave that impulse an enormous stimulus. Lewis Mumford was not far off the mark when he called it the "first attempt, on a comprehensive scale, to make the country itself worthily known to Americans." The historian William Stott argues persuasively that the dominant intellectual mode of the thirties was the documentary. Certainly there was a wholly new passion to tell of things as they actually were, not as wishful thinking might portray them. That passion, a product both of the realism that characterized the new consciousness and the romanticism that characterized Marxism, changed the intellectual and cultural landscape of America almost beyond recognition.

# 35

# The South Stirs

More than any other section of the country the South appeared as "a problem." Poverty and race were the crosses it bore and seemed destined to bear: tragedy and despair in the lower classes— the poor whites and poorer blacks—and illusion in the upper class. Ellen Glasgow wrote that the Southern upper class needed "blood and irony"—blood "because Southern culture has strained too far away from its roots in the earth" and irony as the "safest antidote to sentimental decay." The South was a region where "a congenial hedonism had established . . . a confederacy of the spirit," where "pride, complacency, . . . self-satisfaction, a blind contentment with things as they are, and a deaf aversion from things as they might be . . . stifle both the truth of literature and the truth of life." W. J. Cash described the wretched condition of Southern farmers on the eve of the New Deal and added: "Everybody was either ruined beyond his wildest previous fears or stood in peril of such ruin. . . . Men everywhere walked in a kind of daze."

Violence and violent crime were, as they had been for generations, part of the Southern way of life. In 1935 the Federal Bureau of Investigation published figures which showed that the eleven former Confederate states had a murder rate of 21.9 per 100,000 people in towns with populations between 10,000 and 250,000; it rose to 23.23 in 1937. In the latter year the New England states had a rate of 1.3 in the same category; in the Middle Atlantic states the figure was 3.8; the Rocky Mountain states checked in at 4.7 (two-tenths of a point above the North-Central states), and the Pacific coast tallied 4.2 murders per 100,000. The Southern homicide rate was thus eighteen times as high as that of New England and between five and six times that of the rest of the nation. The black slums of Southern cities accounted for a substantial portion of the homicides; the great majority of black crimes of violence were against other blacks. Violence of whites against blacks and whites against whites was also high. The health of lower-class Southerners, white and black, was far worse than that of similar people in other sections of the country; epidemic diseases such as tuberculosis and diphtheria were common. Sanitation was often primitive in the extreme, especially, as we have noted, in black sections, and poor as medical care was for lower-class whites, it was far worse for blacks, who were almost invariably refused even emergency treatment at white hospitals.

In 1935, 1,831,475 Southerners worked other people's land. Sharecroppers made an average of $312 a year, and hired labor earned $180. James Agee found all the paradoxes of the lower depths of American life in the rural South. Along with their strange, quiet dignity and sense of honor, "you must reckon in," he wrote, "traits, needs, diseases, and above all mere natural habits, differing from our own, of a casualness, apathy, self-interest, unconscious, offhand, and deliberated cruelty, in relation to extra-human life and toward negroes, terrible enough to freeze your blood or to propel you toward murder; and . . . you must reckon them as 'innocent' even of the worst of this." Perhaps that was the saving grace of the rural South—a pervasive innocence, a dark, tribal unknowingness, born of generations of poverty and ignorance. The photographers Walker Evans and Dorothea Lange combined their remarkable talents to show us the proud, worn, patiently enduring, and strangely beautiful faces of Southern tenant farm men and women and children.

Ironically, the South, the most conservative section of the country (despite its long Populist tradition), became the cornerstone of the most radical reformation of our social and cultural institutions since the Founding Fathers drafted the Federal Constitution. As Cash noted, "no section of the country greeted Franklin Roosevelt and the New Deal with more intense and unfeigned enthusiasm than did the South."

The reasons were various. For one thing, no region of the country had experienced such desperate hardship. Southerners, moreover, were singularly ill equipped to analyze or understand what had happened to them. Coolidge and Hoover had been representatives of Wall Street, the bankers and moneymen whom they instinctively feared and hated, whom they had indeed feared and hated since the days of Thomas Jefferson. If Roosevelt was a Yankee, he was a Yankee aristocrat, and that fact touched the old nerve of respect for breeding and "family." It was decidedly in his favor that he was a farmer, even if a "gentleman" farmer—i.e., a "plantation owner."

Associated with no business, scornful of the moneymen, Roosevelt was amply endowed with that expansive charm common to Southern politicians. He was also a Democrat, and Democrats, with the exception of Cleveland and Wilson, had been shut out of the highest office in the land since the Civil War. Finally, he professed admiration for the sainted Jefferson. Since 1800 few Yankees had had a good word to say for the man still referred to reverently in the upper-class South as Mr. Jefferson. On the contrary, they had been tireless in their abuse. Even Theodore Roosevelt, much admired in the South for his mindless militancy, considered Jefferson's administration to have marked the nadir of American politics. His cousin, on the other hand, seldom missed an opportunity to evoke the spirit of the great Virginian. He could have done nothing to endear him more to his Southern constituents.

Many of the specific New Deal measures were not notably popular in the South. The Tennessee Valley Authority, the most spectacular gift of the New Deal to the South, was not welcomed by everyone. There was a deep-grained conservatism in the Southern mind that resisted change of any kind. A typical attitude was that of a white farmer in Tennessee, who told a Federal Writers' Project interviewer, "I hold to the good old ways; that's the best ways, when all is said and done. . . . Take this TV and A, this electricity stuff, they talk about these days. It would come through here if we'd vote it in. Everybody studied it over. But you take this electricity, them wires—why, they's power in them wires. Power to kill abody. Wires will come down then it's mourning for somebody. Yes, we're afraid of that stuff. They's things the good Lord never meant mankind to fuddle with. So we turned the TV and A down."

Yet despite this ingrained conservatism, the New Deal, in numerous direct and indirect ways, brought relief to Southern blacks and whites alike. Sam Mayhew, a middle-aged black man, lived in Seaboard, North Carolina. As he told his story to Bernice Kelly Harris, he had started life as the son of a sharecropper. When an opportunity came for him to go to the Agricultural and Technical College at Greensboro, he worked as a janitor to pay his way through college, hoping to become a brickmason, but before he could complete his college program, his father became so crippled with rheumatism that Mayhew had to go home to help on the farm. Soon he was married, running a cotton gin, and working in a sawmill in the off-season. An accident at the mill resulted in the amputation of his leg. When his wife went insane, Mayhew was left with the task of rearing seven children. His interests became the school and the church. "It was through my instrumentality," he told Bernice Harris, "that the colored people now have a high school here." He was vice-president of the Parent-Teacher Association and was one of the few black voters in the district. Yet all jobs or public offices for which Mayhew felt himself qualified had been denied him. When he applied for a job in the welfare office, he was sent, despite his artificial leg, to dig ditches. All skilled jobs, he was told, were reserved for whites. "Because of my color, I must ditch or work on the road in spite of my college training and in spite of physical handicaps from amputation and high blood pressure." When Mayhew was unable to prevail on local welfare officials to buy him a new artificial leg, he wrote to President Roosevelt "asking him to interfere on my behalf, stating my circumstances and needs." He got a quick reply, assuring him that the matter would be attended to, and soon he had his new leg.

A black sharecropper told a Federal Writers' Project interviewer that the New Deal relief workers understood his plight. "She [the relief worker] knowed right well I wuz tellin' de Gawd's truth, and her eyes kinda flash lak, an' she sez: 'Damn 'em, dey wucks de po' niggers an' white buckra mos' to death in de spring an' summer, and fall, an' den loads 'em on us after stealin' dere share of de crop! An' den dey got de nerve to cuss de relief! Why *dey's* de ones meckin' money offen de government! Damn 'em!' "

Ironically, the farm program of the New Deal brought in the years between 1931 and 1934 a reduction in Southern agricultural land of more than 13,000,000 acres and a drop in farm income. But for many Southerners this decline in acreage was more than balanced by the availability of various forms of public aid. In the words of W. J. Cash, "WPA wages or direct relief payments did more than barely make their condition tolerable for these dispossessed ones; often, in the case of the least ambitious, it actually made their whole life much more tolerable than it had ever been before." In Ned Cobb's description, "Negro workin' on halves with the white man, the government was issuin' checks to both of 'em, a check to the white man and a check to the Negro, both of 'em receivin' checks for takin' the white man's land *out* of cultivation. Under the government rulins. But it started off, they'd send both of them checks to the white man, and the white man was takin' it all and puttin' it in his pocket. The government found it out and called the thing in question and after bonin' the white man about it someway, they just finally quit and sent the nigger his check and the white man his. . . . White man didn't like for the government to pay the nigger for either farmin' his land or *not* farmin'. O, good God, they swore and kicked against that like a mule kickin' in a stable." White resistance to this practice, according to Cobb, took the form of "pasturin' their land for cattle, prohibitin' the poor nigger from workin' that land in crops. Just drivin' the Negro back, let him root pig and die poor."

Southern whites, on the other hand, complained that for many blacks the relief payments were substantially larger than wages usually paid them. One farmer told Harry Hopkins that it was "impossible to get lots of these people to work at all because plenty of able-bodied people are living off the relief funds and doing nothing. These relief funds may even prevent the farmers from getting sufficient labor to gather their crops." A member of the du Pont family similarly complained that "five negroes on my place in South Carolina refused work this spring after I had taken care of them and given them a house rent free and work for three years during bad times, saying they had easy jobs with the Government."

It was evident, Hopkins reported, "that a great many of the planters in the South are opposed to the Government's program of increasing wages and are fighting every move to raise the standards of the workers, which have been pitifully low." To placate such sentiment, it was the practice of the Relief Administration in the South to refuse relief to anyone who was offered a job and turned it down.

In Anderson, South Carolina, the vagrancy laws of the post Civil War Black Codes were revived. The police chief declared that anyone who could not satisfy him that he had a means of support would have to pick cotton or go to jail and then be rented out to a cotton planter to work off his fine. Marginal whites and many blacks who drew more money from direct relief or from undemanding WPA work than they could make in twelve or fourteen hours of backbreaking labor picking cotton not surprisingly preferred public subvention to private drudgery. As it always had, the owning, employing class raised a great hullabaloo, decrying the corruption of its labor force and denouncing alternately the Federal government for making such wickedness possible and the lazy, good-for-nothing blacks and whites who, in taking the easier of two hard choices, simply displayed a human instinct common in all classes and in all ages. Those who live on the labor of others are always full of moral outrage when labor demands a larger share of the profits. Such sentiments invariably appear to the employers as not simply another expression of their own determination to profit, often excessively, at the cost of others but as an expression of those fatal flaws of character so evident in the lower classes, flaws which are taken as conclusive proof that they are destined by fate, or by a wise and benign God, to be workers rather than bosses.

A landlord in a North Carolina rural town told an FWP interviewer, "It's a fact that the government program has done a lot for farmers. I don't know what in the world we would have done without the government help. Some phases of the program don't work out right, it don't seem to me. It ain't right for the sharecroppers to have half the spring check. . . . The landlord furnishes the soybeans or peas, uses his tractor, hires additional labor, pays all the taxes yet the check comes directly to the sharecropper who refuses to pay his half of the beans and other expenses. If he gets his hand on the money he won't let it go . . . it's my land that lies idle, though he reaps half the benefit. . . . Old Benjamin got behind this year, and after staying with me twenty years he left, thinking I had cheated him . . . most of them don't last but one, two, or three years. Any man that has to work labor has a lot to contend with."

Needless to say, the dominant ideas of the South were not congenial to higher education. The writer and editor Lillian Smith deplored the fact that although the South spent "a greater percentage of its total income for higher education than any other region," it had "not one university of the first rank while 9 of the 11 states comprising the Southeastern region have no universities rated by the American Council on Education as capable of giving the Ph.D. degree and no Southern university rated competent to give this degree in civil, chemical, mechanical, electrical or mining engineering or in bacteriology, entomology, geography, plant pathology, plant physiology, social science. . . ." It was also anomalous that the South had one-third of all the women's colleges in the United States, none of which had standards comparable with the "upper group of U.S. women's colleges."

Despite the generally low level of academic attainment in the South, such impulse to reform as existed found its home in a handful of Southern universities, chief among them Vanderbilt in Nashville, Tennessee, and the University of North Carolina at Chapel Hill, where men like Donald Davidson and Howard Odum were poets and sociologists. Odum was born in Georgia. His education included undergraduate work at Emory, the University of Mississippi, Clark University, and Columbia. At the University of North Carolina he was successively or simultaneously director of the School of Public Welfare, director of the Institute for Research in Social Science, and dean of the School of Public Administration. Among his publications were *Cold Blue Moon, Rainbow Round My Shoulder, Wings on My Feet,* and *Southern Regions of the United States,* the last unquestionably the most important scholarly book of the era on the problems facing the South. It immediately became a starting point for future research on the region.

At Vanderbilt, Davidson, a Fugitive and later an Agrarian, was also a brilliant scholar and researcher.

The risks of criticizing any of the sacred institutions of the South remained high. In 1931 Carl Taylor had been dismissed as dean of North Carolina State College of Agriculture and Engineering because of his advocacy of free speech. Joseph Gelbers, a mathematics professor at the University of Birmingham, was kidnapped and beaten almost to death by Dent Williams, a member of the Montgomery elite, because of his involvement with radical politics and especially the Scottsboro case.

Rockwell Kent, hearing of Gelbers's beating, wrote to the liberal Southern journalist John Temple Graves, upbraiding him for not condemning the attack more strongly. Graves wrote back: "Senator Hugo Black told me over half the people he talked to during his recent months in Birmingham thought the flogging of Gelbers a good thing. I know Rhodes Scholars who think so, doctors of medicine who have studied in Paris and Vienna, novelists whose books have sold all over the country. . . . Maybe I'm wrong, but I'm on the scene and you are not, and I know the South and you don't."

Three years later Clarence Cason, who taught journalism at the University of Alabama, committed suicide because, at least in the opinion of his friend W. J. Cash, he couldn't face the hostility of his colleagues over the publication of his book *90° in the Shade,* a bitter criticism of Southern mores.

In 1932 a Tennessean named Myles Horton founded a Southern counterpart to A. J. Muste's Brookwood Labor College. It was Horton's intention to use education "as one of the instruments for bringing about a new social order." Horton was the child of grammar school-teacher parents of Scotch-Irish origin, who traced their ancestry back to the Watauga settlement before the American Revolution, and his Presbyterian background and radical inclinations combined to form his own highly individual brand of Christian socialism, major elements of which were resistance to racial segregation and a devout belief in industrial unions. From Bible classes Horton went on to "community meetings" with farm families from the surrounding mountains. He widened his reading to include William James and John Dewey. After a year at the Union Theological Seminary, where he became acquainted with the Social Gospel teachings of Walter Rauschenbusch and Reinhold Niebuhr, Horton moved on to the University of Chicago to study in the new field of sociology with Robert Park. At Chicago, Horton became acquainted with the writings of Bishop N. F. S. Grundtvig, the shaper of modern Denmark and the apostle of the "folk." A trip to Denmark in 1931 hardened Horton's determination to start a "folk school" for ordinary men and women in the mountains of Tennessee. Back in the United States, Horton sought out Jane Addams for advice on how to start a "rural settlement house." The result was the Highlander Folk School located at Summerfield, Tennessee, and based on the determination to achieve "a genuine democracy" through the participation of the "masses . . . in their own economic and political organizations."

Like Brookwood Labor College, the Highlander Folk School gave much attention to the techniques for organizing various kinds of social and economic groups: to cooperatives; to unions; to various forms of political activity and protest.

After a sobering report on economic conditions in the South, President Roosevelt called the section the nation's number one problem. The result was the Southern Conference for Human Welfare. Mary McLeod Bethune, Hugo Black, and Eleanor Roosevelt were delegates to the conference, along with labor leaders and politicians. Hosea Hudson estimated that some 16,000 people, black and white, attended a mass meeting called by the Workers' Alliance the day before the conference. The principal demand was for a higher pay scale; the WPA paid only $40.40 per month in the South. A resolution calling for punishment for lynchers was also passed.

Since there were to be black as well as white delegates to the conference, the police ran a barrier from the street up the steps, through the door and down the center of the aisle to separate blacks from whites. When Mrs. Roosevelt and Aubrey Williams, head of the National Youth Administration, arrived late for one session and took places on the black side of the aisle, police stepped forward at once to tell them they were breaking the law. "I was told," Eleanor Roosevelt wrote, "that I could not sit on the colored side." Rather than give in, she asked that chairs be placed for her and Williams on the speakers' platform, facing the audience. Simple as the episode was, word of it spread like wildfire: The wife of the President of the United States had defied the South's most basic law. Rumor spread that the whole audience was to be arrested.

In Hosea Hudson's opinion, if the leaders of the conference, black and white, individuals like Mary McLeod Bethune and Hugo Black, had defied the Jim Crow law, the color line would have been broken in the South at that moment. On the other hand, the appointment of Hugo Black, one of the most liberal justices of the Supreme Court, might have been blocked by Southern Senators, and Roosevelt might have lost important support from Southern Democrats.

It is significant that two of the most notable members of the New Deal—Aubrey Williams and Will Alexander—were Southerners. Aubrey Willis Williams was born in 1890 in Springville, Alabama, into a classic ruined Southern family. Williams's grandfather, a Southern planter of strong abolitionist sentiments, had freed 1,000 slaves prior to the Civil War. Williams's father had been reared on a cotton plantation in a family that lost everything in the war, and in his son's words, he "never got over the feeling of having the roots cut from under him and being adrift in the world." Williams's childhood, as he remembered it, was "one of living in many places and many houses, moving around, looking for a cheaper place to live."

From the time he was a child in Birmingham, Alabama, Williams worked, at first in a laundry and then in a department store. He reached the age of twenty-one with only some eighteen months of schooling. Largely self-taught in a family that fiercely kept alive a tradition of culture in the midst of poverty, Wiliams attended Maryville College in

Tennessee with the notion of becoming a Presbyterian minister. From Maryville he went to the University of Cincinnati and then joined the YMCA overseas, working with British and French troops in France. There he decided that he must become an active fighter for the Allied cause and joined the French Foreign Legion. When the United States entered the war, he transferred to the U.S. 1st Division and was given a battlefield commission.

After the war Williams enrolled at the Sorbonne, took a degree from the University of Bordeaux, returned to the University of Cincinnati to complete his degree in social work, and then moved to Wisconsin in 1922 as executive director of the Wisconsin Conference of Social Work. In the depths of the Depression Williams returned to the South to work for the Reconstruction Finance Corporation. It was in this job that he came to the attention of Harry Hopkins, who enlisted him in the Federal Emergency Relief Administration. He and Hopkins had remarkably similar backgrounds and many of the same ideas on how relief should be administered. Even more important, they were in agreement in their determination to see direct state-administered relief replaced by a Federally managed program of public works jobs. When the Civil Works Administration largely replaced the FERA, Williams made jobs for young men his special concern, and his constant agitation for a program for youth helped bring about the creation of the National Youth Administration. His close friendship with Eleanor Roosevelt and her strong support were also a vital factor. When the NYA was created in June, 1935, Williams was appointed its head. Hopkins found that he could not do without Williams in setting up and running the Works Progress Administration, and Williams thus wore two hats for a time, director of the NYA and deputy director of the WPA. Williams appointed Mordecai W. Johnson, president of Howard University, to a position on the NYA advisory committee, and it was Williams who pushed through the appointment of Mary McLeod Bethune, founder of the Bethune-Cookman College and president of the National Council of Negro Women, as head of the Division of Negro Affairs. Bethune, in turn, gathered an able black staff.

When Williams visited Birmingham, his hometown, as director of the National Youth Administration, a luncheon was arranged for project workers in his honor. When Williams discovered that only whites had been invited, he told the unhappy NYA administrator in Birmingham, John Bryan, that he would not attend unless blacks were also invited. When Williams entered the dining hall, he saw at once that blacks were not seated at the tables but were standing along the walls.

"John, God Damnit," he said to Bryan, "you are determined to mistreat these Negro Youth. Well, you won't do it while I am here. You have tables brought in here and chairs for these Negroes to sit down and eat." A perspiring Bryan protested that they had already eaten. Nevertheless, Williams insisted, "[Y]ou have tables and chairs put in here for them and serve them, just as though they had not eaten and don't serve anybody until they are seated."

Opening a black youth center in Birmingham several years later, Williams stated his credo: "I made up my mind long ago to use my power to help those at the bottom of the social and economic ladder in America. I have and will continue to play that part. I don't care who knows it. . . . I want to say as a Southerner I covenant that the black man shall have his share in that better life."

Under Williams's administration, the NYA excelled all other New Deal agencies in the appointment and promotion of black administrators. The *Chicago Sunday Bee,* a black newspaper, noted: "No Federal agencies have been fairer to colored Americans than the N.Y.A.; none as tolerant. It is the N.Y.A. that has distinguished itself by placing Negroes in policy-making positions. The ideas and thoughts of Negroes were sought and used in building the N.Y.A. program from the bottom up. . 41. The N.Y.A. is ahead of all the Federal agencies in working toward the full integration of colored people . . . in American democracy. . . . Aubrey Williams has been to the N.Y.A. what the Prince of Denmark has been to Shakespeare's Hamlet—he gave it life, substance and direction."

When Hosea Hudson got an audience with Williams to complain about the government's failure to pay a WPA worker for time lost searching for his brother, he reported to Nell Painter, "I didn't know whether he's progressive [i.e., Communist] or not. But he was nice. He wasn't rude, nothing like that. I didn't consider he was a racist." He was one of the few Southern whites Hudson had encountered who treated him civilly.

One consequence of Williams's enlightened racial attitudes was that he was under constant attack as unchristian, subversive, and communistic. Harry Hopkins, on the other hand, called him "a very great man," and Henry Wallace wrote that he "understands the very heart of the Christian message as very few people in the United States understand that message . . . pushing for that ultimate balance that centers around the concept of the Fatherhood of God and the brotherhood of man."

To what degree Williams was or considered himself a Marxist is unclear. He was certainly a devout Christian, but obviously more concerned with the Communists' ability and commitment to a just society than with their political affiliations, he welcomed known or suspected Communists to the agencies in which he was involved as director or deputy director. The consequence was that a number of Communists found positions in the Works Progress Administration and in the National Youth Administration, doubtless to the benefit of both agencies.

At the same time Williams never troubled to be discreet. His outspoken and often radical sentiments enraged the opponents of the New Deal and gave them ammunition to use against the administration.

Will Alexander had a background similar to that of Williams. His home state was Alabama, and his deepest commitment was to justice for Southern blacks. He had been active as a YMCA worker, executive director of the Commission on Interracial Cooperation, a trustee of five black colleges, and for four years president of largely black Dillard College in New Orleans. Rexford Tugwell prevailed upon Alexander to be his deputy in the Resettlement Administration. In that role Alexander made it his special concern to see that justice was done to black tenant farmers, many of whom were being forced out of their tenancies by New Deal farm policies. One of his first acts was to appoint a black farm specialist, Joseph H. B. Evans, his administrative assistant and adviser on the problems of black tenant farmers. When the Farm Security Administration was formed, and Alexander appointed to head it, he took Evans with him. Moreover, he insisted that each of the Southern regional directors have a black assistant to advise him.

The ranks of the "new" intellectuals of the South grew impressively. In South Carolina Julia Peterkin, Conrad Aiken, and Du Bose Heyward won national literary laurels. Gerald Johnson, Roark Bradford, and Paul Green were conspicuous figures in the Southern Renaissance. Finally, there were two indisputably major talents, William Faulkner and Thomas Wolfe.

The most terrible fact of Southern life remained the institution of lynching. Angelo Herndon in his autobiography recalled an episode in Birmingham, Alabama, when a black man working for "a rich white woman who lived in an exclusive white neighborhood" was seen by some passersby entering his employer's house. "Suddenly they got the lunatic idea to yell at the top of their lungs that a Negro had raped a white woman." A lynch mob formed in minutes, and the black residents of the area disappeared from the streets. When the police arrived, the woman explained the circumstances, and the crowd drifted off reluctantly, deprived of its prey.

One of the most poignant expressions of Southern lynch law was that of the singer, Billie Holiday:

> Southern trees bear a strange fruit
> Blood on the leaves and blood at the root;
> Black body swinging in the Southern breeze,
> Strange fruit hanging from the poplar trees.
>
> Pastoral scene of the gallant South,
> The bulging eyes and the twisted mouth;
> Scent of magnolia sweet and fresh,
> And the sudden smell of burning flesh.
> Here is a fruit for the crows to pluck.
> For the rain to gather, for the wind to suck,
> For the sun to rot, for the tree to drop,
> Here is a strange and bitter crop.

The Southern historian C. Vann Woodward wrote, "The ultimate horror might be the tragedy of Charles Bon in *Absalom, Absalom!* or that of Joe Christmas of *Light in August* [referring to the lynching of two black men in William Faulkner's novels]. But the ultimate cost has never been reckoned. It is still unpaid, still mounting, and it could run much higher."

It was to confront this tradition that Jessie Daniel Ames built the most effective organization for the eradication of lynching, the Association of Southern Women to Prevent Lynching. Ames was born in Palestine, Texas, in 1883, the third child of Scotch-Irish parents who had migrated from Indiana to work for the railroad. She and her two sisters were converted to Methodism at a revival. The children grew up in a raw town, where both typhoid fever and physical violence were endemic. "Mob rule," Ames wrote later, "is the typhoid fever of the emotional life of the South, as devastating and as shocking in its implications as ever attended any of the physical scourges which . . . undermined our social and economic life." Jessie Daniel's father was a severe Victorian type whose determination to get ahead resulted in his becoming the owner and manager of a local telephone company, which provided a modest degree of support for his wife and children after his death. Jessie believed that his life was shortened by his grief over the death of his son in a fight following a local baseball game. It was the most personally devastating episodes of violence that Jessie Daniel experienced growing up in East Texas.

She married a young army surgeon named Roger Ames. It was a difficult and unhappy alliance from the first. Ames's snobbish parents refused to accept her as a member of the family and did all they could to break up the marriage. When her husband was dispatched to distant army posts, Jessie visited him, but the visits were usually disastrous. "I could not live away from him. I could not live with him. I always returned [to him] in hope and joy; I was sent away in despair." Nevertheless, the couple had three children, the youngest of whom, Lulu, contracted polio and was a virtual invalid, fanatically cared for by her mother. When her husband died of blackwater fever in Guatemala, Jessie Daniel Ames was left a widow at the age of thirty-one. Searching for a career which might engage her unusual energies and budding administrative talents, Ames was inspired by Carrie Chapman Catt to join the women's suffrage movement in Texas. Active in the Methodist Church, she formed an alliance with one of the state's most prominent feminists, Minnie Fisher Cunningham, famous as an orator and a leading figure in Democratic politics. When Eleanor Roosevelt heard Cunningham speak at the second national convention of the League of Women Voters in 1921, she described her as a person who made her listeners feel "that you had no right to be a slacker as a citizen, you had no right not to take part in what was happening to your country as a whole."

Under Cunningham's tutelage, Jessie Ames became an effective speaker and skillful organizer. Women were used by men in the political arena to march in parades and serve hot coffee, but they were "brushed aside at the final and actual decision helplessly looking on while the men go in and in this county undo the labor of all the days," Cunningham declared. The greatest triumph of the women of the state was the defeat of the governor, James "Farmer Jim" E. Ferguson, an opponent of women's suffrage and, equally important, an enemy of Prohibition. In the course of that battle Ames demonstrated her new political skills and emerged as Cunningham's successor in the councils of the Democratic Party. At the same time she became increasingly concerned about the deplorable situation of Southern blacks. "Gradually, it came over me," she wrote, "that someone with enough

background to do it was going to have to get out and tell white Texans—
the women especially—that until we were ready to stand up and say
in public that we would include Negroes in social benefits we might as
well quit." The conviction grew that she had been "called by the
Lord . . . and didn't even know it" to work for the betterment of Southern blacks. Her first step was "interracial" work, a very modest and
discreet upper-middle-class movement, involving a handful of liberal
whites and a few blacks, most of them preachers and doctors. By 1922
Ames was active with the Commission on Interracial Cooperation, one
of the goals of which was to fight the widespread influence of the Ku
Klux Klan. She was appointed director of woman's work for the committee and in that role found herself increasingly preoccupied with
the issue of lynching, which took on a profound symbolic significance
for her. Convinced that it was *the* racial issue above all others, she
formed the Association of Southern Women to Prevent Lynching
(ASWPL) in 1930. Her strategy was simple. The association would be
confined to Southern white women (a decision which offended the
black women actively involved in the Commission on Interracial Cooperation). Its purpose would be to spread the message of the evils of
racial discrimination throughout the South, depending primarily on
the women members of major Protestant denominations—the Methodists, the Southern Methodists, the Presbyterians, and the Baptists.
Women would be asked to sign pledges committing themselves to oppose lynching and to work to spread the word in the name of Christian
brotherhood. Women, it seemed to Ames, were the proper vessels of
the Lord's word because lynchings were typically carried out in their
name. Consequently, they must take the lead in rooting out the most
terrible crime committed in the nation.

The second article of the ASWPL declared that lynching "brings
contempt upon America as the only country where such crimes occur,
discredits our civilization and discounts the Christian religion around
the globe." All twelve "founding mothers" of the Association of Southern Women to Prevent Lynching were officials of Protestant church
groups. In the words of Ames's biographer, Jacquelyn Dowd Hall,
"From its inception, the anti-lynching campaign was rooted firmly in
a tradition of evangelical reform." When the first small cadre of women
met, Will Alexander told them, "Lynching is distinctly a Southern white
institution . . . as much a part of us as mint juleps or hot biscuits, or
camp meetings or evangelists or hookworm, or eloquence."

Ironically, the veneration for Southern womanhood professed by

Southern males protected the women in the ASWPL from much of the abuse that would have been directed at men. Some of the more prominent members did, to be sure, receive threatening or obscene letters, but for the most part male criticism was muted by convention. Some men took the line initially that the things that women did were not of any practical importance in any event. Their involvement in the ASWPL was attributed to their simpleminded goodness of heart. It came under the innocuous heading of "church work." Some husbands, on the other hand, objected strongly and forbade their wives to participate. Bessie Alford was active with her husband's encouragement, but her sister-in-law was not allowed to join the association. "I am married to a man who doesn't see things as I do," she wrote Ames, "and I have enough opposition to meet from him where my work with the negro is concerned that I do not feel like undertaking anything else that he is not in sympathy with and like a good many other southern men, he thinks we women should keep our mouths out of this and let the men take care of it as they think best."

A major reason for excluding men from the ASWPL was that, in Ames's words, "we Southern white women still have a feeling that many things we know we should not know. Consequently, when there are . . . men present we feign ignorance because of our traditional training." Women were not even supposed to discuss the subject of rape in mixed company except in code words and circumlocutions.

The fact was that Ames and her cohorts were as much engaged in altering the Southern notion of "womanhood" as they were in stopping lynching; indeed, in their minds the two were synonymous. "Public opinion has accepted too easily," an ASWPL pamphlet declared, "the claim of lynchers and mobsters that they are acting *solely in defense of womanhood.* Women dare no longer to permit the claim to pass unchallenged nor allow themselves to be the cloak behind which those bent on personal revenge and savagery commit acts of violence and lawlessness." In Ames's words, "the crown of chivalry . . . has been pressed like a crown of thorns on our heads. . . . I have always been curious," she added, "about the . . . white mentality which as far back as I can remember assumes that only segregation and the law against intermarriage keep . . . white women from preferring the arms of Negro men."

In explaining to a group of Presbyterian women the evolution of the Southern notion of womanhood, Ames reminded her listeners that the black American "was cast outside the law. . . . Added to this was—

and is—the peculiarly construed chivalry, which of necessity—if the belief in racial superiority was to be maintained—must place all white women in a category characterized by physical frailty, goodness, purity, and chastity, and all Negro men in a category characterized by brutish build and sex perversion. To establish in the public emotions the conception of the Negro race as inherently and everlastingly inferior, disenfranchisement was secured."

Ames counted on recruiting, in addition to the older church-women, "younger women . . . educated in the increasing numbers of co-educational schools [who] did not accept the dictum of the man-made society."

Lillian Smith, a recruit to the cause, was equally forthright. White women, she wrote, no longer accepted the worn clichés of men, who "went on with their race-economic exploitation, protecting themselves behind rusty shields of as phony a cause as the Anglo-Saxon world has ever witnessed. . . . The lady insurrectionists gathered together in one of our southern cities. . . . They said calmly that they were not afraid of being raped; as for their sacredness, they could take care of themselves; they did not need the chivalry of lynching to protect them and did not want it."

The campaign of the ASWPL was, as much as anything, a process of education for the women involved. Ames herself puzzled over the question of whether white women in "their own minds perceive danger where none exists, or whether the fears have been put in their minds by men's fears." But fear there evidently was. The ASWPL's major argument initially was that the law could be trusted to punish rapists severely. As Ames extended her own study of the problem, she was dismayed to find that white women often "cohabit with Negro men." Kate Davis, a South Carolina member of the association, came to the same startling conclusion: "There are [white] women in all towns who cater to Negro men."

Much of the success of the ASWPL was due to the tireless publicity given by its members to the issue of lynching. It was one that Southerners would much prefer to forget until some especially lurid episode burst into the news. That was the irony of the situation. Since the avowed purpose of lynching was to frighten blacks and deter them from raping white women, it was important to give widespread publicity to each lynching. At the same time lynchings were the darkest stain on the escutcheon of the South. The Southern solution was to avoid scrupulously any general discussion of lynching as a Southern institution. The ASWPL set out, in a sense, to "talk lynching to death" by keeping the subject constantly in the public mind and in the press. The pressures were various and often subtle: Lynching was bad for the image of the South and, above all, bad for business. Jessie Daniel Ames declared: "We have managed to reduce lynchings not because we've grown more law-abiding or respectable but because lynchings became such bad advertising. The South is going after big industry at the moment and a lawless, lynch-mob population isn't going to attract much outside capital. And this is the type of attitude which can be turned to advantage much more speedily than the abstract appeal to brotherly love."

The most effective techniques developed by Ames and the Association of Southern Women to Prevent Lynching were, first, prompt investigations by members of the organization into the actual circumstances of alleged rapes, and, second, immediate action in a specific local area when an episode of the kind that often culminated in lynching occurred. Women in the area would at once alert state and local officials of possible trouble and press for prompt action.

Ames took the lead in investigating specific lynchings, usually accompanied by local members of the association. In a two-year period she personally investigated twenty lynchings that involved alleged rape. By 1941 the ASWPL had investigated forty-six cases. The widely publicized investigations had a dampening effect on the lynch spirit, especially when the investigations were conducted in a plainly unsympathetic spirit by those spotless and innocent creatures whom the lynchings purported to protect. Still, danger was ever present. "Many of the [local] people were surly and belligerent," Ames recalled. "When we take into consideration the fact that some of the lynchings had grown out of politics and crooked business deals, we can understand that the women were by no means safe at all times. They knew of the constant danger, and they didn't forget to pray."

When ASWPL women intervened to try to prevent a lynching, they often showed remarkable ingenuity and guile. Hearing of a prospective lynching in Tennessee, Ames contacted the ASWPL officer nearest the scene. "She went to work immediately," Ames recalled, ". . . funny how a woman could stir up things if she wanted to." She created such distractions that the fleeing black got over the state line into Arkansas.

Another successful ploy of the ASWPL was to write to newspaper editors soliciting their support for the antilynching campaign and pointing out specifically how their news coverage of alleged rape incidents had served, time and again, to inflame public feelings and thereby encourage a lynching spirit. Ames was invited to speak to the annual meeting of the Southern Newspaper Publishers' Association in 1936, one of the few women to have been asked to address that almost exclusively masculine gathering. She spared no feelings and scanted no facts in exhorting the publishers to take responsibility for discouraging lynching both in their editorials and in their news stories.

Starting out with a concern over lynching as a moral issue, as specifically an unchristian act, the ASWPL grew more and more sophisticated with each passing year, coming to recognize the complicated economic and psychological motivations behind the institution. The association's statements of purpose consequently grew bolder and more comprehensive. In 1934 it adopted a resolution, framed by Ames, which declared that "our deliberate conclusion [is] that the crime of lynching is a logical result in every community that pursues the policy of humiliation and degradation of a part of its citizenship because of accident of birth; that exploits and intimidates the weaker element . . . for economic gain . . . that segregates arbitrarily a whole race in unsanitary, ugly sections. . . ."

By 1935 all but one of Mississippi's eighty-two counties were represented in the ASWPL. Two years later eighty-one women's organizations with a membership of more than 4,000,000 had pledged their support to the ASWPL campaign. In addition, by the end of the decade more than 43,000 Southern women had signed personal pledges to work for the elimination of lynching.

Two other remarkable reform-minded Southern women were Lillian Smith and Paula Snelling. Lillian Smith was the director of Laurel Falls Camp for Girls on Old Screamer Mountain near Clayton, Georgia; she also took care of her invalid mother. She joined forces with Snelling, who was a high school mathematics teacher in Macon, Georgia, to edit a Southern literary journal they named *Pseudopedia* (which became in turn the *North Georgia Review*, a less taxing title, and, later, *South Today*). What made the journal, in its various forms, notable was that its editors had, in addition to excellent critical judgment, an entire disregard of the classic Southern pieties. Like Jessie Daniel Ames, they were far more emancipated on the racial issue than their masculine counterparts. "We are not interested in perpetuating that sterile fetishism of the Old South which has so long gripped our section," they announced defiantly in their initial issue. Lillian Smith believed that the insights of Freudian analysis might, indeed must, be applied to that dangerously deranged patient the South. Only by a prolonged and painful analysis could the South begin to cure itself. Like the patient on the analyst's couch, it must have all its illusions and defenses stripped away, one by one, until it came at last face-to-face with its own naked soul. Then the healing could start. Smith applied Karl Menninger's theory of chronic suicide to the South. Menninger had used the term to describe an individual "whose destructive tendencies . . . turn back upon their owner to undermine and cripple certain of his functions"; he thus enters upon "an existence characterized by invalidism, impotence, warping of personality, delusions. . . ." Smith speculated on "the degree to which chronic suicide may be practiced by a cultural group which, borne down upon by powerful sociological and psychological forces, has regressed into decades of self-absorption."

Smith described herself as a "southern woman born in a region of all the earth where race prejudice is sharpest, where it has its bitterest flavor, its deepest roots, where the relationship of the two races has become so intertwined with hate and love and fear and guilt and poverty and greed, with churches and with lynchings, with attraction and repulsion that it has taken on the ambivalent qualities, the subtle conflicts, of a terrible and terrifying illness." From her childhood she had known that a white person was entitled to be "a Christian and Southerner simultaneously; to be a gentlewoman and an arrogant callous creature in the same moment; to believe in freedom, to glow when the word is used, and to practice slavery from morning to night." She deplored "our own sick obsession with skin color" and made the point that when white liberals talked about race relations, they invariably meant a "more harmonious adjustment of the Negro to the white man's pattern." There was no "Negro problem," Smith insisted; there was, instead, a "white problem." Attention should be directed to the "deep-rooted needs that have caused him [the white] to seek those strange regressive satisfactions that are derived from worshipping his own skin-color." Whites "must learn to confess this." It was not enough, she insisted, to deal with specific needs of blacks. Even if these were met, "one by one," it was vain to believe that "somehow in the shuffle this schizophrenic philosophy of death will change into a philosophy of creative living." The white man who refused to face the real nature of his prejudice was "lynching the spirit" of his own children. There were 11,000,000 blacks in America, not one of whom had "his full constitutional rights as a citizen." In the South, she wrote, "the Negro loses out on all counts: education, health, recreation, housing, the vote, jobs both as to pay and kind, civil liberties, right of free movement, right to the courtesies of address which civilized countries accord citizens regardless of race and economic status."

The constant refrain of white liberals to blacks was that "The time is not ripe yet," was "One step at a time," was that militancy would only arouse white resistance. To them Lillian Smith replied that the American black "believes quite simply that as a citizen he has an inalienable right to protest the nation-wide denial of his Constitutional freedoms." Most liberal Southerners seemed to believe that all the problems of race could be solved "by silence and evasion, pep talks, quiet pressures, or by criticism of Negroes who are attempting to pull their race toward freedom. . . ." White Southerners bore the full responsibility for the racial situation "by our faint-heartedness, our covering up of actual conditions, our personal snobbery, our selfish habit of putting private affairs, state politics, business interests and desire to be 'gentlemen' ahead of deep fundamental human needs." Segregation was the basic issue, and all those who argued that the plight of black Americans must be dealt with in the context of segregation were guilty of "lynching the mind and spirit" of blacks every day.

"There are things to do now in the South," the two editors wrote, "things that we all can do to ease the tension felt throughout our region. Somehow we must believe this. Believing it, we shall break the spell we have put upon ourselves. We know that a man can paralyze his own body. Torn by his hates and his loves, his conscience and his desires, his fears, his guilt, a man can lock himself in a grip like death and become a thing like the dead." There were forces at work in the South entirely free of sentiment and illusion, forces of "industry and finance and agriculture, economic exploiting forces which have no doubts, no inner conflicts. . . . Childlike, savagelike, ruthlessly," they go after what they want, while Southern men and women of conscience seem lost in dreams of the past. The "good" Southerners seem frozen into inaction. Friendship with the black might "turn the forces of violence against the Negro himself"; therefore, it is better to do nothing. But there were, in fact, "simple undramatic things" that could be done. "We can give ourselves a first-aid course on the South. We can learn where the racial pressure-points are. We can learn the names of economic groups who have a stake in race tension. . . . We can learn to understand our region, how it functions, what its laws are, how to change them. We can learn how sick it is, the significance of its symptoms, where its strength lies."

A place to start was to stop using demeaning terms for black Southerners—words like "nigger," "darkie," "coon." Stop telling "nigger jokes." Speak of and to blacks as formally and courteously as you would speak to or of whites. Write letters to newspapers suggesting that black jokes be avoided and that "courtesy titles be used for living Negroes as well as dead ones. Spend a little time thinking. Thinking how it must feel to be a Negro in our South today. How it must feel to be jim-crowed on buses, on street cars, in dining cars, in theaters, in elevators, in churches, in schools, hotels, restaurants, in the armed forces, in jobs. . . . You will not lose your friends, nor your prestige, nor your job nor will you cause a race riot by thinking . . . thinking about the Negro and the white man in the South. . . . Write to your newspaper and suggest that photographs of Negroes be published; Negro heroes in the armed forces, Negro artists and scientists, and educators, and others who have achieved to a newsworthy level. . . . Read a Negro's book or his articles; then write him a letter. Write an artist, a singer, an actor and tell him of your appreciation of his work. . . . Subscribe to a Negro magazine or a Negro newspaper. . . . Whenever you have a chance of not being segregated, quietly take it. Such as sitting by a Negro on a bus or street car, or standing by a Negro in an elevator." One might thus proceed gradually from one level to another until finally one had the courage to speak out publicly against all forms of persecution and humiliation.

Among the strategies devised by Lillian Smith and Paula Snelling to break down racial stereotypes were contests on such topics as "an economic, social, religious, or literary theme of concern to the South today" and, reflecting the two women's interest in psychology (and their desire to attract feminine readers), "My Responsibilities as a Mother in Regard to the Emotional Needs of My Child." Another contest proposed the topic "How Can the South Achieve a Real Democracy?" The contests and the journal itself, with its disarming appeals to the best spirits of the South, drew responses from blacks and whites alike, most notably perhaps from black college students at such places as Fisk, Atlanta University, Tuskegee, and Howard. The essays submitted for the modest prizes revealed a new and different South, militant and hopeful, young blacks and whites reaching out through the pages of *Pseudopedia* and its successors for "a meeting of minds" where bodies still dared not meet.

In addition to encouraging black writers to write for their magazine, Smith and Snelling often had blacks review books about blacks by white authors.

Three years after they had started the magazine, Lillian Smith and Paula Snelling invited twenty-two prominent Southerners to Old Screamer Mountain to discuss "a new and different South." Smith wrote about the gathering: "Everybody had this in common: deep concern for a new and different South. Otherwise, we had socialists, one fellow-traveler, . . . good old Democrats, New Dealers, professors who did not think politically but did think socially, a few people who thought in literary terms only. We had wonderful food. Nobody drank too much; nobody got obscene or nasty in his talk, nobody was sexy; you see their brains were electrified by all that was being said. . . . Anyway there was simplicity [in the living arrangements] with sophistication, hilarity with good manners, and it was fun."

It is a fact of no small import that in one of the most active literary periods in our history, two Southern women, a high school mathematics teacher and a social worker, produced in Macon, Georgia, what was arguably the most intelligent critical journal of its day. This is, of course, a proposition that can be easily tested by reading the magazine under its various titles.

Lillian Smith and Paula Snelling were refreshingly free from the ideological wars that possessed their Northern sisters and brothers (although Smith confessed she had been attacked as a Stalinist). They had excellent critical judgment and a passion for justice. That they made a major impact upon what their friend and contributor W. J. Cash called the "mind of the South" cannot be doubted.

It is important to keep in mind that white women such as Lillian Smith and Jessie Daniel Ames saw far more truly into the true nature of white prejudice against blacks than their masculine counterparts. This was undoubtedly due to the fact that white women, as they had since abolitionist days, identified their own dependent and subordinate status with that of blacks. The more intelligent and sensitive of them were horrified at the fact that lynchings were commonly justified as a means of protecting *them,* and they perceived that the opposite was true: It was a device for their own enslavement.

Just at the moment when Lillian Smith, Paula Snelling, and Jessie Daniel Ames were attacking the myth of Southern womanhood, Margaret Mitchell produced *Gone with the Wind,* which was a kind of recapitulation of every hoary Southern myth and at once became a runaway best-seller.

The same year that W. J. Cash's *The Mind of the South* appeared, a white Southerner, William Alexander Percy, published a classic product of that mind entitled *Lanterns on the Levee.* Percy, by the moving testimony of his nephew, the novelist Walker Percy, whom he took in as an orphan and reared as his son, was an exemplary representative of all that was best in the aristocracy of the Old South, "the most extraordinary man I have ever known . . ." Walker Percy wrote. He was courtly, courteous, as they say in the South, to a fault, generous, considerate of others, a minor poet, an amateur scholar of considerable attainment, a man always attentive to the needs of others with a special affection for his black friends. Yet time and again William Percy speaks in the most conventionally patronizing way of black people. "The righteous are usually in a dither over the deplorable state of race relations in the South," he wrote. "I, on the other hand, am usually in a condition of amazed exultation over the excellent state of race relations in the South. It is incredible that two races, centuries apart in emotional and mental discipline, alien in physical characteristics, doomed by war and the Constitution to a single, not a dual, way of life, and to an impractical and unpracticed theory of equality which deludes and embitters, heckled and misguided by pious fools from the North and impious fools from the South—it is incredible, I insist, that two such dissimilar races should live side by side with so little friction, in such comparative peace and amity. This result," Percy added, "is due solely to good manners." Scattered through the book are condescending little stories of the goodness and amiability of blacks, their loyalty toward and affection for their white friends and masters.

To the modern reader the lack of self-consciousness or perhaps the conscious rectitude with which the stories and little asides are laid on the page can only be disconcerting or dismaying, but there is no gainsaying that they mirrored accurately the mind-set of the class and the section that Percy loved passionately. Blacks were "care-free and foolish and innocent," and, of course, only Southerners understood them. Since "Negroes" in their primitive innocence are unduly disposed to violence, white law looks indulgently upon their failings. Where an assault by one white man on another white with intent to do extensive bodily harm must be treated as a serious crime, a felony, such an assault by a black against another of his race is to be considered no more than a misdemeanor requiring a few weeks in jail as punishment; the offenders are "often turned loose at night so they may enjoy the pleasures of domesticity." If there is an improvement to be measured in the relations between the races, Percy wrote, it is "due solely to the white man. It should be further noted that the Negro is losing his most valuable weapon of defense—his good manners."

Percy concludes a discussion of "racial relations" with an exhortation to Southern whites and blacks alike. To the Negro he issues a warning that he "learn to be a white man morally and intellectually" before he can hope to "be one socially and politically." And to the white: The "black man is our brother, a younger brother, not adult, not disciplined, but . . . pitiful and lovable; act as his brother and be patient."

*Lanterns on the Levee* ends on the nostalgic and elegiac note so dear to Southern hearts. The thirties are "this time of doom. A tarnish has fallen over the bright world; dishonor and corruption triumph; my own strong people are turned lotus-eaters [presumably by the New Deal's largess]; defeat is here again, the last, the most abhorrent. But the autumn air is tinged with gold, the spotted sun sleeps in the garden, and the only treasure that's exempt from tarnish is what the jackdaw gathers."

"The 'lyrical longing to be a gentleman'—how it aches in the heart of Southerners!" Lillian Smith wrote. "That it is a sham gentlemanliness we long for is no matter. . . . Driven by our insecurities, aching with unconscious and conscious fears and dreads and frustrations, we feverishly continue to blow ourselves up from miniature dimensions to the magnificent proportions of a super race and a super class." Smith called *Lanterns on the Levee* "a grotesque and comic thing. One could forget it in a great gust of sane and healthy laughter were it not so malevolent in its effects upon mankind."

In Georgia, where he had gone to give a poetry reading at Atlanta University, Langston Hughes went into the railroad station to buy a *New York Times*. A policeman in the station would not allow him to leave by the "white" door. Hughes had to take a roundabout route, crossing the railroad tracks, to regain the street. He left the South with no regrets on a "One-Way Ticket":

> I am fed up
> With Jim Crow laws,
> People who are cruel

And afraid,
Who lynch and run,
Who are scared of me
And me of them.
I pick up my life
And take it away
On a one-way ticket—
Gone up North,
Gone out West,
Gone!

# 36

## The New Deal

By the end of 1938 the New Deal was not so much "over" as "complete." What could be done to change the basic character of American life, to create a more just and equitable society, had been done. It had been a long and bitter fight. In Rexford Tugwell's words, "Every item of 'reform' had to be fought for inch by inch; and the fight grew harder as recovery proceeded and the renewed profits of business could be poured into its lobbies, its control of mass-communication media, and its resistance to change of any sort." So it is perhaps the place to make at least a preliminary assessment of the New Deal's achievements. They were substantial. Those of the PWA under Harold Ickes were the most impressive in sheer material, physical terms. The PWA projects were what we would call today capital-intensive, while the WPA enterprises were labor-intensive. That is to say, the PWA favored large-scale undertakings that employed relatively small numbers of skilled workers. Dams, parkways and highways, bridges, and public buildings such as post offices usually fell under the PWA. A classic PWA project was a scenic highway starting in northern Vermont and running down the Green Mountains to the Berkshires and from there across Connecticut to Bear Mountain on the Hudson.

Two of the President's favorite projects were a memorial to Thomas

Jefferson and a Pan-American building that would symbolize the spirit of friendship and cooperation between the nations of the Americas. Another major PWA project was "the construction of a great bridge . . . to connect San Francisco with Marin"—the Golden Gate Bridge. The Grand Coulee Dam on the Columbia River was a PWA project. PWA money was also used for national defense, notably in building up the navy.

The Passamaquoddy power project was a PWA venture, one of the unhappier ones in which millions of dollars were spent in a largely unsuccessful effort to harness the tides in the Bay of Fundy. Both Roosevelt and Ickes were enthusiastic supporters of slum clearance and large-scale public housing projects. In Atlanta, Georgia, Ickes presided over the ground-breaking ceremonies for the "first slum clearance program ever undertaken by the Federal Government." There were, in fact, two projects, one for whites and one for blacks. Ickes was rushed off to the site of the black project near Atlanta University. "The students," he wrote in his diary, "did a little singing in those wonderful Negro voices of theirs. They were really a fine-looking lot." Ickes gave a brief speech and then blew up an old shack on the site of the project.

The President was enthusiastic about a PWA housing project for blacks in Indianapolis. He had driven through a black area near the housing project and reported with delight that his picture was "in the window of every house." There were also Federally funded housing projects in Bridgeport, Connecticut, and Lackawanna, Pennsylvania, in New York City, and, indeed, in most large U.S. cities.

Two major PWA projects were the Triborough Bridge in New York and the Queens-Midtown Tunnel, which received $58,365,000 in Federal loans and grants.

Among them the Federal Emergency Relief Administration, the Civil Works Administration, and the Works Progress Administration built more than 11,000 structures, including courthouses, firehouses, hospitals, gymnasiums, schools, more than 100 airfields, and 800 parks, and made extensive improvements on more than 30,000 other buildings. They laid out 40,000 miles of new roads and repaired and widened 150,000 miles of old roads. More than 1,400 athletic fields and 1,800 swimming pools were built, 20,000 acres reforested, and 20,000,000 trees and bushes planted. The WPA introduced talking books for the blind, taught some 200,000 illiterates to read, and gave job training to 150,000 more.

In addition, the New Deal became a patron of the arts on a vast scale.

Perhaps most remarkable of all, in the endless array of projects and the billions of dollars disbursed to state or regional officers of the WPA, its predecessor or successor, there were no major scandals involving the misuse of public funds for private advantage.

Among the achievements of the New Deal must be counted the area of conservation. A vast program of tree planting was undertaken in the Dust Bowl region. More than 10,000,000 acres of marginal farmland, much of it seriously damaged by erosion, was returned to forest. Innumerable flood and erosion control programs were initiated, and large areas of natural forest were improved by the corpsmen of the CCC.

The Triple-A and the various agricultural programs (Henry Wallace presided over more than thirty bureaus and agencies) failed to solve the "farm problem." The measure closest to the President's heart—the plan to reduce farm productivity and thereby raise prices, providing a reasonable return to the farmer for his labor—could hardly have been termed a success. Cotton was an example. After six years of efforts to limit production through subsidies for taking acreage out of production, there were 3,000,000 more bales of unsold cotton in 1939 than there had been at the beginning of the program. Nonetheless, a Gallup Poll showed 69 percent of the farmers giving Henry Wallace high marks for his performance as secretary of agriculture at the end of 1937. A tenant farmer told a Federal Writers' Project interviewer, "There ain't no other nation in the world that would have sense enough to think of WPA and all the other A's."

Starting off as the showpiece of the New Deal, a model for the world of land reclamation, flood control, and well-planned industrial and recreational development, the Tennessee Valley Authority became eventually a bureaucratic monster. The TVA did not become, as George Norris and Franklin Roosevelt had hoped it would, a model for other "valley authorities," but it did a world of good for those families that lived within its far-reaching precincts, and it marked a substantial advance in thinking about the interrelatedness of regional problems—watersheds, power supply, economic activity, and recreation. For many Americans, for many years, it symbolized the most positive aspects of large-scale government planning.

The Civilian Conservation Corps remained the most popular of the New Deal programs by a wide margin. A Gallup Poll in the summer of 1936 showed 82 percent of those polled favoring its continuation. Of the Democrats, 92 percent supported the CCC, followed by 79 percent of the Socialists. In April, 1938, a Gallup Poll showed 78 percent of the electorate favored making the Civilian Conservation Corps a permanent agency of the government. The number of young men in some 2,600 camps ranged from 250,000 to 500,000; by the middle of 1936 some 1,600,000 were or had been in camps. The enrollees, as they were called, wore stylish uniforms of forest green with khaki shirts and black ties. An army "overseas" cap of the same color completed the formal dress, used primarily for visiting the nearest town or for home leave. It became the practice of juvenile court judges to offer young men charged with minor crimes the choice of reform schools or the Cs. Most, not surprisingly, chose the Cs. The consequence was that in many of the Eastern camps located near large cities, a number of the enrollees were youths with records of petty crime or, more commonly, graduates of reform schools. The situation was quite different in the West, where unemployed middle-class youths mixed with the sons of working-class families. The CCC projects ranged from timber stand improvement, to flood and erosion control in the form of riprapping of stream and riverbanks, to the building of parks and recreation areas. The corps planted millions of trees—more, it was proudly claimed, than had been planted in the whole prior history of the Republic.

The commitment of the Roosevelts to the Civilian Conservation Corps was demonstrated when two young graduates of the class of 1939 at Harvard gained an audience with Eleanor Roosevelt at her cottage, Val-Kill, on the Hyde Park estate. Frank Davidson and James Lanigan had come to propose that a "leadership training camp" be established in Vermont to train future leaders for the CCC, the idea being that if the corps were to become a permanent agency of the government, then young men who had been enrolled in its camps should be trained to become its administrators. Lanigan and Davidson entertained the First Lady with bowdlerized versions of popular camp songs. The President was dining with Crown Princess Martha of Norway, and Mrs. Roosevelt suggested that the young men go in to meet the President and his guest and sing the songs for them. The President then questioned Davidson and Lanigan about conditions in the camps and their suggestions about improvements. Their response was to propose an advisory committee to look into personnel policies, "especially the mechanics of broadening the recruitment base so that all young

Americans, and not just those in need, might have a chance to serve their country in the spirit of William James' famous essay, 'The Moral Equivalent of War.' " They proposed the establishment of a leadership training camp at Sharon, Vermont, to be called Camp William James. While Mrs. Roosevelt took notes, the President expressed his desire to see "all measures . . . taken to broaden its usefulness, improve its morale and make it serviceable to all its members and to the country," in Davidson's words. The young men were invited to spend the night at Hyde Park, and orders were dispatched to initiate the camp, which, begun in the winter of 1940–41, expired with the beginning of the draft.

In the exhilarating atmosphere of the New Deal the majority of black Americans began, for the first time since Reconstruction, to feel some hope that they might one day claim their rights as citizens of the Republic. There was a new stirring of hope. That Americans danced to black music, visited "black and white" nightclubs, adored black entertainers, and in the North at least began to read black authors were less superficial symptoms than they seemed. Before black Americans could take up the fight against prejudice and repression, they had to emerge from their ghettos (or attract whites to them); the invisible had to become visible.

Horace Cayton, who headed a WPA project studying the social structure of black Chicago, discovered a blues record that ran:

> Please, Mr. President, listen to what
>     I've got to say:
> You can take away all of the alphabet,
>     But please leave that WPA.
> Now I went to the polls and voted
>     And I know I voted the right way—
> So I'm asking, Mr. President,
>     Don't take away that WPA.

As Cayton noted, one consequence of the flood of blacks from the South to Chicago was that large numbers abandoned the Republican Party. "The Negro South Side," he wrote, "became a solid New Deal town, and Negroes were firmly established in the labor movement. But more important, black citizens of Chicago discovered new ways of letting the city know that they were restive about the conditions under which they were forced to live. The black belt would never, and could never, be quite the same again." When Harry Hopkins was ill, he received from a black correspondent a letter which particularly pleased him: "You have done more to help our Great President to help the poor people of my race than any other man in America, and I pray God that you will be spared to live many years to come."

The deficit spending that Roosevelt indulged in so reluctantly had, in practical fact, relatively little success in reducing unemployment. It was estimated that there were nearly 12,000,000 unemployed in 1933; five years later there were approximately 10,000,000 unemployed. Some 20 percent of the work force was unemployed in 1933. This figure dropped by only some 4 percent in 1939 to 16.33—after five years of the New Deal.

World War II and the boom that followed brought virtually full employment and thereby obscured the fact that high unemployment was a more or less permanent condition of modern industrial society. The fact is that ever since the end of the 1940s unemployment has fluctuated between 6 and 11 percent. This problem has been not so much solved as mitigated by unemployment insurance and by raising the level of what is considered a tolerable level of unemployment.

In the last analysis, the parks, the highways, the reforested lands, the bridges, the dams, the housing projects, the conservation measures, the public art and the literature, born out of the throes of economic collapse and despair, were less important than establishing the principle that the Federal government had a responsibility for the well-being of all its citizens that, at the peril of its existence, it dare not ignore. If the resources of the municipalities and states were inadequate to the needs of people, the Federal government, with its much vaster command of resources, must step in. But there was far more to the New Deal than that. The notion that in the depths of Depression, on the brink of disaster, it was possible not merely to attempt to salvage the economy (which, as is often pointed out, the New Deal in practical fact failed to do) but to enhance the lives of all Americans, to make things fairer and finer in the midst of adversity—an extraordinary accomplishment of the imagination. It was, in the ancient phrase, to make bricks without straw; it was to suggest a whole breathtaking range of new possibilities.

The New Deal had to overcome a mountain of provincialism to achieve that fulfillment. That ancient enemy of progress states' rights (so often a code term for "keeping down the niggers") was at last put in its proper place. It was a Democratic hero, Thomas Jefferson, who had opened that Pandora's box; another Democrat, Franklin Roosevelt, clamped the lid back on.

Something remains to be said about the relationship between communism and the New Deal. The New Deal, its enemies charged, was riddled with Communists of a wide variety of shades of red, from "pinkos," as they were called, to "tools of Moscow." A pinko could, of course, be anyone with the mildest liberal sentiments. A Red could be a card-carrying party member or an equally convinced and dedicated Marxist. He or she could be a Trotskyite, a member of the Revolutionary Workers' Party, Walter Lippmann's secretary, a prominent editor with a respectable publishing house, or an employee of any one of a dozen government agencies. A Red could be a fairly open party member or a "deep" or "steel" (tough as steel) member like a relatively inexperienced Elizabeth Bentley or the seasoned veteran Whittaker Chambers.

To say that the New Deal was filled with large and small *c* communists is accurate but misleading. Given the present connotation of the word "communism," it has a pejorative tone (as, of course, it had for the Red hunters of the late forties and early fifties). It would better be phrased "The New Deal was filled with brilliant and idealistic young men and women whose idealism (not surprisingly, in view of the times) often, or commonly, took the form of communism." The fact that there were Communists on the National Labor Relations Board and on the staffs of the various congressional committees charged with overseeing the general area of labor meant that those vital committees demonstrated a fierce dedication to the rights of working-class men and women; they were tireless in exposing the coercive and illegal activities of "capitalists" in the final stages of the war between capital and labor.

In this attempt to assess the nature and the importance of the New Deal it may be instructive to compare Woodrow Wilson's administration with that of Franklin Roosevelt's. Wilson had, in effect, two years to accomplish the reforms that he had promised in his presidential campaign before the exigencies of the European war turned public attention from domestic reform to the burning issue of America's role in the widening conflict.

Roosevelt, deeply influenced by the goals of the Wilson administration which had been aborted by the war, had six years—from 1933 to 1938—or almost three times as long to effect *his* reforms, many of which were Wilson's updated. In Rexford Tugwell's words, "It would almost be true to say that the New Deal of the thirties consisted of postponed items from Wilson's program, abandoned in favor of preparation for war. . . ."

The most important question about the New Deal may well be: Why did it survive? Why, when the Populists went down to defeat, and then the Progressives and the Woodrow Wilson liberals, did the New Deal endure? As the threat of war increased, Josephus Daniels, secretary of the navy under Woodrow Wilson, wrote to warn Wilson's heir apparent of the dangers that American involvement would pose for the New Deal's social programs. Daniels reminded Roosevelt that Wilson in 1916 had said to him, "There are two reasons why I am determined to keep out of war if possible." The first was his reluctance to send young Americans overseas to die in combat. The second was "that if we enter this war, the great interests which control steel, oil, shipping, munition factories, and mines will of necessity become dominant factors, and when the war is over our government will be in their hands. We have been trying and succeeding to a large extent, to unhorse government by privilege. If we go into this war all we have gained will be lost and neither you nor I will live long enough to see our country wrested from the control of monopoly." Daniels, now an old man, repeated Wilson's prophecy to Roosevelt, who, it may be assumed, hardly needed the reminder. "If our country should be drawn into this maelstrom," Daniels said, echoing Wilson's warning, "the benefit of your reform measures will be lost and our country will fall into the same quagmire witnessed in 1921–33." It was certainly not as unreasonable conjecture, and Daniels's warning points up the basis of much of the isolationist sentiment among Progressive Republicans and Democrats alike.

Two answers for the survival of the New Deal suggest themselves. Every important transformation of society has to happen in an earlier version in order that it can happen in its appointed time. There must always be an advance guard of radicals and innovators whose prescriptions are too extreme for society to swallow. Almost invariably reactions set in when everything that has been accomplished seems to have been lost. In fact, it has simply been temporarily eclipsed. That thought was a comfort to Woodrow Wilson in his last years. It was not that the dream of a League of Nations was impossible of achievement; it had simply been too soon. In his hubris, Wilson came to believe he had tried to force the time by the exercise of his own will. Such a concert of nations would come in God's good time; he had been chastened by a higher and wiser power.

So one suspects this was an important element in the survival of the New Deal. Certainly it was Roosevelt's own feeling that the time was ripe, that there was "a tide in the affairs of men, which, taken at the flood, leads on to fortune," and that he had been lucky enough (and skillful enough) to seize upon it. It was also true that he showed great ingenuity in transforming the Democratic Party into a predominantly liberal political organization, thereby avoiding the division of liberal and radical reformers *between* the two major parties, leaving the control of both parties in the hands of their most conservative factions.

Thirty-six years, somewhat more than a generation, from 1902 to 1938, had been required to effect what were on the whole modest and long-overdue reforms, reforms that one suspects could not have been achieved at all without the benefit (if that is the proper word) of the second most devastating crisis in our history and the genius of our ablest and most visionary President.

The reader will not be surprised to learn that historians are still heatedly debating the question of what, in fact, the New Deal *was*. Some historians have even taken the engaging line that *there was no New Deal!* That debate began, of course, during the New Deal and within it as well as outside. A favorite story that was passed about in New Deal circles during the 1936 campaign told of a telephone call to a Democratic headquarters. "We're having an argument," the caller said. "Tell us what the principles of the New Deal are." "Hold the phone," a party official replied. After a long interval he returned to the line to report, "Sorry but we're having an argument, too."

It has been widely noted that in the hardship of the Depression Americans found a new capacity to share what little they had, to offer a helping hand to those less fortunate, to take some consolation in the fact that "everyone was in the same boat." A new sense of what we might call national community was born. That was another accomplishment of the New Deal or, more specifically, of Franklin Roosevelt, whose jaunty spirit made the struggle to solve the country's economic woes seem like a great adventure. One of the women interviewed in Studs Terkel's *Hard Times* recalled the Depression years as a time when everything in life took on a heightened significance: "If one man died, it was like a headline. Life was more important, it seemed to me. . . ."

John Winthrop, on board the *Arabella* headed for New England with his band of Puritans to found a Bible Commonwealth, wrote in his "A Modell of Christian Charity" that it was God's intention "that every man might have need of another, and from hence they might be knit more nearly together in the bonds of brotherly affection. . . . We must be knit together in this work as one man. . . . We must delight in each other; make others' condition our own . . . having always before our eyes our commission and community in the work, our community on the same bond. . . ." That was the nature of the true or "covenanted community." It must be "as a Citie Uppon a Hill," an example to those who came after. Winthrop compared the true community to a human body knit together by the muscles and ligaments of social life, of mutual love and of caring for the needs of others.

The covenanted community produced what a modern sociologist, David Reisman, has called the inner-directed individual—men and women confident of their own values and their own worth, able to function effectively in the world "outside" the community. In the nineteenth century the community, most often represented by a small town, was dissolved or at least much weakened by the acid of individual*ism*, a creed quite contrary to the creed enunciated by John Winthrop. The creed of individualism saw the world as a kind of jungle where the strong survived and prospered and the weak perished or, perhaps more typically, found the meaning of their lives in serving the purposes of the strong and unscrupulous. Nature, in its inscrutable way, put the "fittest" on top. That was simply the way of the world; it was useless to contend against it. In the end it came out best for everyone. Thus were the bonds of community severed. The rich and powerful supped with the Lord; the poor ate the crumbs that fell from the table and drank whatever trickled down.

The history of the United States can be seen as a prolonged contest between the values of community and the code of individualism. Throughout the nineteenth century there were numerous efforts to reassert the values of the community against the disintegrative effects of American life—Robert Dale Owen's New Harmony, the Shakers, the Rappites, the Fourierists, Adin Ballou's Hopedale, Brook Farm, John Humphrey Noyes's Oneida Community, and dozens of others. They were, for the most part, short-lived but nonetheless poignant demonstrations of the perpetual yearning for the true community.

By the third decade of the present century—the 1920s—individualism seemed to have carried the day. We were not one national "community" of common visions and common hopes; there were at least two Americas—the haves and the have-nots—and, indeed, many more. The notion that Americans owed something to one another, that the well-to-do had a responsibility to those less fortunate, that we, as a nation, constituted "one body," knit together by common memories and obligations, was quite foreign to most Americans. We talked grandiloquently about such themes on the Fourth of July, but we did little to represent them as practical realities in the lives of all Americans regardless of race or color or national origins.

The New Deal healed America by making us once more "almost" a community in the only way a vast modern nation can be: by trying, through the agency of the government, to effect a more just and equitable society. The government, as the instrument of our collective wills, accepted, belatedly to be sure, its role as the creator or re-creator of a national community. It was no longer simply a referee between competing interests; it became the keeper of our conscience as a people. It persuaded us that we all were responsible for one another.

There has recently been a revisionist attack on the New Deal as the agent of our present woes. We are being strangled by an enormous bureaucracy, so the argument goes, and weighted down by a staggering national debt. True enough, but nobody ever argued (or at least no one ever *should* have argued) that the New Deal was the final solution to the problems of a modern industrial society. Solutions become problems in a disconcertingly short time. "God fulfills himself in many ways lest one good custom should corrupt the world," James Russell Lowell wrote, or in the words of the British historian E. L. Woodward, "Everything good has to be done over again forever." Those inescapable facts of history cannot shake or shadow the remarkable accomplishments of the New Deal. The Socialists and Communists grumbled that it had not gone far enough; the conservatives, that it had gone so far as to be indistinguishable from socialism or communism. The fact was that it had gone about as far as it could go, and that was much farther than the most optimistic forecaster would have dared predict in the bitter winter of 1932–33, when the issue had simply been one of survival.

# 37

# Religion

A major premise of this work is that it is impossible to understand the course of American history without close attention to the role of religion, specifically that of Protestant Christianity. The German sociologist Max Weber popularized the idea of the Protestant ethic as the foundation of American capitalism. Thrift, piety, and hard work, Weber argued, provided the essential elements in American business enterprise. But thrift, piety, and hard work are common to many cultures that have not produced an effulgent capitalism. The story of American capitalism is far more complicated than Weber's thesis suggests. What the Protestant Reformation did unquestionably produce was a new kind of person who came to be called an individual, a person who, as it turned out, was remarkably well equipped to take advantage of the unparalleled natural and human resources of a virgin continent. That individual, when he channeled his efforts into entrepreneurial activity (rather than into law or the ministry or reform), was seldom thrifty (he joyfully spent money to "make" money) and not notably pious (there were certainly exceptions, the most striking being John D. Rockefeller), but he was hardworking and not particularly scrupulous about how he made his money.

As Weber's rival, the British socialist sociologist R. H. Tawney, has argued, orthodox Protestantism did its best to restrain or at least to tame the generally rapacious spirit of capitalism, and as we have seen throughout this work, it often succeeded. That capitalism was not much worse than it was during the nineteenth and early twentieth centuries was due, as much as anything else, to the devoted labors of innumerable reformers, the great majority of whom, down at least until the second decade of the present century, were zealous Christians, most commonly Christian socialists of one kind or another; they believed that capitalism was the work of the devil and that it was their duty, as Christians, to oppose or at least to reform it. Helen Phelan, head of Merrick House, a settlement house in Cleveland, spoke for that tradition when she declared, "I am old-fashioned enough to have a religious motive for doing the thing I am doing." And Vida Scudder, who helped found the College Settlement Association, in the 1920s described the difference between the new professional social workers and her generation of social workers and reformers as that "between a salaried clergy and the mendicant orders who had become fools for Christ."

Populism was the most successful form of Christian socialism (the Populists routinely opened their conventions by singing the Lord's Prayer). If populism has not always been specifically identified as such, its enemies in the late 1880s and the 1890s had no doubts about its socialist bias. Socialist or not, it was the high tide of American political radicalism, and it was inextricably intertwined with Protestant fundamentalism. That fact may indeed have contributed to its demise. Tainted with racism and xenophobia, it alarmed the more sophisticated middle-class Christian socialists like George Herron and Washington Gladden. One strain of populism mutated into the revived Ku Klux Klan (the Klan's aggressive racism and anti-Catholicism obscured the fact that it was often highly critical of capitalism). The activities of the Klan, with its burning crosses and inflammatory rhetoric about a "White Christian [Protestant] America," contributed to the image of Christianity as obscurantist and reactionary.

In 1926 the Imperial Wizard and Emperor of the Klan wrote: "Nordic Americans for the last generation have found themselves increasingly uncomfortable and finally deeply distressed" at the "moral breakdown that has been going on for two decades. . . . The sacredness of our Sabbath, of our homes, of our chastity, and finally even of our right to teach our children in our own schools fundamental facts and truths were torn away from us."

Gerald L. K. Smith and Huey Long, relatively enlightened on racial issues, were heirs of what we might call the "fundamentalist left wing of populism." Their rhetoric was hardly to be distinguished from that of the great orators of the Populist Party: God would punish the rich and powerful and exalt the poor and weak. It was His will that the vast wealth of the land be shared.

The formation of the new intellectual class in the 1920s was, as we have seen, accompanied by its secularization (or perhaps better, dereligionization). This process reached its culmination in the late 1920s. Protestant Christianity was viewed by the more enlightened as a type of bourgeois social posturing, a bulwark of capitalism, a morass of obsolete and archaic doctrines and dogmas, the last stronghold of puritanical repressions and inhibitions, or, most conclusively, the "opiate of the people" (this was thought to be especially true of Catholicism).

The attitude of the new intellectual class toward traditional organized religion was perhaps best represented by H. L. Mencken and the *American Mercury*. Mencken celebrated all signs of the decay of religion and religious influence. "I can think of no clergyman in any great American city today," he wrote, "whose public dignity and influence are much above those of an ordinary Class I Babbitt. . . . When bishops begin launching thunderbolts against heretics, the towns do not tremble; they laugh. When the elders denounce sin, sin only grows more fashionable." In Mencken's view it was the tenacious survival of "sacerdotal authority . . . and not hookworm, malaria or 100% Americanism" that was chiefly responsible "for the cultural paralysis of the late Confederate States. The South . . . is run by country towns—and in every country town there is some baptist mullah who rules by scaring the peasantry."

At the same time the majority of Americans continued to think of themselves as Christians of one variety or another. The two dominant religious trends of the 1920s were what we might call exhibitionist Christianity and fundamentalist Christianity. Exhibitionist Christianity had its roots in the well-established American tradition of revivalism, which, in turn, had its roots in Jonathan Edwards's Great Awakening and the innumerable frontier and rural revivals that have been a major element in American religious history. Dwight Moody had adapted the revival to an urban setting and in his wake came a series of revivalists— Gipsy Smith, Billy Sunday, and, most spectacular of all, Aimee Semple McPherson. It was McPherson who, perhaps more than any other figure of the decade, defined the character of American religion in the 1920s.

Another episode that served to define the religious atmosphere, at least as it appeared in the popular press, was the so-called Scopes trial. The World's Fundamentalist Convention, meeting at Fort Worth, Texas, in 1924, had vowed an all-out attack on Darwinism in any form. The convention recommended "compulsory measures to force all teachers to sign annually a statement of creed which affirms a firm and steadfast faith in the Genesis account of creation, the historical fact of all Bible miracles, the virgin birth, the bodily resurrection, the imminent second coming of Jesus, the existence of a personal devil and a literal hell." Perhaps with this resolution in mind, a Tennessee legislator introduced a bill to outlaw the teaching of evolution in the state. The legislation was sponsored by John Washington Butler, a former teacher, a farmer, and a man renowned for his kindness and public spirit. The bill he presented to his fellow legislators read in part: "An Act prohibiting the teaching of Evolution Theory in all the Universities, Normals, and all other public schools of the State." It would be unlawful for any teacher "to teach any theory that denies the story of the Divine Creation of man as taught in the Bible, and to teach instead that man has descended from a lower order of animals." He introduced his bill, as he explained, because he believed that "The evolutionist who denies the Biblical story of creation, as well as other Biblical accounts, cannot be a Christian. . . . It goes hand in hand with Modernism, makes Jesus Christ a fakir, robs the Christian of his hope and undermines the foundation of our Government. . . ."

There was only token opposition to the bill in Tennessee. The faculty of the University of Tennessee had little say on the subject. The Tennessee Academy of Science was silent. On January 28, 1925, the lower house passed the bill by a vote of 71 to 5. The next day William Jennings Bryan appeared in Nashville to speak on the topic "Is the Bible True?" His answer, which surprised none of his auditors, was that every word was literally true.

The liberal and reform-minded governor of Tennessee, Austin Peay, signed the bill reluctantly while expressing the hope that it would never be enforced. "Nobody," he wrote, "believes that it is going to be an active statute." In other words, it was intended as nothing more than a pious gesture.

When the Butler Law came to the attention of Roger Baldwin, one of the founders and head of the American Civil Liberties Union,

Baldwin decided to have the ACLU challenge its constitutionality. He appealed to John W. Davis, Democratic presidential candidate recently defeated by Calvin Coolidge, to take the case. When Davis refused, Baldwin advertised in the Tennessee papers for an attorney willing to take the case. He received a reply from George W. Rappelyea, a mining engineer, in Dayton, Tennessee, who had grown up in New York City and was in charge of six coal and iron mines owned by the Cumberland Coal Company. Rappelyea enlisted two young lawyers, and the three men then prevailed on John Thomas Scopes, a recent graduate of the University of Kentucky who had come to Dayton to coach football and teach science, to defy the law. Scopes's arrest would then be arranged. "That will make a big sensation," Rappelyea said. "Why not bring a lot of doctors and preachers here? Let's get H. G. Wells and a lot of big fellows." Scopes was reluctant. He believed that "evolution is easily reconciled with the Bible." Finally the young teacher agreed. "It was just a drugstore discussion that got past control," he said later.

Roger Baldwin agreed to the plan. Scopes was arrested, and Baldwin announced to the papers: "We shall take the Scopes case to the supreme court if necessary to establish that a teacher may tell the truth without being thrown in jail." The World Christian Fundamentalist Association promptly enlisted the most famous fundamentalist of them all, William Jennings Bryan, who announced, "For the first time in my life I'm on the side of the majority." Bryan had shouted in challenge to the evolutionists: "You believe in the age of rocks. I believe in the Rock of Ages." He declared: "I would rather begin with God and reason down than begin with a piece of dirt and reason up." And again: "A teacher receiving pay in dollars on which are stamped 'In God We Trust,' should not be permitted to teach the children there is no God."

John Randolph Neal was appointed chief counsel for Scopes. Dean of the law school at the University of Tennessee, Neal had been fired for assigning James Harvey Robinson's *The Mind in the Making* to his students. Encouraged by, among others, Henry Mencken, Clarence Darrow volunteered to assist Neal. The judge was John T. Raulston, a native of Gizzards Cove, Tennessee, and a lay preacher in the Methodist Episcopal Church. Judge Raulston announced that God "the Author of all truth and justice shall direct every official act of mine," a statement that the defense did not find reassuring.

As the date in July set for the trial approached, public controversy mounted in intensity. It was taken up with special relish in Great Britain as an example of American primitivism. Gilbert Murray, Regius professor of Greek at Oxford, called the trial the "most serious setback to civilization in all history," which seemed a bit excessive. George Bernard Shaw had a good deal to say on the subject, and if H. G. Wells did not rush to Dayton, he expressed his opinion of the lawmakers of Tennessee. Vanderbilt University, a private institution, announced that it would continue to teach evolution. A parade of scientists, legal scholars, and academic philosophers denounced the Butler Law. They were supplemented by liberal ministers and theologians, who declared that Darwinism was not inconsistent with Christianity. Genesis was simply the account by a primitive tribal people of their notion of the creation of the world and was to be treated like the numerous other creation myths of the various world religions.

The Bible Crusaders of America joined forces with the Supreme Kingdom—an organization founded by Edward Young Clarke, former head of the Ku Klux Klan—the World Christian Fundamentalist Association of Minneapolis, and the Bryan Leaguers to support the Tennessee law. Millions of words were thus written and uttered on the subject before the trial itself ever began. Politicians and preachers rivaled, if they did not outstrip, professors and other secular prophets. Both sides of the controversy were free to predict disaster if the opposition prevailed. The ideological differences of the two Americas were thrown into sharp relief. Eleven scientists were recruited by the ACLU, with advice from the American Association for the Advancement of Science, to testify in Dayton.

Professor Arthur O. Lovejoy of Johns Hopkins wrote: "The effort to raise legislative barriers against science is by no means new, and science has always prevailed. Of course, we regret to have the issue arise in this age of progressive thought and developing intelligence. But we shall attempt to meet it in a spirit of fairness and willingness to explain and will depend upon the usual sound sense of the American people for a decision." Lovejoy did not indicate how the American people were to express their "decision."

Dr. Vernon Kellogg, executive director of the National Research Council, which was made up of "all American scientific organizations," "smiled a little," the *New York Times* reported, when asked to explain evolution. "Evolution means continuity, transmutation, development of the new from the old," he replied. "It means blood relationship, a universal genealogy of life. It teaches us the fundamental unity of all life, no matter what the appearance or form. Every living creature, big or little, though it lives a moment or a century, is like every other creature and has a relationship with every creature that ever lived. Since we ourselves are in and of nature—an inseparable part—evolution supplies us many answers to the questions we ask about ourselves."

Dr. Kellogg expressed surprise that the theory of evolution was singled out for a ban. Why not a ban on zoology, botany, and geology, none of which could be properly taught without reference to the principle of evolution? "It cannot be too often declared," Kellogg continued, "that science and evolution as a part of science do not nullify religion. Many competent scientists and evolutionists are convinced religious believers."

The Reverend John R. Straton, a spokesman for the fundamentalists, countered that evolution was simply a theory. There was no conclusive proof that humankind had evolved from the amoeba or some simple, primitive form of life. There were many gaps and unexplained events in the development of human life. Evolution therefore should be presented, if at all, simply as a set of suppositions, unprovable even by scientific methods. Straton believed that only "a God-inspired revival of old-fashioned religion" could save the nation from its demoralization and worldliness.

In the midst of the controversy the school board of Paducah, Kentucky, fired Scopes's sister, a mathematics teacher, because she refused to disavow Darwinism.

Reporters, scientists, fundamentalists, and the merely curious descended on Dayton. For most of the citizens of that rural town, the trial seemed heaven-sent. A Dayton merchant named Darwin hung out a sign that proclaimed: "Darwin is right." In much smaller letters was written: "inside." The front of the Aqua Hotel was painted a garish yellow, and cots were placed in the halls to accommodate the flood of visiting dignitaries. A reporter asked a grizzled old-timer what he thought of the evolution case, and he replied, alarmed, "Land's sake! Who's got it?"

When the orator of the Platte arrived, to much fanfare, he was dressed in striped trousers, a black coat, and a white pith helmet to guard against the dangerous rays of Tennessee's July sun. Bryan and John Washington Butler were photographed together with their hands on a Bible. At a testimonial dinner for Bryan he was introduced as "the greatest man in the world and its leading citizen."

H. L. Mencken, enraptured by the whole affair, arrived, trailing admiring reporters; two movie crews recorded everything even mildly noteworthy. Local wits greeted out-of-towners with such gibes as "Brother, thy tail hangs down behind." A blind man went about with a sign proclaiming him the world's greatest authority on the Bible. The journalist Joseph Wood Krutch was pleased by the willingness of Daytonians to give their views on theology, cosmology, and astrology. They were in sharp contrast with the state's intelligentsia. Bigotry, Krutch noted, was "militant and sincere," while "intelligence is timid and hypocritical."

Mencken, in his articles for the *Baltimore Sun,* used such terms as "morons" and "peasants" to describe the residents of Rhea County. Of Bryan, he wrote: "Once he had one leg in the White House and the nation trembled under his roars. Now he is a tinpot pope in the Coca-Cola belt and a brother to the forlorn pastors who belabor halfwits in galvanized iron tabernacles behind the railroad yards."

When Clarence Darrow arrived, his reputation as a great lawyer, however heretical, was recognized by the prefixing of "Colonel" to his name. His opinions were respectfully solicited by the more enlightened spirits of the town.

William Allen White was well aware of the drama of the encounter between the two heroes of radical America. Although he deplored Bryan's mindless fundamentalism, he understood very well its origins and its significance. Darrow, White noted, "was the antithesis of Bryan, a cynic, a sophisticate and a Sybarite." The physical world was immediate and tangible to Darrow; beauty moved his soul. "In conversation," White wrote, "he was a chuckler who talked in wise saws, cheered meticulously, grinned diabolically." In addition, he shared with a number of the more progressive spirits of the time an infatuation with women which was much more—and much more complex—than simple womanizing. He felt transported by the feminine spirit, the anima; the distinctly female quality of mind and temperament intoxicated him. He had entered into that new world where whatever a man's and a woman's sexual relationship to each other was, they were, above all, *friends.* In White's words, "Until the day he died, Darrow belonged to the great brotherhood of pilgrims who tread the primrose path not idly but with zeal and a deep conviction of their rectitude."

Of the jurors chosen on July 10, nine were farmers; six were Baptists, four were Methodists; two unrecorded; one was illiterate, and three declared that they read only the Bible. While the judge was cooled by a small electric fan, the jurors beat the air futilely with fans bearing a toothpaste advertisement that read: "Do your gums bleed?" It was all Henry Mencken could have wished.

Darrow began his case for the defense by declaring that Scopes was on trial "because the fundamentalists are after everybody who thinks . . . [and] he is here because ignorance and bigotry are rampant. . . ." With a style that evoked memories of his defense of Big Bill Haywood in the bombing trial of the Western Federation of Miners in Caldwell, Idaho, in 1906, Darrow treated the aficionados of court trials to a classic performance. He was sixty-eight, and his adversary, Bryan, was sixty-five. What they were doing was reenacting a drama as old as the Republic: faith versus skepticism; science versus religion; the South and Midwest against the Northeast; rural townfolk against big-city slickers (Darrow had, to be sure, been born in Kinsman, Ohio, but he had long since shed any trace of provincialism).

Darrow described the consequences of attempting to restrain the free circulation of ideas: "Today it is the public school teachers, tomorrow the private. The next day the preachers and lecturers, the magazines, the books, the newspapers. After a while, Your Honor, it is the setting of man against man and creed against creed until . . . we are marching backward to the glorious age of the sixteenth century when bigots lighted faggots to burn the men who dared bring any intelligence and enlightenment and culture to the human mind."

Ben McKenzie was a lawyer for the prosecution whose courtesy title of General indicated his standing in the community. He pulled out all the stops on the Yankee invader theme. "They had better go back to their homes," he declared, "the seats of thugs, thieves, and Haymarket rioters, and educate their criminals than to try to proselyte here in the South. . . ." The defense was trying "to put words into God's mouth, and have Him say that he issued some sort of protoplasm, or soft dish rag, and put it in the ocean and said, 'Old boy, if you wait around about 6,000 years, I will make something out of you.' "

When Bryan finally spoke in the latter days of the trial (which lasted eight days), he denounced the evolutionists for classifying man with the mammals, "with lions and tigers and everything that is bad!" Children taught such notions would "scoff at the religion of their parents! And the parents have a right to say that no teacher paid by their money shall rob their children of faith in God and send them back to their homes, skeptical, infidels or agnostics or atheists. . . . The Bible, the record of the Son of God, Savior of the world, born of the

Virgin Mary, crucified and risen again—that Bible is not going to be driven out of this court by experts who come hundreds of miles to testify that they can reconcile evolution, with its ancestors in the jungle, with man made by God in His image, and put here for His purposes as part of a divine plan." People in the courtroom cheered Bryan's words, and there were periodic shouts of "Amen."

Much time was taken up with legal technicalities that had little to do with evolution, and the court audience dwindled. The judge refused to hear testimony from the scientific experts who had been assembled, a serious blow to the defense that was vigorously protested. Darrow began to bait Judge Raulston, hoping to provoke him into some reaction that would provide the basis for an appeal. He failed. The judge indeed bade fair to outmaneuver Darrow, but Darrow had a final strategy in reserve. He was determined to get Bryan himself on the witness stand and grill him about the literal truth of the Book of Genesis.

The defense managed to have some of the expert scientific testimony read into the trial record. In addition, entered into the record was the testimony of various eminent theologians, perhaps most notably that of Shailer Mathews, dean of the University of Chicago Divinity School. "Genesis and evolution are complementary to each other," Mathews wrote, "Genesis emphasizing the divine first cause, and science the details of the process through which God works. . . . Evolution is not a power or a force; it is a process, a method. God is a power, a force; He necessarily uses processes and methods in displaying His power and exerting force. . . . For science there is no beginning and no ending; all acceptable theories of the earth's origin are theories of rejuvenation rather than of creation from nothing."

After the reading of the testimony of the eminent scientists and theologians into the record, the defense called a startled Bryan to the stand, and Clarence Darrow began his work of destruction. It was one of the strangest and most revealing confrontations in our history, loaded or overloaded with symbolic connotations. Did Bryan indeed take every word of the Bible to be literally true? Bryan affirmed that he did. Did Jonah remain three days in the belly of a whale? God could perform any miracle he wished, Bryan replied. Did Joshua make the sun stand still? On many questions Bryan skillfully evaded a direct answer, and Darrow grew increasingly hectoring in his manner. When did the Flood occur? Was the Bible dating calculated at 4004 B.C. accurate? When one of Bryan's answers brought cheers from the audience, Darrow said caustically, "Great applause from the bleachers."

"From those whom you call 'yokels,'" Bryan replied.

Stung, Darrow denied he had used the word.

"Those are people you insult."

"You insult every man of science and learning in the world because he does not believe in your fool religion."

That was too much. The judge cautioned Darrow. But the remorseless questioning went on. When Bryan protested that the questions had "no other purpose than ridiculing every Christian who believes in the Bible," Darrow replied: "We have the purpose of preventing bigots and ignoramuses from controlling the education of the United States and you know it—and that is all."

The questioning of Bryan by Darrow, a matter strictly speaking, extraneous to the trial itself and improperly allowed by a rattled Judge Raulston, polarized public sentiment more severely than any other event of the trial or the events attendant upon it. Many people who admired and indeed loved Bryan as the embodiment of the democratic faith, the ancient enemy of the capitalists, the champion of rural America were deeply offended by Darrow's treatment of the ancient hero. One Southern editor described it not inaccurately as "a thing of immense cruelty." It was also a serious error on Darrow's part. The judge, after a night's reflection, ordered the exchange stricken from the record, but the damage had been done. Opinion hardened against the defense. Bryan was ravaged by the experience.

The next day the case went to the jury, which took nine minutes to return a verdict of guilty. The judge imposed a fine of $100 on Scopes, who replied with considerable dignity: "Your Honor, I feel that I have been convicted under an unjust statute. I will continue in the future as I have in the past to oppose this law in any way I can. Any other action would be a violation of my ideal of academic freedom—that is, to teach the truth—as guaranteed by our constitution, of personal and religious freedom. I think the fine is unjust." He would refuse to pay the fine and appeal the verdict. The judge set a bond of $500, which Mencken posted. Soon after the trial Scopes confessed to a reporter that he was innocent. He had missed his class on the days when the theory of evolution would normally have been discussed.

The reporters who had swarmed over the town for a fortnight or more hired a band from Chattanooga and put on a dance for the townspeople. Clarence Darrow danced with some of the high school girls. He was clearly the hero. Bryan, tired and ill, slipped away quietly. Five days after the end of the trial he died in his sleep. Mencken's obituary for Bryan read: "Has it been duly marked by historians that William Jennings Bryan's last secular act on this globe of sin was to catch flies?"

While liberal and enlightened sentiment was wholly on the side of Darrow and Darwin, those older Progressives who recalled the glory days mourned the humiliation of the man who had once been a hero to them. Jane Addams had debated against Bryan as a college student. She was in England during the Scopes trial, and she found herself interrogated patronizingly by her liberal and radical English friends. Nothing so retrograde, they assured her, could happen in England. She tried patiently to explain that in the United States, particularly in states or small isolated communities steeped in the tradition of Christian fundamentalism, such conflicts were not uncommon, were, indeed, evidence of the vitality of American democracy, whereby simple, poorly educated people refused to be overawed by intellectuals and "experts." In her characteristic way she entered sympathetically into the minds of the beleaguered fundamentalists, "the so-called narrow-minded men." Addams pointed out that it did not occur to the young Chicago intellectuals living among ghetto immigrants whose ideas were quite as naïve as those of farmers of Tennessee, that they might look as tolerantly on the mountain folk of western Tennessee in *their* rural ghettos.

The State Supreme Court threw out the *Scopes* case entirely, stating, "We see nothing to be gained by prolonging the life of this bizarre case." The indictment was ordered dropped, and the possibility of an appeal to the U.S. Supreme Court blocked. Nothing in a legal or constitutional way resulted from the whole affair. At the same time it could be said that the case had served some purpose. It had provided the kind of spectacle that the American public doted on; it had given a vast amount of publicity to the doctrines of evolution and helped at the same time to make the point that, at least in the opinion of a substantial number of liberal ministers and theologians, there was no necessary conflict between Christianity and evolution. While the fundamentalists pressed their campaign to ban the teaching of evolution in public schools and colleges with renewed vigor for a time, the tide definitely turned against them. Few states followed the example of Tennessee, and some that had passed similar legislation repealed it.

From the time of the Scopes trial the fundamentalists perceived themselves as increasingly beleaguered.

While liberal theology had a unique opportunity to present its own view of the relationship between science and religion, it continued its decline, notably, as we have observed, in the new intellectual class and in the academy. There were, of course, buried or suppressed issues below the surface. There was something, after all, to Bryan's impassioned cry that Christianity itself was on trial. It was religion that came to science, hat in hand, anxious to resolve ancient quarrels and clearly ready to do so primarily on science's terms. The "real experts" were the scientists; the theologians were there to salvage what they could from the debacle.

Clarence Darrow, with his conviction that a price must be paid for every so-called advance of civilization, with his essentially pessimistic view of human nature, of the persistence in history of greed and selfishness and the dangers incident to the pursuit of truth, was in many ways closer to Christian orthodoxy than were his fundamentalist opponents. Certainly his view of man as a fallen creature was more compatible with the Christian doctrine of original sin than the faith of so many of his fellow citizens in the efficacy of science and the inevitability of progress. Darrow had been tormented all his life by the tragic nature of the human condition, of, in essence, history. The ferociousness of his attack on Bryan may well have been the result of his impatience with a version of Christianity that evaded the agonizingly difficult questions that lay at the heart of the human dilemma. Darrow seemed determined to expose the moral and intellectual bankruptcy of a historic branch of American Protestantism that had become an anomaly in the modern world; his rage at poor Bryan was the expression of his own anguished and untiring search for the meaning of existence. Law had little or nothing to do with it. He had a reckless determination to press on without regard to the practical consequences, a determination which alarmed his fellow defense counsel, who were concerned with winning the case and thereby advancing the cause of civil liberties.

The issues, practical and symbolic, in the Scopes trial have proved remarkably enduring. The fundamentalists, left for dead, have revived and recently resumed their attack on "secular humanism," on "liberals" and "professors" and the doctrine of evolution. The arguments are much the same as those paraded by the various factions at the time of the Scopes trial. The scientists and liberal theologians have checked in. Once more the fundamentalists perceive their mission as "saving the Bible" (and Americans in general) from infidelism and skepticism. It does little good to assert that there need be no conflict. The tension will be there as long as the aims of life remain shrouded in mystery.

In their insistence that the Bible contained the essentials of the Christian religion the fundamentalists had hold of an important fact of which many Social Gospelers had lost sight. But it was one thing to assert that the sciences and the social sciences together could not give a convincing account of the nature and destiny of man, of ultimate questions; it was another to fly in the face of a mass of scientific evidence about the geologic origins of the earth.

The 1920s were the heyday of itinerant evangelists. In addition to Cyclone Mack, Billy Sunday, and Gipsy Smith, there was the Singing Evangelist, the Boy Evangelist, the Railroad Evangelist, the Business Man's Evangelist, the Cowboy Evangelist, and the Labor Evangelist. Aimee Semple McPherson was born in 1890 in the province of Ontario, Canada. When she was six weeks old, her mother dedicated her to God's work at a Salvation Army mission. A handsome, shapely girl, Aimee was converted, or reborn, at the age of seventeen through the influence of a Pentecostal minister named Robert James Semple, who finished off the job by marrying his young convert. Aimee traveled from revival to revival throughout the United States and Canada with her husband. Called to missionary work in China, Semple died there, leaving Aimee with an infant daughter. She returned to the United States, where she assisted her mother in Salvation Army work and delivered religious lectures.

In 1912, at the age of twenty-two, Aimee married Harold Stewart McPherson, a bookkeeper. It was not a successful union. Aimee had a long period of illness which she believed was God's punishment for giving up her career as an evangelist. Back in Canada, she resumed her mission, preaching a God of love and the ecstasy that came from a reawakened faith. She soon discovered a gift for healing, and her sermons became increasingly dramatic, featuring public conversions, speaking in tongues, and other familiar revivalistic responses. With her mother, Minnie Kennedy, as her manager, McPherson began a nationwide tour. The handsome young woman, clothed in gleaming white robes and speaking in ecstatic tones, became an overnight sensation. It seemed inevitable that with her talents as a showwoman she should settle in Los Angeles, the self-styled entertainment capital of the world.

McPherson's backdrops were more like stage sets than conventional churches—draperies and colored lights, flowers in abundance, and a "Christian orchestra."

Her first pulpit in Los Angeles was at Victoria Hall; she hung out a banner eight feet high and fifty feet long that proclaimed: "Aimee Semple McPherson—Lady Evangelist—Nightly at 7:30 P.M. Full orchestra, choir, Holy Ghost revival." She was, she told the enraptured men and women who thronged Victoria Hall, "just a little woman, God's handmaiden, the least of all saints." The glory of the success of her mission went not to her, "not even to our marvelous Christian orchestra and this awesome two-hundred voice choir," but to the Almighty.

Glory followed on glory: the Angelus Temple, built of steel and concrete to last through the ages; a radio program beamed from the temple; "a radio station of sacred word and song in Los Angeles, California," which broadcast the *Sunshine Hour;* a five-story Bible school called the Lighthouse of International Foursquare Evangelism, or LIFE. The temple counted 10,000 members, and its float won the Tournament of Roses' first prize in 1924. The rich and famous were as susceptible as the poor and obscure; Hollywood stars proved especially susceptible. Young Anthony Quinn, an aspiring actor, was fourteen when he "met the most magnetic personality I was ever to encounter." The most gifted actresses "all fell short of that first electric shock Aimee Semple McPherson produced in me," he wrote years later.

McPherson began seeing a good deal of Ken Ormiston, her sound engineer at the Angelus Temple and a married man. In January, 1926, she announced that she was taking a long-delayed vacation. It was, in fact, a clandestine journey with Ormiston. The "vacation" ended with a triumphant meeting in the Royal Albert Hall in London on Easter Day. She returned at the end of April to her adoring congregation and was welcomed by the acting mayor of Los Angeles. Three weeks later, on May 18, 1926, she disappeared, and newspaper extras announced: "Evangelist McPherson Believed Drowned." She had last been seen swimming, far out in the ocean. The news of her disappearance was greeted with hysteria. In the auditorium of the Bible school 15,000 of her followers gathered to pray for her, while hundreds more kept an all-night vigil at the beach where she was last seen. Some had to be restrained from joining her in what was presumed to be her watery final resting place. Rumors spread that she would rise from the sea on the third day after her disappearance. Other rumors circulated that she was alive and well. It was reported that she had been seen here or there; that she had been kidnapped by the Mafia; that she was being held for ransom; that an evil-looking man had killed her and eaten her body to destroy the evidence; that she had been devoured by a shark, or, more appropriately biblical, swallowed by a whale. Concessionaires began selling posters showing her rising from the sea. At least one man drowned while swimming in search of her body. Every new rumor spawned another newspaper extra. One by-product of the public attention concentrated on the coastal waters of the Pacific Ocean was that bootleggers' ships, which were accustomed to discharging their cargoes along the beaches south of the city, were driven off, and Los Angeles grew perilously dry.

For a month there was no trace of Aimee Semple McPherson, or none that could be verified. Then her mother received a ransom note demanding $500,000 for the return of her daughter. Minnie, apparently well aware that Aimee had slipped away with Ken Ormiston, kept the note secret. McPherson finally emerged from the Arizona desert on June 23 at the little town of Douglas with a lurid tale of kidnapping and escape. "Woman Evangelist Escapes Abductors," a *New York Times* headline read. "Aimee Tortured for Huge Ransom," the *Los Angeles Examiner* announced more familiarly. But as enterprising reporters poked about, the story seemed more and more suspect. The kidnappers' cabin, from which she professed to have escaped, could not be located within any reasonable radius of Douglas. She was in remarkably good condition to have undergone such an ordeal: Her shoes were hardly scuffed, and there were no signs that she had suffered from a searing sun. The accumulation of evidence that the story was a fabrication, evidence that finally induced the police to file charges against her for obstructing justice, did not shake the faith of the faithful. Her return to California was a triumphal procession with thousands of followers crowding the stations through which her train passed. Fifty thousand cheering believers greeted her when she arrived in Los Angeles. Back at the Angelus Temple she went on the air to assure her listeners that she was alive and well. "God bless you all! I'm just bubbling over with *joy!*" she exclaimed.

Second only to Aimee Semple McPherson as a popular evangelist in Southern California was the Reverend Bob Shuler, the Lord's avenger, who had won fame by catching the Los Angeles police chief in bed with a young woman whose husband and brother were notorious criminals. Not surprisingly, Shuler was among the skeptics who publicly doubted Aimee Semple McPherson's story.

But she and the temple and the Foursquare Gospel Church all survived and, indeed, flourished, and when Aimee Semple McPherson died in 1944 of an overdose of sleeping pills, thousands of the faithful passed by her body at the Angelus Temple. Carey McWilliams, chronicler of California's vagaries, wrote that the whole episode was "a kind of compendium of all the pervading nonsense, cynicism, credulity, speakeasy wit, passion for debunkery, sex-craziness and music-hall pornography of the times."

In the history of religion in America the tale of Aimee Semple McPherson merits no more than a footnote, but it does serve to remind us of the character of that stream of emotional Christianity generally called the Pentecostal, from the descent of the spirit at Pentecost ("And they were all filled with the Holy Ghost, and began to speak with other tongues, as the Spirit gave them utterance" Acts 2:4). The religious life of seventeen-year-old Aimee Kennedy had begun with the ecstatic experience of speaking with tongues. The Pentecostalists might or might not believe in the inerrancy of the Bible, but what was central to their experience was the emotional surrender to the power of the Holy Spirit. And that was a current that, as we have noted, reached back to colonial New England and countless "freshenings of the spirit." The ubiquitousness of revivals and revivalists in the 1920s was evidence of the disposition of Americans to turn everything into entertainment. But it must also be understood as a measure of public demoralization. The state of the nation seemed incomprehensible. The angry and accusatory voices of the two Americas spread confusion and alarm. The revivals, bizarre as they were, provided some relief. The revivalists spoke of love and repentance and damnation, and in doing so, they reattached many Americans to a tradition that seemed imperiled by forces too complex to understand, forces that were generally denominated "modernist," that emanated primarily from New York or its West Coast offspring, Los Angeles.

The principal target of the revivalists was theological liberalism, typically the doctrines of the so-called Social Gospel. The liberal Christian was denounced as both a spineless and a godless Socialist or Communist (Billy Sunday called him a "hog-jowled, weasel-eyed, sponge-columned, jelly-spined, pussy-footing, four-flushing, charlotte-russed Christian").

The fragmentation of the Protestant churches continued. The sociologist Anton Boisen noted that in the small Midwestern town that he studied, a town with a population of scarcely 1,200, there were six different Presbyterian churches, among them the New School Presbyterian, the Old School Presbyterian, the Associate Reformed Presbyterian, and, in the county, two Cumberland Presbyterian churches. The Disciples of Christ, the Methodists, and the Baptists were also strongly represented. Among the thirty-three churches in the town and its environs were three Pentecostal Assemblies of Jesus Christ, two Churches of the Nazarene, an Assembly of God, a Church of God, a Church of Christ, a Foursquare Gospel Church, and a Free Methodist Church.

Substantial numbers of middle-class Americans continued to believe that the mind could control matter, that good health was the result of good thoughts. The Christian Scientists grew in numbers, and other "science of mind" sects held their own. The Church of Latter-Day Saints dominated the state of Utah and was strongly represented in the neighboring states of Idaho and Montana as well as in California. It was especially well prepared to meet the exigencies of the Depression. Since the faithful were organized in "wards," the church through its bishops provided for the needy out of its own stores.

Father Francis X. Talbot, a Jesuit, the Catholic contributor to Harold Stearns's *America Now,* described the dilemma of the American Catholic plainly enough. "There is no blinking the fact that the non-Catholic American has as much difficulty in understanding the Catholic soul and spirit as the Catholic American has in plumbing the intricacies of the minds and emotions of the non-Catholic citizen. The Catholic church is forever being misunderstood and misjudged; and it is continually asserting itself in such ways that it gives cause for new misjudgments. . . . Being materialistic, naturalistic, agnostic, turning rapidly to a neo-paganism, [American society] creates an environment that tends to stifle the Catholic spirituality and supernaturalism. Being capitalistic, idolizing wealth, it weakens the Catholic insistence on authority and absolute truth. Animated by a flair for license of behavior, it vitiates the Catholic concept of chastity and control. Truly the Catholic church must struggle in America to keep itself true to its traditions and ideals."

What is perhaps most striking about the passage, besides its paranoid air, is its easy assumption that non-Catholic America is agnostic and materialistic (as well as "naturalistic" and "liberalistic"). Father Talbot ignored the Protestant America that in the aggregate outnumbered Catholic America by a substantial margin and was hardly less critical of materialism and naturalism.

By the late twenties a number of intellectual bellwethers were beginning to be alarmed by the decline in morals and the general psychic disarray of the new intellectual class. Critics like Walter Lippmann, Herbert Croly, Lincoln Steffens, and Waldo Frank evinced a vague religiosity. Lippmann was plainly describing himself when he wrote of those Americans "no longer moved" by the "stale echoes" of the "romantic age in politics," when people thought that they might create a more just and humane society. Such an individual was "a man back from a crusade to make the world something or other it did not become; he has been tantalized too often by the foam of events, has seen the gas go out of it." Lippmann called for a new "religion of the spirit." He wrote: "In an age when custom is dissolved and authority is broken, the religion of the spirit is not merely a possible way of life. In principle it is the only way which transcends the difficulties. . . . A religion which rests upon particular conclusions in astronomy, biology, and history may be fatally injured by the discovery of new truths. But the religion of the spirit does not depend upon creeds and cosmologies; it has no vested interest in any particular truth. It is concerned not with the organization of matter but with the quality of human desire."

For Lippmann, Frank, and others of a similar inclination, the key word was "spiritual." Americans must achieve a new spiritual quality. Spirituality must replace materialism. The language in which they advocated the new spirituality was reminiscent of the mid-nineteenth-century transcendentalism of Ralph Waldo Emerson and William Ellery Channing. Like the transcendentalists, the champions of new religiosity were attracted by the "world religions," especially Buddhism, and the ideal of "world unity" on some not-very-well-defined spiritual level. John Herman Randall, the bête noire of the fundamentalists, was a prominent figure in the movement, as was Kirtley Mather, the Harvard geology professor who helped prepare Clarence Darrow for his grilling of Bryan at the Scopes trial. Indeed, it is hard not to suspect that the world unity movement was, to a degree, an outgrowth of the trial.

In the fall of 1927 the World Unity Foundation published the first edition of a magazine by that name. Its purpose was "to interpret and record those significant changes in present-day thought [which] mark the trend toward worldwide understanding and a humanized civilization able to release the finer aspirations of mankind. . . . The emergence of new and higher values in philosophy, science, religion, ethics and the arts from the alembic of universal unrest represents the focal point of vision for the World Unity Magazine." The editors were not concerned with "political, economic, sectarian matters . . . or . . . any concrete program." They wished only to respond "to the uprush of the spirit of the age." It was in essence a protest against the "extremes of purposeless culture and self-centered propaganda. . . ." The contributing editors included Havelock Ellis, Kahlil Gibran, Charlotte Perkins Gilman, Alain Locke (the black scholar and patron of Langston Hughes), and Frank Lloyd Wright, along with a scattering of Chinese, Japanese, and Indian scholars and gurus, including Ng Poon Chew. In the lead essay John Herman Randall wrote of the eternal struggle between the "forces of light and darkness, of truth and error, of good and evil." All these could be reduced to a contest between those forces working for unity and those working for disunity. What was necessary, above everything else, was "a fellowship between races and nations and classes and individuals that has never yet been experienced." The principal enemies were *"nationalism,"* a combination of the most obsolete and retrograde notions; *"class-consciousness";* and *"the spirit of religious sectarianism."* Randall concluded: "The great prophets of religion have always voiced their message in universal terms. It is their followers who build ecclesiastical barriers and create creedal boundaries which divide the members of God's human family here upon earth."

The theme of the leading article by Charles Henry Rieber, dean of the University of California at Los Angeles, was that all the great religions shared the same basic doctrines, above all, the Golden Rule: Do unto others as you would have them do unto you.

Mary Siegrist, a popular writer on "spiritual subjects," told the readers of *World Unity:* "In the New Age that is being brought to birth, the Spirit of poetry, of art and of science will move in ever-widening wave-lengths of freedom and its breath will be upon and will inform all men. The vibrations of the vaster rhythms—the Jubilate of creation from the ocean of Cosmic Harmony—will be heard of all the reverently listening ones. . . . The little brothers and sisters of St. Francis . . . will be authentic citizens of the new World State." The result will be "sharpened spiritual powers and enlarged capacities of perceptions. . . ."

Kirtley Mather endorsed prayer, which, he wrote, "puts at the disposal of the Transcendental Spirit a tool, which, however weak or tiny it may be, is nevertheless indispensable in the project of creating a world which will be an adequate expression of the nature of God."

As might be expected from Mather's involvement, a major theme of *World Unity* was the absence of any real conflict between science and religion. A regular department of the magazine was titled "The Wisdom of the Ages" and contained, typically, quotations from the Koran, the Talmud, the Bible, and the Upanishads: "Brahma is He who, dwelling in all things, yet is other than all things, whom all things know, whose body all things are, who controls all things from within—He is your Soul, the Inner Controller, the Immortal."

World Unity was closely allied with the English Oxford Group, a "spiritual" pacifist movement, appealing, Edmund Wilson wrote in a cruel phrase, "to the best people and their butlers."

The onset of the Depression posed a special challenge to the Christian churches. They met in a variety of ways. To many Pentecostalists, Evangelicals, fundamentalists, and millenarians (the categories often overlapped), the onset of the Depression was simply the final chapter of human history. They anticipated the Day of Judgment with the return of Christ to rule 1,000 years on earth. The *Moody Bible Institute Monthly* called on its readers to prepare for the millennium. The organ of the beleaguered Social Gospelers, the *Social Service Bulletin* of the Methodist Federation for Social Service, took a very different line, announcing the demise of capitalism and calling for the creation of a new social order. In Donald Meyer's words, "between these extremes of professional millenarian fundamentalism and professional [earthly] millenarian radicalism, Protestantism as a whole [stood] entangled in the crisis, socially, financially, ethically, and also theologically."

For many churches the most immediate practical concerns came to be helping feed the hungry and find shelter for the homeless. From the Social Gospel wing of Protestantism came an early call for Federal programs to aid the unemployed. The Federal Council of Churches gave its support early in 1931 to a public works program and unemployment insurance. It joined with the National Catholic Welfare Council and the Central Committee of American Rabbis to sponsor a conference on Permanent Preventatives of Unemployment. Increasingly church leaders began to speak of the collapse of capitalism as an accepted fact and to endorse some form of non-Marxist socialism. Again the Methodist district conferences took the lead. In 1932 the New York East Conference unanimously endorsed public ownership of the principal means of production and distribution. The Pittsburgh Conference announced that the "only alternative to the present system is one in which social ownership and control is gradually and widely inaugurated and developed. . . ." A meeting of Methodist directors of religious education referred to the "essential bankruptcy of the present industrial capitalistic regime" as a working assumption.

In a poll taken by the *World Tomorrow*, out of some 20,000 ministers who replied, 28 percent declared themselves advocates of some form of socialism. The Methodists, with 34 percent, led, followed by the Congregationalists and the Evangelicals (33 percent), down to 19 percent for the Presbyterians and 12 percent for the Lutherans. In the larger cities the percentage of Protestant ministers supporting socialism was substantially larger, nearly 50 percent. The editors of the *World Tomorrow* wrote: "Among all the trades, occupations, and professions in the country, few can produce as high a percentage of Socialists as can the ministry." The most prominent leaders of the Protestant churches—Bishop Francis J. McConnell of the Methodists; Sherwood Eddy, international chairman of the YMCA, and Reinhold Niebuhr— endorsed some form of socialism. The most radical wing of Protestantism continued to be the Methodist Federation for Social Service, led throughout most of its existence by Harry Ward, the fiery apostle of the Social Gospel (the historian Donald Meyer has called it the "prophetic headquarters within Methodism"). The Federal Council of Churches was the interdenominational voice of the Social Gospel and "its highest platform."

One response of the Protestant ministry to the Depression was the formation in 1930 of the Fellowship of Socialist Christians. Like secular intellectuals, most of the Protestant ministers of socialist inclination placed their faith in the workers. Niebuhr did so not because he believed that the workers had escaped the taint of original sin but because he believed that the capitalist class had been corrupted by wealth and power and that the very powerlessness of the workers was their strength. The coincidence between the workers' demand for social and economic justice and the urgent need of the larger society for radical reform made them, in his view, the key element in the transformation of American capitalism. However, as distinguished from doctrinaire Marxists, Niebuhr had no illusion that the workers would somehow remain uncorrupted by power if and when they achieved it. Their role was to *initiate the process* rather than to preside over its consequences. In biblical terms, God chooses the "things which are not, to bring to nought the things that are."

The seminaries of the various Protestant churches were hotbeds of radical sentiment. Elizabeth Bentley, as one of her early party assignments, was instructed to sign up a young theology student at the Union Theological Seminary. When Bentley asked him why he wanted to join the party, the man she called Edwin in her autobiography, "with eyes aglow," replied, "The old Christianity is dead, Elizabeth. Christ came to this earth to preach the brotherhood of man, but most people seem to have forgotten. They are too immersed in making money and getting ahead in the world. I've always wanted to be a minister of Christ, but somehow, until I discovered the doctrine of Communism, I was nauseated with the rotten hypocrisy of the average churchgoer, not to mention the attitude of the clergy. . . . I am convinced that Communism is the Christianity of the future, that I, as a potential Christian minister, must *per se* be a Communist, even though it will be a very hard life." He had placed his life in the hands of God, he told Bentley, and he was confident that the Lord would guide him aright.

Vanderbilt Theological Seminary was also a center for Christian radicals. In addition to Howard Kester, Claude Williams, also a Vanderbilt Seminary graduate, was active in the Southern Tenant Farmers' Union. He had been discharged from his Presbyterian parish in Paris, Arkansas, for heretical political opinions and badly beaten by vigilantes after a union meeting. He joined the Communist Party not long afterward.

In many cities the various Protestant churches took the lead in helping their congregations cope with the Depression. They also provided forums for discussions of social and political issues in which the dominant tone was decidedly radical. More conservative churchmen spoke contemptuously of "pink religion," but in Minneapolis the rector of the Wesley Methodist Church, George Mecklenburg, started the Organized Unemployed, Inc. to initiate various cooperative enterprises. It enrolled 7,000 unemployed, who were paid in scrip they had printed themselves. "Capitalism is beginning to sense that there are only two roads that it can follow," Mecklenburg told Frazier Hunt. "One is the trail of co-operative brotherhood; the other is the red road of Communism. There is no middle road. Here in Minneapolis the group of rich men we thought were against us—I mean, against the whole new conception of the Christian's duty toward the common man—well, they're more and more on our side. They figure that the world has made a frightful mess of things and they want to find the way out."

In the Broadway Church in Cleveland hungry and disillusioned men and women gathered to debate the country's future. The minister organized a forum to discuss Russian communism. Another young minister had just returned from Russia, and Frazier Hunt, somewhat of an expert on the basis of his two visits to the Soviet Union, was invited to participate. "The sky is the limit," the minister told him. The topic debated was the degree to which Soviet communism might be applicable to the United States.

Hunt heard a young red-headed minister in a Chicago working-class district tell his congregation that if the church failed to provide leadership in essential reforms, "the world will fail. No honest preacher, priest, or rabbi can dodge the square-cut issue. Something must be done right now toward remaking the sorely pressed world." All that was needed was "a new injection of the real spirit of Jesus, the brave and uncompromising revolutionary leader." Most of the predominant middle-class Protestant suburban churches rallied to the defense of capitalism. In the rural areas, in the small towns of the Middle and Far West, in the rare working-class churches, a radical spirit was manifested.

Sociologist Anton Boisen discovered that the congregations of Pentecostal churches weathered the severe psychological strains of the Depression far better than the members of what he called the "churches of custom," the old-line Protestant denominations—the Methodists, Baptists, Lutherans, Presbyterians, Episcopalians, Congregationalists, Unitarians. There was a far higher percentage of breakdowns and suicides among the members of those denominations than among the Pentecostalists or Holiness sects, which grew rapidly, increasing their combined membership by more than 50 percent (the churches of custom decreased 11 percent in the same period, from 26,000,000 to 23,000,000).

The churches of custom, Boisen argued, were unable to counteract, in most instances, the sense of personal failure that affected the members of the more prosperous middle-class congregations in the depths of the Depression. He divided the middle-class congregations into "types": the "complacent," "difficult," "defeated," and "distressed." The churches attended by these individuals had little, it turned out, to offer them in the way of help or consolation. Their principal interest was in defending or imposing conventional morality. For those suffering various psychic disorders and stresses, the repressive theology of the churches of custom offered cold comfort. On the other hand, the "testifying," the singing and shouting, the emotional outpourings that were the essence of the Pentecostal and Holiness sects gave an outlet to frustration and despair. Problems, mental and physical sufferings, were shared with others. Sins were confessed, and feelings of guilt alleviated. In Boisen's words, the church meetings "may . . . bring new life and hope and tap new sources of power." They accomplished this, in large part, by their otherworldly orientation. They were not, in the main, concerned with social problems. Depression, hardship, suffering were part of the human lot, ordained by the Almighty. The reward for faith was to be found in heaven, not on earth. Such episodes as wars, plagues, and depressions were either the inscrutable punishments of the Lord or mere transitory events. At the same time a deep strain of popular democracy ran like a thread through the Pentecostal and Holiness churches. They were made up, in the main, of the poor, the outcast, the despised, the socially and economically marginal. They were related to the Populists and other "people's" movements and impulses. Their congregations voted for Franklin Roosevelt and his New Deal.

On the other hand, the socialist inclinations of the many Protestant clergy apparently had little influence on their flocks. In the major Protestant denominations only 54 percent of the Baptists voted for Roosevelt in the presidential election of 1936, and the Baptist support was undoubtedly due in large part to the strength of that denomination in the South. Only 47 percent of the Methodists expressed a preference for the President, and the number of his supporters fell rapidly in the other main-line Protestant denominations: Presbyterian and Episcopalian 37 percent and Congregationalists 22 percent.

The most significant development in the Catholic Church in this period was little noticed. Dorothy Day was the daughter of a peripatetic sportswriter. One of her earliest memories was of the San Francisco earthquake. Growing up in a working-class section of Chicago after her parents had moved east, Day identified from childhood with the hard lives of the poor and admired their struggle to endow them with touches of beauty. She remembered all her life the "odor of geranium leaves, tomato plants, marigolds; the smell of lumber, of tar, of roasting coffee; the smell of good bread and rolls and coffee cake coming from the small German bakeries."

At sixteen Dorothy Day enrolled at the University of Illinois. There she read omnivorously and found herself drawn especially to the great

Russian novelists Tolstoy, Dostoyevsky, and Gorky. When the family moved to New York City, she plunged into the exotic life of Greenwich Village. In a bar called Hell Hole she established a reputation as a formidable drinker. There she listened to her friend Eugene O'Neill, already recognized as a prospective genius, recite Francis Thompson's "The Hound of Heaven."

> I fled Him, down the nights and down the days;
>     I fled Him, down the arches of the years;
> I fled Him, down the labyrinthine ways
>     Of my own mind; and in the mist of tears
> I hid from Him, and under running laughter.
>
> . . . . . . . . . . . .
>
> Fear wist not to evade as Love wist to pursue.
>     Still with unhurrying chase,
>     And unperturbed pace,
> Deliberate speed, majestic instancy,
>     Come on the following Feet,
>     And a Voice above their beat—
> "Naught shelters thee, who wilt not shelter Me."

The poem had a special poignance for Dorothy Day. She knew that O'Neill, reared a Catholic, was also fleeing Him as he would all his life, always fleeing, always pursued. When the bar closed, O'Neill and Day would stagger out into the chill night air. She would put O'Neill to bed and lie beside him to warm him with her body's heat. He, she recalled, would ask, "Dorothy, do you want to surrender your virginity?" She always demurred.

For a decade, from 1917 to 1927, Day worked as an increasingly radical journalist, active in various Communist Party activities. In 1924 a Hollywood studio paid her $5,000 for the film rights of a novel, *The Eleventh Virgin*. It was an enormous sum for the time. Day bought a cottage on Staten Island and shared it with a radical friend, Forster Batterham, a biologist who became her lover. She had a child by him, named Tamar, and soon afterward became a Roman Catholic. "I knew that I was going to have my child baptized, cost what it may," she wrote. "I knew that I was not going to have her floundering through many years as I had done, doubting and hesitating, undisciplined and amoral. I felt that it was the greatest thing I could do for my child." The church would be the family she desired. Her Communist friends, prominent among them Mike Gold, gave her the cold shoulder. She had sinned against the party by giving her allegiance to another religion—worst of all, to Catholicism.

In 1932, covering the Communist-led hunger march on Washington as a journalist, Day was overwhelmed by a sense of guilt at having abandoned her political activism for personal salvation. The devotion of the Communists to the cause of the poor and unemployed was a reproach to her. "I stood on the curb and watched them, joy and pride in the courage of this band of men and women mounting in my heart, and with it a bitterness too that since I was now a Catholic with fundamental philosophical differences, I could not be out there with them. I could write, I could protest, to arouse the conscience, but where was the Catholic leadership in the gathering of the bands of men and women together, for the actual works of mercy that the comrades had always made a part of their technique in reaching out to the workers?

"How little, how puny my work had been since becoming a Catholic, I thought. How self-centered, how ingrown, how lacking in a sense of community."

Back in New York she shared her feelings with a young friend, Peter Maurin, a kind of "holy bum" with a vision of community that matched Day's. They decided to set up Houses of Hospitality for the poor and hungry, for, indeed, anyone who wished to serve the Lord in poverty and humility by helping others. They started a penny newspaper called the *Catholic Worker* in the spring of 1933 (distinguished by its unpretentiousness and quality art and graphics). It was also part of their plan to establish farming communes as models for Christian community life. Day had a great gift for drawing people to her, for making them "part of her family." At the same time she was tough and down to earth; a cigarette dangled constantly from her lips. When a young disciple asked her if she had visions, she replied, "Horseshit! Just visions of unpaid bills." She wrote of her work: "Yes, we have lived with the poor, with the workers . . . the unemployed, the sick. . . . We have all known the long loneliness, and we have learned that the only solution is love and that love comes with community." As one of her biographers put it, she made the "radical Christian idealism [of the Catholic Worker movement] seem homey as well." To make the world a home for the lost and homeless was her dream.

As Day described the beginnings of the *Catholic Worker,* "We were just sitting there when Peter Maurin came in. We were just sitting there talking when lines of people began to form, saying, 'We need bread.' We could not say 'Go, be thou filled.' If there was six small loaves and a few fishes, we had to divide them. There was always bread.

"We were just sitting there talking and people moved in on us. Let those who can take it, take it. Some moved out and made room for more. And somehow the walls expanded.

"We were just sitting there talking and someone said, 'Let's all go live on a farm.'"

In the strange workings of history Dorothy Day and her eccentric, marginal Catholic "hippie" communes found their way eventually into the hearts of the lords of the church—bishops and cardinals—and turned them to a deeper concern for the needs of the poor and the requirements of peace.

The Depression and the New Deal served to liberalize the Catholic Church itself; in the presidential election of 1936, 78 percent of all Catholics voted for Roosevelt. Father Charles Coughlin began his radio career as a strong supporter of the New Deal. Catholic labor unions were a major component in the labor movement, and while they were vigorously anti-Communist, they were often radical on specific issues. Although Coughlin's virulent anti-Semitism and increasing hostility to the President finally brought him down, his denunciations of capitalism and his radical stand on many social and economic issues had served, somewhat paradoxically, to move many Catholics to the left. Just as the South, deeply conservative, not to say reactionary, on so many issues, provided the political base for the radical innovations of the New Deal, so American Catholics, also inherently conservative, were equally a mainstay. The loss of either constituency would have imperiled the success of the New Deal.

American Jews had moved, in the generation or more since their arrival in the United States, far from European orthodoxy. There were, to be sure, Orthodox congregations, but even these were a far cry from their Old World counterparts. Conservative and Reform Jews were further removed, and many Jews found their homes in the Ethical Culture movement and in radical politics that rejected religion entirely. Nevertheless, a deep racial consciousness persisted.

Eighty-two percent of American Jews supported Roosevelt, and Jews were prominent in his inner circle of advisers. Sam Rosenman had been one of the early members of that inner circle, a confidant and speech writer. Herbert Lehman had been a close friend and political ally in New York. The prominent Jewish financier Henry Morgenthau, Jr., was a member of Roosevelt's Cabinet and also part of his inner circle. Felix Frankfurter was in the Roosevelt Kitchen Cabinet. Roosevelt admired Louis Brandeis and considered himself in some degree a disciple of his. Benjamin Cohen became another member of the inner circle: The New Deal was filled with brilliant young Jews, many of them protégés of Frankfurter. Roosevelt's enemies called it the "Jew Deal," and anti-Semites marked him as their enemy. But Jewish support for the New Deal went beyond pride in the fact that Jews apeared for the first time as a major influence in the highest circles of government. Jews had a long tradition of concern for social justice. Eastern European Jews had a tradition of radical politics as well. They provided an important part of the leadership of the Communist Party (and all the various deviations of the left), and those for whom the Communist Party was too strong a medicine naturally gravitated to the New Deal.

The most important figure to emerge from what we might call the theological revival stimulated, if not caused, by the Depression was Reinhold Niebuhr. Niebuhr was born in Wright City, Missouri, in 1892. His father was a German immigrant and a minister in the Evangelical Synod of North America, a denomination that combined Lutheran and Calvinistic doctrines. Having decided at the age of ten to become a minister himself, young Niebuhr left public school at fifteen and entered his denomination's seminary. He was graduated five years later, at the age of twenty, an ordained minister. In 1913 Niebuhr was admitted to the Yale Divinity School for two years of graduate study. In that rarefied atmosphere he was acutely conscious of his small-town Midwestern origins. He felt, he wrote a friend, "like a mongrel among thoroughbreds."

The war and the bitter divisions that it created between the Anglophilic East and the isolationist West and, even more painful, the hostility it evoked toward Americans of German ancestry helped turn Niebuhr toward Christian pacifism, with strong socialist overtones. The aggressively atheistic character of Russian Marxism afforded, ironically, some protection from the witch-hunting spirit of the early twenties to Christian socialists and Christian radicals generally. The Red hunters did not know quite how to categorize the Christian socialists.

A pastor in Detroit's Bethel Evangelical Church, Niebuhr became a leading preacher in Sherwood Eddy's crusade on college campuses.

He played a prominent role in the Fellowship for a Christian Social Order, founded in 1921. In 1926, when Detroit automobile manufacturers, alarmed at what they considered the increasing radicalization of their workers, began a campaign aimed at silencing criticism from the liberal churches, Niebuhr took on Henry Ford, denouncing his assembly line speedup and calling his famous $5-a-day wage a fraud on his workers.

In 1928 Niebuhr was appointed to the faculty of the Union Theological Seminary in New York City, where he soon became that institution's leading light and helped make it the best-known liberal Protestant seminary in the country. Four years later his *Moral Man and Immoral Society* officially launched the movement known as Neo-Orthodoxy, although there had certainly been intimations of it as early as 1910, when Shailer Mathews of the Chicago Divinity School protested that the basic teachings of the Gospels were being neglected in the church's concern with social reform. Niebuhr's thesis was as simple as it was startling: "The dream of perpetual peace and brotherhood for human society is one that will never be fully realized." He wrote: "It is because a philosophy of the enlightened mind and a civilization of great technical power cannot solve these ultimate problems of human existence that the frame of meaning established by the traditionally historic religions has become much more relevant to the modern man than seemed possible a century ago. There is in these religions a sense of mystery and meaning which outrages the canons of pure rationality but which makes 'sense' out of life."

Niebuhr insisted that the notion of the fall, of man as a fallen creature, tainted, as Genesis stated, with the original sin of Adam in his disobedience to God's injunctions, must be taken seriously as an irresistible metaphor for man's true nature. At the moment when Genesis was proving an embarrassment to liberal theologians, dismayed by the fundamentalists' attack on the notion of evolution, Niebuhr gave it a special relevance. The story of Adam and Eve was a story not of sexual misbehavior but of disobedience, of human pride and willfulness that set itself against the dictates of the Lord. The heart *was*, as the prophet Jeremiah said, "deceitful above all *things*, and desperately wicked: who can know it?" the prophet added. (The verse called up William Manning's eighteenth-century essay *The Key to Libberty*, in which Manning had argued that "self-love and self-aggrandizement" were the principal impediments to perceiving and following the will of the Almighty.)

With close attention to the Scriptures and the classic teachings of the church, Niebuhr set about to reconstruct contemporary Christian doctrine, making it more relevant to the needs of the time. He stressed repeatedly the naïveté of believing that "moral man" could perfect himself or his society. In *Moral Man and Immoral Society* he pointed out the inherent ambiguity and the psychic tension that followed from the effort to live a moral life in a society and a world which, it might be said, *required* evasions. He called for a new "Christian realism" that accepted the contingent and compromised character of all human actions and yet kept always in view the necessity for the Christian to enlarge constantly the arena in which Christ's compassion for the poor and oppressed was expressed in human actions. He warned, in words that echoed those of the Founding Fathers, of the inevitable abuse of power. If men and women were tainted by original sin, power could only accentuate greed ("self-aggrandizement") and vanity. To Niebuhr "realism" meant taking into account "all factors in social and political situation, which offer resistance to established norms," especially the factors of "self-interest and power."

He wrote: "All life is an expression of power. Human life, as other life, must have power to exist. The relation of life to life is, therefore, a relation of power to power. All truth is spoken from a perspective. It is, therefore, however subtle, a weapon of the ego, individual or collective, against another. It is a tool of conflict. This is the truth in the Marxist theory of ideology and, more profoundly, the Christian doctrine of original sin." It is only the Christ on the cross who is "completely powerless," who reveals to us "the goodness of God and reminds us of the terrible ambiguity of power. Christianity sees in this act on the Cross not only the revelation of the ultimate character of God, but of the essential character of man."

The believers in progress through the use of reason and its handmaiden, science, do not recognize, Niebuhr argued, "that when collective power, whether in the form of imperialism or class domination, exploits weakness, it can never be dislodged unless power is raised against it. If conscience and reason can be insinuated into the resulting struggle they can only qualify but not abolish it." To Niebuhr the "most persistent error of modern educators and moralists is the assumption that our social difficulties are due to the failure of the social sciences to keep pace with the physical sciences which have created our technological civilization."

While, in Niebuhr's view, Marx had developed brilliant tools for social analysis, the materialism and "moral cynicism" of Marxism fatally compromised it. *Moral Man and Immoral Society* was, as much as anything, an extended critique of Marxist utopianism, indeed of all utopian schemes as inevitably authoritarian and manipulative. They all tried, in a manner of speaking, to bypass the problem of original sin; they wished to speed up, by force and coercion, the painfully slow process by means of which the individual's notion of the meaning of brotherhood and sisterhood grew larger and more generous. This was what Niebuhr referred to as their "moral cynicism."

At the same time Niebuhr was equally severe in his criticism of capitalism. The Depression had had the positive effect of destroying "some of our illusions," he argued. "We can no longer buy the highest satisfactions of the individual life at the expense of social injustice. . . . Must we not warn powerful and secure nations and classes that they have an idolatrous idea of their own importance and that as surely as they say, 'I sit as a queen and shall never know sorrow,' so surely shall 'in one moment her sorrow come?' . . . Must we not say to the rich and secure classes of society that their vaunted devotion to the laws and structures of society which guarantee their privileges is tainted with self-interest; and must we not say to the poor that their dream of a propertyless society of perfect justice turns into a nightmare of new injustice because it is based only upon the recognition of the sin which the other commits and knows nothing of the sin the poor man commits when he is no longer poor but has become a commissar? Everywhere life is delivered unto death because it is ensnared in self-delusion and practices every evasion rather than meet the true God." Freedom without community led, Niebuhr wrote, "to man making himself his own end." On the other hand, "no historic community deserves the final devotion of man"; that was owed only to God.

Niebuhr's conviction that the human community was one made him impatient with the isolationist passion of his countrymen. "The plight of Europe is tragic enough," he wrote. "If we cannot see it as a tragedy in which we are all involved, we merely add the cruelty of Pharisees to the cruelty of nationalistic pagans."

The "irony of American history" seemed to Niebuhr to lie in the fact that Americans had little or no understanding of the distortions produced in the individual as well as the collective psyche by the self-righteous use of power. It never occurred to Americans, secure in their rectitude, that they could use power brutally or obtusely. It seemed to him the greatest defect in the American character—and the most dangerous as well as the most unchristian. One thinks again of the strange sentence of Emerson's "Great men, great nations, have not been boasters and buffoons, but perceivers of the terror of life and have manned themselves to face it." Because we were so woefully deficient in knowledge of our past, our innocence was potentially destructive; we failed to recognize any necessary limits to our announced good intentions to remake the world. That greed, ambition, and vainglory might masquerade as benignity was inconceivable to us. One consequence was that we often appeared hypocritical to the rest of the world when, in fact, we were simply naïve.

Niebuhr did what no American thinker or theologian had undertaken since the virtual disappearance of the Classical-Christian Consciousness (marked by the passing from the stage of the Founders); he revived that tradition, explored and extended it, and gave it a modern context. Shailer Mathews, dean of the Divinity School of the University of Chicago, had warned years earlier of the danger of the churches' losing their hold on the fundamentals of the Christian faith in their preoccupation with social reform, but Niebuhr was the first theologian to grasp that nettle. In doing so, he gave new life to a religious establishment the waning powers of which had left it very much on the defensive. Almost single-handedly Reinhold Niebuhr made Christian theology intellectually respectable once more. In consequence, his influence was felt far beyond theological schools and seminaries. Even the academic world lent an ear, although for the most part it simply abstracted such ideas—ambiguity, the contingent nature of all human actions, etc.—as suited it, while ignoring their specifically Christian grounding. The coincidental correspondence between Niebuhr's (or Christianity's) view of human nature and that of Sigmund Freud undoubtedly made certain of Niebuhr's concepts more acceptable to intellectuals.

In the words of Donald Meyer, "As a political religion, Marxism demonstrated that the crisis of Western politics was a crisis of religion, and the crisis of both religion and politics was identical with the fact that politics had become religion. . . . Neo-orthodoxy was what was left after faith in social science, in liberalism, in Marxism . . . was excluded."

# 38

## Education

To those whose notions of progress are primarily statistical, the 1920s saw notable progress in the realm of education. The number of pupils enrolled in kindergarten, primary, and secondary schools increased from 23,278,000 to 28,329,000 by the end of the decade. Kindergarten attendance increased substantially (from 481,000 to 723,000), while high school enrollments rose even more sharply, from 2,200,000 to 4,399,000. At the same time the number of high school graduates more than doubled, from 311,000 in 1920 to 667,000 in 1930, an increase from 16.3 percent of boys and girls of high school age to 28.8 percent. Illiteracy dropped from 6 percent to 4.3, and illiteracy among blacks from 23 percent to 16.4 percent. Junior colleges increased from 52 to 277, divided almost equally between public and private institutions. The number of students enrolled in colleges and universities rose from 589,000, or 4.7 percent of the college-age population, to 1,101,000, or 7.2 percent. Most striking, degrees conferred rose from 53,516 to 138,752. The number of doctorates awarded increased from 560 in 1920 to 2,071 in 1930.

What went on in the classroom was more difficult to measure. The principal changes in curriculum were directed toward a more practical and vocationally oriented education. The effect in public schools of John Dewey's teachings was strongly felt. Columbia University's Teachers College spread its influence across the country through the agency of normal schools or state teachers' colleges, which experienced a rapid growth. Courses in "civics," designed to produce knowledgeable citizens, replaced more traditional courses in history, especially English history, and much was heard of skills rather than information. Latin and Greek and foreign languages generally lost ground in favor of subjects more directly related to life in twentieth-century America.

The magic word was "consolidation." Elementary and secondary schools must be consolidated. A dozen small local schools must be made into one large school. Then the students could have all kinds of advantages, available only in the modern curriculum. Teachers could be experts in a subject but, even more important, in an "age-group." The paving of country roads and the improvement in transportation allowed for the introduction of school buses, a dazzling new phenomenon which whisked children from remote farms and villages to great gleaming new consolidated schools, with their splendid facilities—indoor toilets, cafeterias presided over by dietitians—and their new categories of educators: counselors, athletic coaches, vocational instructors, and child psychologists. In 1930 there were 150,000 one-room schools in the United States. Fifty years later there were fewer than 600, many of those in the Rocky Mountain region.

Higher education remained largely the province of the prosperous middle class, with a scattering of genteel poor and a few able and ambitious representatives of the working class. The private liberal arts colleges continued to do business much as they had done since the introduction of the elective system, largely through the influence of Charles Eliot's Harvard. State colleges and universities were considerably more democratic than private institutions, but much the same routine, lifeless instruction prevailed in both classes of institutions. Indeed, academic specialization made notable strides. Institutions, anxious to preserve or achieve academic respectability, began to exert pressure on their faculties to publish scholarly books and learned articles. Graduate instruction burgeoned, and undergraduate instruction increasingly took its tone and even the organization of its curriculum from the model of graduate study. Great attention was paid to footnotes and bibliographies, a trend that William James had noted and deplored at the turn of the century. Professors strove to be as "scientific" as possible, even though their subject might be Elizabethan literature or the Georgian poets. Enthusiasm was frowned on lest it incline its possessor to be less than objective in his treatment of his subject. Courses were more and more commonly devised to conform to the research interests of professors rather than to the needs of the students. Like James, John Jay Chapman had deplored the aridity of a Harvard education (comparing it to hell) and the disposition to dismiss young instructors who showed too much enthusiasm.

The last flicker of Protestant Christianity in the academic world was represented by the so-called New Humanists, whose principal prophets were Paul Elmer More and Irving Babbitt. Babbitt, a Harvard professor and a disciple of William Graham Sumner, announced: "The remedy for the evils of competition is found in the magnanimity of the strong and successful, and not in any sickly sentimentalizing over the lot of the underdog." While Babbitt and More claimed to be reasserting the principles of the Founding Fathers, the Fathers would have been astonished by the notion that anyone could be naïve enough to believe that the "strong and successful" could be counted on to rectify social "evils." They believed that it was in the nature of power to exploit weakness and that basic principle underlay all their efforts at constitution making; that was the burden of James Madison's *Tenth Federalist Paper,* and the delegates to the Federal Convention in the summer of 1787 were constantly reminded that it was the nature of the rich to exploit the poor. In the words of Gouverneur Morris, one of the most conservative members of the convention, "They always have, they always will."

Babbitt's credentials as a humanist, old or new, were clouded by his support for Mussolini. Babbitt proposed the "doctrine of the right man for the doctrine of the rights of man." A Mussolini might be "needed to save us from the American equivalent of a Lenin," Babbitt wrote. While there were certainly many Americans who shared his exalted view of the Italian dictator, such notions had precious little to do with "humanism." At Princeton More expressed similar, if less intemperate, sentiments. "I saw Paul Elmer More," Burton Rascoe wrote, "an erudite, scholarly, and religious man, adopt a socio-religio-aesthetic idea, the extension of Calvinism, and pursue it to the appalling conclusion, 'The rights of property are more important than the right to life.'" Such a notion was certainly foreign to Calvinism, that of the Geneva divine or its various American expressions, and not entirely fair to More. The fact is that the New Humanism, with its vaguely religious posturings, helped discredit whatever mild religious impulse still existed in the academic world. "My own feeling," Edmund Wilson (who had been a student of Babbitt's at Princeton) wrote Burton Rascoe, "is that Humanism is now a flattened corpse over which the whole army of American intelligence has passed, and it might as well be left for dead."

The general spirit of repression evident in the larger society was felt in the schools and universities. We have already taken note of the Scopes trial. The Florida legislature passed a "Concurrent Resolution" asserting "that it is improper and subversive to the best interest of the people of this State for any professor, teacher or instructor in the public schools or colleges of this State, supported in whole or in part by public taxation, to teach, or permit to be taught, atheism or agnosticism, or to teach as true, Darwinism, or any other hypothesis that links man in blood relationship to any other form of life."

In North Carolina a legislative committee tried to have all subversive books removed from the University of North Carolina library, a list which, in W. J. Cash's words, included the works of "every distinguished man who has lived since 1850."

In 1927 a professor at Winthrop College in South Carolina was fired for "modernism." A teacher at the Pennsylvania State Normal College was ousted for denouncing Coolidge's Nicaraguan policy. A professor at Northwestern was sacked for unorthodox religious views, and at the University of Washington a faculty member was fired for reading to his class Bertrand Russell's essay "What I Believe," which turned out to be not what the trustees of the university believed. The trustees of Amherst College fired its president, the well-known liberal philosopher Alexander Meiklejohn, because they were offended by his efforts to reform that liberal arts institution.

The ignorance of students was frequently demonstrated and deplored. For example, freshmen at the University of Maine believed that Henry James was a train robber, Martin Luther was the son of Moses (who was identified as a Roman emperor), and Shakespeare was the author of *Vanity Fair*.

At the end of the 1920s Abraham Flexner, whose survey of American medical education had led to sweeping reforms, turned his attention to American colleges and universities. He described the great American universities as "composed of three parts: they are secondary schools and colleges for boys and girls; graduate and professional schools for advanced students; 'service' stations for the general public. The three sorts are not distinct; the college is confused with the 'service' station and overlaps the graduate school; the graduate school is partly a college, partly a vocational school, and partly an institution of university grade. . . ." It appeared to Flexner that "in the main the student body lacks intellectual background or outlook. . . . [The] students are in the mass devoid of cultural interests and develop little, for the most part, during their four years at college. . . . Where class instruction is pursued, the classes are usually too large; the young instructor's time is too largely consumed in correcting and grading papers, most of which are badly written." The system of "credits and units" seemed to Flexner "an abominable system, destructive of disinterested and protracted intellectual effort. . . . The hopelessness of America," in Flexner's words, lay "in the inability and unwillingness of those occupying seats of intelligence to distinguish between genuine culture and superficial veneer." Flexner accused university presidents of "Babbittry" and compared them to the "venders of patent medicines." He went on to list some sample Ph.D. dissertations offered by the department of home economics at the University of Chicago—such topics as "Variations in Demand for Clothing at Different Income Levels" and "Trends in Hosiery Advertising." To Flexner the solution was the establishment of exclusively postgraduate institutions run by scholars and scientists devoted "to higher teaching and research." The only tangible result of his study was the establishment of the Institute for Advanced Study at Princeton, headed by Flexner himself.

The criticisms of Robert Hutchins, then president of the University of Chicago, were similar. Most colleges and universities had only the most rudimentary intellectual life. "Undoubtedly," Hutchins wrote, "fine associations, fine buildings, green grass, good food, and exercise are excellent things for anybody." But they could be had at any good resort hotel. The reason why they were advertised "by every college and university," Hutchins added, "is that we have no coherent educational program to announce."

During the twenties all this made little difference. Most students were glad to be neglected by their professors, delighted, indeed, to be free to follow their own inclinations. The twenties were, after all, the decade of the young, and college campuses were convenient places to light the fires of flaming youth. Liquor and sex and sports made an exciting amalgam; short skirts and rolled stockings and rumble seats and bootleg gin, hip flasks, unbuckled galoshes, and fraternities and sororities flourished. Bobbed hair and jazz seemed far more compelling than carefully balanced academic judgments on virtually everything.

Vincent Sheean, who attended the University of Chicago in the early twenties, wrote: "Within those Gothic walls what, after all, had I learned? What did I take away from the pseudo-gothic sanctuary of my pseudo-education? Not much. I had some vague idea of history and philosophy, a bowing acquaintance with English and French literature. I had learned a good deal about snobbery, cruelty, prejudice, injustice and stupidity. I had acquired half a dozen friends—perhaps. I had learned how to dance the fox trot."

A popular song conveyed the atmosphere of the college campus reasonably well:

> C'llegiate, c'llegiate. Yes! we are c'llegiate!
> Nothin in-ter-med-jate, No ma'am.
> Trousers baggy and our clothes look raggy,
> But we're rough and ready, Yea!
>              Hot dog!
> Garters are the things we never wear . . .
> We're col-le-giate! Rah! Rah! Rah! Rah!
> Slickers, knickers, we can't do without;
> And we wouldn't care if there were
>              No suspenders!

In the midst of the hoopla of college life, where men and women alike did their best to emulate the cartoonist John Held's collegians and flappers, the activities of a handful of student socialists and an even smaller number of avowed Communists caused somewhat of an uproar in the national press. It was feared that the Communists, who were generally considered to have loose morals as well as subversive political doctrines, would seduce coeds, both figuratively and literally. *Liberty* magazine, bellwether of the right, published an alarming treatise: "Will the Communists Get Our Girls in College?" The answer, of course, was yes.

The voice of the student radicals was the *New Student,* launched in the early 1920s, which confined itself to such relatively innocuous topics as the "gigantism" of the universities and the "evils of commercialized education." By 1927 its editors confessed that "Where we used to dream of new faith and new communities developing out of the colleges and flowering through a thankful country, now the main hope is that students will be less bored by lecturing. . . ."

Women's colleges went their own way, stressing, as they had from the first, such subjects as biology, physical education, home economics, drama, art, and art history. In addition, they preserved a stronger commitment to reform than did their masculine counterparts. It is significant that the two most interesting experimental ventures in higher education in the 1920s were Sarah Lawrence, a women's college in Bronxville, New York, which opened its doors in 1928, and Bennington College in Bennington, Vermont, which was chartered in 1925 and enrolled students seven years later. Both were protests against traditional academic practices. They eschewed formal instruction and emphasized the individual needs and interests of the students. Discussion groups and fieldwork outside academic walls were stressed. Dance, drama, and the arts were offered long before they found a lodgment in predominantly masculine institutions.

In the sexually stimulated atmosphere of the twenties, intense emotional relationships developed between college women. Such alliances were called smashing. At Vassar Alice Stone Blackwell, Lucy Stone's daughter, wrote that smashing was one of the principal things that injured students' health. It was "an extraordinary habit which they have of falling violently in love with each other, and suffering all the pangs of unrequited attachment, desperate jealousy, etc., etc. with as much energy as if one of them were a man." A young friend at Smith told her she, too, had been a victim. " 'A veteran smasher' attacked her, & captured her, & soon deserted her for someone else; & she used to cry herself to sleep night after night & wake up with a headache in the morning. . . . If the 'smash' is mutual, they monopolize each other & 'spoon' continually, & sleep together & lie awake all night talking instead of going to sleep." It was Alice Blackwell's conclusion that the phenomenon resulted from "massing hundreds of nervous young girls together, & shutting them up from the outside world. They are just at the romantic age, they see only each other, & so their sentimentality has no other outlet."

Besides Sarah Lawrence and Bennington, there were other efforts to counter the general disposition to academic detachment. The New School for Social Research, founded in 1919 primarily for adult education, was a conscious effort to revive the spirit of Johns Hopkins in its golden age. At Antioch College Arthur Morgan introduced a program in which students spent half their time in studies and half in practical tasks in the world beyond the campus, trying thereby to relate their studies to the exigencies of everyday life. In Rome, Georgia, Martha Barry started a school for boys and girls from the lowest strata of white Georgia society; work and learning were combined. For six months a year the sudents worked full-time in the school kitchens, in the laundry, in workshops, in the brick factory, and on the school farm. It was a plan based on Booker T. Washington's Tuskegee, but of course, no black students were admitted.

At the University of Wisconsin, long a pioneer in education designed to serve the needs of the citizens of the state, John Christiansen of the College of Agriculture introduced certain ideas from the Danish folk schools founded by Bishop Grundtvig and devised a two-year curriculum for young farmers. A total of $104 paid for a student's room, tuition, books, and all fees. The only requirements for admission to the program were that a student could read and write. In addition to learning the most up-to-date agricultural techniques, the students were introduced to "new worlds of books, music, lectures, . . . practical sociology and economics, and something of the swiftly changing world they lived in; their whole outlook was broadened and deepened, and they were given a little finer cultural background," in Frazier Hunt's words. They went back to their farms "with new interests and new understandings."

Black colleges remained highly conservative or, perhaps better, cautious on the racial issue and, indeed, on most other matters. Langston Hughes, who had preferred to go to Lincoln, a black university in Pennsylvania, rather than to Harvard, was dismayed to discover that his fellow students preferred white instructors to black. "Over and over" Hughes heard students say "that there was something inherently superior in white teachers that Negro teachers did not have." He was anxious to prove that "the students were wrong, and that Lincoln was fostering—unwittingly, perhaps—an inferiority complex in the very men it wished to train as leaders of the Negro race." Hughes wanted to show "that the color line is no good on campus or off." (Hughes's poll showed that 63 percent of the juniors and seniors at Lincoln preferred an "all-white faculty.")

Tuskegee Institute not only insisted on the most rigid conformity to codes of dress and behavior but acquiesced in the blatant racism of the surrounding white communities; it had, indeed, no other choice. The curriculum was a watered-down version of white institutions of higher learning, with little or nothing taught about the achievements of black Americans or the history of race relations in the United States.

When Horace Cayton finished his graduate work at the University of Chicago, he was offered a job at Tuskegee. It was his first venture into the South, where his roots were deep, and it was as much of a shock in its own way as black Chicago had been. The faculty members, the majority of whom were black (in this respect Tuskegee differed from most black colleges, whose faculties were almost exclusively white), plainly regarded him as a Northern interloper, whose resistance to the pattern of segregation irritated and alarmed them. He found himself conned by a student into paying for a suit for the student's graduation. He discovered that visiting white faculty members were assigned to separate quarters and dined in different dining rooms. When Cayton ordered a sandwich in a local restaurant, two white men protested, and the proprietor took the sandwich back into the kitchen, wrapped it in waxed paper, and told him he would have to eat it outside. Although the faculty members were not allowed to vote, they were assessed a poll tax. When E. Franklin Frazier, a respected black sociologist, refused to pay his poll tax, the college paid it and took it out of his salary.

Cayton's time at Tuskegee enabled him to understand better the migration of blacks from the South to places like Seattle and Chicago. "What awaited them there seemed woefully inadequate," Cayton wrote, "yet I . . . realized that no matter how it seemed it was still better than what they were leaving behind. In the North, at least, there was hope." But there was no sign that either the faculty or administration of Tuskegee or the whites who lived in the area had any inkling of the feeling of ordinary blacks. "The institute," Cayton wrote, "was merely mouthing the worn-out generalities and formulae that the whites wanted to hear. But who was fooling whom?" The president of Tuskegee was Robert Russa Moton, who, in Cayton's view at least, had inherited Booker T. Washington's outmoded ideas.

Howard University was, in the opinion of many blacks, little better. A black doctor told Allen B. Ballard of his experience at Howard. "We got the feeling that the reason the white man hated us so was because he knew that we were not inferior. That was indoctrinated into us very subtly. We called Howard University the capstone of black education."

A handful of black students were admitted to white colleges and universities, more for their athletic prowess than their scholarly attainments. A disproportionate number of such students became all-American football players. But the ranks of the professoriat were firmly closed to black scholars as well as to Jews. Many bright Jews from large Eastern cities, finding that they were discriminated against in private Eastern colleges and universities, moved west and enrolled in such state universities as Iowa, Michigan, Wisconsin, and Minnesota, which were innocent of the quota system of Eastern colleges and universities limiting the number of Jews admitted to a certain (low) percentage of the student body.

During the controversy at Harvard over a quota system for Jewish applicants, eighty-nine-year-old Charles Eliot, the president of Harvard during its heyday, appeared to oppose any quota on Jewish students. Brahmin as he was, Eliot knew that much of Harvard's glory lay less in its proliferation of handsome academic structures (which had burgeoned under his presidency) than in its generous policy of admissions. An informal quota system was, nonetheless, imposed. Walter Lippmann, ambivalent about his own Jewishness, was outraged. At Harvard, he charged in an editorial in the *New York World,* there had been "a change of soul at the top. . . . In the place of Eliot, who embodied the stern but liberal virtues of New England, there sits a man [A. Lawrence Lowell] who has lost his grip on the great tradition which made Harvard one of the true spiritual centers of American life. Harvard, with the prejudices of a summer hotel; Harvard, with the standards of a country club, is not the Harvard of her greatest sons."

One of the most notorious instances of discrimination against black scholars was the case of Ernest Everett Just. Just was born in Charleston, South Carolina, in 1883. His widowed mother was a devoutly religious woman who founded an industrial school for young blacks near Charleston. Just received a scholarship at Kimball Union Academy in New Hampshire and then went on to Dartmouth, the only black student in a class of 287. He got the highest grades ever given a freshman student in Greek, and in his junior year he became a Rufus Choate Scholar, the only one in his class. He was graduated magna cum laude, and his principal Dartmouth professor, William Patten, got Just a job at the Marine Biological Laboratory at Woods Hole, Massachusetts, were he was soon considered a "genius in the design of experiments." But all normal academic channels, including the grants necessary for independent scientific work, were unavailable to Just. Finally he got a job teaching at Howard University, with responsibilities for some 500 biology majors. He had little time for his own work, but his summers at Woods Hole enabled him to complete his *The Biology of the Cell Surface,* which was recognized as a classic work on the subject.

After Just's second marriage to a German philosophy student he had met in Berlin, he planned to spend part of each year in Germany, where there were greater opportunities for him to pursue his research interests, but ironically, the rise of the Nazis with *their* racial animosities drove him and his German wife back to the United States.

Just's mother had taught him faith in the brotherhood of man; his science confirmed it. It was not, he wrote, "so much a Christian doctrine as a fundamental biological law. For biology does not and cannot recognize any specific differences among humans. This is a fact of tremendous significance for the human family. The peace of the world lives here. And the transcendent value of science to man will be measured in just proportion to which we realize the truth." Just perceived the unity of man with nature well in advance of most of his colleagues, who remained committed to a Cartesian world of "rational objectivity." He wrote: "We feel the beauty of Nature because we are part of Nature and because we know that however much in our separate domains we abstract from the unity of Nature, this unity remains. Although we may deal with particulars, we return finally to the whole pattern woven out of these. So in our study of the animal egg: though we resolve it into constituent parts the better to understand it, we hold it as an integrated thing, as a unified system: in it life resides and in its moving surface life manifests itself." Just, in his own physical presence, manifested the unity with nature that he proclaimed, for he was tall, graceful, strikingly handsome, a natural athlete. It was as though he, like other black Americans, had never experienced that Cartesian split between mind and body on which so much Western thought and, above all, Western science had been built. One of the most brilliant biologists of his generation, he was a poet in his perceptions and in his writing; the Greek spirit which had attracted him in college abode with him.

In 1929, when Just was proposed for a senior appointment to faculty of Brown University, the administration found him "quite ideal except for race." The same story was repeated again and again. Ernest Everett Just tested white America at that higher realm where disinterested intelligence and rational objectivity purported to reign. There he achieved much and was denied much. The academic caste that deplored the benighted racial attitudes of the South failed, in the last analysis, far more dismally than the South, if only because far more was properly expected of it.

The Depression years brought a halt to the rapid growth of education. By 1930 there was a slight decline in the number of students enrolled in public primary and secondary schools, and the middle of the decade saw a drop in the percentage of students in school. While the number of degrees conferred rose, the percentage of high school graduates going on to college dropped from 22 percent to 18. In addition, more than 200,000 teachers lost their jobs or couldn't find jobs after graduating from teachers' colleges. In higher education a new sobriety came to prevail. Money for tuition was hard to come by, and with recent graduates unable to get jobs, the incentive to go to college lessened substantially. The number of women entering college, which had tripled in the twenties from some 16,000 to 48,000, rose only to 54,000 in 1932. Presumably parents who could not afford to send all their children to college chose to send sons as prospective wage earners rather than daughters, who would, it was generally assumed, be homemakers.

In addition to an atmosphere of austerity (which did not, to be sure, much affect the more affluent students at private institutions), college and university campuses during the Depression years were pervaded by an air of unreality. In the face of the nation's worst crisis since the Civil War and the anticipation by many people of radical, perhaps revolutionary social change, the academies went on doing business as usual—the same courses; the same curriculum; the same above-the-battle stance; the same posture of objectivity. "It was the intolerance and the complete isolation of our colleges and universities," an angry Frazier Hunt wrote, "that deserved most . . . criticism. Nine professors out of every ten in our liberal arts schools were out of touch with the advancing age. They were not truly 'teachers': they were but priests of outdated and outworn modes. . . . Above all else the professors had to conform. Men with the slightest touch of divine discontent were unwanted. They were unsafe. The constant threat of excommunication by conservative trustees, legislature, and powerful graduates dampened and extinguished any brave spark of true questioning."

The New Deal had, as we have seen, a unique relationship to the academic world. Woodrow Wilson, as an ex-professor and college president, had had a close association with the academic world, and the Inquiry, made up predominantly of professors, had played a central role in drawing the boundary lines between European countries that were embodied in the Versailles Treaty. But Franklin Roosevelt, starting in his last term as governor of New York State, had made, and continued to make, unprecedented use of academic experts and advisers. Indeed, it was like the fulfillment of the dream of Frederic

Howe's generation of young scholars at Johns Hopkins: to put mind to work in the service of society. Some professors, like Felix Frankfurter, continued to profess from their chairs behind ivied walls while advising the administration on a wide variety of issues. Others, like Jerome Frank and William O. Douglas, left their academic posts to accept important and responsible jobs with one government agency or another. Some resigned their tenured academic posts for the uncertain waters of politics. Others simply took extended leaves of absence.

Alarmed conservative alumni and trustees began to take notice of such Washington connections. How could professors discharge their obligation to treat all matters objectively if they were directly, or even indirectly, involved in the radical, socialistic schemes of the New Deal? Walter Lippmann, with his anti-New Deal bias, was one of the most outspoken critics of the ties between the academic world and the Roosevelt administration. In a speech at Harvard, Lippmann declared that "members of university faculties have a particular obligation not to tie themselves to, nor to involve themselves in, the ambitions and purposes of politicians, the parties and movements which are contending for power. . . . For once they engage themselves that way . . . they cease to be scholars because they are no longer disinterested and having lost their own independence, they impair the independence of the university to which they belong."

No longer were scholars, academics, and intellectuals in general supposed to lead the legions of reform, applying their expertise to remedy the ills and inequities of society. Their sole responsibility was to their research, their scholarly monographs, to what was more and more frequently referred to as "pushing back the frontiers of knowledge."

In 1913 Brooks Adams, in his *Theory of Social Revolutions*, had taken the line that the colleges and universities of the United States were owned by the capitalists by right of purchase and could thus be counted on to do nothing to challenge the status quo. The response of the vast majority of professors to the shattering consequences of the Depression seemed to substantiate Adams's charge. The specialized knowledge generated by the universities, Adams had argued, was just the kind of intellectual activity that the business community wanted since it avoided the generalizing inclination that might produce ideas subversive of capitalism itself. With the onset of the Depression Adams's thesis was clearly demonstrated. Professors, however committed to the ideal of scientific objectivity, were, like the rest of the citizenry, not immune to reflections on the apparent downfall of capitalism, but instructed by years of painful experience and constrained by the canons of their profession, they kept radical opinons to themselves. If they joined the Communist Party, as a number of faculty members of large urban universities did, they cloaked their political activities under one of the less conspicuous fronts.

Under the circumstances, it was not surprising that radical student movements soon appeared on most major campuses. Such movements were most conspicuous on big-city campuses. On the West Coast the University of California at Berkeley became a center of radical student activity, referred to disparagingly by the more conservative-minded as the Little Red Schoolhouse. The continuation of the Depression increased the radicalization of college students. In 1934 it was estimated that one-third of the previous year's graduating class had been unable to find jobs. By January, 1935, 2,876,800 young men and women—between 20 and 30 percent of all youth—were unemployed. A popular ditty went:

> I sing in praise of college,
> Of M.A.'s and Ph.D.'s
> But in pursuit of knowledge
> We are starving by degrees.

When the Intercollegiate Socialist Society, which had metamorphosed into the League for Industrial Democracy, held its annual student conference at the Union Theological Seminary in 1931 on the topic "Guiding the Revolution," there were more than 200 representatives from forty-four colleges and universities. The most common student front for the Communist Party was the American Student Union (ASU), most of the national officers of which were covert members of the Young Communist League (YCL). Like all fronts, the ASU had the advantage, from the Communist perspective, of attracting a substantial number of liberal students who were susceptible to manipulation by the Young Communist League and some of whom were recruited into the YCL.

College radicals were encouraged by student strikes at the College of the City of New York and New York University in the spring of 1933 (students at Columbia had already struck), just a few weeks after Roosevelt's inauguration. Richard Dichter wrote in the magazine *Common Sense:* "The strike at Columbia University last year ushered in a new era. It heralded the beginning of a left-wing movement on the campus. Numerous other strikes of a definite political character followed." There was a strike at Commonwealth College in Arkansas, where students walked out of their classes when they were refused representation on the school's governing board.

A central preoccupation of the American Student Union was pacifism, a sentiment shared by the great majority of students. In 1933, 31 percent of a sampling of Columbia students identified themselves as "absolute pacifists"—men who would not bear arms under any circumstances—and 52 percent said they would serve in the armed forces only if the United States were invaded. Only 8 percent said they would be willing to fight for the United States under any circumstances. A national poll of young men reported that 39 percent said they would not participate in any war, while 33 percent said they would fight only if the United States were invaded. In the same year the Oxford Union, following a debate on military preparedness, passed a resolution declaring that under no circumstances would they "fight for King and country." The resolution passed by a vote of 273 to 153, and when Winston Churchill's son, Randolph, a student at Oxford, tried to have the vote expunged at a subsequent stormy meeting, the vote was reaffirmed by an overwhelming 750 to 175. Other British universities followed suit. In the United States plans were made for a nationwide Student Strike Against War, set to take place on April 13.

The reaction of most college and university administrations was to threaten punishment up to and including suspension for those who participated. Despite such efforts, it was estimated that taking part in the strike were 25,000 students, more than half of whom, it might be noted, attended New York City institutions such as the City College of New York, Brooklyn College, and Hunter. The second student strike in 1935 concentrated on securing pledges from students not to bear arms "in any war the United States government may conduct." This time it was estimated that 150,000 students participated in one form of protest or another. Brooklyn College led with 6,000; on the West Coast the University of California at Berkeley enlisted 4,000. The universities of Chicago, Minnesota, and Wisconsin also had large turnouts.

The major setback to the student peace movement came from the Young Communist League members, acting through the American Student Union. On instructions from the Communist Party, they did their best to dampen the peace movement on the ground that if Hitler and the "Fascist nations" of Europe turned on Soviet Russia, the United States must be prepared to come to the defense of the nation which had the responsibility for securing the victory of Marxism over capitalism.

The most conspicuous student front was the American Youth Congress, ostensibly convened by the American Student Union but actually run by the Young Communist League. The AYC profited especially from the interest and support of Eleanor Roosevelt, who was unaware of its domination by the Communists. Mrs. Roosevelt had a special sympathy with the plight of young people. "I felt," she wrote, "that in any effort they made to help themselves or one another the young people should have all the consideration and assistance their elders could possibly give them. . . . I believed . . . that these young people had the right to be heard. They had the right to fight for the things they believed in as citizens of a democracy." When the Dies committee probed the activities of the American Youth Congress, Eleanor Roosevelt attended the hearings, and on one occasion, when a member of the committee was bullying a young witness, she rose conspicuously and seated herself at the press table. The tone of the interrogator at once became more moderate.

The leaders of the AYC were, in Eleanor Roosevelt's words, "an idealistic, hard-working group." When charges surfaced that they were Communists, Mrs. Roosevelt asked them directly if the charges were true. If she was to work with them and support them, she must have an honest answer. "If any of them were communists," she told them, she "would quite understand, for I felt they had grown up at a time of such difficulty as to explain their being attracted to almost any ideas that promised them better conditions. . . . In every case," she wrote later, "when the communist affiliations of the leadership of the American Youth Congress had been established beyond reasonable doubt, they said they had no connection with the communists, had never belonged to any communist organizations, and had no interest in communist ideas." Suppressing her doubts, she continued to encourage and support them, to invite them to the White House, sometimes for several days at a time, and to facilitate their using public buildings for their larger meetings. Of all the actions of Communists or Communist-affiliated groups in the period of the Depression, the deceptions of the leaders of the American Youth Congress perhaps reveal most clearly the insidious nature of the Marxist ethic that the ends justify the means. This was what the young men and women directing the AYC had been taught. To have the ear of the wife of the President of the United States was of inestimable value in the class war. Any lie or evasion was justified in the name of the revolution and the eventual emancipation of the masses. The ideas of truth and falsity were bourgeois notions used by the exploiters to keep the exploited in their places. Just as there was no honor among capitalists, who stole from and cheated each other, the public, and, above all, their workers, Communists should feel no compunctions about an equal ruthlessness on behalf of the oppressed. As a theory of class struggle there was a perverse kind of logic about the proposition, but it broke down quickly in the face of specific persons and the betrayal of their trust.

When the Second World Youth Congress met at Vassar in 1938, Eleanor Roosevelt was a featured speaker. "I have been bombarded with protests from Catholics & others," she wrote to Lorena Hickok, "saying they [the delegates] are communist controlled . . . but I think they are wrong." She confessed that she felt "sad at the sight of all those young people & so earnest & full of hope—54 countries represented—Did you see them in N.Y.?"

Influenced by his wife's sympathy with the causes of young people, the President sent a letter of greeting to the annual convention of the American Student Union in 1938. The mayor of New York and the Board of Higher Education also expressed support for the student group. Bruce Bliven, writing in the *New Republic,* described a convention that was hardly to be distinguished from a monster football rally. The delegates' enthusiasm "reached its peak at the Jamboree in the huge . . . auditorium of the Hippodrome, (seating capacity of 4500) which was filled to its loftiest tier. There were a quintet of white-flanneled cheer leaders, a swing band, and shaggers doing the Campus Stomp ('everybody's doing it, ASU'ing it'). . . . There were ASU feathers and buttons, a brief musical comedy by the Mob Theatre and pretty ushers in academic caps and gown." The cheers were not to beat Yale or Rutgers but for "Democracy to beat Reaction." To a skeptical Bliven it all bordered on the phony. What he did not know, but may have suspected, was that it all was carefully orchestrated by the leaders of the Young Communist League, who were also the leaders of the American Student Union.

When the American Youth Congress met in Washington, Eleanor Roosevelt took the leaders of the congress into her family, helped some of them with loans or small gifts of money, and attended their weddings. Prominent among them was an aging—twenty-eight-year-old—young Jew, Joseph Lash (many of the active youth leaders were Jewish).

During an AYC meeting in the summer of 1939 ten delegates

"slept & ate" at the White House. "Life is interesting these days," Mrs. Roosevelt wrote to Hickok, "so many young people come by my door. . . ."

At the American Youth Congress convention at Madison, Wisconsin, the pro-Soviet students were in firm control. The Russian-German nonaggression pact had been signed, and Russia had outraged world opinion by its invasion of Finland, but a resolution to condemn the invasion was defeated, 322 to 49.

Despite the actions of the Madison convention, Eleanor Roosevelt gave unstinting assistance to the meeting of the youth congress scheduled for Washington. The site was the Labor Department auditorium, which gave the event a mildly official sanction, as, of course, did Mrs. Roosevelt's support. It was evident to her that despite their disavowals, the American Youth Congress leaders were conforming closely to the Soviet line (and, of course, to the indistinguishably similar line of the Communist Party of the United States). On February 10, 1940, the AYC called for a parade, a conference, and a demonstration in Washington to protest American aid to Britain and any American involvement in the European war. Russia and Germany were still allies, and the line to every Communist Party in every country was the same: Oppose all aid to Great Britain; work assiduously for the triumph of Hitler and his ally, Stalin. Such a line was an especially excruciating one for Jews in leadership positions in the American Youth Congress.

Mrs. Roosevelt asked her husband to speak informally with delegates to the congress from the south portico of the White House. The President took the occasion to give the young men and women clustered on the White House lawn in a cold rain a stern lecture on their responsibilities as citizens of a democracy and on the evil that Adolph Hitler had let loose in the world. "The idea that a loan to Finland was an attempt to force America into an imperialist war" was, he declared, "unadulterated twaddle . . . based on ninety percent ignorance." A scattering of boos greeted his admonitions. Mrs. Roosevelt was embarrassed at what seemed to her bad manners, whatever the ideological predispositions of the young people might be, but Roosevelt took the episode in stride, saying to her later with a slightly ironic smile, "Our youngsters are always unpredictable, aren't they?" The next day at the congress, when Eleanor Roosevelt rose to speak, she was greeted with a loud chorus of boos. "I waited until I could be heard," she wrote of the experience, "and then remarked that since they had asked me to speak and I had listened to all the other speakers, I thought in return they had an obligation to listen to me." They heard her out, gave brief and perfunctory applause, and saved their cheers for John L. Lewis, who had recently broken with the President and announced his intention of supporting the Republican candidate for President. "I wish to make it clear," Eleanor Roosevelt wrote in her autobiography, *This I Remember*, "that I felt a great sympathy for these young people, even though they often annoyed me. It was impossible to forget the extraordinary difficulties under which they were growing up." In the words of a journalist present, "The nation probably has not seen in all its history such a debate between a President's wife and a critical, not to say, hostile auditorium full of politically minded youth of all races and creeds."

"Sunday," Mrs. Roosevelt wrote Lorena Hickok, "I spent all day with the Youth Congress, ending with answering questions Sunday night in a way which was not too popular & there was considerable hissing. F.D.R. made them very sore, more by the way he said things than by the things he said & it is especially hard to stand in the rain & 'take it' when you feel as sensitive as youth does. John Lewis grasped his opportunity & walked away with them the next day & I brought them down to earth a bit which wasn't pleasant either. However, when all is said & done it was remarkable to have so many come & talk & listen & I think it was a great experience for them & I learned much myself." But the next year, when the congress denounced aid to a beleaguered Great Britain as "imperialism," Eleanor Roosevelt, convinced that its leaders were doctrinaire Communists, told them that she and they had come to the parting of the ways: "They had condemned everything that meant help for the countries fighting Germany."

Despite the radical political activities of what was, in the final analysis, only a handful of students, American colleges and universities remained bastions of conservatism, both politically and intellectually. Where they might not reasonably have been expected to take the lead in exploring alternatives to capitalism *and* Marxism, they maintained a discreet, objective silence. As for the mass of college and university students, they continued to be more engaged with sports and fraternities than with intellectual matters. The dean of Columbia College wrote: "I am convinced that the youth of college age at the present time are as immature morally and as crude socially as they are undeveloped intellectually."

Aside from student political activity, the most interesting development in the academic world was the resurrection of a small, ancient, and rapidly dwindling liberal arts college in Annapolis, Maryland, named St. John's. In 1937 Stringfellow Barr and Scott Buchanan converted St. John's into an experimental institution with no formal lecture courses. Disciples of Robert Hutchins, Barr and Buchanan had long deplored the fragmented character and excessive specialization of American higher education. Following the Aristotelian theories of Hutchins, the two men developed a curriculum based on the study (and above all, discussion) of the great books—100 classics that had shaped civilization. There were no "courses" at St. John's and only occasional lectures.

After World War II, in the mood of McCarthyism, a group of distinguished ex-Communist professors and sympathizers, which included Sidney Hook of New York University, addressed the *New York Times* on behalf of the Commission on Academic Freedom of the American Committee for Cultural Freedom, recommending that "cultural freedom" be denied Marxist professors. "Where," the professors asked rhetorically, "does the Communist teacher fit into the scheme of academic freedom? The only reasonable answer is: He does not. A member of the Communist party has transgressed the canons of academic responsibility, has engaged his intellect to servility, and is therefore professionally disqualified from performing his functions as scholar and teacher." It was one of the odder documents in our history; not surprisingly, it was seized upon by conservative college and university trustees and boards of directors as an excuse to purge faculties of "Reds," past and present, many of them once colleagues of the professors who had drafted and signed the manifesto on academic non-freedom. How curious that the American academic world, which had earlier been a stronghold of reform, should suddenly declare with the finality of natural law that only professors who professed capitalism could be trusted to tell the truth about the nature of man and society!

# 39

## Medicine

A mid the progress that Americans were so proud of (and that, as we have often observed, was regress for many segments of the society), the practice of medicine regressed, and with it the standing of its practitioners. In the era of the American Revolution doctors such as David Ramsay of South Carolina and Philip Physick and Benjamin Rush of Philadephia were held in great esteem by their countrymen and countrywomen, not only for their revolutionary zeal but for their skills as physicians and their high professional standards. Philadelphia was the center of the new Republic's most advanced medical practice. But medicine proved singularly unsuited for the American free enterprise system. As the nation spread westward, new states and territories failed to follow uniform practices in licensing doctors or setting even the most modest standards for the training of physicians and surgeons. Medical schools were, in the main, private business ventures run as a profit-making sideline by general practitioners. Virtually anyone who was able to pay the fees was admitted, and a certificate of graduation after several years of hit-or-miss instruction entitled him or her to hang out a shingle as an M.D.

There was, moreover, no uniform notion of what constituted proper treatment for the ill. The homeopaths contended with the allopaths;

the osteopaths and the chiropracters vied with both. As the nineteenth century wore on, the journals and newspapers were filled with advertisements for medicines guaranteed to cure everything from warts to cancer. Uncounted gallons of patent medicines and tonics were consumed by the ailing. The tonics commonly contained opium, cocaine, or alcohol, and at least had the virtue of indisputably making the patients, many of whom were teetotalers, feel much better, whereas licensed doctors often killed them by their inept attentions. Surgery, as we have noted earlier, was an area in which a degree of progress was made, but surgical procedures were unsanitary, and the risk of infection and death was so high as to make surgery a desperate measure. Doctors often carried sutures in their pockets with handkerchiefs or plugs of tobacco. Scalpels were not sterilized, and no antiseptic procedures were observed.

When Dr. Benjamin Rush called for "democratic medicine" in the early years of the Republic, he certainly did not have in mind the chaotic condition which prevailed in the profession by the end of the century. Medicine had progressed little, if at all, since the Greeks; indeed, it might be argued that it had retrogressed. If medicine in the eighteenth century was a hit-or-miss affair, it had at least established certain professional standards, and its practitioners were men of a genuinely scientific bent. The same could not be said at the end of the next century.

A combination of circumstances worked to bring a degree of order and professionalism into medicine. The most important factors, undoubtedly, were the discoveries by Louis Pasteur and Robert Koch. Pasteur, as early as 1862, had identified bacteria as elements in the process first of fermentation and then of disease. The idea of vaccination, first used in the eighteenth century to combat smallpox, was extended by Pasteur as a preventative to anthrax and then to hydrophobia. The Pasteur Institute, which opened in Paris in 1888, included a dispensary and extensive research facilities.

Koch, a country practitioner, made microscopic studies of bacteria and identified them as the culprits in a number of infectious diseases, including tuberculosis (in 1882) and Asiatic cholera. The University of Berlin founded the Institute for Infectious Diseases, and Koch was professor there from 1891 to 1904.

With the discoveries of Pasteur and Koch, medicine entered the modern age. Increasingly research replaced abstract hypotheses. Once it had been demonstrated that the work of Pasteur and Koch was "scientific," the means were at hand to create modern medicine, first by establishing standards of simple cleanliness, then by defining an acceptable medical education.

Although Americans were responsible for little, if any, of the basic research that made modern medicine possible, American physicians were quick to perceive the implications and to apply them to the general practice of medicine. The story had been much the same with such inventions as the telegraph: Europeans made the significant discoveries; Americans, the practical applications or "democratizations."

The individual who, more than anyone else, set the tone for the revolution in medicine by his intellect and personality was William Osler, a British physician who was professor of medicine first at McGill University and then, significantly, at Johns Hopkins, where he played the leading role in setting up that institution's medical school. When he left Johns Hopkins in 1904 to return to England (and a knighthood), it had become the foremost medical school in the country and the model by which all others were judged. When the Johns Hopkins Medical School opened its doors in 1893, it began with a four-year program and the requirement that all students seeking admission have college degrees. One of the significant aspects of American medicine was the relationship of general medical practice to research. Osler and William Henry Welch established at Johns Hopkins a tradition that stressed the importance of physicians whose primary interest was research maintaining a close relationship with patients.

The professionalization of nursing was influenced, to a remarkable degree, by one woman, Isabel Hamilton, who came to Johns Hopkins during the Osler era and immediately made her mark both as an efficient administrator, an innovator in nursing and in the training of nurses, and as a woman of unusual charm and strength of character. Tall and handsome, she had a cosmopolitanism that came from two years in Rome at an Episcopal hospital for American and English travelers and a stint as superintendent of nurses at the Illinois Training School in Chicago. Like Osler's, her personal qualities counted as much as her intelligence. In the words of her successor, "had she been a man and in the business world, nothing could have kept her from an active and controlling share in some of the great organizations and combinations of which the world now hears so much."

Under Hamilton's leadership, the type of young woman recruited for nursing became predominantly upper-middle-class. Out of one group of 102, 53 were Episcopalians and 14 Presbyterians. Susie Carroll of Little Rock, Arkansas, was a typical student, described by Hamilton as "a lady by heredity, breeding and culture and qualified by education and natural endowment to learn any vocation appropriate for her sex." Another candidate played the piano and organ and spoke French and German. In Baltimore society Isabel Hamilton "became well known as a delightful representative of the great Hospital and a new profession for women."

Abraham Flexner, born in Louisville, Kentucky, and a graduate of Johns Hopkins who did postgraduate work at Harvard and the University of Berlin, became a member of the staff of the Carnegie Foundation for the Advancement of Teaching. From this post he undertook a study of medical education in the United States. In Flexner's famous *Medical Education in the United States and Canada,* referred to as the *Bulletin Number Four* and published in 1910, he mercilessly exposed the inadequacies of privately run hospitals. His conclusion: "Society reaps at this moment but a small fraction of the advantage which current knowledge has the power to confer." Diseases might be controlled and lives saved on a large scale if the available medical knowledge were taught to doctors and practiced on patients. That was the spur to action. The success of the *Bulletin Number Four* in the reform of medical education was ensured by the enthusiastic support of the American Medical Association. The association had been founded in 1847, when some 250 delegates representing forty medical societies and twenty-eight medical colleges met in Philadelphia. For almost half a century its membership and its influence were modest. By the early years of the twentieth century the remarkable advances in medical research gave the AMA a chance to impose some order on the chaotic medical situation in the United States. A Council on Medical Education and Hospitals was set up in 1904, followed by one on Pharmacy and Chemistry a year later.

The Council on Medical Education of the AMA set four years of high school as a minimum standard for admission to medical school; four years of medical school and a test were required before a license to practice was granted. Science was already a talismanic word. Science was based on research. The notion that medical schools must become centers of research as well as instruction was as inevitable as was the argument that a medical school must have a full-time teaching faculty. It was soon evident that the new research techniques disclosed such a wide range of medical problems that some doctors had to specialize in particular and increasingly narrow fields. One area of specialization after another was added: pediatrics, obstetrics, gynecology, urology, cardiology, neurology, etc. By the same token diagnostic methods became increasingly sophisticated. The use of X rays revolutionized the treatment of broken bones, taking much of the guesswork out of surgery.

In 1906 there were 160 institutions that claimed to be medical schools and issued degrees. By 1915 there were 95, of which 80 percent required at least a year of college. Licensing boards in many states imposed increasingly strict standards; the number of medical schools able to meet them declined along with the number of graduates. By 1922 the number of medical school graduates had fallen from 5,440 in 1906 to 2,529, while the population had risen from 83,000,000 to 110,000,000. Although Flexner had recommended that there be no more than thirty medical schools in the country, more than seventy survived, but the bulk of private foundation money went to seven institutions. In 1936 the Rockefeller General Education Board and other foundations awarded some $60,000,000 to those seven, primarily for research.

Not surprisingly, the costs of a medical education rose astronomically in this period. If the quality of medicine delivered to those who could afford to pay for it rose in spectacular fashion, there were, of course, losers. The number of women admitted to medical schools fell to the infinitesimal. Between 1880 and 1900 women physicians had increased to 5.6 percent of all doctors, some 7,000 in number (in the larger cities the number of women doctors ran much higher: 19.3 percent in Minneapolis and 18.2 percent in Boston). One of the reasons for the increase in women physicians was the unwillingness of many Victorian women to be closely examined by male physicians.

Both the time needed to complete the requirements for a degree and the cost deterred women. An even greater deterrent was the fact that male-dominated medical school faculties were increasingly disposed to refuse to admit highly qualified female candidates on the ground that they would, in most instances, marry and have families before completing their medical education.

Another group that suffered was the blacks, both those who wished to become doctors and those, especially in the South, who could not expect to receive treatment from white doctors. In Mississippi there was 1 black doctor for every 14,634 prospective patients. Moreover, since doctors, especially specialists, tended to congregate in large cities, where there were patients able to pay their fees, where the most modern and up-to-date medical facilities were available, and where life was generally more agreeable, small towns and rural areas suffered from what was, in some respects, an artificially created shortage of doctors.

A doctor in a medical school in Chattanooga, Tennessee, wrote, protesting the strict new standards: "True, our entrance requirements are not the same as those of the University of Pennsylvania or Harvard; nor do we pretend to turn out the same sort of finished product. Yet we prepare worthy, ambitious men who have striven hard with small opportunities and risen above their surroundings to become family doctors to farmers of the south and to the smaller towns of the mining districts. . . . Would you say that such people should be denied physicians? Can the wealthy who are a minority say to the poor majority, you shall not have a doctor?" The answer turned out to be yes. In 1910 Massachusetts had 1 doctor for every 497 persons; South Carolina, 1 doctor per 1,170. In 1920 the number of doctors was down from 173 per 100,000 population in 1900 to 137; in the next ten years it dropped to 125 per 100,000.

With all the remarkable advances in medicine, it remained (and remains) an inexact science; indeed, many of its widely heralded advances turned out to be, if not illusory, at least acompanied by significant losses and setbacks. Much daily medicine consists of the treatment of injuries, of sewing up wounds, setting broken bones, administering routine medicines, and reassuring the ill or the suffering. To systematically withdraw such classic comforts from large portions of the population in order that a relatively small number shall have the finest medical care in the world might be considered a poor bargain. Many argued that it was an undemocratic and an unnecessary one.

The American Medical Association's Council on Pharmacy and Chemistry, meanwhile, set out to establish standards in the patent medicine field as well. Its aim was to force unethical companies out of business and to require all drug companies to work through doctors. Pressure on the drug companies by the AMA resulted in a kind of partnership (some critics suggested a conspiracy) between the drug companies and physicians, a partnership which, while a great improvement over the patent medicine days, was not always in the best interests of the patient.

The most direct beneficiary of the medical advances may have been the hospital. Not much better than charnel houses through much of the nineteenth century, hospitals had served the destitute more than the well-to-do. After the turn of the century the hospital came to be perceived as an antiseptic haven for the ailing. A marvel of cleanliness and efficiency, often with a medical school attached, with laboratories, expert doctors, and highly trained nurses, it became the exemplar and distributor of the new medicine. Doctors encouraged middle-class patients to stay for extended periods. Because many private hospitals were closed to Jews and inhospitable to Catholics (and because there were dietary problems for religious Jews in Gentile hospitals), Jewish hospitals were established as well as Catholic ones. In many instances these hospitals outstripped their rivals, the Jews by their brillance as physicians, the Catholics because, in part, they ran their hospitals as charitable institutions and the nuns who supervised them proved excellent administrators as well as superior nurses.

By 1937 there were 6,189 hospitals in the United States. Of these, 584 were for mental patients, and of the remaining, 969 were denominational institutions. The author of the article on medicine in Harold Stearns's *America Now* was highly critical of the quality of food and care in most hospitals. "Noise in American hospitals," he wrote, "is continuous day and night. . . . Discipline among attendants is sloppy and consideration for the feelings of patients hardly taught at all."

Another consequence of discoveries in the realm of bacteriology was the notion of preventive medicine and, following from it, the development of the field of public health. The health center movement was an important part of the growing concern for public health. By 1920 there were 72 centers in 49 communities. Many big cities had more than one health center. Moreover, 39 had medical clinics attached, and visiting nurses were on the staffs of 34. In 1930 the number of health centers had grown to 1,500, half of which were operated by private agencies and half by county or municipal authorities. They included venereal disease clinics, tuberculosis dispensaries, and settlement houses that provided medical care and advice. Most were in the ghetto areas of industrial cities. A number were in rural areas poorly served by physicians. As immunology progressed, many health centers offered as their main service inoculation against contagious disease.

The American Medical Association, having shown great enterprise and zeal in improving the quality of American medicine (and in the process having greatly elevated the status and the monetary rewards of the profession), went on to demonstrate the principle that power corrupts. Every effort to extend medical care to the less privileged classes—to the poor, the aged, the rural population—or to lower the cost of medical care through various plans of health insurance, public or private, was resisted with every resource at the AMA's command. A measure of the extent of doctors' control of medical services was the decline of midwives. In New York City in 1919 there were 1,700 midwives, many of them foreign-born, who delivered more than 40,000 children, a third of those born in that year. Ten years later only 12,000 babies were delivered by midwives, 12 percent of the births in the city. As the doctors and hospitals gained greater control over deliveries, the cost and the period of time that mothers and their newborn infants stayed in hospitals increased greatly, two weeks being not an unusual time for a middle- or upper-middle-class wife to spend recovering from the ordeal of birth. One suspects that such protracted stays were a kind of conspicuous consumption of hospital services, perceived as one of the privileges of the upper social classes.

A study was made in 1927 of the causes of the deaths of women in childbirth. The study, which covered fifteen states, concluded that of the 2,041 deaths investigated, some 66 percent were preventable. In the preventable deaths, responsibility lay with the physician in 61 percent of the cases and with midwives in only 2.2 percent. In cases of death following surgical procedures, most commonly cesarean sections, 77 percent of the deaths were considered preventable. The death rate in hospital deliveries was more than twice the rate for home deliveries. Moreover, the study also showed that the risk of death was "highly correlated" with economic status and race. The poor, primarily blacks and immigrant women, died in disproportionate numbers; deaths of black mothers were twice the rate for whites. Such statistics supported those who contended that "free enterprise" medicine had failed conspicuously to extend the benefits of new medical and surgical techniques to all Americans. Another conclusion that might be drawn from the study was that such techniques were overused. Birth was clearly an event that suffered from the excessive intervention of the doctor.

The debate over some form of public health insurance had begun in the Progressive era as one of the measures of social reform dear to Progressive hearts. When bills were introduced in various state legislatures to initiate health insurance in the period from 1915 to 1917, there was strong opposition from doctors. In California doctors formed the League for the Preservation of Public Health to oppose health insurance. In the wartime spirit the doctors declared, "It is a dangerous device, invented in Germany, announced by the German Emperor from the throne the same year he started plotting and preparing to conquer the world." Later the argument shifted: Health insurance was part of a Communist plot to destroy the free enterprise system in America. Yet the agitation for some form of insurance persisted, and in 1926 a group consisting of physicians, economists, and public health experts under the title Committee on the Costs of Medical Care, headed by Ray Lyman Wilbur, president of Stanford University, was formed to study the subject. Over the next five years the committee made a number of influential reports. For every dollar spent on health care, roughly thirty cents went to physicians, twenty-three to hospitals, eighteen to medication, twelve to dentists, six to nurses, three to "cultists," and three to public health. Moreover, almost half the families with annual incomes under $1,200 received no medical care in the course of a typical year.

According to the committee, virtually nobody was getting sufficient medical attention, especially, of course, those at the bottom of the economic pile. The committee concluded its report by recommending "group practice and group payment" but opposing compulsory health insurance for everyone. Although group practice and insurance were far closer to "free enterprise" than any compulsory health plan, they were denounced as "mass production" medicine and encountered immediate and bitter opposition from a substantial segment of the medical profession; the New York Times summarized the report under the headline "Socialized Medicine Is Urged in Survey."

The Depression and the New Deal revived the agitation for a general public health program to cover all citizens. In June, 1934, Roosevelt announced the appointment of a Committee on Economic Security, chaired by Frances Perkins. One of the forms of security it was instructed to consider was compulsory health insurance. The AMA was by this time so powerful that everyone on the committee agreed there was little chance of getting any health insurance legislation through Congress. A fight on that issue might well imperil unemployment insurance and "social security" for the aged, so there was general agreement simply to avoid the issue. Morris Fishbein, editor of the American Medical Association's *Journal*, declared that the lines were clearly drawn: "Americanism versus sovietism for the American people. . . . The alignment is clear. On one side the forces representing the great foundations, public health officialdom, social theory—even socialism and communism—inciting to revolution; on the other side, the organized medical profession of this country urging an orderly evolution guided by controlled experimentation." The trouble proved to be that if anything that smacked of experimentation was proposed, it was immediately opposed.

Not only were the resources of the AMA expended in opposition to any legislative measures designed to establish some form of public-assisted medical care, but it was alert to suppress any voluntary physician-sponsored plan for cooperative or group medicine. When Dr. Michael Shadid set up such a plan in Elk City, Oklahoma, in 1929, he encountered immediate opposition from local physicians, who did their best to strip him of his license although he had practiced medicine in the area for twenty years. He was expelled from the county medical association and denied access to hospital facilities controlled by the association. When the Group Health Association was formed in Washington, D.C., by government employees a few years later, the American Medical Association called for legislation against it as "unlicensed, unregulated health insurance." Professional reprisals were threatened against any doctors who participated in the plan, and the hospitals in the Washington area were strong-armed into refusing admitting privileges to doctors involved. While the assistant attoney general, Thurman Arnold, secured an indictment against the AMA for conspiracy in restraint of trade, an indictment later upheld by the Supreme Court, few physicians cared to challenge the power of the association.

When the Resettlement Administration in 1935 began instituting a cooperative medical prepayment plan for farmers in the Dakotas, the AMA sniffed it out and denounced it as a "step toward socialized medicine."

The doctor who wrote the essay on American medicine for Harold Stearns's *America Now* in 1938 declared confidently that the United States was the "leader of the world" in medicine, setting the pace "in research, practice, physical equipment and organization. . . . [and] it occupies the same position that Vienna did before the war; that Paris did before Vienna. . . ." The claim, if somewhat vainglorious, was close to the truth, but historians are still debating the role of the medical profession in the generally acknowledged improvement in the health and longevity of Americans. Some historians of American medicine have argued that the notable improvement in the general health of the population resulted less from the accomplishments of the medical profession than from changes in the larger patterns of American society—e.g., greater personal cleanliness that was at least in part the result of improved standards of living; eradication of child labor; shorter working days and weeks and vastly improved working conditions (by this measure unions, it might be argued, have contributed as much or more to better health and longevity than doctors); retirement at a relatively early age; and better nutrition. Other important factors in reducing death by contagious disease were the quarantining of sick individuals and families at the onset of the infection and extension of inoculation to the general public.

It is undoubtedly true that many Americans who could not afford medical care profited, if often skimpily and belatedly, from the remarkable advances in medicine. It is also the case that the advances in "scientific medicine" were achieved at considerable cost to the classic relationship between doctor and patient.

In the 1930s three Americans won the Nobel Prizes in medicine, the first since 1912. The awards signaled the coming of age of American medicine, not simply as a highly organized and expensive new industry but as a first-class scientific undertaking. The reactionary character of the profession, so evident since the 1920s, should not obscure its genuine achievements.

A field on the borderline of standard medical practice was that of psychiatry. Psychiatry was the medical offshoot of psychology. By the 1920s psychology had a substantial history in the United States. William James had pioneered the study of mental and psychological health, as contrasted with the purely physiological. S. Weir Mitchell, novelist and "alienist" (the initial term for psychiatrist), had done much to draw attention to the field. Henry Adams had complained of the disposition of his friends to introspection. "Nothing was easier," Adams had written at the turn of the century, "than to take one's mind in one's hand, and ask one's psychological friends what they thought of it. . . ." Psychologists, he wrote, had revealed a "subconscious chaos" in the inner man and woman. "The only absolute truth was the subconscious chaos below, which everyone could feel when he sought it."

Freud's theories had received a warm welcome in the United States. Clark University in Worcester, Massachusetts, had become the citadel of Freudian psychology. Emma Goldman had gone there in 1896 during a lecture tour to hear the great Viennese doctor. In Greenwich Village, in the Progressive era, Freudian psychology had been the rage. Walter Lippmann had organized discussions of Freud at Mabel Dodge's literary evenings and written a political treatise based on a

Freudian interpretation of man's political behavior. Freudian psycho-analysis was soon established as the favored form of psychotherapy or psychiatry. Frederic Howe, in despair over the collapse of the dreams of the reformers in the postwar era, consulted a psychiatrist, who told him he must rid himself of guilt and devote more time to cultivating his private life. Increasingly psychoanalysis was developed as a kind of sideline by progressive medical doctors, who believed that many human ailments were "psychosomatic," more in the unsettled mind than in the body. George Draper, Franklin Roosevelt's physician, undertook to analyze, among others, William O. Douglas (he persuaded him that most of his psychological problems were related to his childhood fear of water).

In the emotionally disturbed atmosphere of the twenties psychia-try came into its own. Morever, it became fashionable. So-called ner-vous breakdowns were endemic, and the most common remedy for those who could afford the cost was a stay at a sanatorium, with regular consultations with a psychologist or, better, a psychiatrist. While an M.A. or a Ph.D. was enough to set a clinical psychologist up in business, psychiatry set a far more difficult standard: graduation from medical school plus additional study, including a so-called didactic analysis of the student on the not unreasonable ground that he should understand his own psychological problems before he undertook to cure the prob-lems of others.

By the late 1930s, when Harold Stearns published his anthology America Now, psychiatry was sufficiently well established to merit a chapter in the section on "Health." It was written by a young M.D. who was also a Freudian psychiatrist, Karl Menninger. Menninger argued that psychiatry was on the verge of discoveries about the human personality as revolutionary in their way as the developments in the fields of radio and television transmission. The treatment of "shell-shocked" soldiers in the World War had, Menninger argued, given psychiatry an enormous boost. In probing the roots of human behavior, he noted, psychologists had discovered that it derived from ego grat-ification. Thus what had seemed unselfish behavior—"civic virtue," in the phrase of the Founding Fathers—was revealed "as the expression of a disorder, rather than the wholesome activity of a well-balanced personality. . . ." By the same token was it not likely that "the eman-cipated and unconventional individual, who is expressing his person-ality to the amazement of his social circle, may be the victim of illusion and be really in the throes of a mild mental disorder? Is it possible,"

Menninger asked, "that many of our beliefs, attitudes, emotions, habits, standards, are not as valid as we have assumed them to be, but are of the same stuff of which mental disorder is made?"

Menninger lamented the conservatism of the medical profession, which was reluctant to accept the fact that a patient might have "a psychologically determined physical disease, such as gastric hyperacidity or mucous-colitis," and was consequently unwilling to refer such cases to a psychiatrist.

After reflections on the very considerable influence of Freudian psychology on "literature, art and music," Menninger discussed its effect on "legal and criminal procedures" and, finally, on religion. Since psychiatry was, in a sense, a competing "religion" or way of viewing human nature and the aims of life, conflict between psychiatry and religion appeared inevitable, but Menninger saw signs of "*rapprochement between them.*" Religion had become increasingly interested "in the application of the scientific principles of human personality" to "inspiration and faith." Menninger wrote: "To what extent psychiatry will replace religion is problematical. . . ." In his view, religion would "long continue to supply the healing of the nations. . . ." Psychiatry "would do for the individual what religion has endeavored to do and to some extent has succeeded in doing for the masses." Freud, Menninger concluded, should be ranked with Aristotle, Plato, Leonardo, Columbus, and Newton. "The psychiatry of 1938 is an organized science, art, and profession linked in a three-way combination with medicine, psychology and sociology," the three together producing "a new concept of human beings." While Menninger admitted that much remained to be learned about human nature, he seemed confident that it was only a matter of time before the truth was revealed to patient researchers.

The new intellectual class subscribed to tenets of Freudian psychology, and a number of its members underwent psychoanalysis in the hope of curing themselves of the malaise of the age. Many put their trust in a combination of Marx and Freud, and when they could no longer hold fast to Marx, they clung to Freud more doggedly than ever. Works of art, poems, and novels made use of Freudian concepts (and increasingly Jungian archetypes). Many men and women interpreted Freud's system of the id, the ego, and the superego and the notion of repression as at least implying that all inhibitions should be banished, especially in the realm of sexuality. The experiments in this latter area have not, as we have seen, been strikingly successful.

Freudian psychology proved far more pervasive and enduring

than Marxism and, in time, penetrated popular culture as well as so-called high culture. Phrases like "Oedipus complex," "Freudian slip," and "ego gratification" became part of the language. There is, of course, nothing to indicate (or certainly nothing to prove) that the Freudian interpretation of the human personality is more scientific than any of a half dozen other interpretations. For the new intellectual class, however, it had the useful function of providing an explanation of "things" when traditional religion no longer seemed able to.

The ties between psychiatry and medicine were destined, as Karl Menninger hoped, to grow closer, but the cost of psychoanalysis limited it to the well-to-do, and its claims to the status of a science continued to be challenged.

# 40

## The Popular Arts

I f many areas of American life appeared ambiguous during the 1920s and 1930s, it was plainly the case that the popular arts flourished. They found a handmaiden in technology—the Gramophone, the radio, and the movies. Music, wedded to the Gramophone and the radio, set the whole world dancing. Movies, silent though they might be in their first incarnation, disclosed a dazzling new world of images.

It was entirely appropriate that the United States should become the entertainment center of the world. It was inevitable in a democracy, more affluent than any other nation, that the ancient and implacable bugaboo of the species, boredom, should assert itself with irresistible urgency. When American workingmen fought, during the nineteenth and well into the twentieth century, for a less-than-seventy-hour week, their employers argued that work was a sovereign corrective for the depraved instincts of the working class (or dangerous class) and that if the hours of labor were shortened, those hours would be spent in bars, in crime, or in plotting revolution. When, in fact, the hours of labor grew shorter (and life correspondingly longer) and it became possible to retire from labor entirely with some years of life expectancy remaining, the question was how, indeed, those hours were to be spent. An enormous vacuum of unstructured time was created. Some of that unstructured time was, as the employers had predicted, spent drinking, but more was spent attending baseball games (and drinking) and, later football games (and drinking) and in an ever-widening range and variety of public entertainments.

It turned out that Americans would pay enormous sums simply to avoid being bored. The Gramophone helped. One could crank a handle, have a few minutes of hectic sound, and dance a bit; soon one could listen to a symphony or an opera, Madame Schumann-Heink or Enrico Caruso. However tinny the sound emitted, it dispelled silence. The radio was a magic extension of the Gramophone, and in the twenties it came into its own. For those who could not attend a particular baseball game, it brought a play-by-play account. Each year throughout this era the maestros of radio added new pleasures and delights for an audience that rapidly swelled into the millions. Soon there were "networks," a revealing word. The nation's psyche was being knit together by the networks, each determined to outdo the other in the breadth of its appeal to legions of listeners.

The great "announcers," some of whom, like the first of the breed, Graham McNamee, were aspiring singers, became household words. Their rich, mellifluous voices poured like a soothing syrup over the airwaves, reporting mass spectacles, sporting events, stunts, and disasters. Paul Fleisher changed his name to Paul Douglas, announced into an open grand piano, "Buck Rogers . . . in the twenty-fifth century!", and went on to become a success in the movies. Norman Brokenshire announced the *Chesterfield Hour*. Suddenly the voice was the compelling organ of the body. There were professional screamers, baby criers, animal imitators, and mimics.

Band music was one of the early forms of the "big broadcast" over national networks, and Fred Waring was one of the first bands to win national popularity. Most of the bands broadcast from a hotel ballroom or auditorium, where they were playing "live." The announcer would declare: "From the beautiful Westwood Room of the fabulous Park Sheraton Hotel in New York City, it's the tantalizing rhythms of Fred Waring and his Pennsylvanians."

Vincent Lopez was one of the first bandleaders to broadcast regularly; his base was the Hotel Taft in New York. Guy Lombardo and his Royal Canadians soon became a New Year's Eve fixture. Paul Whiteman, Cab Calloway, the Dorsey brothers, and, by the thirties, Glenn Miller, Benny Goodman, Gene Krupa, Harry James, Ina Ray Hutton and her all-girl band, Hal Kemp, Wayne King, and Ben Bernie ("the old maestro") all were part of the "big broadcast." Jimmy Lunceford, Duke Ellington, and Count Basie were among the few black band-leaders who made it to big-time radio.

The bands were supplemented by variety shows, which featured vocalists, comedians, and dramatic sketches. One of the first popular variety shows was the *Atlantic Spotlight,* emceed by Ben Grauer and featuring Eddie Cantor and Jimmy Durante. Situation comedies and "soap operas" for bored housewives were another addition. *Amos 'n' Andy,* a comedy involving a black cabdriver, Andy, who, with his friend Amos, ran the Fresh-Air Taxi Company, and their friends Kingfish and Madame Queen began in 1926 and soon ran five nights a week. It was written by white writers and acted by white actors, and for almost twenty years was one of the most popular programs on radio.

The Jack Benny show and Fred Allen and his "alley" became features of the airwaves. There were numerous informational and educational shows—the *American Forum;* the *American School of the Air; America's Town Meeting of the Air* chaired by George V. Denny, Jr., to name a few. In 1934 the *Kraft Music Hall,* sponsored by the cheese makers, began its long career, with Paul Whiteman's orchestra and Al Jolson as MC.

In 1930 WXYZ in Detroit began a program for young people based on the pioneer days of the West. The hero was to be "realistic, serious and sober-minded, a man with a righteous purpose, a man who would serve as an example of good living and clean speech." The result was *The Lone Ranger.* To promote the show, a modest network of four stations was formed; it called itself the Mutual Network.

By the 1930s radio broadcasting had hit its stride. Every hour of the day and most hours of the night were crowded with dramatic shows, serials, bands, symphony orchestras, quiz shows like *Beat the Band,* news broadcasts. One of the longest comedy-dramas was *Ma Perkins,* which began in 1933 and remained a fixture for twenty-seven years. Indeed, one of the distinguishing features of the successful radio programs was their durability. Millions of people were born and grew to man- or womanhood listening to *Myrt and Marge, Fibber McGee and Molly,* the *March of Time*—"Time marches on!" was its tag—or the *Lux Radio Theater.* It was the radio tycoons who rescued the Metropolitan Opera when that prestigious institution, devastated by the Depression, was about to go under. When the Columbia Broadcasting System signed up the famous Philharmonic Orchestra, the National Broadcasting Company created the rival NBC symphony under the baton of Arturo

Toscanini. In the words of Louis Reid, "Radio's world-wide scope has provided the broadcasters with the zest to hook up the Vatican one minute and Moscow the next, of following the serenity of Scandinavia with the confusion of Spain, of switching from a celebration of Bach to a celebration of Bacchus, of passing . . . from hosannas to hi-de-hos."

The modern philosopher Marshall McLuhan has declared that "the medium is the message." It can be said with some confidence that since the appearance of man (and woman) on the stage of world history, no medium, no form of public expression, has been as ubiquitous as the American radio in the period from 1920 to 1940. Such ubiquitousness could not fail to affect the nation's collective psyche in important, if subtle, ways. We have spoken from time to time of the disintegrative effects of American life, even of two Americas, but difficult as it may be to assess, we can be sure that the burgeoning of radio as a creator and conveyor of the popular arts was of profound importance in creating a national consciousness and, in doing so, of counterbalancing, if not overcoming, those disintegrative effects. Karl Radek, the Soviet theoretician who told Hamilton Fish Armstrong that a revolution was not apt to take place in a nation of 24,000,000 automobiles, might well have added "and 100,000,000 radios." Who could man the barricades if it meant missing Kay Kyser's *Kollege of Musical Knowledge* or George Denny's *America's Town Meeting of the Air,* scheduled to explore the dangers of revolution in the United States? It is also hard to imagine that Franklin Roosevelt could have exerted such an influence on the American people without his masterful use of the radio. With most of the leading newspapers of the country strongly opposed to him, FDR was able to bypass the press in direct appeals to the nation. The brilliance of that achievement is underlined by the fact that no subsequent President was able to use the medium of radio as effectively as he.

There was, of course, another equally potent tranquilizer—the silver screen. When the ear was sated, the eye had another realm to explore. The richness of imagination available to the ear was a perpetual challenge to wizards of the eye. B. P. Schulberg's ecstatic evocation of the "Motion Picture" at the First Annual Ball of the Screen Club turned out not to be excessive after all: "Marvel of science, mirror of art, product of the ingenuity of man. . . . You are King in the Land of Mechanical Wonders, supreme in the land of daring dreams! . . . You translate the world's sorrows and delineate life's joys. You bear the burden of the earth. . . . You are great. You are the agent of the age. . . ."

If boredom was to be kept at bay, one must doubt that a better instrument could have been devised. The United States had once been considered (or at least considered itself) the hope and inspiration of the world; now it stepped forth as the creator and custodian of its dreams. What dreams! In the sacred darkness of the movie palace (and palaces they assuredly were, from the Alhambra in Baltimore, where stuffed peacocks perched on richly ornamented fake balconies, to Sacramento, California, where the interior heaven of one theater glittered with stars and skillfully projected clouds drifted by) on-screen luminous figures far larger and more compelling than life acted out the buried and not so buried fantasies of the race—of riches, success, courage, hardihood, feminine beauty beyond desire, manhood without flaw. The heroes and heroines did not have names like ordinary folk, but made-up names that lifted them into the realm of myth. Their teeth were not like teeth of common people; they were as flawless as their tailoring, as brilliant as their gestures, as memorable as their smiles.

It was not uncommon for a town with a population of 10,000 to have a movie theater that held a quarter or a third of the population since it was expected that everyone in the community would go at least once a week. The bill thus changed every night or two so that an avid moviegoer could see three or four picture shows a week. The order of the service was as well established as that of a church: first, in the sacrosanct darkness, short subjects, a Pathé or March of Time newsreel and, with the latter, a portentous voice intoning, "Time . . . marches On!"; next, a cartoon, often greeted with an outbreak of applause; coming attractions; on Saturdays, customarily, another episode in the serial, ending with the hero or heroine hanging over a cliff or in some other imminent peril, to be rescued next Saturday. Then came the sing-along. In the more pretentious palaces a Hammond organ rose pneumatically from the orchestra pit, the words of popular songs or old-time favorites were flashed on the silver screen, and the audience sang together. Indeed, the moviegoers went to the movies in the same spirit (though in far greater numbers) that the faithful went to church—religiously.

The movies were initially considered no more than a form of vulgar entertainment for the masses by those Americans with refinement or good taste. Even D. W. Griffith, the acknowledged genius of the new medium, considered it, in the early days, much inferior to the "legitimate" theater. An important aspect of the emergence of the movies as "art" was the appearance of critics who took them seriously. Hugo Münsterberg, the German-born professor of psychology at Harvard, was one of the first. He had few immediate successors. Not until the 1920s were films treated as art by the new intellectual class. "To me," James Agee wrote in 1927 to Dwight Macdonald, "the great thing about the movies is that it's a brand new field. I don't see how much more can be done with writing or with stage. In fact, every kind of recognized 'art' has been worked pretty nearly to the limit. . . . As for the movies, however, their possibilities are infinite—that is, in so far as the possibilities of any art CAN be so. So far as I can see, all that's been done so far is to show that art is really possible on the screen. We've barely begun to stir the fringes of their possibilities, though." Agee was seventeen; Macdonald, a recent graduate of Yale, was twenty-one. They both were entranced by the movies. They became its first serious professional critics.

Keith Brownlow, the most resourceful historian of the early days of the movies, has noted that the silent-film directors were, for the most part, young men "from every conceivable background." One had been a pipeline worker; another, a tramp; another, a blacksmith. Clarence Brown, one of the most gifted, had been an automobile salesman, and W. S. Van Dyke had been, successively, "a lumberjack, gold miner, railroader, and mercenary." Brownlow added: "They had no qualifications but their experiences, but these were often ideal training for the job, preparing them for rough assignments, tough personality problems, and uncomfortable location trips." To the producer David O. Selznick, "They had no affectation, they were full of adventure and the desire to do things. They were fast-moving and impatient and made their pictures very quickly. They were extremely imaginative and extremely knowledgeable. They were a wonderful breed."

The silent days were the days preeminently of comedy, and Mack Sennett was the master of comedy. Sennett was a huge man whose original ambition had been to be an opera singer. He had made his way through circuses, burlesque houses, and vaudeville. Working as an actor for D. W. Griffith, Sennett revealed that his ambition was to play a slapstick policeman, but Griffith was unimpressed. Sennett began writing down story ideas, hoping to sell them for $25 apiece; he graduated to directing under Griffith's aegis. "He was my day school, my adult education program, my university," Sennett wrote of Griffith. In 1912, with $2,500 from two bookie "partners," Sennett headed for

California and started his own studio on a vacant lot, the Keystone. At last he could have his cops, as they came to be known, the Keystone Kops, the most famous minions of the law in history.

Sennett's office was an abandoned water tower, where, ensconced in a huge bathtub, he could oversee actors and directors on the "lot." He would often start a movie with shots of some actual event and then build his movie around that shot, constructing a story line as he went along. Soon he had assembled what was doubtless the greatest collection of slapstick artists in the history of the film: Roscoe "Fatty" Arbuckle, Chester Conklin, Edgar Kennedy, Ben Turpin, Charlie Chase, and, finally, Charlie Chaplin. In the first year of operation, Keystone turned out more than 140 one- and two-reel comedies. The writer Gene Fowler recalled that when a gag failed to make Sennett laugh in the projection room after a day's shooting, it was eliminated or reshot. "He was," Fowler wrote, "the Abraham Lincoln of comedy, by, for, and of the people—his taste was the most infallible audience barometer in the history of motion picture burlesque. He *never* missed." A devotee of crownless hats, frequent baths, champagne with corned beef and raw onions, Sennett was eccentric even for Hollywood, but under his aegis a company of the greatest comedians in the world flourished. Buster Keaton, Harold Lloyd, Arbuckle, and, for a time, Chaplin—all responded to his large, encouraging presence.

Silent film was not simply stories *without* sound (with captions). It was pantomime, movement, gesture; it was specifically and intensely visual. Thus it was not surprising that the great geniuses of the silent film—Chaplin, Keaton, Lloyd, and Arbuckle—were, in essence, the producers, writers, directors, actors, and stuntmen of their own films. It was what distinguished their work from all other films, what made them timeless when most ordinary dramatic films look hopelessly dated. When we think of films like Chaplin's *The Gold Rush*, Keaton's *The General*, and Lloyd's *Safety Last*, it is easier to understand Jack Warner's conviction that no one wanted to hear actors *talk*. What the geniuses did was carry expressive gesture and movement as far as it could be carried; no one has ever equaled, let alone surpassed, them. Because *gesture was what it was all about* (and because they usually controlled the production in every detail), Chaplin and Keaton and the others could spend days on one small bit of business, a luxury that was seldom, if ever, attained again in the history of film. The consequence was that a picture sometimes took years to make. Chester Conklin, a veteran of the Keystone days, recalled that it took more than two years to film *The Gold Rush*.

Mary Pickford and Charlie Chaplin were the two most adored stars of the silent-movie firmament. Both were also producers and gifted directors. In Chaplin's little tramp he created an image so potent it is used today by a great corporation to sell computers. Moreover, he did it with a meticulous attention to detail that was extraordinary, if not unique. Some scenes were shot as many as 100 times until Chaplin got exactly the nuance he wanted. When he was shooting a picture, he often took days off, thinking about some piece of business. Of Chaplin, T. S. Eliot declared: "The egregious merit of Chaplin is that he has escaped in his own way from the realm of the cinema and invented a *rhythm*. Of course, the unexplored possibilities of the cinema for eluding realism must be very great."

Mary Pickford told Keith Brownlow: "I always tried to get laughter into my pictures. Make them laugh, make them cry, and back to laughter. What do people go to the theater for? An emotional exercise. . . . It is not my prerogative as an actress to teach them anything. *They* will teach *me*. *They* will discipline *me*. And that's how it should be because I am a servant of the public." When Pickford felt she could no longer play the roles that the public associated her with, she left the screen. "I didn't want what happened to Chaplin," she added, "to happen to me. When he discarded the little tramp, the little tramp turned around and killed him. The little girl made me. I wasn't waiting for the little girl to kill me."

Charlie Chaplin's only rivals in the world of comedy were Harold Lloyd and Buster Keaton. Like Chaplin, both men functioned as their own directors much of the time, and many of their most brilliant gags were their own creations. In the early years they worked without scripts in a curious combination of spontaneity and laborious planning. The result was a remarkable fluidity.

After some pallid imitations of Chaplin, Lloyd found his own character, the tentative, bespectacled all-American boy, apprehensively confronting the world but determined to overcome his apprehensiveness. Lloyd and Hal Roach had met as $5-a-day extras at Universal Studios. From there, after a brief stint at Keystone, they went on to make their own one- and two-reelers. Beginning in 1917, Lloyd developed the character that made him famous. Like Chaplin and Keaton, Lloyd had the capacity for taking infinite pains with a picture, previewing a film time and again to be sure that gags worked and were properly spaced and timed. Again, like Chaplin and Keaton, he did most of his own stunts, many of them extremely hazardous. Although he made more than 300 films during his career, he is most closely associated with what he called his "thrill pictures," the most famous being *Safety Last,* in which he emulated a human fly crawling up the façade of a ten-story building.

Keaton's childhood was undoubtedly the most bizarre of all. Part of his parents' traveling medicine show, he was born during a cyclone and given his nickname by his father's friend the magician Harry Houdini. "I was a veteran before I went into pictures," Keaton told Keith Brownlow. "I made my first picture when I was twenty-five." Keaton's greatest gift besides his acrobatic skill was the painstaking attention he gave to the creation of extraordinary sight gags and visual effects. His films, like those of Chaplin and Lloyd, took much longer to make than ordinary dramatic movies and generally cost much more.

The comic possibilities shading into the surreal that were inherent in the film were demonstrated in dazzling fashion by Keaton in a 1924 film entitled *Sherlock Junior.* In that remarkable work Keaton, as Dwight Macdonald pointed out, anticipated half a century of filmic invention, including Woody Allen's 1985 film *The Purple Rose of Cairo.* As a movie-struck projectionist Keaton comes out of his booth, walks up to the screen, and enters it as a character in the film that is playing. His parents, his girlfriend, and his rival all become actors in the film.

Considering the generally demoralizing atmosphere of Hollywood, Harold Lloyd's greatest achievements may have been preserving his life and fortune and remaining married to the same wife.

Buster Keaton's story was less happy. When his style of comedy fell out of fashion and his wife, Natalie Talmadge, the sister of the star Norma Talmadge, divorced him, Keaton became an alcoholic and a part-time gag writer for his ex-wife's brother-in-law, Joseph Schenck. Before his death Keaton sobered up, tended to his flock of chickens, and enjoyed a belated fame when his best films were revived. At the height of his career he was rated one of the ten top movie stars in Hollywood, along with cowboy star William Hart, Norma Talmadge, the athletic Douglas Fairbanks, Mary Pickford, Charlie Chaplin, Latin lover Rudolph Valentino, Harold Lloyd, and glamorous Gloria Swanson.

In 1926 a revolution in filmmaking took place. In a desperate effort to shore up its waning fortunes, Warner Brothers introduced a

novelty, the Vitaphone, or talking picture. A year later it completed
the first fell-length feature film with sound, *The Jazz Singer,* with Al
Jolson singing "Mammy." (*The Jazz Singer* was based on the life story
of its star. Jolson—Asa Yoelson—was born in the Russian village of
Srednicke, the son of Naomi and Moses Yoelson. His father, a pious
cantor, was horrified at the thought of his son's leaving the "sanctity
of the synagogue for a career as a public entertainer.") The technique
of the "talking" had been available for more than a decade, but Thomas
Edison had decided that there was "no field for talking pictures." Nonetheless, *The Jazz Singer* was a sensational success, and within a year
every major studio had produced a talkie. In 1927 only 55 theaters
out of 20,500 had sound equipment; two years later there were 9,000.
At the time of the stock market crash weekly movie theater admissions
had risen to 110,000,000 a week (the country's population was
121,000,000). The appearance of talking pictures was hailed at once
by a popular song:

> If I had a talking picture of you,
> I'd play it every time I felt blue,
> I'd sit there in the gloom of my lonely little room;
> I would have three shows a day,
> And a midnight matinee.

John Gilbert was one of the great lovers of the silver screen, but
his high-pitched voice meant the end of his career. Norma Talmadge
was another casualty, "a vision of romance," Anita Loos wrote, "as long
as she kept her mouth shut." Her ineradicable Brooklyn accent was
her downfall. However hard the innovation was on certain stars, "talking pictures brought a tremendous advance in the possibilities of film."
Now scripts, instead of being for the most part rough outlines of plots
interspersed with captions, became more specific and intricate than
plays for the legitimate theater.

The rise of Irving Thalberg, the "boy genius" of Hollywood, was
coincidental with the advent of the talkies. Thalberg, who had been
infatuated with a third Talmadge sister, Constance, "Dutch" to her
friends, developed a bevy of women superstars—among them Greta
Garbo, Myrna Loy, Jean Harlow, Joan Crawford, and his wife, Norma
Shearer. Thalberg's improbable right-hand man at Metro-Goldwyn-
Mayer was Arlie Lewin. The son of Russian immigrant parents, Lewin
had served a brief stint as professor of English at a small Midwestern
college. Lured by the movies, he headed for Hollywood, where Thal-

berg, always on the lookout for eccentric geniuses, promptly signed him up as his assistant.

One of Irving Thalberg's most potent contributions to the silver screen was his skillful development of sex. Mary Pickford, Mabel Normand, Blanche Sweet, and Lillian Gish, stars of the silents, were pretty or strikingly handsome women, but their sexuality was subordinated to a kind of stylized sweetness. Thalberg's new stars were women like Jean Harlow, who projected an unabashed image of sexuality. Jean Harlow's real name was Harlean Carpentier. She had been reared in Kansas City, where an indulgent grandfather had given her an ermine bedspread for her fifth birthday. At the age of sixteen she had married one of the city's wealthy playboys. After the couple had moved to Los Angeles, Harlean, finding housekeeping a dull business, began working as an extra in movies. Thalberg "discovered" her and realized at once that with her he could create a new dimension in screen romance. He christened her Jean Harlow and starred her in a series of hugely successful films, beginning with *Red Headed Woman,* for which Anita Loos wrote the script. Unlike most stars, Harlow treated the film world with a thinly veiled mockery.

Besides raising sex in film to new heights of sophisticated suggestiveness (certainly there had been earlier sex goddesses, Theda Bara being the most famous), Thalberg, according to Anita Loos, developed the preview, whereby films yet to be released were tried out on local audiences. At the end of the film the viewers were asked a series of questions, and portions of the film were often rewritten and refilmed to conform to the audiences' suggestions. It was a practice much ridiculed by those who considered movies a hopelessly inferior art or, perhaps more accurately, craft, but Anita Loos welcomed it. When Thalberg questioned whether audiences were sophisticated enough to "get" her witty and lighthearted dialogue, she challenged him to try it out on preview audiences. They responded enthusiastically. It might thus be said that at least in its early years the preview served to raise rather than lower the quality of Hollywood films by demonstrating that the public was ahead of the filmmakers.

An important by-product of the advent of sound was the musical film. It was as though the musical were the challenge that Hollywood had been waiting for, that the words "extravaganza," "colossal," and "spectacular" were invented for. The choreography was so elaborate, the settings so dazzling, the dance routines of the stars so intricate and compelling that a new order of unreality was created. The so-called story might be jejune in the extreme, the characters flat and unconvincing, the songs merely tinkly (although many were the works of such composers as Jerome Kern, Irving Berlin, George Gershwin, and Cole Porter), but all that mattered little in light of the visual "effects." One set of images followed another; the world dissolved into light and motion; chorus lines, viewed from an aerial perspective, turned into flowers and then back into long-legged chorines of infinite desirability. They floated on vaporous clouds, swam in limpid waters. Busby Berkeley ruled the world; Fred Astaire was the crown prince, Ginger Rogers the queen.

Above all, the musical was a celebration of the scantily clad female form. It was *about* barely draped feminine flesh and particularly about incredible legs that moved with the precision of a single great, alluring machine. The musical offered the viewers an essence or distillation of youthful beauty. The performing life of the chorus girl was as brief as that of the fruit fly, but it was splendid to behold. The musical did not last much longer. It was born on the stage and meant for the stage; its conventions were impossible to sustain in cinema.

By the early thirties Walt Disney had turned the infant animated cartoon into a new art form with the adventures of Mickey Mouse, Donald Duck, and a constantly growing cast of characters. The film critic Louis Reid called *Snow White and the Seven Dwarfs*, which appeared in 1937, "the greatest boon to the movies since sound."

With the arrival of talkies, pairs or groups of comedians virtually replaced the single comedian; they could talk to each other. Visual gags became less important than oral ones (the Marx Brothers bridged the gap between the Chaplin-Keaton days and, say, Bing Crosby and Bob Hope). Laurel and Hardy, the Little Rascals (movement still very important there), the Ritz Brothers, the Three Stooges—what we might call comic ensemble playing came into its own.

The talkies simply did not add aural to the visual but constituted a new medium with a whole different set of possibilities (and limitations). They ended what was in some ways the greatest era of film and began the modern age, a time when the primary task of filmmakers was to saturate the market with films. Once a new medium has established itself as a universal form of entertainment, the public becomes insatiable, and artistic considerations (and all others) have to be subordinated to relentless production schedules. That was the story of Hollywood in the 1930s. To feed the insatiable appetite of the moviegoing public for films of whatever quality, for images however banal or inane that moved on the silver screen, Hollywood was forced to turn out 500 or 600 films a year. The great majority of these were low-budget productions, or B movies (a number of which, incidentally, turned out to be better art and entertainment than the high-budget blockbusters).

The fastest-growing and most exotic region of the country was Southern California. Beginning in 1919, oil was struck first at Huntington Beach, then at Signal Hill and Santa Fe Springs. By 1923 the three fields were producing almost half a million barrels of oil a day among them. In Hell's Half Acre at Santa Fe Springs the derricks were so close together that a man could walk across most of the field stepping from one derrick to another. Mushrooming suburbs sprang up around the oil fields; some lucky individuals struck oil in their yards. Oil derricks bisected the Los Angeles and Beverly Hills skyline, competing with palm trees. By the end of World War I Hollywood had become the nation's and the world's film capital. Mary Pickford and Douglas Fairbanks laid the foundation of the film colony's social life, which soon took on a quality as bizarre as any movie fantasy. Foreign titles, real and bogus, bypassed New York for Hollywood. The Princess Beatriz de Ortego y Braganza of Alhambre Granada, Spain, was wined and dined until it was discovered that she was an enterprising San Francisco typist. But the duke d'Alba was real enough, as were Lord and Lady Mountbatten. Titled Europeans were anxious to appear as actors in Hollywood films. The Baron Henry Arnous de Rivire co-starred with the dog Stongheart. A cousin of the king of Spain, the duke of Ducal, had a small role in Douglas Fairbanks's *The Thief of Baghdad,* and Archduke Leopold of Austria had parts in a number of films. Even prominent socialites like Mrs. Morgan Belmont were prevailed upon to take small parts.

Among the famous hosts and hostesses in the film colony were Edgar and Ruth Selwyn. Selwyn was a producer at MGM, and the Selwyns were known for their high style and good taste. When Anita Loos and Wilson Mizner arrived at their house for a Christmas party in 1931, they found the swimming pool filled with floating gardenias. The party was in honor of the world's (it was said) richest woman, Doris Duke, heir to a tobacco fortune, looking, Anita Loos noted, "like a Persian princess." Among the more or less regular guests of the Selwyns were the ex-king of Spain, the Cole Porters, Elsa Maxwell, and Evelyn McLean, owner of the Hope Diamond. The prince of Wales and the duke and duchess of Sutherland were there when their peregrinations brought them to the United States. The exotic-looking princess de Frasso and her gangster lover Bugsy Siegel, as handsome as a movie star, rubbed elbows with Hollywood's stars. Another familiar figure was Barbara Hutton, the Woolworth heiress, "a white wraith except for heavy eyebrows that made her seem an Etruscan portrait." She was married to Prince Mdivani, a no-count prince, who would soon drift away with a sizable chunk of her fortune, to be followed by, in time, Cary Grant. It was said that Grant was put off by Hutton's insistence on speaking only French to the household staff.

Sex scandals were routine, although most of those involving major stars were hushed up by the studios. When Douglas Fairbanks asked the deposed king of Spain what film star he would like to meet, his ex-majesty replied that he would like to meet Fatty Arbuckle, who had killed Virginia Rappe while she, in Anita Loos's words, "was trying to fight off his unorthodox love-making." That scandal did get out and ended Arbuckle's career. But an atmosphere of sexuality pervaded the industry. Darryl Zanuck, it was said, had a liaison with some star or starlet punctually every afternoon at four o'clock in his office on the studio lot.

The unreal quality of the movie world took a heavy toll on the men and women involved in the "industry." Periods of exhausting activity that would daunt a prizefighter while a film was being shot alternated with intervals of idleness. Alcohol and drugs were commonplace. An actor on the Sennett lot put a number of actors and actresses on junk, among them the popular star Mabel Normand. She and several others died as a consequence. When the former child star Kenneth Anger came to write about the scandals of Hollywood under the title *Hollywood Babylon,* he rated a number of well-known films as one, two, or three suicide movies, based on the number of featured players in them who later committed suicide. The movie *All About Eve* was, by Anger's system, a SSS, "a triple suicide movie": Barbara Bates, George Sanders, and Marilyn Monroe were eventual suicides.

During the Depression Hollywood became a kind of classy relief agency for the better-known writers, who could count on base salaries of $1,500 a week, more than most of them made in a year from their writing. John Dos Passos went to the cinema capital to do "Spanish background," at a huge salary, for Marlene Dietrich. "He writes back that he hates it," Edmund Wilson wrote Malcolm Cowley, "but what a break!"

Since New York and Hollywood were virtually synonymous, it was inevitable that the movie world evince the same radical politics as its Eastern connection. John Howard Lawson was only the most prominent of those writers and directors who were also active members of the Communist Party. Many of them were gathered in the Hollywood Anti-Nazi League, which boasted 4,000 members and which obediently changed its name after the German-Russian nonaggression pact to the Hollywood League for Democratic Action.

The cultural historian would do well to contemplate the fact that the advent of the "talking picture" preceded the Depression by slightly more than a year. Hollywood was dismayed by the crash, assuming that its audiences would dwindle away, but its pessimism proved unwarranted. In the words of Anita Loos, "motion picture houses throughout the nation were jammed. Folks were skimping on the bare necessities of life to buy distraction." Distraction at fifteen or twenty-five cents a ticket seemed to many Americans the only bargain left. The moving pictures were a great pacifier and distracter. Certainly they helped keep boredom (which may be as great an incentive to revolution as injustice) at arm's length.

When any new form of expression presents itself to the members of a particular culture, it has the power to attract the most creative individuals; in the first moment, therefore, work is done that, however crude and awkward technically, can never again be equaled. A purity of vision combines with the exhilaration of the new form to produce remarkable results. This was clearly the case with moving pictures and especially the case, for reasons that are not readily apparent, with comedy of the "silent" days.

The final effect of the movies was perhaps cumulative. They poured forth in such a stream, good, bad, and indifferent, that all the empty spaces in the American consciousness were filled to overflowing; together they constituted a new dimension of reality and made the world smaller in the process. If, in earlier generations, America had been a land of promise, that promise was often ambiguously vague. Now the word "America" summoned up for peoples around the globe a set of images which, wildly conflicting though they might be, had a potency all their own; as surely as it was anything at all, that strange montage was America.

It was calculated in 1938 that more than 85,000,000 people attended the movies each week in the United States. There were an estimated 90,000 movie theaters in the world (showing predominantly American films), almost 20,500 of them in the United States. The importance of the "foreign market" to American filmmakers is perhaps best illustrated by the fate of a movie considered objectionable by the Nazis. When James Whale, the director of such films as *Frankenstein* and *Show Boat,* was hired by Universal to direct Erich Maria Remarque's *The Road Back,* a sequel to the brilliant *All Quiet on the Western Front,* the German consul in Los Angeles wrote to everyone connected with the production to warn that if it were made, all Universal films would be banned in Germany. The movie was withdrawn, and portions considered objectionable to the consul were cut.

In Harold Stearns's symposium *America Now,* published in 1938, a chapter entitled "Amusement: Radio and Movies," preceded chapters on politics, business, economics, education, religion, etc., indicating that Stearns considered radio and the movies the two dominant elements in American life. "In the production of mass entertainment," the author of the article, Louis R. Reid, wrote, ". . . America has achieved a position as startling and significant as the rise of the industrial era following the Civil War. On these inexpensive, easily-accessible and closely-related amusements the public is so dependent that vast commercial, sociologic, technological and—not least—artistic forces have been given powerful play in the nation."

Popular music was primarily the music of Tin Pan Alley, songs of the type Americans had loved to sing since the era of "My Old Kentucky Home." The Gramophone (or Victrola) had given an enormous stimulus to the writing of such songs. Tin Pan Alley had been strongly influenced by Scott Joplin and ragtime. Will Marion Cook was a black songwriter whose popularity rivaled Scott Joplin's. Both his parents had gone to college (his mother was a graduate of Oberlin), and the musically precocious Cook grew up in Washington, D.C. At the age of eight his parents sent him to Berlin to study violin under the master Joseph Joachim. Back in the United States Cook discovered that the concert world of classical music was closed to blacks, and he began setting some of Paul Laurence Dunbar's poems to music. They were an instant success as "coon songs," and his mother protested, "Oh, Will! Will! I've sent you all over the world to study and become a great musician, and you return such a nigger!"

The first all-black revue that opened on Broadway was entitled *Shuffle Along* and featured songs by ex-Sergeant Noble Sissle, who had been the drum major of the black 369th Infantry, and Eubie Blake, who also played in the musical. Starring Florence Mills, *Shuffle Along* was a sensational success with white audiences. Sissle, Claude McKay wrote, "knows his range and canters over it with the ease and grace of an antelope. The Harmony Kings are in the direct line of the Jubilee Singers." The lovely Florence Mills was the "sparkling gold star of the show." James Reese Europe, another hero of the 369th, became one of the first of the big band kings, the rage of Harlem, of Broadway, and of France. In Claude McKay's words, "his heart was shot out during a performance in Boston by a savage buck of his own race."

Tin Pan Alley turned out a constant stream of popular songs, both sentimental and nonsensical. "Three little words; eight little letters, just three little words, That say 'I love you.' " "Yes, we have no bananas, / We have no bananas today." "Life is just a bowl of cherries, / Don't take it serious / It's too mysterious. / You work, you slave, you worry so, / But you can't take your dough / When you go, go, go. / So keep repeating it's the berries. . . ." Then there was Barney Google, "with his goo-goo-googly eyes."

A popular ditty was:

> Just Molly and me
> And baby makes three,
> We're happy in my blue heaven.

There was also:

> Tea for two and two for tea,
> I'm for you and you're for me.

Other hits were "The Love Nest," "Hot Lips," "Burning Kisses," "Sweet Lips," "Kiss Before Dawn," "Baby Face," "I Need Lovin'." The years between 1920 and 1928 witnessed twenty-four Broadway musicals, among them *The Student Prince, No, No, Nannette, Show Boat,* and *Rio Rita,* all of which produced a spate of popular songs.

With the onset of the Depression popular songs often reflected the somber mood of the country. The classic song of the Depression era was "Brother, Can You Spare a Dime?"

> Once I built a railroad, made it run,
> Made it race against time,
> Once I built a railroad,
> Now it's done.
> Brother, can you spare a dime?

Even musicals took on a social tone. The most successful was the garment workers' revue *Pins and Needles*. The opening number set the tone:

> Sing me a song of social significance,
> All other songs are taboo.

A former coed lamented:

> I used to be in a daisy-chain,
> But now I'm a chain-store daisy . . .
> I sell smart but thrifty corsets
> At three-fifty, better grade
> Four, sixty-nine.
> I sell bras and girdles
> To Maudes and Myrtles
> To hold in their plump
> Behind this counter.
> Once I wrote poems
> Put people in tears
> Now I write checks
> For Red Star brassieres
> I used to be in a daisy-chain
> But now I'm a chain-store daisy.

A showstopper was a black number in which parents and friends celebrate the birth of a son, singing that they intend to name him "Franklin D. Roosevelt Jones." "He will not be a dud / Or a stick in the mud / When he's Franklin D. Roosevelt Jones, / Yessiree, yessiree yessireeeeeeee."

Then there was jazz, less to be sung than danced to. Americans had always loved to dance; foreign travelers almost invariably commented on the infatuation of Americans with dancing. Jazz captured America and then captured the world. There were also the blues and gospel and country music. Blues was a relatively recent secular offspring of spirituals. Gospel was black shoutin' music, music of praise to the Lord sung by black congregations, and it, like blues and jazz, was of relatively recent origin. Fortunately we do not have to decide whether jazz came up the Mississippi from New Orleans or down from St. Louis or east from Kansas City; it is enough that it became a permanent constituent of American music.

Country was white Southern music, vaguely derived from English ballads and folk songs preserved in the Southern mountains. It was the mournful music of love and betrayal and, not infrequently, murder. Although it spread into the "southern" Midwest, it remained stubbornly regional.

While black songwriters, as we have seen, wrote Tin Pan Alley songs, the alley was largely a white preserve; jazz was unmistakably black. Original New Orleans bands usually had piano, bass fiddle, banjo, and tuba or drums, with several wind instruments "out in front." Following the example of King Oliver and the early Louis Armstrong band, bands grew larger and larger—trombone, clarinet, drums, cornet, "vibes"—but the improvisational character of the early jazz bands was preserved. White bands learned from black bands, and jazz was one of the few areas of American life where blacks and whites mixed with some degree of freedom.

Robert Palmer, historian of the blues, ascribes their origin to the Mississippi delta near Clarksville, the Stovall plantation, and the Will Dockery plantation. "Now the blues was a Saturday night deal," Joe Dockery, Will's son, told Palmer. "The crap games started about noon Saturday, and then the niggers would start getting drunk. . . . And then they'd have frettin' and fightin' scrapes that night and all the next day." There Charley Patton began playing his own version of the blues. Robert Johnson, another delta bluesman, sang:

> You can call the blues, you can call the blues any old thing you please,
> You can call the blues any old thing you please,
> But the blues ain't nothing but the doggone heart disease.

Muddy Waters, one of the fathers of the blues on the Stovall plantation in Mississippi, sang classic blues for Alan Lomax:

> If I'm feelin' tomorrow
> Like I feel today
> I'm goin' to pack my suitcase
> And make my getaway
> I'm all worried in my mind
> And I never been satisfied
> And I just can't keep from cryin'.

While blues had an origin independent of jazz, it soon became a basic ingredient of jazz and the special province of black women vocalists. To Mezz Mezzrow, Bessie Smith was the mistress of blues singing—"Young Woman Blues," "Reckless Blues," "Empty Bed Blues." Mezzrow described her as "all woman, all the femaleness the world ever saw in one sweet package . . . tall and brown-skinned, with great dimples . . . dripping good looks . . . buxom and massive but stately too, shapely as an hour-glass. . . ." Bessie Smith died in 1937, when a white hospital in Mississippi refused to admit her after she had been badly injured in an automobile accident. Other great blues singers were Billie Holiday, Ethel Waters, Mabs Moberly, and Pearl Bailey. Indeed, one of the most arresting facts about the jazz era was the number of black women involved, both as instrumentalists and vocalists. Linda Dahl's *Stormy Weather* is a history primarily of black jazzwomen. She tells of dozens of now largely forgotten black women instrumentalists, from Billie Pierce, who played piano for the Preservation Hall Jazz Band in the early twenties, to Dolly Adams, who played with the Creole Serenaders and finally formed her own band in the late 1930s, to Lil Hardin and Mary Lou Williams. Lovie Austin inspired Mary Lou Williams, who wrote: "I remember seeing this great woman sitting in the pit and conducting a group of five or six men, her legs crossed, a cigarette in her mouth, playing the show with her right hand and writing music for the next hand with her left. Wow! . . . My entire concept was based on the few times I was around Lovie Austin." It was Lovie Austin who wrote one of Bessie Smith's greatest songs, "Graveyard Blues."

A group of black women singers bridged the gap between blues and gospel, among them "Sister" Rosetta Tharpe, Martha Belle Hall, and Arizona Dranes, a blind pianist-singer. The jazz historian Frank Driggs wrote of Dranes: "It is easy, listening to her play, to see the relationship between gospel, blues, and boogie-woogie. . . ." Dahl counted several hundred black female instrumentalists, bandleaders, and vocalists. While there were a number of white vocalists with the big bands of the thirties, white female instrumentalists, composers, and bandleaders were rare.

As we have seen, blues had a particular potency for black writers and poets. Many of Langston Hughes's poems were written in a blues vernacular. Ralph Ellison was another black writer deeply influenced by the blues mood.

Chicago was famous for the jazz-hungry ofay (white) kids who hung on the fringes of the great black bands and curried favor with their idols. Austin High School was their headquarters. "As they roamed around town in their knee-britches," Mezz Mezzrow wrote, "sniffing for signs of life like a scavenger snagging cigarette butts, they bumped into other defiant, music-starved kids like themselves—Floyd O'Brien, Muggsy Spanier, Eddie Condon, Gene Krupa, . . . Joe Marsala, Bill Davidson, Danny Polo, Jack Teagarden, Jess Stacy, Pee Wee Russell. . . . All these different strands of music kept snaking around in their heads, and these kids finally began to weave them together, working out their own styles and techniques. . . . They started to play hot music themselves. . . ." One result was Husk O'Hare's Wolverines, one of the first white jazz bands. The *American Mercury* was their bible. It seemed to them that they were trying to do in sound what H. L. Mencken and George Jean Nathan were doing with words; the *American Mercury* was literary marijuana.

Richard Voynow was a jazz pianist and manager of the Wolverines, whose most famous member was Bix Beiderbecke. Muggsy Spanier was another young white musician infatuated by the New Orleans style of King Oliver and his Creole Jazz Band. "Jazz was played long before this craze about it came into being," Richard Voynow told the Federal Writers' Project interviewer Sam Ross in the mid-thirties. "Nobody made too big a fuss about it." As Bud Freeman described the evolution of Chicago style, it was a composite of the New Orleans Rhythm Kings (a white band playing in Chicago), "who planted the seed, and then Joe Oliver, Louis Armstrong, Bix, Jimmy Noone . . . and Bessie Smith. Our style, 'Chicago style,' came from all of that."

Mezz Mezzrow ("Mezz" was one of the innumerable names for marijuana) was entranced by jazz and jazz musicians as he was growing up in Pontiac, Michigan. Mezzrow boasted that he learned to play the sax in the Pontiac reformatory: "Took my public-school training in three jails and plenty of poolrooms, went to college in a gang of tea[marijuana]-pads. . . ." Hearing "Livery Stables Blues" played by the Original Dixieland Jazz Band while he was in Pontiac turned him on to jazz. Out of prison, Mezzrow headed for Chicago, one of the great centers of jazz. Chicago was crawling with big-time gamblers and gangsters—Nick the Greek, Big Izzy, Cincy Norton. One of them became famous when he parlayed $7 into $43,000, bought the Boulevard Hotel, and turned it into a four-story whorehouse. At the Roamer Inn, a cathouse, speakeasy, and gambling joint, Mezzrow sat for hours listening to a Creole jazz band, "straight from the bayou."

The DeLuxe Café, at Thirty-fifth and State, was the real center of Chicago night life. It was there Mezzrow first heard such musicians as Sugar Johnnie play the cornet, Sidney Bechet on clarinet and soprano sax, and Lil Hardin, Louis Armstrong's wife, on piano. They played numbers like "Gold Dust," "Skeleton Jungle," "Sassafras," "I Ain't Gonna Give Nobody None of My Jelly Roll," "Apple Sass Rag,"—pieces in which there were elements of ragtime and blues and something else. The clarinets of Jimmie Noone and Johnny Dodds were another inspiration.

Marijuana was the jazzman's tea. "Tea," Mezzrow wrote, "puts a musician in a real masterly sphere, and that's why so many jazzmen have used it. . . . Nothing can mess you up. You hear everything at once and you hear it right."

Leon Bismarck Beiderbecke, Bix for short, had grown up in Davenport, Iowa, "a rawboned, husky, farmboy kind of kid," in Mezzrow's words. The two young men were soon close friends, united by their enthusiasm for jazz. Beiderbecke taught Mezzrow "Riverboat Shuffle" and dazzled him with his horn playing, with a tone "full, big, rich and round, standing out like a pearl. . . ." Beiderbecke was credited with being the inventor of swing through his smooth cornet style and gift for improvisation.

Chicago Heights was another nightclub where black and white musicians met on Sunday afternoons "to groove real holes. . . . Hell . . . we'd sit down and play blues for an hour and a half and we'd have to stop from physical and mental exhaustion although the ideas we'd be getting were absolutely inexhaustible. You know you're in the groove the more you get yourself worked up. . . . When you're in a groove you're lost in what you're doing. . . . Jazz isn't like classical music where you get a chance to describe things. The images you get are very disconnected, more like a dream," George Barnes told Sam Ross.

Muggsy Spanier began playing the drums at the age of thirteen. He borrowed his brother's long pants and stood outside the Dreamland Café in Chicago to listen to King Oliver's band. After his mother had bought him a cornet and he had mastered it, Oliver let him sit in with his band. That was ecstasy for young Spanier. It was "unheard of in those days up North here, a white person playing with Negroes. There were few white guys they'd let sit in with them. . . ."

Like the movies, jazz was an American item of export. Josephine Baker was brought over to Paris by Caroline Dudley, a white woman, in *La Revue Nègre*. The musical created a sensation and made Baker the toast of Paris. In London and Berlin, in Moscow and Tokyo, jazz proved irresistible. Just as the twenties belonged to the silent films (or the silent films to the twenties), they belonged to the great black jazz bands. The thirties saw the birth of swing, a kind of formalized white derivative of jazz. White musicians took jazz, smoothed it out, and made big money. Harry James, the Dorsey brothers, Glenn Miller, Benny Goodman, Woody Herman all were excellent musicians, and they made good music, music for records and the radio. Underneath it black music continued. Some black bands (Jimmie Lunceford, Jimmy Rushing, Louis Armstrong, Duke Ellington) made it into the big band world and continued to do brilliant and innovative things, Ellington especially, but many of the great black jazzmen were reduced to working as day laborers or playing for tips in small jazz clubs. The end of Prohibition was a major blow to jazz. Speakeasies disappeared, and there were far fewer places to play.

While small jazz combos stressed individual riffs and improvisation, the larger bands depended on brilliant arrangers, who were, in fact, composers in all but name. A number of black musicians and bandleaders were arrangers for white bands. Don Redman was one of the most accomplished arrangers, and Fletcher Henderson, besides having his own band, did arranging for other bandleaders.

Not surprisingly, jazz turned out to have serious ideological implications. It was decadent, the ideologues of nazism and communism decided. In Russia the novelist Maxim Gorky alerted the party to the demoralizing effects of jazz. "Listening for a few moments to these wails, one involuntarily imagines an orchestra of sexually driven madmen conducted by a man-stallion brandishing a huge genital member," Gorky wrote. Blacks, he added, "undoubtedly laugh in their sleeves to see how their white masters are evolving toward a savagery which they themselves are leaving behind."

The Nazis denounced jazz as "judeonegroid music." The Soviet solution to the passion of Russians for jazz was to form a state jazz orchestra which was forbidden to play real jazz and which produced an ersatz jazz, purged of any sexual undertones. Its first concert was greeted with "booing, hissing and shouting" and "ended in a near riot." Sergei Prokofiev's work *Lieutenant Kije Suite* was barred because it called for a saxophone, an instrument under a cloud because it was associated with jazz.

Paul Robeson was prevailed upon to denounce jazz and to state that spirituals and blues were the only true black music. Jazz was played by "debased Negroes," he declared, and it "prostituted and ruthlessly perverted the genuine expression of folk life." Jazz was denounced in Russia as a "Jewish Freemasonic Yowl," and stubborn jazz musicians were sent off to labor camps for corrective training; a few lucky ones ended up in a forced labor camp the commandant of which was a secret jazz fanatic. They constituted his private jazz combo.

In the United States the party's response was far more cautious, but there were noticeable tensions over the issue. When Earl Robinson took Huddie Ledbetter (Leadbelly) to a Communist summer camp for adults, Ledbetter's low-down blues songs about "Ella Speed" and "Frankie and Johnny" caused an uproar, which subsided only when Ledbetter sang a song about the Scottsboro boys, followed by "Bourgeois Blues": "the white man, he know how / To throw a colored man a nickel, Just to see him bow. / Oh, Washington, it's a bourgeois town."

A buried and only recently exhumed class of black music was the so-called race record, made for black listeners and sold in the black section (usually the basements) of Southern department stores. Race records featured black bands and singers like Nellie Lutcher, seldom heard by whites.

On a very different level, Marian Anderson, a contralto who had started her career singing in church choirs, became an international concert star, giving more than 100 concerts in Scandinavian countries. Roland Hayes, acclaimed by foreign critics as one of the great tenor voices of the day, also became famous on the European concert stage.

If sports were not precisely a popular art, they were definitely a form of mass entertainment. Although the "play" element was rapidly leached out in favor of commercialization, Americans could not get enough of sports. Baseball was, of course, America's game, and the stars of baseball glittered with a brilliance that no other American heroes could rival. The heroes that Thomas Carlyle wrote about in his essay "Heroes and Hero-Worship" were Old World heroes, famous warriors and war chiefs, statesmen and orators, prophets and saints and kings. The heroes of democratic America played shortstop or outfield or pitched a baseball with blinding speed or wicked guile. Small boys dreamed not of becoming famous generals or notable politicians but of emulating Christy Mathewson or Ty Cobb or Babe Ruth. The two Dempsey-Tunney fights set records for gate receipts and attendance.

The distinction between amateur and professional gradually broke down under the pressure of the democratization of sport. Tennis, the game heretofore of the rich, became a remunerative sport for gifted young men of modest means. One consequence was that the skill with which various previously amateur games were played vastly increased. It was soon evident that not only were "gentlemen" not superior in athletic prowess to members of the lower classes (a cherished article of upper-class faith), but they were, with some notable exceptions, inferior. By the mid-thirties the United States had reaped the benefits of having carried the "democratization of sports" further than any other capitalist country. We were, in the words of John Kieran, the sports columnist of the *New York Times*, "the world leader in sports and organized athletics" (Kieran pointed out what had happened to the Greeks after they obtained a similar ascendancy).

To be fair to upper-class youth, the increased competition that resulted from enlarging the pool of potential athletes some hundreds of times was doubtless the primary factor in improving performances. Sports technology also improved. Running tracks were better made and vaulting poles, bats and gloves, and rackets were substantially improved. Improved diets meant taller and stronger and heavier athletes.

Far less defensible was the disposition to turn collegiate athletics, especially football, into quasi-professional sports. Kieran pointed out that a recent Rose Bowl team had included five married men out of a starting eleven, hardly a representative undergraduate group. Kieran took comfort in the thought that aroused college faculties must soon put a check to the drift toward increasing professionalism in intercollegiate sports.

Between 1924 and 1936 black athletes gradually made their presence felt in intercollegiate and Olympic competition. In 1924 William DeHart Hubbard, a University of Michigan trackman, won the long jump in Paris, the first black athlete to win a gold medal. Feelings ran high during the games, and French crowds on several occasions attacked American athletes, ostensibly because the Untied States had criticized the French for occupying the Ruhr Valley in defiance of the Versailles Treaty.

When the 1928 Olympics were held in Amsterdam, 3,014 athletes, including 290 women, represented forty-six nations. The United States won fifty-six gold, silver, and bronze medals. Germany, joining the games for the first time since 1912, was second with thirty-one medals.

The 1932 Olympics were held in Los Angeles; because of what was considered its inaccessibility and modest facilities, only 1,409 athletes participated, representing thirty-seven nations. Black athletes dominated the dash events. Eddie Tolan, like DeHart Hubbard, was a Michigan student. His principal competition in the 100-meter dash was another black sprinter, Ralph Metcalfe of Marquette University. Tolan, it was judged, beat Metcalfe by two inches. In the 200-meter dash Americans finished one, two, three, with Tolan again the winner.

The 1936 Olympics, held in Berlin, was given a heightened drama by virtue of the fact that Hitler, then at the height of his power, attempted to use the occasion to demonstrate the superiority of the so-called Aryan race. The United States, which had "won" the 1932 games by an overwhelming margin, as calculated by gold, silver, and bronze medals, was Germany's most serious competitor. In Los Angeles in 1932, the year before Hitler became chancellor, the Germans had done poorly, finishing seventh. A "victory" in the overall count of medals would be taken by Germans at least as proof that Der Führer had elevated and revitalized the German spirit in sports as well as in all other respects. It would have enormously important symbolic significance, not only in Germany but in other countries where Fascists hoped to seize power.

The brightest star of the American track and field team was Jesse Owens, a student at Ohio State. Owens, born in Decatur, Alabama, was the son of sharecroppers. His family moved to Cleveland, Ohio, in 1922, when Jesse was nine, and his talent as a track star soon became evident. As a high school student he broke national records in the broad jump, as well as in the 100- and 200-yard dash. Twenty-eight colleges tried to recruit him, but he chose to go to Ohio State. In 1935 he broke five world records and equaled a sixth in a period of forty-five minutes. His record in the long jump was not beaten for twenty-five years. At Berlin Owens easily won the 100-meter dash, with Ralph Metcalfe close behind him. In the 200-meter he was pursued by another black sprinter, Mack Robinson, whose younger brother, Jackie, would be a baseball star at UCLA. Owens then won the long jump and was a member of the winning 400-meter relay team, which set a new world record.

Even more famous than Jesse Owens was a young black boxer named Joe Louis Barrow. The son of Alabama sharecroppers, Louis was the seventh of eight children. His father, Munroe Barrow, was committed to a mental hospital when Louis was only two years old. His mother, believing her husband was dead, moved in with Pat Brooks, a widower with five children of his own. When Brooks got a job in a Ford factory in Detroit, the Barrow and Brooks children moved to that city. By the time he was in his early teens, Joe Louis Barrow had decided that he wanted to be a boxer. When he was badly beaten in his first amateur fight, he dropped the name Barrow and was henceforth Joe Louis. After a period of discouragement Louis began to fight again and won fifty out of fifty-four amateur bouts (forty-three by knockouts), fighting as a light heavyweight. In the course of his fights he attracted the attention of the numbers king of Detroit, John Roxborough. Roxborough in turn enlisted the support of Julian Black, owner of a bar in Chicago's black section. The two men went to the best-known black trainer of the day, Jack Blackburn, and prevailed upon a skeptical Blackburn to become Louis's trainer.

Since Jack Johnson's sensational career, the prejudice against black heavyweights had stymied the careers of a number of promising black fighters. The odds were that white prejudice would thwart Louis's ambition to become the world heavyweight champion. His black backers were tireless in admonishing him to avoid any actions or statements that would inflame white prejudices. Above all, he was never to be seen with a white woman.

From the time that he turned professional on July 4, 1934, to the end of that year, Louis won eleven straight fights. In November, when he knocked out Lee Ramage, an experienced fighter who was a leading contender for the heavyweight title, it was evident that Louis was himself a major contender. In fewer than six months he had emerged from obscurity to national prominence, certainly in boxing circles, if not in the consciousness of the general public. It was the most sensational rise of a fighter in American ring history. A hustling promoter named Mike Jacobs signed up Louis for a hastily contrived organization called the Twentieth Century Club and promoted the young fighter into a bout with the former (very briefly) heavyweight champion Primo Carnera. When there were rumors that riots would occur between Italian-Americans and blacks, whose feelings were already inflamed by Mussolini's invasion of Ethiopia, the New York police commissioner announced: "The American Negro is by nature law-abiding, kindly, well-behaved. He is also happy and fun-loving. If Louis wins, there will likely be singing and shouting and dancing in the streets of Harlem."

When Louis and Carnera met in Yankee Stadium in June, 1935, the black fighter, by now nicknamed the Brown Bomber, had won twenty-two straight fights in less than a year. Louis scored a technical knockout in the sixth round. He later recalled: "This was my first night in New York and this was the night I remember best in all my fighting.

If you was ever a raggedy kid and you come to something like that night, you'd know." Most of the journalistic comments of Louis's victory were like parodies of racism. He was called "a brown cobra," with the "speed of the jungle," a "black panther" (actually he was tan). The *New York Daily Mirror* declared: "In Africa there are tens of thousands of powerful, young savages that with a little teaching could annihilate Mr. Joe Louis."

The next widely publicized Louis fight was with another ex-world champion, the popular Max Baer, an excellent fighter with a confirmed prejudice against training. Paul Gallico, a syndicated sportswriter, described Louis as "a mean man, a truly savage person, a man on whom civilization rested no more securely than a shawl thrown over one's shoulders. . . . I had the feeling that I was in the room with a wild animal."

Louis dispatched Baer with the same deadly efficiency that he had demonstrated in the Carnera bout. Baer was too badly beaten by the fourth round to continue the fight. Jim Braddock, a skilled but aging Irishman who had beaten Baer for the world championship, was Louis's next logical opponent, but Braddock was understandably reluctant to fight Louis, and Louis was persuaded to fight the German Max Schmeling, ranked as the number one contender. When an overconfident and inadequately trained Louis met Schmeling on June 1, 1936, he was an eight-to-one favorite over the German. In the early rounds Louis piled up points, but in the fourth round Schmeling knocked him down with a right. He had noted that Louis had a tendency to drop his left hand, exposing his jaw to a right counter. Schmeling kept exploiting this opening and in the twelfth round knocked Louis out.

Before Louis could fight again, Jesse Owens had astonished the world with his sensational performance at the Olympic Games in Berlin. Louis's next fight was against another ex-champ, Jack Sharkey, and Louis knocked Sharkey out in the third round.

To black Americans every important Louis victory was precious balm for the wounds that white America had inflicted (and continued to inflict upon them). Joe Louis became the most powerful symbolic figure since Frederick Douglass, a man who, at least in the eyes of blacks, gave the lie to the charges of black inferiority. Every victory was the occasion for a night and often days of celebration.

Maya Angelou, in *I Know Why the Caged Bird Sings,* gives a memorable description of blacks gathered in Stamps, Arkansas, listening to a broadcast of a Louis bout: "If Joe lost we were back in slavery and beyond help. It would all be true, the accusations that we were lower types of human beings. . . ." But when he won, it was euphoria: "People drank Coca-Colas like ambrosia and ate candy bars like Christmas. . . . It would take an hour or more before the people would leave the Store and head for home." In the words of his biographer, "in the 1930s Louis was the only black who was a consistent winner in white America. . . . He wasn't just defeating white men, he was *beating them up.*"

When Mike Jacobs finally lured Jim Braddock into the ring with his fighter in June, 1937, before a Chicago crowd of 50,000 spectators, almost half of whom were black, Louis was only twenty-three. He knocked out a game Braddock in the eighth round and became the youngest (and arguably the best) heavyweight champion in ring history.

Among the various strands that were being woven together to change the perception whites had of blacks and blacks had of themselves, Jesse Owens and, above all, Joe Louis, who ruled the highly visible world of heavyweight boxing for ten long years, were among the most potent.

Aside from the popular entertainment aspect of American sports, they served, as we have noted earlier, as a point of entry by immigrants and minorities into the general stream of American life. Since successful athletes were by definition heroes, the achievements of Irish, German, Italian, and, finally, black athletes served to moderate native prejudices. It is hard to think of any other area of American life in which minorities had a similar opportunity to break ethnic and racial stereotypes. On the athletic field only the individual performance counted. In the long, slow process by which black Americans gained a measure of acceptance and, in time, respect, nothing counted as heavily as the skill and grace with which they enacted the society's most cherished common ritual, spectator sports.

# 41 ❧

# Art and Architecture

In the boom of the twenties art became a growth industry. From 1921 to 1930 sixty new museums were started and thirteen museums built, at an estimated cost of more than $16,000,000. The art market burgeoned, and even established (and usually dead) American artists began to command high prices. In 1922 Winslow Homer's "Eight Bells" was bought for $50,000, the highest price paid for the work of an American painter, and it was soon topped by $60,000 for George Inness's "Spirit of Autumn." At the same time several great private collections "went public." The Lillie Bliss collection became the nucleus of the Museum of Modern Art in New York. The terrible-tempered Dr. Barnes of Philadelphia, whose fortune had been made in Argyrol, formed one of the world's great collections, which he guarded jealously. Gertrude Whitney started a museum devoted to contemporary American art. In Baltimore Etta Cone and her sister, cousins of Leo and Gertrude Stein, formed a brilliant collection of Impressionist and Postimpressionist painting. Duncan Phillips, heir to the magnesia fortune, opened a gallery in his Washington home.

One of the famous patronesses of the arts was Mrs. C. C. Rumsey, the widow of a rich young polo-playing sculptor, who had been killed in an automobile accident in 1922. In 1925 she launched a grandiose scheme to form an "Artel of the Arts," which she described as "an intellectual legion in today's life which, ridiculing philistine sophistry and time-eaten platitudes, pursues those spiritual essentials upon which the great cultures of the past were built. The Artel of the Arts aspires to new ideas in art and literature, not for the newness sake, but for the sake of a revolutionary principle. It advocates a more noble and sincere civilization than the one we have today. It emphasizes the idea of the essential, not the form. . . . The Artel of the Arts becomes in its metaphysical aspects, as it were, a religious community of the future." The Old World was "in the grip of a reckless mobocracy," while the New had evolved into a soulless "bureaucratic machine with money interest on one side and organized labor on the other." The artel was launched in the renovated Harriman stables on Long Island, with such guests as the sculptor Constantin Brancusi; Guilio Gatti-Casazza, the impresario of the Metropolitan Opera; two Russian princesses; Ivan Narodny, a Russian mystic who had exerted a strong influence on his hostess; and Bob Chanler, the socialite-painter and a famous giver of parties in his own right. The Artel featured a cello performance of Bach, some English ballads, an " 'aesthetic' dance by three awkward girls," in Burton Rascoe's disenchanted description, and a creaky reading by ancient Edwin Markham of "The Man with the Hoe," after which the venture sank quietly out of sight. It was not the first or the last of such enterprises.

It seems safe to say that never in the history of art had there been such conflicts over what constituted the proper subjects or techniques for the artist. Even before the Armory Show there were intimations of revolt against academic art. American painters and sculptors had been taking their cues from Europe for a generation or more. Certainly the impact of impressionism and Postimpressionism had been felt in the United States before the aesthetic shock treatment of the Armory Show. The contention over what constituted art was loud, bitter, and prolonged. There were the Dadaists, preoccupied by the task of exploring, à la Freud, the subconscious, and their first cousins the Surrealists. There were the Expressionists, mostly Germans and Scandinavians. There were the Fauves, or Wild Beasts, closely allied with the Expressionists; there were the Futurists, with their headquarters in Italy and with strong Fascist tendencies, the Synchronists, and the Simultanists. Constructivism was closely allied with cubism.

Marcel Duchamp, whose "Nude Descending a Staircase" (termed an "explosion in a shingle factory" by one critic), had been the most sensational painting in the 1913 Armory Show, spent several years in the United States and exerted a strong influence on a group of young American painters that included Charles Demuth, Charles Sheeler, and Joseph Stella. Demuth, born in 1883 in Lancaster, Pennsylvania, studied with William Chase and Thomas Anschutz before the obligatory interlude in Europe. Duchamp wrote that Demuth "had a curious smile, reflecting an incessant curiosity for every manifestation life offered." Demuth was a close friend of the poet William Carlos Williams, and he painted a picture based on Williams's poem "The Great Figure":

> Among the rain
> And lights
> I saw the figure 5
> In gold
> On a red
> foretruck
> moving
> tense
> unheeded
> to gong clangs
> siren howls
> and wheels rumbling
> through the dark city

Charles Sheeler was born in Philadelphia in 1883. He studied at the Pennsylvania Academy of Fine Arts with Chase, and became a photographer as well as a painter. While he was still a student, Sheeler made two trips to Europe with his master to acquaint himself with the work of the modern European painters. He exhibited in the Armory Show, which Chase had done so much to arrange. Drawing on his skills as a photographer and clearly influenced by the Cubists, Sheeler began to paint a series of industrial buildings in which flat, gleaming surfaces were symmetrically arranged. The most famous were those of the Ford assembly plant at River Rouge. The effect was one of simplicity and clarity, with no hint of the presence of "workers." Like Edward Hopper's city landscapes, Sheeler achieved an eerie quality by omitting all disorderly human beings. The result was what has been called in recent decades "magic realism," an apparent realism with haunting overtones.

Joseph Stella, born in 1877, was an Italian immigrant who came to the United States when he was nineteen. Already influenced by the Futurists, he found New York a city "rich with so many new motives to be translated into a new art. Steel and electricity had created a new world. A new drama had surged . . . [and] a new polyphony was ringing all around with the scintillating, highly colored lights. The steel had leaped to hyperbolic altitudes and expanded to vast latitudes with the skyscrapers and with bridges made for the conjunction of worlds." His famous "Brooklyn Bridge" was painted in 1922. Stella then undertook a series of paintings entitled "New York Interpreted," using light and shadow in monochromic palette. A number of his paintings depicted the play of light in the nighttime city.

As Stella's comments indicate, the city—typically New York or Chicago—became a primary subject for many artists. The Ashcan school of John Sloan, George Luks, and William Glackens had already staked out an artistic claim to the city. The Cubists and Constructionists found the city ideally suited to their styles. The so-called Fourteenth Street school, including Reginald Marsh, Morris Kantor, and the brothers Raphael and Moses Soyer, followed in the Ashcan tradition. The Missourian Thomas Hart Benson felt the powerful attraction of the metropolis as well. He wrote: "The buildings of our great cities, for all that is evil about them, that is cheap and tawdry in their surface decoration, for all that they are practically devoted to, are, nevertheless, evidence of a new spirit awakening within us, which cries for expression. They symbolize the end of that era where everything was calculated for profit, for they are not just buildings, but strivings for dramatic effect and form. And in many instances they achieve it." Benton was thrilled by "the beauty of these great structures, lifted above the dirt and squalor at their feet into our bright American sky." The land had been "gutted, the people . . . squeezed, tricked, and wheedled into mortgaging their lives and hopes." The minerals beneath the earth had been pillaged and "the forests mercilessly stripped for short-range profit. Out of all this our great cities have risen, full of life, Meccas for all the cunning and merciless schemers . . . packed to the top with sordid and vicious self-seeking, but possessed as well of a dark and strange beauty."

Even John Marin, lyrical watercolorist of the Maine coast, turned his attention to the city. Marin "disintegrated" the city. To him "landscapes and buildings had a vital life of their own. Thus the whole city is alive; buildings, people, all are alive," he wrote. ". . . at times one is afraid to look at them [the skyscrapers] and feels like running away." At other times he was enthralled. "I see great forces at work, great movements; the large buildings and the small buildings; the warring of the great and the small; influences of one mass on another greater or smaller mass."

One of the premier painters of the city came to be Edward Hopper. Hopper, who, like Marin and indeed so many other modern American painters, had passionately recorded the changing light and moody seascapes of New England, now made the loneliness of cities his major theme, evoking time and again the image of empty streets on Sunday morning, a lonely diner in a mercilessly lit all-night restaurant, a tired, pensive usher in an empty movie theater, a woman in a barren city room looking out on blank façades. Infatuated with nature, Hopper hinted at its absence in spaces empty of human life. While the painters of the Ashcan school and their successors, the short-lived Fourteenth Avenue school, filled the teeming streets with tenderloin types—chorines and pimps, soapbox orators and assorted hustlers—Hopper emptied his and thereby caught what was perhaps the more essential character of the city, if only by the fact that he was able to suggest the relationship of city to country in large part by his handling of light.

Charles Burchfield was a native of Salem, Ohio. He evinced that passionate mysticism so evident in the Midwest. For Burchfield, houses, trees, and natural forms were as animate as human beings, filled with mysterious powers, haunted by the lives lived in and among them. He took his text from Sherwood Anderson's *Winesburg, Ohio*. Like Anderson, Burchfield was accused of defaming his hometown by his gloomy renditions of it. He defended himself vigorously: "I was not indicting Salem, Ohio, but simply giving way to a mental mood, and sought out the scenes that would express it—where I could find, I created, which is perfectly legitimate. Much, however, I hated justly and would like to go on hating to my last breath—modern industrialism, the deplorable conditions in certain industrial fields such as steel-working and mining sections, American smugness and intolerance, and conceited provincialism—to mention only a few of our major evils." If he presented the decadence of small towns "in all their garish and crude primitiveness and unlovely decay," he wrote, "it was merely through a desire to be honest about them."

Burchfield and Hopper were friends and admired each other's

work. Hopper wrote of Burchfield: "Some have read an ironic basis in some of his paintings but I believe this is caused by the coincidence of his coming to the fore at a time when in our literature, the American small towns and cities were being lampooned so viciously; so that any straightforward and honest presentation of the American scene was thought of necessity to be satirical." The fact is that different as their styles are, there is a similar tone in much of the work of Hopper and Burchfield. It is a tone of loss, of loneliness and decay. Houses and façades assume personalities.

In the midst of the "art wars" came the Great Depression (a worldwide phenomenon, it must be remembered), which imposed a new layer of ideological dogma over an already confusing scene. What, the Marxists asked, was the role of the painter in revolutionary times? Clearly it was the same as that of the writer or musician: to produce revolutionary art. In form or in content or both? What was decadent art? Was art that depicted the decadence of the bourgeoisie decadent or revolutionary? Was "realism" the only acceptable form of a "people's art"? If we assume, as I suspect we must, that the visual arts are in the main sensitive registers of the collective psyche of a society, we are forced to the conclusion that the angry debate over what constituted art reflected, as many critics of both the right and the left contended, disintegration of the "old order" of European civilization. Certainly that was loudly proclaimed as the essential meaning of Dadaism: The only proper response of the artist to a crazy world was crazy art.

Artists, as we have noted, were no more immune to the siren call of communism than authors and playwrights. When the American Artists' Congress met in New York in February, 1936, among the more prominent artists present were Stuart Davis, George Biddle, David Siqueiros, and Rockwell Kent, all of whom addressed the congress. Kent urged union leaders to commission murals for their union halls, and Joseph Curran's National Maritime Union was among the unions that had artists decorate their headquarters.

Of all the various contending schools, the most important, at least from a historian's view, is that of the Regionalists. Thomas Hart Benton was dean (or king) of the Regionalists. Benton had the good fortune to live a long, active, and contentious life (he died at the age of eighty-six). He published a splended autobiography, *An Artist in America,* in 1937, when he was forty-eight. When it was reprinted in 1951, he added a substantial postscript, containing mainly acidulous comments on the current art scene. Then, when it was reissued in 1968, sixteen years later, he was able to add further reflections. He also wrote *An American in Art*, subtitled *A Professional and Technical Autobiography;* it was published in 1969.

Benton was born in Neosho, Missouri, in 1889. For a certainty he was Missouri-born and Missouri-bred. His great-uncle Thomas Hart Benton had brawled with Andrew Jackson, been Missouri's first Senator, served in the U.S. Senate for thirty years, and written a massive abridgment of that body's debates. Benton's father was also an "American original," in Harriet Martineau's phrase. "Colonel (by courtesy) M. E. Benton was a great eater, drinker, and talker," his son wrote. "He was stubborn and there was nothing on earth that could hurry him. . . . He was addicted to odd and inexplicable ways of self-communication. His refuge was the outhouse and once ensconced there no call or alarm could budge him. . . . Our dinner table was always surrounded with arguing, expository men who . . . talked long over fat cigars, the ends of which they chewed." As a boy young Benton sat openmouthed watching Champ Clark and William Jennings Bryan eat breakfast in his home, "half a potato and an egg at a bite." His father had "the grand drive, the expansiveness, the *go* that electrifies existence." Young Tom traveled all over the state with him, politicking from the time he was eight, attending political rallies and revival meetings. He read *Pilgrim's Progress, Plutarch's Lives,* the *Life of Thomas Jefferson,* and his great-uncle's *Thirty Years' View.*

By the time Benton went to Chicago in 1907 he was drawing constantly, to the dismay of his parents. "I was a variant of our stock," he wrote, adding, "There was throughout the great valley of the Mississippi, from the eighteen eighties up to the Great War, the most complete denial of aesthetic sensibility that has probably ever been known. . . . The ideals and practices of the go-getter" were ranked "above all other human interests." Like innumerable other small-town boys, Benton suffered from "the shrewd and narrow practicality of the dominant classes,—the business and professional men, the lawyers and bankers and merchants."

Intending to be a "big-time" newspaperman, Benton found irresistible the "rich, sensual joy of smearing streaks of color" on a canvas. Paris was still a necessity, and he spent three years there, studying the old masters, refining his own technique, and talking and talking about the ends of art. He met Gertrude and Leo Stein and experimented with George Seurat's pointillism. John Marin and Jo Davidson, the sculptor, along with the Mexican painter Diego Rivera, were also studying in Paris. El Greco became a major influence on the Young Missourian.

Back in the United States, Benton tried a stint as an actor, became an habitué of Alfred Stieglitz's gallery at 291 Fifth Avenue, and subsequently a member of the People's Art Guild, founded "to bring art to the workers." Soon he was a conspicuous figure in the art world's "left," a friend of such radical artists and journalists as Bob Minor, John Sloan, and Mike Gold. By the end of the World War, in which he enlisted in the navy, Benton had decided that painting American themes would be his métier.

Perhaps the most important intellectual influence on Benton was the work of the Midwestern historian Frederick Jackson Turner, who maintained in his famous essay "The Significance of the Frontier in American History" that the real story of America was the story of the westward-moving frontier. That was the story Benton set out to paint. When his resources permitted, he traveled the country by bus and train. Appointed to the faculty of the Art Students League, Benton was commissioned along with the Mexican muralist José Clemente Orozco to do murals for the New School for Social Research. Benton's mural, entitled "Modern America," was the first large-scale mural in the United States done in the classic fresco style with egg tempera on wet plaster. It depicted the seamier side of American life—frontier revival meeting, burlesque shows, black jazz combos, corpulent businessmen, hustlers, and acrobats. Such themes were a far cry from earlier renderings, which had featured classical figures in the style of Lorado Taft. Benton found himself embroiled in a rancorous controversy, attacked from the right and the left. The right denounced his often unflattering vignettes, and the left berated him for "chauvinism," for not depicting workers sympathetically, for failing to demonstrate class consciousness. Above all, the mural did not demonstrate the "international solidarity" of the working classes. A meeting of the New York chapter of the John Reed Club, called to discuss the New School mural and another that Benton had painted for the library of the Whitney Museum, ended in a brawl reminiscent of those that his great-uncle had participated in so enthusiastically on the Tennessee frontier almost a century earlier.

Benton, who considered himself a small *c* communist, thereupon gave up on the New York art community and cast his lot with the Middle West. He met John Steuart Curry in the midst of the brouhaha and discovered a kindred spirit. Like Benton, Curry wanted to paint pictures that would appeal to a large general public, not because he was avid for fame but because he believed, like Benton, that in a democracy painting should be a popular rather than an esoteric art.

Indiana commissioned Benton to do a mural on the state's history. It was to be 200 feet long and 12 feet high. Benton completed it in six months, and it was included in the Indiana exhibition at the Chicago world's fair in 1933. Typically Benton included a scene of the Ku Klux Klan as well as less reprehensible aspects of the state's history.

Controversy followed Benton to Kansas City, where he was commissioned to paint a mural depicting the history of his home state. During the planning and painting of the Missouri mural Benton traveled around the state. "I met all kinds of people. I played the harmonica and wore a pink shirt to country dances," he wrote. "I went on hunting and fishing parties. I attended an uproarious three-day, old settler's drunk in the depths of the Ozarks. I took in the honky-tonks of the country and the night clubs of Kansas City and St. Louis." All those things he put in his mural. "A storm broke over me," he wrote, "and my illusions about a good many Missouri things were broken with it. I saw that realism was not by any means a completely shared Missouri virtue, and that the habit of calling things by their right names and representing them in their factual character was not wholly agreeable to so many people as I supposed." Missouri, in its own way, Benton discovered, was as benighted as New York. "One illusion," he wrote "has been knocked out of me for good—that is, that the cultivated people of the Middle West are less intellectually provincial than those of New York. . . . Those who affect art with a big 'A' do so with their eyes on Europe just as they do in New York. They lisp the same tiresome, meaningless aesthetic jargon. In their society are to be found the same fairies, the same Marxist fellow travelers, the same 'educated' ladies purring linguistic affectations. The same damn bores that you find in the penthouses and studios of Greenwich Village hang onto the shirts of art in the Middle West."

By the mid-twenties Benton's mature style had emerged. The fluid, elongated figures and chiaroscuro were vaguely reminiscent of El Greco. The scenes were predominantly rural farmers, cotton pickers, Missouri riverboats, hay and rice and wheatfields being harvested, black men and mules plowing the red Missouri soil.

Benton borrowed themes of jealous love and murder from country music. He painted square dancers and obese politicians making backroom deals. In a conscious updating of George Caleb Bingham's scenes of democratic politics, Benton showed similar gatherings. He drew on his brief movie career to depict a Hollywood movie set. Two of his best-known paintings transposed biblical stories and classical myths to Midwestern farms. "Susanna and the Elders" showed a senuous female nude—Susanna—on the bank of a stream with the "Elders," two farmers, peering at her from behind a tree. The story was from the Apocrypha; it told of two elders who try to seduce Susanna and, when they are rebuffed, claim she incited them. Young Daniel defends her and exposes the falsehoods of the elders. Among other things, the painting is about the sexual hypocrisy of rural life, in which the pious often violate the code they profess.

"Persephone," a kind of companion piece, was painted years later. Once again a voluptuous nude is the central figure, this time reclining asleep. Persephone, daughter of Demeter and Zeus, was the Greek goddess of fertility and the wife of Hades (Pluto), lord of the underworld, who had abducted her. She was required to spend four months of the year in hell, during which time all growing things withered. When she returned, it was spring and the earth bore its fruits. A lecherous old man, Hades, is viewing her youthful beauty before he bears her away.

Benton's commanding presence and talent for controversy made him a conspicuous figure in the art world. He unabashedly enjoyed his popular acclaim. "Like movie stars, baseball players and loquacious senators, I was soon a figure recognizable in Pullman cars, hotel lobbies and night clubs," he wrote. "I became a regular public character. I signed my name for armies of autograph hunters. I posed with beauty queens. . . . I was continuously photographed and written about by the columnists."

Grant Wood, the second member of the Regionalist trio, was born in 1891 in the little town of Anamosa, Iowa, north of Cedar Rapids. His mother was a schoolteacher who played the organ in the local church; his father, superintendent of the Sunday school, died at the age of forty-six when Grant was ten. His mother moved to Cedar Rapids to live with her parents. Wood's recollections of his childhood were dominated by his stern and demanding father and austere aunts and older relatives. Like most Midwestern small-town and farm boys with literary or artistic inclinations, Grant Wood thought first of flight. With encouragement from a sympathetic teacher he developed his early precociousness in drawing and painting, and when he graduated from high school, he headed for Minneapolis, where he began taking courses at the Minneapolis School of Design and Handicraft. He found the crafts as alluring as painting; he explored woodworking and jewelry making in the spirit of Art Nouveau. After a brief stint in the army during the war Wood returned to Cedar Rapids to help support his mother and got a position teaching art in the public schools.

In 1920 Wood visited Paris with a friend, Marvin Cone, and returned at the end of the summer with a beard and a noticeably bohemian air. Three years later he took a sabbatical and spent the year in France. There he experimented with the styles of the Impressionists and Postimpressionists. Back home, Wood became the town's resident painter, recording the faces and places of the town's leading businessmen. He also found congenial spirits in a budding young journalist, William Shirer, and in MacKinlay Kantor, a reporter for the town paper.

At the age of forty Wood painted "American Gothic." It was an American icon of such potency that it at once took its place with Gilbert Stuart's portrait of Washington and Matthew Brady's photograph of Lincoln. Whether it was art or not was clearly irrelevant. It was an imaginative achievement of a high order. The two faces summarized a substantial portion of American history, especially that of the Puritan Midwest. The man's face, direct and shrewd and joyless, spoke more eloquently than volumes of exposition of the psychological cost of opening a continent and wresting a living from an often uncongenial soil. The surprising thing was that Americans saw themselves (or their parents and grandparents) in the two strong but graceless figures. Stimulated by the success of "American Gothic," Wood turned out a number of notable canvases in the last decade of his life.

John Steuart Curry was the youngest of the three Regionalists whose names were associated. Curry was born on a farm near Dunavant, Kansas, in 1897. His mother loved art, albeit of a traditional kind, and was the first person to direct his attention to her favorite, Peter Paul Rubens, who became an important influence in the development of Curry's style. His father was a graduate of Kansas State University. Curry showed an early talent for drawing and decided while he was still a boy that he wished to become a commercial artist and illustrator.

After a brief stint at the Kansas City Art Institute and two years at the Chicago Art Institute he served in the United States Army during the World War. Following the war he began a career as an illustrator of stories in Wild West magazines. Deciding that he wanted to be a serious painter, Curry spent a year in Paris, where he experimented with various modern styles and then returned to study at the Art Students League. By 1928 he was ready to try to make his living as a painter. His decision to paint scenes associated with his home state of Kansas coincided with the growing interest in the nation's past and especially a concern for the role of the farmer and of the land in our history.

To Curry the radical crusading spirit of abolitionism was still alive, and one of his first notable paintings was a giant figure of John Brown, calling up his legions to do battle against slavery. One familiar Curry painting showed his mother and father in the plain living of their farmhouse with the barns and cattle visible though the window. Another depicted a Kansas farm family fleeing to their storm cellar in the face of an approaching tornado. An early painting, "Baptism in Kansas," portrayed a baptism by immersion in the water tank of a Kansas farm. It was shown at the Corcoran Gallery in Washington and attracted favorable attention as a classic American subject. The most striking features of the painting were two doves representing the descent of the Holy Spirit, in marked contrast with the somber faces of the farm men and women gathered for the ceremony.

In 1931 Curry, fascinated with the circus and seeking "native themes," traveled for a season with the Ringling Brothers, painting elephants, clowns, and trapeze artists. Soon he was receiving commissions for murals in government buildings, one for the Supreme Court in Washington. In 1936 when the first issue of *Life* magazine appeared, Curry was the artist chosen by the editors to represent "Art in America." (Benton had already received the American equivalent of a knighthood by appearing on the cover of *Time* magazine.) The same year the University of Wisconsin offered Curry the novel position of artist in residence, one of the first, if not *the* first, such appointment to a major university. His duties, in *Life*'s words, would be "to mingle with undergraduates, ramble over the Wisconsin farmland, occasionally drop remarks about the Appreciation of Art to students." It was not a successful experiment. Curry was given to corrosive periods of self-doubt. His health began to fail, and by the outbreak of World War II, modernism or internationalism had reasserted itself. The Regionalists had become old hat.

Benton, Wood, and Curry complemented each other; their personalities (as reflected in their paintings) represented different facets of the character of the American Midwest. Benton displayed a rough-edged realism that tried at the same time to lift its subject to a mythic plane, relating it to classic human themes. Wood imposed a surreal order on the natural world and viewed the human one with a sly and sardonic eye. In the broken and uneven surfaces of Curry's paintings (as far as one could well get from Wood's immaculate canvases), one feels the perpetual strain and tension that lay below the seemingly ordinary encounters of farm folk.

"We were different in our temperaments and many of our ideas," Benton wrote of himself, Curry, and Wood, "but we were all alike in that we were all in revolt against the unhappy effects which the Armory Show of 1913 had had on American painting. We objected to the new Parisian aesthetics which was more and more turning away from the living world of active men and women into an academic world of empty pattern. We wanted an American art which was not empty. . . . We symbolized aesthetically what the majority of Americans had in mind— America itself. Our success was a popular success. Even where some American citizens did not agree with the nature of our images, instanced in the objections to my state-sponsored murals in Indiana and Missouri, they understood them. . . . We came to our conclusions separately but we ended with similar convictions that we must find our aesthetic values, not in thinking, but in penetrating the meaning and forms of life as lived. For us this meant . . . American life and American life as known and felt by ordinary Americans."

The last years of both Wood's and Curry's lives were years of despondency. Wood had intermittent moods of self-doubt. Dying of cancer of the liver, he told Benton that when he recovered, he planned to change his name, find some refuge, and begin to paint in an entirely different style. Curry also felt the indifference of the art world to his work and, in Benton's words, the "actual scorn" of his students. Visiting with him in the last year of his life, Benton tried to bolster his morale. "You must feel pretty good now, after all your struggles, to know that you have come to a permanent place in American art. It's a long way from a Kansas farm to fame like yours."

"I don't know about that," Curry replied, "maybe I'd have done better to stay on the farm. No one seems interested in my pictures. Nobody thinks I can paint. If I *am* any good, I have lived at the wrong time." Benton noted that one of the saddest experiences of his life had been to see Curry and Wood "so well known, and, when compared with most artists, enormously successful, finish their lives in ill health and occasional moods of deep despondency." He consoled himself with the thought the regionalism had lasted some twenty years, a "considerably longer period than any other artistic movement of our time. . . ."

The fact was that Wood and Curry fitted in very well with the realism—the direct and unabashed warts-and-all view of American life—proclaimed by the new consciousness. They also represented what has been called the documentary style, recording the daily lives of ordinary men and women.

In addition, all three did a number of murals in what we might call the era of murals, the 1930s. Indeed, Benton identified the Regionalists most strongly with the Mexican school—primarily Rivera, Orozco, and Siqueiros. It is ironic that those painters and critics who were virtually unanimous in condemning the American Regionalists often expressed unstinting admiration for their Mexican counterparts. Granted that the Mexicans may well have been more powerful painters, their immunity from the hostile criticism directed at Benton et al. seems to have been due, as much as anything else, to the fact that the content of their work was specifically and consistently "revolutionary." Mexicans and Americans alike studied in Paris, experimented with virtually all the currently fashionable styles, particularly cubism, and turned back to realism, or popular public art.

Ironically, in the era of murals the greatest mural in the United States was painted by Orozco in the Dartmouth College Library, a library built in the neo-Georgian style of Independence Hall. In the basement of the building Orozco painted murals depicting the destruction of the Aztec civilization by the invading Spaniards and the rise of the industrial age. A central panel showed skeleton professors in academic robes delivering the stillborn skeleton of knowledge. In the final panel a livid and militant Christ has chopped down the cross. Despite the howls of enraged alumni, the murals were preserved.

The most striking architectural accomplishments of the twenties were those skyscrapers that caught the imaginations of so many artists. The Tribune Tower in Chicago, designed by Raymond Hood, was a skyscraper topped with conventional architectural ornament, in this case elements suggesting a multistoried Gothic cathedral. By the time he designed the American Radiator Building in New York, Hood had fallen under the spell of the so-called international style. In the Daily News Building in New York he designed one of the first of those monolithic slabs that came to dominate the New York skyline. The Empire State Building, designed by the firm of Shreve, Lamb & Harmon, was started in 1929, the year of the crash. Rising 1,250 feet above the antlike humans below, it was capped by an Art Deco spire from which King Kong swatted attacking airplanes while holding Fay Wray in an enormous paw.

It was appropriate that the most ambitious venture in the building of imperial towers should be undertaken by the nation's most famous capitalist. In the center of Manhattan John D. Rockefeller, Jr., began (or took over) Rockefeller Center, a complex of stores, buildings, restaurants, a vast theater, and a skating rink, occupying three adjacent city blocks and dominated by the RCA tower in the center. The interior design and architectural embellishments were essentially Art Deco. Diego Rivera was commissioned to paint the central mural of the complex. His theme was the coming revolution, and, being a Trotskyite, he chose as the hero of U.S. communism Jay Lovestone, managing to enrage everyone except, of course, Lovestone's handful of followers. The Rockefellers, ardently supported by the Communists, ordered the mural removed in May, 1933.

The glass and steel monoliths thrusting spectacularly into the sky were like modern towers of Babel. They bespoke the hubris of triumphant capitalism, confident to arrogance, one pinnacle trying to outreach the other like the fourteen feudal lords of San Gimignano in Tuscany.

Despite the prevailing winds of internationalism, Frank Lloyd Wright remained the dominant theorist of American architecture. While he continued to design brilliantly innovative homes—the Millard House in Pasadena, California, the Kaufmann House, "Falling Water," in Pennsylvania, and the splendid Barnsdall House in Los Angeles—his interests turned increasingly to public structures and to urban planning, a notion increasingly popular. The idea of planned communities was not new. It was, in fact, as old as civilization. In America it was as old as the "planned" villages of New England and the innumerable utopian communities of the nineteenth century. Frederick Law Olmsted, the architect of Central Park, the father of the American park move-

ment, and the godfather of suburbia, was a fervent believer in planning. His son, Frederick Law Olmsted, Jr., was an architect and an
advocate of planned communities. The best-known planned communities were undoubtedly the industrial villages or company towns built
by nineteenth-century manufacturers for their workers, starting with
Lowell and Lawrence, Massachusetts, and running up through Pullman, Illinois, a model town built by George Pullman for his employees.
In more recent times the Norton Grinding Company in Worcester,
Massachusetts, had built Indian Hill, a community for its workers.
World War I stimulated the building of a number of towns for workers
in defense industries—Allwood in Passaic, New Jersey, by the Brighton
Mills Company; Goodyear Heights in Akron, Ohio, and Alcoa, Ten-
nessee, home for employees of the Aluminum Company of America.
In Beloit, Wisconsin, Fairbanks-Morse built Eclipse Park—300 Dutch
colonial houses—on fifty-three acres near its factory. And as we have
seen, the greenbelt "villages" were built under the aegis of the New
Deal.

In Wright's view, the chaotic and unplanned growth of American
cities was in defiance of every humane principle of building. "To look
at the plan of any great city," he wrote, "is to look at a cross-section
of some fibrous tumor." To Wright the city rose, "Tier upon tier, the
soulless Shelf, the interminable empty crevice along the winding ways
of the windy unhealthy canyon. The heartless grip of the selfish, grasping, universal stricture. Box on box beside boxes. Black shadows below
with artificial lights burning all day long in little caverns and squared
cells. Prison cubicles." The city was built on "rent," rent for land, for
money, and, finally, for ideas. "The city itself is become a form of
anxious rent, the citizen's own life rented, he and his family evicted if
he is in arrears or the system goes smash. Should this anxious lockstep
of his fall out with the landlord, the moneylord, or the machinelord,
he is a total loss."

Wright was in practical fact a Henry George single taxer who saw
rent for land as the enslaver of men and women and wished to abolish
it in his model Broadacre City. There every dweller could develop the
"full harmony of his being" in a combination of farming, intellectual
activity, and industrial labor. The family would be reconstituted as the
basis of the social order. The individual domestic house was to be the
basic unit of Broadacre City. The family head would work part-time
at farming and part-time in nearby factories, making his house "a
harmonious whole, as appropriate to him as his purse, to his ground

as to his God." Like his hero Jefferson, Wright hated banks, "the pillared 'Temples-of-the-Unearned-Increment.'" Broadacre City would have no vast department stores, teeming with customers buying expensive things they did not need; instead, there would be a "great Roadside Market," where each part-time farmer had his own stall and where craftsmen sold their handiwork.

Another conspicuous feature of Broadacre was the "Community Center," an alluring "automotive objective," with a zoo, a racetrack and golf course, an aquarium, a planetarium, art galleries, restaurants, and theaters. Instead of "experts," every man and women would be informed through an education which prized and rewarded individuality. "In any genuine democracy," Wright wrote, "were education adequate, the expert would be kept in a cage as some abnormality to be publicly exhibited as a warning." Schools should be decentralized; "The *big* American knowledge factory, the *big* school, the *big* anything was always a self-defeating institution." The goal of education should be the "Perfect correlation of the faculties, active and potential. . . . Eye and hand, body and what we call Mind thus becoming more and more sensitive to Nature. . . . Spiritually and physically the Broadacre boys and girls would become the coefficients of a *naturally* creative humanity."

To advance the principles of Broadacre City, Wright founded his own utopian community, thinly disguised as a design center. There, at Taliesin, he established the fellowship of apprentices. "So we begin this Working Fellowship as a kind of daily work-life," he wrote. The apprentices constructed their own dwelling spaces on Wrightian principles; they talked and worked, farmed, formed an orchestra and a chorus, and strove, under Wright's direction, to develop as "well-correlated" individuals. No one could smoke; the use of pepper was forbidden.

Frank Lloyd Wright was a fascinating compendium of half the utopian visions America was so fertile in. The generational line reached back to Robert Dale Owen and New Harmony, to Bronson Alcott and Fruitlands, to Brook Farm, and, above all, to John Humphrey Noyes and his Oneida Community. There was a strong element of Emerson's self-reliance and Walt Whitman's religion of individualism. The family and the farm were basic. The machine and the manipulation of money were the enemies of the harmonious and integrated life, of humanity.

The most serious challenge to the Frank Lloyd Wright school of architecture came from the German Bauhaus refugees, especially Walter Gropius, Ludwig Miës van der Rohe, Rudolf Schindler, and Marcel Breuer. The Bauhaus dogma, a reaction against the Beaux-Arts tradition with a heavy load of radical political and social theory, was that ornamentation was decadent and corrupt. Houses were "machines for living." They should be fashioned from such "honest industrial" materials as steel and concrete and "form should follow function," or, rather, function should dictate the external form. The Bauhaus doctrine was a kind of architectural Puritanism, rectilinear and austere. When machines were first made in America, they were treated as art objects, painted brilliant colors, and decorated with intricate scrolls and gold lettering. In part through the influence of the Italian futurists, the machine was now seen as beautiful in and of itself; it was said that art should imitate and explicate the machine. That was the ideal of socialist efficiency.

Frank Lloyd Wright was horrified at such a bleak and alien doctrine. He refused even to speak to Gropius, whose teachings he deplored. But the capitalists took to the international style, to steel and glass towers, like ducks to water. They employed "Marxist" architectural principles to raise monuments to capitalism. Where Wright labored to wed architecture to nature, houses to the landscape, the Bauhaus group defied nature, proclaiming "scientific" dialectical materialism as a superior value. For the courtyard of the Harvard graduate school resident halls, Gropius designed a "World Tree" made of stainless steel. For architects of the Wright persuasion, it was a perfect symbol of the barren and alien temper of the Bauhaus school.

Starting with the Armory Show, European art had challenged Americans, forcing them to reconsider many of their basic artistic tenets. American artists had to fight for their own souls. The pessimism and despair that infected so much European art in the period between the wars were profoundly antithetic to the American temperament and were in the main rejected, however much superficial stylistic elements were adapted to American themes.

By the end of this period refugee artists like Hans Hofmann and Josef Albers had begun to exert a strong influence on the younger generation of American painters, among them Benton's student and protégé Jackson Pollock. Among Hofmann's students were Larry Rivers, Louise Nevelson, and Helen Frankenthaler.

By the end of the war New York was ready to replace Paris as the art capital of the world.

In the architecture of the postwar era the "planned community" of Levittown on Long Island broke emphatically with the Bauhaus ideal of large urban apartment complexes. However architectually undistinguished Levittown and its imitators were, they were far superior to the urban housing "projects" that sprang up during the New Deal years.

# 42

# The Literary Scene

The period of American history covered by this volume might well be termed the "Age of Literature," since it brought the most notable (or remarkable) effusion of literary activity since the 1850s.

Theodore Dreiser and Sherwood Anderson, as leaders of the literary liberation movement, were the presiding elders. Willa Cather, Edith Wharton, Ellen Glasgow, and, on a less exalted level, Gertrude Atherton published some of their best work in the first decade of this era.

Gertrude Stein occupied an unique position as the doyenne of American letters while living in Paris. She was reputed to have been William James's favorite student in psychology. She had also been a promising student of brain surgery at Johns Hopkins Hospital in Baltimore. In 1909 she published *Three Lives,* a book that has almost as important a place in the history of the twentieth-century literary consciousness as Theodore Dreiser's *Sister Carrie,* which was published for the first time in an inadequate edition in 1900. The "lives" were of three women. The first is "The Good Anna," the shrewd immigrant servant—"small, square, german woman"—of a New England spinster, Miss Mathilda. It is a simple and apparently artless tale of Anna's life with Miss Mathilda, a succession of lesser servants, and Miss Mathilda's dogs. When Miss Mathilda, whose care has absorbed Anna's whole life, goes abroad, Anna falls ill and dies. The life is a poignant study of service and dependence.

The second "life" is that of a black woman, Melanctha Herbert, her friend Rose Johnson, and her older friend Jane Harden. "Rose Johnson was a real black, tall, well built, sullen, stupid, childlike, good looking negress. She laughed when she was happy and grumbled and was sullen with everything that troubled. . . . Melanctha Herbert was a graceful, pale yellow, intelligent attractive negress . . . [who] always loved too hard and much too often. She was always full with mystery and subtle movements and denials and vague distrusts and complicated disillusions. Then Melanctha would be sudden and impulsive and un-bounded in some faith, and then she would suffer and be strong in her repression." The main theme of the story concerns Melanctha's relationship with a young black doctor, Jefferson Campbell. In the end they drift apart, and Melanctha, abandoned by her friends and pro-foundly "blue," becomes ill and dies of consumption (tuberculosis) while still a young woman. "Melanctha" is the most ambitious and the most striking of the *Three Lives*. It was the most successful attempt by a white writer to enter sympathetically in the life of a black woman since Harriet Beecher Stowe's *Uncle Tom's Cabin*. James Weldon John-son considered it the first effort of a white writer to tell the story of love between two black characters, treating them as "normal members of the human family."

"The Gentle Lena" was about another German immigrant serving girl and her arranged marriage to Herman Kreder. It was a grim and loveless relationship in which Lena gradually sickened and died. The three women lived lives full of a kind of suppressed pathos; none had any understanding of her relationship to the larger world.

Sherwood Anderson, finding he could not make a living as a writer, went back to his work as an advertising man in 1917. "I will be corrupt, but God give me this grace . . . let me in some way keep an honest mind. When I am being corrupt, perverting the speech of men, let me remain aware of what I am doing." It seemed to him that the danger was "believing your own bunk"; that was "the real sin against the Holy Ghost." He laughed at himself and at the agency and it was at once perceived and resented by his fellow workers. "It is the way you come into the office, the way you walk. It is a certain expression on your face. It is as though you were always laughing at yourself and us," his boss, who was also a friend, said to him.

"But I am laughing. It is the only thing I can do to save myself. I am like you. I am caught in a trap. If I did not laugh I would be often on the point of suicide." It was not said lightly. During the period that Anderson worked for one advertising agency five people working in the copy department had committed suicide.

In 1914 Anderson's brother, who was, in his own way, as interesting and appealing a figure as Anderson himself and had a major influence on his work, had brought Gertrude Stein's *Tender Buttons* with him to a party to read aloud. People laughed at the odd syntax, but Anderson's brother declared, "It gives words an oddly new intimate flavor and at the same time makes familiar words seem almost like strangers. . . ." Anderson, alerted by his brother's comments, found the book equally seductive. What every artist yearned for was the ability to create with words "a whole new world of sensation . . ." Anderson wrote, "he would like to call back into life all of the dead and sleeping senses." He wanted words "that have a taste on the lips, that have a perfume to the nostrils, rattling words that one can throw into a box and shake . . . [and that] have a distinct arresting effect upon the eye. . . ." These were the words that Gertrude Stein had liberated to work in new ways upon the reader's consciousness.

In June, 1921, the editors of the *Dial* gave Sherwood Anderson a $2,000 prize for his achievements in the field of the American short story, which, to be sure, he had revolutionized, much as Theodore Dreiser had revolutionized the novel. He decided to use some of his prize for a trip to Europe. In Paris Sylvia Beach introduced him to Gertrude Stein, who already knew his work. He had heard Stein described as "a languid woman lying on a couch, smoking cigarettes, sipping absinthes perhaps and looking out upon the world with tired, disdainful eyes." When he finally met her, he found instead "a woman of striking vigor, a subtle and powerful mind, a discrimination in the arts such as I have found in no other American born man or woman, and a charmingly brilliant conversationalist." The two hit it off at once. Stein asked him to write an introduction to a book of hers about to be published. Anderson was delighted by the request. It gave him an opportunity to acknowledge his debt to her. "For me," Anderson wrote, "the work of Gertrude Stein consists in rebuilding, an entire new recasting of life, in the city of words." She was an artist who had passed up the "privilege of writing the great American novel" to "go live among the little housekeeping words. . . . Would it not be a lovely and charmingly ironic gesture of the odds if, in the end, the work of this artist were to prove the most lasting and important of all the word slingers of our generation!"

Later Anderson wrote: "Stein is great because she is a releaser of talent. She is a pathfinder. She has been a great, a tremendous influence among writers because she has dared, in the face of ridicule and misunderstanding, to try to awaken in all of us who write a new feeling for words." It was not just the impressive persona of Stein, her wit or her perceptiveness, that so attracted Anderson. It was equally the setting—"your room in the house there in Paris"—and, as he wrote her, her unexpected Americanness: "You would be surprised to know just how altogether American I found you. You see, dear friend, I believe in this damn mixed-up country of ours. In an odd way I'm in love with it. And you get into it, in my sense of it, quite tremendously."

Stein, for her part, wrote: "There are four men so far in American letters who have essential intelligence. They are Fenimore Cooper, William Dean Howells, Mark Twain and Sherwood Anderson." The account of Anderson's childhood in *A Story Teller's Story* seemed to her "without any equal in quality in anything that has been done up to this time by any one writing to-day," and she wrote him what is probably the most famous valentine in literary history:

> I knew too that through them I knew too that he was through.
> I knew too that he threw them, I knew too that they were through,
> I knew too I knew too, I knew I knew them.
> I knew to them . . .
> Very fine is my valentine.
> Very fine and very mine.
> Very mine is my valentine very mine and very fine.
> Very fine is my valentine and mine, very fine very mine
> And mine is my valentine.

In 1927 Anderson bought the Marion, Virginia, newspaper, and decided to become a small-town newspaper editor. "It's been the greatest sport I ever got into," he wrote Stein. Living in Virginia, Anderson felt the presence of the heroes of the Civil War. "I sleep and dream. Robert E. Lee comes into my room. Jackson comes, Longstreet, Grant, Sheridan.

"These men come into my bedroom, in dreams and talk of the war, of what got them into it, how they felt, what they think they meant by it.

"They come in there, into my bedroom, talking and I know their voices."

Anderson found himself agreeing with his critics that "all of my tales were of one sort . . . they were stories of escape. . . ." Indeed, it seemed to him "that the real tale of American lives is as yet just that, . . . eternal fleeing from something." American men were children who never grew up, who played "with railroads, whole railroad systems, chains of newspapers, great oil companies, steel companies, chains of retail stores . . . playing with gigantic toys."

Ben Hecht told Anderson that he boe a charmed life caused, in large part, by his "profound egotism. It is colossal. When you are snubbed, you do not know it. When someone condemns your work, you simply put him down as a fool. Some of us have to go through terrible times of doubt of our talents, but you never have to. . . . You will always be loved more than you deserve. Your egotism. . . . Why, man, it is so colossal that you will always be going around wearing an air of modesty and even humility. You will even believe you are actually humble. Lord God, but you are a lucky one!"

"For all my egotism," Anderson wrote, "I know I am but a minor figure." But looking back on his life, he felt compelled to exclaim: " 'Oh thou fortunate one!' Lucky to have been born an American in what may well turn out to have been America's happiest period, to have been born poor and in a small town where community life was intimate and close, to have had to work as a laborer both in factories and on farms, thus to have known whence came the food that nourished my body and what toil went into its production. . . ."

With the crash and the Great Depression, as we have seen, Anderson threw himself into radical politics with characteristic enthusiasm. "My own feeling now is," he wrote in 1932, "that if it is necessary in order to bring about the end of a money civilization and set up something new, healthy and strong, we of the so-called artist class have to be submerged. Let us be submerged. Down with us. A little poverty and shaking down won't hurt us and I believe in my own class, the artist's class. I believe in our ability to survive. The world is old. Changes have swept over the world before. . . . If the movement to free all men from the rule of money means the submerging of our class, let us be submerged. Down with us. . . . We'll survive. We'll swim. We will in the long run be healthier and better if we get it in the neck now along with the workers."

In 1934 Gertrude Stein came to the United States on a lecture tour. By now she had become a public curiosity, and people flocked to hear her in somewhat the same spirit that they had turned out to take note of Oscar Wilde on his American tour. She renewed her love affair with America. "It's a lovely American continent, and it is very lovely that we should be wandering around in it," she wrote Anderson, "just as we are and bumping up against each other and not just as we are. I like it a lot, I don't think one could like anything better. . . ." She and Alice B. Toklas couldn't decide what they liked best. "I guess we like it all best and really I can see a possible future of wandering around this land . . . it is a lovely land so white and blue and lovely. . . ."

Stein and Toklas rented a car, drove around Chicago, and got lost. It was "wildly exciting," and they determined to "take to the road" and drive to Texas. From Texas they traveled to San Francisco through the San Joaquin Valley and Yosemite and decided that they wanted "to come back and drive and drive. . . ."

Stein wrote:

> There are many that I know and they know it.
> They are all of them repeating and I hear it. I love it
> and I tell it. I love it and now I will write it.
> This is now a history of my love of it. I can hear it
> and I love it and I write it. They repeat it.
> They live it and I see it and I hear it. They live it
> and I hear it and I see it and I love it
> and now and always I will write it.
> There are many kinds of men and women
> and I know it. They repeat it and I hear it
> and I love it. This is now a history of the way they do it.
> This is now a history of the way I love it.

After Anderson's death of peritonitis in March, 1941, Gertrude Stein wrote an appreciation of him for the magazine *Story*. For her his most essential quality had been "a sweetness, and sweetness is rare. Once or twice somebody is sweet, but everything in Sherwood was made of this sweetness." He was like grape sugar, she wrote. "One cannot cry . . . and one cannot die when they are like that, so one does not cry for Sherwood nor does Sherwood die.

"No."

If Anderson was all "sweetness," his literary coadjutor, Dreiser, was all odd, uncomfortable awkwardness. "He was," Hutchins Hapgood wrote, "a passionate propagandist for what he might call realistic writing, though I am not sure he ever used the word realistic. He hated the sweet and conventional bondage which for the most part held American literary expression. . . . He despised the well-to-do. . . ." But

Dreiser, in Hapgood's view, was crippled by an aesthetic blindness. In his large, showy apartment on Fifty-seventh Street in New York City, "a young woman and a white Russian wolfhound supplied the only pleasing color." Later, when Dreiser lived at the Hotel Ansonia, visitors were admitted by him, "dressed in a long white linen garment, into a small, bare room containing a table and some hard chairs"; the atmosphere reminded Hapgood of a dentist's office. Dreiser worked at a huge desk made from a piano. On one of his Thursday evenings Claude Bowers encountered "a dozen Congo Negroes, all but naked in costumes representing various animals and birds. . . ."

For a time Dreiser took refuge on a farm at Mount Kisco. When Bowers visited him there, he found Dreiser out walking with Max Eastman. That evening, talking in Dreiser's cottage, the novelist poured out his bitterness against politicians and the "capitalist press." The United States, he declared, was headed toward an unabashed plutocracy that would in time turn into a totalitarian state. He saw in the hostility toward radicals and dissenters the beginnings of totalitarianism. He was equally disenchanted with the younger generation. "I can truthfully say," he wrote in 1921, "that I cannot detect, in the postwar activities or interests, social, intellectual or otherwise, of the younger or other generations of Americans, poor, rich, or middle class, any least indication of the breaking of hampering shackles of any kind—intellectual, social, monetary, or what you will."

The year 1925 clearly belonged to Dreiser. His last novel, *The Genius*, had been published in 1915 and had had a generally cool reception. Since then he had been, one might say, in semiretirement as a novelist, although he turned out a substantial quantity of writing as the admired smasher of conventions, a monument of the new literary age. Now he came forth with a novel that was an instant success. The theme of *An American Tragedy* had haunted Dreiser for years. There had been three separate widely publicized incidents—Carlyle Harris in 1893, Chester Gillette in 1906, and Clarence Richeson in 1911—in which ambitious young men had had affairs with "lower-class" girls. When they subsequently had opportunities for socially advantageous marriages, they had discovered that their "girlfriends" were pregnant. Fearful of losing marriages that they believed were essential to their careers, they had murdered their pregnant lovers. To Dreiser it was a classic American story, a conflict between the passions of the heart and the terrible American pressure for success. It was the kind of tragedy that could happen, Dreiser believed, only in a supposedly "classless" society where fear of "failure" and longing for "success" overshadowed all natural human relationships. Dreiser wrote of Chester Gillette that Gillette *"was really doing the kind of thing* [abandoning the poor girl for the rich one] *which Americans should and would have said was the wise and moral thing to do had he not committed murder."* Dreiser confessed to similar dreams in his youth. He had envied the rich and wished "that I was famous or the member of a wealthy family, and that I might meet some one of the beautiful girls I imagined I saw there and have her fall in love with me."

The hero of Dreiser's novel, Clyde Griffiths, is the shy, poetic, but ambitious son of fundamentalist street preachers. Griffiths pays court to an attractive young woman named Roberta. Deeply involved with her, he meets and is favorably considered by Sondra, a girl from a wealthy and socially prominent family. Trying to break off his relationship with Roberta, he discovers that she is pregnant. After several unsuccessful attempts at an abortion Clyde lures Roberta on a canoe trip in a remote region and drowns her. He is apprehended, indicted for Roberta's murder, convicted, and electrocuted.

The success of *An American Tragedy,* the most popular of Dreiser's novels, strengthened his reputation as the dean of American letters. "Theodore Dreiser . . . had been fighting our battles since his first book, *Sister Carrie . . .*" Malcolm Cowley wrote. Cowley compared Dreiser's mind to "an attic in an earthquake, full of big trunks that slithered about and popped open one after another, so that he sometimes spoke as a Social Darwinist, sometimes as a Marxist, sometimes as almost a fascist, and sometimes as a sentimental reformer." He had an "uncalculating candor that gave him a large sort of bumbling dignity," Cowley added.

Sherwood Anderson wrote to much the same effect: "I was profoundly grateful to Dreiser. I dedicated a book to him. . . . No more awkward writer ever lived. He can write sentences that fairly jar the teeth out of your head. . . . In his hands words go sick and lame. . . . He is a great novelist. He builds and builds slowly, patiently. Something arises, huge, significant, real. He does not play cheap scurvy tricks on life. . . . Theodore Dreiser is a great figure."

During the twenties a number of young novelists and poets, most of whom had seen service, if not combat, in the World War, burst on the literary scene in spectacular fashion, notably Scott Fitzgerald, Ernest Hemingway, John Dos Passos, and William Faulkner (Thomas Wolfe and John Steinbeck followed in their train by a decade).

Princeton, oddly enough, contributed a gaggle of writers, critics, and poets, of whom Fitzgerald and Dos Passos were the most famous and Edmund Wilson was the most ubiquitous. Another member of the circle was the poet John Peale Bishop. Princeton was the last stronghold of what Edmund Wilson later called "a sort of eighteenth-century humanism." Woodrow Wilson's influence still lingered in the tutorial system. Professor (later Dean) Christian Gauss cared equally about students and about literature. Most of the professors were gentlemen, native to the East or thoroughly Easternized Midwesterners, converts to the genteel tradition, more catholic than the Catholics. Beside Gauss himself, the principal luminary of the literature department was Paul Elmer More, champion of the New Humanism, a creed, it seems fair to say, invented by professors for professors. It was the dogma of the cloister, with a strong emphasis on manners, traditions, decorum, religion, good breeding, or the simulation of it. It was an ideal doctrine for self-consciously literary undergraduates. Harvard, as Malcolm Cowley pointed out, had its own variation, inspired by Irving Babbitt (More and Babbitt often seemed interchangeable academic parts). As we have seen in the case of William James, one gifted teacher can animate the whole inert mass of a modern university. Christian Gauss was apparently such a teacher. If Paul Elmer More's ideas were archaic, they were at least *ideas*. The two men fanned the creative fires in their students.

Francis Scott Key Fitzgerald was born in 1896 in St. Paul, Minnesota. His father, who valued his own upper-class Eastern antecedents, sent him to a private school, and he then attended the Newman Academy (a Catholic boarding school near New York City). Fitzgerald's mother was the daughter of an Irish immigrant, and her son always felt torn between the Irish Catholic middle-class world and his father's social pretensions. At Princeton, with his charm and good looks and a precocious talent for writing, he soon became the center of the college literary group.

When Edmund Wilson was graduated ahead of Fitzgerald, the two friends corresponded faithfully. Before he left Princeton to accept a commission as a second lieutenant, Fitzgerald had already found the note that would make him the spokesman of his generation. It was elegiac, somewhat in the tone of Pound's and Eliot's poems, full of yearning for a lost good (perhaps the Catholic faith of his mother) and of fascination for the rich and the world of high society. He wrote to Wilson from Princeton: "God! How I miss my youth. . . . I don't think you ever realized at Princeton the childlike simplicity that lay behind all my petty sophistication and my lack of a real sense of honor." He also wrote of "my romantic Chestertonian orthodoxy," a reference to the British Catholic poet, critic, and novelist. A poem echoed the tone:

> Oh might I rise again! Might I
> Throw off the throbs of that old wine—
> See the new morning mass the sky
> With fairy towers, line on line—
> Find each mirage in the high air
> A symbol, not a dream again!
> But old monotony is there—
> Long, long avenues of rain.

The poem had hints of Amy Lowell and the imagists and what might not unreasonably be considered a premature touch of nostalgia. When Fitzgerald received his army commission, he departed from the "cool sophistries of the shattered world" of collegiate life and the "short, swift chain of Princeton intellectuals, Brooks's clothes, clean ears, and, withal, a lack of mental priggishness." Sent from one stateside training camp to another, he started work on a novel entitled, with startling appropriateness, *The Romantic Egotist*. At an officers' club dance near Montgomery, Alabama, he fell head over heels in love with beautiful Zelda Sayre. She was far more than the typical Southern belle (if there was such a thing). She was talented and ambitious, longed to dance and write professionally, and was, it turned out, highly neurotic as well. The engagement of Francis Scott Key Fitzgerald to Zelda Sayre was, as they say, a storybook romance. Fitzgerald rewrote *The Romantic Egotist* as *This Side of Paradise*. It was published in March, 1920, when he was twenty-four, and made him instantly rich and famous. In addition to the royalties on the book, he began selling short stories at $1,000 a crack. A month later he and Zelda were married in a spectacular wedding and were soon caught up in an endless round of parties. The parties, Fitzgerald wrote later, in essence, were a means of discharging the "nervous energy" that was to him the decisive characteristic of his generation. "In the morning," he wrote, "you were never violently sorry—you made no resolutions, but if you had overdone it and your heart was slightly out of order, you went on the wagon for a few days . . . and waited until an accumulation of nervous boredom projected you into another party." Boredom was the nightmare, the horror to be avoided at all costs, and boredom was, of course, inevitable, when life was lived at such a frantic pace. *The Beautiful and Damned,* which appeared in 1922, was a chronicle of the jazz age when life seemed to move to that wild beat. Already the Fitzgeralds were being consumed by their own images. They escaped to Europe, then drifted back to New York. Zelda became pregnant, and Scott bore her off to St. Paul, hoping that amid familiar scenes they could lead some kind of normal life. But he wrote his publisher: "Loafing puts me in this particularly obnoxious and abominable gloom. My 3rd novel, if I ever write another, will I am sure be black as death with gloom. I should like to sit down with ½ a dozen chosen companions and drink myself to death but I am sick alike of life, liquor and literature. If it wasn't for Zelda I think I'd disappear out of sight. . . ." From St. Paul the Fitzgeralds moved to Long Island and began the round of parties and hectic social life that provided the material for his next and most successful novel.

Having retreated from Long Island to a French villa in the south of France, Fitzgerald began to make progress with a new novel. "My book is really wonderful," he wrote Wilson, "so is the air & the sea. I have got my health back. . . ." To John Peale Bishop he wrote: "The cheerfulest things in my life are first Zelda and second the hope that my book has something extraordinary about it. I want to be extravagantly admired again. Zelda and I sometimes indulge in terrible four day rows that always start with a drinking party but we're still enormously in love and about the only truly happy married people I know."

When *The Great Gatsby* appeared, it received all the acclaim that Fitzgerald could have hoped for. He sent an extravagantly inscribed copy to Gertrude Stein. She replied warmly. His dedication to her showed, she wrote, that "you have a background of beauty and tenderness and that is a comfort. The next good thing is that you write naturally in sentences and that too is a comfort. You write naturally in sentences and one can read all of them and that among other things is a comfort. . . . You make a modern world and a modern orgy strangely enough it was never done until you did it in *This Side of Paradise.*"

Bunny Wilson also congratulated Fitzgerald. "It is undoubtedly in some ways the best thing you have done—the best planned, the best sustained, the best written. In fact, it amounts to a complete new departure in your work." Having said that much, Wilson who could never leave a good criticism alone, went on to criticize the book, declaring that Fitzgerald should undertake in his next book "a more sympathetic theme."

Fitzgerald also sent a copy of *The Great Gatsby* to Edith Wharton with an admiring dedication, and she, too, responded: "I am touched at your sending me a copy, for I feel that to your generation which has taken such a flying leap into the future, I must represent the literary equivalent of tufted furniture & gas chandeliers . . . let me say at once how much I like Gatsby or rather His Book, & how great a leap you have taken this time—in advance upon your previous work." The brilliant touches in the book, she added, "make me augur still greater things!"

Not long after the publication of *The Great Gatsby*, Fitzgerald wrote a short story entitled "The Rich Boy," soon included in a collection called *All the Sad Young Men*. It was the saga of a young man named Anson Hunter and contains Fitzgerald's most succinct observations on the life of the rich in America. "Even the intelligent and impassioned reporters of life," he wrote, "have made the country of the rich as unreal as fairy-land.

"Let me tell you about the very rich. They are different from you and me. They possess and enjoy early, and it does something to them, makes them soft where we are hard, and cynical where we are trustful, in a way that, unless you were born rich, it is very difficult to understand. They think, deep in their hearts, that they are better than we are because we had to discover the compensations and refuges of life for ourselves. . . . They are different. The only way that I can describe young Anson Hunter is to approach him as if he were a foreigner. . . . Anson accepted without reservation the world of high finance and high extravagance, of divorce and dissipation, of snobbery and privilege. Most of our lives end as a compromise—it was as a compromise that his began."

Back from another European hegira, the Fitzgeralds rented a "brand-new suburban house" in Great Neck, Long Island, where they gave a succession of parties that featured jazz and booze and "pranks." Fitzgerald meanwhile turned out a number of short stories, most of them hackwork to put bread on the table (or gin on the sideboard). The *Saturday Evening Post* paid him $4,000 a story, the equivalent of perhaps $30,000 in today's currency, but Zelda had a nervous breakdown and was confined in a sanatorium. Writing to comfort Fitzgerald, Edmund Wilson noted, "I know from my own experience that these breakdowns where people seem to go off their heads aren't necessarily serious. . . ." He told Fitzgerald that he thought it was a great mistake for American writers to live abroad as the Fitzgeralds had done so much. Writers should live in America, "hard as America can be to live in."

When Malcolm Cowley visited the Fitzgeralds in the spring of 1933 at the Bayard Turnbull farm near Baltimore, he found Fitzgerald on the wagon but Zelda far gone in schizophrenia. "That girl had everything," Fitzgerald said to Cowley. "She was the belle of Montgomery, the daughter of the chief justice of the Alabama Supreme Court. We met at the governor's ball. Everybody in Alabama knew about her, everybody that counted. She had beauty, talent, family, she could do anything that she wanted to, and she's thrown it all away." It sounded like a character in one of his stories, Cowley replied. "Sometimes I don't know whether Zelda isn't a character that I created myself. And you know, she's cuckoo, she's crazy as a loon. I'm madly in love with her." Fitzgerald went on to talk about his childhood. "I have a streak of pure vulgarity that I like to cultivate. One side of me is peasant and one aristocratic. My mother was a rich peasant, Molly McQuillan. She kept telling me, 'All this family is a lot of shit. You have to know where the money is coming from.' She was as realistic as Karl Marx. . . . My father belonged to the same Baltimore family as Francis Scott Key. What if they tore down the monument to the author of 'The Star Spangled Banner' and instead built one for me because I died for communism—a monument to the author of *The Great Gatsby?*" Fitzgerald was finishing *Tender Is the Night*. He had written 400,000 words and thrown most of them away, but he pronounced it "good, good, good." Cowley, Fitzgerald declared rudely, couldn't write a book "half as good as *The Great Gatsby*. I tell you that's a book you can't touch."

Zelda Fitzgerald pulled herself together long enough to write a first-rate, if somewhat overwritten, novel, *Save Me the Waltz*, the saga of a spoiled Southern belle. Soon she was back in the sanitorium. Fitzgerald drifted to Hollywood, desolated and despairing, to work in films, which had always fascinated him. His writing suffered; he drank to excess, and his health deteriorated. He died on December 21, 1940, three months before Sherwood Anderson. He was forty-four years old.

The other young literary prince of the twenties was also a Midwesterner. Ernest Hemingway was three years younger than Fitzgerald. Born in the Chicago suburb of Oak Park, son of a prosperous and outdoors-loving doctor, Hemingway was taken each summer of his boyhood by his father to the woods of northern Michigan, where he acquired a lifelong attachment to hunting, fishing, camping, canoeing, and similar masculine diversions. Hunting especially came to have a symbolic significance for Hemingway, hunting and blood sports, notoriously, of course, bullfighting. He also developed a keen interest in writing while still in high school, and after graduation in 1917 went to work for the *Kansas City Star* as a reporter. Thwarted by his father in his initial efforts to enlist in the army at the outbreak of the war, Hemingway finally got an appointment to the Red Cross ambulance service, which shipped him to Italy (Cowley and Dos Passos also enlisted in the Red Cross). Shortly after his arrival he was badly wounded by a mortar shell and spent three months in hospital in Milan. Discharged, he returned to Oak Park, determined to pursue a career as a writer. Working for an advertising firm, Hemingway hung around gyms and wrote poems and short stories. Most important, he met Sherwood Anderson and found a friend and counselor in the older man.

"I remember him coming up the stairs, a magnificent broad-shouldered man, shouting as he came," Anderson wrote. With his unfailing kindness to younger writers, Anderson criticized Hemingway's work and shared his enthusiasm for Gertrude Stein and for Mark Twain's *Huckleberry Finn*. With encouragement from Anderson, Hemingway developed a sparse and austere style in which the burden of the story was usually carried by dialogue. He had a remarkable ability to capture the tone and rhythm of ordinary speech, much as Robert Frost did in his poems. Stein's use of repetition in speech, which she carried to a deliberate extreme, made a strong impression on him.

Ironically, when Anderson met Hemingway, the older man had given up his struggle to make a living by his writing and was working for an advertising agency. Anderson's contacts with Hemingway stirred him to abandon again the business for the literary world. Having encouraged Hemingway to go to Paris, where so many young writers and artists were finding stimulation, Anderson gave Hemingway and his wife a letter of introduction to Gertrude Stein. In Paris Hemingway began to produce the short stories, many of them of the Michigan woods, that initially made his fame. He became a fixture of Gertrude Stein's salon and the troop leader of the American literary colony. When Burton Rascoe visited Paris, he found Hemingway very much in evidence. Hemingway's first novel, *The Sun Also Rises*, was published in 1926. The title page bore Gertrude Stein's comment to Hemingway: "You are all a lost generation." It was followed by mournful verses from Ecclesiastes: "One generation passeth away, and another generation cometh: but the earth abideth for ever. The sun also ariseth, and the sun goeth down, and hasteth to his place where he arose. . . . All the rivers run into the sea; yet the sea is not full. . . ."

Like *This Side of Paradise,* the note is elegiac. Human beings are vain and foolish, but the earth endures. *The Sun Also Rises* is the story of Jake, an expatriate American bearing the physical and psychological wounds of the war, and his friends, chief among them Robert Cohn, a young Jew, "once middleweight boxing champion of Princeton," and the fascinating lost Lady Brett Ashley. There is little plot. Jake and Brett love each other, but their love is complicated by his wounds. Cohn, like all the young men in Jake's circle, is desperately in love with Brett. When they travel to Spain in their flight from boredom, Brett seduces a handsome young bullfighter. That relationship, doomed from the first, ends in tragedy, and at the novel's end Jake and Brett face a mutual impoverishment of emotion. They are sitting characteristically at a bar. Jake says: " 'Some people have God. . . . Quite a lot.'

" 'He never worked very well with me.'

" 'Should we have another Martini?'

"The barman shook up two more Martinis and poured them out into fresh glasses.

" 'Where will we have lunch?' I asked Brett. The bar was cool. You could feel the heat outside through the window."

They go to a restaurant recommended by the bartender and drink and talk some more. After lunch they get a taxi and ride aimlessly about.

" 'O, Jake,' Brett said, 'we could have had such a damned good time together.'

"Ahead was a mounted policeman in khaki directing traffic. He raised his baton. The car slowed suddenly pressing Brett against me.

" 'Yes,' I said. 'Isn't it pretty to think so?' "

*The Sun Also Rises* was almost as successful, both monetarily and critically, as *This Side of Paradise* and *The Great Gatsby* had been. Edmund Wilson called it a "knockout—perhaps the best piece of fiction that any American of this new crop has done." Hemingway, with his love of sporting analogies, saw himself as the challenger and Fitzgerald as the fading champ. By this time the two were rather uneasy friends in Paris. Fitzgerald's considerable ego was tempered by a genuine sweetness of disposition, at least when he was sober (drunk he could be dangerously homicidal), while Hemingway was a bully at heart.

*A Farewell to Arms* was Hemingway's belated war novel; most of his contemporaries had published their war novels immediately after the war and their "lost" novels later. Hemingway reversed the order. *A Farewell to Arms,* it should be said, is only marginally about the war, in some ways less about war than *The Sun Also Rises.* It is primarily an old-fashioned love story about the romance between an American soldier, wounded in the Italian theater of operations and the English nurse, Catherine Barkley, who takes care of him and who dies in childbirth at the end of the novel. The story, as they say, was in the telling of it, and in the telling Hemingway was at his dazzling best in evoking mood by dialogue. It was immediately the ambition of every would-be young writer to write like Ernest Hemingway, and soon most of them did.

One thing Hemingway did supremely well, and it won him the admiration, if not the affection, of every one of his contemporaries who put pen to paper. Trying to write, he "found the greatest difficulty aside from knowing truly what you really felt, rather than what you were supposed to feel, and had been taught to feel, was to put down what really happened in action; what the actual things were which produced the emotion that you experienced. . . ." That was a task essential to the new consciousness. It set aside all larger issues of meaning and value, issues that had so often produced only windy rhetoric, and concentrated on the form and character and, above all, the truthful rendering of the particular moment or event, charging bull or speeding bullet.

Rather in the manner of Fitzgerald, Hemingway lived a life hardly to be distinguished from the characters in his novels. When Hamilton Fish Armstrong visited Madrid, he found Hemingway there with a coterie of companions. After absorbing as much beer and shrimp as they could hold, the party went on to Botin's, where Jake had taken Brett in *The Sun Also Rises.* At the upstairs restaurant there was a huge square oven that, it was said, hadn't gone out since the days of Cervantes. It usually contained a whole lamb or a suckling pig. A thick bean soup, fish, pork, melon, and white wine for the four of them came to sixteen pesetas, some forty cents apiece. From Botin's the friends headed for a flamenco dance hall. Walking along the Puerto del Sol, Hemingway used his jacket to demonstrate on passing taxis the difference between good and bad veronicas. At the hall Hemingway drew the dancers, who collected around him in a haze of cheap powder and perfume, displaying their charms "in a friendly and matter-of-fact way." Armstrong was charmed by Hemingway. "Since," Armstrong wrote, "there was no animal or bird to shoot and no fish to catch he was not in competition with anyone" and thus "did not display the noisy belligerence that sometimes disconcerted his friends."

Hemingway and Fitzgerald epitomized the era. Hemingway had his hideaway, not much hidden because it soon attracted a stream of friends and hangers-on, at Key West. He had discarded his first wife, Hadley, and had a new wife, Pauline, and an infant son, Patrick. He was toying with Catholicism, which disconcerted his friends, among them John Herrmann and Josephine Herbst, who moved to Key West.

Hemingway turned savagely on Anderson in a book called *The Torrents of Spring* and then had the gall to write a letter explaining that he felt he had to do it, in Anderson's words, "to bring to an end, once and for all the notion that there was any worth in my own work." He told Anderson that he hated to have to do it because of his personal friendship for him. He had done it in the interest of literature. "It was," Anderson wrote, "a kind of funeral oration delivered over my grave. It was so raw, so pretentious, so patronizing that in a repellent way it was amusing. . . ."

In her autobiography, called typically, *The Autobiography of Alice B. Toklas*, Gertrude Stein wrote that she and Anderson had "formed" Hemingway and "were both a little proud and a little ashamed of the work of their minds." After his attack on Anderson Hemingway avoided the man who had done so much to forward his literary career. Stein and Anderson "admitted that Hemingway was yellow," but they also agreed that with all his shortcomings they had a weakness for him because he was "such a good pupil," a man who took from others without acknowledgment and without even understanding what he took.

What was common to Fitzgerald and Hemingway was what we might call the autobiographical style. Following their example, writers began to write about themselves, that most compelling of all topics. The novel came to be about the novelist. Walt Whitman had written "Song of Myself" in *Leaves of Grass;* American writers had not in the main followed his lead. Now they did. Theodore Dreiser had broken the sex barrier with *Sister Carrie,* and Sherwood Anderson had widened the breach with *Winesburg, Ohio.* Anderson in the process had pioneered the autobiographical novel (*Windy McPherson's Son* and *Winesburg, Ohio*). What followed was the literary expression of individualism in novel form. Whatever could be done with that genre, F. Scott Fitzgerald, Ernest Hemingway, and later, Thomas Wolfe did.

If Fitzgerald and Hemingway were, preeminently, the voices of the Lost Generation, of perhaps inordinately sensitive young men and women bearing the psychic wounds of the war and its aftermath, Sinclair Lewis and John Dos Passos were the heirs of Dreiser's realism. Sinclair Lewis's *Main Street*, for all its realism, was a merciless satire on small-town America, its pretensions, its narrowness of mind and spirit, its piety and boosterism. However real it might have been, some critics with small-town origins questioned its humanity. But *Main Street* fitted too well with the prevailing mood of cynicism to be anything but successful.

In 1922 Sinclair Lewis published *Babbitt*, which, like *Main Street*, gave a new word to the American vocabulary. It was again a merciless satire on small-town ideas and attitudes, a work closely observed but without charity. Frazier Hunt, himself a small-town boy, complained that Lewis had simply yielded to urban clichés of small-town life. Walter Lippmann was among the skeptics. He called Lewis "a revolted provincial." *Babbitt* was a mere rubber stamp. "Had his gift been in a different medium," Lippmann wrote of Lewis in one of those devastating thrusts that authors never forgive, "he could have manufactured wax flowers that would make a man with hay fever sneeze."

Sinclair Lewis continued to document various aspects of the American scene. *Arrowsmith*, published in 1925, dealt with the world of medical research, and *Elmer Gantry* was a cruel portrait of a revivalist. As we have noted earlier, Lewis's novel about fascism's coming to the United States under the guise of democracy—*It Can't Happen Here*—made him, briefly, a hero of the left, the advances of which he rejected. For years he labored on a "labor" novel. He consulted Eugene Debs before the latter's death and conferred with Carl Haessler, among others. When the Barre, Vermont, marble workers went on strike, Lewis, living in Woodstock, allowed Budd Schulberg, then a Dartmouth undergraduate and a leader in the Dartmouth chapter of the Young Communist League to enlist his uneasy support, but when Schulberg brought him to Dartmouth to meet with the members of the YCL, their insolent and hectoring questions enraged Lewis and, in Schulberg's view at least, helped to drive him farther to the right.

Lewis's friend the journalist Vincent Sheean wrote that Lewis was, "of all the writers or artists of his approximate age, the one who had most amply developed and exactly applied the gifts he possessed." It was perhaps a fair enough evaluation, if it might be added that the gifts were essentially modest ones. Lewis had a kind of dogged American taste for the practical, for specific details. Sheean reported that he made cardboard models of the towns his characters lived in and labeled the buildings and the streets with the names used in the novel.

John Dos Passos had a parentage more bizarre than that of any character in his novels. His father was a brilliant, philandering, highly successful Portuguese businessman; his mother, a highborn Southern lady, was his father's mistress, and Dos Passos was the illegitimate offspring of that unlikely union. Acknowledged and supported by his father (including his Princeton education), Dos Passos had an abnormal set of phobias and anxieties even for a generation as driven as his own. Like Hemingway, he found his way into battle in Italy in the World War through the American Red Cross, and the two young men, both so ambitious and talented, became close friends. Dos Passos's war novel, *Three Soldiers*, was published in 1921, the same year as his friend E. E. Cummings's *The Enormous Room*, also a war novel. Dos Passos borrowed from (or shared) Cummings's contempt for capitals and punctuation marks. The free-form and unorthodox syntax of Dos Passos's novels concealed an often rather pedestrian view of the world. *Manhattan Transfer*, which appeared in 1925, set out to re-create the disorder, confusion, and stirring life of America's greatest city.

In *The Big Money*, Dos Passos used, as we have seen, the idea of two nations, one the older, truer nation of haters of injustice, the new one of "strangers . . . their hired men sit on the judge's bench they sit back with their feet on the tables under the dome of the State House they are ignorant of our beliefs they have the dollars the guns the armed forces the power plants

"they have built the electricchair and hired the executioner to throw the switch.

"all right we are two nations."

The philosophical problem with Dos Passos's formulation is that he implies that the "strangers" are the new rich, the newcomers ignorant of the old values. Their hired men are presumably the Irish bosses who dominate the state's politics. But this conception hardly conforms to the notion of two warring classes—capitalists and workers. The two nations appear to be those who hold to the original faith in freedom and equality and those who believe in the "big money."

By the time Dos Passos had completed *The Big Money*, he had acquired a definite Marxist perspective, but his commitment to old-fashioned morality gave rise to strong misgivings. He was, for example, one of the first important American literary figures to express misgivings about the Moscow treason trials. He shared his doubts with Edmund Wilson. Wilson replied that it seemed to him "a mistake to form any too definite opinion because we really know nothing about it." When Dos Passos compared Stalin to Napoleon, Wilson defended the Russian dictator as "a convinced marxist and old Bolshevik. . . . Stalin, whatever his limitations, is still working for socialism in Russia." Friends of revolution in the United States should not play into the hands of the enemies of Russia by joining in the criticism of the treason trials. "One doesn't want to give aid and comfort," Wilson wrote Dos Passos, "to people who have hopped on the shootings in Russia as a means of discrediting socialism." Dos Passos believed that an American brand of communism (or Marxian socialism) could be achieved in the United States without the revolutionary upheaval that had characterized the Russian Revolution. Wilson replied that he could "just barely imagine this happening since Upton Sinclair nearly got elected [governor of California], but," he added, "it is hard to imagine it happening without a certain amount of civil war."

Dos Passos certainly undertook the most demanding task of his literary generation—a trilogy that purported to be an autobiography of America. He called it, somewhat grandiloquently, *U.S.A.* One of his most effective literary devices was his so-called newsreels, excerpts from newspapers designed to set the historical context for his characters, who seemed to be moved far more by external events than by their own free will.

While not perhaps a major figure in the American literary Valhalla, John Dos Passos, one suspects, has an assured place as the tireless and often brilliant chronicler of post World War I America.

In the thirties a young California writer checked in with two bona fide proletarian novels. John Steinbeck was born in the farming town of Salinas, California, in 1902, and studied at Stanford before turning his attention to the writing of novels. His first three passed unnoticed, but in 1935 *Tortilla Flat*, a novel about the Mexican community of Monterey written in the realistic (or documentary) style of a Sinclair Lewis about a colorful but unknown segment of American life, brought Steinbeck considerable critical acclaim. The next year saw the publication of what was perhaps his best novel, *In Dubious Battle*, the story of Jim Nolan, a young man who joins the Communist Party because, in Nolan's words, "My whole family has been ruined by this [capitalist] system. My old man, my father, was slugged so much he went punch-drunk." The party organizer to whom Nolan appeals for membership describes the life that awaits him: "Look, Jim, I want to give you a picture of what it's like to be a Party member. You'll have a chance to vote on every decison, but once the vote's in, you'll have to obey. When we have the money we try to give field workers [organizers] twenty dollars a month to eat on. I don't remember a time we ever had the money. Now listen to the work: In the field you'll have to work along-side the men, and you'll have to do the Party work after that, sometimes sixteen, eighteen hours a day. You'll have to get your food where you can. Do you think you could do that?"

Jim replies in the affirmative, and Harry Nilson goes on to ques-tion him further. Why does he want to join the party? Jim has served time in jail. There he met some party men. "They talked to me. Every-thing's been a mess, all my life. Their lives weren't messes. They were working toward something. I want to work toward something. I feel dead. I thought I might live again." Jim's words were curiously like those of Whittaker Chambers in his autobiography, *Witness,* and, in-deed, like those of many other real-life Communists who sought to explain their motives in joining the party.

With a companion, Mac, an experienced organizer, Jim is sent to organize apple pickers. Strikes, police beatings, and killings, vigilantes working for the growers—all the familiar ingredients of the efforts to organize the California farmworkers—are in Steinbeck's novel. As pro-letarian novels went, *In Dubious Battle* was one of the better ones despite Steinbeck's rather leaden prose. It was followed by a famous novella, *Of Mice and Men,* the story of the friendship of two itinerant workers, one of them huge, feebleminded Lenny.

In 1939 Steinbeck published *The Grapes of Wrath,* the story of the migration of the Joad family from the Dust Bowl to California—a book which also qualified as a proletarian novel, became a best-seller, and earned Steinbeck the Pulitzer Prize.

As though stimulated to greater productivity by the challenge of the younger writers, the "old" writers published some of their best novels in the twenties. Willa Cather published *A Lost Lady* in 1923. Her war novel, *One of Ours,* published the year before, won the Pulitzer Prize of 1923. *A Lost Lady* is about Mrs. Forrester, the beautiful and charming young wife of an older man, and the admiration of her by Niel Herbert. The locale is Sweet Water in the Black Hills of Nebraska. Told briefly in a minor key, the novel is about the disappearance of an older and more gracious order. When her husband suffers a stroke that makes him an invalid and requires all his wife's time and care, she "maintained her old reserve. She had asked nothing and accepted nothing. Her demeanor toward the townspeople was always the same; easy, cordial, and impersonal."

*A Lost Lady* appeared a year after *Babbitt;* it is interesting to compare the two novels. Willa Cather was all her life a shrewd observer of small-town life. Sweetwater is a town as narrow and pinched in its own way as Babbitt's hometown, but Cather's novel is far richer in its treatment of Mrs. Forrester's relationship to the townspeople and to her devoted admirer, Niel Herbert.

*A Lost Lady* was followed, in 1925, by *The Professor's House.* Perhaps the most somber or disconsolate of her novels, it was also the most autobiographical, one suspects, since the professor, St. Peter, is the same age as Willa Cather—fifty-two—when she wrote the novel. He decides he has to learn to "live without delight." "Theoretically he knew that life is possible, maybe even pleasant, without joy, without passionate griefs. But it never occurred to him that he might have to live like that." His most promising young student, Tom Outland, is killed in the war, and his own life is correspondingly diminished. He says to another student, "Art and religion (they are the same thing in the end, of course) have given man the only happiness he has ever had." Cather sold the serial rights to *The Professor's House* for $10,000 and bought herself a mink coat.

Reading the novel, one cannot help feeling that Cather could not free herself from the cloud that the war and its consequent demoralization had brought upon her, so while she wrote still in what we might call the old style of a novel with other imagined figures in it, she suffered from the personalizing of literature and of history itself.

In *My Mortal Enemy* (1926), Myra Driscoll gives up her family fortune to marry for love, but poverty and hardship turn her into an embittered woman who in the last years of her life asks, "Why must I die like this, alone with my mortal enemy [her husband]?" She regrets that she gave up her fortune for love. "It was money I needed. We've thrown our lives away." She turns to Catholicism for solace and, clutching a crucifix, makes her way to a cliff overlooking the sea.

In her next novel, *Death Comes for the Archbishop,* Cather turned away from the modern world, which seemed so bleak to her, and back to the land of the Southwest, to New Mexico, which had been such a healing experience for her long before. She chose as the subject of her novel the lives of two French Catholic missionaries, real figures—Archbishop Jean Baptiste Lamy, the first bishop of New Mexico, and his friend and vicar general Joseph Machebeuf. Lamy became for her "a sort of invisible friend," a man who embodied "something fearless and fine and very, very well-bred-something that spoke of race." The novel was the simple story of the relationship of Lamy and Machebeuf to each other and to the beautiful but austere landscape Cather loved. "Only on the bright edges of the world, on the great grass plains or the sagebrush desert" could one find such luminous air. "Something soft and wild and free, something that whispered to the ear on the pillow, lightened the heart, softly, softly picked the lock, slid the bolts, and released the prisoned spirit of man into the wind, into the blue and gold, into the morning, into the morning."

Unquestionably she had in mind, in the love of the two men for each other, her own long friendship with Edith Lewis. Love, faith, and the land. The writing of the novel was a time of serenity and joy for Cather; it reconciled her to the world and restored her spirits. First serialized, it was published by Alfred Knopf in 1927 and at once recognized as one of her major works.

Like Willa Cather, Ellen Glasgow went through a period of deep personal disappointment, indeed despair, in the aftermath of the war. Her war novel, *The Builders*, had been a disappointment both financially and artistically. Two successive novels were little better. Then, in 1925, the same year as *An American Tragedy*, she published perhaps her finest novel, *Barren Ground*, the story of Dorinda Oakley and her life and adventures in Pedlar's Mill, Virginia, and in New York City. Dorinda's grandfather, John Calvin Abernathy, "lived with learning, prudence, and piety until he was not far from a hundred." His daughter, Eudora, "fell a victim of one of those natural instincts which Presbyterian theology has damned but never wholly exterminated, and married a member of the 'poor white' class, who had nothing more to recommend him than the eyes of a dumb poet and the head of a youthful John the Baptist, . . ." Dorinda was the offspring of Joshua Oakley, the poor white, and Eudora Abernathy, child of Virginia aristocracy.

After a devastating betrayal by charming but weak Jason Greylock, Dorinda, pregnant and desperate, flees to New York, hoping to get a job there and have her child. It seems to her, when she flees, that the land is the enemy: "She had never lost the feeling that the land contained a terrible force, whether for good or evil she could not tell, and there were hours when the loneliness seemed to rise in a crested wave and surge over her." She saw her mother driven by the farm to the edge of despair. "Though she spent every bit of her strength there was nothing to show for her struggle. Like the land which took everything and gave back nothing, the farm had drained her vitality without altering its general aspect of decay."

In New York Dorinda realizes that she has fled from the element that has most nourished her. She tells her friend and benefactor that she must go back, "I told him we had to get our living from barren ground. . . . The old feeling that the land thought and felt, that it possessed a secret personal life of its own, brushed her mood. . . ."

Like Willa Cather's *Death Comes for the Archbishop*, *Barren Ground* became for Ellen Glasgow "almost a vehicle of liberation. After years of tragedy and the sense of defeat that tragedy breeds in the mind, I had won my way to the other side of the wilderness, and had discovered, with astonishment, that I was another and a very different person." Her earliest determination as a writer had been to "write of the South not sentimentally, as a conquered province, but dispassionately, as part of the larger world."

In *Barren Ground* the major themes are the contrast between rural and urban life, the nature of community, the land as the source of all strength and beauty, and, perhaps above all, the ties of family. "Filial devotion," Glasgow wrote of a son who looked after his ill but "undeserving" old father, "was both esteemed and practised in that pre-Freudian age, before self-sacrifice had been dethroned from its precarious seat among the virtues; and to give up one's career for a few months, at most for a possible year, appeared dutiful rather than dangerous to a generation that knew not psychoanalysis."

W. J. Cash credited *Barren Ground* with being "the first real novel, as opposed to romances, the South had brought forth; certainly the first wholly genuine picture of the people who make up and always have made up the body of the South."

In 1932 Glasgow published *The Sheltered Life*, a novel about age and youth, about General Archibald and his granddaughter, Jenny Blair, and Jenny's relations with George and Eva Birdsong. John Welch, a young doctor, believes in the omnipotence of science, but the old general finds a world in which science presides over "only a stark and colourless spectacle. . . . A thin-lipped world of facts without faith, of bones without flesh." Yet, the old man reflects, passion was "even in the old, a simple problem of lowering your blood pressure and abandoning salt." The general had had one ardent, if unfulfilled, romance. Except for that "defeated passion in his youth, he had lived entirely upon the shifting surface of facts. He had been a good citizen, a successful lawyer, a faithful husband, an indulgent father; he had been, indeed, everything but himself."

At the end of the novel Jenny Blair, a beautiful young woman of eighteen, cannot resist seducing the husband of her friend and patroness Eva Birdsong and brings tragedy to the Birdsongs and to her own family. "Oh, Grandfather, I didn't mean anything," she cries at the novel's end. "I didn't mean anything in the world!" *The Sheltered Life* is one of Glasgow's better novels and one of the best of the thirties.

Edith Wharton continued to explore the theme of the old New York aristocracy (which she certainly did not sentimentalize) and its encounter with new money. "A frivolous society," she wrote, "can only acquire dramatic significance through what its frivolity destroys." *The Age of Innocence*, which was published in 1920, won the Pulitzer Prize.

Newland Archer is the hero of *The Age of Innocence*. He is in love with Ellen Olenska, an American woman who has had a tragic marriage to a dissolute nobleman and whose reputation is clouded with scandal. Giving her up for a respectable marriage and a conventional career, Archer comes, after his wife's death, to Paris with his son to reflect upon the meaning of having given up what he most desired in life. It is a sacrifice his son could not have understood, Archer realizes; the times have changed.

*Old New York*, published four years after *The Age of Innocence*, was made up of four vignettes or novellas, each dealing with a decade— the forties through the seventies—of nineteenth-century New York social life. "False Dawn" tells of the Raycie family and young Lewis Raycie, who, sent to Italy by his father to buy third-rate "Christian Art," came home with then-unappreciated Piero della Francescas and Giottos.

"The Old Maid" is the story of the Ralstons, an "old family," who lived "in simplicity and affluence." The theme of "The Spark" (the sixties) is the Delane family and the relationship between Hayley Delane and his wife. Delane "shared cheerfully in all the amusements of his little set—rode, played polo, hunted and drove his four-in-hand with the best of them." The only unorthodox element in his life is the memory he cherishes of a friend he met during the Civil War, an unforgettable figure of gaiety and benevolence. Puzzled by the identity of Delane's friend, the narrator discovers by chance that it was Walt Whitman. He reads Delane some of Whitman's poetry. Delane replies: "Old Walt—that was what all the fellows used to call him. He was a great chap; I'll never forget him.—I rather wish, though, . . . you hadn't told me that he wrote all that rubbish."

"New Year's Day" is about the fascinating Lizzie Hazeldean's fall from grace in New York society because of rumors which, although without foundation, tarnished her reputation. To the narrator she was the victim of an age in which a young woman's only function was "to please." "Marriage alone could save such a girl from starvation. . . . The self sufficing little society of that vanished New York attached no great importance to wealth, but regarded poverty as so distasteful that it simply took no notice of it."

It seemed to Edith Wharton, surveying the contemporary literary scene, that the novelists of her age had labored to turn the "wooden dolls of that literary generation into struggling, suffering human beings; but we have been avenged, and more than avenged, not only by life but by the novelists, and I hope the latter will see before long that it is as hard to get dramatic interest out of a mob of irresponsible criminals as out of the Puritan marionettes who formed our stock in trade. Authentic human nature lies somewhere between the two. . . ."

In 1925 Wharton received the first honorary degree awarded by Yale University to a woman. By the time of her death she had written some fifty books, including travel accounts and critical essays. Her biographer was understandably startled (or shocked) to find among her unpublished manuscripts a vivid erotic passage describing father-daughter incest.

As the South had its own social customs and "mind," it had its own literary renaissance or "naissance" centered, oddly enough, at Vanderbilt University in Nashville, in the border state of Tennessee. There students and some of the younger English literature faculty banded together to form what they called, rather self-consciously, the Fugitives.

As Allen Tate recalled the origin of the Fugitives, he was talking to Donald Davidson, a young English instructor, on the steps of College Hall on the Vanderbilt campus in the fall of 1921 when Davidson invited him to meet with some friends "to read poems and to discuss 'philosophy.' " John Crowe Ransom was another young professor who was a member of the small group of campus literati. Their host and the leader of the little group was Dr. Sidney Mttron Hirsch, "a mystic and a Rosicrucian," whose "shining pince-nez stood upon his handsome nose," while "curled Assyrian hair topped a massive brow." The sources of the Fugitives ran from G. K. Chesterton and Hilaire Belloc to T. S. Eliot, William Yeats, and Robert Frost. Allen Tate wrote of their "almost superstitious distrust of the physical sciences and the mystical reverence for authority. . . ."

The Fugitives yearned for what they believed to have been the graces of the Old South: respect for tradition, benevolence and courtesy to those who were dependent (women and blacks), respect for the land, and opposition to materialism, industrialism, and all the disorders of the modern world. Although they wrote essays, short stories, and even novels, their preferred mode of expression was poetry. Their poetry abounded in words like "gone," "past," "dark," "regret," "ancestors." In their nostalgia for a lost good they shared a tone common to the age, but in their defense of tradition and religion, especially religion, they placed themselves in direct opposition to the dominant intellectual tone of their Northern compatriots. In the North the literary world shared Edmund Wilson's conviction that "religion . . . has become impossible." The Fugitives, some of whom were soon to be metamorphosed into the Agrarians, considered the established churches for the most part hopeless, but they shared a belief in a religious or spiritual dimension to life which it was fatal to ignore and which was desperately needed to oppose extravagant claims of science.

John Crowe Ransom's "Antique Harvesters" sounds the familiar note of loss and decay:

> Tawny are the leaves turned but they still hold,
> And it is harvest; what shall this land produce?
> A meager hill of kernels, a runnel of juice;
> Declension looks from our land, it is old,
> Therefore let us assemble, dry, gray, spare,
> And mild as yellow air.

Another of the Fugitive poets was Donald Davidson. His "Prologue: The Long Street" ends:

> So long, forever so.
> Forever, night after night, to say good-bye
> Across the portals of an iron age
> And close the ivory gate with hopeless stare
> Down the long street and up and down again . . .
> Again, old man? How shall we meet again . . .
> Tonight, for lights bloom up uncertainly for us,
> Or in this dead coming let smoke and dark take leave
> Of dead men under a pall, nameless and choked?

Davidson's poem "On a Replica of the Parthenon" ends:

> And gods, like men, to soot revert.
> Gone is the mild, the serene air.
> The golden years are come too late.
> Pursue not wisdom or virtue here,
> But what blind motion, what dim last
> Regret of men who slew their past
> Raised up this bribe against their fate.

Allen Tate was perhaps the best of the Fugitive poets. His "Ode to the Confederate Dead" epitomized the respect for the ancestors that was so central to the Southern creed:

> Row after row with strict impunity
> The headstones yield their names to the element,
> The wind whirrs without recollection;
> In the riven troughs the splayed leaves
> Pile up, of nature the casual sacrament
> To the seasonal eternity of death;
> Then driven by the fierce scrutiny
> Of heaven to their election in the vast breath,
> They sought the rumor of mortality.
> . . . . . . . . . . . . . . . . . . . . . . . . . . . . . . .
>         Now that the salt of their blood
> Stiffens the saltier oblivion of the sea,
> Seals the malignant purity of the flood,
> What shall we who count our days and bow
> Our heads with a commemorial woe
> In the ribboned coats of grim felicity,
> What shall we say of the bones, unclean,
> Whose verdurous anonymity will grow?
> * * * * * * * * * * * * * * * * * * * * * * * *
> What shall we say who have knowledge
> Carried to the heart? Shall we take the act
> To the grave? Shall we, more hopeful, set up the grave
> In the house? The ravenous grave?
>         Leave now
> The shut gate and the decomposing wall:
> The gentle serpent, green in the mulberry bush,
> Riots with his tongue through the hush—
> Sentinel of the grave who counts us all!

Equally representative is a poem of Tate's prompted by a news item about the bacchanalian party in New York thrown by Flo Ziegfeld, at which a nude chorus girl bathed in a tub of wine:

In a lean house spawned on baked limestone
Blood history is the murmur of grasshoppers
Eastward of the dawn. Have you a daughter,
Daughters are the seeds of occupations,
Of aspirities, such as will, deeds, mortgages,
Duels, estates, statesmen, pioneers, embezzlers,
Eminent Virginians, reminiscences, bastards,
The bar-sinister hushed, effaced by the porcelain
                                        tub.
A daughter is the fruit of occupation;
Let her not read history lest knowledge
Of her fathers instruct her to be a noted bawd.
Vittoria was herself, the contemporary strumpet
A plain bitch . . .
Year after year the blood of Christ will sleep
In the holy tree, the branches sagged without bloom;
Then the plant o'erflowing the stale vegetation,
In May the creek swells with the anemone,
The Lord God wastes his substance towards the ocean.
In Christ we have lived, on the flood of Christ
                                        borne up. . . .

One of the most productive members of the group was Merrill Moore, who was to write 50,000 sonnets in eighteen years. Another addition to the circle was a tall, thin youth, who walked with "a sliding shuffle, as if his bones didn't belong to one another." The "long quivering nose, large brown eyes, and a long chin—all topped by curly red hair"—belonged to Robert Penn Warren, Red to his friends. He was sixteen years old, with all the stigmata of a prodigy.

As in every other aspect of the South, the racial issue affected the Fugitives. Their inability to face up to the situation of blacks in the South in the end deprived their work of the kind of relevance that can come only from squarely facing the most urgent realities of the time. Langston Hughes, traveling through the South and reading his poetry at black colleges, was rebuffed by the Fugitives. When young black faculty members at Fisk College in Atlanta were approached by one of the Fugitives with the idea of having common meetings, the idea was vetoed by Tate. Since blacks and whites could not intermarry in the South, interracial literary gatherings were taboo.

Nonetheless, the basic ideas of the Fugitives proved remarkably enduring, at least in the South. By the end of the decade the Fugitives, meeting at a symposium in Nashville, had transformed themselves into the better-known Agrarians by contributing to a manifesto entitled "I'll

Take My Stand." Many of the original Fugitive ideas were reaffirmed, along with a new emphasis on regionalism, on the notion that Americans should value and strengthen regional traditions and not be drawn into one homogenized cultural blob directed from New York. It was the Agrarians' intention "to support a Southern way of life against what may be called the American or prevailing way; and all as much as agreed that the best terms in which to represent the distinction are contained in the phrase, Agrarian *versus* Industrial." As put by one of the Agrarians, Andrew Lytle, it was "impossible for any culture to be sound and healthy without a proper respect and a proper regard for the soil, no matter how many urban dwellers think that their victuals came from groceries and delicatessens and their milk from tin cans."

The Agrarians attracted attention and won recruits to their cause by traveling about to colleges and universities and debating the issue. Sherwood Anderson heard them at the University of Virginia and thought "the whole thing rather pathetic." He was amazed at the patience of the audience. "Do not go about debating other professors," he told them. "Get some big industrialist to take you on." They did, but the trouble was the industrialists won, or that was the common opinion. When Anderson met John Crowe Ransom at a writers' conference at the University of Colorado in Boulder, Ransom admitted that some of the Agrarians had taken a disturbing turn toward a kind of fascism which involved "continual subjugation of the Negro and hatred of the Jews." The community was to be paramount, and if the community was racist and reactionary, "you did not oppose it."

The Agrarians and the Communists agreed on one point only, but it was an important point: that industrialism had brought with it terrible inequities and widespread dehumanization. In their concern for the land and their emphasis on how removed America's increasingly urbanized population was from the sources of its material existence, the Agrarians anticipated the present-day (1980s) environmental movement. They were certainly right in their skepticism about the claims of science as well and in their concern with tradition, with religion, and the graces of good living. Religion, in their view, was essential because it staked out the realm of the ultimately unknowable, the infinitely mysterious dimensions of man's spiritual life, of faith, reverence, loyalty, fidelity, and love. Secular religions like communism were, the Agrarians believed, deaf and blind to a whole range of human experience, past and present. Their image of man was shallow and superficial and suffered surpassingly from that ancient bane named by the Greeks hubris: vanity and presumption and an unwillingness to recognize the compromised and contingent character of all human enterprises. On the other hand, the Agrarians were engaged in the basically hopeless task of retrieving the myth of the antebellum South. Their tone was nostalgic, and they refused to face the morally destructive consequences of slavery. It thus followed that they appeared increasingly archaic and irrelevant. It was unfortunate that their obtuseness on the racial issue rendered the genuine truths they proclaimed nugatory. Edmund Wilson wrote to John Peale Bishop that Allen Tate was "falling foul of everybody of his own generation" by charging them "with romanticism, impressionism, Bohemianism, and all the stock crimes which [Paul Elmer] More and [Irving] Babbitt, looking out, at the beginning of the century, from their academic shelters, supposed people who produced literature to be guilty of." Wilson himself gave little weight to Agrarianism or the New Humanism (the Southerners preferred to call it the New Realism), but he did credit it with being "the only systematic attempt . . . to deal with large political, social, moral, and aesthetic questions, in relation to each other, in a monumental and logical way." Nonetheless, he believed that "their system is going to sink through its preoccupation with American small-town morality of the day before yesterday, its little sympathy with or insight into humanity, and its incomprehension of art. . . ."

The Agrarians were not unchallenged in the South. W. T. Couch, director of the University of North Carolina Press, took issue with them. Defending Erskine Caldwell, who had been accused by the Agrarians of exploiting the poor mountain people of Tennessee, Couch argued that "the South must recognize that evils of the kind Mr. Caldwell describes actually exist in this region, and must do what it can to correct them." It seemed highly inconsistent for the Agrarians to "assert that virtue is derived from the soil, but see no virtue in the Negro and the poor white who are closest to the soil." One critic, reviewing Donald Davidson's *The Attack on Leviathan*, noted that the manifesto of the Southern Agrarians, while "not without charm to admirers of fervid prose, . . . lacked the ring of reality; it failed to command belief," and Lillian Smith called them mockingly the "United Writers of the Confederacy."

An important Southern writer of the period was Julia Mood Peterkin. Born in Laurens County, South Carolina, into an old planter family, Julia Mood was graduated from Converse College in Spartenburg, South Carolina, and seven years later, when she was almost an old maid by Southern standards, married William Peterkin, a wealthy plantation owner. She was a tall, striking-looking redhead. After her marriage she settled down to be mistress of Lang Syne, the Peterkin plantation, with a work force of more than 400 blacks, most of whom lived on the plantation and farmed for "shares," and a number of whom were Gullahs, originally from the Sea Islands off the Georgia-Carolina cast. Intimately involved in the lives of the sharecroppers, she made herself a student of their ways. The nurse of her only son, William, was an old Gullah woman, Maum Lavinia Berry. Raising turkeys, setter dogs, pigeons, and a variety of roses as well as being a member of a ladies' musical club occupied Julia Peterkin for some twenty years of a thoroughly domestic existence. Then a series of disasters afflicted the Peterkins and Lang Syne. William Peterkin's appendix ruptured, serious complications followed, and he became a virtual invalid. The hogs, which constituted one of the plantation's principal cash crops, died off from swine flu, and the black foreman of the plantation, on whom Peterkin depended heavily, had to have his legs amputated after they had become infected. As a form of solace Julia Peterkin resumed the study of music and began writing sketches of plantation life. When Carl Sandburg visited Charleston, South Carolina, in 1920, to lecture to the Poetry Society, his host took him to visit the Peterkins at Lang Syne. After an evening of singing, in which Sandburg and some of the plantation's black farmers exchanged folk songs, Peterkin mentioned that she had written some short stories. Sandburg asked to see them; he was so impressed that he urged her to send them to Henry Mencken, then editor of the *Smart Set*. Mencken published one, and Emily Clark, editor of the *Reviewer* in Richmond, Virginia, was soon publishing a number of others. The publisher Alfred Knopf suggested they be woven into a novel, and the result was *Green Thursday*, published in 1924.

Despite her family background and her own position in South Carolina society, Peterkin anticipated resentment and hostility from her "own South Carolina audience," she wrote to Emily Clark and to Joel Spingarn, the benefactor of the NAACP, who asked for stories to publish in the magazine *Crisis*. "My nearest of kin and my natural protectors think (they say) that to publish my raw crude things in *The Crisis* will win me the scorn of both black and white. That sounds bad. I am not sure I could bear it. . . . In time I shall achieve courage. I shall. Courage to face every aunt, uncle, cousin. But now, somehow, since they talked to me, I'm low-spirited. Down-hearted." She wrote

Emily Clark: "In this part of the world, my book has not met with much sympathy, but that does not surprise me at all. I said things that no nice South Carolina lady ever says, and so I must be disciplined a bit even by my friends." But others praised the book. Spingarn assured her that nothing "so stark, taut, poignant, has come out of the South in fifty years." Most gratifying of all was the praise of W. E. B. Du Bois in a review in the *Crisis*. He called it a "beautiful book" and said of Peterkin, "She is a Southern white woman but she has the eye and ear to see beauty and to know truth."

Like Willa Cather and Ellen Glasgow, Julia Peterkin was deeply preoccupied with the earth as fact and symbol. "There is hardly a sign," she wrote in *Green Thursday*, "of the black twisted roots. There is not a trace to be seen of their silent, tense struggle as they grope deep down in the earth. There is nothing to show how they reach and grapple and hold, or how in the darkness down among the worms they work out mysterious chemistries that change damp clay into beauty."

*Black April* is the story of the black foreman April who rules his master's plantation with an iron hand. Finally he goes too far. An old woman "conjures" on him. He has a serious accident, a wound becomes infected, and he dies. The story of April's dominance and decline is told through the eyes of a young black boy, Breeze. *Black April* is a story of pride and arrogance brought down in defeat and humiliation. It ends with April's death, his legs having been amputated in a vain effort to save his life. April demands to be buried in "a man-size box— You un'erstan'?—A man-size box—I-been-six-feet-fo'-Uncle-six feet-fo'!"

*Black April* brought more critical praise. "Now, I walk on air!" she wrote a friend. "Let the S.C. ladies gnash their teeth as much as they like! Let the heathen rage! Somebody *does* believe in me!" She was pleased by a review written by Donald Davidson, a leader of the Fugitive group, who called it "perhaps the first genuine novel in English of the Negro as a human being," while Julian Harris, the son of Joel Chandler Harris, wrote in the *Columbus* (Georgia) *Enquirer-Sun* that Peterkin deserved the Pulitzer Prize. Other Southern writers encouraged her. Du Bose Heyward, a fellow South Carolinian, was a warm supporter. She was given a fellowship to the MacDowell Colony in Peterborough, New Hampshire, and there she completed her most finished and most popular novel, *Scarlet Sister Mary*.

Scarlet Sister Mary is Mary Pinesett, the liveliest and most audacious person on the plantation, who, before she reforms, has children by nine different fathers. Much of the book tells of her relationship with two very different brothers who courted her—the reckless and faithless July and his upright brother, June. It is July whom Mary chooses, knowing that he will bring her nothing but grief. The black community tries in vain to turn their erring sister from her wicked ways. Called before the congregation, she tells them defiantly: " 'I know yunnuh talks about me behind my back, but I don' mind. Talk all you want to. I ain't no member o de church. I been baptized an' I been a member four different times in my life. A member, de same as you. When I git old an' tired seein' pleasure, I'm gwine to seek and pray an' be a member again.'

"She looked around and smiled.

" 'If I was fat or either old, I might would settle down, but, tank Gawd, ain' neither one. Not yet.' "

If the novel is about the tension between natural human instincts and the constraints of civilization, it is also about the eternal tension between Southern men and Southern women, white or black. Mary suffers betrayal by July and gives herself, often casually, to other men, but she retains her independence and her pride while the more proper and conventional women in the community generally lose both.

When *Scarlett Sister Mary* appeared, it received a chorus of praise. Robert Herrick wrote in the *New Republic* that it was "something more than a novel—the revelation of a race which has lived with the whites for hundreds of years, without becoming known beneath the skin." It got the supreme accolade: It was banned in Boston.

What Julia Peterkin did with great skill was to take classic Southern themes (which were certainly more than Southern) of family, community, authority, loyalty, courage, devotion to the land, religious faith, etc., and depict these qualities in the Lang Syne blacks.

William Faulkner, born in 1897, in New Albany, Mississippi, announced his presence on the literary scene by publishing three novels before the end of the twenties. Faulkner had served in the Royal Canadian Air Force during the war and been seriously wounded. After he was discharged, he returned to Oxford, Mississippi, to attend the University of Mississippi, and made that town his home after he left the university.

*Soldier's Pay*, the story of a badly injured veteran's attempt to cope with the world, was published in 1926, and *Mosquitoes*, a not particularly successful attempt at satire, a year later.

*The Sound and the Fury* tells, in flashbacks and stream of consciousness interjections, the story of the Compson family—Quentin and his sister, Candace, or Caddy, for whom Quentin has incestuous longings; Jason, his coldly realistic brother, and Benjy, an idiot brother—and of the blacks among whom they lived: Luster, Benjy's rather simple-minded attendant; Frony, the daughter of Dilsey; and Dilsey herself, cook and nourisher, who ran the "whole family."

Quentin Compson is one who "loved death above all, who loved only death, loved and lived in an almost perverted anticipation of death as a lover loves and deliberately refrains from the willing friendly tender incredible body of his beloved, until he can no longer bear not the refraining but the restraint and so flings himself, relinquishing, drowning."

Quentin goes off to Harvard and experiences the North in painful contrast with his homeland in Jefferson County, Kentucky. Jason filches from his mother's estate; Caddy makes a disastrous marriage. Much of the novel revolves around Benjy, a castrate and an idiot, and Luster and Dilsey.

In its weavings back and forth through time, its changing voices and tenses, the novel demands the reader's close attention; no résumé could more than hint at its potency. Faulkner combined the mythic, the symbolic, the bizarre with the closest observation of the minutiae of daily existence with an ear for the subtlest intonations of the human voice. The melding of the two—the universal, cosmic, symbolic, mythic dimension and the mundane—is to be found only in the greatest works of the imagination. It is manifestly evident in Herman Melville's *Moby Dick*, Hawthorne's novels, and Eugene O'Neill's plays.

*The Sound and the Fury* was followed by Faulkner's most sensational novel, *Sanctuary*, written, by the author's account, to make money. Published in 1931, *Sanctuary* was both a commercial and an artistic success. It was, in essence, the story of a Southern belle, Temple Drake, vain and impetuous, who is kidnapped by bootleggers, is raped under the supervision of the malevolent Popeye, and confined to a brothel in Memphis. The novel is an exploration of the relationship (or absence of a relationship) between the white upper class and "poor whites." It is also a parable of how the darkest horrors lie close to wealth and social position. In a dialogue between Temple Drake and the wife of one of the bootleggers, the wife expresses her scorn for Drake's world, a world without the knowledge of the desperate struggle for survival and the nature of evil. "Oh, I know your sort," the woman says. "Honest women. Too good to have anything to do with common people. . . . Take all you can get and give nothing. . . . Do you know what you've got into now?" What Temple Drake had gotten into was a world as alien as outer space, and what followed was murder, lynching, and execution, with a Memphis whorehouse as the stage.

Faulkner's novel *As I Lay Dying* (1930) is a tragic farce about the Bundren family's efforts to bring their dead mother back to Jefferson County for burial. The Bundrens are both touching and absurd in their blundering and often frustrated efforts to express their grief for their mother by "doing the right thing."

Between *Sanctuary* and *Light in August* (1932), Faulkner wrote the long short story (or novella) "Spotted Horses." It is Faulkner at his most accomplished. Flem Snopes, whose name is a synonym for unscrupulous schemes, turns up in Frenchman's Bend with a Texan and a string of semiwild horses, a scraggly bunch of unmanageable brutes. Everyone in town knows that the creatures are the embodiment of trouble and knows that despite such foreknowledge, Snopes and his companion will sell them at a handsome profit. Seemingly uncongenial subjects, the horses acquire a spectacular life and potency of their own. Faulkner's prose captures their frantic rushes more faithfully than any movie camera could. After the Texan has auctioned off all the ponies, he departs, leaving their new owners to claim them, but the crazed animals escape from their corral and scatter over half a dozen counties.

"Spotted Horses" was followed by "The Bear," first published in 1935 and later incorporated in *Go Down, Moses*, where it was supplemented by so-called Section 4. "The Bear" tells the story of a ritual hunt for a bear known as Old Ben. The central figure is sixteen-year-old Isaac or Ike McCaslin. Included in the hunt are characters from other Faulkner novels, General Compson and Major de Spain and old Ikkemotubbe, a Chickasaw chief. To Isaac McCaslin, "they were going not to hunt bear and deer but to keep a yearly rendezvous with the bear which they did not even intend to kill." The bear was not so much a mortal beast as a symbol of the "doomed wilderness whose edges were constantly and punily being gnawed at by men with plows and axes. . . ." He was "an anachronism indomitable and apotheosis of the old wild life . . . the old bear, solitary, indomitable, and alone; widowered childless and absolved of mortality—old Priam reft of his old wife and out-lived all his sons." Sam Fathers is the ancient black custodian, hunter and friend of the bear. Like the bear, he "was old. He had no children, no people, none of his blood anywhere above the earth that he would ever meet again. And even if he were to, he could not have touched it, spoken to it, because for seventy years now he had had to be a negro. It was almost over now and he was glad." Sam and the bear are bound together, shaped out of the same earth, "in the solitary brotherhood of an old and childless Negro's alien blood, and the wild and invincible spirit of an old bear. . . ."

At last the fierce old hound Lion brings Ben to bay. The bear is killed, but not before he fatally wounds Lion. Sam Fathers dies as well. He has seen and lived enough.

In Section 4 of "The Bear," Isaac McCaslin goes over an old, barely decipherable family ledger, reflecting on his family's history. His musings are more reflections on the South, on life and death. More cogently than perhaps anywhere else, Faulkner enunciates his own credo in Isaac McCaslin's intermittent dialogue with his McCaslin cousin: *"Truth is one. It doesn't change. It covers all things which touch the heart— honor and pride and pity and justice and courage and love . . . and what the heart holds to becomes truth, as far as we know the truth. Do you see now?"*

Like the characters in his novels, Faulkner had the Southern gift for wild buffoonery, clownish behavior, and the playing of roles. He went to Hollywood to work on a script of one of his novels and soon found the life of a scriptwriter, which involved punching a time clock, unsupportable. He petitioned to be allowed to work at home. In view of his eminence as a "serious writer," permission was given, but when the producer tried to contact Faulkner at his Hollywood apartment, he found that he had returned to Oxford, Mississippi, the only place he knew as "home." On infrequent forays to New York to consult with his publisher, Faulkner delighted in the role of Southern yokel. He was not a writer, he insisted, but a farmer. Visiting Japan, Faulkner told a group of his Japanese admirers, "I'm a countryman. My life is farm land and horses and the raising of grain and feed. I took up writing simply because I liked it . . . but just to be a writer is not my life; my life is a farmer, so in that sense, I'm not a writer because that doesn't come first."

As he had with so many other young writers, Sherwood Anderson befriended and encouraged Faulkner. During Anderson's "Southern period," when he lived in New Orleans, Faulkner appeared at Anderson's apartment, a small man wearing a huge, bulging overcoat. He would be spending some time in New Orleans, he told Anderson, and while he looked for a place to stay, he would like to leave his "things" with Anderson. The things turned out to be six or seven gallons of "moon liquor."

William Faulkner was the most protean of the novelists of this era (perhaps, indeed, of any other). He made himself the master of the darker passions of the human heart—hate, envy, greed, vanity, physical and psychic violence—and their byproducts—incest, rape, and murder—as well as its nobler impulses—honor, fortitude, courage, endurance, trust, and love. The conflict between the ancient virtues of the ancestors and the degenerate inclinations of modern times was a major theme. In reversion to the great nineteenth-century novelists by his specific depiction of physical landscapes and of social classes and, perhaps most strikingly, races, he invented a county and intricate genealogies. Yoknapatawpha County, he calculated, covered some 2,400 square miles and contained 15,611 inhabitants, 6,298 of whom were white and the rest black, all of them his subjects.

Whether Faulkner was in any sense an orthodox Christian is uncertain; what is evident is that he constantly made use of the rich symbolism of Christianity and of the themes of suffering, crucifixion, repentance, and forgiveness. He found black religion compelling, and the black figures in his novels are men and women, especially women, of depth and complexity. In *The Sound and the Fury* Faulkner draws an unforgettable portrait of Dilsey. On April 8, 1928, she emerges from her cabin into a gloomy, threatening day, a ruined monument to endurance, "as though muscle and tissue had been courage or fortitude which the days or the years had consumed until only the indomitable skeleton was left rising like a ruin or a landmark above the somnolent guts, above the collapsed face . . . lifted into the driving day with an expression at once fatalistic and of a child's astonished disappointment. . . ." Blacks are not, indeed, just sympathetically drawn characters. In a number of the novels they are central figures bearing a special, often symbolic significance, frequently seen (as the abolitionists saw them) as suffering Christ figures. They are the ones who hold life together, bearers of the enduring wisdom of those close to the center of human experience.

Throughout this work we have spoken of two separate and sharply contrasting streams of thought or intellectual tradition in American history: the Secular-Democratic Consciousness (essentially the Jefferson notion of man as good and society as perfectible through reason and science) and the Classical-Christian Consciousness, which was far more skeptical about man's nature, believed in original sin as a fact or metaphor, viewed history as a tragic drama and all "progress" as limited and contingent. The Fugitives, and then the Agrarians, held fast to many of the main elements of the Classical-Christian Consciousness. More to the point, virtually every important Southern writer (and there were soon dozens of them), however careful he or she might be to disassociate himself or herself from the Agrarians, worked within the philosophical framework of the Classical-Christian Consciousness. We could thus readily construct a kind of checklist for Southern writers: the land; the family; community; loyalty; courage; tradition; faith. Writers as varied as Ellen Glasgow and William Faulkner explored these same themes. While some Southern writers slipped off into the slough of racist and quasi-Fascist fantasies, others perpetuated or revived an intellectual tradition as old as the Founding Fathers. By doing so, they would come, in time, to dominate the American literary scene.

Thomas Wolfe was in the South but hardly of it. Born at the turn of the century in Asheville, North Carolina, he turned out in his brief and haunted life (he died in 1938) a succession of evocative, if often florid (in that sense he was thoroughly Southern), novels about the anguish of growing up in America. He was a huge man with vast and insatiable appetites. Wolfe, Sherwood Anderson wrote, had "a determination, half-physical, all his big body in it, like a man striving to push his way through a stone wall."

Educated at the University of North Carolina and the star of George Pierce Baker's drama class at Harvard, Wolfe wrote *Look Homeward, Angel* in twenty furious months of labor. Published in 1929, it made him famous.

In *Look Homeward, Angel* Eugene Gant, the son of a patiently enduring mother and a bitter, raging, alcoholic father, sets out to unriddle the meaning of America like so many young men before him. "He felt suddenly the devastating impermanence of the nation. Only the earth endured—the gigantic American earth, bearing upon its awful breast a world of flimsy rickets. Only the earth endured—the broad terrific earth that had no ghosts to haunt it. . . . Within its hills he had been held a prisoner; upon its plain he walked, alone, a stranger.

"O God! O God! We have been an exile in another land and a stranger in our own." And later he reflected that he did not care under what form of government he lived: Republican, Democrat, Tory, Socialist, or Bolshevist. . . . He did not want to reform the world, or to make it a better place to live in: his whole conviction was that the world was full of pleasant places, enchanted places, if he could only go and find them." Like the characters of Faulkner's novels, Gant-Wolfe carried the curse of his ancestry, full of darkness and despair.

*Look Homeward, Angel* was followed in 1935 by *Of Time and the River*, a continuation of the story of Eugene Gant.

*The Web and the Rock*, an effort to break out of the autobiographical mode, appeared in 1939, a year after Wolfe's death, and out of a vast accumulation of manuscript two more posthumous books were winnowed: *You Can't Go Home Again* and *The Hills Beyond*.

As Whitman had carried the self—the inviolate individual measuring the world—perhaps as far as it could be carried in poetry, Wolfe exhausted the possibilities of the autobiographical novel of the self, which is not to say, perhaps unfortunately, that he dissuaded other young men and from following in his footsteps. But Paula Snelling was right in her criticism of the posthumously published *The Web and the Rock*. Wolfe was struck in a particular time warp—that of the young man searching for the meaning of his life in the meaning of America—and he could do nothing but repeat that theme. He could not grow up or go beyond it, so he died at the age of thirty-eight after a decade of such furious writing that it was perhaps accurate to say that he had written himself to death. And while on the surface it seemed that he had escaped the Southern syndrome—the painful journey to the past, the elegiac reflecting on lost glories, the gloom over modern corruptions—that escape is more illusion than fact. There is, in all his novels, a sense of loss, loss of community, of friendship, of family, of the endlessly turning earth; the whistle of the childhood-remembered train in the vanishing distance, a note of sadness and regret for what is gone; the inability to return. *You Can't Go Home Again* ends on what is perhaps the most poignant falling note in modern literature.

In addition to the novels by well-known authors that we have noted, two other novels deserve mention. Henry Roth, born in 1906, wrote *Call It Sleep* when he was in his mid-twenties. It is a gripping (and harrowing) story of Roth's own childhood on the New York Lower East Side. It belongs to three characteristic genres of the American novel: the autobiographical novel; the proletarian novel dealing with the underside of American life; and what we might call the one-shot novel, the novel which records a man (or woman's) anguish and joy in growing up in America in a single work that exhausts all the writer has to say. Having written *Call It Sleep*, Roth retired to a poultry farm in a remote area of rural Maine and never wrote another novel.

Zora Neale Hurston was part of the Harlem Renaissance. She was born in 1901 in Eatonville, Florida, a small all-black town that became the setting for three of her four novels. A graduate of Barnard College and an anthropology student under Franz Boas at Columbia, she was a protégée of Charlotte Mason, who dominated a decade or more of her life and supplied her with funds for her anthropological researches in the South. The requirement, as with all of Mrs. Mason's protégées, was that she write her a letter daily. After a disastrous collaboration with Langston Hughes on a play that was never produced, Zola Hurston went very much her own way. Her most successful novel, *Their Eyes Were Watching God*, was not published until 1937, when she was in her late thirties. It is a substantial achievement, one of the best novels written by a black author of either sex in this century. It is also a strongly "feminist" novel that is interesting to compare, in its attitude toward black men, with the novels of such women as Edith Wharton, Ellen Glasgow, and Gertrude Atherton.

"Ships at a distance have every man's wish on board," the novel begins. "For some they come in with the tide. For others they sail forever on the horizon, never out of sight, never landing until the Watcher turns his eyes away in resignation, his dreams mocked to death by Time. That is the life of men.

"Now, women forget all those things they don't want to remember, and remember everything they don't want to forget. The dream is the truth. Then they act and do things accordingly."

The novel is the story of Janie Mae Crawford, a black woman; of her conventional marriage to Logan Killicks, who expects her to be a submissive and dutiful wife, and of her escape, marriage, widowhood, and passionate romance with the carefree Tea Cup. Janie learns the ways of men and the world from her grandmother. The white man "throw down de load and tell de nigger to pick it up. He pick it up because he have to, but he don't tote it. He hand it to his womenfolks. De nigger woman is de mule uh de world so fur as Ah can see." Janie, still a child, determines to have a different destiny. When Killicks tries to force her to do all the laborious domestic work, she tells him defiantly, "Ah'm just as stiff as you is stout. If you can stand not to chop and tote wood Ah reckon you can stand not to git no dinner."

Janie runs off with Joe Starks, like Hurston's father the strong-willed founder of a black town. While she is treated like a lady, the "spirit of the marriage left the bedroom and took to living in the parlor"; she becomes restless and unhappy. After Joe's death from cancer Janie finds herself free and realizes that she had been "saving up her feelings for some man she had never seen." That man turns out to be Tea Cup, a young black man with the reputation of a hell

raiser. After an idyllic interlude the novel ends in melodramatic tragedy. But in its deeply felt and vividly realized portrayal of black life it
has a secure place as a minor masterpiece, and Hurston as the precursor
of a remarkable group of present-day black women writers.

An interesting literary phenomenon of the thirties was the Hollywood Relief Association for Starving Writers, or more simply and
accurately, serious writers employed by major studios, which held its
meetings, according to Budd Schulberg, at the Stanley Rose Book
Store. It was there that Nathanael West, a kind of Jewish Faulkner,
gestated his remarkable "Hollywood" novel *The Day of the Locust.* Other
regulars, when they were in Los Angeles (L.A.) refurbishing their
coffers, were John O'Hara, Scott Fitzgerald, Erskine Caldwell, Dashiell
Hammett, Tess Slesinger, Dorothy Parker, and William Saroyan. It
was as lively a literary circle as the Republic could boast, dominated
by a severely Marxist view of the world, from which Saroyan and West
were the principal dissenters; West was tolerated for his clearly superior
wit and intelligence, Saroyan for his boyish, if tiring, ebullience. Among
other things, the Stanley Rose Book Store symbolized the uneasy bi-
coastal alliance between the country's most gifted writers and the film
industry, a classic love-hate relationship.

Like all other branches of literature, the theater burgeoned during
this period. The movement had begun in Greenwich Village and Provincetown in the years prior to the outbreak of the war. In fewer than
ten years the Provincetown Players produced ninety-three plays, written by forty-seven playwrights.

Of all that considerable company, one playwright emerged as
indisputably the most talented. The twenties found Eugene O'Neill at
the height of his powers as a dramatist. Like Faulkner, O'Neill explored
the darker recesses of the psyche. He, too, was strongly attracted to
such themes as adultery, incest, murder, and the degeneration of old
families.

O'Neill was born in New York City in 1888, the son of one of the
best-known actors of the day, James O'Neill, and Ella O'Neill, who
became a drug addict while O'Neill was still a young man. An Irish
Catholic, O'Neill attended Princeton for a year and then moved on to
Harvard to participate in George Pierce Baker's famous drama workshop. With a hunger for experience comparable to that of Thomas
Wolfe, O'Neill was a heavy drinker; he was nicknamed Ego by his

Princeton classmates because of his preoccupation with his own states of mind. O'Neill married the beautiful Kathleen Jenkins when he was twenty-one in defiance of both his and her parents. A few months later he set out on a gold-mining expedition to Honduras with the ostensible goal of making his fortune. A son was born in his absence. His wife obtained a divorce, and O'Neill never saw his son until the boy was eleven years old.

O'Neill's next adventure was as a sailor on a Norwegian vessel, one of the last sailing ships in international commerce, bound for Buenos Aires. There he worked briefly for the Singer Sewing Machine Company, acquiring, in the process, a lifelong distaste for machines. Back in New York he frequented working-class bars, feasted on Jack London, Joseph Conrad, and Rudyard Kipling, and frequently recited Kipling's poems and, notably, Francis Thompson's "The Hound of Heaven," which, the reader may recall, helped convert Dorothy Day to a Catholicism which O'Neill had abandoned.

After a brief but ardent romance with Louise Bryant (who insisted that her love for Jack Reed did not preclude love for O'Neill), O'Neill fell deeply in love with Agnes Boulton, a young widow with a year-and-a-half-old daughter, and entered into one of the most productive periods in the life of any dramatist. In a period of fifteen years—between 1919 and 1934—O'Neill wrote twenty-five plays, almost two a year.

*The Emperor Jones*, produced in the fall of 1920, was based on a story that O'Neill had heard in a bar about a Haitian, named Vilbren Guillaume Sam, who, convinced that he could be killed only by a silver bullet, had seized and held power in Haiti for almost six months. *The Emperor Jones* was the story of Brutus Jones, head of an island kingdom, pursued by fear of a death foretold on jungle drums. The critic Alexander Woollcott praised it as a "striking and dramatic study of panic fear." It was O'Neill's first major box-office success.

It was followed a year later (two other plays were produced in the interim) by his second major success, *Anna Christie*. Drawn from O'Neill's maritime adventures, it was the story of a young Swedish immigrant girl, seduced by her cousin on a Minnesota farm. Finding a job as a nurse in the city, she is once more sexually exploited and becomes a prostitute. In the final act she is reconciled with her father, who has abandoned her, and becomes a respectable married woman. Greta Garbo made the role famous in the movie version.

*The Hairy Ape*, produced some four months after *Anna Christie*, was another hit. In 1924 five O'Neill plays opened. *All God's Chillun Got Wings*, starring Paul Robeson, and *Desire Under the Elms* were the most important.

*All God's Chillun* is a play about a white girl, Ella Downey, and a black boy, Jim Harris, who live in adjacent Irish and black ghettos. As children they play unselfconsciously together in the streets, but in high school the color barrier abruptly separates them. When Jim makes a special effort to graduate from high school, he risks his friendship with his pal Joe, who accuses him of "denyin' you's a nigger." Jim appeases Joe by agreeing, "We're both niggers." When Ella breaks free of her relationship with Mickey, an Irish tough, a prizefighter and mobster, she and Jim renew their childhood friendship. Jim is laboring against heavy odds to graduate from college. They fall in love, and realizing the impossibility of their situation, Jim cries, "We'll go abroad where a man is a man—where it don't make that difference—where people are kind and wise to see the soul under skins." His only desire is to shield and care for her, "to become your slave!—your black slave that adores you as sacred!" They marry and leave for Europe. When they return two years later, Jim Harris's mother, who opposed the marriage, faces their return with apprehension. Jim's militant sister, Hattie, believes they were "cowards to run away. . . . We don't deserve happiness till we've fought the fight of our race and won it." Jim agrees with Hattie that he must go to law school and become a lawyer, but Ella has misgivings about his ability to do so, misgivings that are based on her feelings that he is racially inferior. Clearly she can't face the possibility of Jim's failing and of his family and friends seeing the failure as somehow being a racial failure. Under constant social pressure Ella starts to lose her sanity; she is obsessed by the conviction that she is turning black. In desperation Jim turns to Hattie for strength and comfort while Ella does all she can to prevent him from passing the bar examinations. The play ends with both Jim and Ella locked in a desperate and hopeless embrace. Published in the first issue of the *American Mercury* in February, 1924, and produced a few months later, the play shocked (and doubtlessly titillated) audiences with its bold treatment of an interracial romance and tragic ending.

The central themes of *Desire Under the Elms* are greed and lust. The year is 1850, and the main characters are the Cabots, an old New England family gone to seed—Ephraim Cabot and his sons, Simeon, Peter, and Eben. Elm trees "brood oppressively over the house." The trees "have developed from their intimate contact with the life of man in the house an appalling humanness. . . . They are like exhausted women resting their sagging breasts and hands and hair on its roof. . . ."

The play opens with the brothers discussing their desire to go to California and start new lives there, but the old house, the farm, and his tyrannical old father hold Eben.

Ephraim meanwhile succumbs to the local temptress and marries. Abbie sets out to seduce Eben, in order to have a child by him, convince Ephraim that the child is his, and thereby to inherit Ephraim's wealth. But Abbie falls passionately in love with Eben, and when their child is born, she kills it, hoping thereby to prove her devotion to him. The horrified Eben informs the police and decides he must share the guilt and punishment.

Brooks Atkinson called the play "an ode to greed and lust and murder without remorse" and speculated that it "may turn out to be the greatest play written by an American."

O'Neill's next important play was *Strange Interlude*, a long, thoroughly modern drama of a charming woman's tireless acquisition of men. Nina Leeds, the daughter of Professor Henry Leeds, is an emancipated modern woman. The most striking novelty in the play was the technique of asides. The characters spoke to each other, often in stilted tones, and then spoke their real thoughts and feelings. The play opens with Charles Marsden, a student of the professor's and a sometime suitor of Nina, reflecting on his frustrated longings for Nina: "[T]o the devil with sex! our impotent pose of today to beat the loud drum on fornication! . . . boasters . . . eunuchs parading with the phallus! . . . giving themselves away . . . whom do they fool . . . ?"

Later, as Nina listens to her father, whom she dominates, she reflects: "The Professor of Dead Languages is talking again . . . a dead man lectures on the past of the living . . . since I was born I have been in his class, loving-attentive, pupil-daughter Nina . . . my ears numb with spiritless messages from the dead. . . ." Nina, yearning for some passionate involvement, has affairs with numerous young men, but she acquires as a husband the rather passive and dutiful Sam Evans, hoping to have a child by him. Pregnant, she learns that there is insanity in his family when Evans's mother urges her to have an abortion. After her abortion, still determined to have a baby, she persuades Dr. Edmund Darrell, her husband's close friend, to father a child. Her husband is surprised and delighted to learn that she is pregnant and only too ready to think the child is his. Nina now has three men in her web. She thinks: "My three men! . . . I feel their desires converge in me! . . . to form one complete beautiful male desire which I absorb . . . and am whole . . . they dissolve in me, their life is my life . . . I am pregnant with the three. . . . Husband! . . . lover! . . . father!" And the son she has wrested from Darrell. When the son, Gordon, named after Nina's fiancé killed in the war, grows up, he is deeply attached to Evans and resentful of his mother's obvious devotion to Darrell. The remaining acts deal with Nina's management of her men. As she grows older, she comes to feel that her "account with God the Father is settled . . . afternoons of happiness paid for with years of pain . . . love, passion, ecstasy . . . in what far-off life were they alive! . . . [T]he only living life is in the past and future . . . the present is an interlude . . . strange interlude in which we call on past and future to bear witness we are living. . . ."

*Strange Interlude* is a kind of Proustian reflection on the brevity, or indeed the illusion, of happiness. Love is intimately connected to sexual passion, and sexual passion is transient. The pain of the present can be diminished by the better memories of the past and hopes for the future.

*Mourning Becomes Electra* was even longer and more ambitious than *Strange Interlude*. It was presented as a trilogy—"Homecoming," "The Hunted," and "The Haunted"—successive performances lasting almost nine hours. As in *Desire Under the Elms*, the time was the mid nineteenth century, and the place New England. Once more a house, the Greek Revival Mannon mansion—"pagan temple front stuck like a mask on Puritan gray ugliness!"—is a character in the play. The principal characters are Ezra Mannon, a judge turned general in the Civil War, a cold, hard, proud man; his beautiful and dissatisfied wife, Christine; their daughter, Lavinia; and Captain Adam Brant, Christine's lover (and, as it turns out, nephew).

Christine prevails on Brant to conspire with her to kill her husband, Ezra, when he returns from the army. She gives him poison. Lavinia finds out. When Christine's son, Orin, arrives home soon after his father's death, Lavinia tells him the grim truth. They follow their mother to a tryst with Brant and, after Christine has left, Orin kills Brant, exclaiming that he is convinced he, Orin, has really killed his father. He then tells his mother and assures her that he will take both Brant's and his father's place. His mother kills herself, and Lavinia and Orin go away together, hoping to forget the tragedies.

They go to the South Sea islands where Orin had dreamed of sailing to with his mother, and there Lavinia is transformed from a grim Puritan maiden to a voluptuous young woman. "I loved those islands," she tells a suitor. "They finished setting me free. There was something there mysterious and beautiful—a good spirit of love—coming out of the land and the sea. It made me forget death. There was no hereafter. There was only this world . . . the fires at night and the drum throbbing in my heart."

Orin develops incestuous desires for Lavinia, and when she rebuffs him, he shoots himself. Lavinia boards up the Mannon mansion and retires to it to live the rest of her life as a kind of bitter penance. In synopsis, the play sounds rather like an Italian opera, but O'Neill invests his drama with a tragic power that lifts it above the merely melodramatic.

If the American stage belonged to Eugene O'Neill in the twenties, the stage of the thirties was claimed by a much less gifted playwright, but one much more in harmony with the radical temper of the decade. Clifford Odets was the son of a Jewish immigrant from Latvia who had become a successful printer. He left high school at the age of fifteen after a quarrel with his parents to pursue the uncertain career of an actor. After an apprenticeship with the Theatre Guild, he joined the Group Theatre when it was formed by Howard Clurman. Howard Clurman wrote of Clifford Odets that "he wanted to belong to the largest possible group of humble, struggling men prepared to make a great common effort to build a better world. . . . He was driven by a powerful emotional impetus, like a lover on the threshold of an elopement."

In addition to writing and acting, Clifford Odets taught other actors the Stanislavsky method, an approach to acting developed by the Russian actor and director, which emphasized naturalness and spontaneity, getting under the skin of the character being portrayed.

In February, 1934, the taxi drivers of New York City went out on strike. The strike began when Sam Orner, a popular young driver, was summarily dismissed because he had not made enough money on his shift for the cab company. Fired, he turned to several other drivers and said, "Well, boys, how long are we going to take this?" He touched a responsive chord. Within twenty-four hours most cabdrivers were on strike, and Orner was president of the Taxi Drivers' Union of Greater New York. Union halls were set up in all five boroughs, and one of the city's most violent strikes was in progress. In a strike that lasted forty days 40,000 men and 19,000 taxicabs were involved. Cabs were burned. Scabs were beaten, drivers and strikebreakers were killed, and when Orner addressed a mass meeting in St. Nicholas Arena at Sixtieth Street and Central Park West, the police mounted machine guns on a roof across the street. Odets was taken to a strike meeting in the Village organized by Orner. The most dramatic meeting, the one on which Odets based his play *Waiting for Lefty,* came in a strike meeting at the Hunts Point Palace when efforts were being made to break the strike. Orner was delayed by someone who, he was convinced, had put knockout drops in his beer. Meanwhile, the meeting started, and certain cabbies, encouraged by management agents, urged an end to the strike. Others shouted, "No vote till we hear from Orner." Orner was found unconscious, revived, and brought to the meeting hall, where he managed to scotch the effort to end the strike before the major demands of the cabbies had been met.

When Clifford Odets wrote the play based on the strike, he used the incident with the difference that Orner, now "Lefty," was found dead, presumably murdered by company thugs.

When Odets took *Waiting for Lefty* to the Group Theatre, Lee Strasberg opposed its production. The play was too simple and blatant, Strasberg declared. It was propaganda, not art. Odets rounded up half a dozen Group actors, rented a hall, and prepared to produce the play himself as a benefit performance for the *New Theatre* magazine. On Sunday, January 6, 1935, *Waiting for Lefty* was put on after a dance group had performed.

Harold Clurman wrote of that evening: "The first scene of *Lefty* had not played two minutes when a shock of delighted recognition struck the audience like a tidal wave. . . . The actors no longer performed; they were being carried along as if by an exultancy of communication such as I had never witnessed in the theatre before. Audience and actors became one." What followed was closer to a religious revival than an evening of theater. Odets, so transported that he lost the sense that he was author of the play, jumped to his feet with others in the audience to applaud. *"The proscenium arch disappeared,"* he wrote.

Harry Fatt, the despotic boss, represents capitalism. "The audience should be kept constantly aware of him," Odets wrote, "the ugly menace which hangs over the lives of the people who act out their own dramas. . . . He might walk insolently in and around the unseeing players." Agate, Lefty's lieutenant, so called because he has a glass eye, on hearing the news that Lefty has been found murdered by company hit men, cries: "Hear it, boys, hear it? Hell, listen to me! Coast to coast! HELLO AMERICA! HELLO. WE'RE STORMBIRDS OF THE WORKING-CLASS.

WORKERS OF THE WORLD . . . OUR BONES AND BLOOD! And when we die they'll know what we did to make a new world! Christ, cut us up in little pieces. We'll die for what is right! put fruit trees where our ashes are! (*To the audience*): Well, what's the answer?"

"All: STRIKE!

"Agate: LOUDER!

"All: STRIKE!

"Agate and Others on Stage: AGAIN!

"All: STRIKE, STRIKE, STRIKE!!!"

When the audience joined tumultuously in the cry of "Strike," Harold Clurman wrote: "It was the birth cry of the thirties. Our youth had found its voice. It was a call to join the good fight for a greater measure of life in a world free of economic fear. . . . The audience was delirious. It stormed the stage. . . . People went from the theatre dazed and happy; a new awareness and confidence had entered their lives." Many members of the audience later recalled staying up all night in their excitement, "walking in the street instead of on the sidewalk, kissing and hugging one another, talking and laughing, some even weeping—all too excited to go to sleep," as Odets biographer Margaret Brenman-Gibson put it. According to Brenman-Gibson, *Waiting for Lefty* was performed more frequently all over the world and banned more frequently than "any other play in all of theatre history."

Odet's next successful play, *Awake and Sing*, was a far richer work than *Waiting for Lefty*. An affectionate portrait of a middle-class Jewish family, it made brilliant use of the characters' idiomatic speech and Jewish intonations. For many Jews it was a revelation of the potency of their own tradition, so closely associated with the Yiddish art theater. For Gentiles it was a fascinating glimpse into an almost totally unfamiliar world. Like *Waiting for Lefty*, it introduced a new theme but, more important, a new mode or genre into the theatrical and literary world. It was thus both a measure of assimilation (since tens of thousands of Gentiles attended the various productions) and a foretaste of a Jewish literature which would almost preempt the American literary scene following the Second World War.

And then there were the poets. T. S. Eliot continued to be the most influential single figure, although as American writers and intellectuals turned sharply to the left, Eliot and, even more notably, Ezra Pound drifted to the right; Pound became, along with Wallace Stevens, a warm admirer of Mussolini. Eliot wrote "The Hollow Men" in 1925 in much the same mood of stylized despair he had popularized in "The Waste Land."

> We are the hollow men
> We are the stuffed men
> Leaning together
> Headpiece filled with straw. Alas!
> Our dried voices, when
> We whisper together
> Are quiet and meaningless
> As wind in dry grass
> Or rats' feet over broken glass
> In our dry cellar
>
> Shape without form, shade without colour.
> Paralysed force, gesture without motion;
>
> Those who have crossed
> With direct eyes, to death's other Kingdom
> Remember us—if at all—not as lost
> Violent souls, but only
> As the hollow men
> The stuffed men.

The poem ended:

> *This is the way the world ends*
> *This is the way the world ends*
> *This is the way the world ends*
> *Not with a bang but a*
> *whimper.*

"Lines for an Old Man," published in 1935, maintained the same tone:

> The tiger in the tiger-pit
> Is not more irritable than I.
> The whipping tail is not more still
> Than when I smell the enemy
> Writhing in the essential blood
> Or dangling from the friendly tree.
> When I lay bare the tooth of wit
> The hissing over the archèd tongue
> Is more affectionate than hate,
> More bitter than the love of youth,

> And inaccessible by the young.
> Reflected from my golden eye
> The dullard knows that he is mad.
> Tell me if I am not glad!

Eliot also wrote essays specifying his disenchantment with the spirit of the times. "The Catholic," he wrote, in a succinct enunciation of his credo after his conversion to Anglo-Catholicism, "should have high ideals—or rather, I should say *absolute* ideals—and moderate expectations: the heretic, whether he call himself fascist, communist, or democrat or rationalist, always has low ideals and great expectations. For I say that all ambitions of an earthly paradise are informed by low ideals." Eliot was convinced that "any general scheme of international harmony put forward as a substitute for religious unity is likely to be more of a menace than a hope . . . and like every structure built only on human reason, will eventully fall beneath the impact of human passions, leaving only a bitter and unnecessary disillusionment. It is only the Catholic who cannot be disillusioned." Like Reinhold Niebuhr, whom in his thinking he closely resembled, Eliot warned of committing oneself "to any one form of temporal order."

He also wrote two verse dramas, as we have noted earlier. Besides *Murder in the Cathedral*, produced by the Federal Theatre, Eliot completed *The Family Reunion* in 1939. At its end Agatha Monchensey, preparing to become a missionary, says:

> This way the pilgrimage
> of expiation
> Round and round the circle
> Completing the charm
> So the knot be unknotted
> The cross be uncrossed
> The crooked made straight
> And the curse ended
> By intercession
> By pilgrimage. . . .

Ezra Pound began his long, ambitious cycle of the *Cantos*, of which Hemingway wrote that the "*Cantos* . . . will last as long as there is any literature." Like Pound's earlier work, it abounded in classical allusions. Almost willfully obscure, the *Cantos* were sprinkled with Greek, Latin, and Italian phrases. From the seventh *Canto*:

> Square even shoulders and the satin skin,
> Gone cheeks of the old dancing woman,
>     Still the old dead dry talk, gassed out—
> It is ten years gone, makes stiff about her a glass,
> A petrifaction of air.
>     The old room of the tawdry class asserts itself;
> The young men, never!
>     Only the husk of talk.
> O voi che siete in piccioletta barca,
> Dido choked up with sobs, for her Sicheus
> Lies heavy in my arms, dead weight
>     Drowning, with tears, new Eros.

Difficult, but unmistakably poetry.

Robert Frost continued to write his austere celebrations of rural New England. His principal concessions to the troubled times were "A Lone Striker" and "Build Soil—A Political Pastoral" ("As delivered at Columbia, May 31, 1932, before the National party conventions of that year"). "A Lone Striker" contained a characteristic amendment—"Without Prejudice to Industry":

> The swinging mill bell changed its rate
> To tolling like the count of fate,
> And though at that the tardy ran,
> One failed to make the closing gate.
> There was a law of God or man
> That on the one who came too late
> The gate for half an hour be locked,
> His time be lost, his pittance docked.
> He stood rebuked and unemployed.

The locked-out worker knows a better place, "a wood. . . . He knew a path that wanted walking;/He knew a spring that wanted drinking;/A thought that wanted further thinking. . . ." If the day came

> When industry seemed to die
> Because he left it in the lurch,
> Or even merely seemed to pine
> For want of his approval, why
> Come get him—they knew where to search.

"Build Soil" is Frost's reply to those who chided him for not writing "socially responsible" poetry:

> To advertise our farms to city buyers,
> Or else write something to improve food prices,
> Get in a poem toward the next election. . . .
>
> "The times seem revolutionary bad."
> "The question is," the poet replies,
>             Whether they've reached a depth
> Of desperation that would warrant poetry's
> Leaving love's alternations, joy and grief,
> The weather's alternations, summer and winter,
> Our age-long themes, for the uncertainty
> Of judging who is a contemporary liar. . . .
> I prefer to sing safely in the realm
> Of types, composite and imagined people:
> To affirm there is such a thing as evil
> Personified, but to ask to be excused
> From saying on a jury, "Here's the guilty."

Frost concluded: "You see the beauty of my proposal is/It needn't wait on general revolution./I bid you to a one-man revolution—/The only revolution that is coming."

Frost attested elsewhere he had "never been radical when young for fear of being conservative when old." As he grew older, he grew "more sure of everything I knew was true." Gradually he acquired the reputation of being "America's poet" (Eliot and Pound lived abroad and eschewed popularity in any event). He became a kind of latter-day Longfellow, enjoyed by thousands of readers and listeners who found modern poetry much too arcane. He thus provided a link with the older tradition—Whittier, Bryant, Lowell, Emerson—of poetry as a form of public speech.

The most brilliant of the rising generation of poets, in the opinion of many critics, was star-crossed Hart Crane. Crane was born in 1899 in Garrettsville, Ohio. He grew up in Cleveland and moved to New York when he was seventeen years old, under the guardianship of a family friend. After a vain attempt to enlist in the army, Crane returned to Cleveland to work in his father's candy factory. Back in New York, working for an advertising agency, Crane found a sponsor in Waldo Frank and through Frank's support received a grant of $1,000 from Otto Kahn to enable him to work full-time on his ambitious plan for a poem that took the Brooklyn Bridge as a symbol of the nation. Crane, who was an alcoholic and a homosexual, was also a young man of great charm and obvious talent. He became a kind of literary-community project. In addition to Waldo Frank's efforts in his behalf, Malcolm and Peggy Cowley befriended him, as did Allen Tate and his novelist wife, Caroline Gordon, and Katherine Anne Porter. Deciding that Oaxaca, Mexico, would provide an ideal environment for Crane to write, Peggy Cowley spirited Crane off. It was not a successful experiment, and on the ship returning to the United States, Crane ended his life by jumping overboard.

Although Crane is chiefly associated with *The Bridge*, he wrote a number of enduring poems. The volume *White Buildings*, dedicated to Waldo Frank, contains some of Crane's finest poems. It begins with the unforgettable lines of "Legend":

> As silent as a mirror is believed
> Realities plunge in silence by . . .
> I am not ready for repentance;
> Nor to match regrets. For the moth
> Bends no more than the still
> Imploring flame. And tremorous
> In the white falling flakes
> Kisses are,—
> The only worth all granting.

*The Bridge* is divided into two sections. The first—"Ave Maria"—seeks out the meaning of the nation's past. The second—"Cape Hatteras" to "Atlantis"—seeks to adumbrate the country's future. The bridge is the symbol of the connecting tissue between the material and spiritual aspects of the nation. Crane wrote to Frank that the "bridge in becoming a ship, a world, a woman, a tremendous harp (as it does finally) seems to really have a career. I have attempted to induce the same feelings of elation, etc.—like being carried forward and upward simultaneously—both in imagery, rhythm and repetition that one experiences in walking across my beloved Brooklyn Bridge." A bridge, he wrote to Frank in another letter, "is an act of faith besides being a communication." It was a "symbol of consciousness spanning time and space."

For Crane the bridge symbolized, among other things, the incredible courage and perseverance of its designer, John Roebling, killed in an accident, and his son, Washington Roebling, who, with his sight and hearing impaired, supervised, over some thirteen years, the building of the bridge: In the course of construction more than twenty workers died. It was that remarkable melding of technical brilliance and moral courage that expressed the noblest achievements of Americans as builders. The introductory verse begins:

> And Thee, across the harbor, silver-paced
> As though the sun took step of thee, yet left
> Some motion ever unspent in thy stride—
> Implicitly thy freedom staying thee!

And ends:

> O sleepless as the river under thee,
> Vaulting the sea, the prairies' dreaming sod,
> Unto us the lowliest sometime sweep, descend
> And of the curveship lend a myth to God.

Following is a soliloquy, "Ave Maria," by Christopher Columbus on the theme of questing and discovery, discovery of self as well as un-revealed worlds. The arrival of Columbus shatters the primal inno-cence of America but begins also a process of redemption of the Old World by the New.

"Harbor Dawn" introduces Pocohontas, and Crane moves be-tween that Indian princess and modern America, using Pocohontas as an image of America.

The next section takes Rip Van Winkle as a figure linking past and present:

> Macadam, gun-grey as the tunny's belt,
> Leaps from Far Rockaway to Golden Gate:
> Listen! the miles a hurdy-gurdy grinds—
> Down gold arpeggios mile on mile unwinds.

The Mississippi River, the *Twentieth Century Limited*, tramps de-bating the nature of the land. An Indian sachem, Maquokeeta, in the section entitled "The Dance," is evoked to "dance us back the tribal orn." The serpent and the eagle symbolize the primitive world:

> We danced, O Brave, we danced beyond their farms,
> In cobalt desert closures made our vows . . .
> Now is the strong prayer folded in thine arms,
> The serpent with the eagle in the boughs.

Finally, in "Indiana," a pioneer couple settle in that state after a fruitless search for California gold. Their son, Larry, decides to go to sea, and his mother laments:

Come back to Indiana—not too late!
   (Or will you be a ranger to the end?—
Good-bye . . . Good-by . . . oh, I shall always wait
   You, Larry, traveller—
       stranger,
         son
           —my friend—

"Cape Hatteras," "Three Songs," "Quaker Hill," "The Tunnel," and "Atlantis" made up the second half of *The Bridge*. Much of the latter portion of the poem is a reflection on the effect of the machine on modern man and praise of Whitman as the appropriate spirit to preserve us from its darker consequences.

                            Yes, Walt,
Afoot again, and onward without halt,—
Not soon, nor suddenly,—No, never to let go
   My hand
     In yours,
       Walt Whitman—
         so—

It is in "Atlantis" that Crane returns to the bridge most directly, this time the bridge as an enormous harp plucked by the winds.

   So to thine Everpresence, beyond time,
   Like spears ensanguined of one tolling star
   That bleeds infinity—the orphic strong,
   Sidereal phalanxes, leap and converge:
   One Song, one Bridge of Fire! . . .

In trying to make the Brooklyn Bridge, marvel that it is, bear the weight of all American dreams and hopes as well as those of the poet (so far as they differed), Crane may, as his critics have suggested, have strained himself beyond his resources. But it was certainly a gallant and unique effort.

A poet who, like Frost and Faulkner, went his own defiant, lonely way, was the Californian Robinson Jeffers. Jeffers and his wife, Una, made their home on the wild coast of Big Sur below Monterey Bay. Jeffers built himself a kind of Viking tower of river rocks and, as in the title of one of his long narrative poems, "gave his heart to the hawks" that swirled above the rugged coastline. Looking rather like a hawk himself, with hooded eyes and an aquiline nose, Jeffers summoned up the ancient gods, the gods of the Greeks and Norsemen, and wrote of the dark side of life, clearly preferring hawks to humans, or at least the common run. Incest, murder, repentance, and revenge, somewhat in the spirit of Eugene O'Neill, were the recurrent themes of his longer poems; the transitoriness of life and the enduringness of nature were the subjects of his shorter verse. George Santayana had urged Californians to invent a philosophy worthy of the state's scenic grandeur; "these primeval solitudes" must lift from their shoulders the remnants of the "Genteel Tradition." As the poet William Everson pointed out in his *Archetype West*, Robinson Jeffers responded to the challenge. "The son of a Presbyterian theologian," Everson wrote, "[Jeffers] had gained in his nature the long Calvinist distrust of human aspiration." With this he combined a "pantheistic insight of a divine cosmos. . . ." The result was "a religious passion," an obsessive concern with the drama of man's encounter both with external nature and with his own inner nature.

In his introduction to his *Selected Poems*, Jeffers recalled the impact of Nietzsche's phrase "The poets? The poets lie too much." It became Jeffers's passion "not to feign any emotion that I did not feel; not to pretend to believe in optimism or pessimism, or unreversible progress; not to say anything because it was popular, or generally accepted, or fashionable in intellectual circles, unless I myself believed it; and not to believe it too easily." The Monterey mountains attracted him because there he saw life "purged of its ephemeral accretions. Men were riding after cattle, or plowing the headland, hovered over by white seagulls, as they have done for thousands of years. . . ."

The poem "Rock and Hawk" may be the most explicit expression of Jeffers's vision:

> Here is a symbol in which
> Many high tragic thoughts
> Watch their own eyes.
>
> This gray rock, standing tall
> On the headland, where the seawind
> Lets no tree grow,
>
> Earthquake-proved, and signatured
> By ages of storms: on its peak
> A falcon has perched.

I think, here is your emblem
To hang in the future sky;
Not the cross, not the hive,

But this; bright power, dark peace:
Fierce consciousness joined with final
Disinterestedness;

Life with calm death; the falcon's
Realist eyes and act
Married to the massive
Mysticism of stone,
Which failure cannot cast down
Nor success make proud.

In the twenties Jeffers wrote the bitter poem "Shine, Perishing Republic":

While this America settles in the mold of its vulgarity,
    heavily thickening to empire,
And protest, only a bubble in the molten mass, pops and
    sighs out, and the mass hardens,
I sadly smiling remember that the flower fades to
    make fruit, the fruit rots to make earth.
  * * * * * * * * * * * * * * * * * * * * * * * * * * * * *
You making haste haste on decay: not blameworthy; life
    is good, be it stubbornly long or suddenly
A mortal splendor: meteors are not needed less than mountains:
    shine, perishing republic.

His children, Jeffers hopes, will "keep their distance from the thickening center; corruption."

A decade or more later, when the world seemed ready to succumb to tyranny and violence on a vast new scale, Jeffers wrote: "Shine Republic."

The quality of these trees, green height; of the sky,
    shining, of water, a clear flow, of the rock, hardness
And reticence: each is noble in its quality. The love of
    freedom has been the quality of Western man.

There is a stubborn torch that flames from Marathon to
    Concord, its dangerous beauty binding three ages
Into one time; the waves of barbarism and civilization
    have eclipsed but have never quenched it.

For the Greeks the love of beauty, for Rome of ruling;
  for the present age the passionate love of discovery;
But in one noble passion we are one; and Washington, Luther,
  Tacitus, Aeschylus, one kind of man.

And you, America, that passion made you. You were not
  born to prosperity, you were born to love freedom.
You did not say "en masse," you said "independence." But
  we cannot have all the luxuries and freedom also.

Freedom is poor and laborious; that torch is not safe
  but hungry, and often requires blood for its fuel . . .
But keep the tradition, conserve the forms, the observances,
  keep the spot sore. Be great, carve deep your heel-marks.

The states of the next age will no doubt remember you, and
  edge their love of freedom with contempt of luxury.

Edith Wharton died in 1937; Thomas Wolfe a year later at the age of thirty-eight. Scott Fitzgerald and Nathanael West died in 1940 (West in an automobile accident); Sherwood Anderson died in 1941; Dreiser and Ellen Glasgow in 1945; Willa Cather two years later; Edna St. Vincent Millay in 1950; Sinclair Lewis in 1951; Eugene O'Neill in 1953. Only Faulkner and Hemingway remained. Hemingway committed suicide in 1961, and Faulkner died a year later at the relatively ripe old age (for an author) of sixty-five.

Within sixteen years—1937–1953—most of the writers who had shone so brightly in the American literary firmament through the first half of the twentieth century were gone. Their deaths marked the end of a remarkable era in American letters.

# 43

## The Clouds of War

The year 1938 was significant for four major reasons: the passage of the last major piece of New Deal social legislation; the acceptance by the administration of Federal spending as an antidote for recession; Roosevelt's effort to "purge" Congress of conservative Senators and Congressmen who had opposed his programs; and, finally and most important, a shift in the President's attention from domestic issues to crises around the globe that, in his view, threatened world peace.

Annoyed by the growing opposition in Congress to his proposed measures and egged on by his gadfly, Thomas Corcoran, Roosevelt decided to wage a vigorous campaign in the midterm elections of 1938 to rid Congress of conservative Democrats. "It was up to him now," Corcoran said to Ickes, "to show whether he was going out like Herbert Hoover or like Andrew Jackson." Marked for what the press was soon referring to as the "purge" were such conservatives as Senator Cotton Ed Smith of South Carolina; Senator Alva Adams of Colorado; Senator Pat McCarran, the czar of Nevada; Senator Millard Tydings of Maryland; and Congressman John O'Connor of New York, the powerful and reactionary chairman of the House Rules Committee.

"The Boss has stirred up a hornet's nest by getting into these primary fights," Vice-President Garner complained to James Farley.

"There are twenty men—Democrats—in the Senate who will vote against anything he wants because they are mad clean through, Jim. I think you ought to take exception to the President's attitude."

Farley replied, "John, I just can't do that unless I resign from the Cabinet and the Democratic Committee. I don't like this purge any better than you do, but the situation won't be helped by my breaking with the Boss."

Corcoran, Ickes, and Hopkins, nicknamed the Elimination Committee, were considered the principal architects of the purges. It was not done in a vengeful spirit so much as with the intention of ensuring for the future a Democratic Party liberal in spirit. Roosevelt was aware how inherently conservative most Democratic regulars were, especially those from the South. Most of them were devout Democrats, who would no more think of abandoning their party than a devout Catholic would think of abandoning the church. They thus were inclined to support their party and its leadership, however outraged their feelings. Party regularity was the foundation stone of politics. As we have seen, many of these Democrats grew increasingly restless and resentful. Some kicked over the traces completely and, without relinquishing any of their zeal for party, went openly into the opposition. In Texas Lyndon Johnson had demonstrated the popularity of the President by winning a seat in Congress primarily by supporting Roosevelt's court plan. The temptation to try to strengthen the New Deal orientation of the Democratic Party against the day when Roosevelt would no longer be President and the magic of his name and personality could no longer be counted on to bring the recalcitrant into line was irresistible.

Roosevelt, it may be recalled, told Harry Hopkins in 1934 that he had at best only eight years to achieve the basic goals of the New Deal. The critical question was how to ensure the permanence of the New Deal reforms. There had been other, earlier reforms—those of his cousin and of Woodrow Wilson, most notably—that had been wiped out by tides of reaction. Roosevelt saw his task as not simply forcing liberal or radical legislation through Congress but of changing the fundamental character of the Democratic Party; that was the only way to preserve the hard-won victories, *his* hard-won victories. Roosevelt was well aware of the precarious nature of his "alliance," of the fact that he had *no reliable political constituency*. The Progressive Republicans were clearly a dying breed. The Republican old guard had recaptured the party and constituted his most determined opposition. The Democratic Party was still dominated by the South, which was profoundly, constitutionally conservative, if not reactionary. Roosevelt had made, to be sure, important converts among the older Southern politicians, men like Alben Barkley, and among the rising generation, men like young Lyndon Johnson, Claude Pepper of Florida, and Maury Maverick of Texas. But for every Maverick there were three or four Martin Dieses, determined enemies of the New Deal and all its works.

Although most Americans continued to think of themselves as conservative, Roosevelt had clearly created a liberal temper or mood in the country, and he was obsessed with the problem of how to translate that temper into long-range political goals. He foresaw a world conflict in which the United States, in his view, must inevitably be involved. Would there be, in the aftermath of that impending conflict, a reactionary swing such as that which had followed the end of the World War? Would all the achievements of the New Deal be swept away? In the period from the succession of Theodore Roosevelt to the presidency in 1902 to the entry of the United States into the European war, Progressive Republicans, with the erratic support of liberal Democrats (and vice versa), had made important, if transitory, reforms. But the collapse of that alliance had revealed how fragile it was at best. It seemed to Franklin Roosevelt that with the defeat of his cousin Theodore by the Taft forces in 1912, the Republican Party had become uncompromisingly the party of the business interests. The best that could be said of the Democratic Party was that despite its innate conservatism and its complete hopelessness on the racial issue, it was not essentially an instrument of the business interests. It was tied to the big-city bosses with their primarily immigrant constituencies and, in a sense, to the land (although the Midwest was, of course, filled with Republican farmers). Weak vessel though it might be, it was all that there was to work with. It must be made, one way or another, the party of liberalism, the party of the "common man," the "workers," the "people," as opposed to the "interests." The party of Thomas Jefferson and Andrew Jackson must become the keeper of the New Deal grail. The liberal temper of the country must have a genuinely liberal party to represent it; otherwise, as so often in the past, it would have *no place to go.*

Certainly there were disturbing signs of a reactionary trend. The House Un-American Activities Committee was set up in June, 1938. "Our world grew older after 1938," Len De Caux wrote. "The Dies committee blew the brassy trumpet of reaction. In CIO some softly echoed its call, to trade the Spirit of the CIO for the Spirit of Anti-communism."

While there was strong anti-Communist sentiment in many parts of the country and in certain segments of society (and more or less covert Nazi sympathies in some groups), Americans seemed to have no difficulty in distinguishing between Nazi Germany and Soviet Russia. Asked which side they would favor if the two nations went to war, 83 percent cast their votes for Russia, and when Americans were first asked by George Gallup what they thought the principal targets of the Dies committee—the House Committee on Un-American Activities—should be, 72 percent replied "War propaganda and Nazi activities in the U.S." Only 26 percent listed "Communist activities in the U.S."

It was, of course, natural that Harry Hopkins, with presidential ambitions himself, was anxious to rid the party of those who, it must have been assumed, would be his bitterest opponents. So there were, in effect, two incentives: (1) to complete the restructuring of the Democratic Party as the party of liberalism and reform and (2) to help smooth the way for Hopkins (or some other unequivocally New Deal Democrat) as Roosevelt's successor in 1940. The latter objective could not, of course, be stated, but it was plainly in Hopkins's mind and in the minds of his enemies. In Florida administration support for Senator Claude Pepper, in the face of a very active campaign against him in the state primary by a conservative Democrat, helped give Pepper the victory, but administration backing for a supporter of the administration is routine in American politics. The administration's efforts to evict uncongenial tenants of Congress was a very different matter; that smacked of Federal intrusion into local political matters.

Hugh Johnson, more and more critical of the New Deal, called the architects of the "purge" the "White House Janizaries," a reference to the murderous palace guard of the Ottoman Empire. In any event, the effort at purging Congress backfired. The midterm elections represented the most serious setback for the New Deal since its beginning. Of those marked for elimination, only O'Connor of New York was defeated. The Republicans won 81 new seats in the House. Thirteen governorships went to the Republicans. Philip La Follette, the son of Bob La Follette, was defeated in Wisconsin, and Frank Murphy lost his bid for another term in Michigan. Robert Taft, the son of William Howard Taft, was elected to the Senate from Ohio. While the Democrats held on to a majority in both chambers, the returns indicated a rough road ahead. By the fall of 1938 voter approval of the President had declined from 62 percent six months earlier to 55 percent. The narrowness of the liberal or New Deal consensus is suggested by a Gallup Poll taken in February, 1939. Democrats were asked the question if Roosevelt were not a candidate in 1940, would they prefer "a conservative type of candidate or a New Dealer." Of the Democrats polled, 52 percent declared they would prefer "a conservative type," while only 48 percent favored a New Dealer.

Moreover, it was soon evident that the House Un-American Activities Committee's primary target was the New Deal. Hallie Flanagan, the brilliant head of the Federal Theatre, was one of the first witnesses called by the Dies committee, and she was followed by Aubrey Williams, who was interrogated about Communists in the NYA and the WPA. When the Dies committee came out with its list of suspicious organizations, its critics were delighted to find that among the contributors to one or another of the organizations were the secretaries of the army and navy, Stimson and Knox, and Sara Delano Roosevelt, the President's mother.

It was also the case that, according to Whittaker Chambers, by 1938 "the Soviet espionage apparatus in Washington had penetrated the State Department, the Treasury Department, the Bureau of Standards and the Aberdeen Proving Ground in Maryland. In the State Department, it had two active sources and two contacts. . . ." Some were members of the Communist Party, and others fellow travelers. One "underground apparatus" was headed by Elizabeth Bentley. The principal source in the State Department was Alger Hiss, assistant secretary of state to Francis Sayre, Woodrow Wilson's son-in-law. Hiss was considered one of the most brilliant of the young New Dealers; every door was open to him. Henry Julian Wadleigh was the "No. 2 source" in the State Department, while the Treasury Department was "covered" by Harry Dexter White, who was assistant to Henry Morgenthau. The source at the Aberdeen Proving Ground was Vincent Reno, who was working on a highly secret bombsight. Under the name Lance Clark, Reno had been a party organizer in the radical county of Sheridan, Montana. Part of the Washington apparatus involved two photographic workshops where papers taken from various government departments and agencies could be photographed for transmission to Russian agents.

Charles Kramer, who was on the staff of the AAA, the NYA, and the La Follette subcommittee of the Senate on civil liberties was, according to Whittaker Chambers, a member of the Communist Party. Nathan Witt, who from 1937 to 1940 was on the legal staff of the National Labor Relations Board, was a member of the Ware Group, named after Harold Ware, who had been killed in an automobile accident in 1936. Lee Pressman was a member of the Ware Group. Pressman later named several members of the group (in addition to himself), but Chambers estimated that there were as many as sixty or seventy others.

Henry Julian Wadleigh was the son of an Episcopal minister with an M.A. from Oxford and a Bachelor of Science degree from London. He began his New Deal career in the Federal Farm Bureau, moved on to the State Department and then to the Department of Agriculture. During his tour in the State Department, from 1936 on, he passed on some 400 State Department documents to Whittaker Chambers. Henry Collins was treasurer of the Ware Group. John Abt, Pressman, and Witt all were Harvard graduates.

"Besides . . . purely military information," Elizabeth Bentley wrote, "we had a steady flow of political reports from the Treasury which included material from the Office of Strategic Services, the State Department, the Navy, the Army, and even a limited amount of data from the Department of Justice. We knew what was going on in the inner chambers of the United States government, up to and including the White House."

At the height of her operation Bentley was transmitting some forty rolls of microfilm a week to Russian agents. Her "infant prodigy" was William Remington, a graduate of Dartmouth College and Columbia University. Remington not only was the youngest member of Bentley's apparatus, but was an "all-American boy," a tall, handsome, blue-eyed blond, a high school track star and brilliant student. He had won his party spurs in the dangerous field of sharecropper organizing in the South; he and his wife, Bing, both were ardent Communists. Remington was on the War Production Board, where he had access to secret data on aircraft production.

Mary Price, Walter Lippmann's secretary, brought into Elizabeth Bentley's apparatus Duncan C. Lee, grandson of General Robert E. Lee, who had been born in China of missionary parents. Lee, a rising star in the law firm of William "Wild Bill" Donovan, was active in the Institute of Public Relations.

In Whittaker Chambers's words, "The important point about the Washington apparatuses is that, in the 1930's the revolutionary mood had become so acute throughout the whole world that the Communist Party could recruit its agents, not here and there, but by the scores within the Government of the United States. And they were precisely among the most literate, intellectually eager and energetic young men in a nation which by all its traditions . . . was farthest removed from the revolutionary struggles of Europe."

For a scholar and intellectual like Chambers, the description of the United States as "a nation which by all its traditions . . . was farthest removed from the revolutionary struggles of Europe" seems singularly obtuse. The nation had been born in revolution, in Wyndham Lewis's words, in the spirit of "radical universalism," and had maintained a strong tradition of radical reform since its infancy.

When Franklin Roosevelt finally consented to address the highly conservative Daughters of the American Revolution (whose refusal to allow the black singer Marian Anderson to give a concert in its Washington auditorium had led to Eleanor Roosevelt's resignation from that society), he urged them to "remember always that all of us, you and I especially, are descended from immigrants and revolutionists." Roosevelt was a far better historian than Whittaker Chambers.

The situation in Great Britain was an instructive contrast with the United States. There the Labor Party had the misfortune to come to power in 1928 on the eve of worldwide depression. The blame fell on it as, in the United States, it did on Hoover and the Republicans, and the Laborites were ousted by the Conservatives. The British Communists and socialists were thus forced to bide their time and anticipate their New Deal after the war, when, they believed, British and European capitalism would finally collapse and Labor and the left would take over, redirecting the British economy along socialist lines. Labor did indeed come to power after the war, but capitalism in Europe revived under the benign influence of the Marshall Plan, and the Labor Party, demoralized by that unexpected turn of events and lacking popular support, was able to make only modest changes in the British economy. In the United States a fierce conservative reaction against the New Deal took place after the war.

Time and tribulation brought Hopkins and Ickes closer together as the years of the New Deal passed. The Democratic ex-social worker and the old Progressive Republican found that they saw eye to eye on most issues. They joined forces to press the President to push ahead with his program of social legislation. While others grew fainthearted at the prospect of vast expenditures and huge deficits, they cheerfully persevered. "Harry," Ickes noted in his diary in April, 1938, "is pretty disgusted with the way some supposed New Dealers have been acting. Harry is a man who sticks to his guns and isn't afraid either of a fight or a licking." That, of course, was the way Ickes liked to think of himself. He was pleased to hear that Hopkins had been "speaking of me in very friendly and complimentary terms." In fact, improbable as it seemed to practical politicians like Jim Farley, Hopkins was beginning to think of himself as a possible successor to Roosevelt in 1940, when, it was widely assumed, Roosevelt's term of office would be ended by the unwritten rule that no President should serve more than two terms.

Ickes himself was not immune to the presidential bug; he noted frequently in his journal that this or that political figure had told him he was presidential timber. But word in the inner circle was that Hopkins was Roosevelt's anointed. Henry Wallace, it was generally conceded, was too eccentric, too fuzzy to be a strong candidate, and Cordell Hull declined to enter the lists. Ickes was considered too "combative." Farley had all the right political connections, and was undoubtedly the favorite of the Democratic rank and file, the party workers and political bosses, but he was innately conservative. His loyalty was to the President, and he viewed much of the New Deal legislation with horror. As chief executive he could be counted on to placate business and jettison what he could of the New Deal or at least do nothing to extend it.

What was clearly most important to Roosevelt was the perpetuation of the New Deal. For that task Hopkins was a natural choice; Farley, a "dangerous" contender. Roosevelt appointed Hopkins secretary of commerce at the end of 1938, thereby removing him from his controversial post as administrator of the WPA, and Hopkins told close friends that his presidential ambitions had the "green light" from the President. Eleanor Roosevelt did her bit by noting in her column, "My Day," that Hopkins "seems to work because he has an inner conviction that a job needs to be done and that he must do it. I think he would be that way about any job he undertook." Yet Hopkins was an odd choice. He had come under heavier fire than any other member of Roosevelt's administration. His name was anathema to conservative Democrats, representing all that they most disliked about the New Deal. Never robust, he had had a major operation for cancer, with half his stomach removed. That Roosevelt should have settled on Hopkins as his candidate for the presidency, with all the practical political problems that his choice must necessarily entail, is the best indicator of the strength of his commitment to a long-term program of reform, or, more simply, the perpetuation of the New Deal. Hopkins had, of course, changed greatly from the rather arrogant and acerbic head of the Federal Emergency Relief Administration who had not bothered to hide his contempt for run-of-the-mill politicians.

The response of the newspapers to the news of Hopkins's appointment as secretary of commerce was predictable. "Surely this is the most incomprehensible, as well as one of the least defensible, appointments the President has made in his six and one-half years in the White House," the *Chicago Daily News* exclaimed. Averell Harriman, a friend of Hopkins's and chairman of the Business Advisory Council, while acknowledging that the "business community was somewhat surprised and shocked" at the news, gave his support to the appointment, as did Bernard Baruch. The *Kiplinger Newsletter* took the appointment as evidence that Hopkins wished to be President and that Roosevelt had given him his imprimatur: "It means he will use the Secretaryship as a buildup. He is sick of the WPA, and the bad smell about it, the social work reputation. He wants to show he is a big man, a broad man, can administer business."

Spurred by ambition, Hopkins now practiced his considerable charms on Congressmen and Senators of both parties, aware that his unique relationship with the President gave him great power. In addition, he plainly liked to mingle with the rich and the socially prominent, whom he had once scorned. There was more than a hint of disapproval in Eleanor Roosevelt's comment "What surprised some of us was the fact that Harry seemed to get so much genuine pleasure out of contact with gay but more or less artificial society. People who could give him luxuries and the kind of party in which he probably never before had had the slightest interest became important to him. I did not like this side of Harry as much as the side I first knew, but deep down he was a fine person who had the courage to bear pain and who loved his country. . . ."

Roosevelt told Ickes that he thought Hopkins was a good secretary of commerce "because he gets along well with the big businessmen with whom he comes in contact. . . . There is something debonair and easy-going about him that makes him personally attractive; he seems to like to accept invitations to expensive homes; he loves horse racing and poker and women. . . ."

As secretary of commerce Hopkins did his best to sound like a friend of business. Speaking in Des Moines, Iowa, he claimed the state as his birthplace and assured his listeners that the emphasis of the New Deal had shifted "from reform to recovery" and that "this Administration is now determined to promote that recovery with all the vigor and power at its command." Labor, Hopkins added, "must fully realize that under our economic system businessmen have to make money to hire workers." The presidential ambition was so evident that Jim Farley, with his own presidential ambitions, called it "Hopkins' Acceptance Speech," and Ickes wrote: "another lost liberal."

Ickes noted in his diary that various progressive friends were urging him to consider himself the strongest candidate to succeed the President; he persisted in the line that the country was "much more radical than the Administration." The implication was clear that Roosevelt was not radical enough for the country but that Ickes, in 1940, would be. He anticipated that "in all probability a very fierce battle will be waged at the polls in 1940 with a far more radical and much more determined electorate trying to get control of the Government as against concentrated wealth." In such a case Ickes thought he would be a logical candidate for the liberal or radical wing of the Democratic Party, certainly a far likelier prospect than Hopkins. The fact that the President himself had said that the elections of 1940 "might determine the destinies of the Government for many years to come," encouraged Ickes to think that FDR might have him in mind as a likely successor.

Farley, concerned over the increasing prominence of Hopkins, who, for many Americans hostile to the New Deal, represented its worst "giveaway" aspects and its reputed indifference to money, told him he was the "most unpopular man in the Administration" and the "greatest handicap to the President," as Hopkins reported it to Morgenthau. But Roosevelt stressed his support by taking Hopkins on a campaign swing through the drought states. The trip included the inspection of a reservoir in Wyoming and an arsenal in Utah, an airport in Portland and an island in San Francisco Bay.

In San Francisco the Symphony Orchestra Unit of the Federal Music Project played a concert for Hopkins, and in Los Angeles Hopkins told a group of businessmen: "I have never liked poverty. I have never believed that with our capitalistic system people have to be poor. I think it is an outrage that we should permit hundreds and hundreds of thousands of people to be ill clad, to live in miserable homes, not have enough to eat, not to be able to send their children to school for the only reason that they are poor. I don't believe that ever again in America are we going to permit the things to happen that have happened in the past to people. We are never going back again, in my opinion, to the days of putting old people in the alms houses, when a decent dignified pension at home will keep them there. . . ." The American system was "an ideal instrument to increase this national income of ours . . . up to 100 billion or 120 billion." Hopkins concluded: "The capitalistic system lends itself to providing a national income that will give real security for all."

The global crises that preoccupied the President included both Europe and the Far East. The most significant events of 1938 in Europe were the crisis in Czechoslovakia and Hitler's stepped-up persecution of the Jews. When his assault on the Jews first became known, there had been a worldwide outcry. Hitler's response was to order a boycott of Jewish businesses and the services of Jewish professionals as retribution for the foreign criticism of German actions. If that continued, he implied, there would be further punishment of the Jews.

In 1938 the Nuremberg Laws took away the civil rights of Jews and left them completely at the mercy of their persecutors, public and private alike. In November, 1938, Nazi bands terrorized Jewish sections of Germany's major cities, smashing windows of Jewish stores and setting synagogues afire. A number of Jews were murdered, many were beaten, and 25,000 were shipped off to concentration camps. The glass-strewn streets gave the well-planned outbreak the name of *Kristallnacht*. Roosevelt expressed the indignation of the United States government by recalling the American ambassador, but no effort was made to facilitate the immigration of German Jews to the United States; they fell under the restrictive provisions of the so-called Quota Laws, which severely limited the entry of Central Europeans. While Hitler had attacked the Jews unmercifully in his autobiographical *Mein Kampf* and called for their persecution, *Kristallnacht* marked the beginning of an all-out campaign against German and Austrian Jews, indeed European Jews in general. Roosevelt told newsmen, "I myself could scarcely believe that such things could occur in a twentieth-century civilization." Some 15,000 German and Austrian refugees, most of them Jews in the United States on visitors' visas, were given permission to remain.

The vastness of the tragedy of the Third Reich can hardly be described. One facet of that tragedy was Hitler's war against German intellectuals, many of whom were Jews. German culture was, after all, a common heritage of immense richness. In the words of Anthony Heilbut, German intellectuals, whether "Jew or radical or simple patriot, . . . had all been devotees of German culture." In addition to artists, writers, and intellectuals, Hitler forced into exile an estimated 43 percent of all German academics, including 47 percent of all social scientists. Many of the persecuted academics were not Jewish. To be a German became a reproach. "They [the Germans] are a shitty people," Bertolt Brecht declared. He believed "everything bad in me" was German. Klaus Mann, son of the novelist Thomas Mann, abjured his native language. "Why remain loyal to your mother tongue when the Fascists are itching to cut out your radical tongue and kill your Jewish mother?"

The refugees came to America with mixed feelings. Many of the newcomers viewed Americans as a crude and semibarbaric people. They made exceptions for a few American figures, notably Walt Whitman, and they were, like all Europeans, fascinated by blacks. Klaus Mann wrote that black Americans alone "possessed a spontaneous and yet consciously developed artistic style . . . a new rhythmic experience, a new histrionic style, a new melody." A German refugee, Eugene van Groma, founded the American Negro Ballet in 1934.

However dim a view the refugees may have had of American culture, the experience of freedom was, for most of them, enormously exhilarating. "I can't explain what kind of feeling I had," Jacques Lipchitz, the sculptor, wrote of his first view of New York Harbor. "It was like I came from death to life."

The list of Jewish writers, intellectuals, and academics who came to the United States during the Hitler years is an extraordinary one: Theodor Adorno, Hannah Arendt, Rudolf Arnheim, Marcel Breuer, Erik Erikson, Hojo Holborn, Paul Lazarsfeld, Claude Lévi-Strauss, Eugen Rosenstock-Huessy, the Manns (Klaus, Heinrich, Erika, and Thomas), Herbert Marcuse, Hans Morgenthau, Erwin Panofsky, Leo Strauss, Leo Szilard, Hans Bethe, Edward Teller, and hundreds of others. The sciences, art, music, architecture, literature, philosophy, the theater, the movies—there was no aspect of American culture or scholarship that was not enhanced by that immigration.

Adjustment was not easy, and in an America still mired in the Depression, jobs were hard to come by. Hans Morgenthau, the historian, got a job as an elevator operator. Hans Hofmann, who had been a physics student, became an avant-garde painter.

The Emergency Committee in Aid of Displaced Foreign Scholars found jobs for 288 academics in 145 schools and colleges, among them a few black colleges in the South. The Rosenwald Foundation gave a grant that enabled 47 more to find positions. The New School for Social Research, founded by Alvin Johnson in 1919, became an enclave of radical refugee scholars, especially in the social sciences.

Josef Albers and a number of other refugees distinguished in the arts joined the faculty of Black Mountain College near Asheville, North Carolina, and made it for a time the most vital institution of higher education in the United States. George Grosz, one of Germany's best-known artists, became a teacher at the Art Students League in New York. Erik Fromm and Erik Erikson established themselves as two of the most influential psychologists in America. The Austrian philosopher Rudolf Carnap helped popularize logical positivism in the United States.

Included among the Bauhaus figures who came to the United States was Walter Gropius, who received an appointment at Harvard. Ludwig Miës van der Rohe had been one of the most prominent figures in the Bauhaus and had designed a monument to the Communist hero and heroine of the abortive uprising of Vienna workers. In the United States he became a leader in the field of industrial design.

In music Paul Hindemith taught at Yale and wrote music for Whitman's "When Lilacs Last in the Dooryard Bloom'd," and Darius Milhaud taught at Mills College in California. Igor Stravinsky wrote *Ebony Concerto* for the bandleader Woody Herman. Arnold Schoenberg, the master of twelve-tone music, composed a libretto in English and the music for MGM's *The Good Earth*, starring Luise Rainer and Paul Muni.

One of the most controversial émigré composers was Hanns Eisler. Eisler was a well-known Communist who was often referred to as the "world's leading composer of music and songs for workers." He was praised extravagantly by the *Daily Worker*: "As [the workers] march, thousands of voices eagerly catch up in militant determined song their struggles and their fight for liberation. In the pulsating, stirring rhythms of these revolutionary songs they forge their common challenge, which hurls itself in a volume of sound against the walls of their ruling-class enemies. Behind this music stands Hanns Eisler—foremost revolutionary composer."

The *Red Song Book* was popular at party meetings and social functions. It included a Hanns Eisler song that went:

> Oh, you who are missing,
> Oh, comrades in dungeons,

You're with us, you're with us,
   This day of vengeance.
No Fascists can daunt us,
   No terror can halt;
All lands will take flame
   With the fire or revolt.
The Comintern calls you,
   Raise high the Soviet banner,
In steeled ranks to battle
   Raise sickle and hammer. . . .

When Eisler, having found a temporary refuge in Cuba, tried to get a visa to come to the United States, American anti-Communists raised a hue and cry. Among those supporting Eisler's immigration into the United States were Dorothy Thompson, Malcolm Cowley, Clifford Odets, Harold Clurman, and Eleanor Roosevelt.

All in all, the immigration of German and Austrian intellectuals was the most remarkable episode in the long history of European immigration to America. It recalled the era of the 1848s, when hundreds of European revolutionaries came to the United States in the aftermath of the reactionary counterrevolution, the most famous of those refugees being Carl Schurz. The effects on American cultural and intellectual life were profound. Without such refugee scientists as Albert Einstein, Leo Szilard, Edward Teller, and the Italian Enrico Fermi, the Germans might well have perfected an atomic bomb before the United States, with consequences too appalling to contemplate.

The adjustment of the refugees to the United States was complicated by the left-wing politics of many of them, Brecht being perhaps the best known; by native American anti-Semitism; and by the Depression itself. Moreover, the European invasion pointed up the relative lack of sophistication in American cultural and intellectual life. The ease with which émigré artists and scholars established their authority and the extent of their influence was disconcerting. Nor is it clear that despite its vastly greater sophistication, the influence was always salutory. What is plain enough was that it encountered little resistance from a strong and confident indigenous culture. Such classic American figures as Whitman, William James, John Jay Chapman, and Charles Sanders Peirce had no successors and few disciples. Although it is too recent a phenomenon to assess very confidently—a number of the young émigré scholars are still alive—it undeniably had the effect of helping create in the United States a far more cosmopolitan culture. At the same time it reinforced an already evident arrogance in the new intellectual class, which considered itself superior to the common run of Americans. While the tradition of European, especially German, scholarship strengthened graduate study in the United States, it simultaneously drew energy and talent away from undergraduate instruction and left it, more than ever, a stepchild of the academic world.

Since World War II the New Deal and Roosevelt have been accused of not having done enough to assist refugees from the Nazis to reach a haven in this country. Some historians have stressed the fact that impediments were actually placed in the way of refugees seeking asylum in the United States, but as we have noted, Roosevelt was always skating on thin ice in isolationist and anti-Semitic America. The situation was, in many ways, similar to Roosevelt's position vis-à-vis American blacks. He could do only so much for blacks without risking the erosion of his political base in the white South. His administration could do only so much for refugees without inflaming the isolationists. Jews and blacks indicated by their support of the President that they were profoundly grateful for what he did accomplish and well aware of the political obstacles that stood in the way of doing more. Moreover, what critics of Roosevelt often lose sight of are the moral implications of the fact that the major efforts at rescuing German Jews were focused on those Jewish intellectuals and scholars with worldwide reputations. There was no pretense that any substantial number of ordinary Jews could be rescued from Hitler's "final solution."

When Senator Robert Wagner introduced a bill to allow 200,000 Jewish children to be admitted to the United States outside the quotas, the bill was never reported out of committee. A refugee ship, the *St. Louis*, carried 930 Jews from Hamburg to Cuba, where authorities refused them permission to land. When the ship sailed on to Miami, the refugees were once more turned away and forced to sail back to Europe. "We had it in our power to rescue this doomed people and we did not lift a hand to do it," Freda Kirchwey wrote in the *Nation* in 1943, referring not to the refugees on the *St. Louis* alone but to German Jews generally.

Early in 1938 Hitler summoned Chancellor Kurt von Schuschnigg of Austria to Berchtesgaden to harangue him about his resistance to national socialism and the Nazis in Austria. Schuschnigg's acquiescence to Hitler's demands for the inclusion of Nazis in the Austrian Cabinet was followed by German annexation of Austria a month later.

Hitler then turned his attention to Czechoslovakia. It had been clear for a year or more that the French and British would not come to the aid of that small democratic nation if Hitler invaded it. The French foreign minister, Georges Bonnet, told Walter Lippmann in November, 1937, that the British had indicated very plainly that they would not fight to save Czechoslovakia from Hitler's armies.

Hitler's first move was to demand autonomy for the Germans in Czechoslovakia, primarily those in the Sudetenland. For a time war seemed imminent as the Czechs rejected Hitler's demands and called for the mobilization of 400,000 soldiers. Germany responded by calling up 750,000 reservists, while Hitler toured German fortifications and the British announced that its fleet would be concentrated in British waters by September. The French began to call up reservists, and it was estimated that more than 1,000,000 men were under arms in the nations most directly concerned.

The British prime minister, Neville Chamberlain, desperately anxious to avoid war, proposed a meeting with Hitler. At Berchtesgaden Hitler repeated his demand for the annexation of predominantly German areas on the basis of self-determination, insisting that he was fully prepared to go to war to attain his goal. French Premier Edouard Daladier joined Chamberlain in London, where they agreed to try to persuade the Czechs to accept the German demands. Under intense pressure the Czechs yielded. Hitler indicated he was still not satisfied. Chamberlain returned to Germany in September for a second meeting with Hitler. This time Chamberlain refused to make further concessions and returned home, urging resistance to Hitler. Roosevelt joined in an appeal to the German dictator as well as to Mussolini to make a final effort to avoid war.

The principal obstacle to the United States' bringing any substantial economic pressure to bear against the aggressors was the Neutrality Act. "We'll be on the side of Hitler by invoking the act," Roosevelt said to Texas Senator Tom Connally. "If we could get rid of the arms embargo, it wouldn't be so bad." But Borah and his allies in the Senate dug in for a last-ditch fight. When Roosevelt invited the isolationist contingent to the White House, Borah said bluntly, "We are not going to have a war." Still, Roosevelt persisted, sending an appeal to Hitler and Mussolini on April 15, urging them to disavow any designs on a list of thirty-one countries, among them Syria and Palestine. Hitler relayed the message to the Reichstag and poured out his scorn. Syria and Palestine could not respond to his query on whether they felt threatened by Germany since they were occupied by French and British troops, he pointed out. Mussolini referred contemptuously to Roosevelt's "Messiah-like messages."

On September 29, 1938, in Munich, there was a meeting attended by Mussolini, Hitler, Chamberlain, and Daladier. Most of Hitler's demands were agreed to: France and Britain guaranteed the borders of the dismembered Czechoslovakia. Poland got the area of Teschen, which was populated by fewer than 100,000 Poles out of a population of 240,000. The area ceded by Czechoslovakia to Germany covered some 10,000 square miles with a population of some 3,500,000, of whom some 700,000 were Czechs. Hungary, with claims of its own, was given part of Slovakia and Ruthenia, about 5,000 square miles with more than 1,000,000 inhabitants. Czechoslovakia lost approximately a third of its population and territory. "This is the last territorial claim I have to make in Europe," Hitler declared in one of the more cynical statements in history. Chamberlain came home announcing to a skeptical world that he had achieved "peace with honor . . . peace in our time." But Winston Churchill warned his fellow members of the House of Commons: "Do not suppose that this is the end. This is only the beginning of the reckoning. This is only the first sip, the first foretaste of a bitter cup which will be proffered to us year by year unless, by a supreme recovery of moral health and martial vigor, we arise again and take our stand for freedom as in the olden time."

To friends of democratic government the fate of Czechoslovakia seemed especially tragic. Thomas Masaryk and Eduard Beneš were two of the most enlightened politicians in Europe. To Hamilton Fish Armstrong they complemented each other perfectly. Masaryk, a "philosopher and a Platonist," in Armstrong's words, was "quizzical, dry, mild in speech but audacious in crises," with a deep knowledge of history, while Beneš, "springy mentally and physically," reacted "intuitively as well as logically to each new problem." At Geneva Beneš had worked in a disinterested spirit to strengthen the League of Nations. The Geneva Protocol, which served as a kind of model for the Kellogg-Briand Pact, was largely his handiwork. It not only ruled out wars of aggression but declared war itself to be illegal as a means of settling international conflicts.

Armstrong noted that Masaryk's "modesty and indeed shyness made it difficult to recall that he had won so many victories not merely in the realm of intellectual dispute but in desperate political battles in the world arena. The quietness with which he spoke heightened the impression he gave of nobility, even grandeur." Masaryk died on the eve of the dismemberment of the nation he had worked so hard to create. Beneš left for the United States after Munich.

To Walter Lippmann, looking back from the perspective of time, it seemed that Chamberlain's acquiescence in the dismantling of Czechoslovakia was less appeasement than an effort to encourage Hitler to turn his attention to the conquest of Russia. "In sacrificing Czechoslovakia to Hitler, Britain and France were really sacrificing their alliance with Russia. They sought security by abandoning the Russian connection at Munich, in a last vain hope that Germany and Russia would fight and exhaust one another."

Roosevelt's angry response to Chamberlain's visit to Berchtesgaden was that it was an "international outrage." American sentiment was strongly pro-Czech. Not only were there many Czechs in the United States, especially in the Midwest, but the democratic nation seemed one of the few positive results of the World War and the Versailles Treaty. France and Britain, Roosevelt wrote, had "washed the blood from their Judas Iscariot hands." The President was convinced that there would be "an inevitable conflict within the next five years. Perhaps when it comes the United States will be in a position to pick up the pieces of European civilization and help them to save what remains of the wreck—not a cheerful prospect," he wrote his old friend William Phillips.

Harry Hopkins was hobnobbing with Bernard Baruch at Hobcaw Barony in South Carolina on the Pee Dee and Waccamaw rivers when word came of Hitler's occupation of Czechoslovakia. Baruch expressed no surprise. His British friend Winston Churchill had written a year before: "War is coming very soon. We will be in it and you will be in it. You will be running the show over there, but I will be on the sidelines over here."

Joseph Stalin was well aware that there was a strong inclination in the European nations to do whatever they could to pit the Nazis against the Russians in the hope that they would do each other in. He believed that in any crisis the capitalist countries, however much they might talk of popular fronts and collective security, would readily sacrifice Russia to protect their interests. This view was strengthened by the obvious reluctance of France, Great Britain, and indeed the United States as well to take a strong stand against either Germany or Japan. Stalin's paranoia even went so far as to include the suspicion that France and Great Britain might join forces with Germany in an attack on Russia.

The Munich Agreement of September 29, which accepted what was in effect the dissolution of Czechoslovakia, seemed to Stalin to confirm his fears. The lesson that he drew was that collective security, never a very healthy creature, was now dead and it was every man for himself, or every nation for itself. His conclusion was that he must make whatever accommodation with Germany was necessary to reduce the danger of an attack by Hitler.

This was also the reading of Alexander Kirk, Bohlen, and the embassy staff directly charged with Soviet watching. The question was how could these suspicions be best conveyed to Washington. When Kirk's dispatches began to warn of the possibility of such a development, the rather disapproving response of the State Department was that the embassy analysts "seem to feel that no foreign government mapping out its foreign policies should place a dependence upon sustained Soviet cooperation or should consider Soviet gestures of friendship as other than opportunistic moves taken in order to meet some international exigency," which was, of course, exactly what the embassy staff thought and what, in fact, Bullitt had stated almost five years earlier at the time of his disillusionment.

Stalin, meanwhile, called for a conference of Rumania, France, Poland, Turkey, Britain, and Russia to discuss collective action in the event of a German attack on Poland or Rumania. The British rebuffed Stalin and unilaterally guaranteed Poland and Rumania against German attack. In doing so, the British, from having been too timid, now appeared too bold. They had surrendered all possibility of bargain or maneuver vis-à-vis Russia.

A dramatic change in Russian foreign policy was foreshadowed by the sacking of Maxim Litvinov, the architect of collective security and the popular front, and his replacement as commissioner for foreign affairs by the more compliant Yacheslav Molotov. Kirk and Bohlen were uncertain whether the change represented the beginning of an approach to Germany or, on the other hand, by simply raising that possibility, was intended to put pressure on the British to join the Russians in a bolder anti-Fascist front. Litvinov was a Jew, and in the reorganization of the Soviet Foreign Office, most Jews were eliminated, suggesting again that Stalin might be getting ready to do business with Hitler. What the State Department did not know and what Charles Bohlen could not tell them was that he had a secret source of information in the German Embassy. The embassy had leased a dacha some ten miles from the city. There two scrawny horses were owned jointly by the Americans, a member of the German Embassy, and a member of the British Embassy. The German, Hans Heinrich Herwarth von Bittenfeld, an aristocrat called Johnny Herwarth by his American friends, Bohlen, and a young Englishman, Fitzroy-MacLean, were constant companions, riding, playing tennis, skiing and skating in the winter. Herwarth had little sympathy with Hitler and the Nazis, and one day, when he and Bohlen were riding together, he told the startled American that he had information which indicated that "something was up," presumably Russian-German negotiations. (Herwarth, it turned out, was one-quarter Jewish and a member of the secret resistance among the German aristocracy to the Nazis.) An appointment had been made for the German ambassador to confer with Molotov. From that point on Bohlen, hardly believing his luck, got from Herwarth regular reports, which he forwarded to the United States Department of State while carefully guarding the source of the information. On May 20, 1939, Charles Bohlen and the new U.S. chargé d'affaires, Grummon, wired Washington that the German foreign minister, Joachim von Ribbentrop, had told the German ambassador that in the opinion of the German government, "Communism has ceased to exist in the Soviet Union; that the Communist International was no longer a factor of importance, and consequently it was felt that no real ideological barrier remained between Germany and Russia." The Russians, unaware that Hitler had declared Russian communism at an end, responded with unmistakable signals of their own. It was a brilliant coup for Bohlen, one that had fallen into his lap by virtue of his friendship with his counterpart in the German Embassy. Bohlen followed it with further wires incorporating fresh information and a wealth of specifics that finally convinced the most skeptical department officials that he was on to something. Hull called in the British and French ambassadors and informed them of the impending pact. They, in turn, informed their governments, which, having no very high opinion of American intelligence and, furthermore, not wishing to believe what was very bad news indeed, ignored the report.

Week after week the cautious negotiations went on. On July 1 Bohlen wired Washington that the talks between Molotov and the German ambassador were approaching a conclusion, which would apparently take the form of a nonaggression pact between the two countries. Germany would thereby be free to pursue its ambitions in Europe without the threat of having to fight a two-front war. Stalin, on the other hand, distrusting France and Great Britain, believed he had insured his country against the nightmare of an assault by Hitler's formidable army. In retrospect, it all seemed logical, if not exactly inevitable. What was most surprising was that no one had anticipated it. With discussions in their final stage British and French delegations arrived in Leningrad on July 10 to draft a mutual defense pact with the Soviet Union. Their hearts were plainly not in their task, and their reception by Molotov was decidedly cool. On August 15, at a reception at the German Embassy, Herwarth drew Bohlen aside, an extremely risky act under the circumstances, and informed him that the Russian-German nonaggression pact was, for all practical purposes, completed. On August 23 Ribbentrop arrived in Moscow to be greeted by a band that had belatedly rehearsed the Nazi anthem the "Horst Wessel Lied." The next morning the pact was announced to a dumbfounded world. Even Marshal Kliment Voroshilov, who was busy negotiating with the British and French, was caught by surprise. Only the President, Cordell Hull, and those members of the administration privy to Bohlen's reports were prepared for the news.

Communist parties in every major Western country were thrown into alarm and confusion. "I felt like I had been hit by a bolt of lightning," Steve Nelson wrote. "The very heart of our policies and struggles over the last decade had been the fight against the spread of fascism, and in that fight the Soviet Union had played a central role." But gradually Nelson became reconciled. The Soviet Union had, after all, made evident its desire to form an alliance with the Western capitalist countries against the menace of Hitler and Mussolini. Those nations had been cool to Stalin's advances. "It seemed to me," Nelson wrote years after the fact, "that the Western countries were willing to let Hitler advance, hoping he would move first to the east against the Soviet Union. . . . In any case it did not appear that the Soviets would be able to count on Western support if Hitler invaded. Consequently I could understand the Soviet Union's desire to secure itself from hostilities and buy time to develop its defenses. But I was devastated by the morning paper with its shocking photo of Foreign Minister Molotov and Stalin toasting Hitler at the signing of the pact." That seemed, even to the faithful, carrying things too far.

Elizabeth Bentley, who had originally joined the American League Against War and Fascism to fight fascism in all its forms and found herself at the head of one of the party's underground "apparatuses" in Washington, was one of those to whom the pact was a blow. But her NKVD lover explained that the Soviet Union was "surrounded by a vicious group of capitalist nations waiting to pounce on her and crush her. The situation at the present time is such that if she hadn't signed the pact, Hitler would certainly have attacked her. Not only is she totally unprepared to fight but neither the United States nor Great Britain would have come to her aid, for all their noble speeches. In fact, they would have been glad to see her destroyed." That certainly was true of Britain and France. The United States was a somewhat different matter, since Franklin Roosevelt was determined to use every means and support every ally in his effort to stop the spread of fascism.

For many members of the Communist Party in the United States the nonaggression pact was the end of innocence. They bailed out. "The Party's standing, which was quite good on the West Coast, started to slide," Nelson wrote. "It wasn't that we hated fascism any less but people saw us as the mechanical pawns of Soviet foreign policy. How could we vociferously oppose fascism for all these years and suddenly mute our criticisms? Some people left the Party over this change of policy, and others quietly withdrew from activities or simply stopped coming around to meetings. . . . We were hurt particularly among intellectuals and the Jewish community. Left-wing Jews were as sectarian as the other members of the party and suffered the consequences. . . . Jewish Communists had long been engaged in factional fighting with the Socialists, who were stronger in the Jewish community. Now they found themselves isolated."

It was relatively easy for intellectuals, to whom the party's appeal was essentially ideological, to bail out. This was especially the case with writers whose books were proscribed for deviating from Marxist-Leninist dogma or the latest interpretation of that dogma. They usually disembarked with alacrity amid mutual recriminations. For party organizers in the South, for men and women everywhere who had been beaten and jailed for their convictions, it was a different matter. To "defect"—the word itself was loaded with negative connotations—was to admit that the struggle and the suffering that had been endured in the name of a brighter and better day for humanity in general had been wasted, expended for nothing or, worse than nothing, in a fatally flawed cause. It is small wonder, this being the case, that those men and women who had sacrificed most for the new order were most reluctant to leave the church of the party. They had become hardened, in some interior place, to normal doubts and misgivings. The impulse to question was sealed off and gradually died for lack of the air and sunshine of skepticism. Just as the believer in any religion comes at some point to accept certain doctrines as being mysteriously beyond understanding, the faithful party member forbore to question the ultimate authority, the Comintern.

The alarming turn of events in Europe gave dramatic emphasis to the debate over the issue of America's role in the growing international crisis. The country seemed, to some observers, locked in a schizophrenic struggle with its own conscience. By January, 1939, 62 percent of Americans thought there would be a European war started by Germany, and 57 percent thought that in such an event the United States would be drawn in. To the question "If France and England go to war against Germany do you think the United States can stay out?" 57 percent said yes, while a substantial 43 percent said no. President Roosevelt alarmed the isolationists by declaring that "there are many ways short of war, but stronger and more effective than mere words, of bringing home to aggressor governments the aggregate sentiments of our own people."

Walter Lippmann was dismayed by the strength of the isolationist sentiment in the country. He himself had flirted with isolationism, largely, to be sure, on the ground that isolationism was the settled temper of the country and it was futile to contend with it. But now, with all Europe succumbing to Hitler's armies and Britain alone holding out, it seemed to him folly to hang back. Americans, he declared, had been "duped by a falsification of history . . . [and] miseducated by a swarm of innocent but ignorant historians, by reckless demagogues, and by foreign interests, into believing that America entered the other war because of British propaganda, the loans of the bankers, the machinations of President Wilson's advisers [of whom, of course, Lippmann was one of the most prominent], and a drummed up patriotic ecstasy." He warned his readers that "the democracies must not delude themselves with the idea that there is any bloodless, inexpensive substitute for the willingness to go to war. . . . For more than three years Europe has been denouncing aggression and retreating before it. . . ." The result was a growing boldness on the part of the aggressors, who were convinced that they could do what they wished without serious opposition.

Yet Lippmann and many Americans of a similar persuasion, for all their calls for a realistic assessment of the world crisis, clung to some curious illusions. Lippmann insisted that the United States need not send any substantial numbers of soldiers abroad. American warships and airplanes could be counted on to vanquish the enemy in Europe or, if necessary, in the Pacific. Superior American technology and industrial might could be counted on to carry the day with a minimum investment of American lives. "Our most effective part . . . is now, and for any predictable future," he wrote, "to hold the seas and to be the arsenal of those fighting aggression." He had said much the same thing on the eve of the United States' entry into the European war in 1917. Although thousands of American lives had been sacrificed on the battlefields of France and Belgium in the closing months of the war, our losses had been modest compared with the other nations involved.

Meanwhile, Japan, under the spurious banner of the Greater East Asia Co-Prosperity Sphere, strengthened its hold on China and pushed its imperial designs in Southeast Asia. A world that had entered the twentieth century with a kind of Darwinian faith in inevitable progress, with hopes for a just and peaceful international order—to many, an essentially socialistic order—seemed, instead of realizing those hopes, to be on the verge of a new Dark Age.

When Oswald Garrison Villard concluded his autobiography in 1939, he found it "far from easy to retain one's courage when bitterness, hatred, and medieval cruelty have entered into men's hearts and brute force . . . rules the world. Much of the great promise of my youth has been dispelled," he added. "All that hope and belief that we, in a country of unlimited riches and inexhaustible lands, were destined to be a tranquil, happy, uniquely prosperous people safe from all the quarrels and embroilments of the Old World, have vanished. Our social problems have become those of the old countries—by our own folly and shortsightedness. We have wasted our natural resources, deliberately and needlessly invited class strife engendered by special privilege, by unequal economic conditions, by unfair governmental favoritism." Villard speculated: "Crass materialism, the armaments race, and war [will] end not only the creation of the American Revolution, but will destroy all democracy, and civilization itself."

He added: "Finally, in this hour of diabolical, unchristian, psychopathic, anti-Semitic barbarism, I must state the simple truth that if I had not had the support and encouragement of many Jews I could not have carried on in the measure that I did. Their idealism, their liberalism, their patriotism, their devotion to the cause of freedom in the time-honored American way, heartened me in the hardest hours. . . . I have never appealed to them for aid for the Negro, for the sick, the poor, the distressed, or for any philanthrophy and been rebuffed. . . . My pen may have some skill, but I could not begin to measure the debt that this country owes to its Jews and to millions of its first-born citizens, first for a jealous guarding of American rights and liberties to which the native-born have too often been indifferent; second, for preserving at all times a great reservoir of idealism and liberalism, and, thirdly, for keeping alive a passionate desire for knowledge in every field, which has steadily quickened American life and notably its colleges."

Villard asked: "How can one keep one's faith?" "How present a cheerful mien to those coming after?" The values that his grandfather (William Lloyd Garrison), his mother, and he himself had fought for and for which he had made the *Nation* a spokesman were, he believed, indestructible. It was only in the short run that things seemed gloomy. If humanity were to survive, those ideals must reassert themselves.

Hutchins Hapgood, who was finishing his autobiography, *A Victorian in the Modern World*, at the same time, had similar reflections. He was reminded of his friend Lincoln Steffens's letter, written from Paris in 1919 at the time of the peace conference, in which Steffens had declared that he was watching the Allied leaders "make the next war." They had indeed made it, as many witnesses to that travesty besides Steffens had discerned. "And now! Now as I finish the record of my entire life," Hapgood wrote, "the total values of that life, as written in foregoing pages, are vitally threatened—an imminent danger for civilization which will certainly become an accomplished fact, if democracy does not re-assert itself with greater purity, force and completeness than ever before. . . ."

# The Election of 1940

On September 1, 1939, President Roosevelt was awakened at three in the morning by a telephone call. It was William Bullitt calling from Paris. He had just heard from the American ambassador to Poland, Anthony Biddle. Seven German divisions, supported by bombers, had entered Poland.

"Well, Bill, it's come at last, God help us all," Roosevelt replied.

Word was soon received from the American embassies in London and Paris that Great Britain and France would declare war on Germany, although there was nothing they could do to assist Poland. Roosevelt had a strange feeling of déjà vu—it all had happened before. During the World War, when he had been assistant secretary of the navy, there had been a telephone at his bedside with a line to the Navy Department. The phone "time after time," he recalled, "brought me other tragic news in the night—the same rush messages were sent around—the same lights snapped on in nerve centers of government. I had *in fact* been through it all before."

France was confident that its famous Maginot Line was impregnable and presumably thought that magic would prevent the Germans from falling on it through Belgium, as they had done twenty-five years earlier. The British were as unprepared for war as they had been in 1914.

The Russians, anxious to hasten the dismemberment of Poland and determined to get their share, moved into eastern Poland on September 17, occupying the area agreed to by the Germans. The Russians next occupied Estonia and then Lithuania and Latvia without resistance, to protect "our friends," as Stalin put it. In less than a month all organized resistance in Poland collapsed.

"I hope the United States will keep out of this war," Roosevelt declared in a fireside chat on September 3, 1939. "I believe that it will, and I give you assurance and reassurance that every effort of your Government will be directed toward that end. As long as it remains within my power to prevent, there will be no black-out of peace in the United States." He reasserted the American commitment to neutrality. In contrast with the outbreak of the "European war" in August, 1914, there was little public sentiment in favor of Germany. The various nationalities and ethnic groups that had identifed with Germany or the Central Powers at the beginning of the earlier conflict had had two decades to become more thoroughly integrated into American society. Equally important, Americans of Polish, Czech, and other Slavic origins were incensed by Hitler's invasions of their respective homelands. In 1914 many radicals and socialists had denounced the war as a struggle between capitalist nations fighting over the division of colonial spoils. Now the issues seemed far more clear-cut. France and Great Britain had, if anything, gone too far in their efforts to preserve peace. Hitler's villainy was pointed up by his persecution of the Jews, his ruthless destruction of Czechoslovakia, and his invasion of Poland. A Gallup Poll indicated that while 82 percent of Americans wished for an Allied victory, only 2 percent favored Germany.

Roosevelt, determined to do everything in his power to aid the Allied cause, called Congress into a special session on September 21, to make amendments in the Neutrality Act that would permit the United States to provide France and Great Britain with war matériel. The President, meanwhile, took special pains with his speech to the legislators at the beginning of the session. "I give you my deep and unalterable conviction that by repeal of the embargo the United States will more probably remain at peace than if the law remains as it stands today," he told the joint session of the House and Senate. American ships, he assured Congress, would not be allowed to enter the war zone, and Americans would be forbidden to cross the ocean aboard ships of the belligerents. What Roosevelt proposed was suspension of the arms embargo and a policy of cash and carry—that is, weapons and munitions were to be paid for in cash (rather than through loans, as in World War I) and to be carried away in Allied shipping. The isolationists were up in arms immediately. It was a strange moment in the nation's history. Their names read like a roster of old Progressives; led by Borah, they included Hiram Johnson, Theodore Roosevelt's running mate on the Bull Moose ticket of 1912, and Philip La Follette, heir to his father's liberal legacy in Wisconsin. The America Firsters rallied around the banner of the Lone Eagle, America's premier hero, Colonel Charles A. Lindbergh, who proposed seizing all foreign assets in the United States to pay the debts of the last war. "As long as European powers maintain their influence in our hemisphere," he declared, "we are likely to find ourselves involved in their troubles." Lindbergh was fascinated with the efficiency of the German Air Force and he had found its leader, Hermann Göring, a congenial spirit.

In a shrewd move Roosevelt prevailed on William Allen White, dean of Midwestern journalists and politicians, to organize a Non-Partisan Committee for Peace Through Revision of the Neutrality Act. "Things move with such terrific speed these days," the President wrote White, "that it is essential to us to think in broader terms and, in effect, to warn the American people that they, too, should think of conceivable consequences without scaring the American people into thinking that they are going to be dragged into war." Catholic leaders were appealed to for their support, and labor was recruited for the campaign to amend the Neutrality Act with the unstated assumption that providing arms for the Allies would result in the employment of hundreds of thousands of union members.

In October, 1939, Albert Einstein sent Roosevelt a letter, reinforced by one from the German refugee physicist Leo Szilard, warning that German scientists were at work splitting the atom, a process which, if successful, would release enormous amounts of energy. "This new phenomenon would also lead to the construction of bombs, and it's conceivable—though much less certain—that extremely powerful bombs of a new type may be constructed." Einstein's messenger was a Jewish friend and economist, Alexander Sachs. When Roosevelt failed to respond, Sachs insisted on reading the letter aloud to be sure he had the President's attention. "Alex," the President responded, "what you are after is to see that the Nazis don't blow us up."

"Precisely," Sachs answered.

Roosevelt lost little time in appointing an advisory committee on nuclear fission made up of scientists and military officers.

Vannevar Bush, head of the Carnegie Institution, asked for a meeting with the President to discuss the role of the scientific community in preparations for the war which many Americans now believed was inevitable. Bush represented James B. Conant, president of Harvard, and Karl Compton, president of the Massachusetts Institute of Technology. He recommended the establishment of a National Defense Research Committee. Roosevelt endorsed the idea at once and announced its formation soon afterward. He instructed the committee on nuclear fission to report to the Committee and instructed the Committee itself to pay particular attention to the subject of atomic fission.

One of the unexpected residual benefits of the New Deal was that the United States, despite the dogged and tireless obstructionist tactics of the isolationists, did achieve a modest degree of preparedness by using WPA funds to build aircraft carriers and airplane plants. After Hitler's anschluss in Austria, Roosevelt had sent Hopkins to California to survey the aircraft factories in the state and their capacity for turning out planes. Hopkins's estimate was 2,600 per year, which Roosevelt thought much too low. Anticipating a war on a global scale in which, in his view, the United States must inevitably become involved, Roosevelt hoped that by extensive use of aircraft, especially bombers based in Britain and France, the United States could avoid a heavy involvement of ground troops. He concluded that the aircraft industry must be expanded to a productive capacity of 15,000 planes within two years. In addition, Roosevelt decided to build three more aircraft plants with PWA funds, designed to manufacture another 16,000 planes. In fact, planes became his obsession. When Hitler invaded Poland and France and Britain declared war on Germany, Roosevelt pressed the secretary of war and the army general staff to make the most advanced American planes available to those countries, pointing out that to have them tested in combat would provide invaluable information about their performance.

Russia, meanwhile, made demands on the Finns that they refused to accept, and at the end of November, 1939, Russian troops crossed the Finnish border. The Finns, like the Czechs, were admired in the United States. They, too, had achieved independence as one of the happier consequences of the Versailles Treaty. They were, furthermore, the only European nation to have paid its war debts in full. As a consequence, there was widespread indignation in the United States at the Russian invasion. Roosevelt spoke for most of his countrymen when he denounced the "dreadful rape of Finland." But when the Finns requested a loan to buy arms to hold off their enormous adversary, the Neutrality Act tied the President's hands. The isolationists in Congress were obdurate. An indignant Roosevelt told his Cabinet that Congress was "a bunch of Uriah Heeps . . . who did not realize that what was going on in Europe would inevitably affect this county."

The deficiencies of the Red Army were dramatically demonstrated by the Russian invasion. The initial attacks were thrown back by the much smaller Finnish army, with heavy losses to the Soviet troops. In February, 1940, the Russians threw such numbers of new divisions into the assault that the Finns were forced to capitulate, giving up an area near Leningrad as well as Hanko and accepting the destruction of the Mannerheim Line, which had cost so many Russian lives.

While outraged by the Russian attack on Finland, Charles Bohlen came after the war to the conviction that the attack "very probably saved the Soviet Union from defeat by Germany." His reasoning was that by demonstrating the inefficiency and general demoralization of the Russian Army, it enabled Stalin to institute the reforms that made it a formidable force, capable of throwing back the German invasion when it came.

With Poland overrun in a blitzkrieg that gave an alarming demonstration of the power and efficiency of the German war machine, with its emphasis on highly mobile tanks, Hitler proposed peace to the French and British; when they rebuffed him, he settled into the sitzkrieg or, as it was soon called, the phony war. The French felt confident that even Hitler's awesome armored divisions could not pierce the famous Maginot Line, which had been built at enormous cost as an impenetrable barrier to invasion from the east. The line extended from Switzerland to Belgium. Walter Lippmann was in Paris during the period of the phony war. He was taken to visit a sector of the Maginot Line. For three days he toured the defense positions—a series of underground tunnels and concrete strongpoints. The line stopped at the Belgian frontier. What about the area from there to the North Sea? he asked General Maurice Gamelin. "Oh, we've got to have an open side," Gamelin replied, "because we need a *champs de bataille*," a field of battle, where the French could "attack the German army and destroy it. The Maginot Line will narrow the gap through which they can come, and thus enable us to destroy them more easily."

When Lippmann visited Joseph Kennedy, the United States ambassador in London, Kennedy gave a gloomy recitation of impending disasters. The Spanish Army, seasoned by its victory over the Loyalists, could defeat the French single-handedly. The British fleet would be impotent in the face of German submarines. "Russia is useless, Rumania can't fight. The Japanese will attack in the East." The only sensible course for the British to take was to concede Eastern Europe to Hitler. Democracy in Europe was dead or dying.

During the phony war common wisdom had it that Hitler had swallowed all of Europe he could digest. In time what appeared to be a military stalemate—the Allies had no real hope of making Hitler disgorge his conquests—would be converted into an unfortunate but necessary peace. "The White House is very quiet," Roosevelt wrote to Kennedy in London. "There is a general feeling of sitting quiet and waiting to see what the morrow will bring forth."

Only slightly less present in the minds of Americans than the second European war was the question of whether the President would seek a third term in office. Many Americans recoiled from the notion. By retiring at the end of his second term in office, the country's first President and "Father" had established what was perhaps the nation's most enduring tradition: No President should serve more than two terms. On the other hand, as some of Roosevelt's bolder supporters had begun to point out, no President had retired in the face of a crisis such as that which confronted the nation, the beginnings of a "world war" of incalculable consequences. The problem was that for eight years one man had so filled the consciousness of Americans that it was almost impossible to imagine his absence. There was no individual in sight, Democrat or Republican, capable in the minds of most Americans of filling that vast space. The basic question was simple in the extreme: If not Roosevelt, who? He had rescued the country from what had appeared almost certain disaster (at least in the eyes of those who adored him). And now, although the United States was not a belligerent in the strange war or nonwar that was in progress, Roosevelt had somehow assumed the leadership of what was coming to be called the free world. It was obvious to any close observer (though it could not be said out loud) that the defeat of the Axis powers or, specifically, the checking of Hitler's inordinate ambition to rule the world must depend, in the last analysis, on the participation of the United States, indirectly if possible, directly if necessary, on the Allied side. The serious individual and collective weaknesses of the Allies were, to be sure, not yet fully apparent, but the alarming strength of the Third Reich was abundantly evident. If it was, for many Americans, unthinkable for the President to seek a third term in the face of an heretofore unchallenged precedent, to many others it was equally unthinkable to face a perilous future without that trusted and familiar hand at the wheel. Gallup Polls purported to show that 78 percent of the Democrats favored Roosevelt's nomination; his next closest rival drew only 10 percent.

The President told Claude Bowers that it was "not good for a party to revolve around any one man." The British Liberal Party had disintegrated, in his view, because it had become the personal property of David Lloyd George. "Principles became subordinate to personalities. I don't want that to happen to the Democratic Party," he added. Bowers came away with the impression that Roosevelt favored Cordell Hull, "with his fine mind and character and beautiful face. . . . He would not be a militant campaigner, but we could nominate a running mate to stir up the animals," the President added. Roosevelt might have preferred Henry Wallace; Wallace was just such a visionary idealist as the President. But Roosevelt was enough of a realist to know that Wallace, as a presidential candidate, was out of the question. That the best alternative, at least in Roosevelt's view, was Harry Hopkins, whose health was bad and who looked like a walking cadaver, is an accurate measure of the precariousness of the New Deal and the depletion of its ranks by death, defection, and simple attrition.

In his State of the Union address in January, 1940, Roosevelt was plainly preoccupied by the war. "There is a vast difference," he told Congress and the nation, "between keeping out of war and pretending that war is none of our business. We must see the effect on our own future if all the small nations of the world have their independence snatched from them. . . . It becomes clearer and clearer that the future world will be a shabby and dangerous place to live in . . . yes, even for Americans to live in—if it is ruled by force in the hands of a few. . . . I hope that we shall have fewer American ostriches in our midst; it is not good for the ultimate health of ostriches to bury their heads in sand."

The strength of American isolationism early in 1940 was a fairly accurate measure of the trauma of the 1914–1918 war. The European conflict had torn the nation like no event since the Civil War. It had raised and then dashed the extravagant hopes that Woodrow Wilson felt obliged to arouse in order to justify our entry into the war. "Never again" was an irresistible slogan for a bitter and disillusioned people, but it was nonetheless a foolish and deluded one. It was based on the ancient dream that America could somehow be better than the world allowed, pure and uncorrupted. It was an attempt to escape from the terrors and dilemmas of history into that consoling womb of innocence that had always attracted Americans. Roosevelt knew as much; he described his efforts to make such unpalatable facts evident to his countrymen as "walking on eggs," a task as exacting as breaking down the accumulated prejudices and stereotypes which had more than once threatened his program of domestic legislation, the New Deal.

In addition to the isolationists, Roosevelt had to contend with the Communists, who protested loudly at any indication of a military buildup by the United States or any proposal to help the Allies with arms and munitions. The President told the American Youth Congress at the White House "pilgrimage" in February, 1940: "The Soviet Union, as everyone who has had the courage to face the fact knows, is run by a dictatorship as absolute as any other dictatorship in the world. It has allied itself with another dictatorship and it has invaded a neighbor so infinitesimally small that it could do no possible harm to the Soviet Union." Repeating this statement, Charles Bohlen added, significantly, "The President was learning some of the hard facts about the Bolsheviks." The clear implication was that Roosevelt and a number of those about him, perhaps most conspicuously his wife, had been naïve in their views about the real nature of the Soviet system and the men who ran it. However mistaken such an attitude may have been, it was certainly a sounder basis for dealing with Russia than an inveterate hostility. The fact was that Roosevelt had expressed his friendly disposition toward the Soviet Union, initially, by recognizing it and then by sending Bill Bullitt, known to be sympathetic to the Soviets, as the first United States ambassador, with the mission of trying to create an atmosphere of trust and cooperation with the Russian people.

The President's own political intentions were inscrutable. It seemed clear he was tired. Friends who had not seen him for many months were alarmed by his grayness and frequent air of weariness. He talked of going back to Hyde Park when his term of office was over. "I have to have a rest," he told Daniel Tobin of the Teamsters' Union. "I want to have a rest." He sounded like a weary child, oppressed, as he certainly was, by the weight of the world. Indeed, it was a miracle that he had survived the trials of office. The movement from his bed to a wheelchair was an exhausting struggle; a dozen times a day he was forced to heave his aging, crippled body about. On top of that brutal daily physical testing there were the manifold and unending burdens of office: a constant stream of people to be seen, decisions to be made or deferred, correspondence to be read and answered, newspapermen to be pampered and cajoled, and the ever-present fact that the country, still in the grip of the most prolonged depression in its history, was now faced with global problems on an unprecedented scale.

Roosevelt would not have been human if his indomitable spirit had not faltered and his faith had not flagged. However enamored of his office, he must have longed in the depths of his soul for quiet and repose. Yet he knew as well as any of his fellow citizens that having put his foot on the path, he dared not stop or turn back. Events have their own momentum; the wisest and most powerful individuals affect them only fitfully. Roosevelt's fate or destiny was to be the first three-term and then four-term President in the nation's history, and presumably the last. If he had doubts and uncertainties, events swept him along in their train. In Europe the phony war ended abruptly. On April 9 the Nazis blitzed Denmark and landed an occupation force in Norway. A month later the blitzkrieg struck at Holland and Belgium, swinging around the end of the Maginot Line in a startling reprise of the attack that had begun the European war in 1914. The same day Neville Chamberlain resigned as the British prime minister and was succeeded by Winston Churchill, who told his countrymen that they must be prepared to endure "blood, toil, tears and sweat." From Belgium the German panzer forces pushed across the Somme and Aisne-Marne Canal into France, while Mussolini, eager to get some of the spoils, attacked the southern flank of the latter country.

Franklin Roosevelt, Jr., was graduating from the University of Virginia Law School, and his father had agreed to make the commencement address. When word came of Mussolini's invasion of France, Roosevelt added to his speech the famous words "On this tenth day of June 1940 the hand that held the dagger has struck it into the back of its neighbor." Hull's advisers had urged that the President omit the sentence when he sent it to Hull for his suggestions. That he restored it was an accurate measure of Roosevelt's feelings not just about Mussolini but about the Axis powers and their policy of ruthless aggression against their neighbors. There could be no more equivocating. "We will pursue two obvious and simultaneous courses," he declared. "We will extend to the opponents of force the material resources of this nation; and at the same time we will harness and speed up the use of those resources in order that we ourselves in the Americas may have equipment and training equal to the task of any emergency and every defense. All roads leading to the accomplishment of these objectives must be kept clear of obstructions. We will not slow down or detour. Signs and signals call for speed—full speed ahead."

The fall of Belgium forced the evacuation of Dunkirk by 338,226 British and French troops, including a substantial portion of the British Army; the men were carried off under German strafing in 861 vessels from destroyers to small pleasure boats.

On June 14, less than ten days after the invasion of France had begun, German troops entered Paris, and three days later Marshal Henri Philippe Pétain asked for armistice terms. On July 2, 1940, Pétain established a dictatorial government, under German supervision, at Vichy. The French surrender, or armistice, was signed by Marshal Pétain in the same railway car in the forest of Compiègne in which the German surrender had been signed in 1918. Hitler did a little jig of triumph on emerging from the railway car. France, the humiliator of Germany, had been humbled in turn on the same spot.

American military experts believed it was only a matter of time before the Germans launched an invasion of the British Isles and Great Britain suffered the fate of its ally. The American ambassador, Joe Kennedy, expressed his doubts that Britain could withstand an invasion. Roosevelt himself considered Britain's chances of turning the Germans back no better than one in three. The isolationists in Congress were undeterred. Although Congress blocked an effort by Roosevelt to supply the British with twenty torpedo boats and reaffirmed its opposition to loans, it approved a massive military and naval buildup, voting $1,800,000,000 for "national defense." Roosevelt announced a goal of 50,000 war planes a year. In addition, he showed considerable ingenuity (and some deviousness) in channeling military supplies to Great Britain on one pretext or another.

In June, shortly before the Democratic Convention, Roosevelt replaced his secretaries of war and the navy with outstanding Republicans. Harry Woodring, the secretary of war, was an old-fashioned isolationist and Anglophobe who doggedly opposed aid to Great Britain. Roosevelt asked for his resignation, to the alarm of the isolationists in Congress and out. He also forced the resignation of Chares Edison, secretary of the navy. He replaced Woodring with Henry Stimson, a pro-British upper-class Progressive Republican and lawyer, the friend and benefactor of, among many others, Felix Frankfurter. Stimson had been secretary of state under Hoover; he had also long been an advocate of collective security against Japan and Hitler and Mussolini.

Frank Knox (publisher of the *Chicago Daily News* and Alf Landon's running mate in 1936), long a power in Republican circles, was made secretary of the navy. The appointments dramatized the nonpartisan approach of the administration to the accelerating crisis in Europe. There was unquestionably more support for the French and British in Eastern upper-class Republican circles than in many segments of the Democratic Party. The appointment of Stimson was reassuring to such Republicans. Knox, an outspoken critic of the New Deal, was popular in the Middle West.

As the 1940 presidential campaign approached, it became clear that the Republicans would base much of their strategy on the charge that the Roosevelt administration had failed to prepare the nation adequately for defense against an invader. Governor Harold Stassen of Minnesota sounded that note, declaring, "We are tragically unprepared. We are too woefully weak to give the Allies that material assistance this nation wants to give them. We're sadly wanting in the state of our defenses of this hemisphere." The leading Republican candidates, in addition to Stassen, were Senator Robert Taft of Ohio, the able scion of the Taft dynasty of that state, New York County District Attorney Thomas E. Dewey, and Senator Arthur Vandenberg of Michigan.

The Republicans met in Philadelphia on June 28, and when Tom Dewey, the demon prosecutor, and Robert Taft, hero of the conservatives, became deadlocked, the party managers finally settled on Wendell Willkie, the Indiana native who had been president of one of the nation's largest utility holding companies, Commonwealth and Southern. A socialist in his youth, Willkie, a large, amiable man who looked a bit like an overgrown boy from a Booth Tarkington novel, had been a supporter of the New Deal in its early days and indeed promised, if elected, to preserve much of it but to run it more efficiently. "Any man who is not something of a Socialist before he is forty has no heart; any man who is still a Socialist after he is forty has no head," Willkie had declared.

Senator Charles McNary of Oregon, famous as the cosponsor of the perennial McNary-Haughen farm bill, the precursor of the AAA, was nominated for Vice-President.

The old guard Republicans regarded Willkie, the converted Midwesterner, with ill-concealed suspicion. Senator James Watson spoke for them when he declared, "I don't mind the church converting a whore, but I don't like her to lead the choir the first night!" When Frances Perkins read the Republican platform in 1940, she discovered that it had, in effect, adopted the New Deal social security programs. "God's Holy name be praised!" she exclaimed. "No matter who gets elected we've won."

A few weeks before the Democratic Convention Roosevelt decided to break the no-third-term tradition and run again, despite the opposition of some of his closest advisers and indications from Jim Farley that such a decision would bring an end to their relationship. Farley had become disenchanted with Roosevelt. To him the New Deal seemed increasingly "socialistic" in its aims. Emergency measures, undertaken to stimulate the economy or to prevent starvation, showed signs of becoming permanent government programs. Farley's background as a lower-middle-class Irish Catholic made him often feel out of place among the liberal intellectuals who made up Roosevelt's inner circle. His determination to leave the administration proved proof against Roosevelt's blandishments. The President explained that he had decided to run because not to have "would have destroyed my effectiveness as the leader of the nation in the efforts of this country to cope with the terrible catastrophe raging in Europe." Each day brought a new crisis, and for the nation to endure both a change in the form of an untested chief executive and the kind of hiatus in leadership that must result from the interval between the presidential elections in November and the swearing in of a new President more than two months later seemed too great a risk to run. Hopkins, whose health had deteriorated alarmingly, suppressed his disappointment, if he felt any, and rallied behind the President.

Roosevelt felt that he had come to the parting of the ways with Jack Garner, who had already hinted that he would not be available to run on a third-term ticket with the President. Roosevelt asked Farley his opinion of Henry Wallace as a running mate. To Farley Wallace was a "wild-eyed fellow" who would be a definite liability.

Roosevelt wished to have the convention appear to draft him when the Democrats met in Chicago on July 16. He stayed in Washington, writing his acceptance speech, while Harry Hopkins directed the strategy from the same room at the Blackstone Hotel where Warren Harding's nomination had been cooked up twenty years earlier. It was the first time that Farley had not been in charge of that operation. Now he was a rival candidate, his alienation from Roosevelt complete. The Stevens Hotel housed the official Democratic headquarters. "All the leaders in the country," Farley later wrote, "began trekking to the unofficial Roosevelt headquarters in a Blackstone Hotel suite. . . . Many never came in to see me at all. A few came in to pay their respects to me, and some of those were timidly ill at ease. Others were swinging aboard the Roosevelt band wagon. . . ." Farley found Hopkins's manner "arrogant rather than ingratiating. He offered [the delegates] nothing and demanded blind obedience. Murmurings of mutiny grew until the delegates were downright ugly. . . ." But they "lacked a rallying point of revolt and were forced to surrender, grumbling and glumly, on the never genuine threat that Roosevelt might not run and thus leave the party without the greatest vote getter."

Certainly the delegates were not in the best frame of mind. Many of them did not want Roosevelt—some because of the no-third-term tradition; others because they were disenchanted in one degree or another with the New Deal or with FDR himself. But they had been outmaneuvered and found themselves without a choice. "This convention is bleeding to death," Ickes wired. "Your reputation and prestige may bleed to death with it." Frances Perkins, unnerved by the strength of anti-Roosevelt feeling, called to urge him to come to Chicago to practice his familiar magic on the mutinous delegates. He refused: "No, no, I have given it full consideration. I thought it all through both ways. I know I am right, Frances. It will be worse if I go. People will get promises out of me that I ought not to make. If I don't make promises, I will make new enemies. If I do make promises, they'll be mistakes. I'll be pinned down on things I don't want to be pinned down on *now*." He suggested his wife. "You know Eleanor always makes people feel right," he told Perkins. "She has a fine way with her." Eleanor Roosevelt departed for Chicago.

The second night of the convention Alben Barkley delivered the keynote address and ended his speech by reading a message from the President stating that he had no desire to run for another term and that the delegates should consider themselves "free to vote for any candidate." The mayor of Chicago, Ed Kelly, had filled the convention hall with followers, who poured into the aisles, chanting, "We want Roosevelt! Illinois wants Roosevelt!" The convention resisted the effort to stampede it. Garner, Farley, and Millard Tydings, the Maryland Senator and war hero whom Roosevelt had tried to purge in 1938, were nominated, but on the first ballot Roosevelt got 946 votes to 72 for Farley and 61 for Garner. Farley, in his last gesture for his chief, made his way to the podium to propose that the nomination be made unanimous. The most serious test—the vice-presidential choice—lay ahead.

When Frances Perkins called to consult with the President about his choice of a running mate, the question was apparently still uncertain in his mind. He was inclined to Wallace. "Frances, don't you think he'd be good?" He knew she was close to the Wallaces, and she assented.

"Yes, I think Wallace will be all right." Was he sure? she asked.

He went over the others—Hull, Farley, Hopkins—then said again, "I think Wallace is the one. . . . He is the kind of a man I like to have around. He is good to work with and he knows a lot, you can trust his information. He digs to the bottom of things and gets the facts. He is honest as the day is long. He thinks right. He has the general ideas we have. He is the kind of man who can do something in politics. He can help the people with their political thinking."

How was he going to persuade the already rebellious delegates to accept Wallace, who, to many of them, epitomized all they most disliked about the New Deal? Perkins should tell Hopkins and then call Eleanor Roosevelt; she might be able to put it over. Hopkins predicted a "cat and dog fight" to get the delegates to accept Wallace. "Well," Roosevelt responded, "I suppose all the conservatives in America are going to bring pressure on the convention to beat Henry. The fellow they want is either Jesse Jones or William Bankhead. I'm going to tell them I won't run with either of these men or with any other reactionary—I've told them that before and I'll tell them again."

The President drafted a message to that effect to be read to the delegates: "Under the circumstances, I cannot in all honor, and will not, merely for political expediency, go along with the cheap bargaining and political maneuvering which have brought about party dissension in this Convention. . . . By declining the honor of the nomination for the Presidency, I can restore that opportunity to the Convention. I so do."

Pa Watson was appalled. "He's all excited in there now," he told Sam Rosenman, who had been charged with reviewing the President's draft. He would feel different in the morning. "Besides, the country needs him. I don't give a damn who's Vice-President and neither does the country. The only thing that's important to this country is that fellow in there. There isn't anyone in the United States who can lead this country in the next four years as well as he can." Roosevelt was prevailed upon not to send the message. Instead, the word was passed informally to party leaders.

When Wallace's name was put in nomination, the delegates burst into boos and hisses. Wallace was sitting in the rear of the hall with his wife, Ilo; he looked stunned. "His mouth was half-open, in that unbelieving half-openness. He was stooped a bit forward," Perkins wrote, "listening, but his eyes were way off. I could have spoken to him, and I'm sure he would not have heard me. He had a face of utter, blank suffering." Perkins moved in front of him as though to protect him from the furious delegates. His wife looked equally crushed, "reeling." "You could see it. Her brain was reeling inside her head. The antagonism was crushing." Eleanor Roosevelt took Ilo's hand.

Harold Ickes wired that he might be an acceptable alternative. "Dear old Harold," Roosevelt said. "He'd get fewer votes even than Wallace in that convention."

After various vice-presidential candidates had been nominated, Eleanor Roosevelt spoke to the convention. She urged the delegates to "rise above considerations which are narrow and partisan. This is a time when it is the United States we fight for." Jim Farley, listening intently and gauging the reaction of the delegates, believed that she had carried the day for the Iowan, but despite all the pressure the Roosevelt forces could bring to bear, Wallace had only 500 of the necessary 551 votes at the end of the balloting. At that point Michigan and Massachusetts, which had abstained, cast their votes for Wallace. The final tally was 627 votes for the secretary of agriculture. Rexford Tugwell called Wallace's nomination the "Roosevelt gambit for the preservation of the New Deal in spite of the bosses' reluctance."

Roosevelt was delighted by the news and sent word that he would address the delegates by radio from Washington. As he spoke, a spotlight shone on a huge portrait suspended from the ceiling of the hall. "Lying awake, as I have many nights, I have asked myself whether I have the right, as Commander-in-Chief of the Army and Navy, to call men and women to serve their country or train themselves to serve, and, at the same time, decline to serve my country in my own personal capacity, if I am called upon to do so by the people of my country. . . . Today, all my private plans, all private lives, have been in a sense repealed by an overriding public danger. In the face of that public danger all those who can be of service to the Republic have no choice but to offer themselves for service in those capacities for which they may be fitted. . . . I had made plans for myself, plans for a private life . . . but my conscience will not let me turn my back on a call to service."

The time had come for a direct challenge to the isolationists. Roosevelt reaffirmed his determination to support Great Britain in its desperate struggle against the armies of Hitler. "I would not undo, if I could," Roosevelt declared, "the efforts I made to prevent war. . . . I do not recant the sentiments of sympathy with all free peoples resisting such aggression, or begrudge the material aid that we have given to them. I do not regret my consistent endeavor to awaken this country to the menace for us and all we hold dear. . . . As long as I am President, I will do all I can to insure that that foreign policy remains our foreign policy."

Jim Farley, angry at his defeat, "took a walk" and resigned as chairman of the Democratic National Committee. Edward Flynn took the job, with the understanding that the hard-line New Dealers like Hopkins and Wallace be kept under wraps.

Norman Thomas ran, of course, on the Socialist ticket, as he had done since 1924, and Roger Babson of Massachusetts on the Prohibition ticket. Earl Browder was the candidate of the Communist Party. Thomas, who believed that the New Deal had stolen much of the Socialist program from him, ridiculed Willkie as the "Me too" candidate. "He agreed with Mr. Roosevelt's entire program of social reform and said it is leading to disaster," Thomas noted.

Walter Lippmann announced his support for Willkie. In a remarkable replay of his attitude toward Wilson when the latter resisted entering the European war in support of the Allies long after Lippmann had begun calling for American participation, Lippmann became increasingly disenchanted with the President. Roosevelt was, in the journalist's view, weak and vacillating, taking the nation's isolationist pulse rather than providing the strong leadership that Lippmann believed the country needed. He fired off frequent letters of advice to the Republican candidate. The confused and drifting temper of the public opinion, he told Willkie, was due to the fact that the voters wanted the "assurance of a strong, competent man. Roosevelt is not a strong, competent man, and that is where you can beat him if you take 'the hard line' and summon the people rather than vaguely trying to please them all."

In spite of the fact that William Allen White declared himself "fond" of the President, he remained true to his Republican faith and gave his wholehearted support to Wendell Willkie. Like Walter Lippmann, he became a kind of unofficial adviser, urging Willkie to "attack the fundamental domestic policy of the New Deal" and warn the voters of the dangers of excessive government planning which turned men into wooden figures, "powerless human sheep . . . a social and political eunuch. The people are ready to hear this. They are yearning for new leadership."

Undoubtedly the most dramatic defection from Democratic ranks was that of John L. Lewis. The break between the President and Lewis was signaled by an article in *Collier's*, in which Lewis declared, "Political malignity, springing from a determination to destroy all who cannot be controlled, has conducted an organized campaign to stir a fury of rage against us, both at home and on the firing lines abroad. No other labor executive or union has been subjected to any such bitter, cruel and sustained attack." At the CIO convention Lewis tried to whip up enthusiasm for the old Progressive war-horse and isolationist Burton K. Wheeler as an alternative to Roosevelt. Lewis's supporters broke loose after his speech with a wild demonstration, but the Hillman delegates were conspicuous by their nonparticipation. It was only five years since Lewis had ushered in the new age of union power and prominence by socking Big Bill Hutcheson on the nose. Now the ranks of labor were split over the reelection of the man who had, next to Lewis himself, been the hero of the working class. The glory days were over. The war between capital and labor, which had torn the country since the Great Strikes of 1877, had finally ended; there would be more battles and skirmishes, to be sure, but the right of workers to organize and to bargain collectively for a larger share of capitalist pie would never again be seriously challenged. By the same token "Labor" with a capital *L* and the "Workers" with a capital *W* would never again fire the imaginations of intellectuals and reformers as they had in earlier decades, most dramatically in the decade of the 1930s.

As publicity director for the CIO Len De Caux was with Lewis in a Washington radio station when Lewis and Hiram Johnson made a national broadcast for Wendell Willkie. De Caux reflected upon the irony of the occasion: Hiram Johnson, the champion of the Progressives, running mate of Theodore Roosevelt in the Bull Moose days, paired with the most famous labor leader of the day in opposition to Franklin Roosevelt and the New Deal.

In an act of astonishing hubris an angry Lewis announced that if Wendell Willkie were not elected President, he, Lewis, would resign his long-held office as president of the United Mine Workers. To Len De Caux, "the Willkie ploy was Lewis's device for bowing out."

At the same time that he was enchanting the Communists with his denunciation of Roosevelt's imperialist war, Lewis was conspiring for their downfall. He supported a resolution at the CIO convention that read: "We neither accept nor desire—and we firmly reject—consideration of any policies emanating fom totalitarianism, dictatorships, and foreign ideologies such as Nazism, and fascism. They have no place in this great modern labor movement."

The resolution was bitter medicine for those delegates who were Communists. Lee Pressman had been prevailed upon to submit the resolution. To Len De Caux it was a "degrading moment." Pressman's face was that of "a troubled man," a man saying to himself, "See, I don't shrink. This I must do. I do it!" No one rose to protest. Philip Murray, presiding, declared the voice vote unanimous. The submission of the left, in the opinion of De Caux, "helped preserve formal CIO unity for many progressive purposes."

In the midst of the presidential campaign there was a sudden alarm. One of Henry Wallace's liabilities in the minds of many of those close to the President was his alleged involvement in spiritualism. A Washington rumor was that the price of corn was determined by his medium's answer to the questions he directed at the spirits. The Republican National Committee got its hands on correspondence between Wallace and his medium with the intention of making it public and thereby damaging the Democratic ticket. The Democrats' own intelligence network discovered the plan, and Roosevelt was shown copies of the letters. He showed them to William Douglas and asked, "How does one get rid of his Vice-Presidential running mate?" Douglas looked into the matter and reported that there would have to be another convention.

"My God" was Roosevelt's response.

As Hopkins and Douglas left the Oval Room, Hopkins said, "This may kill the Old Man."

But fortune smiled on the Democrats. They got word of Willkie's affair with a young woman in New York, and a deal was struck: no Wallace letters; no exposure of Willkie's peccadillo.

The America First Committee, formed to spearhead the isolationists, was a strangely mixed bag: old Socialists like Norman Thomas, last-ditch pacifists like Robert Hutchins, native Fascists like Gerald L. K. Smith, old Progressives like William Borah, Burton K. Wheeler, and Gerald Nye; and Charles and Mary Beard, the reformer-historians. John L. Lewis's daughter, Kathryn, was a prominent member of the America First Committee. The Communists joined in the chorus: "The Yanks are not coming!" The hard core of Communists held fast to the Soviet line. "We paid for it, though," Steve Nelson reflected later.

The Republican-Communist alliance did not escape the notice of the President. In a speech in Brooklyn Roosevelt declared: "Something evil is happening in this country when a full page advertisement against this administration, paid for by Republican supporters, appears—where, of all places?—in the *Daily Worker*, the newspaper of the Communist Party.

"Something evil is happening in this country when vast quantities of Republican campaign literature are distributed by organizations that make no secret of their admiration for the dictatorship form of government."

While Willkie had billed himself as an internationalist and "one-worlder," the pull of Midwestern isolationism proved too strong to resist. In addition, Willkie, long on a kind of engaging homespun charm—Harold Ickes coined the unforgettable phrase a "barefoot boy from Wall Street"—was not a man of notably strong character. He began denouncing Roosevelt as a warmonger. That he had touched a responsive chord was indicated by the fact that he began, for the first time in the campaign, to gain ground on the President in the opinion polls.

Isolationism was the only issue on which America Firsters and Communists were in agreement. In a Gallup Poll 83 percent of Americans expressed opposition to direct American involvement in the war. The *New Masses* published a statement of the League of American Writers with the names of 300 members who opposed the involvement of the United States in the war. The California chapter included John Steinbeck, Upton Sinclair, and Donald Ogden Stewart. To Waldo Frank in the summer of 1940 it seemed as though the birds of cynicism and uninvolvement had come home to roost. He was especially dismayed over the attitude of the youth of America, who, in his words, smoldered "in a sullen quandary." They seemed to live in a "schizoid world," oscillating between "the isolation of the Youth Congress . . . based upon the false assumption that American institutions can survive in a fascist world," and the illusion that "socialism, by some miracle, will 'capture' the fascist revolution when it is completed." In an article in the *Nation* entitled "American Inventory," Frank announced his final disenchantment with the Communists, who were "wrong, criminally, because they are dishonest" in their dream of falling heir to the ruins of a "fascist world," rendered impotent by war. It seemed to Frank that the nation had been corrupted "by the prostrate pragmatism of Professor Dewey and by the empirical rationalism of all our liberal schools. . . ." These forces had militated against the "creative mind." Frank wrote: "As our world dies, perhaps our cultural life will find in its new trial a new passion and depth, and that knowledge of human tragedy which is the fire of creation." This could come only by upholding "the sanctity of man [and] the channeling of the religious energy of human growth into new democratic forms. . . ." All this was vague enough but suggested the way the intellectual wind was blowing.

In a somber counterpoit to the American presidential campaign, Great Britain fought for its life. On August 8, the Luftwaffe began an all-out aerial assault on the island nation. Some 2,600 fighters and bombers were assigned to prepare the way for a German invasion. Day and night German bombers flew sorties against British shipping, against airfields, against factories, and against major cities. The outnumbered British sent up their newly developed fighter planes, the Spitfires, to oppose the German planes. The Germans took heavy casualties. Each day newspapers printed the tallies on which the nation's survival was assumed to depend. The dramatic struggle was soon known as the Battle of Britain; it reached its denouement on September 15, when the British claimed to have shot down 183 German fighters and bombers. While the figure was later found to be a more modest 56, it was still too much for the Luftwaffe to tolerate. The German attacks dropped sharply, and on October 11 Winston Churchill proclaimed a British victory of a kind. At the cost of 915 British fighters, the Germans had suffered losses, according to the prime minister, of 2,698. In fact, the Germans had lost 1,733 planes, but they were unable to sustain the all-out assault. If they had planned an air and sea invasion, they were forced to abandon it. The intensity and drama of the battle, on the outcome of which many Americans believed the future of the United States and the world itself depended, gave the presidential campaign an eerie quality and, it must be assumed, helped the President substantially.

Recalling the terrible years of 1916 and 1917, when German submarines sank uncounted tons of British shipping, Winston Churchill, pleading for help from America, told Roosevelt that if the United States refused to sell Great Britain fifty old destroyers, relics of the earlier war, he doubted that his nation could survive. "The whole fate of the war may be decided by this minor and easily remediable factor. Mr. President, with great respect, I must tell you . . . this is a thing to do now." Churchill's proposal that the United States "lend" Britain the destroyers in return for American leases on British air and sea bases in the Western Hemisphere helped neutralize the isolationists. "Congress is going to raise hell about this," Roosevelt said to Grace Tully, "but even another day's delay may mean the end of civilization." Wendell Willkie supported the destroyer agreement, and it was concluded in September.

Funds had also been approved for a 70 percent increase in the size of the navy and the building of a modern air force, but the question of how to provide the manpower to sail the ships, fly the airplanes, and defend the nation in the event of war was a touchy issue. Roosevelt remembered very vividly the resistance to conscription at the entry of the United States into the First World War and the repression called forth by that resistance. The nation, in a real sense, had still not recovered from that trauma. Much of the isolationist sentiment derived from it. Treading cautiously, Roosevelt appointed a committee to make recommendations about the best way to fill up the ranks of the armed forces. Headed by the distinguished lawyer Grenville Clark, the committee, as expected, recommended a draft, with generous exemptions for "conscientious objectors," whose beliefs made them unwilling to take up arms. Once again Willkie supported Roosevelt's decision to give effect to the committee's recommendations by instituting a draft as the most equitable way of providing the human cadres required to bring the nation into a state of preparedness for war. A majority of the Republican Congressmen opposed the draft. Burton K. Wheeler spoke for them when he declared: "Enact peacetime conscription and no longer will this be a free land—no longer will a citizen be able to say he disagrees with a government edict. Hushed whispers will replace free speech—secret meetings in dark places will supplant free assemblage—labor and industry, men and women will be shackled by the chains they have themselves forged."

Passed on September 16, the Selective Service Act, also known as the Burke-Wadsworth bill, provided for an army of no more than 900,000 to be recruited and trained for a year "unless Congress declares that the national security is imperilled, when such service may be extended by the President to such time as may be necessary in the interest of national defense."

Roosevelt set October 16 as the date for young men to register for the draft. The drawing of the first draft numbers took place two weeks later (a week before the election). The President participated in the drawing ceremony, in which a blindfolded Stimson reached into a large jar, pulled out a number, and handed it to FDR, who opened it and declared resonately: "The first number which has been handed to me is number one five eight."

Working with his writers on a speech to be delivered at Boston, the President received a telegram from an apprehensive Edward Flynn. The most frequent concern Flynn heard expressed by voters around the country was over American involvement in the war. He urged the President to include in his speech a specific disavowal of any intention to send American soldiers overseas. Roosevelt responded to the suggestion impatiently. "How often do they expect me to say that?" he asked Robert E. Sherwood. "It's in the Democratic platform and I've repeated it a hundred times."

"I know it, Mr. President," Sherwood replied, "but they don't seem to have heard you the first time. Evidently you've got to say it again— and again—and again."

Roosevelt yielded reluctantly. He may well have had in mind Wilson's repeated assurances in the campaign of 1916 that he would never involve American boys in *that* European war. He would add, after his promise to the parents of young men drafted into the services to take good care of their sons, another pledge: "And while I am talking to you mothers and fathers, I give you one more assurance.

"I have said this before, but I shall say it again and again and again.

"Your boys are not going to be sent into any foreign wars."

Rosenman proposed that he add "except in case of attack."

"Of course we'll fight if we're attacked. If somebody attacks us, then it isn't a foreign war, is it?"

The night of the election Harry Hopkins visited Hyde Park to find Roosevelt established in the dining room amid a bewildering array of charts for tallying the incoming votes, and ticker tape machines and telephones tied in to Democratic campaign headquarters in New York City. The early returns ran strongly to Willkie, but Roosevelt retained his cheerful optimism. By ten o'clock it was clear that Roosevelt was winning, and an hour later Flynn claimed victory. The Hyde Park neighbors gathered in a torchlight procession, one of them holding aloft a sign that read "SAFE ON 3RD."

Roosevelt received only 55 percent of the popular vote, but he took thirty-eight states with 449 electoral votes to ten states for Willkie with 82 electoral votes. Norman Thomas got his usual 100,000-plus votes, Babson 57,812, and Browder 48,579 (a decrease from the 80,181 he had received in 1936). The principal losers in the presidential campaign of 1940 were the Communists. They were required to defend the Russian-German nonaggression pact, Germany's invasion of Poland, the division of Poland between Germany and Russia, and Russia's assault on Finland. Moreover, since Germany and Russia were allies, the Communists were required to oppose all American defense measures on the ground that any friend of Great Britain was an enemy of Germany and its ally Russia. An endorsement of American neutrality would have been relatively innocuous, but the strident denunciation of all measures designed to check the Axis powers was too much to swallow. What the signing of the nonaggression pact had begun—the disillusionment of all those large and small *c* communists capable of disillusionment—the presidential campaign of 1940 completed. Communism and the Communist Party, USA, would never again be an important factor in American life.

With the election over, Roosevelt felt less inhibited in stressing the theme that Britain's war was our war as well. "We must be the great arsenal of democracy," he declared in a fireside chat in December, 1940. "For us this is an emergency as serious as war itself. We must apply ourselves to our task with the same resolution, the same sense of urgency, the same spirit of patriotism and sacrifice as we would show were we at war." He repeated his conviction that the United States could stay out of a shooting war. "There is far less chance of the United States getting into war, if we do all we can now to support the nations defending themselves against attack by the Axis than if we acquiesce in their defeat, submit tamely to an Axis victory, and wait our turn to be the object of attack in another war later on." The argument was virtually the same that Woodrow Wilson had used in the preparedness phase of the First World War.

# 45

# War

A month after the presidential election Roosevelt received an urgent communication from Churchill: "The moment approaches when we shall no longer be able to pay cash for shipping and other supplies." Roosevelt's solution was what he called lend-lease. At a press conference on December 17, 1940, he unveiled his scheme. "Suppose my neighbor's home catches fire, and I have a length of garden hose four or five hundred feet away. If I can take my garden hose and connect it up with his hydrant, I may help him put out the fire. Now what do I do? I don't say to him before that operation, 'Neighbor, my garden hose cost me fifteen dollars; you have to pay me fifteen dollars for it.' No! What is the transaction that goes on? I don't want fifteen dollars—I want my garden hose after the fire is over."

In his annual message to Congress on January 6, 1941, the President outlined his plan and dismissed the notion that the Axis powers could consider it a breach of America's neutrality. "Such aid is not an act of war, even if a dictator should unilaterally proclaim it so to be. When the dictators are ready to make war upon us, they will not wait for an act of war on our part. They did not wait for Norway or Belgium or the Netherlands to commit an act of war." The Allies were fighting for freedom everywhere, for a world "founded upon four essential human freedoms . . . freedom of speech and expression, freedom of religion, freedom from want and freedom from fear—everywhere in the world."

HR 1776, entitled "An Act to Further Promote the Defense of the United States and Other Purposes," went to Congress on January 10. The Committee to Defend America by Aiding the Allies rallied to its support while the isolationists, led by the America Firsters, rushed to do battle against it. Wendell Willkie gave it his support, telling a Senate committee, "I struggled as hard as I could to beat Franklin Roosevelt, and I tried to keep from pulling any of my punches. He was elected President. He is my President now." Burton Wheeler denounced lend-lease as the "New Deal's triple-A foreign policy," which would "plow under every fourth American boy." Roosevelt's reply was heated. "That is really the rottenest thing that has ever been said in public life in my generation," he told a reporter, adding, "Quote me on that."

After two months of often acrimonious debate the Lend-Lease Act was passed by a large margin in March, 1941. Churchill called it the "most unsordid act in the history of any nation." The pedagogue-President had educated his constituent pupils patiently and tactfully, bringing the country, in the main, to his position: that the Allies were fighting a critically important war against what was uncontestably the most malignant combination of forces in modern history. That it should have taken so long a time and demanded such forensic skills testified to the depth of American disillusionment with the outcome of the earlier war "to make the world safe for democracy." The two conflicts were, in some respects, deceptively similar. Once again Germany was the principal villain, but the Germany that led the Axis powers in 1940 was a far more dangerous nation than that of the kaiser. The European war that began in 1914 with the murder of Archduke Franz Ferdinand at Sarajevo could be accurately characterized as a capitalist-imperialist struggle of a corrupt and decadent order in which the upper classes, swollen with greed and arrogance, fought to preserve or extend their privileges and vindicate their national honor. Although it was a war unsurpassed in the horror of its fighting and in the terrible toll of the dead and maimed, it took place, nonetheless, within the context of a civilization that, whatever its faults (and they were surely grievous), accepted, if it did not always honor them, certain ancient values. The Germany of Adolf Hitler was, in the profoundest sense of the word, an outlaw nation led by a murderous psychopath, a man who prided himself on standing outside the bounds of decency and humanity. That Americans should have thought for a moment that they could endure the triumph of such a monstrous evil without themselves taking up arms against it is surely a wonder; it says a great deal about our collective view of life or perhaps our incomprehension of the reality of evil in the world. The isolationists were, after all, neither stupid nor wicked men. They were intelligent and loyal Americans, acting, as they believed, in the interests of their beloved country. Many of them were men distinguished throughout long and useful lives by their devotion to the common good, to the happiness and well-being of their fellow citizens.

After the presidential election Harry Hopkins, ailing and with no official position, moved into the White House as Roosevelt's closest aide. He lived in a suite of rooms and paid rent, a kind of minister without portfolio. His first important assignment was to go to England to confer with Churchill about Anglo-American cooperation and to find out what reat Britain needed most to sustain it in a war which, in Roosevelt's view, was as much America's war as Britain's.

In his position as first lord of the admiralty Winston Churchill had begun a correspondence with Roosevelt on the prospects of holding off the Germans. He had signed himself "Naval Person." Now the correspondence flourished, with Churchill as calling himself "Former Naval Person." While Joseph Kennedy continued to send dispatches of the gloomiest nature, predicting the fall of Britain before a German invasion, Churchill assured Roosevelt that his nation was determined to resist to the last man and, most important, had the capability to do so, especially with help from the United States.

Roosevelt announced to the press that he was sending Hopkins to England "so that he can talk to Churchill like an Iowa farmer," a sly poke at Hopkins's efforts to stress his Midwestern origins, which were, to be sure, smalltown but hardly rural. The meeting turned out to be highly congenial. Churchill, who had been warned by Felix Frankfurter that Hopkins was excessively sensitive in regard to Roosevelt's standing as a world leader, was fulsome in praise of his American counterpart, although he hardly needed such prompting; he and Roosevelt were, after all, "old salts." Almost equally important, Churchill and Hopkins hit it off well. Later Churchill, in writing of their first meeting, called Hopkins "that extraordinary man, who played, and was to play, a sometimes decisive part in the whole movement of the war. His was a soul that flamed out of a frail and failing body. He was a crumbling lighthouse from which there shone the beams that led great fleets to harbour. He had also the gift of sardonic humour." And to Roosevelt Churchill wrote: "I am most grateful to you for sending so remarkable an envoy who enjoys so high a measure of your intimacy and confidence." Hopkins, for his part, fell completely under the spell of Churchill's formidable personality, assuring Roosevelt that "He is the one and only person over here with whom you need to have a full meeting of minds." Hopkins was convinced that a speedy meeting between the two leaders was "essential." He added in a wire, "This island needs our help now, Mr. President, with everything we can give them," and he assured his British hosts that the "President is one with your Prime Minister in his determination to break the ruthless power of that sinful psychopath of Berlin."

With France having surrendered to the Nazis and Britain itself under the threat of an imminent amphibious assault, Churchill sometimes seemed to Hopkins more preoccupied with Great Britain's colonial possessions than with its existence. England was like a drowning man who clings to a bar of gold that is dragging him down to destruction. "I know perfectly well," Hopkins told Churchill and the chiefs of staff of the British forces, "that all of you here in Britain are determined to go on fighting to hold the Middle East at all costs and it's difficult for you to understand the American attitude. But you have got to remember that we in the United States just simply do not understand your problems in the Middle East, and the interests of the Moslem World, and the interrelationship of your problems in Egypt and India."

In the spring of 1941 the President seemed vacillating and uncertain to at least some of his Cabinet members. Harold Ickes professed to find "a growing discontent with the President's lack of leadership. He still has the country if he will take it and lead it. But he won't have it much longer unless he does something. It won't be sufficient for him to make another speech and then go into a state of innocuous desuetude again." Hopkins, Ickes grumbled, was unwilling to oppose the President on anything for fear of losing "his place under the President's bed."

The fact was that Roosevelt was tormented by the memory of Woodrow Wilson. His uncertainty was indicated by the fact that he postponed a scheduled speech on Pan-American relations on the ground that he was too sick to deliver it, an illness that Missy LeHand described as a "case of sheer exasperation." When he got down to drafting it with the aid of Sherwood and Rosenman, he found that Sherwood had inserted the sentence "I hereby proclaim that an unlimited national emergency exists." A startled Roosevelt exclaimed: "What's *this*? Hasn't somebody been taking liberties?" Sherwood said that he had been urged by Hopkins to put in the sentence. Cordell Hull was dubious, but it stayed in. When FDR delivered the talk in the East Room of the White House, he declared: "Our patrols are helping now to ensure delivery of the needed supplies to Britain. All additional measures necessary to deliver the goods will be taken. Any and all further methods or combinations of methods which can and should be utilized are being devised by our military and naval technicians who, with me, will work out and put into effect such new and additional safeguards as may be needed.

"I will say that the delivery of needed supplies to Britain is imperative. I say this can be done; it must be done; it will be done."

Having spoken so boldly, Roosevelt waited apprehensively for the public reaction. He was delighted when the ratio of letters and telegrams ran 95 percent favorable. He had dared hope for only 50 percent support. Yet he drew back at a press conference. He had no intention of invoking the emergency powers. He still hoped to avoid war. When a German U-boat sank the American freighter SS *Robin Moor* on May 21, Roosevelt ordered all German and Italian assets in the United States frozen and their consulates closed on the ground that they were being used for espionage.

A critical issue was that of having American naval ships protect convoys of merchant ships carrying war materials to Great Britain. If American supplies were sunk in the Atlantic by German U-boats, they were obviously of little use to the Allies. But Roosevelt was reluctant to order American naval vessels to take on such a mission; he was well aware that it would be counted as another step on the way to all-out war. Pressed by Stimson and Knox, he procrastinated, although he agreed to have American planes and ships radio to British warships the locations of German U-boats and naval vessels. A few weeks later, on May 24, 1941, Ensign Leonard Smith, flying a patrol mission in a Catalina, spotted the huge German battleship *Bismarck*, which, having recently sunk the British heavy cruiser *Hood*, was "hiding out" in the South Atlantic. Smith's sighting was relayed to the Royal Navy, which closed in with ships and planes and sank the *Bismarck* in one of the most important naval engagements of the war.

Meanwhile, there were indications that the German-Russian alliance was deteriorating. In August, 1940, Germany had adjusted the borders between Hungary and Rumania without informing the Russians, and a month later Hitler concluded a mutual defense treaty with Italy and Japan. Stalin suspected it was a move directed at Russia, but the Germans assured him that the United States was the target. Matters were not improved when Molotov traveled to Berlin in November for discussions with Hitler. The meetings were not a success. Molotov had been stiff and unyielding, displaying the characteristic Russian paranoia. Hitler tried unsuccessfully to charm him and was as much offended by Molotov's personal unresponsiveness as by his rigidity on particular issues. The day after Molotov had left Berlin, Hitler gave orders to start planning for Barbarossa, the code name for an attack on Russia.

On June 22, 1941, Germany invaded Russia. The shock and alarm of Stalin and those around him who had been the architects of the nonaggression pact were only slightly greater than those of experts and scholars of international relations around the world. Charles Bohlen, unhappy in an assignment to the American Embassy in Tokyo, was among those Soviet experts who were caught by surprise. He was astonished that Hitler, already engaged on the "western front" with Britain, should have opened the "second front" against Russia that the nonaggression pact was designed to avoid. Hitler, as well as the Allies, could forget the lessons of history, it seemed. That Hitler intended all along to destroy bolshevism can hardly be doubted; it was his timing that raised eyebrows and that carried the seeds of the destruction of his splendid German armies and of Hitler himself. But for the moment he seemed invincible on all fronts. France was prostrate, and Britain, still bombarded by the Luftwaffe, in a perilous state. Hitler was confident that his soldiers could smash the unwieldy Russian legions as quickly and decisively as they had routed the Poles and the French, considered far superior to the Russians in training and equipment. In tanks and in planes—the feared Stuka dive-bombers, the Messerschmitts and the Focke-Wulf long-distance bombers—in the tactics of the new mechanized forces, the Germans were so superior to the Russians as to beggar comparison.

The Germans advanced swiftly, and it seemed a foregone conclusion that Russia could hold out for only a few months; Secretary of War Stimson made the estimate of a maximum of three months. There was little sympathy for Russia in the United States. That country had, after all, encouraged and supported Hitler's adventures in Europe and participated, vulturelike, in the dismemberment of Poland. Now it was reaping the rewards of its perfidy. The invasion provided a "temporary breather" for Great Britain. Stimson's advisers, he wrote Roosevelt, "were unanimously of the belief that this precious and unforeseen period of respite should be used to push with the utmost vigor our movements in the Atlantic theater of operations."

The Communist Party of the United States immediately sent down the new line to its bewildered but dutiful members. What had been an imperialist war yesterday became a noble struggle against fascism today (it had, of course, prior to the German-Russian nonaggression pact, been a laudable popular front against fascism). All the dedicated hewers to the party line raised a clamor for the United States to come to the assistance of the heroic Russians, who had been shamelessly cheated and deceived by the German dictator. For those party members and fellow travelers who had fallen reluctantly into line with the nonaggression pact, the German attack on Russia was the end of a nightmare. All those homebred Communists still capable of understanding the notion of morality, private or public (and there were undoubtedly many), had suffered considerable agony of spirit over Stalin's embracing of Hitler. That dilemma at least was resolved by Hitler's invasion.

With Germany's invasion of Russia, the Soviets became applicants for American aid. The Russian ambassador to England, Ivan Maisky, during his visit to England to confer with Churchill, conveyed Stalin's request for a second front against Hitler in northern France. "A front in the North of France," Stalin argued, "besides diverting Hitler's forces from the East would make impossible the invasion of Britain by Hitler." When Harry Hopkins met Maisky in England, the Russian repeated his plea for a second front. According to Maisky, Hopkins replied: "We in the USA are a non-belligerent country now, and cannot do anything to help you in regard to a second front. But as regards supplies, things are different. . . . We are providing Britain with much in the way of armaments, raw materials, ships and so on. We could give you quite a lot. . . . But what do you require?" Maisky's response was that Hopkins should go to Moscow and talk to Stalin.

The President lost no time in offering a helping hand to the Russians. "I deem it of paramount importance for the safety and security of America that all reasonable munitions help be provided for Russia," he wrote Henry Stimson. When Hopkins suggested that a trip to confer with Stalin might be fruitful, Roosevelt quickly concurred. Hopkins, ailing as he was, departed for the USSR. Stalin impressed

Hopkins by his physical presence—"a football coach's dream of a tackle," he wrote. "He talked as he knew his troops were shooting—straight and hard. . . . He shook my hand briefly, firmly, courteously. He smiled warmly. There was no waste of word, gesture, nor mannerism. It was like talking to a perfectly coordinated machine, an intelligent machine. . . . There is no small talk in him. His humor is keen." Stalin's needs were considerable: a million rifles, machine guns, antiaircraft, gasoline, and aluminum. "Give us antiaircraft guns and the aluminum and we can fight for three or four years," he told Hopkins. He also urged Hopkins to try to prevail on Roosevelt to declare war against Germany. "He repeatedly said," Hopkins noted, "that the President of the United States had more influence with the common people of the world today than any other force." Perhaps Hopkins's most important service was to convince Roosevelt that Russia was determined to stay in the war. Churchill persisted in his opinion that the Soviets must capitulate in a few months.

In July, when Japan invaded Indochina, Roosevelt issued a warning to the Japanese ambassador. If his nation persisted in trying to seize the oil resources of Southeast Asian countries, the United States would join the Dutch and British in sanctions against Japan, and "an exceedingly serious situation would immediately result." Roosevelt then froze some $131,000,000 of Japanese assets in the United States and cut off a trade with Japan that brought in 80 percent of the island nation's oil. Ickes described Roosevelt's policy as not drawing "the noose tight. He thought it better to . . . give it a jerk now and then." Japan was left, in the words of Charles Bohlen, with three alternatives: "One course was to abandon all imperialist pursuits on the continent of Asia, to withdraw from Indochina and China and make a deal with the United States in order to ensure the resumption of oil imports. The second alternative was to accept slow strangulation. The third alternative was to fight."

If we accept Bohlen's analysis, it might well be argued that the United States forced Japan to attack it. Of course, it did not appear that way to the State Department and to the President. Something had, they felt, to be done to check the voracious and apparently insatiable appetite of the Japanese for gobbling up all of Southeast Asia and the Pacific islands. Rather as Hitler completely underestimated the endurance of the Russian people, an endurance which had little to do with communism or Marxism, Roosevelt took too light a view of the Japanese war-making potential. It was ironic that Franklin Roosevelt's cousin Theodore had made a far more realistic assessment of Japanese naval and military power in the early years of the century than FDR did with, presumably, a much more sophisticated and extensive intelligence network to keep him informed. It is not saying too much to assert that while a major aim of the first Roosevelt's foreign policy was to give Japan no cause for making war on the United States, the second Roosevelt seemed determined to provoke a conflict.

Charles Bohlen pointed out another problem in American policy toward Japan. Many Americans, among them politically influential people, felt a strong emotional attachment to China and considered Japan a ruthless dictatorship which was feeding on the helpless body of China. What we might call the missionary lobby, made up in large part of ex-missionaries and their offspring, was especially active on behalf of China and in expressions of hostility toward Japan. In Bohlen's words, "The immense sympathy for China . . . limited Roosevelt's ability to talk with Tokyo." More basic was the more or less subconscious underlying conviction that the Japanese, despite their aggressions against large and small Asian nations, were not a first-class military and naval power on a par with the United States and European nations. It was thus the case that while Japan had grown vastly stronger in military technology and war-making potential since the beginning of the century, it had, in the intervening years, lost ground in the West's perception of its military and naval might. In short, it was taken more casually (and with much more hostility) in 1941 than it had been in 1906 after the Russo-Japanese War.

The Selective Service Act, or the draft, was due to expire in August, 1941. General George Marshall, the army chief of staff, and the President both thought it essential to extend the period of service, but there were rebellious mutterings from the ranks of those who had been drafted. The case of the national guardsmen was especially touchy. They were weekend soldiers with jobs and, in many instances, families. They had simply been "Federalized," snatched up for service willy-nilly, and most of them looked forward eagerly to a return to civilian life. The word "OHIO" began to appear ominously on walls and fences; it was short for "Over the Hill in October"—in other words, a threat of mass desertions. All the isolationist and pacifist sentiment in the country crystallized against the extension of the draft. It passed the Senate by a comfortable margin, but in the House the margin was one vote, 203 to 202.

With the United States in the war for all practical purposes, Roosevelt decided he needed to meet and talk with Churchill in secret. Setting out for an ostensible cruise in the yacht *Potomac* in the middle of August, Roosevelt transferred to the cruiser *Augusta* off Martha's Vineyard and rendezvoused with Churchill off Argentia, Newfoundland. Churchill came aboard the *Augusta*, and the two leaders of what was now called the free world sat down to discuss its future.

Churchill and Roosevelt had met last in 1918, when Roosevelt was assistant secretary of the navy and Churchill a leading Member of Parliament, but Churchill, not surprisingly, did not remember the meeting. The two leaders hit it off like two schoolboys. They had the same capacity for taking delight in social situations; they each had a flair, a gift for friendship, a rollicking sense of humor, an ebullience, a common devotion to the ocean and to nautical matters in general. One had the omnipresent cigar: the other, the jaunty cigarette.

At the Atlantic Conference Churchill urged Roosevelt to join formally in the war against the Axis and also to issue a warning to Japan that the West would not endure further extensions of that nation's empire. Roosevelt tactfully but firmly gave Churchill a lecture on American isolationism. In support of his argument he was able to cite the fact that Congress had extended the draft for another nineteen months by only a single vote.

On Sunday, August 10, Roosevelt and a party of sailors and officers from the *Augusta* attended an Anglican service on board the *Prince of Wales*. The combined crews sang "Onward Christian Soldiers" and "For Those in Peril on the Sea." Churchill wept unabashedly and recalled: "It was a great hour to live." Nearly half of those who sang were soon to die in the torpedoing of the battleship.

The Atlantic Conference marked the beginning of a warm friendship between the two leaders. "It is fun to be in the same decade with you," Roosevelt once cabled Churchill. "Fun" was the determinative word. Life was fun; power was fun; politics were fun. Churchill compared Roosevelt's temperament to champagne. He addressed Roosevelt as "Mr. President," while Roosevelt called him "Winston." As Eleanor Roosevelt put it, it was "a fortunate friendship. The war would have been harder to win without it, and the two men might not have gone through it so well if they had not had that personal pleasure in meeting and confidence in each other's integrity and ability."

The most notable fruit of the conference was the Atlantic Charter, which included Roosevelt's Four Freedoms. In the spirit of the Fourteen Points of his Democratic predecessor, Woodow Wilson, the charter pledged the two nations to the principle of self-determination for all peoples and to the ideal of an equitable distribution of the world's goods among all its peoples. Both nations renounced imperial ambitions. Roosevelt did his best to extract from the prime minister some hint that Great Britain might give its colonies independence in the aftermath of a successful war against the Axis powers, but Churchill was no more disposed to discuss such a proposition seriously than the British delegates who had gathered in Paris to draft the Versailles Treaty and had startled their American counterparts by their devotion to the "Empire."

The news of the Roosevelt-Churchill meeting infuriated isolationists, but most of the nation and much of the world were thrilled by the dramatic encounter of the two leaders. A Gallup Poll showed, however, that 74 percent of the country wanted the United States to stay out of the war, although the movement of the nation toward involvement had developed its own irresistible momentum.

Although Churchill and Roosevelt got along "famously" on the personal level, there were frequent differences of opinion and deep ideological divisions. Roosevelt told William Douglas that he was offended by the way in which Churchill referred to colonial or non-Western people. To Churchill the Chinese were the "pigtails." He wrote: "I believe that as civilized nations become more powerful they will get more ruthless, and the time will come when the world will impatiently bear the existence of barbaric nations who may at any time arm themselves and menace civilized nations. . . . I believe in the ultimate partition of China—I mean ultimate. I hope we shall not have to do it in our day. The Aryan stock is bound to triumph."

Such ideas seemed to Roosevelt "barbaric," and they served to remind him of the substratum of racial arrogance that underlay the otherwise humane and tolerant British people. Although Roosevelt had been nurtured in a thoroughly WASP environment, where a common article of faith was the genetic superiority of Anglo-Saxons over "lesser races," his own innate tact and sensitivity toward the feelings of others preserved him from blatant racism. Knowing the sensitiveness of Oriental people toward Western colonialism, Roosevelt felt, in William Douglas's words, that Americans must be "discreet and courteous in their relations with the colored people of Asia." Moreover, he pressed

Churchill to give India its independence to the point that the prime minister showed his irritation. "Winnie's world is different from mine," Roosevelt declared in frustration.

A few weeks after the Atlantic Conference the navy destroyer *Greer* pursued a German submarine near Iceland. The intention of its captain was to track the submarine by sonar while radioing the British its position so that they could hunt it down. The submarine commander, well aware of the nature of the dangerous game, fired a torpedo at the *Greer*. The *Greer* dropped depth charges. The Germans fired another torpedo, and the *Greer* turned away. A few days later, after the death of his mother at the age of eighty-seven, Roosevelt referred to the encounter in a fireside chat, calling the submarine the aggressor. He accused the Germans of "piracy—legally and morally. . . . We sought no shooting war with Hitler. We do not seek it now." But the United States was determined to "keep open the line of legitimate commerce. . . . When you see a rattlesnake poised to strike, you do not wait until it has struck before you crush him. These Nazi submarines and raiders are the rattlesnakes of the Atlantic. . . . " The navy, to protect itself, must now "shoot on sight." Again the isolationists protested heatedly that Roosevelt's policy was a *de facto* declaration of war, a war that the American people had repeatedly indicated they did not want. And so the strange game went on: war by accretion; war by inches; war with the reluctant acquiescence of the nation.

The Germans were not slow to respond. If U-boats were to be crushed on sight like rattlesnakes, they were ready to strike without warning. A month after the *Greer*, the destroyer *Kearny* was hit by a torpedo and eleven of its crew were killed. On Navy Day, announcing the U-boat attack, Roosevelt declared: "The U.S.S. *Kearny* is not just a Navy ship. She belongs to every man, woman and child in this Nation." A bit thick, but it was a desperate and emotional time, and some hyperbole was justified.

Four days later the *Reuben James* was sunk 600 miles west of Iceland; 115 officers and men lost their lives in the frigid waters of the North Atlantic. Yet Roosevelt felt instinctively that the American people were still not ready to accept a formal declaration of war against the Axis powers.

Hitler had much to gain and nothing to lose by an indefinite extension of the war that was not a war. If America could not make up its mind, so much the better: It could not muster its full force against the Axis powers; it could not dispatch its bombers over German cities or its battleships against the remnants of the German Navy. It could not challenge Italy's control of the Mediterranean or help defend the British Isles against invasion. Roosevelt was, in practical fact, at the mercy of Hitler in the sense that he needed some dramatic act of provocation in order to be confident of entering the war with a united nation behind him. He was acutely aware of Wilson's fate and determined to do his best to avoid it. In the words of Robert Sherwood, "He had no more tricks left. The hat from which he had pulled so many rabbits was empty." But for a child of fortune the game is never lost. If the Germans were unwilling to provide Roosevelt with an unequivocal *casus belli*, an appropriate cause of war, the Japanese, it turned out, were willing to oblige.

Adolf Hitler had hoped that his unpredictable ally Japan would aid the Nazi cause by attacking the British possessions in Southeast Asia, but Japan had its own objectives. In the face of the growing tension between the United States and Japan the Japanese premier, Prince Fumimaro Konoye, proposed that he and Roosevelt meet in the waters of Hawaii in order to try to compose the differences between the two countries and avoid war. Roosevelt was favorably disposed to the notion, but Cordell Hull persuaded him that it would be a mistake. Konoye, who felt that he was risking assassination by the war party in Japan for even suggesting such a meeting, lost face as a result of Roosevelt's refusal to meet, and he resigned, to be replaced by the much more militant Hideki Tojo. Roosevelt, alarmed by Konoye's resignation, huddled with Hull, Marshall, Stimson, and Harold Stark, chief of naval operations. Konoye himself tried to reassure the United States through Ambassador Joseph Grew that the new Cabinet did not mean a more aggressive policy on the part of Japan.

When the decision was made, in view of the increasingly tense relationship with Japan, to move the Pacific Fleet to Pearl Harbor, at Honolulu, Hawaii, the admiral of the fleet, James O. Richardson, protested vigorously on the ground that it would be vulnerable to attack by planes based on Japanese aircraft carriers. He was relieved of his command and replaced by Admiral Husband E. Kimmel.

Ambassador Grew, dean of the Western diplomatic corps in Tokyo, warned that an ancient Japanese tradition called for surprise attack as the initial act of war, and in Tokyo a drunken Japanese naval officer told the Peruvian military attaché that the Japanese had plans to attack the American fleet at Pearl Harbor in the event of war between the two countries. The Peruvian informed the American Embassy, which passed word on to Washington, where it was duly filed away and ignored since American intelligence was convinced that the Japanese did not have the capability of attacking Pearl Harbor.

As rumors of a possible surprise attack by the Japanese continued to circulate, Cordell Hull urged the President, vacationing at Warm Springs, to return to Washington. Hull had been meeting almost daily with the Japanese envoys, Kichisaburo Nomura and Saburo Kurusu, and on December 4 an alarmed Roosevelt made the unusual request of congressional leaders that Congress not recess for more than three days. American intelligence had broken the Japanese code, an achievement which was not unambiguous since it gave the Americans the dangerous illusion that they were fully informed of Japanese military plans.

At a Cabinet meeting on December 6 Hull told those present that in his opinion, the Japanese were not negotiating in good faith. They didn't "mean business. I'm sure they don't mean to do anything. With every hour that passes, I have become more convinced that they are not playing in the open, that what they say is equivocal and has two meanings to it. . . . They are the worst people I ever saw." Throughout a desultory conversation "there was never a flicker of expression by anybody," Frances Perkins recalled, "that the Japanese might at that time engage in war with the United States." Roosevelt sent a message to Emperor Hirohito urging further talks. "Both of us for the sake of the peoples not only of our own great countries but for the sake of humanity in neighboring territories, have a sacred duty to restore traditional amity and prevent further death and destruction to the world," the telegram read. The appeal must have seemed the height of hypocrisy to those Japanese who read it. In their view, Roosevelt had, in Ickes's phrase, "drawn the noose" so tight that it threatened to choke them to death.

The same day, December 6, a long message to the Japanese Embassy was decoded and passed on to Roosevelt. When he read it, he handed it to Hopkins with the remark "This means war." To Hopkins's half-serious suggestion that this being the case, the United States should strike first, Roosevelt replied: "No, we can't do that. We are a democracy and a peaceful people. . . . We have a good record."

December 7 was an unseasonably warm day in Washington. Hopkins, recovering from several weeks of hospitalization, had lunch in the Oval Office with the President. "We were talking about things far removed from war," he wrote later, "when at about 1:40 Secretary

Knox called and said they had picked up a radio message from Honolulu from the Commander-in-Chief of our forces there advising all our stations that an air raid was on and that it was 'no drill.' " Hopkins and Roosevelt did not take the report very seriously. There was obviously a mistake. The Japanese could hardly attack Honolulu. Roosevelt reasserted his desire to keep the nation out of war. If the Japanese had actually attacked, the matter would be out of his hands. Twenty-five minutes later the President, still unaware of the seriousness of the Japanese assault, called Hull to tell him of the report and to suggest that he nevertheless go through with a scheduled meeting with the Japanese envoys. At 2:28 Roosevelt received a call from Admiral Stark giving him some notion of the seriousness of the Japanese bombing attacks, but the information passed on by Stark still gave no notion of the devastating effects of the raid. At a hastily called meeting attended by Stimson, Knox, Stark, and Marshall, the atmosphere was, in Hopkins's words, "not too tense because I think that all of us believed that in the last analysis the enemy was Hitler and that he could never be defeated without force of arms; that sooner or later we were bound to be in the war and that Japan had given us an opportunity."

When Churchill called from England, Roosevelt "told him that we were all in the same boat now." He would go to Congress the next day for a declaration of war on the Axis powers. Churchill responded that he would also ask Parliament for a declaration of war against Japan the next morning. Again in Hopkins's words, "The President ordered the Japanese Embassy and all consulates in the United States to be protected and ordered all Japanese citizens to be picked up and placed under careful surveillance." This was to be done by the Department of Justice.

A Cabinet meeting was called, and a somber Roosevelt declared the crisis the most severe the nation had faced since Lincoln called his Cabinet together after the firing on Fort Sumter. After the Cabinet members had departed, the President met with congressional leaders, among them Hiram Johnson. It must have been an odd moment for Johnson, who, almost twenty-five years before, had bitterly opposed another Democratic President's appeal to Congress for a declaration of war. Now the worst that he had feared had come to pass. All the Neutrality Acts which he had strongly supported had been unavailing; the nightmare had again become an actuality. There was some desultory conversation, and the legislators left. Hull and Sumner Welles wanted the President to give a long account of Japanese-American relations in his address to Congress, but Roosevelt, with his surer instinct, decided to keep his message as brief and as dramatic as he could make it. He called Grace Tully to his study. "I'm going before Congress tomorrow, and I'd like to dictate my message. It will be short."

The next morning Eleanor Roosevelt went with her husband to Congress to hear him deliver the war message. "I was living through again . . . the day that President Wilson addressed the Congress to announce our entry into World War I. Now the President of the United States was my husband, and for the second time in my life I heard a president tell the Congress that this nation was engaged in a war. I was deeply unhappy." She thought of her four sons, all at the age for military service. She reflected on the long, difficult process by which Americans had come to face the reality of the world conflict. "With war all about us, we still lived on an 'island' where most people felt that war was an impossibility. Wishful thinking is one of our besetting sins. . . . One could no longer do anything but face the fact that this country was in a war; from here on, difficult and dangerous as the future looked, it presented a clearer challenge than the long uncertainty of the past."

The President read his message from a small black notebook: "Yesterday, December 7, 1941—a date which will live in infamy—the United States was suddenly and deliberately attacked by naval and air forces of the Empire of Japan.

"The United States was at peace with that Nation and, at the solicitation of Japan, was still in conversation with its Government and its Emperor looking toward the maintenance of peace in the Pacific. . . .

"The attack . . . caused severe damage to American naval and military forces. Very many American lives have been lost."

Roosevelt went on to list the other simultaneous attacks of the Japanese: Malaya; Hong Kong; Guam; the Philippines; Wake Island; Midway. "As Commander-in-Chief of the Army and Navy, I have directed that all measures be taken for our defense," he said.

At the end he said: "With confidence in our armed forces—with the unbounded determination of our people—we will gain the inevitable triumph—so help us God."

The President concluded by asking Congress to declare that "a state of war has existed between the United States and the Japanese Empire." The House voted with one dissent, that of Jeannette Rankin of Montana, a friend of Jane Addams's and a founder of the Women's

International League for Peace and Freedom, who had also voted against the United States declaration of war against the Central Powers in 1917.

Josephine Herbst wrote in her diary: "Today all talk on street echoes war, and words Japs, etc. from all sides and at the hour Roosevelt broadcast war, girls and men pouring out of the Automat on 14th Street, huddled around taxicabs to hear the radio . . . at last there *is* War again, so awaited by so many people, with all life suspended in so many ways so long as if it were not worth beginning vast dreams when destruction or violence was so near at hand. It is ten years since Mike Gold said to me, this is no time to write, general war is coming next year, it was said again all through 1934, every time there was a crisis, first Manchukuo, then Ethiopia, and later on, drop by drop, it came, everyone saying this is the war, now coming, and it was coming, too, just as we grow older without truly appreciating it, and near our dying without exactly knowing how."

On December 11 Japan and Germany declared war on the United States. Hitler did so with reluctance. He had wished to avoid drawing the United States into the war. He hated, despised, and feared Franklin Roosevelt, and now Roosevelt would become his nemesis.

It was no wonder that the isolationists wept in their beers and cursed their fate. No wonder that they expended extraordinary ingenuity in "proving" that the President had, in effect, maneuvered the Japanese into attacking Pearl Harbor in order to provide him with the necessary and ultimate rabbit. Pearl Harbor seemed to men like Burton Wheeler and Charles Lindbergh too bad to be true.

It may seem bizarre to speak of an event as devastating as the attack on Pearl Harbor, which resulted in the loss of 2,403 men killed, more than 1,000 wounded and the virtual destruction of the Pacific Fleet (19 ships sunk or damaged, 265 planes destroyed on the ground), as a stroke of good fortune, but we are talking of the survival of freedom and some modest degree of decency in the world, of the threat of virtually universal tyranny on a heretofore unimagined scale. So measured, the price was a relatively modest one to pay for bringing the United States into the strife as a nation united in its determination to defeat the Axis powers and, above all, to end the monstrous regime of Adolf Hitler.

Franklin Roosevelt had believed that in the last analysis Japanese military leaders would draw back from an attack that, in view of the strength of the American fleet in the Pacific, must be suicidal. He believed that a policy of firmness, the dispatch of the Pacific Fleet from San Diego to Pearl Harbor, and the withholding of vital supplies of oil would bring the Japanese to their senses. To Roosevelt Hitler-led Germany was the paramount threat to the civilized world. Italy, and Japan as well, were, in a sense, side issues. His policies were directed toward neutralizing the Japanese while throwing the nation's industrial weight onto the scales against Germany and Italy.

The Japanese were well aware of all these factors. The shifting of the Pacific Fleet to Pearl Harbor, intended to discourage Japanese aggression in that area, instead provided the military planners with what they thought was a once-in-a-lifetime opportunity to cripple seriously the Pacific Fleet and with it the capacity of the United States to wage war successfully in that quarter of the globe. Only with such a daring stroke could the Japanese hope for victory or, if not a conclusive victory, a stalemate in which the United States would have to abandon its opposition to the Greater East Asia Co-Prosperity Sphere and accept Japan as an equal in the Pacific Basin.

The Japanese bombardment of Pearl Harbor was one of the most dramatic achievements in military history. Brilliantly planned and executed, it reminded an astonished world of that nation's feudal tradition, which honored martial prowess above all other attributes and put a premium on cunning and surprise. It also had great significance on the symbolic level. The journalist Murobuse Koshin had written that the Japanese must *"worship or overcome"* the United States. Pearl Harbor, whatever else it was, was perhaps preeminently a liberation of the Japanese imagination from the oppressive weight of the United States. That Japan in the end succumbed to the fateful bombs that dropped on Hiroshima and Nagasaki was less significant than the fact that in Freudian terms, it "killed the father" at Pearl Harbor by destroying the most visible symbol of American omnipotence—the great Pacific Fleet. Whatever defeats and setbacks the Japanese might subsequently experience during the course of the war, they had dealt the awesome giant a blow from which he recovered with the greatest difficulty and which he would never forget. In doing so, they had changed Americans' apprehension of the Japanese as surely as the bombing had changed the Japanese image of America.

Advocates of the theory that Roosevelt deliberately invited the Japanese to make their attack on Pearl Harbor, first by placing the fleet there and then by doing nothing to alert its commander to the danger of an attack, of which he presumably knew from intercepted Japanese messages, have a naïve notion of the efficiency of intelligence systems. As Roberta Wohlstetter pointed out in her book *Pearl Harbor: Warning and Decision*, all intelligence systems receive a vast amount of miscellaneous information (Wohlstetter calls it "noise), which can be sorted out only in terms of certain assumptions about enemy intentions and capabilities. Once the United States intelligence officers had concluded that an attack on Pearl Harbor was not within the capabilities of the Japanese Navy, all information coming into the intelligence system that pointed to such an operation was disregarded. The only "noise" taken seriously (and thus converted into information or intelligence) was that which confirmed existing hypotheses about Japanese intentions and capabilities.

One of the first reactions of Americans to the shock of Pearl Harbor was to turn on Japanese-Americans, most of whom lived in California, with the charge that they were a potential fifth column; it was assumed that they would give aid to their ancestral land in the event that Japan invaded the West Coast, a possibility which, in the aftermath of Pearl Harbor, did not seem as farfetched as it does in retrospect. The Japanese in California had made themselves vulnerable by collecting in enclaves that remained aloof from the Caucasians who surrounded them. They did so partly because of racial prejudice against them, but it was due also to the fact that they were an intensely proud and militant people with an ancient warrior culture of extraordinary richness—men and women who, in many instances, considered their white American neighbors a crude and barbarous race. Most Japanese-Americans preserved close ties with their homeland, and some anticipated returning to Japan in their old age. Many identified, as we would say today, more with Japan than with the United States and took pride in its spectacular rise as a world power. As for white Californians, they had been kept in a state of agitation for some fifty years over the "yellow peril," that favorite hobgoblin of the Hearst press. Although there was clearly no military threat from China, hostility toward Chinese in California had been a staple of that state's politics and the Chinese themselves had been the whipping boy of demagogically inclined politicians since the 1880s. In the aftermath of the Russo-Japanese War the threat of a Japanese invasion of the American Southwest, either through Mexico and up the Mississippi Valley or along the line of the Rio Grande, had been taken seriously, not simply by the sensational yellow press but by U.S. military planners and, as it turned out, by the Japanese themselves. Homer Lea's *The Valor of Ignorance*, with its prediction of an attack by the Japanese on the United States starting with an invasion of the Philippines at Mindanao, had been a best-seller in California. Theodore Roosevelt, as we have noted, took the threat of a Japanese attack seriously enough to summon the San Francisco school board to Washington to persuade it that excluding Japanese children from the public schools of that city might provoke an attack on the United States by Japan. Movies, magazines, and newspapers had kept the fear of Japan alive. The attack on Pearl Harbor and the speedy capture of the Philippines seemed like the fulfillment of the gloomiest predictions. Under the circumstances it is not surprising that California and United States officials, in fear of an attack, overreacted. It would have been strange if the panic response had been other than it was. Walter Lippmann, after conferring with the army commander in California, announced to his readers that the entire Pacific coast was "in imminent danger of a combined attack from within and without." In the event of an invasion "organized sabotage by Japanese-Americans and un-naturalized Japanese nationals might be expected."

Granted all that, the manner in which the indiscriminate rounding up of Japanese was conducted left a dark stain on the nation's record. The German-American Bund, an organization of mostly young men of German ancestry firmly committed to Hitler, was treated with much more circumspection. The best that can be said for the treatment of the Japanese in the euphemistically named relocation camps is that they were run, for the most part, by decent and humane men, a number of them Quakers, and that the occupants of the camps were by and large well fed and well treated. Many camps, through the resource-fulness of the men and women confined in them, became notable centers of cultural and artistic activity. After the war, through a combination of guilt on the part of white Americans over their treatment of their Japanese fellow citizens, the brilliant performance in battle of the Nisei battalion in the U.S. Army, and a determination on the part of Japanese-Americans themselves to find a place in the dominant white society, the rapid integration of Japanese-Americans and their out-standing accomplishments came to constitute one of the most impressive chapters in the history of immigration in America.

# 46

# The Evaluation of Roosevelt

As promised, *A People's History of the United States* has been conceived as ending with the Japanese bombing of Pearl Harbor. The reasons are manifold: mercy for the reader as well as for the aging historian; the notion that the conclusion (though not the end) of the New Deal makes an appropriate conclusion for the history; the fact that most Americans have lived through all or a substantial part of the post-World War II era and thus can be their own historians; and, finally, and perhaps most important, my belief that the two overriding themes in our history are, one, the abolition of slavery and the achievement of equality for black Americans and, two, the resolution of the war between capital and labor. While the drama of the civil rights–black power movement had still to unfold, it is my conviction that the groundwork for black equality in white America was laid in the twenties and thirties, in part by the Communist Party and in part by the New Deal and, of course, by such black leaders as A. Philip Randolph, James Weldon Johnson, Charles Sidney Johnson, Mary McLeod Bethune, and hundreds of others.

However, since this history is, to put the matter as grandiloquently (and presumptuously) as possible, my last will and testament to the American people, I feel entitled to add a codicil and at least to sketch in the interval between the entry of the United States into World War II and the present day.

There was, first of all, of course, the war itself, almost incomprehensibly vast and terrible in death and suffering. Even before the entry of the United States into the war Roosevelt had been the *de facto* head of the Allies and then, with the capitulation of France, of an Anglo-American alliance: with the German attack on Russia in June, 1941, he became the dominant figure in a British, American, and Russian alliance. The central element in the alliance was the personal friendship between Churchill and Roosevelt, but there was never any question of who the dominant figure was. Churchill was a veteran conservative politician in the British tradition. He had been an outspoken enemy of the Russian Revolution since the earliest days of the Bolsheviks. His principal preoccupation often seemed to be the preservation of the British Empire. Brilliant though Churchill might be as a wartime leader of the British people, Roosevelt considered him a relic of the past, politically speaking. The President was determined to act as a kind of mediator between Churchill and Stalin. Of all the Western statesmen, Stalin, according to the testimony of Harry Hopkins, came closest to trusting Roosevelt.

Seen from the perspective of the world, the war *for* the world became a contest between good (in the person of Franklin Delano Roosevelt) and a man who was the actual embodiment of evil. For Hitler, who planned to rule the world, Roosevelt was *the* enemy, a figure who came to loom larger and larger in Hitler's feverish imagination, the thwarter of all his plans, the destroyer of his dreams of universal empire, his nemesis. They had come to power within a few weeks of each other. "I have not come into the world," Hitler wrote, "to make men better, but to make use of their weaknesses." In *Mein Kampf* he had written: "Yes, we *are* barbarians! We want to be barbarians! It is an honourable title. We shall rejuvenate the world. This world is near its end." National socialism would usher in a new era in world history. "After National Socialism has lasted some time, it will be impossible to imagine a form of life different from ours."

In July, 1941, shortly after his armies had invaded Russia for what he was confident would be a brief and victorious campaign, Hitler consented to have his dinner table conversations transcribed. For somewhat more than a year this was faithfully done.

Hitler began on July 5 with a distinction "between the Fascist popular movement and the popular movement in Russia. The Fascist movement is a spontaneous return to the traditions of ancient Rome. The Russian movement has an essential tendency toward anarchy. . . . What matters is that Bolshevism must be exterminated. . . . Moscow, as the center of the doctrine, must disappear from the earth's surface. . . . " A few days later he amplified his argument. "The heaviest blow that ever struck humanity was the coming of Christianity. Bolshevism is Christianity's illegitimate child. Both are the inventions of the Jews. The deliberate lie in the matter of religion was introduced into the world by Christianity. Bolshevism practices a lie of the same nature when it claims to bring liberty to men, whereas in reality it seeks only to enslave them. . . . What repulsive hypocrisy, that arrant Freemason, Roosevelt, displays when he speaks of Christianity!" Hitler exclaimed.

With the entry of the United States into the war in December, 1941, Hitler's obsession with Roosevelt grew. The American President had "a sick brain . . . was typically hebraic." Hitler repeated his hope that Britain would make a separate peace with Germany, leading to a collapse of the American economy, which, in Hitler's view, had been saved from disaster only by the outbreak of the war. He instructed the German radio stations, which broadcast in English to Great Britain, to stress "the drunkard Churchill and the criminal Roosevelt on every possible occasion." He was persuaded that Roosevelt was Jewish (Roosevelt, indeed, spoke of ancient Jewish blood). He told his dinner companions that "all half-caste families—even if they have but a minute quantity of Jewish blood in their veins—produce regularly, generation by generation, at least one pure Jew. Roosevelt affords the best possible proof of the truth of this opinion. Roosevelt, who in his handling of political issues and in his general attitude, behaves like a tortuous, pettifogging Jew. . . . The completely negroid appearance of his wife is also a clear indication that she, too, is a half-caste," Hitler added.

The tide of the war turned decisively with the stubborn Russian resistance at Stalingrad, where suffering fearfully, the Russians held out against repeated German onslaughts, taking and inflicting terrible losses. When an officer read out figures on Russian troop strength, Hitler, according to General Franz Halder, "flew at him with clenched fists and foam in the corners of his mouth, and forbade the reading of such idiotic twaddle." One of his secretaries wrote, "After Stalingrad, Hitler could not listen to music any more . . . [and] world events and events at the front were never mentioned: everything to do with the war was taboo."

In addition to providing the leadership in the alliance in the global war against the Axis powers, Roosevelt was determined to do all in his power to lay the foundations for a peaceful postwar world. According to his wife, he was convinced that the world would be "considerably more socialistic after the war" and that Churchill, with his colonial notions and dogged hostility toward the Soviets, might find it difficult to adjust to the new conditions. When they met at Teheran, Roosevelt said to Stalin, "So much depends in the future on how we learn to live together. Do you think it will be possible for the United States and the USSR to see things in similar ways?" Stalin replied: "You have come a long way in the United States from your original concept of government and its responsibilities, and your original way of life. I think it is quite possible that we here in the USSR, as our resources develop and people can have an easier life, will find ourselves growing nearer to some of your concepts and you may be finding yourselves accepting some of ours."

A cause of suspicion and ill will on the part of the Russians was the stream of promises for greater material assistance, for assault landings and new fronts, that were made to the Russians but not fulfilled. When the promises were made, the Allied commands knew they were impossible to accomplish, but the rationale was that they might encourage Russia to remain in the war rather than make a peace with Germany, which would free the Germans for an all-out assault on the West. It was certainly not a moral or even an intelligently expedient policy. When one promise after another went unfulfilled, Stalin became convinced that his capitalist allies were remaining aloof from the severest fighting in the hopes that Russia would bleed to death in its desperate struggle to repel the German invaders. A fateful foundation was thus laid for future suspicion and distrust. On the other hand, it could be said that the Allies had no reason to place any confidence in a nation, an ally by virtue of desperate need, which had shown what appeared to Western eyes a cynical disregard for the basic principles of international morality.

Before the meeting of the three wartime leaders at Yalta Roosevelt talked frequently with his wife about the importance of the opportunity to strengthen the personal relationship between himself and the Russian dictator, but his hopes were disappointed. It seemed clear to him after Yalta that Stalin could not be trusted, and, in Mrs. Roosevelt's words, "he wrote him a number of extremely stern messages." Nonetheless, he continued to believe that an understanding with the Russians was essential.

The President called the Dumbarton Oaks Conference in the fall of 1944 to begin the process which he hoped would result in the United Nations. He was determined to prepare the nation for the acceptance of such an international body. "The American people have to be brought along slowly," he told William Douglas. As for the Security Council veto, to which many advocates of a league objected on the grounds that it was undemocratic and that it simply ratified big power politics, Roosevelt responded: "If the United States and Russia can work together, the United Nations will be a success. If they cannot work together, the UN will fail—veto or no veto."

In 1944, with the end of the war in sight and Allied forces victorious on every front, the quadrennial presidential election rolled around once more. Four years earlier, with the nation clearly on the eve of war, changing leadership seemed to a majority of Americans unwise. The same feeling prevailed again; if a third term had been controversial, a fourth seemed inevitable. Wallace was jettisoned as Vice-President and replaced by the Democratic regular and strong New Dealer, Harry Truman.

William Allen White debated with his friend Henry Allen the President's motives in seeking a *fourth* term. Allen believed it was a simple lust for power. White had a gentler interpretation. "I think he wants to sit in, to win hand after hand, and maybe take quite a pot with him as he passes through the portals of history. . . . "

The mark of death was on Roosevelt during the campaign. The great, powerful torso had a crumpled look about it, and every movement was an effort. The closest to the President realized that his days were numbered, yet no one could speak his or her thoughts.

Thomas Dewey was Roosevelt's Republican rival; he garnered a respectable number of votes, some 22,000,000 to Roosevelt's 25,000,000, but only 99 electoral votes to 432 for Roosevelt.

A few days before the inauguration Frances Perkins tried to bring up the matter of resignation with the President. She was shocked at his appearance. "As I sat down beside him," she wrote, "I had a sense of his enormous fatigue. He had the pallor, the deep gray color, of a man who had long been ill. He looked like an invalid who has been allowed to see guests for the first time and the guests have stayed too long. . . . His lips were blue. His hand shook."

When she asked his permission to resign, he said, "Not now! Do stay and don't say anything. You are all right." His voice was weary beyond expression. It seemed an effort even to speak. "Frances, you have done awfully well. I know what you have been through. I know what you have accomplished. Thank you." He put his hand on hers. "There were tears in our eyes." she wrote. All her resolution crumpled; she felt only love and concern and gratitude.

At the inauguration Perkins found herself beside the President in the White House. (The taking of the oath had been moved inside, in keeping with wartime austerity and out of regard for Roosevelt's uncertain health.) As it came time for him to take the oath, he turned and said to her, "Frances, I can't." She replied: "Mr. President, you must." He took the oath and then recalled the words of Endicott Peabody from his schoolboy days at Groton: "Things in life will not always run smoothly. Sometimes we will be rising toward the heights—then all will seem to reverse itself and start downward. The great fact to remember is that the trend of civilization itself is forever upward; that a line drawn through the middle of the peaks and valleys of the centuries always has an upward trend."

At the reception following the inauguration Mrs. Woodrow Wilson said to Frances Perkins that the President looked "exactly as my husband did when he went into his decline."

"Don't say that to another soul," Perkins replied. "He has a great and terrible job to do, and he's got to do it even if it kills him."

A few weeks later Roosevelt departed for the ardors of the Yalta Conference, hoping to draw Stalin and Soviet Union into a peace agreement that would heal the divisions between Russia and the West. It was not to be. Back in Washington he found every act an effort. Warm Springs beckoned and he returned there as to home, hoping perhaps to muster the strength to live out the war, to experience the sweetness of the victory he had poured his life into. But the great heart broke on April 12, 1945; he died of a cerebral hemorrhage. There was a special poignance in the fact that Lucy Mercer was with him when he died. It had, after all, been a love affair of more than twenty years' duration.

Hitler was in the Führerbunker, sixty feet below ground in the final hours of the collapse of the Reich that had been designed to last for 1,000 years, issuing orders that there was no one to carry out. Roosevelt's death was reported to him; the news pulled him for a moment out of a drugged stupor. His enemy was dead, Roosevelt, the "sick . . . crippled . . . criminal Jew," no longer lived to plague him. Hope revived. Perhaps it was not too late. Perhaps the shattered German armies could be reconstituted, the war won after all. The delusion was the measure of the obsession. The German armies continued to disintegrate, and Hitler took his own life by poison on April 30. A week later articles of surrender were signed by Field Marshal Alfred Jodl. The European war was over.

As Hitler and Roosevelt had come to power a few weeks apart, so they now died a few weeks apart, thirteen years later. Almost too patly, good had triumphed over evil. If the world was not precisely free again, *it was free to be free,* free to set about that endless task, free of the most terrible challenge to freedom in all history. More than any other individual, Franklin Roosevelt was the architect of that freedom. He had perceived the menace of Hitler in the first moment of the dictator's triumph and had, with infinite patience, brought his countrymen and countrywomen to the point where they were ready at last to do what he all along knew must someday be done.

Claude Bowers was ambassador in Chile when word came of Roosevelt's death. "Never in Chilean history," he wrote, "had the death of any foreigner so touched the emotions of the people; they knew that Roosevelt had been their friend." The Chilean cardinal offered the cathedral for a memorial service for the dead President, an offer without precedent since Roosevelt had been a Protestant. The highest officials of the country joined in the mourning. "But even more impressive to me," Bowers wrote, "were the delegations of workers who came from the factories in their work clothes to express their sympathy; and still more touching the delegations of small schoolchildren bearing flowers."

It was much the same story in every nation that had been part of the alliance against Hitler and Mussolini—deep grief and a sense of loss. Not since Lincoln's assassination had the people of the world so grieved over the death of an American President.

Frances Perkins went to the White House to comfort Eleanor Roosevelt. She was not surprised to find her composed and self-possessed. Her belongings were being packed so that the Trumans could move in promptly, and the two women who had perhaps known Roosevelt best and who each in her own way had loved him deeply sat on a bench at the end of a hall, "like two schoolgirls and talked about FD." Perkins had prayed long, seeking comfort where she had found it so often before, but his presence was still powerfully about, and she longed for "a good laugh with him over the confusions of the human race" or to see him "put his subtle and delicate hand into the mess of human passions and jealousies and bring out some kind of voluntary and creative order." She recalled the observation of Plato " 'that creation is the victory of persuasion, not the victory of force.' I always thought FD was an extraordinary illustration of that," she later wrote a friend, recounting her visit.

To Perkins Roosevelt was the "most complicated human being I have ever known." Henry Morgenthau found him "an extraordinarily difficult person to describe . . . a man of bewildering complexity of moods and motives."

The more ideologically inclined among Roosevelt's inner circle of advisers were often disconcerted by Roosevelt's intensely personal approach to large social issues: He supported old-age pensions, it was said, because he had three old neighbors in their eighties who had ended up in the poorhouse when they lost their farm. The story infuriated the Communist writer Mauritz Hallgren, who thought Roosevelt should have come to the conclusion by an analysis of the cruel indifference of capitalism to human suffering. But the apparent personal response was often misleading; Roosevelt loved to illustrate the need for a piece of legislation by a homely story. He was not nearly so naïve as Hallgren thought. At the same time people *were* clearly more important to him than ideas. "Roosevelt," Raymond Moley wrote, "is interested in people. He wants people to like him and the combination is almost irresistible." Nonetheless, there was always, in Moley's view, "the suggestion of some inner watchfulness, some subtle incompleteness that makes intimacy impossible."

Roosevelt's curiosity seemed limitless. A reporter noted that he always had a supply of blank pieces of paper which he called "chits." Whenever any question occurred to him, he wrote it down on one of the slips and later sent it off to the individual or agency he thought best able to answer it.

"Curious" and "open" were both essential aspects of his character. Moley gives a classic instance. While Roosevelt was taking a brief Warm Springs vacation prior to his inauguration in 1933, two young "Reds" appeared with the firmly expressed intention of seeing the President-elect and telling him of their plans for the salvation of the country. There was immediate alarm. The Secret Service men as well as the local police were notified. An aide assured the Reds that while it was out of the question for them to see the President-elect, their plan would be delivered to him. But they refused to abandon their intention of talking with Roosevelt personally. When the aide appealed to FDR for suggestions on how to get them out of town, Roosevelt said he would be glad to talk with them. In Moley's words, "Roosevelt invited them to tell him all about their ideas. . . ." Soon they had their plan spread out on the table. "The visitors and Roosevelt were fascinated by one another. They talked, and he talked. The discussion went on and on. . . . After two solid hours of this the 'Reds' went away. . . . And Roosevelt, himself, gave every evidence of feeling that he'd had an absorbingly interesting, informative, and not at all extraordinary experience." Moley cited the incident as an example of the President's complete lack of self-consciousness as well as his receptivity to ideas however eccentric or by whomever advanced.

What was perhaps most remarkable of all about Roosevelt, and one of the qualities hardest to measure, was his complete unconventionality. It was demonstrated most dramatically by the extraordinary variety of people he surrounded himself with and the relationships he built and maintained with most of them through some of the most critical years in the nation's history.

What has been done even if its "rightness" or efficacy is challenged, has been done. But the climate in which it was done is often hard to recapture; the doubts, the uncertainties, the countervailing arguments, the very different conventions and ways of doing things inherited from the past can never be very precisely reconstructed. Such is peculiarly the case with the New Deal. While the President was never unaware of political considerations, he always kept them in perspective. They seldom inhibited him in pursuing his goals. They might limit and define what could be done, notably in the case of the pervasive isolationism of the country, but the goals were never lost sight of, and as Frances Perkins put it, he was "never discouraged." If one approach failed, he turned to another. In the realm of politics there was always more than one way to skin a cat.

"Instinct," "hunches," "intuitions,"—such words appear frequently in the efforts of Roosevelt's closest associates to describe the process by which he arrived at decisions. "Clairvoyant" was the word Perkins came back to. "If Roosevelt had been a less clairvoyant person, less able to see so many things and so many facets of everything, he wouldn't have had such a hard time with himself," in Perkins's opinion. As President, seeing so much, so much darkness as well as so much light, "he suffered more intellectually and spiritually," Perkins believed, "than a person with a less diverse, less sensitive and less understanding mind."

In an era of bitterly conflicting ideologies, panaceas, and prescriptions for salvation, Franklin Roosevelt sailed serenely along, never losing sight of his goal—a more just and equitable America—and unshaken in his conviction that such a society could be achieved and, indeed, that he, and only he, could achieve it. For a man by no means insensitive to ideas, he showed a remarkable capacity for never becoming their prisoner. In one of Rexford Tugwell's most incisive passages, he noted that Roosevelt "was not a made President, but a born one. He came," he added, "to the manipulation of powerful forces and vast interests as naturally as I had to studying them. . . . No monarch . . . can have given more sense of a serene presiding, of gathering up into himself, or really representing, a whole people. He had a right to his leeways, he had a right to use everyone in his own way, he had every right to manipulate the palpables and the impalpables. He would only do it for his country's good. He was part of a guided ordering of affairs. He had the secure innocence that comes of resting on a broader bosom than most of us ever find."

We have been presented so often with the picture of Roosevelt the pragmatist, uncommonly skillful in manipulating people to achieve some particular practical end, that it is hard to realize that he was equally, or indeed more, an extravagant dreamer and visionary. For example, the middle of a speech designed to lay out the goals of his administration, he stated one of his most dearly held and thoroughly impractical schemes (dreams): to put unemployed city dwellers back on the land. Along with providing work for the unemployed, Americans "must frankly recognize the overbalance of population in our industrial centers and, by engaging on a national scale in redistribution, endeavor to provide a better use of the land for those best fitted for the land." It was an idea, in essence the notion of resettlement, that he returned to frequently and that he, of course, tried to give practical effect to in the Resettlement Administration. In the general confusion of New Deal ventures, the efforts at resettlement, almost uniformly failures, were lumped with other less than successful undertakings. It was not widely recognized how visionary the whole project was and, at the same time, how revealing of Roosevelt's own view of the world. The fact that he refused to identify himself with any kind of programmatic radicalism obscured what we might call his radical idealism, a temper that clearly derived from the old Progressives, from his cousin Theodore, and, perhaps most of all, from Woodrow Wilson. The old Progressives had been immunized against the "essential Wilson," the Wilson of the Fourteen Points and the League of Nations, by their stubborn Midwestern isolationism. They had completely rejected (and defeated) the aspect of Wilson that had captured the imaginations of the internationalists, men like Herbert Hoover, Colonel Edward House, and Newton D. Baker. Roosevelt's desire to resettle unemployed city dwellers on prosperous and productive farms (he was confident that they would be eager to go) was a kind of small-scale domestic equivalent of Wilson's plan to bring peace and order to the world. It was equally impractical and equally American.

Another case in point is the Civilian Conservation Corps, an idea at least half a century ahead of its time. We have become so accustomed to thinking of the CCC simply as "one of the most popular and successful" New Deal programs that we are inclined to lose sight of how idealistic and visionary it in fact was. It was, of course, closely related to Roosevelt's interest in resettlement. The CCC enrollees were being "temporarily resettled." It was Roosevelt's hope that once introduced to the joys of life in the great open spaces of the nation, the campers, the majority of them from cities, would discover an affinity for rural life and settle on the land after their novitiates with the CCC had ended. The fact that the CCC had no particular ideological reference point— it was not a part of a Socialist or Communist platform (the Communists, in fact, attacked it wrathfully as a capitalist quasi-militaristic regimentation of the nation's youth)—obscured its visionary radicalism. It masqueraded as just another relief measure, and the country accepted it as that. That Roosevelt had quite another vision of it was demonstrated by the particular pleasure he took in visiting the camps themselves. The speed with which the three Cs were initiated was another clue to its importance in Roosevelt's vision of the nation's future. Before Congress could catch its breath or collect its wits, it was an accomplished fact, and the first recruits had begun to filter into hastily constructed camps.

To William O. Douglas the most appealing thing about Roosevelt was his love of the land and his appreciation of the life and problems of the farmer. "He was the 'squire' who cherished the topsoil, the fields, and the forests and saw in soil conservation as well as in the wilderness the salvation of America. . . . The shelterbelts he built still stand as monuments to his conservation instincts, especially in North and South Dakota." The shelterbelt was a New Deal invention. Two rows of trees were planted thirty to sixty feet apart. In Douglas's words, "as the trees grew, the space between the two rows became a tangle of wildwood. Birds were attracted, and rabbits and deer as well. The shelterbelts helped make the Great Plains abundant in wildlife. They caught the drifting snows of winter; the spring melt watered the land."

Reviving the spirit of his cousin Theodore, Roosevelt told the listeners to one of his fireside chats, "The history of every nation is eventually written in the way in which it cares for its soil." One of his dreams was to restore the Great Plains to the grassland it once had been. In 1938 he threw the weight of his office behind the creation of the Olympic National Park in Washington State, a unique rain forest with great stands of western hemlock and Douglas fir. The following year he began negotiations with Daniel Willard, head of the Baltimore & Ohio Railroad, "for the Chesapeake & Ohio property running along the C&O canal for 180 miles to become the great C&O Canal National Historical Park."

Rexford Tugwell's judgment was that Roosevelt "attained a kind of victory, as Lincoln did, but it was far from a clean-cut or final one; and it might have gone to pieces if the vast digression of the war had not swallowed up and hid all of its half-failures and distressing withdrawals." Tugwell, like most intellectuals, wished to live in a world where there were only "clean-cut" and "final" victories. The "half failure" of the New Deal was that it never really "solved" the Depression. Its essential half success was that it rescued the country, by general agreement, from something bordering on chaos, and it did so as much by force of the President's character as by any combination of programs designed to end it. The "distressing withdrawals" were an obvious reference to the fact that Roosevelt did not follow the line prescribed by his Brain Trust to achieve a "holistic," "organic" economy, characterized by "concentration and control"—in effect, a managed, socialist economy. The New Deal, Tugwell wrote, "was a Roosevelt construction, not that of a Brain Trust, of an inherited tradition, of Brandeis and Frankfurter, or of anyone else or any other group."

Ogden Mills spoke for conservative politicians and wealthy financiers when he accused Roosevelt of "fostering revolution under the guise of recovery and reform." The charge had a considerable measure of truth. Long before he was President, long before the Depression, Roosevelt had made clear his "nationalism"—that is to say, his conviction that it was the responsibility of the Federal government to take whatever measures were necessary for the common good, uninhibited by any theory of constitutional limitations or states' rights. It was not, certainly, that Roosevelt was committed to proceeding *un*constitutionally or was cavalier about the constitutional constraints on executive power; it was rather that his study of the Constitution and, perhaps more important, of the political theories of the drafters of that document convinced him they had intended the powers of the Federal government to be boldly and broadly used. It was not the Founders, but the twisted and self-serving interpretations that had been placed on their handiwork, that were at fault.

Finally, it must be kept firmly in mind what is so easy to forget: that Roosevelt, more than any prominent American leader and far more than any European political figure, perceived from the first the significance of the rise of fascism in Italy and, far more dangerously, in Germany and that he armed the nation, materially and psychologically, to face it. To Eleanor Roosevelt the two crises of her husband's presidency were closely related. The New Deal provided the context in which the Second World War could be carried to a successful conclusion. "If he had not successfully handled the one," she wrote, "he could never have handled the other, because no leader can do anything unless the people are willing to follow him."

Perhaps when all is said and done, Franklin Delano Roosevelt, far from being the complex and mysterious figure historians seem determined to make him, was a disarmingly simple man at heart; at heart rather than at mind. At heart he was a devout upper-class Episcopalian, a man with strong religious convictions who sought to manifest those convictions in the world, "on earth as it is in heaven," who sincerely wished to relieve want and suffering and to lay the political foundations for a more just and humane society, not simply in the United States but in the world. He was kind, generous, thoughtful, loving. He loved life and people and gaiety, laughter, the precise specific land, nature. Just as the Lord used him, a frail vessel, as the instrument of His will, he in turn used those around him, as he believed, not to his own ends but the Almighty's. This Roosevelt I find the most reassuring of all the various Roosevelts his friends and, subsequently, historians have offered us or tried to impose on us. It seems, finally, to have been the Roosevelt that the patient, tireless Tugwell "discovered." Tugwell wrote: "As some of us gradually came to understand, he had in mind a comprehensive welfare concept, infused with a stiff tincture of morality. These were, in most respects, like those of the progressives who had preceded him. . . . He wanted all Americans to grow up healthy and vigorous and to be practically educated. He wanted business men to work within a set of understood rules. Beyond this he wanted people free to vote, to worship, to behave as they wished so long as a moral code was respected; and he wanted officials to behave as though office were a public trust."

Rexford Tugwell took the line that when Roosevelt died and the war ended, the Democratic regulars were firmly ensconced "in all the strategic places of power." From these vantage points "they proceeded at once to oust from the administration all the remaining Rooseveltians, to institute a new 'red hunt,' and to drive into political exile all those who might furnish any opposition. Truman, the bosses' man, allowed it all to happen."

Tugwell's melodramatic account considerably overstates the case or misstates it. Roosevelt had, after all, created such a powerful political aura that virtually every ambitious Democratic politician for the next thirty or forty years eagerly sought to identify himself or, occasionally, herself with it. Roosevelt became a magic and talismanic name guaranteed to ward off defeat at the polls. It became a reference point, an affirmation of faith. It was more than a specific program or programs. It was an attitude of concern for the less fortunate, a determination to create a more equitable society, a hunger for social justice, a conviction that poverty, prejudice, and the hardships attendant upon old age and illness were, beyond a certain irreducible minimum, not inevitable conditions of all societies but things that could and must be ameliorated by the whole society collectively through its agent, the government—a government that was not an impartial arbiter between competing interests but an active instrument of the common will with a responsibility for promoting, with all the means available to it, the common good.

Perhaps the most important New Deal legacy of all, in the light of our history, was the achievement of peace or, at the least, a truce in the war between capital and labor. Labor was "empowered," as we say today, and capital chastened. Americans discovered what many prophetic voices had long proclaimed: that capital's and labor's common interests were stronger than their divisions.

Eleanor Roosevelt had another life to lead with her husband's death. "On the whole," she wrote at the end of her autobiographical volume, *This I Remember*, " . . . I think I lived [the years of the presidency] very impersonally. It was almost as though I had erected someone a little outside of myself who was the president's wife. I was lost somewhere deep down inside myself. That is the way I felt and worked until I left the White House." It was an extraordinary flash of self-revelation that revealed the range of her intelligence and the depth of her sensibility, so often hidden beneath her simple courtesy and artless style. Her life was a demonstration of the power of simple goodness. Few figures in public view have endured so much obloquy, been so denounced and ridiculed (as well, of course, as loved and revered), but through it all she preserved, undiminished, an exceptional sweetness of disposition. In everything she did there was a kind of innocence, the innocence of a saint who takes the world as she finds it, loves it, and wishes to improve it. To enter her presence was, in a real sense, to experience grace.

Walter White, the head for many years of the NAACP, became one of Eleanor Roosevelt's closest friends. He wrote in his autobiography that it was often simply an awareness of Eleanor Roosevelt's existence that kept him from hating all white people.

# Postwar America:
# Suppressing the Left

On August 6, 1945, two months after the surrender of Germany, an atomic bomb was dropped on the city of Hiroshima. Four square miles of the city were destroyed, and more than 160,000 people were killed or seriously injured. The war with Japan was over, and the atomic age had begun.

The philosopher George Santayana pronounced one of the most often repeated aphorisms of modern times when he wrote, "Those who cannot remember the past are condemned to repeat it." After World War II the Allied powers, with the leadership of the United States, set about to rehabilitate the defeated enemy nations rather than punish them as the Allies had punished the Central Powers after World I. It was, of course, not an entirely disinterested act. There were already serious tensions between Russia and those nations under its domination and the so-called free world (which, if imperfectly free, was free by comparison with the Soviet bloc). One of the main purposes of the policy of rehabilitating the enemy was to prevent those nations from falling under the spell (and domination) of Russian communism. The story of the Marshall Plan in Europe and the joint Allied occupation of Japan (which was primarily an American enterprise) is one of the more encouraging cases of enlightened self-interest that history discloses. If the rehabilitation of the enemy (and those nations that had suffered most in the war) was, in part, a consequence or by-product of the burgeoning cold war, it was nonetheless exemplary.

The seventh volume of this work is titled *America Enters the World.* We entered spectacularly with Theodore Roosevelt's peacemaking intervention in the Russo-Japanese War. We, in a sense, confirmed that act with our reluctant entry into the European war in 1917 and, above all, with Wilson's declaration of the Fourteen Points. The Versailles Treaty and the events that followed it brought profound disillusionment. We withdrew into the deepest mood of isolationism in our history (the Founding Fathers had, after all, hoped to redeem the world). We emerged from the Second World War an imperial power determined to contest with Communist Russia for the domination of the world. We did not, of course, put it so directly. We proclaimed that it was our sacred duty to protect the world, whether it wished to be protected or not, from the spread of godless communism. However exalted our motives may have been, the result was a naked power struggle with no holds barred. Righteousness wedded to power is a dangerous combination; the consequence was that we and the Soviet Union developed weapons terrible enough to blow up the world in the name of saving it from each other.

The war had been unsettling in many ways. The alliance of capitalist America with Communist Russia made a jumble of ideological positions, and the cold war, following so closely on the heels of the wartime alliance, further confused issues so that the war ran like a fault line across the consciousness of American intellectuals. Some ex-Communists became recanters, turned on their former comrades, and denounced communism and all its works with as much fervor as the most dyed-in-the-wool reactionary. Meanwhile, the Communist Party itself was virtually dismantled.

In May, 1945, Steve Nelson was helping a friend in Oakland build a chimney for his house when he heard over the radio the news that Jacques Duclos, the leading French Communist theoretician, had denounced the Communist Political Association, the new name for the American branch of the party, for various heresies and deviations. "I was deeply shocked and confused," Nelson confessed. William Foster immediately conformed to the new line; Earl Browder resisted and was deposed. "The Party . . . " Nelson reflected, "was never the same again." Max Shachtman, a prominent Marxist, wrote at the end of the war: "What we are witnessing, in the International, is the *death of a theory.* It is clear that *nobody* now defends the 'workers' state' theory, certainly not in the old way and with the old arguments; nobody *can* defend it. . . . The war is over. The proletarian revolution did not come and did not triumph in Europe—an unhappy statement, but one that must be made."

Even before the war was over, the FBI confronted Josephine Herbst with her sins of the thirties. "It is reported," the bureau said, "that in Madrid, in 1937, you broadcast in behalf of the Spanish Loyalists," that she had signed a petition in 1932 "protesting the violation of civil liberties in Detroit; that you wrote a piece on Cuba for the *New Masses.*" The two young FBI agents, "gentle, clerklike," and uncomprehending, were dealing with matters of whose human and historical complexity they had not the faintest comprehension. Herbst was fired from her job with the German section of the U.S. propaganda agency with no explanation. The terror had begun, quietly and inconspicuously, with a minor administrator in a not particularly important agency. Malcolm Cowley, who worked in the Office of Facts and Figures, was also forced to resign, and there were dozens of similar firings.

While some former Communists made the welkin ring with their confessions and accusations, others simply "forgot" the thirties. The story was told that when a young inquirer at a postwar social gathering asked John Dos Passos a question about the thirties, his wife intervened. "John does not remember much about that period," she said protectively. Dos Passos remained silent. Whether the story is true or apocryphal, it makes the point. Dos Passos's alienation from the Communist Party had begun well before the war, but for him, as for many of his generation, the postwar discontinuities were too extreme to cope with; it was easier (and perhaps safer) to "forget."

Josephine Herbst was distressed at the disposition of many of her radical friends to try to expunge the past. Already the inclination of the reformed sinner to the *mea culpa* was evident. Herbst resisted it. "We are not only what we are today," she wrote, "but what we were yesterday and if you burn your immediate past there is nothing left but ashes which are all very well for those heads that like nothing better than to be sprinkled with ashes."

In a reprise of the Red hunts that had followed World War I, new Red hunts began. The most sensational case involved the beau ideal of liberal politics Alger Hiss and a pudgy, unattractive editor of *Time* magazine named Whittaker Chambers. Chambers accused Hiss of having been a member of the Harold Ware Group, a group of espionage agents of which Chambers himself had been a member and whose contact was Elizabeth Bentley.

"In accusing Hiss of Communism, I had attacked an architect of the U.N., and the partisans of peace fell upon me like combat troops," Chambers wrote in his autobiography, *Witness*. "I had attacked an intellectual and a 'liberal.' . . . From their roosts in the great cities, and certain collegiate eyries, the left-wing intellectuals of almost every feather . . . swooped and hovered in flocks like fluttered sea fowl . . . and gave vent to hoarse cries and defilements."

The language is revealing. Reading it, one feels that all of Chambers's bottled-up resentments had found expression. He was the victim, and the foul fowls, disturbing the air with their shrieks and defiling the ground, were his liberal enemies. It was not so much the information on subversion that Chambers reiterated in his book but the tone of ineffable self-righteousness with which he put it forth that offended "liberals" (and delighted conservatives). "Liberals" fought back out of the ill-articulated feeling that Chambers and his allies were in fact attacking, by indirection at least, the New Deal and every piece of progressive social legislation that had been passed under its aegis. But the book was one thing, and Chambers's simple unadorned testimony before various committees of Congress and before the courts was another.

In the rallying of liberal forces the pressures on Henry Luce to fire Whittaker Chambers from *Time* magazine did not come from right-wing political groups or yet from an aroused public opinion. It was exerted primarily by members in good standing of what we call today the establishment. According to Chambers, Luce expressed himself puzzled by the "implacable clamor of the most enlightened people against me [Chambers]." Luce said: "By any Marxian pattern of how classes behave the upper class should be for you and the lower classes should be against you. But it is the upper class that is most violent against you. How do you explain that?"

A Russian guest whom Chambers called Smetana replied: "You don't understand the class structure of American society or you would not ask such a question. In the United States, the working class are Democrats. The middle class are Republicans. The upper class are Communists." It was a clever answer that pleased Chambers, but it was not entirely satisfactory. More broadly interpreted, it did point up the fact that among those Americans who had both social position and inherited wealth, there was, as we have noted in numerous instances,

a tradition of concern for social justice that went back to the early years
of the Republic and that was perhaps most evident during the Progressive era. The various branches of the Roosevelt family were part
of it; John Jay Chapman was an exemplar, along with Florence Kelley
and Frances Perkins, the Pinchot brothers, Willard Straight, Henry
Stimson, and, from the South, Cordell Hull and Will Alexander. These
sons and daughters of the upper class were heavily reinforced, of
course, by middle-class reformers in the abolitionist tradition, men and
women like Henry George, Jane Addams, and David and Jane Cunningham Croly, parents of Herbert Croly. What was distinctive about
the 1930s was that a large proportion of such people were gathered
into the Communist fold, in part because it was the only fold in any
way adequate to express their extreme doubts about the existing economic system. To them Whittaker Chambers, with his ineffably lower-
class manners and appearance, his paranoia, his religious zeal and
right-wing zealotry, was an anathema.

Alger Hiss was transformed into a symbolic figure by right and
left alike. It might be argued that he got, in a substantial measure,
what he deserved, but thousands of other Americans, against whom
no charge of treason could be justly leveled, suffered severe persecution for having held in the thirties ideas that had become objectionable in the fifties.

If the psychology of the Communist hunters and persecutors is
clear enough—a desire to expunge America's flirtation with communism from the historical record and pretend it never happened (or
that it was the aberration of a few wicked or misled "un-Americans")—
the psychology of those who resisted to the bitter end the fact that a
significant number of Americans had passed information of varying
degrees of importance to Soviet agents is harder to explain. Perhaps
less effort has been devoted to explaining it because most of the prospective "explainers" are those very liberal intellectuals who doggedly
resisted knowing the truth. The Alger Hiss case is a kind of key to the
American psyche. Those Americans who maintained through thick
and thin that Alger Hiss was an upstanding liberal, innocent of the
charges against him, and that Whittaker Chambers was a psychopathic
liar did so by suspending those very standards by which they professed
to be guided: rationality and objectivity. Any relatively dispassionate
reading of the testimony at the various congressional hearings and at
the trials themselves convinces the reader of Hiss's guilt. In addition,
a vast amount of corroborative evidence was then and subsequently

deduced, so that there may indeed today be few people who still cling to the conviction of his innocence. The question remains: Why were otherwise intelligent and rational people unable to accept the fact that Alger Hiss had been an important member of an underground Communist apparatus that passed classified government information to Soviet agents (not all of it was even classified, and arguments on how much use the information was to our Russian allies continue)?

One obvious answer was that virtually all the liberals in question had been, to one degree or another, caught up in the vast network of activities engineered, guided, and directed by the Communist Party. Anyone with strong social concerns could hardly have escaped being identified with one front or another, from the Scottsboro boys and the Harlan County miners to medical supplies for the Spanish Loyalists. Those all were good causes, good causes then and good causes now. That the same kind of people, people from the same schools and colleges and clubs, from "good families," people with education and "advantages," friends and acquaintances, could have slipped over the line into activities considered "bad"—that is to say, treasonable—was difficult, indeed, in many instances, impossible, to accept. It raised troubling questions about gullibility and far more basic questions about good and evil, questions too complex and even frightening for well-intentioned American liberals to confront. It was easier to suppress such questions than to face them. Then there was the fact that Chambers was indubitably from the wrong side of the tracks. He had never finished college, he was disheveled and unkempt; his tailoring was hopeless; he was a Dostoyevskian figure from the underground. With his messianic zeal and self-evident paranoia, he was not an encouraging figure. He worked for *Time* magazine, which was generally considered a bastion of reaction, and finally, he had come forth essentially as a man who had experienced a religious conversion and, in consequence, felt himself bound to expose evil. He thus became the symbol of a severely judgmental religious tradition and an instrument in the hands of those forces that liberals considered most retrograde in American life, fundamentalist Christians and reactionary politicians.

The "evil" that Chambers believed he was exposing was not simply or even primarily the spy apparatus of which he had been a part; he says, quite convincingly, that he wished to leave all that in obscurity and only revealed it reluctantly under pressure to vindicate himself. He saw his mission as exposing not only the Antichrist, international communism, but secularism in general, of which communism was only the most virulent manifestation. Chambers's real message was that his friend Alger Hiss (and all the other Hisses) were heretics. The danger of communism was not so much that it would take over the world (although Chambers certainly feared that, too) as that it, along with associated heresies, was poisoning the roots of American life.

The ex-Communists and ex-communists (the fellow travelers) who retreated to the sanctuary of liberalism after the war understood that, consciously or subconsciously. They understood that all those Americans who were participants in what I have called the Secular-Democratic Consciousness, those who believed in the exclusively "material" character of the world, in science and in reason as the sole arbiters of human affairs, who believed that man was "good" and progress more or less inevitable, were, in a sense, on trial with Hiss. If Hiss was guilty and, most alarming of all, revealed as guilty by a representative of all they deplored, something was dreadfully askew in the universe. All presuppositions about man in time—the purpose and meaning of human existence—must be reexamined. It is hardly surprising that embattled liberals had little taste for such a demanding exercise; it was easier to shut their eyes and cover their ears and vilify Chambers.

As for those engaged in passing on information to the Russians (it may be doubted that they considered it espionage), they took comfort after June, 1941, from the fact that the Russians were our allies against the "accumulated evil of the world." In their view they were simply hastening the day of the victory over fascism/nazism. The means by which most of them were prevailed upon to carry on such activities make grim reading, but the fact seems to be that they broke no laws except those of morality, and the "secrets" they passed on to Russian couriers certainly did nothing to imperil the security of the United States. Many were concerned with such mundane matters as agricultural output. Nevertheless, the members of the Communist espionage apparatus for a certainty did themselves and their country at the least a serious disservice. More serious than that, they tainted the atmosphere, so to speak. That is to say, their relatively mild treacheries gave credence to the notion that all Americans who succumbed to communism were traitors to their country. The spies thus aided and abetted the inquisitors.

The principal persecutors of ex-C(c)ommunists were the members of the House Un-American Activities Committee (HUAC), sometimes called the Dies committee after its rancorous and reactionary chairman. Dies's successor as the number one Red hunter was the porcine Senator from Wisconsin, of all places, Joseph McCarthy. Special attention was given by HUAC to older, foreign-born radicals. One of Rockwell Kent's old friends, Norman Tallentire, had worked in the coal mines of Great Britain at the age of thirteen and then come to the United States to work as a party and union organizer. He had lived in the United States for thirty-three years and suffered from a severe heart condition. He died of a heart attack on Ellis Island while fighting deportation proceedings.

Kent himself had a successful dairy at Au Sable Forks in New York, but in the McCarthy era his customers stopped buying his milk, and he was forced to give away the dairy with its cows and equipment. His passport was canceled, and Kent, who had roamed the world from Greenland and Newfoundland to Alaska and Brazil in search of subjects for his paintings, was not allowed to travel out of the United States. He sued, and after three years of expensive litigation the Supreme Court declared in his favor. Writing to the old cartoonist of the *New Masses* William Gropper, Kent noted, "I think it is a hell of a time to have lived into. It is disillusioning and dreadful what these times have done to people—or, rather, to have become aware of people's vulnerability to fear."

Paul Robeson was blacklisted in the United States, and when he tried to go abroad for concert engagements, his passport was also lifted, so that one of the greatest artists of the day was denied the right to practice his art or earn his living because he adhered to political opinions that had been held by hundreds of thousands of thoroughly respectable Americans a decade earlier.

Steve Nelson and his wife and two young children were in Pittsburgh in 1948 when the great retrospective anti-Communist movement began its vengeful course. "Before we left in 1957," he wrote, "we saw hundreds of men and women fired from their jobs, driven out of town, deported, or jailed. Moreover, the movements these people participated in were, by and large, crushed. Radicals in labor unions were curbed, progressive fraternal organizations intimidated, and the Communist Party hounded into impotency."

The persecutors said, in effect, to the persecuted: "Your ideas about the future of humanity were different from ours, and we are going to punish you for that; we are going to punish you with public exposure, with bullying and humiliation, with loss of esteem, with degradation, with accusations of treason, often with loss of jobs and the opportunity to work at your chosen occupation or profession. Moreover, without any respect for the historical context in which these acts and opinions took place, without regard for what might be called an ideological statute of limitations (that is to say, that opinions quite commonly change during a normal lifetime as a consequence of changing circumstances in the world), we are going to punish you today for what you thought yesterday." It is hard to imagine a more unjust, immoral, and, finally, unconstitutional procedure. People who were actually charged with no crime were driven to despair and sometimes to suicide by implication and innuendo.

There appear to have been two motivations in what Elinor Langer has called "the war of the 50's [late forties might be closer] against the 30's." The first, I suspect, was a largely subconscious motivation. The new intellectual class that took shape during the twenties had poured scorn on the booboisie, the rubes, the yokels, the benighted dwellers in small towns, the Rotarians, the Legionnaires, the Christians, in short, on the great mass of their countrymen. The Communists had been equally vehement a decade later in denouncing the bourgeoisie, the middle class—in other words, most Americans (poll after poll showed that virtually all Americans identified themselves as part of that remarkably compendious class). All that had not gone entirely unnoticed by the rank and file. Now they had their innings.

There was another discernible element among the ringleaders and masters of ceremonies of the meanest show on earth. They were the politicos, in large part the Roosevelt haters, the New Deal haters, those who wished to annul or undo what had been done. If the New Deal, the Jew Deal, could be revealed to the world as filled with Communists and traitors, if the new intellectual class could be exposed as Communist to the core, perhaps the clock could be turned back to some illusory "good old days," before the United States had been corrupted by foreign, atheistic notions. At the very least, retrospective vengeance could be wreaked against all who had deviated from the norms of Americanism set by the American Legion and had joined one of the groups now included on the attorney general's list of subversive organizations. Thus began one of the most dismal chapters in American history, perhaps *the* most dismal. The Communist Party no longer existed under its own name. It had dwindled to a handful of the doggedly faithful; its great days were a thing of the past; if it had ever been a menace (and numerous anti-Communists have exhausted their ingenuity, entirely unsuccessfully, I believe, trying to prove that case), it certainly was not in the postwar era.

It might be well to review here the nature of communism in the Depression era. First there is the matter of the individual party members (and fellow travelers). A prominent enemy of communism on the left has recently complained that historians who have spoken well of communism in the thirties have supported their arguments primarily by emphasizing the often estimable character and heroic accomplishments of individual Communists, men like Hosea Hudson and Ned Cobb. Surely that is relevant evidence. While it is true that communism as a political movement was *less* than the sum of those men and women involved in it, by the same token, it was *far more* than its preposterous theories and groundless dreams. Without close attention to the actions and motives of individual Communists, we can have only a very inadequate notion of the nature of American communism.

Len De Caux in his autobiography makes the legitimate point that "under a constant searchlight of redbaiting hostility from press, employers, and opposing union factions, the 'communists' had to meet higher standards than most union leaders in respect to honesty, democracy, business-like operation, militancy and results." He added: "The most fully employed persons I met during the depression were the communists." "They worked 10 or 12 hours a day—maybe 16, if you counted yakking time. Most got no pay. A few full-timers had theoretical salaries, more theory than salary. . . . Most worked for love, or spite, if you prefer. Work they did. They were in on every protest I saw or heard of. If they didn't start things themselves, they were Johnnies-on-the-spot. . . . They organized block committees, mass meetings, demonstrations. . . . The communists made immediate demands. More relief, in cash and jobs. Public works at union wages. Hot lunches for school children. An end to evictions . . . . They demanded jobless and social security. They fought in the way most open to the dispossessed—by raising hell to force concessions from rulers. In doing this, the communist didn't fail to emphasize that capitalism was proving a lousy system, and should be replaced."

In the words of Sidney Lens, the Communists "passed out leaflets, held meetings, led strikes with a zeal no other force could muster. And we were willing to make personal sacrifices in a way that the staid leadership of labor was not. Whatever one may think of communist political foibles," Lens wrote, "individual members faced hardships, beatings and the threat of jail with great courage. . . . From late 1929 to 1932 twenty-three men and women were shot in strikes and unemployment demonstrations led by communists." He added: "Apart from the tendency to get married without marriage licenses, the moral code of the radicals I knew—including myself and Lillian [his wife]—was somewhat sterner than that of most people. Our relationships were emotionally strong, and though there were no legal ties or taboos on sex, infidelity was probably less frequent than it was among the public at large." Sidney and Lillian Lens survived by working in restaurants, he as short-order cook, she as a waitress. After work, he recalled, "we would distribute leaflets, visit contacts."

Such instances could be multiplied thousands of times over. Selfless labors in the cause of the poor and oppressed were at least as characteristic of party members as acrimonious factional squabbles and servile obedience to orders from Moscow.

Those non-Communists who worked most closely with the party and knew its members best were commonly in agreement on their good qualities as well as their less admirable ones. "The Communists—the best of them—were devoted people," Norman Thomas wrote, "able in organizing labor and the unemployed. One often wanted to work with them. But their tactics were completely unscrupulous." Dorothy Day had been deeply involved with the Communist Party before her conversion to Catholicism. In the words of her biographer William Miller, "she regarded the Communists she had known as good people. In their generosity and self-sacrifice in the cause of human values, they were unlike any other people she knew."

Even more important than the character of the individuals who made up the party were the achievements of the party and its innumerable auxiliaries. First and foremost was their espousal of the cause of black Americans, the high points of which were undoubtedly the cases of the Scottsboro boys and Angelo Herndon. But those were only the best known. The history of the International Labor Defense is made up of hundreds of cases in which the civil rights of blacks and union organizers (and Communists, to be sure) were argued before the courts with skill and tenacity and, often, success. The party raised millions of dollars for such cases and supplemented in critically important ways, if it did not outdo, the American Civil Liberties Union in its defense of the rights of those whose rights had been denied.

In many of the most conclusive battles of the labor movement the Communist Party provided critically important cadres of experienced union organizers for the Congress of Industrial Organizations. It thereby played a crucial role in ending the war between capital and labor with, if not victory for labor, at least a rough kind of justice and the beginning of a new era in the relations between those two ancient foes. In the final phases of that war, the strike at Flint, Michigan, against General Motors was a crucial campaign, and so narrow was the victory that it is hard not to believe that without the active participation of the Communists it might well have failed. A failure would have been a major, if not a conclusive, setback for the infant CIO and the cause of industrial organization in general. A case by case study of the most important strikes in the period from 1933 to 1940 reveals a similar pattern of Communist participation. To Len De Caux the history books were "full of hypocrisy, evasions, and lies about the communists in the CIO and elsewhere. The lies are from union factions that fought the left for their union cards, or 'piecards.' The evasions are to cover the past of the reds who became antireds and sometimes to protect the communists. . . . Everyone in labor or progressive politics played footsy with the communists at some time or in some way. A rule of the game was that the communist player should not proclaim his communism. That way the respectable, if caught at it, could say with shocked innocence, 'Good gracious, we never knew he was a communist!' . . . Some camouflage was necessary as communists moved into battle for progressive causes. It was expected, if not demanded, by the allies they battled alongside. . . . All the CIO leaders worked, or played, with communists. . . . " Dubinsky was the one exception Le Caux allowed. The leader of the Ladies' Garment Workers was so bruised by his fight for control of his union that he never forgot or forgave.

The final, bitter irony was that when those unions that had welcomed, indeed sought out, the help of the Communists in organizing the autoworkers, the miners, steel and textile workers, and the longshoremen had become powerful and effective organizations that had brought many benefits to their members, in the hysterical atmosphere created by the cold war they turned on the "Reds," many of them older men in their late forties and fifties, and drove them out of the unions they had played such a vital role in organizing. Hosea Hudson was one such victim. He was ousted as president of the steelworkers' local he had helped to found. The order was: "Get that Hosie Hudson out of there, that God damn communist! He's nothing but a communist!" The black workers went along. "They didn't know no better," he told Nell Painter.

The Unemployed Councils organized by the Communists were without doubt the most effective "people's" organization in the Depression era, perhaps in our history. Ironically, by giving the poor and unemployed a means of expressing themselves through common action, the Unemployed Councils helped defuse radical sentiment rather than inflame it. It could indeed be argued that much of the good that the Communists did was, in a manner of speaking, inadvertent. "We . . . might not have been making much headway, but I thought we were getting on the right track, doing the right thing. That's what kept people moving on," Steve Nelson wrote.

The Communists intended to lay the groundwork for the revolution, for example, by "educating the workers in forms of mass action." Instead, they helped the bewildered recipients of welfare to cope with the often obtuse bureaucracies set up to keep them from starving. Claude McKay, opposed to the Communist Party as he was, readily admitted that it had played the leading role in organizing the unemployed and the WPA workers.

Too much emphasis can hardly be placed on the role of the Communist Party as a rallying point (prior, of course, to the Russian-German nonaggression pact) for the opponents of fascism. In isolationist America the party, through dozens of fronts, organized opposition first to Mussolini and then to Hitler.

Besides treating blacks as equals, the greatest contribution of the Communists to the health and well-being of the Republic may have been their nutty exaltation of the "worker" into the hope of mankind and, collectively, the ruler of the world. Bizarre as this notion appears in retrospect, it did focus attention on the plight of laboring men and women in the United States, just as the party's dedication to the principle of racial equality focused attention on the terrible consequences of racial prejudice. The result was that writers, artists, professors, and radical intellectuals generally—all those drawn to the party—devoted themselves wholeheartedly to the workers' cause. While this effort produced mostly bad literature, it produced excellent propaganda. It helped create a "social atmosphere" or "climate of opinion" favorable to the claims of labor.

If to this we add the fact that the Communist Party (along with its various factions) represented the only substantial resistance in the United States to the growth of fascism, it seems fair to say that its influence on the era was positive, if not essential.

Attempting to wean his friend John Dos Passos from his growing "Marxophobia," Edmund Wilson listed some of the accomplishments of the Communists. He wrote that "you ought to give the Communists, with all their shortcomings, credit for playing a valuable role as agitators. It seems to me that during these recent years their influence has been felt through the whole length of American politics. They have put fundamental questions up to the rest of the world and have worried people into trying to find answers. You speak disapprovingly of intellectuals, theories, etc.; but aren't you giving evidence, in your present disillusion about the Communists and Russia, of having cherished a typical intellectual illusion? I don't think you ought to be so shocked at discovering that political movements are failing in practice to live up to their pretensions. They never have and, when the whole world is socialist, will continue to fail to do so. I don't think you ought to let yourself be driven into Marxophobia by the present literary popularity of Marxism. . . . " And a month later Wilson played a variation on the theme of the ubiquitousness of Marxist thought: "We live in a world now which had been profoundly permeated with Marxism—Washington as well as Moscow—(since Tugwell went to Russia, took his cue from the Five-Year Plan, etc.). What is needed is to see Marx and Lenin as part of the humanistic tradition."

From a Steve Nelson, working in the anthracite fields of Pennsylvania or the coal mines of Illinois or Kentucky to help people who desperately needed help, to blacks like Hosea Hudson and Ned Cobb, the party reached where few others ventured.

Of all the peoples in the world, Americans may well have the shortest memories. Indeed, it often seems as if they wish to "disremember." Above all, they wished to "disremember" the thirties. Thoreau's observation on Americans—"One generation abandons the enterprises of another like stranded vessels"—applies with particular force to the America of the 1930's.

So we were treated to the unedifying spectacle of retroactive revenge, featuring the enthusiastic bashing of eggheads. All in all, it was the grimmest episode in our history, far worse than the Salem witchcraft trials. It made trimmers and cowards of many decent people and heroes of a few. It was a rite of expiation, the ritual murder of selected victims to propitiate the household gods of nineteenth-century America; it helped us "disremember" by annihilating an important and dramatic segment of our history. Moreover, the politics of revenge in the period following World War II had the coincidental effect of obscuring the strong socialist and anarchist traditions that had been so prominent in the United States in the decades following the Civil War. The readers of earlier volumes of this work will be well aware of the strength of American radicalism in those years—socialisms, anarchisms, the single taxers, Bellamy's nationalists, and, above all, populism. In burying the thirties we obscured the whole long and noble tradition of American radicalism, back to and including the American Revolution itself.

In this attempt to put American communism into perspective, a review of the complex of ideas out of which it came may be helpful. The utopian impulse, strongly represented by communism, dates back to John Winthrop's *A Modell of Christian Charity,* written by the Puritan leader aboard the *Arbella* on the way to establish a Bible commonwealth at Massachusetts Bay. It was the mission of the little Puritan band, Winthrop argued, to redeem Christendom. They (Puritans) must be "as a Citie Uppon a Hill," so that those who came after would model themselves upon the first settlers, sent by God into the wilderness to create a new order of Christian piety—the convenanted community.

Winthrop's theme became the basis of the Protestant Passion for redemption. The Scottish, the English, and specifically the French Enlightenments complemented the Protestant Passion by aspiring to a perfected society achieved through reason and science (reason applied to the natural world).

At the time of the American Revolution the Apocalypse was widely anticipated. Elias Boudinot, a Pennsylvania patriot and president of the Continental Congress for a term, left his considerable fortune to hasten the millennium by converting the Jews and the Indians (considered by him and many others to be the Lost Tribes of Israel), and the poet laureate of the new Republic Philip Freneau predicted that America would become "A new Jerusalem, sent down from heaven," to "grace our happy earth,—perhaps this land, / Whose ample bosom shall receive, though late, / Myriads of saints, with their immortal king, / To live and reign on earth a thousand years, / Thence called Millenium. . . . "

Thomas Jefferson was the prophet of the American variation of the Enlightenment. To Jefferson and his followers the French Revolution promised utopia. As Carl Becker pointed out in his *The Heavenly City of the Eighteenth-Century Philosophers,* the philosophers of the French Enlightenment—Condorcet, Voltaire, Rousseau, Diderot—in their dream of a perfected society were, in essence, transferring the hope of St. Augustine's heavenly city to earth. Instead of perfection in the hereafter, perfection was to be achieved here and now. Religion was superstition, and superstition had prevented society from being perfected.

The initial enthusiasm with which virtually all Americans greeted the revolution by their recent allies against a decadent monarchy soon was mitigated by the bloody excesses of the far left—the Jacobins and the followers of Robespierre and Danton. The ferociously anticlerical nature of the French Revolution, its bloody elimination or exile of many of its earlier heroes, among them the revered Lafayette, and its faith in reason and science turned more conservative Americans off. At the same time it seemed only to increase the ardor of the radical supporters of Thomas Jefferson, the Jeffersonian Republicans, as they came to be called (having nothing to do, of course, with the Republican Party of the 1850s). News of each new atrocity was greeted with enthusiasm by the American Jacobins, who called each other "Citizen" and "Citizeness." Enemies of the Federalist Party declared their allegiance to France, wore the tricolors of the revolution as cockades in their hats, waved the tricolor flag, and sported miniature guillotines. In all these extravagant demonstrations of devotion to a cause of which they had little real comprehension, Jefferson was their cautious coadjutor, the hero of the Jacobin societies and the Democratic clubs, where the members sang the "Marseillaise" and drank to the overthrow of monarchs and aristocrats. Was not the French Revolution the offspring of the American Revolution and the prospective parent of numerous revolutions to come, until the people everywhere, the "many," triumphed over their rulers, the "few"?

When Jefferson was elected President in 1800, it was said old ladies hid their Bibles, fearing that the atheistic Virginian would send his agents to destroy them. A hundred and thirty some years later, American intellectuals, liberals and radicals alike, showed the same irrational enthusiasm for rationalism and revolution that they had displayed in the period from 1789 until there was such an accumulation of evidence that the French Revolution had gone awry that even the most obtuse Jeffersonians—now "Democrats" instead of "Republicans"—could no longer delude themselves, a period, incidentally, of about twenty-five years. But the general sentiments that underlay the revolutionary ardor of Jefferson and his followers found their lodgment in what I have called the Secular-Democratic Consciousness. That particular philosophical pot simmered away throughout our subsequent history as a nation, joining forces intermittently with the more potent Protestant Passion for the Redemption of America and the World (through the abolition of slavery, support of the rights of women, the prohibition of spirituous liquors, and all the other lesser panaceas that have attracted us) until, in the aftermath of the Great Depression, it all suddenly boiled over in a new brew of universal revolution. Those men and women who joined the Communist Party in fact or in spirit in the decade from 1929 to 1939 were, though few were aware of the fact, reviving an ancient American tradition.

It is interesting to reflect further upon the fact that two Christian heresies bear a striking similarity to Marxian communism. One is the Pelagian heresy named after the monk Pelagius of the fifth century A.D. Pelagius, who preached his doctrines in Africa and Palestine, contested the orthodox view of man as tainted by original sin. Or at least he insisted that perfection was possible for all human beings (he was thus, of course, the father of so-called Christian perfectionism which we have already taken notice of). Manichaeanism was founded by the Persian Mani, who propounded the doctrine of dualism—that the world was a battleground between the forces of good and evil. Manichaeanism proved remarkably enduring. Revived again and again in various forms in the Christian Church, it flourished in times of crisis and demoralization such as the period of the so-called Babylonian Captivity, when two Popes ruled, one in Rome and one in Avignon.

Finally, there was (and is) the notion of the imminent millennium, when human history as we know it will end in the Second Coming of Christ to reign 1,000 years on earth in universal peace and harmony.

In Marxism the notion that the state will "wither away" after an interval of the "dictatorship of the proletariat" and all peoples will live in a world free of oppression and competition corresponds neatly with the Christian hope of the millennium.

The Marxian faith in human perfectibility, inherited from the philosophers of the French Enlightenment, has its equivalent in Pelagianism, and Marx's division of the world into bad capitalists and good workers suggests the Manichaean division of the world into a clear-cut contest between good and evil.

Perhaps in the last analysis we can best understand international communism as a judgment on the callousness and indifference of Western Christendom (or industrial capitalism) to the suffering and injustice that it had inflicted on the great mass of people living within its precincts. By the same token the nations of Western Europe and, even more, the United States have been the principal beneficiaries of Soviet communism because communism challenged them to create more equitable societies and they were ultimately forced to respond. Most European nations did so at a heavy cost, having first endured harsh and repressive dictatorships of the right. The United States is, in the main, the most fortunate legatee of communism because, as Karl Radek, the Bolshevik theoretician, predicted, when challenged, it achieved a modest degree of social justice without sacrificing (or sacrificing only briefly and partially) those liberties guaranteed by the Constitution.

When the subject is seen in this light, it particularly behooves the United States to do everything within its power to achieve a reconciliation with the Soviets. However much we may deplore the absence of freedoms precious to us in countries under Soviet domination, we must recognize that their absence is, in large measure, the price that we forced those nations to pay for economic equality. The bottom line, as they say, is that the working classes in Communist societies have a fairer share of the national wealth, meager as it may be in some instances, than they had under previous regimes or economic systems.

To put it another way, if we consider the length and bitterness of the war between capital and labor and the fact that from the Great Strikes of 1877 to the end of the New Deal most thoughtful men and women believed that that war could end only in a revolutionary upheaval, we may understand that in all likelihood *Russia had our revolution for us.* And for that we should be grateful.

Communists through the twenties and thirties were far from being evil or treacherous individuals; they were dreamers of the utopian dream, stirred by a selfless passion for the redemption of the world on Marxian principles. That they should have looked to Moscow or Joseph Stalin for salvation was no more bizarre when one stops to think of it than believing that salvation would come through temperance and a vegetarian diet. Or emancipation. Or spiritualism and free love. Or Woodrow Wilson's Fourteen Points and the League of Nations. In the words of the British critic Wyndham Lewis, "Liberalism substituted itself for Christianity, and, dying, it designat[ed] communism as its heir."

Certainly communism represented a failure of intellect (and, to an extent, of moral clarity) among Americans most zealous for a solution to the world's ills, but it was a failure so selfless and so well intentioned that it is difficult not to sympathize with it. We might well wish that it had been other than it was—more rational (which was, after all, its principal claim), more humane, more honest with itself and others, less rancorous, less disputatious, less given to mind-numbing rhetoric. But history is not cut to the historian's order, and considering the requirements of the times and the contingent character of all human enterprises, the various denominations of communists served their country well.

The end of communism-cum-Enlightenment as a persuasive account of historical man, of reality, surely marks one of the intellectual turning points in history. Human nature being what it is, there is, of course, no guarantee that we will not, in the future, drag it out, refurbish it, and once more proclaim it the hope of mankind. Meantime, we can only be grateful for its demise while doing our best to do it justice. The fracture line that runs across our consciousness must be healed. We must incorporate the Depression era, and the Communists with it, into our history so that we and the Russians may anticipate a common future.

# 48

# The Path to the Future

One of the most striking postwar developments was the Supreme Court's enunciation of what has come to be called the nationalization of civil liberties and civil rights. It appeared to the casual observer that the Court, quite on its own, had reached the conclusion— after almost two centuries of reflection in the form of innumerable decisions—that the Founding Fathers, by incorporating the first ten amendments in the Constitution, had intended to make the Federal government or, specifically, the Supreme Court the final arbiter on all matters having to do with civil rights of the nation's citizens. That adoption of the concept had been delayed so long was eloquent testimony to the ubiquitousness of the states' rights doctrine, in its more extreme forms one of the most mischievous notions in the history of political ideas.

The most important case, of course, was *Brown* v. *Board of Education of Topeka,* which declared in 1954 that all public schools must be desegregated with "deliberate speed." In that case Felix Frankfurter did much to absolve himself of his often excessively conservative decisions by helping secure an unanimous decision in favor of the plaintiffs.

After the desegregation decision of the Supreme Court, Justice

Hugo Black's law class at the University of Alabama refused to invite him to attend its fiftieth reunion in 1956; his colleague Bill Douglas described him as "crushed." A Southern Congressman intercepted Douglas on a Washington Street and shouted, "Why didn't I kill that son-of-a-bitch Black? We were in the Army together. In the same company. I could easily have shot him—and no one would have known the difference. I was a fool, a goddamn silly fool."

With our predilection for electing generals to the highest office in the land, we chose able and amiable Dwight Eisenhower as President in 1952 over "egghead" Adlai Stevenson. Eisenhower, a nonpolitical figure, presided benignly over a nation astonished and delighted by its own prosperity. The fifties had been preceded by three "difficult decades." The twenties were times of hedonistic self-indulgence and moral and spiritual disarray, of wild prosperity and cruel repression. The thirties were a decade of profound and unsettling disaster and, with the New Deal, unprecedented change in many basic American attitudes and assumptions about the nature of society. The forties were the decade of the war and of the "disremembering" of the thirties. Depressions had commonly followed wars, but World War II not only "cured" the Depression but produced worldwide prosperity. In doing so, it refuted the ideologues of the left and the right. Capitalism did not collapse after the war, as the Communists had insisted it must according to the scientific laws of Marxism, but entered a new and dazzling era of expansion, caused in large part by the enlightened policies of the victors, primarily the United States, which demonstrated that it was possible to learn, at least occasionally, from history. The revival of what I think we may fairly call New Deal capitalism—that is to say, capital tamed and domesticated by the New Deal—refuted the ideologues of the right, who insisted that Franklin Roosevelt had transformed the nation into a communist or at least socialist imitation of the Soviet Union, destroyed "business confidence," and killed capitalism. Following the Democratic President, Harry Truman, the Republican, Dwight Eisenhower, untroubled by social theories, ratified the New Deal simply by accepting it. A kindly, reasonably intelligent, avuncular man, he admired successful businessmen, played golf with tycoons and revivalists, and left office with an imperishable warning against the greedy ambitions of the "military-industrial complex."

Eisenhower also witnessed and gave cautious support to the beginning of the civil rights movement, not so much because he believed in the cause of black Americans as because he believed in upholding the law which the Supreme Court had declared in the case of *Brown* v. *Board of Education*. That was the first step. On December 1, 1955, Rosa Parks refused to go to the back of the bus in Montgomery, Alabama, and the strike of Montgomery blacks against the city transportation system began. Rosa Parks has sometimes been depicted as a tired black domestic servant whose feet hurt her. She was, in fact, a member of the small but active Montgomery chapter of the NAACP. At the recommendation of Martin Luther King, Sr. she had attended one of Myles Horton's workshops at the Highlander Folk School. There she had mingled with white Southerners as friends and social equals, talked with them and eaten with them, and learned peaceful techniques of social protest. That experience had helped nerve her for her symbolic act of defiance. What she did not know when she performed that act was whether her instinct was correct that Montgomery blacks had experienced sufficient humiliation to come to her support. As it turned out, they had.

It was also the case that a direct line ran from Abraham Lincoln's abolitionist friend "dear old double 'd' Addams" to Rosa Parks. It ran through Addams's devoted daughter, Jane, and through Hull House to Myles Horton and the Highlander Folk School in Tennessee, one of those strange currents of history which are the channels of our redemption, which are always there, though not always noted or understood.

If the retrospective revenge of the House Un-American Activities Committee era was the negative side of postwar America, the civil rights–black power movement was the positive side, the most compelling drama of the period. Its roots lay in hundreds of discrete episodes that ranged from the Harlem Renaissance to the trials of Scottsboro boys, from Jesse Owens's triumphs in the Berlin Olympics of 1936 and Joe Louis's awesome victories in the boxing ring to Eleanor Roosevelt's first tentative embrace of Mary McLeod Bethune. "Sit-in" took a new meaning as courageous young black men and women sat in in segregated theaters and restaurants and as white students ventured into the South to give witness to their solidarity, to be beaten and jailed, to risk their lives, and, in three cases, to lose them. The new medium of television helped dramatize the black cause. White and black Americans joined in the march from Selma to Montgomery, Alabama. Black Muslims provided a unique religion and identity for hundreds of thousands of black Americans. The Black Panthers enacted in the form of guerrilla theater black rage and white fear. Stokeley Carmichael spoke of black power, and Rap Brown reminded his white countrymen who accused black activists of violent rhetoric and destructive actions that "violence . . . is as American as cherry pie." Baseball, the first sports barrier for blacks, was breached in 1947 by Jackie Robinson, with the support of Branch Rickey, and hundreds of astonishingly gifted black athletes poured through the breach until they threatened to take over the professional sports world. It was as though the game of basketball had been invented to demonstrate the remarkable grace and agility of black Americans.

So at long last, after unaccountable misery and persecution, black Americans began to claim their rights as citizens of the Republic. Black culture, black literature, black poetry, and notably black music already constituted a major component of the broader American culture; now blacks began to penetrate hitherto unassailable white strongholds in business and the professions, in labor unions and social organizations.

W. E. B. Du Bois said at the end of the nineteenth century that the overriding issue of the new century would be the place of black people in white America. It took so long and there were so many setbacks, disappointments, and delays that Du Bois, whose *The Souls of Black Folk* was testament and scripture for every black man and woman who dreamed of justice, despaired at the end of his life. He gave up on white "capitalist" America, became a Communist, and moved to Africa, so seriously did we fail him and so grievously did we wound him.

We have given considerable attention to the formation of the new consciousness. The Great Depression, with its grim rigors, dampened, if it did not entirely extinguish, the new consciousness. Communism, with its own Puritanism, its aesthetic of art for the masses, and its censorious temper was directly counter to the major tenets of what we have called the new consciousness, with its exaltation of the sponta-neous and the natural. Such art was declared decadent and bourgeois— most dreaded denunciation of all. Marxism was rational and scientific. For a time the two currents appeared to merge in the Harlem Ren-aissance: then, gradually, Marxism established its dominance over writ-ers, artists and intellectuals. Black writers like Richard Wright and Claude McKay who would not tolerate being told what to write about and how to write about "proletarian" topics broke bitterly with the Communist Party. Many writers simply drifted away, and some of the less talented bowed to the party; but sooner or later all the more important writers who had once been under the party's spell broke free. The general effect of the party's heavy doctrinal hand had been decidedly discouraging. Beyond that, it seemed frivolous to celebrate the senses and the instincts when simple bodily well-being was threatened. The Second World War also called for austerity, self-denial, sacrifice, loyalty to the flag. The dark forces let loose by fascism, or whatever we wish to call it, were like some gigantic, universal id, rising with shocking and unprecedented violence out of humanity's collective subconscious. Fascism gave a bad name to spontaneity; suddenly reason, logic, objectivity, science were in the ascendancy. The university became their sanctuary and citadel. Even the Puritans enjoyed a degree of popularity. The Harvard historian Samuel Eliot Morison, who had been thrilled by Teddy Roosevelt's call to battle under the Progressive banner and flirted with Emma Goldman's brand of anarchism while he was Harmsworth professor at Oxford, led the Puritan revival, followed by his student Perry Miller. They praised the Puritans for their rational intellects and their devotion to learning; neither of them remarked the similarity of the Puritans, with their scheme of orthodoxies, to present-day Marxists.

Meanwhile, as we say, the academic world exploded. Higher education became one of the nation's major "growth industries," with millions of students and hundreds of thousands of professors and administrators. But there was no comparable growth in the intellectual horizons of the academy. "Instruction" took the place of education. Learning went on in the same deadening manner of which Charles Francis Adams had complained in the Harvard of the 1850s. The most conspicuous difference was that the so-called social sciences—sociology, economics, political science, psychology, and anthropology—came into the ascendancy. Science, now tied to national defense and showered with government largess, grew vast and ubiquitous. Professors, busy "pushing forward the frontiers of knowledge," had little time to consider the needs of their students. As more intellectuals and professors (not necessarily the same thing) found a marvelously secure home in the academy (once they had published the required amount), the gap between the "man in the street" and the men in the cloistered world of the university grew ever wider. The preacherly function which had its roots in the Protestant passion for learning, as we have already noted, gave way to the priestly function. The academy became so entirely secularized that at least in most public institutions religion was not admitted as a subject of serious study. The result was spiritual sterility in the intellectual world and yahoo religion. That students should have become alienated in such an environment was perhaps inevitable.

Their response was a dramatic one. If the new consciousness slumbered or smoldered through the decades of the thirties, forties, and fifties, it burst into flame in the 1960s and 1970s, and again it was inspired by and identified itself with black consciousness. It first appeared among middle-class college students, and with the stimulus of the increasingly unpopular Vietnam War, it spread like wildfire across the nation's campuses. It was the first youth movement in our history, and it clearly depended upon the enormous growth in higher education that followed World War II. Students invented or reinvented the new consciousness that had flowered in the first two decades of the twentieth century and then withered under the economic devastation of the Great Depression and the wartime discipline of the Second World War. Once again the instinctual life was exalted above the rational life.

Virtually every aspect of American life was affected; in a measure, changed. Americans became more aware of areas of blight, of the crippling effects of prejudice on the prejudiced as well as on their victims; they perceived injustices and inequities that had previously passed unnoticed. The middle-class young, who identified most closely with the fight of black Americans for the justice and equality promised by the Declaration of Independence and so long deferred, began to question the received wisdom of their elders. The most dramatic form that questioning took was what came to be called the free speech movement. One of its leaders, Mario Savio, never fails to remind us that it was a direct outgrowth of the civil rights movement. Young white students, who sat in and marched with young blacks in Mississippi or Alabama, returned to their comfortable middle-class existences, to their homes and colleges, with new questions about the meaning and requirements of justice. The questions were given a heightened urgency by the accelerating American involvement in Southeast Asia, where we had undertaken to "contain" communism. Young Americans began to question our right to kill Vietnamese in the name of stopping the advance of communism. We had too much to do to put our own house in order, they argued.

The dominant culture produced a counterculture, which had many facets. It had its own style of dress, its own music—Bob Dylan, the Beatles, rock and roll—its own "age," the Age of Aquarius. The music was startlingly different from any other popular music in our history. It was "talking music," poetry set to music, a poetry and music of lament over the harsh, wounding character of American life. It was in a kind of code, with songs like the "Yellow Submarine" telling in Aesopian language of drug "trips." Flower children burned money in the Haight-Ashbury district of San Francisco to dramatize their contempt for the materialistic society around them. Mario Savio attacked the impersonality of the education "industry" and the indifference of the professors to the needs and concerns of their students, declaring that with the free speech movement, the Berkeley campus of the University of California had become, for the first time, "a community of love." "Love," in fact, was the key word. One thought of Hutchins Hapgood and the early Greenwich Village mood or those pioneers of love Victoria Woodhull and Angela Heywood; of Sherwood Anderson, who longed for "the end of a money civilization" and in its place "something new, healthy and strong." It had seemed to Anderson that "in our civilization" one had to "fight hard to get a bit of . . . curiously elusive joy. . . . Do you suppose it's because of money?"

When Paul Kellogg, editor of the liberal journal *Survey*, wrote to various writers and critics in the early 1920s soliciting their views on how to create "a liveable world," Anderson had replied, "I want men and women who, at any physical cost to themselves and others, will refuse to continue work as we understand the word work." With "such surplus energy loose among us, we may begin to do some of the things that now seem entirely out of our reach. We may begin to make towns, houses, books, pictures, gardens, even cities that have beauty and meaning. . . . So you see I want a body of healthy young men and women to agree to quit working, to loaf, to refuse to be hurried or to try to get on in the world. . . . Something of the sort must happen if we are ever to bring color and flair into our modern life." It was almost as though the counterculture had read Anderson and taken him to heart. Prominent among the elements of the counterculture was the rediscovery of the crafts. Tens of thousands of mostly middle-class young men and women revived the crafts of pottery, blown and stained glass, woodwork and leatherwork in a thousand variations. Organic gardens sprouted on vacant city lots. Crafts and craft fairs became a multimillion-dollar "industry"; an opening was made in the machine-tooled façade of American society, a poignant gesture toward a softer, more gracious way of life.

That was a remarkable achievement. We are sometimes inclined to think of the late sixties and early seventies primarily in terms of violent student demonstrations against the Vietnam War. But much more was going on. One of its most important forms was the commune. It has been estimated that between 3,000,000 and 4,000,000 young Americans lived at one time or another in communal groups during the period between 1965 and 1975, and a substantial number still do. As the reader of these volumes is well aware, utopian communities, communes, have figured, if not prominently, at least arrestingly, in American history from the original "commune," the Puritan Massachusetts Bay Colony, through innumerable "covenanted" communities, to Brook Farm, John Humphrey Noyes's Oneida Community, and California's Fountain Grove. But since the disappearance of the covenanted community no more than a few thousand Americans had been involved in such ventures. Now millions of the nation's "privileged youth" abandoned the luxury of suburbia for the usually rather squalid confines of some forest retreat where the arduousness of frontier life was re-created—from carrying water of uncertain purity from the nearest stream or pond to cooking "natural" food over open fires or, in more extreme instances, eating it raw.

Throughout this work I have spoken often of the disintegrative effects of American life and compared the continental United States to a kind of vast vacuum chamber, where atomized individuals float freely but often desperately in our vast lonely spaces. Just when it seemed that the classic small American community or town was obsolete, young men and women began to reinvent it. They reinhabited small towns, but more dramatically, they started their own communities. Naïve and ephemeral as most of these undertakings were, they were a kind of collective cry for help from young men and women who wished passionately to belong to human groups. Whatever several million people stake their lives on requires to be taken seriously by the historian. It may have little or no meaning "historically"—that is to say, it may vanish without a trace—but symptomatically it tells us something we ignore at our peril. In this instance, its message appears to be that even Americans can stand only so much individualism, that we yearn to belong to coherent human groups, to communities, that we will believe in something even if it is something as commonplace as the value of living together with others and sharing their joys and tribulations. We may be sure, I believe, that these needs—for community, for celebration, for openness, for grace and joy—are deep and enduring human needs, not just American needs but *especially* American needs; our society, which has done so well in other, more material ways, has not done well in these, and these needs must be in some way attended to. Competition, "success" (whatever that strange, insatiable beast is), power, aggressiveness—in every generation thousands, perhaps tens of thousands of Americans have yearned for a better, fairer way of living.

Ihab Hassan, professor of English literature at Wesleyan University, may well have had the counterculture in mind when he wrote: "It is possible that certain areas of our literary, social, and dream life may turn out to be secret laboratories in which man is experimenting with the values on which his future depends. A novel and radical mode of self-consciousness may be in the making. The really 'new frontier' of the age cannot be defined politically. It will be defined, superficially, by our patterns of work and leisure; and beyond that, by a revolution in our instinctual lives comparable to the industrial revolution of the last century. Ultimately, the new frontier will be a religious one. It will be religious in the sense that the over-weening concerns of the Self, which fills hugely the void of the modern world, will be modified on terms that the new self can honor. Ultimately, a new ground for transcendence—neither the State nor perhaps Christianity—will have to be discovered."

In a somewhat similar spirit the British historian Michael Howard has observed: "After a prolonged stay in the United States . . . I returned to England with two impressions. The first was the sheer richness of contemporary American culture. America leads the world in every branch of science and technology, every field of scholarship and the arts. New York City is in a state of continuous creative ferment, while across the country a score of smaller cities [and, one might add, towns] compete, like Italian Renaissance states in conspicuous cultural display, each trying to outdistance the others with its orchestras, its museums, its universities, its civic center, and, not least, its restaurants." If Professor Howard somewhat overstates the case, the basic point is sound enough. The cultural desert of the "Bozarts" that Henry Mencken and the artists and intellectuals of the 1920s so derided no longer exists. Not all this cultural activity is, to be sure, of the highest quality, nor need it be. We produce more art than we can consume. Yet it does represent a profound change in the atmosphere of American life. We are closer than ever before to having a common culture that serves to soften the harsher contours of our national life.

In this attempt to think about the future of America, it may well be that a black anthropologist, John Langston Gwaltney, has given us a valuable clue by reminding white Americans that black Americans view the world very differently. Gwaltney, whose respondents are members of what he calls a "core black culture," has been remarkably skillful in drawing out their perceptions of the falsities and hypocrisies of the dominant white world. In the words echoed by many other respondents, Bernard Vanderstell said: "Black people think that they are at the mercy of life or that they must teach their children to be ready to stand whatever life brings. White people think they can be victors, even in death, and this no black person of the blacks [true black person] can understand. . . . White men have inherited a position of command and that means that they cannot admit that anything is beyond them, so they must pretend to capabilities that they do not possess. Subconsciously they fear that if they admit to being anything less than omnipotent they will become impotent; their power will crumple away. These ideas are certainly present in Christian doctrine—'the fear of the Lord is the beginning of wisdom,' etc.—but whites have chosen, in the main, to ignore them and blacks have taken them with great seriousness."

John Langstaff, a dignified elderly black, stressed the same theme. Whites want "that which in the nature of things is impossible. They believe that there must be a man who is more manly than a good man can be, and that there is a beautiful woman who is more beautiful than all the other beautiful women. They really think that everything and every people, except us, can be whatever they would like it to be. . . . They are never contented because they are always looking for a happiness which is greater than happiness. They want to find love where they have sown only hate and selfishness. They want to run and never tire, to satisfy their thirsts and hungers and not be full. They cannot see that the sickness which they all suffer comes from greed, a kind of childish believing that when they close their minds, the world is not what it always was and always will be."

Eleanor Roosevelt expressed a similar sentiment when she noted that Americans were the world's greatest "wishful thinkers." Can such a people, so nurtured in optimism, perceive, in Ralph Waldo Emerson's words, the "terror of life" and become "manned to face it"? Perhaps the real hope of the future lies not in "equality" between whites and blacks in America but in white understanding and acceptance as their own of "black reality." D. H. Lawrence in an introduction to Edward Dahlberg's *Bottom Dogs*, published in 1930, wrote that "the real pioneer . . . fought like hell and suffered until the soul was ground out of him: and then, nine times out of ten, failed, was beaten." There was little to suggest "the amazing Odyssey of the brute fight with savage conditions of the western continent. . . . Americans will not stand for the pioneer stuff, except in small sentimental doses. They know too well the grimness of it, the savage fight and savage failure which broke the back of the country but which also broke something in the human soul. The spirit and the will survived: but something in the soul perished; the softness, the floweriness, the natural tenderness. How could it survive the sheer brutality of the fight with that American wilderness, which is so big, vast, and obdurate? The savage America was conquered and subdued at the expense of the instinctive and intuitive sympathy of the human soul. The fight was too brutal."

Lawrence went on to contrast America with Europe. Americans, he noted, believed "that man should behave in a kind and benevolent manner. But this is a social belief and a social gesture, rather than an individual flow. The flow from the heart, the warmth of fellow-feeling which has animated Europe and been the best of her humanity, individual, spontaneous, flowing in thousands of little, passionate currents often conflicting, this seems unable to persist on the American soil. Instead you get the social creed of benevolence and uniformity, a mass *will*, and an inward individual retraction, an isolation, an amorphous separateness like grains of sand, each grain isolated upon its own will, its own indomitableness, its implacability." It seemed to Lawrence that the phenomenon—"the deep psychic change which [I] call the breaking of the heart, the collapse of the flow of spontaneous warmth between a man and his fellows"—was happening all over the world, the terrible isolation of modern man.

We have frequently noted the psychic strains in America; how families, especially immigrant families, have been torn apart, generation from generation, parent from child, brothers from sisters: how communities have collapsed under social or economic pressures and "classes" become increasingly separate, socially and geographically; how neighborhoods have changed in a decade or so and towns been absorbed in metropolitan suburbs. All these changes have imposed severe psychological burdens upon us: They have dulled our instincts for community, weakened our capacity for love and tenderness, they have, in Lawrence's phrase, broken our hearts. So the healing of hearts and the restoring of souls may be the next great task.

W. E. B. Du Bois called his great book *The Souls of Black Folk*. It is as though in some strange way the soul missing in white America has been preserved as a common legacy in black America, as though, in short, black America might give white America the soul that had been lost in the unimaginable rigors of breaking America. At least it is tempting to think so. Of course, it is not white America's soul that black America has been keeping; it is its own, its precious achievement accomplished in the face of suffering and hardship beyond the telling. White America, well aware, in Harriet Beecher Stowe's words, of its "cold Northern temper," has periodically yearned for black soul. Many abolitionists believed it would penetrate white America in the aftermath of slavery. In the period of the Harlem Renaissance American intellectuals hoped to claim it as an essential part of the new consciousness. Black Americans have given it to jazz and blues and gospel music, to rock and roll and virtually every form of musical expression, and, dramatically, to professional sports.

In Ralph Ellison's words, "all Negroes affirm certain feelings of identity, certain foods, certain types of dancing, music, religious experiences, certain tragic attitudes toward experience and toward our situation as Americans. . . . I think that the mixture of the marvelous and the terrible is a basic condition of human life and that the persistence of human ideals represents the marvelous pulling itself up out of the chaos of the universe. In the fairy tale, beauty must be awakened by the beast, the beastly man can only regain his humanity through love."

That remains the final challenge: the restoration of the American soul by those despised and degraded Americans who hold it in trust, not just for a white Americans but for the human race.

I must confess what is doubtless apparent enough: that the intent of this work is broader than simply a narrative history of the United States. It is my view that the scheme of psychotherapy that consists, typically, of a therapist and a patient, a patient presumably suffering from some emotional difficulty or other out of a fairly wide range made available by our society, is severely limited in its therapeutic value. This has been acknowledged by some psychotherapists, who now engage in sessions with two or more members of the family of the patient on the not unreasonable ground that his or her problem may be tied up somehow with those close personal relationships. By the same logic, it seems to me that history, which provides the broadest context for the individual sufferer, is, by that fact, the ultimate or most comprehensive therapy. In other words, it is in history that we are revealed "in the concrete reality of our historical being," wherein we may be healed and reconciled. What we have said and done in our history, in our "autobiography," as Eugen Rosenstock-Huessy puts it, is in large part what (and who) we are. So my ambition has been to lead the reader into a larger and more spacious realm than any that we can dwell in simply as contemporaries. It has been my hope that the reader not only would find the history of the United States instructive but would perceive it to be "philosophy teaching by examples." In other words, the remarkable range of human potentialities would be demonstrated, on the one hand, and the limited, contingent and providential nature of history/life be made evident, on the other. I must also be at some pains to insist that I have no illusion that I have told the truth, the whole truth, and nothing but the truth. I have done my best to tell "nothing but the truth," but I am constantly aware that a historian can encompass only a fraction of it at best. History, in the last analysis, is no more understandable than (or just as mysterious as) life, because it is the same as life; it is life. If we could explain history, we could obviously explain life, and vice versa.

By the same token there is, of course, no explanation in the strict sense of anything in history. There are hypotheses, conjectures, and assumptions. But the notion that history is, in some way, a sequence of "causes" and "effects" is not only without evidence but is contradicted by everything we know about it. The fact that we can never predict what will happen in the future (except by lucky guess) means that, conversely, we can never fully explain what has happened in the past. That is the most encouraging fact for the narrative historian. He can rest secure in the knowledge that he has done his duty when he has done his best to tell *what happened*. In view of this inescapable fact, it might not be unreasonable to ask why, then, write history at all. Because history is our collective memory, and without memory we are apt to commit even more and more dangerous blunders than we commit with a substantial knowledge of history to draw on.

My master, Eugen Rosenstock-Huessy, identified three forms of historical writing—"grateful history," whereby the historian expresses his gratitude for the best of what we have inherited through the courage and wisdom of our forebears; "reconciling history," through which we try to heal divisions in our society by telling of our past with sufficient compassion and regard for all warring factions that proponents can feel that justice has been done to the causes they fought and often bled for; and, finally, "fruitful history," which opens new paths into the future and suggests new possibilities. I have been presumptuous enough to try in this work to accomplish all three—to write, one might say, three-in-one history.

It seemed to me that in undertaking to write this history, I was under a particular obligation to tell the bad as well as the good. We had too long solaced ourselves with spurious and inflated history, obscuring or ignoring our cruelities and injustices; the great, grim, brute force of our past, the heartbreak and the terror of it. It was that "terror," in its peculiarly American forms, that it seemed to me I must ask my readers to confront. I feared that they would find it a depressing experience, but surprisingly, for me and apparently for them as well, trying to tell the truth seemed to deepen and, in a curious way, exalt our history so that it became more moving, more dramatic and compelling than I could have imagined. It became a "new life" for me and, I trust, offered a new one to my readers, and the reason was transparently evident. It was because, more or less inadvertently, I had written not simply old-fashioned archaic "narrative history" in defiance of the current canons of my profession but an equally old-fashioned, archaic "biographical" history. It is, after all, the lives of those people about whom it has been my good fortune to write that has given my history whatever life it has. It was Walt Whitman who called on America to "learn to better dwell on her choicest possession, the legacy of her good and faithful men." I believe that the tendency of history, of all human institutions is downward, toward complacency, decadence, obtuseness, and coldness of heart, and that we are saved only by the often obscure but heroic efforts of men and women whose passion it has been to redeem the world. Reinhold Niebuhr suggests that we can best avoid the equally dismal pitfalls of self-adulation and self-hate by understanding that our remarkable accomplishments have been, first, "on behalf of humanity" in general and, secondly, the consequence of "grace," that they have been bestowed on us, as trustees for mankind, by a beneficent Providence, in Niebuhr's words, "by grace of a virgin continent, and advancing frontier, and an expanding economy. . . . " That we have sinned, in some ways exceedingly, is to say no more than that we are human. It is essential to acknowledge our sins and allow them to chasten our pride, but it is more important to rectify them than to dwell on them. As the contemporary journalist Peter Marin has written, "All men, like all nations, are tested twice in the moral realm: first by what they do, then by what they make of what they do. The condition of guilt, a sense of one's own guilt, denotes a kind of second chance;

men are, as if by a kind of grace, given a chance to repay to the living what it is they find themselves owing the dead."

Let me remind the reader of some of the major themes in this work.

The Protestant Reformation re-formed the intellectual and psychological world of the faithful. It created a new human type, the "individual," a person free from the constraints of traditional society, a person guided by faith and, above all, by will, a person able to join with like-minded "individuals" to form new "covenanted communities." In the community the individual was fully realized and supported. This new human type came to the American wilderness in the form of the Puritan settler and, in a modification of that type, by the ideal of the English country gentleman to Virginia and, subsequently, to the other Southern colonies.

In the New World, freed of the inhibitions of Old England, both types—Puritan and Virginia gentleman—discovered new potentialities. The tradition of British political liberties, especially Thomas Hooker's injunction "laws they are not which public approbation hath not made so," and the conviction that there must be "no taxation without representation" led, one suspects inevitably, to resistance to the distant power of Great Britain and to independence. The faith of the Scottish, English, and, to a lesser degree, French Enlightenments in a rational and orderly world encouraged the Founding Fathers to try the novel experiment of a republican government with a considerable measure of democracy built into it. A purer strain of Enlightenment thought (primarily French this time) resulted in the Declaration of Independence, a very curious document that declared that all men were born equal, a proposition impossible to prove and taking a long time to achieve even approximately. The Founding Fathers subscribed to a set of propositions about the nature of man and society that I have called the Classical-Christian Consciousness. The Jeffersonian-Enlightenment cluster of ideas I have called the Secular-Democratic Consciousness. The Classical-Christian Consciousness, with its acute awareness of human fallibility, fashioned the Federal Constitution on the basis of that consciousness at the last possible moment before it was overwhelmed by the Secular-Democratic Consciousness in the person of Thomas Jefferson. The Secular-Democratic Consciousness was subsequently reinforced by Darwinism, which was taken by many Americans as a kind of confirmation of the general doctrines of the Enlightenment; the Classical-Christian Consciousness thereafter was kept alive primarily by a few individuals—John Quincy Adams, George Templeton Strong, Abraham Lincoln, John Jay Chapman, William Graham Sumner, Henry and Brooks Adams and William James among others. Its present primary lodgment is in the South; Southern writers have given it its most effective literary expression, from Faulkner through, in the postwar period, such writers as Flannery O'Connor, Eudora Welty, Carson McCullers, Walker Percy, and Wendell Berry. The South thus has a legitimate claim to have honored and preserved one of our essential traditions.

The Secular-Democratic Consciousness perhaps found its final form in the Communist Party and its affiliated organizations. It is still alive, but it is not well, various diagnosticians tell us.

Inadequate as the Secular-Democratic Consciousness is in its notion of human nature, we can ill afford to lose it because it has been characterized throughout its history by a utopian vision and a passion for reform. The Classical-Christian Consciousness, on the other hand, has often shown itself relatively indifferent to the issues of social justice and reform, frequently taking the line that poverty, for example, is always with us; that since man is tainted by original sin, reform in the long run is either self-defeating or an active and potentially destructive intervention in those divinely ordained natural laws which function best when left alone.

I believe that we badly need a combination or a melding of the two consciousnesses. We need a deeper and wiser view of the "nature and destiny of man," to use the title of one of Reinhold Niebuhr's books, without for a moment relaxing the fight for peace and social justice. Indeed, I believe not only that the two views of man and society are readily reconcilable but that the Secular-Democratic Consciousness is derived from the Classical-Christian Consciousness; that it was produced, as communism was in the twentieth century, by the indifference of the ruling classes in Britain and later the United States to the needs of the lower or, as they were called, "dangerous" classes.

The abolition of slavery and the achievement of "equality" socially, economically, and politically by black Americans have been one of the two major themes of this work.

The resolution or the making of peace in the war between capital and labor has been the other major theme.

The subsidiary themes of this work have included the central role of religion in American history, specifically the Protestant passion for redemption, appearing in dozens of particular reform movements such as abolition, the women's rights movement, and, perhaps most strikingly, in temperance or prohibition, and our "missionary" mission to convert the world and to transform it, a theme closely related to the general theme of redemption.

The revolt of the intellectuals from religion and the formation of an intellectual "class" and a new consciousness.

The central and essential role of women and of various ethnic minorities—immigrants.

The "wildness," and eccentricity, the rawness, crudity, and plain vulgarity that have characterized much of our history.

The long and strong tradition in America of native radicalism cropping out in a variety of forms—populism and socialism, most notably. These movements have either been essentially Christian (populism) or had an important Christian branch or division (socialism).

The tension between the community and the individual and the interplay between the "landscape of ideas and the physical landscape."

America in the world, our entry and withdrawal, but our inescapable involvement with the world both by virtue of the fact that we are less a traditional nation than a congress of nations—United States and united nations—and by the ties of immigrants to their native lands, ties which point up our mission as a transnational nation.

Another theme has been the high anxiety that Americans in all generations and every class have had to endure as the price of being an American.

The great, empty geographical spaces of America have been filled up, "civilized," inhabited. But Americans still have lonely interior spaces to fill and seem disconcertingly uncertain how to fill them. With art perhaps (we have tried sex, without very encouraging results), with the rediscovered pleasures of family life and restored communities. With veneration. With respect and gratitude for our ancestors. With history, without which we are missing an essential part of our collective memory.

Robert Frost has said that we believe the future into existence. It does not take place inevitably or "naturally" or "scientifically"; it takes place out of our hopes and dreams, out of our faith, out of our determination that there be a future worthy of the best in our past. We are the inheritors of all the treasures of mind and spirit that our forebears in this and every other land have willed to us. George Eliot wrote in *Middlemarch:* "The growing good of the world is partly dependent upon unhistoric acts; and that things are not so ill with you and me as they might be is half owing to the number who have lived faithfully a hidden life, and rest in unvisited tombs." So respect and gratitude for the accumulation of the good, if often obscure, lives that make up the ground of history, of our common past, and the determination to pass on that inheritance improved by our loyalty to the precepts of the fathers and mothers. The "ephebic oath" taken by the graduating class of the College of the City of New York read: "We, men of the class of February, 1913, today receiving the arms of the city as a symbol of her faith in us, take this oath of devotion to her: We will never bring disgrace upon these . . . arms by an act of dishonesty or cowardice. We will never desert our suffering comrades in the ranks. . . . We will strive ever to do our whole duty as citizens, and . . . to transmit this city not only not less but greater, better, and more beautiful than it was transmitted to us." The Founding Fathers spoke constantly of their obligation to the "millions yet unborn," those men and women who would come later to fill up the United States. So are we, too, inheritors, custodians, legatees. That is the true story of history, Lincoln's "mystic chords of memory" that bind us together in all our diversity, that make us one people, multiform, indivisible, and free.

Rosenstock-Huessy's most important book is titled *Out of Revolution: The Autobiography of Western Man*. The author makes the essential point that the modern world was born out of a series of revolutions that began with the English Civil War in 1642, also called the Puritan Revolution, during the period of the so-called interregnum. The interregnum, like the late 1960s, spawned a marvelous and remarkable progeny of Christian utopian/communist movements. The Diggers planted vegetables in parks and public lands to feed the hungry (a group with the same name in self-conscious imitation appeared in San Francisco in the late 1960s). The Fifth Monarchy men and women believed the Second Coming had come and gathered together in communities of the faithful.

The Glorious Revolution of 1689 ratified the more positive achievements of the Puritan Revolution in the famous Bill of Rights, which William of Orange accepted as the condition of succeeding James II. The American Revolution was a self-conscious attempt to claim for Americans the rights that Englishmen had won in those two revolutions, one bloody and violent, one peaceful. The American Revolution broadened the British concept of rights to include the democratic participation of all Americans, without regard to class or wealth, in the political life of the nation.

Every true revolution, Rosenstock-Huessy has pointed out, seeks to re-create the world. This was certainly true of our own revolution. Wyndham Lewis stresses the "radical universalism" of the Founding Fathers.

The French Revolution carried things substantially further (and not always for the best) by unseating the ancient regime in the name of liberty, equality, and fraternity. The Russian Revolution staked its claim on the theory that the primary instrument of repression and exploitation was essentially economic and that only by the overthrow of the money power in the form of capitalism could a just society be created. The Chinese, proclaiming perpetual revolution, have been the first Communist nation to adopt substantial elements of capitalism. Every modern society has had to incorporate the most positive elements of each revolution or face its own revolution. By the same token the revolutions that proclaimed a new and redemptive social order and began by dumping everything "old" into the refuse pile of history (which most of them wished to annul or escape from) had to make peace with the most positive and enduring aspects of the old order. We are now, Rosenstock-Huessy argued, at the end of the three-centuries-long process of revolution out of which the modern world was born. We are in a postrevolutionary era. We do not need any more revolutions; we are ready to move to the next stage of human history. The future of the world (and even its existence) depends, in large part, upon Americans' comprehending this relatively simple, fundamental fact. Russian communism or third world communism or world communism poses no ideological threat to the United States. Our problems are, so to speak, all in our minds, as, of course, are the Russians'.

At the time of the Mexican War Walt Whitman wrote an essay entitled "Some Calm Hints on an Important Contingency": "If we could teach mankind nothing better than the old lesson of wars, recriminations and hatred—if we cannot march forward to our mission with bloodless hands, and treading not upon the slain—the life and essential glory of our high example is dissolved utterly away. Our policy is peace; our system of government recommends itself to the world in the strength of its own gentle benefits, not by the enforcement of physical strength. . . . "

The Founding Fathers, well aware of the reality of original sin and the contingent nature of all human undertakings, suppressed their misgivings and set about devising a government based on a skeptical view of human beings as greedy, ambitious, self-aggrandizing, eager to exploit each other and almost certain to abuse power. They tried to frame a government that took into account our propensity for doing mischief and preferring our own well-being to that of our neighbors, however the Scriptures might exhort us to the contrary. They certainly believed that there was some essential degree of good in human nature but that the good could be counted on to take care of itself (it would, it was hoped, manifest itself in civic virtue, an unselfish concern for the public good). When they finished, they were not without doubts about the document they had labored over so long and so intelligently (and in such hot weather). Not everyone could be pleased; it was at best a compromise. Few of them expected it to last very long; most of them came to believe before they died that the Union (and the Constitution, of course, with it) would shatter over the issue of slavery (how could they have anticipated a Lincoln?).

By the greatest of good fortune the Republic survived first a devastating civil war and then a great depression, which fastened its grip upon the country for the better part of a decade in a crisis equaled only by the Civil War (who could have anticipated a Roosevelt?). I like to think that the Founding Fathers would be (or are) pleasantly surprised that their handiwork has endured so long (and, on the whole, what with one thing and another, reasonably well). Benjamin Franklin, the reader may (or may not) recall, did not wish the President to have a salary on the ground that adding a monetary incentive to the inevitable attractions of power would induce unscrupulous men to contest for the office. He believed that the United States would in time have a king, on the not unreasonable ground that nations throughout history had demonstrated a strong predilection for kings.

In any event we have not only survived but managed to become what I am sure the Founding Fathers would have deplored (or do deplore)—that is to say, a menace to the rest of the world, or at least we are perceived by the rest of the world as a menace only slightly less to be feared than the other leading brand. That, of course, is not our view of ourselves; we are full of our famous rectitude and self-righteousness, confident that it is our mission to save the world from its own error and folly in the form of communism or socialism. The Founding Fathers knew very well that self-righteousness wedded to power is a marriage fraught with potential disaster. Our real problem at the moment is not how to save the world but how to keep from destroying it with our constantly and loudly professed good intentions, which haven taken the unexpected and ominous form of 5,000-plus nuclear missiles, each capable of destroying millions of our fellows on what William James called "this only partially habitable planet." That is obviously the overriding problem beside which all other problems pale. If we are to have the opportunity to continue the long, slow, painful process of improving the world, a modest bit at a time—constantly mindful of the words of the British historian E. L. Woodward: "Everything good has to be done over and over again forever"—the world, which we are apparently prepared to destroy in the name of righteousness, must survive. The experiment of creating the "cosmic man" (and woman) obviously cannot continue if we blow up the laboratory.

It was Arnold Toynbee's view that "the difference between the Liberal and Communist way of Western life might be expected to diminish progressively . . . until the . . . feud that was obsessing nearly half the human race might have become no more than an academic issue in the life of an oecumenical society a hundred years later."

One of the major themes of this work has been the strange madness of America which, since John Winthrop's *Citie uppon a Hill,"* has sought the redemption of the world. The Founding Fathers, despite their skepticism about human nature and their belief in original sin, dreamed of the "emancipation of a world," and in every generation we have yearned for the reconciliation of mankind. More than any other people of the world we have been obsessed by the dream of a redeemed humanity, a universal brotherhood. Every dominating figure in our history has participated, in some degree, in that vision. That is our destiny; that or the destruction of the world.

In accepting the National Book Award for *The Invisible Man* in 1952, Ralph Ellison recalled the struggle of Menelaus with Proteus. The daughter of Menelaus warns him that Proteus will turn into various shapes to elude and test him, but he must hold him fast to subdue him finally. To Ellison Proteus stood "for both America and for the inheritance of illusion through which all men must fight to achieve reality; the offended god stands for our sins against those principles we all hold sacred. The way home we seek is that condition of man's being at home in the world which is called love, and which we term democracy. Our task then is always to challenge the apparent forms of reality—this is, the fixed manners and values of the few, and to struggle with it until it reveals its mad, vari-implicated chaos, its false faces . . . until it surrenders its insight, its truth." With all its bitter divisions and agonizing trials, "American experience is of a whole," Ellison declared. "Its truth lies in its diversity and swiftness of change. . . . Whenever we as Americans have faced serious crises we have returned to fundamentals. . . . " My principal hope for this work is that it is, in the last analysis, about those fundamentals.

# Acknowledgments

As in previous volumes I have relied in this on "primary sources" so far as possible—journals, diaries, letters, and, in the more recent volumes, autobiographies, the latter category exemplified by such works as Henry Adams's *Education*, Lincoln Steffens's and Oscar Ameringer's autobiographies and, more recent works such as Len De Caux's *Labor Radical: From the Wobblies to CIO, a Personal History*, Steve Nelson's autobiography, and Allen Ballard's quasi-autobiography, *One More Day's Journey*. Elinor Langer's biography of Josephine Herbst was also very useful, as were Nell Irvin Painter's *Narrative of Hosea Hudson* and John Langston Gwaltney's remarkable *Drylongso*, undoubtedly the best "reading" of black Americans' view of their white countrymen.

In this volume I have been more dependent on monographs than in other volumes, and while I have identified these works in the text itself, some deserve special mention. Among them are Jacquelyn Dowd Hall's *Revolt Against Chivalry: Jessie Daniel Ames and the Women's Campaign Against Lynching*, Louis Joughlin's and Edmund M. Morgan's *The Legacy of Sacco and Vanzetti*, Dan T. Carter's *Scottsboro: A Tragedy of the American South*, Lowell Dyson's *Red Harvest: The Communist Party and American Farmers*, and Mark Naison's *Communists in Harlem During the Depression*.

Donald Meyer's *The Protestant Search for Social Realism* remains the best treatment of Reinhold Neibuhr and the rise of Neo-Orthodoxy.

In addition, a number of individuals were helpful. Lucy Haessler made available material on her husband, Carl, a prominent figure of the left. David and Edith Jenkins read and criticized chapters having to do with the role of the Communist Party. David Williams gave important assistance on the chapters covering the early days of the CIO. John Hope Franklin rescued me from certain errors. Daniel Rhodes read the chapter on "Art and Architecture" and made helpful suggestions.

Finally, Frances Rydell gave the manuscript her usual devoted attention.

# Index

AAA (*see* Agricultural Adjustment Act)

Abbeville (South Carolina) lynch mobs, 93–94

Aberdeen Proving Ground, 1029

Abolition of slavery, 1142

Abolitionists, 220, 222, 595

Abt, John, 1030

Abyssinian Baptist Church, New York City, 657

Acheson, Dean, 421, 446, 673, 696

Actors and acting, 1012–1014
 Stanislavsky method, 1012

Adamic, Louis, 516

Adams, Alva, 1025

Adams, Brooks, 175, 675, 682, 890

Adams, Charles Francis, 346, 348

Adams, Franklin P., 29

Adams, Henry, 479, 914

Adams, John, 96

Addams, Jane, 55–56, 113, 220, 414, 648, 650
 Scopes trial, 862

Addes, George, 710, 726, 728, 741, 745

Advertising and selling, 24
 advances in, 24–25

Advisory Committee on Agriculture, 378, 393

Africa, Back to Africa movement, 214
 Marcus Garvey and, 239

African art, 240

African cultural heritage, 592

African Methodist Episcopal Church, 93

Afro-American Federation of Labor, 590

Age of Flaming Youth, 39, 52

Agee, James, 923

Agrarians, 995–996, 1003–1004

Agricultural Adjustment Act (AAA), 441, 601
 achievements, 842
 Supreme Court decision against, 660

Agricultural Advisory Commission, 378, 393

Agriculture, 175
 New South, 76
 productivity, 176
 (*See also* Farms and farming)

Aiken, Conrad, 825

Aiken, J. W., 324

Aircraft industry, expanded under New Deal, 1053

Alanne, Vieno Severi, 195
Albania, 62
Albers, Josef, 964, 1037
Albright, Ivan Le Lorraine, 809
Alcott, Bronson, 963
Alexander, Will, 97, 99, 425, 548, 582, 822,
 825
Alfonso, King of Spain, 767–768
Algren, Nelson, 793–795
Alienation, 535
Aliens, arrest of, 6
 (See also Migratory workers)
Alinsky, Saul, 708
All God's Chillun (O'Neill), 1009
Allen, Henry, 11
Allen, Jay, 767
Allen, Woody, 926
Alsberg, Henry Garfield, 792
Amalgamated Clothing Workers Union, 63,
 112, 709
Amalgamated Textile Workers of America,
 209
America and the Young Intellectual (Stearns),
 447
America Comes of Age (Siegfried), 24
America Enters the World (Smith), 1109
America First Committee, 1052, 1067–
 1068
 isolationists and, 1067–1068
American Artists Congress, 952
American Bankers Association: attacks on
 FDR, 648
American Bar Association, 111
American Car and Foundry Company,
 408
American Civil Liberties Union, 725, 743,
 1118
 founded by Roger Baldwin, 3
 Scopes trial, 854–855
American Communist Party (see Communist
 Party)
American Fascisti Order, 542
American Federation of Labor (AFL), 12–14,
 112, 121, 210, 413, 570
 CIO suspended by, 745
 craft unions, 763
 industrial unions and, 707, 713
 leaders, 707, 709
 National Recovery Administration, 455
 racial discrimination, 261
American Fund for Public Service, 532
"American Gothic," Wood, 957

American Jitters, The (Wilson), 36
American League Against War and Fascism,
 529, 656
American Legion, 7–8, 541, 1116
 communists and, 582
American Liberty League, 606
American Medical Association, 644, 801,
 907–914
 and drug companies, 909
 opposition to health insurance, 910–913
American Mercury, 16, 20, 32–36, 40, 535, 853
 editorial policies, 32–36
 founding of, 32
American Negro Labor Congress, 199
American Party Convention, 113–114
American Revolution, 1144
American Student Union (ASU), 897–898
 Communist influence, 900–901
 FDR support for, 900–901
American Telephone and Telegraph Com-
 pany, 20
American Tragedy (Dreiser), 972–973
American Writers Congress, 522–523, 526
American Youth Congress, 899, 1057
 Communist influence, 899
 deception of leaders, 899–900
 Eleanor Roosevelt and, 899–901
Americans
 anxiety, 1143
 disintegrative effects of American life, 921,
 1134, 1137
 hope and optimism, 461
 postwar refugees in Europe, 28–29
Ameringer, Oscar, 5–6, 12, 14, 205, 208,
 289–291, 420, 638, 714–715, 717
Ames, Jessie Daniel, 95, 826–832
 background, 826–827
Amherst College, 102
Amis, B. D., 551
Amsterdam News, 199–200, 555, 776
Anarchists and anarchism, 118, 120, 1131
Ancestors: respect and gratitude for, 1143–
 1144
Anderson, Marian, 248, 355, 941, 1031
Anderson, Maxwell, 41, 138, 802
Anderson, Paul, 653
Anderson, Sherwood, 28, 49, 192–193, 250,
 252, 340–341, 380, 401, 507, 520, 535,
 791, 966–971, 979, 982, 995, 1133
 egotism, 970
 letter to Hoover on Bonus Marchers, 341
 Gertrude Stein and, 967–971

Anderson (Indiana) UAW unionization, 742–744
Angelou, Maya, 945
Anschluss between Germany and Austria, 57–59
Anschutz, Thomas, 949
Anstrom, Otto, 190
Anthony, Susan B., 38
Anti-Catholicism, 3
  election of 1924, 106–107
Antioch College, 890
Anti-Semitism, 3, 691
  attacks on FDR, 606
Aragon, Louis, 256, 509, 526
Arbuckle, Roscoe "Fatty," 924, 931
Architecture, 960–965
  Bauhaus school, 462, 963, 1037
  internationalism, 961
  skyscrapers, 960–961
  urban planning, 961–962
  Frank Lloyd Wright, 961–962
Armory Art Show in 1913, 948–949, 959, 964
Arms embargo, 482, 1040
  repeal of, 1052
Armstrong, Hamilton Fish, 35, 172, 178, 307, 372, 375–376, 483
  interview with Hitler, 490–491
  interview with Mussolini, 491–492
  on post World War I Europe, 56–69
  trip to Moscow, 501
  visit to Berlin in 1933, 489–490
Armstrong, Louis, 939–940
Arnold, Thurman, 421, 913
Art and artists, 947–965, 1143
  architecture, 960–965
  Armory Show of 1913, 948–949, 959, 964
  art market, 947
  Ashcan school, 950–951
  Communist influence, 948, 952
  conflicts over subjects and techniques, 948
  effect of Depression, 952
  European influences, 948, 963
  Federal Art Project, 805–811
  Fourteenth Street school, 950–951
  government sponsorship, 798
  modern industrialism and, 25
  museums, 947
  New Deal patronage, 789–812
  New York City, art capital of the world, 964
  Regionalists, 952–960
  revolutionary art, 952
Art Deco, 25, 402, 961

Art Students League in New York, 1037
Art Week, 810–811
Arvin, Newton, 507
Asch, Nathan, 138
Association of Southern Women to Prevent Lynching, 826–832
Astor, Vincent, 395, 425–426
Atheism or agnosticism, 73, 887
Athens Manufacturing Company, 83
Atherton, Gertrude, 966
Atlanta, Communists, 543
Atlanta Constitution, 319
Atlanta University, 223
Atlantic Charter, 1083
Atlantic Conference, 1082–1083
Atlantic Monthly Press, 23
Atom bombs, 1052, 1108
Attorney General's list of subversive organizations, 1116
Auden, W. H., 771, 776–777, 802
Austin, Rev. J. C., 570
Austria, 58–59
  Communist uprisings, 164–168
  Hitler's annexation of, 1039–1040
Author's League, 791
Autobiography (Steffens), 28
Autobiography of an Ex-Colored Man, The (Johnson), 226
Auto-Lite strike, 704–705
Auto Workers Union, 727–750
  Communist-dominated, 704
  (See also United Autoworkers Union)
Automation, 382
Automobiles, 173
  ownership of, 175–176
Axis powers, 1057–1058
  ruthless aggression by, 1058
  (See also Germany, Nazis)
Ayres, Tom, 194

Babbitt, Irving, 886
Babbitt (Lewis), 16
Babel, Isaac, 526
Babson, Roger, 1065, 1072
Bailey, Pearl, 219, 937
Baker, George Pierce, 1004, 1007
Baker, Josephine, 939
Baker, Newton D., 273–274, 321, 326, 331, 354, 385, 408
  candidate for Presidency, 326
Baker, Ray Stannard, 421

Baldwin, Roger, 2–3, 190, 495, 532, 656, 743, 854–855
  founded American Civil Liberties Union, 3
Baldwin, Stanley, 167
Ballard, Allen, 216–219
Ballou, Adin, 849
Ballou, Robert, 213
Band music, 919
  black band leaders, 920
Bank for International Settlements, 484
Bank holiday, 437–438
  fireside chat, 437
  proclamation, 434–435
  results of, 438
Bank of America, 174
Bankhead-Jones Farm Tenant Act, 695
Banking Act, 647
Banks and banking, 3, 175–176, 640
  bank holidays, 426, 429–430
  concentration of economic power, 640
  Emergency Banking Act, 438
  failures, 15, 306, 426
  Federal Home Loan Banks, 304–305
  financial crisis, 426–431
  reaction against FDR, 604–605
  Senate investigation, 428
Barbershops: black, 214–215
Barkley, Alben, 74, 327, 1027, 1062
Barnes, Djuna, 43
Baron, Rosa, 130
Barr, Alfred, 806
Barr, Stringfellow, 903
Barre, Vermont, marble workers strike, 521–522, 983
Barrett, Janie Porter, 98
Barron's business journal, 432
Barth, Karl, 66
Barton, Ralph, 51
Baruch, Bernard, 26, 278, 286, 388, 407–408, 418–419, 445, 1033, 1042
  campaign of 1932, 391, 395
Baseball, 941
  black players, 1130
Bates, Ruby, 543–544, 555–556
Battle of the Overpass, 749
Bauhaus school of architecture, 462, 963, 1037
Bavaria, 66
Beal, Fred, 193
Beard, Charles, 3, 61, 302
Beauty shops, black, 214–215
Beaverbrook, Lord Max, 69

Beecher family, 38, 53
Beer and wine, made legal, 439
Beiderbecke, Bix, 938–939
Belgium: Lindbergh's welcome, 156
  Nazi invasion, 1058–1059
Bellamy, Edward, 369, 394, 630
Bemis, Edward, 2
Beneš, Eduard, 1041–1042
Benét, William Rose, 45, 131
Bennett, Frank, 502
Bennett, Gwendolyn, 247
Bennett, Harry, 722, 746–747, 749
Bennington College, 890
Bentley, Elizabeth, 528–530, 873
  head of Washington "Apparatus," 1029–1031, 1045–1046
Bentley, Milo, 584–585
Benton, Thomas Hart, 950, 952–960
  murals, 954–955
Bercovici, Konrad, 47
Berenson, Bernard, 110
Berger, Meta, 656
Berkman, Alexander, 29, 141
Berle, Adolf A., 385–387, 389, 464, 639
  campaign of 1932, 393–394, 397
Berlin: international set, 64
Berry, Abner, 201
Berry, Martha, 890
Bessie, Alvah, 774
Bethlehem Steel, 645–646, 751
Bethune, Mary McLeod, 98, 672, 821–823, 1093, 1129
Bethune-Cookman College, 98
Biddle, Anthony, 1050
Biddle, George, 806
Big business, 640
  Lincoln Steffens on, 21–22
  policy of sabotaging New Deal, 609–610
Big Ivy, Tennessee, 78, 92
Big Money, The (Dos Passos), 138, 140
Bilbo, Theodore, 317
Bill of Rights, 1144
Birmingham, Alabama: black Communists, 577
  Communism, 539–541
  registering to vote campaign, 586–587
Birth control, 5
Bishop, John Peale, 51, 141, 447, 508
Bismarck, German battleship, 1077
Black, Hugo, 447–448, 451, 608, 646, 691, 820, 1128

Black Americans, 211–262
  abolition of slavery, 1142
  abused and exploited, 88
  accepted in Soviet Union, 255–256
  achievement of equality, 1142
  alcoholism, 218
  *American Mercury* and, 35
  athletes, 892, 942–946
  attitude of poor whites toward blacks, 81–
    82, 1136–1137
  attraction for whites, 248–249
  barbershops and beauty parlors, 214–215
  black businesses, 92
  black elite, 215
  black men and white women, 249–250,
    549
  Black Rennaissance, 243–245
  black "style," 255
  black-white relationships, 249–250, 1136–
    1137
  burial societies, 92
  Camp Hill uprisings, 581–582
  churches, 212–213
  class distinctions, 253
  colleges for, 891–892
  Communist Party and, 575–596, 1118
    campaign to attract blacks, 198–203
  Communist union organizers
    Herndon, Angelo, 575
    Hudson, Hosea, 575–580
    Williams, Frank, 575–576
  contributions to American culture, 798
  crime committed against, 89–90
  Crow, Jim, laws, 88, 199, 822
  culture, 212, 219–220, 255, 1130
  discrimination against, 227, 261
    black scholars, 893–894
    Reuther, Walter, 750
  disfranchised, 91
  education, 87, 253
  election of 1936, 672–673
  equality for, 1093
  fad for things black, 249
  fear and, 89
  fear of black insurrection, 96
  fear of Communists and, 71–72
  Federal Writers' Project, 793
  field Negroes, 217
  hair and skin color, 214–215
  Harlem Renaissance (*see* Harlem Renais-
    sance)
  health and illness, 217, 220

Black Americans (*cont.*):
  historians, 793
  inferior to whites myth, 546
  insurance companies, 92
  integration of whites and blacks, 201
  intellectual superiority of Northern blacks,
    217
  intellectuals, 217, 221–262
  intelligentsia, 230
  interracial marriages, 227
  Ku Klux Klan hostility to, 3
  leaders, 587, 1093
    Hudson, Hosea, 578
    Johnson, James Weldon, 4
    Williams, Frank, 575–576
  life-styles, 92–93
  literary works by white authors, 251–
    252
  lynching, 93–96
  meaning of being a "black," 252
  medical doctors, 908–909
  middle-class, 579
  migration North, 211–212, 216, 892
  miscegenation, 226
  music and musicians, 212–213, 216, 218–
    219, 933–941, 1130
  nationalism, 219
  Negro national anthem, 224
  New Deal programs, 424–425, 672–673
  New Negro, 238
  New Negro literature, 246
  New York City, 221–222
  "nigger baiting," 75
  "numbers" game, 220–221
  organizations and savings clubs, 217
  outbreaks between Italians and, 657–658
  ownership of farms, 91
  in policy-making positions, 824
  poets and poetry, 226–231
  poverty and hunger, 86
  prejudice against, 228
  promiscuity of black males, 75
  Protestant Christianity, 92
  prostitutes and pimps, 92
  Pullman porters, 259–262
  racial inferiority feelings, 550, 578–579
  racial prejudice, 215–216
  racial stereotypes, 835–836
  "radical" Negro organizations, 71
  registration drives, 586–587
  relationship between black and white
    churchwomen, 98–100

Black Americans (*cont.*):
  religion, 92–93
  return to Africa, 214, 239
  rural, 212, 579
  sexual relations between blacks and whites,
      250–251, 549
  sexuality, 253
  soldiers, 71
  in Spanish Civil War, 772–773
  in sports, 892, 942–946, 1130
  Stalin's film project, 593–594
  tenants and sharecroppers, 81–83
  theater projects, 802–803
  unemployment, 217, 312–313
  union organizers and organizing, 72, 722
  unionization of black workers, 258–261
  westward movement, 215–216
  white attitudes toward, 71, 87–89, 249–250
  white perceptions of, 254
  white prejudice, 215–216, 254, 832–836
  women, 202, 247–248, 251
      relationships with white churchwomen,
          98–100
      sexual aggression by white men, 90–91
  world travelers, 255–257
  writers and intellectuals, 222–223, 228–
      237, 524, 793, 1130
      break with Communist Party, 1130–1131
      Communist Party members, 594–595
      New Deal and, 587
Black Belt, 324, 566, 570, 576
Black Hills, 179–180
Black Mountain College, 1037
Black Muslims, 1129
"Black Nation" approach, 201
Black Panthers, 1129
Black sharecroppers' union, 582–586
Blackwell, Alice, 124, 145
Blackwell, Henry, 124
Blankfort, Michael, 802
Blease, Coleman, 74, 93
Bliven, Bruce, 433–434, 900
Bloor, Mother, 189, 197, 293, 295
Blum, Leon, 788
Bodenheim, Maxwell, 44, 48, 516, 794
Bogan, Louise, 51
Bohemianism, 535
Bohlen, Charles "Chip," 496–498, 788,
      1043–1045
      on Japanese-American relations, 1080–
          1081
      Moscow trials, 781, 783, 787

Boisen, Anton, 868, 874–875
Boll weevil, 78
Bolsheviks and Bolshevism, 2, 7, 781, 1095
  denunciations of, 14
  Latin America, 168
  menace of, 55
  "old" Bolsheviks, 782–783, 787
  socialism and, 3
Bonds, Margaret, 248
Bontemps, Arna, 242, 245, 793
Bonus Army March on Washington (1932),
      337–339
  Communist participation, 338
  exodus from Washington, 338–340
  second expedition, 455–456
Bonus for soldiers, 330
Books: Book-of-the-Month Club, 536
  censorship, 887
  study of Great Books, 903
Boom period (twenties), 14–17
  money mania, 17
Bootlegging, 35
Borah, William, 116, 123, 169, 183, 320, 363,
      637, 688, 1040, 1052, 1067
Boredom: flight from, 918, 922, 932, 980
Borodin, Mikhail, 165, 166–167
Bosch, John, 293–295
Boston: Puritanism, 139
  Sacco-Vanzetti case, 132–133
*Boston* (Sinclair), 138, 140
*Boston Herald*, 101, 127
"Boston marriages," 479
Boudinot, Elias, 1122
Bowers, Claude, 44–45, 106, 160, 269, 286, 329
  ambassador to Chile, 1099
  ambassador to Spain, 419
  Democratic Convention (1932), 318
  interest in Jefferson, 363
  keynote address, 269–270
  FDR and, 364, 640
Bowles, Eva, 98
Boyd, Ernest, 45
Boyesen, Bayard, 29
Bradford, Gamaliel, 103–104
Bradford, Roack, 825
Brain Trust, 376, 423, 1104
  campaign of 1932, 391–405
  "economic jam sessions," 387–388
Brandeis, Louis, 390, 421–422, 452, 682–
      683, 879
  Court-packing fight, 682–683, 685
  criticism of, 645

Brandeis, Louis (*cont.*):
  influence on FDR, 368
  New Deal legislation, 639
Brandeis, Mrs. Louis, 121
Braun, Otto, 490
Brecht, Bertolt, 1036, 1038
*Bridge of San Luis Rey, The* (Wilder), 511
Bridges, Harry, 613–617, 758
  deportation of, 616, 693–694
Briggs, Cyril, 199–200, 556
Brill, Abraham, 45
Brisbane, Arthur, 172–173
Broadacre City, 962–963
Brodsky, Joseph, 555
Brody, John, 500
Bromfield, Louis, 447
Brook Farm, 849, 1134
Brooklyn Bridge, 1019–1021
Brooks, Abigail, 346
Brooks, Van Wyck, 48, 521
Brookwood Labor College, 209, 719–721,
  821
*Broom* (magazine), 32
Brophy, John, 187, 710, 714, 716
Brotherhood, universal, 1147
Brotherhood of Locomotive Engineers, 716
Brotherhood of Sleeping Car Porters, 259,
  261
Broun, Heywood, 128, 335, 401, 515
Browder, Earl, 198, 204, 523, 580, 656, 717,
  751, 773, 786, 801, 1065, 1072, 1109
  nominated President, 668, 1065, 1072
Brown, Charlotte Hawkins, 98, 100
Brown, John, 36
*Brown v. Board of Education of Topeka*, 1127
Brownlow, Keith, 923, 925–926
Brownsville, Pennsylvania, strike, 187–188
Brüning, Heinrich, 490
Bryan, John, 823–824
Bryan, William Jennings, 37, 106–109, 328
  Scopes trial, 854–857, 859–863
  silver issue, 446
Bryant, Louise, 232, 495, 1008
Bryn Mawr College, 528, 720–721
Buchanan, Scott, 903
Budenny, Semyon, 497
Budenz, Louis, 725–726
Budget balancing, 26, 334, 697–698
  deficit spending or, 698–699
  New Deal legislation, 439
Bukharin, Nikolai I., 195–196, 203, 498, 782
Bulgaria, Communist threat, 57

Bull Moose Convention in 1912, 112, 367
Bullard, F. Lauriston, 127
Bullitt, Louise Bryant Reed, 232, 495, 1008
Bullitt, William, 68–69, 232, 445–446, 656–
  657, 781, 1043, 1057
  appointed ambassador to Soviet Union,
    495–497
  disappointment with Soviets, 499–500, 781
  1919 expedition to Russia, 495, 499
  on Peace Commission, 495
  recognition of Soviet Union, 494
  Wilson and, 495–496
Bureau of Standards, Communist influence,
  1029
Burchfield, Charles, 951–952
Burke, Betty, 754–756
Burke, Donald, 539, 550
Burke, Fielding, 193
Burke, Kenneth, 44, 524
Burnham, James, 786
Burroughs, Nannie H., 248
Bush, Vannevar, 1053
Business and businessmen, 19–26, 174
  alliance with politics, 309–310, 389, 448,
    460
  attacks on FDR, 604–606, 640, 659, 674–
    676
  big business control of U.S., 309–310
  boom (twenties), 20–21
  demand for culture, 24
  disenchantment with leadership, 309
  growth in American, 174–175
  partnership with government, 389, 448
  rejection of New Deal, 674–677
  research, 22–23
  role of, 20–21, 389
  FDR's deference to, 659, 667
  FDR's policies, 448–449
  value of educated executives, 24–25
Business ethics, 25
*Business the Civilizer* (Calkins), 23
Butler, John Washington, 854, 857
Butler, Nicholas Murray, 325
Butler, Pierce, 684
Byrd, Harry, 332, 408
Byrd, Richard E., 150–151, 157
Byrd, William, 79
Byrnes, James F., 74, 528

Cahill, Holger, 792, 810
Cain, James M., 33
Caldwell, Charles, 96

Caldwell, Erskine, 996
California: bank holiday, 438
  political movements, 629–633
  repressive spirit, 9
  unionization of farm workers, 759–763
Calkins, Earnest Elmo, 20, 23–25
Callahan, William Washington, 559–560
Calles, Plutarco, 169–171
Calverton, V. F., 532–533
Camp Hill affair: black uprising, 581
  impact on black community, 586
Can You Hear Their Voices? (Flanagan and
  Clifford), 799–801
Canby, Henry Seidel, 790
Cannery and Agricultural Workers Industrial
  Union, 760–761
Cannon, Bishop James, 269
Cantwell, Robert, 315, 514, 536, 797
Capital and labor, war between, 11–14, 677,
  761, 846, 1093, 1125, 1142
Capital punishment, 142
Capitalism, 17, 24, 286
  effect of bank holiday, 438
  effect of depression, 310–311, 438
  expansion after World War II, 1128
  inequities of, 188
  Marx's predictions, 310
  natural resources exploited by, 175
  Niebuhr's criticism of, 882–883
  ownership of colleges and universities, 896
  Protestant ethic and, 851
  revolution leading to overthrow of, 506
  FDR's actions, 649
  Soviet plan to overthrow, 499
  struggle between Communism and, 507
  threat to, 435
  triumphant in twenties, 27
Capone, Al, 39
Capper, Arthur, 4
Cardozo, Justice Benjamin, 2, 421, 434, 682
Carey, James, 710, 719
Carmer, Carl, 75, 556
Carmichael, Stokeley, 1129
Carnap, Rudolf, 1037
Carnegie Foundation for the Advancement
  of Teaching, 907
Carnot, Sadi, 141–142
Carrel, Alexis, 163
Carroll, Earl, 46
Cash, W. J., 7, 73, 82–83, 91–92, 193, 653,
  814, 821, 837
Cather, Willa, 535, 966, 986–988, 1024

Catholic Church, 868–869
  anti-Catholicism issue, 106–107, 269, 699
  Depression and, 875–878
  fear of, 699
  Ku Klux Klan and, 3
  problems in Mexico, 170–171
Catholic Worker movement, 877–878
Cattlemen, 10
  grazing lands, 465
Cayton, Horace, 220, 245, 250, 256–257,
  300–301, 566, 591, 793, 844, 891–892
CCC (see Civilian Conservation Corps)
Cecil, Viscount, 483
Centennial Exposition of 1876, 461
Century of Progress Exposition in Chicago,
  461–462
Cermak, Anton, 329, 332
  assassination of, 425–426
Chafee, Zechariah, 1–2
Chalmers, Allan Knight, 560–563, 571
Chamberlain, John, 786
Chamberlain, Neville, 1040, 1058
  Munich meeting, 1041
  "peace in our time," 1041–1042
Chamberlin, Clarence, 150
Chambers, Whittaker, 185, 188, 527–529,
  799, 1110–1114
  on Soviet espionage apparatus, 1029–1031
Chamber of Commerce, 7, 21
  attacks on New Deal, 605
Chandler, Robert Winthrop, 46–47
Channing, William Ellery, 869
Chaplin, Charlie, 32, 924–926
Chapman, John Jay, 479, 886
Chase, Stuart, 500, 630
Chase, William, 949
Cheever, John, 794–795
Cherry, Prophet, 213
Chesnut, Mary, 72
Chestnutt, Charles, 226–227
Cheyny, Ralph, 138
Chiang Kai-shek, 165–166
Chicago, 70
  bank holiday, 426–427
  black Americans, 216, 219–220
  black culture, 219–220
  campaign of 1932, 402
  Democratic Convention in 1932, 317–341
  demonstrations and protests, 591
  Depression and, 590
  gangsters, 161
  jazz and jazz musicians, 937–939

Chicago (*cont.*):
New Negroes, 219
packing plants strikes, 754–756
racial conflict, 219
unemployed, 313–314
*Chicago Tribune*, 64
Chicago World's Columbian Exposition, 223
Child Health Conference, 283
Child labor, 449, 640
abolition of, 413
amendment, 19, 696–697
prohibition, 453
Childs, Marquis, 443, 468
China: American policy, 1081
Communist uprisings, 164–168
Kuomintang, 165, 167
Chinese-American relations, 700
Japanese invasion, 700
Chinese revolution, 164–166, 1145
Christensen, Parley P., 184
Christian Scientists, 868
Christian utopian/communist movements, 1144
fundamentalist, 853
revivalism, 853–854
Christiansen, John, 891
*Christmas Carol, A.* (Dickens), 472
Christy, Howard Chandler, 345
Chrysler Corporation, 462
unionization, 742
Church of Latter-Day Saints, 868
Churchill, Winston (novelist), 30, 69
Churchill, Winston, 286, 1041–1042, 1058, 1059
Atlantic Conference, 1082–1083
Hopkins talks with, 1075–1076
lend-lease program, 1070
racial arrogance, 1083
FDR and, 1073–1075, 1082–1083, 1096
ideological divisions, 1083
personal friendship, 1094
Christianity, 853, 1095, 1124
CIO (*see* Congress of Industrial Organization)
*Citie Upon a Hill* (Winthrop), 849, 1122, 1147
Cities, urban planning, 961–962
Citizen League for Fair Play, 589
Citizens' Alliance, 705–706
Citizens League, terrorist tactics, 743
Citron, Alice, 202
Civil liberties, 1127
Civil Liberties Union, 2

Civil rights issues, 644, 1093, 1127, 1129, 1132
Constitution and, 695
Civil War, 1146
legacy of, 677–678
Civil Works Administration (CWA), 463, 598, 613, 806–807
achievements, 841
criticism of, 598–599
Civilian Conservation Corps (CCC), 439, 617, 699, 1103
achievements, 842–843
jobs and projects, 598
inspection of, 459
opposed by labor, 441
projects, 636
FDR's message to Congress, 440–441
segregated camps, 603
veterans enrolled in, 456
Clara Ward Singers, 219
Clark, Champ, 352
Clark, Mrs. Champ, 275
Clark, Eleanor and Eunice, 528
Clark, Emily, 997–998
Clark, Grenville, 1070
Clark, Lance, 1029
Clark University in Worcester, Mass., 914
Class differences, 1111–1112
black Communists, 579
Classical-Christian Consciousness, 1003–1004, 1141–1142
Clemenceau, Georges, 141, 487
Clurman, Howard, 1012–1014
Coad, Mack, 306, 593
Coad, Ned, 88, 91, 582–585, 1117
world-wide attention, 585–586
Coal mines and mining, 11–12, 70
labor conditions, 11–13
organization of miners, 455
unemployment, 12
Coal strikes, 517
Harlan County, Kentucky, 517–518
Pineville, 518–519
Cobb, Irvin, 632
Cohen, Benjamin V., 424, 464, 879
Cohen, Elliot, 341
Cohen, Jack, 396
Cohen, John S., 327
Cohen, Morris, 688–689
Cohn, Harry, 633
Coit, Lillie Hitchcock, 808
Colby, Bainbridge, 107

Cold war, 1109
Coleman, McAllister, 724
Coli, François, 155–156
Collective bargaining, 115, 303, 336, 448,
    697, 703
  labor's right to, 449
  NIRA and, 455
Colleges and universities, 73, 885–889
  Communist influence, 889
  consequences of Depression, 896
  conservatism, 902
  Flexner's survey of, 887–888
  radical student movements, 897–903
  Southern, 819–820
Collins, Herbert, 26, 285
Collins, Ware, 1030
Colored (see Black Americans)
Columbia University, 385
  Communist shop unit, 530
  student strikes, 897
Comintern, 182–183, 196, 199, 203, 1047
  on Hitler, 494
  jazz condemned by, 552
  new popular front policy, 656
  opposition to fascism, 655
  U.S. policy, 324
Commercial art, 22
Commission on Interracial Cooperation
    (CIC), 97, 99, 828
Committee for Industrial Organization, 713–
    714, 745
  (See also Congress of Industrial Organiza-
    tion (CIO)
Committee for the Nation, 445
Commonwealth Land Party, 113
Communes, 1134
  utopian communities, 1134
Communist International, 182
Communist Party, 167–168, 182–210
  accomplishments, 595, 1120–1121
  American Communist Party, 184–185, 655
  Black America and, 575–596
    appealing aspects, 588
    black writers broke with, 1130–1131
    campaign to attract blacks, 198–203, 539
  Central Committee, 528
  comradeship and participation, 1002–1003
  covert activities, 530
  critics and journalists, 515–516
  cultural organization of workers, 512
  Depression and, 310–311
  devotion to causes, 531

Communist Party (cont.):
  dismantling of, 1109–1126
  doctrinal deviation, 534
  effect of German attack on Russia, 1079
  election of 1936, 668
  election of 1940, 1065
  factional infighting, 203–205, 210
  fellow travelers, 505
  Fifteenth Congress, 20
  financial contributions, 531–533
    philanthropic foundations, 532
  Fourth Congress of the Third Interna-
    tional, 231
  fronts, 505–506
  goals, 190
  heresies and deviations, 1109
  homosexuality and lesbianism, 531
  influence in New Deal, 668
  instructions from Moscow, 190–191
  intellectuals and, 505–538
  International Labor Defense (ILD), 516,
    520, 540, 546–550, 564–565, 568–569
  Jews in leadership roles, 879
  labor conflicts, 516–517
  literary and artistic organizations, 511–512
  meetings and committees, 508
  menace to American democracy, 129
  name changed, 1109, 1116
  National Convention in 1932, 324
  non-communist left, 208–210
  organization of, 205–210, 751
  organizers, Southern, 539
    black sharecroppers, 581
  proletarian and revolutionary leaders, 508
  proletarian literature, 512
  raised consciousness of American blacks,
    595
  recruitment within government, 464, 1031
  resistance to growth of fascism, 493, 1120
  Russian-German non-aggression pact, 1120
  Sacco-Vanzetti case, 142–143
  Scottsboro Boys case, 564
  Secular-Democratic Consciousness, 1142
  Seventh World Congress in 1935, 726
  sex and marriage, 531
  Soviet line, 901
  student fronts, 897–903
  unemployed workers organized by, 310–
    316
  whites and blacks working .ogether, 595
  (See also Workers' Party)
Communist Political Association, 1109

Communists and communism, 6, 11, 73, 112,
     182, 317, 400
  advantages, 602
  American Communist Party, 184–185, 655
  analysis of, 533–538
  anti-Communist sentiment, 1028
  American beneficiaries of, 1124–1125
  attraction for artists and writers, 533–536
  black Communists, 579–580
  charges of being, 18
  collapse of capitalism, 185
  confessions and accusations, 1110–1111
  CIO, 718, 745, 1067
  defections, 785, 1067
  Depression era, 1117
  election of 1940, 1072
  exaltation of "workers," 1120
  farmers and, 194–195
  fear of blacks and, 71–72
  Federal Project No. 1, 791–813
  Federal Theatre project, 800
  "forgot" the thirties, 1110, 1117
  front organizations, 119, 194–195, 718
  future in U.S., 537
  intellectuals and, 505–538
  involved in unionization, 751–752
  involvement of women, 527–531
  jazz denounced by, 941
  liberal intellectuals and, 1112–1114
  literary and poetic movement, 536
  Manichaeanism and, 1124
  nature of communism, 1117
  New Deal and, 458, 846, 850
  non-Communist liberals, 499–500
  opposed CCC, 441
  opposition to war buildup, 1057
  Pelagian heresy and, 1124
  persecutors, 1114–1116
  proletarian and revolutionary leaders, 508
  reaction to Soviet-German nonaggression
       pact, 1045–1046
  Red hunters, 846, 1110–1111
  religious element, 508, 534
  Republican-Communist alliance, 1068
  rush to Washington, 419–420
  ruthless and cynical exploitation, 778
  Sacco-Vanzetti case, 119, 129–132, 135, 546–547
  Scottsboro Boys defense, 556–557
  Southern members, 539
  Spanish Civil War, 771–780
  spy apparatus, 1029–1031, 1045–1046,
       1112–1114

Communists and communism (cont.):
  strikes led by, 190–191, 763
  struggle between capitalism and, 185, 507
  sympathizers, 8
  third period doctrines, 654–655, 778
  treasonable activities, 1113–1114
  Trotskyites vs. Stalinists, 775
  Unemployed Councils, 591, 771
  (See also Unemployed Councils)
  union organizers, 192–193, 455, 714–715,
       1117–1118
     Southern blacks, 588
     White, 588
  union participation, 726, 751–752
  utopian dream, 1125
Community: covenanted, 849, 1134, 1141
  individualism vs., 849
  national, 848–849
  needs for, 1134–1135
  Puritan settlers, 1141
  utopian, 963, 1134
Community arts centers, 809–810
Competition, 535
Compton, Karl, 1053
Conant, James B., 1053
Cone Mills, 84–85
Conference for Progressive Labor Action, 210
Conference for Progressive Political Action,
     111–112
Congress, U.S.: farm relief, 294
  Hawley-Smoot tariff bill, 287
  hearings on state of the economy, 407
  Neutrality Act amendments, 1051–1052
  New Deal legislation, 437–462
  FDR's defeats in, 456
  FDR purge of conservative Democrats,
       1025–1028
  special session (1937), 698–699
Congress of Industrial Organizations (CIO),
     703–726
  AFL suspension of, 745
  auto workers and, 727–750
  Chicago packing plants, 756
  Communist influence, 717–718, 745, 753
  Communist union leaders, 714–715, 751
  convention in 1940, 1066–1067
  formation, 713–714
  General Motors unionization, 727–750
  growth of, 722–726, 744
  industrial unions, 764
  no racial discrimination, 752
  organizing drives, 752

Congress of Industrial Organizations (*cont.*):
  strikes, 751–766
  union activity in the South, 757
Connally, Thomas, 429, 1040
Connelly, Marc, 251
Conroy, Jack, 513–514, 524, 536
Consciousness: "black" consciousness, 254,
    1132
  Classical-Christian Consciousness, 1003–
    1004, 1141–1142
  new consciousness, 28, 49, 252, 254, 279,
    1130, 1132
  Secular-Democratic Consciousness, 114,
    1003, 1123, 1141–1142
  subconsciousness and, 31
Conservation and reforestation programs,
    380, 410, 444, 842, 1103–1104
Conservatism, 9
Conservative Democrats, 600, 604
Conservative Southern Congressmen, 610, 815
Constitution, 1, 22, 1127, 1141, 1146
  amendments, 13
  interpretations of, 1104–1105
  FDR's views, 680, 686
  (*See also* Founding Fathers)
Constitutional Convention, 372
Constitutional rights of American citizens, 1–3
Convoys of merchant ships, 1077–1078
Cook, George Cram "Jig", 30
Cook, Nancy, 360, 477
Coolahan, Tom, 48
Coolidge, Calvin, 15, 40, 139, 282–284
  Bolshevik threat in Latin America, 168
  business favored by, 178–181
  Cabinet members, 178
  Coolidge boom, 172, 277, 284–285
  defeat in Congress, 116
  domestic and foreign programs, 115
  early life and education, 101–103
  effect of Hoover's nomination, 278
  election of 1920, 101
  election of 1924, 101–116
  election of 1928, 179–180
  foreign policy, 115, 168–172
  handling of Boston police strike, 102
  "I do not choose to run," 179–180
  inaugural address, 115
  Lindbergh's welcome home, 156–158
  nominated President, 106
  personality and traits, 173–174, 178, 180
  political career, 102–103
  popular with electorate, 104

Coolidge, Calvin (*cont.*):
  presidency, 103
  prosperity, 172
  public faith in, 114–115
  stock market speculation, 173–175
  Vice-President, 101
Cooper, Henry, 97
Cooperative Central Exchange, 197
Cooperative Unity Alliance, 197
Copland, Aaron, 805
Copper strike, 10
Coral Gables, Florida, 172–173
Corcoran, Thomas, 174, 421–422, 424, 464,
    480, 490, 669–670, 675, 1025–1026
Costigan, Edward, 303–304, 429
Cotton Club, 237
Cotton crops, 15, 76–78, 594
  boll weevil decimated, 78
Couch, W. T., 996
Coughlin, Father Charles, 337, 627–629,
    661, 665, 878
Council of Foreign Affairs, 375
Counterculture, 1132–1135
Couric, Gertha, 79–80
Court-packing fight, 682–695
  Congressional reactions, 690–691
  defeat for President, 691
  opposition to bill, 686–688
  supporters, 688–689
Couzens, James, 485
Covarrubias, Miquel, 47, 244
Cowley, Malcolm 42, 44, 137, 162, 208, 294,
    315–316, 373, 401, 424, 602, 1019
  on Bonus Marchers, 339–340
  communism, 507–508, 510–511, 515, 518–
    520, 523, 527–528, 531, 533–534
  forced to resign, 1110
Cowley, Peggy, 51, 516, 1019
Cox, Edward Eugene, 757
Cox, James, 107, 326, 485
Cox, Father James R., 337
Coxey, General Jacob, 112, 324, 337
Coxey's March on Washington, 324, 337
Coyle, Albert, 500, 716
Crafts and craft fairs, 1133
Crane, Hart, 51, 516, 1018–1021
Crane, Winthrop Murray, 102
Crawford, Anthony, 228
Creel, George, 5, 45, 335–336, 368, 421, 464,
    468, 479, 686
  political movements in California, 629
Crichton, Kyle, 515

Crime and violence: organized crime, 38–39
  in South, 814–815
*Crisis* magazine of NAACP, 222, 245–246
Crissinger, D. R., 176
Cristadora House, New York City, 380
Crocker, William H., 397
Croly, Herbert, 30, 60, 62, 122, 226, 273,
  280, 350, 458–459
Crosswaith, Frank, 259–260, 590
Crowder, Henry, 257
Cuba–U.S. trade, 601
Cuban poets, 256
Cullen, Countee, 246, 253
Cultural activity, 1135
  black, 1130
  businesses and, 24
  counterculture, 1132–1135
  internationalization of, 31
  richness of contemporary, 1135
Cummings, e. e., 48, 984
Cummings, Homer, 408, 434, 615, 635, 685
Cunard, Nancy, 48, 255–257
Cunningham, Minnie Fisher, 827
Curley, James Michael, 419, 454
Curran, Joseph, 710, 952
Curry, John Steuart, 955–960
Cutting, Bronson, 409–410, 456, 520
CWA (*see* Civil Works Administration)
Cynicism, 162
Czechoslovakia, 56, 59
  dismembering of, 1041–1043
  Hitler's occupation of, 1036, 1039–1043

Dadaists, French, 32, 64
Dahlberg, Edward, 1137–1138
*Daily Worker*, 194, 208, 592, 717, 1037
Daladier, Edouard, 617, 1040–1041
Dali, Salvador, 47
Daly, Alice Lorraine, 195–196
Dana, Richard Henry, 153, 510
Dance and dancing, 9, 35, 46, 49, 805
  fox-trot, 30
Daniel, Will, 292–293
Daniels, Josephus, 107, 267, 320, 354, 557,
  847
Darrow, Clarence, 8–9, 185, 547, 553, 632,
  858–863
Darwin, Charles, 120, 125
Darwinism, 73
  attack on, 854–857
  social, 208
  (*See also* Scopes trial)

Daugherty, Harry M., 13, 105, 116
Daughters of the American Revolution
  (DAR), 7–8, 1031
Davidson, Donald, 820, 991–993, 996, 998
Davidson, Jo, 21, 47
Davies, Joseph E., 442, 781, 783
Davis, Benjamin, 566–567, 579–580, 592
Davis, Elmer, 335
Davis, John W., 110–111, 114, 319, 326, 332,
  606, 853
Davis, Kid, 556
Davis, Noel, 150–151
Davis, Norman, 481
Davis, Stuart, 811
Dawes, Charles, 106, 263
Dawes Plan, 67–68
Day, Dorothy, 42, 875–878, 1008, 1118
  *Catholic Worker*, 877–878
  Communist Party activities, 876
Debs, Eugene V., 12, 121–122, 464, 983
Debts (*see* War debts)
"Debunking," 162
De Caux, Len, 707–726, 1066–1067
  editor of *CIO News*, 714
  sit-down strikes, 734, 739–740, 744–745,
    753
Declaration of Independence, 1132, 1141
Deficit spending, 845
Deflation policy, 10
  gold standard and, 445
De Leon, Daniel, 186
Dell, Floyd, 39, 49–50, 229, 535
Dellums, C. L., 260, 262
Democracy: problems of, 18–19
  viability of, 18
Democratic Party, 363, 679
  alliance between big-city bosses and South,
    678
  character of, 1026–1027
  conservatives, 600
    FDR purge, 1025–1028
  dominated by South, 618, 1026–1027
  liberal spirit, 848, 1026
  liberalism and reform, 1028
  National Convention in 1912, 352
  National Convention in 1920, 370
  National Convention in 1924, 106–110
    anti-Catholicism, 106–107
    Ku Klux Klan role, 106–107
    racial issues, 112
  National Convention in 1928, 269–271
  National Convention in 1932, 317–341, 391

Democratic Party (*cont.*):
  platform, 334–335
  National Convention in 1936, 75, 659–681
  National Convention in 1940, 1061–1064
  opposition to Roosevelt, 606, 848
  party of progress and reform, 363
  progressive wing, 321
  Solid South, 111, 364, 618, 1025–1028
Demonstrations and protests, 312–313, 422
Dempsey-Tunney fight, 181
Demuth, Charles, 949
Denmark, Nazi invasion, 1058
Dennis, Lawrence, 493
Department of Agriculture, 410
  Communist members, 464
Department of Interior, 410–412
  Ickes in charge, 465
  responsibilities, 411–412
Department of Justice, 1–2
Department of Labor: immigration laws,
    466–467
  investigative unit, 467
  Women's Bureau, 100
Department of State: Communist influence,
    1029–1030
  repressive spirit, 2–3
Depression, 1146
  American capacity to share, 848–849
  barter associations, 301
  blame Republicans, 309, 327
  block committees, 312
  business and politics, 309–310
  Communist Party and, 310–311
  Communists and communism, 291–295,
    299, 1117
  consequence of, 318, 379
  cured by World War II, 1025, 1128
  devastating drought (1930), 288
  disenchantment with business leadership,
    309, 327
  economic crises, 406
  education, 894–903
  effects on "success ethic," 298–299
  European countries, 305–306
  events of 1934 and, 597–617
  evictions, 300, 312–313
  farm prices depressed, 291–295, 460
  Federal programs, 304–305, 692
  Hoover's economic theories, 282–316
  hunger and starvation, 288–289
  increased library circulation, 301
  migrants, 289

Depression (*cont.*):
  New Deal programs and, 692
    (*See also* New Deal)
  role of churches, 871–878
  role of Federal Government, 390, 429
  Roosevelt's view of, 373
  selling apples, 299
  unemployment, 289–290, 295–298, 460
    (*See also* Unemployed Councils)
  Wall Street crash, 284–287
Dern, George, 410, 412
Detroit, bank moratorium, 426
De Voto, Bernard, 138
Dewey, John, 3, 113, 136, 165, 209, 335, 786,
    800, 821
Dewey, Thomas E., 696, 1060, 1097
Dewson, Mary "Molly," 412–413, 422
Díaz, Adolfo, 168, 171
Dickens, Charles, 472
Dickerman, Marion, 360
Dictatorial powers, 432
Dictatorships, 435
Dies, Martin, 692–694, 1027, 1114
  House Un-American Activities Committee,
    692–693, 812, 1027–1028, 1114, 1129
  inquisitorial tactics, 804, 812
Dillion, Francis, 727
Dimitrov, Georgi, 617, 655
Disarmament Conference in Geneva in 1933,
    482, 486–487
Disenchantment of youth, 40
Disintegrative effects of American life, 921,
    1134, 1137
Disney, Walt, 929
Dissent, 312–313
  suppression of, 422
Divine, Father, 213
Divorce, 5, 531
  rate, 34–35
Doak, William N., 466
Documentary: dominant intellectual mode, 813
Dodd, William, 654
Dodge, Horace, 173
Dodge, Mable, 29
Doheny, Edward, 105, 109
Domingo, W. A., 200
Donovan, William "Wild Bill," 1030
Dorsey, Hugh, 572–573
Dos Passos, John, 27, 30–31, 128, 130–131,
    135, 138, 140, 208, 229, 401, 517, 520–
    521, 526, 764, 811, 931, 983–985
  communism, 507, 1110

Dos Passos, John (cont.):
  Sacco-Vanzetti case, 138, 140
  Spanish Civil War, 775–776, 778
  two Americas, 52
Douglas, Lewis, 439–440, 445–446, 608, 673
  director of budget, 419
Douglas, Paul, 335, 500, 919
Douglas, William O., 23, 74, 357, 373, 381,
    418, 421–422, 478, 601, 915, 1128
  on FDR, 1103
  Securities and Exchange Commission, 469,
    697
  Supreme Court appointment, 692
Douglass, Frederick, 226, 551, 574, 945
Draft of young men, 1070–1071
  Selective Service Act, 1081–1082
Draper, Dr. George, 357, 359, 915
Draper, Hal, 655
Draper, Muriel, 237, 244
Dreams, 162
Dreiser, Theodore, 28, 36, 44–45, 48, 51, 110,
    407, 500, 516–518, 535–536, 569, 632,
    791, 966, 971–973, 982–983, 1024
  An American Tragedy, 972–973
  Scottsboro Boys defense, 552
Dreyfus, Captain, 141
Droughts, Southern states (1930), 288
Dryden, John, 513
Dubinsky, David, 261, 708–710, 720, 745,
    1119
Du Bois, W. E. B., 96–97, 219, 222, 249–
    250, 998, 1130, 1137–1138
Du Bois, Yolande, 246
Duchamp, Marcel, 949
Duclos, Jacques, 1109
Dulles, Allen, 481
Dulles, John Foster, 646
Dunbar, Paul Laurence, 223–224, 235, 923
Dunbarton Oaks Conference, 1097
Dunkirk, evacuation of, 1059
Dunne, Bill, 540–541
duPont, Irenée, 606
duPont, Pierre S., 395
duPont family, major GM stockholder, 739
Duranty, Walter, 327, 501
Dust Bowl, 842
Dust storms, 460–461
Dylan, Bob, 1132
Dyson, Lowell, 194–195

Earle, George, 671
Early, Stephen, 358, 475

Eastman, Crystal, 231
Eastman, Max, 229, 231, 253, 811, 972
Eccles, Marriner S., 647, 698
Economic conditions; election of 1928 and,
    278–279
  warning signals (1927), 177
"Economic royalists," 666, 672
Edison, Charles, 1059
Education, 884–893
  academic freedom and Communist teach-
    ers, 903
  colleges and universities, 885–889, 1131
  black, 891–894
  conservatives, 896
  curriculum, 884–885
    for young farmers, 891
  discrimination against black scholars, 893–894
  effect of Depression years, 894–903
  enrollments, 884, 895
  general spirit of repression, 887
  higher education, 885–891, 1131
    faculties, 885–886
    Flexner's survey of, 887–888
    growth in, 1131–1132
    quota system for Jews, 893
    women's colleges, 889–890
  medical, 906–908
  New Humanists, 886–887
  reforms, 29
  religion and, 1131
Edwards, Johnathan, 853
Egypt (Ohio) coalfields, 11–12
Einstein, Albert, 1038, 1052
Eisenhower, Dwight D., 339, 678, 1128–1129
Eisenstein, Sergei, 536
Eisler, Hanns, 1037
Election of 1912, 352
Election of 1920, 101, 370
Election of 1924, 104–114
Election of 1928, 263–281, 310
  Catholic issue, 269, 273–275
  Democratic platforms, 270–271
  Hoover nominated, 263
  Smith nominated by Democrats, 267–271
  Southern Baptists opposed Smith, 273–274
Election of 1930, 303
Election of 1932, 317–341
  attack on Hoover, 398–400
  campaign, 391–405
  political and economic proposals, 396
  FDR's margin of victory, 404
  whistle-stop campaign, 395–396

Election of 1934, 610, 628, 634
Election of 1936, 659–681
  inauguration of FDR, 680
  landslide victory, 675–676
Election of 1938, 1025–1027
Election of 1940, 1034, 1050–1060
Election of 1944, 1097
Electricity, growth in use of, 175
Electro Auto-Lite stride in Toledo, 728
Eliot, Charles, 893
Eliot, T. S., 53–54, 62, 802, 925, 1014–1016
Elks, 7–8
Ellington, Duke, 552, 589, 940
Ellison, Ralph, 248, 254–255, 793–794, 1138,
  1147–1148
Emancipation Proclamation, 226–227
Embree, Charles, 513
Embree, Edwin, 425
Emergency Banking Act, 438
Emergency Relief Administration, 442–443
Emerson, Ralph Waldo, 23, 53, 869
Emporia (Kansas), KKK in, 3–5
Emspak, Julius, 710, 719
End Poverty in America (EPIA), 611–612
End Poverty in California (EPIC), 631–633
Energy projects, 444
Engels, Friedrich, 534
England: Lindbergh's hero's welcome, 156–
  157
English Oxford Group, 871
Enlightenment, 208, 1122
Entertainments, 918–946
EPIA (see End Poverty in America)
EPIC (see End Poverty in California)
Environmental movement, 995
Epstein, Abraham, 17
Erie Canal, 383
Erikson, Erik, 1037
Ernst, Morris, 571
Estonia, 1051
Ethel Traphagen's School of Design, 24
Ethical Culture movement, 878
Ethiopia: Italian invasion, 657, 681
European crises, 1035–1048
  economic crisis, 285, 307
European nations, 55–69
Evangelists, 864, 871
Evans, Elizabeth Glendower, 121
Evans, Hiram Wesley, 4
Evolution theory, 856–857
  prohibiting study of, 854, 862–863
  (See also Scopes trial)

Executive Mansion at Albany, 378–379
Expatriate Americans, 48, 161
  return from Europe, 447
Ezekiel, Mordecai, 392

Fair Labor Standards Board, 696–697
Fairbanks, Douglas, 930–931
Fall, Albert, 105
Family and clan, 1143
  continuity of, 17
Far East crises, 1035, 1048
  threat of war, 670–671
Farewell to Arms, A (Hemingway), 40, 980–
  981
Faris, Herman, 113–114
Farley, James A., 278, 383–384, 475, 673,
  1025–1026
  campaign of 1932, 391, 396, 402, 404
  Democratic Convention (1932), 319, 328,
    331–332
  opposition to FDR's third term, 1061–1063
  presidential ambitions, 1032
  resigned from Democratic National Com-
    mittee, 1065
Farm communities: economic conditions, 10,
  76, 175–176
Farm Credit Administration, 443
Farm-Labor alliance, 6
Farm-Labor Reconstruction League, 6
Farm Mortgage Act, 443, 445
Farm Mortgage moratorium, 690
Farm Mortgage Refinancing Act, 600
Farm Security Administration, 74, 695, 808
Farm workers in California: Communist in-
  volvement, 760–762
  Communist leaders, 763
  Mexican workers, 760–762
  unionization of, 759–763
Farmer-Labor Party, 184, 196, 337, 665
  National Committee, 318, 324
Farmer-Laborites, 112
Farmers' Alliances, 194
Farmers Holiday Association, 291–295
Farms and farming: Agricultural Adjustment
    Act, 441, 601, 660, 842
  Communist organization of, 194–197,
    757–763
  contour plowing, 16
  crop rotation, 16
  Depression effects, 291–295
  diversified crops, 16
  dust storms, 460–461

Farms and farming (*cont.*):
  economic welfare, 14
  farming methods, 15–16
  foreclosures, 291–295
  general farm strike, 292–293
  Marxist farm organizations, 196–197
  migratory workers, 6, 161, 695
  mules on Southern farms, 79
  New Deal legislation, 443, 695–696
  operated by women, 79–80
  poor white tenant farmers, 77–78
  prices and wages, 14–15
  productivity, 176
  radicalism, 194
  FDR's policies, 384
  scientific farming, 15–16
  sharecropers and tenant farmers, 78
  soil conservation, 16
  South, 76–77
  surpluses, 15
  wages, 14–16
  worsening situation, 14–15
Farrell, James T., 138, 514, 524, 782
Farrington, Frank, 715
Fascists and fascism, 491–493, 1094, 1131
  anti-fascist groups, 617
  capitalism and, 493
  Communist opposition to, 655
  dangers of, 1105
  fight against, 1045–1046
  in Italy, 56–63
  Italian-American Fascists, 493
  menace of, 617, 784–785
  Moscow trials and, 784–785
Father Devine, 213
Faulkner, William, 825–826, 999–1003
  Sherwood Anderson and, 1002
Fauset, Jessie, 226, 246, 249
Fay, Larry, 38–39
Fear and repression: of black insurrection, 96
  country's mood of, 3–7
  Federal government catered to, 1
  principal causes of, 671
Federal Art Project, 805–811
  programs of teaching and instruction, 809–810
Federal Bureau of Investigation, 1110
Federal Council of Churches, 871
Federal Deposit Insurance Act, 604
Federal Emergency Relief Administration (FERA), 441–442, 460, 463, 598
  achievements, 841

Federal government (*see* Government)
Federal Project No. 1, 789–813
  Communist influence, 811–813
  Federal Theatre, 792
  Federal Writer's Project, 789–798
Federal Reserve Act, 408
Federal Reserve Board, 176, 278, 429
  policy of deflation, 10
  reserve requirements, 647
Federal Theatre Project (FTP), 792, 798–804
  Communist influence, 799, 804
  critical response, 803
  groups involved in, 804
  Living Newspaper, 800–801
  newspaper attacks on, 803
  number of employees, 803
  variety of productions, 802–803
Federal Theatre Circus, 803
Federal Trade Commission, 443
Federal works program, 336
Federal Writers' Project, 76, 79, 83, 756, 789–798
  Communist influence, 795, 812
  ex-slave narratives, 793
  state guidebook series, 792–797, 812
Federated Press, 532, 714, 717–718
  Communist influence, 717–718
Felicani, Aldino, 120
Fellow travelers, Communist Party, 505
FERA (*see* Federal Emergency Relief Administration)
Ferber, Edna, 29, 48, 64
Ferguson, Otis, 44
Fermi, Enrico, 1038
Filene, E. A., 22
Film and Photo League, 525
Films (*see* Movies and movie-making)
Financial crisis (1933), 426–431
Financing companies, 175
Finland: Soviet invasion, 901, 1053–1054, 1072
Finnish farmers, 197
Firestone, Harvey, 174
Firestone rubber plant, 722
First Amendment, 573
Fischer, Louis, 501, 573
Fishbein, Morris, 912
Fisher, Rudolph, 243
Fisher, Vardis, 51
Fisk University, 99, 200–201, 223
Fitzgerald, F. Scott, 45, 48–51, 61, 162, 973–978
  marriage to Zelda Sayre, 975–978

Flanagan, Hallie, 511–512, 530, 1029
  Dies committee charges, 804
  Federal Theatre Project, 792, 798–804
Flexner, Abraham: study of medical education, 907
  survey of colleges and universities, 887–888
Flood control, 440, 444, 600–601, 842
Floods: Mississippi River, 181
Florida: real estate boom, 172–173
Flower children, 1133
Flynn, Edward J., 278, 1065
  election of 1940, 1071–1072
  political analysis, 679
Flynn, Elizabeth Gurley, 532
Folklore and songs, 793–794, 805
Food, purchased for needy, 460
Football, 942
For Whom the Bell Tolls (Hemingway), 778
Forbes, Charles R., 105
Ford, Ford Madox, 42, 48
Ford, Henry, 173, 364, 453, 746–749
  $5-a-day minimum wage, 22
  Hoover backed by, 400
  tractors and cars built in Soviet Union, 501–502
    Gorky plant, 502–504
Ford Motor Company, 173
  attempts to stymie union, 746–749
  River Rouge plant, 730, 746, 749
  spy and intimidation system, 722
  UAW-CIO recognized by, 749
Ford, James W., 200–201, 324, 556, 668
  Scottsboro Boys defense, 553
Foreign affairs, 481–504, 700
  aggression, punishment of, 701
  Japanese aggression, 660
  tariff issue, 482
  Quarantine Speech, 700–701
  war threat, 700–701
Foreign Affairs magazine, 62, 372, 375
Foreign Service, 496
Foreman, Charles, 425
Forestry Service, 411
Forster, E. M., 526
Forsythe, Margaret, 656
Forsythe, Robert, 515
Fortas, Abe, 601
Fortune, T. Thomas, 227
Fortune magazine, 62
Fosdick, Harry Emerson, 555, 571

Foster, William Z., 112, 186, 192, 196–197, 204, 263, 311, 401, 493, 532, 540–541, 717–718, 1109
  nominated President, 324
Founding Fathers, 363, 370–371, 432, 1141–1144
  Classical-Christian Consciousness, 1141
  government devised by, 1146–1147
  radical universalism of, 1145
Fourteen Points, 64
Fourteenth Amendment, 573
Fourteenth Street school, 950–951
France, Anatole, 122–123, 136, 138
France, 33, 483, 788
  acceptance of blacks, 256–257
  Czechs and Hitler's demands, 1040–1041
  disarmament problem, 487
  economic chaos, 307
  fascism, 491
  German invasion, 1058
  Kellogg-Briand pact, 171–172
  Lindbergh's welcome, 155–159
  Maginot Line, 492, 1051, 1054, 1058
  Mussolini's invasion of, 1058
  mutual defense pact with Soviets, 1045–1046
  occupation of Ruhr, 65–66
  relations with Germany, 65–66
  surrender, 1059
  war debts, 484–485
  World War II, 1050
Franco, Gen. Francisco, 768, 772, 777
Franco-Japanese relations, 700
Franco-Soviet pact, 655
Frank, Jerome, 896
Frank, Waldo, 39–40, 103, 229, 252, 280, 341, 791, 812
  communism, 507, 515, 518–521, 523, 526
  Hart Crane and, 1018–1019
  disenchantment with Communists, 1068–1069
  Moscow trials, 786
  on religion, 869
  Scottsboro Boys defense, 552
Frankensteen, Richard, 728, 741, 745, 747–749
Frankfurter, Felix, 1–3, 8, 13, 29, 111, 113–114, 879, 896
  court-packing bill, 685–686, 689
  "hot dogs," 691
  ideal of service, 421
  influence, 464
  law clerks recommended by, 421–425
  on new society, 318

Frankfurter, Felix (*cont.*):
  newspaper attacks on, 423
  nominated for Supreme Court, 691
  protégés, 421–425
  recognition of Soviet Union, 183
  FDR supporter and adviser, 388–389
  on FDR's victory in 1932, 404
  Sacco-Vanzetti case, 126, 128–129, 133
Frankfurter, Marion, 133–134
Franklin, Benjamin, 371, 1146
  on wealth, 371
Franklin, Sidney, 767–768, 776
Frazier-Lemke Act, 639, 690
"Free enterprise," 26
Free love, 5
Free speech movement, 1132–1133
Free world, 1108
Freeman, Douglas Southall, 557, 562
Freeman, Joseph, 231, 512–513
Freidel, Frank, 407
French Dadaists, 32, 64
French Enlightenments, 1141
French Revolution, 1122–1123, 1145
French-Soviet relations, 654–655
Freud, Sigmund, 45, 52, 495
  influence, 916–917
Frick, Henry, 141, 187
Fromm, Erich, 1037
Frost, Robert, 1017–1018, 1143
Fugitive group, 992–998, 1003–1004
  (*See also* Agrarians)
Fuhr, Lee, 529
Fuller, Alvin T., 123, 127–129, 131, 136, 139
  Fundamentalism, 852–853
Fundamentalists, 9, 871
  Scopes trial, 862–863
Funk, Garland, 260
Future trends, 1127–1148
  hopes and dreams, 1143–1144

Gallup, George, polls, 649–650, 662, 670
  (*See also* Polls and polling)
Gangsters: in Chicago, 161
Garden city movement, 638–639
Garfield, James, 325
Garland, Charles, 532
Garman, Charles, 102
Garner, John "Cactus Jack," 326, 329, 331–
  332, 395, 418, 686, 1025–1026, 1081
  opposed sit-down strike, 734–735
  poker-playing companions, 469
  Vice-President nomination, 332

Garsson, Murray, 467
Garvey, Marcus, 198–199, 213–214, 239, 593,
  658
Gastonia, North Carolina, textile strike, 191–
  193, 529
Gauss, Christian, 506
Gay, Charles, 697–698
*Gazette* (Emporia, Kansas), 4, 11
Gelbers, Joseph, 586, 595, 820
General Electric Company, 20, 383
General Motors, 10, 174, 462, 722
  effect of the strike, 742
  Flint plant, 730
  labor problems, 10
  negotiations, 734–736
  sit-down strike, 732–745
    UAW victory, 739–740
    vigilante committees, 743
  spies, 731
  union recognized by, 739
  unionization of, 727–750
Generation gap, 48
Geneva Protocol, 1041
George, Henry, 53, 369, 394, 630
George V, King of England, 156
Gerard, James W., 26
German-American Bund, 1092
German Expressionists, 64
German refugees: in America, 1036
German-Soviet nonaggression pact, 783, 788,
  901, 1042–1046, 1072, 1078–1079, 1120
  reaction of Communists, 1045–1046
Germany, 33–34, 55
  aggression, 660
  Allied occupation force, 65
  anschluss between Austria and, 57–59
  blitzkrieg, 1054–1055
  Communist party, 68, 488
  declared war on U.S., 1089
  Disarmament Conference in Geneva, 487
  foreign relations, 1044
  Hitler's rise to power, 436, 487–491
  international set in Berlin, 64
  invasion of Russia, 1094
  Jewish persecution, 487–492
  mutual defense pact with Soviets, 1045–1046
  mutual defense treaty with Italy, 1078
  mutual defense treaty with Japan, 1078
  National Socialists, 64–65
  1925 election, 68
  phony war, 1054–1055
  postwar, 63–67

Germany (*cont.*):
  public sentiment for, 1051
  Reichstag fire, 488
  reparations, 67–68
  Ruhr occupation, 65
  Russia invaded by, 1078–1079
  Socialist trade unions, 489
  Soviet-German nonaggression pact, 783,
    788, 901, 1042–1046, 1078–1079,
    1120
  storm troopers, 488–489
  surrender in 1945, 1108
  terrorist gangs, 63–64
  Versailles Treaty limitations, 486–487
  vindictiveness of Europeans toward, 55–56
  (*See also* Hitler, Adolph; Nazis)
Germany-Japanese relations, 654
Gershwin, George, 53
Giannini, A. P., 174
Gibbons, Floyd, 64
Gibran, Kahlil, 870
Gibson, Hugh, 282
Gifford, Walter, 305
Gillespie, Dizzy, 219
Gilman, Charlotte Perkins, 91, 631
Giovannitti, Arturo, 63
Girdler, Tom, 752
Gitlow, Ben, 184–186, 191–192, 196, 203–
  204, 263, 314, 316, 324, 532
  Trotskyite heresies, 324
Gladden, Washington, 53
Glasgow, Ellen, 966, 988–990, 998, 1024
Glass, Carter, 332, 418, 687
Gold, Ben, 192, 710
Gold, Mike, 131, 186–188, 230, 511, 527,
  591, 655, 802, 954, 1089
Gold and silver, 435, 445–447
  drain in 1933, 407
  purchase plan, 447
  ratio between silver and, 447
  reserves, 429
  FDR's policy on, 445–447
  setting price of, 447
Gold standard, 26, 306
  abandoned by FDR, 445–446, 460, 484–485
  Thomas amendment, 446
Goldman, Emma, 14, 29, 113, 143–144, 537,
  606, 741, 914, 1131
Goldmark, Josephine, 416
Goldstein, Benjamin, 557
Gomez, Manuel, 525
Gompers, Samuel, 14, 258, 413, 597

Gone with the Wind (Mitchell), 592
Good and evil in world, 533, 1094, 1099
Goodavich, Sophie, 209–210
Goodenough, Carolyn, 133
Goodyear Tire and Rubber Company, 722–726
  strike, 722–726
Gordon, Caroline, 42
Gordon, Eugene, 552, 564
Gordon, Taylor, 47, 237, 244–245, 515
Gore, Howard M., 178
Göring, Hermann, 436, 489, 1052
Gorman, Francis, 706
Gould, Joe, 44
Government: partnership between business
  and, 449–450, 460
  regulatory power, 394
  repressive spirit, 3–7
  responsibility for public welfare, 845
  responsibility to achieve more just and hu-
    mane society, 452
  supported employers against unions, 13
Governmental reorganization bill, 698
Grace, Eugene, 453
Grady, Henry, 70
Graft and corruption: Harding administra-
  tion, 105
Graham, Martha, 805
Gramaphone (or Victrola), 918–919, 933
Granich, Irwin (*see* Gold, Mike)
Grant, Robert, 128
Graves, Bibb, 560, 562–563
Graves, John Temple, 95, 820
Graves, Morris, 811
Gray, Gilda, 38
Grey, Ralph, 581–582
Great Britain, 483
  alliances, 654
  Battle of Britain, 1069–1070
  communists and socialists, 1031
  economic crisis, 285
  fascism, 491
  general strike (1926), 68
  Hitler's invasion of Austria, 1040
  Labor Party, 1031
  lend-lease program, 1070
  relations with Japan, 69, 700
  Russian-German nonaggression pact,
    1045–1046
  Scottsboro Boys, 553, 855–856
  unemployment compensation, 382
  war debts, 484–485
  World War II, 1050

Great Depression (*See* Depression)
*Great Gatsby, The* (Fitzgerald), 976–977
Great Plains: shelterbelts, 1103–1104
Great Society, 318
Greater East Asia Co-Prosperity Sphere, 1048, 1090
Greece, 59
  post World War I, 56
Greed, sanctification of, 422
Greek-Christian culture, 23
Green, Fitzhugh, 157–159
Green, Lucille, 258
Green, Paul, 225, 251, 520, 551–552, 825
Green, William, 14, 261, 413, 453–454, 693, 712
  opposed New Deal legislation, 441
  opposed UAW, 739
*Green Pastures* (Green), 225, 251
Greenbelt towns, 638, 962
Greenwich Village, New York City: artists and writers, 42
  eccentricity, 43–44
  parties and party-givers, 44–48
  Provincetown Players, 1007
  sex, 48–51
  tourist-scandalizing, 42
Greenwood, Marion, 531
Grew, Joseph, 1085
Gridiron Club's 1934 dinner, 473
Griffith, D. W., 922–923
Grinnell College, 380
Groma, Eugene van, 1036
Gropius, Walter, 964, 1037
Gropper, William, 131, 1115
Gross, Ethel, 380–381
Grosz, George, 1037
Groton school, 342–343
Gruening, Ernest, 635
Guffey, Joseph, 351–352
Guide Lamp (Anderson, Indiana) strike, 742–743
Guidebooks, state, 792–797, 812
Guinan, Texas, 38
Gurdjieff, Georges, 243
Guthrie, Woody, 714, 762
Gwaltney, John Langston, 90–91, 1135–1136

Haessler, Carl, 714–718, 733
Haile Selassie, 658
Haines Normal and Industrial Institute, Augusta, Georgia, 98
Hair, bobbed, 9
Haiti: poets, 256
  U.S. occupation, 171, 256

Hall, Gus, 718
Hall, Jacquelyn Dowd, 95
Hall, Otto, 183, 201
Hallgren, Mauritz A., 299, 1100
Hamid, Sufi, Abdul, 589–590
Hamilton, Alexander, 269–270, 363–365
Hamilton, Isabel, 906–907
Hammond, Lily Hardy, 98
Hampton Institute, 552
Hand, Learned, 18, 30, 113, 129, 135–136, 424
Handy, W. C., 242
Hanfstaengl, Ernst "Putzi," 490
Hankow (China): revolutionary center, 164–166
Hanseon, Florence Curtis, 717
Hapgood, Hutchins, 28–30, 48–49, 66, 113, 131, 536–537, 971–972, 1049, 1133
Hapgood, Neith, 28–30
Hapgood, Norman, 8
Hapgood, Powers, 131, 715–716, 723, 728, 736
  labor organizer, 707
"Happy Days Are Here Again," 329, 438, 454
Hardin, Lil, 937, 939
Harding, Warren G., 13, 40, 101, 174
  obituary, 101
  scandals, 105
Harlan County (Kentucky) coal strikes, 517–518
Harlem, New York City
  Communist Party, 592
  "drag balls," 47
  educational problems, 202
  numbers game, 220–221
  nightlife, 237
  race riot in 1935, 589
  strong attraction for whites, 248–249
Harlem Literary group, 247–248
Harlem Renaissance, 199, 221–222, 226, 232, 234, 243–249, 257, 1129–1130, 1138
  black women, 247–251
  Langston Hughes, 234–243
  Zora Neale Hurston, 1005
  James Weldon Johnson, 243
  new consciousness, 254
  white writers and artists, 237, 251–252
Harper, William, 2
Harriman, Averell, 1033
Harriman, Florence "Daisy," 132, 328
Harris, Abram, 261

Harris, Lem, 190, 195, 293–294
Harrisburg (Pennsylvania): demonstration by
    unemployed, 316
Harrison, George M., 261
Harrison, Hubert H., 214, 243
Hart, Albert Bushnell, 380
Harvard University, 2, 126, 222, 885–886
    Board of Overseers, 2
    Business School, 25
    clubs, 345
    Crimson (college newspaper), 344
    "Jewish quota," 126
    Law School, 8, 421
Harvey, T. H., 9
Harvey, William H., 325
Haskin, Sara Estelle, 98
Hassan, Ihab, 1135
Hathaway, Charles, 112, 717
Hathaway, Clarence, 656
Hauptmann, Bruno, 163
Hawes, Harry, 275
Hawley-Smoot tariff bill, 287
Hay, John, 307, 479
Hayes, Alfred, 296
Hayes, Roland, 941
Haymarket anarchists, 141
Haynes, Elizabeth Ross, 99
Hays, Arthur Garfield, 112, 135, 571
Haywood, Big Bill, 29
Haywood, Harry, 201
Health, 51
    lower-class Southerners, 815
Health insurance, 644
    opposition from doctors, 910–911
Healy, Dora, 80
Hearst, William Randolph, 172, 329, 332,
    397, 399, 491
    Federal Theatre denounced by, 803
    opposition to FDR, 668–669
Hecht, Ben, 970
Hedonism, 49, 103, 178
Heflin, Thomas, 519, 563
Hellman, Lillian, 48, 776
Hemingway, Ernest, 40, 48, 52, 61–62, 978–983
    attack on Anderson, 982
    Spanish Civil War, 767–768, 776–778
Henderson, Donald, 758–759
Henderson, Fletcher, 552
Henderson, Mrs. Leon, 125
Herald Tribune, 19
Herbst, Josephine, 40–43, 48, 51, 63, 125,
    134, 311, 500, 522, 524, 733

Herbst, Josephine (cont.):
    communist leanings, 509, 527, 1110
    lesbianism, 531
    Moscow trials, 785–786
    Russian visit, 501
    Spanish Civil War, 774–775, 778–779
    visit to Germany in 1935, 654
Herman, Woody, 1037
Herndon, Angelo, 539–542, 565–574, 773,
    825
    arrest and imprisonment, 565–567
    Communist organizer, 540–543, 565
    International Labor Defense, 565, 568–569
    Scottsboro Boys defense, 551
    trip to New York, 569–571
Herndon, Milton, 773
Herrick, Myron, 155, 162
Herrin, Illinois, 5
Herriot, Georges, 67
Herrmann, John, 41, 48, 51, 134, 316, 500,
    509
    joined Communist Party, 527
Herron, George, 258, 852
Herwarth, Johnny, 1044
Heyward, DuBoise, 251, 825, 998
Hibbard, Cornella, 593
Hibbard, West, 593
Hibben, Paxton, 130, 131
Hickerson, Harold, 138
Hickok, Guy, 28
Hickok, Lorena, 460–461, 478–479, 661,
    900–902
Hicks, Granville, 137, 510–511, 522–523,
    775
    communist, 507
Hicks, Mary, 76–77
Highlander Folk School, 821, 1129
Hill, Lister, 697
Hillman, Sidney, 205, 260, 532, 709, 713
Hindemith, Paul, 1037
Hindenburg, Paul von, 68, 436, 487–489
Hirohito, Emperor, 1086
Hirsch, Alfred, 516
Hirsch, Dr. Sidney Mttron, 991
Hiss, Alger, 421, 527, 601, 1029, 1110–1114
Hiss, David, 421
Historical Records Survey, 793
History and historical writing: "biographical"
    history, 1142
    Classical-Christian Consciousness, 1003
    collective memory, 1139
    forms of, 1139–1140

History and historical writing (*cont.*):
intellectual tradition, 1003–1004
major themes, 1141–1148
movement to "debunk," 533
narrative, 1138–1142
New Deal importance, 848
psychotherapy and, 1138–1139
FDR's interest in, 362–365
Secular-Democratic Consciousness, 1003
World War I, 1094
Hitler, Adolf, 306, 1075, 1085
alliance with Mussolini, 681
annexation of Austria, 1039–1040
collapse of Reich, 1098–1099
death of, 1099
Fascist popular movement, 1094
invasion of Rhineland, 702
meeting with Chamberlain, 1040
*Mein Kampf*, 66, 1094
Munich meeting, 1041
1936 Olympics, 943
objectives, 491
obsession with FDR, 1094–1095
persecution of Jews, 1035, 1051
phony war, 1054–1055
putsch started by, 66
rise to power, 64–65, 68, 436, 487, 746
threat to civilized world, 1089–1090, 1099
Versailles Treaty denounced by, 654
war against German intellectuals, 1035–
1036
Hoare, Sir Samuel, 157
Hofmann, Hans, 964, 1036
Hofstadter, Richard, 434
Holding company bill, 646
Holiday, Billie, 219, 826, 937
Holiness sects, 874
"Holistic" theorists, 641
Holland, Nazi invasion, 1058
Holly Grove, Arkansas, 86–87
Holmes, Oliver Wendell, 20, 390, 421
Holstein, Caspar, 221
Home Owners Loan Act, 445, 601
*Home to Harlem* (McKay), 232–234
Homer, Winslow, 947
Homestead strike, 141
Honduras, U.S. occupation, 171
Hood, Raymond, 960–961
Hook, Sidney, 903
Hooker, Thomas, 1141
Hoover, Herbert, 177, 407
acceptance speech, 265–266

Hoover, Herbert (*cont.*):
administrative ability, 282–283
ambition to be President, 179–180
campaign of 1928, 263, 275–278
campaign of 1932, 398
defeat in 1932, 404–405
Depression and, 282–316, 390
discredited leadership, 405–406
economic troubles, 278–279, 300
flood relief operations, 181
nominated President, 263, 318
ordered eviction of Bonus Army, 339–340
personality and traits, 282–283
program, 283–284
Republican National Convention, 665
requests joint statement with FDR, 427–429
FDR and, 407, 448
secretary of commerce, 179
on "Voluntaryism," 275–276
welfare programs, 304–305
Hoover, Irwin "Ike," 278, 429
Hoover, J. Edgar, 258
Hope, John, 71, 97
Hope, Lugenia, 98–99
Hopkins, Harry, 366, 379–381, 390, 422,
460, 597, 609–610, 1042
American aid for Soviets, 1079–1080
appointment with Mussolini, 491
Dies and, 693
distribution of money through the states,
459
election of 1940, 1071–1072
health problems, 845, 1056, 1061–1062,
1086
Ickes and, 635, 1031–1032
influence, 664
intimate of FDR, 463
power, 1033
presidential ambitions, 608, 1028, 1032,
1034
on presidential trip, 651
purge of conservative Democrats, 1026
Roosevelt family Christmas, 472
secretary of commerce, 1032–1034
social work background, 442–443
Soviet aims and, 500
state guidebook series, 792
talks with Churchill, 1075–1076
Temporary Emergency Relief Administration, 422
Hopkins, Mary Alden, 34
Hopper, Edward, 949–952

Hornsby, Sadie, 83
Horton, James Edwin, Jr., 553–555, 559
Horton, Myles, 821, 1129
Houdini, Harry, 29
Houghton, Alanson B., 156
House, Col. Edward M., 35, 68, 318, 397, 635
    Democratic Convention (1932), 318–321
    effect of isolationist policy, 483
House, John, 723
House of Morgan, 19, 26, 111, 170
    defaulted loans, 177
House Un-American Activities Committee, 692–693, 804, 812, 1027–1028, 1114, 1129
    New Deal opposition, 1029
Houseman, John, 800, 802, 804
Housing projects, 845
    federally subsidized, 699
    Levittown, Long Island, 965
    planned communities, 961–962, 965
    public housing projects, 841
    "subsistence homesteads," 611–612
Houston, Charles, 261
Houston, David, 411
Howard, Charles P., 707, 713
Howard, Michael, 1135
Howard, Perry, 259
Howard, Roy, 605
Howard University, 222, 412, 892
Howe, Frederick, 29–31, 112, 208, 420, 896
Howe, Julia Ward, 121
Howe, Louis McHenry, 107, 352, 378, 384
    campaign of 1932, 391, 402, 404
    chief secretary, 418
    Democratic Convention (1932), 318
    family background, 353
    friendship with FDR, 352–353, 463
    illness and death, 662–664
    lived at White House, 470
    political instincts, 353
Howe, Mark DeWolfe, 421
Howe, Quincy, 518
Howell, Clark, 319
Huddleston, George, 169, 549
Hudson, Hosea, 72, 89, 312, 531, 586–587, 593, 699, 751–752, 821–822, 824, 1117, 1119
    Communist union organizer, 575–580
    learning to read, 580
Hudson, Colonel and Rev. John H., 566

Hudson, William, 379
Hughes, Charles Evans, 1, 119, 157, 162, 351, 397, 680, 682, 689
    presented Cross of Honor to Lindbergh, 159–161
    secretary of state, 168, 178
Hughes, Langston, 47, 234–239, 243, 245, 247–249, 259, 573–574, 593, 937, 994
    in Africa, 239
    on Berlin, 306
    black writer, 253
    celebrity in Russia, 256
    dedicated Communist, 784
    hostile toward New Deal, 587–588
    jazz and blues themes, 241–242
    in Moscow, 593–594
    "One-Way Ticket," 839
    in Paris, 239–240
    poems, 238–243, 253, 839
    romantic affairs, 251
    Scottsboro Boys, 551–552
    Spanish Civil War, 770, 773, 776–777
    travels abroad, 255–256
Hughes, Rupert, 632
Hull, Cordell, 408–409, 419, 445, 485, 615, 635, 656, 1032, 1044, 1056, 1085
    international cooperation, 484
Hungary: post war, 56–57, 1041
Hunger marches, 313–314
Hunt, Frazier, 16–17, 63–65, 103, 113, 292, 874, 895
    on New Deal, 458–459
Hurley, Patrick, 338–339
Hurston, Zora Neale, 247, 1005–1006
Hutcheson, William "Big Bill," 13, 713
    punched by John L. Lewis, 712–713, 744
Hutchins, Grace, 528
Hutchins, Robert, 26, 126, 607, 888, 903, 1067
Hutton, Barbara, 931
Huxley, Aldous, 526
Hyde Park, 356–357
    conservation work, 359

Ickes, Harold, 113, 402, 409–410, 425, 1068
    court-packing fight, 683
    creation of jobs, 459
    diary, 411, 459, 466
    Dies and, 693
    election of 1936, 659–681
    Hopkins and, 1031–1032

Ickes, Harold (*cont.*):
  interest in Indians, 465
  presidential ambitions, 1032, 1034
  PWA, 453
  purge of conservative Democrats, 1026
  on Eleanor Roosevelt, 479
  on FDR, 457, 469–475, 1076
  secretary of interior, 465
  on Henry Wallace, 465
Ideas and ideologies: election of 1936, 679
ILD (*see* International Labor Defense)
Immigration and immigrants, 14
  alien immigrants, 161
  role of, 1143
Immigration laws, 466–467
Immigration Service, 466–467
Imperialism, Yankee, 169, 171
*In Search of Roosevelt* (Tugwell), 371
Independent Progressive Party, 105, 111, 113
Index of American Design, 809
Indians, 72
  FDR visit with, 603
  under Department of Interior, 465
Individualism vs. community, 849
Industrial system, 178, 640, 995
  collective bargaining, 115, 303, 336, 448
  exploitation of men, women and children, 608–609
  government planning for, 394
  reforms, 414
  replace competition with cooperation, 449–450
Ingersoll, Jerry, 190
Initiative and referendum movement, 18–19
Inness, George, 947
Insurance companies, 175
  health insurance (*see* Health insurance)
  social, 602
  unemployment and old-age, 601–602
Intellectuals, 221–262, 1003–1004
  artists and, 21
  black, 217, 221–262
  communism and, 505–538, 1112–1115
  in Department of Agriculture, 464
  German and Austrian, 1035–1038
  idealization of the worker, 742
  immigration of German and Austrian, 1035–1039
  left-wing politics, 1038
  Moscow trials, 780–784
  movement to the left, 506–507

Intellectuals (*cont.*)
  new class, 853
  new consciousness, 1143
  "new" intellectuals in the South, 825
  revolt against capitalism, 32
  FDR and, 373
  in the twenties, 27–28
Intelligence systems, 1091
Interest rates, 10, 15
Intermediate Credit Act of 1923, 15
International Fur Workers' Union, 192
International Labor Defense, 516, 520, 539, 540, 546–550, 564–565
  defense of Scottsboro Boys, 546–550
  Angelo Herndon case, 564–565, 568–569
  legal arm of Communist Party, 546, 548–550, 553, 564
  NAACP vs. 547–549
International Ladies Garment Workers Union, 9–10, 112, 710, 720, 726, 1119
International Legal Defense, 539
International Longshoremen's Association, 613–617, 710
International monetary system, 176
International set, 68
  in Berlin, 64
International Union of Revolutionary Writers, 523
Internationalism, 320, 367, 428, 481–482
  America's role in, 1047–1048, 1143
  FDR predilections toward, 481–482
Irwin, William A., 453
Isolationists, 72, 320–321, 393, 481–482, 847, 1040, 1052, 1103
  attack on Pearl Harbor, 1089
  opposed lend-lease, 1074
  opposition to America's involvement in war, 1067–1068
  and refugees from Nazis, 1039
  strength of, 1047, 1056–1057
*It Can't Happen Here* (Lewis), 526, 802, 983
Italian Futurists, 32
Italian radicals, 63
Italians: outbreaks between blacks and, 657–658
Italy, 55
  fascism, 56–63
  invasion of Ethiopia, 681
  Mussolini and fascism, 59–63, 491–493
*Izvestia*, 782, 785

Jackman, Harold, 249
Jackson, Gardner, 120, 125, 135
Jacksonville, Florida, 222–223
James, Edward, 131–132
James, Clifford, 582–584
James, William, 53, 131, 208–209, 439, 479,
    821, 914, 1147
Japan: American policy, 700, 1080–1081
    declaration of war by U.S., 1087–1088
    expansion in Far East, 700–702, 1048
    Greater East Asia Co-Prosperity Sphere,
        1048, 1090
    growing tensions between U.S. and, 1085–
        1091
    Manchurian conquest, 306–307, 481
    Nazi ally, 1085
    Pearl Harbor attack, 1085–1092
        (See also Japanese attack on Pearl Harbor)
    relations with Great Britain, 69
    war-making potential, 1081
Japanese-Americans, 1091–1092
Japanese attack on Pearl Harbor: casualties,
    1089
    meeting with Japanese envoys, 1086–1087
    Pacific Fleet transferred to Pearl Harbor,
        1085–1086, 1090
    reactions of Americans, 1091–1092
    FDR's address to Congress, 1087–1088
    U.S. declaration of war on Axis powers, 1087
Jardine, William M., 178
Jazz, 9, 45, 49, 212
    denounced by Nazi and Communists, 552, 940
Jazz Age, 52, 162
Jeffers, Robinson, 1021–1024
Jefferson, Thomas, 269–270, 373, 816, 841,
    1122–1123
    influence on FDR, 362–365
    redistribution of land, 371
    rehabilitation of, 362–365
    Secular-Democratic Consciousness, 1141
Jefferson and Hamilton (Bowers), 363
Jefferson Centennial Commission, 364
Jelliffe, Russell and Rowena, 236
Jews, 17
    anti-Semitism, 3
    Hitler persecution of, 1035–1036
    Jewish religion, 878–879
    Ku Klux Klan and, 3
    refugees from Nazis, 1036–1039
    FDR and, 691
    quota system for students, 893
Jim Crow laws, 88, 199, 219, 822

Jobless Party, 337
John, Augustus, 47
John Reed Clubs, 508–509
Johns, Frank, 113–114
Johns, Orrick, 44, 299, 516, 811
Johns, Peggy Baird, 516
Johns Hopkins Medical School, 906
Johnson, Alvin, 1037
Johnson, Caleb, 250
Johnson, Carrie Parks, 98–99
Johnson, Charles Sidney, 1093
Johnson, Charles Spurgeon, 246
Johnson, Fenton, 246
Johnson, Gerald, 32, 35, 73, 825
Johnson, Hiram, 171, 320, 397, 409–410,
    482, 484–485, 615, 1052, 1066
    World Court Treaty, 648
Johnson, Hugh, 388, 418, 440, 597, 615–
    616, 701, 1028
    criticism of, 607
    head of NRA, 452–453
    Huey Long attacked by, 627
    National Industrial Recovery Act, 448
Johnson, J. Rosamond, 224, 237, 244
Johnson, James Weldon, 4, 96–97, 222–227,
    1093
    foreign service posts, 225–226
    musical activities, 224–227
Johnson, James William (later James Weldon
    Johnson), 222–224
Johnson, Lyndon B., 690, 1026–1027
Johnson, Mordecai, W., 823
Johnson, Tom, 30, 386, 420
Johnson Act of 1934, 484
Jolson, Al, 927
Jones, Bishop R. E., 97
Jones, Bobby, 29
Jones, Mother, 12, 43
Jordan, David Star, 8
Josephson, Matthew, 26, 32, 401–402
Joughin, Louis, 117, 137, 144
Journalists, 26
Judd, Zebulon, 550
Judiciary reorganization bill, 687
Julian, Hubert, 658
Julius Rosenwald Foundation, 97
Jungle, The (Sinclair), 754
Junkyards, 176
Just, Ernest Everett, 893–894
Justice department, 1–2
    infiltration of radical organizations, 2
Justice, sense of, 23

Kahn, Albert, 502
Kamenev, Leo, 168, 195, 203, 780
Kansas: Ku Klux Klan in, 3–5
  Progressives, 11
Károlyi, Count Michael, 2
Kaufman, George S., 29
Kazin, Alfred, 140, 335
Keaton, Buster, 924–926
Keller, Helen, 113, 229
Kelley, Florence, 13, 414–415
Kelley, Nicholas, 708
Kellock, Katherine, 792, 796, 798
Kellogg, Frank, 3, 168–169, 178
Kellogg, Paul, 382, 415, 424
Kellogg, Dr. Vernon, 856–857
Kellogg-Briand Pact, 67, 171–172, 307, 1041
Kelly, Edward, 402, 1062
Kelly, William H. "Kid," 595
Kelsey-Hayes Wheel Company, 729–730
Kemal, Mustafa, 56, 395–396
Kennan, George, 496–498
Kennedy, Joseph P., 395–396, 601, 628,
  1059
  Ambassador to Britain, 1055, 1075
Kent, Frank, 103, 606
Kent, Rockwell, 507, 522, 807, 820, 952,
  1115
Kerr, Angus, 12
Kerr, Clark, 632
Kerr, Florence, 798
Key West, Florida, 48
Kieran, John, 942
Kimmel, Husband E., 1085
King, Carol Weiss, 573
King, Charles, 411
King, Edward, 510
King, Jere, 558
King's Henchman, The (Millay and Taylor), 45
Kirby, Rollin, 334
Kirk, Alexander, 788, 1043
Kirov, Sergei Mironovich, 657
Knights of Labor, 187, 764
Knox, Bernard, 774
Knox, Frank, 665, 1060, 1077
Knoxville, Tennessee, 83
Knudsen, William S., 722, 738–739
Knutson, Alfred, 112, 194–195
Koch, Robert, 905
Kollontai, Madame Aleksandra, 307–308
Koltsov, Mikhail, 778
Konop, Thomas F., 688
Konoye, Prince Fumimaro, 1085

Kramer, Charles, 1029
Kramer, Victoria, 754
Kreymbourg, Alfred, 802
Krock, Arthur, 408–409
  influence on FDR, 473
Kropotkin, Prince Piotr, 120, 125, 143
Krutch, Joseph Wood, 45, 533–534, 858
Ku Klux Klan, 35, 161, 422, 541, 852
  anti-Catholicism and racism, 3–7
  anti-Smith campaign, 274–275
  bigotry, malice and terror, 4
  Democratic Convention of 1924, 106–107
  membership, 6–7
  militantly Protestant, 7
  penetrated Republican Party, 4–5
  White Supremacy, 7
Kuniyoshi, Yasuo, 811
Kuusinen, Otto, 198

Labor and capital, war between, 11–14, 677,
    761, 846, 1093, 1125, 1142
Labor unions, 703–723
  American Federation of Labor, 703, 707
  benefits for nonunion members, 764
  blacks organized by, 589–590, 722
  Catholic members, 710
  "closed" unions, 13
  coal industry, 11–12
  Communist dominated, 191–193, 703, 709,
    726, 757
  company, 455
  conflict between capital and labor, 11–14
  cooperating with employers, 709
  decline in membership, 9–10, 703
  discrimination against blacks and immi-
    grants, 13
  effect of prosperity, 14
  employers' attempts to destroy, 13
  election of 1924, 111–112
  fair labor standards bill, 696
  Gallup polls, 765
  government-employers-labor councils, 710
  independent, 707
  industrial vs. craft unions, 711–713
  leaders, 33
    Communist, 1117–1118
    conservative, 12–13, 765
  National Labor Relations Act, 643
  NRA labor codes, 703–704, 706
  organizing activities, 704
  planning and running strikes, 721–722
  reformers, 13

Labor unions (*cont.*):
  repressive action by authorities, 10–11
  right to collective bargaining, 449
    (*See also* Collective bargaining)
  right to organize, 449, 766
  rights of workers vs. rights of owners, 10
  social life and, 12
  Southern, 84–85
  steel industry, 751–754
  strikes, 10–11, 703
    (*See also* Strikes)
  threats to, 12
  unfair practices, 449
  union songs, 723–724
  unionization of American workers, 525–526
  vigilante committees, 725
  weaknesses, 703
Labor's Bill of Rights, 449
Laborsaving machines, 12
Ladies Garment Workers (*see* International Ladies Garment Workers Union)
*Lady Chatterley's Lover* (Lawrence), 3
La Follette, Philip, 301–302, 1028
La Follette, Robert, 13, 112–114, 303–304, 318, 439
  candidate for President, 184, 196
La Guardia, Fiorello, 113, 657, 793
Lamont, Thomas, 19, 26, 170, 429–430
Land reclamation, 444, 601
Landis, James, 421, 694
Landon, Alfred, 665, 673
Laney, Lucy Craft, 98
Langer, Elinor, 41, 776–779, 1116
Langstaff, John, 1136
Langston, Charles Howard, 234–235
*Lanterns on the Levee* (Percy), 837–838
Lash, Joseph, 355, 900
Laski, Harold, 20, 29, 128, 421, 691
Latin America: Bolshevik threat, 168
  Coolidge's policy, 169–170
Latvia, 1051
Law, Oliver, 772
Lawrence, D. G., 3
Lawrence, D. H., 1136–1137
Lawrence (Massachusetts) strike, 209
Lawson, John Howard, 524–525, 568, 633
Lawyers, New Deal programs, 422
Lea, Homer, 165
Leaders and leadership, 161, 575–576
  black, 578, 587, 1093
"Leading economic indicators," 460

League of American Writers, 523, 526–527, 786, 811–812
League of Nations, 35, 58–59, 64, 307, 320, 372, 483, 1041
  abstention of U.S. from, 483
  Italian invasion of Ethiopia, 657, 681
  Japanese sanctions, 700
  Roosevelt advocate of, 399, 481
League of Women Voters, 827
Lee, Duncan C., 1030
Left, the, 182–210, 1109–1126
  Communist Party, 182–208
  intellectuals movement to, 506–507
  non-Communist, 208–210
  postwar America, 1108
  suppressing, 1109–1126
Le Gallienne, Eva, 42
LeHand, Marguerite "Missy," 333, 372, 378, 426, 470, 477
Lehman, Herbert, 273, 878
Leibowitz, Samuel, 553–567, 562
Leisure class, 21
Leiter, Joseph, 11
Lemke, William, 665
Lend-lease, 1073–1075
Lenin, Vladimir, 125, 167, 497, 534, 781–782
  death and struggle for succession, 195–196
  interest in American farmers, 189–190, 194
  New Economic Policy, 183–184, 499
Lens, Sidney, 297, 522, 532, 714, 1117
Le Sueur, Meridel, 534
Levittown (Long Island) "planned community," 965
Lewis, Acquilla, 12
Lewis, John Frederick, Jr., 532
Lewis, John L., 13, 187, 192, 261, 517, 669, 707–716, 766, 902
  defection from Democratic ranks, 1066–1067
  leadership, 708
  organizing blacks, 590
  punched Big Bill Hutcheson, 712–713
  role in negotiations, 708
  steel strike, 752–753
  unionization by industry vs. craft, 711–713
  UAW supported by, 732, 738–741
Lewis, Kathryn, 745
Lewis, Sinclair, 16, 48, 51, 61, 64, 285, 415, 516, 521, 535–536, 802, 983–984
  Nobel Prize for literature, 526

Lewis, Wyndham, 103, 1125, 1145
Liberals and radicals, 27, 55, 533, 1125
  election of 1936, 673
*Liberator*, 229–231, 588
  radical literary journal, 229
Liberty League, 668–669, 694
Liberty Party, 318, 325
"Lift every voice and sing," 224, 226
Lincoln, Abraham, 38
Lincoln University, 240–241
Lindbergh, Charles A., 26, 146–163, 1052
  army air training, 148–149
  arrival in Paris, 154–156
  barnstorming, 148–149
  education and family background, 146–147
  heroes welcome, 155–163
  kidnapping and death of son, 163
  marriage to Anne Morrow, 162–163
  *The Spirit of St. Louis* (book), 153, 163
  *The Spirit of St. Louis* (plane), 149–155
  transatlantic flight, 149–155
  weather reports, 151–153
Lindbergh, Evangeline Lodge Land, 146, 157
Lindley, Ernest, 322, 375, 384, 403, 486
Lindsay, Vachel, 42, 240
Lindsey, Judge Benjamin, 5, 420–421
Lippmann, Walter, 3, 18, 26, 34, 110–111,
      113–114, 128–129, 136–137, 528
  America's role in international crises,
      1047–1048
  anti-interventionists, 170
  anti-New Deal bias, 896
  backed Newton D. Baker, 326–327
  capital vs. labor, 19–20
  on Coolidge's policy in Latin America,
      169–170
  critic of Mussolini, 62
  on economy in 1932, 402
  election of 1928, 265, 271–274
  election of 1936, 673
  on foreign affairs, 701–702
  on Frankfurter, 388
  on Herbert Hoover, 287
  influence on FDR, 473
  on morals, 279–280
  on New Deal measures, 457
  phony war, 1054–1055
  on power of majorities, 18–19
  on quota system, 893
  reform legislation, 642
  religion of spirit, 869
  on FDR, 334–335, 359, 473, 486

Lippmann, Walter (*cont.*):
  support for Willkie, 1065–1066
  on Versailles Treaty, 68
Lipchitz, Jacques, 1036
Literary scene, 966–1024
  autobiographical style, 982–983, 1005
  Harlem Renaissance, 1005–1006
  (*See also* Harlem Renaissance)
  individualism, 982–983
  playwrights, 1007–1012
  poets and poetry, 1014–1024
  proletarian novels, 523–524, 1005
  scriptwriters, 1007
  Southern literary renaissance, 991–1007
  theatre, 1007–1012
*Literature and Revolution* (Trotsky), 507
Literary creativity, 28
*Literary Digest* poll, 673–674, 676
Lithuania, 1051
Litvinov, Maksim, 494, 656, 1043
  Roosevelt-Litvinov agreement, 788
Liveright, Horace, 45, 47–48
Living Newspaper, 800–801
Lloyd, Harold, 924–926
Lloyd, Henry Demarest, 54, 394
Lobbying campaigns, 646
Locarno Pact, 67
Locke, Alain, 222, 238, 240, 246, 552, 870
Lodge, Henry Cabot, 105
Lomax, John, 793
London, Jack, 510
London, England: ex-patriates in, 46
London Economic Conference, 608
Loneliness and isolation, 535
Long, Breckinridge, 396
Long, Huey, 323, 325–327, 329–330, 395,
      618–628
  accomplishments, 652
  assassination, 651
  attacked oil companies, 619–621, 625
  attacks on, 627–628
  campaign tactics, 622
  challenge to the Democrats, 628
  early life and family background, 618–619
  elected Senator in 1930, 626
  impeachment proceedings, 624–625
  poor and underprivileged causes, 653
  Populist principles, 621–622
  Railroad Commission member, 620–621
  roads and highway system, 623–624
  Share Our Wealth movement, 618, 626–627
  World Court opposition, 647

Longshoremen's strike in 1934, 613–617
  attacks on Communists, 616
  deportation of Harry Bridges, 616, 693–684
  general strike, 614–616
  mass picketing, 614
Longworth, Nicholas, 364
*Looking Backward* (Bellamy), 630
Loos, Anita, 48, 173, 928
Lost Generation, 52
Louis, Joe, 943–946, 1129
  symbolic figure, 945–946
Louisiana: bank holiday, 426
  oil wells, 70
Louisiana State University, 624
"Love," counterculture and, 1133
Lovejoy, Arthur O., 856
Lovestone, Jay, 184, 196, 203–204, 718, 745, 961
Lovett, Robert Morss, 137
Lowell, A. Lawrence, 126, 128–129, 139
Lowell, Amy, 975
Lowell, James Russell, 139, 850
Lowenthal, Max, 388
Luce, Henry, 649, 1111
Ludendorff, General Erich, 66
Ludwig, Emil, 373
Lumpkin, Grace, 131, 193, 528
Lynch, Charles, 95
Lynch, Marvin, 545, 554
Lynching, 71, 76, 93–96, 825–832
  anti-lynching campaign, 96–97, 825–832
    education for women, 830
    investigation of specific lynchings, 831–832
    purpose of lynching, 830–831
    Southern notion of "womanhood," 829–839
  Association of Southern Women to Prevent Lynching, 826–832
  interracial cooperation, 94–95, 828
  lynch mobs, 95
  myth of Southern womanhood, 828–830, 836
  psychological roots, 95
  rape and, 95–97
  ritual, 96
Lynd, Helen and Robert, 301
Lyons, Eugene, 122, 186

McAdoo, William, 106–109, 111, 397
  Democratic Convention (1932), 318, 320
  unions' support of, 111–112

MacArthur, Douglas, 338–339
McCarran, Pat, 1025
McCarthy, Joseph, 1115
McCarthy, Mary, 528
McCloskey, Edward, 339
McClure, Sam, 32, 60
*McClure's Magazine*, 60
McConnell, Dorothy, 656
McCormick, Anne O'Hare, 61, 395, 461
McCracken, Henry Noble, 799
Macdonald, Dwight, 923, 926
MacDonald, Ramsay, 69
MacDowell Colony in Peterborough, New Hampshire, 998
McGrady, Edward F., 317
McHenry, Dean E., 632
Machines: laborsaving, 12
MacIntire, Ross, 651
McIntyre, Marvin, 475
Mack, John, 329
Mackay, Clarence, 160
McKay, Claude, 199, 208, 213–214, 220, 228–234, 237, 253, 587, 589, 786, 1130
  disenchantment with communism, 812
  editor of *Liberator*, 231
  Moscow visit, 231–232
  poetry, 229–230
  trips abroad, 256–257
McKinley, William, 141, 344–345
McLaughlin, John P., 616
MacLeish, Archibald, 362, 406
McLuhan, Marshall, 921
Macmillan, Harold, 68
McNamee, Graham, 919
McNary-Haugen farm relief bill, 15, 179, 264, 1060
McPherson, Aimee Semple, 853–869
  disappearance and kidnapping, 865–866
  Angelus Temple in Los Angeles, 865
McReynolds, James Clark, 682–685
Madison, James, 362–363, 370, 886
Madrid: Spanish Civil War, 767–768, 770–771
Maginot Line, 492, 1051, 1054, 1058
*Main Street* (Lewis), 16, 983–984
Maisky, Ivan, 1079
Malatesta, Enrico, 120
Malraux, André, 526
Manchuria: Japanese invasion, 306–307
Mangione, Jerre, 44, 48, 51, 74, 82, 213, 251, 509, 526, 733, 797
Manifesto of writers, 520–521

Manichaeanism, 1124
Manley, Joseph, 112
Mann, Klaus, 1036
Mann, Thomas, 1036
Marcantonio, Vito, 571–572
Marin, John, 950
Marin, Peter, 1142
Marinoff, Fania, 47, 237
Maritime union: (See International Long-
    shoremen's Association)
Markham, Edwin, 666
Marriages: Communist, 531
    "companionate marriage," 5
Marshall, Thurgood, 571
Marshall Plan, 1031, 1108
Martin, Homer, 726–728, 745–746
Martin, Peter, 525
Marx, Karl, 120, 125, 506–507, 534–535
    dialectical materialism, 208
    predictions, 310
    utopian schemes, 882
Marx, Wilhelm, 68
Marxism, 785
    collapse of Capitalism, 1128
    faith in human perfectibility, 1124
    Freudian psychology and, 916–917
Masaryk, Thomas, 1041
Mason, Charlotte, 238, 247, 562, 1006
Mass production, 21, 394
Masses (magazine), 229
Massing, Hede, 530–531
Massingill, Edwin, 76
Materialism, 4, 20, 113, 280
    accomplishments, 21
    spirituality to replace, 869
    success, 535
Mather, Kirtley, 869–871
Mathews, Shailer, 880, 883
Matthews, Brander, 225, 227
Matthews, Herbert, 777
Maugham, Somerset, 47
Maurer, James H., 263, 324
Maverick, Maury, 1027
May Day parade: in 1934, 602
Mayer, Louis B., 633
Mayfield, Henry, 580, 593
Mazarin, Cardinal Jules, 652
Mazzini, Giuseppe, 120
Meader, Lee, 47
Mecklenburg, George, 873
Medicine, 904–917
    American Medical Association, 907–914

Medicine (cont.):
    black doctors, 908–909
    emotionally disturbed, 915–916
    Flexner's study of medical education, 907–
        908
    group practice and group payment, 913
    history of, 904–905
    hospitals, 909–912
    medical schools, 904–908
    nurses and nursing, 906–907
    patent medicines, 905, 909
    preventive, 910
    psychiatry, 914–917
    religion and, 916–917
    research, 905–906
    women physicians, 908–909
Mein Kampf (Hitler), 66, 1094
Mellon, Andrew, 26, 176, 179
    secretary of treasury, 179
Memphis, U.S. Navy flagship, 156–157
Mencken, Henry L., 2, 13, 20, 32, 45, 48,
    105, 121, 335, 513, 535, 853
    American Mercury founded by, 16, 20, 32–
        36, 40
    obituary of Warren G. Harding, 101
    political foe of FDR, 473
    Scopes trial, 857–861
Menninger, Karl, 915–917
Mercer, Lucy Page, 355, 1098
Mergers and amalgamations, 175
Merriam, Charles, 409
Merriam, Frank, 632–633
Merrick, George, 172
Merrick, Solomon, 172
Messenger (magazine), 261
Methodist Federation for Social Service, 871–
    872
Methodists: racial relations, 98
Mexican painters, 954, 960
    muralists, 806
Mexican workers, 72
    Chicago packing plants, 756
    unionization of, 760–762
Mexico: American oil companies, 169–170
    Bolshevik threat, 168–171
    military intervention, 169
    negotiations with Catholic Church, 170–171
Meyer, Eugene, 429
Mezzrow, Mezz, 938
Michigan: bank moratorium, 426
Middle-class Americans, 23, 52–53
Middle East, 1076

Midwest, 70, 72
Migratory workers, 6, 161, 695
  unionization of, 760
Milhaud, Darius, 1037
Military-industrial complex, warnings
    against, 1128
Millay, Edna St. Vincent, 39, 45, 51, 128,
    135, 138, 208, 520
Millennium, 1122, 1124
Miller, B. M. of Alabama, 553
Miller, Earl, 385
Miller, Henry, 243
Miller, Loren, 593
Miller, Nathan, 346, 453
Miller, Perry, 1131
Millowners, 82–83
  benevolent paternalism, 82–83
  towns and houses owned by, 83
Mills, Florence, 933–934
Mills, Ogden, 307, 325, 429, 1104
Mills Brothers, 552
Millworkers, 82–85
  stretchout, 84–86
Milton Academy, 371
Minneapolis: strikes, 705
Minor, Robert, 204, 551, 570, 954
Minorities, 1143
  (See also Black Americans; Migratory work-
      ers; Women)
Mississippi Valley, 15
  floods, 181
Mitchel, John Purroy, 381
Mitchell, H. K., 757–759
Mitchell, Margaret, 836
Mizner, Addison, 173
Mizner, Wilson, 173
Model T Ford, 30, 173
Moley, Raymond, 321, 328, 334, 366, 370,
    376, 384–390
  adviser and confidant of FDR, 463–464,
      471, 474, 476
  on bank holiday, 438
  Brain Trust member, 384, 389
  cabinet members screened by, 407–419
  campaign of 1932, 391, 393, 397–398
  chief of staff, 418
  defection from New Deal, 608
  election of 1936, 667
  on foreign debts, 482
  New Deal beginnings, 407–419, 424–435,
      438–440, 446
  on reform legislation, 642

Moley, Raymond (cont.):
  resignation from State Department, 486
  on FDR, 605, 1100
  speechwriting, 609
  at World Economic Conference, 485–486
Molotov, Yacheslav, 1043–1044, 1078
Monetary reforms, 408
Monopoly: drive against, 336
Montana: rural radicalism, 194
Montgomery, Olen, 543, 562
Montgomery (Alabama) bus strike, 1129
Monticello: rehabilitation of, 364
Moody, Dwight, 853
Mooney, Tom (labor leader), 9, 586
Moore, Audley, 202
Moore, Ida, 84–86
Moore, Marianne, 791
Moore, Merrill, 994
Moore, Otis, 358
Moore, Richard B., 200–201, 593
Moore, Walter, 732
Moors, John F., 128
Moral Man and Immoral Society (Niebuhr),
    880–882
Morale of American people, 461
Morals and morality, 18, 27, 279–280
More, Paul Elmer, 886
Morehouse College, 97
Morgan, Arthur, 476
Morgan, J. P., 26, 174, 177
Morgenthau, Elinor, 477
Morgenthau, Hans, 1036
Morgenthau, Henry, Jr., 278, 378, 380, 390,
    407, 447, 468–469, 879
  on balanced budget, 698–699
  campaign of 1932, 392–394
  recognition of Soviet Union, 494
  on FDR, 1100
  secretary of the treasury, 446
  wheat purchase for needy, 460
Morison, Samuel Eliot, 121, 1131
Morris, Gouverneur, 372
Morrow, Anne, 162–163
Morrow, Dwight, 29, 162, 170
  ambassador to Mexico, 170
Mortimer, Wyndham, 312–313, 514, 704,
    713–714, 716
  UAW, 728, 731–732, 739, 741–742, 745
Moscow: Chinese Communists revolution,
    164–166
  McKay's tour, 231–232
  mecca for American blacks, 256

Moscow: Chinese Communists revolution (*cont.*):
tenth anniversary of revolution, 167
(*See also* Soviet Union)
Moscow Ballet, 498
*Moscow News*, 186
Moscow trials, 780–788
consequence of, 786
Moses, Robert, 417
Moskowitz, Belle, 267–268, 328, 378, 416
Mosley, Archie, 593
Mosley, Sir Oswald, 491
Mother Jones, 12, 43
Motley, Willard, 793
Moton, Robert Sussa, 97, 558, 892
Mott, Lucretia, 38
Mount Holyoke College, 8, 413–414
Movies, and movie-making, 918–933
alcohol and drugs, 931
comedians, 923–924, 929
Communist influence, 932–933
critics, 923
Depression era, 931–932
effect of, 932–933
emergence as "art," 923
"foreign market," 933
Hollywood, 929–930
hosts and hostesses in film colony, 930–931
motion picture theaters, 922
musical films, 928–929
negroes, 592
scriptwriters, 1007
sex in, 928
sex scandals, 931
silent films
comedies, 923–924
directors, 923
stories with captions, 924
super stars, 926–928
talkies, 926–927
workers' movies, 525
Muckrakers, 522, 630
Mumford, Lewis, 130, 335, 520, 812
Munich agreement, 1041, 1043
Munitions manufacturers, 484
Mural art, 806–807
Murphy, Al, 575–576
Murphy, Carl, 595
Murphy, Frank, 693, 734–735, 738, 741–742, 1028
Supreme Court appointment, 692
Murray, Alfalfa Bill, 326, 328

Murray, Philip, 709–710, 716, 751
Muscle Shoals, 444
Museum of Modern Art in New York, 793, 806, 947
Music and musicians, 49, 53, 805, 933–941
black, 212–213, 940
all-black revue, 933–934
black bands, 940
black church music, 219
black songwriters, 933, 936
black women vocalists, 936–937
blues, gospel and country music, 218, 935–937
Broadway musicals, 934–935
Chicago, 937–938
jazz, 935–936
swing, 940
Tin Pan Alley, 933–934, 936
Mussolini, Benito, 2, 28, 59–63, 491–493, 542, 886
alliance with Hitler, 681
critics of, 61–63
dictatorial powers, 67–68
Franco supported by, 768
Hitler and, 491–492
invasion of Ethiopia, 657
invasion of France, 1058
Munich meeting, 1041
postwar dictator, 60
U.S. reaction to, 60–61
Muste, A. J., 208–210, 719, 721, 785, 821

Naison, Mark, 202
Nast, Condé, 47
Nathan, George Jean, 32
*American Mercury*, 40
*Nation*, 548, 1049
National Association for the Advancement of Colored People (NAACP), 96, 222, 1107
Scottsboro Boys defense, 547–548
treatment of rural blacks, 596
unionization of Pullman car porters, 261
National Association of Colored Women, 98
National Catholic Welfare Council, 871
National Committee for the Defense of Political Prisoners, 311, 516, 527
National Consumers' League, 414
National Council of Negro Women, 98, 823
National Defense Research Committee, 1053
National Endowment for the Arts, 798
National Endowment for the Humanities, 798

National Industrial Recovery Act (NIRA), 448, 450, 613
  code for automobile industry, 727
  fireside chats, 449, 451
  opposition to, 449–452
  policy of cooperative business-government planning, 450
  Section 7 (a), 643, 703–704, 706, 708
  Section 8, 644
  Section 9 (c) declared unconstitutional, 634
  Supreme Court decisions, 452, 634, 639–640, 643
  Title II, 440, 459
National Labor Relations Act, 643
National Labor Relations Board, 766
  Communist influence, 1030
  steel strike, 754
National Miners Union, 517, 798
National Negro Congress, 591
  A. Philip Randolph and, 591
National Park Service, 441
National Recovery Administration (NRA), 399
  codes for industry, 452–455, 460
  criticism, 4, 597, 607, 641
  destruction of, 641
  hour and wage codes, 452–453
  parades, 454
  partnership of business, government and labor, 668
National Socialist German Workers Party (see Nazis)
National Socialists, 487
National Training School, 580
National Urban League, 258
National Youth Administration: Aubrey Williams, 822–825
  Communist influence, 825
National Youth Authority, 699
Nationalism, 55, 394
Nations, Gilbert O., 113–114
Nativism, 3
Naval construction programs, 699
Naval engagements, 1077–1078
Naval warfare, 1084
Nazis, 68, 305
  concentration camps, 1035
  Hitler's rise to power, 487–491
  persecution of Jews, 1035
  (See also Germany, Hitler, Adolph)
Neal, John Randolph, 855
Nearing, Scott, 387–388, 532

Nebraska Aircraft Corporation, 147
Needle Trades Industrial Union, 726
Neel, Alice, 43–44
Negro (see Black Americans)
Negro History Week, 202
Negro Labor Committee, 589
Negro World, 214, 243, 593
Negro Youth Theatre, 802
Nelson, Steve, 184–186, 204, 306, 311–314, 493, 1045–1046, 1109
  on anti-Communist movement, 1115
  Spanish Civil War, 771–772, 778–780
  union activities in California, 762
Neruda, Pablo, 255–256
Nesbit, Evelyn, 46
Neutrality and war, 660
  commitment to, 1051
  Neutrality Act, 1040
    amendments to, 1051–1052
  Neutrality Laws of 1935 and 1936, 483–484
Nevelson, Louise, 964
New Bedford textile strike, 191, 522
New consciousness, 28, 49, 252, 254, 279
  black consciousness and, 1132
  black soul, 1137–1138
  effect of Communism, 1130
  formation of, 1130
New Deal, 223, 334, 375, 840–850
  academic world and, 895
  accomplishments, 456, 463, 479
  aircraft industry expanded, 1053
  art projects, 789–813
  bank moratorium, 426
  beginnings, 406–436
  blacks and women in, 424–425
  blacks' attitude toward, 587, 672–673
  blacks helped by, 844–845
  business community rejection of, 674–677
  cabinet members, 407–410
  capital vs. labor, 1106
  capitalism, 1128
  Catholic Church and, 878
  Civilian Conservation Corps, 1103
  Communist influence, 1116
  Communists and, 506, 655–656, 846
  conclusion of, 1093
  decline in popularity, 635
  defections from, 606–608
  defense of, 674–675
  distributing money through the states, 459
  early days, 406–436

New Deal (cont.):
 economic crises, 406–436
 enemies of, 1027
 farm program, 817–818
 financial crisis, 426–431
 first New Dealers, 642
 individualism vs. community, 849
 innovative character, 445
 jobs for Roosevelt's inner circle, 418–425
 lawyer preachers, 422
 legislation, 437–462, 479, 648
 national community, 848–849
 New Dealers, 405–436
 origins of programs, 389–390
 permanence of reforms, 1026
 platform resolutions and, 370
 reformer-journalists, 421
 Resettlement Administration, 1102
 revisionist attack on, 850
 FDR urged to assume dictatorial powers,
  32
 Second, 641–642
  social issues, 641–642
 social legislation, 628, 639–658, 1031–1032
 social programs, 389, 667, 847
 "socialistic," charges, 664–665
 Southerners helped by, 816–817
 special session of Congress, 437–462
 stimulating recovery, 460
 Supreme Court decisions against, 680,
  682–695
 survival of, 847–848
 Washington life, 423–424
New Economic Policy (Soviet), 499
New England, 72
 homes for itinerant intellectuals, 29
 movement of immigrants, 34
New Freedom, Wilson policy, 320, 334
New Harmony, 631, 849, 963
New Humanism, 996
New Masses, 187, 222, 548, 591, 779
New Nationalism, 334
New Negro, The (Locke), 222
New Negro movement, 228
New Orleans, Louisiana, 212
 jazz, 936–937
 longshoremens strike, 542
 Scottsboro Boys defense, 551
New Realism, 996
"New Religion of Humanism," 143
New Republic, 44, 61, 136, 222, 511, 548
New School for Social Research, 890, 1037

New York Age, 227, 230
New York City, 70, 72
 architecture, 961
 black Americans, 216, 221–222
 black culture, 221–222
 Communist-front organizations, 532
 Communist-inspired demonstrations, 314
 Communist May Day parade in 1934, 602–
  603
 Communist organizing, 588–589
 creative ferment, 1135
 Federal Theatre Project, 800
 furrier's strike (1926), 191
 life-style, 40–41
 Lindbergh's ticker-tape parade, 159–161
 literary scene, 40–45
 May Day parades, 314, 316, 602–603
 numbers game, 220–221
 race riot, 589
 Republican Party, 351
 Rockefeller Center, 961
 Scottsboro Boys defense, 550–551
New York City Consumers League, 415
New York Herald Tribune, 109
New York Post, 351
New York Public Library: Schomburg Collec-
  tion of Negro Literature, 237
New York State: FDR as Governor, 377–390
New York State Industrial Commission, 10
New York Stock Exchange, 438
 Whitney scandal, 696
New York Times, 66, 116, 151, 177, 351, 436
New York World, 19, 29, 334
Newman, Dean, 83
Newspaper Guild, 515
Newspapers, 95
 opposition to FDR, 669
Nicaragua, 168–169
 U.S. intervention, 171, 263
 U.S. policy, 168–169
Nicholai, Bishop of Orthodox see of Ochrida,
  57
Nicholson, Harold, 163
Niebuhr, Reinhold, 335, 821, 872, 879–883,
  1192
 criticism of capitalism, 882
Nightwood (Barnes), 43
Nin, Andrés, 775
1920's, 1–26, 1128
 (See also Twenties)
1927 events, 164–181
 Communist Revolution in China, 164–166

1927 events (*cont.*):
  Coolidge's foreign policy, 168–172
  Dempsey-Tunney fight, 181
  economic boom, 172
  Florida real estate boom, 172–173
  Lindbergh's flight, 164
  Sacco-Vanzetti case, 164
  significant events, 164–181
  stock market speculation, 173–175
1930 events, 1128
1932 presidential campaign, 391–405
  FDR prior to, 342–361
1933 events, 406–436
1934 events, 597–617
1935 events, 634–658
1936 election, 659–681
1938 events, 1025
1940 events, 1128
  election of 1940, 1050–1072
1950 events, 1128
NIRA (*see* National Industrial Recovery Act)
Nonpartisan League, 184, 194–196, 665
Norman, Montagu, 176
Norris, Clarence, 543, 546, 552, 561, 563
Norris, George, 326, 667
Norris, Kathleen, 632
*Norris v. Alabama*, 560, 564
North Dakota: Nonpartisan League, 6
  rural radicalism, 194
*North Georgia Review*, 832
North-South differences, 72–73
  black migration from South, 211–212
Norway: Nazi occupation force, 1058
Noyes, John Humphrey, 631, 849, 963, 1134
NRA (*see* National Recovery Administration)
Nuclear fission: committee on, 1053
Nuclear missiles, 1147
Numbers game, 220–221
Nungesser, Charles, 155–156
Nye, Gerald, 848

O'Brien, Robert, 101
O'Connor, John, 1025
Odets, Clifford, 1012–1014
Odlum, Howard, 820
Office of Indian Affairs, 411
Oglethorpe University, Atlanta, 322
Oil and gas: Louisiana, 70
Oklahoma: farms and farming, 15
  KKK in, 5–6
Older, Fremont, 9
Oliver, Frank, 274

Oliver, King, 936, 938–939
Olmsted, Frederick Law, 961–962
Olympic National Park, 1104
Olympics, 942–943
  1936 Olympics in Berlin, 943
Oneida Community, 849, 963, 1134
O'Neill, Eugene, 208, 252, 876, 1007–1012
Open Door policy, 307
Open shop, 13
Optimism of American people, 8, 461
Orators and speeches, 12
Orientals: objects of hatred and persecution, 3
Orozco, José Clemente, 806–808, 959–960
Orwell, George, 776
Osler, William, 906
Ottinger, Albert, 273
*Our America* (Frank), 39
*Out of Revolution: The Autobiography of Western Man* (Rosenstock-Huessay), 1144–1145
Ovington, Mary White, 97
Owen, Chandler, 258–259
Owen, Robert Dale, 631, 849, 963
Owen, Ruth Bryan, 328, 412
Owens, Jesse, 943–946, 1129
Oxley, Lawrence A., 425

Pace, John, 338
Pacific Fleet: transferred to Pearl Harbor, 1085, 1090
Pacifists and Pacifism, 8, 41, 209
Page, Myra, 193
Painter, Nell Irvin, 575–580, 586, 751, 824
Palmer, Alice Freeman, 100
Palmer, A. Mitchell, 258
Panama, 171
*Panay*, USS 1, 702
Papists, 6
Parades: inaugural, 432–433
Paris: Americans in, 31–32, 48
  international conference of radical writers, 617
  left-wing intellectuals, 591
  Lindbergh landing at Le Bourget Field, 154–155
  Pact of Paris, 171
Paris Peace Conference, 18, 307
Park, Robert, 220, 821
Parker, Charles, 196
Parker, Dorothy, 776
Parks, Rosa, 1129
Parran, Dr. Thomas, 390

Parrington, Vernon, 387
Parrish, Maxfield, 30
Parties and party-givers, 44–48
  Hollywood "orgies," 48
  nude bathing parties, 48
Passaic (New Jersey): textile workers strike
  (1925), 191
Passamaquoddy power project, 841
Pasteur, Louis, 905
Pasternak, Boris, 526, 593
Patmos Group, 66
Patterson, Heywood, 543, 545–546, 549, 555,
  560–561, 563
Patterson, Janie, 549
Patterson, Roscoe, 610
Patterson, William, 201, 556
Patton, George, 339
Payne-Aldrich Tariff, 350
Paz, Octavio, 169
Peabody, Rev. Endicott, 343–344, 349, 434,
  696, 1098
Peace movements, 898
Pearl Harbor: Japanese attack, 1085–1087,
  1090
  reactions of Americans, 1091–1092
Peek, George N., 422
Pegler, Westbrook, 468, 515
Peirce, Charles Sanders, 53, 208
Pelagian heresy, 1124
Pelley, William Dudley, 492
Pendergast, Tom, 330
Pentecostalists, 871
*People's History of the United States, A* (Smith),
  1093
Pepper, Claude, 697, 1027–1028
Pepper, John, 184
Percy, Walker, 837
Percy, William Alexander, 181, 837–838
Pergain, Marie, 518
Perkins, Frances, 10, 13, 267–268, 274, 352,
  354, 372, 410, 412, 616–617, 806,
  1061
  attacks on, 468, 606, 692–694
  blacks appointed by, 424–425
  career as public official, 416–418
  compulsory health insurance, 912
  Department of Labor, 434, 466–468
  election of 1940, 1062–1063
  family background and education, 412–
    415
  friction between members of Congress and,
    468

Perkins, Frances (*cont.*):
  honorary degrees, 648
  impeachment threat, 617
  labor commissioner, 378–382, 385, 390
  labor opposition, 693
  labor standards, 640
  lobbyist, 415–416
  marriage, 415–416
  National Industrial Recovery Act, 448
  New Deal programs, 439, 467–468
  politicians critical of, 468
  position on Industrial Commission, 416
  reform of Immigration Service, 467
  relief programs, 440
  religious convictions, 468
  on Roosevelt family, 356–357, 1100–1101
    death of FDR, 1099–1100
  secretary of labor, 412–418
  sit-down strikes, 734–736
  Al Smith and, 416
  social security legislation, 644–645
  unemployment and old-age insurance,
    601–602
  wish to resign, 1097–1098
Perkins, Susanna, 806
Pershing, George, 193
Pétain, Marshal Henri Philippe, 1059
Peterkin, Julia Mood, 252, 825, 996–999
Pettigrew, Richard F., 194–195
Phelps, Williams Lyon, 33
Phelps Stokes Fund, 97
Philadelphia, 70
  black Americans, 213, 216–217
  slum section, 218
Philadelphia Board of Trade, 466
*Philadelphia Evening Bulletin*, 8
Philanthropic foundations: disposed to Com-
  munist causes, 532
Philippines: Japanese invasion, 1092
Phillips, Duncan, 947
Phillips, William, 354, 419, 522, 786, 1042
Piatokov, Y. L., 781
Picasso, 31, 40
Pickens, William, 112–113
Pickford, Mary, 925, 930
Pilnyak, Boris, 536
Pinchot, Amos, 112, 113
Pinchot, Gifford, 316, 366, 411, 424
Pinkerton agents as strike breakers, 13–14
Pioneer spirit, 162
Pittman, Key, 445, 485
Plantation owners, 82–83

Platt, Charles, 30
Poetic Theatre, 802
Poets and poetry, 1012–1024
    blacks, 226–231
Poincaré, Henri, 67
Poland, 1041
    German attack on, 1043, 1050
    Soviet invasion, 1050
Political movements, 618–633
    Father Charles Coughlin, 627–629
    Huey Long, 618–628
    program to End Poverty in California
        (EPIC), 631–633
    technocrats, 629–630
    Townsend Plan, 629
    Utopians, 630
Political parties, 318
    (See also Democratic Party; Republican
        Party)
Politicians: criticism of, 162
    Southern, 74
    target of American Mercury, 32–33
Pollock, Jackson, 811, 964
Polls and polling: court-packing plan, 695
    Gallup, 649–650, 662, 670
    Literary Digest, 673–674, 676
    Spanish Civil War, 769
    on unions, 765
Poor whites, 82
    registering to vote, 587
    (See also Whites)
Popular arts: movies, 918–933
    music, 933–941
    sports, 941–946
Popular government, 18–19
Populist movement, 38, 852–853, 1122
Populist Party, 194, 210, 678
Porgy (Heyward), 593
Porter, Katherine Anne, 41–42, 501, 527,
    778
    Moscow trials, 785–786
    Sacco-Vanzetti case, 120, 130–135
Posetta, Rose, 720–726
    UAW campaign, 728–729, 733, 739
Post World War I, repressive spirit, 1–9
Post World War II, 1108–1126
    rehabilitation of the enemy, 1108–1109
    suppressing the left, 1109–1126
Poston, Ted, 793
Pound, Ezra, 1014, 1016–1017
Pound, Dean Roscoe, 1, 8, 421–422
Powell, Adam Clayton, Jr., 589, 657

Powell, Ozzie, 543, 562–563
Power, use made of, 19
Power plants, unionization of, 742
Powys, Llewelyn, 45
Poyntz, Juliet Stuart, 528–529
Pravda, 785
Preface to Morals, A (Lippmann), 279–280
Prejudice and injustices, 1132
Pressman, Lee, 716, 1030, 1067
Price, Mary, 528, 1030
Price, Victoria, 543–545, 554–556, 559–560
Price controls, 455
Prince of Wales, 47
Princeton, writers critics and poets, 974–975
Private property, protecting institution of,
    609
Producers News, 293
Productivity, growth in, 175
Progressive Party, 1, 194, 301
Progressive Republicans, 351, 409, 1026–
    1027
Progressives, 18, 112–113, 116, 184
    rush to Washington, 419–420
    support for Wilson, 482
Prohibition era, 36–39, 212, 220, 271–272,
    422
    drinking parties, 30
    enforcement difficult, 37
    gangsters and organized crime, 37–39
    repeal of Eighteenth Amendment, 325
    speakeasies and nightclubs, 37–38
Prohibition Party, 113–114, 324, 664, 1065
Prohme, Bill, 166
Prohme, Rayna, 165–168, 527
Proletarian literature, 512–515
    novels, 523–524, 1005
Proletarian Party, 718
"Proletarian" topics, 1130
Promise of American Life, The (Croly), 350, 458
Propaganda: disseminated by Department of
        Justice, 2
    Soviet, 593
Property, rights of, 604, 694, 733, 886
    protecting, 609
Prosperity (1924–1929), 14, 176–177, 180
Prostitutes and pimps, 9
    black, 92
Protestant Christianity, 92, 851–853
Protestant churches, 874
    Depression and, 873
    fragmentation of, 868
    socialist inclinations of clergy, 875

Protestant ethic, 371, 851
Protestant Passion for learning, 1131, 1142–1143
Protestant Passion for redemption, 1122–1123, 1142–1143
Protestant Reformation, 851, 1141
Protestantism, 851
  capitalism and, 852
  fundamentalism, 27, 32, 52, 852–853
Provincetown Playhouse in Greenwich Village, 30
*Pseudopedia*, 832
Psychiatry and medicine, 30–31, 914–917
Psychoanalysis, 915
Psychohistorians, 144, 495
Psychotherapy and history, 1138–1139
Public health movement, 910, 912
Public opinion, 279
*Public Opinion* (Lippmann), 18
Public ownership of municipal utilities, 2
Public power policy, 384, 444
Public Utility Holding Company Act, 646
Public Works Administration (PWA), 425, 453
  achievements, 840–841
Public Works Art Project, 806–809
Public works projects, 304–305, 439–440, 598–609, 635
  opponents, 440
Pullman porters union, 259–262
Pulpwood, 79
Puritan revival, 1131
Puritan Revolution, 1144
"Puritanical" America, 27, 39, 52
Puritanism, 34, 36, 103, 139
  Massachusetts Bay Colony, 1134
Putnam, Phelps, 520
PWA (*see* Public Works Administration)

Quill, "Red Mike," 710

Race riots, 591
Racial prejudices, 161, 576, 669
  Scottsboro Boys case, 564–565
Racial problems of the South, 97
  aid of Southern white churchwomen, 98–100
  lynching (*see* Lynching)
Radek, Karl, 175, 195, 256, 498, 537–538, 781–782, 785, 921, 1125
Radical movements, 2, 677–678
  philosophy of progress, 493
  revival of radical spirit, 143

Radical movements (*cont.*):
  students, 889, 897–903
Radicals and reformers, 2–3, 55, 161, 182–210
  American, 1121–1122
  fascism and, 493
  Paris conference of radical writers, 617
  students, 889, 897–903
Radio broadcasting, 319
  band music, 920
  FDR, 396, 921
  soap operas, 920
  variety shows, 920
Railroad Pensions Act, 648
Railroad Retirement Board Act of 1934, 639
Railroad strikes, 10–11
  repressive action by authorities, 11
Railway Labor Act, 690
Raleigh, W. T., 112
*Raleigh News and Observer*, 557
Ralston, Samuel, 109
Rand School of Economics, 258
Randall, John Herman, 870
Randolph, A. Philip, 94, 257–262, 570, 1093
  Pullman porters organized by, 260–262
Rankin, Jeannette, 1088
Ransom, John Crowe, 991–992, 995
Rappelyea, George W., 855
Rascoe, Burton, 15–16, 26, 37, 43, 45, 47–48, 53, 285, 297
Raskob, John J., 272, 278, 328, 395, 606
Raulston, John T., 855, 860
Rauschenbusch, Walter, 821
Rayburn, Sam, 331, 646
Reactionary tendency of the country, 422, 1027–1028
Recession of 1924, 14
Recession of 1937, 697–699
Reclamation, 444, 601
Reconstruction Finance Corporation, 305, 601, 627
Red menace (*see* Communists and communism)
*Red Song Book*, 1037–1038
"Red violence," 129
Redeemed humanity, 1146–1147
Reed, David A., 317, 427
Reed, John, 189, 229, 232, 236, 495, 1008
Reed, Stanley, 692
Reeve, Ella, 189
Reforestation of land, 384
  marginal farmland, 444, 465
  FDR's interest in, 440

Reforms and reformers, 3, 113, 677–678, 743, 1026, 1142–1143
   middle-class, 1112
   in New Deal, 419
   social workers and, 852
   union movement, 13
Regionalism, 995
Regionalist school of art, 952–960
Rehabilitating the enemy, 1108–1109
Registering to vote, 586–587
Reid, Ogden and Helen, 19
Reinhardt, Max, 45
Relief measures, 439–440
   New Deal programs, 439
Religion, 851–883, 995
   attitude of new intellectual class, 853
   blacks, 92–93
   central role in American life, 1142
   evangelists, 864–869
   German search for new directions, 66–67
   Jewish, 878–879
   liberal Christians, 867–868
   medicine and, 916–917
   moral decline and, 869
   Pentecostal, 867
   "pink religion," 873
   Protestant Christianity, 92, 851–853
   Protestant Passion for Redemption, 1122–1123, 1142–1143
   relationship betweem black and white churchwomen, 98–100
   response to the Depression, 871–878
   revivalism, 853, 867
   Scopes trial, 854–864
   theological revival, 879–883
Remington, William, 1030
Renan, Ernest, 120
Reno, Milo, 291–295
Reno, Vincent, 1029
Reparations payments, 306
Reporters and columnists, 473
Repressive spirit, 1–7, 887
   in Federal government, 7
   postwar America, 1108–1126
   "red menace" threat, 11
Republic Steel, 752–753
Republican-Communist alliance, 1068
Republican Party, 23, 363, 678–679
   conservatives, 610
   election of 1920, 101
   election of 1928, 263, 269–270
   election of 1940, 1060–1061

Republican Party (cont.):
   National Convention in 1924, 105–106
   National Convention in 1932, 318, 325
   National Convention in 1936, 665
   in New York, 351
   party of business interests, 363, 1027
   Progressive wing, 179, 1026
   (See also Progressive Republicans)
Research, 22–23
Resettlement Administration, 637–638, 695, 1102
   medical prepayment plan, 913
Reuther, May (Walter's wife), 720, 729–730
Reuther, Roy, 719, 730–731, 736, 746
   Flint plant of GM organized by, 730–731
Reuther, Sophie (Victor's wife), 209, 729, 743–744, 749
Reuther, Victor, 209, 657, 719, 729–730, 733, 736–737, 740, 744, 746, 749
   trip to Berlin, 488–489
   trip to Russia, 502–503
Reuther, Walter, 719, 743, 746
   achievements, 749–750
   brutal beating of, 746–748
   campaigned for Norman Thomas, 719
   drive to unionize River Rouge Ford plant, 746–750
   in Gorky automobile plant, 488–489, 502–503, 719
   Kelsey-Hayes strike, 729–730
   leadership role, 719–720, 729–731, 743, 746–750
   sit-down strikes, 732–750
   trip to Berlin, 488–489
   trip to Russia, 502–503
Revels, Hiram R., 215
Revivals and revivalists, 853, 867
Revolutions, 565
   characteristics, 308
   modern world and, 1144–1145
   strikes and, 763
   threat of, 317–318, 599
Rexroth, Kenneth, 794–795
Reynolds, Verne L., 324
Rhapsody in Blue (Gershwin), 53
Rhodes, Daniel, 807–808
Rice, Elmer, 800, 803
Richardson, James O., 1085
Richberg, Donald, 388, 448, 607–608, 611, 685
Richmond News-Leader, 557
Richmond Times-Dispatch, 562–563

Ridge, Lola, 131, 135, 138
Rieber, Charles Henry, 870
Riis, Jacob, 366
Ringling, John, 244
Ríos, Fernando de los, 767
Rist, Charles, 176
Ritchie, Albert, 326, 408, 473
Rivera, Diego, 806, 954, 960–961
Rivers, Larry, 964
Roach, Hal, 925
Robber barons, 26
Robbins, Warren Delano, 485
Robert Marshall Foundation, 533
Roberts, Justice Owen, 571, 573, 682
Robertson, Will, 543, 562
Robeson, Paul, 243, 248, 592, 940, 1115
Robinson, Bill "Bojangles," 47
Robinson, Corinne Roosevelt, 345
Robinson, Jackie, 1130
Robinson, Joseph, 628
Robinson, Reid, 758
Robles Pazos, José, 775–776, 778
Robots and automation, 382
Roche, Josephine, 421
Rockefeller, John D., 2, 26
Rocky Mountain West, 72
Roebling, John and Washington, 1019
Rogers, Ward, 757–758
Rogers, Will, 109, 438
Rogers Act of 1924, 496
Rolland, Romain, 136
Rollins, William, 514
Romain, Jacques, 248
Rome (New York) copper strike, 10
Roosevelt, Anna, 355
Roosevelt, Eleanor, 115, 330, 333, 345–360,
    372, 379, 1136
  American Youth Congress meeting, 900–
    902
  analysis of FDR's character, 374–375
  Mary McLeod Bethune and, 1129
  blacks and, 672
  children, 479
  CCC and, 843–844
  death of FDR, 1099–1100
  Democratic Convention in 1940, 1063–
    1064
  Democratic Party politics, 360
  education, 347
  eyes and ears for FDR, 378, 383, 385, 390,
    395, 477
  first inauguration, 431–434

Roosevelt, Eleanor (cont.):
  newspaper comments, 433–434
  Lorena Hickok and, 479
  on Hopkins, 1032–1033
  hostility toward, 433–434, 605
  and Louis Howe, 355–356, 662–664
  liberal views and independence, 347, 356,
    478
  marriage to FDR, 347–349, 476–477
  public career, 356
  relationship between FDR and, 476–
    477
  relationship with women, 478–479
  resignation from DAR, 1031
  on FDR's illness, 358–359
  on FDR's Presidency, 1105
  at Southern Conference for Human Wel-
    fare, 821–822
  Soviet aims and, 500
  supported Al Smith, 267–268
  sweetness of disposition, 1107
  This I Remember, 1106
  trip through Tennessee Valley, 444
  Wallace's nomination, 1063–1064
  World Court issue, 647
  Yalta Conference, 1096
Roosevelt, Elliott, 346, 355
Roosevelt, Franklin Delano (FDR)
  administrative ability, 353
  advisers and staff, 278, 320–321, 377–390,
    463–468, 642, 895–896
    poker-playing companions, 468–469
  on American neutrality, 1051
  appeal to blacks, 672–673
  appearance, 351
  Art Week, 810–811
  assistance for Nazi refugees, 1039
  assistant secretary of the navy under Wil-
    son, 342, 353–354, 1050
  attacks on, 604–606, 640, 648–649
    anti-semitic character, 606
    by business community, 640
    stories spread by enemies, 400–401
  attempted assassination, 426
  attitude toward Communists, 1057
  bank holiday proclamation, 434–435
  Brain Trust, 323, 385–390, 1104
  budget balancing, 334
  Cabinet, 407–410, 463–464, 879
    swearing in ceremonies, 434
  campaign of 1932, 342–361, 391–405
  campaign of 1936, 669–672

Roosevelt, Franklin Delano (*cont.*):
  Caribbean cruise, 425, 699
  character and personality, 321, 323–327, 344, 358–361, 365–366, 373, 378–379, 385, 403, 469–470, 474–475, 479, 612, 1100–1102
    attitude of concern, 1106
    charm and political charisma, 365
    dreamer and visionary, 641, 1102
    enthusiasm and zest for life, 379, 469, 471
    faith in common man, 459
    liberal temper or mood, 1027
    receptivity to ideas, 641, 1101
  children, 354–355, 478
  Churchill and, 1073–1075, 1094
    Atlantic Conference, 1082–1083
    differences of opinion, 1083
    personal friendship, 1094
  Communist opinion of, 580
  court-packing fight, 682–695
  criticism of, 334–336, 599, 607, 1039
  death, 1098
  decision-making, 389
  declaration of war, 1087
  defeats in Congress, 456
  Democratic Convention of 1924, 107–110
  Democratic Convention of 1928, 107–108
    nominated Al Smith, 107–108, 319, 342
  Democratic Convention of 1932, 317–341
  Democratic Convention of 1940, 1061–1064
  dictatorship charge, 699
  Dumbarton Oaks Conference, 1097
  early life, 342–361
  education, 342–344, 348
    Columbia Law School, 348
    at Groton, 343–344
    at Harvard, 343–345
  as educator and leader, 667–668
  Eleanor and, 347–349, 476–477
    bonds of mutual interest, 355, 475–476
  election of 1900, 344
  election of 1928, 267, 271
  election of 1934, 610
  election of 1936, 659–681
    landslide victory, 675–676
  election of 1940, 1050–1072
  emergency powers, 1077
  evaluation of, 1093–1107
  family background, 342–343

Roosevelt, Franklin Delano (*cont.*):
  on farm problems, 384, 397
  fear of alienating Southern Congressmen, 587
  fireside chats, 437–438, 449, 451, 1051, 1072
    bank holiday, 437–438
    National Industrial Recovery Act, 449
  foreign policy, 372, 429
  foundation for peaceful postwar world, 1096
  Four Freedoms, 1074, 1083
  fourth term, 1058, 1097–1098
  Gallup polls, 649–650
  goals, 392
  Governor of New York State, 272–273, 277–278, 342, 377–390
    campaigning for second term, 383
    Executive Mansion in Albany, 384
    farm policies, 384
    public power policy, 384
    reforestation of land, 384
  head of Anglo-American alliance, 1094
  health and illness, 358–359, 660, 699, 1057–1058, 1097–1098
    burdens of office, 1058
    effect of illness, 358–361
    nervousness, 640
    polio and rehabilitation, 342, 357–361
    restless activity, 368
  Herbert Hoover and, 282, 407, 427
  Louis Howe and, 352–353, 663–665
  Hyde Park home, 356–357, 359
  ideas and visions, 369–371, 376, 386–387, 451, 641, 1102
  influences on, 362–370
  inner circle, 897, 1061, 1100
  inspection of CCC camps, 459
  interest in Jefferson, 363–365
  internationalist, 481
  Japanese policy, 1080–1081
  Kitchen Cabinet, 418
  labor reforms, 390
  on labor unions, 765
  legislative programs, 324, 597–617
    (*See also* New Deal)
  liberal supporters, 659
  Lippmann's assessment of, 327
  Litvinov agreement, 788
  marriage to Eleanor, 347–349
  mediator between Stalin and Churchill, 1094

Roosevelt, Franklin Delano (*cont.*):
  Lucy Mercer affair, 355, 1098
  messages to Congress, 440
    on December 8, 1941, 1088–1089
  moral leadership, 461, 1105–1106
  New Deal, 323, 334, 840–850
    (*See also* New Deal)
  nomination in 1932, 329–330
  North Dakota primary, 319
  outings and expeditions, 425, 471, 699
  philosophy, 323, 362–376, 390
  political ambitions, 349
  political background, 319–321
  presidential train trip to Pacific Northwest,
    603–604
  press conferences, 470, 472–473
  primaries won by, 325
  progress to presidency, 366–370, 377
  public career, 351
  public works programs, 390
  qualifications for Presidency, 334–335
  radical advisers, 642
  radio broadcasts, 396, 437–438, 457, 921
  reaction to challenge, 375
  reforestation interests, 384, 440
  reforms, 604–605, 644
  relationship to women, 372–373
  relationship with mother, 357–358
  relationships with subordinates, 474–475
  religious faith, 361, 365, 374–375, 475,
    1105
  second Administration, 680–681
  Al Smith nominated by, 107–108, 319, 342
  social legislation, 382, 389
  Soviet Union, recognition of, 494
  special session of Congress in 1933, 437–
    462
  speeches and speech-writing, 321–322,
    391, 397, 666–667, 674, 1031, 1076–
    1077
    acceptance speeches, 330, 333–334,
      1064–1065
    disavowal to send American soldiers
      overseas, 1071
    first inaugural address in 1933, 430–432
    "forgotten man" speech, 321–322
    Quarantine Speech, 700–701
    State of the Union address in 1935, 612
    State of the Union address in 1940, 1056
  Stalin and, 1094, 1098
  stamp collection, 471, 495
  state legislator, 349–352, 366–367

Roosevelt, Franklin Delano (*cont.*):
  storytelling by, 472
  study of history, 362–365, 373
  supporter of Al Smith, 319
  third term in office, 1055–1056, 1058,
    1061
  unemployment insurance programs, 381–
    382
  vacation trip aboard *U.S.S. Houston*, 651
  Vice-President candidate in 1920, 342
  voter approval of, 1029
  Warm Springs, Georgia, 107, 272, 358, 471
  welfare concepts, 1105
  White House, 469–476
  Yalta Conference, 1096, 1098
Roosevelt, James, 352, 354, 478
Roosevelt, Sara Delano, 345, 349–350, 372,
    375
  overprotective mother, 358
  relationship with son, 357–358
Roosevelt, Theodore (TR), 20, 27, 114–115,
    174, 333
  Bull Moose campaign in 1912, 409, 448
  police commissioner in New York City, 366
  progressive nationalism, 350–351
  FDR and, 345, 348, 365–368
  Sagamore Hill home, 343
Root, E. Merrill, 137
Root, Elihu, 172
Roper, Daniel Calhoun, 412, 610
Rose, Don, 577, 580
Rosenberg, Dr. Alfred, 489
Rosengarten, Theodore, 88, 91, 583
Rosenman, Samuel I., 278, 330, 333, 389,
    392, 589, 672, 685, 701, 878, 1077
  intimate of FDR, 463
Rosenstock-Huessy, Eugen, 66–67, 533, 1139
  modern world and revolutions, 1144–1145
Rotarians, 7–8
Roth, Henry, 1005
Rothschild banking house, 3
Rubinstein, Helena, 47
Rudd, Wayland, 593–594
Ruini, Professor M., 62
Rukeyser, Muriel, 528, 790, 798
Rumania, 56, 1043
Rumsey, Mrs. C. C., 947–948
Rural areas, 16, 52, 579
  black union organizers, 581
Rural Electrification Administration, 647
Rush, Dr. Benjamin, 904–905
Rushton, John, 502–503

Russak, Martin, 524
Russell, Bertrand, 48, 250
Russell, Charles Edward, 112, 205, 208, 421, 467, 522, 535, 788
Russell Sage Foundation, 379
Russia, 73
  Americans' fascination with, 307–308
  industrial system, 308
  training young people, 308
  (*See also* Soviet Union)
Russian Famine Relief Committee, 190
Russian-German nonaggression pact, 783, 788, 901, 1042–1046, 1072
Russian Revolution, 182–183, 495, 1145
Rutherberg, Charles, 184, 196
Ryan, Thomas Fortune, 364
Ryan Airlines in San Diego, 149
Rykov, Alelssey I., 782–783

Sacco, Nicola, 117
  character, 124–125
  family background, 119–120
Sacco-Vanzetti case, 117–145, 505
  anarchism, 141–142
  bombs and bombings, 132
  books and pamphlets, 120–121
  commission to review case, 128
  Communists and, 119, 142–143
  death sentence and execution, 117–118, 127–129, 132–138
  Defense Committee, 128–129, 133
  defense fund, 120
  demonstrations and picketing, 129–132, 135, 136
  denial of appeals, 117, 127–128
  foreign support for, 122–123
  guilt or innocence, 142–144
  holdup and murders, 117–118
  indictment, 117, 119
  motion for new trial, 117, 121, 126–127
  "New York gang" and "Boston gang," 131
  psychological impact on intellectuals, 137–139
  radical spirit, 119, 143
  significance of, 141–145
  support for, 120–123
  union participation, 121
  victims of capitalist conspiracy, 126–127
Sachs, Alexander, 1052–1053
Saint-Gaudens, Augustus, 30
St. John's college, 903
Salvemini, Gaetano, 60, 492

San Francisco, 48
  bomb explosion in 1916, 9
  Haight-Ashbury district, 1133
  Longshoremen's strike in 1934, 613–617
  murals painted on tower, 808–809
  FDR speech, 397–398
Sandburg, Carl, 208, 229
Sandino, Agustino, 171
Santayana, George, 1108
Saroyan, William, 48, 1007
Sarah Lawrence college, 890
*Saturday Review of Literature,* 790
Savage, Augusta, 248
Savio, Mario, 1132–1133
Sayre, Francis, 1029
*Scarlet Sister Mary* (Peterkin), 998–999
Schacht, Dr. Hjalmar, 176
Schechter case, 639–640
Schoenberg, Arnold, 1037
Schomburg, Arthur A., 232, 253–254
School desegregation, 1127
  *Brown v. Board of Education,* 1127
Schulberg, Budd, 522, 983, 1007
Schultz, Dutch, 39, 220
Schultz, Sigrid and Mamma, 64
Schurz, Carl, 1038
Schuschnigg, Chancellor Kurt von, 1039
Schwab, Charles M., 645
Scientific attitude and scientific method, 22
  national defense and, 1131
  science vs. religion, 859–860
  theory of evolution, 856–857
Scopes, John Thomas, 855
Scopes trial, 854–864
  arrest of Scopes, 855
  attack on Darwinism, 854, 856
  William Jennings Bryan, 854–863
  Butler Act, 854
  Clarence Darrow, 858–863
  evolution theory, 854, 856–857, 863
  fundamentalists, 857–859, 863–864
  science versus religion, 859–860
Scott, Howard, 629–630
Scottsboro Boys, 543–565, 1113, 1129
  alleged rape, 544–545
  appeals, 546, 553, 560
  black colleges and, 552–553
  blacks excluded from juries, 553–554, 559–560
  communism issue, 556–557, 560
  Communist Party statements, 546–547
  defense teams, 548

Scottsboro Boys (*cont.*):
first trial, 544–546
guilty verdict, 555, 561–562
death in electric chair, 555
International Legal Defense (ILD), 539–
540, 548–550, 553, 564
Samuel Leibowitz hired to defend, 553
lynching threats, 544
mothers' activities in behalf of, 549, 564,
595–596
pardons, 561–562
racial injustice, 563–564
second trial, 549, 553
third trial, 559
Scottsboro Defense Fund, 552
Scripps-Howard newspaper chain, 605
Script-writers in Hollywood, 1007
Search-warrants, 2
Seattle (Washington), black Americans, 215–
216
Seaver, Edwin, 534
Second International Conference of Revolu-
tionary Writers, 509
Second International Writers Congress in
Paris in 1937, 573
Secular-Democratic Consciousness, 114, 1003,
1123, 1141–1142
utopian vision and passion for reform,
1142
Securities and Exchange Commission, 478
Joseph P. Kennedy first chairman, 601
Truth in Securities Act, 443
Seldes, George, 64
Seldes, Gilbert, 493
Selective Service Act, 1070–1071, 1081–1082
Selma, march from Montgomery, 1129
Selznick, David O., 923
Seminaries, radical views, 873
Senate Foreign Relations Committee, 485
Sennett, Mack, 923–924
*Seven Arts* magazine, 229
Sex and morals, 48–51
Mencken on, 50–51
Sex education, 5
Sexual relations, 5, 9
blacks, 253
between blacks and whites, 250–251
Seymour, Whitney North, Jr., 570, 572–573
Sforza, Count Carlo, 60, 492
Shachtman, Max, 1109
Shahn, Ben, 138, 808
Shakers, 849

Sharecroppers and tenant farmers, 78, 81,
588, 815
government programs, 816–819
organized by communists, 581–582
Shaw, George Bernard, 856
Sheean, Vincent, 165–168, 284–285, 527,
983–984
Sheeler, Charles, 32, 949–950
Shelterbelts, 1103–1104
Sherwood, Robert E., 1071, 1077
Shouse, Jouett, 327, 606
Shuler, Rev. Bob, 866–867
"Sidewalks of New York, The," 329
Siegel, Eli, 42
Siegfried, André, 24
Siegrist, Mary, 870
Silone, Ignazio, 526
Silver policy, 446
Simons, Bud, 732–733
Sinclair, Harry, 105
Sinclair, Upton, 138–140, 208, 510, 749, 754,
1068
campaign of abuse and innuendo, 633
program to End Poverty in California
(EPIC), 631–633, 665
supporters, 632–633
Singer, Paris, 172–173
Single Tax Party, 113
Sioux City (Iowa) strike, 292–293
Siqueiros, David, 807, 960
Sissle, Noble, 933–934
Sisson, Thomas, 96–97
*Sister Carrie* (Dreiser), 28
Sit-down strikes, 732–750
Anderson, Indiana, 742–743
agreement reached, 739
effect of, 742–743
Firestone strike, 744
Fisher Body plant, 732–734
injunction to vacate, 732–733
government negotiations, 735–738
public opinion and, 738, 741
techniques, 736–741
UAW victory, 740
(*See also* United Auto Workers)
Skvirsky, Boris E., 494
Slavery, abolition of, 1093
Slesinger, Tess, 48
Sloan, Alfred P., 734–735
Sloan, John, 47, 954
Slum clearance, 699
*Smart Set*, 40

Smedley, Agnes, 527–528
Smith, Alfred E., 160, 185, 408
  acceptance speech, 271–272
  anti-Catholic opposition, 273
  defeat, 277
  Democratic candidate in 1924, 106
  Democratic Convention in 1932, 319
  governor of New York, 267–268
  nominated president in 1928 by FDR, 107–
    108, 329, 342
  presidential ambitions, 377
  primary victories, 325–327
  FDR and, 319, 331, 606, 661–662
  Southerners opposed to, 269
  urges FDR to run for governor, 377–378
Smith, Bennie, 262
Smith, Bessie, 47, 219, 936–937
Smith, "Cotton Ed," 75, 1025
Smith, Gerald L. K., 651, 665
Smith, Homer, 594
Smith, John T., 739
Smith, Kate, 30
Smith, Lillian, 819, 830–836, 966
  white prejudice against blacks, 832–836
Smith, Tommy, 47, 48, 250
Smithfield, Alabama, 89
Snelling, Paula, 832–836
Social changes, 23
Social gospel, 864, 871
  target of revivalists, 867–868
Social justice, 414
  UAW and, 750
Social protest, techniques of, 1129
Social reforms, 17, 28, 678–679
  ideal of unselfish service, 18
  through political action, 750
Social sciences, 1131
Social security legislation, 602, 634, 644–645,
  690
Social security programs, 336
Social Welfare department, 698–699
Social workers, 17–18
Socialist Labor Party, 113–114, 664
Socialist Party, 182–183, 185, 194–195, 208,
  532, 1065
  election of 1928, 263
  election of 1936, 664
  national convention in 1932, 324, 401
Socialists and socialism, 3, 6, 8, 14, 17, 26,
  112, 182, 434, 664–665, 719, 1121
  Christian Socialists, 852
  endorsed by clergy, 872

Socialists and socialism (cont.):
  New Deal and, 850
  non-Marxist, 58–59
  non-Russian, 464
  philosophy, 17
  in Washington, 419–420
Soil conservation work, 440, 601
Sokoloff, Nikolai, 792
Soong Ching-ling, 165
Sorenson, Charles E., 502
Soul of Black Folk, The (Du Bois), 1137
South and Southerners, 814–839
  agriculture, 76, 78–80
  aliens, 73–74
  antebellum, 70
  black migration North, 70–71, 211–212
  black-white relations, 71, 93–96
  colleges and universities, 819–820
  Communist Party in, 568
  CIO organizing drives, 752
  defeat and poverty, 70
  Democratic Party, 678
  economic conditions, 821–822
  education, 819–821
  farm problems, 15, 79–80
  fear of blacks and Communists, 71–72
  feminine heroism, 75
  industry, 70, 83
  labor unions, 84–85, 193, 757
  landlords, 80–81
  legacy of slavery, 71
  literary renaissance, 991–1007
  lynchings, 93–96, 825–832
  mill hands and millowners, 82–84
  "new" intellectuals, 825
  New South, 70, 74
  Northern capitalists and, 72–73
  plantation owners, 82–84
  politics and politicians, 74, 1026
  poor white tenant farmers, 77–78
  poverty and hunger, 82, 86, 815
  promiscuity of black males, 76
  racial prejudice, 576
  racial problems, 71–72, 97, 558
  relationship between black and white
    churchwomen, 98–100
  relief payments, 817–819
  FDR and New Deal, 815–816
  social distinctions, 82
  Solid South, 111
  Southern womanhood, 75–76, 79–80
  Southerners in New York, 42

South and Southerners (*cont.*):
  Southerners in FDR's cabinet, 408
  tenants and sharecroppers, 76–78, 81–83, 91
  Tennessee Valley Authority, 816
  in the twenties, 70–100
  violence and crime, 76, 814–815
  working conditions, 84–86
  writers, 991–1007, 1142
South Braintree (Massachusetts), Sacco-Vanzetti case, 117–118
South Dakota, rural radicalism, 194
*South Today,* 832
Southern Conference for Human Welfare, 821–822
Southern Newpaper Publishers Association, 832
Southern Sociological Congress, 97
Southern Tenant Farmers Union, 757–758
  Communist influence, 758–759
Souvestre, Marie, 347
Soviet-German nonaggression pact, 783, 788, 901, 1042–1046, 1078–1079
  reaction of communists, 1045–1046
Soviet Union, 129
  acceptance of blacks, 255–256, 593
  aims of Soviet policy, 499–500
  American aid, 1079, 1096
  American technology and "know-how," 501–502, 594
  American tourists, 500–501
    blacks, 255–256, 593
  anti-religion campaign, 494
  danger of attack by Hitler, 1043
  double-standard of truth, 785
  effect on European politics, 55
  espionage network, 168, 1030
  famine in 1933, 499
  fellow travelers, 183
  Five-Year Plan, 203, 502
  foreign policy, 1042–1044
  German invasion in 1941, 1043, 1078–1079
  ignorance of outside world, 308
  industrialization, 503–504
  invasion of Poland, 1051, 1053–1054
  leaders, 787
  modernization of agriculture, 190
  Moscow trials for treason, 780–788
    consequences of, 786–788
    investigation of, 786–787
    validity of, 784

Soviet Union (*cont.*):
  New Economic Policy (NEP), 499
  people, 501, 787
  purges and public trials, 657, 780–788
  Red Army deficiencies, 782–784, 1054
  relations with U.S., 494–504, 601, 1079, 1096, 1109, 1125
  Russian Jews in, 3
  second front against Hitler, 1079
  tenth anniversary of the revolution, 167
  U.S. recognition of, 183, 494, 594, 788
  (*See also* Communist Party; Communists and communism)
Spanish Civil War, 767–780
  casualty rate, 777–778
  International Brigade, 771, 774–775, 777
  Lincoln-Washington Battalion, 773, 777
  meaning of, 779–780
  Soviet support, 768, 774–775
  struggle against fascism and Nazism, 768, 773–774
  volunteers, 770–771
Spanish Loyalists, 768–770, 777, 780
Spanish republican government, 768, 777
Spargo, John, 10, 17
Speakeasy era, 37, 52
Spears, Jane, 585
Speculation in stock market, 278–279
Speed, Jane, 557
Spencer, Herbert, 120
Spender, Stephen, 255
Spingarn, Joel, 997–998
*Spirit of St. Louis, The* (Lindbergh), 153, 163
*Spirit of St. Louis, The* (plane), 149–155
  first airmail stamp, 159
Spirituality, to replace materialism, 869
Spirituals, 212
Sports, 941–946
  amateur and professional, 941–942
  black athletes, 592–593, 942–946
  football, 942
  Olympic competition, 942–943
  point of entry into American life, 946
  racial discrimination, 592–593
Sproul, Robert Gordon, 632
Stalin, Joseph, 195, 324, 497, 579, 782
  American Communist Party and, 203–204
  black film project, 593–594
  Five-Year Plan, 203, 502
  German invasion of Soviet Union, 1043, 1078–1079
  opposition to, 787

Stalin, Joseph (*cont.*):
 Red Army reforms, 1054
 FDR and, 1094
 Russian-German negotiations, 1042–1045
 Stalin-Trotsky battle, 195–196, 203–205
 Teheran Conference, 1096
 third period dogma, 654
 trials for treason against, 780–788
 Yalta Conference, 1096
Stalingrad, Russian resistance at, 1095
Standard of living, 16, 279
Standard Oil Company, 619–621, 625, 652
Standard University, 8
*Stars Fell on Alabama* (Carmer), 75
Stassen, Harold, 1060
State Department (*see* Department of State)
State guidebooks, 795–797
States' rights doctrine, 19, 363, 365, 845,
 1127
Stearns, Harold, 447, 913, 915, 933
Steel, Ronald, 19
Steel industry: CIO organizing drives, 751–
 752
 FDR and steel strike, 754
 steel code, 453–454
 unionization of, 455, 751–754
Steel Workers Organizing Committee, 718–
 719, 752
Steffens, Ella Winter, 21–22, 255, 592
Steffens, Lincoln, 9, 21, 28–29, 32, 61, 208,
 255, 309, 366, 401, 419, 522, 592, 1049
 appearance, 516
 on big business, 21–22
 expedition to Russia in 1919, 495, 499
 predictions for new struggles, 21–22
 on revolutionary spirit, 14
 Theodore Roosevelt and, 470
Stein, Gertrude, 52, 966–968
 Hemingway and, 979
 influence among writers, 968–969
 lecture tour of U.S., 971
Steinbeck, John, 297, 984–986, 1068
Steiner, Edward, 380
Stella, Joseph, 949–950
Stengel, Hans, 51–52
Stevens, Mary, 585
Stevens, Wallace, 658, 1015
Stevenson, Adlai, 1128
Stewart, Donald Ogden, 784, 1068
Stiles, Lela, 329
Stimson, Henry, 170, 307, 423, 428, 1059–
 1060, 1071, 1077–1079

Stimson, Henry (*cont.*):
 doctrine of nonrecognition, 481
Stock, Ernest, 42
Stock market crash in 1929, 285–286
 end of era, 335–336
 mid-twenties boom, 16–17
 speculation, 173–175, 278–279, 284–285
 Truth in Securities Act, 443
 warning signals, 176, 177
Stoddard, Henry, 107, 111, 114, 180
Stolberg, Benjamin, 317
Stone, Harland, 116, 682
Stone, Lucy, 124
Storey, Moorfield, 122, 126
Stotesbury, E. T., 174
Stowe, Harriet Beecher, 222, 510
Strachey, John, 526, 558
*Strange Interlude* (O'Neill), 1010–1011
Strasberg, Lee, 1013
Stratton, Samuel, 128
Straus, Jesse Isidor, 379, 397
Stravinsky, Igor, 1037
Stresemann, Gustav, 64
Strikes, 10–11, 455, 703
 Akron, Ohio, 722–726
 Auto-Lite strike, 704–705
 Chicago packing plants, 754–756
 Communist-led, 190–192, 1119
 communist writers and, 521–522
 company spies, 722
 farm workers in California, 759–763
 Ford Motor Co., 746–749
 General Motors, 732–739
 number of, 763
 planning and running, 721–722
 sit-down strikes, 732–739
 strategies, 722–725
 stretch-out system, 84–86
 strikebreakers, 12, 724
 student, 897–898
 textile workers, 190–194, 706–707
 violence and hostility, 764
 (*See also* Labor unions)
Strong, Anna Louise, 186, 573
Strong, Benjamin, 176
Student demonstrations against Vietnam
 War, 1133–1134
Student Strike Against War, 898
Subsistence Homestead Corporation, 637–
 638
Subversives, 1, 8
 State Department charges, 2–3

Subversives (*cont.*):
  (*See also* House Un-American Activities
    Committee)
Sudetenland, 1040
Suicides, in the twenties, 51–52
Sullivan, Mark, 473
Summer, Charles, 122
Summers, Hatton, 686
Summers, Dr.Thomas Osmund, 223
Sumner, William Graham, 321
*Sun Also Rises, The* (Hemingway), 980–981
Sun Yat-sen, 165
Sun Yat-sen, Madame, 166, 528
Sunday, Billy, 864, 867
Supreme Court
  age and health of justices, 689
  Agricultural Adjustment Act, 660
  *Brown v. Board of Education*, 1127, 1129
  civil liberties and civil rights, 1127
  court-packing fight, 682–695
  Four Horsemen, 682
  Herndon case, 570–571, 573
  interpreting the Constitution, 691
  labor decisions, 13
  New Deal legislation declared unconstitu-
    tional, 634, 639–640, 680
  retirement plan, 687
  Scottsboro Boys case, 553, 560
  wages and hours decision, 689–690
Surrealists, 64
Sutherland, Justice George, 177, 682
Swanson, Claude, 171, 332, 412
Sweatshops, 450
Swope, Gerard, 383, 453
Swope, Herbert Bayard, 26, 268, 484–485
Sydney, Iolanthe, 245
Szilard, Leo, 1038, 1052

Taft, Robert, 1028, 1060
Taft, William Howard, 36, 126, 174, 177, 653
Taggard, Genevieve, 41
Talbot, Rev. Francis X., S.J., 868
Tallapoosa County, Alabama, 581
Taliesin, utopian community, 963
Talmadge, Eugene, 568–569, 706–707
Tammany Hall, 268–269, 325
Tarbell, Ida, 32, 60–61, 421, 522, 791
Tariff issue, 26, 287, 307, 482, 484–485
  campaign of 1932, 393
Tate, Allen, 42, 47, 506, 520, 991–994, 996
Tate, Wilmer, 725
Tax reform measures, 645–646

Taylor, Charles E., 194–195, 204
Taylor, Deems, 45
Taylor, Francis Henry, 810
Taylor, Frederick, 22
Taylor, Graham, 414–415
Taylor, W. J., 196
Taylor Grazing Act, 465
Teagle, Walter, 453
Teapot Dome oil scandal, 105, 115
Technocrats, 629–630
Teetotalism, 38
Teheran Conference, 1096
Teller, Edward, 1038
Temperance movement, 38
Temporary Emergency Relief Administration
  (TERA), 379, 390
*Ten Days that Shook the World* (Reed), 236
Tenant farmers and sharecroppers, 78
  union activity, 757–759
Tennessee Valley Authority, 444–445, 476,
  816, 842
Terkel, Studs, 791
Terrorist gangs in Germany, 63–64
Textile Labor Relations Board, 707
Textile workers strikes, 190–194, 706–707
Thalberg, Irving, 927–928
Thalmann, Ernst, 68
Tharpe, Sister Rosetta, 219
Thaw, Harry K., 46
Thayer, Charles, 497–498
Thayer, Webster, 118, 126–127, 139
Theaters: Federal Theatre Project, 798–804
  "guerrilla theater," 630
  repertory, 42
  Suitcase Theater, 590
  workers, 525
Theatre Guild, 1012
Theater of Action, 511, 525
*Theory of Social Revolutions* (Adams), 675, 682, 896
*This I Remember* (Roosevelt), 1106
Thomas, J. Parnell, 812
Thomas, Norman, 488, 1118
  America First Committee, 1067
  American Fund for Public Service, 532
  Anderson (Indiana) strike, 743
  on Communists, 1118
  election of 1932, 719
  election of 1940, 1072
  leader of Socialist Party, 208, 464
  on Lippmann, 20
  presidential nomination, 263, 335, 401,
    664, 1065, 1072

Thompson, Dorothy, 64, 285, 490, 516, 526, 530
Thompson, Francis, 876, 1008
Thompson, Louise, 202, 247, 251, 593–594, 776
Thompson, Malvina, 477
*Three Soldiers* (Dos Passos), 31
Thurman, Howard, 558
Thurman, Wallace, 245, 247
Tillich, Paul, 66
*Time* magazine, 468, 649, 749, 1110–1111
Tindley, Charles A., 218–219
Title II programs, 440
  (*See also* National Industrial Recovery Act)
Tobacco, 76–77, 79
Tobin, Daniel, 711
Todhunter School, 360
Tojo, Hideki, 1085
Toklas, Alice B., 971
Tolson, Melvin, 513–514
Tolstoy, Leo, 120
Toomer, Nathan Eugene "Jean," 208, 243
Totten, Ashley L., 259, 262
Tourgee, Albion, 510
Townsend, Dr. Francis Everett, 629, 665
Townsend Plan, 629, 633
Toynbee, Arnold, 1147
Trade organizations, 449, 451
Trade Union Educational League, 192
Trade Union Unity League, 704
Trade unions, 580
  outlawed in Germany, 489
  (*See also* Labor unions)
Transcendentalism, 869
*transition* (magazine), 41
Travis, Bob, 731–732, 739–741, 743
Treasury Department, Communist influence, 1029–1030
Trent, Lucia, 137–138
Tresca, Carlo, 121, 537, 786
Trilling, Lionel, 786
Trotsky, Leon, 167–168, 498, 507, 782
  cleared of charges, 786
  Stalin-Trotsky battle, 195–196, 203–205
  struggle for power, 195–196
Trotskyites, 718, 775, 786
  heresies, 324
Truman, Harry, 275, 610, 1106, 1128
  Vice-President nomination, 1097
Truth, Sojourner, 100
Truth in Securities Act, 443
*Tucson Citizen*, 9

Tugwell, Rexford, 356, 424, 801
  adviser and confidant of FDR, 464
  Agricultural Adjustment Act, 441
  campaign of 1932, 392–393, 398–399, 401
  on decision to recognize Soviet Union, 494
  deficiencies as administrator, 637–638
  expert on agricultural economics, 385–387, 389, 418
  greenbelt towns, 638
  on Herbert Hoover, 265, 283, 340
  member of FDR's Brain Trust, 323
  NIRA and, 448
  NRA destruction, 641
  New Deal Legislation, 438
  presidential ambitions, 608
  on FDR, 359–361, 367–371, 475–476, 605, 1104–1106
  Subsistence Homestead Corporation, 637–638
Tully, Grace, 372, 378, 388, 470
Tunney, Gene, 181
Turner, Frederick Jackson, 954
Turner, Nat, 71, 551
Tuscaloosa (Alabama) communists, 558–559
Tuskegee Institute, 97–98, 254, 891–892
Twenties, 1–26, 1128
  age of parties, 45–48
  boom period, 14–17
  labor unions, 9–11
  lack of challenges, 162
  literary and intellectual culture, 52–53
  money mania, 17
  psychic costs of living in, 51
  "Red menace," 11
  repressive spirit, 1
  south and southerners, 70–100
  terrible disillusionment, 52
  triumphant capitalism, 27
"Two Americas," 27
  repressive spirit, 1, 27
  workers, intellectuals, writers and artists, 27
*Two Years Before the Mast* (Dana), 153, 510
Tydings, Millard, 1025, 1062
Tyrrell, Lord, 62

UAW (*see* United Auto Workers)
Un-Americanism and subversion, 1, 4, 18
  (*See also* House Un-American Activities Committee)
*Uncle Tom's Cabin* (Stowe), 214, 222, 510

Unemployed Councils, 294, 311–315, 540–543, 771, 791, 1119–1120
  Communist activities, 301
  protests and demonstrations, 591
Unemployed Writers Association (UWA), 791
Unemployment: block aid, 300
  Communist influences, 311–314
  compensation, 700
  demonstrations and protests, 312–316, 406
  Depression years, 295–296
  New Deal programs, 439–440, 442, 845
  New York State programs, 379
  relief programs, 304
  technological, 12
  white-collar workers, 296
  work programs, 442
  working-class, 297–298
Unemployment insurance plans, 611
  employer-initiated, 383
Union movement (see Labor unions)
Union Party, 665
Union Theological Seminary, 873, 880
United Auto Workers (UAW), 720, 727–759
  Battle of the Overpass, 748–749
  Battle of the Running Bulls, 737, 748
  Chevrolet No. 4, 738–740
  Communist members, 727–729
  CIO support for, 727, 731–732, 739–740
  convention in 1936 in South Bend, 728
  employers antiunion educational campaign, 729
  factional infighting, 727–728, 745–746
  Fisher Body Plant No. 1, 731–734, 738
  Ford strikes, 746–749
  General Motors unionization, 727–750
    Flint plant, 730–731
    recognition of union, 740
    sit-down strikes, 732–745
  growth of, 729, 744
  Kelsey-Hayes Wheel strike, 729–730
  liberal politics, 750
  Homer Martin, president, 727–728
  NIRA, Section 7 (a), 727
  organizing campaigns, 728–750
  public relations, 733
  raids by AFL, 727–728
  Reuther brothers, 730–749
  sit-down strikes, 729–749
    judges injunction defied, 738
  social reform through political action, 750
  unionization of automobile industry, 729–759

United Auto Workers (cont.):
  Unity Caucus, 728–729
  (See also Labor unions; Strikes)
United Cigar stores, 26
United Electrical Workers, 710
United Farmer, 195
United Farmers Educational League, 194
United Mine Workers union, 187, 192, 517, 669, 707–716
  John L. Lewis, 707–716
  Philip Murray, 710
United Nations, 1097
  Security Council veto, 1097
United Rubber Workers, 724, 744
United States Geological Survey, 411
United States Steel, 174, 751
United Textile Worker's Union, 84
University Commission on Southern Race Questions, 97
University of California, 632
University of California at Berkeley, 1133
University of Chicago, 2, 26, 220
University of North Carolina, 820
University of Wisconsin, 147, 891
Untermeyer, Louis, 208
Up from Slavery (Washington), 226
Upper-class Americans, 52
  concern for social justice, 1112
Upshaw, William, 324
USA trilogy (Dos Passos), 138
Utility holding companies, 175
Utopian communities, 630, 963, 1122, 1134

Val-Kill project at Hyde Park, 465
  furniture manufacturing, 477
Van Davanter, Willis, 682–683, 690
Vandenberg, Arthur, 1060
Vanderbilt, Cornelius, Jr., 532, 820
Vanderbilt University, 856
  Southern literary renaissance, 991
van der Rohe, Ludwig Miës, 964, 1037
Vanderstell, Bernard, 1136
Van Doren, Carl, 45
Van Doren, Mark, 45
Van Hise, Charles R., 394
Van Vechten, Carl, 45, 47, 237, 244, 252
Vanity Fair, 39–40
Vanzetti, Bartolomeo, 117, 120
  atheism, 118–119
  intellectual, 118–120
  on justice, 145
  letters, 124

Vanzetti, Bartolomeo (*cont.*):
 tribute to Sacco, 125
 (*See also* Sacco-Vanzetti case)
Vanzetti, Luigia, 120
Vardaman, J. K., 71
Vassar College, 528–529
Veblen, Thorstein, 387
Vermont, home of itinerant intellectuals, 29
Versailles Treaty, 18, 63, 68, 164, 320, 768,
 1042, 1053, 1109
 opposed by Germans, 64–65
 reduction in German armies, 486–487
Victorianism, 49
Vienna, 58–59
 Communist uprisings, 166–167
Viereck, George Sylvester, 492
Vietnam War, 1132
 student demonstrations, 1133–1134
Villard, Oswald Garrison, 101, 113, 227, 279,
 326
 on social problems, 1048–1049
Virginia, settlers, 1141
Vishinsky, Andrey Y., 783
Visual arts, 805–808
 in public buildings, 806–807
Volstead Act, 38, 325
von Hindenburg, Paul, 68, 436, 487–489
von Papen, Franz, 436
Voroshilov, Marshal Kliment, 498, 1045
Vorse, Mary Heaton, 193, 518, 528, 554–
 555, 733, 758
Voyez, George, 192
Voynow, Richard, 938

Wading River, Long Island, 29
Wadleigh, Henry Julian, 1029–1030
Wages and hours, 10, 13, 413, 640, 697
 Black bill, 447–448
 Supreme Court decision, 689–690
Wagner, Robert E., 303–304, 439, 672–673,
 1039
 Wagner Act, importance of, 766
 NIRA, 448
 National Labor Relations Act, 643
*Waiting for Lefty* (Odets), 1013–1014
Walker, A'Lelia, 244, 249
Walker, Charles Rumford, 517–518
Walker, Frank, 599
Walker, Mayor Jimmy, 48, 160
Walker, Madam C. J., 215
Wall Street crash, 285–286
 speculative boom, 284–285

Wall Street crash (*cont.*):
 Whitney scandal, 696
 (*See also* Stock market crash)
*Wall Street Journal*, 174
Wallace, George, 558
Wallace, Henry C., 417, 460, 464–465, 801,
 1064, 1097
 Agricultural Adjustment Act, 407, 441
 Brain Trust member, 392
 Coolidge's secretary of agriculture, 178,
 276
 election of 1940, 1061–1064
 presidential ambitions, 608, 1032, 1056,
 1064
 secretary of agriculture, 411–412, 464–
 465
 religious mystic, 465, 1067
 vice-president nomination, 1064, 1097
Wallace, W. J., 113
Wallas, Graham, 19, 129
Waller, Fats, 552
Walling, William English, 112
Walsh, David I., 698–699
Walsh, Frank, 45
Walsh, Thomas, 1, 105, 118, 328, 408
Walsh-Healy, or Public Contract Act, 640
Walton, "Jack," 6
Wanamaker, Rodman, 151
War between capital and labor, 1125
 resolution of, 677, 761, 846, 1093, 1142
War debts, 784–785
 amounts owed by European countries,
 485
 reparations and, 484
War Production Board, 1030
Warbasse, J. P., 197
Warburg, Felix, 364
Warburg, James, 445–446, 484, 608
Ward, Harry, 656
Ware, Harold "Hal," 189, 293, 295, 527,
 1030
Ware Group, 1030, 1110–1111
Waring, Fred, 919
Warm Springs, Georgia, 107, 272, 471
 death of FDR, 1098
 treatment of polio victims, 358
Warner, Jack, 924, 927
Warren, Charles, 116
Warren, George, 447
Warren, Robert Penn, 994
Washington, Booker T., 99, 222, 225, 227
Washington, Margaret, 99

Washington, D.C.
  Bonus Army March in 1932, 337–339
  Coxey's March, 324
  idealistic young men in, 420–424
  Lindbergh's hero welcome, 157–158
  mecca for reformers, 420
  National Hunger March, 314–315
  Scottsboro Boys protest march, 556
Washington "apparatus," Communist spy operation, 1029–1031, 1045–1046, 1112–1114
Washington Conference of 1922, 486
Wasserman, Jakob, 45
*Waste Land, The* (Eliot), 53
Waters, Ethel, 937
Waters, Walter W., 337
Watson, Forbes, 806–807
Weaver, Robert C., 425
Webb, Beatrice, 347
Weber, Max, 851
Webster, Milton P., 260, 262
Wechsler, Herbert, 573
Weems, Charles, 543, 546, 562–563
Weinstone, William, 183, 204
Welch, William Henry, 906
Welles, Gideon, 411
Welles, Orson, 802
Welles, Sumner, 419
Wellesley College, 100
Wells, H. G., 553, 653, 855–856
West, Nathanael, 1007, 1024
West, Rebecca, 653–654
West, black migration to, 215–216
West Coast, 70
Wetmore, Douglas, 223–224
Wharton, Edith, 966, 977, 990–991, 1024
Wharton School of Finance and Commerce, 387
Wheat, 14
  bought for needy, 460
Wheeler, Burton K., 2, 113, 326, 445, 646, 686, 1066, 1070
White, Harry Dexter, 1029
White, Maude, 202
White, Nancy, 90–91
White, Stanford, 46
White, Walter, 251, 547–548, 562, 1107
White, William Allen, 3–4, 8, 103, 172, 405
  on Coolidge boom, 177–178
  "freedom of utterance," 11
  opposed KKK, 3–4
  on prohibition issue, 272

White, William Allen (*cont.*):
  on railroad strikes, 11
  on FDR, 457, 473, 600
  on FDR seeking fourth term, 1097
White House, 463–480
  center of Roosevelt administration, 479
  cocktail hour, 470–471
  decor, 477
  food and drink, 472
  press conferences, 470
  Eleanor Roosevelt and, 472
  Roosevelt changes in, 434
  routine, 469–476
  social events, 469
White Supremacy, 7
"White Terror," 1
Whites
  black-white relationships, 71, 87–88, 595, 1136–1137
  blacks and whites working together, 595
  fear of black insurrection, 96
  perceptions of blacks, 254
  prejudice against blacks, 832–836
  race relations, 833–835
  recruiting for Communist Party, 577
  registering to vote, 587
  relationship between white men and white women, 90
  sexual aggression of black women, 90
Whitlock, Brand, 28
Whitman, Walt, 36, 919, 982, 1142, 1145
Whitney, Gertrude, 947
Whitney, Parkhurst, 36
Whitney, Richard, 286, 696
Whitney Museum of Art, 43, 809, 954
Whittemore, Mrs. E. M., 9
Wigmore, John H., 126
Wilbur, Ray Lyman, 263
Wilder, Thornton, 511
Willard, Frances, 38
Williams, Aubrey, 432, 597, 822–825, 1029
  appointment of black administrators, 824–825
  enlightened racial attitudes, 824
  National Youth Administration head, 822–823
  Eleanor Roosevelt and, 823
Williams, Bonita, 202
Williams, Dent, 820
Williams, Eugene, 544, 562
Williams, Frank, 540, 575–576
Williams, Harold, 201

Williams, John Sharp, 84
Williams, William Carlos, 791
Willison, George, 794
Willkie, Wendell, 742, 1067–1068
  election of 1940, 1060, 1072
  lend-lease supported by, 1074
  Republican presidential candidate, 1060–1061
  support for, 1065–1066
Wilson, Dooley, 802
Wilson, Edmund, 51, 229, 285, 517, 974–975
  arbiter of literary scene, 43
  Communist Party member, 174–175, 208–209, 506–507, 520–521, 526–527, 534–535, 785
  defection from Communist Party, 785
  description of inaugural parade, 433
  effect of boom, 285
  effects of Depression, 298–299
  on Edna St. Vincent Millay, 39–40
  on optimism and morale of Americans, 36
  party-giver, 47–48
  return from Europe, 447
  on Sacco-Vanzetti case, 141
  Soviet trials, 782
Wilson, M. L., 386, 393
Wilson, Paul, 415
Wilson, Woodrow, 18, 27, 160, 320, 780, 1076
  academic world and, 895
  administration, 846–847
  appointed FDR assistant secretary of the navy, 253
  death of, 35–36
  Fourteen Points, 1083, 1102, 1109
  government and business, 448
  New Freedom, 334
  Progressive movement and, 482
  reforms, 1026
  FDR and, 253, 351–352, 369
Winter, Ella (see Steffens, Ella Winter)
Winterset (Anderson), 138
Winthrop, John, 848–849, 1122, 1147
Wisconsin, LaFolette's program, 301–303
Wise, James Waterman, 656
Wise, Rabbi Stephen, 8, 335
Witch-hunting, 1, 422
Witt, Nathan, 1030
Wolf, Friedrich, 523, 525
Wolfe, Thomas, 825, 1004–1005
Woll, Matthew, 711
Woman's Christian Temperance Union, 38

Women
  black, 202, 247–248
    class differences, 251
    sexual aggression by white men, 90
  colleges, 889–890
  education of, 35, 889–890
  involvement in Communism, 527–531
  in New Deal agencies, 425
  physicians, 908–909
  in politics, 416–417
  relationship between black and white churchwomen, 98–100
  relationship between white men and women, 90–91
  role of, 1143
  Southern womanhood, 75–76
  union organization and, 385
Women and Economics (Gilman), 91
Women's International League for Peace and Freedom, 650
Women's rights movement, 124, 1143
Wood, Grant, 956–960
  "American Gothic," 957
  murals, 958
Woodin, William, 408, 434–435, 437–438, 445, 449
Woodring, Harry, 1059
Woodrow Wilson Foundation, 64
Woodward, Ellen, 798
Woodward, E. L., 850, 1147
Wooley, Mary (president of Mount Holyoke College), 8, 413
Woollcott, Alexander, 29, 64
Work, Merrill, 200–201
Work ethic, 34
Work relief plan, 597–599
Workers, 27
  rights of, 10
  romanticization of, 741
Workers' Alliance, 821
Workers Defense Conference of New England, 119
Workers Defense Union of New York, 119
Workers Ex-Servicemen League, 338
Workers Film and Photo League, 511
Workers' Party (Communists), 183, 185–186, 189, 196, 210
  election of 1928, 263
Working-class, hardship and repression, 27
Working conditions, 10, 13
  (See also Wages and hours)

Works Progress Administration, 463
  (*See also* Works Projects Administration)
Works Projects Administration (WPA), 463,
    612–614, 635–637, 699
  achievements, 840–842
  amendments, 636
  Communist influence, 825
  Federal Art Project, 807
  under Harry Hopkins, 637
*World*, 3, 110, 160, 170–171
World affairs, 481–504
World Christian Fundamentalist Association,
    854–856
World Court, 647, 692
World Economic Conference in London in
    1933, 484–486
World revolution, 788
World unity movement, 869–871
World War I, 1074
World War II, 1025–1049, 1073–1092,
    1131
  cured the Depression, 1128
  disillusionment following, 1109
  effect on unemployment, 845, 1128
  global crises, 1035–1048
  Nazi conquests, 1039–1047
  preparedness for war, 1050–1072
  threats to world peace, 1025–1049
World's Columbian Exposition of 1893,
    461
WPA (*see* Works Projects Administration)
Wright, Andrew, 543, 561, 563
Wright, Clifford, 809
Wright, Frank Lloyd, 961–962
Wright, Leroy, 544, 546
Wright, Richard, 212, 248, 251, 509, 524,
    793, 1130
Wright, Stanton McDonald, 811
Wright brothers, 147
Writers and artists, 27
  Americans in Europe, 31
  appeal of communism, 533–536
  black intellectuals and, 222–223, 228–237,
    793, 1130

Writers and artists (*cont.*):
  campaign of 1932, 400–402
  Communist critics, 511
  Communist front organizations, 508–510
  Communist influence, 791, 811–812
  Federal assistance, 789–790
  Federal Writers' Project, 789–798
  manifesto, 520–521
  projects employing, 789–813
  public attitude toward, 790
  scriptwriters, 1007
  Second International Conference of Revo-
    lutionary Writers in Kharkov, 509
  Second International Writers Congress in
    Paris, July 1937, 573
Wylie, Elinor, 44, 131, 229
Wyzanski, Charles, 440, 639

Yagoda, G. G., 783
Yale Law School, 421
Yalta Conference, 1096
Yankee Imperialism, 169, 171
Yerby, Frank, 793
Yergan, Max, 590
Yokinen, August, 198
Young, Brigham, 24
Young, J. Kyle, 581–582
Young, Owen D., 24–26, 320, 395, 408
Young, Roy, 278
Young Communist League, 197, 592, 771,
    897, 898–899, 983
Young Women's Christian Association
    (YWCA), 9
  racial reforms, 98–100
Young Workers League, 184
Youngstown steel strike, 753–754
Youth, 161
  revolt of, 39
Yugoslavia, post war, 56–57, 62

Zangara, Giuseppe, 426
Zinoviev, Grigori, 195–196, 203, 780–781,
    785
Zola, Emile, 120

# About the Author

Page Smith was educated at the Gilman School in Baltimore, Dartmouth College, and Harvard University. He has taught at the University of California at Los Angeles and at Santa Cruz, where he was provost of Cowell College. He is now professor emeritus of that university, as well as codirector of the William James Association. Dr. Smith is the author of *The Historian and History; Daughters of the Promised Land: Women in American History; As a City upon a Hill: The Town in American History;* the highly acclaimed two-volume biography *John Adams,* which was a selection of the Book-of-the-Month Club, a National Book Award Nominee, and a Bancroft winner; *As New Age Now Begins* and *The Shaping of America,* both Main Selections of the Book-of-the-Month Club. *Redeeming the Time* continues Dr. Smith's extensive *People's History of the United States,* of which *A New Age Now Begins, The Shaping of America, The Nation Comes of Age, Trial by Fire, The Rise of Industrial America,* and *America Enters the World* are the preceding volumes. Page Smith lives in Santa Cruz, California.